PRAISE FOR THE ULTIMATE SCHOLARSHIP BOOK BY GEN AND KELLY TANABE

"Upbeat, well-organized and engaging, this comprehensive tool is an exceptional investment for the college-bound."

—*Publishers Weekly*

"Gen and Kelly Tanabe are by far the best experts on winning scholarships. Not only will their books help you find scholarships that you qualify for, they will show you how to win them. Soon after applying the strategies in their book, I won a $1,000 scholarship. I couldn't have done it without them. The Tanabes can help you win scholarships too!"

—*Doug Wong, University of California, San Diego*

"A present for anxious parents."

—*The Honolulu Advertiser*

"Upbeat tone and clear, practical advice."

—*Book News*

"Unlike other authors, the Tanabes use their experiences and those of other students to guide high school and college students and their parents through the scholarship and financial aid process."

—*Palo Alto Daily News*

"If the Tanabes could earn over $100,000 in scholarships and graduate from an Ivy League institution owing nothing, others can, too."

—*Star-Bulletin*

"This is a helpful, well-organized guide. A good resource for all students."

—*KLIATT*

"A common sense approach to scholarship searches. *The Ultimate Scholarship Book* gives a down to earth step by step method of finding, applying for and winning scholarships. The scholarship list has many opportunities for students to showcase their talents for financial reward."

—*Lynda McGee, College Counselor, Downtown Magnets High School, Los Angeles*

"This guide (has) ... practical tips on where to find scholarships; how to write effective applications, resumes and winning essays; and how to get glowing recommendations and ace scholarship interviews."

—*C.E. King, Iowa State University, Choice Magazine*

"Getting into college is only half of the game. How to pay for it offers the second big challenge. Whether they qualify for financial need or are just looking for ways to help their parents with this heavy burden, all students will profit from *The Ultimate Scholarship Book* which both outlines the process of finding financial help for college as well as it provides an extensive and up to date list of current scholarship sources.

"Take these important tips from two experienced writers who are nationally recognized for their expertise on all facets of the college application process. Both members of this impressive husband and wife team paid for their Harvard educations by following the precepts which they share with you now in this easy to read guidebook."

—*David Miller, Director of College Counseling, Stevenson School, Pebble Beach, California*

Dedication

To our families for shaping who we are.

To Harvard for four of the best years of our lives.

To the many students and friends who made this book possible by sharing their scholarship experiences, secrets, successes and failures.

To all the students and parents who understand that paying for college is a challenging but worthwhile endeavor.

The Ultimate Scholarship Book 2020

Billions of Dollars in Scholarships, Grants and Prizes

Gen and Kelly Tanabe

Winners of over $100,000 in college scholarships and award-winning authors of *Get Free Cash for College* and *How to Write a Winning Scholarship Essay*

- Comprehensive scholarship directory to over 1.5 million awards worth more than $2 billion
- Scholarships for high school and college students of every background, talent and achievement level
- Easy to use indexes to quickly find the best matching scholarships

The Ultimate Scholarship Book 2020: Billions of Dollars in Scholarships, Grants and Prizes

By Gen and Kelly Tanabe

Published by SuperCollege, LLC
2713 Newlands Avenue
Belmont, CA 94002
650-618-2221
editor@supercollege.com
www.supercollege.com

Credits: Cover: Monica Thomas, www.tlcgraphics.com. Cover photograph: ©iStockphoto.com/Bubaone. Layout: The Roberts Group, www.editorialservice.com. Back cover photograph: Alvin Gee, www.alvingee.com.

The Ultimate Scholarship Book is the #1 bestselling scholarship guide based on Nielsen/BookScan sales data of the 2019 editions of comparable titles.

Special Sales: For information on using SuperCollege books in the classroom or special prices for bulk quantities, please contact our Special Sales Department at sales@supercollege.com.

ISBN-13: 978-1-61760-147-7
ISBN-10: 1-61760-147-0

Manufactured in the United States of America
10 9 8 7 6 5 4 3 2 1

Library of Congress Cataloging-in-Publication Data

Tanabe, Gen S.
The ultimate scholarship book 2020: billions of dollars in scholarships, grants, and prizes / Gen Tanabe and Kelly Tanabe.
p. cm.
Includes indexes.
ISBN-13: 978-1-61760-147-7 (alk. paper)
ISBN-10: 1-61760-147-0 (alk. paper)
1. Scholarships--United States--Directories. I. Tanabe, Kelly Y. II. Title.
LB2338.T36 2019
378.3'402573--dc22

2019014761

CONTENTS

How to Use the Ultimate Scholarship Book

chapter 1

A Scholarship Book That's Better Than a Website

Is it crazy to say that a bound stack of paper and glue is superior to the high speed bits and bytes of a scholarship website? Absolutely not! Because it is true.

Let us explain.

Unless you're starting out, you've probably used a scholarship website. Typically you fill out a profile questionnaire to provide information about yourself before hitting the "search" button. So far, this seems much easier than using a book.

Until you get your results.

No matter what website you use, there will be an unusually large number of scholarships that aren't good matches. After reading the eligibility requirements, you will discover that only a small handful are worth your time to apply.

You've just discovered the first major weakness of every scholarship website: your life (background, experiences, goals, talents, awards, interests and accomplishments) cannot be defined or summarized by a computer-generated questionnaire.

Your Life is MORE Than a 30-Question Profile

The simple truth is that no computer can match you to scholarships as well as you can. You are a complex individual with a variety of passions, interests and goals. Nothing—person or machine—knows you better than you know yourself.

And think about that profile form. That's the only information the computer has about you. But what if you don't know all the answers? Are you really set on becoming an orthopedic surgeon, or did that just sound cool? Even worse, you are limited by the choices provided on that profile questionnaire. Imagine that you wrote a poem that was published in your town's community newspaper. Should you select "poet" as a future career? Will that trigger a great poetry scholarship? Or maybe under hobbies, you should select "writing and journalism"? Of course, that might trigger a flood of journalism scholarships that wouldn't apply to you. Or maybe, even though your school doesn't have a poetry club, you should still tell the computer that you are a member of one in order to trick it into showing you a sweet poetry award?

Do you see where we're going?

The very fact that you need to give the computer information about yourself while only using the choices the computer provides, without any clue about how those answers will affect your results, almost guarantees that you are going to miss out on some good scholarships. How do you know that because you answered a single question in the way that you did, that you are not missing out on some fantastic scholarship opportunities?

The answer is, you don't.

About Your Authors

What makes us qualified to write *The Ultimate Scholarship Book*? Primarily it's because at one time we were exactly where you are now. We needed money to pay for college, and scholarships turned out to be our only answer. Not only did we do pretty well (winning more than $100,000 in free cash for college) but since then, we've continued to help thousands of students do the same.

Here's our story:

Kelly grew up in Los Angeles and when she got accepted to Harvard (which costs about $70,000 per year!), her family just didn't have the money to pay for it. Gen grew up in Hawaii and faced a similar financial crunch when he got into Harvard. In fact, his father even tried to bribe him to attend his state university by offering him a new car if he would give up his idea of attending the ivy-league college. Even considering the cost of a brand new car, it would have been cheaper for Gen's family to make car payments than pay Harvard tuition!

Since we both had our hearts set on attending a very expensive college that our families could not afford, we had little choice but to become fanatics about applying for scholarships. While we made a lot of beginner mistakes and it was by no means a quick or easy process, we were ultimately successful in winning more than $100,000 in scholarships. It was only because of this money that we were able to attend Harvard and were both able to graduate from college debt free.

As you may have guessed by now, we met while at college. We were actually next door neighbors in the dorm, and we were married a few years after we graduated from Harvard. Knowing first-hand how hard it can be for families to pay for college, we decided to share what we had learned as a result of our own pursuits to find funds for tuition. Our first books were about how to win scholarships and get financial aid. In fact, you can find *1001 Ways to Pay for College* and *How to Write a Winning Scholarship Essay* in bookstores. But despite the success of these books, we found that whenever we spoke to groups of students or parents, the number one question they asked was, "Do you know of scholarships for such-and-such a student?"

At the same time, we were also noticing a growing dissatisfaction from students who only relied on websites for scholarship information. This was somewhat of a mystery to us since we knew of thousands of great scholarships that were available. Why weren't these awards being found? Why wasn't every student applying for these scholarships?

All of this led to our decision to build our own database of scholarships and publish the results in *The Ultimate Scholarship Book*. We have a team of researchers who help us investigate scholarships, verify awards and ensure that the scholarships that make it into the book are the best and most up-to-date possible.

So that's our story and why we feel so passionate about what we write in this book. It's not just a collection of words on paper; it's really the collective experience and intelligence of our own quest for scholarships along with thousands of hours of research by our scholarship staff.

How This Book Overcomes the Disadvantages of Websites

A book has certain advantages over websites; for example, a book can work for you without the necessity of input. In many ways, a book is more flexible than a computer site because you are not penalized for not having an answer to a specific question that is worded in a narrow and inflexible way. Likewise, you are not forced to fit yourself into a predetermined, inflexible category. A book also lets you do the matching, a tool which we have found to be far better than outsourcing that work to some machine.

The Ultimate Scholarship Book is designed to be browsed. Spend an hour with this book and you will be able to evaluate hundreds of scholarships quickly and efficiently. By scanning the descriptions, you (not some computer) can decide if you have the right combination of background, interests or skills to qualify. By seeing all of the possibilities, you remain in control of how you prioritize which awards are right for you.

Now it is true that this is a slower process than using a website. But the trade-off is that it is far more accurate, and accuracy is what it's all about. You're not trying to find hundreds of awards that you may or may not win. Who has time to apply for that many scholarships anyway?! Your goal is to find the best awards that you have highest chances of winning. So while you'll invest more time in the finding of scholarships by using a book, we guarantee that the payoff (which in this case is literally thousands of extra dollars in scholarships) will be worth it.

If the time aspect of using a book versus a website still bothers you, here's one more thought. You can use books practically anywhere—especially when you have downtime. In other words, you can transform the natural wasted time during your day into highly productive scholarship time.

A Dirty Secret of Websites: They're Out-of-Date

It's natural to assume that anything online is more current than something printed on paper. But is this really true? Use a few scholarship websites and you'll soon realize that many are horribly out of date. Does it make you angry? Do you want to demand a refund? Of course not! Most scholarship websites are free services! Now it is true that many so-called "free" websites do actually make money by reselling your information; and once they get this from your profile form, you are of little value to the site. This is very annoying. However, we digress. Our point is that as a free service, there is really very little incentive for the website to maintain a high level of accuracy in their data. You really do get what you pay for with most scholarship websites!

It's a lot different with a book. There are two strong incentives that ensure the data in this book is up-to-date and accurate. The first is that we know once we commit something to paper, it's permanent. That creates a very strong desire to get it right the first time. This degree of permanence—the finality of words on paper—is a huge responsibility for us. Once the book goes to press, it is very difficult and expensive to update a mistake. The second powerful incentive is that you're paying hard earned money for this book! It's not free. Because of this, you expect to receive only the best product. If we don't deliver, we'll hear from you!

Together, these two incentives guarantee that each award in this book has been checked and re-checked. We have a small army of researchers whose only job is to verify each award in the book before it goes to press. We also send out letters twice a year to every scholarship listed to ask the providers themselves to verify and update their information. The end result is that this book is extremely accurate and up-to-date.

We also never keep this book in print for longer than a year—which is what we have found to be the typical time in which scholarships change. So as long as you are buying this book new, you are guaranteed to have the latest information possible.

Given how diligent and thorough our researchers are and the rigorous process we apply to every award we publish, we would happily pit this book against any website!

Another Dirty Secret of Websites: They Don't Actually List Millions of Awards

Here's a controversial statement: Websites often claim to list millions of awards worth billions of dollars, but the truth is that these numbers are just marketing hype. To arrive at these numbers, the websites use the most liberal definitions possible. For example, the Coca-Cola Foundation awards $3 million per year to 150 high school seniors. So the website counts their single listing of the Coca-Cola Foundation Scholarship as being 150 awards valued at $3 million. Or consider that the Jack Kent Cooke Foundation awards forty scholarships for $40,000 each. The total value of $1.6 million is added to the website's sum even though you can only win up to $40,000 of this amount. The results are highly inflated numbers.

Now before we claim the high road in this debate, we have to admit that we do the exact same thing! Take a look at the front cover of this book. Our numbers are just as impressive as many scholarship websites. But unlike the websites, we don't hide reality. All you need to do is pick up our book and see how thick it is to know how many awards we have inside. But you can't do this with a website. There is no way to know (and the website will never tell you) how many actual awards they have. They want you to think that they have millions when in reality they often contain no more—and often much less—than what you'll find in this book!

The Bottom Line: Books Can Beat Websites

It should be obvious by now that we are just a little bothered when we hear that websites—just because they are online—are superior to books.

It's just not truc.

This is not to say that websites don't have any value. They absolutely do and inside this book, we list a number of websites that we think are worth your time. However, you need to understand that you must go beyond websites if you hope to find the best scholarships. In fact, you need to go beyond books too! The entire next chapter is dedicated to places in which to find scholarships other than books and websites. We highly recommend that you explore all these sources in order to find the best scholarships for you.

Why Choose *This* Book?

We know that there are other books that provide directories of scholarships, so why choose this one?

- Discover the best scholarships for you with awards in the humanities, academics, public service, extracurricular activities, talents, athletics, religion, ethnicity, social science and science based on career goals and more.
- Find scholarships that are not based on grades.
- Get all the information you need in one place with the application details, eligibility requirements, deadlines, contact information and website addresses.
- Find scholarships you can use at any college.
- Avoid wasting money on scholarship competitions that require a fee to enter.
- Save time and find the best scholarships that fit you with the easy-to-use indexes.
- Access the most up-to-date information that has been checked and double-checked.
- Learn not only how to find scholarships but how to win them! Get insider advice from judges and scholarship winners.

Common Scholarship Myths Busted

Now that we've cleared up some of the misconceptions about books and websites, let's debunk some of the common scholarship myths. We hate these myths because not only are they untrue, but they often prevent students from applying for scholarships.

Myth: You need to be financially destitute to be eligible to apply for scholarships.

Busted: While it is true that financial need is a consideration for some scholarships, the definition of "need" varies considerably. Given the cost of a college education, many families who consider themselves to be "middle class" actually qualify for some need-based scholarships. In addition, there are many scholarships where financial need is not even a factor. These "merit-based" scholarships are based on achievements, skills, career goals, family background and a host of other considerations that have nothing to do with a family's financial situation. You could actually be the son or daughter of Bill Gates and still win a "merit-based" scholarship.

Myth: You can only win scholarships as a high school senior.

Busted: It is never too early or too late to apply for scholarships. There are awards for students as young as seventh grade. If you win, the money is usually held in an account until it is time for you to actually go to college. But even if there are not as many awards for younger students as there are for seniors, it doesn't mean it's not important to look. Finding awards that you can apply for next year or even two years from now is a huge advantage. Keep a list of these awards since you are going to be super busy as a senior (think college apps and AP classes!) and you are going to be so thankful when you can just refer to your file of previously found awards and don't have to spend time searching. At the same time, you also don't want to stop applying for scholarships after you graduate from high school. There are many awards for college students. Once you are in college, you should continue to apply for scholarships, especially those geared toward specific majors and careers.

Myth: Only star athletes get college scholarships.

Busted: While star running backs receiving full-tuition scholarships are often what make the news, the majority of scholarships awarded by colleges are not for athletics. As you will see in this book, there are literally thousands of scholarships for those of us who don't know the difference between a touchdown and a touchback. Even if you are an athlete, you might also be surprised to know that many colleges give scholarships to student athletes who may not be destined to become the next Kevin Durant. The needs of a college's athletic program depend on the level of their competition. You may find that at one college your soccer skill wouldn't earn you a place on the team as a bench warmer; but at another school, you might not only be a starter but also earn a half-tuition scholarship.

Myth: You need straight A's to win money for college.

Busted: While straight A's certainly don't hurt, most students mistakenly assume that grades are the primary determinate for selecting scholarship winners. This is just not true. Most scholarships are based on criteria other than grades and reward specific skills or talents such as linguistic, athletic or artistic ability. Even for scholarships in which grades are considered, GPAs are often not the most important factor. What's more relevant is that you best match the qualities the scholarship committee seeks. Don't let the lack of a perfect transcript prevent you from applying for scholarships.

Myth: You should get involved in as many extracurricular activities as possible to win a scholarship.

Busted: Scholarship competitions are not pie eating contests where you win through volume. They are more like baking contests in which you create an exquisite dessert with an appearance and flavor that matches the tastes of the judges. Scholarships are won by quality, not quantity. Scholarship judges are looking for students who have made quality contributions. For example, for a public service scholarship, the judges would be more impressed if you organized a school-wide volunteer day than if you were a member of 20 volunteer organizations but did little to distinguish yourself in any one of them.

Myth: If you qualify for financial aid, you don't need to apply for scholarships.

Busted: Financial aid and scholarships are not mutually exclusive but complimentary. You need to do both—apply for financial aid and scholarships—at the same time! Relying only on financial aid is dangerous. First, financial aid is "need based" which means if you're a middle or upper middle class family, you may not receive any free money (i.e. grants) but only student loans which you need to pay back. Even if you do qualify for grants, it may not be enough. The maximum Pell Grant, for example, is $6,195 per year, which is still far short of what tuition plus room and board costs at most schools. While financial aid is important, we consider scholarships to be far superior. With few, if any, strings attached, scholarships represent free cash that does not have to be paid back and which you can use at almost any school. Best of all, you can win scholarships regardless of your family's income!

Myth: You should apply to every scholarship that you find.

Busted: When you turn 35, you technically are eligible to run for President of the United States. This hardly means you should start packing your bags for the White House. Let's apply that same logic to scholarships. Just because you are technically eligible for a scholarship does not mean you should start filling out the paperwork for it. Why? You have a limited amount of time to spend on scholarship applications. It is necessary to allocate your time to those that you have the best chance of winning. You may find that you are eligible for 500 scholarships. Unless you're willing to make applying to scholarships your full-time avocation, it's unlikely that you can apply for more than several dozen awards. Thus, you need to be selective about which scholarships fit you the best. One caveat: This does not mean that you should only apply to two or three scholarships. You should still apply to as many scholarships as you can—just make sure you have them prioritized.

How a Solid Scholarship Strategy Helps Win You Money

Back in high school, Kelly applied for a scholarship from her father's employer. She was confident she would win since academically she had both high grades and test scores—which she diligently listed on the application. After turning in her application, she eagerly waited for the check to arrive. But the check never came. In fact, when Kelly found out who did win, she was surprised to learn that he had lower grades and lower test scores. What happened? How did this guy win instead of Kelly?

The answer was that Kelly relied solely on grades and test scores to win while the other applicant clearly used the entire application to stand out. That was when Kelly learned the importance of having a strategy.

So what does it take to win a scholarship?

The answer is that scholarship winners are not superstars. Rather, they are the students who have prepared—those young men and women that have invested the time to create applications that highlight their strengths. It's really sad to see students who don't apply for scholarships because they mistakenly assume that they don't have a chance to win.

Unlike a lottery, scholarships are not based on luck. To win scholarships, you need to show the scholarship judges how you fit the award. Often this is through the scholarship application, essay and interview. In fact, almost all scholarship competitions come down to one key factor—how well you can show that you fit the purpose of the scholarship. In this respect, you have power over the outcome. Through what you choose to highlight (and ignore) in the scholarship application, you are able to construct a case for why you deserve to win.

In the following chapters we will lay out what we found to be the keys to a winning strategy. Now turn the page and let's get started!

Where to Find the Best Scholarships

chapter 2

Scholarships Beyond this Book

We know you bought this book because it's the largest and most up-to-date directory of scholarships available. However, we do want to show you how to find even more scholarships above and beyond the ones listed in this book.

We learned how to find scholarships through trial and often painful error. For example, when we first started to search for scholarships, we spent a lot of time tracking down scholarships that we later discovered were listed in our high school counseling office. But we did learn from each mistake and slowly developed an efficient strategy for finding scholarships.

Our approach to finding scholarships consists of two important steps. First, you must create a list of as many scholarships as possible that fit you. Second, once you have a big list of scholarships, prioritize the awards. Here is where you will do some detective work that will show you which scholarships are worth your time to fill out.

By following this two-step approach, you will end up with a prioritized list of scholarships that are closely matched to your background and achievements. So, even before you fill out a single scholarship application form, you will have greatly improved your chances of winning. Plus, you saved time by not wasting energy on awards that you won't win.

Start Your Scholarship Search in Your Own Backyard

When we began looking for scholarships, we made what is perhaps the biggest mistake of the novice scholarship hunter—we started by looking as far away as possible. We were mesmerized by the big prizes of the large (and often well-publicized) national awards. We thought, "If I won just one of these national scholarship competitions, I'd be set and could end my search." This turned out to be a big mistake and an even bigger time-waster. It seemed that everyone and his brother, sister and cousin were also applying to these competitions. The Coca-Cola scholarship competition, for example, receives more than 100,000 applications each year.

It turned out that the last place we looked for scholarships was our most lucrative source. Best of all, this place turned out to be in our own backyard!

What are backyard scholarships and where do you find them? Think about all the civic groups, clubs, businesses, churches and organizations in your community. Each of these is a potential source for scholarships. (If you are already in college, you have two communities: your hometown and the city in which you go to school.) Since these awards are usually only available to students in your community, the competition is a lot less fierce.

You may be thinking, "What good is a $500 Lions Club scholarship when my college costs 20 grand a year?" It's true that local scholarships don't award the huge prizes that some of the national competitions do. You already know that we won over $100,000 in scholarships. What we haven't told you is that the majority of this money came from local scholarships! We literally won $500 here and $1,500 there. By the time we graduated from Harvard and added up all the awards, it turned out to be a huge amount. Plus, some of the local scholarships that we won were "renewable," which meant that we received that money each year we were in college. So a $500 renewable scholarship was really worth $2,000 over four years.

If you still can't get excited because these local awards seem small compared to the cost of tuition, try this exercise: Take the amount of the award and divide it by the time you invested in the application. For the $500 Lions Club award, let's say that you spent one hour each night for three days to complete the application and write the essay. Take $500 and divide it by three hours. That works out to a little over $166 per hour. (Now imagine that the award was for $1,000 instead. That would make it $333 per hour!) Not bad by any measure. If you can find a job that pays you more than $166 an hour, then take it and forget applying to scholarships. If not, get back to applying for scholarships–even the little ones!

Let's get specific and look at all of the places in your backyard to find scholarships.

✓ High school counselor or college financial aid officer

If you are a high school student, start with your counselor. Ask if he or she has a list of scholarship opportunities. Most counselors have a binder filled with local scholarships. It's helpful if before your meeting, you prepare information about your family's financial background as well as special interests or talents you have that would make you eligible for scholarships. Don't forget that your own high school will have a variety of scholarships from such places as the parent-teacher organization, alumni group and athletic booster clubs.

If you are a college student, make an appointment with your school's financial aid office. Before the appointment, think about what interests and talents you have and what field you may want to enter after graduation. Take a copy of your Free Application for Federal Student Aid (FAFSA) as background (https://studentaid.ed.gov). Mention any special circumstances about your family's financial situation. Ask the financial aid officer for recommendations of scholarships offered by the college or by community organizations.

Also, if you have already declared a major, check with the department's administrative assistant or chair for any awards that you might be eligible to win.

It's important whenever you speak to a counselor (either in high school or college) that you inquire about any scholarships that require nomination. Often these scholarships are easier to win since the applicant pool is smaller. You have nothing to lose by asking, and if anything, it shows how serious you are about financing your education.

High school websites

You may not visit your school's website daily, but when you are looking for scholarships, it pays to search the site for lists of scholarships. Most high schools post scholarship opportunities for students on their websites. (You may have to dig down a few levels to find this list.)

Other high school websites

If your school does not post scholarship opportunities, surf over to the websites of other high schools in the area. You'll find that many offer a wealth of scholarship resources.

Nearby colleges

While your college has great scholarship resources, wouldn't it be great if you had double or triple these resources? You can. Simply seek the resources of other local colleges. Ask permission first, but you'll find that most neighboring schools are more than willing to help you. If you are in high school, nothing prevents you from visiting a local college and asking for scholarship information. Because you are a prospective student, the college will often be happy to provide whatever assistance it can.

Student clubs and organizations

Here's a reason to enjoy your extracurricular activities even more. One benefit of participating may be a scholarship sponsored by the organization. Inquire with the officers or advisors of the organization about scholarship funds. Bands, newspapers, academic clubs, athletic organizations and service organizations often have scholarships that are awarded to outstanding members. If the organization has a national parent organization (e.g. National Honor Society) visit the national organization website. There are often awards that are given by the parent organization for members of local chapters.

Community organizations

Maybe you've wondered why community organizations have so many breakfast fundraisers—one reason is that some provide money for scholarships.

You usually don't have to be a member of these organizations to apply. In fact, many community groups sponsor scholarships that are open to all students who live in the area. As we have mentioned, college students really have two communities: their hometown and where they go to college. Don't neglect either of these places.

How do you find these organizations? Many local government websites list them. Visit the websites for your town, city and state. Also visit or call your community association or center. You can search online to look up organizations and a calendar of annual events that are sponsored by various civic groups. Finally, don't forget to pay a visit to the public library and ask the reference librarian for help. Here is a brief list of some of the more common civic groups to track down:

- Altrusa
- American Legion and American Legion Auxiliary
- American Red Cross
- Association of Junior Leagues International
- Boys and Girls Clubs
- Boy Scouts and Girl Scouts
- Circle K
- Civitan
- Elks Club
- Lions Club
- 4-H Clubs
- Fraternal Order of Eagles
- Friends of the Library
- Kiwanis International
- Knights of Columbus
- National Exchange Club
- National Grange
- Optimist International
- Performing Arts Center
- Rotary Club
- Rotaract and Interact
- Ruritan
- Sertoma International

- Soroptimist International of the Americas
- U.S. Jaycees
- USA Freedom Corps
- Veterans of Foreign Wars
- YMCA and YWCA
- Zonta International

Local businesses

Businesses like to return some of their profits to employees and students in the community. Many offer scholarships as a way to reward students who both study and work. Ask your manager if your employer has a scholarship fund and how you can apply. Some companies—particularly large conglomerates that have offices, distributorships or factories in your community—offer scholarships that all students in the community are eligible to win. Check with the chamber of commerce for a list of the largest companies in the area. You can call the public relations or community outreach department in these companies to inquire about any scholarship opportunities. Visit the large department and chain stores in the area and ask the store manager or customer service manager about scholarships.

Parents' employer

Your parents may hate their jobs, but they'll love the fact that many companies award scholarships to the children of employees as a benefit. They should speak with someone in the human resources department or with their direct managers about scholarships and other educational programs offered by their company.

Parents' or grandparents' military service

If your parents or grandparents served in the U.S. Armed Forces, you may qualify for a scholarship from a military association. Each branch of the service and even specific divisions within each branch have associations. Speak with your parents and grandparents about their military service and see if they belong to or know of these military associations.

Your employer

Flipping burgers may have an up side. Even if you work only part-time, you may qualify for an educational scholarship given by your employer. For example, McDonald's offers the National Employee Scholarship to reward the accomplishments of its student-employees. If you have a full- or part-time job, ask your employer about scholarships.

Parents' union

Don't know if your parents are in a union? Ask and find out. Some unions sponsor scholarships for the children of their members. Ask your parents to speak with the union officers about scholarships and other educational programs sponsored by their union.

Interest clubs

Performing arts centers, city orchestras, equestrian associations and amateur sports leagues are just a few of the many special interest clubs that may offer scholarships. While some limit their awards to members, many simply look for students who are interested in what they support. A city performing arts center, for example, may offer an award for a talented performing artist in the community.

Professional sports teams

They may not have won a World Series since the 1950s, but don't discount them as a viable scholarship source. Many local professional athletic teams offer community awards (and not necessarily for athletes) as a way to contribute to the cities in which they are based.

Church or religious organizations

Religious organizations may provide scholarships for members. If you or your parents are members of a religious organization, check with the leaders to see if a scholarship is offered.

Local government

Some cities and counties provide scholarships specifically designated for local students. Often, local city council members and state representatives sponsor a scholarship fund. Even if you didn't vote for them, call their offices and ask if they offer a scholarship.

Local newspaper

Local newspapers often print announcements about students who win scholarships. Keep a record of the scholarships featured or go to the library or look online at back issues of the newspaper. Check last year's spring issues (between March and June) for announcements of scholarship recipients. Contact the sponsoring organizations to see if you're eligible to enter the next competition.

Is There a Magic Number of Scholarships?

We often are asked, "How many scholarships should I apply to?" The truth is that there is no magic number of scholarships for which you should apply. But you should avoid the extremes. Don't select only a couple of scholarships with the intention of spending countless hours crafting the perfect application. While it is true that to win you need to turn in quality applications, there is also a certain amount of subjective decision making. So even with the perfect application, you may not win. This means that you need to apply to more than a few scholarships. On the other hand, don't apply for 75 awards, sending in the same application to each. You'll just waste your time. You need to strike a balance between quantity and quality.

Searching Beyond Your Backyard

Once you have exhausted the opportunities in the community, it is time to broaden your search. Although the applicant pool is often larger with national awards, you shouldn't rule them out. Because many national award programs have marketing budgets, finding these awards may actually be easier than local awards. Most national awards will be advertised and the following places will help you track them down:

Internet

Forget the time-wasting social networks, and let's use the Internet for something productive. We recommend that you use as many online scholarship databases as possible as long as they are free. There are enough quality free databases that you should not have to pay for any online search. Here are a few we recommend:

- SuperCollege (www.supercollege.com)
- moolahSPOT (www.moolahspot.com)
- Sallie Mae (www.salliemae.com/scholarships)
- FastWeb (www.fastweb.com)
- CollegeXpress (www.collegexpress.com)
- The College Board (www.collegeboard.com)
- Scholarships.com (www.scholarships.com)
- AdventuresinEducation (www.adventuresineducation.org)
- CollegeNet (www.collegenet.com)

Just remember that while many online databases claim to have billions of dollars in scholarships listed, they represent only a tiny fraction of what is available. We have personally used nearly every free scholarship database on the Internet and know from experience that none of them (including our own at www.supercollege.com) lists every scholarship that you might win. Think of these databases as starting points, and remember that they are not the only places to find awards.

Professional associations

There is an association for every profession you can imagine. Whether you want to be a doctor, teacher or helicopter pilot, there are professional organizations that exist not only to advance the profession, but also to encourage students to enter that field by awarding grants and scholarships.

To find these associations, contact people who are already in the profession. If you think you want to become a computer programmer, ask computer programmers about the associations to which they belong. Also look at the trade magazines that exist for the profession since they have advertisements for various professional organizations.

Another way to find associations is through books like *The Encyclopedia of Associations*. This multi-volume set found at most college libraries lists nearly every professional association in the United States. Once you find these associations, contact them or visit their websites to see if they offer scholarships.

Professional associations often provide scholarships for upper-level college students, graduate school or advanced training. But even high school students who know what they want to do after college can find money from associations.

Big business

If you've never received a personal "thank you" from large companies like Coca-Cola, Tylenol or Microsoft, here it is. A lot of these have charitable foundations that award scholarships. Companies give these awards to give something back to the community (and the positive PR sure doesn't hurt either). When you visit company websites, look for links to their foundations, which often manage the scholarship programs.

Many companies offer similar types of scholarships. What if you're a student film maker? Think about all the companies that make money or sell products to you from cameras to editing software to tripods. Are you into industrial music? What special equipment or instruments do you use? Consider the companies that will benefit from more people using their products and services. Some companies also offer awards to attract future employees. For example, Microsoft, the software company, sponsors a scholarship program for student programmers. Be sure to investigate companies that employ people in your field of study—especially if it is highly competitive—to see if they offer scholarships.

Colleges

You may think that checks only travel from your pocket to your college to pay for tuition. But colleges actually give a lot of money to students. Some of this money comes from the college itself while other money is from generous donations of alumni. Every college administers a number of scholarships, some based on financial need and some based on merit. What many students don't know is that often a student's application for admission is also used by the college to determine if he or she may win a scholarship. This is one reason it is worth the submission of any optional essay suggested on a college application. Even if the essay does not impact your admission, it could be used to award you some scholarship dollars.

Don't Look for Scholarships Alone

One of the biggest mistakes we made when looking for scholarships was that we did so alone. Maybe we didn't want to share what we found with our friends and thereby increase competition, or perhaps we just didn't see the benefits of working in groups. Whatever the reason, it probably cost us a ton of money.

Since then we've met thousands of students who have won scholarships. Of these the most successful are those who did not look for scholarships alone. In fact, they made it the biggest group project imaginable.

Take for example the three guys we met in Los Angeles. Essentially, all three young men are going to college for free because they were able to win way more money than they could ever use! How did they do it? They formed a "scholarship group". Every Saturday morning they met at Starbucks and one of their parents agreed to pick up the tab for Frappuccinos. The only rule was that each had to bring at least two new scholarships. What happened was that one guy might find an award that was not right for him but was perfect for someone else in the group. This sharing of information was a tremendous advantage over laboring individually and literally tripled their chances of finding scholarships.

Another benefit was that working in a group kept these guys motivated. There certainly must have been weeks when searches were fruitless and the scholarship pickings were slim. The guys might have been tempted to give up, but being in a group brings with it a sense of responsibility not to disappoint the other members of the unit. Searching for scholarships alone is very difficult and it's so easy to just quit. But when you work in a group, you keep one another motivated and you have a natural support base that keeps you going when you feel like quitting.

So did these guys increase the competition by sharing scholarships? In some cases they did. But this was far outweighed by the sheer number of scholarships that they found collectively that they never would have found working alone.

As a general rule, students who worked with others discovered that by sharing the awards they found and pooling their resources, they were able to find more scholarships in less time than they would have found individually. The end result was that these students had more scholarships to apply to and more time to focus on their applications. Hence, they won more money.

Let this be a lesson to all of us. Look around you and find others who are also hunting for scholarships. Convince them that the way to really win lots of free money for college is to work in groups.

Prioritize the Scholarships You Find

Until now, we have focused on where to find scholarships. If you invest time exploring these areas, you should have a fairly long list of potential scholarships. It may be tempting to start cranking out applications. We actually have a name for the methodology used by students that apply to anything and everything they find—it's called the "shotgun" approach and it never works. Just because you find an award for which you qualify does not mean that you should immediately apply. You want to focus your energies (and limited time) only on those awards that you have the best chance of winning.

It would save a lot of time if you knew beforehand which scholarships you'd win and which you wouldn't. With this information, you'd only spend time applying for the scholarships that you knew would result in cash in your pocket. While there is no way to be 100 percent certain that you'll win any scholarship, you can do some research and make an educated guess.

Here are the steps you should take with each scholarship to determine if you have a reasonable chance of winning it. By prioritizing your list based on these criteria, you'll be able to focus time on awards that you have the best odds of winning while not wasting time on the ones where being a match is a long shot.

Step 1 Learn the Purpose

Nobody, and we mean nobody, gives away money without a reason. Every sponsor of a scholarship has a concrete reason for giving away their hard-earned cash to students like you. For example, a teachers' organization might award a scholarship to encourage students to enter the teaching profession. An environmental group might sponsor a scholarship with the purpose of promoting environmental awareness, or it might reward students who have done environmental work in school. A local bank might give money to a student who has done a great deal of public service as a way to give back to the community in which it does business.

Your job is to uncover the purpose of every scholarship on your list. If you're lucky, it will be stated in the description of the award. Look at the eligibility requirements to see what kind of questions the scholarship sponsors are asking. Is there a GPA requirement? If there is and it's relatively high, academic achievement is probably important. If the GPA requirement is low, then grades are probably not important. Does the application ask for a list of extracurricular activities? If so, they are probably a significant part of the selection criteria. Do you need to submit an essay on a specific topic or a project to demonstrate proficiency in a field of study? All these requirements are clues about what the scholarship judges think will (and won't) be important.

For example, the sole purpose of a public service scholarship may be to reward a student's philanthropic acts. If that is the case, the application will most likely be focused on descriptions of a student's selfless deeds. On the other hand, a scholarship given by a major corporation may be based on a combination of grades, leadership and character.

If you cannot determine the purpose of the scholarship by reading its description and eligibility requirements, then you need to look for the purpose of the group that sponsors the award. For example, even if the scholarship description does not directly state it, you can be sure that an award given by an organization that is composed of local physicians will probably prefer that the winner have a connection with medicine or an intention to enter the medical field.

The membership of the organization can be a big clue. Just as your friends are a reflection of who you are, most clubs and organizations want to reach students who are similar to their membership. If you don't know much about the organization, contact them to learn background information regarding the history, purpose or contributions of the group. Visit the organization's website. Read their brochures or publications. The more you know about why the organization is giving the award, the better you'll understand how you may or may not fit.

Somewhere on your list of potential scholarships, note in a few words its purpose. You'll be using this information in the next step which is to determine if you can make a case that you are the type of person the scholarship committee is looking for.

Beware of Scholarship Scams

While the great majority of scholarship providers and services have philanthropic intentions, not all do. There are some scholarship services and even scholarships themselves that you need to avoid. According to the Federal Trade Commission, in one year there were more than 175,000 cases reported of scholarship scams, costing consumers $22 million. And this is a low estimate since most scholarship scams go unreported!

While we were fortunate to have not been victims of a scholarship scam, we have to admit that the offers we received were tempting. We both received letters in high school and college from companies that promised to help us find and win "unclaimed" scholarships. The pitch was tempting: There is money out there that no one is claiming. All we needed to do was purchase their service to get a list of these awards. Had we done so, we would have been $400 poorer and certainly none the richer. In this chapter, we will describe some of the common scams that you may encounter. You must avoid these offers, no matter how glamorous they seem.

The key to avoiding a scholarship scam is to understand the motivation of the people behind these scams. Those who operate financial aid rip-offs know that paying for college is something that makes you extremely nervous. They also know that most people don't have extensive experience when it comes to scholarships and may therefore believe that there are such things as "hidden" or "unclaimed" scholarships. These charlatans take advantage of your fears and discomfort by offering an easy answer with a price tag that seems small compared to the promised benefits. Be aware that you are vulnerable to these kinds of inducements. Think about it this way. If you have a weakness for buying clothes, you need to be extra vigilant when you are at the shopping mall. Similarly, because you need money for college, you are more susceptible to tempting scholarship offers. Acknowledging that these fears make you a target of scam artists is the first step to spotting their traps.

Step 2 Think Like a Judge

Once you know the purpose of the scholarship, you need to see if you are a match for the organization that sponsors it. At this point students often make one of two mistakes. Either they 1) overestimate how well they fit the purpose or, more commonly, 2) underestimate their qualifications and don't apply. After working with thousands of students, we have learned that students more often underestimate their abilities than overestimate. Try to be realistic, but also don't sell yourself short. Remember that scholarship judges are not looking for the perfect match. There are a lot of factors that will influence their decision, and many of these things—like personality, character and motivation—are difficult to measure.

Let's look at an example. If you are your school's star journalist, naturally you should apply for journalism scholarships. But if all you have done is write a single letter to the editor, then spend your time applying to scholarships that better match what you have accomplished. You can still apply for a journalism scholarship, especially if you only recently realized that you want to become a journalist, but you will be at a disadvantage compared to the other applicants and therefore should prioritize this award below other awards on your to-do list.

As you go through your list of scholarships, move to the bottom those which are the weakest matches to the goal of the scholarships. Make those awards that fit you best your highest priority. These are the ones that you want to focus on first.

Step 3 Take a Reality Check

Scholarship deadlines are not like tax deadlines, where there is a single day when all forms are due. The deadlines for scholarships vary. Be aware of these crucial dates. Unless you plan carefully, you may miss out on a scholarship simply because you don't have the time to create a decent application. Sandwiched among studying, sleeping and everything else in your busy life, there is limited time to spend on applying for scholarships. If you find a great scholarship that is due next week but requires a yet to-be-written original composition that would take a month, you should probably pass on the competition. If you know that, given the amount of time available, you won't be able to do an acceptable job, it's better to pass and move on to awards in which you have the time to put together a winning application. Remember too that you may be able to apply for the award next year.

Review Your List Daily

After you prioritize your scholarships with the ones you feel fit you best at the top of the list, push yourself to apply to as many as you can, working from top to bottom. You probably won't get to the end. This is okay since you have the least chance of winning the awards at the bottom anyway. By prioritizing and working methodically down your list, you will have hedged your bets by making sure that your first applications are for the scholarships that you have the best chance of winning while also not limiting yourself to only a handful of awards.

How to Win the Scholarships You Find

Chapter 3

Attacking the Scholarship Application

At first glance, scholarship applications look easy—most are only a single page in length. Piece of cake, right? Don't let their diminutive size fool you. The application is a vital part of winning any scholarship. Scholarship judges must sift through hundreds or even thousands of applications, and the application form is what they use to determine which applicants continue to the next stage. It's crucial that you ace your application to make this first cut.

In this chapter, we'll look at strategies you can use to transform an ordinary scholarship application form into a screaming testament of why you deserve to win free cash for college.

Five Steps to Crafting a Winning Application

Step 1 Strategically Choose What to List

Imagine that you need to give a speech to two groups of people. Without knowing who your audience is, you would have a difficult time composing a speech that would appeal to them, right? It would make a huge difference if one were a group of mathematicians and the other a group of fashion designers. To grab the attention of each of these audiences, you'd need to adjust your speech accordingly. References to mathematical theorems would hardly go over well with the designers, just as the mathematicians probably couldn't care less about how black the "new" black really is.

In much the same way, you need to decide what to highlight on your scholarship application based on the purpose of the award. When you know what the scholarship judges are looking for, it makes it easier to decide what to include or omit. As we mentioned earlier, organizations don't give away scholarships and expect nothing in return. Behind their philanthropic motives lies an ulterior motive—to promote their organization's purpose. If you prioritized your list of scholarships correctly, you've already uncovered the purpose for each award. Now look at all your activities, interests, hobbies and achievements. Ask yourself which ones fit the purpose of each award and would make a positive impression on the scholarship judges.

Let's imagine that you are applying for an award given by an organization of professional journalists. In visiting their website, you learn that print and broadcast journalists join this group because they are passionate about the profession of journalism and want to encourage public awareness about the importance of a free press. Immediately, you know that you need to highlight those experiences that demonstrate your zeal for journalism and, if applicable, your belief in the value of a free press.

Among your activities and accomplishments are the following:

- Soccer team captain
- Vice President of the Writers' Club
- Key Club treasurer
- Columnist for your high school newspaper
- English essay contest winner
- Summer job working at a pet store
- Summer internship at a radio station

As you look at this list, you can eliminate some activities outright. Your involvement on the soccer team, with the Key Club, and your job at the pet store are not relevant and don't show how you fit with the purpose of the scholarship.

However, even looking at what's left, you still have to decide which ones to list first. As you think about the purpose of the scholarship, you remember that in the Writers' Club you participated in a workshop that helped a local elementary school start its own newspaper. Since this achievement almost perfectly matches the mission of our hypothetical journalism organization, use your limited space in the application to list it first and to add an explanation.

You might write something like this:

```
Writers' Club, Vice President, organized "Writing Counts"
workshop at Whitman Elementary School, which resulted in the
launch of the school's first student-run newspaper.
```

Think of the impact this would have on the scholarship judges. "Look here, Mark!" one journalist on the judging committee would say. "This student does what we do! Definitely someone we should interview!"

When choosing accomplishments to list, don't be afraid to eliminate any that don't fit—even good ones. You have limited space in which to cram a lot of information. As you fill out the application, you may find that you are trying to squeeze in too many details or simply too many things. You need to be ruthless in trimming down what you submit to the judges. Make sure to include the accomplishments that *best fit* the purpose of the award.

At the same time you are picking which things to include in your application, be sure to also be aware of what might be offensive to the organization's members. Just imagine what would happen if you thoughtlessly mentioned that you were the author of an economics project entitled "How Labor Unions Make the U.S. Unable to Compete and Lower Our Standard of Living" to judges who are members of the International Brotherhood of Teamsters.

Clearly you can't use the same list of activities and accomplishments for every scholarship. You must take the time to craft a unique list that matches what each of the scholarships is intended to reward.

Create a Timeline

Every scholarship has a deadline. Even though you have created a prioritized list of awards, you need also be aware of the deadlines. In fact, the due date for an award may also influence how you prioritize it. It's also helpful to set yourself deadlines and create a schedule for applying. Set deadlines for when you will have the application forms completed, essays written and any required recommendations submitted. Post this schedule where you can see it every day. We also recommend that you share it with your parents. Moms and dads are great at nagging (we mean reminding) you to meet deadlines, so you might as well use their nagging (we mean motivating) skills to your advantage.

Step 2 List Important Accomplishments First

In movies, the most dare-devilish car chase, the most harrowing showdown and the most poignant romantic revelations are usually saved until the end. While this works for Hollywood, it does not for scholarship applications. Since scholarship judges review so many applications and the space on the form is limited, you must learn to highlight your most impressive points first.

If you have listed four extracurricular activities, assume that some judges won't read beyond the first two. This doesn't mean that all judges will be this rushed, but there are always some who are. It's extremely important that you prioritize the information that you present and rank your accomplishments according to the following criteria—which should not come as too much of a surprise.

Fit: The most important factor in ordering your achievements is how they fit with the purpose of the scholarship. This is, after all, why these kind people want to hand you some free dough. Emphasize accomplishments that match the purpose of the scholarship. If you are applying for an award that rewards athleticism, stress how well you've done in a particular sport before listing your volunteer activities.

Scope: Next prioritize your accomplishments by their scope, or how much of an impact they have made. How many people have been affected by your work? To what extent has your accomplishment affected your community? Did your contribution produce measurable results? In simple terms, put the big stuff before the small stuff.

Uniqueness: Since your application will be compared to those of perhaps thousands of others, include accomplishments that are uncommon. Give priority to those that are unique or difficult to win. Being on your school's honor roll is certainly an achievement, but it is an honor that many others have received. Try to select honors that fewer students have received—you want to stand out in order to be selected.

Timeliness: This is the least-important criterion, but if you get stuck and aren't sure how to arrange some of your accomplishments, put the more recent achievements first. Having won an election in the past year is more relevant than having won one three years ago. Some students ask us if they should list junior high or even elementary school achievements. Generally, stick to accomplishments from high school if you're a high school student and to college if you're a college student. An exception is if your accomplishment is extremely impressive and relevant—such as publishing your own book in the eighth grade. Of course, if you run out of recent achievements and there is still space on the form, go ahead and reach back to the past—but try to limit yourself to only one or two items.

You want your application to be as unforgettable as the best Hollywood movies. The only difference between your work and Spielberg's—besides the millions of dollars—is that you need to place the grand finale first.

You Can Recycle Your Applications

The first scholarship for which you apply will take the most time. But with each application you complete, it will get easier. This is because for each successive application, you can draw on the materials you developed for the previous one. To complete your first application, you need to think about your activities and recall achievements that you have forgotten. If there is an essay component, you will need to find a topic and craft an articulate essay. When you work on your second application, you can benefit from the work you've already done for the first. As you're building your timeline, look for scholarships in which you can recycle information from one application to another.

Recycling will save you time. In addition, you can improve on your work each time that you use it. For example, the second time you answer a question about your plans after graduation, you can craft your response more effectively than the first. As you recycle information, don't just reuse it—improve it!

Step 3 Spin Your Application to Impress the Judges

Politicians are notorious for telling voters what they want to hear. Good politicians never lie, but they do put a flattering "spin" on their words depending on whom they're addressing. While you must never lie on your application forms, you do want to present yourself in the best possible way so that you appeal to your audience. In other words, employ a little spin.

We know that some politicians have a difficult time distinguishing between lying and spinning. You shouldn't. Let's say you are applying for a scholarship that rewards students who are interested in promoting literacy. You have been a volunteer at your local library where, aside from typical page duties each week, you also read stories to a dozen children for story time. Here are three ways you could describe this activity on your application:

Non-spin description:

```
Library volunteer.
```

Lie:

```
Library reading program founder. Started a national program
that reaches thousands of children every day to promote
literacy.
```

Spin:

```
Library volunteer. Promoted literacy among children through
weekly after-school reading program at public library.
```

At one extreme, you can see that a lie exaggerates well beyond the truth. At the other extreme, the non-spin description is not very impressive because it does not explain how the activity relates to the purpose of the scholarship. The spin version is just right. It does not stretch the truth, but it does make clear how this activity fits within the context of the purpose of the scholarship. It focuses on what is important to the judges while at the same time, it ignores other aspects of your job that are not relevant—such as shelving books.

To take this example one step further, let's say that now you are applying for a scholarship that rewards student leaders. One of your other responsibilities as a library volunteer is to maintain the schedule for volunteers and help with the recruitment of new volunteers. Your description for this scholarship might read something like this:

```
Library volunteer. In charge of volunteer schedule and re-
cruitment of new members.
```

Notice how you have "spun" your activity so that it highlights a different aspect of what you did and better shows the judges how you fit their criteria. In the application, you should use the opportunity to spin your accomplishments to match the purpose of the award.

To be able to spin effectively, you need to know your audience. When you prioritized your scholarships earlier, you should have discovered the purpose of each scholarship. Remember that in most cases the scholarship judges want to give their money to students who are the best reflections of themselves. For example, the Future Teachers of America judges will want to fund students who seem the most committed to pursuing a teaching career. The American Congress of Surveying and Mapping judges, on the other hand, want to award their money to students who have the strongest interest in cartography.

Step 4 Write to Impress

The inspiring words of Martin Luther King Jr.'s "I Have a Dream" speech were punctuated with his dramatic, emotion-filled voice, hopeful expression and confident presence. His delivery would not have been as forceful had he spoken in a drab, monotone, with hands stuffed into his pockets and eyes lowered to avoid contact with the audience. Nor would his dramatic presentation have been as effective had his message been unimportant. The lesson? Both content and delivery count. While you don't have the opportunity for person-to-person delivery with your scholarship applications, you can and should present information in a compelling way. Here are some time-tested writing strategies for creating a positive impression through your applications:

Showcase Your Smarts. There's a reason why your parents wanted you to study and do well in school. In addition to the correlation between studying and success in college, almost all scholarship judges (even those of athletic awards) are impressed by academic achievement. College is, after all, about learning (at least that's what you want your parents to believe).

As you are completing your applications, keep in mind that while you may be applying for a public service scholarship, you should also include at least one academic achievement. For example, it does not hurt to list on an athletic scholarship form that you also came in second place at the science fair. This should not be the first thing you list, but it should be included somewhere to show the committee that you have brains in addition to brawn.

Extracurricular Activities and Hobbies Show Your Passion. If your only activity were studying, your life would be severely lacking in excitement. Scholarship organizers recognize this and thus the criteria for many scholarships include extracurricular activities or hobbies. Scholarship committees want evidence that you do more than read textbooks, take exams and watch

Youtube. They want to know that you have other interests. This makes you a more well-rounded person.

As always, when completing your applications, select extracurricular activities and hobbies that fit with the scholarship's mission. If you are applying for a music scholarship, describe how you've been involved in your school's orchestra or how you've taken violin lessons. By showing that you not only have taken classes in music theory but have also been involved with music outside of your studies, the scholarship committee will get a more complete picture of your love for music. Remember to use your activities and hobbies to illustrate your passion for a subject.

Leadership Is Always Better Than Membership. If you've ever tried to motivate a group of peers to do anything (without taking the easy way out—bribery) you know that it takes courage, intelligence and creativity to be a leader. Because of this, many scholarships give extra points to reward leadership. Scholarship judges want to know that the dollars will be awarded to someone who will not only make a difference in the future but who will also be a leader and motivate others to do the same. Think of it this way: If you were a successful businessperson trying to encourage entrepreneurship, wouldn't you want to give your money to a young person who is not only an entrepreneur but who also motivates others to become entrepreneurs?

Describing leadership in your activities or hobbies will also help set you apart from the other applicants. Many students are involved with environmental groups, but what if you are the only one to actually help increase recycling on your campus? Wouldn't that make your application a standout?

To show scholarship judges that you are a leader, list any activities in which you took responsibility for a specific project. Use action verbs when describing your work:

- Organized band fundraiser to purchase new instruments
- Led a weeklong nature tour in Yosemite Valley
- Founded first website to list volunteer activities
- Directed independent musical performance

Remember that you don't need to be an elected officer to be a leader. Many students have organized special projects, led teams or helped run events. Even if you didn't have an official title, you can include these experiences. Here's an example:

```
Environmental Action Committee Member. Spearheaded subcom-
mittee on reducing waste and increasing recycling on campus.
```

When describing your leadership, include both formal and informal ways you have led groups. This shows the scholarship committee that you are a worthy investment.

Honors and Awards Validate Your Strengths. There's a reason why all trophies are gold and gaudy. They shout to the world in a deafening roar, "Yes, this glittery gold miniature figure means I am the best!" For applications that ask for your honors and awards, impart some of that victorious roar and attitude. In no way are we recommending that you ship your golden statuettes off with your applications. We are saying that you should highlight honors and awards in a way that gets the scholarship committee to pay attention to your application. What makes an award impressive is scope. Not a minty mouthwash, scope in this case is the impact and influence of the award. You worked for the award and earned every golden inch of it. Show the committee that they don't just hand these statuettes out to anybody. One way to do this is to point out how many awards are given:

```
English Achievement Award. Presented to two outstanding ju-
niors each year.
```

By itself, the English Achievement Award does not tell the scholarship committee very much. Maybe half the people in your class were given the award. By revealing the scope of the award (particularly if it was given to only a few) it becomes much more impressive.

In competitions that reach beyond your school, it is important to qualify your awards. For example, while everyone at your school may know that the Left Brain Achievement Award is given to creative art students, the rest of the world does not.

Don't write:

```
Left Brain Achievement Award.
```

Do write:

```
Left Brain Achievement Award. Recognized as an outstanding
creative talent in art as conferred upon by vote of art de-
partment faculty.
```

You've worked hard to earn the honors and awards that you have received, and you should not hesitate to use them in your applications to help you win scholarships.

Know when to leave a space blank. An official mom rule from childhood is this: "If you don't have anything nice to say, don't say it." While this is a good lesson on self-restraint, it does not always hold true for scholarship applications. In general, it is not a good idea to leave any area blank. You don't need to fill the entire space, but you should make an effort to list something in every section. However, before you try to explain how the handmade certificate that your mom presented you for being Offspring of the Year qualifies as an "award," realize that there are limits. If you've never held a job, don't list anything under work experience. If, however, you painted your grandmother's house one summer and got paid for it, you might consider listing it if you don't have any other options.

Perfect every sentence. Succinct and terse, scholarship application forms bear the well-earned reputation for having less space than you need. Often offering only a page or less, scholarship and award forms leave little room for much more than just the facts. As you are completing your applications, remember to abbreviate where appropriate and keep your sentences short. Often judges are scanning the application form. If they want an essay, they will ask for one. However, you do not want to take instructions so literally that you miss their intent. For instance, if the instructions say to list your awards, don't feel like you can't add explanation if you need to. And, as always, be selective in what you list. If you have three great awards, it is better to use your space to list those three with short explanations rather than cram in all 15 awards that you've won in your life. (No argument can be made for the timeliness of your Perfect Attendance Award from kindergarten.) You are trying to present the most relevant information that shows the scholarship judges why you deserve their money. Use the space to explain how each award, job or activity relates to the scholarship.

Also, feel free to interpret some instructions. Work experience does not have to be limited to traditional jobs. Maybe you started your own freelance design business or cut lawns on the weekends—those count! The same goes for leadership positions. Who said that leadership has to be an elected position within an organization? Just be sure to explain the entry if the relationship is not totally clear. Here's an example:

```
Volunteer Wilderness Guide. Led clients through seven-day
trek in Catskills. Responsible for all aspects of the trip
including group safety.
```

Always remember that the application is you. A scholarship application is more than just a form. In the eyes of the scholarship judges, it is *you*. It may not be fair, but in many cases the application is the only thing that the judges will have as a measurement standard. The last thing you want to be is a dry list of academic and extracurricular achievements. You are a living, breathing person. Throughout the application, take every opportunity—no matter how small—to show the judges who you really are. Use descriptions and vocabulary that reveal your passion and commitment. Always remember that the application is a reflection of you.

Step 5 Separate Yourself from the Competition

Think of the scholarship competition as a reverse police lineup where you want to stand out and be picked by the people behind the one-way mirror. You want the judge to say without hesitation, "That's the one!" The only way this will happen is if your application is noticed and doesn't get lost in the stack. One of the best ways to accomplish this is to know what you're up against—in other words, think about who else will be in the lineup with you.

Try to anticipate your competition—even if it's just an educated guess. Depending on to whom the scholarship is offered, you may have a limited or broad pool of competitors. If the award is confined to your school, you may know everyone who will enter on a first-name basis. If it's national, all you may know is that all the applicants have a similar interest in a broad field. For a medical scholarship, for instance, the applicants might be students interested in becoming doctors or nurses. More important than the scope of the competition is the type of students who will apply. One of the biggest challenges in any competition is to break away from the pack. If 500 pre-med students are applying for a $10,000 scholarship from a medical association, you need to make sure that your application stands out from those of the 499 other applicants. If you are lucky, you may have done something that few have done. (Inventing a new vaccine in your spare time would certainly set you apart!) Unfortunately, most of us will have to distinguish ourselves in more subtle ways, such as through the explanation of our activities and accomplishments.

Say you are applying for a scholarship given by a national medical association that seeks to promote the medical sciences. It just so happens that you are considering a pre-med major and you have interned at a local hospital. If you hadn't read this book, you might have listed under activities something like this entry:

```
Summer Internship at Beth Israel Children's Hospital.
```

But you did read this book! So you know that this is a great activity to elaborate on since it demonstrates your commitment to medicine and shows that you truly are interested in entering the medical field. You also know that you need to stand out from the competition; and as great as this activity is, you know that a lot of other applicants also will have volunteered at hospitals. So instead of simply listing the internship, you add detail to make the experience more unique. You could write it this way:

```
Summer Internship at Beth Israel Children's Hospital; as-
sisted with clinical trial of new allergy medication.
```

This description is much more unique and memorable. By providing details, you can illustrate to the judges how your volunteer work is different from that of other students. Remember that you can add short descriptions in most applications even if the instructions do not explicitly ask for them.

If you can anticipate who your competition will be and what they might write in their applications, you will be able to find a way to go one step further to distinguish yourself from the crowd. Even the simple act of adding a one-sentence description to an activity can make the difference between standing out or being overlooked.

Now that you know the five steps to insure that your application is a winner, here is our Top Ten list of application form do's and don'ts which will serve as a final reminder of how to create that stunning application!

Be a Neat Freak

You may have dirty laundry strewn across your room and a pile of papers large enough to be classified as its own life form, but you don't want the scholarship judges to know that. When it comes to applications, neatness does count. We would not ordinarily be neatness zealots—we admit to having our own mountains of life-imbibed papers—but submitting an application with globs of correction fluid, scratched out words or illegible hieroglyphics will severely diminish your message. Think how much less impressive the Mona Lisa would be if da Vinci had painted it on a dirty old bed sheet. You may have the most incredible thoughts to convey in your applications, but if your form is filled with errors, none of it will matter. In a sea of hundreds and even thousands of other applications, you don't want yours to be penalized by sloppy presentation.

Top Ten Application Do's and Don'ts

With money on the table, it's much better to learn from others' successes and mistakes before you risk your own fortunes. From interviews with students and scholarship judges and firsthand experience reviewing scholarship applications, we've developed our Top Ten list of scholarship application do's and don'ts. Let's shed the negative energy first and start with the don'ts.

Don'ts

1. DON'T prioritize quantity over quality. It's not the quantity of your accomplishments that is important. It's the quality of your contributions.
2. DON'T stretch the truth. Tall tales are prohibited.
3. DON'T squeeze to the point of illegibility. Scholarship applications afford minimal space. It's impossible to fit in everything that you want to say. Don't try by sacrificing legibility.
4. DON'T write when you have nothing to say. If you don't have something meaningful to present, leave it blank.
5. DON'T create white-out globs. If it's that sloppy, start over.
6. DON'T procrastinate. Don't think you can finish your applications the night before they're due.
7. DON'T settle for less than perfect. You can have imperfections. Just don't let the selection committee know.
8. DON'T miss deadlines. No matter the reason, if you miss the deadline, you won't win the scholarship.
9. DON'T turn in incomplete applications. Make sure your application is finished before sending it.
10. DON'T underestimate what you can convey. Scholarship applications

may appear to be short and simple. Don't undervalue them. In a small space, you can create a powerful story of why you should win.

And now the good stuff.

Do's

1. DO understand the scholarship's mission. Know why they're giving out the dough.
2. DO remember who your audience is. You need to address animal rights activists and retired dentists differently.
3. DO show how you fit with the scholarship's mission. You're not going to win unless you have what the selection committee wants.
4. DO be proud of your accomplishments. Don't be afraid to brag.
5. DO focus on leadership and contributions. Make your contributions known.
6. DO make your application stand out.
7. DO practice to make sure everything fits. Make practice copies of the original form before you begin filling it out. Then use your spare copies for trial and error. If you apply electronically, edit so everything fits.
8. DO get editors. They'll help you create the best, error-free applications you can.
9. DO include a resume. Whether they ask for it or not, make sure you include a tailored scholarship resume. See the next chapter for how to create a great resume.
10. DO make copies or take photos of your finished applications for reference. Save them for next year when you do this all over again.

Double Check Your App

Once you've completed your applications, check and double-check for accuracy. Look at every line and every question to make sure you've filled out all the information that is requested on the form. Make sure you have someone else take a look at your application. A second set of eyes may catch mistakes that you invariably will miss. Remember that presentation affects how scholarship judges view applications. You want to convey that you are serious about winning the scholarship by submitting an application that is complete and error-free.

Finally, before submitting your application, save or print a copy. If for some reason your application form is lost, you have a copy to resend. Plus, by saving this year's applications, you have recycling possibilities (especially the essays: you'll see what we mean in Chapter 4!) and a great starting place for next year's scholarships.

How to Write a Winning Scholarship Essay

chapter
4

The Essay Can Make or Break Your Chances of Winning

Here's a situation repeated a million times each year. A student receives a scholarship application and quickly glances over the form. It looks pretty straightforward, so it's tossed into the "to do" pile. The day before it's due, the student finally gets around to filling it out. Breezing through the application form, the student is about to celebrate finishing when he or she encounters the final requirement. It reads as follows:

```
In 1894 Donald VonLudwig came to America with 10 cents in
his pocket and within a decade built an empire. Write an
800-word essay on how you would incorporate the lessons
of VonLudwig's success into your life.
```

Uh, oh. Life just got harder. Meet the dreaded scholarship essay. The hypothetical student described above—the one we are poking fun at—was one of us! After a few experiences like this one, (which were usually accompanied by all night writing sessions), we learned to work on the essay first and never underestimate how much time it requires.

For most scholarship competitions, it is the essay that will make or break your chances of winning. Why? Because the essay offers you the best chance to show the scholarship judges why you deserve to win. While your application form will get you to the semifinals, it is the essay that will carry you into the winner's circle.

Since the essay is so important, you must not assume that you can crank out a quality essay the night before it's due. A quality essay will take both time and effort. In this chapter we will take you step by step through the process of crafting a winning essay—don't worry, it's easier than you may have imagined. Plus, you will read examples of essays that won thousands of dollars in scholarships. From these, you can see firsthand how the strategies presented in this chapter are actually put to use in real life.

All Essays Ask the Same Underlying Question

Regardless of the specific wording, the underlying question for almost all essay questions is the same: "Why do you deserve to win?" (Your answer should *not* be, "Because I need the money!")

Think about these questions: The Future Teachers of America scholarship asks you to write about the "future of education". The Veterans of Foreign Wars asks you to define "patriotism". The National Sculpture Society asks you to "describe your extracurricular passions". Believe it or not, all these seemingly different questions are asking for the same answer: Why do you deserve to win our money?

Your answers to each must address this underlying question. When writing the Future Teachers of America essay, you can discuss the general state of education and quote a few facts and figures, but you'd better be sure to include how you personally fit into the future of education. If you are planning to be a teacher, you might elaborate on how you will contribute to shaping students' lives. Similarly use the topic of patriotism to impress the VFW judges with not only what you perceive patriotism to be but also how you have actually acted upon those beliefs. And if you answer the National Sculpture Society question with an essay on how much you love to play the guitar, then you really don't deserve to win!

Six Steps to Writing a Winning Scholarship Essay

By now you should be tired of hearing us repeat our mantra of knowing the purpose of the scholarship. You have used this to guide your selection of those scholarships you are most likely to win and how to complete the application form for them. It shouldn't surprise you that you must also use it to guide your essay. Remember, when you are writing about why you deserve to win, the answer and all the examples that you use should show how you fulfill that mission of the scholarship. With this in mind, let's begin our six steps to writing a winning scholarship essay.

Step 1 Find the Right Topic and Approach

You will encounter two types of essay questions. The first asks you to write about a specific topic. For example, "Why is it important to protect our natural environment?" The second type of question gives you a very broad topic such as, "Tell us about yourself." In the first case you don't need to think about a topic, but you do need to develop an approach to answering the question. In the latter you need to come up with both a topic and an approach. Let's look at how this is done, starting with the more difficult task of finding a topic.

Finding a Topic

Let's imagine that you are applying for a scholarship that presents an essay question so broad that you can essentially choose your own topic. To get the ideas flowing, you should use that idea-generating technique you learned in fifth grade—brainstorming. Take out a notebook or start a new file on your computer and just start listing possible topics and themes. Ask yourself questions like these:

- What was a significant event in my life?
- What teacher, relative or friend has influenced who I am?
- What have I learned from my experiences?
- What are my goals for the future?
- Where will I be ten years from now?
- What motivates me to achieve my goals?

When brainstorming, don't be critical of the topics you unearth—just let the creativity flow. Ask parents and friends for suggestions.

Once you have a list of topics, you can start to eliminate those that don't help you answer the question of why you deserve to win. For example, if you apply to a scholarship that rewards public service, you would not want to write about the time you got lost in the woods for three days and had to survive on a single candy bar and wild roots. While that might make an interesting and exciting essay, it does not show the scholarship judges why you are the epitome of public service. This topic, however, may come in handy when you need to write an essay for a scholarship based on character or leadership or why you love Snickers bars.

After you whittle down your list to a few topics that will help show why you deserve to win this particular scholarship, then choose the topic that is the most interesting to you or that you care about the most. It seems self-evident, but surprisingly many students do not select topics that excite them. Why is it important to pick a topic that you are passionate about? Because if you truly like your topic, you will write a better essay. In fact, your enthusiasm and excitement will naturally permeate your writing, which will make it interesting and memorable. It's so much easier to stay motivated writing about something you enjoy rather than something you find boring.

How to Develop a Unique Approach

Whether you have to think of a topic yourself or one is given to you, the next task is to figure out how you are going to approach it. For any given topic there are probably a hundred ways you could address the subject matter in an essay. Most topics are also way too large to completely cover in an 800- to 1,000-word essay, so you are going to have to narrow it down and only share a small part of the larger story. All this involves coming up with an approach to what you will present in your essay—an approach that must convince the judges that you deserve to win their money.

Let's take a look at writing about the traumatic experience of being lost in the woods for three days. You choose this topic since the scholarship wants to reward students with strong character and leadership and this is an experience that you believe shows both. But how do you write about it? If you just retell the story of the ordeal, it will not help the judges see why such an experience reveals the quality of your character or leadership. You need to dig deeper and think about how this experience revealed your strengths. To do this, ask yourself questions like these:

- What does this topic reveal about me?
- How has my life been changed by this experience?
- Why did I do what I did?
- What is the lesson that I learned from this experience?
- What aspect of this topic is most important to making my point?

In thinking about your experience alone in the woods, you may realize that on the second day you came close to breaking down and losing all hope of being rescued. This was the critical point where you had to make a decision to give up or push forward. You decide to focus your essay only on this small sliver of time, what went through your mind and how you decided that you were not going to give up. The details of how you got lost and of your eventual rescue would be unimportant and may be mentioned in only a sentence or two. Focusing your essay on just the second day—and more particularly on how you were able to conquer your fears and not lose hope—would clearly demonstrate to the judges that even under extreme pressure, your true character was revealed. Since you also need to address the leadership aspect, you decide to focus on how you took charge of your fears on the second day. To do this, your essay will describe specific actions you took to lead yourself successfully through this ordeal.

Finding the right approach is just as important as finding the right topic. This is especially true if you answer a question that provides a specific topic. With every scholarship applicant writing about the same topic, you need to be sure that your approach persuasively shows the judges why you deserve to win more than anyone else.

Step 2 Share a Slice of Life

Now that you have a topic and an idea for your approach, you need to decide how you are going to convey your message on paper. Keep in mind that scholarship judges are going to read hundreds if not thousands of essays. Often the essays will be on similar topics, particularly if the topic was given in the scholarship application. Therefore, you need to make sure that your writing is original. The best way to do this is to share a "slice of your life" in the essay.

Imagine that you are writing about your summer trip to Europe. Travel is a very common topic. If you decide to write about how your trip made you realize people from around the world are really quite similar, then you run the real risk of sounding just like every other travel essay. The same would be true for writing about sports. If you tell the story of how your team rallied and came from behind to win the game, you can be sure that it will sound like many other essays about sports. To make sure your essay is original, you need to share a "slice of life." Find one incident that happened during your travels or pick one particular moment in the game and use that to make your point. By focusing on a single day, hour or moment, you greatly reduce your chances of having an essay that sounds like everyone else's. Plus, essays that share a slice of life are usually a lot more interesting and memorable.

Let's look at an example. What if you choose to write about how your mom has been your role model? Moms are one of the most popular role models for essays (and they should be, considering the pain of childbirth). How do you make your mom distinct from all the other applicants writing about their moms? Go ahead and take a moment to think about your mom. Be very specific. Can you find one character trait or incident that really influenced you? Let's say your mom has an obsession with collecting porcelain figurines and this passion led to you becoming interested in collecting baseball cards. Because of this, you are now considering a career in sports management. Now we have something! Imagine that first day when you realized how much your mom loved collecting figurines. Maybe you even bought her one as a present and now she cherishes it above all others. Perhaps it was that moment that jump-started your love for baseball cards, which has now developed into a full blown obsession with sports to the point that you intend to make it a career. You've just succeeded in turning a very popular topic—Mom—into an entirely original essay by finding that slice of life. No two people share the exact same slice of life, so by finding one to share, you are almost always guaranteed to have an original essay.

Want another example? Let's set the stage. Imagine that you are applying to a scholarship for students who major in psychology. The question posed on the application is this: "Tell us about an influential person who inspired you to pursue psychology." As you brainstorm, you list the authors of books you've read and some professors whose classes you have enjoyed. But how many students will be writing about these same people? You could even wager money that every other essay will be about Freud!

As you brainstorm, you recall the worst fight you have ever had with your best friend Susan. As you think about this fight that nearly destroyed a 10-year friendship, you realize that it was one of the first times you applied classroom knowledge to a real life experience. In analyzing the fight, you realize that those psychology principles you studied have practical applications beyond the textbook. So for your essay you decide to write about the fight and how it made you even more committed than ever to become a psychology major.

You don't have to look far to find originality. We all have experiences that are unique to us. Even common experiences can be made original, depending on how you approach them. So don't exclude a topic just because it is common. By spending some time thinking about how you will write about it, you may be surprised at how original it could be.

Step 3 Stop Thinking, Start Writing

The most challenging part of writing a scholarship essay is getting started. Our advice: Just start writing. The first words you put down on paper may not be brilliant, but don't worry. You can always return to edit your work. It's easier to edit words you've already written than words that don't exist.

Do you think you have a bad case of writer's block? If so, the cure may surprise you. The best cure for writer's block is to just start writing!

We all have different writing styles, but certain points should be kept in mind as you are writing something that is focused on winning over a scholarship committee. Think about these things as you craft that winning essay:

Write for the Scholarship Judges. Let's pretend you're a stand-up comedian who has two performances booked: one at the trendiest club in town where all cool college students congregate and the other at a retirement home. As a skilled comedian, you would prepare different material aimed at the different audiences. The college crowd would be able to relate to jokes about relationships and dating, while your jokes about dentures and arthritis would probably—and this is a hunch—go over better with the senior citizens. The same goes for writing your essays. Since many are given by specialized organizations or for specific purposes, you need to write an essay that is appropriate for the audience. Think about who is going to read your essay. Is your audience natural science professors, circus performers or used car salesmen? Write your essay so it appeals to that audience. This should guide not only your selection of topics but also your word choice, language and tone.

Be Yourself. While you want to present yourself in a way that attracts the attention of the scholarship judges, you don't want to portray yourself as someone you are not. It's okay to present selected highlights from your life that fit with the award, but it's not ethical to exaggerate or outright lie. If you apply for a scholarship to promote the protection of animals, don't write about your deep compassion for helping animals when you've never ventured closer than 10 feet to one because of your allergies. Feel comfortable about everything you write, and don't go overboard trying to mold yourself into being the student you think the scholarship judges want to read about. If you've done your job of picking scholarships that match you best, you already know that you are a good fit. Your task in the essay is to demonstrate this to the judges.

Personalize Your Essay. Think of the scholarship judges as an audience that has come to see your Broadway show. You are the star. To keep them satisfied, give them what they want. In other words, the scholarship judges want to know about your life and experiences. When you write your essay, write about what has happened to you personally or about how you personally have been affected by something. If you are writing about drug abuse for an essay about a problem that faces college students today, do more than recite the latest national drug use statistics and the benefits of drug rehabilitation programs. Otherwise, your essay may be informative, but it won't be interesting. Instead, write about how a friend nearly overdosed on drugs, how others tried to pressure you into trying drugs or about your volunteer work at a rehabilitation clinic. Instantly, your essay will be more interesting and memorable. Plus, the judges really do want to learn more about you, and the only way for them to do this is if you share something about yourself in your essay.

Make Sure You Have a Point. Try this exercise: See if you can encapsulate the point of your essay into a single sentence. If you can't, you don't have a main point. So, you'd better get one! You may think this is obvious, but many students' essays don't have a main point. Use that most basic lesson from Composition 101: Have a thesis statement that states the main point of your essay. Let's say you are writing about growing up in the country. You might structure your essay around the idea that growing up in the country gave you a strong work ethic. This is the essay's main point. You can describe all the flat land and brush you like, but unless these descriptions help to support your point, you don't have a quality essay.

Support Your Statement. Once you put your main point out there, you can't abandon it. Like a baby learning to walk, you have to support your thesis statement because it can't stand on its own. This means you have to provide reasons why your statement is true. You can do this by giving detailed and vivid examples from your personal experiences and accomplishments.

Use Examples and Illustrations. When a reader can visualize what you are writing, it helps to make an impression. Anecdotes and stories accomplish this very effectively. Examples and illustrations also make your ideas clearer. If you want to be a doctor, explain how you became interested in becoming one. You might describe the impact of getting a stethoscope from your father when you were a child. Or maybe you can write about your first day volunteering at the hospital. Examples help readers picture what you are saying and even relate to your experiences. The scholarship judge may have never volunteered at a hospital; but by reading your example, that judge can easily understand how such an experience could be so influential. The one danger of examples is that you need to be sure to keep them concise. It is often too easy to write a long and detailed example when only a few sentences are sufficient. Remember, in an example you are not retelling an entire story but just pulling out a few highlights to illustrate the point you are trying to make.

Show Activity. If you were forced to sit in an empty room with nothing but a bare wall to stare at, you would probably get bored pretty quickly. The same goes for an essay. Don't force the scholarship judges to read an essay that does nothing. Your essay needs activity and movement to bring it to life. This may consist of dialogue, action, stories and thoughts. The last thing you want to do is bore your readers. With action, you won't have to worry about that!

Highlight Your Growth. You may not have grown an inch since seventh grade, but scholarship judges will look for your growth in other ways. They want to see evidence of emotional and intellectual growth, what your strengths are and how you have developed them. Strengths may include—but certainly aren't limited to—mastery of an academic course, musical talent, a desire to help others, athletic ability, leadership of a group and more. Overcoming adversity or facing a challenge may also demonstrate your growth.

Be Positive. You don't need to break out the pompoms and do a cheer, but you need to convey a positive attitude in your essay. Scholarship committees want to see optimism, excitement and confidence. They prefer not to read essays that are overly pessimistic, antagonistic or critical. This doesn't mean that you have to put a happy spin on every word written or that you can't write about a serious topic or problem. For example, if you were a judge reading the following essays about the very serious topic of teen pregnancy, to which author's education fund would you rather make a contribution?

Thesis 1:
We could reduce the number of pregnant teens if we shifted our efforts away from scare tactics to providing responsible sex education combined with frank discussions regarding the responsibilities of caring for a child.

Thesis 2:
Teen pregnancy is incurable. Teenagers will always act irresponsibly and it would be futile for us to believe that we can control this behavior.

Scholarship committees favor authors who not only recognize problems but also present potential solutions. Leave being pessimistic to adults. You are young, with your entire future ahead of you. Your optimism is what makes you so exciting and why organizations want to give you money to pursue your passion for changing the world. Don't shy away from this opportunity.

Be Concise. The scholarship essay may not have the strict limits of a college admission essay, but that does not give you a license to be verbose. Keep your essay tight, focused and within the recommended length of the scholarship guidelines. If no parameters are given, one or two pages should suffice. You certainly want the readers to get through the entirety of your masterpiece. Remember that most scholarship selection committees are composed of volunteers who are under no obligation to read your entire essay. Make your main points quickly and keep your essay as brief and to the point as possible.

Step 4 Don't Neglect Your Introduction and Conclusion

Studies have found that the most important parts of a speech are the first and last minutes. In between, listeners fade in and out rather than constantly pay attention. It is the introduction and conclusion that leave a lasting impact. This holds true for scholarship essays as well. You need to have a memorable introduction and conclusion. If you don't, the readers may not make it past your introductory paragraph or they may discount your quality essay after reading a lackluster ending. Spend extra time making sure these two parts deliver the message you want. Here are some tips to create knockout introductions and conclusions:

For Introductions

Create action or movement. Think of the introduction as the high-speed car chase at the beginning of a movie that catches the audience's attention.

Pose a question. Questions draw the readers' attention for two reasons. First, they think about how they would answer the query as you have posed it. Second, they are curious to see how you will answer or present solutions to the question in your essay.

Describe. If you can create a vivid image for readers, they will be more likely to want to read on.

For Conclusions

Be thoughtful. Your conclusion should make the second most powerful statement in your essay because this is what your readers will remember. (The most powerful statement should be in your introduction.)

Leave a parting thought. The scholarship committee members have already read your essay (we hope), so you don't need to rehash what you have already said. It's okay to summarize in one sentence, but you want to do more than just "wrap it up". You have one final opportunity to make an impression, so add a parting thought. This should be one last observation or idea that ties into the main point of your essay.

Don't be too quick to end. Too many students tack on a meaningless conclusion or even worse, don't have one at all. Have a decent conclusion that goes with the rest of your essay. Never end your essay with the two words, "The End."

Step 5 Find Editors

Despite what you may think, you're not infallible. Stop gasping—it's true. This means it's important to get someone else to edit your work. Roommates, friends, family members, teachers, professors or advisors make great editors. When you get another person to read your essay, he or she will find errors that eluded you, as well as parts that are unclear to someone reading your essay for the first time. Ask your editors to make sure your ideas are clear, that you answer the question appropriately and that your essay is interesting. Take their suggestions seriously. The more input you get from others and the more times you rewrite your work, the better.

You want your essay to be like silk—smooth and elegant. When you read your work, make sure the connections between ideas are logical and the flow of your writing is understandable. (This is where editors can be extremely helpful.) Also check that you have not included any unnecessary details that might obscure the main point of your essay. Be careful to include any information that is vital to your thesis. Your goal is to produce an essay with clear points and supporting examples that logically flow together.

You also want to make sure that your spelling and grammar are perfect. Again, the best way to do this is to have someone else read your work. If you don't have time to ask someone, then do it yourself—but do it carefully. Read your essay at least once with the sole purpose of looking for spelling and grammatical mistakes. (Your computer's spell check is not 100 percent reliable and won't catch when you accidentally describe how you bake bread with one cup of "flower" instead of "flour.") Try reading your work out loud to listen for grammatical mistakes.

Step 6 Recycle Your Essays

This has no relation to aluminum cans or newspapers. In this case recycling means reusing essays you have written for college applications, classes or even other scholarships. Because colleges and scholarship committees usually ask very broad questions, this is generally doable and saves you a tremendous amount of time. Later in this chapter you will read an example essay. You may be surprised to learn that the author recycled her essay with minimal changes to answer such differing questions as these: "Tell us about one of your dreams," "What is something you believe in strongly?" and "What past experience continues to influence you today?"

However, be careful not to recycle an essay when it just doesn't fit. It's better to spend the extra time to write an appropriate essay than to submit one that doesn't match the scholarship or answer the question.

Seven Sins of the Scholarship Essay

Instead of writing an essay, one student placed the sheet of paper on the floor and tap danced on it. She then wrote that she hoped the scuff marks on the paper were evidence of her enthusiasm. In the judges' eyes, this was a silly stunt and, of course, her application was sent to the rejection pile. While you may not make such an egregious error, there are common mistakes that you need to avoid. Most of these lessons were learned the hard way—through actual experience.

1. DON'T Write a Sob Story

Everyone who applies for a scholarship needs money. Many have overcome obstacles and personal hardships. However, few scholarships are designed to reward students based on the "quantity" of hardships. Scholarship judges are not looking to give their money to those who have suffered the most. On the contrary, they want to give money to students who came up with a plan to succeed despite an obstacle. Therefore, if you are writing about the hardships you have faced, be sure that you spend as much time, if not more, describing how you have overcome or plan to rise above those challenges.

2. DON'T Use the Shotgun Approach

A common mistake is to write one essay and submit it without any changes to dozens of scholarships—hoping that maybe one will be a winner. While we do recommend that you recycle your essays, you should not just copy your essays and blast them out to every scholarship committee. This simply does not work. Unless the scholarships have identical questions, missions and goals, your essay cannot be reused verbatim. Spend the time to craft an essay for each scholarship, and you will win more than if you write just one and blindly send it off to many awards.

3. DON'T Be Afraid to Get Words on Paper

One common cause of writer's block is the fear of beginning. When you sit down to write, don't be afraid to write a draft, or even ideas for a draft, that are not perfect. You will have time to revise your work. What you want to do is get words on paper. They can be wonderfully intelligent words or they can be vague concepts. The point is that you should just write. Too many students wait until the last minute and get stuck at the starting line.

4. DON'T Try to Be Someone Else

Since you want to be the one the scholarship judges are seeking to reward with money, you need to highlight achievements and strengths that match the criteria of the scholarship. But you don't want to lie about yourself or try to be someone you are not. Besides being dishonest, the scholarship judges will probably pick up on your affectation and hold it against you.

5. DON'T Try to Impress with Feats of Literary Gymnastics

You won't get any bonus points for overusing clichés, quotes or words you don't understand. Too many students think that quotes and clichés will impress scholarship judges; but unless they are used sparingly and appropriately, they will win you no favors. (Remember that quotes and clichés are not your words and are therefore not original.) The same goes for overusing the thesaurus.

Do experiment with words that are less familiar to you, but do not make the thesaurus your co-author. It's better to use simple words correctly than to make blunders with complicated ones.

6. DON'T Stray Too Far from the Topic

A mistake that many students make is that they don't actually answer the question. This is especially true with recycled essays. Make sure that your essays, whether written from scratch or recycled from others, address the question asked.

7. DON'T Write Your Stats

A common mistake is to repeat your statistics from your application form. Often these essays begin with "My name is" and go on to list classes, GPAs and extracurricular activities. All this information is found in your application. On top of that, it's boring. If you are going to write about a class or activity, make it interesting by focusing on a specific class or activity.

Example Winning Scholarship Essays

It's one thing to study the theory behind the pheromones of love, but it is entirely a different thing to experience the euphoria, quickened heartbeat and walking-on-clouds feeling that goes with love. In a similar way, you have seen the theory behind writing a powerful scholarship essay. It is now time to see this theory in action.

The following two essays were written by students who won scholarships. In each essay you will see how winning principles are put to use. The results are essays that inspire, provoke and most important, win money. As with any example essay, please remember that this is not necessarily the way your essay should be written. Use these sample essays as illustrations of how a good essay might look. Your essay will naturally be different and unique to your own style and personality.

Winning Essay: My Two Dads

This essay was written by Gregory James Yee, a graduate of Whitney High School in Cerritos, California. Although Gregory is a student at Stanford University, he wrote this essay as part of his application to the University of Southern California. Besides garnering an acceptance to USC, this essay also earned him a $7,500 per year Trustee Scholarship. Remember that many colleges use your college application to automatically consider you for scholarships they offer.

The topic of the essay is Gregory's musical talent, which was discovered early in his life. At the age of two, he could hum *The Star-Spangled Banner* in perfect rhythm and pitch; and at age four, he began piano lessons. Throughout his 15 years of lessons, he won numerous awards, including the Raissa Tselentis Award given to one student nationwide for outstanding performance in the Advanced Bach category of the National Guild Audition. He is also a composer.

My Two Dads

I have two fathers. My first and biological father is the one who taught me how to drive a car, throw a baseball and find the area under a curve using integral calculus, among the innumerable other common duties of a good dad. He has been there for me through the ups of my successful piano career and the downs of my first breakup, and has always offered his insightful hand of guidance. My second father is who I connect with on a different level; he is the only person I know who thinks like I do. My second dad is my music composition teacher, Tony Fox, and he shares the one passion that has been a part of my life since the age of two: music.

Tony is a hardworking professor who can spend hours illustrating the meaning of a particular chord in a famous classical composition or ease an extraordinarily stressful situation with his colorful wit. He may appear intimidating to a new student at USC as the Assistant Band Director, but once someone mentions music, there is no one more adept, more creative or more dedicated to making music for the world to hear than Tony.

Tony has touched my life in a way few people have experienced. At my lessons with him, I bring compositions I am in the progress of perfecting, and with a few words of his guidance, I can almost see the changes needed before he mentions them. Almost instantly after I ask a question – such as which chord progression works best at a certain point in the music or why a certain counter melody sounds so beautiful—we agree on what is best for the music. It is almost as if we know what the other is thinking and merely state aloud our thoughts just in case one or the other is caught off guard. It is truly rare to find two people who agree with each other on what it is exactly that makes compositions aesthetically pleasing. Last year when I was working on a composition, I ran into a discouraging roadblock that could have delayed my progress significantly. No one in my family and none of my friends could help.

However, as soon as I shared the piece with Tony, he made some suggestions and together we made the necessary amendments to the music. The result was a finished project, a beautiful mosaic of our collective design, and it was debuted last year by my high school wind ensemble. When I first heard my music performed, I thought back to the hours I had spent tinkering at my piano and Tony's thoughtful guidance. This is how Tony and I relate. It's a common frequency upon which the most advanced radio cannot even begin to comprehend.

Tony has filled in areas of my life where few people, including my real father, could understand. He is the teacher of lessons big and small, from looking into the eyes of those whose hands I shake to recognizing that time is the most valuable gift one can give or receive. Whereas many of my peers have only one father, I have been fortunate enough to have two of them.

Why This Essay Won

An accomplished musician like Gregory could have written an essay that was simply a retelling of all the musical awards he had won. Instead, Gregory gives insight into what music means to him and takes us into his mind to see the creative and learning process at work. Writing about what he goes through to create a composition allows even those of us who are tone deaf to experience vicariously what it is like to create music.

Notice how Gregory uses powerful imagery to show us how he interacts with his music teacher and overcomes difficulties while composing. Gregory also subtly includes some of his most important musical accomplishments. Although he listed many of his awards in his application, this essay takes us beyond those achievements and really lets us see the wonderful person behind those awards.

Winning Essay: Leadership

Donald H. Matsuda, Jr. is the kind of person who doesn't just act. He inspires others to act as well. In his application for the Truman Scholarship, Donald shared how he directed community leaders and health professionals to start a series of health insurance drives. This is one of the essays that he wrote to become one of 80 Truman Scholars in the country.

From Sacramento and a graduate of Stanford University, Donald also founded the San Mateo Children's Health Insurance Program, directed the United Students for Veterans' Health and founded the Nepal Pediatric Clinical Internship.

Leadership

A few years ago, I saw a shocking headline on the front page of the New York Times that read: "Forty-Four Million Americans Without Health Insurance." Upon reading the article, I was stunned to discover that one-third of these uninsured Americans were children. Such figures made it clear to me that work needed to be done to remedy this problem, and I was ready to take action.

At this time, I was working at the Health for All Clinic as a public health and community outreach intern, and I decided to approach the director about this problem. He clearly agreed that immediate action needed to be taken to control the growing numbers of America's uninsured. However, he admitted that the clinic did not have the time, energy or the funds to invest in such an ambitious endeavor. I was not discouraged by his response. Instead, I saw this challenge as an opportunity to gain firsthand experience as a change agent in the field of public policy.

After completing extensive research, I discovered a unique program called Healthy Families. The ultimate goal of this government program is to provide low-cost insurance coverage to children who do not qualify for traditional insurance plans. I decided to develop my own project from scratch, proposing to launch a sustainable series of Healthy Families insurance drives at the Health for All Clinic. I applied for funding through the Haas Center for Public Service Fellowship program, and the clinic director signed on as my community partner for the project.

During the next six months, I worked very closely with the clinic staff to organize and plan this series of insurance drives. I recruited various ethnic community leaders and healthcare professionals to help generate support for the program and assembled several advertising campaigns in the surrounding communities. The clinic director and I also developed a workshop on immigrant health to attract more diverse populations to our insurance drives. After holding three Healthy Families drives, the clinic managed to sign up over 150 children for this program. The director was elated by this turnout and established an entire Healthy Families division to build upon the success of this project. Upon completion of this project, I started directing other insurance drives with the hope of improving the health and well-being of America's children.

Why This Essay Won

Donald's essay only scratches the surface of his accomplishments, which is exactly how it should be. Instead of listing every leadership role he has ever had, Donald explains how he created a health care program in his community. He begins with his motivation for starting the program and then recounts the initial skepticism that he faced when he first proposed the idea. Donald's essay describes the various difficulties and ultimate success of his project.

Notice that Donald does not describe a typical leadership role, one in which he was elected as a leader. This is an excellent example of how you can take a project in which you played a significant role and show how it demonstrates your leadership abilities. Remember, leadership is not just an elected position.

Where to Find More Winning Scholarship Essays

We believe that reading real essays is the best way for you to really see what works, and these essays are certainly a start. Unfortunately, we could not include more than two examples in this book. If you want more scholarship essay examples, take a look at our book, *How to Write a Winning Scholarship Essay*. In it you will find 30 additional winning essays from students who tested the waters of many topics and wrote in a variety of styles. Also, take a look at our website, SuperCollege (www.supercollege.com), where we post additional example essays. We think you'll be inspired.

The Scholarship Resume

Chapter 5

Write Your Own One-Page Autobiography

If you want to say that your life is a book, then be ready to follow with the analogy that your scholarship resume is the *CliffsNotes* summary. A scholarship resume is your opportunity to tout your greatest achievements and life's accomplishments. The only catch is that you are limited to one page. Some scholarship committees require resumes as a part of the application process so that they can use them to get a quick overview of your achievements. Others don't, but including a resume will always enhance your application.

A scholarship resume is not the same as one that you would use to get a job. It's unlikely that your work experience (if you have any) will be the focus. However, the principles and format are the same. A good resume that scores you a job shows employers that you have the right combination of work experience and skills to be their next hire. Similarly, your scholarship resume should show the committee why you are the most qualified student to win their award.

Think of the scholarship resume as a "cheat sheet" that you give to the judges. By looking at your resume, the judges get a quick overview of your achievements and interests. The resume is not an exhaustive list of everything you have done. It rather highlights and summarizes the most impressive and relevant achievements.

To make sure that it really focuses on the crème de la crème, your resume should fit on a single sheet of paper. This is sometimes harder than it sounds.

Here is the information you need for a scholarship resume:

- **Contact information:** Your vital statistics, including name, address, phone number and email.

- **Education:** Schools you've attended beginning with high school, expected or actual graduation dates.
- **Academic achievements:** Relevant coursework, awards and honors received.
- **Extracurricular experience.** Relevant extracurricular activities, locations and dates of participation, job titles, responsibilities and accomplishments.
- **Work experience:** Where and when you've worked, job titles, responsibilities and accomplishments on the job.
- **Skills and interests:** Additional relevant technical, lingual or other skills or talents that do not fit in the categories above.

Don't worry if your resume presents the same information that's in the application form. Some judges will read only the application or your resume, so it's important your key points are in both. However, in the resume, try to expand on areas that you were not able to cover fully in the application.

Example Resume that Worked

There are many good ways to format a resume. Most important, your resume should be easy to skim and be organized in a logical manner. Here is an example of a well-written scholarship resume. Remember that there are other equally good formats in which to present this information.

Melissa Lee
1000 University Drive
San Francisco, CA 94134
(415) 555-5555
melissa@email.com

Education
University of San Francisco; San Francisco, CA
B.A. candidate in sociology. Expected graduation in 2023. Honor roll.

Lowell High School; San Francisco, CA
Graduated in 2019 with highest honors. Principal's Honor Roll, 4 years.

Activities and Awards
SF Educational Project; San Francisco, CA
Program Assistant. Recruited and trained 120 students for various community service projects in semester-long program. Managed and evaluated student journals, lesson plans and program participation.
2017-present.

Lowell High School Newspaper; San Francisco, CA
Editor-In-Chief. Recruited and managed staff of 50. Oversaw all editorial and business functions.
Newspaper was a finalist for the prestigious Examiner Award for excellence in student journalism. 2015-2019.

Evangelical Church; San Francisco, CA
Teacher. Prepared and taught weekly lessons for third grade Sunday School class. Received dedication to service award from congregation. 2015-2019.

Asian Dance Troupe; San Francisco, CA
Member. Performed at community functions and special events. 2017-present.

Employment
Palo Alto Daily News; Palo Alto, CA
Editorial Assistant. Researched and wrote eight feature articles on such topics as education reform, teen suicide and summer fashion. Led series of teen-reader response panels. Summer 2019.

Russian Hill Public Library; San Francisco, CA
Library Page. Received "Page of the Month" Award for outstanding performance. Summers 2017-2018.

Interests
Fluent in Mandarin and HTML. Interests include journal writing, creative writing, photography, swimming and aerobics.

Some points to note about this resume:

- Notice how this resume is concise and very easy to read. By limiting herself to a single page, Melissa makes sure that even if you just scan her resume, you will pick up her key strengths.
- See how each description includes examples of leadership as well as awards or special recognition.
- Melissa conveys the impact of her work by pointing out concrete results (which you should also do on the application form).
- Notice how her description of summer jobs highlights some of her key accomplishments.
- The final section adds a nice balance by describing some of her other hobbies and interests.

Elements of a Powerful Resume

Your resume should be descriptive enough for the judges to understand each item but not so wordy that they can't find what they need. It should be neatly organized and easy to follow. Having reviewed hundreds of resumes, here are some simple strategies that we've developed to help you:

Include only the important information. Remember to incorporate only the most relevant items and use what you know about the scholarship organization to guide how you prioritize what you share in your resume. Only include things that support your fit with the scholarship's mission. For each piece of information, ask yourself these two questions: Will including this aid the selection committee in seeing that I am a match for the award? Is this information necessary to convince them that I should receive the award?

Focus on responsibilities and achievements. In describing your experiences in work and activities, focus on the responsibilities you held and highlight measurable or unique successes such as starting a project, reaching goals or implementing one of your ideas. For example, if you were the treasurer of the Literary Club, you would want to include that you were responsible for managing a $10,000 annual budget.

Demonstrate in your resume how you showed leadership. Leadership could include leading a project or team, instructing others or mentoring your peers. What's more important than your title or where you worked is the quality of your involvement. Explaining your successes and your role as a leader will provide concrete evidence of your contribution.

Be proud. Your resume is your time to shine. Don't be afraid to draw attention to all that you've accomplished. If you played a key role in a project, say so. If you exceeded your goals, advertise it. No one else is going to do your bragging for you.

Use action verbs. When you are describing your achievements, use action verbs such as these: founded, organized, achieved, created, developed, directed and (our personal favorite) initiated.

Don't tell tall stories. On the flip side of being proud is being untruthful. It's important that you describe yourself in the most glowing way possible, but stay connected with the truth. If you developed a new filing system at your job, don't claim that you single-handedly led a corporate revolution. With your complete scholarship application, selection committees can see through a resume that is exaggerated and doesn't match the rest of the application, essay and recommendations.

Get editors. After the hundredth time reading your resume, you'll probably not notice an error that someone reading it for the first time will catch. Get others to read and edit your resume. Editors can let you know if something doesn't make sense, offer you alternative wording and help correct your boo-boos. Some good choices for editors may be teachers or professors, work supervisors or parents. Work supervisors may be especially helpful since part of their job is to review resumes of job applicants. Your school may also offer resume help in the counseling department or career services office.

Avoid creating an eye test. In trying to squeeze all the information onto a single page, don't make your font size so small that the words are illegible. Try to leave space between paragraphs. The judges may have tired, weary eyes from reading all those applications. Don't strain them even more.

Strive for perfection. It's a given that your resume should be error-free. There's no excuse for mistakes on a one-page document that is meant to exemplify your life's work.

Include Your Resume in Every Application

Once you have a resume, include it with every scholarship application. In addition, you should also give it to your recommenders so that they have a "cheat sheet" that highlights your accomplishments when it comes time to write those letters of recommendations. They will no doubt want to mention some of your successes to make their letters on point and personal. Remember, your resume is *you*!

Getting Great Recommendations

Chapter 6

Letters of Recommendation Count

If you need a reason to kiss up to your teachers or professors, here's one: recommendations. Scholarships sometime require that you submit recommendations from teachers, professors, school administrators, employers or others who can vouch for your accomplishments. Scholarship judges use these testaments to get another perspective of your character and accomplishments. Viewed together with your application and essay, the recommendation helps the judges get a more complete picture of who you are. Plus, it's always impressive when someone else extols your virtues.

Many students believe that they have no control over the recommendation part of their application. This isn't true. You actually can have a lot of input regarding the letters that your recommenders write. In this chapter we will explore several ways—all perfectly ethical—to ensure that you get great recommendations.

A recommendation is an important opportunity for someone else to tell scholarship judges why you deserve to win. You may assume that because others do the actual writing, recommendations are completely out of your control. Banish that thought. The secret is to not only pick the right people but to also provide them with all of the information they need to turn out a great letter of recommendation. Many applicants overlook this fact. But not you, right? Armed with superb recommendations, your scholarship application is sure to rise to the top.

Find People to Say Nice Things about You

Your first task is to find recommenders. Unfortunately, Mom, Dad and anyone else related to you is excluded. So, how do you get those recommendations without familial ties to sing your praises?

First, think about all the people in your life who can speak meaningfully about you and your accomplishments. Your list may include teachers, professors, advisors, school administrators, employers, religious leaders, coaches or leaders of organizations and activities in which you are involved. While some scholarships require recommendations from specific people (like a teacher or professor), most are pretty liberal and allow you to select anyone who knows you.

Second, once you have a list of potential recommenders, analyze which of these people could present information about you that best matches the goals of the scholarships.

If you apply for an academic scholarship, you'll want at least one teacher or professor to write a recommendation. If you apply for an athletic scholarship, a coach would be a good choice. Select people who are able to write about the things that are most important to the scholarship judges. A good exercise is to imagine what your potential recommender would write and whether or not this would enhance your case for winning the scholarship.

After considering these two questions, you should be left with only a few people from which to choose. If you can't decide between two equally qualified people, choose the one who knows you the best as a person. For example, if you got A's in three classes and are trying to decide which professor to ask for a recommendation, pick the one who can write *more* than a testament to your academic ability. This is important because a recommendation that contains comments on your character is extremely memorable. Maybe one of the professors knows you well enough to include a few sentences on your drive to succeed or your family background. Ideally, your recommender is able to describe not only your performance in the classroom but also the values and character traits that make you special.

Give Your Recommender the Chance to Say "No"

Once you've selected those you'd like to write your recommendations, ask them to do so—early. A general rule is to allow at least three weeks before the recommendation is due. Explain that you are applying for scholarships and are required to submit recommendations from people who know you and who can comment on some of your achievements.

It's important to ask the person a question like this: "Do you feel comfortable writing a recommendation letter for me?" This allows the person the opportunity to decline your request if he or she doesn't feel comfortable or doesn't have the time. If you get a negative or hesitant response, don't assume that it's because he or she has a low opinion of you. It could simply be that the person doesn't know you well enough or is too busy to write a thoughtful recommendation. It's much better to have the recommender decline to write a letter than to get one that is rushed or not entirely positive. In most cases, however, potential recommenders are flattered and happy to oblige.

Don't Play the Name Game

From being recognized by strangers to getting preferential reservations at the hottest restaurants, there are a lot of perks to being famous. You might think that this special treatment carries over to recommendations, and that scholarship judges will be star-struck by a letter from someone with a fancy title. However, don't assume that just because you ask someone well known to write your recommendations that you are a shoo-in for the scholarship. In fact, you might be surprised to learn that doing so could actually hurt your chances of winning.

So the question is this: "Should I try to find someone famous to write a letter of recommendation for me?" The answer comes down to the principles outlined above. How well does the person know you, and can he or she write about you in a way that presents you as a viable candidate for the scholarship? If the answer is "yes," then by all means ask the person to help you. However, if you don't know the person very well or if what he or she will write could lack a connection to the qualities that the scholarship committee is looking for, it's better to forgo the value of high name recognition and ask someone who can address what's most important in a letter of recommendation.

For example, if you work as a summer intern for your state senator, you may think that a letter from such a political luminary would give your application the star power to set it apart from others with recommendations from mere mortals. However, if you spent more time photocopying or stuffing envelopes than you did developing keen political strategies, and you saw the senator as many times as you have fingers on your left hand, chances are that he or she would have very few meaningful things to say about your performance. "A skilled photocopier" and "brewed a mean cup of coffee" are not compliments you want sent to the scholarship judges.

If you ask someone well known to write your recommendations, make sure that he or she really knows you and can speak about your accomplishments personally and meaningfully. The quality of what is said in the recommendations is much more important than whose signature is at the bottom of the page.

Do the Grunt Work for Your Recommenders

Once you've selected your recommenders, give them everything they need to get the job done. Since they are doing you a favor, make the process as easy as possible for them. This is also where you can most influence what they write and actually direct what accomplishments they highlight. But before we delve into the specifics, here is an overview of what you need to provide each recommender:

Cover letter: This describes the scholarships you are applying for. In the letter, you should list deadlines and give the recommenders direct guidance on what to write. More on this in a bit.

Resume: A resume provides a quick overview of your most important achievements in an easy to follow one-page format. It is also what your recommenders will use as they cite your important achievements.

Recommendation form: Some scholarships provide an actual form that your recommenders need to complete. Fill in the parts that you can, such as your name and address.

Pre-addressed, stamped envelopes: Read the application materials to find out if you need to submit your recommendations separately or with the rest of your application. For letters that are to be mailed separately, provide your recommenders with envelopes that are stamped and have the scholarship's mailing address on them. If you are supposed to submit the letters with your application, provide your recommenders with envelopes on which you have written your name. Many recommenders prefer to write letters that are confidential and that you don't get to read. Once you have everything, place it in a folder or envelope and label it with your recommender's name.

Give Your Recommenders a Script

Because you know yourself better than anyone else, you would probably receive the best recommendations if you sat down and wrote them yourself. Unfortunately, this practice is frowned upon by scholarship judges. Short of writing your own recommendations, you can influence how they turn out by providing your recommenders with detailed descriptions of your accomplishments that can help them decide which aspects of you to highlight in their letters. This is best done through the cover letter that you send to the prospective recommender.

Your cover letter provides your recommenders with all the information that they need to write your recommendations, including details about the scholarships and suggestions for what you'd like the recommendations to address. Since the cover letter also includes other essentials like deadlines, mailing or submitting instructions and a thank you, you will not sound as if you are giving orders but rather that you are providing helpful assistance. In fact, your recommenders will appreciate your reminding them what's important and what they should include.

Here are the elements to include in your cover letter:

Details on the scholarships: List the scholarships for which you will use their letters. Give a brief one-paragraph description of the mission of each of the awards and what qualities the scholarship committee seeks. This information will help your recommenders understand which of your qualities are important to convey and who will read the letters.

How you fit the scholarship: This is the most important part of your cover letter because it's your chance to remind your recommenders of your accomplishments and to offer suggestions for what to write. Make sure that you highlight how you match the goals of the scholarships. For example, if you are applying for a scholarship for future teachers, include information about your student teaching experience and the coursework you've taken in education. Leave out the fact that you were on the tennis team.

Deadlines: Inform your recommenders of how long they have to compose the letters. If time permits, ask them to mail the letters a week before the actual deadlines.

What to do with the letters when they're done: Give your recommenders instructions about what to do with the completed letters. You may want to offer to pick them up, or you might explain that you have included addressed, stamped envelopes so that the letters can be mailed. If the letters are to be submitted electronically, provide these details.

Thank you: Recommendations may take several hours to complete, and your recommenders are very busy people. Don't forget to say thank you in advance for writing you a great letter of recommendation.

To illustrate the power of a good cover letter, read the example on the following page as if you were a recommender. Remember that this is only one example and your cover letter will naturally be different. However, regardless of your individual writing style, your cover letter should include the same points as the following example.

Some notes about this cover letter:

- Beth describes each scholarship she is applying for, its goal and deadline, and why she feels she is a match for the award.
- The heart of the cover letter is here, where Beth gives a quick summary of information she suggests her professor include in the letter.
- Beth provides instructions about what to do with the letters when completed.
- This is a well-written cover letter that is brief and easy to understand.

Dear Dr. Louis,

Thank you again for writing my scholarship recommendations. I want to do my best to be competitive for these awards. They are very important for my family as they will help me to pay for my education. Here are the scholarships I am applying for:

SuperCollege.com Scholarship Deadline: July 31
This is a national scholarship based on academic and non-academic achievement, including extracurricular activities and honors. I believe I'm a match for this scholarship because of my commitment to academics (I currently have a 3.85 grade point average) and because of the volunteer work I do with the Youth Literacy Project and the PLUS program.

Quill & Scroll Scholarship Deadline: April 20
This scholarship is for students who want to pursue a career in journalism. As you know, I am an editor for our school newspaper, contributing a column each week on issues that affect our student body. Journalism is the field I want to enter after graduation.

Community Scholarship Deadline: May 5
This scholarship is for students who have given back to their communities through public service. I have always been committed to public service. Outside of class, I not only formed the Youth Literacy Project but have also volunteered with the PLUS program.

To help you with your recommendation, I've enclosed a resume. Also, here are some highlights of specific accomplishments that I was hoping you might comment on in your letter:

* The essay I wrote for your class that won the Young Hemingway competition

* How I formed the Youth Literacy Project with you as the project's advisor

* My three years of volunteer work with the PLUS program

* The weekly column I've written for the newspaper on school issues

After you've finished, please return the recommendations to me in the envelopes I've enclosed. If you have any questions, please feel free to contact me at 555-5555. Again, thank you very much for taking the time to help me.

Sincerely,

Beth

Don't Let Your Recommenders Miss Deadlines

All recommenders have one thing in common: Too much to do and not enough time. It's important that you check with your recommender a couple of weeks before the letters are due. You need to monitor the progress of your recommendations. You may find that they're complete and already in the mail. A more common discovery is that they won't have been touched. Be polite yet diligent when you ask about the progress. It's crucial that you work with your recommenders to get the letters in on time.

The "You Can't Spell Success Without U" Mug

You now have everything you need to receive stellar recommendations. It's important to remember that even if it is a part of their job description, your recommenders are spending their time to help you. Remember this as you ask others to write recommendation letters and be sure to let them know that you appreciate their efforts.

Sometimes, a thank you gift is appropriate. Every time my (Kelly) mother wants to say thank you to a friend or acquaintance, she writes a note and gives a small token gift. My favorite is the "You Can't Spell Success Without U" mug because of its campy play on words.

Whether or not you select an equally campy token of appreciation, it's important that you thank your recommenders. After all, they are dedicating their free time to help you win funds for college.

Ace the Scholarship Interview

Chapter 7

The Face-to-Face Encounter

A judge for the Rotary International Ambassadorial Scholarship shared with us the following true story. For the last phase of the scholarship competition for his region, the finalists met with the selection committee for an interview. The interview was very important and was the final step in determining who would win the $25,000 scholarship.

One finalist was an Ivy League student who flew across the country for the interview. Within the first five minutes, it was painfully clear to all the judges that the applicant didn't have the foggiest idea what the Rotary Club stood for. It's as if the applicant thought that his resume and Ivy League pedigree would make him a winner. As you can guess, this applicant had a very disappointing flight back to his college. Lesson number one for the scholarship interview: At the very least, know what the organization stands for.

Many students dread the interview. If your heart beats faster or your palms moisten when you think about the prospect of sitting face to face with the judges, you are not alone. While the other parts of the scholarship application take time and effort, they can be done in the privacy of your home. Interviews, on the other hand, require interaction with—gasp—a real live human.

The good news is that the interview is usually the final step in the scholarship application process and if you make it that far, you're a serious contender. In this chapter, we show you what most scholarship committees are looking for and how you should prepare to deliver a winning interview. We also show you how to make the most of your nervousness and how to turn it into an asset rather than a liability.

There are two secrets for doing well in scholarship interviews. The first is this: Remind yourself over and over again that scholarship interviewers are real people. Repeat it until you believe it. As such, your goal is to have as normal a conversation as possible, despite the fact that thousands of dollars may hang in the balance. It's essential that you treat interviewers as real people, interact with them and ask them questions.

The second secret is just as important: The best way to have successful interviews is to train for them. The more you practice interviewing, the more comfortable you'll be during the real thing. Don't worry—we'll tell you what kinds of questions to expect and how to perfect your answers.

Why Human Interaction Is Necessary

The first step to delivering a knockout interview is to understand why some scholarships require interviews in the first place. With the popularity of technology like e-mail and text messaging, there seems to be less need for human interaction. (Believe it or not, there was a time when telephones were answered by a person instead of a maze of touchtone options.)

For some scholarship committees, a few pieces of paper with scores and autobiographical writing are not enough to get a full picture of who the applicants really are. They are giving away a lot of cash and the judges are responsible for making sure they are giving it to the most deserving students possible.

Scholarship judges use interviews as a way to learn how you compare in person versus on paper. Having been on both sides of the interview table, we can attest to the fact that the person you expect based on the written application is not always the person you meet at the interview. It's important to know that the purpose of interviews is not to interrogate you, but rather for the scholarship committee to get to know you better and probe deeper into the reason that you deserve their money.

Interviewers Are Real People Too

If you've ever met someone famous, you've probably realized that while celebrities' faces may grace the covers of magazines and they have houses big enough to merit their own ZIP code, they eat, drink and sleep and have likes and dislikes just like other people. The same thing holds true for interviewers.

Interviewers can be high-profile professors or high-powered businesspeople, but they are all passionate about some topics and bored with others. They enjoy speaking about themselves and getting to know more about you. Acknowledging this will help keep your nerves under control. Throughout the interview, remind yourself that your interviewer is human, and strive to make the interview a conversation, not an interrogation.

Interview Homework

You'd never walk into a test and expect to do well without studying the material. The same is true for interviews. Don't attempt them without doing your homework. There is basic information you need to know before starting your interviews so that you appear informed and knowledgeable. It's not difficult information to obtain, and it goes a long way in demonstrating that you care enough about winning to have put in some effort. Here are some things you should know before any interview:

Purpose of the scholarship: What is the organization hoping to accomplish by awarding the scholarship? Whether it's promoting students to enter a certain career area, encouraging a hobby or interest or rewarding students for leadership, every scholarship has a mission.

Criteria for selecting the winner: From the scholarship materials, you can get information about what the judges are hoping to find in a winner. From the kinds of information they request in the application to the topic of the essay question, each piece is a clue about what is important to the judges. Scholarships can be based on academic achievement, nonacademic achievement or leadership, to name a few criteria. Understand what kind of student the organization is seeking and stress that side of yourself during the interview.

Background of the awarding organization: Do a little digging on the organization itself. Check out its website or publications. Attend a meeting or speak with someone who's a member. From this detective work, you will get a better idea of who the organization's members are and what they are trying to achieve. It can also be a great topic of conversation during the interview.

Background of your interviewer: If possible, find out as much as you can about who will be interviewing you. In many cases, you may know little more than their names and occupations, but if you can, find out more. You already have one piece of important information about your interviewers: You know that they are passionate about the organization and its mission. They wouldn't be volunteering their time to conduct interviews if they weren't.

Use Your Detective Work to Create an Advantage

Once you've done your detective work on the above topics, it's time to use the information you've uncovered. For example, if you are in front of a group of doctors and they ask you about your activities, you would be better off discussing your work at the local hospital than your success on the baseball diamond. As much as possible, focus the conversation on areas where your activities, goals, interests and achievements match the goal of the awarding organization. By discussing what matters most to the scholarship judges, you will insure that this will be a memorable conversation—one that will set you apart from the other applicants that are interviewed.

By knowing something about your interviewers beforehand, you can think of topics and questions that will be interesting to them. Most interviewers allow some time for you to ask questions. Here again your detective work will come in handy since you can ask them about their background or the history of the organization. By asking intelligent questions (i.e. not the ones that can be answered by simply reading the group's mission statement) you will demonstrate that you've done your homework.

You'll also give interviewers something interesting to talk about—either themselves or their organization. The more information you can get before the interview, the better you will perform. Having this background material will also allow you to answer unexpected questions better and come up with thoughtful questions for the judges if you are put on the spot.

You Are Not the Center of the Universe

Despite what Mom or Dad says, the Earth revolves around the sun, not you. It helps to remember this in your interviews. Your life may be the most interesting ever lived, but this is still no excuse for speaking only about yourself for the duration of the interview.

The secret to successful interviews is simply this: They should be *interactive*. The surest way to bore your interviewers is to spend the entire time speaking only about yourself. You may have had the unfortunate experience of being on the receiving end of a conversation like this if you have a friend who speaks nonstop about herself and who never seems to be interested in your life or what you have to say. Don't you just hate this kind of conversation? So will your scholarship interviewers.

To prevent a self-centered monologue, constantly look for ways to interact with your interviewers. In addition to answering questions, ask some yourself. Ask about their experiences in school or with the organization. Inquire about their thoughts on some of the questions they pose to you. Take time to learn about your interviewers' experiences and perspectives.

Also, speak about topics that interest your interviewers. You can tell which topics intrigue them by their reactions and body language. From the detective work you've done, you also have an idea of what they are passionate about.

Try to make your interviews a two-way conversation instead of a one-way monologue. Engage your interviewers and keep them interested. If you do this, they will remember your interview as a great conversation and you as a wonderful, intelligent person deserving of their award.

Look and Sound the Part

Studies on the effectiveness of speeches have shown that how you sound and how you look when you present your material is more important than what you actually say. From that, we can learn that it is positively essential that you make a good visual presentation. Here are some tips to make sure that you look and sound your best, an important complement to what you actually say to the judges:

Dress appropriately: A backward-turned baseball cap and baggy jeans slung down to your thighs may be standard fare for the mall (at least they were last season), but they are not appropriate for interviews.

You probably don't have to wear a suit unless you find out through your research that the organization is very conservative, but you should dress appropriately. No-no's include the following: hats, bare midriffs, short skirts or shorts, open-toe shoes and iron-free wrinkles. Think about covering obtrusive tattoos or removing extra ear/nose/tongue/eyebrow rings. Don't dress so formally that you feel uncomfortable, but dress nicely. It may not seem fair, but your dress will affect the impression you make and influence the decision of the judges. Save making a statement of your individuality for a time when money is not in question.

Sit up straight: During interviews, do not slouch. Sitting up straight conveys confidence, leadership and intelligence. It communicates that you are interested in the conversation. Plus, it makes you look taller.

Speak in a positive tone of voice: One thing that keeps interviewers engaged is your tone. Make sure to speak in a positive one. This will not only maintain your interviewers' interest but will also suggest that you have an optimistic outlook. Of course, don't try so hard that you sound fake.

Don't be monotonous: If you've ever had a teacher or professor who speaks at the same rate and tone without variation, you know that this is the surest reason for a nap. Don't give your interviewers heavy eyelids. Record yourself and pay attention to your tone of voice. There should be natural variation in your timbre.

Speak at a natural pace: If you're like most people, the more nervous you are, the faster you speak. Be aware of this so that you don't speed talk through your interview.

Make natural gestures: Let your hands and face convey action and emotions. Use them as tools to illustrate anecdotes and punctuate important points.

Make eye contact: Eye contact engages interviewers and conveys self-assurance and honesty. If it is a group interview, make eye contact with all your interviewers—don't just focus on one. Maintaining good eye contact can be difficult, but just imagine little dollar signs in your interviewers' eyes and you shouldn't have any trouble. Ka-ching!

Smile: There's nothing more depressing than having a conversation with someone who never smiles. Don't smile nonstop, but show some teeth at least once in a while. If you use these tips, you will have a flawless look and sound to match what you're saying. All these attributes together create a powerful portrait of who you are. Unfortunately, not all these things come naturally, and you'll need to practice so that they can become unconscious actions.

The Practice Interview

One of the best ways to prepare for an interview is to do a dress rehearsal. This allows you to run through answering questions you might be asked and to practice honing your interview skills, including demeanor and style. You will feel more comfortable when it comes time for the actual interview. If anything will help you deliver a winning interview, it's practice. It may be difficult, but force yourself to set aside some time to run through a practice session at least once. Here's how:

Find a mock interviewer. Bribe or coerce a friend or family member to be your mock interviewer. Parents or teachers often make the best interviewers because they are closest in age and perspective to most actual scholarship interviewers.

Prep your mock interviewer. Share with your interviewer highlights from this chapter such as the purpose of scholarship interviews, what skills you want to practice and typical interview questions, which are described in the next section. If you're having trouble with eye contact, for example, ask them to take special notice of where you are looking when you speak and to make suggestions for correcting this.

Video yourself. Use your phone to video yourself so that you can review your mock interview afterward. Position it behind your interviewer so you can observe how you appear from their perspective.

Do the dress rehearsal. Grab two chairs and go for it. Answer questions and interact with your mock interviewer as if you were at the real thing. Get feedback. After you are finished, get constructive criticism from your mock interviewer. Find out what you did well and what you need to work on. What were the best parts of the interview? Which of your answers were strong, and which were weak? When did you capture or lose your mock interviewer's attention? Was your conversation one-way or two-way?

Review the video. Evaluate your performance. If you can, watch or listen to the video with your mock interviewer so you can get additional feedback. Listen carefully to how you answer questions so you can improve on them. Pay attention to your tone of voice. Watch your body language to see what you are unconsciously communicating.

Do it again. If you have the time and your mock interviewer has the energy or you can find another mock interviewer, do a second interview. If you can't find anyone, do it solo. Practice your answers, and focus on making some of the weaker ones more interesting. The bottom line is the more you practice, the better you'll do.

How to Answer to the Most Common Interview Questions

The best way to ace an exam would be to know the questions beforehand. The same is true for interview questions. From interviewing dozens of judges and applicants as well as having judged dozens of scholarship competitions ourselves, we've developed a list of commonly asked questions along with suggestions for answering them. This list is by no means comprehensive. There is no way to predict every question you will be asked, and in your actual interviews, the questions may not be worded in exactly the same way. However, the answer that interviewers are seeking is often the same.

Before your interviews, take the time to review this list. Add more questions particular to the specific scholarship to which you are applying. Practice answering these questions to yourself and in your mock interviews with friends and family. You will find that the answers you prepare to these questions will be invaluable during your real interviews. Even though the questions you are asked may be different, the thought that you put in now will help you formulate better answers. To the interviewer, you will sound incredibly articulate and thoughtful. Let's take a look at those questions.

Why did you choose your major?

- For major-based scholarships and even for general scholarships, interviewers want to know what motivated you to select the major, and they want a sense of how dedicated you are to that area of study. Make sure you have reasons for your decision. Keep in mind that an anecdote will provide color to your answer.
- If you are still in high school, you will probably be asked about your intended major. Make sure you have reasons for considering this major.

Why do you want to enter this career field?

- For scholarships that promote a specific career field, interviewers want to know your inspiration for entering the field and how committed you are to it. You will need to articulate the reasons and experiences that prompted your interest in this career and also anything you have done to prepare yourself for associated studies in this area.
- Be prepared to discuss your plans for after graduation, i.e. how will you use your education in the field you have chosen. You may be asked what kind of job you plan to have and why you would like it.
- Know something about the news in the field associated with the scholarship. For example, if you are applying for an information technology award, read up on the trends in the IT industry. There may be some major changes occurring that you will be asked to comment on.

What are your plans after graduation?

- You are not expected to know precisely what you'll do after graduation, but you need to be able to respond to this common question. Speak about what you are thinking about doing once you have that diploma in hand. The more specific you can be, the better.
- Provide reasons for your plans. Explain the process in which you developed your plans and what your motivation is.
- It's okay to discuss a couple of possible paths you may take, but don't bring up six very different options. Even if you are deciding among investment banking, the Peace Corps, banana farming and seminary, don't say so. The interviewer will think that you don't have a clear direction of what you want to do. This may very well be true, but it's not something you want to share. Select the one or two possible paths that you are most likely to take.

Why do you think you should win this scholarship?

- Focus your answer on characteristics and achievements that match the mission of the scholarship. For example, if the scholarship is for biology majors, discuss your accomplishments in the field of biology. Your answer may include personal qualities as well as specific accomplishments.
- Be confident but not arrogant. For this type of question, be careful about balancing pride and modesty in your answer. You want to be confident enough to have reasons why you should win the scholarship, but you don't want to sound overly boastful. To avoid sounding pompous, don't say that you are better than all the other applicants or put down your competition. Instead, focus on your strengths independent of the other people who are applying.
- Have three reasons. Three is the magic number that is not too many or too few. To answer this question just right, offer three explanations for why you fulfill the mission of the scholarship.

Tell me about times when you've been a leader.

- Interviewers ask this type of question (although sometimes worded a little differently) to gauge your leadership ability and your accomplishments as a leader. They want to award scholarships to students who will be leaders in the future. When you answer, try to discuss leadership you've shown that matches what the scholarship is meant to achieve.
- Don't just rattle off the leadership positions you've held. Instead, give qualitative descriptions of what you accomplished as a leader. Did your group meet its goals? Did you start something new? How did you

shape the morale of the group you led? For this kind of question, anecdotes and short stories are a good way to illustrate how you've been effective.

- Remember that leadership doesn't have to be a formally elected position. You can describe how you've informally led a special project or group. You could even define how you are a leader among your siblings.
- Be prepared to discuss what kind of leader you are. Your interviewer may ask about your approach to leadership or your philosophy on being a good leader. Have examples ready that show how you like to lead. For example, do you lead by example? Do you focus on motivating others and getting their buy-in?

What are your strengths? Weaknesses?

- As you are applying for jobs, you will answer this question more times than you will shake hands. It is a common job interview question that you may also get asked in scholarship interviews. Be prepared with three strengths and three weaknesses. Be honest about your weaknesses.
- Your strengths should match the mission of the scholarship and should highlight skills and accomplishments that match the characteristics the judges are seeking.
- You should be able to put a positive spin on your weaknesses. (And you'd better say you have some!) For example, your perfectionism could make you frustrated when things don't go the way you plan but could also make you a very motivated person. Your love of sports could detract from your studies but could provide a needed break and be representative of your belief in balance for your life. Just make sure that the spin you put on your weakness is appropriate and that your weakness is really a weakness.

Where do you see yourself ten years from now?

- We know that nobody knows exactly what he or she is going to be doing in ten years. The interviewers don't need specific details. They just want a general idea of what your long-term goals are and what you aspire to become. If you have several possibilities, at least one should be in line with the goals of the scholarship.
- Try to be as specific as possible without sounding unrealistic. For example, you can say that you would like to be working at a high-tech company in marketing, but leave out that you plan to have a daughter Sawyer, son Parker and dog Skip. Too much detail will make your dreams sound too naive.

Tell me about yourself. Or, is there anything you want to add?

- The most difficult questions are often the most open-ended. You have the freedom to say anything. For these kinds of questions, go back to the mission of the scholarship and shape your answer to reflect the characteristics that the judges are seeking in the winner. Practice answering this question several times because it is the one that stumps applicants the most.
- Have three things to say about yourself that match the goal of the scholarship. For example, you could discuss three personal traits you have, such as motivation, leadership skills and interpersonal skills. Or, you could discuss three skills applicable to academics, such as analytical skills, problem-solving skills and your love of a good challenge.
- The alternative, "Is there anything you want to add?" is typically asked at the end of the interview. In this case, make your response brief but meaningful. Highlight the most important thing you want your interviewer to remember.

Other Questions

In addition to these, here are some more common questions:

- What do you think you personally can contribute to this field?
- How do you plan to use what you have studied after graduation?
- Do you plan to continue your studies in graduate school?
- What do you want to specifically focus on within this field of study?
- Do you plan to do a thesis or senior project?
- Who are your role models in the field?
- What do you see as the future of this field?
- How do you see yourself growing in your career?
- What can you add to this field?
- What do you think are the most challenging aspects of this field?
- What is your ideal job after graduating from college?
- Tell me about a time that you overcame adversity.
- What are your opinions about (fill in political or field-related issue)?
- Tell me about your family.
- What do you hope to gain from college?
- Who is a role model for you?

- What is your favorite book? Why?
- What is the most challenging thing you have done?

Remember that with all these questions your goal is to demonstrate that you are the best fit for the scholarship. Be sure to practice these with your mock interviewer. The more comfortable and confident you feel answering these questions, the better you'll do in your interviews.

Questions for the Questioner

There is a huge difference between an interview and an interrogation. In an interview, you also ask questions. Make certain that your interview does not become an interrogation. Ask questions yourself throughout the conversation. Remember that you want to keep the conversation two-way.

Toward the end of your interview, you will probably have the opportunity to ask additional questions. Take this opportunity. If you don't ask any questions, it will appear that you are uninterested in the conversation or haven't put much thought into your interview. Take time before the interview to develop a list of questions you may want to ask. Of course you don't have to ask all your questions, but you need to be prepared to ask a few.

To get you started, we've developed some suggestions. Adapt these questions to the specific scholarship you are applying for and personalize them.

- How did you get involved with this organization?
- How did you enter this field? What was your motivation?
- Who do you see as your mentors in this field?
- What do you think are the most exciting things about your career?
- What advice do you have for someone starting out?
- What do you see as the greatest challenges for this field?
- What do you think will be the greatest advancements in ten years?
- What effect do you think technology will have on this field?
- I read that there is a (insert trend) in this field. What do you think?

The best questions are those that come from your detective work. Let's say that in researching an organization you discover that they recently launched a new program to research a cure for diabetes. Inquiring about this new program would be a perfect question to ask. It not only shows that you have done your homework, but it is also a subject about which the organization is deeply concerned.

Use Time to Your Advantage

The best time to ask Mom or Dad for something is when they're in a good mood. It's all about timing. Timing is also important in interviews. If you have more than one scholarship interview, time them strategically. Schedule less important and less demanding interviews first. This will allow you the opportunity to practice before your more difficult interviews. You will improve your skills as you do more interviews. It makes sense to hone your skills on the less important ones first.

If you are one of a series of applicants who will be interviewed, choose the order that fits you best. If you like to get things over with, try to be interviewed in the beginning. If you need more time to prepare yourself mentally, select a time near the end. We recommend that you don't choose to go first because the judges will use your interview as a benchmark for the rest. They may not recognize you as the best applicant even though it turns out to be true.

The Long-Distance Interview

If you've ever been in a long-distance relationship, you know there's a reason why most don't last. You simply can't communicate over the telephone in the same way you can in person. Scholarship interviews are the same. You may find that an interview will not be face to face but over the telephone instead. If this happens, here are some strategies to help bridge the distance:

Find a quiet place to do the interview where you won't be interrupted. You need to be able to give your full attention to the conversation you are having.

Know who's on the other end of the line. You may interview with a panel of people. Write down each of their names and positions when they first introduce themselves to you. They will be impressed when you are able to respond to them individually and thank each of them by name.

Use notes from your practice interviews. One of the advantages of doing an interview over the telephone is that you can refer to notes without your interviewers knowing. Take advantage of this.

Look and sound like you would in person. Pretend that your interviewers are in the room with you, and use the same gestures and facial expressions that you would if you were meeting in person. It may sound strange, but your interviewers will actually be able to hear through your voice when you are smiling, when you are paying attention and when you are enthusiastic about what you're saying. Don't do your interview lying down in your bed or slouched back in a recliner.

Don't use an unreliable phone. Speaker phones often echo and pick up distracting surrounding noise. If you use a cell phone, make sure you have good reception and a charged battery.

Turn off call waiting. Nothing is more annoying than hearing the call waiting beep while you are trying to focus and deliver an important thought. (And, this may sound obvious, never click over to take a second call.) Use the techniques of regular interviews. You'd be surprised how much is translated over the telephone. Don't neglect good speaking and delivery points just because the interviewers can't see you!

Secrets to the Group Interview

So it's you on one side of the table and a panel of six on the other side. It's certainly not the most natural way to have a conversation. How do you stay calm when you are interviewed by a council of judges?

Think of the group as individuals. Instead of thinking it's you versus the team, think of each of the interviewers as an individual. Try to connect with each person separately.

Try to get everyone's name if you can. Have a piece of paper handy that you can use to jot down everyone's name and role so that you can refer to them in the conversation. You want to be able to target your answers to each of the constituents. If you are interviewing with a panel of employees from a company and you know that Ms. Sweeny works in accounting while Mr. Duff works in human resources, you can speak about your analytical skills to appeal to Ms. Sweeny and your people skills to appeal to Mr. Duff.

Make eye contact. Look into the eyes of each of the panelists. Don't stare, but show them that you are confident. Be careful not to focus on only one member of the group.

Respect the hierarchy. You may find that there is a leader in the group like the scholarship chair or the CEO of the company. Pay a little more attention to stroke the ego of the person or persons in charge. They are used to it, they expect it and a little kissing up never hurt anyone.

Include everyone. In any group situation, there are usually one or two more vocal members who take the lead. Don't focus all your attention only on the loud ones. Spread your attention among the panelists as evenly as possible.

The Disaster Interview

Even if you do your interview homework and diligently practice mock interviewing, you may still find that you and your interviewer(s) just don't connect or that you just don't seem to have the right answers. For students who spend some time preparing, this is a very rare occurrence. Interviewers are not trying to trick you or make you feel bad. They are simply trying to find out more about you and your fit with the award. Still, if you think that you've bombed, here are some things to keep in mind:

Avoid should have, would have, could have. Don't replay the interview in your head again and again, thinking of all the things you should have said.

It's too easy to look back and have the best answers. Instead, use what you've learned to avoid making the same mistakes in your next interview.

There are no right answers. Remember that in reality there really are no right answers. Your answers may not have been perfect, but that doesn't mean that they were wrong. There are countless ways to answer the same question.

The toughest judge is you. Realize that you are your own greatest critic. While you may think that you completely bombed an interview, your interviewer will most likely not have as harsh an opinion.

The Post-Interview

After you complete your interviews, follow up with a thank you note. Remember that interviewers are typically volunteers and have made the time to meet with you. If you feel that there is very important information that you forgot to share in your interview, mention it briefly in your thank you note. If not, a simple note will suffice. You will leave a polite, lasting impression on your interviewer(s).

Final Thoughts

Chapter 8

How to Keep the Money You Win

When you learn to skydive, your first lesson does not start with jumping out of an airplane. First you go through training in which you learn techniques and safety measures—on the ground. Only after practicing on the ground can you take to the sky. In your scholarship education, you have just completed the ground training and are ready to take the plunge. As you move from the *strategies* for applying for scholarships to actually *applying* for them, we have a few words of advice on how to keep the dollars you earn and how to stay motivated.

Let's jump ahead to after you win a cache of scholarship dollars. It would be nice once the scholarship checks were written if you could run off for that well-deserved trip to the Bahamas. Alas, there are restrictions on how you can spend the cash and how you must maintain your scholarship. (Besides, everyone knows that Hawaii is the place to go.) Here are some tips to keep in mind:

Get to know your scholarship and financial aid administrators. These people will be able to answer questions about your award and make sure you are spending it in the way that you should.

Give the scholarship committee members proof if they want it. Some awards require that you provide proof of enrollment or transcripts. Send the committee whatever they need.

Be aware of your award's requirements and what happens if something changes. How long does the award last? What happens if you take a leave of absence, study part time, study abroad, transfer schools or quit your studies? College is full of possibilities! Do you have to maintain a minimum grade point average or take courses in a certain field?

Know if there are special requirements for athletic scholarships. If you've won an athletic scholarship, you are most likely required to play the sport. (You didn't get that full ride scholarship for nothing!) Understand the implications of what would happen if you were not able to play because of circumstances such as an injury or not meeting academic requirements.

Find out if the award is a cash cow (renewable). If an award is renewable, you are eligible to get it every year that you are in school. If so, find out what you need to do, and when you need to do it, to renew your scholarship. Some awards just require a copy of your transcript, while others require you to submit an entirely new application.

Understand restrictions for spending the dough. Some awards are limited to tuition. Others can be used for books, travel or even living expenses. Some provide the money directly to your school; others provide a check made out to you. Be aware of what you can spend the money on and what sort of records you need to keep.

Learn the tax implications of your award. Speak with the award administrator or your pals at the IRS (www.irs.gov or 800-829-1040). Be aware of requirements after you graduate. Some awards such as ROTC scholarships require employment after graduation. Because these arrangements can drastically affect your future, learn about the requirements now.

Keep the awarding organization up to date on your progress as a student. Write the organization a thank you note, and keep them updated on your progress at the end of the year. This is not only good manners, but it will also help ensure that the award is around in the future.

Parting Words

I (Gen) remember when I won the Sterling Scholarship, one of the highest honors for students in Hawaii. The awards ceremony was televised live throughout the state. For weeks before submitting my application, I prepared for the competition, compiling a 50-page application book, practicing for the eight hours of interviews and enlisting the help of no less than three teachers from my high school. Even though the scholarship was only $1,000, my parents still keep the trophy on display and share with unwitting visitors the videotape of my triumph. I realize now that I was able to put in such extensive effort because of my outlook on the award. I knew whether I won or lost, I would gain the experience of building a portfolio, becoming a skilled interviewee, working closely with my teachers and meeting some incredible students.

While scholarships are primarily a source of funding for your education, approach them in the same way you do your favorite sport or hobby. I also played for my school's tennis team—and lost just about every match. Yet, I continued because I enjoyed the sport and found the skills a challenge. If you approach your scholarships in this manner, you'll probably win more of them and have fun in the process. Treat them like a chore, and you'll hate every minute, neglecting to put in the effort required to win.

The bottom line is that if you are going to take the time to apply, you should take the time to win. The secrets, tips and strategies in this book will put you within striking distance. Follow them and you'll win more and more often. This book is unique in that it really is two books in one. Now that you know how to win, it's time to begin finding scholarships to put these strategies to use. The second half of this book is a complete listing of scholarships and awards and is indexed by various criteria so you can quickly find those that match your interests and qualifications. And, because we know you just can't get enough of us, we also encourage you to visit our website, SuperCollege.com, for the most up-to-date information on scholarships and financial aid.

We both wish you the best of luck.

A SPECIAL REQUEST

As you jump headlong into the wonderful world of scholarships, we have a special request. We would love to hear about your experiences with scholarships and how this book has helped you. Please send us a note after you've finished raking in your free cash for college.

Gen and Kelly Tanabe
c/o SuperCollege
2713 Newlands Avenue
Belmont, CA 94002

Onward! Flip the page and start finding scholarships. It's time to put all the strategies and tips you've just learned to work for you!

The Ultimate Scholarship Directory

Now it's time to put into action all that you learned in the first half of the book. We've done the hard work of scouring the country to find the best scholarships that you can win. We've made a special effort to select awards with broad eligibility requirements, which means you'll find plenty of scholarships that fit your background, goals and interests.

Before you jump into the directory, spend a few moments to learn how the scholarships are organized so you don't miss out on any awards for which you might be a good fit.

To help find the awards that match you best, we've conveniently organized our directory of scholarships into eight major categories.

Below is the complete list of categories and descriptions of the types of awards you'll find in each one. Remember to also use the various indexes in the back of the book to help you zero in on more scholarships.

General

This section lists scholarships that have the broadest eligibility requirements. Included are awards based on **academics**, **leadership** and **community service** to name a few. While some of the scholarships have GPA requirements, you'll be surprised at how many are not based on grades. Some are even awarded by random drawing.

Humanities / Arts

This section includes awards for students interested in **English** and **writing** as well as **foreign language** and **area studies**. It also includes all of the **visual and performing arts** such as **dancing**, **singing**, **acting**, **music**, **drawing**, **painting**, **sculpture**, **photography** and **graphic art**.

Social Sciences

This section deals with the study of the human aspects of the world. Often called the "soft sciences" it includes:

- Anthropology
- Accounting / Finance
- Archaeology
- Business Management
- Communications
- Criminology
- Economics
- Education / Teaching
- Geography
- History
- Hospitality / Travel
- International Relations
- Journalism / Broadcasting
- Law / Legal Studies
- Marketing / Sales
- Political Science
- Psychology
- Public Administration / Social Work
- Sociology
- Urban Studies

Sciences

Typically known as the "hard sciences," this category includes:

- Aerospace / Aviation
- Agriculture / Horticulture / Animals
- Anatomy
- Architecture
- Astronomy
- Biological Sciences / Life Sciences
- Biochemistry
- Chemistry
- Computer and Information Science
- Dentistry
- Earth and Planetary Sciences
- Ecology
- Engineering
- Forestry / Wildlife
- Geology
- Health Professions / Medicine
- Mathematics
- Neuroscience
- Nursing
- Oceanography
- Paleontology
- Pathology

- Pharmacology
- Physics
- Zoology

State of Residence

Here's your opportunity to get something back from your (or your parents') state tax dollars. Every state offers scholarships and grants for their residents. Some states even offer awards to out-of-state students who study in their states. Be sure to look at both your home state as well as any of the states you are planning to go to college in to find the most awards.

Membership

Many large **companies**, **unions**, **organizations** and **religious organizations** give awards to their members. If you or your parents are members of any of the groups in this category, you may qualify for a scholarship.

Ethnicity /Race/Gender/Family Situation/Sexual Orientation

There are a lot of awards for members of minority and nonminority ethnic groups, women and students with unique family situations.

Disability / Illness

This section has awards for students with physical, hearing, vision, mental and learning disabilities. It also includes awards for students who have been afflicted with certain illnesses.

"Take Off the Blinders" to Find the Most Scholarships

Now that you know the categories, the best way to find scholarships is to jump right in and head to the sections that fit you best.

Do you remember when your elementary school teacher used to say, "Take off the mental blinders"? Ours did to encourage us to think broadly. In the same way, we want to encourage you to "take off the scholarship blinders" and not think about yourself too narrowly. Consider your accomplishments, activities, goals and background as broadly as possible. Look through some of the categories even if you don't immediately see a fit. You might discover that you actually fit one of the leadership scholarships even if you haven't held a formal leadership position. Or you may find an award in the sciences category in a field that you love but never realized was a science.

Don't be afraid to be forward-thinking. Write down any scholarships that fit, even if you have to wait a year to apply. The awards we have selected are from the larger organizations and businesses, so you can be certain that they are going to be around for a long time.

We are really excited that you can now put everything that you learned to good use to help you find and win some free cash for college.

Happy scholarship hunting!

GENERAL

(1) • $1,000 JumpStart Scholarship

College JumpStart Scholarship Fund
4546 B10 El Camino Real, No. 325, Los Altos, CA 94022
http://www.jumpstart-scholarship.net
Purpose: To recognize students who are committed to using education to better their life and that of their family and/or community.
Eligibility: Applicants must be 10th, 11th or 12th grade high school, college or adult students. Applicants may study any major and attend any college in the U.S. Applicants must be legal residents of the U.S. and complete the online application form including the required personal statement. The award may be used for tuition, room and board, books or any related educational expense.
Target applicant(s): High school students. College students. Adult students.
Amount: $1,000.
Number of awards: 3.
Deadline: April 15, October 17.
How to apply: Applications are available online.
Exclusive: Visit www.UltimateScholarshipBook.com and enter code CO120 for updates on this award.

(2) • $1,000 Moolahspot Scholarship

MoolahSPOT
2713 Newlands Avenue, Belmont, CA 94002
http://www.moolahspot.com/index.cfm?scholarship=1
Purpose: To help students pay for college or graduate school.
Eligibility: Students must be at least 16 years or older and plan to attend or currently attend college or graduate school. Applicants may study any major or plan to enter any career field at any accredited college or graduate school. A short personal statement is required.
Target applicant(s): High school students. College students. Adult students.
Amount: $1,000.
Number of awards: Varies.
Deadline: April 30, August 31, December 31.
How to apply: Applications are only available online.
Exclusive: Visit www.UltimateScholarshipBook.com and enter code MO220 for updates on this award.

(3) • $1,000 Plan for College Sweepstakes

Sallie Mae
Sallie Mae, 300 Continental Drive, Newark, DE 19713
https://salliemae.com/scholarshipsearch
Purpose: To help students pay for college, Sallie Mae is awarding this $1,000 Plan for College Sweepstakes.
Eligibility: Enter to win $1,000 when you register for Sallie Mae's free college planning tools, resources and calculators. It's fast, easy, free and no essay required.
Target applicant(s): High school students. College students. Adult students.
Amount: $1,000.
Number of awards: 1 per month.
Deadline: January 31.
How to apply: Applications are available online.
Exclusive: Visit www.UltimateScholarshipBook.com and enter code SA320 for updates on this award.

(4) • $1,000 Scholarship Detective Launch Scholarship

http://www.scholarshipdetective.com/scholarship/
Purpose: To help college and adult students pay for college or graduate school.
Eligibility: Applicants must be high school, college or graduate students (including adult students) who are U.S. citizens or permanent residents. Students may study any major. The funds may be used to attend an accredited U.S. institution for undergraduate or graduate education.
Target applicant(s): High school students. College students. Adult students.
Amount: $1,000.
Number of awards: 2.
Deadline: May 31, August 31, December 31.
How to apply: Applications are available online.
Exclusive: Visit www.UltimateScholarshipBook.com and enter code SC420 for updates on this award.

(5) • 1 for 2 Education Foundation Scholarship

1 For 2 Education Foundation
4337 E. Grand River, Suite 198, Howell, MI 48843
Email: info@1for2edu.org
http://www.1for2edu.com
Purpose: To support highly motivated students who agree to "pay it forward."
Eligibility: Applicants must be enrolling as full-time students at an accredited four-year college or university and maintain a 3.0 GPA. Recipients agree to provide scholarships in the future.
Target applicant(s): High school students. College students. Graduate school students. Adult students.
Amount: $50,000.
Number of awards: 2.
Deadline: April 30.
How to apply: Applications are available online.
Exclusive: Visit www.UltimateScholarshipBook.com and enter code 1 520 for updates on this award.

(6) • 100th Infantry Battalion Memorial Scholarship Fund

Hawaii Community Foundation - Scholarships
827 Fort Street Mall, Honolulu, HI 96813
Phone: 888-731-3863
Email: scholarships@hcf-hawaii.org
https://www.hawaiicommunityfoundation.org
Purpose: To support students who promote the legacy of the 100th Infantry Battalion of World War II.
Eligibility: Applicants must be full-time undergraduate or graduate students at a two- or four-year college or university. They must be a direct descendant of a 100th Infantry Battalion World War II veteran and demonstrate excellence in academics and community service. A minimum 3.0 GPA is required. Students do not need to be a Hawaii resident.
Target applicant(s): High school students. College students. Graduate school students. Adult students.
Minimum GPA: 3.0
Amount: Varies.
Number of awards: Varies.
Deadline: January 31.
How to apply: Applications are available online. An application form, transcript and two letters of recommendation are required.

Exclusive: Visit www.UltimateScholarshipBook.com and enter code HA620 for updates on this award.

(7) • 1Dental Scholarship

1Dental.com
2501 Parkview Drive, Suite 210, Fort Worth, TX 76102
Phone: 800-372-7615
Email: scholarships@1dental.com
http://www.1dental.com/scholarship/
Purpose: To support students in higher education.
Eligibility: Applicants must be currently enrolled high school seniors, college or graduate school students who are also U.S. citizens. Applicants must answer a 30-question survey.
Target applicant(s): High school students. College students. Graduate school students. Adult students.
Amount: $1,000.
Number of awards: 1.
Deadline: December 21.
How to apply: Apply by submitting the essay by email along with your full name, address, phone number, name of high school or college you are attending, school address, current GPA and grade level.
Exclusive: Visit www.UltimateScholarshipBook.com and enter code 1D720 for updates on this award.

(8) • 1st Marine Division Association Scholarship

1st Marine Division Association Inc.
P.O. Box 9000, Box #902, Oceanside, CA 92051
Phone: 760-763-3268
Email: june.oldbreed@fmda.us
http://www.1stmarinedivisionassociation.org
Purpose: To provide financial aid to undergraduate students who are the dependents of deceased or disabled veterans of the 1st Marine Division.
Eligibility: Applicants must be dependents of honorably discharged veterans of the 1st Marine Division or units attached to or supporting the Division who are now deceased or totally and permanently disabled for any reason. Applicants must attend an accredited university as full-time undergraduate students.
Target applicant(s): College students. Adult students.
Amount: Up to $1,750.
Number of awards: Varies.
Scholarship may be renewable.
Deadline: Varies.
How to apply: Applications are available online.
Exclusive: Visit www.UltimateScholarshipBook.com and enter code 1S820 for updates on this award.

(9) • A Voice for Animals Essay Contest

Humane Education Network
P.O. Box 7434, Menlo Park, CA 94026
Phone: (650) 854-8921
http://www.hennet.org/contest.php
Purpose: To support students who wish to have a voice for animals.
Eligibility: Applicants must be high school students who plan to study any major. Applicants must write an essay as part of their application.
Target applicant(s): High school students.
Amount: Varies.
Number of awards: Varies.
Deadline: April 30.
How to apply: Applications are available online.

Exclusive: Visit www.UltimateScholarshipBook.com and enter code HU920 for updates on this award.

(10) • A-OK Student Reward Program

Navy Exchange
3280 Virginia Beach Boulevard, Virginia Beach, VA 23452-5724
Phone: 800-628-3924
https://www.mynavyexchange.com/
Purpose: To assist children of active-duty Navy members in paying for their college educations.
Eligibility: Applicants must be full-time students in first through 12th grade who are dependents of active-duty military members, reservists or retirees and have a B or higher grade point average.
Target applicant(s): Junior high students or younger. High school students.
Minimum GPA: 3.0
Amount: $500-$2,500.
Number of awards: 4.
Deadline: Quarterly.
How to apply: Applications are available from the Navy Exchange.
Exclusive: Visit www.UltimateScholarshipBook.com and enter code NA1020 for updates on this award.

(11) • AAU Karate Scholarship

AAU National Headquarters
c/o AAU Karate Scholarship, P.O. Box 22409, Lake Buena Vista, FL 32830
Phone: 407-828-3704
Email: jennifer@aausports.org
http://www.aaukarate.org
Purpose: To reward a young man or woman who participated in AAU Karate for no less than four years.
Eligibility: Applicants must be enrolled in an accredited college or university or plan to attend an accredited college or university in the fall.
Target applicant(s): High school students. College students. Adult students.
Amount: $1,000.
Number of awards: 2.
Deadline: May 5.
How to apply: Applications are available online. An application form, an essay, a letter of recommendation and transcripts are required.
Exclusive: Visit www.UltimateScholarshipBook.com and enter code AA1120 for updates on this award.

(12) • AAUS Student Scholarships

American Academy of Underwater Sciences
101 Bienville Boulevard, Dauphin Island, AL 36528
Phone: 251-591-3775
Email: aaus@disl.org
http://www.aaus.org/aaus_scholarships_information
Purpose: To support students involved in collegiate research in which diving is a principle research tool.
Eligibility: Applicants must be a current member of AAUS and attending an undergraduate or a graduate level program. Selection is based on the project proposal submitted by the applicant. The proposal must describe the benefits of the project and how the funds will be used.
Target applicant(s): College students. Graduate school students. Adult students.
Amount: Up to $3,000.
Number of awards: Varies.

Deadline: June 30.
How to apply: Applications are available online and include a written project proposal and at least one letter of recommendation.
Exclusive: Visit www.UltimateScholarshipBook.com and enter code AM1220 for updates on this award.

(13) • ACJA/Lambda Alpha Epsilon Scholarship

American Criminal Justice Association
P.O. Box 601047, Sacramento, CA 95860-1047
Phone: 916-484-6553
Email: acjalae@aol.com
http://www.acjalae.org
Purpose: To assist criminal justice students.
Eligibility: Applicants must be undergraduate or graduate students who are studying criminal justice. Students must be ACJA/LAE members, but they may submit a membership form at the time of application. Applicants must have completed at least two semesters or three quarters of their education while earning at least a 3.0 GPA. Applicants must submit transcripts, letters of enrollment and goals statements.
Target applicant(s): High school students. College students. Graduate school students. Adult students.
Minimum GPA: 3.0
Amount: Varies.
Number of awards: Varies.
Deadline: December 31.
How to apply: Applications are available online and by written request.
Exclusive: Visit www.UltimateScholarshipBook.com and enter code AM1320 for updates on this award.

(14) • ACT Student Champions

ACT
Phone: 319-337-1270
http://www.act.org/content/act/en/public-affairs/college-and-career-readiness-champions.html
Purpose: To reward students who have made exemplary college and career readiness efforts.
Eligibility: Applicants must be graduating high school seniors who have taken the ACT. Students must have a composite ACT score of 22 or have earned a minimum 3.0 grade point average. Applicants must demonstrate that they have overcome challenges and are tenacious in their pursuit of goals.
Target applicant(s): High school students.
Minimum GPA: 3.0
Amount: $500.
Number of awards: 50.
Deadline: October 31.
How to apply: Applications are available online.
Exclusive: Visit www.UltimateScholarshipBook.com and enter code AC1420 for updates on this award.

(15) • Admiral Mike Boorda Loan Program

Navy-Marine Corps Relief Society
875 North Randolph Street, Suite 225, Arlington, VA 22203
Phone: 703-696-4960
Email: education@nmcrs.org
http://www.nmcrs.org/pages/education-loans-and-scholarships
Purpose: To help eligible Navy and Marine Corps members.
Eligibility: Applicants must be enrolled or planning to enroll as full-time undergraduate students at an eligible post-secondary, technical or vocational institution. Applicants must have a minimum 2.0 GPA and be active duty servicemembers accepted to the Enlisted Commissioning Program, the Marine Enlisted Commissioning Education Program or the Medical Enlisted Commissioning Program.
Target applicant(s): College students. Adult students.
Minimum GPA: 2.0
Amount: $500-$3,000.
Number of awards: Varies.
Scholarship may be renewable.
Deadline: June 1.
How to apply: Applications are available online.
Exclusive: Visit www.UltimateScholarshipBook.com and enter code NA1520 for updates on this award.

(16) • Adult Skills Education Award

Imagine America Foundation
12001 Sunrise Valley Drive, Suite 203, Reston, VA 20191
Phone: 571-267-3010
Email: Leed@imagine-america.org
https://www.imagine-america.org/students/scholarships-education/
Purpose: To support adult learners with tuition assistance and college scholarships to career colleges.
Eligibility: Applicants must be U.S. citizens or permanent residents enrolling in a participating career college. Applicants must also either have a high school diploma, GED or pass an Ability to Benefit test. The minimum age requirement for application is 19. Applicants must also complete the NCCT Educational Success Potential Assessment. Selection is based on the overall strength of the application.
Target applicant(s): College students. Graduate school students. Adult students.
Amount: $1,000.
Number of awards: Varies.
Deadline: June 30.
How to apply: Applications are available online.
Exclusive: Visit www.UltimateScholarshipBook.com and enter code IM1620 for updates on this award.

(17) • Adzuna Student of the Year

Adzuna
40 Vanston Place, London, SW6 1AX
https://www.adzuna.com/student-of-the-year
Purpose: To help students who write about their dream job.
Eligibility: Applicants must be currently enrolled in an accredited post-secondary institution as an undergraduate or graduate student. Students must write an essay discussing what their dream job is and why they are the perfect candidate for that job.
Target applicant(s): College students. Graduate school students. Adult students.
Amount: $5,000.
Number of awards: 1.
Deadline: December 31.
How to apply: Applications are available online.
Exclusive: Visit www.UltimateScholarshipBook.com and enter code AD1720 for updates on this award.

(18) • AFCEA ROTC Scholarships

Armed Forces Communications and Electronics Association (AFCEA)
4400 Fair Lakes Court, Fairfax, VA 22033
Phone: 703-631-6149

http://www.afcea.org
Purpose: To assist ROTC sophomores or juniors who are majoring in aerospace engineering, electronics, computer science, computer engineering, physics or mathematics.
Eligibility: Applicants must major in electrical or aerospace engineering, electronics, computer science, computer engineering, physics or mathematics at an accredited U.S. four-year college or university. Applicants must also be enrolled full-time as college sophomores or juniors and be nominated by professors of military science, naval science or aerospace studies. Applicants must be U.S. citizens enrolled in ROTC, have good moral character, demonstrate academic excellence and the potential to serve as an officer in the U.S. Armed Forces and have financial need.
Target applicant(s): College students. Adult students.
Minimum GPA: 3.0
Amount: $2,000-$3,000.
Number of awards: Varies.
Deadline: February 22.
How to apply: Applications are available online.
Exclusive: Visit www.UltimateScholarshipBook.com and enter code AR1820 for updates on this award.

---

(19) • AFSA National Essay Contest

American Foreign Service Association (AFSA)
2101 East Street NW, Washington, DC 20037
Phone: 202-944-5504
Email: dec@afsa.org
http://www.afsa.org
Purpose: To support students interested in writing an essay on foreign service.
Eligibility: Applicants must be U.S. Citizens, high school students and have parents who are not members of the Foreign Service. Students must attend a public, private, parochial school, home school or participate in a high school correspondence program in any of the 50 states, the District of Columbia or U.S. territories or must be U.S. citizens attending schools overseas. The current award is $2,500 to the student and all expenses paid trip to Washington, DC, for the winner and parents.
Target applicant(s): High school students.
Amount: $2,500.
Number of awards: 1.
Deadline: March 15.
How to apply: The registration form is available online. Applicants must write a 750- to 1,000-word essay on the topic provided.
Exclusive: Visit www.UltimateScholarshipBook.com and enter code AM1920 for updates on this award.

---

(20) • Ag Day Essay Contest

Agriculture Council of America
11020 King Street, Suite 205, Overland Park, KS 66210
Phone: 913-491-1895
Email: jenam@nama.org
https://www.agday.org/essay-contest
Purpose: To support agricultural awareness while encouraging students to pursue higher education.
Eligibility: Applicants must be in 9th to 12th grade during the current school year and be a U.S. citizen. The contest requires an essay or video response to the given prompt on the website.
Target applicant(s): High school students.
Amount: $1,000.
Number of awards: 2.
Deadline: January 31.
How to apply: Applications are available online.
Exclusive: Visit www.UltimateScholarshipBook.com and enter code AG2020 for updates on this award.

---

(21) • AHHS Foundation Scholarship

American Hackney Horse Society
4059 Iron Works Parkway A-3, Lexington, KY 40511-8462
Phone: 859-255-8694
Email: ahhscsl@qx.net
http://hackneysociety.com/
Purpose: To aid incoming college freshmen who promote the Hackney industry.
Eligibility: The applicant must be a high school senior or recent graduate. Selection is based on academic achievement, financial need, community service, involvement with Hackney Horses and the letters of recommendation.
Target applicant(s): High school students.
Amount: $2,500.
Number of awards: Varies.
Deadline: July 15.
How to apply: Applications are available online and include a personal essay, an official transcript and three letters of recommendation. A personal interview may also be required.
Exclusive: Visit www.UltimateScholarshipBook.com and enter code AM2120 for updates on this award.

---

(22) • Air Force ROTC ASCP

Air Force Reserve Officer Training Corps
HQ AFROTC/DOR, 60 West Maxwell Boulevard, Maxwell AFB, AL 36112-6501
Phone: 866-423-7682
https://www.afrotc.com/scholarships
Purpose: To allow active duty Air Force personnel to earn a commission while completing their bachelor's degree.
Eligibility: Applicants must be active-duty Air Force personnel who are U.S. citizens under the age of 31, with the exception of nurses, who must be under the age of 42. They must also meet all testing and waiver requirements and be recommended by their commanding officer. Applicants must have at least 24 hours of graded college course work with at least a 3.0 cumulative GPA and have a minimum ACT composite score of 26 or an SAT combined Reading and Math score of 1180 or an AFOQT Academic Aptitude score of 55.
Target applicant(s): High school students. College students. Adult students.
Minimum GPA: 3.0
Amount: Up to $18,000 plus textbook allowance and stipend.
Number of awards: Varies.
Scholarship may be renewable.
Deadline: October 15.
How to apply: Application details are available online.
Exclusive: Visit www.UltimateScholarshipBook.com and enter code AI2220 for updates on this award.

---

(23) • Air Force ROTC High School Scholarship Program

Air Force Reserve Officer Training Corps
HQ AFROTC/DOR, 60 West Maxwell Boulevard, Maxwell AFB, AL 36112-6501
Phone: 866-423-7682
https://www.afrotc.com/scholarships

Purpose: To help students with financial need who are also interested in joining the Air Force in order to pay for college.
Eligibility: Applicants must pass the physical fitness assessment and demonstrate academic achievement or outstanding leadership skills. There are three types of award: one that pays full tuition, most fees and a book allowance, one that pays tuition and fees up to $18,000 and a book allowance and one that pays the equivalent of in-state tuition and a book allowance. In return for the scholarship, recipients must serve in the Air Force. Applicants must have minimum ACT score of 24 or minimum SAT score of 1100. GPA minimum requirement is 3.0.
Target applicant(s): High school students.
Minimum GPA: 3.0
Amount: Up to full tuition plus fees, books and stipend.
Number of awards: Varies.
Scholarship may be renewable.
Deadline: December 1.
How to apply: Applications are available online.
Exclusive: Visit www.UltimateScholarshipBook.com and enter code AI2320 for updates on this award.

---

(24) • Air Force ROTC In-College Program

Air Force Reserve Officer Training Corps
HQ AFROTC/DOR, 60 West Maxwell Boulevard, Maxwell AFB, AL 36112-6501
Phone: 866-423-7682
https://www.afrotc.com/scholarships
Purpose: To promote the Air Force ROTC program.
Eligibility: Applicants must be U.S. citizens who have passed the Air Force Officer Qualifying Test, the Air Force ROTC Physical Fitness Test and a Department of Defense medical examination. Students must also be college freshmen or sophomores and have a GPA of 2.5 or higher.
Target applicant(s): College students. Adult students.
Minimum GPA: 2.5
Amount: Varies.
Number of awards: Varies.
Scholarship may be renewable.
Deadline: December 1.
How to apply: Applications are available from your school's Air Force ROTC detachment.
Exclusive: Visit www.UltimateScholarshipBook.com and enter code AI2420 for updates on this award.

---

(25) • Air Force ROTC Professional Officer Course-Early Release Program

Air Force Reserve Officer Training Corps
HQ AFROTC/DOR, 60 West Maxwell Boulevard, Maxwell AFB, AL 36112-6501
Phone: 866-423-7682
https://www.afrotc.com/scholarships
Purpose: To allow active duty Air Force personnel the opportunity for early release in order to complete their bachelor's degrees.
Eligibility: Applicants must be active-duty Air Force personnel who are U.S. citizens under the age of 31, with the exception of nurses, who must be under the age of 42. They must also meet all testing and waiver requirements, be recommended by their commanding officer and not be within one year of receiving their degree.
Target applicant(s): College students. Adult students.
Minimum GPA: 2.5
Amount: Varies.
Number of awards: Varies.
Scholarship may be renewable.
Deadline: October 15.
How to apply: Application details are available online.
Exclusive: Visit www.UltimateScholarshipBook.com and enter code AI2520 for updates on this award.

---

(26) • Air Force ROTC SOAR Program

Air Force Reserve Officer Training Corps
HQ AFROTC/DOR, 60 West Maxwell Boulevard, Maxwell AFB, AL 36112-6501
Phone: 866-423-7682
https://www.afrotc.com/scholarships
Purpose: To give active duty Air Force personnel the opportunity to earn their commissions while completing their bachelor's degrees.
Eligibility: Applicants must be active-duty Air Force personnel who are U.S. citizens under the age of 31, with the exception of nurses, who must be under the age of 47. They must also meet all testing and waiver requirements and be recommended by their commanding officer. Students must have at least 24 hours of graded college course work with at least a 3.0 cumulative GPA and have a minimum ACT composite score of 25 or an SAT combined Reading and Math score of 1180 or an AFOQT Academic Aptitude score of 55.
Target applicant(s): College students. Adult students.
Minimum GPA: 3.0
Amount: Up to $18,000 plus textbook allowance and stipend.
Number of awards: Varies.
Scholarship may be renewable.
Deadline: October 15.
How to apply: Application details are available online.
Exclusive: Visit www.UltimateScholarshipBook.com and enter code AI2620 for updates on this award.

---

(27) • Airmen Memorial Foundation Scholarship Program

Air Force Sergeants Association
5211 Auth Road, Suitland, MD 20746
Phone: 301-899-3500
Email: staff@hqafsa.org
http://www.hqafsa.org
Purpose: To assist dependents of Air Force enlisted personnel in obtaining higher education.
Eligibility: Applicants must be dependents of Air Force enlisted personnel who are attending high school or college. They must have a GPA of 3.5 or higher and be accepted to the college of their choice.
Target applicant(s): High school students. College students. Adult students.
Minimum GPA: 3.5
Amount: Up to $2,000.
Number of awards: Varies.
Deadline: March 31.
How to apply: Applications are available online.
Exclusive: Visit www.UltimateScholarshipBook.com and enter code AI2720 for updates on this award.

---

(28) • Akash Kuruvilla Memorial Scholarship

Akash Kuruvilla Memorial Scholarship Fund Inc.
P.O. Box 140900, Gainesville, FL 32614
Email: akmsfinfo@gmail.com
https://www.akmscholarship.com

Purpose: To continue the legacy of Akash Jacob Kuruvilla.
Eligibility: Applicants must be entering or current full-time college students at an accredited U.S. four-year college or university. They must demonstrate academic achievement, leadership, integrity and excellence in diversity. Selection is based on character, financial need and the applicant's potential to impact his or her community.
Target applicant(s): High school students. College students. Adult students.
Amount: $1,000.
Number of awards: 2.
Deadline: June 28.
How to apply: Applications are available online. An application form, essay, personal statement, one recommendation letter and resume are required.
Exclusive: Visit www.UltimateScholarshipBook.com and enter code AK2820 for updates on this award.

(29) · All-American Scholars (Cheerleading)

Pop Warner Little Scholars, Inc.
586 Middletown Boulevard, Suite C-100, Langhorne, PA 19047
Phone: 215-752-2691
http://www.popwarner.com/
Purpose: To recognize Pop Warner participants for their academic accomplishments.
Eligibility: Applicant must be a participant in the Pop Warner program as a cheerleader, be in grade 5 or higher and maintain a 96 percent grade point average or higher. Selection will be based on academic achievement and additional non-sport related activities and achievements.
Target applicant(s): Junior high students or younger. High school students.
Minimum GPA: 3.8
Amount: Varies.
Number of awards: Varies.
Deadline: Varies.
How to apply: Applications are available online.
Exclusive: Visit www.UltimateScholarshipBook.com and enter code PO2920 for updates on this award.

(30) · All-American Scholars (Football)

Pop Warner Little Scholars, Inc.
586 Middletown Boulevard, Suite C-100, Langhorne, PA 19047
Phone: 215-752-2691
http://www.popwarner.com/
Purpose: To recognize Pop Warner participants for their academic accomplishments.
Eligibility: Applicants must be a participant in the Pop Warner program as a football player, be in grade 5 or higher and maintain a 96 percent grade point average or higher. Selection will be based on academic achievement and additional non-sport related activities and achievements.
Target applicant(s): Junior high students or younger. High school students.
Minimum GPA: 3.8
Amount: Varies.
Number of awards: Varies.
Deadline: Varies.
How to apply: Applications are available online.
Exclusive: Visit www.UltimateScholarshipBook.com and enter code PO3020 for updates on this award.

(31) · Alpha Kappa Alpha Financial Need Scholars

Alpha Kappa Alpha Educational Advancement Foundation Inc.
5656 S. Stony Island Avenue, Chicago, IL 60637
Phone: 800-653-6528
Email: akaeaf@akaeaf.net
https://akaeaf.org/scholarships
Purpose: To assist undergraduate and graduate students who have overcome hardship to achieve educational goals.
Eligibility: Applicants must be studying full-time at the sophomore level or higher at an accredited institution and have a GPA of 2.5 or higher. Students must also demonstrate leadership, volunteer, civic or academic service. The program is open to students without regard to sex, race, creed, color, ethnicity, religion, sexual orientation or disability. Students do NOT need to be members of Alpha Kappa Alpha. Deadline is April 15 for undergraduate students and August 15 for graduate students.
Target applicant(s): College students. Graduate school students. Adult students.
Minimum GPA: 2.5
Amount: Varies.
Number of awards: Varies.
Deadline: April 15 and August 15.
How to apply: Applications are available online. An application form, personal statement and three letters of recommendation are required.
Exclusive: Visit www.UltimateScholarshipBook.com and enter code AL3120 for updates on this award.

(32) · Alphonso Deal Scholarship Award

National Black Police Association
NBPA Scholarship Award, 3100 Main Street #256, Dallas, TX 75226
Phone: 855-879-6272
http://www.blackpolice.org/scholarships.html
Purpose: To support students who plan careers in law enforcement.
Eligibility: Applicants must be collegebound high school seniors planning to study law enforcement or a field related to the criminal justice system who are U.S. citizens and are recommended by their high school principal, counselor or teacher.
Target applicant(s): High school students.
Amount: Varies.
Number of awards: Varies.
Deadline: May 19.
How to apply: Applications are available online.
Exclusive: Visit www.UltimateScholarshipBook.com and enter code NA3220 for updates on this award.

(33) · America's 911 Foundation Scholarship

America's 911 Foundation, Inc.
13630 Barnhouse Place, Leesburg, VA 20176
Phone: 703-771-0118
http://www.americas911foundation.org
Purpose: To support students who are children of a first responder.
Eligibility: Applicants must be a child of an active duty or volunteer first responder. Students must be accepted to a college or university.
Target applicant(s): High school students. College students. Graduate school students. Adult students.
Amount: $2,000.
Number of awards: 15.
Deadline: March 19.
How to apply: Applications are available online.

Exclusive: Visit www.UltimateScholarshipBook.com and enter code AM3320 for updates on this award.

(34) • American Bar Association Law Day Art Contest

American Bar Association (ABA)
321 North Clark Street, Chicago, IL 60654
Phone: 312-988-5000
http://www.americanbar.org
Purpose: To encourage students to learn about the legal system.
Eligibility: Applicants must be high school students in grades 9-12 or the equivalent within the United States. Students must create an art piece representing the theme for Law Day.
Target applicant(s): High school students.
Amount: $750.
Number of awards: 2.
Deadline: March 31.
How to apply: Applications are available online.
Exclusive: Visit www.UltimateScholarshipBook.com and enter code AM3420 for updates on this award.

(35) • American Darts Organization Memorial Scholarships

American Darts Organization
Youth Scholarship Fund, 8900 Melodic Court, Elk Grove, CA 95624
Phone: 844-883-2787
Email: thermae@surewest.net
http://www.adoyouthdarts.com/
Purpose: To support participants in the American Darts Organization Youth Playoff Program.
Eligibility: Applicants must be ADO members, and they must have been at least quarter-finalists in the ADO Youth Playoff Program. Students must be under 21 years old on December 1 of the year in which they intend to start school. They must be enrolled or accepted in a degree-granting program on a full-time basis with at least a 2.0 GPA.
Target applicant(s): High school students. College students.
Minimum GPA: 2.0
Amount: $500-$1,500.
Number of awards: 8.
Deadline: June 30.
How to apply: Applications are available online.
Exclusive: Visit www.UltimateScholarshipBook.com and enter code AM3520 for updates on this award.

(36) • American Fire Sprinkler Association High School Senior Scholarship Contest

American Fire Sprinkler Association
12750 Merit Drive, Suite 350, Dallas, TX 75251
Phone: 214-349-5965
Email: scholarship@firesprinkler.org
http://www.afsascholarship.org
Purpose: To provide financial aid to high school seniors and introduce them to the fire sprinkler industry.
Eligibility: Applicants must be high school seniors who plan to attend a U.S. college, university or certified trade school. Students must read the "Fire Sprinkler Essay" available online and then take an online quiz. Applicants receive one entry in the scholarship drawing for each question answered correctly.
Target applicant(s): High school students.
Amount: $2,000.
Number of awards: 10.
Scholarship may be renewable.
Deadline: April 1.
How to apply: Applications are available online.
Exclusive: Visit www.UltimateScholarshipBook.com and enter code AM3620 for updates on this award.

(37) • American Legion Baseball Scholarship

American Legion Baseball
700 N. Pennsylvania Street, P.O. Box 1055, Indianapolis, IN 46206
Phone: 317-630-1203
Email: baseball@legion.org
https://www.legion.org/scholarships/baseball
Purpose: To award scholarships to members of American Legion-affiliated baseball teams.
Eligibility: Applicants must have graduated high school and be nominated by a head coach or team manager. One player per department (state) will be selected. Nominations should be sent to the local Department Headquarters. Scholarships may be used to further education at any accredited college, university or other institution of higher education.
Target applicant(s): College students. Adult students.
Amount: $2,500-$5,000.
Number of awards: 9.
Deadline: July 15.
How to apply: Applications are available online.
Exclusive: Visit www.UltimateScholarshipBook.com and enter code AM3720 for updates on this award.

(38) • American Legion Legacy Scholarships

American Legion
700 North Pennsylvania Street, P.O. Box 1055, Indianapolis, IN 46206
Phone: 317-630-1202
https://www.legion.org/scholarships
Purpose: To support the children of deceased U.S. military personnel.
Eligibility: Applicants must be the children or adopted children of a parent who was in the U.S. military and died in active duty on or after September 11, 2001. Students must be high school seniors or high school graduates pursuing or planning to pursue undergraduate study in the U.S.
Target applicant(s): High school students. College students. Adult students.
Amount: Up to $20,000.
Number of awards: Varies.
Deadline: March 15.
How to apply: Applications are available online.
Exclusive: Visit www.UltimateScholarshipBook.com and enter code AM3820 for updates on this award.

(39) • American Society of Crime Laboratory Directors Scholarship Program

American Society of Crime Laboratory Directors
139A Technology Drive, Garner, NC 27529
Phone: 919-773-2600
http://www.ascld.org
Purpose: To help students who are enrolled in a forensics-related degree program and who plan to pursue a career in the forensics field.
Eligibility: Applicants must be rising undergraduate juniors, rising undergraduate seniors or graduate students who are enrolled in a degree

program in forensic science, forensic chemistry or a related physical or natural science. They must attend an accredited university and must be interested in pursuing a career in the field of forensics. Preference is given to students who are enrolled in degree programs accredited by the Forensic Science Education Program Accreditation Commission (FEPAC). Selection is based on overall academic achievement, achievement in forensics coursework, personal statement, level of interest in forensics careers and recommendation letter.
Target applicant(s): College students. Graduate school students. Adult students.
Amount: $1,000.
Number of awards: Varies.
Deadline: April 15.
How to apply: Applications are available online. An application form, transcripts, personal statement and one recommendation letter are required.
Exclusive: Visit www.UltimateScholarshipBook.com and enter code AM3920 for updates on this award.

---

(40) · Americanism Essay Contest

Fleet Reserve Association (FRA)
FRA Scholarship Administrator, 125 N. West Street, Alexandria, VA 22314
Phone: 800-372-1924
Email: news-fra@fra.org
http://www.fra.org
Purpose: To recognize outstanding student essayists.
Eligibility: Applicants must be in grades 7 through 12 and must be sponsored by a Fleet Reserve Association (FRA) branch or Ladies Auxiliary unit. They must submit an essay on a sponsor-determined topic. Selection is based on the overall strength of the essay.
Target applicant(s): Junior high students or younger. High school students.
Amount: $2,500-$5,000.
Number of awards: Varies.
Deadline: December 1.
How to apply: Entry instructions are available online - look under "events and programs" link. An essay and cover sheet are required.
Exclusive: Visit www.UltimateScholarshipBook.com and enter code FL4020 for updates on this award.

---

(41) · Americorps National Civilian Community Corps

AmeriCorps
1201 New York Avenue NW, Washington, DC 20525
Phone: 202-606-5000
Email: questions@americorps.org
http://www.americorps.gov
Purpose: To strengthen communities and develop leaders through community service.
Eligibility: Applicants must be U.S. citizens who are between 18 and 24 years of age. Recipients must live on one of five AmeriCorps campuses in Denver, Colorado; Sacramento, California; Baltimore, Maryland; Vinton, Iowa or Vicksburg, Mississippi. Applicants must commit to 10 months of service on projects in areas such as education, public safety, the environment and other unmet needs. The projects are located within the region of one of the four campuses.
Target applicant(s): High school students. College students. Graduate school students. Adult students.
Amount: $5,775.
Number of awards: Varies.
Deadline: Varies.
How to apply: Applications are available online.
Exclusive: Visit www.UltimateScholarshipBook.com and enter code AM4120 for updates on this award.

---

(42) · Americorps Vista

AmeriCorps
1201 New York Avenue NW, Washington, DC 20525
Phone: 202-606-5000
Email: questions@americorps.org
http://www.americorps.gov
Purpose: To provide education assistance in exchange for community service.
Eligibility: Applicants must be United States citizens who are at least 17 years of age. They must be available to serve full-time for one year at a nonprofit organization or local government agency with an objective that may include to fight illiteracy, improve health services, create businesses or strengthen community groups.
Target applicant(s): High school students. College students. Graduate school students. Adult students.
Amount: Varies.
Number of awards: Varies.
Deadline: Varies.
How to apply: Applications are available online.
Exclusive: Visit www.UltimateScholarshipBook.com and enter code AM4220 for updates on this award.

---

(43) · AMVETS National Scholarships for Entering College Freshman

AMVETS National Headquarters
4647 Forbes Boulevard, Lanham, MD 20706-4380
Phone: 877-726-8387
Email: thilton@amvets.org
http://www.amvets.org
Purpose: To provide education assistance for graduating JROTC cadets.
Eligibility: Applicants must be high school seniors with a minimum GPA of 3.0 or documented extenuating circumstances. They must be United States citizens and children or grandchildren of U.S. veterans. They must show academic potential and financial need.
Target applicant(s): High school students.
Minimum GPA: 3.0
Amount: $1,000.
Number of awards: 1.
Deadline: May 1.
How to apply: Applications are available online.
Exclusive: Visit www.UltimateScholarshipBook.com and enter code AM4320 for updates on this award.

---

(44) · AMVETS National Scholarships for Veterans

AMVETS National Headquarters
4647 Forbes Boulevard, Lanham, MD 20706-4380
Phone: 877-726-8387
Email: thilton@amvets.org
http://www.amvets.org
Purpose: To provide financial assistance for veterans.
Eligibility: Applicants must be United States citizens and veterans who demonstrate financial need. They must have been honorably discharged or be on active duty and eligible for release. They must agree to allow AMVET to publicize their award if selected.
Target applicant(s): College students. Adult students.
Amount: $1,000-$12,000.

Number of awards: Varies.
Deadline: May 1.
How to apply: Applications are available online.
Exclusive: Visit www.UltimateScholarshipBook.com and enter code AM4420 for updates on this award.

(45) • Anchor Scholarship Foundation Scholarship

Anchor Scholarship Foundation
4966 Euclid Road, Suite 109, Virginia Beach, VA 23462
Phone: 757-671-3200
Email: ScholarshipAdmin@AnchorScholarship.com
http://www.anchorscholarship.com
Purpose: To assist the dependents of current and former members of the Naval Surface Forces, Atlantic and Naval Surface Forces, Pacific.
Eligibility: Applicants must be high school seniors or college students planning to attend or currently attending an accredited, four-year college or university full-time. Applicants must also be dependents of service members who are on active duty or retired and have served a minimum of six years in a unit under the administrative control of Commander, Naval Surface Forces, U.S. Atlantic Fleet or U.S. Pacific Fleet. The award is based on academics, extracurricular activities, character, all-around ability and financial need.
Target applicant(s): High school students. College students. Adult students.
Amount: Varies.
Number of awards: Varies.
Deadline: March 1.
How to apply: Applications are available online.
Exclusive: Visit www.UltimateScholarshipBook.com and enter code AN4520 for updates on this award.

(46) • Annual Community Volunteer Scholarship

Dealhack
140 Broadview Avenue, Suite 31, Toronto, ON Canada M4M
https://dealhack.com/scholarship
Purpose: To assist students with exceptional volunteer involvement.
Eligibility: Applicants must be enrolled as full-time students at a college or university in the U.S. or Canada. Students must demonstrate outstanding community volunteer involvement.
Target applicant(s): High school students. College students. Graduate school students. Adult students.
Amount: $1,500.
Number of awards: 1.
Deadline: June 30.
How to apply: Applications are available online.
Exclusive: Visit www.UltimateScholarshipBook.com and enter code DE4620 for updates on this award.

(47) • Applying for the College Success Scholarship

Study.com
100 View Street #202, Mountain View, CA 94041
https://study.com/pages/Academic_Awards_Home.html
Purpose: To support students who are pursuing a higher education.
Eligibility: Applicants must be citizens of the United States who are either graduating high school seniors or students currently enrolled at an accredited college or university. Students must have a minimum of 30 semester hours or 40 quarter hours remaining in their program until graduation.
Target applicant(s): High school students. College students. Adult students.
Amount: $1,000.
Number of awards: 1.
Deadline: April 1.
How to apply: Applications are available online.
Exclusive: Visit www.UltimateScholarshipBook.com and enter code ST4720 for updates on this award.

(48) • Armed Services YMCA Annual Essay Contest

Armed Services YMCA
7405 Alban Station Court, Suite B215, Springfield, VA 22150-2318
Phone: 703-313-9600
Email: essaycontest@asymca.org
http://www.asymca.org
Purpose: To promote reading among children of service members and civilian Department of Defense employees.
Eligibility: Applicants must be K-12 students who are children of active duty or Reserve/Guard military personnel. Entrants up to eighth grade should write an essay of 300 words or less. High school entrants should write an essay of 500 words or less.
Target applicant(s): Junior high students or younger. High school students.
Amount: Varies.
Number of awards: Varies.
Deadline: Varies.
How to apply: Applications are available online.
Exclusive: Visit www.UltimateScholarshipBook.com and enter code AR4820 for updates on this award.

(49) • Army Emergency Relief's MG James Ursano Scholarship Program

Army Emergency Relief (AER)
200 Stovall Street Rm. 5S33, Alexandria, VA 22332
Phone: 703-428-0035
Email: education@aerhq.org
https://www.aerhq.org/Apply-for-Scholarship
Purpose: To assist the children of Army families with their undergraduate education, vocational training and service academy education.
Eligibility: Applicants must be dependent children of Army soldiers who are unmarried and under the age of 22. Students must also be registered with the Defense Eligibility Enrollment Reporting System, have a minimum 2.0 GPA and be enrolled and accepted or pending acceptance as full-time students in post-secondary educational institutions. Awards are based primarily on financial need.
Target applicant(s): High school students. College students.
Minimum GPA: 2.0
Amount: Varies.
Number of awards: Varies.
Scholarship may be renewable.
Deadline: April 1.
How to apply: Applications are available online and by mail.
Exclusive: Visit www.UltimateScholarshipBook.com and enter code AR4920 for updates on this award.

(50) • Army Nurse Corps Association Scholarships

Army Nurse Corps Association (ANCA)
Scholarship Program, P.O. Box 458, Lisbon, MD 21765
Phone: 210-650-3534
Email: education@e-anca.org
http://e-anca.org/Scholarships

Purpose: To support nursing and nurse anesthesia students who are or plan to become affiliated with the U.S. Army.
Eligibility: Applicants must be enrolled in a bachelor's or graduate degree program in nursing or nurse anesthesia. They must be in the U.S. Army, planning to enter the U.S. Army or be the parent, spouse or child of a U.S. Army officer. They cannot already be receiving funding from any source that is associated with the U.S. Army. Selection is based on the overall strength of the application.
Target applicant(s): College students. Graduate school students. Adult students.
Amount: Varies.
Number of awards: Varies.
Deadline: Varies.
How to apply: Applications are available online. An application form, personal statement, endorsement from student's academic dean, official transcript and military service documents (if applicable) are required.
Exclusive: Visit www.UltimateScholarshipBook.com and enter code AR5020 for updates on this award.

(51) • Army ROTC Advanced Course

U.S. Army
Human Resources Command, 1600 Spearhead Division Avenue, Department #410, Fort Knox, KY 40122-5401
Phone: 888-276-9472
Email: askhrc.army@us.army.mil
https://www.goarmy.com
Purpose: To prepare ROTC members for service as officers.
Eligibility: Applicants must be rising college juniors who have completed the ROTC Basic Course or Leader's Training Course who have made a commitment to serve as an officer in the Army after they graduate. Students must take an ROTC class or lab each semester of their final two years of school and attend a summer leadership camp.
Target applicant(s): College students. Adult students.
Amount: Varies.
Number of awards: Varies.
Scholarship may be renewable.
Deadline: Varies.
How to apply: Applications are available from your school's military science department.
Exclusive: Visit www.UltimateScholarshipBook.com and enter code U.5120 for updates on this award.

(52) • Army ROTC Four-Year Scholarship Program

Headquarters
U.S. Army Cadet Command, 55 Patch Road, Fort Monroe, VA 23651
Email: atccps@monroe.army.mil
http://www.goarmy.com/rotc
Purpose: To bolster the ranks of the Army, Army Reserve and Army National Guard by providing monetary assistance to eligible student candidates.
Eligibility: Applicants must be U.S. citizens and high school seniors, graduates or college freshmen with at least four years of college remaining who wish to attend one of 600 colleges and earn a commission. Recipients must serve in the Army for four to eight years after graduation.
Target applicant(s): High school students.
Minimum GPA: 2.5
Amount: Up to full tuition.
Number of awards: Varies.
Scholarship may be renewable.
Deadline: Varies.
How to apply: Applications are available online.
Exclusive: Visit www.UltimateScholarshipBook.com and enter code HE5220 for updates on this award.

(53) • Army ROTC Green To Gold Scholarship Program

Headquarters
U.S. Army Cadet Command, 55 Patch Road, Fort Monroe, VA 23651
Email: atccps@monroe.army.mil
http://www.goarmy.com/rotc
Purpose: To provide scholarship funds for Army enlisted soldiers.
Eligibility: Applicants must be active duty enlisted members of the Army who wish to complete their baccalaureate degree requirements and obtain a commission. Recipients are required to serve in the U.S. Army. Applicants must also meet numerous U.S. Army related requirements, be a high school graduate or equivalent, have a minimum GPA of 2.5 (high school or college) and be a U.S. citizen under age 31.
Target applicant(s): High school students. College students. Adult students.
Minimum GPA: 2.5
Amount: Varies.
Number of awards: Varies.
Deadline: February 1.
How to apply: Applications are available online.
Exclusive: Visit www.UltimateScholarshipBook.com and enter code HE5320 for updates on this award.

(54) • Arnold Fencing Classic Scholarship

Arnold Schwarzenegger Fencing Classic
5770 Westbourne Avenue, Columbus, OH 43213
Phone: 614-330-2445
Email: arnold@royalarts.org
http://www.arnoldfencingclassic.com
Purpose: To support youth fencers as they pursue higher education.
Eligibility: Applicants must be competing in the Arnold Fencing Classic, be a U.S. citizen and be between the ages of 13 and 18 years old. Selection is based on competitive participation and success in fencing, academic achievement, personal essay and letter of recommendation.
Target applicant(s): Junior high students or younger. High school students. College students.
Amount: $2,500.
Number of awards: 1.
Deadline: February 12.
How to apply: Applications are available online or may be submitted via email. The application includes a school transcript, personal essay, letter of recommendation, a fencing bio and the completed registration for at least one event at the Arnold Fencing Classic.
Exclusive: Visit www.UltimateScholarshipBook.com and enter code AR5420 for updates on this award.

(55) • Arnold Sports Festival Columbus Rotary Scholarship

Columbus Weightlifting Club
Beyond Limits Reynoldsburg, 6925 Americana Parkway, Suite A, Reynoldsburg, OH 43068
Phone: 614-986-8020
Email: arnold@columbusweightlifting.org
https://www.columbusweightlifting.org/

Purpose: To support an athlete competing in the Arnold Weightlifting Championships who intends to pursue post-secondary education.
Eligibility: Applicants must show "positive-impact involvement" consistent with capacity and circumstances and improvement and/or success in community involvement. The applicant must also demonstrate good moral character.
Target applicant(s): Junior high students or younger. High school students. College students. Adult students.
Amount: $2,000.
Number of awards: 1.
Deadline: February 15.
How to apply: Applications are available online. An application form and one letter of recommendation are required.
Exclusive: Visit www.UltimateScholarshipBook.com and enter code CO5520 for updates on this award.

(56) • Ashley Soule Conroy Foundation Scholarship

Ashley Soule Conroy Foundation
Three Lakeway Center, 3838 North Causeway Boulevard, Suite 3130, Metairie, LA 70002
http://www.ashleysfoundation.org
Purpose: To support undergraduate students in pursuing study abroad.
Eligibility: Applicants must commit to at least one semester of full-time study abroad outside of the U.S. A minimum GPA of 3.0 is required. Students must be currently attending a four-year college and have earned at least 30 credits or completed one year of college. Selection is primarily based on demonstration of financial need, academic achievement and employment history.
Target applicant(s): College students. Adult students.
Minimum GPA: 3.0
Amount: $3,000.
Number of awards: 2.
Deadline: July 1, December 1.
How to apply: Applications are available online.
Exclusive: Visit www.UltimateScholarshipBook.com and enter code AS5620 for updates on this award.

(57) • Athnet Sports Recruiting Scholarship

Athnet
450 Geary Street, Unit 201, San Francisco, CA 94102
Phone: 800-974-2171
http://www.athleticscholarships.net/sports-scholarships.htm
Purpose: To support student athletes in pursuing post-secondary education.
Eligibility: Applicants must be graduating seniors or current college students. Students must submit an essay explaining how sports have impacted their life.
Target applicant(s): High school students. College students. Adult students.
Amount: $1,000.
Number of awards: 1.
Deadline: June 1.
How to apply: Applications are available online.
Exclusive: Visit www.UltimateScholarshipBook.com and enter code AT5720 for updates on this award.

(58) • AU Student Essay Contest

Americans United for Separation of Church and State
Attn.: Essay Contest Submission, 1901 L Street NW, Suite 400, Washington, DC 20036
Phone: 202-466-3234 x427
Email: campus@au.org
http://www.austudents.org/essaycontest/
Purpose: To emphasize the importance of the separation of church and state.
Eligibility: Applicants must be current high school juniors or seniors in the U.S. Students must submit an essay discussing potential violations of church-state separations as found in the topics listed on the website.
Target applicant(s): High school students.
Amount: $1,500.
Number of awards: 3.
Deadline: April 15.
How to apply: Applications are available online.
Exclusive: Visit www.UltimateScholarshipBook.com and enter code AM5820 for updates on this award.

(59) • AWSEF Scholarship

USA Water Ski and Wake Sports Foundation
1251 Holy Cow Road, Polk City, FL 33868
Phone: 863-324-2472
Email: usa-wsf@waterskihalloffame.com
http://www.usawaterskifoundation.org/
Purpose: To support those involved in USA Water Ski.
Eligibility: Applicants must be full-time undergraduates at a two- or four-year college as incoming sophomores to incoming seniors. Applicants must also be active members of USA Water Ski all divisions: AWSA-ABC-AKA-WSDA-NSSA-NCWSA-NCWSRA-USAWB-HYD. Students should submit an application, two reference letters, an essay and a transcript.
Target applicant(s): College students. Adult students.
Amount: Varies.
Number of awards: Varies.
Scholarship may be renewable.
Deadline: March 15.
How to apply: Applications are available online.
Exclusive: Visit www.UltimateScholarshipBook.com and enter code US5920 for updates on this award.

(60) • AXA Achievement Scholarships

AXA Achievement Scholarship
c/o Scholarship America, One Scholarship Way, St. Peter, MN 56082
Phone: 800-537-4180
Email: axaachievement@scholarshipamerica.org
https://us.axa.com/axa-foundation/about.html
Purpose: To provide financial assistance to ambitious students.
Eligibility: Applicants must be U.S. citizens or legal residents who are current high school seniors and are planning to enroll full-time in an accredited college or university in the fall following their graduation. They must show ambition and drive evidenced by outstanding achievement in school, community or workplace activities. A recommendation from an unrelated adult who can vouch for the student's achievement is required.
Target applicant(s): High school students.
Amount: $2,500.
Number of awards: Up to 12.
Deadline: December 15.
How to apply: Applications are available online.
Exclusive: Visit www.UltimateScholarshipBook.com and enter code AX6020 for updates on this award.

(61) · Babe Ruth League Scholarships

Babe Ruth League Inc.
1770 Brunswick Avenue, P.O. Box 5000, Trenton, NJ 08638
http://www.baberuthleague.org
Purpose: To provide educational assistance to players in the Babe Ruth Baseball and Softball divisions.
Eligibility: Applicants must be members or former members of the Babe Ruth Baseball or Softball leagues. They must be graduating seniors. A short essay, copy of high school transcript and a letter of recommendation are required.
Target applicant(s): High school students. College students. Adult students.
Amount: Varies.
Number of awards: Varies.
Deadline: June 30.
How to apply: Applications are available online.
Exclusive: Visit www.UltimateScholarshipBook.com and enter code BA6120 for updates on this award.

(62) · BankMobile Financial Literacy Scholarship

BankMobile
401 Park Avenue South, New York, NY 10016
Phone: 917-543-3254
Email: scholarship@bankmobile.com
https://www.bankmobile.com/scholarship
Purpose: To support student financial literacy.
Eligibility: Applicants must be undergraduate or graduate level students, U.S. citizens, and have a minimum 3.0 GPA. Students must submit an essay explaining the importance of financial literacy in both their lives and their career. Special consideration is given to applicants who are actively promoting financial literacy within their community.
Target applicant(s): College students. Graduate school students. Adult students.
Minimum GPA: 3.0
Amount: $1,500.
Number of awards: 1.
Deadline: July 19.
How to apply: Applications are available online and must include an official transcript (high school or college) and the essay.
Exclusive: Visit www.UltimateScholarshipBook.com and enter code BA6220 for updates on this award.

(63) · Barbara Bolding/Jim Grew Scholarship

USA Water Ski and Wake Sports Foundation
1251 Holy Cow Road, Polk City, FL 33868
Phone: 863-324-2472
Email: usa-wsf@waterskihalloffame.com
http://www.usawaterskifoundation.org/
Purpose: To support students who are active members of USA Water Ski.
Eligibility: Students must be incoming freshman through senior students in an undergraduate program. Applicants do not have to be collegiate water ski competitors but do have to be members of USA Water Ski. Selection is based on number of years as a member, academic achievement, financial need, school and community activities and individual contributions to the sport. A short essay is required.
Target applicant(s): High school students. College students. Adult students.
Amount: $5,000.
Number of awards: 1.
Scholarship may be renewable.
Deadline: March 15.
How to apply: Applications are available online and must include two letters of reference.
Exclusive: Visit www.UltimateScholarshipBook.com and enter code US6320 for updates on this award.

(64) · Barbizon's College Tuition Scholarship

Barbizon Modeling & Acting Centers
4950 W. Kennedy Boulevard, Suite 200, Tampa, FL 33609
Phone: 888-999-9404
http://www.barbizonmodeling.com/scholarships/
Purpose: To support students who wish to continue their education.
Eligibility: Applicants must be legal U.S. residents who are planning to attend an accredited college or university. Students must fill out an entry form for the sweepstakes and must be accepted at an accredited college or university within three years of graduation.
Target applicant(s): High school students.
Amount: $100,000.
Number of awards: 1.
Deadline: December 31.
How to apply: Applications are available online.
Exclusive: Visit www.UltimateScholarshipBook.com and enter code BA6420 for updates on this award.

(65) · Be the Boss Scholarship

GoSkills
555 Bryant Street, #901, Palo Alto, CA 94301
Phone: 650-822-7732
Email: support@goskills.com
https://www.goskills.com/scholarship
Purpose: To encourage women to start their own online business.
Eligibility: Applicants must be female high school or college students interested in starting their own online business. Students must submit their business plan to apply.
Target applicant(s): High school students. College students. Graduate school students. Adult students.
Amount: $2,000.
Number of awards: 2.
Deadline: September 15, March 15.
How to apply: Applications are available online.
Exclusive: Visit www.UltimateScholarshipBook.com and enter code GO6520 for updates on this award.

(66) · Bellhops' Moving Forward Scholarship

Bellhops Inc.
1100 Market Street, Suite 502, Chattanooga, TN 37402
Phone: 888-836-3939
Email: scholarship@getbellhops.com
https://www.getbellhops.com/scholarship/
Purpose: To help students pursue higher education.
Eligibility: Applicants must be graduating high school seniors or current college students. Students must complete application and essay as well as provide academic transcripts and a photo. Applicants must have a grade point average of 3.0 or higher.
Target applicant(s): High school students. College students. Adult students.
Minimum GPA: 3.0
Amount: $3,000.
Number of awards: 1.

Deadline: September 15.
How to apply: Applications are available online.
Exclusive: Visit www.UltimateScholarshipBook.com and enter code BE6620 for updates on this award.

(67) · Beyond the Boroughs Scholarship

Beyond The Boroughs
282 Katonah Avenue, Suite 122, Katonah, NY 10536
Phone: 914-458-2926
http://www.beyondtheboroughs.org
Purpose: To support students with financial need in pursuing a bachelor's degree.
Eligibility: Applicants must be accepted to an accredited four-year college. A minimum GPA of 2.5 is required. Selection is primarily based on demonstration of financial need, academic achievement, work history and extracurricular involvement.
Target applicant(s): High school students. College students. Adult students.
Minimum GPA: 2.5
Amount: $20,000.
Number of awards: Varies.
Scholarship may be renewable.
Deadline: March 15.
How to apply: Applications are available online.
Exclusive: Visit www.UltimateScholarshipBook.com and enter code BE6720 for updates on this award.

(68) · Bob Bennett Memorial Scholarship

Unity One Credit Union
6701 Burlington Boulevard, Fort Worth, TX 76131
Phone: 817-306- 3100
http://www.unityone.org
Purpose: To support students pursuing a higher education.
Eligibility: Applicants must be either graduating high school seniors or current college students. Students must write an essay as part of their application.
Target applicant(s): High school students. College students. Adult students.
Amount: $250-$1,000.
Number of awards: 3.
Deadline: April 27.
How to apply: Applications are available online.
Exclusive: Visit www.UltimateScholarshipBook.com and enter code UN6820 for updates on this award.

(69) · Bob Warnicke Scholarship

Bob Warnicke Memorial Scholarship Fund
USA BMX/BMX Canada, 1645 W. Sunrise Boulevard, Gilbert, AZ 85233
Phone: 480-961-1903
Email: administration@nbl.org
http://www.usabmx.com
Purpose: To help students who have participated in BMX racing events.
Eligibility: Applicants must be members, have a current NBL competition license or official's license and have participated in BMX racing events for at least a year. Students must also be high school graduates and plan to or currently attend a postsecondary institution full- or part-time.
Target applicant(s): High school students. College students. Adult students.
Amount: Varies.
Number of awards: Varies.
Deadline: March 6.
How to apply: Applications are available online, by mail or by phone.
Exclusive: Visit www.UltimateScholarshipBook.com and enter code BO6920 for updates on this award.

(70) · Bonner Scholars Program

Bonner Foundation
10 Mercer Street, Princeton, NJ 08540
Phone: 609-924-6663
Email: info@bonner.org
http://www.bonner.org
Purpose: To award four-year community service scholarships to students planning to attend one of 75 participating colleges.
Eligibility: Students must complete annual service requirements as stipulated by the organization. Awards are geared toward students demonstrating significant financial need. Scholarship recipients are named Bonner Scholars.
Target applicant(s): High school students.
Amount: Varies.
Number of awards: Varies.
Deadline: Varies.
How to apply: Contact the admission office at each participating school to request an application.
Exclusive: Visit www.UltimateScholarshipBook.com and enter code BO7020 for updates on this award.

(71) · Boomer Benefits Scholarship

Boomer Benefits
5650 N. Riverside Drive #200, Fort Worth, TX 76137
Phone: 855-732-9055
http://boomerbenefits.com
Purpose: To support adult students who are at least 50 years of age in returning to school to complete their degree.
Eligibility: Applicants must be enrolled in an undergraduate or graduate degree program at an accredited educational institution. A minimum GPA of 3.0 is required. Selection is primarily based on demonstration of academic achievement and community service.
Target applicant(s): Adult students.
Minimum GPA: 3.0
Amount: $1,000.
Number of awards: 1.
Deadline: July 15.
How to apply: Applications are available online.
Exclusive: Visit www.UltimateScholarshipBook.com and enter code BO7120 for updates on this award.

(72) · Brainly Everyone Knows Something Scholarship

Brainly Inc.
161 Bowery 2nd Floor, New York, NY 10002
Email: contact@brainly.com
https://brainly.com/app/scholarship
Purpose: To support students who are users of Brainly and are pursuing a college education.
Eligibility: Applicants must be graduating high school seniors at least 16 years of age and they must write an essay as part of their application. Students must have a Brainly account and be a citizen of the United States. Applicants must have enrolled in an accredited college or university within the U.S. by the fall of the upcoming school year.

Target applicant(s): High school students.
Amount: $1,000.
Number of awards: 1.
Deadline: May 31.
How to apply: Applications are available online.
Exclusive: Visit www.UltimateScholarshipBook.com and enter code BR7220 for updates on this award.

(73) • Bridging the Dream Scholarship Program for Graduate Students

Sallie Mae Bridging the Dream
Scholarship America, One Scholarship Way, Saint Peter, MN 56082
Phone: 800-537-4180
Email: bridgingthedream@scholarshipamerica.org
http://www.salliemae.com/bridgingthedreamgrad
Purpose: To support students who wish to continue their education into graduate school.
Eligibility: Applicants must be U.S. citizens or permanent residents of the U.S., Puerto Rico or the District of Columbia. Students must be a current college senior, a prospective graduate student or currently enrolled in postsecondary graduate school. A minimum 3.0 GPA is required. Awards are for postgraduate study in law, business, medicine, dentistry or other graduate fields.
Target applicant(s): College students. Graduate school students. Adult students.
Minimum GPA: 3.0
Amount: $20,000.
Number of awards: 4.
Deadline: February 15.
How to apply: Applications are available online.
Exclusive: Visit www.UltimateScholarshipBook.com and enter code SA7320 for updates on this award.

(74) • Bright!Tax Global Scholar Initiative

Bright!Tax
244 Fifth Avenue, New York, NY 10001
Phone: 212-465-2528
Email: inquiries@brighttax.com
http://www.brighttax.com/scholarships.html
Purpose: To support students wishing to study abroad.
Eligibility: Applicants must be U.S. citizens who want to study abroad for at least one full semester at an accredited institution. Selection is based on academic and extracurricular achievement, community involvement, future ambitions and financial need. Scholarship is awarded on a ongoing basis with no deadlines.
Target applicant(s): High school students. College students. Graduate school students. Adult students.
Amount: $1,000.
Number of awards: Minimum of 2.
Deadline: Rolling.
How to apply: Applications are available online.
Exclusive: Visit www.UltimateScholarshipBook.com and enter code BR7420 for updates on this award.

(75) • Brownells/NRA Outstanding Achievement Youth Award

National Rifle Association
11250 Waples Mill Road, Fairfax, VA 22030
Phone: 800-672-3888
Email: grantprogram@nrahq.org
https://awards.nra.org/awards/
Purpose: To recognize NRA Junior Members who actively participate in shooting sports.
Eligibility: Applicants must be NRA Junior Members (or Regular or Life Members under 21 years old) and have completed five core and five elective requirements. Core requirements are being current members of the NRA, attending and completing an NRA Basic Firearm Training Course, earning a rating in a shooting discipline and submitting an essay.
Target applicant(s): High school students.
Amount: $2,000-$5,000.
Number of awards: 3.
Deadline: May 1.
How to apply: Applications are available online.
Exclusive: Visit www.UltimateScholarshipBook.com and enter code NA7520 for updates on this award.

(76) • Bruce Lee Scholarship

U.S. Pan Asian American Chamber of Commerce
1329 18th Street NW, Washington, DC 20036
Phone: 800-696-7818
Email: info@uspaacc.com
http://uspaacc.com/
Purpose: To support the higher education goals of students of all ethnic backgrounds.
Eligibility: Applicants must be U.S. citizens or permanent residents and be high school seniors who will pursue post-secondary educations at an accredited institution in the U.S. Students do not need to be Asian Americans. Selection is based on character, the ability to persevere over adversity, academic excellence with at least a 3.3 GPA, community service involvement and financial need. Applicants must be able to attend the Excellence Awards and Scholarships Dinner during the CelebrAsian Annual Conference (in May).
Target applicant(s): High school students.
Minimum GPA: 3.3
Amount: Varies.
Number of awards: Varies.
Deadline: March 17.
How to apply: Applications are available online.
Exclusive: Visit www.UltimateScholarshipBook.com and enter code U.7620 for updates on this award.

(77) • Buddy Pelletier Surfing Foundation Scholarship

Buddy Pelletier Surfing Foundation Fund
BPSF Scholarship Committee, Attn: Lynne Pelletier, 5121 Chalk Street, Morehead City, NC 28557
Phone: 252-241-7115
Email: buddypelletier@hotmail.com
http://www.buddypelletier.com
Purpose: To support the education and humanitarian needs of the East Coast surfing community.
Eligibility: Applicants must be members of the East Coast surfing community. Rising high school seniors, current undergraduate college students and returning students may apply regardless of age. Two letters of recommendation and a 500-word essay are required. Previous applicants and winners may reapply each year.
Target applicant(s): High school students. College students. Adult students.
Amount: $1,000.
Number of awards: Varies.
Deadline: June 1.

How to apply: Applications are available online.
Exclusive: Visit www.UltimateScholarshipBook.com and enter code BU7720 for updates on this award.

---

(78) • Burger King Scholars Program

Burger King Scholars Program
5505 Blue Lagoon Drive, Miami, FL 33126
Phone: 305-378-3000
Email: bdorado@whopper.com
http://www.bkmclamorefoundation.org
Purpose: To provide financial assistance for high school seniors who have part-time jobs.
Eligibility: Applicants may apply from public, private, vocational, technical, parochial and alternative high schools in the United States, Canada and Puerto Rico and must be U.S. or Canadian residents. Students must also have a minimum 2.5 GPA, work part-time an average of 15 hours per week unless there are extenuating circumstances, participate in community service or other activities, demonstrate financial need and plan to enroll in an accredited two- or four-year college, university or vocational/technical school by the fall term of the graduating year. Applicants do NOT need to work at Burger King, but Burger King employees are eligible.
Target applicant(s): High school students.
Minimum GPA: 2.5
Amount: $1,000-$50,000.
Number of awards: Varies.
Deadline: December 15.
How to apply: Applications are available online and may only be completed online.
Exclusive: Visit www.UltimateScholarshipBook.com and enter code BU7820 for updates on this award.

---

(79) • C.I.P. Scholarship

College Is Power
1025 Alameda de las Pulgas, No. 215, Belmont, CA 94002
http://www.collegeispower.com/scholarship.cfm
Purpose: To assist adult students age 18 and over with college expenses.
Eligibility: Applicants must be adult students currently attending or planning to attend a two-year or four-year college or university within the next 12 months. Students must be 18 years or older and U.S. citizens or permanent residents. The award may be used for full- or part-time study at either on-campus or online schools.
Target applicant(s): High school students. College students. Adult students.
Amount: $1,000.
Number of awards: Varies.
Deadline: May 31, August 31, December 31.
How to apply: Applications are available online.
Exclusive: Visit www.UltimateScholarshipBook.com and enter code CO7920 for updates on this award.

---

(80) • CAPT Ernest G. "Scotty" Campbell, USN (Ret) and Renee Campbell Scholarship

Navy League Foundation
2300 Wilson Boulevard, Suite 200, Arlington, VA 22201
Phone: 800-356-5760
Email: smcfarland@navyleague.org
https://www.navyleague.org
Purpose: To support students who are either dependents or direct descendants of a member of the U.S. Marine Corps, U.S. Navy or U.S.-Flag Merchant Marines or who are active members of the U.S. Naval Sea Cadet Corps.
Eligibility: Applicants must be U.S citizens who are current high school seniors and who will be entering an accredited institution of higher learning after graduating. Only dependents or direct descendants of a member of the U.S. Marine Corps, U.S. Navy or U.S.-Flag Merchant Marines or who are active members of the U.S. Naval Sea Cadet Corps are eligible to apply. A minimum GPA of 3.0 is required. Financial need must also be demonstrated. Selection is based on the overall strength of the application.
Target applicant(s): High school students.
Minimum GPA: 3.0
Amount: $10,000.
Number of awards: 1.
Deadline: March 1.
How to apply: Applications are available online.
Exclusive: Visit www.UltimateScholarshipBook.com and enter code NA8020 for updates on this award.

---

(81) • Capt. James J. Regan Scholarship

Explorers Learning for Life
1325 West Walnut Hill Lane, P.O. Box 152225, Irving, TX 75015-2225
Phone: 855-806-9992
Email: exploring@lflmail.org
http://www.exploring.org/scholarships/
Purpose: To support students who are Law Enforcement Explorers.
Eligibility: Students must be at least in their senior year of high school. Applicants must submit three letters of recommendation and an essay.
Target applicant(s): High school students. College students. Adult students.
Amount: $500.
Number of awards: 2.
Deadline: March 31.
How to apply: Applications are available online.
Exclusive: Visit www.UltimateScholarshipBook.com and enter code EX8120 for updates on this award.

---

(82) • Captain Caliendo College Assistance Fund

U.S. Coast Guard Chief Petty Officers Association
CCCAF Scholarship Committee, 5520-G Hempstead Way,
Springfield, VA 22151-4009
Phone: 703-941-0395
Email: cgcpoa@aol.com
http://www.uscgcpoa.org
Purpose: To provide financial assistance for children of CPOA/CGEA members.
Eligibility: Applicants must be dependents of a living or deceased USCG CPOA/CGEA member who are under the age of 24 as of March 1 of the award year. The age limit does not apply to disabled children. Proof of acceptance or enrollment in an institution of higher learning is required.
Target applicant(s): High school students. College students.
Amount: $1,000-$5,000.
Number of awards: 3.
Deadline: April 1.
How to apply: Applications are available online. An essay not exceeding 500 words is required.
Exclusive: Visit www.UltimateScholarshipBook.com and enter code U.8220 for updates on this award.

(83) · Car Covers $1,000 Scholarship

CarCovers.com
671 Willow Pass Road, Suite 1, Pittsburg, CA 94565
Phone: 800-385-3603
http://www.carcovers.com/resources/scholarship/
Purpose: To support undergraduate and graduate students in funding their education.
Eligibility: Applicants must submit an essay describing ways to extend the service life of cars. Selection is based on the overall strength of the submission.
Target applicant(s): College students. Graduate school students. Adult students.
Amount: $1,000.
Number of awards: 1.
Deadline: December 15.
How to apply: Applications are available online.
Exclusive: Visit www.UltimateScholarshipBook.com and enter code CA8320 for updates on this award.

(84) · CareerFitter Scholarship

CareerFitter.com
P.O. Box 124, Pisgah Forest, NC 28768
http://www.careerfitter.com
Purpose: To support students in pursuing their college educations.
Eligibility: Applicants must be planning to enroll or already enrolled in accredited college or graduate school program. Students must take a career test on Career Fitter's website and include the results on their application. Selection is based on the overall strength of the application.
Target applicant(s): High school students. College students. Graduate school students. Adult students.
Minimum GPA: 2.4
Amount: $500.
Number of awards: Varies.
Scholarship may be renewable.
Deadline: September 15.
How to apply: Applications are available online.
Exclusive: Visit www.UltimateScholarshipBook.com and enter code CA8420 for updates on this award.

(85) · Carson Scholars

Carson Scholars Fund
305 W Chesapeake Avenue, Suite 310, Towson, MD 21204
Phone: 877-773-7236
Email: katie@carsonscholars.org
http://carsonscholars.org/scholarships/
Purpose: To recognize students who demonstrate academic excellence and commitment to the community.
Eligibility: Applicants must be nominated by their school. They must be in grades 4 through 11 and have a GPA of 3.75 or higher in English, reading, language arts, math, science, social studies and foreign language. They must have participated in some form of voluntary community service beyond what is required by their school. Scholarship recipients must attend a four-year college or university upon graduation to receive funds.
Target applicant(s): Junior high students or younger. High school students.
Minimum GPA: 3.75
Amount: $1,000.
Number of awards: Varies.
Deadline: January 8.
How to apply: Applications are available from the schools of those nominated. Only one student per school may be nominated.
Exclusive: Visit www.UltimateScholarshipBook.com and enter code CA8520 for updates on this award.

(86) · CCA Christian Cheer Nationals

Christian Cheerleaders of America
P.O. Box 49, Bethania, NC 27010
Phone: 877-243-3722
Email: info@cheercca.com
http://www.cheercca.com
Purpose: To support cheerleaders who participate in cheer through Christian Cheerleaders of America.
Eligibility: Applicants must be a junior or senior in high school, participate in Christian Cheerleaders of America and be nominated by the cheer coach. The student should have a 3.0 GPA or higher. Selection is based on academic achievement and Christian service.
Target applicant(s): High school students.
Minimum GPA: 3.0
Amount: Varies.
Number of awards: Varies.
Deadline: February 15.
How to apply: Nomination forms are available online.
Exclusive: Visit www.UltimateScholarshipBook.com and enter code CH8620 for updates on this award.

(87) · Cecilia Colledge Memorial Fund Award

U.S. Figure Skating
20 First Street, Colorado Springs, CO 80906
Phone: 719-635-5200
Email: info@usfigureskating.org
http://www.usfsa.org
Purpose: To support successful novice U.S. Figure Skaters.
Eligibility: Award is given to the skater with the highest program components score at the U.S. Figure Skating Championships in the novice ladies and novice men's event.
Target applicant(s): Junior high students or younger. High school students. College students. Adult students.
Amount: Varies.
Number of awards: 2.
Deadline: Varies.
How to apply: Award is given at the U.S. Figure Skating Championships.
Exclusive: Visit www.UltimateScholarshipBook.com and enter code U.8720 for updates on this award.

(88) · Center for Alcohol Policy (CAP) Essay Contest

Center for Alcohol Policy
1101 King Street, Suite 600-A, Alexandria, VA 22314
Phone: 703-519-3090
http://www.centerforalcoholpolicy.org/essay-contest/
Purpose: To reward students, academics, attorneys, policymakers and members of the general public for outstanding essays regarding alcohol policy.
Eligibility: Applicants must be at least 18 years old. Students must submit an essay analyzing different alcohol regulations. Selection is based on the strength of analysis, thoroughness of research and quality of writing.
Target applicant(s): High school students. College students. Adult students.
Amount: $1,000-$5,000.

Number of awards: 3.
Deadline: December 7.
How to apply: Applications are available online.
Exclusive: Visit www.UltimateScholarshipBook.com and enter code CE8820 for updates on this award.

(89) · Challenge Scholarship

National Strength and Conditioning Association (NSCA) Foundation
1885 Bob Johnson Drive, Colorado Springs, CO 80906
Phone: 800-815-6826
http://www.nsca.com/foundation/
Purpose: To support NSCA members pursuing studies related to strength and conditioning.
Eligibility: Applicants must be NSCA members for one year before applying and be pursuing careers in strength and conditioning. Students must submit an essay detailing their course of study, career goals and financial need. Applications are evaluated based on grades, courses, experience, honors, recommendations and involvement in the community and with NSCA.
Target applicant(s): High school students. College students. Graduate school students. Adult students.
Amount: $1,500.
Number of awards: Varies.
Deadline: October 15.
How to apply: Applications are available with membership.
Exclusive: Visit www.UltimateScholarshipBook.com and enter code NA8920 for updates on this award.

(90) · Charles T. Stoner Law Scholarship

Women's Basketball Coaches Association
4646 Lawrenceville Highway, Lilburn, GA 30047
Phone: 770-279-8027
Email: dtrujillo@wbca.org
https://wbca.org/recognize/player-awards
Purpose: To aid a female collegiate basketball player in her pursuit of a career in law.
Eligibility: Applicants must be a senior, collegiate women's basketball player who plans on pursuing a career in law and must be nominated by their collegiate head coach.
Target applicant(s): College students. Adult students.
Amount: $1,000.
Number of awards: 1.
Deadline: December 3.
How to apply: Applicants must be nominated by their collegiate head coach who are WBCA members. Nomination forms are available online. The nomination form, a letter of recommendation, academic major and GPA and present season statistics will all be considered.
Exclusive: Visit www.UltimateScholarshipBook.com and enter code WO9020 for updates on this award.

(91) · Charlie Logan Scholarship Program for Seamen

Seafarers International Union of North America
Seafarers Health and Benefits Plan, Scholarship Program, 5201 Auth Way, Camp Springs, MD 20746
Phone: 301-899-0675
http://www.seafarers.org
Purpose: To offer scholarships to members of the SIU.
Eligibility: Applicants must be active seamen who are high school graduates or its equivalent, are eligible to receive Seafarers Plan benefits and have credit for two years (730 days) of employment with an employer who is obligated to make contributions to the Seafarers' Plan on the employee's behalf prior to the date of application. Recipients may attend any U.S. accredited institution (college or trade school). Selection is based on high school equivalency scores or secondary school records, college transcripts, if any, SAT/ACT scores, references on character or personality and autobiography. The $6,000 scholarships are for two-year study, and the $20,000 scholarship is for four-year study.
Target applicant(s): College students. Adult students.
Amount: $6,000-$20,000.
Number of awards: Varies.
Scholarship may be renewable.
Deadline: April 15.
How to apply: Applications are available by written request.
Exclusive: Visit www.UltimateScholarshipBook.com and enter code SE9120 for updates on this award.

(92) · Chief Master Sergeants of the Air Force Scholarships

Air Force Sergeants Association
5211 Auth Road, Suitland, MD 20746
Phone: 301-899-3500
Email: staff@hqafsa.org
http://www.hqafsa.org
Purpose: To provide financial assistance to the families of Air Force enlistees.
Eligibility: Applicants must be dependents of enlisted Air Force members, either on active duty or retired. They must meet the eligibility requirements and participate in the Airmen Memorial Foundation Scholarship Program. An unweighted GPA of 3.5 or higher is required. Extenuating circumstances are considered.
Target applicant(s): High school students. College students. Adult students.
Minimum GPA: 3.5
Amount: Varies.
Number of awards: Varies.
Deadline: March 31.
How to apply: Applications are available online.
Exclusive: Visit www.UltimateScholarshipBook.com and enter code AI9220 for updates on this award.

(93) · Chief Petty Officer Scholarship Fund

Chief Petty Officer Scholarship Fund
328 Office Square Lane, Suite 101A, Virginia Beach, VA 23462
Phone: 757-233-9136
Email: cposfboard@cposf.org
http://www.cposf.org
Purpose: To aid the families of Chief Petty Officers of the U.S. Navy.
Eligibility: Applicants must be spouses or children of active, retired or reserve Chief, Senior Chief or Master Chief Petty Officers of the U.S. Navy. They must be high school graduates or have earned a GED and plan to attend a college or university to earn an AA, BA or BS degree. Current college students may also apply. Selection criteria include scholastic proficiency, character and all-around ability.
Target applicant(s): High school students. College students. Adult students.
Amount: Varies.
Number of awards: Varies.
Deadline: April 1.

How to apply: Applications are available online. An application form, three letters of recommendation, a copy of your dependents ID card and a personal statement are required.
Exclusive: Visit www.UltimateScholarshipBook.com and enter code CH9320 for updates on this award.

(94) • Children of Warriors National Presidents' Scholarship

American Legion Auxiliary
8945 N. Meridian Street, Indianapolis, IN 46260
Phone: 317-569-4500
Email: alahq@legion-aux.org
https://www.alaforveterans.org/scholarships/
Purpose: To award scholarships to children, grandchildren and great-grandchildren of veterans who served in the Armed Forces.
Eligibility: Applicants must be the children, grandchildren or great-grandchildren of veterans who served in the Armed Forces for membership in The American Legion, be high school seniors and complete 50 hours of community service. Selection is based on character, application/essay, scholastic achievement, leadership and financial need.
Target applicant(s): High school students.
Amount: $5,000.
Number of awards: 15.
Deadline: March 1.
How to apply: Applications are available online. Applicants should submit applications, four recommendation letters, essays, proof of volunteering, transcripts, ACT or SAT scores and parent's or grandparent's military service description.
Exclusive: Visit www.UltimateScholarshipBook.com and enter code AM9420 for updates on this award.

(95) • Chinese American Citizens Alliance Foundation Essay Contest

Chinese American Citizens Alliance
1044 Stockton Street, San Francisco, CA 94108
Phone: 415-829-9332
Email: info@cacanational.org
http://www.cacanational.org
Purpose: To provide a forum for expression for future leaders of the United States.
Eligibility: Applicants must be high school students in grades 9 through 12. Students do NOT need to be Chinese Americans. They must write a 500-word essay on a topic chosen by the Chinese American Citizens Alliance. The essay must be written on a given date at the student's local lodge or other designated location.
Target applicant(s): High school students.
Amount: Up to $1,000.
Number of awards: 13.
Deadline: March 4.
How to apply: Applications are available online. An application form and essay are required.
Exclusive: Visit www.UltimateScholarshipBook.com and enter code CH9520 for updates on this award.

(96) • Christophers Video Contest for College Students

Christophers
5 Hanover Square, 22nd Floor, New York, NY 10004
Phone: 212-759-4050
Email: youth@christophers.org
http://www.christophers.org
Purpose: To support college students who believe in The Christophers' mission that any one person can make a difference.
Eligibility: Applicants must be current undergraduate or graduate level college students and U.S. citizens. Selection is based on the video submitted and how well it depicts the theme of "One Person Can Make a Difference."
Target applicant(s): College students. Graduate school students. Adult students.
Amount: $500-$2,000.
Number of awards: 3.
Deadline: December 17.
How to apply: Applications are available online. Students must also submit a video of five minutes or less communicating the theme.
Exclusive: Visit www.UltimateScholarshipBook.com and enter code CH9620 for updates on this award.

(97) • CIA Undergraduate Scholarship Program

Central Intelligence Agency
Office of Public Affairs, Washington, DC 20505
Phone: 703-482-0623
https://www.cia.gov/careers/student-opportunities
Purpose: To encourage students to pursue careers with the CIA.
Eligibility: Applicants must be high school seniors or college freshmen or sophomores. High school students must have an SAT score of 1500 or higher or an ACT score of 21 or higher, while all applicants must have a GPA of at least 3.0. Applicants must demonstrate financial need, defined as a household income of less than $70,000 for a family of four or $80,000 for a family of five or more. They must meet all criteria for regular CIA employees, including security checks and medical examinations. Applicants must commit to a work experience each summer during college and agree to CIA employment for 1.5 times the length of their CIA-sponsored scholarship.
Target applicant(s): High school students. College students. Adult students.
Minimum GPA: 3.0
Amount: Varies.
Number of awards: Varies.
Scholarship may be renewable.
Deadline: August 31.
How to apply: Applications are available online. A resume, SAT/ACT scores, family income information, copy of FAFSA or Student Aid Report, transcript and two letters of recommendation are required.
Exclusive: Visit www.UltimateScholarshipBook.com and enter code CE9720 for updates on this award.

(98) • CJ Pony Parts Scholarship Video Contest

CJ Pony Parts
7461 Allentown Boulevard, Harrisburg, PA 17112
Phone: 800-888-6473
http://www.cjponyparts.com
Purpose: To support graduating seniors and undergraduate students in pursuing post-secondary education.
Eligibility: Applicants must be U.S. residents who will be enrolling in classes for the upcoming semester. Students must submit a video addressing an automotive related topic. Selection is based on the overall strength of the submission.
Target applicant(s): High school students. College students. Adult students.
Amount: $500.

Number of awards: 2.
Deadline: April 15, October 15.
How to apply: Applications are available online.
Exclusive: Visit www.UltimateScholarshipBook.com and enter code CJ9820 for updates on this award.

(99) • Clean Water Scholarship Competition

Waterlogic
Phone: 866-917-7873
Email: info@waterlogicusa.com
https://www.waterlogic.com/en-us/scholarship-competition/
Purpose: To support students pursuing a higher education who have demonstrated a sincere interest in increasing global access to clean water.
Eligibility: Applicants must be U.S. citizens entering college for the upcoming fall semester or be currently enrolled as undergraduate students with a 3.0 GPA. Students must write an essay as part of their application.
Target applicant(s): High school students. College students. Adult students.
Minimum GPA: 3.0
Amount: $1,500.
Number of awards: 1.
Deadline: May 31.
How to apply: Applications are available online.
Exclusive: Visit www.UltimateScholarshipBook.com and enter code WA9920 for updates on this award.

(100) • CLEP Scholarship

Study.com
100 View Street #202, Mountain View, CA 94041
https://study.com/pages/Academic_Awards_Home.html
Purpose: To support students pursuing CLEP credit.
Eligibility: Applicants must be a U.S. citizen or permanent resident and be planning on taking the College Level Examination Program (CLEP) exam prior to April of the following year.
Target applicant(s): High school students. College students. Adult students.
Amount: Up to $500.
Number of awards: 3.
Deadline: April 1.
How to apply: Applications are available online.
Exclusive: Visit www.UltimateScholarshipBook.com and enter code ST10020 for updates on this award.

(101) • Clubs of America Scholarship Award for Career Success

Clubs of America
484 Wegner Road, Lakemoor, IL 60051
Phone: 800-258-2872
https://www.greatclubs.com/scholarship/
Purpose: To support undergraduate students in funding their education.
Eligibility: Applicants must be enrolled at an accredited U.S. educational institution. A minimum GPA of 3.0 is required. Students must submit an essay explaining their career goals. Selection is based on the overall strength of the submission.
Target applicant(s): College students. Adult students.
Minimum GPA: 3.0
Amount: $1,000.
Number of awards: 1.
Deadline: August 31.
How to apply: Applications are available online.
Exclusive: Visit www.UltimateScholarshipBook.com and enter code CL10120 for updates on this award.

(102) • CMP Scholarships

Civilian Marksmanship Program
P.O. Box 576, Port Clinton, OH 43452
Phone: 419-635-2141
Email: kwilliams@thecmp.org
http://thecmp.org/
Purpose: To aid students who have participated in marksmanship competitions with their higher education costs.
Eligibility: Applicants must be a U.S. Citizen, represent good moral character, have a 3.0 or higher GPA and participate in rifle or pistol marksmanship competitions. Selection is based on academic achievement, a letter of recommendation and a personal letter to the committee explaining how the scholarship will help you to reach your goals and marksmanship participation and success.
Target applicant(s): High school students.
Minimum GPA: 3.0
Amount: $1,000.
Number of awards: Varies.
Deadline: March 20.
How to apply: Applications are available online and must include the letter to the committee, one letter of recommendation, a transcript and documentation of marksmanship activity.
Exclusive: Visit www.UltimateScholarshipBook.com and enter code CI10220 for updates on this award.

(103) • CNO Naval History Essay Contest

United States Naval Institute (USNI)
291 Wood Road, Annapolis, MD 21402
Phone: 410-268-6110
https://www.usni.org/essay-contests
Purpose: To promote sea services and naval history.
Eligibility: Applicants must be active duty military, reservists, veterans, government civilian personnel or civilians. Students may be professional historians or rising historians. Applicants must write an essay discussing a naval historical topic and how lessons from the past can be applied to today.
Target applicant(s): College students. Adult students.
Amount: $5,000.
Number of awards: 6.
Deadline: June 30.
How to apply: Applications are available online.
Exclusive: Visit www.UltimateScholarshipBook.com and enter code UN10320 for updates on this award.

(104) • CoachTube Scholarship

CoachTube
600 Congress Avenue, 14th Floor, Austin, TX 78701
Phone: 888-331-7273
Email: ask@coachtube.com
https://coachtube.com/scholarship
Purpose: To support athletes and their families pursuing a college education.
Eligibility: Applicants must be either high school senior student athletes, coaches who are continuing their education or parents who have kids involved in sports.

Target applicant(s): High school students. College students. Adult students.
Amount: $1,000.
Number of awards: Varies.
Deadline: April 27.
How to apply: Applications are available online.
Exclusive: Visit www.UltimateScholarshipBook.com and enter code CO10420 for updates on this award.

(105) · Coast Guard College Student Pre-Commissioning Initiative

U.S. Coast Guard
2703 Martin Luther King Jr. Avenue SE, Washington, DC 20593-7000
Phone: 877-663-8724
http://www.gocoastguard.com
Purpose: To train future Coast Guard officers for success.
Eligibility: Applicants must be between 19 and 27 years of age and be college sophomores or juniors with at least 60 credits completed toward their degrees. They must be enrolled in a four-year degree program at a Coast Guard-approved institution with at least a 25 percent minority population. Students must be U.S. citizens, have a 2.5 or higher GPA and meet all physical requirements of the Coast Guard. Applicants must have a minimum score of 1100 on the SAT, 23 on the ACT or 109 on the ASVAB.
Target applicant(s): College students. Adult students.
Minimum GPA: 2.5
Amount: Tuition plus salary.
Number of awards: Varies.
Scholarship may be renewable.
Deadline: October 3, January 9.
How to apply: Applications are available online. An application form, physical exam results, immunization record, copy of Social Security card and driver's license, transcript, test results, proof of enrollment and tuition statement are required.
Exclusive: Visit www.UltimateScholarshipBook.com and enter code U.10520 for updates on this award.

(106) · Coast Guard Foundation Scholarship Fund

Coast Guard Foundation
394 Taugwonk Road, Stonington, CT 06378
Phone: 860-535-0786
Email: info@cgfdn.org
http://www.coastguardfoundation.org/how/scholarships
Purpose: To provide financial assistance to children of Coast Guard members.
Eligibility: Applicants must be unmarried dependent children of U.S. Coast Guard members, living, retired or deceased or Coast Guard reservists on extended active duty. They must be high school seniors or full-time undergraduate students in a four-year program or vocational/technical program. They must be under 23 years old.
Target applicant(s): High school students. College students.
Amount: Varies.
Number of awards: Varies.
Scholarship may be renewable.
Deadline: April 15.
How to apply: Applications are available online.
Exclusive: Visit www.UltimateScholarshipBook.com and enter code CO10620 for updates on this award.

(107) · Coca-Cola All-State Community College Academic Team

Coca-Cola Scholars Foundation
P.O. Box 442, Atlanta, GA 30301
Phone: 800-306-2653
Email: Scholars@coca-cola.com
http://www.coca-colascholarsfoundation.org/apply/
Purpose: To assist community college students with college expenses.
Eligibility: Applicants must be enrolled in community college, have a minimum GPA of 3.5 on a four-point scale and be on track to earn an associate's or bachelor's degree. Students attending community college in the U.S. do NOT need to be members of Phi Theta Kappa. Fifty students will win a $1,500 scholarship, fifty students will win a $1,250 scholarship and fifty students will win a $1,000 scholarship.
Target applicant(s): College students. Adult students.
Minimum GPA: 3.5
Amount: $1,000-$1,500.
Number of awards: 150.
Deadline: December 6.
How to apply: Applications are available online. Nomination from the designated nominator at your school is required. A list of nominators is available at http://www.ptk.org.
Exclusive: Visit www.UltimateScholarshipBook.com and enter code CO10720 for updates on this award.

(108) · Coca-Cola Scholars Program

Coca-Cola Scholars Foundation
P.O. Box 442, Atlanta, GA 30301
Phone: 800-306-2653
Email: Scholars@coca-cola.com
http://www.coca-colascholarsfoundation.org/apply/
Purpose: Begun in 1986 to celebrate the Coca-Cola Centennial, the program is designed to contribute to the nation's future and to assist a wide range of students.
Eligibility: Applicants must be high school seniors in the U.S., be U.S. citizens, nationals or permanent residents and must use the awards at an accredited U.S. college or university. Selection is based on the transcript, school profile, school and non-school related clubs and organizations, honors and awards and volunteer service. Application period typically reopens on August 1st of each year.
Target applicant(s): High school students.
Amount: $20,000.
Number of awards: 150.
Scholarship may be renewable.
Deadline: October 31.
How to apply: Applications are available online.
Exclusive: Visit www.UltimateScholarshipBook.com and enter code CO10820 for updates on this award.

(109) · College Prep Scholarship for High School Juniors

QuestBridge
120 Hawthorne Avenue, Suite 103, Palo Alto, CA 94301
Phone: 888-275-2054
Email: questions@questbridge.org
http://www.questbridge.org
Purpose: To equip outstanding low-income high school juniors with the knowledge necessary to compete for admission to leading colleges.
Eligibility: Applicants must be high school juniors who have a strong academic record and an annual household income of less than $60,000.

Many past award recipients have also been part of the first generation in their family to attend college. Scholarships are open to all qualified students, regardless of race or ethnicity.
Target applicant(s): High school students.
Amount: Varies.
Number of awards: Varies.
Deadline: March 22.
How to apply: Applications are available on the QuestBridge website in February. An application form, transcript and one teacher recommendation are required.
Exclusive: Visit www.UltimateScholarshipBook.com and enter code QU10920 for updates on this award.

(110) • CollegeNET Scholarships

CollegeNET Scholarship Review Committee
805 SW Broadway, Suite 1600 , Portland, OR 97205
Phone: 503-973-5200
Email: scholarship@collegenet.com
http://www.collegenet.com
Purpose: To assist college applicants.
Eligibility: Applicants must sign up at the website and visit and participate in forums. Recipients are determined by votes on the website.
Target applicant(s): High school students. College students. Adult students.
Amount: Varies.
Number of awards: Varies.
Deadline: Weekly.
How to apply: Applications are available online.
Exclusive: Visit www.UltimateScholarshipBook.com and enter code CO11020 for updates on this award.

(111) • Collegiate Championship Award Program

U.S. Figure Skating
20 First Street, Colorado Springs, CO 80906
Phone: 719-635-5200
Email: info@usfigureskating.org
http://www.usfsa.org
Purpose: To aid eligible collegiate figure skaters with their college tuition.
Eligibility: The award is presented to the senior ladies champion and senior men's champion at the U.S. Collegiate Figure Skating Championships.
Target applicant(s): College students. Adult students.
Amount: $5,000.
Number of awards: 2.
Deadline: Varies.
How to apply: The award is presented at the U.S. Collegiate Figure Skating Championships.
Exclusive: Visit www.UltimateScholarshipBook.com and enter code U.11120 for updates on this award.

(112) • Come 2 Iowa (C2IA) Senior Scholarship

Iowa Student Loan
6775 Vista Drive, West Des Moines, IA 50266-9305
Phone: 515-273-7656
Email: scholarship@studentloan.org
http://www.IowaStudentLoan.org/Come2Iowa
Purpose: To help students with expenses related to their pursuit of post-secondary education.
Eligibility: Applicants must be high school seniors who are at least 13 years of age. Students must be a permanent resident of and enrolled in a high school located in one of the following states: Illinois, Minnesota, Missouri, Nebraska, South Dakota or Wisconsin. Applicants must be planning to attend college at an institution located in Iowa. Selection is based on the overall strength of the application.
Target applicant(s): High school students.
Amount: $1,000.
Number of awards: 5.
Deadline: May 31.
How to apply: Application information is available online. Two online financial literacy tutorials, an online financial literacy assessment and a short essay are required.
Exclusive: Visit www.UltimateScholarshipBook.com and enter code IO11220 for updates on this award.

(113) • Congress Bundestag Youth Exchange Program

Congress Bundestag Youth Exchange Program
http://www.usagermanyscholarship.org
Purpose: To aid high school students who wish to study abroad in Germany.
Eligibility: Applicants must be U.S. citizens or permanent residents and be current high school students who will be between the ages of 15 and 18 at the beginning of the exchange program. They must have a GPA of 3.0 or higher on a four-point scale. Previous knowledge of the German language is not required. Selection is based on academic achievement, written and oral communication skills and temperamental suitability for adjusting to different cultures.
Target applicant(s): High school students.
Minimum GPA: 3.0
Amount: Varies.
Number of awards: Varies.
Deadline: December 12.
How to apply: Applications are available online. An application form and supporting materials are required.
Exclusive: Visit www.UltimateScholarshipBook.com and enter code CO11320 for updates on this award.

(114) • Congressional Medal of Honor Society Scholarships

Congressional Medal of Honor Society
40 Patriots Point Road, Mount Pleasant, SC 29464
Phone: 843-884-8862
Email: medalhq@earthlink.net
http://www.cmohs.org
Purpose: To provide education assistance to children of Congressional Medal of Honor recipients.
Eligibility: Applicants must be ROTC undergraduate students of the Air Force, Army, Navy or Marine Corps and must demonstrate leadership and a commitment to serve in the United States Armed Forces. Applicants must also be enrolled as sophomores or juniors. Applicants must have a minimum 3.5 GPA.
Target applicant(s): College students. Adult students.
Minimum GPA: 3.5
Amount: Varies.
Number of awards: Varies.
Deadline: February 19.
How to apply: Applications are available from the Congressional Medal of Honor Society.

Exclusive: Visit www.UltimateScholarshipBook.com and enter code CO11420 for updates on this award.

(115) • Connections Scholarship

Spokeo
556 South Fair Oaks Avenue, Suite #101-179, Pasadena, CA 91105
Phone: 877-913-3088
https://www.spokeo.com
Purpose: To support students who write an essay on forming connections.
Eligibility: Applicants must be U.S. citizens, recent high school graduates who will enroll as freshmen in the spring or current college students enrolled at an accredited institution who have a GPA of 3.0 or higher. Selection is based on the strength of the required essay submission.
Target applicant(s): High school students. College students. Adult students.
Minimum GPA: 3.0
Amount: $1,000.
Number of awards: 1.
Deadline: June 30.
How to apply: Applications are available online.
Exclusive: Visit www.UltimateScholarshipBook.com and enter code SP11520 for updates on this award.

(116) • Coolidge Scholarship

Calvin Coolidge Memorial Foundation Inc.
P.O. Box 97, Plymouth, VT 05056
Phone: 802-672-3389
Email: coolidgescholars@coolidgefoundation.org
https://coolidgescholars.org/
Purpose: To reward high school juniors who have achieved academic excellence and have an interest in public policy.
Eligibility: Applicants must be U.S. citizens planning on enrolling full-time in an accredited U.S. college or university. Students must apply during their junior year in high school. Selection is based on academic excellence, interest in public policy and appreciation for Coolidge values and demonstrated humility and leadership.
Target applicant(s): High school students.
Amount: Full tuition.
Number of awards: 2.
Deadline: January 24.
How to apply: Applications are available online through the website and include an essay, a transcript, a resume and two letters of recommendation.
Exclusive: Visit www.UltimateScholarshipBook.com and enter code CA11620 for updates on this award.

(117) • Copyright Awareness Scholarship

Music Publishers Association of the United States
243 5th Avenue, Suite 236, New York, NY 10016
Email: scholarship@mpa.org
http://www.mpa.org
Purpose: To support students interested in educating their peers via video about the laws surrounding intellectual property and copyright.
Eligibility: Applicants must be legal residents of the U.S. and be currently enrolled at a college, university or trade school in the United States. They must be between 13 and 25 years of age. A video submission that accurately illustrates the applicant's viewpoint of the importance of Intellectual Property and Copyright Law is required. Selection is based on the overall quality of the video submission.
Target applicant(s): Junior high students or younger. High school students. College students. Graduate school students.
Amount: $2,000-$5,000.
Number of awards: 3.
Deadline: May 21.
How to apply: Application with video submission must be submitted online.
Exclusive: Visit www.UltimateScholarshipBook.com and enter code MU11720 for updates on this award.

(118) • Corporate Culture Scholarship

Investor's Podcast
https://www.theinvestorspodcast.com/corporate-culture/
Purpose: To encourage awareness of sustainable profitability.
Eligibility: Applicants must be current undergraduate or graduate students enrolled at any North American university. Students must write an essay relating to corporate culture and their ideal workplace culture.
Target applicant(s): College students. Graduate school students. Adult students.
Amount: $1,000.
Number of awards: 1.
Deadline: October 1.
How to apply: Applications are available online.
Exclusive: Visit www.UltimateScholarshipBook.com and enter code IN11820 for updates on this award.

(119) • Cottage & Bungalow Scholarship

Cottage & Bungalow
P.O. Box 384, Tullahoma, TN 37388
Phone: 844-677-6604
Email: scholarships@cottageandbungalow.com
https://www.cottageandbungalow.com/scholarship.html
Purpose: To support creativity in education.
Eligibility: Applicants must be legal U.S. students or hold a valid student visa and be at least 18 years of age. Students must be currently enrolled or enrolling in an accredited U.S. institution as a full-time undergraduate or graduate student. Applicants must submit an essay describing the importance of creativity in education.
Target applicant(s): High school students. College students. Graduate school students. Adult students.
Amount: $500.
Number of awards: 1.
Deadline: January 15.
How to apply: Applications are available online.
Exclusive: Visit www.UltimateScholarshipBook.com and enter code CO11920 for updates on this award.

(120) • Cottage Inn Scholarship

Cottage Inn
4390 Concourse Drive, Ann Arbor, MI 48108
Phone: 734-663-2470
Email: info@cottageinn.com
http://www.cottageinn.com/cottage-inn-scholarship/
Purpose: To reward those who embrace education.
Eligibility: Applicants must be U.S. residents and be enrolled in or accepted into an accredited college or university in the U.S. Students will need to submit an essay. Minimum 3.0 GPA required.

Target applicant(s): High school students. College students. Graduate school students. Adult students.
Minimum GPA: 3.0
Amount: $500-$2,500.
Number of awards: 3.
Deadline: May 31.
How to apply: Applications are available online and must include an official transcript and an acceptance letter to the college or university you will be attending.
Exclusive: Visit www.UltimateScholarshipBook.com and enter code CO12020 for updates on this award.

---

(121) • Countdown to College Scholarship

Potential Magazine
61 Market Place, Montgomery, AL 36117
Phone: 334-518-7810
http://potentialmagazine.com
Purpose: To support high school students in pursuing post-secondary education.
Eligibility: Applicants must be subscribed to the Countdown to College eNewsletter.
Target applicant(s): High school students.
Amount: $500.
Number of awards: 1.
Deadline: May 4.
How to apply: Applications are available online.
Exclusive: Visit www.UltimateScholarshipBook.com and enter code PO12120 for updates on this award.

---

(122) • Couponing in College

Dealspotr
Zipfworks, Inc., 1601 Cloverfield Boulevard, Suite 1050N, Santa Monica, CA 90404
https://dealspotr.com/scholarship
Purpose: To promote awareness of budgeting and saving money in college.
Eligibility: Applicants must be residents of the United States and currently enrolled in a college or university. Students must write an essay pertaining to best strategies for using coupons in college. Applicants must have a valid .edu email address.
Target applicant(s): College students. Adult students.
Amount: $2,000.
Number of awards: 1.
Deadline: October 27.
How to apply: Applications are available online.
Exclusive: Visit www.UltimateScholarshipBook.com and enter code DE12220 for updates on this award.

---

(123) • Courage to Grow Scholarship

Courage to Grow Scholarship
P.O. Box 2507, Chelan, WA 98816
Phone: 509-731-3056
Email: support@couragetogrowscholarship.com
http://www.couragetogrowscholarship.com
Purpose: To assist high school and college students.
Eligibility: Applicants must be high school seniors or college students with a minimum GPA of 2.5 and must also be U.S. citizens.
Target applicant(s): High school students. College students. Adult students.
Minimum GPA: 2.5
Amount: $500.
Number of awards: 1 per month.
Deadline: Monthly.
How to apply: Applications are available online.
Exclusive: Visit www.UltimateScholarshipBook.com and enter code CO12320 for updates on this award.

---

(124) • Courageous Persuaders Video Contest

Courageous Persuaders
Email: sherp@dada.org
http://courageouspersuaders.com/official-rules/
Purpose: To reward students who understand the dangers of underage drinking and texting while driving.
Eligibility: Applicants may enter as an individual or as a team. Students must be a high school student, in grades 9-12 (ages 19 and under) and a United States or Canadian citizen attending a United States (or U.S. territories) or Canadian high school. Students must submit a 30-second commercial about the dangers of underage drinking or the dangers of texting while driving.
Target applicant(s): High school students.
Amount: $3,000.
Number of awards: 18.
Deadline: February 9.
How to apply: Applications are available online.
Exclusive: Visit www.UltimateScholarshipBook.com and enter code CO12420 for updates on this award.

---

(125) • CourseHorse Learner's Scholarship

CourseHorse
220 E. 23rd Street, Suite 500, New York, NY 10010
Phone: 914-227-2800
https://coursehorse.com/scholarship
Purpose: To support current and incoming college students in funding their education.
Eligibility: Applicants must be 25 years of age or younger. Students must submit a video or blog explaining what learning means to them. Selection is based on the overall strength of the submission.
Target applicant(s): High school students. College students.
Amount: $1,000.
Number of awards: 1.
Deadline: June 15.
How to apply: Applications are available online.
Exclusive: Visit www.UltimateScholarshipBook.com and enter code CO12520 for updates on this award.

---

(126) • CPI Champion of Service Award

College Preparatory Invitational
P.O. Box 566357, Miami, FL 33256-6357
Phone: 786-369-9040
Email: info@collegeprepinvitational.com
http://www.collegeprepinvitational.com
Purpose: To support young riders and promote higher education as a foundation to future success.
Eligibility: Applicants must be participants in the College Preparatory Invitational, be students in grades 8 through 12, have a 3.0 GPA or higher and have served a minimum of 36 hours of community service within the last 16 months. The scholarship is awarded to the applicant with the highest number of community hours served.

Target applicant(s): Junior high students or younger. High school students.
Minimum GPA: 3.0
Amount: $500.
Number of awards: 1.
Deadline: Varies.
How to apply: To apply, send a letter with the organization's letterhead documenting service hours performed, a copy of the IRS letter of recognition of exemption of the organization and current school transcript via certified mail.
Exclusive: Visit www.UltimateScholarshipBook.com and enter code CO12620 for updates on this award.

(127) · CPI Essay Award

College Preparatory Invitational
P.O. Box 566357, Miami, FL 33256-6357
Phone: 786-369-9040
Email: info@collegeprepinvitational.com
http://www.collegeprepinvitational.com
Purpose: To aid riders as they pursue higher education.
Eligibility: Applicants must participate in the College Preparatory Invitational and be students in grades 8 through 12. Selection is based on the style, grammar, spelling and creativity of a personal essay.
Target applicant(s): Junior high students or younger. High school students.
Amount: $500.
Deadline: Varies.
How to apply: Applications are available online.
Exclusive: Visit www.UltimateScholarshipBook.com and enter code CO12720 for updates on this award.

(128) · CPI Highest Point Hunt Seat Rider

College Preparatory Invitational
P.O. Box 566357, Miami, FL 33256-6357
Phone: 786-369-9040
Email: info@collegeprepinvitational.com
http://www.collegeprepinvitational.com
Purpose: To support young riders and promote higher education as a foundation to future success.
Eligibility: Applicants must attend the College Preparatory Invitational and be students in grades 8 through 12. The scholarship is awarded to the rider with the highest point score.
Target applicant(s): Junior high students or younger. High school students.
Amount: $500.
Number of awards: 1.
Deadline: Varies.
How to apply: Applications are available online.
Exclusive: Visit www.UltimateScholarshipBook.com and enter code CO12820 for updates on this award.

(129) · CPI Written Horsemanship Test Award

College Preparatory Invitational
P.O. Box 566357, Miami, FL 33256-6357
Phone: 786-369-9040
Email: info@collegeprepinvitational.com
http://www.collegeprepinvitational.com
Purpose: To support young riders and promote higher education as a foundation to future success.
Eligibility: Applicants must be participants in the College Preparatory Invitational and be students in grades 8 through 12. Students will take an online test on horsemanship, and the top five will be invited to take a written exam during the invitational.
Target applicant(s): Junior high students or younger. High school students.
Amount: $500.
Number of awards: 1.
Deadline: December 1 (FL), February 1 (TX).
How to apply: Applicants are required to take an online test on a given date. Information is available online regarding a link to the exam.
Exclusive: Visit www.UltimateScholarshipBook.com and enter code CO12920 for updates on this award.

(130) · Create Real Impact Contest

Impact Teen Drivers
Attn.: Create Real Impact Contest, P.O. Box 161209, Sacramento, CA 95816
Phone: 916-733-7432
Email: info@impactteendrivers.org
http://www.createrealimpact.com
Purpose: To raise awareness of the dangers of distracted driving and poor decision making.
Eligibility: Applicants must be legal U.S. residents who are between the ages of 14 and 22. They must be enrolled full-time at an accredited secondary or post-secondary school. They must submit an original, videotaped creative project that offers a solution to the problem of distracted driving. Selection is based on project concept, message effectiveness and creativity.
Target applicant(s): High school students. College students. Graduate school students.
Amount: $500 and $1,500.
Number of awards: 13.
Deadline: March 22.
How to apply: Contest entry instructions are available online. A videotaped creative project is required.
Exclusive: Visit www.UltimateScholarshipBook.com and enter code IM13020 for updates on this award.

(131) · Create-a-Greeting-Card Scholarship

Gallery Collection
Prudent Publishing, 65 Challenger Road, P.O. Box 150, Ridgefield Park, NJ 07660
Phone: 800-950-7064
Email: service@gallerycollection.com
https://www.gallerycollection.com/greeting-cards-scholarship.htm
Purpose: To reward high school, college students and members of the United States armed forces who enter a contest to create a Christmas card, holiday card, birthday card or all-occasion greeting card.
Eligibility: Applicants must be U.S. citizens or legal residents who are at least 14 years old. The submission must include original artwork or photographs. Those members of the United States armed forces must not be older than 34. Selection is based on the overall quality of the submission including creativity, uniqueness and suitability.
Target applicant(s): High school students. College students. Adult students.
Amount: $1,000-$10,000.
Number of awards: 2.
Deadline: March 1.
How to apply: Applications and submissions may be made online or mailed directly to the scholarship administrator at the Gallery

Collection. Entry form and greeting card submission are required. Online submissions are preferred.
Exclusive: Visit www.UltimateScholarshipBook.com and enter code GA13120 for updates on this award.

(132) • Credit Sesame Financial Literacy Scholarship

Credit Sesame
607 A West Dana Street, Mountain View, CA 94041
https://www.creditsesame.com/scholarship/
Purpose: To encourage students to have financial literacy.
Eligibility: Applicants must be current students at a four year college or university or enrolling in one in the upcoming school year. Students must be at least 17 years of age and reside in the U.S. Applicants must complete the application and an essay in English.
Target applicant(s): High school students. College students. Adult students.
Amount: $1,000.
Number of awards: 1.
Deadline: July 31.
How to apply: Applications are available online.
Exclusive: Visit www.UltimateScholarshipBook.com and enter code CR13220 for updates on this award.

(133) • Crescent Electric Supply Company

Crescent Electric Supply Company
P.O. Box 500, East Dubuque, IL 61025-4420
Phone: 815-747-3145
http://www.cesco.com/content/EnergySaverScholarship
Purpose: To support students who support reducing their carbon footprint.
Eligibility: Applicants must be a graduating high school senior or a freshman, sophomore or junior in college. Students must be between the ages of 16 and 22. Applicants must post a photograph on social media that shows how they reduce their carbon footprint.
Target applicant(s): High school students. College students.
Amount: $1,000.
Number of awards: 1.
Deadline: August 8.
How to apply: Applications are available online.
Exclusive: Visit www.UltimateScholarshipBook.com and enter code CR13320 for updates on this award.

(134) • Curt Greene Memorial Scholarship

Harness Horse Youth Foundation
16575 Carey Road, Westfield, IN 46074
Phone: 317-867-5877
Email: ellen@hhyf.org
http://www.hhyf.org
Purpose: To support students who are interested in harness racing.
Eligibility: Students must demonstrate financial need, and must be enrolled or planning to enroll full-time (minimum of 12 credit hours) in an undergraduate program. Applicants must submit an essay and two letters of reference.
Target applicant(s): High school students. College students.
Minimum GPA: 2.5
Amount: $2,500.
Number of awards: Varies.
Deadline: April 30.
How to apply: Applications are available online.
Exclusive: Visit www.UltimateScholarshipBook.com and enter code HA13420 for updates on this award.

(135) • Curwen-Guidry-Blackburn Scholarship Fund

Southern Bowling Congress
9817 Miller Road, Sherwood, AR 72120
Phone: 501-425-2299
Email: dclements858@sbcglobal.net
http://www.southernbowlingcongress.org/
Purpose: To aid any senior youth bowler in Southern Bowling Congress member states in their education.
Eligibility: Students must be high school seniors and currently bowling in a USBC Certified Youth League. Students must reside in a Southern Bowling Congress member state which includes Alabama, Arkansas, Florida, Georgia, Kentucky, Louisiana, Mississippi, Tennessee and Texas. Applicants must have bowled in a USBC Certified Youth League three of four years in high school and have bowled 75 percent of the league schedule. Students must have a minimum grade point average of 2.5 on a 4.0 scale and achieved an ACT composite score of 20 or SAT composite score of 1410.
Target applicant(s): High school students.
Minimum GPA: 2.5
Amount: $750.
Number of awards: 1.
Deadline: March 15.
How to apply: Applications are available online. An application form, official high school grade and credits transcript with a minimum of six semesters of information that includes ACT and/or SAT scores and a personal letter of recommendation from high school principal or counselor are required.
Exclusive: Visit www.UltimateScholarshipBook.com and enter code SO13520 for updates on this award.

(136) • Daedalian Foundation Matching Scholarship Program

Daedalian Foundation
P.O. Box 249, Randolph AFB, TX 78148
Phone: 210-945-2111
Email: info@daedalians.org
http://daedalians.org/programs/scholarships/
Purpose: To aid undergraduates who are studying to become military pilots.
Eligibility: Applicants must be rising or current undergraduates attending a four-year institution and must have a demonstrated interest in pursuing a career in military aviation. Selection is based on the overall strength of the application.
Target applicant(s): High school students. College students. Adult students.
Amount: Varies.
Number of awards: Varies.
Deadline: Varies.
How to apply: Applications are available online. An application form and applicant photo are required.
Exclusive: Visit www.UltimateScholarshipBook.com and enter code DA13620 for updates on this award.

(137) • Daughters of the Cincinnati Scholarship

Daughters of the Cincinnati
National Headquarters, 20 West 44th Street #508, New York, NY 10036

Phone: 212-991-9945
Email: scholarships@daughters1894.org
http://daughters1894.org/
Purpose: To support daughters of Armed Services commissioned officers.
Eligibility: Applicants must be daughters of career officers in the United States Army, Navy, Air Force, Coast Guard or Marine Corps (active, retired or deceased). Daughters of reserve officers or enlisted personnel cannot apply. Applicants must also be high school seniors.
Target applicant(s): High school students.
Amount: $16,000-$20,000 paid over 4 years.
Number of awards: Varies.
Scholarship may be renewable.
Deadline: March 15.
How to apply: More details are available by contacting the organization. An essay, a secondary school report, a letter of recommendation and a Student Aid Report are required.
Exclusive: Visit www.UltimateScholarshipBook.com and enter code DA13720 for updates on this award.

(138) • Davidson Fellows Scholarships

Davidson Institute for Talent Development
9665 Gateway Drive, Suite B , Reno, NV 89521
Phone: 775-852-3483
Email: DavidsonFellows@davidsongifted.org
http://www.davidsongifted.org/
Purpose: To reward young people for their works in mathematics, science, technology, music, literature, philosophy or "outside the box."
Eligibility: Applicants must be under the age of 18 and be able to attend the awards reception in Washington, DC. In addition to the monetary award, the institute will pay for travel and lodging expenses. Three nominator forms, three copies of a 15-minute DVD and additional materials are required.
Target applicant(s): Junior high students or younger. High school students.
Amount: $10,000-$50,000.
Number of awards: Varies.
Deadline: February 8.
How to apply: Applications are available online.
Exclusive: Visit www.UltimateScholarshipBook.com and enter code DA13820 for updates on this award.

(139) • Davis-Putter Scholarship Fund

Davis-Putter Scholarship Fund
P.O. Box 7307, New York, NY 10116
Email: information@davisputter.org
http://www.davisputter.org
Purpose: To assist students who are both academically capable and who aid the progressive movement for peace and justice both on campus and in their communities.
Eligibility: Applicants must be undergraduate or graduate students who participate in the progressive movement, acting in the interests of issues such as expansion of civil rights and international solidarity, among others. Applicants must also have demonstrated financial need as well as a solid academic record.
Target applicant(s): College students. Graduate school students. Adult students.
Amount: Up to $10,000.
Number of awards: Varies.
Deadline: April 1.
How to apply: Applications are available online.
Exclusive: Visit www.UltimateScholarshipBook.com and enter code DA13920 for updates on this award.

(140) • Delete Cyberbullying Scholarship Award

Delete Cyberbullying
2261 Market Street #291, San Francisco, CA 94114
Email: help@deletecyberbullying.org
http://www.deletecyberbullying.org
Purpose: To get students committed to the cause of deleting cyberbullying.
Eligibility: Applicants must be a U.S. citizen or permanent resident and attending or planning to attend an accredited U.S. college or university for undergraduate or graduate studies. Applicants must also be a high school, college or graduate student or a student planning to enter college.
Target applicant(s): High school students. College students. Graduate school students. Adult students.
Amount: $1,000.
Number of awards: 1.
Deadline: June 30.
How to apply: Applications are available online. An application form and an essay are required.
Exclusive: Visit www.UltimateScholarshipBook.com and enter code DE14020 for updates on this award.

(141) • Dell Scholars Program

Michael and Susan Dell Foundation
P.O. Box 163867, Austin, TX 78716
Phone: 512-329-0799
Email: apply@dellscholars.org
http://www.dellscholars.org
Purpose: To support underprivileged high school seniors.
Eligibility: Students must be participants in an approved college readiness program, and they must have at least a 2.4 GPA. Applicants must be pursuing a bachelor's degree in the fall directly after graduation. Students must also be U.S. citizens or permanent residents and demonstrate financial need. Selection is based on "individual determination to succeed," future goals, hardships that have been overcome, self motivation and financial need.
Target applicant(s): High school students.
Minimum GPA: 2.4
Amount: Varies.
Number of awards: Varies.
Scholarship may be renewable.
Deadline: January 15.
How to apply: Applications are available online. An online application is required.
Exclusive: Visit www.UltimateScholarshipBook.com and enter code MI14120 for updates on this award.

(142) • Delta Theta Chi Sorority National Memorial Scholarship

Delta Theta Chi Sorority
Attn: Cindi Cook, 2614 S. Lulu, Wichita, KS 67216
http://www.deltathetachi.org/Scholarships.html
Purpose: To support the pursuit of higher education.
Eligibility: Applicants must provide transcripts for the past four years. Students graduating high school or current undergraduate freshmen must provide official documentation of grade point average, SAT and/or ACT scores. Applicants must complete application in full, including the essay, and provide at least one letter of reference.

Target applicant(s): High school students. College students. Graduate school students. Adult students.
Amount: $2,600.
Number of awards: 2.
Deadline: February 1.
How to apply: Applications are available online.
Exclusive: Visit www.UltimateScholarshipBook.com and enter code DE14220 for updates on this award.

---

(143) • DevMountain Scholarship

DevMountain
Phone: 844-433-8686
https://scholarship.devmountain.com/
Purpose: To assist students who create a short video.
Eligibility: Applicants must be legal residents of the U.S. except for Puerto Rico who are at least 18 years old and who reside in the U.S. Students must be enrolling in the upcoming school semester and must create a short video as part of their application.
Target applicant(s): College students. Graduate school students. Adult students.
Amount: $2,500.
Number of awards: 1.
Deadline: October 31.
How to apply: Applications are available online.
Exclusive: Visit www.UltimateScholarshipBook.com and enter code DE14320 for updates on this award.

---

(144) • Dietspotlight.com Scholarship

DietSpotlight.com
75 Valencia Avenue, Suite 1000, Coral Gables, FL 33134
https://www.dietspotlight.com/scholarship/essay/
Purpose: To encourage students who are pursuing a health-related degree to create an obesity conscious community.
Eligibility: Applicants must be enrolled in a health-related degree program and submit a personal essay using between 900-1,500 words. Students must provide their name and address along with the essay in a Word or PDF format to be considered.
Target applicant(s): College students. Adult students.
Amount: $3,000.
Number of awards: 4.
Deadline: December 31.
How to apply: Applications are available online.
Exclusive: Visit www.UltimateScholarshipBook.com and enter code DI14420 for updates on this award.

---

(145) • Digital Privacy Scholarship

Digital Responsibility
3561 Homestead Road #113, Santa Clara, CA 95051-5161
Email: scholarship@digitalresponsibility.org
http://www.digitalresponsibility.org
Purpose: To help students understand why it's important to be cautious about what they post on the Internet.
Eligibility: Applicants must be a high school freshman, sophomore, junior or senior or a current or entering college or graduate school student of any level. Home schooled students are also eligible. There is no age limit. Students must also be a U.S. citizen or legal resident.
Target applicant(s): High school students. College students. Graduate school students. Adult students.
Amount: $1,000.
Number of awards: 1.
Deadline: June 30.
How to apply: Applications are available online.
Exclusive: Visit www.UltimateScholarshipBook.com and enter code DI14520 for updates on this award.

---

(146) • Dinah Shore Scholarship

Ladies Professional Golf Association
100 International Golf Drive, Daytona Beach, FL 32124-1092
Phone: 386-274-6200
Email: info@lpgafoundation.org
http://www.lpga.com/lpga-foundation/scholarships
Purpose: To honor the late Dinah Shore.
Eligibility: Applicants must be female high school seniors who have been accepted into a full-time course of study at an accredited U.S. institution of higher learning. They must have played golf regularly for the past two years but not played on a competitive collegiate golf team. A minimum GPA of 3.2 is required.
Target applicant(s): High school students.
Minimum GPA: 3.2
Amount: $5,000.
Number of awards: 1.
Deadline: May 15.
How to apply: Applications are available online.
Exclusive: Visit www.UltimateScholarshipBook.com and enter code LA14620 for updates on this award.

---

(147) • DirectTextbook.com Scholarship Essay Contest

DirectTextbook.com
1525 Chemeketa Street NE, Salem, OR 97301
Phone: 503-779-4056
Email: service@directtextbook.com
https://www.directtextbook.com/
Purpose: To support students who write an essay.
Eligibility: Applicants must be U.S. citizens enrolled in a two- or four-year institution in the fall semester. Students must have a grade point average of 2.5 or higher. Applicants must provide completed application and essay.
Target applicant(s): College students. Adult students.
Minimum GPA: 2.5
Amount: $1,000-$5,000.
Number of awards: 3.
Deadline: August 1.
How to apply: Applications are available online.
Exclusive: Visit www.UltimateScholarshipBook.com and enter code DI14720 for updates on this award.

---

(148) • Diverse Minds Writing Challenge

B'nai B'rith International
4605 Lankershim Boulevard, Suite 710, North Hollywood, CA 91602
Phone: 323-308-0195
Email: diverseminds@bnaibrith.org
http://www.bnaibrith.org/diverse-minds.html
Purpose: To reward students for promoting equality among all citizens.
Eligibility: Applicants must be high school students in grades 9-12 residing in one of the five New York City boroughs (Manhattan, Bronx,

Brooklyn, Staten Island and Queens) and must create a children's book that discusses the topics of tolerance and diversity.
Target applicant(s): High school students.
Amount: $1,000-$5,000.
Number of awards: 3.
Deadline: August 24.
How to apply: Entries must be submitted by email or regular mail and must include a cover letter with name and contact information of author(s), name of school and teacher and a brief biographical note.
Exclusive: Visit www.UltimateScholarshipBook.com and enter code B'14820 for updates on this award.

(149) · Dixie Boys Baseball Scholarship Program

Dixie Boys Baseball
P.O. Box 8263, Dothan, AL 36304
Phone: 334-793-3331
Email: jjones29@sw.rr.com
http://baseball.dixie.org
Purpose: To help high school seniors who have participated in a franchised Dixie Boys Baseball Inc. program.
Eligibility: Applicants must plan to pursue undergraduate studies at a college or university. An application, financial statement, two recommendation letters, proof of baseball participation, transcript and essay are required. Selection is based on class rankings, strong school and community leadership and financial need. Programs are located in Alabama, Arkansas, Florida, Georgia, Louisiana, Mississippi, North Carolina, South Carolina, Tennessee, Texas and Virginia.
Target applicant(s): High school students.
Amount: $1,250.
Number of awards: 11.
Deadline: April 1.
How to apply: Applications are available online.
Exclusive: Visit www.UltimateScholarshipBook.com and enter code DI14920 for updates on this award.

(150) · Dixie Softball Scholarships

Dixie Softball Inc.
Doug Garrett, Chairman, Dixie Softball Scholarship Committee, 106 Woodlake Drive, Pineville, LA 71360
Phone: 318-451-4344
Email: dayprodoug@suddenlink.net
http://softball.dixie.org/site/
Purpose: To support Dixie softball participants as they seek to further their education beyond high school.
Eligibility: Applicants must be female Dixie Softball participants, be high school seniors and have played softball for at least two seasons. Selection is based on financial need, academic achievement and future goals.
Target applicant(s): High school students.
Amount: $1,500.
Number of awards: 8.
Deadline: February 1.
How to apply: Applications are available online and must include the following: copy of most recent tax return, letter from parent or guardian explaining financial need, verification letter from Dixie Softball league official, photo and personal letter describing goals, activities and achievements.
Exclusive: Visit www.UltimateScholarshipBook.com and enter code DI15020 for updates on this award.

(151) · Dixie Youth Scholarship Program

Dixie Youth Baseball, Inc.
Johnny Berthelot, Chairman Scholarship Committee, 110 South Bolivar Street, Suite 207, Marshall, TX 75670
Phone: 903-927-2255
Email: dyb@dixie.org
http://youth.dixie.org/
Purpose: To help high school seniors who have participated in a franchised Dixie Youth Baseball league.
Eligibility: Applicants must have been registered on a Dixie Youth Baseball team participating in a franchised Dixie Youth Baseball Inc. league prior to reaching age thirteen. Selection is based on financial need, scholastic record and citizenship. Programs are located in Alabama, Arkansas, Florida, Georgia, Louisiana, Mississippi, North Carolina, South Carolina, Tennessee, Texas and Virginia.
Target applicant(s): High school students.
Amount: $2,000.
Number of awards: Varies.
Deadline: February 1.
How to apply: Contact your local league officials or a district, state or national director for an application, and applications are also available online.
Exclusive: Visit www.UltimateScholarshipBook.com and enter code DI15120 for updates on this award.

(152) · Dizzy Dean Scholarship

Dizzy Dean Baseball Inc.
2470 Highway 51 South, Hernando, MS 38632
Phone: 662-429-7790
Email: dphil10513@aol.com
http://dizzydeanbbinc.org/
Purpose: To aid members of the Dizzy Dean Baseball/Softball program in pursuing their college education.
Eligibility: Applicants must have played on a Dizzy Dean Baseball/Softball program for four years. Students must also be graduating seniors and be able to provide a high school transcript, copy of diploma and a copy of parent/guardian prior years' federal income tax form.
Target applicant(s): High school students.
Amount: Varies.
Number of awards: Varies.
Scholarship may be renewable.
Deadline: June 15.
How to apply: Applications are available online.
Exclusive: Visit www.UltimateScholarshipBook.com and enter code DI15220 for updates on this award.

(153) · Dollars for Scholars Scholarship

Citizens' Scholarship Foundation of America
One Scholarship Way, St. Peter, MN 56082
Phone: 800-537-4180
Email: dollarsforscholars@scholarshipamerica.org
http://www.scholarshipamerica.org
Purpose: To encourage students to aim for and achieve loftier educational goals.
Eligibility: Applicants must be members of a local Dollars for Scholars chapter. There are more than 1,200 Dollars for Scholars chapters that award more than $29 million in awards each year.
Target applicant(s): High school students.
Amount: Varies.
Number of awards: Varies.

Deadline: Varies.
How to apply: Contact your local Dollars for Scholars chapter for more information. A list of chapters is available online.
Exclusive: Visit www.UltimateScholarshipBook.com and enter code CI15320 for updates on this award.

(154) • Dolphin Scholarships

Dolphin Scholarship Foundation
4966 Euclid Road, Suite 109, Virginia Beach, VA 23462
Phone: 757-671-3200
Email: scholars@dolphinscholarship.org
http://www.dolphinscholarship.org
Purpose: To assist the children of members of the Navy Submarine Force and other Navy submarine support personnel.
Eligibility: Applicants must be the unmarried children or stepchildren of navy submariners or navy members who have served in submarine support activities and must be under 24 years old at the time of the application deadline. The parents must have been part of the Submarine Force for at least eight years, have served in submarine support activities for at least 10 years or died on active duty while in the Submarine Force. The children of submariners who served less than the required number of years due to injury or illness occurring in the line of duty may also be eligible. Applicants must also be high school seniors or college students planning to attend or currently attending an accredited four-year college, working for a bachelor's degree.
Target applicant(s): High school students. College students.
Amount: $2,000-$3,400 per year.
Number of awards: 25-30.
Scholarship may be renewable.
Deadline: March 15.
How to apply: Applications are available online.
Exclusive: Visit www.UltimateScholarshipBook.com and enter code DO15420 for updates on this award.

(155) • Don't Text and Drive Scholarship

Digital Responsibility
3561 Homestead Road #113, Santa Clara, CA 95051-5161
Email: scholarship@digitalresponsibility.org
http://www.digitalresponsibility.org
Purpose: To help students understand the risks of texting while driving.
Eligibility: Applicants must be a high school freshman, sophomore, junior or senior or a current or entering college or graduate school student of any level. Home schooled students are also eligible. There is no age limit. Students must also be a U.S. citizen or legal resident.
Target applicant(s): High school students. College students. Graduate school students. Adult students.
Amount: $1,000.
Number of awards: 1.
Deadline: September 30.
How to apply: Applications are available online.
Exclusive: Visit www.UltimateScholarshipBook.com and enter code DI15520 for updates on this award.

(156) • DoSomething.org Seasonal Scholarships

Do Something (Scholarships)
19 West 21st Street, Floor 8, New York, NY 10010
Phone: 212-254-2390
Email: scholarships@dosomething.org
https://www.dosomething.org/us/about/easy-scholarships
Purpose: To assist students who participate in a social issue campaign.
Eligibility: Applicants must be age 25 or younger and be U.S. or Canadian citizens. There is a new scholarship each quarter. Selection is based on a random drawing of all students who participate in the campaign.
Target applicant(s): Junior high students or younger. High school students. College students. Graduate school students.
Amount: Varies.
Number of awards: Varies.
Deadline: Varies.
How to apply: Applications are available online.
Exclusive: Visit www.UltimateScholarshipBook.com and enter code DO15620 for updates on this award.

(157) • Dr. Aileen W. Tobin Scholarship

U.S. Army Ordnance Corps Association
P.O. Box 5251, Ft. Lee, VA 23801
Phone: 410-272-8540
http://usaoca.org/index.php/scholarship-information/
Purpose: To honor the memory of LTG Joseph M. Heiser.
Eligibility: Applicants must be active or reserve Ordnance soldiers or OCA members or members or their immediate family. They must write a 300- to 500- word essay about the reasons they are seeking the grant and why they feel they deserve it and a 1,000- to 1,500-word essay on the missions, heritage or history of the U.S. Army Ordnance Corps.
Target applicant(s): High school students. College students. Adult students.
Amount: Varies.
Number of awards: Varies.
Deadline: June 30.
How to apply: Applications are available online.
Exclusive: Visit www.UltimateScholarshipBook.com and enter code U.15720 for updates on this award.

(158) • Dr. Alma S. Adams Scholarship

Truth Initiative
900 G Street, NW, Fourth Floor, Washington, DC 20001
Phone: 202-454-5555
Email: adamsscholarship@truthinititative.org
http://truthinitiative.org/Adams-Scholarship
Purpose: To support students who have a passion to help reduce the use of tobacco products in priority underserved populations.
Eligibility: Applicants must be U.S. citizens or legal residents. Students should be pursuing a degree in public health, communications, social work, education, liberal arts or related field and have a minimum GPA of 2.0. Applicants must provide proof of community service activities such as (but not limited to) activism, outreach or peer counseling in tobacco prevention or control. Financial need is considered.
Target applicant(s): College students. Graduate school students. Adult students.
Minimum GPA: 2.0
Amount: $5,000.
Number of awards: 2.
Deadline: April 30.
How to apply: Applications are available online and must include a SAR report.
Exclusive: Visit www.UltimateScholarshipBook.com and enter code TR15820 for updates on this award.

(159) • Dr. Arnita Young Boswell Scholarship

National Hook-Up of Black Women Inc.
1809 East 71st Street, Suite 205, Chicago, IL 60649
Phone: 773-667-7061
Email: nhbwdir@aol.com
http://www.nhbwinc.com/scholarship.html
Purpose: To reward adult students for their academic achievement.
Eligibility: Applicants must be African American undergraduate students with a minimum GPA of 2.75. Selection is based on academic accomplishments as well as involvement in school and community activities and an essay.
Target applicant(s): College students. Adult students.
Minimum GPA: 2.75
Amount: $1,000.
Number of awards: Varies.
Scholarship may be renewable.
Deadline: March 31.
How to apply: Applications are available by mail and must be requested by March 1.
Exclusive: Visit www.UltimateScholarshipBook.com and enter code NA15920 for updates on this award.

(160) • Dr. Wynetta A. Frazier Sister to Sister Scholarship

National Hook-Up of Black Women Inc.
1809 East 71st Street, Suite 205, Chicago, IL 60649
Phone: 773-667-7061
Email: nhbwdir@aol.com
http://www.nhbwinc.com/scholarship.html
Purpose: To assist women who are returning to school without the support of a spouse or family.
Eligibility: Applicants must be at least 21 years of age and may have taken a break in their educations to seek employment, care for their children or because of financial burden. Students must have confirmation of acceptance to college or university for pursuit of a bachelor's degree and must demonstrate mastery of written communication skills.
Target applicant(s): Adult students.
Amount: Varies.
Number of awards: Varies.
Deadline: March 1.
How to apply: Applications are available by mail.
Exclusive: Visit www.UltimateScholarshipBook.com and enter code NA16020 for updates on this award.

(161) • Dwight F. Davis Memorial Scholarship

United States Tennis Association Foundation
70 W. Red Oak Lane, White Plains, NY 10604
Phone: 914-696-7223
Email: foundation@usta.com
http://www.ustafoundation.com/
Purpose: To support youth tennis players who represent the sport with distinction.
Eligibility: Applicants must be high school seniors who have participated in an organized youth tennis program. Students must excel in academics, have participated in extracurricular activities and have participated in various community service projects.
Target applicant(s): High school students.
Amount: $10,000.
Number of awards: 2.
Scholarship may be renewable.
Deadline: February 27.
How to apply: Applications are available online.
Exclusive: Visit www.UltimateScholarshipBook.com and enter code UN16120 for updates on this award.

(162) • Dwight Mosley Scholarship Award

United States Tennis Association Foundation
70 W. Red Oak Lane, White Plains, NY 10604
Phone: 914-696-7223
Email: foundation@usta.com
http://www.ustafoundation.com/
Purpose: To support youth tennis players of ethnically diverse backgrounds who have excelled both on and off the court.
Eligibility: Applicants must be USTA ranked high school seniors who are of an ethnically diverse background and who have participated extensively in an organized youth community tennis program. Selection is based on academic excellence and exemplary sportsmanship on and off the court.
Target applicant(s): High school students.
Amount: $10,000.
Number of awards: 2.
Scholarship may be renewable.
Deadline: February 27.
How to apply: Applications are available online.
Exclusive: Visit www.UltimateScholarshipBook.com and enter code UN16220 for updates on this award.

(163) • E-waste Scholarship

Digital Responsibility
3561 Homestead Road #113, Santa Clara, CA 95051-5161
Email: scholarship@digitalresponsibility.org
http://www.digitalresponsibility.org
Purpose: To help students understand the impact of e-waste and what can be done to reduce e-waste.
Eligibility: Applicants must be a high school, college, graduate or home schooled students. There is no age limit. Students must also be a U.S. citizen or legal resident. A 140-character message about e-waste is required to apply. The top 10 applications will be selected as finalists; finalists will be asked to write a full length 500- to 1,000-word essay about e-waste. Only online applications are accepted.
Target applicant(s): High school students. College students. Graduate school students. Adult students.
Amount: $1,000.
Number of awards: 1.
Deadline: April 30.
How to apply: Applications are available online.
Exclusive: Visit www.UltimateScholarshipBook.com and enter code DI16320 for updates on this award.

(164) • Earl Anthony Memorial Scholarships

United States Bowling Congress
Attn.: Alberta E. Crowe Star of Tomorrow, 621 Six Flags Drive, Arlington, TX 76011
Phone: 800-514-2695
Email: contactus@ibcyouth.com
https://www.bowl.com/Youth/Youth_Home/Scholarships/
Purpose: To recognize USBC members for community involvement and academic achievement.
Eligibility: Applicants must be USBC members in good standing who are high school seniors or current college students. They must have a

GPA of 3.0 or higher. Community involvement, academic achievement and financial need are considered.
Target applicant(s): High school students. College students. Adult students.
Minimum GPA: 3.0
Amount: $5,000.
Number of awards: 5.
Deadline: Varies.
How to apply: Applications are available online.
Exclusive: Visit www.UltimateScholarshipBook.com and enter code UN16420 for updates on this award.

(165) · Easton/NFAA Scholarship Program

National Field Archery Association
800 Archery Lane, Yankton, SD 57078
Phone: 605-260-9279
Email: info@nfaausa.com
https://www.nfaausa.com
Purpose: To help those students who have participated in National Field Archery Association events continue their education beyond high school.
Eligibility: Applicants must be high school students or a student enrolled in a two-year or four-year college or university. High school students applying to be full time students at a technical training college are also eligible to apply. Applicants must also be current members of NFAA or the NAA/USA Archery. The student must have a minimum GPA of 2.0 in high school or 2.5 in college. Selection is based on academic achievements, level of participation in NFAA and USAT rankings.
Target applicant(s): High school students. College students. Graduate school students. Adult students.
Minimum GPA: 2.0 for high school students, 2.5 for college students
Amount: Varies.
Number of awards: Varies.
Deadline: December 31.
How to apply: Applications are available online.
Exclusive: Visit www.UltimateScholarshipBook.com and enter code NA16520 for updates on this award.

(166) · eCampus Tours Scholarship Giveaway

Edsouth
eCampusTours, P.O. Box 36014, Knoxville, TN 37930
Phone: 865-342-0670
Email: info@ecampustours.com
http://www.ecampustours.com
Purpose: To assist students in paying for college.
Eligibility: Eligible students include U.S. citizens, U.S. nationals and permanent residents or students enrolled in a U.S. institution of higher education. Winners must be enrolled in an eligible institution of higher education, as stipulated in the eligibility requirements, within one year of winning the award. Scholarship awards will be paid directly to the college.
Target applicant(s): High school students. College students. Graduate school students. Adult students.
Amount: $1,000.
Number of awards: 2.
Deadline: March 31.
How to apply: Applications are available online or by mail. Registration with eCampusTours is required.
Exclusive: Visit www.UltimateScholarshipBook.com and enter code ED16620 for updates on this award.

(167) · Ed Frickey Memorial Scholarship

American Hackney Horse Society
4059 Iron Works Parkway A-3, Lexington, KY 40511-8462
Phone: 859-255-8694
Email: ahhscsl@qx.net
http://hackneysociety.com/
Purpose: To support those students who have participated in the American Hackney Horse Society.
Eligibility: Students must be a college sophomore, junior or senior and have been involved with American Hackney Horses or Ponies. Selection is based on academic success, financial need, community service and extracurricular activities.
Target applicant(s): College students. Adult students.
Amount: $2,500.
Number of awards: 1.
Deadline: July 15.
How to apply: Applications are available online and must include an official transcript, IRS Form 1040, personal essay and three letters of reference. An interview may also be required.
Exclusive: Visit www.UltimateScholarshipBook.com and enter code AM16720 for updates on this award.

(168) · Educational Advancement Foundation Merit Scholarship

Alpha Kappa Alpha Educational Advancement Foundation Inc.
5656 S. Stony Island Avenue, Chicago, IL 60637
Phone: 800-653-6528
Email: akaeaf@akaeaf.net
https://akaeaf.org/scholarships
Purpose: To support academically talented students.
Eligibility: Applicants must be full-time college students at the sophomore level or higher, including graduate students, at an accredited school. They must have a GPA of at least 3.0 and demonstrate community involvement and service. The program is open to students without regard to sex, race, creed, color, ethnicity, religion, sexual orientation or disability. Students do NOT need to be members of Alpha Kappa Alpha. The application deadline is April 15 for undergraduates and August 15 for graduates.
Target applicant(s): College students. Graduate school students. Adult students.
Minimum GPA: 3.0
Amount: Varies.
Number of awards: Varies.
Deadline: April 15 (undergraduates) and August 15 (graduates).
How to apply: Applications are available online. An application form, personal statement and three letters of recommendation are required.
Exclusive: Visit www.UltimateScholarshipBook.com and enter code AL16820 for updates on this award.

(169) · Educational Scholarship Award / George and Rosemary Murray Scholarship Award

25th Infantry Division Association (TIDA)
P.O. Box 7, Flourtown, PA 19031-0007
http://www.25thida.org
Purpose: To aid in the education of the members of the 25th Infantry Division Association or the children and grandchildren of active and former members of the association.
Eligibility: Applicants must be high school seniors who are the child or grandchild of an active association member, the child of a former member who died during combat with the Division or an active member

who will be discharged before the end of the award year. Applicants must be entering a four-year college or university as a freshman. Selection is based on future plans, school activities, interests, financial status and academic achievement.
Target applicant(s): High school students.
Amount: Up to $1,500.
Number of awards: Varies.
Deadline: February 28.
How to apply: Applications are available throughout the year in Tropic Lightning Flashes, the quarterly newsletter of the 25th Infantry Division Association.
Exclusive: Visit www.UltimateScholarshipBook.com and enter code 2516920 for updates on this award.

(170) • Educator.com Scholarship

Educator.com
Email: scholarship@educator.com
https://www.educator.com/scholarship/
Purpose: To support students pursuing post-secondary education.
Eligibility: Applicants must be graduating high school seniors or currently enrolled undergraduates. Students must provide transcripts and an essay.
Target applicant(s): High school students. College students. Adult students.
Amount: $500-$1,000.
Number of awards: 5.
Deadline: August 31.
How to apply: Applications are available online.
Exclusive: Visit www.UltimateScholarshipBook.com and enter code ED17020 for updates on this award.

(171) • EOD Memorial Scholarship

Explosive Ordnance Disposal (EOD) Memorial Committee
P.O. Box 594, Niceville, FL 32588
Phone: 850-729-2401
Email: admin@eodmemorial.org
http://www.eodmemorial.org
Purpose: To support those connected to Explosive Ordnance Disposal (EOD) technicians.
Eligibility: Applicants must be accepted or enrolled as full-time undergraduates in a U.S. accredited two-year, four-year or vocational school. Students must also be the family member of an active duty, guard/reserve, retired or deceased EOD technician. The award is based on academic achievement, community involvement and financial need. Applicants should submit the Free Application for Federal Student Aid form.
Target applicant(s): High school students. College students. Adult students.
Amount: Varies.
Number of awards: Varies.
Deadline: February 24.
How to apply: Applications are available online.
Exclusive: Visit www.UltimateScholarshipBook.com and enter code EX17120 for updates on this award.

(172) • Ethnic Minority and Women's Enhancement Scholarship

National Collegiate Athletic Association
700 W. Washington Street, P.O. Box 6222, Indianapolis, IN 46206
Phone: 317-917-6222
Email: lthomas@ncaa.org
http://www.ncaa.org/about/resources/ncaa-scholarships-and-grants
Purpose: To assist minority and female students in intercollegiate athletics with postgraduate scholarships at the NCAA national office.
Eligibility: Applicants must be planning to attend a sports administration program and plan to pursue a career in intercollegiate athletics such as athletic administration, coaching or athletic training.
Target applicant(s): College students. Adult students.
Minimum GPA: 3.2
Amount: $7,500.
Number of awards: 26.
Deadline: February 15.
How to apply: Application details are available online.
Exclusive: Visit www.UltimateScholarshipBook.com and enter code NA17220 for updates on this award.

(173) • Eve Kraft Education and College Scholarship

United States Tennis Association Foundation
70 W. Red Oak Lane, White Plains, NY 10604
Phone: 914-696-7223
Email: foundation@usta.com
http://www.ustafoundation.com/
Purpose: To support youth tennis participants who have come from an economically disadvantaged community.
Eligibility: Applicants must be high school seniors who have participated in an organized youth tennis program and who reside in an economically disadvantaged community. Selection is based on academic excellence and community service.
Target applicant(s): High school students.
Amount: $2,500.
Number of awards: 2.
Deadline: February 27.
How to apply: Applications are available online.
Exclusive: Visit www.UltimateScholarshipBook.com and enter code UN17320 for updates on this award.

(174) • Explore the World Scholarship

Hostelling International USA
8401 Colesville Road, Suite 600, Silver Spring, MD 20910
http://www.hiusa.org/travel-scholarships
Purpose: To support students who wish to study abroad or participate in service abroad.
Eligibility: Applicants must be between 18 and 30 years of age and a U.S. citizen or permanent resident. Students should be able to prove financial need, live in one of the metropolitan areas listed on the website and plan to travel abroad on an education, volunteer or service learning trip.
Target applicant(s): High school students. College students. Adult students.
Amount: $2,000.
Number of awards: 104.
Deadline: March 2.
How to apply: Applications are available online.
Exclusive: Visit www.UltimateScholarshipBook.com and enter code HO17420 for updates on this award.

(175) • Families of Freedom Scholarship Fund

Families of Freedom c/o Scholarship America
One Scholarship Way, P.O. Box 297, St. Peter, MN 56082
Phone: 877-862-0136

Email: familiesoffreedom@scholarshipamerica.org
http://www.familiesoffreedom.org
Purpose: To support dependents of victims of the 9/11 attacks.
Eligibility: Applicants must be dependent children, spouses or domestic partners of 9/11 victims. Children of victims must enroll in a postsecondary program by age 24 and must continue studies uninterrupted after their 24th birthday to continue to receive assistance. Financial need is required.
Target applicant(s): High school students. College students. Graduate school students. Adult students.
Amount: Varies.
Number of awards: Varies.
Scholarship may be renewable.
Deadline: May 15.
How to apply: Applications are available online. An application form, copy of most recent tax return, transcript and copy of school billing statement are required.
Exclusive: Visit www.UltimateScholarshipBook.com and enter code FA17520 for updates on this award.

---

(176) · Family Travel Forum Teen Travel Writing Scholarship

Family Travel Forum
135 West 20th Street, 5th Floor, New York, NY 10011
Phone: 212-595-6074
Email: editorial@travelbigo.com
http://scholarship.familytravelforum.com
Purpose: To aid college-bound students who have written the best travel essays.
Eligibility: Applicants must be members of the MyFamilyTravels.com online community and be between the ages of 13 and 18. They must be in grades 8 through 12 and must be attending a U.S. or Canadian high school, U.S. or Canadian junior high school, U.S. home school or an American school located outside of the U.S. They must submit an essay about a significant travel experience that occurred within the past five years and that happened when the applicant was between the ages of 12 and 18. Selection is based on originality, quality of storytelling and grammar.
Target applicant(s): Junior high students or younger. High school students.
Amount: $1,000.
Number of awards: 3.
Deadline: July 14.
How to apply: Application instructions are available online. An essay submission form and essay are required.
Exclusive: Visit www.UltimateScholarshipBook.com and enter code FA17620 for updates on this award.

---

(177) · Final Fantasy Fan Scholarship

Epic Action LLC
2225 E. Bayshore Road, Suite 200, Palo Alto, CA 94303
https://www.finalfantasyxvapp.com/scholarship
Purpose: To support students who are Final Fantasy gamers.
Eligibility: Applicants must be passionate players of the Final Fantasy game franchise who are enrolled in or are enrolling in post-secondary education. Students must write an essay describing their experience with Final Fantasy games and the impact on their lives.
Target applicant(s): High school students. College students. Graduate school students. Adult students.
Amount: $1,000.
Deadline: December 15.
How to apply: Applications are available online.
Exclusive: Visit www.UltimateScholarshipBook.com and enter code EP17720 for updates on this award.

---

(178) · First Cavalry Division Association Scholarship

Foundation of the First Cavalry Division Association
Alumni Of The First Team, 302 North Main Street, Copperas Cove, TX 76522
Phone: 254-547-6537
Email: firstcav@1cda.org
http://www.1cda.org
Purpose: To assist the children of First Cavalry troopers who have become disabled or who died while serving in the Division.
Eligibility: Applicants must be First Cavalry Division troopers who have become totally disabled while serving in the division or active duty members, their spouses or children. Applicants may also be the spouses or children of First Cavalry Division troopers who have died while serving in the division.
Target applicant(s): High school students. College students. Adult students.
Amount: $1,200 per year.
Number of awards: Varies.
Deadline: Varies.
How to apply: Applications are available by request.
Exclusive: Visit www.UltimateScholarshipBook.com and enter code FO17820 for updates on this award.

---

(179) · FMAA Scholarship Program

Flag Manufacturers Association of America
994 Old Eagle School Road, Suite 1019, Wayne, PA 19087
Phone: 610-971-4850
http://www.fmaa-usa.com/about/scholarship.php
Purpose: To support graduating high school seniors who create a video on the United States flag.
Eligibility: Applicants must create a video essay discussing what the United States flag means to them as a young American in today's world. Students must post their one and a half to two minute video online.
Target applicant(s): High school students.
Amount: Up to $3,000.
Number of awards: 5.
Deadline: May 30.
How to apply: Applications are available online.
Exclusive: Visit www.UltimateScholarshipBook.com and enter code FL17920 for updates on this award.

---

(180) · FMC Skaters Scholarship

Facility Management Corporation (FMC) Ice Sports
100 Schoosett Street, Building 3, Pembroke, MA 02359
Phone: 888-747-5283
Email: customercare@fmcicesports.com
http://www.fmcicesports.com
Purpose: To support ice sport participants and recreational ice skaters seeking to further their education beyond high school.
Eligibility: Applicants must be a New England resident, a senior in high school and skate at an FMC arena. Selection is based on academic achievement, extracurricular activities, community service and accomplishments and leadership on the ice.
Target applicant(s): High school students.
Amount: Varies.
Number of awards: Varies.

Deadline: May 1.
How to apply: Applications are available online. Along with the application form, students must submit a high school transcript, one letter of recommendation, a student resume and a personal essay.
Exclusive: Visit www.UltimateScholarshipBook.com and enter code FA18020 for updates on this award.

(181) · Folds of Honor Higher Education Scholarship

Folds of Honor
5800 N. Patriot Drive, Owasso, OK 74055
Email: scholarships@foldsofhonor.org
https://www.foldsofhonor.org/resources/scholarships/
Purpose: To support spouses and children of American military service members pursuing higher education.
Eligibility: Applicants must be spouses or children of U.S. service members who were killed in action, lost a limb, died while on active duty or who has at least a 10 percent combined service-connected evaluation. Students must be currently attending or recently accepted into an accredited degree program or vocation program.
Target applicant(s): High school students. College students. Adult students.
Amount: $5,000.
Number of awards: Varies.
Deadline: March 31.
How to apply: Applications are available online.
Exclusive: Visit www.UltimateScholarshipBook.com and enter code FO18120 for updates on this award.

(182) · Foot Locker Scholar Athletes

Foot Locker Scholar Athletes
19 West 21st Street, Floor 8, New York, NY 10010
Email: footlocker@dosomething.org
http://www.footlockerscholarathletes.com
Purpose: To honor high school athletes who demonstrate good sportsmanship and contribute to their community.
Eligibility: Applicants must be high school seniors who plan to enter a four-year college in the upcoming fall semester. Students must demonstrate leadership, academic excellence, good sportsmanship and strong moral character. Applicants must also have a minimum 3.0 GPA, be U.S. citizens or permanent legal residents and currently be involved in high school, intramural or community-based sports.
Target applicant(s): High school students.
Minimum GPA: 3.0
Amount: $5,000 per year.
Number of awards: 20.
Scholarship may be renewable.
Deadline: December 14.
How to apply: Applications are available online.
Exclusive: Visit www.UltimateScholarshipBook.com and enter code FO18220 for updates on this award.

(183) · Foreclosure.com Scholarship Program

Foreclosure.com
1095 Broken Sound Parkway, NW, Suite 200, Boca Raton, FL 33487
Phone: 561-988-9669 x 7387
Email: scholarship@foreclosure.com
http://www.foreclosure.com/scholarship/
Purpose: To support current undergraduate college students who are interested in addressing critical issues facing the nation, namely issues involving real estate/housing.
Eligibility: Applicants must be U.S. citizens 13 years of age or older who are currently enrolled as undergraduate college students. They must write an essay between 800 and 2,000 words providing creative solutions to a given topic involving critical issues facing the nation centered around real estate/housing. Selection is based upon the overall strength of the essay and application.
Target applicant(s): College students. Adult students.
Amount: $1,000-$5,000.
Number of awards: 5.
Deadline: December 15.
How to apply: Applications are available online. An application form and essay are required.
Exclusive: Visit www.UltimateScholarshipBook.com and enter code FO18320 for updates on this award.

(184) · Form.com Scholarship

Form.com
161 Forbes Road, Braintree, MA 02184
Email: scholarship@form.com
https://form.com/resources/scholarship-program/
Purpose: To help the next generation of leaders meet their educational goals.
Eligibility: Applicants must be 18 years of age or older and legal residents of the U.S., the United Kingdom, Canada or Australia. Students must be enrolling in or currently enrolled in an accredited university and must write an original essay pertaining to one of the given prompts.
Target applicant(s): High school students. College students. Graduate school students. Adult students.
Amount: $1,500.
Number of awards: 1.
Deadline: December 17.
How to apply: Applications are available online.
Exclusive: Visit www.UltimateScholarshipBook.com and enter code FO18420 for updates on this award.

(185) · Fostering the Entrepreneurial Spirit: A Contest for High School Students

Ed Snider Center for Enterprise and Markets
4568 Van Munching Hall, College Park, MD 20742
Phone: 301-405-7036
Email: info@enterpriselit.org
http://www.enterpriselit.org
Purpose: To promote the entrepreneurial spirit in high school students through works of literature.
Eligibility: Applicants must be in grades 9-12. Students will work in teams of two to four and choose a work of literature that emphasizes the struggles and achievements of a person seeking to become an entrepreneur. The book will then be compared to real-life entrepreneurs. Teams will submit an essay outlining the main character and his/her contributions to the theme of the book including works cited and also a video that visually demonstrates what was learned during the project.
Target applicant(s): High school students.
Amount: $200-$1,500.
Number of awards: 8.
Deadline: May 2.
How to apply: Applications are available online and include an essay and video.

Exclusive: Visit www.UltimateScholarshipBook.com and enter code ED18520 for updates on this award.

(186) • Foundation for Blended and Online Learning Scholarship

Foundation for Blended and Online Learning
Scholarship America, One Scholarship Way, Saint Peter, MN 56082
https://scholarsapply.org/fbol-scholarship
Purpose: To support students pursuing degrees through online education.
Eligibility: Applicants must be high school seniors who have completed at least five blended or online courses during the past two years and who plan to enroll full-time at an accredited two- or four-year institution for an undergraduate degree.
Target applicant(s): High school students.
Amount: $10,000.
Number of awards: 30.
Scholarship may be renewable.
Deadline: April 30.
How to apply: Applications are available online.
Exclusive: Visit www.UltimateScholarshipBook.com and enter code FO18620 for updates on this award.

(187) • Fraternal Order of Eagles Memorial Foundation

Fraternal Order of Eagles
1623 Gateway Circle S., Grove City, OH 43123
Phone: 614-883-2200
Email: help@foe.com
http://www.foe.com
Purpose: To provide financial support for post-secondary education to the children of Eagles.
Eligibility: Applicants must be the children of Eagles who lost their lives while serving in the military or in the commission of their daily employment. Applicants must have a 2.0 minimum GPA, be under the age of 25, unmarried and non-self supporting.
Target applicant(s): High school students. College students. Graduate school students.
Minimum GPA: 2.0
Amount: Varies.
Number of awards: Varies.
Scholarship may be renewable.
Deadline: Varies.
How to apply: Eligible juniors in high school will be sent a form requesting post high school plans, and eligible seniors will be mailed the scholarship application form.
Exclusive: Visit www.UltimateScholarshipBook.com and enter code FR18720 for updates on this award.

(188) • Free Speech Essay Contest

Foundation for Individual Rights in Education
510 Walnut Street, Suite 1250, Philadelphia, PA 19106
Phone: 215-717-3473
Email: highschooloutreach@thefire.org
http://www.thefire.org/contest
Purpose: To encourage students to promote the freedom of speech.
Eligibility: Applicants must be juniors or seniors in U.S. high schools including home-schools or U.S. citizens attending overseas schools. Students must submit an essay pertaining to the topic of free speech and censorship.
Target applicant(s): High school students.
Amount: Up to $10,000.
Number of awards: 9.
Deadline: December 31.
How to apply: Applications are available online.
Exclusive: Visit www.UltimateScholarshipBook.com and enter code FO18820 for updates on this award.

(189) • Freedom of Speech PSA Contest

National Association of Broadcasters
1771 N Street NW, Washington, DC 20036
Phone: 202-429-5428
Email: nab@nab.org
http://www.nab.org
Purpose: To reward part-time or full-time undergraduate or graduate students who can effectively illustrate what freedom of speech means to them and what part it plays in the world today in a 30-second public service announcement.
Eligibility: Applicants must be part-time or full-time graduate or undergraduate students currently attending a college, university or technical/community college. They must create a 30-second public service announcement while enrolled answering the question, "What does freedom of speech mean to me?" Announcements may be created for television or radio. Selection is based upon quality of submission.
Target applicant(s): College students. Graduate school students. Adult students.
Amount: $1,000-$3,000.
Number of awards: 4.
Deadline: April 30.
How to apply: Applications are available online.
Exclusive: Visit www.UltimateScholarshipBook.com and enter code NA18920 for updates on this award.

(190) • Fulbright Grants

U.S. Department of State
Office of Academic Exchange Programs, Bureau of Educational and Cultural Affairs, U.S. Department of State, SA-44, 301 4th Street SW, Room 234, Washington, DC 20547
Phone: 202-632-3238
Email: fulbright@state.gov
https://us.fulbrightonline.org/
Purpose: To increase the understanding between the people of the United States and the people of other countries.
Eligibility: Applicants must be graduating college seniors, graduate students, young professionals and artists. Funds are generally used to support students in university teaching, advanced research, graduate study or teaching in elementary and secondary schools.
Target applicant(s): Graduate school students. Adult students.
Amount: Varies.
Number of awards: Varies.
Deadline: October 15.
How to apply: Applications are available online.
Exclusive: Visit www.UltimateScholarshipBook.com and enter code U.19020 for updates on this award.

(191) • G2 Crowd Entrepreneurial Scholarship

G2 Crowd
20 N. Upper Wacker, Chicago, IL 60606

Phone: 847-748-7559
https://learn.g2crowd.com/scholarship
Purpose: To support entrepreneurial-minded students.
Eligibility: Applicants must be enrolling in or currently enrolled as a full-time student at an accredited U.S. university and hold a minimum GPA of 2.5. Students must write an essay pertaining to entrepreneurialism.
Target applicant(s): High school students. College students. Adult students.
Minimum GPA: 2.5
Amount: $5,000.
Number of awards: 12.
Deadline: August 16.
How to apply: Applications are available online.
Exclusive: Visit www.UltimateScholarshipBook.com and enter code G219120 for updates on this award.

(192) • GE-Reagan Foundation Scholarship Program

Ronald Reagan Presidential Foundation
40 Presidential Drive, Suite 200, Simi Valley, CA 93065
Phone: 844-402-0354
Email: ge-reagan@scholarshipamerica.org
https://www.scholarsapply.org/ge-reagan/
Purpose: To reward students who demonstrate leadership, drive, integrity and citizenship.
Eligibility: Applicants must be high school seniors and pursue a bachelor's degree at an accredited U.S. college or university the following fall. Students must demonstrate strong academic performance (3.0 or greater GPA or equivalent), demonstrate financial need and be a U.S. citizen. Funds may be used for student tuition and room and board.
Target applicant(s): High school students.
Minimum GPA: 3.0
Amount: $10,000.
Number of awards: Varies.
Scholarship may be renewable.
Deadline: January 4.
How to apply: Applications are available online. The competition will close earlier than the deadline once 25,000 applications are received.
Exclusive: Visit www.UltimateScholarshipBook.com and enter code RO19220 for updates on this award.

(193) • Gen and Kelly Tanabe Student Scholarship

Gen and Kelly Tanabe Scholarship Program
2713 Newlands Avenue, Belmont, CA 94002
Phone: 650-618-2221
Email: scholarships@gkscholarship.com
http://www.genkellyscholarship.com
Purpose: To assist high school, college and graduate school students with educational expenses.
Eligibility: Applicants must be 9th-12th grade high school students, college students or graduate school students who are legal U.S. residents. Students may study any major and attend any college in the U.S.
Target applicant(s): High school students. College students. Adult students.
Amount: $1,000.
Deadline: July 31, December 31.
How to apply: Applications are available online.
Exclusive: Visit www.UltimateScholarshipBook.com and enter code GE19320 for updates on this award.

(194) • Gene Carte Student Paper Competition

American Society of Criminology Gene Carte Student Paper Competition
Daniel Ragan, Department of Sociology, University of New Mexico, 1915 Roma N.E., Suite 1103, MSCO5 3080, Albuquerque, NM 87131
Phone: 602-543-6601
Email: dragan@unm.edu
http://www.asc41.com
Purpose: To recognize outstanding student works in criminology.
Eligibility: Applicants must be full-time undergraduate or graduate students. The writing competition requires applicants to write on a topic directly related to criminology and must be accompanied by a letter signed by the dean or department chair. Other paper formatting requirements are listed on the website. The first place winner also receives a travel award.
Target applicant(s): College students. Graduate school students. Adult students.
Amount: $200-$500.
Number of awards: Up to 3.
Deadline: April 15.
How to apply: There is no application form. Paper must be mailed in. The paper specifications are on the website.
Exclusive: Visit www.UltimateScholarshipBook.com and enter code AM19420 for updates on this award.

(195) • General Henry H. Arnold Education Grant Program

Air Force Aid Society
Education Assistance Department, 241 18th Street S, Suite 202, Arlington, VA 22202
Phone: 703-972-2647
Email: ed@afas-hq.org
https://www.afas.org/how-we-help/education-support/
Purpose: To help Air Force family members realize their academic goals.
Eligibility: Applicants must be the dependent sons and daughters of Air Force members, spouses of active duty members or surviving spouses of Air Force members who died while on active duty or in retired status. They must also be high school seniors or college students enrolled or accepted as full-time undergraduates for the following school year and maintain a minimum 2.0 GPA.
Target applicant(s): High school students. College students.
Minimum GPA: 2.0
Amount: $500-$4,000.
Number of awards: Varies.
Scholarship may be renewable.
Deadline: March 10.
How to apply: Applications are available online.
Exclusive: Visit www.UltimateScholarshipBook.com and enter code AI19520 for updates on this award.

(196) • George Blair Ambassador Scholarship

USA Water Ski and Wake Sports Foundation
1251 Holy Cow Road, Polk City, FL 33868
Phone: 863-324-2472
Email: usa-wsf@waterskihalloffame.com
http://www.usawaterskifoundation.org/
Purpose: To aid young water skiers with their college expenses so that they can not only pursue a college education but continue with water skiing.

Eligibility: Applicants must be incoming freshmen through senior level college students who are current active members of USA Water Ski. Students do not have to be collegiate water ski competitors. Selection is based on the number of years as an active member, academic success, financial need, school and community activities and individual contributions to the sport. A short essay is required.
Target applicant(s): High school students. College students. Adult students.
Amount: $2,200.
Number of awards: 1.
Deadline: March 15.
How to apply: Applications are available online and must include two letters of recommendation.
Exclusive: Visit www.UltimateScholarshipBook.com and enter code US19620 for updates on this award.

(197) • George Montgomery/NRA Youth Wildlife Art Contest

National Rifle Association
11250 Waples Mill Road, Fairfax, VA 22030
Phone: 800-672-3888
Email: grantprogram@nrahq.org
https://awards.nra.org/awards/
Purpose: To support young artists and encourage awareness of local game birds and animals.
Eligibility: Applicants must be in grades 1 through 12 and submit an original artwork depicting any North American game bird or animal that may be legally hunted or trapped. NRA membership is not required. Art is divided into categories based on grade level and is judged on effort, creativity, anatomical accuracy and composition.
Target applicant(s): Junior high students or younger. High school students.
Amount: Up to $1,000.
Number of awards: Varies.
Deadline: November 3.
How to apply: Application information is available online. A statement of authenticity signed by a parent, guardian or teacher must be submitted along with the artwork.
Exclusive: Visit www.UltimateScholarshipBook.com and enter code NA19720 for updates on this award.

(198) • George S. and Stella M. Knight Essay Contest

National Society, Sons of the American Revolution
1000 South Fourth Street, Louisville, KY 40203
Phone: 502-589-1776
Email: sdelong1@san.rr.com
http://www.sar.org
Purpose: To reward students who have written outstanding essays on the American Revolution, the U.S. Constitution or the Declaration of Independence.
Eligibility: Applicants must be U.S. citizens or legal residents. Students must be high school sophomores, juniors or seniors. Applicants must submit an 800- to 1,200-word essay on some topic that is related to the Declaration of Independence, the American Revolution or the U.S. Constitution. Selection is based on the overall strength of the essay.
Target applicant(s): High school students.
Amount: $1,000-$5,000.
Number of awards: 3.
Deadline: December 31.
How to apply: Applications are available online.
Exclusive: Visit www.UltimateScholarshipBook.com and enter code NA19820 for updates on this award.

(199) • Gift for Life Scholarships

United States Bowling Congress
Attn.: Alberta E. Crowe Star of Tomorrow, 621 Six Flags Drive, Arlington, TX 76011
Phone: 800-514-2695
Email: contactus@ibcyouth.com
https://www.bowl.com/Youth/Youth_Home/Scholarships/
Purpose: To provide financial assistance to high school students with financial need.
Eligibility: Applicants must be USBC Youth members who are current high school students in grades 9-12. They must have a GPA of 2.5 or higher and demonstrate financial need. Two awards each year are reserved for children of fire department, emergency rescue or police personnel. Candidates may win once per year up until graduation.
Target applicant(s): High school students.
Minimum GPA: 2.5
Amount: $1,000.
Number of awards: 6.
Deadline: December 1.
How to apply: Applications are available online.
Exclusive: Visit www.UltimateScholarshipBook.com and enter code UN19920 for updates on this award.

(200) • Global Citizen Scholarship

EF Educational Tours
EF Center Boston, Two Education Circle, Cambridge, MA 02141
Phone: 800-665-5364
Email: EF.Global.Citizen@ef.com
http://www.eftours.com
Purpose: To help students reflect on their place in the world through writing and then have a chance to experience it first-hand.
Eligibility: Applicants must be college-bound high school students in the U.S. or Canada nominated by their schools and must write an essay or create a video or digital media project on a topic related to global citizenship. The award involves a paid educational trip to Europe.
Target applicant(s): High school students.
Amount: Educational tour expenses.
Number of awards: Varies.
Deadline: November 7.
How to apply: Applications are available online on the EF Tours Facebook page.
Exclusive: Visit www.UltimateScholarshipBook.com and enter code EF20020 for updates on this award.

(201) • Gloria Barron Prize for Young Heroes

Barron Prize
P.O. Box 1470, Boulder, CO 80306
http://www.barronprize.org
Purpose: To reward young people who have organized and led extraordinary service projects.
Eligibility: Applicants must be residents of the U.S. or Canada between the ages of 8 and 18. Students must be currently working on a service project or have completed a service project within the past year. Selection is primarily based on demonstration of generosity, tenacity and positive impact on the world.
Target applicant(s): Junior high students or younger. High school students.

Amount: $5,000.
Number of awards: 15.
Deadline: April 15.
How to apply: Applications are available online.
Exclusive: Visit www.UltimateScholarshipBook.com and enter code BA20120 for updates on this award.

(202) • GM Genius

How I Decide Foundation
401 City Avenue, Suite 915, Bala Cynwyd, PA 19004
Phone: 610-668-1484
https://www.gmgenius.com
Purpose: To support education-based decision making.
Eligibility: Applicants must 13 to 19 years of age and legal residents of the U.S. or Canada. Students must sign up for a free account at the website in order to compete for scholarship prizes.
Target applicant(s): Junior high students or younger. High school students.
Amount: $10,000.
Number of awards: 3.
Deadline: December 25.
How to apply: Applications are available online.
Exclusive: Visit www.UltimateScholarshipBook.com and enter code HO20220 for updates on this award.

(203) • GMR Transcription Academic Scholarship

GMR Transcription Services
2552 Walnut Avenue, Suite 110, Tustin, CA 92780
Phone: 714-202-9653
https://www.gmrtranscription.com/scholarship/scholarshiphome.aspx
Purpose: To help students offset the costs of continuing education.
Eligibility: Applicants must be enrolled as full-time students at an accredited college or university. Students must have a minimum 3.0 grade point average. Applicants must submit essays and complete a qualification quiz.
Target applicant(s): High school students. College students. Adult students.
Minimum GPA: 3.0
Amount: $500.
Number of awards: 2.
Deadline: December 15.
How to apply: Applications are available online.
Exclusive: Visit www.UltimateScholarshipBook.com and enter code GM20320 for updates on this award.

(204) • GNC Nutritional Research Grant

National Strength and Conditioning Association (NSCA) Foundation
1885 Bob Johnson Drive, Colorado Springs, CO 80906
Phone: 800-815-6826
http://www.nsca.com/foundation/
Purpose: To fund nutrition-based research.
Eligibility: Applicants must be graduate students and be NSCA members for one year before applying and pursuing careers in strength and conditioning. Students must also plan a research project that falls within the mission of the NSCA and submit a proposal describing the rationale, purpose and methods of the planned research. Applications are evaluated based on grades, courses, experience, honors, recommendations and involvement in the community and with NSCA.
Target applicant(s): College students. Graduate school students. Adult students.
Amount: $2,500.
Number of awards: 1.
Deadline: March 15.
How to apply: Applications are available with membership.
Exclusive: Visit www.UltimateScholarshipBook.com and enter code NA20420 for updates on this award.

(205) • Go! Overseas Study Abroad Scholarship

Go! Overseas Study Abroad Scholarship
2040 Bancroft Way, Suite 200, Berkeley, CA 94704
Phone: 415-796-6456
Email: scholarship@gooverseas.com
http://www.gooverseas.com/study-abroad/
Purpose: To aid students who have been accepted into a study abroad program.
Eligibility: Applicants must be current college or graduate students who have been accepted into a study abroad program for the coming academic year. Selection is based on application creativity and display of analytical thinking.
Target applicant(s): College students. Graduate school students. Adult students.
Amount: $500.
Number of awards: 2.
Deadline: May 6 (fall) and December 2 (spring).
How to apply: Applications are available online. An application form and essay are required.
Exclusive: Visit www.UltimateScholarshipBook.com and enter code GO20520 for updates on this award.

(206) • Go! Volunteer Abroad Scholarship

Go! Overseas Volunteer Abroad Scholarship
2040 Bancroft Way, Suite 200, Berkeley, CA 94704
Phone: 415-796-6456
Email: volunteerscholarship@gooverseas.com
http://www.gooverseas.com/scholarships/volunteer-abroad-application
Purpose: To aid people who have been accepted into a volunteer abroad program.
Eligibility: Applicants must be accepted into a volunteer abroad program. Selection is based on application creativity and display of analytical thinking.
Target applicant(s): College students. Graduate school students. Adult students.
Amount: $500.
Number of awards: 1.
Deadline: December 2.
How to apply: Applications are available online. An application form and essay are required.
Exclusive: Visit www.UltimateScholarshipBook.com and enter code GO20620 for updates on this award.

(207) • GoBankingRates

GOBankingRates
1700 E. Walnut, Lost Angeles, CA 90245
Email: info@gobankingrates.com
https://www.gobankingrates.com/scholarships/
Purpose: To assist with the expense of post-secondary education.

Eligibility: Applicants must be legal U.S. residents at least 18 years of age and a graduating high school senior or currently enrolled freshman, sophomore or junior at an accredited U.S. college or university. Students must submit an essay along with their application.
Target applicant(s): High school students. College students. Adult students.
Amount: $2,500.
Number of awards: 1.
Deadline: June 15.
How to apply: Applications are available online.
Exclusive: Visit www.UltimateScholarshipBook.com and enter code GO20720 for updates on this award.

(208) • Goedeker's Appliances Annual College Book Scholarship

Goedeker's
13850 Manchester Road, Ballwin, MO 63011
Email: scholarship@goedekers.com
http://www.goedekers.com/college-scholarship
Purpose: To offset the cost of higher education.
Eligibility: Applicants must be currently enrolled or enrolling in an undergraduate or graduate college and have a minimum grade point average of 3.0.
Target applicant(s): High school students. College students. Graduate school students. Adult students.
Minimum GPA: 3.0
Amount: $500.
Number of awards: 3.
Deadline: July 8.
How to apply: Applications are available online.
Exclusive: Visit www.UltimateScholarshipBook.com and enter code GO20820 for updates on this award.

(209) • Goedeker's Appliances Annual Public Service College Book Scholarship

Goedeker's
13850 Manchester Road, Ballwin, MO 63011
Email: scholarship@goedekers.com
http://www.goedekers.com/college-scholarship
Purpose: To support the families of our troops.
Eligibility: Applicants must be U.S. citizens and public service employees or family members of a public service employee including military, fire fighters and police who are currently enrolled or enrolling in an accredited college.
Target applicant(s): High school students. College students. Graduate school students. Adult students.
Amount: $500.
Number of awards: 3.
Deadline: July 8.
How to apply: Applications are available online.
Exclusive: Visit www.UltimateScholarshipBook.com and enter code GO20920 for updates on this award.

(210) • Golden Door Scholars

Golden Door Scholars
1423 Red Ventures Drive, Fort Mill, SC 29707
Email: info@goldendoorscholars.org
https://www.goldendoorscholars.org/
Purpose: To assist DACA students pursuing higher education.
Eligibility: Applicants must be approved DACA students with strong academic records who are enrolling in an undergraduate program or who are current high school seniors or undergraduate students. Students pursuing engineering, computer science, technology or math are given preference.
Target applicant(s): High school students. College students. Adult students.
Amount: Varies.
Number of awards: Varies.
Deadline: October 25.
How to apply: Applications are available online.
Exclusive: Visit www.UltimateScholarshipBook.com and enter code GO21020 for updates on this award.

(211) • Good Neighbor Scholarship

Leading by Legacy Foundation
1020 Park Drive #807, Flossmoor, IL 60422
Phone: 708-922-0196
Email: scholarship@leadingbylegacy.org
http://www.leadingbylegacy.org/
Purpose: To assist high school seniors.
Eligibility: Applicants must have a GPA of 2.5 or higher, demonstrate leadership, actively participate in community service and have an SAT score of 800 or higher or ACT score of 17 or higher.
Target applicant(s): High school students.
Minimum GPA: 2.5
Amount: $500-$1,000.
Number of awards: 4.
Deadline: May 1.
How to apply: Applications are available online and must be returned by mail.
Exclusive: Visit www.UltimateScholarshipBook.com and enter code LE21120 for updates on this award.

(212) • Goodshop Scholarship

Goodshop
550 Montgomery Street, 9th floor, San Francisco, CA 94111
Email: information@goodshop.com
https://www.goodsearch.com/scholarship/
Purpose: To support students who write about causes they support.
Eligibility: Applicants must write an essay on the topic provided.
Target applicant(s): High school students. College students. Graduate school students. Adult students.
Amount: $500-$1,000.
Number of awards: 2.
Deadline: December 31.
How to apply: Applications are available online.
Exclusive: Visit www.UltimateScholarshipBook.com and enter code GO21220 for updates on this award.

(213) • Google SVA Scholarship

Student Veterans of America
1625 K Street North West, Suite 320, Washington, DC 20006
Phone: 202-223-4710
http://studentveterans.org/programs/scholarships
Purpose: To support students who are veterans and are pursuing a degree in computer science.
Eligibility: Applicants must be veterans who are currently enrolled as a full-time undergraduate or graduate student at a four-year university. Students must exhibit a strong academic performance and be pursuing

a degree in either computer science or computer engineering. Applicants must currently be in good standing with their military branch or have an honorable discharge.
Target applicant(s): College students. Graduate school students. Adult students.
Amount: $10,000.
Number of awards: 8.
Deadline: November 14.
How to apply: Applications are available online.
Exclusive: Visit www.UltimateScholarshipBook.com and enter code ST21320 for updates on this award.

---

(214) • Gordon Law Group Need-Based Scholarship

Gordon Law Group
400 Central Avenue, Suite 340, Northfield, IL 60093
Phone: 847-580-1279
https://www.gordonlawltd.com/gordon-law-group-scholarship/
Purpose: To support students who write an essay on income taxes.
Eligibility: Applicants must be U.S. citizens or permanent residents enrolling as full-time students in the fall at any accredited community college, four-year institution or law school. Students must complete the online application and essay on the given topic found on the webpage.
Target applicant(s): High school students. College students. Graduate school students. Adult students.
Amount: $1,000.
Number of awards: 1.
Deadline: July 15.
How to apply: Applications are available online.
Exclusive: Visit www.UltimateScholarshipBook.com and enter code GO21420 for updates on this award.

---

(215) • Graduate Research Grant - Master and Doctoral

National Strength and Conditioning Association (NSCA) Foundation
1885 Bob Johnson Drive, Colorado Springs, CO 80906
Phone: 800-815-6826
http://www.nsca.com/foundation/
Purpose: To support research in strength and conditioning.
Eligibility: Applicants must be master's or doctoral students and submit a proposal for a research project in the field of strength and conditioning that fulfills the mission of the NSCA. Students must be NSCA members for one year before applying and pursuing careers in strength and conditioning. Applications are evaluated based on grades, courses, experience, honors, recommendations and involvement in the community and with NSCA.
Target applicant(s): Graduate school students. Adult students.
Amount: Up to $15,000.
Number of awards: Varies.
Deadline: March 15.
How to apply: Applications are available with membership.
Exclusive: Visit www.UltimateScholarshipBook.com and enter code NA21520 for updates on this award.

---

(216) • Grasshopper Entrepreneur Scholarship

Grasshopper
197 First Avenue, Suite 200, Needham, MA 02494
Phone: 800-820-8210
Email: scholarships@grasshopper.com
https://grasshopper.com/entrepreneur-scholarship/
Purpose: To assist incoming first-year or current college students in undergraduate or graduate degree programs.
Eligibility: Applicants must attend an accredited American college, university or trade school. An essay of 500-700 words on the entrepreneurial-related topic provided is required.
Target applicant(s): High school students. College students. Graduate school students. Adult students.
Amount: $5,000.
Number of awards: 1.
Deadline: April 30.
How to apply: Applications are available online.
Exclusive: Visit www.UltimateScholarshipBook.com and enter code GR21620 for updates on this award.

---

(217) • H&P Veterans Helping Veterans Scholarship

Hill & Ponton
605 E. Robinson Street, Suite 635, Orlando, FL 32801
https://www.hillandponton.com/veterans-scholarship/
Purpose: To support veterans pursuing post-secondary education.
Eligibility: Applicants must be veterans of the U.S. armed forces. Students must plan to use their education to help fellow veterans. Applicants must complete statement explaining how their education will be used to assist veterans.
Target applicant(s): College students. Adult students.
Amount: $1,000.
Number of awards: 4.
Deadline: May 1.
How to apply: Applications are available online.
Exclusive: Visit www.UltimateScholarshipBook.com and enter code HI21720 for updates on this award.

---

(218) • H. U. Lee Scholarship

H.U. Lee Memorial Foundation
6210 Baseline Road, Little Rock, AR 72209
Phone: 501-568-2821 x2263
Email: hulf@ataonline.com
http://www.huleefoundation.org
Purpose: To support the advancement of discipline, respect and courtesy through Taekwondo.
Eligibility: Applicants must be current high school seniors graduating from an accredited high school with a minimum 3.0 GPA. Students must have received a letter of acceptance from an accredited U.S. college for full-time study beginning no later than September 30. Applicants must have a minimum combined score of 1100 on the SAT and/or 27 on the ACT, must have registered with Selective Service if required and have no convictions of drug possession or distribution.
Target applicant(s): High school students.
Minimum GPA: 3.0
Amount: Varies.
Number of awards: Varies.
Deadline: February 15.
How to apply: Applications are available through the student's instructor. An application form, a sealed copy of high school transcripts with signature of school's director of admissions across the sealed envelope, two recommendation letters and an essay are required.
Exclusive: Visit www.UltimateScholarshipBook.com and enter code H.21820 for updates on this award.

(219) • Hagan Scholarship

Hagan Scholarship Foundation
P.O. Box 1225, Columbia, MO 65205
Email: scholarships@hsfmo.org
https://haganscholarships.org

Purpose: To help high-achieving, dedicated students who live in smaller counties.
Eligibility: Applicants must be U.S. citizens and be graduating seniors from a public high school located in a county with fewer than 50,000 residents. Students must be enrolling in a four-year college or university the first semester following high school graduation. Applicants must work 240 hours in the year prior to the start of each academic year.
Target applicant(s): High school students.
Minimum GPA: 3.5
Amount: Varies.
Number of awards: 300.
Deadline: November 15.
How to apply: Applications are available online.
Exclusive: Visit www.UltimateScholarshipBook.com and enter code HA21920 for updates on this award.

(220) • Halloween Express Scholarship Contest

Halloween Express
302 North Main Street, Owentown, KY 40359
Phone: 502-484-0551
http://www.halloweenexpress.com/scholarship.php

Purpose: To support students who write about a history or pop culture topic provided.
Eligibility: Applicants must be at least 18 years or older, have been accepted to an accredited college or university and submit a 500- to 2,500-word essay based on topic provided.
Target applicant(s): High school students. College students. Adult students.
Amount: $1,000.
Number of awards: 1.
Deadline: October 31.
How to apply: Applications are available online.
Exclusive: Visit www.UltimateScholarshipBook.com and enter code HA22020 for updates on this award.

(221) • Hamilton Award

Alexander Hamilton Scholars
200 1st Avenue West Suite 201, Seattle, WA 98119
Phone: 206-774-0764
Email: program@hamiltonscholars.org
http://www.hamiltonscholars.org

Purpose: To reward the academic, personal, service and entrepreneurial accomplishments of students.
Eligibility: Applicants must be high-achieving, service-focused high school juniors with grit, perseverance and demonstrated need. Students must be committed to participating in a rigorous five-year curriculum designed to provide a comprehensive network of support and practical guidance to Alexander Hamilton Scholars as they transition from high school to college and college to career.
Target applicant(s): High school students.
Amount: $500.
Number of awards: 35.
Deadline: January 16.
How to apply: Applications are available online.
Exclusive: Visit www.UltimateScholarshipBook.com and enter code AL22120 for updates on this award.

(222) • Hanscom Air Force Base Spouses' Club Scholarship

Hanscom Officers' Spouses' Club
75 Grenier Street, Box 8888, Hanscom AFB, MA 01731
Phone: 781-538-5361
Email: scholarship@hanscomsc.org
http://www.hanscomsc.org

Purpose: To aid dependents of past and present members of the military.
Eligibility: Applicants must be children or spouses of retired, deceased or current active duty members of any branch of the military. They must hold a valid military ID card. Children of military members must be high school seniors.
Target applicant(s): High school students. College students. Adult students.
Amount: Varies.
Number of awards: Varies.
Deadline: March 29.
How to apply: Applications are available online. An application form and copy of military ID are required.
Exclusive: Visit www.UltimateScholarshipBook.com and enter code HA22220 for updates on this award.

(223) • Harry Vold "Duke of the Chutes" Scholarship Award

National Intercollegiate Rodeo Association
2033 Walla Walla Avenue, Walla Walla, WA 99362
Phone: 509-529-4402
Email: rodeo@collegerodeo.com
http://www.collegerodeo.com/

Purpose: To support college-level student members of NIRA who have exhibited traits exemplified by Harold Vold.
Eligibility: Selection is based on the representation by the applicant of the following traits: courteousness, loyalty, faithfulness, honesty, kindness and generosity. In addition, the applicant must show patriotism and dedication to the sport of rodeo.
Target applicant(s): College students. Graduate school students. Adult students.
Amount: $2,500.
Number of awards: 1.
Deadline: May 25.
How to apply: Applications are available online and must include an official transcript and two letters of recommendation.
Exclusive: Visit www.UltimateScholarshipBook.com and enter code NA22320 for updates on this award.

(224) • Hayek Fund for Scholars

Institute for Humane Studies at George Mason University
3434 Washington Boulevard, MS 1C5, Arlington, VA 22201
Phone: 800-697-8799
Email: ihs@gmu.edu
http://www.theihs.org

Purpose: To make awards to graduate students and untenured faculty members for career-enhancing activities.
Eligibility: Applicants must be graduate students or untenured faculty members and must submit a cover letter explaining how participation will advance their liberty-advancing careers. Applicants must also submit an abstract of the paper they are going to present (if applicable), an

itemized expense list and resume. Students may attend any university but must be alumni of IHS programs and events.
Target applicant(s): Graduate school students. Adult students.
Amount: Up to $750.
Number of awards: Varies.
Deadline: Rolling.
How to apply: There is no application form.
Exclusive: Visit www.UltimateScholarshipBook.com and enter code IN22420 for updates on this award.

(225) • HD Hogan Rodeo Scholarship

HD Hogan Memorial Rodeo Scholarship Fund
407 S. X Road, Aurora, NE 68818
http://www.circlehdrodeo.org/scholarship
Purpose: To aid students in continuing their education and their rodeo careers in college.
Eligibility: Applicants must be a current high school senior and current rodeo participant. Selection is based solely on the essay about what being an American means to you and also what the sport of rodeo means to you.
Target applicant(s): High school students.
Amount: Varies.
Number of awards: Varies.
Deadline: July 1.
How to apply: Applications are in the form of the essay that must be mailed.
Exclusive: Visit www.UltimateScholarshipBook.com and enter code HD22520 for updates on this award.

(226) • Helen Gee Chin Scholarship Foundation Scholarship

Helen Gee Chin Scholarship Foundation
66 Winchester Street, Newton Highlands, MA 02461
Phone: 617-527-8890
Email: hgc@calvinchin.com
http://www.hgcscholarshipfoundation.org
Purpose: To promote academic achievement and inspire individuals to become students of the Chinese martial arts.
Eligibility: Applicants must be a U.S. citizen, plan to attend an accredited U.S. four year college or university as a full-time student for the entire academic year and have a B GPA. Applicants must have studied for at least five years one or more of the Chinese martial arts including Kung Fu, Wu Shu or Tai Chi. Selection is based on achievement in academics and martial arts, recommendations, work experience, educational and career goals and leadership in school and community activities.
Target applicant(s): High school students. College students. Adult students.
Minimum GPA: 3.0
Amount: $1,000-$3,000.
Number of awards: At least 2.
Deadline: June 15.
How to apply: Applications are available online. An application form, an essay, official transcripts covering the previous two years, a recommendation letter from current or most recent Sifu and a recommendation letter from a teacher, counselor or advisor are required.
Exclusive: Visit www.UltimateScholarshipBook.com and enter code HE22620 for updates on this award.

(227) • Helen McLoraine Figure Skating Scholarship

U.S. Figure Skating
20 First Street, Colorado Springs, CO 80906
Phone: 719-635-5200
Email: info@usfigureskating.org
http://www.usfsa.org
Purpose: To assist amateur and professional skaters seeking a college education.
Eligibility: Applicants must be a high school senior or college undergraduate and have competed in a U.S. Figure Skating qualifying competition. Synchronized skating is not eligible. Selection is based on academic success, honors, demonstrated leadership in extracurricular activities, work experience, goals and the essay.
Target applicant(s): High school students. College students. Adult students.
Amount: $4,000-$8,000.
Number of awards: Varies.
Deadline: February 17.
How to apply: Applications are available online and include an official transcript, competition documentation and an IRS 1040 tax form for the past two years.
Exclusive: Visit www.UltimateScholarshipBook.com and enter code U.22720 for updates on this award.

(228) • High School Scholarship

National Strength and Conditioning Association (NSCA) Foundation
1885 Bob Johnson Drive, Colorado Springs, CO 80906
Phone: 800-815-6826
http://www.nsca.com/foundation/
Purpose: To support high school students entering the strength and conditioning field.
Eligibility: Applicants must be high school seniors planning to graduate with a degree related to strength and conditioning with a current 3.0 GPA. Students must be NSCA members, although applicants may enroll at the time of application, and pursuing a career in strength and conditioning. Applications are evaluated based on grades, courses, experience, honors, recommendations and involvement in the community and with NSCA.
Target applicant(s): High school students.
Minimum GPA: 3.0
Amount: $1,500.
Number of awards: Varies.
Deadline: October 15.
How to apply: Applications are available by contacting the organization.
Exclusive: Visit www.UltimateScholarshipBook.com and enter code NA22820 for updates on this award.

(229) • HireInfluence Scholarship

HireInfluence Inc.
2002 Timberloch Place, Suite 200, The Woodlands, TX
Phone: 800-535-4732
Email: scholarships@hireinfluence.com
https://hireinfluence.com/scholarship/
Purpose: To support future leaders and entrepreneurs.
Eligibility: Applicants must be between 18 and 25 years of age. Students must be a current high school student or currently enrolled in an accredited college or university in the U.S. or Canada. A minimum 2.0 GPA is required.

Target applicant(s): High school students. College students. Graduate school students.
Minimum GPA: 2.0
Amount: $500.
Number of awards: 1.
Deadline: May 31.
How to apply: Applications are available online.
Exclusive: Visit www.UltimateScholarshipBook.com and enter code HI22920 for updates on this award.

(230) • Hit the Books Scholarship

CoffeeForLess.com
250 South 18th Street, Suite 802, Philadelphia, PA 19103
Phone: 800-261-2859
Email: info@coffeeforless.com
https://www.coffeeforless.com/scholarship/
Purpose: To support college students between 18 and 25 years of age with college expenses through an essay contest that includes their passion for coffee in the content.
Eligibility: Applicants must be enrolled in an accredited institution of higher learning and must be 18-25 years of age. An essay of up to 500 words must be submitted on how education is important in their lives and how the scholarship money will impact their educational goals. Awards are given twice a year. Selection is based on the overall strength of the essay, a creative way to include the applicant's passion for coffee in the content of his/her essay and financial need.
Target applicant(s): High school students. College students. Graduate school students.
Amount: $500.
Number of awards: 2.
Deadline: August 25 and January 31.
How to apply: Applications are submitted via e-mail. An application form, essay and proof of enrollment are required.
Exclusive: Visit www.UltimateScholarshipBook.com and enter code CO23020 for updates on this award.

(231) • Horatio Alger Association Scholarship Program

Horatio Alger Association
Attn.: Scholarship Department, 99 Canal Center Plaza, Suite 320, Alexandria, VA 22314
Phone: 703-684-9444
Email: association@horatioalger.org
https://scholars.horatioalger.org/
Purpose: To assist students who are committed to pursuing a bachelor's degree and have demonstrated integrity, financial need, academic achievement and community involvement.
Eligibility: Applicants must enter college the fall following their high school graduation, have at least a 2.0 GPA, be in need of financial aid ($55,000 or less adjusted gross income per family is preferred) and be involved in extracurricular and community activities. Students applying from Louisiana, Montana and Idaho have additional state specific requirements.
Target applicant(s): High school students.
Minimum GPA: 2.0
Amount: $25,000.
Number of awards: 106.
Deadline: October 25.
How to apply: Applications are available online.
Exclusive: Visit www.UltimateScholarshipBook.com and enter code HO23120 for updates on this award.

(232) • Humane Studies Fellowships

Institute for Humane Studies at George Mason University
3434 Washington Boulevard, MS 1C5, Arlington, VA 22201
Phone: 800-697-8799
Email: ihs@gmu.edu
http://www.theihs.org
Purpose: To award scholarships to students who are interested in the classical liberal/libertarian tradition of individual rights and market economies and wish to apply these principles in their work.
Eligibility: Applicants must be graduate students who are in any field and at any stage before completion of the Ph.D., law students, MBA students or other professional students. The fellowships can be used for study in the U.S. or abroad. Applicants must also be enrolled as full-time students at an accredited degree-granting institution. Students must be alumni of IHS programs and events.
Target applicant(s): Graduate school students. Adult students.
Amount: Up to $15,000.
Number of awards: Varies.
Scholarship may be renewable.
Deadline: February 8.
How to apply: Applications are available online. There is a $25 application fee that is waived by applying by January 5.
Exclusive: Visit www.UltimateScholarshipBook.com and enter code IN23220 for updates on this award.

(233) • IAFC Foundation Scholarship

International Association of Fire Chiefs Foundation
4025 Fair Ridge Drive, Suite 300, Fairfax, VA 22033-2868
Phone: 571-344-5410
Email: iafcfoun@msn.com
http://www.iafcf.org
Purpose: To assist students in fire sciences or related academic programs.
Eligibility: Applicants must be active members with a minimum of three years volunteer work, two years paid work or a combination of paid and volunteer work of three years with a state, county, provincial, municipal, community, industrial or federal fire department who will use the scholarship at an accredited institution of higher education. Students must submit application forms, statements, a list of credits and a transcript. Preference is given to those demonstrating need, desire and initiative.
Target applicant(s): College students. Adult students.
Amount: Varies.
Number of awards: Varies.
Deadline: April 30.
How to apply: Applications are available online.
Exclusive: Visit www.UltimateScholarshipBook.com and enter code IN23320 for updates on this award.

(234) • IAPMO Essay Scholarship Contest

International Association of Plumbing and Mechanical Officials (IAPMO)
4755 E. Philadelphia Street, Ontario, CA 91761
Phone: 909-472-4100
Email: gaby.davis@iapmo.org
http://www.iapmo.org
Purpose: To share the "importance the plumbing and mechanical industry plays in our everyday lives."
Eligibility: Applicants must be current high school seniors or enrolled or accepted as full-time students in an accredited technical school,

community college, trade school, four-year accredited college or university or an apprentice program.
Target applicant(s): High school students. College students. Adult students.
Amount: $500-$1,000.
Number of awards: 3.
Deadline: May 1.
How to apply: Applications are available online. An essay of 800 to 1,600 words on the topic provided is required.
Exclusive: Visit www.UltimateScholarshipBook.com and enter code IN23420 for updates on this award.

---

(235) • IEA Founders College Scholarship Awards

Interscholastic Equestrian Association
467 Main Street, Melrose, MA 02176
Phone: 877-743-3432
Email: info@rideiea.org
http://www.rideiea.org/opportunities/for-riders.html
Purpose: To recognize the top participants in the Interscholastic Equestrian Association's National Final Competitions.
Eligibility: Students must be a high school senior, compete in either the IEA Hunt Seat National Finals or the IEA Western National Finals and place in the top two in their category.
Target applicant(s): High school students.
Amount: Up to $1,100.
Number of awards: Varies.
Deadline: Varies.
How to apply: Participant must qualify during their IEA Zone Final Competition.
Exclusive: Visit www.UltimateScholarshipBook.com and enter code IN23520 for updates on this award.

---

(236) • IEA Zone Specific Scholarships

Interscholastic Equestrian Association
467 Main Street, Melrose, MA 02176
Phone: 877-743-3432
Email: info@rideiea.org
http://www.rideiea.org/opportunities/for-riders.html
Purpose: To support high school seniors in each Interscholastic Equestrian Association zone as they further their education beyond high school.
Eligibility: Students must be active participants in an IEA zone, display outstanding sportsmanship, maintain academic excellence and portray and overall role model to the IEA membership. Each zone has varied selection criteria.
Target applicant(s): High school students.
Amount: Varies.
Number of awards: Varies.
Deadline: Varies.
How to apply: All zone applications are available online. Most zones require letters of recommendation, high school transcript and an essay.
Exclusive: Visit www.UltimateScholarshipBook.com and enter code IN23620 for updates on this award.

---

(237) • Ike Foundation Scholarship

Ike Foundation
348 Palatine Road, Elmer, NJ 08318
Phone: 856-466-7798
https://theikefoundation.org
Purpose: To support students involved in the sport of fishing.
Eligibility: Applicants must be U.S. citizens or permanent residents and high school seniors who are planning to enroll full-time in a two- or four-year institution. Students must have a minimum GPA of 3.2 and demonstrate an interest in fishing and/or conservation. Applicants must submit an original essay along with their application materials.
Target applicant(s): High school students.
Minimum GPA: 3.2
Amount: $5,000.
Number of awards: 5.
Deadline: April 1.
How to apply: Applications are available online.
Exclusive: Visit www.UltimateScholarshipBook.com and enter code IK23720 for updates on this award.

---

(238) • IMCEA Scholarships

IMCEA Headquarters - Scholarships
14080 Nacogdoches Road, #329, San Antonio, TX 78247-1944
Phone: 940-463-5145
Email: imcea@imcea.com
https://imcea.org/awards/scholarship-info/
Purpose: To provide scholarships for high school students and military welfare and recreation professionals seeking to further their educations.
Eligibility: High school or college applicants must be children of IMCEA members. Candidates must provide information about their activities, honors and awards and submit an essay on the provided topic.
Target applicant(s): High school students. College students. Graduate school students. Adult students.
Amount: $1,000.
Number of awards: 2.
Deadline: June 1.
How to apply: Applications are available online and an official transcript must also be submitted.
Exclusive: Visit www.UltimateScholarshipBook.com and enter code IM23820 for updates on this award.

---

(239) • Indianhead Division Scholarships

Second Indianhead Division Association
P.O. Box 218, Fox Lake, IL 60020-0218
Phone: 512-295-5324
Email: warriorvet@verizon.net
http://www.2ida.org
Purpose: To support the children and grandchildren of veterans from the Second Indianhead Division Association.
Eligibility: Applicants' parents or grandparents must have been members of the association for at least three years, or they must have been killed while serving with the Second Infantry Division.
Target applicant(s): High school students. College students. Adult students.
Amount: Varies.
Number of awards: Varies.
Scholarship may be renewable.
Deadline: June 1.
How to apply: Applications are available by phone.
Exclusive: Visit www.UltimateScholarshipBook.com and enter code SE23920 for updates on this award.

---

(240) • Individual Scholarship Program

International Surfing Association
5580 La Jolla Boulevard, #145, La Jolla, CA 92037
Phone: 858-551-8580

Email: info@isasurf.org
http://www.isasurf.org/
Purpose: To aid student surfers who plan to pursue higher education after high school.
Eligibility: Applicants must be U18 junior surfers. Selection is based on financial need and the ability of the applicant to represent themselves as a positive role model both within the sport of surfing and at school.
Target applicant(s): Junior high students or younger. High school students.
Amount: Varies.
Number of awards: Varies.
Deadline: April 30.
How to apply: Applications are available online and must include the following: a recent report card, one letter of recommendation, a personal essay, a budget plan and four photos (family, school, surfing and headshot).
Exclusive: Visit www.UltimateScholarshipBook.com and enter code IN24020 for updates on this award.

(241) • Innovative Architects Essay Contest

Innovative Architects
3122 Hill Street, Duluth, GA 30096
Phone: 770-623-5734
Email: scholarships@innovativearchitects.com
https://www.innovativearchitects.com/scholarship.aspx
Purpose: To assist students who write an essay on boldness.
Eligibility: Applicants must be U.S. citizens or residents who are enrolled in a U.S. college or university. Students must write an essay discussing what the term "bold" means to them and give an example of a time when they were bold.
Target applicant(s): High school students. College students. Graduate school students. Adult students.
Amount: $1,000.
Number of awards: 1.
Deadline: January 31.
How to apply: Applications are available online.
Exclusive: Visit www.UltimateScholarshipBook.com and enter code IN24120 for updates on this award.

(242) • International Association of Fire Chiefs Foundation Fire Explorer Scholarships

Explorers Learning for Life
1325 West Walnut Hill Lane, P.O. Box 152225, Irving, TX 75015-2225
Phone: 855-806-9992
Email: exploring@lflmail.org
http://www.exploring.org/scholarships/
Purpose: To support students who are pursuing careers in fire sciences.
Eligibility: Students must be graduating high school seniors, active fire service Explorers and members of a fire department. Applicants must submit three letters of recommendation and an essay.
Target applicant(s): High school students.
Amount: $500.
Number of awards: Varies.
Deadline: April 30.
How to apply: Applications are available online.
Exclusive: Visit www.UltimateScholarshipBook.com and enter code EX24220 for updates on this award.

(243) • International Bipolar Foundation Essay Contest

International Bipolar Foundation
8755 Aero Drive, Suite 310, San Diego, CA 92123
Phone: 585-598-5967
http://www.ibpf.org/
Purpose: To support students affected by bipolar disorder.
Eligibility: Applicants must be students age 13 to 19 years. Students must write an original research essay on a notable figure with bipolar disorder.
Target applicant(s): Junior high students or younger. High school students.
Amount: $1,000.
Number of awards: 3.
Deadline: November 1.
How to apply: Applications are available online.
Exclusive: Visit www.UltimateScholarshipBook.com and enter code IN24320 for updates on this award.

(244) • Irlet Anderson Scholarship Award

National Organization of Black Law Enforcement Executives (NOBLE)
Pamela C. Chapman, 4609-F Pinecrest Office Park Drive, Alexandria, VA 22312
Phone: 703-658-1529
http://www.noblenatl.org
Purpose: To support students who are committed to a career in criminal justice or law enforcement.
Eligibility: Applicants must be U.S. citizens who are graduating seniors in high school, are studying any of the social sciences and are committed to becoming sworn law enforcement officers or special agents or work in a related field. Students must demonstrate financial need, be accepted to an accredited institution and have a GPA of 3.8 or higher.
Target applicant(s): High school students.
Minimum GPA: 3.8
Amount: $2,500.
Number of awards: 1.
Deadline: April 15.
How to apply: Applications are available online.
Exclusive: Visit www.UltimateScholarshipBook.com and enter code NA24420 for updates on this award.

(245) • ISIA Education Foundation Scholarship

Ice Skating Institute of America (ISIA) Education Foundation
6000 Custer Road, Building 9, Plano, TX 75023
Phone: 972-735-8800
Email: ISI@skateisi.org
http://www.skateisi.com
Purpose: To encourage skaters to make athletic and educational achievements.
Eligibility: Applicants must have completed at least three years of high school with a minimum 3.0 GPA during the last two years and enroll as full-time undergraduate students. Applicants must also have been members of the Ice Skating Institute (ISI), have participated in the ISI Recreational Skater Program for at least four years and have completed 120 hours of volunteer service. Applicants must also submit two evaluation forms and an essay of 500 words or less explaining why they should receive the award.
Target applicant(s): High school students. College students. Adult students.
Minimum GPA: 3.0

Amount: $4,000.
Number of awards: Varies.
Deadline: March 1.
How to apply: Applications are available online.
Exclusive: Visit www.UltimateScholarshipBook.com and enter code IC24520 for updates on this award.

(246) · IVLA Scholarship

International Virtual Learning Academy
2657 Windmill Parkway #142, Henderson, NV 89074
Email: info@internationalvla.com
https://internationalvla.com/college-scholarship-from-ivla/
Purpose: To support students who write about technology.
Eligibility: Applicants must be U.S. residents accepted to an accredited U.S. college, university or trade school or graduating high school senior. Students must have a minimum GPA of 2.5 and write an essay pertaining to technology's effect on education.
Target applicant(s): High school students. College students. Adult students.
Minimum GPA: 2.5
Amount: $1,000.
Number of awards: 1.
Deadline: April 30.
How to apply: Applications are available online.
Exclusive: Visit www.UltimateScholarshipBook.com and enter code IN24620 for updates on this award.

(247) · Jack Kent Cooke Foundation College Scholarship Program

Jack Kent Cooke Foundation
44325 Woodridge Parkway, Lansdowne, VA 20176
Phone: 800-941-3300
Email: scholarships@jkcf.org
http://www.jkcf.org
Purpose: To assist high school seniors with financial need.
Eligibility: Applicants must plan to graduate from a U.S. high school in the spring and plan to enroll in an accredited four-year college beginning in the fall following application. Students must have a minimum 3.5 GPA and have standardized test scores in the top 15 percent: SAT combined critical reading and math score of 1200 or above and/or ACT composite score of 26 or above. Applicants must also demonstrate significant unmet financial need. Family incomes up to $95,000 are considered. However, the majority of recipients will be eligible to receive a Pell grant.
Target applicant(s): High school students.
Minimum GPA: 3.5
Amount: Up to $40,000 per year for four years.
Number of awards: Up to 40.
Scholarship may be renewable.
Deadline: Late November.
How to apply: Applications are available online.
Exclusive: Visit www.UltimateScholarshipBook.com and enter code JA24720 for updates on this award.

(248) · James M & Erma T Freemont Foundation Scholarship Program

James M. & Erma T. Freemont Foundation
P.O. Box 82563, Hapeville, GA 30354
http://www.freemontfoundation.com
Purpose: To support students who demonstrate involvement and leadership.
Eligibility: Applicants must be graduating high school seniors, undergraduate or graduate students. Students must demonstrate outstanding academic achievement, leadership and volunteerism in their community and participation in extracurricular school activities.
Target applicant(s): High school students. College students. Graduate school students. Adult students.
Amount: Varies.
Number of awards: Varies.
Deadline: February 2.
How to apply: Applications are available online.
Exclusive: Visit www.UltimateScholarshipBook.com and enter code JA24820 for updates on this award.

(249) · James M. and Virginia M. Smyth Scholarship

Community Foundation for Greater Atlanta Inc.
50 Hurt Plaza, Suite 449, Atlanta, GA 30303
Phone: 404-688-5525
Email: info@cfgreateratlanta.org
http://www.cfgreateratlanta.org/community-impact/scholarships/
Purpose: To support students who are pursuing undergraduate degrees.
Eligibility: Students must have at least a 3.0 GPA, and they must have community service experience. Applicants must plan to obtain a degree in the arts and sciences, music, ministry or human services. Preference will be given to students from the following states: Missouri, Mississippi, Georgia, Illinois, Oklahoma, Texas and Tennessee. Applicants must demonstrate financial need. Adult students may also apply.
Target applicant(s): High school students. College students. Adult students.
Minimum GPA: 3.0
Amount: $2,000.
Number of awards: 12-15.
Scholarship may be renewable.
Deadline: March 15.
How to apply: Applications are available online.
Exclusive: Visit www.UltimateScholarshipBook.com and enter code CO24920 for updates on this award.

(250) · Jean Downes Scholarship

USA Water Ski and Wake Sports Foundation
1251 Holy Cow Road, Polk City, FL 33868
Phone: 863-324-2472
Email: usa-wsf@waterskihalloffame.com
http://www.usawaterskifoundation.org/
Purpose: To support current active members of USA Water Ski in pursuit of their educational goals.
Eligibility: Applicants must be U.S. citizens and be studying full-time at a two-year or four-year accredited college as an incoming freshman, sophomore, junior or senior. Applicants must attend their chosen college for the full year during the year of receipt of the scholarship. Selection is based on applicant's academic achievement, need, work record and school and community activities as well as their contributions to the sport of water skiing.
Target applicant(s): College students. Adult students.
Amount: $1,500.
Number of awards: 1.
Deadline: March 15.
How to apply: Applications are available online. An application form, 500-word essay and two recommendation letters are required.
Exclusive: Visit www.UltimateScholarshipBook.com and enter code US25020 for updates on this award.

(251) • Jeanne E. Bray Memorial Scholarship

National Rifle Association
11250 Waples Mill Road, Fairfax, VA 22030
Phone: 800-672-3888
Email: grantprogram@nrahq.org
https://awards.nra.org/awards/
Purpose: To aid children of public law enforcement officers obtain a college education.
Eligibility: Applicants must be a dependent child of any current, retired or deceased law enforcement officer. The parent should also be a member of the NRA.
Target applicant(s): High school students. College students. Adult students.
Amount: Up to $5,000.
Number of awards: Varies.
Scholarship may be renewable.
Deadline: November 15.
How to apply: Applications are available online.
Exclusive: Visit www.UltimateScholarshipBook.com and enter code NA25120 for updates on this award.

(252) • Jennifer Odom/David Kammerer Memorial Scholarship

USA Water Ski and Wake Sports Foundation
1251 Holy Cow Road, Polk City, FL 33868
Phone: 863-324-2472
Email: usa-wsf@waterskihalloffame.com
http://www.usawaterskifoundation.org/
Purpose: To support current active members of USA Water Ski with their educational goals.
Eligibility: Applicants must be U.S. citizens and incoming freshmen, sophomores, juniors or seniors enrolled full-time at an accredited two-year or four-year college. Applicants must remain enrolled full-time during the year of receipt of the scholarship. Selection is based on the applicant's academic achievement, need, school and community activities and work record as well as their contributions to the sport of water skiing.
Target applicant(s): College students. Adult students.
Amount: $1,500.
Number of awards: 1.
Deadline: March 15.
How to apply: Applications are available online. An application form, 500-word essay and two letters of recommendation are required.
Exclusive: Visit www.UltimateScholarshipBook.com and enter code US25220 for updates on this award.

(253) • John F. Duffy Scholarship/Grant Program

California Peace Officers' Memorial Foundation
1700 I Street, Suite 100, Sacramento, CA 95811
Email: cpomf@camemorial.org
http://www.camemorial.org
Purpose: To provide financial assistance to survivors of California peace officers who have died in the line of duty.
Eligibility: Applicants must be spouses, children, stepchildren or adopted children of peace officers who died in the line of duty and are enrolled on the California memorial monument. They must carry no less than six units per quarter or eight units per semester at an accredited college or university, and they must maintain a 2.0 or higher GPA.
Target applicant(s): High school students. College students. Graduate school students. Adult students.
Minimum GPA: 2.0
Amount: Up to $4,000.
Number of awards: Varies.
Deadline: June 1.
How to apply: Applications are available online.
Exclusive: Visit www.UltimateScholarshipBook.com and enter code CA25320 for updates on this award.

(254) • John J. Smith Graduate School Scholarship

National Intercollegiate Rodeo Association
2033 Walla Walla Avenue, Walla Walla, WA 99362
Phone: 509-529-4402
Email: rodeo@collegerodeo.com
http://www.collegerodeo.com/
Purpose: To support students who have participated in the National Intercollegiate Rodeo Association as they continue on into graduate level coursework.
Eligibility: Applicants must be current graduate level college students or be entering into a graduate program and be current NIRA members.
Target applicant(s): College students. Graduate school students. Adult students.
Amount: $2,000.
Number of awards: 1.
Deadline: May 20.
How to apply: Applications are available online. The following are to be included with the application: cover letter, proof of acceptance into a graduate level program, an official college transcript and two letters of recommendation.
Exclusive: Visit www.UltimateScholarshipBook.com and enter code NA25420 for updates on this award.

(255) • Jon C. Ladda Memorial Foundation Scholarship

Jon C. Ladda Memorial Foundation
P.O. Box 55, Unionville, CT 06085
Email: info@jonladda.org
http://www.jonladda.org
Purpose: To provide financial assistance to children of Naval Academy graduates and Navy members who have died or become disabled while on active duty.
Eligibility: Applicants must be children of United States Naval Academy graduates or Navy members who served in the submarine service. The Navy member or Academy graduate must have died on active duty or have 100 percent disability and be medically retired. Applicants must also be accepted and enroll in an accredited institution of higher learning.
Target applicant(s): High school students. College students. Adult students.
Amount: Varies.
Number of awards: Varies.
Scholarship may be renewable.
Deadline: March 15.
How to apply: Applications are available by mail.
Exclusive: Visit www.UltimateScholarshipBook.com and enter code JO25520 for updates on this award.

(256) • Jonathan Jasper Wright Award

National Association of Blacks in Criminal Justice
1801 Fayetteville Street, 106 Whiting Criminal Justice Building, P.O. Box 20011-C, Durham, NC 27707

Phone: 919-683-1801
Email: Office@NABCJ.org
http://www.nabcj.org
Purpose: To reward regional and national leadership in the field of criminal justice.
Eligibility: Award recipients will be involved in affecting policy change. Nominator should be a member of NABCJ.
Target applicant(s): College students. Graduate school students. Adult students.
Amount: Varies.
Number of awards: 1.
Deadline: March 15.
How to apply: Nomination applications are available online.
Exclusive: Visit www.UltimateScholarshipBook.com and enter code NA25620 for updates on this award.

(257) • Joseph P. and Helen T. Cribbins Scholarship

Association of the United States Army
2425 Wilson Boulevard, Arlington, VA 22201
Phone: 703-841-4300
Email: Membersupport@ausa.org
https://www.ausa.org/resources/scholarships
Purpose: To aid U.S. army soldiers who are studying engineering or a related subject.
Eligibility: Applicants must be active duty or honorably discharged enlisted soldiers in the U.S. Army or one of its affiliate entities (Army Reserve, National Guard, etc.). They must be accepted or enrolled at an accredited college or university and majoring in or planning to major in engineering or a related subject. Selection is based on the overall strength of the application.
Target applicant(s): High school students. College students. Adult students.
Amount: $2,000.
Number of awards: Varies.
Deadline: July 1.
How to apply: Applications are available online. An application form, two recommendation letters, applicant autobiography, an official transcript, a course of study outline, certificates of completion for other training courses (if applicable) and a copy of form DD-214 (for discharged soldiers) are required.
Exclusive: Visit www.UltimateScholarshipBook.com and enter code AS25720 for updates on this award.

(258) • Josephine De Karman Fellowship

Josephine De Karman Fellowship Trust
P.O. Box 3389, San Dimas, CA 91773
Phone: 909-592-0607
Email: info@dekarman.org
http://www.dekarman.org
Purpose: To recognize students who demonstrate academic achievement.
Eligibility: Applicants must be undergraduate students entering their senior year or Ph.D. candidates nearing completion of their degree (all requirements except for the dissertation must be completed by January 31). Applicants may not be post-doctoral students. Special consideration is given to doctoral students in the humanities. The award is open to international students living in the U.S.
Target applicant(s): College students. Adult students.
Amount: $14,000-$22,000.
Number of awards: 8.
Deadline: January 31.
How to apply: Applications are available online.
Exclusive: Visit www.UltimateScholarshipBook.com and enter code JO25820 for updates on this award.

(259) • Judith Haupt Member's Child Scholarship

Navy Wives Clubs of America (NWCA)
P.O. Box 54022, NSA Mid-South, Millington, TN 38053-6022
Phone: 866-511-6922
Email: scholarships@navywivesclubsofamerica.org
http://www.navywivesclubsofamerica.org
Purpose: To aid college students who are the adult children of members of the Navy Wives Clubs of America (NWCA).
Eligibility: Applicants must be unmarried college students who are the adult children of NWCA members. They cannot be carrying a military ID card and must have been accepted into a college no later than the application due date. Selection is based on academic merit and financial need.
Target applicant(s): High school students. College students. Adult students.
Amount: Varies.
Number of awards: 1.
Deadline: May 30.
How to apply: Applications are available online. An application form and an official transcript are required.
Exclusive: Visit www.UltimateScholarshipBook.com and enter code NA25920 for updates on this award.

(260) • Junior 3-Position Air Rifle National Championship Scholarships

American Legion
Attn.: Americanism and Children and Youth Division, P.O. Box 1055, Indianapolis, IN 46206
Phone: 317-630-1249
Email: acy@legion.org
http://www.legion.org
Purpose: To reward outstanding young marksmen and women.
Eligibility: Applicants must be 18 years of age or younger. They must qualify for and compete in the Junior Air Rifle National Championship. Winners receive a $2,500 scholarship. Championships are held in August.
Target applicant(s): Junior high students or younger. High school students.
Amount: $2,500.
Number of awards: 2.
Deadline: July 18.
How to apply: Applications are available from your local American Legion chapter.
Exclusive: Visit www.UltimateScholarshipBook.com and enter code AM26020 for updates on this award.

(261) • Kathern F. Gruber Scholarship Program

Blinded Veterans Association (BVA)
125 N. West Street, 3rd Floor, Alexandria, VA 22314
Phone: 202-371-8880
Email: bva@bva.org
http://www.bva.org
Purpose: To assist the spouses, children and grandchildren of blinded veterans with their higher-learning goals.
Eligibility: Applicants must be the spouses, children or grandchildren of a blind veteran and be accepted or enrolled at an accredited, higher learning institution.

Target applicant(s): High school students. College students. Graduate school students. Adult students.
Amount: $2,000.
Number of awards: 6.
Deadline: April 21.
How to apply: Contact the BVA for application materials.
Exclusive: Visit www.UltimateScholarshipBook.com and enter code BL26120 for updates on this award.

---

(262) • Keller Law Offices Scholarship for Higher Education

Keller Law Offices
310 S. 4th Avenue #1130, Minneapolis, MN 55415
Phone: 952-913-1421
http://www.kellerlawoffices.com/keller-higher-education-scholarship/
Purpose: To support students who write an essay.
Eligibility: Applicants must be U.S. citizens or legal residents who are high school seniors or currently enrolled college students. Students will need to submit a 500- to 1,000-word essay on the given topic found on the webpage. Selection is based on financial need, academic performance and quality of the written essay.
Target applicant(s): High school students. College students. Graduate school students. Adult students.
Amount: $1,000.
Number of awards: 1.
Deadline: July 15.
How to apply: Applications are available online.
Exclusive: Visit www.UltimateScholarshipBook.com and enter code KE26220 for updates on this award.

---

(263) • Kevin Higgins College Scholarship

US Rugby Foundation
2131 Pan American Plaza, San Diego, CA 92101
Phone: 619-233-0765
Email: bvizard@usrugbyfoundation.com
http://www.usrugbyfoundation.org
Purpose: To support those high school rugby players who plan on continuing to play rugby at the collegiate level.
Eligibility: Applicants must be a U.S. high school senior rugby player, have a 2.5 or better GPA and plan to continue playing rugby at the collegiate level. Selection is based on character recommendations, community service, rugby potential and the personal statement. Financial need will be considered.
Target applicant(s): High school students.
Minimum GPA: 2.5
Amount: $1,000.
Number of awards: Up to 10.
Deadline: July 31.
How to apply: Applications are available online and should include an official transcript, at least one letter of recommendation, a rugby resume, a copy of the previous year's taxes and the personal statement.
Exclusive: Visit www.UltimateScholarshipBook.com and enter code US26320 for updates on this award.

---

(264) • Keyvan Samini Scholarship

Keyvan Samini Scholarship Program
100 Spectrum Center Drive, Suite 900, Irvine, CA 92618
Phone: 949-407-7585
Email: apply@keyvansaminischolarship.com
https://keyvansaminischolarship.com/
Purpose: To support students with promise and initiative.
Eligibility: Applicants must be U.S. citizens or permanent residents who are enrolling as an undergraduate or graduate at an accredited U.S. college or university. Students must have a minimum GPA of 2.5 and have not received a grade of less than a "C" in any course.
Target applicant(s): High school students. College students. Graduate school students. Adult students.
Minimum GPA: 2.5
Amount: $1,000.
Number of awards: 2.
Deadline: February 15.
How to apply: Applications are available online.
Exclusive: Visit www.UltimateScholarshipBook.com and enter code KE26420 for updates on this award.

---

(265) • La Fra Scholarship

Ladies Auxiliary of the Fleet Reserve Association
Gini Larson PNP, National Scholarship Chairman, 2187 Capeheart Street, Ingleside, TX 78362-6222
Phone: 361-442-5707
Email: loveduck@aol.com
http://www.la-fra.org
Purpose: To support the female descendants of sea personnel.
Eligibility: Students must have a father or grandfather who was in the Marine Corps, Coast Guard, Navy, Fleet Reserve, Coast Guard Reserve or Fleet Marine Corps Reserve.
Target applicant(s): High school students. College students. Graduate school students. Adult students.
Amount: Varies.
Number of awards: Varies.
Deadline: April 15.
How to apply: Applications are available online.
Exclusive: Visit www.UltimateScholarshipBook.com and enter code LA26520 for updates on this award.

---

(266) • LA Tutors Innovation in Education Scholarship

LA Tutors
9454 Wilshire Boulevard, Suite 600, Beverly Hills, CA 90212
Phone: 424-335-0067
Email: contact@latutors123.com
http://www.latutors123.com/scholarship/
Purpose: To reward innovation.
Eligibility: Applicants must be a high school or college student within the U.S. or Canada. A minimum 3.0 GPA is required. Students must be a citizen of, permanent resident of or hold a valid student visa in the U.S. or Canada. Applicants will have designed an innovative project that makes the difference in the lives of others. The project can include a website, series of blogs, an app, fundraising event, etc. An essay describing the goal of the project and providing supporting documentation is required. The contest is monthly.
Target applicant(s): High school students. College students. Graduate school students. Adult students.
Minimum GPA: 3.0
Amount: $500.
Number of awards: 12.
Deadline: Monthly.
How to apply: Application is available online.
Exclusive: Visit www.UltimateScholarshipBook.com and enter code LA26620 for updates on this award.

(267) • Law Office of Matthew L Sharp Need-Based Scholarship

Law Office of Matthew L. Sharp
432 Ridge Street, Reno, NV 89501
Phone: 775-324-1500
http://mattsharplaw.com/law-office-matthew-l-sharp-annual-scholarship/
Purpose: To support students with financial need to pursue post-secondary education.
Eligibility: Applicants must be U.S. citizens or permanent residents enrolling as full-time students in the fall at an accredited college or university, community college or law school. Students must complete application and submit a PSA video.
Target applicant(s): High school students. College students. Graduate school students. Adult students.
Amount: $1,000.
Number of awards: 1.
Deadline: July 15.
How to apply: Applications are available online.
Exclusive: Visit www.UltimateScholarshipBook.com and enter code LA26720 for updates on this award.

(268) • Leaders and Achievers Scholarship Program

Comcast Corporation
Comcast Center, 1701 JFK Boulevard, Philadelphia, PA 19103
Phone: 855-670-4787
Email: comcast@applyists.com
http://corporate.comcast.com/
Purpose: To provide one-time scholarship awards to graduating high school seniors. Emphasis is on students who take leadership roles in school and community service and improvement.
Eligibility: Students must be high school seniors with a minimum 3.0 GPA, be nominated by their high school principal or guidance counselor and attend school in a Comcast community. See the website for a list of eligible communities by state. Comcast employees, their families or other Comcast affiliates are not eligible to apply.
Target applicant(s): High school students.
Minimum GPA: 3.0
Amount: $2,500.
Number of awards: 800.
Deadline: December 7.
How to apply: Applications are available from the nominating principal or counselor.
Exclusive: Visit www.UltimateScholarshipBook.com and enter code CO26820 for updates on this award.

(269) • Leadership Essay Contest

United States Naval Institute (USNI)
291 Wood Road, Annapolis, MD 21402
Phone: 410-268-6110
https://www.usni.org/essay-contests
Purpose: To promote awareness of sea services.
Eligibility: Applicants must be junior officers, O-4 and below from the U.S. Navy, Marine Corps or Coast Guard. Students must write an essay discussing leadership.
Target applicant(s): Adult students.
Amount: $5,000.
Number of awards: 3.
Deadline: September 30.
How to apply: Applications are available online.
Exclusive: Visit www.UltimateScholarshipBook.com and enter code UN26920 for updates on this award.

(270) • Leesa Social Impact Scholarship

Leesa
3704 Pacific Avenue, Suite 200, Virginia Beach, VA 23451
Phone: 844-335-3372
Email: scholarship@leesa.com
https://www.leesa.com/pages/scholarship
Purpose: To support exceptional students interested in social action.
Eligibility: Applicants must be accepted to or currently enrolled at an accredited college or university and have a minimum GPA of 3.0. Students must demonstrate a commitment to social action. Applicants must submit a video describing the role that social action has had upon their lives.
Target applicant(s): High school students. College students. Graduate school students. Adult students.
Minimum GPA: 3.0
Amount: $10,000.
Number of awards: 4.
Deadline: May 15, November 15.
How to apply: Applications are available online.
Exclusive: Visit www.UltimateScholarshipBook.com and enter code LE27020 for updates on this award.

(271) • Lemelson-MIT Student Prize

Lemelson-MIT
222 Third Street, Suite 300, Cambridge, MA 02142
http://lemelson.mit.edu/studentprize
Purpose: To support inventive students pursuing graduate degrees.
Eligibility: Applicants must be a full-time advanced degree student at a U.S. college or university. Students must submit at least two tested prototype inventions that represent one or more of the following economic sectors: healthcare, transportation, food and agriculture or consumer devices. Applicants must be a named inventor on all inventions entered into the competition and consider environmental sustainability as part of their work.
Target applicant(s): Graduate school students. Adult students.
Amount: Varies.
Number of awards: Varies.
Deadline: Varies.
How to apply: Applications are available online.
Exclusive: Visit www.UltimateScholarshipBook.com and enter code LE27120 for updates on this award.

(272) • Leo Hamel Fine Jewelers Scholarship

Leo Hamel Fine Jewelers
1851 San Diego Avenue, Suite 130, San Diego, CA 92110
Phone: 619-299-1500
https://www.leohamel.com/scholarships
Purpose: To support students who are wanting to further their education.
Eligibility: Applicants must be a graduating high school senior or undergraduate level college student. Multiple drawings held throughout the year.
Target applicant(s): High school students. College students. Adult students.
Amount: $1,000.
Number of awards: 1-4.
Deadline: January 3.

How to apply: Applications are available online.
Exclusive: Visit www.UltimateScholarshipBook.com and enter code LE27220 for updates on this award.

(273) • Letters About Literature Contest

Letters About Literature
C. Gourley, Project Manager, 81 Oliver Street, Wilkes-Barre, PA 18705
Phone: 202-707-5221
Email: cfbook@loc.gov
http://www.read.gov/letters/
Purpose: To encourage young people to read.
Eligibility: Applicants must be U.S. legal residents. They must be students in grades 4 through 12 and must be at least nine years old by the September 1 that precedes the contest deadline. They must submit a personal letter to an author about how that author's book or work has impacted them. Selection is based on letter originality, grammar and organization.
Target applicant(s): Junior high students or younger. High school students.
Amount: $200-$1,000.
Number of awards: 6.
Deadline: December 2 and January 9.
How to apply: Entry instructions are available online. An entry coupon and letter are required.
Exclusive: Visit www.UltimateScholarshipBook.com and enter code LE27320 for updates on this award.

(274) • Life Lessons Scholarship Program

Life and Health Insurance Foundation for Education
1655 N. Fort Myer Drive, Suite 610, Arlington, VA 22209
Phone: 202-464-5000
Email: info@lifehappens.org
http://www.lifehappens.org
Purpose: To support students who have been affected financially and emotionally by the death of a parent.
Eligibility: Applicants must submit either a 500-word essay or a three-minute video describing the impact of losing a parent at a young age. The grand prize winner of the video contest is selected by an online public vote.
Target applicant(s): High school students. College students.
Amount: Up to $15,000.
Number of awards: 31.
Deadline: March 1.
How to apply: Applications are available online.
Exclusive: Visit www.UltimateScholarshipBook.com and enter code LI27420 for updates on this award.

(275) • Live Más Scholarship

Taco Bell Foundation
Email: info@livemasscholarship.com
http://www.livemasscholarship.com
Purpose: To reward the next generation of innovators, creators and dreamers.
Eligibility: Applicants must be a legal resident of the 50 United States and the District of Columbia, at least 16 years of age and no older than 24 years of age, and on track to apply for or currently enrolled in an accredited post-high school/post-secondary educational programs (including accredited two-and four-year colleges, universities, vocational-technical and trade schools).
Target applicant(s): High school students. College students. Graduate school students.
Amount: $5,000-$25,000.
Number of awards: 100.
Deadline: March 18.
How to apply: Submit a video (2 minutes or less in length) that tells us the story of your life's passion. It could be a short film, animation or just a simple testimonial. This is not about how well you can make a film – we just want you to show us your passion and explain why you should be considered for a Live Más Scholarship.
Exclusive: Visit www.UltimateScholarshipBook.com and enter code TA27520 for updates on this award.

(276) • LiveCareer

LiveCareer
Caribe Plaza 6th Floor, Palmeras Street #53, San Juan, PR 00901
Email: scholarship@livecareer.com
http://www.livecareer.com/education-opportunities
Purpose: To support students with the cost of their education on the path to their career.
Eligibility: Applicants must write an attention-grabbing cover letter for their dream job at their dream company. Students must be currently enrolled full-time college or university students or scheduled to be enrolled full-time in a college or university for the semester they would receive the scholarship. Applicants must be at least 18 years of age and should be legal residents of the United States.
Target applicant(s): High school students. College students. Graduate school students. Adult students.
Amount: $1,500.
Number of awards: 3.
Deadline: April 3.
How to apply: Applications are available online.
Exclusive: Visit www.UltimateScholarshipBook.com and enter code LI27620 for updates on this award.

(277) • Lou Manzione Scholarship

Atlantic Amateur Hockey Association
Attn.: Tom Koester, President, P.O. Box 213, Lafayette Hill, PA 19444
Email: info@atlantic-district.org
http://www.atlantic-district.org
Purpose: To aid hockey students who are planning to continue their education beyond high school.
Eligibility: Applicants must be a high school senior in New Jersey, Pennsylvania or Delaware and registered with USA Hockey. Selection is based on the personal essay, scholastic achievement, the coach and teacher recommendations and extracurricular activities.
Target applicant(s): High school students.
Amount: $1,000.
Number of awards: 2.
Deadline: February 1.
How to apply: Applications are available online.
Exclusive: Visit www.UltimateScholarshipBook.com and enter code AT27720 for updates on this award.

(278) • LULAC National Scholastic Achievement Awards

League of United Latin American Citizens
1133 19th Street NW, Suite 1000, Washington, DC 20036
Phone: 202-835-9646

Email: scholarships@lnesc.org
http://www.lnesc.org
Purpose: To aid students of all ethnic backgrounds attending colleges, universities and graduate schools.
Eligibility: Applicants do not need to be Hispanic or Latino to apply. Applicants must have applied to or be enrolled in a college, university or graduate school and be U.S. citizens or legal residents. Students must also have a minimum 3.5 GPA and if entering freshmen a minimum ACT score of 29 or minimum SAT score of 1350. Eligible candidates cannot be related to scholarship committee members, the Council President or contributors to the Council funds. Since applications must be sent from local LULAC Councils, students without LULAC Councils in their states are ineligible.
Target applicant(s): High school students. College students. Graduate school students. Adult students.
Minimum GPA: 3.5
Amount: $2,000.
Number of awards: Varies.
Deadline: March 31.
How to apply: Applications are available online.
Exclusive: Visit www.UltimateScholarshipBook.com and enter code LE27820 for updates on this award.

---

(279) · Marian Wood Baird College Scholarship

United States Tennis Association Foundation
70 W. Red Oak Lane, White Plains, NY 10604
Phone: 914-696-7223
Email: foundation@usta.com
http://www.ustafoundation.com/
Purpose: To support youth tennis players who have excelled both on and off the court.
Eligibility: Applicants must be high school seniors who have participated extensively in an organized community tennis program. Students must also excel academically, demonstrate leadership skills and exemplify good sportsmanship both on and off the court.
Target applicant(s): High school students.
Amount: Up to $15,000.
Number of awards: 1.
Scholarship may be renewable.
Deadline: February 27.
How to apply: Applications are available online.
Exclusive: Visit www.UltimateScholarshipBook.com and enter code UN27920 for updates on this award.

---

(280) · Marine Corps League Scholarships

Marine Corps League
P.O. Box 3070, Merrifield, VA 22116
Phone: 800-625-1775
http://www.mclnational.org
Purpose: To provide educational opportunities to spouses and descendants of Marine Corps League members.
Eligibility: Applicants must be Marine Corp League or Auxiliary members in good standing, their spouses or their descendants, children of Marines who died in the line of duty or honorably discharged Marines who need rehabilitation training that is not being subsidized by government programs.
Target applicant(s): High school students. College students. Adult students.
Minimum GPA: 3.0
Amount: Varies.
Number of awards: Varies.
Scholarship may be renewable.
Deadline: July 15.
How to apply: Applications are available online.
Exclusive: Visit www.UltimateScholarshipBook.com and enter code MA28020 for updates on this award.

---

(281) · Marine Corps Scholarship Foundation Scholarship

Marine Corps Scholarship Foundation
P.O. Box 3008, Princeton, NJ 08543-3008
Phone: 800-292-7777
Email: mcsfnj@mcsf.org
https://www.mcsf.org
Purpose: To provide financial assistance to sons and daughters of U.S. Marines and children of former Marines in their pursuit of higher education.
Eligibility: Applicants must be children of one of the following: an active duty or reserve U. S. Marine, a U.S. Marine who has received an Honorable Discharge, Medical Discharge or was killed while serving in the U.S. Marine Corps, an active duty or reserve U.S. Navy Corpsman who is serving, or has served, with the U.S. Marine Corps or a U.S. Navy Corpsman who has served with the U.S. Marine Corps and has received an Honorable Discharge, Medical Discharge or was killed while serving in the U.S. Navy. Applicants can also be grandchildren of one of the following: A U.S. Marine who served with the 4th Marine Division during World War II and is/was a member of their association, a U.S. Marine who served with the 6th Marine Division during World War II and is/was a member of their association or a U.S. Marine who served in the 531 Gray Ghost Squadron and is/was a member of their association. Applicants must be either high school graduates or undergraduate students. There is a family income limit.
Target applicant(s): High school students. College students. Adult students.
Minimum GPA: 2.0
Amount: Varies.
Number of awards: Varies.
Deadline: March 1.
How to apply: Applications are available online.
Exclusive: Visit www.UltimateScholarshipBook.com and enter code MA28120 for updates on this award.

---

(282) · Markley Scholarship

National Association for Campus Activities
13 Harbison Way, Columbia, SC 29212
Phone: 803-732-6222
Email: info@naca.org
https://www.naca.org/FOUNDATION/Pages/Scholarships.aspx
Purpose: To support undergraduate and graduate students who have made exceptional contributions in the field of student activities. The focus is on involvement with NACA Central, along with contributions to other activities-based organizations.
Eligibility: Applicants must attend a college/university in the former NACA South Central Region (AR, LA, NM, OK, TX); must be enrolled as juniors, seniors or graduate students at a four-year institution or as sophomores at a two-year institution and must have a minimum 2.5 GPA.
Target applicant(s): College students. Graduate school students. Adult students.
Minimum GPA: 2.5
Amount: Varies.
Number of awards: Up to 2.

Deadline: September 30.
How to apply: Applications are available online. Only electronic applications and supporting documents submitted through the online scholarship application will be accepted.
Exclusive: Visit www.UltimateScholarshipBook.com and enter code NA28220 for updates on this award.

(283) · Marsh Scholarship Fund

Eastern Surfing Association
11 Long Point Road, Stony Creek, CT 06405
Phone: 386-672-4905
Email: scholastics@surfesa.org
http://www.surfesa.org
Purpose: To assist Eastern Surfing Association (ESA) student surfers.
Eligibility: Applicants must be current ESA members. Transcripts, a recommendation letter, purpose letters and applications are required. The award is based on academics and citizenship, not athletic ability.
Target applicant(s): High school students. College students. Graduate school students. Adult students.
Amount: Varies.
Number of awards: Varies.
Deadline: June 15.
How to apply: Applications are available online and by email.
Exclusive: Visit www.UltimateScholarshipBook.com and enter code EA28320 for updates on this award.

(284) · Marshall Memorial Fellowship

German Marshall Fund of the United States
1744 R Street NW, Washington, DC 20009
Phone: 202-683-2650
Email: info@gmfus.org
http://www.gmfus.org/transatlantic-leadership-initiatives/marshall-memorial-fellowship
Purpose: To provide fellowships for future community leaders to travel in Europe and to explore its societies, institutions and people.
Eligibility: Applicants must be nominated by a recognized leader in their communities or professional fields. They must be between 28 and 40 years of age and demonstrate achievement within their profession, civic involvement and leadership. They must be U.S. citizens or permanent residents or be permanent citizens of one of the 38 countries listed on the scholarship page. European applicants will visit the United States for their fellowship opportunities. Candidates should have little or no previous experience traveling through Europe. Fellows visit five or six cities and meet with policy makers, business professionals and other community leaders.
Target applicant(s): College students. Graduate school students. Adult students.
Amount: Varies.
Number of awards: 75.
Deadline: September 28.
How to apply: Applications are available online.
Exclusive: Visit www.UltimateScholarshipBook.com and enter code GE28420 for updates on this award.

(285) · Marshall Scholar

Marshall Aid Commemoration Commission
Email: info@marshallscholarship.org
http://www.marshallscholarship.org
Purpose: Established in 1953 and financed by the British government, the scholarships are designed to bring academically distinguished Americans to study in the United Kingdom to increase understanding and appreciation of the British society and academic values.
Eligibility: Applicants must be U.S. citizens who expect to earn a degree from an accredited four-year college or university in the U.S. with a minimum 3.7 GPA. Students may apply in one of eight regions in the U.S.
Target applicant(s): College students. Graduate school students. Adult students.
Minimum GPA: 3.7
Amount: Varies.
Number of awards: up to 40.
Deadline: October 2.
How to apply: Contact your regional center at the address listed on the website.
Exclusive: Visit www.UltimateScholarshipBook.com and enter code MA28520 for updates on this award.

(286) · Mary Church Terrell Award

National Association of Blacks in Criminal Justice
1801 Fayetteville Street, 106 Whiting Criminal Justice Building, P.O. Box 20011-C, Durham, NC 27707
Phone: 919-683-1801
Email: Office@NABCJ.org
http://www.nabcj.org
Purpose: To reward activism for positive change in criminal justice on city and state levels.
Eligibility: The nominator should be a member of NABCJ. This award is given to an individual who has initiated relationships with churches, courts, councils and assemblies.
Target applicant(s): High school students. College students. Adult students.
Amount: Varies.
Number of awards: Varies.
Deadline: March 15.
How to apply: Nomination applications are available online.
Exclusive: Visit www.UltimateScholarshipBook.com and enter code NA28620 for updates on this award.

(287) · Mary Paolozzi Member's Scholarship

Navy Wives Clubs of America (NWCA)
P.O. Box 54022, NSA Mid-South, Millington, TN 38053-6022
Phone: 866-511-6922
Email: scholarships@navywivesclubsofamerica.org
http://www.navywivesclubsofamerica.org
Purpose: To aid students who are members of the Navy Wives Clubs of America (NWCA).
Eligibility: Applicants must have been accepted into a college no later than the application due date. Selection is based on academic merit and financial need.
Target applicant(s): High school students. College students. Graduate school students. Adult students.
Amount: Varies.
Number of awards: 1.
Deadline: May 30.
How to apply: Applications are available online. An application form, official transcript and tax form copies are required.
Exclusive: Visit www.UltimateScholarshipBook.com and enter code NA28720 for updates on this award.

(288) • Matinee Voice-over Scholarship

Matinee Multilingual
132-134 Oxford Road, United Kingdom, Reading, RG1 7NL
Phone: 44 (0) 118 958 4934
Email: scholarship@matinee.co.uk
http://www.matinee.co.uk/matinee-voice-over-scholarship/
Purpose: To support students who understand the importance of multilingual employees in today's corporate environment.
Eligibility: Applicants must submit a 250+ word blog on the importance of being able to communicate in multiple languages for today's multinational companies and the benefits it can bring to those businesses that make the effort to localize their website content. Winners are selected based on quality of writing, number of blog views and number of retweets with a blog link. Special consideration is given to applicants majoring in English.
Target applicant(s): High school students. College students. Graduate school students. Adult students.
Amount: $1,000.
Number of awards: 1.
Deadline: January 5.
How to apply: Application information available online. Applications are in the form of a blog.
Exclusive: Visit www.UltimateScholarshipBook.com and enter code MA28820 for updates on this award.

(289) • Medal of Honor AFCEA ROTC Scholarships

Armed Forces Communications and Electronics Association (AFCEA)
4400 Fair Lakes Court, Fairfax, VA 22033
Phone: 703-631-6149
http://www.afcea.org
Purpose: To support students who are members of the ROTC and committed to serving in the United States armed forces.
Eligibility: Applicants must be enrolled in college full-time, and they must be in their sophomore or junior year. Students must have at least a 3.0 GPA.
Target applicant(s): College students. Adult students.
Minimum GPA: 3.0
Amount: $5,000.
Number of awards: 4.
Deadline: February 17.
How to apply: Applications are available online.
Exclusive: Visit www.UltimateScholarshipBook.com and enter code AR28920 for updates on this award.

(290) • Medger Evers Award

National Association of Blacks in Criminal Justice
1801 Fayetteville Street, 106 Whiting Criminal Justice Building, P.O. Box 20011-C, Durham, NC 27707
Phone: 919-683-1801
Email: Office@NABCJ.org
http://www.nabcj.org
Purpose: To reward efforts to ensure that all people, including those in institutions, receive equal justice under the law.
Eligibility: This award honors the slain civil rights leader. Nominator should be a member of NABCJ.
Target applicant(s): College students. Graduate school students. Adult students.
Amount: Varies.
Number of awards: 1.
Deadline: March 15.
How to apply: Nomination applications are available online.
Exclusive: Visit www.UltimateScholarshipBook.com and enter code NA29020 for updates on this award.

(291) • Mediacom World Class Scholarship Program

Mediacom
3737 Westown Parkway, Suite A, West Des Moines, IA 50266
Email: scholarship@mediacomcc.com
http://www.mediacomworldclass.com
Purpose: To aid students in Mediacom service areas.
Eligibility: Applicants must be graduating high school seniors. Those who have earned college credits may apply as long as they have not yet graduated high school. Applicants may not be children of Mediacom employees and must live in areas serviced by Mediacom.
Target applicant(s): High school students.
Amount: $1,000.
Number of awards: Varies.
Deadline: February 15.
How to apply: Applications are available online. An application form, essay, transcript and two reference forms are required.
Exclusive: Visit www.UltimateScholarshipBook.com and enter code ME29120 for updates on this award.

(292) • Memorial Fund Scholarships

U.S. Figure Skating
20 First Street, Colorado Springs, CO 80906
Phone: 719-635-5200
Email: info@usfigureskating.org
http://www.usfsa.org
Purpose: To support students who have a continuing interest in figure skating.
Eligibility: Applicants must be pursuing a college degree, be a current member of U.S. Figure Skating, have competed at the sectional level, be participating in volunteer work in skating if no longer skating and have a 3.0 or higher GPA. Selection is based on financial need, academic success and continuing participation in competitive figure skating or U.S. Figure Skating.
Target applicant(s): High school students. College students. Adult students.
Minimum GPA: 3.0
Amount: Varies.
Number of awards: Varies.
Deadline: Varies.
How to apply: Applications are available online.
Exclusive: Visit www.UltimateScholarshipBook.com and enter code U.29220 for updates on this award.

(293) • Memorial Scholarship Fund

Third Marine Division Association
Patrick J. Conroy, Secretary MSF, 8935 Darrow Road, #227, Twinsburg, OH 44087-0227
Phone: 352-726-2767
Email: scholarship@caltrap.org
http://www.caltrap.com
Purpose: To assist veterans and their families.
Eligibility: Applicants must be the children of Marines (Corpsman or other) who served with the Third Marine Division or in support of the Division at any time and who have been members of the Third Marine Division Association for at least two years. Applicants must be 16-23

and unmarried dependents. Applicants must attend school in the U.S. or Canada. Applicants must have and maintain a minimum 2.5 GPA.
Target applicant(s): High school students. College students.
Minimum GPA: 2.5
Amount: Varies.
Number of awards: Varies.
Scholarship may be renewable.
Deadline: April 18.
How to apply: Applications are available by written request after September 1.
Exclusive: Visit www.UltimateScholarshipBook.com and enter code TH29320 for updates on this award.

(294) • Mensa Education and Research Foundation Scholarship Program

Mensa Education and Research Foundation
1229 Corporate Drive West, Arlington, TX 76006
Phone: 817-607-5577
Email: info@mensafoundation.org
http://www.mensafoundation.org
Purpose: To support students seeking higher education.
Eligibility: Applicants do not need to be members of Mensa but must be residents of a participating American Mensa Local Group's area. They must be enrolled in a degree program at an accredited U.S. college or university in the academic year after application. They must write an essay explaining career, academic or vocational goals.
Target applicant(s): High school students. College students. Adult students.
Amount: Varies.
Number of awards: Varies.
Deadline: January 15.
How to apply: Applications are available online in September. Please do not write to the organization to request an application. An application form and essay are required.
Exclusive: Visit www.UltimateScholarshipBook.com and enter code ME29420 for updates on this award.

(295) • Metro Youth Football Association Scholarship

Metro Youth Football Association
P.O. Box 2171, Cedar Rapids, IA 52406
Phone: 319-393-8696
Email: info@metroyouthfootball.com
http://www.metroyouthfootball.com/scholarship
Purpose: To aid college-bound Metro Youth Tackle Football participants.
Eligibility: Applicants must be graduating high school seniors. They must be current or former Metro Youth Tackle Football (MYTF) participants. They must be current high school football players who have a GPA of 2.5 or higher and have plans to pursue post-secondary education. Selection is based on good citizenship, character and leadership potential.
Target applicant(s): High school students.
Minimum GPA: 2.5
Amount: $2,000.
Number of awards: 2.
Deadline: Varies.
How to apply: Applications are available online. An application form, essay and one recommendation letter are required.
Exclusive: Visit www.UltimateScholarshipBook.com and enter code ME29520 for updates on this award.

(296) • Mike and Gail Donley Spouse Scholarship

Air Force Association
1501 Lee Highway, Arlington, VA 22209
Phone: 800-727-3337
Email: lcross@afa.org
http://www.afa.org
Purpose: To aid U.S. Air Force spouses who wish to pursue undergraduate and graduate degrees.
Eligibility: Applicants must be the spouses of active duty members of the U.S. Air Force, Air National Guard or Air Force Reserve. They must be accepted or enrolled at an accredited college or university and have a GPA of 3.5 or higher. Applicants who are themselves Air Force members or in ROTC are not eligible. Selection is based on the overall strength of the application.
Target applicant(s): High school students. College students. Graduate school students. Adult students.
Minimum GPA: 3.5
Amount: $2,500.
Number of awards: 12.
Deadline: April 30.
How to apply: Applications are available online. An application form, official transcript, personal essay, applicant photo, proof of college acceptance (rising freshmen only) and two letters of recommendation are required.
Exclusive: Visit www.UltimateScholarshipBook.com and enter code AI29620 for updates on this award.

(297) • Military Award Program (MAP)

Imagine America Foundation
12001 Sunrise Valley Drive, Suite 203, Reston, VA 20191
Phone: 571-267-3010
Email: Leed@imagine-america.org
https://www.imagine-america.org/students/scholarships-education/
Purpose: To help those who have served in the military with their education and make the transition from military to civilian life.
Eligibility: Applicants must be enrolling into a participating college and be active duty, reservist, honorably discharged or retired veterans of the U.S. military. They must be likely to enroll in and successfully complete their postsecondary education and may not be a previous recipient of any other Imagine America Foundation scholarships/awards. Applicants must also have financial need.
Target applicant(s): College students. Adult students.
Amount: $1,000.
Number of awards: Varies.
Deadline: Varies.
How to apply: Applications are available online.
Exclusive: Visit www.UltimateScholarshipBook.com and enter code IM29720 for updates on this award.

(298) • Military Family Support Trust Scholarships

Military Family Support Trust
1010 American Eagle Boulevard, Box 301, Sun City Center, FL 33573
Phone: 813-634-4675
Email: president@mfst.us
http://mfst.us/
Purpose: To provide financial assistance to children and grandchildren of military members and others who have served their country.
Eligibility: Applicants must be children or grandchildren of current or former military members, federal employees of GS-7 or higher equivalent

officer grade, foreign services officers (FSO-8 and below) and honorably discharged or retired foreign military officers of Allied Nations living in the U.S. The applicant must be a high school senior who has been recommended by his or her principal and have a minimum score of 21 on the ACT or 1500 on the three-part SAT. The minimum GPA required is 3.0. The award is renewable for four years.
Target applicant(s): High school students.
Minimum GPA: 3.0
Amount: $2,000-$12,000.
Number of awards: 17.
Scholarship may be renewable.
Deadline: February 1.
How to apply: Applications are available online.
Exclusive: Visit www.UltimateScholarshipBook.com and enter code MI29820 for updates on this award.

(299) · MILK United States Student Scholarship

Milk Books
Ironbank, Suite 404, 150 Karangahape Road, Auckland, 1010
Phone: 424-389-3485
Email: scholarships@milkbooks.com
https://www.milkbooks.com/scholarship/united-states/
Purpose: To encourage students to be creative thinkers.
Eligibility: Applicants must be attending an educational college or university within the United States that have partnered with MILK Books. Students must either write or illustrate what creativity means as part of the application process.
Target applicant(s): High school students. College students. Adult students.
Amount: $3,000.
Number of awards: 1.
Deadline: May 31.
How to apply: Applications are available online.
Exclusive: Visit www.UltimateScholarshipBook.com and enter code MI29920 for updates on this award.

(300) · Montgomery GI Bill - Active Duty

North Dakota Department of Veterans Affairs
4201 38th Street South, Suite 104, Fargo, ND 58104-7535
Phone: 701-239-7165
http://www.nd.gov/veterans/benefit-type/education-training
Purpose: To provide educational benefits to veterans.
Eligibility: Applicants must have an Honorable Discharge and high school diploma and meet other service requirements. The bill provides up to 36 months of educational benefits to veterans for college, technical or vocational courses, correspondence courses, apprenticeship/job training or flight training, high-tech training, licensing and certification tests, entrepreneurship training and certain entrance examinations. In most cases the award must be used within 10 years of being discharged.
Target applicant(s): College students. Graduate school students. Adult students.
Amount: Varies.
Number of awards: Varies.
Deadline: None.
How to apply: Applications are available online.
Exclusive: Visit www.UltimateScholarshipBook.com and enter code NO30020 for updates on this award.

(301) · Montgomery GI Bill - Selected Reserve

North Dakota Department of Veterans Affairs
4201 38th Street South, Suite 104, Fargo, ND 58104-7535
Phone: 701-239-7165
http://www.nd.gov/veterans/benefit-type/education-training
Purpose: To support members of the United States military Selected Reserve.
Eligibility: Applicants must have a six-year commitment to the Selected Reserve signed after June 30, 1985. The Selected Reserve includes the Army Reserve, Navy Reserve, Air Force Reserve, Marine Corps Reserve and Coast Guard Reserve and the Army National Guard and the Air National Guard. Applicants must have completed basic military training, meet the requirements to receive a high school diploma or equivalency certificate and may use the funds for degree programs, certificate or correspondence courses, cooperative training, independent study programs, apprenticeship/on-the-job training and vocational flight training programs.
Target applicant(s): High school students. College students. Graduate school students. Adult students.
Amount: Varies.
Number of awards: Varies.
Scholarship may be renewable.
Deadline: Varies.
How to apply: Applications are available online.
Exclusive: Visit www.UltimateScholarshipBook.com and enter code NO30120 for updates on this award.

(302) · Montgomery GI Bill Tuition Assistance Top-Up

North Dakota Department of Veterans Affairs
4201 38th Street South, Suite 104, Fargo, ND 58104-7535
Phone: 701-239-7165
http://www.nd.gov/veterans/benefit-type/education-training
Purpose: To support students who are receiving tuition assistance from the military that doesn't cover the full cost of courses.
Eligibility: Applicants must be eligible for MGIB-Active Duty benefits, and they must have served on active duty in the United States military for at least two years.
Target applicant(s): College students. Graduate school students. Adult students.
Amount: Varies.
Number of awards: Varies.
Scholarship may be renewable.
Deadline: Varies.
How to apply: Applications are available online. Contact your education services officer or education counselor for more information.
Exclusive: Visit www.UltimateScholarshipBook.com and enter code NO30220 for updates on this award.

(303) · Most Valuable Student Scholarships

Elks National Foundation Headquarters
2750 North Lakeview Avenue, Chicago, IL 60614
Phone: 773-755-4732
Email: scholarship@elks.org
https://www.elks.org/scholars/
Purpose: To support high school seniors who have demonstrated scholarship, leadership and financial need.
Eligibility: Applicants must be graduating high school seniors who are U.S. citizens and who plan to pursue a four-year degree on a full-time basis at a U.S. college or university. Male and female students compete separately.

Target applicant(s): High school students.
Amount: $1,000-$12,500.
Number of awards: 500.
Scholarship may be renewable.
Deadline: November 15.
How to apply: Contact the scholarship chairman of your local Lodge or the Elks association of your state.
Exclusive: Visit www.UltimateScholarshipBook.com and enter code EL30320 for updates on this award.

---

(304) · MyProjectorLamps Scholarship

MyProjectorLamps
Suite 250, 1000 Lincoln Road, Miami Beach, FL 33139
http://www.myprojectorlamps.com/scholarships.html
Purpose: To support high school seniors and college students.
Eligibility: Applicants must be at least 16 years old and currently attend an accredited high school or college. Students must also be high school seniors or college undergraduate students with a minimum GPA of 3.0 or higher.
Target applicant(s): High school students. College students. Adult students.
Minimum GPA: 3.0
Amount: $500.
Number of awards: 2.
Deadline: April 15; October 31.
How to apply: Application information is available online. An essay on the provided topic is required.
Exclusive: Visit www.UltimateScholarshipBook.com and enter code MY30420 for updates on this award.

---

(305) · NABF Scholarship Program

National Amateur Baseball Federation
Awards Committee Chairman, P.O. Box 705, Bowie, MD 20718
Phone: 301-464-5460
Email: nabf1914@aol.com
http://www.nabf.com/scholarships
Purpose: To support students who have been involved with the federation.
Eligibility: Applicants must be enrolled in an accredited college or university, must have participated in a federation event and must be sponsored by a member association. Selection is based on grades, financial need and previous awards.
Target applicant(s): High school students. College students. Adult students.
Amount: Varies.
Number of awards: Varies.
Deadline: Varies.
How to apply: Applications are available online.
Exclusive: Visit www.UltimateScholarshipBook.com and enter code NA30520 for updates on this award.

---

(306) · NACOP Scholarship

National Association of Chiefs of Police
NACOP Scholarship Program, 6350 Horizon Drive, Titusville, FL 32780
Phone: 321-264-0911
Email: kimc@aphf.org
http://www.nacoponline.org
Purpose: To recognize law enforcement individuals.
Eligibility: Applicants must be disabled officers wishing to retrain through education or the collegebound children of a disabled officer. Students must maintain a 2.0 GPA and be enrolled in a minimum of six credit hours.
Target applicant(s): High school students. College students. Adult students.
Minimum GPA: 2.0
Amount: $500.
Number of awards: Varies.
Deadline: Varies.
How to apply: Applications are available by written request.
Exclusive: Visit www.UltimateScholarshipBook.com and enter code NA30620 for updates on this award.

---

(307) · Naked Nutrition College Scholarship Program

Naked Nutrition
Phone: 877-432-5068
Email: scholarship@nkdnutrition.com
https://nkdnutrition.com/pages/academic-scholarship
Purpose: To support the next generation of leaders with their educational expenses.
Eligibility: Applicants must show academic excellence, community involvement and personal character and be accepted or enrolled at a college or university.
Target applicant(s): High school students. College students. Adult students.
Amount: Up to $1,500.
Number of awards: 1.
Deadline: August 1.
How to apply: Applications are available online.
Exclusive: Visit www.UltimateScholarshipBook.com and enter code NA30720 for updates on this award.

---

(308) · NATA Scholarship

National Athletic Trainers' Association
National Athletic Trainer's Association Research and Education Foundation Inc., 2952 Stemmons Freeway, Dallas, TX 75247
Phone: 214-637-6282
Email: barbaran@nata.org
http://www.nata.org
Purpose: To encourage study among athletic trainers.
Eligibility: Applicants must be at least a junior in college and scholarships are available for undergraduate, master's and doctoral levels. Students must have a minimum 3.2 GPA and be sponsored by a certified athletic trainer and be a member of the NATA. There is an earlier deadline to start the application online.
Target applicant(s): College students. Graduate school students. Adult students.
Minimum GPA: 3.2
Amount: $2,300.
Number of awards: 50-75.
Deadline: January 13.
How to apply: Applications are available online.
Exclusive: Visit www.UltimateScholarshipBook.com and enter code NA30820 for updates on this award.

---

(309) · National College Match Program

QuestBridge
120 Hawthorne Avenue, Suite 103, Palo Alto, CA 94301
Phone: 888-275-2054

Email: questions@questbridge.org
http://www.questbridge.org
Purpose: To connect outstanding low-income high school seniors with admission and full four-year scholarships to some of the nation's most selective colleges.
Eligibility: Applicants must have demonstrated academic excellence in the face of economic obstacles. Students of all races and ethnicities are encouraged to apply. Many past award recipients have been among the first generation in their families to attend college.
Target applicant(s): High school students.
Amount: Full tuition plus room and board.
Number of awards: Varies.
Scholarship may be renewable.
Deadline: September 27.
How to apply: Applications are available on the QuestBridge website in August of each year. An application form, two teacher recommendations, one counselor recommendation (Secondary School Report), a transcript and SAT and/or ACT score reports are required.
Exclusive: Visit www.UltimateScholarshipBook.com and enter code QU30920 for updates on this award.

(310) • National Intercollegiate Rodeo Foundation Scholarship

National Intercollegiate Rodeo Association
2033 Walla Walla Avenue, Walla Walla, WA 99362
Phone: 509-529-4402
Email: rodeo@collegerodeo.com
http://www.collegerodeo.com/
Purpose: To support student members of NIRA.
Eligibility: Applicants must be current college students, have at least a 3.0 GPA and be state financial assistance qualified or show evidence of financial need. Selection is based on academic achievement, financial need and the essay.
Target applicant(s): College students. Adult students.
Minimum GPA: 3.0
Amount: $1,500.
Number of awards: 1.
Deadline: May 22.
How to apply: Applications are available online and must be submitted with an official transcript, financial verification and at least one but no more than three letters of recommendation and an essay.
Exclusive: Visit www.UltimateScholarshipBook.com and enter code NA31020 for updates on this award.

(311) • National Marbles Tournament Scholarship

National Marbles Tournament
Matt Corley, 10908 Bornedale Drive, Hyattsville, MD 20783
Phone: 301-801-0795
Email: matt.corley@nationalmarblestournament.org
https://www.nationalmarblestournament.org/
Purpose: To assist "mibsters," or marble shooters.
Eligibility: Applicants must win first place in a local marble tournament and then compete in the National Marbles Tournament held each summer in New Jersey. Students must be between 7 and 14 years old.
Target applicant(s): Junior high students or younger. High school students.
Amount: Varies.
Number of awards: Varies.
Deadline: Varies.
How to apply: Information on the tournament is available online.
Exclusive: Visit www.UltimateScholarshipBook.com and enter code NA31120 for updates on this award.

(312) • National Merit Scholarship Program and National Achievement Scholarship Program

National Merit Scholarship Corporation
1560 Sherman Avenue, Suite 200, Evanston, IL 60201-4897
Phone: 847-866-5100
http://www.nationalmerit.org
Purpose: To provide scholarships through a merit-based academic competition.
Eligibility: Applicants must be enrolled full-time in high school, progressing normally toward completion and planning to enter college no later than the fall following completion of high school, be U.S. citizens or permanent legal residents in the process of becoming U.S. citizens and take the PSAT/NMSQT no later than the 11th grade. Participation in the program is based on performance on the exam.
Target applicant(s): High school students.
Amount: $2,500.
Number of awards: Varies.
Scholarship may be renewable.
Deadline: October PSAT test date.
How to apply: Application is made by taking the PSAT/NMSQT test.
Exclusive: Visit www.UltimateScholarshipBook.com and enter code NA31220 for updates on this award.

(313) • National Oratorical Contest

American Legion
Attn.: Americanism and Children and Youth Division, P.O. Box 1055, Indianapolis, IN 46206
Phone: 317-630-1249
Email: acy@legion.org
http://www.legion.org
Purpose: To reward students for their knowledge of government and oral presentation skills.
Eligibility: Applicants must be high school students under the age of 20 who are U.S. citizens or legal residents. Students first give an oration within their state and winners compete at the national level. The oration must be related to the Constitution of the United States focusing on the duties and obligations citizens have to the government. It must be in English and be between eight and ten minutes. There is also an assigned topic which is posted on the website, and it should be between three and five minutes.
Target applicant(s): High school students.
Amount: $1,500-$18,000.
Number of awards: Varies.
Deadline: Local American Legion department must select winners by March 18.
How to apply: Applications are available from your local American Legion post or state headquarters. Deadlines for local competitions are set by the local Posts.
Exclusive: Visit www.UltimateScholarshipBook.com and enter code AM31320 for updates on this award.

(314) • National Scholarship Program

National Scholastic Surfing Association
P.O. Box 495, Huntington Beach, CA 92648
Phone: 714-906-7423
Email: jaragon@nssa.org
http://www.nssa.org

Purpose: To assist NSSA members in their pursuit of post-high school education.
Eligibility: Applicants must be competitive student NSSA members and have a minimum 3.0 GPA in the current school year. Scholastic achievement, leadership, service, career goals and recommendations are considered.
Target applicant(s): High school students. College students. Adult students.
Minimum GPA: 3.0
Amount: Varies.
Number of awards: Varies.
Deadline: Varies.
How to apply: Applications are available with organization membership.
Exclusive: Visit www.UltimateScholarshipBook.com and enter code NA31420 for updates on this award.

(315) • National Sportsmanship Award

Interscholastic Equestrian Association
467 Main Street, Melrose, MA 02176
Phone: 877-743-3432
Email: info@rideiea.org
http://www.rideiea.org/opportunities/for-riders.html
Purpose: To help riders pursue a college education.
Eligibility: Students must earn a Sportsmanship Award at a local, regional or zone IEA competition during the school year and maintain a 3.0 GPA. Selection is based on academic achievement, extracurricular involvement, equestrian participation and characteristics that portray good sportsmanship and a role model.
Target applicant(s): Junior high students or younger. High school students.
Minimum GPA: 3.0
Amount: $500-$1,000.
Number of awards: 8.
Deadline: Varies.
How to apply: Riders who have earned a Sportsmanship Award at a lower level will be given an application for the national award. The application includes a 250-word essay, personal resume, copy of official transcript and three letters of recommendation.
Exclusive: Visit www.UltimateScholarshipBook.com and enter code IN31520 for updates on this award.

(316) • National Table Tennis Scholarship

National College Table Tennis Association
154 Mill Run Lane, Saint Peters, MO 63376-7106
Phone: 800-581-6770
Email: info@nctta.org
http://www.nctta.org/
Purpose: To support table tennis athletes by providing financial support for their higher education expenses.
Eligibility: Applicants must be attending or plan on attending an active NCTTA school and plan on being active on the collegiate team. Students must be full time and have at least a 2.0 GPA. Selection is based on table tennis skill, academic achievement, financial need and a personal essay. The essay should explain your involvement and contributions to the sport of table tennis.
Target applicant(s): High school students. College students. Adult students.
Minimum GPA: 2.0
Amount: $1,000.
Number of awards: Varies.
Deadline: May 15.
How to apply: Applications are available online and must include an official transcript.
Exclusive: Visit www.UltimateScholarshipBook.com and enter code NA31620 for updates on this award.

(317) • National Veterans Stipend

Institute of Scrap Recycling Industries
1615 L Street, Suite 600, Washington, DC 20036
Phone: 202-662-8500
http://www.isri.org/about-isri/recycling-research-foundation
Purpose: To support veterans who are seeking higher education.
Eligibility: Applicants must be U.S. citizens, a veteran of the military and pursuing an undergraduate degree. The foundation understands that not all expenses may be covered through existing government and scholarship aid, and thus will pay a stipend of up to $8,000 ($2,000 per year, renewable for up to four years). A minimum 2.5 GPA is required.
Target applicant(s): High school students. College students. Adult students.
Minimum GPA: 2.5
Amount: $2,000.
Number of awards: 1.
Scholarship may be renewable.
Deadline: June 30.
How to apply: Applications are available online
Exclusive: Visit www.UltimateScholarshipBook.com and enter code IN31720 for updates on this award.

(318) • Naval Enlisted Reserve Association Scholarships

Naval Enlisted Reserve Association
6703 Farragut Avenue, Falls Church, VA 22042-2189
Phone: 800-776-9020
Email: members@nera.org
http://www.nera.org
Purpose: To recognize the service and sacrifices made by Navy, Marine and Coast Guard members, retirees and their families.
Eligibility: Applicants must be members of the Naval Enlisted Reserve Association in good standing or their spouses, children or grandchildren. Children and grandchildren of members must be single and under 23 years of age on the application deadline. Applicants must be graduating high school seniors or students who are already pursuing an undergraduate degree.
Target applicant(s): High school students. College students. Adult students.
Amount: $2,500-$3,000.
Number of awards: 6.
Deadline: June 16.
How to apply: Applications are available online.
Exclusive: Visit www.UltimateScholarshipBook.com and enter code NA31820 for updates on this award.

(319) • Naval Helicopter Association Scholarship

Naval Helicopter Association
P.O. Box 180578, Coronado, CA 92178-0578
Phone: 619-435-7139
Email: nhascholars@hotmail.com
http://www.nhascholarshipfund.org
Purpose: To assist those who wish to pursue educational goals.

Eligibility: Applicants must be members of or dependents of members of the association or have an affiliation with naval aviation. Students may pursue undergraduate degrees in any field.
Target applicant(s): High school students. College students. Graduate school students. Adult students.
Amount: $2,000-$3,000.
Number of awards: Varies.
Deadline: January 31.
How to apply: Applications are available by mail.
Exclusive: Visit www.UltimateScholarshipBook.com and enter code NA31920 for updates on this award.

(320) · Naval Intelligence Essay Contest

United States Naval Institute (USNI)
291 Wood Road, Annapolis, MD 21402
Phone: 410-268-6110
https://www.usni.org/essay-contests
Purpose: To promote sea services.
Eligibility: Applicants must be active duty military, reservists, veterans, government civilian personnel or civilians. Students must write an essay discussing the history of Naval Intelligence and how lessons from the past can be applied to today.
Target applicant(s): College students. Adult students.
Amount: $5,000.
Number of awards: 3.
Deadline: July 31.
How to apply: Applications are available online.
Exclusive: Visit www.UltimateScholarshipBook.com and enter code UN32020 for updates on this award.

(321) · Navin Narayan College Scholarship

American Red Cross Youth
2025 E Street NW, Washington, DC 20006
Phone: 202-303-4498
Email: syyin.nyc@gmail.com
http://www.redcrossyouth.org
Purpose: The scholarship is named after Navin Narayan, a former youth volunteer with the Red Cross who died from cancer at the age of 23. In his honor, the Red Cross awards this scholarship to youth volunteers who have made significant humanitarian contributions to the organization and who have also achieved academic excellence in high school.
Eligibility: Applicants must plan to attend a four-year college or university and have volunteered a minimum of two years with the Red Cross.
Target applicant(s): High school students.
Amount: $1,000.
Number of awards: 1.
Deadline: April 1.
How to apply: Application forms are available online.
Exclusive: Visit www.UltimateScholarshipBook.com and enter code AM32120 for updates on this award.

(322) · Navy College Fund

U.S. Navy Personnel
5720 Integrity Drive, Millington, TN 38055
Phone: 866-827-5672
Email: bupers_webmaster@navy.mil
http://www.public.navy.mil/bupers-npc/
Purpose: To encourage entry into the Navy for recruits who have skills and specialties for which there is a critical shortage.
Eligibility: Applicants must be Navy recruits who are qualified for training in selected Navy ratings as non-prior service enlistees and agree to serve on active duty for at least three years. They must have graduated from high school, be 17 to 35 years old, agree to a $1,200 pay reduction and receive an "Honorable" Character of Service.
Target applicant(s): High school students. College students. Adult students.
Amount: Varies.
Number of awards: Varies.
Scholarship may be renewable.
Deadline: Varies.
How to apply: Applications are available from Navy recruiters.
Exclusive: Visit www.UltimateScholarshipBook.com and enter code U.32220 for updates on this award.

(323) · Navy Supply Corps Foundation Scholarship

Navy Supply Corps Foundation Inc.
3651 Mars Hill Road, Suite 200B, Watkinsville, GA 30677
Phone: 706-354-4111
Email: foundation@usnscf.com
http://www.usnscf.com
Purpose: To provide financial aid for undergraduate studies to family members of Supply Corp members and enlisted Navy personnel.
Eligibility: Applicants must be family members of a Navy Supply Corps officer or an enlisted member, active duty, reservist or retired. Awards are based on character, leadership, academic performance and financial need.
Target applicant(s): Junior high students or younger. High school students. College students. Adult students.
Amount: Varies.
Number of awards: Varies.
Deadline: March 13.
How to apply: Applications are available online.
Exclusive: Visit www.UltimateScholarshipBook.com and enter code NA32320 for updates on this award.

(324) · Navy-Marine Corps ROTC College Program

U.S. Navy Naval Reserve Officers Training Corps (NROTC)
Naval Service Training Command Officer Development, NAS Pensacola, 250 Dallas Street, Pensacola, FL 32508-5220
Phone: 800-628-7682
Email: pnsc_nrotc_cgo@navy.mil
http://www.nrotc.navy.mil/scholarships.html
Purpose: To provide education opportunities for NROTC students.
Eligibility: Applicants must be accepted to or attending a college with an NROTC program. They must complete naval science and other specified university courses and attend a summer training session. Scholarships are available for two or four years, depending on time of application.
Target applicant(s): College students. Adult students.
Amount: Up to full tuition plus stipend and allowance.
Number of awards: Varies.
Scholarship may be renewable.
Deadline: End of January.
How to apply: Applications are available online.
Exclusive: Visit www.UltimateScholarshipBook.com and enter code U.32420 for updates on this award.

(325) · Navy-Marine Corps ROTC Four-Year Scholarships

U.S. Navy Naval Reserve Officers Training Corps (NROTC)

Naval Service Training Command Officer Development, NAS Pensacola, 250 Dallas Street, Pensacola, FL 32508-5220
Phone: 800-628-7682
Email: pnsc_nrotc_cgo@navy.mil
http://www.nrotc.navy.mil/scholarships.html
Purpose: To provide education opportunities for ROTC members.
Eligibility: Applicants must plan to attend an eligible college or university. They must commit to eight years of military service, four of which must be on active duty. The scholarship pays full tuition and fees plus a stipend for textbooks.
Target applicant(s): High school students.
Amount: Tuition plus stipend.
Number of awards: Varies.
Scholarship may be renewable.
Deadline: May 31.
How to apply: Applications are available online.
Exclusive: Visit www.UltimateScholarshipBook.com and enter code U.32520 for updates on this award.

---

(326) • Navy-Marine Corps ROTC Two-Year Scholarships

U.S. Navy Naval Reserve Officers Training Corps (NROTC)
Naval Service Training Command Officer Development, NAS Pensacola, 250 Dallas Street, Pensacola, FL 32508-5220
Phone: 800-628-7682
Email: pnsc_nrotc_cgo@navy.mil
http://www.nrotc.navy.mil/scholarships.html
Purpose: To provide education opportunities for NROTC students.
Eligibility: Applicants must be attending a college with an NROTC program as a freshman or sophomore. They must complete naval science and other specified university courses and attend a summer training session. They must also attend a Naval Science Institute program during the summer between their sophomore and junior year.
Target applicant(s): College students. Adult students.
Amount: Varies.
Number of awards: Varies.
Scholarship may be renewable.
Deadline: May 31.
How to apply: Applications are available online.
Exclusive: Visit www.UltimateScholarshipBook.com and enter code U.32620 for updates on this award.

---

(327) • Navy/Marine Corps/Coast Guard (NMCCG) Enlisted Dependent Spouse Scholarship

Navy Wives Clubs of America (NWCA)
P.O. Box 54022, NSA Mid-South, Millington, TN 38053-6022
Phone: 866-511-6922
Email: scholarships@navywivesclubsofamerica.org
http://www.navywivesclubsofamerica.org
Purpose: To provide financial assistance to spouses of certain military members.
Eligibility: Applicants must be spouses of enlisted Navy, Marine Corps or Coast Guard personnel. They must be accepted to an institution of higher learning by May 30 of the year of application.
Target applicant(s): High school students. College students. Graduate school students. Adult students.
Amount: Varies.
Number of awards: 2.
Deadline: May 30.
How to apply: Applications are available online. Financial information and a transcript are required.
Exclusive: Visit www.UltimateScholarshipBook.com and enter code NA32720 for updates on this award.

---

(328) • NCAA Division I Degree Completion Award Program

National Collegiate Athletic Association
700 W. Washington Street, P.O. Box 6222, Indianapolis, IN 46206
Phone: 317-917-6222
Email: lthomas@ncaa.org
http://www.ncaa.org/about/resources/ncaa-scholarships-and-grants
Purpose: To aid athletes who have exhausted their student aid.
Eligibility: Applicants must have competed at a NCAA Division I institution and received athletics-related aid. They must be within 30 semester hours or 45 quarter hours of completing their degrees. Funds are awarded to 40 to 45 percent of applicants. Recipients are chosen by consultants from seven Division I member institutions.
Target applicant(s): College students. Adult students.
Amount: Full tuition and fees.
Number of awards: Varies.
Deadline: May 19.
How to apply: Applications are available online. An application form, copy of tax forms, transcript, personal statement, list of extracurricular activities and leadership roles and statement from the director of athletics is required.
Exclusive: Visit www.UltimateScholarshipBook.com and enter code NA32820 for updates on this award.

---

(329) • NCAA Division II Degree Completion Award Program

National Collegiate Athletic Association
700 W. Washington Street, P.O. Box 6222, Indianapolis, IN 46206
Phone: 317-917-6222
Email: lthomas@ncaa.org
http://www.ncaa.org/about/resources/ncaa-scholarships-and-grants
Purpose: To assist student-athletes who are no longer eligible for athletics-based aid.
Eligibility: Applicants must have exhausted athletics eligibility at an NCAA Division II school within the past calendar year. They must be within their first 10 semesters or 15 quarters of full-time attendance and must have received athletics-related aid from the institution. Applicants must be within 32 semester or 48 quarter hours of earning their first undergraduate degree and have a GPA of 2.5 or higher.
Target applicant(s): High school students. College students. Adult students.
Minimum GPA: 2.5
Amount: Varies.
Number of awards: Varies.
Deadline: March 30.
How to apply: Applications are available online. An application form, personal statement, financial aid information, endorsement from director of athletics, senior woman administrator or coach and transcript are required.
Exclusive: Visit www.UltimateScholarshipBook.com and enter code NA32920 for updates on this award.

---

(330) • NCAA Postgraduate Scholarship

National Collegiate Athletic Association
700 W. Washington Street, P.O. Box 6222, Indianapolis, IN 46206

Phone: 317-917-6222
Email: lthomas@ncaa.org
http://www.ncaa.org/about/resources/ncaa-scholarships-and-grants
Purpose: To reward student athletes who perform well in both sports and academics.
Eligibility: Student athletes must show achievement in their last year of varsity-level intercollegiate athletics at an NCAA school. Applicants must be nominated by the faculty athletic representative or athletic director and be enrolling as a full- or part-time graduate student. Students must also have a minimum 3.2 GPA.
Target applicant(s): College students. Adult students.
Minimum GPA: 3.2
Amount: $7,500.
Number of awards: Up to 174.
Deadline: January 27 (fall), March 31 (winter), June 9 (spring).
How to apply: Applications are available online.
Exclusive: Visit www.UltimateScholarshipBook.com and enter code NA33020 for updates on this award.

(331) • Newman Civic Fellow Awards

Campus Compact
45 Temple Place, Boston, MA 02111
Phone: 617-357-1881
Email: campus@compact.org
http://www.compact.org
Purpose: To provide scholarships and opportunities for civic mentoring to students with financial need.
Eligibility: Emphasis is on students who have demonstrated leadership abilities and significant interest in civic responsibility. Students must attend one of the 1,000 Campus Compact member institutions and be nominated by the Campus Compact member president. Applicants must be sophomores or juniors at four-year colleges or must attend a two-year college.
Target applicant(s): College students. Graduate school students. Adult students.
Amount: Varies.
Number of awards: Varies.
Deadline: February.
How to apply: Nominations must be made by the Campus Compact member president.
Exclusive: Visit www.UltimateScholarshipBook.com and enter code CA33120 for updates on this award.

(332) • Nicholas A. Pennipede Memorial Scholarship

Eye Associates
10120 West 119th Street, Overland Park, KS 66213
http://www.seetheclarity.com/about/scholarship/
Purpose: To support students with a dedication to serving their community.
Eligibility: Applicants must be accepted to a college or university as an undergraduate freshman or have been accepted to an optometry school and are enrolling as an optometry freshman. Students must write an essay discussing how they will use their education to serve a community and provide proof of enrollment along with the application materials.
Target applicant(s): High school students. College students. Adult students.
Amount: $1,000.
Number of awards: 1.
Deadline: September 15.
How to apply: Applications are available online.
Exclusive: Visit www.UltimateScholarshipBook.com and enter code EY33220 for updates on this award.

(333) • Nicholas Virgilio Haiku and Senryu Contest

Haiku Society of America
NVHA Haiku Contest, c/o George Vallianos, 16 Sandringham Terrace, Cherry Hill, NJ 08003
http://www.hsa-haiku.org/hsa-contests.htm
Purpose: To reward students for excellent haiku poetry.
Eligibility: Applicants must be in grades 7 through 12. Students must submit up to three original, previously unpublished haiku. Selection is based on the overall strength of the submission.
Target applicant(s): Junior high students or younger. High school students.
Amount: $50.
Number of awards: 6.
Deadline: March 25.
How to apply: Applications are available online.
Exclusive: Visit www.UltimateScholarshipBook.com and enter code HA33320 for updates on this award.

(334) • Non-Commissioned Officers Association Scholarships

Non-Commissioned Officers Association
9330 Corporate Drive, Suite 701, Selma, TX 78154
Phone: 800-662-2620
Email: membsvc@ncoausa.org
http://www.ncoausa.org
Purpose: The scholarships are given to help the children and spouses of members of the Non-Commissioned Officers Association.
Eligibility: Students must be children or spouses of members of the Non-Commissioned Officers Association. Children must be under 25 to receive the scholarship.
Target applicant(s): High school students. College students. Adult students.
Amount: Varies.
Number of awards: Varies.
Scholarship may be renewable.
Deadline: March 31.
How to apply: Applications are available online.
Exclusive: Visit www.UltimateScholarshipBook.com and enter code NO33420 for updates on this award.

(335) • Noodle Pros GRE Scholarship

StudySoup
1381 9th Avenue, San Francisco, CA 94122
Phone: 415-658-9115
https://studysoup.com/scholarships/
Purpose: To offset the expense of pursuing graduate education.
Eligibility: Applicants must be current college sophomores or above with a GPA of at least 3.0. Students must be members of a pre-professional organization.
Target applicant(s): College students. Adult students.
Minimum GPA: 3.0
Amount: $500.
Number of awards: 1.
Deadline: October 1.
How to apply: Applications are available online.

Exclusive: Visit www.UltimateScholarshipBook.com and enter code ST33520 for updates on this award.

(336) • NROTC Nurse Corps Scholarship

U.S. Navy Naval Reserve Officers Training Corps (NROTC)
Naval Service Training Command Officer Development, NAS Pensacola, 250 Dallas Street, Pensacola, FL 32508-5220
Phone: 800-628-7682
Email: pnsc_nrotc_cgo@navy.mil
http://www.nrotc.navy.mil/scholarships.html

Purpose: To aid students who are planning to pursue nursing degrees at an NROTC college or university.

Eligibility: Applicants must be in the second semester of their junior year of high school. They must plan to attend an NROTC college or university that offers the bachelor's degree in nursing. They must be in the top 10 percent of their class or have a combined critical reading and math SAT score of 1080 or higher or have a combined English and math ACT score of 43 or higher. Selection is based on the overall strength of the application.

Target applicant(s): High school students.

Amount: Varies.

Number of awards: Varies.

Scholarship may be renewable.

Deadline: May 31.

How to apply: Applications are available online. An application form, official transcript, standardized test scores and three references are required.

Exclusive: Visit www.UltimateScholarshipBook.com and enter code U.33620 for updates on this award.

(337) • NROTC Scholarship Program

Naval Service Training Command Officer Development
NAS Pensacola, 250 Dallas Street, Pensacola, FL 32508-5220
Phone: 800-NAV-ROTC
Email: pnsc_nrotc_cgo@navy.mil
http://www.nrotc.navy.mil

Purpose: To prepare young men and women for leadership roles in the Navy and Marine Corps.

Eligibility: Applicants must be U.S. citizens who are at least 17 years old as of September 1 of their first year of college, no older than 23 on June 30 of that first year and must be younger than 27 at the time of anticipated graduation. Students must attend an NROTC college and have no moral or personal convictions against military service. Those interested in the Navy program, including Nurse-option, must have an SAT critical reading score of 530 and a math score of 520 or an ACT score of 22 in English and 22 in math. For the Marine Corps option, students must have an SAT composite score of 1000 or an ACT composite score of 22. Applicants must also meet all Navy or Marine Corps physical standards.

Target applicant(s): High school students. College students.

Amount: Full tuition and fees, books, uniforms and monthly stipend.

Number of awards: Varies.

Scholarship may be renewable.

Deadline: January 31.

How to apply: Applications are available online. Contact information for regional offices is available online.

Exclusive: Visit www.UltimateScholarshipBook.com and enter code NA33720 for updates on this award.

(338) • NSCA Scholarship

National Sporting Clays Association
5931 Roft Road, San Antonio, TX 78253
Phone: 800-877-5338
http://www.nssa-nsca.org

Purpose: To aid high school senior sporting clay participants to reach their career goals by helping to fund their college expenses.

Eligibility: Applicants must be a high school senior, have at least a 2.5 GPA, be an NSCA participant and plan to attend a four-year degree program in college. Selection is based on scholarship, citizenship and NSCA participation.

Target applicant(s): High school students.

Minimum GPA: 2.5

Amount: $5,000.

Number of awards: 1.

Scholarship may be renewable.

Deadline: April 30.

How to apply: Applications are available online and must include an essay, one letter of recommendation, a transcript and a copy of shooting history and accomplishments.

Exclusive: Visit www.UltimateScholarshipBook.com and enter code NA33820 for updates on this award.

(339) • NSCC Scholarship Funds

Naval Sea Cadet Corps
2300 Wilson Boulevard, Suite 200, Arlington, VA 22201-3308
Phone: 800-356-5760
Email: scholarships@navyleague.org
http://www.seacadets.org

Purpose: To provide financial assistance for Sea Cadets.

Eligibility: Applicants must have been Sea Cadets for at least two years and be members at the time of application. They must have attained the rate of NSCC E-3 or higher and be recommended by their commanding officers, NSCC Committee Chairmen and principals or counselors. They must have a B+ or higher GPA and present evidence of acceptance to an accredited institution of higher learning. SAT or ACT scores and class rank are considered.

Target applicant(s): High school students.

Minimum GPA: 3.3

Amount: $1,000-$5,000.

Number of awards: 15.

Deadline: May 1.

How to apply: Applications are available online.

Exclusive: Visit www.UltimateScholarshipBook.com and enter code NA33920 for updates on this award.

(340) • NWTF Academic Scholarship Program

National Wild Turkey Federation (NWTF)
770 Augusta Road, Edgefield, SC 29824-0530
Phone: 800-843-6983
Email: scholarshipinfo@nwtf.net
http://www.nwtf.org

Purpose: To support those students committed to conservation and preserving our hunting heritage.

Eligibility: Applicants must be a senior, have a 3.0 or higher GPA, plan to attend a institution of higher education after high school, be a member of National Wild Turkey Federation and actively participate in hunting sports. Selection is based on scholastic achievement, leadership abilities, community service and commitment to conservation.

Target applicant(s): High school students.

Minimum GPA: 3.0
Amount: $250-$10,000.
Number of awards: Varies.
Deadline: January 1.
How to apply: Applications are available online and require a personal essay and three letters of reference.
Exclusive: Visit www.UltimateScholarshipBook.com and enter code NA34020 for updates on this award.

(341) • Odenza Marketing Group Scholarship

Odenza Vacations
4664 Lougheed Highway, Suite 230, Burnaby, BC V5C5T5
Phone: 877-297-2661
http://www.odenzascholarships.com
Purpose: To aid current and future college students who are between the ages of 16 and 25.
Eligibility: Applicants must be U.S. or Canadian citizens who have at least one full year of college study remaining. They must have a GPA of 2.5 or higher. Selection is based on the overall strength of the essays submitted.
Target applicant(s): High school students. College students. Graduate school students.
Minimum GPA: 2.5
Amount: $500.
Number of awards: Varies.
Deadline: March 30, September 30.
How to apply: Applications are available online. An application form and two essays are required.
Exclusive: Visit www.UltimateScholarshipBook.com and enter code OD34120 for updates on this award.

(342) • Odenza Marketing Group Volunteer Award

Odenza Vacations
4664 Lougheed Highway, Suite 230, Burnaby, BC V5C5T5
Phone: 877-297-2661
http://www.odenzascholarships.com
Purpose: To support graduating seniors and undergraduate students in pursuing post-secondary education.
Eligibility: Applicants must submit two essays regarding topics of their choice. Students must be citizens of the U.S. or Canada who will be enrolled at a post-secondary education by the fall of the year in which the award is granted. Applicants already enrolled in college must have one full year of studies remaining. A minimum GPA of 2.5 is required. Selection is based on the overall strength of the essays.
Target applicant(s): High school students. College students.
Minimum GPA: 2.5
Amount: $500.
Number of awards: 1.
Deadline: September 30.
How to apply: Applications are available online.
Exclusive: Visit www.UltimateScholarshipBook.com and enter code OD34220 for updates on this award.

(343) • ODS Youth Interscholastic Merit Scholarship

Oregon Dressage Society
P.O. Box 959, Hillsboro, OR 97123-0959
Phone: 503-681-2337
Email: J-G.McCabe@Juno.com
http://www.oregondressage.com
Purpose: To aid well-rounded Oregon Dressage Society high school youth members as they begin attending the college of their choice.
Eligibility: Applicants must be current ODS High School Dressage team members, have been members for at least two years and have been accepted to a college or university. Selection is based on experience as a leader and role model, community service, academic achievements, a personal essay and the letters of reference.
Target applicant(s): High school students.
Amount: Varies.
Number of awards: Varies.
Deadline: April 1.
How to apply: Application is available online. Application requirements include an application form, a personal essay, a high school transcript and at least two letters of reference.
Exclusive: Visit www.UltimateScholarshipBook.com and enter code OR34320 for updates on this award.

(344) • Off to College High School Scholarship

Abodo
551 West Main Street, Madison, WI 53703
https://www.abodo.com/blog/high-school-scholarship/
Purpose: To support students headed to college for the first time.
Eligibility: Applicants must be graduating high school seniors at least 18 years of age who will attend an accredited college or university for the upcoming fall semester. An essay must be written as part of the application process.
Target applicant(s): High school students.
Amount: $500.
Number of awards: 1.
Deadline: August 31.
How to apply: Applications are available online.
Exclusive: Visit www.UltimateScholarshipBook.com and enter code AB34420 for updates on this award.

(345) • Off to College Scholarship Sweepstakes

SunTrust
P.O. Box 27172, Richmond, VA 23261-7172
Phone: 800-786-8787
https://offtocollegesweepstakes.suntrust.com
Purpose: To assist a student for the first year of expenses at any accredited college.
Eligibility: Applicants must be high school seniors who are at least 13 years old and plan to attend a college accredited by the U.S. Department of Education the following fall. U.S. residency is required. Financial need and academic achievement are not considered. Note that this is a sweepstakes drawing every two weeks from October until mid-May.
Target applicant(s): High school students.
Amount: Varies.
Number of awards: Varies.
Deadline: May 14.
How to apply: Applications are available online. Mail-in entries are also accepted. Contact information is required.
Exclusive: Visit www.UltimateScholarshipBook.com and enter code SU34520 for updates on this award.

(346) • Open Listings "Take Big Risks" Scholarship

Open Listings
2000 Hyperion Avenue
Los Angeles, CA 90027
Phone: 800-501-2077

Email: support@openlistings.com
https://www.openlistings.com/blog/scholarship/
Purpose: To support students who post a video about taking risks.
Eligibility: Applicants must be outstanding students who exemplify the Open Listings core value to take big risks they believe in. Students must be residents of the United States who are at least 18 years of age and must submit a video as part of their application. Applicants must currently be either a graduating high school senior or a current student at an accredited college or university.
Target applicant(s): High school students. College students. Adult students.
Amount: $1,500.
Number of awards: 1.
Deadline: January 31, July 31.
How to apply: Applications are available online.
Exclusive: Visit www.UltimateScholarshipBook.com and enter code OP34620 for updates on this award.

(347) • OpenWater Student Scholarship

OpenWater
4401 Fairfax Drive, Suite 200, Arlington, VA 22203
https://www.getopenwater.com/scholarship/
Purpose: To encourage the next generation of entrepreneurs.
Eligibility: Applicants must be permanent residents of the U.S. and enrolling or currently enrolled as a full-time student seeking a bachelor's degree with a minimum grade point average of 3.3. Students must have a minimum ACT score of 24 or SAT score of 1680 and demonstrate leadership and good citizenship.
Target applicant(s): High school students. College students. Adult students.
Minimum GPA: 3.3
Amount: $1,500.
Number of awards: 1.
Deadline: December 31.
How to apply: Applications are available online.
Exclusive: Visit www.UltimateScholarshipBook.com and enter code OP34720 for updates on this award.

(348) • Out-of-the-Box Thinking Scholarship

Litter-Robot
2900 Auburn Court, Auburn Hills, MI 48326
Phone: 877-250-7729
Email: marketing@litter-robot.com
https://www.litter-robot.com/scholarship
Purpose: To encourage students who have a passion for pets and creating innovative ideas for pet care.
Eligibility: Applicants must be a current high school, undergraduate or graduate student in the U.S. An essay, pitch or summary about a pet innovation idea and how it was conceptualized is required.
Target applicant(s): High school students. College students. Graduate school students. Adult students.
Amount: $250-$1,250.
Number of awards: 3.
Deadline: July 31.
How to apply: Applications are available online.
Exclusive: Visit www.UltimateScholarshipBook.com and enter code LI34820 for updates on this award.

(349) • Outdoorsy

Outdoorsy
1475 Folsom Street, 3rd Floor, San Francisco, CA 94705
Phone: 415-930-4841
https://www.outdoorsy.com/#scholarship
Purpose: To support students who have taken trips.
Eligibility: Applicants must be at least 18 years old and plan to attend an accredited college or university at the undergraduate or graduate level in the next academic year. Students must write an essay on one of the topics provided. Selection is based on "authentic content, unique insights, writing quality, style, creativity, accuracy and adherence to the written requirements."
Target applicant(s): High school students. College students. Graduate school students. Adult students.
Amount: $1,000.
Number of awards: 4.
Deadline: February 28 and August 31.
How to apply: Applications are available online.
Exclusive: Visit www.UltimateScholarshipBook.com and enter code OU34920 for updates on this award.

(350) • OZY Genius Awards

OZY Media
33 Irving Place, New York, NY 10003
Email: genius@ozy.com
http://www.ozygenius.com
Purpose: To encourage students who have a dream of accomplishing a major project.
Eligibility: Applicants must a current undergraduate level student at an accredited college or university in the United States. Students must be at least 18 years of age. Applicants should have a major project (book to write, start-up to launch, film, medical research, political goal) that they wish to accomplish and must submit a short video or image depicting the project in addition to the application.
Target applicant(s): College students. Adult students.
Amount: $10,000.
Number of awards: 10.
Deadline: December 31.
How to apply: Applications are available online.
Exclusive: Visit www.UltimateScholarshipBook.com and enter code OZ35020 for updates on this award.

(351) • Paul and Daisy Soros Fellowships for New Americans

Paul and Daisy Soros
224 W. 57th Street, New York, NY 10019
Phone: 212-547-6926
Email: pdsoros_fellows@sorosny.org
http://www.pdsoros.org
Purpose: Named after Hungarian immigrants, the Paul and Daisy Soros Fellowships are designed to assist the graduate studies of immigrant children.
Eligibility: Applicants must be immigrants who are resident aliens, have been naturalized or are the children of two parents who have been naturalized. The potential winner of a fellowship must already have a bachelor's degree or be a college senior and must not be over the age of 30 by the application deadline.
Target applicant(s): College students. Graduate school students. Adult students.
Amount: Up to $90,000 over 2 years.

Number of awards: 30.
Scholarship may be renewable.
Deadline: November 1.
How to apply: Applications are available online and should be submitted online.
Exclusive: Visit www.UltimateScholarshipBook.com and enter code PA35120 for updates on this award.

(352) • Pauline Langkamp Memorial Scholarship

Navy Wives Clubs of America (NWCA)
P.O. Box 54022, NSA Mid-South, Millington, TN 38053-6022
Phone: 866-511-6922
Email: scholarships@navywivesclubsofamerica.org
http://www.navywivesclubsofamerica.org
Purpose: To aid college students who are the adult children of members of the Navy Wives Clubs of America (NWCA).
Eligibility: Applicants must be the child of an NWCA member. They must not be carrying a military ID card and must be enrolled or planning to enroll at an accredited postsecondary institution. High school seniors must have been accepted into a college or university no later than the application due date. Selection is based on academic merit and financial need.
Target applicant(s): High school students. College students. Adult students.
Amount: Varies.
Number of awards: 1.
Deadline: May 30.
How to apply: Applications are available online. An application form and an official transcript are required.
Exclusive: Visit www.UltimateScholarshipBook.com and enter code NA35220 for updates on this award.

(353) • Pedro Zamora Young Leaders Scholarship

National AIDS Memorial Grove
870 Market Street, Suite 965, San Francisco, CA 94102
Phone: 415-765-0446
Email: mkennedy@aidsmemorial.org
http://www.aidsmemorial.org
Purpose: To support students with a commitment to ending HIV/AIDS.
Eligibility: Applicants must complete the application with a personal statement and a written essay describing their service or leadership in the fight against HIV/AIDS. Students must provide a letter of recommendation and transcripts demonstrating a minimum grade point average of 2.5.
Target applicant(s): High school students. College students. Adult students.
Minimum GPA: 2.5
Amount: $5,000.
Number of awards: 10.
Deadline: May 31.
How to apply: Applications are available online.
Exclusive: Visit www.UltimateScholarshipBook.com and enter code NA35320 for updates on this award.

(354) • PGA WORKS Golf Management University Scholarship

PGA of America
100 Avenue of the Champions, Palm Beach, FL 33418
Phone: 561-624-8400
Email: pgaworks@scholarshipamerica.org
https://www.pga.com/pga-america
Purpose: To support students pursuing a PGA Golf Management University Program degree.
Eligibility: Applicants must be high school seniors, have graduated high school or be a current undergraduate level student. Students must attend a PGA Golf Management University listed on the sponsor's website and enroll in full-time undergraduate study. Applicants must be pursuing a PGA Golf Management University Program degree and plan to pursue a PGA of America membership.
Target applicant(s): High school students. College students. Adult students.
Amount: $8,000.
Number of awards: 10.
Deadline: January 31.
How to apply: Applications are available online.
Exclusive: Visit www.UltimateScholarshipBook.com and enter code PG35420 for updates on this award.

(355) • Phoenix Marathon Foundation Scholarship

Phoenix Marathon Foundation
3850 E. Baseline Road, Suite 106, Mesa, AZ 85206
http://thephoenixmarathon.com
Purpose: To support graduating seniors who have participated in running-related athletics in pursuing post-secondary education.
Eligibility: Selection is based on the overall strength of the application.
Target applicant(s): High school students.
Amount: $1,000.
Number of awards: Varies.
Scholarship may be renewable.
Deadline: December 31.
How to apply: Applications are available online.
Exclusive: Visit www.UltimateScholarshipBook.com and enter code PH35520 for updates on this award.

(356) • Photo Essay Scholarship Contest

DirectTextbook.com
1525 Chemeketa Street NE, Salem, OR 97301
Phone: 503-779-4056
Email: service@directtextbook.com
https://www.directtextbook.com/
Purpose: To assist students who submit photos.
Eligibility: Applicants must be U.S. citizens who are current two- or four-year college students and who have a minimum 2.0 GPA. Students must submit a photo based on the theme given.
Target applicant(s): High school students. College students. Adult students.
Minimum GPA: 2.0
Amount: $500.
Number of awards: 6.
Deadline: January 16.
How to apply: Applications are available online.
Exclusive: Visit www.UltimateScholarshipBook.com and enter code DI35620 for updates on this award.

(357) • Photography Scholarship Contest

Negative Population Growth
2861 Duke Street, Suite 36, Alexandria, VA 22314
Phone: 703-370-9510

http://www.npg.org
Purpose: To support students who draw attention to the dangers of population growth.
Eligibility: Applicants must submit a photograph of a U.S. environmental feature along with a short explanation of how population growth is putting the environmental future at risk. Selection is based on the overall strength of the submission.
Target applicant(s): High school students. College students. Adult students.
Amount: $1,500.
Number of awards: 5.
Deadline: April 11.
How to apply: Applications are available online.
Exclusive: Visit www.UltimateScholarshipBook.com and enter code NE35720 for updates on this award.

---

(358) · Pilot International Scholarship

Pilot International Foundation
102 Preston Court, Macon, GA 31210
Phone: 478-743-2245
http://www.pilotinternational.org
Purpose: To support students who are preparing for a career that focuses on caring for others.
Eligibility: Applicants must be an undergraduate student and pursuing a career that focuses on helping others.
Target applicant(s): College students. Adult students.
Amount: Up to $1,500.
Number of awards: Varies.
Scholarship may be renewable.
Deadline: March 15.
How to apply: Applications are available online.
Exclusive: Visit www.UltimateScholarshipBook.com and enter code PI35820 for updates on this award.

---

(359) · Pilot Pen G2 Overachievers Student Grant

Pilot Pen
3855 Regent Boulevard, Jacksonville, FL 32224
Phone: 904-645-9999
http://g2overachievers.com/enter
Purpose: To support students involved in community and public service.
Eligibility: Applicants must be ages 13 to 19 years old. Students must demonstrate exceptional academics and a dedication to serving others and must write an essay describing how they are working to help others outside of the classroom.
Target applicant(s): Junior high students or younger. High school students.
Amount: $15,000.
Number of awards: 1.
Deadline: December 31.
How to apply: Applications are available online.
Exclusive: Visit www.UltimateScholarshipBook.com and enter code PI35920 for updates on this award.

---

(360) · Pony Alumni Scholarship

Pony Baseball/Softball
1951 Pony Place, P.O. Box 225, Washington, PA 15301
Phone: 724-225-1060
Email: info@pony.org
http://www.pony.org
Purpose: To support those students who have played on a Pony League, Colt League and/or Palomino League team for at least two years as they continue their education beyond high school.
Eligibility: Applicants must have played on one of the leagues for at least two years prior to submitting the application. Applicants must be a senior in high school and submit the application prior to May 1 of their senior year.
Target applicant(s): High school students.
Amount: Varies.
Number of awards: 8.
Deadline: May 1.
How to apply: Applications are available online. The application consists of the application form as well as sending in a school and community activities form, an essay on the supplied topic, a secondary school transcript, test results from the ACT, SAT or TOEFL, a copy of a letter of acceptance to the college, a notarized letter confirming participation in an affiliated league and two letters of recommendation.
Exclusive: Visit www.UltimateScholarshipBook.com and enter code PO36020 for updates on this award.

---

(361) · Power Poetry Scholarships

Power Poetry
295 East 8th Street, Suite 3W, New York, NY 10009
Phone: 347-460-6741
Email: help@powerpoetry.org
http://www.powerpoetry.org
Purpose: To reward students who write a slam poem.
Eligibility: Applicants must be 25 or younger and a U.S. citizen. Students submit their poem online.
Target applicant(s): Junior high students or younger. High school students. College students. Graduate school students.
Amount: $1,000.
Number of awards: 1.
Deadline: Varies.
How to apply: Applicants must join the website and submit their poem online.
Exclusive: Visit www.UltimateScholarshipBook.com and enter code PO36120 for updates on this award.

---

(362) · Promocodes Cost-Conscious Student Scholarship

Promocodes
321 Santa Monica Boulevard, Suite 300, Santa Monica, CA 90401
Phone: 424-214-5470
Email: scholarships@promocodes.com
https://www.promocodes.com/scholarships
Purpose: To reward thrifty students with good financial sense.
Eligibility: Applicants must be U.S. citizens or permanent residents ages 18 or older currently attending an accredited two- or four-year U.S. institution. Students must create a video describing what they have done to save for their future.
Target applicant(s): College students. Graduate school students. Adult students.
Amount: $5,000.
Number of awards: 1.
Deadline: August 31.
How to apply: Applications are available online.
Exclusive: Visit www.UltimateScholarshipBook.com and enter code PR36220 for updates on this award.

(363) · Prudential Spirit of Community Awards

Prudential Spirit of Community Awards
Prudential Financial Inc., 751 Broad Street, 16th Floor, Newark, NJ 07102
Phone: 973-802-4568
Email: spirit@prudential.com
https://spirit.prudential.com/awards/how-to-apply
Purpose: To recognize students for their self-initiated community service.
Eligibility: Applicants must be a student in grades 5-12 and a legal resident of one of the 50 states of the U.S. or District of Columbia and be engaged in a volunteer activity.
Target applicant(s): Junior high students or younger. High school students.
Amount: Varies.
Number of awards: Varies.
Deadline: November 7.
How to apply: Applications are available online.
Exclusive: Visit www.UltimateScholarshipBook.com and enter code PR36320 for updates on this award.

(364) · QASymphony Software Testing Scholarship

QASymphony
550 Pharr Road, Atlanta, GA 30305
Phone: 844-798-4386
Email: marketing@qasymphony.com
https://www.qasymphony.com/scholarship/
Purpose: To assist students interested in software development pursue higher education.
Eligibility: Applicants must be graduating seniors accepted into a college or university or current students at a post-secondary institution. Students must complete application and essay about the importance of software development or testing.
Target applicant(s): High school students. College students. Adult students.
Amount: $1,000.
Number of awards: 1.
Deadline: November 1.
How to apply: Applications are available online.
Exclusive: Visit www.UltimateScholarshipBook.com and enter code QA36420 for updates on this award.

(365) · Quickship Essay Contest

Quickship
940 Calle Amanecer, Suite H, San Clemente, CA 92673
Phone: 888-273-3084
http://www.quikshiptoner.com/catalog/scholarship_program.php
Purpose: To support students interested in emerging technologies.
Eligibility: Applicants must be U.S. residents and students enrolled in an undergraduate or graduate degree program at an accredited institution in the fall or spring.
Target applicant(s): College students. Graduate school students. Adult students.
Amount: $1,500.
Number of awards: 1.
Deadline: December 15.
How to apply: Applications are available online.
Exclusive: Visit www.UltimateScholarshipBook.com and enter code QU36520 for updates on this award.

(366) · Race Entry Student Scholarship

Race Entry LLC
2250 N. University Parkway #4812, Provo, UT 84604-1590
Phone: 866-304-9944
https://www.raceentry.com/race-to-inspire-scholarship
Purpose: To support runners in pursuing post-secondary education.
Eligibility: Applicants must be enrolled at an accredited U.S. educational institution in the fall of the year in which the award is granted. Students must submit an essay explaining what inspires them to run. Selection is based on the overall strength of the submission.
Target applicant(s): High school students. College students. Adult students.
Amount: $500.
Number of awards: 1.
Deadline: August 15.
How to apply: Applications are available online.
Exclusive: Visit www.UltimateScholarshipBook.com and enter code RA36620 for updates on this award.

(367) · Rawhide Scholarship

National Intercollegiate Rodeo Association
2033 Walla Walla Avenue, Walla Walla, WA 99362
Phone: 509-529-4402
Email: rodeo@collegerodeo.com
http://www.collegerodeo.com/
Purpose: To aid students who exemplify the Rodeo Athletes on Wellness (Rawhide) principles.
Eligibility: Students must be current NIRA members, be college undergraduates and be academically eligible. Selection is based on the applicant's representation of the principles of positive choices, commitment to personal fitness, balance between rodeo and other commitments and having academic and career goals. Applicants should be involved in community service, have been in leadership roles and have a dedication to rodeo.
Target applicant(s): College students. Adult students.
Amount: $500.
Number of awards: Varies.
Deadline: May 22.
How to apply: Applications are available online.
Exclusive: Visit www.UltimateScholarshipBook.com and enter code NA36720 for updates on this award.

(368) · RealtyHop Scholarship

RealtyHop
355 Madison Avenue, 4th Floor, New York, NY 10017
https://www.realtyhop.com/resources/scholarship
Purpose: To support students who demonstrate ambition, diligence, leadership and an entrepreneurial spirit.
Eligibility: Applicants must be graduating high school seniors or currently enrolled undergraduates seeking a bachelor's or associate's degree. Students must submit their application including an essay via their school email address.
Target applicant(s): High school students. College students. Adult students.
Amount: $1,000.
Number of awards: 2.
Deadline: April 30, August 31.
How to apply: Applications are available online.
Exclusive: Visit www.UltimateScholarshipBook.com and enter code RE36820 for updates on this award.

(369) • Redfin Scholarship

Redfin
1099 Stewart Street, Suite 600, Seattle, WA 98101
https://www.redfin.com/resources/scholarship
Purpose: To support the pursuit of higher education.
Eligibility: Applicants must be U.S. residents. Students must have a minimum grade point average of 3.5 and be graduating high school seniors enrolling in an accredited post-secondary institution or current freshmen, sophomores or juniors at an accredited college or university.
Target applicant(s): High school students. College students. Adult students.
Minimum GPA: 3.5
Amount: $2,500.
Number of awards: 2.
Deadline: January 31.
How to apply: Applications are available online.
Exclusive: Visit www.UltimateScholarshipBook.com and enter code RE36920 for updates on this award.

(370) • Rentberry Scholarship Program

Rentberry Inc.
201 Spear Street, Suite 1100, San Francisco, CA 84105
Phone: 415-795-7171
https://rentberry.com/scholarship
Purpose: To help students pay for their housing expenses.
Eligibility: Applicants must be 18 years or older and currently enrolled in an accredited U.S. college or university. Students must write an essay describing the neighborhood in which they were raised.
Target applicant(s): College students. Graduate school students. Adult students.
Amount: $1,000.
Number of awards: 1.
Deadline: June 1.
How to apply: Applications are available online.
Exclusive: Visit www.UltimateScholarshipBook.com and enter code RE37020 for updates on this award.

(371) • RentHop Apartment Scholarship

RentHop
101 Avenue of Americas, 18th Floor, New York, NY 10013
Phone: 913-982-6682
Email: college-scholarship@renthrop.com
https://www.renthop.com/college_scholarship
Purpose: To support undergraduate students who display an entrepreneurial spirit as they pursue their college education.
Eligibility: Applicants must be a graduating high school senior or an undergraduate pursuing a bachelor's or an associate's degree. Students will need to submit a 500-word essay on the topic provided.
Target applicant(s): High school students. College students. Adult students.
Amount: $1,000.
Number of awards: 1.
Deadline: August 31.
How to apply: An application consists of the essay being emailed to RentHop via a school email address. If applicant doesn't have a school email address, proof of enrollment will need to be provided.
Exclusive: Visit www.UltimateScholarshipBook.com and enter code RE37120 for updates on this award.

(372) • Resume Companion $1,000 Scholarship

Resume Companion
427 N. Tatnall Street #95492, Wilmington, DE 19801-2230
Phone: 866-936-4904
Email: scholarship@resumecompanion.com
https://resumecompanion.com/scholarship/
Purpose: To assist students who write resumes.
Eligibility: Applicants must be enrolled or planning to enroll full-time in a U.S. college or university and must write a resume about a fictional or non-fictional character from the past or present.
Target applicant(s): High school students. College students. Adult students.
Amount: $1,000.
Number of awards: 1.
Deadline: July 14.
How to apply: Resumes must be emailed to scholarship@resumecompanion.com including the name of the applicant and university. Selection is based on the "protocols of how a professional resume should be written" and entertainment value of the resume.
Exclusive: Visit www.UltimateScholarshipBook.com and enter code RE37220 for updates on this award.

(373) • Return 2 College Scholarship

R2C Scholarship Program
http://www.return2college.com/awardprogram.cfm
Purpose: To provide financial assistance for college and adult students with college or graduate school expenses.
Eligibility: Applicants must be college or adult students currently attending or planning to attend a two-year or four-year college or graduate school within the next 12 months. Students must be 17 years or older and U.S. citizens or permanent residents. The award may be used for full- or part-time study at either on-campus or online schools.
Target applicant(s): High school students. College students. Adult students.
Amount: $1,000.
Number of awards: Varies.
Deadline: January 31, April 30, September 30.
How to apply: Applications are available online.
Exclusive: Visit www.UltimateScholarshipBook.com and enter code R237320 for updates on this award.

(374) • Rhodes Scholar

Rhodes Scholarship Trust
Attn.: Elliot F. Gerson, 8229 Boone Boulevard, Suite 240, Vienna, VA 22182
Phone: 703-821-5960
Email: amsec@rhodesscholar.org
http://www.rhodesscholar.org
Purpose: To recognize qualities of young people who will contribute to the "world's fight."
Eligibility: Applicants must be U.S. citizens between the ages of 18 and 24 and have a bachelor's degree at the time of the award. The awards provides for two to three years of study at the University of Oxford including educational costs and other expenses. Selection is extremely competitive and is based on literary and scholastic achievements, athletic achievement and character.
Target applicant(s): College students.
Amount: Full tuition plus stipend.
Number of awards: 32.
Deadline: October 4.

How to apply: Applications are available online.
Exclusive: Visit www.UltimateScholarshipBook.com and enter code RH37420 for updates on this award.

(375) • Roller Skating Foundation Scholarship, High School Student Category

Roller Skating Foundation
6905 Corporate Drive, Indianapolis, IN 46278
Phone: 317-347-2626
Email: foundation@rollerskating.com
http://www.rollerskating.org
Purpose: To aid college-bound high school seniors.
Eligibility: Applicants must be high school seniors who plan to enroll at an accredited college or university in the fall following high school graduation. They must have a GPA of 3.4 or higher on a four-point scale and must be the child of an owner or employee of a RSA skating center or RSA affiliated member. They must have composite standardized test scores that are in the 85th percentile or higher. Selection is based on the overall strength of the application.
Target applicant(s): High school students.
Minimum GPA: 3.4
Amount: $2,000-$4,000.
Number of awards: 2.
Deadline: February 28.
How to apply: Applications are available online. An application form, transcript, personal essay, three recommendation letters and income tax information are required.
Exclusive: Visit www.UltimateScholarshipBook.com and enter code RO37520 for updates on this award.

(376) • Ron and Gayle Hershberger Award

U.S. Figure Skating
20 First Street, Colorado Springs, CO 80906
Phone: 719-635-5200
Email: info@usfigureskating.org
http://www.usfsa.org
Purpose: To recognize music and artistry in the program of junior U.S. Figure Skaters.
Eligibility: The award is presented to the junior competitor at the U.S. Figure Skating Championships with the highest combined total of short program and free skate program component marks.
Target applicant(s): Junior high students or younger. High school students.
Amount: Varies.
Number of awards: 1.
Deadline: Varies.
How to apply: The award is presented at the U.S. Figure Skating Championships.
Exclusive: Visit www.UltimateScholarshipBook.com and enter code U.37620 for updates on this award.

(377) • Rosalind P. Walter College Scholarship

United States Tennis Association Foundation
70 W. Red Oak Lane, White Plains, NY 10604
Phone: 914-696-7223
Email: foundation@usta.com
http://www.ustafoundation.com/
Purpose: To support young tennis participants who believe in always putting forth a best effort and giving back to the community.
Eligibility: Applicants must be high school seniors who have participated in an organized youth tennis program. Selection is based on high academic achievement, good character and community involvement.
Target applicant(s): High school students.
Amount: $10,000.
Number of awards: 2.
Scholarship may be renewable.
Deadline: February 27.
How to apply: Applications are available online.
Exclusive: Visit www.UltimateScholarshipBook.com and enter code UN37720 for updates on this award.

(378) • Rover Sitter Scholarship

A Place for Rover, Inc.
2101 4th Avenue #400, Seattle, WA 98121
https://www.rover.com/college-scholarship/
Purpose: To support students who are pet sitters.
Eligibility: Applicants must be residents of the United States at least 18 years of age and be existing pet care providers on Rover.com. Applicants must be graduating high school seniors with a minimum grade point average of 3.0 or current undergraduate or graduate students with a 2.5 or better grade point average.
Target applicant(s): High school students. College students. Graduate school students. Adult students.
Minimum GPA: 3.0 for high school seniors, 2.5 for undergraduate and graduate students
Amount: $500.
Number of awards: 1.
Deadline: May 1.
How to apply: Applications are available online.
Exclusive: Visit www.UltimateScholarshipBook.com and enter code A 37820 for updates on this award.

(379) • Samuel Huntington Public Service Award

Samuel Huntington Fund
Attn: Amy Stacy, National Grid, 40 Sylvan Road, Waltham, MA 02451
Phone: 508-389-2000
Email: amy.stacy@nationalgrid.com
https://www.nationalgridus.com
Purpose: To assist students who wish to perform one year of humanitarian service immediately upon graduation.
Eligibility: Applicants must be graduating college seniors, and must intend to perform one year of public service in the U.S. or abroad. The service may be individual work or through charitable, religious, educational, governmental or other public service organizations.
Target applicant(s): College students. Adult students.
Amount: $15,000.
Number of awards: Up to 3.
Deadline: January 17.
How to apply: Applications are available online.
Exclusive: Visit www.UltimateScholarshipBook.com and enter code SA37920 for updates on this award.

(380) • SanDisk Foundation Scholarship Program

SanDisk Foundation Scholarship Program
c/o International Scholarship and Tuition Services Inc. (ISTS), 1321 Murfreesboro Road, Suite 800, Nashville, TN 37217
Phone: 855-670-ISTS
Email: contactus@applyists.com

http://www.sandisk.com/about-sandisk/corporate-responsibility/community/scholars-program/
Purpose: To assist students who have demonstrated leadership or entrepreneurial interests.
Eligibility: Applicants must be a high school senior or college freshman, sophomore or junior and must attend or plan to attend a full-time undergraduate program. Students must also demonstrate financial need. Up to 27 $2,500 renewable awards will given to students from the general public, up to three $2,500 renewable awards will be given to dependents of SanDisk employees and two students will be chosen as SanDisk Scholars and awarded full tuition scholarships for up to four years.
Target applicant(s): High school students. College students. Adult students.
Amount: $2,500 to full tuition.
Number of awards: Varies.
Scholarship may be renewable.
Deadline: April 1.
How to apply: Applications are available online. An application form and an essay are required.
Exclusive: Visit www.UltimateScholarshipBook.com and enter code SA38020 for updates on this award.

---

(381) • SASS Scholarship Foundation Scholarships

Single Action Shooting Society (SASS)
215 Cowboy Way, Edgewood, NM 87015
Phone: 505-843-1320
Email: misty@sassnet.com
http://www.sassscholarship.org/
Purpose: To support students who have participated in SASS by helping with higher education costs.
Eligibility: Applicants must be a high school senior or college undergraduate, have at least a 2.0 GPA and have been active in SASS for at least one year. Selection is based on academic achievement, leadership, character, extracurricular activities and commitment to cowboy action shooting.
Target applicant(s): High school students. College students. Adult students.
Minimum GPA: 2.0
Amount: $2,000.
Number of awards: Varies.
Scholarship may be renewable.
Deadline: March 1.
How to apply: Applications are available online and must also include an official transcript, an essay on the provided topic, five letters of recommendation, a personal statement of goals and a photo of the applicant in full cowboy attire.
Exclusive: Visit www.UltimateScholarshipBook.com and enter code SI38120 for updates on this award.

---

(382) • Scholars Helping Collars Scholarship

P.L.A.Y.
246 2nd Street, Unit A, San Francisco, CA 94105
Phone: (855) 300-7529
http://www.petplay.com
Purpose: To reward graduating seniors with a passion for animal welfare.
Eligibility: Applicants must have a history of volunteer work to help animals in need. Students must submit an essay about how that volunteer work has impacted their lives and the importance of animal welfare. Selection is based on the overall strength of the submission.
Target applicant(s): High school students.
Amount: $1,000.
Number of awards: 3.
Deadline: February 28.
How to apply: Applications are available online.
Exclusive: Visit www.UltimateScholarshipBook.com and enter code P.38220 for updates on this award.

---

(383) • Scholarship America Dream Award

Scholarship America Dream Award
One Scholarship Way, Saint Peter, MN 56082
Phone: 507-931-1682
Email: dreamaward@scholarshipamerica.org
https://scholarshipamerica.org/dreamaward/
Purpose: To assist students in their second year or higher of post-secondary education.
Eligibility: Applicants must be U.S. citizens or permanent or legal residents who received a high school diploma from a U.S. school. Students must be planning to complete a minimum of one full year of post-secondary education and be planning to enroll as full-time undergraduates at the sophomore level or higher for the coming academic year. Applicants must have a grade point average of 3.0 or better.
Target applicant(s): College students. Adult students.
Minimum GPA: 3.0
Amount: $5,000-$15,000.
Number of awards: Varies.
Scholarship may be renewable.
Deadline: October 15.
How to apply: Applications are available online.
Exclusive: Visit www.UltimateScholarshipBook.com and enter code SC38320 for updates on this award.

---

(384) • Scholarship for International Students

Deserve
1010 Doyle Street, Suite 200, Menlo Park, CA 94025
Phone: 800-418-7353
Email: hello@deserve.com
https://www.deserve.com/scholarship/
Purpose: To assist international students in the U.S.
Eligibility: Applicants must be studying in the U.S. on an F1, J1 or M1 visa and must be accepted to study or continue studying at an eligible college or university. Students must score in the top 15 percent on a standardized U.S. college entrance exam and must have a 3.0 GPA or higher.
Target applicant(s): College students. Graduate school students. Adult students.
Minimum GPA: 3.0
Amount: $5,000.
Number of awards: 10.
Deadline: September 30.
How to apply: Applications are available online. Recipients are randomly selected.
Exclusive: Visit www.UltimateScholarshipBook.com and enter code DE38420 for updates on this award.

---

(385) • Scholarships for Military Children

Defense Commissary Agency (DeCA)
1300 E Avenue, Fort Lee, VA 23801-1800
Phone: 804-734-8000
Email: militaryscholar@scholarshipmanagers.com
http://www.militaryscholar.org

Purpose: To provide educational opportunities for children of military personnel.
Eligibility: Applicants must be unmarried dependents under the age of 21 (23 if full-time students) of active duty, reserve, retired or deceased members of the military. They must be enrolled in the Defense Enrollment Eligibility Reporting System database. Applicants must be enrolled or plan to enroll in a full-time undergraduate degree-seeking program and have a minimum GPA of 3.0. Community or junior college students must be in a program that will allow transfer directly into a four-year program. Applicants also must not be accepted to a U.S. Military Academy or be the recipients of full scholarships at any accredited institution.
Target applicant(s): High school students. College students.
Minimum GPA: 3.0
Amount: $2,000.
Number of awards: Varies.
Deadline: February 13.
How to apply: Applications are available online or from military commissaries.
Exclusive: Visit www.UltimateScholarshipBook.com and enter code DE38520 for updates on this award.

(386) · Scholarships for Student Leaders

National Association for Campus Activities
13 Harbison Way, Columbia, SC 29212
Phone: 803-732-6222
Email: info@naca.org
https://www.naca.org/FOUNDATION/Pages/Scholarships.aspx
Purpose: The NACA foundation is committed to developing professionals in the field of campus activities.
Eligibility: Applicants must be current undergraduate students who hold a significant campus leadership position, have made significant contributions to their campus communities and have demonstrated leadership skills and abilities.
Target applicant(s): College students. Adult students.
Amount: Varies.
Number of awards: Varies.
Deadline: December 31.
How to apply: Applications are available online.
Exclusive: Visit www.UltimateScholarshipBook.com and enter code NA38620 for updates on this award.

(387) · Scholastic Honors Team

U.S. Figure Skating
20 First Street, Colorado Springs, CO 80906
Phone: 719-635-5200
Email: info@usfigureskating.org
http://www.usfsa.org
Purpose: To support high school U.S. Figure Skating members who are distinguished in both figure skating and high school academics.
Eligibility: Students must be a current member of U.S. Figure Skating, entering the junior or senior year of high school, have at least a 3.4 GPA and have competed in a U.S. Figure Skating qualifying competition. Selection is based on academic performance and honors, community and extracurricular involvement, skating achievements and the essay.
Target applicant(s): High school students.
Minimum GPA: 3.4
Amount: $2,500.
Number of awards: Varies.
Deadline: September 9.
How to apply: Applications are available online and must include a high school transcript, SAT/ACT results, photo and essay.
Exclusive: Visit www.UltimateScholarshipBook.com and enter code U.38720 for updates on this award.

(388) · Seabee Memorial Scholarship

Seabee Memorial Scholarship Association
P.O. Box 391, Springfield, VA 22150
Phone: 703-690-7672
Email: smsa@seabee.org
http://www.seabee.org
Purpose: To provide scholarships for the children of Seabees, both past and present, active, reserve or retired.
Eligibility: Applicants must be sons, daughters, step-children or grandchildren of Regular, Reserve, Retired or deceased officers or enlisted members who have served or are now serving with the Naval Construction Force or Naval Civil Engineer Corps, or who have served but have been honorably discharged. Applicants must be a senior in high school or a high school graduate. Selection is based on scholastic record, citizenship, financial need and leadership. Scholarships are for undergraduate degree programs only.
Target applicant(s): High school students. College students. Adult students.
Amount: Varies.
Number of awards: Varies.
Deadline: April 15.
How to apply: Applications are available online or by written request.
Exclusive: Visit www.UltimateScholarshipBook.com and enter code SE38820 for updates on this award.

(389) · Second Chance Scholarship Contest

American Fire Sprinkler Association
12750 Merit Drive, Suite 350, Dallas, TX 75251
Phone: 214-349-5965
Email: scholarship@firesprinkler.org
http://www.afsascholarship.org
Purpose: To help U.S. students pay for higher education.
Eligibility: Applicants must be U.S. citizens or legal residents and be high school graduates or GED recipients. They must be enrolled at an institution of higher learning no later than the spring semester of the upcoming academic year. American Fire Sprinkler Association (AFSA) staff and board member relatives are ineligible, as are past contest winners. Selection is made by random drawing from the pool of contest entrants.
Target applicant(s): College students. Graduate school students. Adult students.
Amount: $1,000.
Number of awards: 5.
Deadline: August 31.
How to apply: Contest entrants must read an informational article on fire sprinklers before taking a ten-question multiple choice test on the material covered in the article. The number of correct responses on the test is equal to the number of entries that will be made in the entrant's name, giving each entrant up to 10 entries to the random drawing that will determine the winners of the contest.
Exclusive: Visit www.UltimateScholarshipBook.com and enter code AM38920 for updates on this award.

(390) • SelectBlinds.com College Scholarship

SelectBlinds.com
7420 South Kyrene Road, Suite 119, Tempe, AZ 85204
http://www.selectblinds.com/scholarship.html
Purpose: To help students who enter a submission related to window coverings.
Eligibility: Applicants must submit an original idea in the form of an image, photograph, video or other creativity means that addresses one of the following: what is the most creative thing you can do with window coverings, or invent a new technology for window coverings. Students must also answer a short essay. Applicants must be residents of the United States, currently registered at an accredited high school or college and hold a 2.5 or better grade point average.
Target applicant(s): High school students. College students. Adult students.
Minimum GPA: 2.5
Amount: $1,000.
Number of awards: 1.
Deadline: June 14.
How to apply: Applications are available online.
Exclusive: Visit www.UltimateScholarshipBook.com and enter code SE39020 for updates on this award.

(391) • Shepherd Scholarship

Ancient and Accepted Scottish Rite of Freemansonry Southern Jurisdiction
1733 16th Street NW, Washington, DC 20009-3103
Phone: 202-232-3579
Email: scholarships@scottishrite.org
https://scottishrite.org/brothers-in-the-community/scholarships/
Purpose: To provide financial assistance to students pursuing degrees in fields associated with service to country.
Eligibility: Applicants must have accepted enrollment in a U.S. institution of higher learning. Up to four letters of recommendation will be considered. Selection is based on "dedication, ambition, academic preparation, financial need and promise of outstanding performance at the advanced level." Applicants must have a minimum GPA of 3.0 and a Masonic background which includes one of the following is required: member of a Masonic youth organization, member of Scottish Rite or son, daughter, granddaughter or grandson of a current or past member of the Southern Jurisdiction of Scottish Rite in good standing.
Target applicant(s): High school students. College students. Adult students.
Minimum GPA: 3.0
Amount: $2,000.
Number of awards: Varies.
Scholarship may be renewable.
Deadline: March 31.
How to apply: Applications are available online. An application form, transcript and up to four letters of recommendation are required.
Exclusive: Visit www.UltimateScholarshipBook.com and enter code AN39120 for updates on this award.

(392) • Sheryl A. Horak Memorial Scholarship

Explorers Learning for Life
1325 West Walnut Hill Lane, P.O. Box 152225, Irving, TX 75015-2225
Phone: 855-806-9992
Email: exploring@lflmail.org
http://www.exploring.org/scholarships/
Purpose: To support students who are pursuing careers in law enforcement.
Eligibility: Students must be in their senior year of high school, and they must be members of a Law Enforcement Explorer post. Applicants must submit three letters of recommendation and an essay.
Target applicant(s): High school students. College students. Adult students.
Amount: $1,000.
Number of awards: 1.
Deadline: March 31.
How to apply: Applications are available online.
Exclusive: Visit www.UltimateScholarshipBook.com and enter code EX39220 for updates on this award.

(393) • Simon Youth Foundation Community Scholarship

Simon Youth Foundation
225 W. Washington Street, Indianapolis, IN 46204
Phone: 800-509-3676
Email: syf@simon.com
http://www.syf.org/scholarships/
Purpose: To assist promising students who live in communities with Simon properties.
Eligibility: Applicants must be high school seniors who plan to attend an accredited two- or four-year college, university or technical/vocational school full-time. Scholarships are awarded without regard to race, color, creed, religion, gender, disability or national origin, and recipients are selected on the basis of financial need, academic record, potential to succeed, participation in school and community activities, honors, work experience, a statement of career and educational goals and an outside appraisal. Awards are given at every Simon mall in the U.S.
Target applicant(s): High school students.
Amount: $1,500.
Number of awards: Varies.
Deadline: Varies.
How to apply: Applications are available online. Only the first 3,000 applications that the organization receives are considered.
Exclusive: Visit www.UltimateScholarshipBook.com and enter code SI39320 for updates on this award.

(394) • Six Star Scholarship Contest

Iovate Health Sciences USA Inc.
3880 Jeffrey Boulevard, Blasdell, NY 14219
Phone: 905-678-3119
http://www.sixstarpro.com/scholarship/
Purpose: To support students who excel in athletics and academics.
Eligibility: Applicants must be residents of the United States, attend a college or university and be between 18 and 22 years of age. Students must have a 3.0 GPA and write an essay or submit a video as part of their application. Applicants must excel in athletics and academics.
Target applicant(s): High school students. College students.
Minimum GPA: 3.0
Amount: $15,000.
Number of awards: 2.
Deadline: April 30.
How to apply: Applications are available online.
Exclusive: Visit www.UltimateScholarshipBook.com and enter code IO39420 for updates on this award.

(395) · Sixt Scholars Program

Sixt Rent a Car
1501 NW 49th Street, Suite 100, Fort Lauderdale, FL 33309
Phone: 954-703-2359
Email: noemi.montejo@sixt.com
https://www.sixt.com/sixt-scholars

Purpose: To assist high-school seniors who involved in extracurricular activities.

Eligibility: Applicants must have a minimum 3.7 GPA on a 4.0 scale, be a graduating high school senior in the U.S. and plan to enroll in full-time in a two- or four-year university. Only the first 500 applicants will be considered. Selection is based on factors including financial need and extracurricular activities.

Target applicant(s): High school students.
Minimum GPA: 3.7
Amount: $5,000.
Number of awards: 5.
Deadline: November 30.
How to apply: Application available online and must include a high school transcript.
Exclusive: Visit www.UltimateScholarshipBook.com and enter code SI39520 for updates on this award.

(396) · Ski Butlers Scholarship Fund

Ski Butlers
Phone: 877-754-7754
http://www.skibutlers.com

Purpose: To support undergraduate, graduate or postgraduate students with a passion for skiing in funding their education.

Eligibility: Applicants must be attending an accredited U.S. educational institution. Students must submit an essay about their passion for skiing. Selection is based on the overall strength of the application.

Target applicant(s): College students. Graduate school students. Adult students.
Amount: $2,000.
Number of awards: 1.
Deadline: January 31.
How to apply: Applications are available online.
Exclusive: Visit www.UltimateScholarshipBook.com and enter code SK39620 for updates on this award.

(397) · Sleeknote Scholarship

Sleeknote
Jens Baggesens Vej 90A, 8200 Aarhus, Denmark,
Email: mail@sleeknote.com
https://sleeknote.com/scholarship

Purpose: To help students who create a video essay.

Eligibility: Applicants must be currently enrolled in a high school, university or college and able to submit their application in English. Students must create a short original video essay discussing their chosen field of study and future plans.

Target applicant(s): High school students. College students. Graduate school students. Adult students.
Amount: $1,000.
Number of awards: 2.
Deadline: January 20.
How to apply: Applications are available online.
Exclusive: Visit www.UltimateScholarshipBook.com and enter code SL39720 for updates on this award.

(398) · Small Business Scholarship

Cover Wallet
100 Avenue of the Americas, Third Floor, 646-844-9933, New York, NY 10013
Email: info@coverwallet.com
https://www.coverwallet.com/small-business-insurance-scholarship

Purpose: To assist students who write about small business.

Eligibility: Applicants must be 18 years old or have the permission of their legal guardian. Students must submit application materials and an essay discussing risks of small business.

Target applicant(s): High school students. College students. Adult students.
Amount: $500.
Number of awards: 1.
Deadline: August 31.
How to apply: Applications are available online.
Exclusive: Visit www.UltimateScholarshipBook.com and enter code CO39820 for updates on this award.

(399) · Soliant's Sunrise Scholarship

Soliant Consulting
Phone: 800-528-0170
Email: scholarship@soliantconsulting.com
http://www.soliantconsulting.com/philanthropy

Purpose: To reward students who understand how businesses can be both philanthropic and profitable.

Eligibility: Applicants must be incoming freshmen or current undergraduate students at an accredited two-year or four-year college or university in the United States. A minimum 3.0 GPA is required. Students will need to submit a 500-word essay on the provided topic.

Target applicant(s): High school students. College students. Adult students.
Minimum GPA: 3.0
Amount: $1,000.
Number of awards: 1.
Deadline: August 31.
How to apply: Applications are available online.
Exclusive: Visit www.UltimateScholarshipBook.com and enter code SO39920 for updates on this award.

(400) · Sons of Union Veterans of the Civil War Scholarships

Sons of Union Veterans of the Civil War
Executive Director David W. Demmy, Sr., 1 Lincoln Circle at Reservoir Park, Suite 240 (National Civil War Museum), Harrisburg, PA 17103-2411
Phone: 610-948-1278
Email: jertell@comcast.net
http://www.suvcw.org

Purpose: To assist students connected with the Sons of Union Veterans of the Civil War in obtaining higher education.

Eligibility: Male applicants must be members or associates of the Sons of Union Veterans of the Civil War. Female applicants must be daughters or granddaughters of members or associates and must be current members of the Women's Relief Corps, Ladies of the Grand Army of the Republic, Daughters of Union Veterans of the Civil War 1861-1865 or Auxiliary to the Sons of Union Veterans of the Civil War. All applicants must rank in the upper quarter of their graduating class, have a record of school and community service and provide three letters of recommendation.

Target applicant(s): High school students. College students. Adult students.
Amount: $2,500.
Number of awards: 2.
Deadline: March 31.
How to apply: Applications are available online.
Exclusive: Visit www.UltimateScholarshipBook.com and enter code SO40020 for updates on this award.

(401) · Southern Region/Elmer Stailing Scholarship

USA Water Ski and Wake Sports Foundation
1251 Holy Cow Road, Polk City, FL 33868
Phone: 863-324-2472
Email: usa-wsf@waterskihalloffame.com
http://www.usawaterskifoundation.org/
Purpose: To support current active members of USA Water Ski in their educational goals.
Eligibility: Applicants must be U.S. citizens and be incoming freshmen, sophomores, juniors or seniors at an accredited two-year or four-year college. Applicants must continue to be enrolled full-time at their college during the year of receipt of the scholarship. Selection is based on the applicant's academic achievement, work record, need and school and community activities as well as their contributions to the sport of water skiing.
Target applicant(s): College students. Adult students.
Amount: $2,000.
Number of awards: 1.
Deadline: March 15.
How to apply: Applications are available online. An application form, 500-word essay and two recommendation letters are required.
Exclusive: Visit www.UltimateScholarshipBook.com and enter code US40120 for updates on this award.

(402) · Spark Energy

Spark Energy
12140 Wickchester Lane, Suite 100, Houston, TX 77079
Email: scholarship@sparkenergy.com
https://www.sparkenergy.com
Purpose: To assist graduating high school students who write about a "spark."
Eligibility: Applicants must be graduating high school seniors with a minimum GPA or 3.5 who have been accepted to a four-year college or university. Students must provide transcripts and essay along with their application.
Target applicant(s): High school students.
Minimum GPA: 3.5
Amount: $3,000.
Number of awards: 1.
Deadline: August 31.
How to apply: Applications are available online.
Exclusive: Visit www.UltimateScholarshipBook.com and enter code SP40220 for updates on this award.

(403) · Spirit of Anne Frank Awards

Anne Frank Center USA
44 Park Place, New York, NY 10007
Phone: 212-431-7993
Email: info@annefrank.com
https://www.annefrank.com/scholarships
Purpose: To reward students who lead the way in combating prejudice and injustice in their communities.
Eligibility: Students should be high school seniors, be U.S. citizens and plan on attending a four-year college or university in the fall of the upcoming academic year. Applicants must submit a 1,000-word essay characterizing their efforts and dedication toward achieving lasting change with regards to prejudice and intolerance.
Target applicant(s): High school students.
Amount: $1,000-$10,000.
Number of awards: Up to 5.
Deadline: March 16.
How to apply: Applications are available online and must be submitted along with the essay and two letters of recommendation.
Exclusive: Visit www.UltimateScholarshipBook.com and enter code AN40320 for updates on this award.

(404) · Spirit of Giving Scholarship

Wine Country Gift Baskets
Phone: 800-394-0394
Email: scholarship@winecountrygiftbaskets.com
https://www.winecountrygiftbaskets.com/information/scholarship.asp
Purpose: To encourage acts of kindness, service and giving.
Eligibility: Applicants must be high school seniors or currently enrolled students in an accredited U.S. certificate program, college, trade school or university who will be attending the program in the following year. Students must submit an essay relating to giving and service to others.
Target applicant(s): High school students. College students. Adult students.
Amount: $1,000.
Number of awards: 3.
Deadline: July 31.
How to apply: Applications are available online.
Exclusive: Visit www.UltimateScholarshipBook.com and enter code WI40420 for updates on this award.

(405) · Sports Unlimited Scholarship

Sports Unlimited
346 Godshall Drive, Harleysville, PA 19438
Phone: 610-994-9701
https://www.sportsunlimitedinc.com/
Purpose: To support student athletes in pursuing post-secondary education.
Eligibility: Applicants must be graduating seniors or college freshmen or sophomores. Students must submit an essay explaining how to improve a piece of sports equipment.
Target applicant(s): High school students. College students. Adult students.
Amount: $1,000.
Number of awards: 1.
Deadline: April 25.
How to apply: Applications are available online.
Exclusive: Visit www.UltimateScholarshipBook.com and enter code SP40520 for updates on this award.

(406) · Stamps Scholars

Stamps Family Charitable Foundation Inc.
P.O. Box 98374, Atlanta, GA 30359-2074
Email: info@stampsfoundation.org
https://www.stampsfoundation.org/

Purpose: To support students pursuing higher education with their related expenses.
Eligibility: Applicants must be currently enrolled high school seniors, undergraduates or graduate students attending an accredited college or university. Selection is based on the overall strength of the application as well as the following: academic achievement, leadership ability, integrity, perseverance, extracurricular activities and community involvement.
Target applicant(s): High school students. College students. Graduate school students. Adult students.
Amount: Varies.
Number of awards: Varies.
Deadline: Varies.
How to apply: Applications are available online. An application form, official transcripts and SAT and/or ACT scores are required.
Exclusive: Visit www.UltimateScholarshipBook.com and enter code ST40620 for updates on this award.

(407) • Standout Student College Scholarship

College Peas LLC
Lake Forest, IL 60045
Phone: 847-681-0698
http://www.collegepeas.com
Purpose: To aid college-bound high school students who have interests that make them stand out from their peers.
Eligibility: Applicants must be current high school students, have a GPA of 2.0 or higher on a four-point scale and have plans to enroll full-time at a four-year postsecondary institution after graduation. They must submit an essay describing a unique interest or skill that teens typically do not have.
Target applicant(s): High school students.
Minimum GPA: 2.0
Amount: $400.
Number of awards: Varies.
Deadline: Varies.
How to apply: Applications are available online. An application form and essay are required.
Exclusive: Visit www.UltimateScholarshipBook.com and enter code CO40720 for updates on this award.

(408) • Stephen J. Brady STOP Hunger Scholarship

Sodexo Foundation
9801 Washingtonian Boulevard, Gaithersburg, MD 20878
Phone: 800-763-3946
Email: stophunger@sodexofoundation.org
http://us.stop-hunger.org
Purpose: To aid students who have been active in the movement to eradicate hunger.
Eligibility: Applicants must be U.S. citizens or permanent residents. They must be students in kindergarten through graduate school who are enrolled at an accredited U.S. institution. They must have been active in at least one unpaid volunteer effort to end hunger during the past 12 months. Sodexo employees and previous recipients of this award are ineligible. Selection is based on the overall strength of the application.
Target applicant(s): Junior high students or younger. High school students. College students. Graduate school students. Adult students.
Amount: $1,000-$5,000.
Number of awards: Up to 25.
Deadline: December 5.
How to apply: Applications are available online. An application form and supporting materials are required.
Exclusive: Visit www.UltimateScholarshipBook.com and enter code SO40820 for updates on this award.

(409) • Stokes Educational Scholarship Program

National Security Agency (NSA)
Attn: MB3, Stokes Program, 9800 Savage Road, Suite 6272, Ft. George G. Meade, MD 20755-6000
Phone: 410-854-4725
https://www.intelligencecareers.gov/icstudents.html?Agency=NSA
Purpose: To recruit those with skills useful to the NSA, especially minority high school students.
Eligibility: Students must be seniors at the time of application, be U.S. citizens, have a 3.0 GPA, have a minimum ACT score of 25 or a minimum SAT score of 1200 and demonstrate leadership skills. Applicants must be planning to major in computer science or computer/electrical engineering.
Target applicant(s): High school students.
Minimum GPA: 3.0
Amount: Up to $30,000.
Number of awards: Varies.
Scholarship may be renewable.
Deadline: October 31.
How to apply: Applications are available online.
Exclusive: Visit www.UltimateScholarshipBook.com and enter code NA40920 for updates on this award.

(410) • Stop-painting.com Scholarship

InSite Solutions, LLC
3660 Rogers Road #298, Wake Forest, NC 27587
Phone: (919) 569-6765
Email: lara@stop-painting.com
http://stop-painting.com/post/scholarships.asp
Purpose: To support students in their pursuit of higher education so that they may then pursue successful professional careers.
Eligibility: Applicants must be a senior in high school or a student currently attending an accredited college or university. An essay (800 to 1,000 words) about a provided topic related to the importance of organization is required.
Target applicant(s): High school students. College students. Adult students.
Amount: $1,000.
Number of awards: 1.
Deadline: March 31.
How to apply: Applications are available online and include short-answer questions as well as an essay.
Exclusive: Visit www.UltimateScholarshipBook.com and enter code IN41020 for updates on this award.

(411) • Strom & Associates Annual Scholarship

Strom & Associates
180 N. LaSalle, Suite #2510, Chicago, IL 60601
Phone: 866-371-7511
https://stromlawyers.com/strom-associates-annual-scholarship/
Purpose: To support students who submit a video.
Eligibility: Applicants must be U.S. citizens or permanent residents. Students must be enrolling as full-time students in the fall at an accredited college or university, community college or law school. Applicants must complete the application and submit a 1,500 word essay on the given topic on the webpage. Proof of enrollment will be required of the recipient.

Target applicant(s): High school students. College students. Graduate school students. Adult students.
Amount: $1,500.
Number of awards: 1.
Deadline: July 15.
How to apply: Applications are available online.
Exclusive: Visit www.UltimateScholarshipBook.com and enter code ST41120 for updates on this award.

(412) • Stuck at Prom Scholarship

Henkel Consumer Adhesives
32150 Just Imagine Drive, Avon, OH 44011-1355
http://stuckatprom.com/
Purpose: To reward students for their creativity with duct tape.
Eligibility: Applicants must attend a high school prom as a couple in the spring wearing the most original attire that they make from duct tape. Both members of the couple do not have to attend the same school. Photographs of past winners are available on the website.
Target applicant(s): High school students.
Amount: $1,000-$10,000.
Number of awards: Varies.
Deadline: May 31.
How to apply: Applications are available online. Contact information, release form and prom picture are required.
Exclusive: Visit www.UltimateScholarshipBook.com and enter code HE41220 for updates on this award.

(413) • Student Activist Awards

Freedom from Religion Foundation
P.O. Box 750, Madison, WI 53701
Phone: 608-256-8900
Email: info@ffrf.org
https://ffrf.org/outreach/awards
Purpose: To assist high school and college student activists.
Eligibility: Selection is based on activism for free thought or separation of church and state.
Target applicant(s): High school students. College students. Adult students.
Amount: $1,000.
Number of awards: Varies.
Deadline: Varies.
How to apply: Contact the organization for more information.
Exclusive: Visit www.UltimateScholarshipBook.com and enter code FR41320 for updates on this award.

(414) • Student Paper Competition

American Criminal Justice Association
P.O. Box 601047, Sacramento, CA 95860-1047
Phone: 916-484-6553
Email: acjalae@aol.com
http://www.acjalae.org
Purpose: To encourage scholarship in criminal justice students.
Eligibility: Applicants must be student members (undergraduate or graduate) of the American Criminal Justice Association-Lambda Alpha Epsilon and submit an original paper on criminology, law enforcement, juvenile justice, courts, corrections, prevention, planning and evaluation or career development and education in the field of criminal justice. Students may apply for membership along with their paper submission. Applicants should submit applications and three copies of the paper.
Target applicant(s): College students. Graduate school students. Adult students.
Amount: $50-$150.
Number of awards: 9.
Deadline: December 31.
How to apply: Applications are available by contacting the Executive Secretary.
Exclusive: Visit www.UltimateScholarshipBook.com and enter code AM41420 for updates on this award.

(415) • Student Transportation Video Contest

American Road and Transportation Builders Association
1219 28th Street, NW, Washington, DC 20007
Phone: 202-289-4434
Email: lshair@artba.org
http://www.artba.org
Purpose: To support students from elementary through graduate school interested in the transportation industry in the United States.
Eligibility: Applicants must be currently enrolled elementary through graduate school students. They must produce a 2-4 minute video on some aspect of the transportation industry in the United States. Selection is based on creativity and the overall strength of the video.
Target applicant(s): Junior high students or younger. High school students. College students. Graduate school students. Adult students.
Amount: $500.
Number of awards: 2.
Deadline: August 15.
How to apply: Videos must be uploaded to You Tube and a link to the video sent to ARTBA by the submission deadline. Submission forms are available online. A submission form, waiver, link to the video, enrollment verification and photo release form are required.
Exclusive: Visit www.UltimateScholarshipBook.com and enter code AM41520 for updates on this award.

(416) • Student View Scholarship

Student Insights
136 Justice Drive, Valencia, PA 16059
Phone: 724-612-3685
Email: jbecker@studentinsights.com
http://studentinsights.com
Purpose: To support graduating high school seniors regardless of academic achievement or need.
Eligibility: Applicants must complete an online survey and then they will be entered into a random drawing for an award.
Target applicant(s): High school students.
Amount: Up to $4,000.
Number of awards: 13.
Deadline: April 22.
How to apply: Applications are available online.
Exclusive: Visit www.UltimateScholarshipBook.com and enter code ST41620 for updates on this award.

(417) • Student-Caregiver Scholarship

Caring.com
2600 South El Camino Real, Suite 300, San Mateo, CA 94403
Email: scholarship@caring.com
https://www.caring.com/local/assisted-living-facilities#scholarship
Purpose: To support students who also serve as family caregivers.
Eligibility: Applicants must be U.S. citizens or permanent residents who are graduating high school seniors or currently enrolled full-time

students at in an accredited two- or four-year college in the U.S. Students must be caring for a family member and must submit an essay or video addressing their caregiver situation.
Target applicant(s): High school students. College students. Adult students.
Amount: $1,500.
Number of awards: 2.
Deadline: June 30.
How to apply: Applications are available online.
Exclusive: Visit www.UltimateScholarshipBook.com and enter code CA41720 for updates on this award.

(418) • Study Abroad Grants

Honor Society of Phi Kappa Phi
7576 Goodwood Boulevard, Baton Rouge, LA 70806
Phone: 800-804-9880
Email: awards@phikappaphi.org
http://www.phikappaphi.org
Purpose: To provide scholarships for undergraduate students who will study abroad.
Eligibility: Applicants do not have to be members of Phi Kappa Phi but must attend an institution with a Phi Kappa Phi chapter, have between 30 and 90 credit hours and have at least two semesters remaining at their home institution upon return. Students must have been accepted into a study abroad program that demonstrates their academic preparation, career choice and the welfare of others. They must have a GPA of 3.75 or higher.
Target applicant(s): College students. Adult students.
Minimum GPA: 3.75
Amount: $1,000.
Number of awards: 75.
Deadline: February 15, September 15.
How to apply: Applications are available online. An application form, personal statement, transcript, letter of acceptance and two letters of recommendation are required.
Exclusive: Visit www.UltimateScholarshipBook.com and enter code HO41820 for updates on this award.

(419) • StudySoup Future Innovator Scholarship

StudySoup
1381 9th Avenue, San Francisco, CA 94122
Phone: 415-658-9115
https://studysoup.com/scholarships/
Purpose: To reward students who have exemplified StudySoup's core values.
Eligibility: Applicants must be at least 13 years of age and be currently attending high school (or equivalent) or be currently attending an accredited university or college in either an undergraduate or graduate level program. Students must submit short essays that show how they represent one or more of StudySoup's core values of: Be a Knight, Make an Impact and Succeed Together. Awarded monthly.
Target applicant(s): High school students. College students. Graduate school students. Adult students.
Amount: $1,000.
Number of awards: 12.
Deadline: Monthly.
How to apply: Applications are available online.
Exclusive: Visit www.UltimateScholarshipBook.com and enter code ST41920 for updates on this award.

(420) • StudySoup Student Side Hustlers Scholarship Program

StudySoup
1381 9th Avenue, San Francisco, CA 94122
Phone: 415-658-9115
https://studysoup.com/scholarships/
Purpose: To support students who have a side business to earn income while in school.
Eligibility: Applicants must be at least 16 years of age and currently students at a high school or accredited college or university. Students must demonstrate initiative and entrepreneurship.
Target applicant(s): College students. Adult students.
Amount: $1,000.
Number of awards: 1.
Deadline: February 1.
How to apply: Applications are available online.
Exclusive: Visit www.UltimateScholarshipBook.com and enter code ST42020 for updates on this award.

(421) • Subic Bay-Cubi Point Scholarship 2

Navy League Foundation
2300 Wilson Boulevard, Suite 200, Arlington, VA 22201
Phone: 800-356-5760
Email: smcfarland@navyleague.org
https://www.navyleague.org
Purpose: To support students who are either dependents or direct descendants of a member of the U.S. Marine Corps, U.S. Navy or U.S.-Flag Merchant Marines or who are active members of the U.S. Naval Sea Cadet Corps.
Eligibility: Applicants must be U.S citizens who are current high school seniors and who are entering an accredited institution of higher learning in the fall after graduating. Only dependents or direct descendants of a member of the U.S. Marine Corps, U.S. Navy or U.S.-Flag Merchant Marines or who are active members of the U.S. Naval Sea Cadet Corps are eligible to apply. A minimum GPA of 3.0 is required. Financial need must also be demonstrated. Selection is based on the overall strength of the application.
Target applicant(s): High school students.
Minimum GPA: 3.0
Amount: $10,000.
Number of awards: 1.
Deadline: March 1.
How to apply: Applications are available online.
Exclusive: Visit www.UltimateScholarshipBook.com and enter code NA42120 for updates on this award.

(422) • Summer Graduate Research Fellowships

Institute for Humane Studies at George Mason University
3434 Washington Boulevard, MS 1C5, Arlington, VA 22201
Phone: 800-697-8799
Email: ihs@gmu.edu
http://www.theihs.org
Purpose: To support graduate students who are interested in scholarly research in the classical liberal tradition.
Eligibility: Applicants must be graduate students in areas related to the classical liberal tradition and should be focusing on a discrete writing project. Selection is based on resume, GRE or LSAT scores and graduate transcripts, writing sample and research proposal and bibliography for thesis chapter or publishable paper.
Target applicant(s): Graduate school students. Adult students.

Amount: $5,000 stipend + travel and housing allowance.
Number of awards: Varies.
Deadline: Varies.
How to apply: Applications are available online.
Exclusive: Visit www.UltimateScholarshipBook.com and enter code IN42220 for updates on this award.

---

(423) • SuperCollege Scholarship

SuperCollege.com
Scholarship Dept. 673, 2713 Newlands Avenue, Belmont, CA 94002
Email: supercollege@supercollege.com
http://www.supercollege.com/scholarship/
Purpose: SuperCollege donates a percentage of the proceeds from the sales of its books to award scholarships to high school, college, graduate and adult students.
Eligibility: Applicants must be high school students, college undergraduates, graduate students or adult students residing in the U.S. and attending or planning to attend any accredited college or university within the next 12 months. The scholarship may be used to pay for tuition, books, room and board, computers or any education-related expenses.
Target applicant(s): High school students. College students. Adult students.
Amount: $1,000.
Number of awards: 1.
Deadline: Monthly.
How to apply: Applications are available online.
Exclusive: Visit www.UltimateScholarshipBook.com and enter code SU42320 for updates on this award.

---

(424) • Supplemental Education Grant (SEG)

Coast Guard Mutual Assistance (CGMA)
4200 Wilson Boulevard, Coast Guard Stop 7180, Arlington, VA 20598-7180
Phone: 202-493-6621
http://www.cgmahq.org
Purpose: To encourage students who are pursuing education to prepare them for their future career.
Eligibility: Applicants must be Coast Guard members applying for themselves or their dependents. Students must be either enrolled in a college or university undergraduate or graduate program, pursuing a multi-course VoTech program approved by the Department of Veteran Affairs or Department of Education that would prepare them for their career, pursuing a GED or completing a correspondence course for a college, university or VoTech program.
Target applicant(s): College students. Adult students.
Amount: $500 per calendar year.
Number of awards: Varies.
Scholarship may be renewable.
Deadline: Varies.
How to apply: Applications are available online.
Exclusive: Visit www.UltimateScholarshipBook.com and enter code CO42420 for updates on this award.

---

(425) • Sweet Karen Alumni Scholarship

Harness Horse Youth Foundation
16575 Carey Road, Westfield, IN 46074
Phone: 317-867-5877
Email: ellen@hhyf.org
http://www.hhyf.org
Purpose: To help students interested in harness horses with their higher education expenses.
Eligibility: Applicants must be at least a high school senior and be planning to enroll as a full-time student or enrolled as a full-time undergraduate student at their selected college, university or trade school. Students must have participated in a Harness Horse Youth Foundation program to include the following events: Harness Racing Youth League event, Family Weekend and/or Leadership Program from 1999 to present.
Target applicant(s): High school students. College students.
Amount: Up to $1,500.
Number of awards: Varies.
Deadline: April 30.
How to apply: Applications are available online. An application form, financial information and an essay are required.
Exclusive: Visit www.UltimateScholarshipBook.com and enter code HA42520 for updates on this award.

---

(426) • Tailhook Educational Foundation Scholarship

Tailhook Association
The Tailhook Educational Foundation, 9696 Businesspark Avenue, San Diego, CA 92131-1643
Phone: 800-269-8267
Email: thookassn@aol.com
https://www.tailhook.net/
Purpose: To assist the members of and the children of the members of the United States Navy carrier aviation.
Eligibility: Applicants must be high school graduates who are accepted at an undergraduate institution and are the natural or adopted children of current or former Naval Aviators, Naval Flight Officers or Naval Aircrewmen. Applicants may also be individuals or children of individuals who are serving or have served on board a U.S. Navy Aircraft Carrier in the ship's company or the air wing. Educational and extracurricular achievements, merit and citizenship will be considered.
Target applicant(s): High school students. College students. Adult students.
Amount: Varies.
Number of awards: Varies.
Deadline: March 1.
How to apply: Applications are available online.
Exclusive: Visit www.UltimateScholarshipBook.com and enter code TA42620 for updates on this award.

---

(427) • Team Development Scholarships

National Collegiate Water Ski Association
A Sport Division of US Water Ski, 1251 Holy Cow Road, Polk City, FL 33868-8200
http://www.ncwsa.com/scholarships/
Purpose: To aid student water skiers with the continuing pursuit of their educational goals.
Eligibility: Applicants must be a U.S. citizen and a member of USA Water Ski. Selection varies by region and may be based on applicant's academic achievement, need, work record and community and school activities as well as contributions to the sport of water skiing as a skier or worker at tournaments.
Target applicant(s): College students. Adult students.
Amount: $1,500.
Number of awards: 4.
Deadline: Varies.
How to apply: Applications are available from each regional director.

Exclusive: Visit www.UltimateScholarshipBook.com and enter code NA42720 for updates on this award.

(428) • Technology Addiction Awareness Scholarship

Digital Responsibility
3561 Homestead Road #113, Santa Clara, CA 95051-5161
Email: scholarship@digitalresponsibility.org
http://www.digitalresponsibility.org
Purpose: To help students understand the negative effects of too much screen time.
Eligibility: Applicant must be a high school, college, graduate or home schooled student who is a U.S. citizen or legal resident. A 140-character message about technology addiction is required to apply. The top 10 applications will be selected as finalists; finalists will be asked to write a full length 500- to 1,000-word essay about technology addiction. Only online applications are accepted.
Target applicant(s): High school students. College students. Graduate school students. Adult students.
Amount: $1,000.
Number of awards: 1.
Deadline: January 30.
How to apply: Applications are available online.
Exclusive: Visit www.UltimateScholarshipBook.com and enter code DI42820 for updates on this award.

(429) • Telluride Association Summer Programs

Telluride Association
217 West Avenue, Ithaca, NY 14850
Phone: 607-273-5011
Email: tasp-queries@tellurideassociation.org
http://www.tellurideassociation.org
Purpose: Summer program to provide high school students with a college-level, intellectually enriching experience.
Eligibility: Applicants must be high school juniors. The association seeks applicants from a variety of socio-economic backgrounds and provides for their tuition and room and board during summer programs in New York and Michigan. Students are invited to apply either by receiving a score on the PSAT/NMSQT that is usually in the top 1 percent or by nomination by a teacher or counselor.
Target applicant(s): High school students.
Amount: Summer program tuition and fees.
Number of awards: Varies.
Deadline: January 24.
How to apply: Applications are sent to nominated students.
Exclusive: Visit www.UltimateScholarshipBook.com and enter code TE42920 for updates on this award.

(430) • TicketCity Annual College Scholarship Program

TicketCity
5912 Balcones Drive, Suite 102, Austin, TX 78731
Email: scholarship@ticketcity.com
http://www.ticketcity.com/ticketcity-annual-college-scholarship-program.html
Purpose: To help a student with their educational expenses.
Eligibility: Applicants must be U.S. citizens and be enrolled full-time as a freshman, sophomore or junior at an accredited U.S. four-year university. Students must have a GPA of 2.5 or higher. Selection is based on the strength of the application and overall creativity of applicant's essay.
Target applicant(s): College students. Adult students.
Minimum GPA: 2.5
Amount: $3,000.
Number of awards: 1.
Deadline: December 1.
How to apply: Applications are available online. An application and an essay which includes a picture or short video are required.
Exclusive: Visit www.UltimateScholarshipBook.com and enter code TI43020 for updates on this award.

(431) • Tim Olson Memorial Scholarship

USA Water Ski and Wake Sports Foundation
1251 Holy Cow Road, Polk City, FL 33868
Phone: 863-324-2472
Email: usa-wsf@waterskihalloffame.com
http://www.usawaterskifoundation.org/
Purpose: To aid current active members of USA Water Ski with the continuing pursuit of their educational goals.
Eligibility: Applicants must be U.S. citizens and be incoming freshmen, sophomores, juniors or seniors at a two-year or four-year accredited college and enrolled full-time. Applicants must remain enrolled full-time at their chosen college during the year of receipt of the scholarship. Selection is based on the applicant's academic achievement record, need, community and school activities and work record as well as their contributions to the sport of water skiing.
Target applicant(s): College students. Adult students.
Amount: $1,500.
Number of awards: 1.
Deadline: March 15.
How to apply: Applications are available online. An application form, two letters of recommendation and a 500-word essay are required.
Exclusive: Visit www.UltimateScholarshipBook.com and enter code US43120 for updates on this award.

(432) • Tortuga Backpacks Study Abroad

Tortuga Backpacks LLC
Phone: 310-692-4680
http://www.tortugabackpacks.com/pages/study-abroad-scholarship
Purpose: To support students who wish to experience the world beyond their college campus through a study abroad program.
Eligibility: Applicants must be either a U.S. citizen, a permanent resident or studying in the U.S. on a student visa. Students must also be in a full-time undergraduate program at a four-year college or university and have applied to or been accepted into a study abroad program.
Target applicant(s): College students. Adult students.
Amount: $1,000.
Number of awards: 1.
Deadline: May 20 (fall) and December 20 (spring).
How to apply: Applications available online.
Exclusive: Visit www.UltimateScholarshipBook.com and enter code TO43220 for updates on this award.

(433) • Toyota Teen Driver Video Challenge

Toyota Teen Driver
One Discovery Place, Silver Spring, MD 20910
Phone: 800-323-9084
http://www.teendrive365inschool.com/teens/video-challenge
Purpose: To support teens who are interested in persuading their peers to drive safely.

Eligibility: Applicants must be at least 13 years old, in grades 9-12 and legal residents of the United States. Applicants must work by themselves or in teams of two to four members. Students must create a 30- to 60-second video aimed at teenage drivers about how important it is to drive safely. Selection of winners will be based on the creativity, content and presentation of the video.
Target applicant(s): High school students.
Amount: Up to $15,000.
Number of awards: 9.
Deadline: February 28.
How to apply: Applications are available online.
Exclusive: Visit www.UltimateScholarshipBook.com and enter code TO43320 for updates on this award.

(434) · Trapshooting Hall of Fame College Scholarships

Trapshooting Hall of Fame
P.O. Box 281, Vandalia, OH 45377
Phone: 937-660-5663
http://www.traphof.org/Hall-Info/Scholarship-Information/
Purpose: To support high school seniors who have participated in trapshooting.
Eligibility: Applicants must be high school seniors and members of Amateur Trapshooting Association. Selection is based on an essay explaining the need for the scholarship, prior shooting experience and accomplishments.
Target applicant(s): High school students.
Amount: $5,000.
Number of awards: Varies.
Deadline: June 15.
How to apply: Applications are available online and must include the essay, one letter of recommendation and a listing of your shooting history and accomplishments.
Exclusive: Visit www.UltimateScholarshipBook.com and enter code TR43420 for updates on this award.

(435) · Travel Video Contest

InternationalStudent.com
224 First Street, Neptune, FL 32266
http://www.internationalstudent.com
Purpose: To support students who wish to pursue an international education or study abroad program.
Eligibility: Applicants must be at least 18 years old, be enrolled or currently enrolling in a college or university abroad. Students must submit a video describing a desired trip if they are currently studying abroad or describing a proposed study abroad if they are currently studying in their home country. Applicants must create a video that does not exceed four minutes, submit a fully completed online entry form and be prepared to document the entire experience in a weekly blog, if selected.
Target applicant(s): High school students. College students. Adult students.
Amount: $4,000.
Number of awards: 1.
Deadline: October 14.
How to apply: Applications are available online.
Exclusive: Visit www.UltimateScholarshipBook.com and enter code IN43520 for updates on this award.

(436) · Triple-Impact Competitor Scholarship

Positive Coaching Alliance
1001 N. Rengstorff Avenue, Suite 100, Mountain View, CA 94043
Phone: 650-210-0815
Email: jennie_wulbrun@positivecoach.org
http://www.positivecoach.org
Purpose: To reward high school juniors who participate in sports.
Eligibility: Students must have a GPA of 2.5 and provide testimonials from a coach, a school administrator and a fellow teammate or competitor.
Target applicant(s): High school students.
Minimum GPA: 2.5
Amount: $2,000.
Number of awards: Varies.
Deadline: May 31.
How to apply: Applications are available online.
Exclusive: Visit www.UltimateScholarshipBook.com and enter code PO43620 for updates on this award.

(437) · Tripz.com

Tripz.com
3422 Old Capitol Trail, Suite 193, Wilmington, DE 27101
Phone: 866-479-2819
https://www.tripz.com/scholarship.php
Purpose: To support students with an interest in promoting their communities.
Eligibility: Applicants must be U.S. citizens in their junior or senior year of high school or currently enrolled college students and have a minimum 2.5 GPA. Students must write an essay pertaining to tourism in their community.
Target applicant(s): High school students. College students. Adult students.
Minimum GPA: 2.5
Amount: $1,000.
Number of awards: 1.
Deadline: May 31.
How to apply: Applications are available online.
Exclusive: Visit www.UltimateScholarshipBook.com and enter code TR43720 for updates on this award.

(438) · Truman Scholar

Truman Scholarship Foundation
712 Jackson Place NW, Washington, DC 20006
Phone: 202-395-4831
Email: office@truman.gov
http://www.truman.gov
Purpose: To provide college junior leaders who plan to pursue careers in government, non-profits, education or other public service with financial support for graduate study and leadership training.
Eligibility: Applicants must be juniors, attending an accredited U.S. college or university and be nominated by the institution. Students may not apply directly. Applicants must be U.S. citizens or U.S. nationals, complete an application and write a policy recommendation.
Target applicant(s): College students. Adult students.
Amount: Up to $30,000.
Number of awards: 55-65.
Deadline: February 7.
How to apply: See your school's Truman Faculty Representative or contact the foundation.

Exclusive: Visit www.UltimateScholarshipBook.com and enter code TR43820 for updates on this award.

(439) • Tuition Giveaway

Dr. Pepper/Seven Up Inc.
Attn.: Consumer Relations, 5301 Legacy Drive, Plano, TX 75024
Phone: 800-696-5891
https://www.drpeppertuition.com/
Purpose: To assist full-time students with higher education costs.
Eligibility: Applicants must be U.S. residents age 18 and older. Applicants between the ages of 18 and 24 must get votes in order to submit a video and are eligible for up to $100,000 in tuition.
Target applicant(s): High school students. College students.
Amount: $2,500-$100,000.
Number of awards: 16.
Deadline: October 18.
How to apply: Application information is available online.
Exclusive: Visit www.UltimateScholarshipBook.com and enter code DR43920 for updates on this award.

(440) • Tweet for Success Scholarship Contest

DialMyCalls
1070 E. Indiantown Road, Suite 212, Jupiter, FL 33477
http://www.dialmycalls.com/scholarship.html
Purpose: To assist students who tweet about education.
Eligibility: Applicants must be high school graduates or GED equivalent and must be enrolled or planning to enroll in an accredited two- or four-year college. Students must also be legal U.S. residents and have a minimum 2.0 GPA.
Target applicant(s): College students. Adult students.
Minimum GPA: 2.0
Amount: $500.
Number of awards: 4.
Deadline: May 31.
How to apply: Applications are available online.
Exclusive: Visit www.UltimateScholarshipBook.com and enter code DI44020 for updates on this award.

(441) • U.S. Bank Scholarship Program

U.S. Bank
c/o U.S. Bank Office of Corporate Citizenship, 1420 Kettner Boulevard, 7th Floor, San Diego, CA 92101
Phone: 800-242-1200
http://www.usbank.com/community/financial-education/scholarship.html
Purpose: To support graduating high school seniors who plan to attend college.
Eligibility: Applicants must be high school seniors who plan to attend or current college freshmen, sophomores or juniors attending full-time at an accredited two- or four-year college and be U.S. citizens or permanent residents. Recipients are selected through a random drawing.
Target applicant(s): High school students. College students. Adult students.
Amount: $20,000.
Number of awards: Varies.
Deadline: October 27.
How to apply: Applications are only available online.
Exclusive: Visit www.UltimateScholarshipBook.com and enter code U.44120 for updates on this award.

(442) • U.S. JCI Senate Scholarship Grants

U.S. JCI Senate
106 Wedgewood Drive, Carrollton, GA 30117
Email: tom@smipc.net
http://www.usjcisenate.org
Purpose: To support high school students who wish to further their education.
Eligibility: Applicants must be high school seniors and U.S. citizens who are graduating from a U.S. accredited high school or state approved home school or GED program. Winners must attend college full-time to receive funds. Applications are judged at the state level.
Target applicant(s): High school students.
Amount: $1,000.
Number of awards: Varies.
Deadline: January 9.
How to apply: Applications are available from your school's guidance office.
Exclusive: Visit www.UltimateScholarshipBook.com and enter code U.44220 for updates on this award.

(443) • U.S. News Path to College Scholarship Program

U.S. News & World Report
U.S. News Path to College Scholarship, Scholarship America, One Scholarship Way, Saint Peter, MN 56082
Phone: 507-931-1682
Email: usnews@scholarshipamerica.org
https://www.usnews.com/education/scholarship
Purpose: To support students who plan on entering college upon graduation from high school.
Eligibility: Applicants must be attending a U.S. public or private high school and plan to enroll full-time at an accredited four-year college or university in the U.S. immediately following graduation. A minimum GPA of a 3.0 is required. Applicants must be U.S. citizens.
Target applicant(s): High school students.
Minimum GPA: 3.0
Amount: $2,500.
Number of awards: 2.
Deadline: June 2.
How to apply: Applications are available online.
Exclusive: Visit www.UltimateScholarshipBook.com and enter code U.44320 for updates on this award.

(444) • U.S. PIRG Fellowship

National Association of State Public Interest Research Groups
294 Washington Street, Suite 500, Boston, MA 02108
Phone: 617-747-4370
https://jobs.uspirg.org/fellowship.html
Purpose: To prepare future leaders for public service.
Eligibility: Applicants must commit to the two-year program. Students must demonstrate academic excellence, leadership experience and superior communication skills.
Target applicant(s): Graduate school students. Adult students.
Amount: $26,500.
Number of awards: Varies.
Deadline: Varies.
How to apply: Applications are available online.
Exclusive: Visit www.UltimateScholarshipBook.com and enter code NA44420 for updates on this award.

(445) • U.S. Veterans Magazine Scholarship

U.S. Veterans Magazine
18 Technology Drive, Suite 170, Irvine, CA 92618
Phone: 855-411-8786
https://www.usveteransmagazine.com/scholarship-opportunity/
Purpose: To support students who are veterans or children of veterans.
Eligibility: Applicants must be U.S. legal residents, veterans or children of veterans. Students must submit an essay, graphic or creative presentation on their college experience and future goals. Selection is based upon the applicant's genuine desire and goal of using the scholarship to help advance in their field and an overall passion for knowledge.
Target applicant(s): College students. Graduate school students. Adult students.
Amount: $500.
Number of awards: 1.
Deadline: August 15.
How to apply: Applications are available online.
Exclusive: Visit www.UltimateScholarshipBook.com and enter code U.44520 for updates on this award.

(446) • UDT-SEAL Scholarship

Naval Special Warfare Foundation
1619 D Street, Virginia Beach, VA 23459
Phone: 757-363-7490
Email: info@navySEALfoundation.org
https://www.navysealfoundation.org/
Purpose: To assist the dependents of UDT-SEAL Association members.
Eligibility: Students must be single dependents of a UDT-SEAL Association member who has served in or is serving in the U.S. Armed Forces and the Naval Special Warfare community. Members must have paid UDT-SEAL Association dues for last four consecutive years. Selection is based on academic achievement, a written essay and extracurricular involvement.
Target applicant(s): High school students. College students.
Amount: Varies.
Number of awards: Varies.
Deadline: March 15.
How to apply: Applications are available by contacting the NWSF.
Exclusive: Visit www.UltimateScholarshipBook.com and enter code NA44620 for updates on this award.

(447) • Undergraduate Transfer Scholarship

Jack Kent Cooke Foundation Undergraduate Transfer Scholarship
44325 Woodridge Parkway, Lansdowne, VA 20176
Phone: 800-941-3300
Email: scholarships@jkcf.org
http://www.jkcf.org
Purpose: To help community college students transfer to and attend four-year universities.
Eligibility: Applicants must be a current student at an accredited U.S. community college or two-year institution with sophomore status by December 31 of the application year or a recent graduate. Students must plan to enroll full time in a baccalaureate program at an accredited college or university in the following fall and have a cumulative undergraduate grade point average of 3.5 or better on a 4.0 scale. Applicants must also demonstrate significant unmet financial need. Family income of up to $95,000 will be considered. However, the majority of scholarship recipients will be eligible to receive a Pell grant.
Target applicant(s): College students. Adult students.
Minimum GPA: 3.5
Amount: Up to $40,000.
Number of awards: About 85.
Scholarship may be renewable.
Deadline: Late November.
How to apply: Applications are available online.
Exclusive: Visit www.UltimateScholarshipBook.com and enter code JA44720 for updates on this award.

(448) • United Daughters of the Confederacy Scholarships

United Daughters of the Confederacy
328 North Boulevard, Richmond, VA 23220
Phone: 804-355-1636
Email: hqudc@rcn.com
http://www.hqudc.org
Purpose: To support the descendants of Confederates.
Eligibility: Applicants must be lineal descendants of Confederates or other eligible descendants and have a minimum 3.0 GPA.
Target applicant(s): High school students. College students. Graduate school students. Adult students.
Minimum GPA: 3.0
Amount: Varies.
Number of awards: Varies.
Scholarship may be renewable.
Deadline: Varies.
How to apply: Contact any Division Second Vice President as listed on the website.
Exclusive: Visit www.UltimateScholarshipBook.com and enter code UN44820 for updates on this award.

(449) • United States Hispanic Leadership Institute Denny's Hungry for Education

United States Hispanic Leadership Institute Denny's Hunger for Education
Email: hungryforeducation@dennys.com
http://www.dennyshungryforeducation.com
Purpose: To support students who have ideas for fighting childhood hunger.
Eligibility: Applicants must be high school seniors or college students, be citizens of the United States or be living in the United States legally and have a 2.5 GPA. Students must write an essay as part of their application and have ideas on ending childhood hunger. Applicants may apply regardless or race or national origin.
Target applicant(s): High school students. College students. Adult students.
Minimum GPA: 2.5
Amount: $1,000.
Number of awards: 8.
Deadline: December 31.
How to apply: Applications are available online.
Exclusive: Visit www.UltimateScholarshipBook.com and enter code UN44920 for updates on this award.

(450) • Unpakt College Scholarship

Unpakt
555 W. 25th Street, Floor 3, New York, NY 10001
Phone: 212-677-5333
Email: scholarship@unpakt.com
http://www.unpakt.com/scholarship

Purpose: To support students who write about their future.
Eligibility: Applicants must be currently enrolled college students or recent graduates. Students must submit an application and essay discussing where they plan to move after graduation to start their professional life and why.
Target applicant(s): High school students. College students. Adult students.
Amount: $1,000.
Number of awards: 3.
Deadline: December 15.
How to apply: Applications are available online.
Exclusive: Visit www.UltimateScholarshipBook.com and enter code UN45020 for updates on this award.

(451) • Urban Fellows Program

New York City Department of Personnel
1 Centre Street, Room 2425, New York, NY 10007
Phone: 212-386-0058
http://www.nyc.gov/html/dcas/html/work/urbanfellows.shtml
Purpose: To support high-achieving students pursue government and public service.
Eligibility: Applicants must have received their bachelor's degree within the last two years. Students must commit full-time to the nine-month Fellowship and suspend any graduate study or outside work. Applicants must be eligible to work in the U.S.
Target applicant(s): Graduate school students. Adult students.
Amount: $30,000.
Number of awards: Varies.
Deadline: January 15.
How to apply: Applications are available online.
Exclusive: Visit www.UltimateScholarshipBook.com and enter code NE45120 for updates on this award.

(452) • USA Roller Sports Scholarship Fund

USA Roller Sports
Educational Scholarship Fund, 4730 South Street, Lincoln, NE 68506
Phone: 402-483-7551
Email: matteberry@usarollersports.org
http://www.teamusa.org/USA-Roller-Sports
Purpose: To support U.S. Roller Sports athletes in paying for educational costs in preparation for accomplishment of career goals.
Eligibility: Applicants must be U.S. citizens or legal residents as well as current USARS members who have held a membership for a minimum of three years. Applicants must also have participated in USARS Sanctioned National Championships. Students must be at least 17 years of age and in their final year of high school or must be high school graduates. A minimum GPA in the final year of high school of 3.0 is required. Eligible applicants must be currently enrolled or plan to enroll in a college or trade school seeking a degree or certificate and be of good academic standing. Selection is based on membership status, eligibility to compete, academic achievement and financial need.
Target applicant(s): High school students. College students. Adult students.
Minimum GPA: 3.0
Amount: $1,000-$2,000.
Number of awards: 3.
Deadline: September 15.
How to apply: Applications are available online.
Exclusive: Visit www.UltimateScholarshipBook.com and enter code US45220 for updates on this award.

(453) • USAR Scholarship

USA Racquetball
2812 West Colorado Avenue, Suite 200, Colorado Springs, CO 80904-2906
Phone: 719-635-5396
Email: Peggine@usra.org
http://www.teamusa.org/USA-Racquetball
Purpose: To support USAR members who are aspiring collegiate athletes.
Eligibility: Applicants must be current USAR members and be graduating high school seniors or college undergraduates.
Target applicant(s): High school students. College students. Adult students.
Amount: Varies.
Number of awards: Varies.
Deadline: March 1.
How to apply: Applications are available online.
Exclusive: Visit www.UltimateScholarshipBook.com and enter code US45320 for updates on this award.

(454) • USBC Alberta E. Crowe Star of Tomorrow

United States Bowling Congress
Attn.: Alberta E. Crowe Star of Tomorrow, 621 Six Flags Drive, Arlington, TX 76011
Phone: 800-514-2695
Email: contactus@ibcyouth.com
https://www.bowl.com/Youth/Youth_Home/Scholarships/
Purpose: To recognize star qualities in female students in high school or college who are competitive bowlers.
Eligibility: Applicants must be female high school seniors or college students 22 years of age or younger and USBC members who compete in certified events. They must hold an average of 175 or higher and must not have competed in professional tournaments except for Pro-AM's. They must also have a GPA of 2.5 or higher.
Target applicant(s): High school students. College students.
Minimum GPA: 2.5
Amount: $6,000.
Number of awards: 1.
Deadline: December 1.
How to apply: Applications are available online.
Exclusive: Visit www.UltimateScholarshipBook.com and enter code UN45420 for updates on this award.

(455) • USBC Annual Zeb Scholarship

United States Bowling Congress
Attn.: Alberta E. Crowe Star of Tomorrow, 621 Six Flags Drive, Arlington, TX 76011
Phone: 800-514-2695
Email: contactus@ibcyouth.com
https://www.bowl.com/Youth/Youth_Home/Scholarships/
Purpose: To reward USBC Youth members with high academic achievement who have participated in community service.
Eligibility: Applicants must be high school juniors or seniors who are USBC Youth members in good standing. They must have a GPA of 2.0 or higher and must not have competed in any professional bowling tournament except for Pro-Am's.
Target applicant(s): High school students.
Minimum GPA: 2.0
Amount: $2,500 plus travel.
Number of awards: 1.

Deadline: Varies.
How to apply: Applications are available online.
Exclusive: Visit www.UltimateScholarshipBook.com and enter code UN45520 for updates on this award.

(456) • USBC Chuck Hall Star of Tomorrow

United States Bowling Congress
Attn.: Alberta E. Crowe Star of Tomorrow, 621 Six Flags Drive, Arlington, TX 76011
Phone: 800-514-2695
Email: contactus@ibcyouth.com
https://www.bowl.com/Youth/Youth_Home/Scholarships/
Purpose: To recognize star qualities in male high school and college students who are competitive bowlers.
Eligibility: Applicants must be United States Bowling Congress members who compete in certified events and are high school seniors or college students with a GPA of 3.0 or higher. They must not have competed in a professional bowling tournament except for Pro-AM's.
Target applicant(s): High school students. College students. Adult students.
Minimum GPA: 3.0
Amount: $6,000.
Number of awards: 1.
Scholarship may be renewable.
Deadline: December 1.
How to apply: Applications are available online.
Exclusive: Visit www.UltimateScholarshipBook.com and enter code UN45620 for updates on this award.

(457) • USBC Youth Ambassador of the Year

United States Bowling Congress
Attn.: Alberta E. Crowe Star of Tomorrow, 621 Six Flags Drive, Arlington, TX 76011
Phone: 800-514-2695
Email: contactus@ibcyouth.com
https://www.bowl.com/Youth/Youth_Home/Scholarships/
Purpose: To recognize contributions to the sport of bowling, academic achievement and community service.
Eligibility: Students must be USBC Youth members who will be 18 years of age or older by August 1 of the year of their selection. They must also be high school seniors and be nominated by a USBC member. The award is given to one male and one female student each year.
Target applicant(s): High school students.
Amount: $1,500.
Number of awards: 2.
Deadline: December 1.
How to apply: Applications are available online.
Exclusive: Visit www.UltimateScholarshipBook.com and enter code UN45720 for updates on this award.

(458) • USHJA Making a Difference in Education Scholarship

United States Hunter Jumper Association Foundation (USHJA)
3870 Cigar Lane, Lexington , KY 40511
Phone: 859-225-6700
Email: foundation@ushja.org
http://www.ushjafoundation.org/grantsscholarship.aspx
Purpose: To help students who choose to rise to the challenge of pursuing a college degree.
Eligibility: Applicants must be a current member of the USHJA/USEF, must be a U.S. citizen or legal resident, must either be in the top 20 percent in class rank or have a 3.0 GPA and demonstrate financial need. Students must be entering a college or trade school in the fall as a freshman, sophomore, junior or senior. Selection is made by the zone committee and is based on financial need, academic achievement, community service, leadership and the personal essay.
Target applicant(s): High school students. College students. Adult students.
Minimum GPA: 3.0
Amount: Varies.
Number of awards: Varies.
Deadline: Varies.
How to apply: Applications are available online and include a photo, the application form, a copy of the FAFSA, a high school and college transcript (if already in college), three letters of reference and the personal essay.
Exclusive: Visit www.UltimateScholarshipBook.com and enter code UN45820 for updates on this award.

(459) • USMA Blake Family Metric Scholarship Award

U.S. Metric Association
P.O. Box 471, Windsor, CO 80550-0471
Phone: 779-537-5611
http://www.us-metric.org/usma-blake-family-foundation-metric-awards
Purpose: To support students who help promote metric awareness and usage.
Eligibility: Applicants must be high school seniors who plan to enter college in the fall after graduation. Selection is based on involvement in promoting metric awareness and usage in the U.S. An additional award is available to a non-student.
Target applicant(s): High school students.
Amount: $2,500.
Number of awards: 1.
Deadline: March 15.
How to apply: Applications are available online.
Exclusive: Visit www.UltimateScholarshipBook.com and enter code U.45920 for updates on this award.

(460) • USTA Foundation College Education Scholarship

United States Tennis Association Foundation
70 W. Red Oak Lane, White Plains, NY 10604
Phone: 914-696-7223
Email: foundation@usta.com
http://www.ustafoundation.com/
Purpose: To support youth tennis players who are planning on attending a two- or four-year college or university.
Eligibility: Applicants must be high school seniors who have actively participated in an organized youth tennis program. Selection is based on academic achievement and community service.
Target applicant(s): High school students.
Amount: $2,500.
Number of awards: 1.
Scholarship may be renewable.
Deadline: February 27.
How to apply: Applications are available online.
Exclusive: Visit www.UltimateScholarshipBook.com and enter code UN46020 for updates on this award.

(461) • VA Essay Scholarship

VA Mortgage Center
2101 Chapel Plaza Court, Suite 107, Columbia, MO 65203
Phone: 800-405-6682
https://www.enhancelives.com/

Purpose: To reward students who are members of the military community as they pursue a college education.
Eligibility: Students must be a surviving spouse or child of a deceased veteran from the U.S. military, be currently enrolled or planning to enroll in a college or university by the spring semester of the following school year. Students must also be comfortable sharing personal stories and aspirations with the Veteran's United Foundation and willing and able to provide requested documentation in a timely manner.
Target applicant(s): College students. Adult students.
Amount: $20,000.
Number of awards: Up to 5.
Deadline: Varies.
How to apply: Applications are available online.
Exclusive: Visit www.UltimateScholarshipBook.com and enter code VA46120 for updates on this award.

(462) • Verbal Ink Transcription Services Scholarship

Verbal Ink
11835 West Olympic Boulevard, Suite 1020E, Los Angeles, CA 90064
Phone: 877-983-7225
http://verbalink.com

Purpose: To support graduating high school seniors and college freshmen in pursuing post-secondary education.
Eligibility: Applicants must enrolled full-time at an accredited educational institution for the upcoming semester. A minimum GPA of 3.0 is required. Students must submit an essay regarding the importance of language.
Target applicant(s): High school students. College students. Adult students.
Minimum GPA: 3.0
Amount: $1,500.
Number of awards: 1.
Deadline: April 15.
How to apply: Applications are available online.
Exclusive: Visit www.UltimateScholarshipBook.com and enter code VE46220 for updates on this award.

(463) • Veterans Caucus Scholarship

Veterans Caucus of the American Academy of Physician Assistants
P.O. Box 362, Danville, PA 17821-0362
Email: fbrace@veteranscaucus.org
http://www.veteranscaucus.org

Purpose: To aid U.S. military veterans who are enrolled in a physician assistant training program.
Eligibility: Applicants must be U.S. military veterans. They must be enrolled in an accredited physician assistant (PA) training program. Selection is based on the overall strength of the application.
Target applicant(s): College students. Graduate school students. Adult students.
Amount: Varies.
Number of awards: 11.
Deadline: March 1.
How to apply: Applications are available online. An application form and personal statement are required.
Exclusive: Visit www.UltimateScholarshipBook.com and enter code VE46320 for updates on this award.

(464) • Viber Mobile Technology Scholarship

Viber
Email: scholarships@viber.com
https://account.viber.com/en/scholarship

Purpose: To support students who write about technology.
Eligibility: Applicants must be currently enrolled at an accredited college or university. Students must also be a U.S. citizen or permanent legal resident. Applicants must write a 400-500 word essay on the given technology topic on the webpage that will be judged on originality, facts and how engaging the paper is. Students must also submit a 50-100 word personal introduction.
Target applicant(s): College students. Graduate school students. Adult students.
Amount: $1,000.
Number of awards: 3.
Deadline: June 1.
How to apply: Applications are submitted via email and must include the essay and personal introduction.
Exclusive: Visit www.UltimateScholarshipBook.com and enter code VI46420 for updates on this award.

(465) • Vivint Smart Home Scholarship

Vivint Smart Home
4931 North 300 W, Provo, UT 84604
Email: scholarship@vivint.com
https://www.vivint.com/scholarship

Purpose: To help students who create a video submission.
Eligibility: Applicants must be graduating high school seniors or currently enrolled college students who are legal residents of the U.S. Students must create a video as part of their submission materials.
Target applicant(s): High school students. College students. Graduate school students. Adult students.
Amount: $1,000.
Number of awards: 5.
Deadline: May 1.
How to apply: Applications are available online.
Exclusive: Visit www.UltimateScholarshipBook.com and enter code VI46520 for updates on this award.

(466) • Voice of Democracy Audio Essay Contests

Veterans of Foreign Wars
406 W. 34th Street, Kansas City, MO 64111
Phone: 816-968-1117
Email: kharmer@vfw.org
https://www.vfw.org/community/youth-and-education

Purpose: To encourage patriotism with students creating audio essays expressing their opinion on a patriotic theme.
Eligibility: Applicants must submit a three- to five-minute audio essay on tape or CD focused on a yearly theme. Students must be in the 9th to 12th grade in a public, private or parochial high school, home study program or overseas U.S. military school. Foreign exchange students are not eligible for the contest, and students who are age 20 or older also may not enter. Previous first place winners on the state level are ineligible.
Target applicant(s): High school students.
Amount: $1,000-$30,000.
Number of awards: Varies.
Deadline: October 31.

How to apply: Applications are available online but must be submitted to a local VFW post.
Exclusive: Visit www.UltimateScholarshipBook.com and enter code VE46620 for updates on this award.

(467) • VRG Scholarship

Vegetarian Resource Group
P.O. Box 1463, Baltimore, MD 21203
Phone: 410-366-8343
Email: vrg@vrg.org
http://www.vrg.org
Purpose: To reward high school seniors who promote vegetarianism.
Eligibility: Applicants must be graduating U.S. high school students who have promoted vegetarianism in their schools or communities. Vegetarians do not eat meat, fish or fowl. The award is based on compassion, courage and commitment to promoting a "peaceful world through a vegetarian diet or lifestyle." Applicants should submit transcripts and at least three recommendations.
Target applicant(s): High school students.
Amount: $5,000-$10,000.
Number of awards: 3.
Deadline: February 20.
How to apply: Applications are available online, by mail, by phone or by email. A typed document containing the application's information will be accepted.
Exclusive: Visit www.UltimateScholarshipBook.com and enter code VE46720 for updates on this award.

(468) • W. H. Howie McClennan Scholarship

International Association of Fire Fighters
1750 New York Avenue, NW, Washington, DC 20006
Phone: 202-737-8484
http://www.iaff.org
Purpose: To provide scholarships for the children of firefighters who died in the line of duty.
Eligibility: Applicants must be the children (natural or legally-adopted) of firefighters who died in the line of duty. Applicant's parent must have been a member in good standing of the International Association of Fire Fighters, AFL-CIO/CLC at time of death. Selection is based on financial need, academic record and promise.
Target applicant(s): High school students. College students. Adult students.
Amount: $2,500.
Number of awards: 1.
Scholarship may be renewable.
Deadline: February 1.
How to apply: Applications are available by written request.
Exclusive: Visit www.UltimateScholarshipBook.com and enter code IN46820 for updates on this award.

(469) • Wade Trophy

Women's Basketball Coaches Association
4646 Lawrenceville Highway, Lilburn, GA 30047
Phone: 770-279-8027
Email: dtrujillo@wbca.org
https://wbca.org/recognize/player-awards
Purpose: To recognize the best women's college basketball player in the country who exceeds expectations on and off the court.
Eligibility: Applicants must be academically eligible NCAA Division I players and members of the WBCA NCAA Division I Coaches' All-American Team. Eligibility is limited to sophomore, junior and senior players.
Target applicant(s): College students. Adult students.
Amount: Varies.
Number of awards: Varies.
Deadline: Varies.
How to apply: There is no formal application process. Eligible applicants are selected by the Wade Trophy Committee at the beginning of the basketball season.
Exclusive: Visit www.UltimateScholarshipBook.com and enter code WO46920 for updates on this award.

(470) • Walter Byers Postgraduate Scholarship Program

National Collegiate Athletic Association
700 W. Washington Street, P.O. Box 6222, Indianapolis, IN 46206
Phone: 317-917-6222
Email: lthomas@ncaa.org
http://www.ncaa.org/about/resources/ncaa-scholarships-and-grants
Purpose: To encourage academic excellence of student athletes by recognizing outstanding academic achievement and success in postgraduate studies.
Eligibility: Applicants must have a cumulative GPA of 3.5 or higher in their undergraduate work and have competed in intercollegiate athletics at a NCAA member institution as a member of a varsity team. Applicants should be a graduating senior or be enrolled in graduate studies. If not already in a graduate program, the applicant should have the intent of pursuing a graduate degree within five years at a properly accredited, nonprofit educational institution. Scholarship funds can also apply to a professional degree program at an accredited law school, medical school or the equivalent. Applicants must be able to demonstrate that athletic participation and community service have guided them to build superior character and leadership as well as helping to influence personal and intellectual growth.
Target applicant(s): College students. Graduate school students. Adult students.
Minimum GPA: 3.5
Amount: $24,000.
Number of awards: 2.
Scholarship may be renewable.
Deadline: January 15.
How to apply: Applicants must be nominated by a faculty athletics representative using the online application form. Applications also include a personal essay detailing future personal and academic goals. Included with the packet is a listing of involvement in activities and honors, as well as four recommendations.
Exclusive: Visit www.UltimateScholarshipBook.com and enter code NA47020 for updates on this award.

(471) • Watson Travel Fellowship

Thomas J. Watson Fellowship
11 Park Place, Suite 1503, New York, NY 10007
Phone: 212-245-8859
Email: tjw@watsonfellowship.org
http://watson.foundation/fellowships/tj
Purpose: To award one-year grants for independent study and travel outside the U.S. to graduating college seniors.
Eligibility: Only graduating seniors from the participating colleges are eligible to apply. A list of these colleges is available online. Applicants must first be nominated by their college or university. An interview

with a representative will follow. Recipients must graduate before the fellowship can begin.
Target applicant(s): College students. Adult students.
Amount: Up to $30,000.
Number of awards: Varies.
Deadline: November.
How to apply: Interested students should contact their local Watson liaison to begin the application process. Once nominated, applicants must complete an online application form, project proposal and personal statement. A photo, transcripts and letters of recommendation are also required.
Exclusive: Visit www.UltimateScholarshipBook.com and enter code TH47120 for updates on this award.

(472) · WBCA Coaches' All-America

Women's Basketball Coaches Association
4646 Lawrenceville Highway, Lilburn, GA 30047
Phone: 770-279-8027
Email: dtrujillo@wbca.org
https://wbca.org/recognize/player-awards
Purpose: To recognize the 10 best women's or girl's basketball players at the NCAA Division I, NCAA Division II, NCAA Division III, NAIA, Junior/Community College and high school levels.
Eligibility: Applicants at the collegiate level must be eligible college women's basketball players whose coaches are members of the WBCA. Applicants at the high school level must be seniors. Selection at all levels is based on current season statistics and achievements, impact on the team, team success, sportsmanship and academic eligibility.
Target applicant(s): High school students. College students. Adult students.
Amount: Varies.
Number of awards: 10.
Deadline: Varies.
How to apply: Applicants must be nominated using the online nomination form.
Exclusive: Visit www.UltimateScholarshipBook.com and enter code WO47220 for updates on this award.

(473) · Wells Fargo Veterans Scholarship Program

Wells Fargo Veterans Scholarship Program, Scholarship America
One Scholarship Way, Saint Peter, MN 56082
Phone: 800-537-4180
Email: wellsfargoveterans@scholarshipamerica.org
http://www.scholarsapply.org/wellsfargoveterans
Purpose: To reward those who have served in the United States military.
Eligibility: Applicants must be honorably-discharged veterans or spouses of disabled veterans who have graduated high school (or obtained a GED) and who have served in the U.S. military. Students must have at least a 2.5 GPA and plan to enroll full-time in an accredited two- or four-year college, university or vocational school the following fall. Award will increase with renewal to encourage completion of program.
Target applicant(s): High school students. College students. Graduate school students. Adult students.
Minimum GPA: 2.5
Amount: Up to $7,000.
Number of awards: Up to 15.
Scholarship may be renewable.
Deadline: February 28.
How to apply: Applications are available online.
Exclusive: Visit www.UltimateScholarshipBook.com and enter code WE47320 for updates on this award.

(474) · Wendy's High School Heisman Award

Wendy's Restaurants
One Dave Thomas Boulevard, Dublin, OH 43017
Phone: 800-205-6367
Email: jdeets@scholarshipamerican.org
http://www.wendysheisman.com
Purpose: To recognize high school students who excel in academics, athletics and student leadership.
Eligibility: Applicants must be entering their high school senior year and participate in one of 43 officially sanctioned sports. Eligible students have a minimum 3.0 GPA. Selection is based on academic achievement, community service and athletic accomplishments.
Target applicant(s): High school students.
Minimum GPA: 3.0
Amount: $1,000-$10,000.
Number of awards: 100.
Deadline: October 3.
How to apply: Application forms are available online.
Exclusive: Visit www.UltimateScholarshipBook.com and enter code WE47420 for updates on this award.

(475) · Western Region/Big Al Wagner Scholarship

USA Water Ski and Wake Sports Foundation
1251 Holy Cow Road, Polk City, FL 33868
Phone: 863-324-2472
Email: usa-wsf@waterskihalloffame.com
http://www.usawaterskifoundation.org/
Purpose: To help current active members of USA Water Ski pursue their educational goals.
Eligibility: Applicants must be U.S. citizens who are incoming freshmen, sophomores, juniors or seniors at a two-year or four-year accredited college. Applicants must be enrolled full-time at their chosen college and must attend for the full year during the year of receipt of the scholarship. Selection is based on academic achievement, need, school and community activities and work record as well as contributions to the sport of water skiing.
Target applicant(s): College students. Adult students.
Amount: $1,500.
Number of awards: 1.
Deadline: March 15.
How to apply: Applications are available online. An application form, two letters of reference and a 500-word essay are required.
Exclusive: Visit www.UltimateScholarshipBook.com and enter code US47520 for updates on this award.

(476) · White House Fellows Program

White House
1600 Pennsylvania Avenue NW, Washington, DC 20500
Phone: 202-395-4522
Email: whitehousefellows@who.eop.gov
https://www.whitehouse.gov/get-involved/fellows/apply/
Purpose: To provide motivated students with first-hand experience working at high levels of federal government.
Eligibility: Applicants must be U.S. citizens who have completed their undergraduate education and demonstrate early professional achievement and evidence of leadership skills. Students must demonstrate commitment to public service and the ability to work as part of a team and provide three recommendations along with the application.
Target applicant(s): Graduate school students. Adult students.
Amount: Varies.

Number of awards: Varies.
Deadline: January 10.
How to apply: Applications are available online.
Exclusive: Visit www.UltimateScholarshipBook.com and enter code WH47620 for updates on this award.

(477) • William J. "Billy" Goaziou Scholarships

US Youth Soccer
9220 World Cup Way, Frisco, TX 75033
Phone: 800-476-2237
Email: jmagleby@usyouthsoccer.org
http://www.usyouthsoccer.org/
Purpose: To aid high school senior soccer players who plan on continuing their education beyond high school.
Eligibility: Applicants must be high school seniors who have participated in a U.S. Youth Soccer program during the past two years. Students must have at least a 3.0 GPA. Selection is based on community service and the desire to give back to the game of soccer.
Target applicant(s): High school students.
Minimum GPA: 3.0
Amount: $1,000.
Number of awards: 2.
Deadline: April 10.
How to apply: Applications are available online and must also include an official transcript and two letters of recommendation.
Exclusive: Visit www.UltimateScholarshipBook.com and enter code US47720 for updates on this award.

(478) • William L. Hastie Award

National Association of Blacks in Criminal Justice
1801 Fayetteville Street, 106 Whiting Criminal Justice Building, P.O. Box 20011-C, Durham, NC 27707
Phone: 919-683-1801
Email: Office@NABCJ.org
http://www.nabcj.org
Purpose: To reward demonstrations of national leadership in criminal justice and the pursuit of policy change within the field.
Eligibility: The award honors the first African American appointed to the bench in 1937 by President Franklin Roosevelt. Nominator should be a member of NABCJ.
Target applicant(s): High school students. College students. Adult students.
Amount: Varies.
Number of awards: 1.
Deadline: March 15.
How to apply: Nomination applications are available online.
Exclusive: Visit www.UltimateScholarshipBook.com and enter code NA47820 for updates on this award.

(479) • Women Divers Hall of Fame Scholarships and Grants

Women Divers Hall of Fame
43 Mackey Avenue, Port Washington, NY 10050
Email: scholarships@wdhof.org
http://www.wdhof.org/wdhof-scholarshipDesc.aspx
Purpose: To support those of all ages who are pursuing careers involving diving.
Eligibility: Applicants must be interested in a career that involves diving. Several scholarships and grants are available, and each has various requirements. Not all are for women only.
Target applicant(s): Junior high students or younger. High school students. College students. Graduate school students. Adult students.
Amount: Up to $2,000.
Number of awards: Varies.
Deadline: November 18.
How to apply: All applications are online and all require a resume, essay and two letters of recommendation.
Exclusive: Visit www.UltimateScholarshipBook.com and enter code WO47920 for updates on this award.

(480) • Women Marines Association Scholarship Program

Women Marines Association
Scholarships, Dottie Stover-Kendrick, P.O. Box 134, Stilwell, KS 66085
Phone: 888-525-1943
Email: scholarship@womenmarines.org
https://www.womenmarines.org/scholarships
Purpose: To aid Marines and their families.
Eligibility: Applicants must be sponsored by a Women Marines Association member. They must have served or be serving in the Marine Corps or Reserve, be a direct descendant, sibling or descendant of a sibling of a member of the Marines or have completed two years in a Marine JROTC program. A minimum GPA of 3.0 is required.
Target applicant(s): High school students. College students. Adult students.
Minimum GPA: 3.0
Amount: $1,500-$3,000.
Number of awards: Varies.
Deadline: February 28.
How to apply: Applications are available online. An application form, copy of sponsor's membership card, photo, three letters of recommendation, proof of Marine or ROTC status or relationship to a Marine and proof of draft registration (for males) are required.
Exclusive: Visit www.UltimateScholarshipBook.com and enter code WO48020 for updates on this award.

(481) • Women's Army Corps Veterans Association Scholarship

Women's Army Corps Veterans Association
P.O. Box 5577, Fort McClellan, AL 36205
http://www.armywomen.org
Purpose: To support relatives of army service women based upon academic achievement and leadership as revealed by co-curricular activities and community involvement.
Eligibility: Applicants must be the child, grandchild, niece or nephew of an Army Service Woman. Students must have a GPA of 3.5 or higher and show academic promise. Students must be graduating seniors and U.S. citizens.
Target applicant(s): High school students.
Minimum GPA: 3.5
Amount: $1,500.
Number of awards: Varies.
Deadline: May 1.
How to apply: Applications are available online.
Exclusive: Visit www.UltimateScholarshipBook.com and enter code WO48120 for updates on this award.

(482) · Women's Overseas Service League Scholarships for Women

Women's Overseas Service League
Scholarship Committee, P.O. Box 124, Cedar Knoll, NJ 07927-0124
Email: kelsey@openix.com
http://www.wosl.org/index.htm
Purpose: To assist women in the military and other public service careers.
Eligibility: Applicants must demonstrate a commitment to advancement in their careers and must have completed at least 12 semester or 18 quarter hours of study at an institution of higher learning and be working toward a degree. Students must agree to enroll for at least six semester or nine quarter hours each academic period. A GPA of 2.5 or higher is required.
Target applicant(s): College students. Adult students.
Minimum GPA: 2.5
Amount: $500-$1,000.
Number of awards: Varies.
Scholarship may be renewable.
Deadline: March 1.
How to apply: Applications are available online. An application form, statement of financial need, resume, three letters of reference, essay and transcript are required.
Exclusive: Visit www.UltimateScholarshipBook.com and enter code WO48220 for updates on this award.

(483) · Women's Western Golf Foundation Scholarship

Women's Western Golf Foundation
Mrs. Richard Willis, Scholarship Selection Director, 393 Ramsay Road, Deerfield, IL 60015
Phone: 608-274-0173
Email: dkdink@aol.com
http://www.wwga.org/WWGA.org/Foundation.html
Purpose: To support female students who are involved in golf.
Eligibility: Applicants must be in their senior year of high school. Students must demonstrate academic excellence, good character and financial need. Recipients must maintain a 3.0 GPA for award renewal.
Target applicant(s): High school students.
Amount: $2,000.
Number of awards: Varies.
Scholarship may be renewable.
Deadline: March 1.
How to apply: Applications are available by mail.
Exclusive: Visit www.UltimateScholarshipBook.com and enter code WO48320 for updates on this award.

(484) · Wpromote Digital Marketing Scholarship

Wpromote
2100 East Grand Avenue, First Floor, El Segundo, CA 90245
Email: scholarships@wpromote.com
https://www.wpromote.com/scholarship
Purpose: To support students interested in digital marketing.
Eligibility: Applicants must be legal U.S. residents and currently enrolled full-time at an accredited university in the U.S. Students must be seeking an undergraduate or graduate degree and hold a 3.0 or higher grade point average. Applicants must complete essay and submit a photo on social media.
Target applicant(s): College students. Graduate school students. Adult students.
Minimum GPA: 3.0
Amount: Varies.
Number of awards: 1.
Deadline: May 31.
How to apply: Applications are available online.
Exclusive: Visit www.UltimateScholarshipBook.com and enter code WP48420 for updates on this award.

(485) · Young People for Fellowship

People For the American Way Foundation
Young People For, 1101 15th Street NW, Suite 600, Washington, DC 20005
Phone: 202-467-4999
Email: mhall@pfaw.org
http://www.youngpeoplefor.org
Purpose: To encourage and cultivate young progressive leaders.
Eligibility: Applicants must be undergraduate students and be interested in promoting social change on their campuses and in their communities. Selection is based on the overall strength of the application.
Target applicant(s): College students. Adult students.
Amount: Varies.
Number of awards: Varies.
Deadline: December 31.
How to apply: Applications are available online. An application form is required.
Exclusive: Visit www.UltimateScholarshipBook.com and enter code PE48520 for updates on this award.

(486) · Young Scholars Program

Jack Kent Cooke Foundation Young Scholars Program
301 ACT Drive, P.O. Box 4030, Iowa City, IA 52243
Phone: 800-941-3300
Email: scholarships@jkcf.org
http://www.jkcf.org
Purpose: To help high-achieving students with financial need and provide them with educational opportunities throughout high school.
Eligibility: Applicants must have financial need, be in the 7th grade and plan to attend high school in the United States. Academic achievement and intelligence are important, and students must display strong academic records, academic awards and honors and submit a strong letter of recommendation. A GPA of 3.65 is usually required, but exceptions are made for students with unique talents or learning differences. The award is also based on students' will to succeed, leadership and public service, critical thinking ability and participation in the arts and humanities. During two summers, recipients must participate in a Young Scholars Week and Young Scholars Reunion in Washington, DC.
Target applicant(s): Junior high students or younger.
Minimum GPA: 3.65
Amount: Varies.
Number of awards: 60.
Scholarship may be renewable.
Deadline: April 5.
How to apply: Applications are available online and at regional talent centers. An application form, parental release, financial and tax forms, school report, teacher recommendation, personal recommendation and survey form are required.
Exclusive: Visit www.UltimateScholarshipBook.com and enter code JA48620 for updates on this award.

(487) • Young Women's Leadership Retreat Scholarship Essay Contest

Network of Enlightened Women
1360 E. Capitol Street NE, Washington, DC 20003
Phone: 423-838-4477
Email: amber@enlightenedwomen.org
https://enlightenedwomen.org/calling-high-school-juniors-seniors-young-womens-leadership-retreat-scholarship-essay-contest-now-open/
Purpose: To inspire female high school students to reflect on leadership.
Eligibility: Applicants must be female and legal residents of the U.S. currently enrolled as a high school junior or senior. Students must write an essay discussing the opportunities and challenges of emerging technology and social media on current and future leaders.
Target applicant(s): High school students.
Amount: $1,000.
Number of awards: 1.
Deadline: April 30.
How to apply: Applications are available online.
Exclusive: Visit www.UltimateScholarshipBook.com and enter code NE48720 for updates on this award.

(488) • Youth Education Summit

Friends of NRA
Field Operations Division, Event Support Coordinator, 11250 Waples Mill Road, Fairfax, VA 22030
Phone: 703-267-1351
Email: yes@nrahq.org
http://www.friendsofnra.org/
Purpose: To help young men and women learn more about their role in civic affairs.
Eligibility: Students must be a high school sophomore or junior and have at least a 3.0 GPA. Membership in the NRA is not required. Most applicants have strong interests in shooting sports, American history, government or the military. Students from Alaska, North Carolina, Oregon, Texas, Virginia and West Virginia must attend the state Y.E.S. program before being considered for the national summit.
Target applicant(s): High school students.
Minimum GPA: 3.0
Amount: Varies.
Number of awards: Varies.
Deadline: January 13.
How to apply: Applications are available online and include a three-page essay, a short personal statement, a high school transcript and three letters of recommendation.
Exclusive: Visit www.UltimateScholarshipBook.com and enter code FR48820 for updates on this award.

(489) • Zale Parry Scholarship

Academy of Underwater Arts and Sciences
27 West Anapamu Street #317, Santa Barbara, CA 93101
Phone: 919-369-0583
http://www.auas-nogi.org/
Purpose: To support students pursuing a career in ocean exploration, diving equipment technology, hyperbaric research or marine conservation.
Eligibility: Applicants must be enrolled in undergraduate or graduate level studies and must be a certified diver. Selection is based on merit.
Target applicant(s): College students. Graduate school students. Adult students.
Amount: $6,000.
Number of awards: Varies.
Deadline: August 31.
How to apply: Applications are available online and must include two letters of reference, a resume and an essay.
Exclusive: Visit www.UltimateScholarshipBook.com and enter code AC48920 for updates on this award.

(490) • Zen Bei Butoku Kai Scholarship

Zen Bei Butoku- Kai International
301 McCormick Avenue, Capitola, CA 95010
Email: senseilj@yahoo.com
http://zenbeibutokukai.com/index.php/scholarship/
Purpose: To aid students of the martial arts with college expenses.
Eligibility: Applicants must have studied a martial art for more than two years and currently be practicing. Selection is based on the merit of a required paper between 3,000 and 10,000 words describing how martial arts training has affected the applicant's personal growth.
Target applicant(s): College students. Adult students.
Amount: Varies.
Number of awards: Varies.
Deadline: Varies.
How to apply: Applicants must request scholarship funds via regular mail by providing name, address, purpose of funds and amount of funds requested. Applicants should also provide martial arts training history to include dates of training, instructor, style of martial arts, history of the martial art being studied and any letter of recommendation from instructors.
Exclusive: Visit www.UltimateScholarshipBook.com and enter code ZE49020 for updates on this award.

(491) • ZipRecruiter $3,000 Scholarship Challenge

ZipRecruiter
1453 3rd Street Promenade #335, 11th Floor, Santa Monica, CA 90401
Phone: 404-936-1644
https://www.ziprecruiter.com/scholarship
Purpose: To promote the use of creativity in the career search.
Eligibility: Applicants must be college students at least 18 years of age who are legal residents of the United States or its territories and possessions. Students are to write an essay on the topic provided. A minimum 2.5 GPA is required.
Target applicant(s): High school students. College students. Adult students.
Minimum GPA: 2.5
Amount: $3,000.
Number of awards: 1.
Deadline: September 30.
How to apply: Applications are available online.
Exclusive: Visit www.UltimateScholarshipBook.com and enter code ZI49120 for updates on this award.

HUMANITIES/ARTS

(492) • ACES Copy Editing Scholarships

American Copy Editor's Society
Eugene S. Pulliam National Journalism Center, 3909 N. Meridian Street, Indianapolis, IN 46208
Email: alex@copydesk.org
http://www.copydesk.org
Purpose: To support students who are interested in copy editing.
Eligibility: Applicants must be college juniors, seniors or graduate students. Graduating students who will take full-time copy editing jobs or internships are eligible. They must demonstrate interest in and aptitude for copy editing.
Target applicant(s): College students. Graduate school students. Adult students.
Amount: $1,000-$2,500.
Number of awards: 5.
Deadline: November 15.
How to apply: Applications are available online. An application form, list of course work related to copy editing, list of copy editing experience, two letters of recommendation, copies of 5 to 10 headlines written by applicant and a copy of a story edited by applicant are required.
Exclusive: Visit www.UltimateScholarshipBook.com and enter code AM49220 for updates on this award.

(493) • ACES Education Fund Scholarship

American Copy Editor's Society
Eugene S. Pulliam National Journalism Center, 3909 N. Meridian Street, Indianapolis, IN 46208
Email: alex@copydesk.org
http://www.copydesk.org
Purpose: To support students pursuing a career in editing written materials.
Eligibility: Applicants must be currently enrolled juniors, seniors or graduate students seeking a degree at a college or university. Students must provide an academic resume along with three references. Applicants must write an original essay as well as sample headlines with the given prompts.
Target applicant(s): College students. Graduate school students. Adult students.
Amount: $1,500.
Number of awards: 4.
Deadline: November 15.
How to apply: Applications are available online.
Exclusive: Visit www.UltimateScholarshipBook.com and enter code AM49320 for updates on this award.

(494) • ACL/NJCL National Greek Examination Scholarship

American Classical League
Scholarship Awards, 860 NW Washington Boulevard, Suite A, Hamilton, OH 45013
Phone: 513-529-7741
Email: info@aclclassics.org
https://www.aclclassics.org/pages/scholarships
Purpose: To support outstanding students of Greek.
Eligibility: Applicants must be high school seniors who have earned purple or blue ribbons in the upper level National Greek Exam. They must agree to earn six credits in Greek during their freshman year in college.
Target applicant(s): High school students.
Amount: $1,000.
Number of awards: 1.
Deadline: Varies.
How to apply: Applications are sent to teachers of eligible students by mail.
Exclusive: Visit www.UltimateScholarshipBook.com and enter code AM49420 for updates on this award.

(495) • ACL/NJCL National Latin Examination Scholarships

American Classical League
Scholarship Awards, 860 NW Washington Boulevard, Suite A, Hamilton, OH 45013
Phone: 513-529-7741
Email: info@aclclassics.org
https://www.aclclassics.org/pages/scholarships
Purpose: To support outstanding students of Latin.
Eligibility: Applicants must be Latin students and gold medal winners in the National Latin Exam Awards. They must also be high school seniors and must agree to take at least one Latin or classical Greek course each semester of their first year of college.
Target applicant(s): High school students.
Amount: $2,000.
Number of awards: Varies.
Scholarship may be renewable.
Deadline: Varies.
How to apply: Applications are mailed to NLE gold medal winners who are high school seniors.
Exclusive: Visit www.UltimateScholarshipBook.com and enter code AM49520 for updates on this award.

(496) • Actors Fund - Career Transition for Dancers Scholarship Program

Actors Fund - Career Transition for Dancers
729 Seventh Avenue, 10th Floor, New York, NY 10019
Phone: 212-221-7300
Email: pschwadron@actorsfund.org
http://www.actorsfund.org/services-and-programs/career-transition-dancers
Purpose: To provide educational grants for dancers seeking second careers.
Eligibility: Applicants must provide documentation of 100 weeks or more of paid employment as a dance performer in the U.S. over at least seven years. For work not performed under union jurisdiction, applicants must also provide documentation of total gross earnings of at least $56,000. Choreographers and dance teachers are not eligible for this program.
Target applicant(s): College students. Graduate school students. Adult students.
Amount: $2,000.
Number of awards: Varies.
Deadline: Varies.
How to apply: Applicants must call to confirm their eligibility.
Exclusive: Visit www.UltimateScholarshipBook.com and enter code AC49620 for updates on this award.

(497) • Adobe Creativity Scholarships

Adobe
Institute of International Education, 530 Bush Street, Suite 1000, San Francisco, CA 94108
Phone: 415-362-6520
https://www.adobe.com/
Purpose: To support young people in pursuing a degree in a creative field.
Eligibility: Applicants must be Adobe Youth Voices alumni, Adobe Youth Voices award winners and finalists or Project 1324 Creative Challenge winners. Students must submit high school transcripts, portfolio of creative work and letters of reference. Selection is based on the overall strength of the application.
Target applicant(s): High school students. College students. Adult students.
Amount: Varies.
Number of awards: Varies.
Scholarship may be renewable.
Deadline: March 13.
How to apply: Applications are available online.
Exclusive: Visit www.UltimateScholarshipBook.com and enter code AD49720 for updates on this award.

(498) • Alert1 Student for Seniors Scholarship

AlertOne Services LLC
1000 Commerce Park Drive, Suite 300, Williamsport, PA 17701
Phone: 866-836-0848
http://www.alert-1.com/scholarship
Purpose: To support students who are interested in a career supporting the senior industry.
Eligibility: Applicants must be citizens of the United States attending an accredited college or university within the United States as of the fall of the upcoming school year.
Target applicant(s): High school students. College students. Graduate school students. Adult students.
Amount: $250.
Number of awards: 1.
Deadline: January 10.
How to apply: Applications are available online.
Exclusive: Visit www.UltimateScholarshipBook.com and enter code AL49820 for updates on this award.

(499) • Alexia Foundation Student Grants

Alexia Foundation
P.O. Box 87 , Bloomingdale, NJ 07403
Phone: 631-354-4960
Email: grants@alexiafoundation.org
http://www.alexiafoundation.org/
Purpose: To support students in producing photojournalism projects that promote world peace and cultural understanding.
Eligibility: Applicants must be enrolled as full-time undergraduate or graduate students in an accredited college or university in the United States or abroad. Professional photographers are not eligible. Selection is based on photographic skill as well as the strength of the proposal.
Target applicant(s): College students. Graduate school students. Adult students.
Amount: Up to full tuition.
Number of awards: Varies.
Deadline: February 14.
How to apply: Application submission must be completed online. A synopsis, proposal, resume and digital portfolio are required.
Exclusive: Visit www.UltimateScholarshipBook.com and enter code AL49920 for updates on this award.

(500) • AMCA Music Scholarship

Associated Male Choruses of America
Weldon Wilson, Scholarship Chair, 5143 S. 40th Street, St. Cloud, MN 56301
Phone: 320-260-1081
Email: scholarships@amcofa-sing.org
http://www.amcofa-sing.org/scholarships.html
Purpose: To promote the study of chorus and music studies in college.
Eligibility: Applicants must be full-time students obtaining their bachelor's degree in a music-related field (with preference given to voice or choral concentrations) and be sponsored by a chorus of the Associated Male Choruses of America. Applicants must submit references and a personal letter.
Target applicant(s): College students. Adult students.
Amount: $1,000-$1,200.
Number of awards: Varies.
Deadline: March 1.
How to apply: Applications are available online or by contacting your local AMCA chorus.
Exclusive: Visit www.UltimateScholarshipBook.com and enter code AS50020 for updates on this award.

(501) • American Theatre Organ Society Scholarships

American Theatre Organ Society
Carlton B. Smith, Director, 2175 N. Irwin Street, Indianapolis, IN 46219
Phone: 317-356-1240
Email: smith@atos.org
http://www.atos.org
Purpose: To provide students with an opportunity to study with professional theatre organ teachers or to further their organ performance education in college.
Eligibility: Applicants must be between the ages of 13 and 22 as of July 1 and either working toward college organ performance degrees or be studying with professional organ instructors. Students' names must be submitted by their present organ instructor or the school's music department head. An essay is also required.
Target applicant(s): Junior high students or younger. High school students. College students.
Amount: Up to $1,500.
Number of awards: Varies.
Deadline: April 15.
How to apply: Applications are available online.
Exclusive: Visit www.UltimateScholarshipBook.com and enter code AM50120 for updates on this award.

(502) • Amy Lowell Poetry Travelling Scholarship

Choate, Hall and Stewart
Two International Place, Boston, MA 02110
Phone: 617-248-5253
Email: amylowell@choate.com
http://www.amylowell.org
Purpose: To support travel abroad for American-born poets.
Eligibility: Applicants should submit applications, curriculum vitae and poetry samples. Recipients should not accept another scholarship

during the scholarship year, must travel outside North America and should have three poems by the end of scholarship year.
Target applicant(s): High school students. College students. Graduate school students. Adult students.
Amount: $54,000.
Number of awards: 1-2.
Deadline: October 15.
How to apply: Applications are available online.
Exclusive: Visit www.UltimateScholarshipBook.com and enter code CH50220 for updates on this award.

---

(503) • Annual Music Student Scholarships

School Band and Orchestra Magazine
6000 South Eastern Avenue, Suite J-14, Las Vegas, NV 89119
Phone: 702-932-5585
Email: pgalileos@symphonypublishing.com
http://sbomagazine.com/essay-contest.html
Purpose: To support music students.
Eligibility: Applicants must be public, private or home school students in grades 4 through 12, be music students and write an essay on the given topic. Five scholarships are awarded to students in grades 4 through 8, and five are awarded to students in grades 9 through 12. Schools of winners will receive merchandise prizes.
Target applicant(s): Junior high students or younger. High school students.
Amount: $1,000.
Number of awards: 10.
Deadline: July 31.
How to apply: Applications are available online. An essay, contact information, school contact information and instrument played are required.
Exclusive: Visit www.UltimateScholarshipBook.com and enter code SC50320 for updates on this award.

---

(504) • Anthem Essay Contest

Ayn Rand Institute
P.O. Box 57044, Irvine, CA 92619
Phone: 949-222-6550
Email: essays@aynrand.org
https://www.aynrand.org/contests
Purpose: To honor high school students who distinguish themselves in their understanding of Ayn Rand's novel *Anthem*.
Eligibility: Applicants must be eighth to twelfth grade students who submit a 600-1,200-word essay that will be judged on both style and content, with an emphasis on writing that is clear, articulate and logically organized. Winning essays must demonstrate an outstanding grasp of the philosophic meaning of *Anthem*.
Target applicant(s): Junior high students or younger. High school students.
Amount: $25-$2,000.
Number of awards: 59.
Deadline: April 25.
How to apply: Essay is required for the contest. There is no application.
Exclusive: Visit www.UltimateScholarshipBook.com and enter code AY50420 for updates on this award.

---

(505) • Art Awards

Scholastic Art and Writing Awards
557 Broadway, New York, NY 10012
Phone: 212-343-6100
Email: info@artandwriting.org
http://www.artandwriting.org/scholarships/
Purpose: To reward America's best student artists.
Eligibility: Applicants must be in grades 7 through 12 in American or Canadian schools and must submit artwork in one of the following categories: art portfolio, animation, ceramics and glass, computer art, design, digital imagery, drawing, mixed media, painting, photography, photography portfolio, printmaking, sculpture or video and film. There are regional and national levels.
Target applicant(s): Junior high students or younger. High school students.
Amount: Varies.
Number of awards: Varies.
Deadline: Varies.
How to apply: Applications are available online. The deadlines vary by state but start in December. There is an online form to find out the deadline for your state.
Exclusive: Visit www.UltimateScholarshipBook.com and enter code SC50520 for updates on this award.

---

(506) • ASCAP Foundation Morton Gould Young Composer Awards

ASCAP Foundation
One Lincoln Plaza, New York, NY 10023
Phone: 212-621-6219
https://www.ascapfoundation.org/programs-and-grants
Purpose: To encourage young composers early in their careers.
Eligibility: Applicants must be composers who have not turned 30 before January 1 of the current year. They must be U.S. citizens or permanent residents or enrolled students with a student visa. Applicants must submit an original composition.
Target applicant(s): Junior high students or younger. High school students. College students. Graduate school students. Adult students.
Amount: Varies.
Number of awards: Varies.
Deadline: February 2.
How to apply: Applications are available online.
Exclusive: Visit www.UltimateScholarshipBook.com and enter code AS50620 for updates on this award.

---

(507) • Atlas Shrugged Essay Contest

Ayn Rand Institute
P.O. Box 57044, Irvine, CA 92619
Phone: 949-222-6550
Email: essays@aynrand.org
https://www.aynrand.org/students/essay-contests
Purpose: To honor students who distinguish themselves in their understanding of Ayn Rand's novel *Atlas Shrugged*.
Eligibility: Applicants must be high school seniors, college undergraduates or graduate students who submit an 800-1,600-word essay which will be judged on both style and content with an emphasis on writing that is clear, articulate and logically organized. Winning essays must demonstrate an outstanding grasp of the philosophic meaning of *Atlas Shrugged*.
Target applicant(s): High school students. College students. Graduate school students. Adult students.
Amount: $100-$25,000.
Number of awards: 59.
Deadline: September 19.
How to apply: Essay is required for the contest. There is no application.

Exclusive: Visit www.UltimateScholarshipBook.com and enter code AY50720 for updates on this award.

(508) • Bentley/Ankrom Theatre Education Scholarship

Florida Thespians
Lindsay Warfield, Director, Steinbrenner High School, 5575 W Lutz Lake Fern Road, Lutz, FL 33558
http://flthespian.com/
Purpose: To support young thespians majoring in theatre education.
Eligibility: Applicants must be members of the International Thespian Society and seriously plan to pursue theatre as a career. They must also be senior high school students majoring in theatre education and must audition to receive this award. Applicants must have a minimum 3.0 GPA and an SAT combined score of 1800 or greater or an ACT score of 26 or greater. Applicants must be approved by their Thespian Troupe director to apply. Selection is based on the overall strength of the application and audition.
Target applicant(s): High school students.
Minimum GPA: 3.0
Amount: $1,000.
Number of awards: 1.
Deadline: March 28.
How to apply: Applications are available online to troupe directors only. An application and audition are required.
Exclusive: Visit www.UltimateScholarshipBook.com and enter code FL50820 for updates on this award.

(509) • Bill Gove Scholarship

National Speakers Association
Attn: Scholarship Committee, 1500 S. Priest Drive, Tempe, AZ 85281
Phone: 480-968-2552
Email: Jessica@NSAspeaker.org
http://www.nsaspeaker.org/recognition/
Purpose: To encourage study in the field of professional speaking.
Eligibility: Applicants must be full-time students majoring or minoring in speech. Selection is based on application, essay, recommendation and college transcript.
Target applicant(s): College students. Graduate school students. Adult students.
Amount: $5,000.
Number of awards: 1.
Deadline: May 19.
How to apply: Applications are available online or by written request.
Exclusive: Visit www.UltimateScholarshipBook.com and enter code NA50920 for updates on this award.

(510) • Bill Walsh Scholarship

American Copy Editors Society
3909 N. Meridian Street, Indianapolis, IN 46208
https://aceseditors.org/awards/scholarships
Purpose: To reward students dedicated to editing and the craft of language.
Eligibility: Applicants must be currently enrolled juniors, seniors or graduate students seeking a college or university degree. Students must provide an academic resume, three references, an original essay, an editing sample and a headline sample using the given prompts.
Target applicant(s): College students. Graduate school students. Adult students.
Amount: $3,000.
Number of awards: 1.
Deadline: November 15.
How to apply: Applications are available online.
Exclusive: Visit www.UltimateScholarshipBook.com and enter code AM51020 for updates on this award.

(511) • Bridging Scholarships for Study Abroad in Japan

American Association of Teachers of Japanese
Bridging Project Clearinghouse, Campus Box 366, 1424 Broadway, University of Colorado, Boulder, CO 80309-0366
Phone: 303-492-5487
Email: aatj@aatj.org
http://www.aatj.org/
Purpose: To assist students with travel and living expenses while studying in Japan.
Eligibility: Applicants must be undergraduates, U.S. citizens and be enrolled in a U.S. college. Study in Japan must be for at least three months and take place during the academic year (summer programs are not eligible). Students must submit a letter of recommendation and an essay on their interest in studying in Japan.
Target applicant(s): College students. Adult students.
Amount: $2,500-$4,000.
Number of awards: Varies.
Deadline: April 11, October 11.
How to apply: Applications are available online.
Exclusive: Visit www.UltimateScholarshipBook.com and enter code AM51120 for updates on this award.

(512) • CardsDirect Future Designer Scholarship

CardsDirect
12750 Merit Drove, Suite 900, Dallas, TX 75251
Phone: 866-700-5030
Email: scholarship@cardsdirect.com
https://www.cardsdirect.com/scholarship.aspx
Purpose: To support aspiring card designers.
Eligibility: Applicants must be at least 17 years old and accepted at or already enrolled in any accredited post-secondary institution as a full-time student. Students must submit an original design for a holiday card.
Target applicant(s): High school students. College students. Graduate school students. Adult students.
Amount: $2,500.
Number of awards: 2.
Deadline: November 1.
How to apply: Applications are available online.
Exclusive: Visit www.UltimateScholarshipBook.com and enter code CA51220 for updates on this award.

(513) • Career Center

Actors' Fund of America/The Career Center
729 Seventh Avenue , 10th Floor, New York, NY 10019
Phone: 800-221-7303
Email: info@actorsfund.org
http://www.actorsfund.org
Purpose: To assist members of the entertainment industry with finding sideline work and pursuing new careers.
Eligibility: Applicants must be members in good standing of an entertainment industry union and others who have earned $6,500 in each of three of the last five years or $5,000 in each of five of the last

10 years. Those who do not have earnings can substitute 12 weeks of documented industry work.
Target applicant(s): Junior high students or younger. High school students. College students. Graduate school students. Adult students.
Amount: Varies.
Number of awards: Varies.
Deadline: Varies.
How to apply: Applicants must attend an Actors' Work Program Orientation to learn more about the program.
Exclusive: Visit www.UltimateScholarshipBook.com and enter code AC51320 for updates on this award.

(514) • Carl A. Ross Student Paper Award

Appalachian Studies Association
Carl A. Ross Student Paper Award, Casey LaFrance, Chair of the Selection Committee, One John Marshall Drive, Huntington, WV 25755
Phone: 304-696-2904
Email: TC-Lafrance@wiu.edu
http://appalachianstudies.org/awards/
Purpose: To promote Appalachian studies.
Eligibility: Applicants must submit a 12- to 30-page research paper on an Appalachian studies topic. Selections will be made from two categories: middle/high school and undergraduate/graduate.
Target applicant(s): Junior high students or younger. High school students. College students. Graduate school students. Adult students.
Amount: $100.
Number of awards: 2.
Deadline: January 15.
How to apply: Submission of research paper is the application.
Exclusive: Visit www.UltimateScholarshipBook.com and enter code AP51420 for updates on this award.

(515) • Carrie Crystal Stuckert Memorial Art Scholarship

Dream Pool Foundation
P.O. Box 2020, Greenfield, WI 53220
Phone: 414-303-2827
http://www.dreampoolfoundation.org/scholarship_app.html
Purpose: To support undergraduate students in pursuing a degree in the visual arts.
Eligibility: Applicants must be visual arts or art therapy majors. Students must submit two letters of recommendation (at least one from an art teacher) and an personal statement regarding their reasons for pursuing a visual arts degree and professional goals. Selection is primarily based on demonstration of community service and extracurricular involvement.
Target applicant(s): College students. Adult students.
Amount: $1,000-$2,000.
Number of awards: 4.
Deadline: April 24.
How to apply: Applications are available online.
Exclusive: Visit www.UltimateScholarshipBook.com and enter code DR51520 for updates on this award.

(516) • Cavett Robert Scholarship

National Speakers Association
Attn: Scholarship Committee, 1500 S. Priest Drive, Tempe, AZ 85281
Phone: 480-968-2552
Email: Jessica@NSAspeaker.org
http://www.nsaspeaker.org/recognition/
Purpose: To encourage study in the field of professional speaking.
Eligibility: Applicants must be full-time students majoring or minoring in speech. Selection is based on application, essay, recommendation and college transcript.
Target applicant(s): College students. Graduate school students. Adult students.
Amount: Varies.
Number of awards: Varies.
Deadline: Varies.
How to apply: Applications are available online or by written request.
Exclusive: Visit www.UltimateScholarshipBook.com and enter code NA51620 for updates on this award.

(517) • Clauder Competition Prize

Portland Stage Company
Attn.: Literary Manager, P.O. Box 1458, Portland, ME 04104
Phone: 207-774-1043
Email: clauder@portlandstage.org
http://www.portlandstage.com
Purpose: To support playwrights.
Eligibility: Applicants must live or attend school in Connecticut, Maine, Massachusetts, New Hampshire, Rhode Island or Vermont. This requirement may be waived for playwrights who have previously lived in New England and produce material relevant to the area. They must submit a full-length play that is an original work and has not been produced or published.
Target applicant(s): High school students. College students. Graduate school students. Adult students.
Amount: Up to $3,000.
Number of awards: Varies.
Deadline: Varies.
How to apply: No application form is required.
Exclusive: Visit www.UltimateScholarshipBook.com and enter code PO51720 for updates on this award.

(518) • COIT Clean Gif Scholarship

Coit Services, Inc.
897 Hinckley Road, Burlingame, CA 94010
Phone: 800-367-2648
Email: coit.scholarship.2017@gmail.com
http://www.coit.com/scholarship
Purpose: To encourage students who create a GIF about cleaning.
Eligibility: Applicants must be enrolled in an undergraduate or graduate program in the United States or Canada and must create a lightly animated GIF.
Target applicant(s): High school students. College students. Graduate school students. Adult students.
Amount: $2,000.
Number of awards: 1.
Deadline: August 31.
How to apply: Applications are available online.
Exclusive: Visit www.UltimateScholarshipBook.com and enter code CO51820 for updates on this award.

(519) • College Television Awards

Academy of Television Arts and Sciences Foundation
5220 Lankershim Boulevard, North Hollywood, CA 91601
Phone: 818-754-2800

Email: ctasupport@televisionacademy.com
http://www.emmys.org
Purpose: To reward college student film or video producers.
Eligibility: Applicants must produce an original film or video in one of the following categories: drama, comedy, music, documentary, news, magazine show, traditional or computer-generated animation, children's programming or commercials. Professionals may not be involved in the production of the piece, including producers, directors, camera operators, lighting or sound technicians and production managers. Applicants must also be full-time students who have produced their video for course credit at an American college or university from January 1 to December 31 of the current year.
Target applicant(s): College students. Graduate school students. Adult students.
Amount: Varies.
Number of awards: Varies.
Deadline: October 19.
How to apply: Applications are available online from September 1 to January 15 and are also sent to college film and television departments.
Exclusive: Visit www.UltimateScholarshipBook.com and enter code AC51920 for updates on this award.

(520) · Corporate Leadership Scholarships

Gravure Education Foundation
P.O. Box 25617, Rochester, NY 14625
Phone: 315-589-8879
Email: lwshatch@gaa.org
http://www.gaa.org/gravure-education-foundation
Purpose: To provide scholarships to undergraduate and graduate students pursuing degrees in printing or graphic arts.
Eligibility: Applicants must be enrolled full-time at a GEF Learning Resource Center at Arizona State University, California Polytechnic State University, Clemson University, Murray State, Rochester Institute of Technology, University of Wisconsin - Stout or Western Michigan University. Students must major in printing, graphic arts or graphic communications and be undergraduate or graduate students at the time of award. Applicants must have a minimum 3.0 GPA.
Target applicant(s): College students. Graduate school students. Adult students.
Minimum GPA: 3.0
Amount: $1,500.
Number of awards: 8.
Deadline: April 28.
How to apply: Applications are available online.
Exclusive: Visit www.UltimateScholarshipBook.com and enter code GR52020 for updates on this award.

(521) · Council on International Educational Exchange (CIEE) Scholarships

Council on International Educational Exchange
7 Custom House Street, 3rd Floor, Portland, ME 04101
Phone: 800-40-STUDY
Email: scholarships@ciee.org
http://www.ciee.org
Purpose: To make the study abroad program available to a wider audience and to provide assistance to CIEE Study Center (CSC) members who have demonstrated academic talent and financial need in order to study abroad.
Eligibility: Applicants must plan to participate in a CIEE study abroad program. Financial need is strongly considered along with other materials from the study abroad application. Other eligibility requirements vary according to the specific scholarship. If awarded a scholarship, applicants are required to submit a one-page essay on their experiences after returning.
Target applicant(s): College students. Adult students.
Amount: Up to $4,000.
Number of awards: Varies.
Deadline: March 1 and October 1.
How to apply: Applications are available online.
Exclusive: Visit www.UltimateScholarshipBook.com and enter code CO52120 for updates on this award.

(522) · Creative Arts/Design Scholarship

Foundation for Outdoor Advertising Research and Education (FOARE)
The Family Scholarship Endowment, c/o Thomas M. Smith & Associates, 4601 Tilden Street NW, Washington, DC 20016
http://oaaa.org/AboutOAAA/FOARE/FOAREScholarshipProgram.aspx
Purpose: To support students who are pursuing a degree in creative arts or design.
Eligibility: Applicants must be accepted for enrollment or enrolled at an accredited educational institution. Students must submit a design portfolio. Selection is primarily based on demonstration of financial need, career goals, academic achievement, community service and extracurricular involvement.
Target applicant(s): High school students. College students. Graduate school students. Adult students.
Amount: $3,000.
Number of awards: 1.
Deadline: June 12.
How to apply: Applications are available online.
Exclusive: Visit www.UltimateScholarshipBook.com and enter code FO52220 for updates on this award.

(523) · DAAD/AICGS Research Fellowship Program

American Institute for Contemporary German Studies - (AICGS)
1755 Massachusetts Avenue NW, Suite 700, Washington, DC 20036-2121
Phone: 202-332-9312
Email: sdieper@aicgs.org
http://www.aicgs.org
Purpose: To bring scholars and specialists working on Germany, Europe and/or transatlantic relations to AICGS for research stays.
Eligibility: Applicants must have a Ph.D. or be enrolled in a Ph.D. program and hold U.S. or German citizenship. The grant provides a research stay of two months at AICGS.
Target applicant(s): Graduate school students. Adult students.
Amount: Up to $4,725 monthly stipend.
Number of awards: Varies.
Deadline: February 28, August 31.
How to apply: Apply via email to jwindell@aicgs.org.
Exclusive: Visit www.UltimateScholarshipBook.com and enter code AM52320 for updates on this award.

(524) · Disney/ABC Television Writing Program

Disney/ABC Television Group
Talent Development and Diversity, 500 South Buena Vista Street, Burbank, CA 91521-4016
Email: abcwritingfellowship@disney.com
http://www.abctalentdevelopment.com

Purpose: To help writers develop skills for careers in television writing.
Eligibility: Applicants must be age 21 or older. They must be able to work in the U.S. legally. Professional writing experience is not necessary, but applicants must have strong spec script writing skills. Selection is based on the overall strength of the application.
Target applicant(s): College students. Graduate school students. Adult students.
Amount: $50,000.
Number of awards: Varies.
Deadline: Varies.
How to apply: Applications are available online. An application form and spec script samples are required.
Exclusive: Visit www.UltimateScholarshipBook.com and enter code DI52420 for updates on this award.

(525) • DL English Scholarship

Planning and Visual Education Partnership (PAVE) c/o Kroger Company
PAVE Entries Attn.: Ken Pray, 1014 Vine Street, Cincinnati, OH 45202
Email: info@paveglobal.org
http://paveglobal.org/Competitions.aspx?typeid=26
Purpose: To support students who are working in retail design, retail planning and visual merchandising.
Eligibility: Applicants must be enrolled in a program working towards a degree in the retail design industry. Students must have at least a 3.0 GPA and be full-time students enrolled in at least 12 credit hours. Students must be studying within the following states: Arizona, California, Nevada, New Mexico, Oregon, Utah or Washington.
Target applicant(s): College students. Adult students.
Minimum GPA: 3.0
Amount: $2,500.
Number of awards: Varies.
Deadline: March 1.
How to apply: Applications are available online.
Exclusive: Visit www.UltimateScholarshipBook.com and enter code PL52520 for updates on this award.

(526) • Doodle 4 Google

Google Doodle 4 Google
1600 Amphitheatre Parkway, Mountain View, CA 94043
Phone: 650-253-0000
Email: doodle4google-team@google.com
http://www.google.com/doodle4google
Purpose: To encourage creativity in United States school students through a logo contest.
Eligibility: Participants must be elementary or secondary school students in the 50 U.S. states or the District of Columbia who have registered for the contest. They must be U.S. residents who have obtained parental consent to enter. Employees, interns, contractors and office-holders of Google Inc. and their immediate families are not eligible.
Target applicant(s): Junior high students or younger. High school students.
Amount: Up to $30,000.
Number of awards: Varies.
Deadline: March 2.
How to apply: Applications are available from participating schools.
Exclusive: Visit www.UltimateScholarshipBook.com and enter code GO52620 for updates on this award.

(527) • Dr. Randy Pausch Scholarship Fund

Academy of Interactive Arts and Sciences (AIAS)
c/o Randy Pausch Scholarship, 9800 S. La Cienega Boulevard, 14th Floor, Inglewood, CA 90301
Phone: 310-484-2560
Email: gabriel@interactive.org
http://www.interactive.org
Purpose: To support students pursuing careers in game design, development and production.
Eligibility: Applicants must be full-time students who are currently enrolled in an accredited college or university at the undergraduate or graduate level. They must plan to enter the video game industry and have a GPA of 3.3 or higher. Selection is based on application, required documentation, service, leadership, character and financial need.
Target applicant(s): College students. Graduate school students. Adult students.
Minimum GPA: 3.3
Amount: $2,500.
Number of awards: 2.
Deadline: April 28.
How to apply: Applications are available online. An application form, verification of enrollment, personal statement, two letters of recommendation and transcript are required.
Exclusive: Visit www.UltimateScholarshipBook.com and enter code AC52720 for updates on this award.

(528) • Dream Dorm Design Challenge

Serena & Lily
10 Liberty Ship Way, Suite 350, Sausalito, CA 94965
Phone: 866-597-2742
Email: university@serenaandlily.com
http://www.serenaandlily.com/dream-dorm-room-design-challenge.html
Purpose: To encourage students interested in design.
Eligibility: Applicants must be enrolling or currently enrolled in a post-secondary institution. Students must provide a rendering of their dream dorm room including swatches, spatial plans and color scheme. Applicants must provide an outline of their design inspiration and a brief essay.
Target applicant(s): College students. Graduate school students. Adult students.
Amount: $2,000.
Number of awards: 1.
Deadline: March 31.
How to apply: Application instructions are available online.
Exclusive: Visit www.UltimateScholarshipBook.com and enter code SE52820 for updates on this award.

(529) • Dumbarton Oaks Fellowships

Dumbarton Oaks
1703 32nd Street NW , Washington, DC 20007
Phone: 202-339-6413
Email: FellowshipPrograms@doaks.org
http://www.doaks.org
Purpose: To provide fellowships to scholars engaged in Byzantine studies, Pre-Columbian studies and garden and landscape studies.
Eligibility: Applicants must hold a doctorate (or appropriate final degree) or have established themselves in their field and wish to pursue their own research or expect to have the Ph.D. in hand prior to taking up residence at Dumbarton Oaks. The fellowships are in the following

areas: Byzantine Studies (including related aspects of late Roman, early Christian, western medieval, Slavic and Near Eastern Studies), Pre-Columbian Studies (of Mexico, Central America and Andean South America) and garden and landscape studies. Fellowships are based on demonstrated scholarly ability and preparation (including knowledge of the required languages), interest and value of the study or project and its relevance to Dumbarton Oaks.
Target applicant(s): Graduate school students. Adult students.
Amount: Up to $35,000 plus allowance and health benefits.
Number of awards: Varies.
Deadline: November 1.
How to apply: Applicants must submit ten complete, collated sets of the application letter, proposal and personal and professional data. Applicants must also submit three recommendation letters.
Exclusive: Visit www.UltimateScholarshipBook.com and enter code DU52920 for updates on this award.

---

(530) • Earl Nightengale Scholarship

National Speakers Association
Attn: Scholarship Committee, 1500 S. Priest Drive, Tempe, AZ 85281
Phone: 480-968-2552
Email: Jessica@NSAspeaker.org
http://www.nsaspeaker.org/recognition/
Purpose: To encourage study in the field of professional speaking.
Eligibility: Applicants must be entering full-time undergraduate juniors, seniors or graduate students who wish to become professional speakers. Selection is based on application, essay, recommendation and college transcript.
Target applicant(s): College students. Graduate school students. Adult students.
Amount: $5,000.
Number of awards: 1.
Deadline: May 19.
How to apply: Applications are available online.
Exclusive: Visit www.UltimateScholarshipBook.com and enter code NA53020 for updates on this award.

---

(531) • Edna Meudt Memorial Award and the Florence Kahn Memorial Award

National Federation of State Poetry Societies
NFSPS College/University-Level Competition, Shirley Blackwell, P.O. Box 1352, Los Lumas, NM 87031
Phone: 801-484-3113
Email: SBSenior@juno.com
http://nfsps.com/
Purpose: To recognize the importance of poetry on the nation's culture.
Eligibility: Applicants can be college students at any level. Applicants must submit 10 original, unpublished poems.
Target applicant(s): High school students. College students. Adult students.
Amount: $500.
Number of awards: 2.
Deadline: January 31.
How to apply: Applications are available online.
Exclusive: Visit www.UltimateScholarshipBook.com and enter code NA53120 for updates on this award.

---

(532) • Fashion Scholarship Fund Scholarships

Fashion Scholarship Fund
1501 Broadway, Suite 1810, New York, NY 10036
Phone: 212-278-0008
Email: hharrison@fashionscholarshipfund.org
http://www.ymafsf.org/
Purpose: To support students attending FSF member schools across the United States.
Eligibility: Applicants must attend Fashion Scholarship Fund member schools and universities and have a demonstrated interest in fashion. Applicants must also be enrolled as full-time, current college sophomores, juniors or seniors with an overall GPA of 3.0 or above. Selection is based on merit with consideration given to GPA, the quality of a case study project, job experience, community service, personal essay and interview.
Target applicant(s): College students. Adult students.
Minimum GPA: 3.0
Amount: $5,000.
Number of awards: About 100.
Deadline: Varies.
How to apply: Applications are available online. Application, case study project, transcript, personal essay and interview are required.
Exclusive: Visit www.UltimateScholarshipBook.com and enter code FA53220 for updates on this award.

---

(533) • Federal Junior Duck Stamp Program and Scholarship Competition

U.S. Fish and Wildlife Service Headquarters
Junior Duck Stamp Program, 5275 Leesburg Pike, MS: MB, Falls Church, VA 22041-3803
Phone: 703-358-1714
Email: Suzanne_Fellows@fws.gov
http://www.fws.gov/juniorduck
Purpose: To encourage students to paint waterfowl and learn about the importance of habitat and wildlife conservation.
Eligibility: Applicants must be in kindergarten to 12th grade and submit their artwork to their state or local department. Students must be U.S. citizens, resident aliens or nationals. The first place national winner has their art made into the next Federal Junior Duck Stamp and travels with a parent to the next First Day of Sale event for their stamp.
Target applicant(s): Junior high students or younger. High school students.
Amount: Varies.
Number of awards: Varies.
Deadline: March 15.
How to apply: Applications are available online.
Exclusive: Visit www.UltimateScholarshipBook.com and enter code U.53320 for updates on this award.

---

(534) • Feldco Windows, Siding and Doors Scholarship

Feldco
9932 South Western Avenue, Chicago, IL 60643
Phone: 708-437-4133
Email: scholarship@4feldco.com
http://www.4feldco.com/scholarship
Purpose: To support students working towards a college education.
Eligibility: Applicants must be U.S. citizens and current high school seniors or undergraduate college students. Students must write an essay on an assigned topic given on the scholarship webpage.

Target applicant(s): High school students. College students. Adult students.
Amount: $1,000.
Number of awards: 1.
Deadline: January 15.
How to apply: Applications are available online.
Exclusive: Visit www.UltimateScholarshipBook.com and enter code FE53420 for updates on this award.

(535) · Fellowships for Regular Program in Greece

American School of Classical Studies at Athens
6-8 Charlton Street, Princeton, NJ 08540-5232
Phone: 609-683-0800
Email: ascsa@ascsa.org
http://www.ascsa.edu.gr
Purpose: The institution is devoted to allowing advanced graduate students enrolled in North American colleges and institutions to study the classics and related fields of language, literature, art, history, archaeology and philosophy of Greece and the Greek world.
Eligibility: Applicants must have completed at least one to two years of graduate study and must take exams in ancient Greek language, history and either literature or art and archaeology. Students must be able to read French, German, ancient Greek and Latin with an ability to also read modern Greek and Italian considered helpful. Applicants must be graduate students who are preparing for an advanced degree in classical and ancient Mediterranean studies or a related field. The fellowships provide study in Athens or Greece for nine months and may not be used for costs at the student's home institution.
Target applicant(s): Graduate school students. Adult students.
Amount: $11,500 plus housing, board and fees.
Number of awards: Up to 12.
Deadline: January 15.
How to apply: Applications are available online.
Exclusive: Visit www.UltimateScholarshipBook.com and enter code AM53520 for updates on this award.

(536) · Fellowships/Grants to Study in Scandinavia

American-Scandinavian Foundation
58 Park Avenue, New York, NY 10016
Phone: 212-779-3587
Email: info@amscan.org
http://www.amscan.org
Purpose: To encourage research projects related to Scandinavia.
Eligibility: Applicant must be a United States citizen or permanent resident who has completed their undergraduate education by the start of their project in Scandinavia. Applicant must have a well-defined research or study project that makes a stay in Scandinavia essential and should have some ability in the language of the host country. First priority will be given to an applicant who has not previously received an ASF award.
Target applicant(s): College students. Graduate school students. Adult students.
Amount: $5,000-$23,000.
Number of awards: Varies.
Scholarship may be renewable.
Deadline: November 1.
How to apply: Applications are available online and by written request.
Exclusive: Visit www.UltimateScholarshipBook.com and enter code AM53620 for updates on this award.

(537) · FFTA Scholarship Competition

Flexographic Technical Association
900 Marconi Avenue, Ronkonkoma, NY 11779
Phone: 631-737-6020
Email: education@flexography.org
https://www.flexography.org/honors-awards/scholarships/
Purpose: To advance the state of the flexographic industry.
Eligibility: Applicants must demonstrate interest in a career in flexography and must be high school seniors with plans to attend a post-secondary institution or be presently enrolled at a post-secondary institution offering a course of study in flexography. Applicants must exhibit exemplary performance in their studies, particularly in the area of graphic communications and must have a minimum 3.0 GPA.
Target applicant(s): High school students. College students. Adult students.
Minimum GPA: 3.0
Amount: $3,000.
Number of awards: Varies.
Scholarship may be renewable.
Deadline: March 27.
How to apply: Applications are available online.
Exclusive: Visit www.UltimateScholarshipBook.com and enter code FL53720 for updates on this award.

(538) · Finlandia Foundation National Student Scholarships Program

Finlandia Foundation
470 W. Walnut Street, Pasadena, CA 91103
Phone: 626-795-2081
Email: ffnoffice@mac.com
http://www.finlandiafoundation.org
Purpose: To support undergraduate and graduate students in Finland and the United States for conducting studies or research related to Finnish culture and society.
Eligibility: Applicants must be full-time undergraduate or graduate students enrolled in a college or university in the U.S. or Finland and must plan research on Finnish culture in the U.S. They must be studying at the sophomore level or higher and have a minimum GPA of 3.0. Financial need, course of study and citizenship are considered in evaluating applications. Students may not receive funds for two consecutive years.
Target applicant(s): High school students. College students. Graduate school students. Adult students.
Minimum GPA: 3.0
Amount: $1,000-$3,000.
Number of awards: Varies.
Deadline: February 1.
How to apply: Applications are available online. Application form and cover letter are required.
Exclusive: Visit www.UltimateScholarshipBook.com and enter code FI53820 for updates on this award.

(539) · Florida Thespians College Scholarship

Florida Thespians
Lindsay Warfield, Director, Steinbrenner High School, 5575 W Lutz Lake Fern Road, Lutz, FL 33558
http://flthespian.com/
Purpose: To support young thespians who have actively participated at the district level and are qualified to attend the state competition.
Eligibility: Applicants must be members of the International Thespian Society and seriously plan to pursue theatre as a career. They must be

high school juniors or seniors who are declared theatre majors or are registered for theatre classes. Applicants must have a minimum 3.0 GPA. Seniors must have an SAT combined score of 1800 or greater or an ACT score of 26 or greater. Junior applicants must have received an Excellent or Superior in any individual events at the district level. Applicants must audition for the awards. Awards are given in three theatre-related areas including acting, musical theatre and design/technical management. Applicants must be approved by their Thespian Troupe director to apply. An additional bonus is available for those who choose to attend college in Florida. Selection is based on the overall strength of the application and audition.
Target applicant(s): High school students.
Minimum GPA: 3.0
Amount: $750.
Number of awards: 10.
Deadline: March 28.
How to apply: Applications are available online for troupe directors only. Application and audition are required.
Exclusive: Visit www.UltimateScholarshipBook.com and enter code FL53920 for updates on this award.

(540) • Fountainhead Essay Contest

Ayn Rand Institute
P.O. Box 57044, Irvine, CA 92619
Phone: 949-222-6550
Email: essays@aynrand.org
https://www.aynrand.org/students/essay-contests
Purpose: To honor high school students who distinguish themselves in their understanding of Ayn Rand's novel *The Fountainhead.*
Eligibility: Applicants must be high school juniors or seniors who submit a 800-1,600 word essay which will be judged on both style and content with an emphasis on writing that is clear, articulate and logically organized. Winning essays must demonstrate an outstanding grasp of the philosophic and psychological meaning of *The Fountainhead.*
Target applicant(s): High school students.
Amount: $50-$10,000.
Number of awards: 59.
Deadline: April 25.
How to apply: Essay is required for the contest. There is no application.
Exclusive: Visit www.UltimateScholarshipBook.com and enter code AY54020 for updates on this award.

(541) • Frame My Future Scholarship Contest

Church Hill Classics
594 Pepper Street, Monroe, CT 06468
Phone: 800-477-9005
Email: info@diplomaframe.com
http://www.diplomaframe.com
Purpose: To help success-driven students attain their higher education goals.
Eligibility: Applicants must be high school seniors or current college students who plan to enroll full-time for the following academic year. Students must be residents of the United States, including APO/FPO addresses but excluding Puerto Rico. Employees of Church Hill Classics and affiliated companies, their family members and individuals living in the same household are not eligible.
Target applicant(s): High school students. College students. Graduate school students. Adult students.
Amount: $500-$5,000.
Number of awards: 3.
Deadline: March 1.
How to apply: Applications must be submitted online. An entry form and original piece of artwork are required.
Exclusive: Visit www.UltimateScholarshipBook.com and enter code CH54120 for updates on this award.

(542) • Gaming Scholarship

Into the AM
Phone: 888-438-5443
Email: scholarships@intotheam.com
https://www.intotheam.com/pages/gaming-industry-scholarship
Purpose: To support students who wish to pursue a career in the gaming industry.
Eligibility: Applicants must be high school seniors or current college students attending full-time at a two- or four-year college, university, vocational or technical school in the United States. Students must have a passion for video games and the gaming industry. Applicants may apply once per calendar year. Students must submit a 500- to 1,000-word essay on the provided topic related to gaming.
Target applicant(s): High school students. College students. Graduate school students. Adult students.
Amount: $1,000.
Number of awards: 2.
Deadline: May 15 and December 15.
How to apply: Applications are available online.
Exclusive: Visit www.UltimateScholarshipBook.com and enter code IN54220 for updates on this award.

(543) • GEF Resource Center Scholarships

Gravure Education Foundation
P.O. Box 25617, Rochester, NY 14625
Phone: 315-589-8879
Email: lwshatch@gaa.org
http://www.gaa.org/gravure-education-foundation
Purpose: To award scholarships to undergraduate and graduate students majoring in printing, graphic arts or graphic communications.
Eligibility: Applicants must be enrolled at one of the following GEF Learning Resource Centers: Arizona State University, California Polytechnic State University, Clemson University, Murray State University, Rochester Institute of Technology, University of Wisconsin - Stout or Western Michigan University. Must have at least a 3.0 GPA.
Target applicant(s): High school students. College students. Graduate school students. Adult students.
Minimum GPA: 3.0
Amount: Varies.
Number of awards: 8.
Deadline: April 28.
How to apply: Applications are available online.
Exclusive: Visit www.UltimateScholarshipBook.com and enter code GR54320 for updates on this award.

(544) • Gilman International Scholarship

Institute of International Education Gilman Scholarship Program
1800 West Loop South, Suite 250, Houston, TX 77027
Phone: 832-369-3484
Email: gilman@iie.org
https://www.gilmanscholarship.org/
Purpose: To support students with financial need who are planning to study abroad.
Eligibility: Students must be recipients of a Pell Grant. They must be currently attending a two-year or four-year college in the United States.

Recipients must study abroad for at least four weeks in any country excluding Cuba and the countries on the Travel Warning list.
Target applicant(s): High school students. College students. Adult students.
Amount: Up to $5,000.
Number of awards: Over 2,900.
Deadline: April 15, August 1, October 15.
How to apply: Applications are available online.
Exclusive: Visit www.UltimateScholarshipBook.com and enter code IN54420 for updates on this award.

(545) · Girls Impact the World Film Festival

Harvard College Social Innovation Collaborative (SIC)
Connecther, 12301 Zeller Lane, Austin, TX 78753
Email: filmfest@connecther.org
http://www.connecther.org/
Purpose: To support high school and undergraduate college students in bringing awareness to global women's issues through a film contest.
Eligibility: Applicants must be current high school or undergraduate college students 25 years of age or under and must not be a resident of Cuba, Iran, North Korea, Sudan or Syria. Applicants must create three- to five-minute short films that either raise awareness about current global issues affecting women or propose solutions to such challenges. Selection is based upon the overall strength of the film.
Target applicant(s): High school students. College students.
Amount: Varies.
Number of awards: Varies.
Deadline: January 20.
How to apply: Film submissions should be made online. A submission form, short film and proof of enrollment are required.
Exclusive: Visit www.UltimateScholarshipBook.com and enter code HA54520 for updates on this award.

(546) · Glenn Miller Scholarship Competition

Glenn Miller Birthplace Society
107 East Main Street, P.O. Box 61, Clarinda, IA 51632
Phone: 712-542-2461
Email: gmbs@heartland.net
http://glennmiller.org
Purpose: To honor Glenn Miller by recognizing future musical leaders.
Eligibility: Applicants may apply as instrumentalists or vocalists. They must be high school seniors or college freshmen who plan to focus on music in their future lives. Applicants must submit an audition CD or tape in addition to an application form. High school seniors may reapply as college freshmen as long as they weren't first-place winners the previous year.
Target applicant(s): High school students. College students. Adult students.
Amount: $1,000-$3,000.
Number of awards: 6.
Deadline: March 1.
How to apply: Applications are available online.
Exclusive: Visit www.UltimateScholarshipBook.com and enter code GL54620 for updates on this award.

(547) · Gravure Publishing Council Scholarship

Gravure Education Foundation
P.O. Box 25617, Rochester, NY 14625
Phone: 315-589-8879
Email: lwshatch@gaa.org
http://www.gaa.org/gravure-education-foundation
Purpose: To support undergraduate students to help them enter the printing industry.
Eligibility: Applicants must major in printing, graphic arts or graphic communications and be at least a junior at the time the scholarship is awarded. Applicants should be interested in promoting gravure as the preferred method in high-quality printing.
Target applicant(s): College students. Graduate school students. Adult students.
Minimum GPA: 3.0
Amount: $1,500.
Number of awards: 1.
Deadline: April 28.
How to apply: Applications are available online.
Exclusive: Visit www.UltimateScholarshipBook.com and enter code GR54720 for updates on this award.

(548) · Harvie Jordan Scholarship

American Translators Association
225 Reinekers Lane, Suite 590, Alexandria, VA 22314
Phone: 703-683-6100
Email: ata@atanet.org
http://www.atanet.org
Purpose: To support members of the Spanish Language Division of the American Translators Association.
Eligibility: Applicants must have been ATA Spanish Language Division members for at least two years. They must also be able to show that they have made important contributions to translation and interpretation.
Target applicant(s): College students. Graduate school students. Adult students.
Amount: Paid registration to ATA Conference.
Number of awards: Varies.
Deadline: September 21.
How to apply: Applications are available online.
Exclusive: Visit www.UltimateScholarshipBook.com and enter code AM54820 for updates on this award.

(549) · Heinlein Society Scholarship Program

Heinlein Society
3553 Atlantic Avenue #341, Long Beach, CA 90807-5606
Email: scholarships@heinleinsociety.org
http://www.heinleinsociety.org/scholarship-program/
Purpose: To reward students who are attending a four-year college.
Eligibility: Applicants must be full-time undergraduate students at an accredited college. One scholarship is awarded to a woman majoring in engineering, math or physical sciences (physics/chemistry). Two scholarships are awarded to male or female students majoring in science fiction as literature. Students must submit a 500- to 1,000-word essay on one of the topics listed on the website.
Target applicant(s): College students. Adult students.
Amount: $1,250.
Number of awards: 3.
Deadline: May 15.
How to apply: Applications are available online and must be submitted with a brief bio including future goals and the required essay.
Exclusive: Visit www.UltimateScholarshipBook.com and enter code HE54920 for updates on this award.

(550) • Henry Luce Foundation/ACLS Dissertation Fellowships in American Art

American Council of Learned Societies (ACLS)
633 Third Avenue, New York, NY 10017-6795
Phone: 212-697-1505
Email: mgoldfeder@acls.org
https://www.acls.org/
Purpose: To support Ph.D. candidates working on art history dissertations.
Eligibility: Applicants must be Ph.D. candidates in an art history department in the U.S. who are working on dissertations about American visual arts history. All the Ph.D. requirements should be met except the dissertation before taking the fellowship. Applicants should submit an application, a proposal, a bibliography, illustrations (optional), a publications list (optional), three reference letters and an official transcript of graduate record. The fellowship lasts for a year.
Target applicant(s): Graduate school students. Adult students.
Amount: $30,000 plus up to $4,000 travel allowance.
Number of awards: Varies.
Deadline: October 26.
How to apply: Applications are available online.
Exclusive: Visit www.UltimateScholarshipBook.com and enter code AM55020 for updates on this award.

(551) • Herb Alpert Young Jazz Composer Awards

ASCAP Foundation
One Lincoln Plaza, New York, NY 10023
Phone: 212-621-6219
https://www.ascapfoundation.org/programs-and-grants
Purpose: To recognize the talent of young jazz composers.
Eligibility: Applicants must be under the age of 30 and U.S. citizens or permanent residents. They must submit one original composition, including a score and performance, if possible.
Target applicant(s): Junior high students or younger. High school students. College students. Graduate school students. Adult students.
Amount: Varies.
Number of awards: Varies.
Deadline: December 1.
How to apply: Applications are available online.
Exclusive: Visit www.UltimateScholarshipBook.com and enter code AS55120 for updates on this award.

(552) • Hub Foundation

Hub Foundation
3130 Crow Canyon Place, Suite 205, San Ramon, CA 94583
Phone: 925-271-5332
Email: information@hub-foundation.org
https://hub-foundation.org/scholarships
Purpose: To support Muslim students and those studying Islam.
Eligibility: Applicants must be graduate students or undergraduate students in their junior or senior year whose studies focus on or include Islam and Muslim perspectives including religious studies, Middle Eastern studies, sociology, political science and anthropology. Students must have a minimum 3.5 grade point average.
Target applicant(s): College students. Graduate school students. Adult students.
Minimum GPA: 3.5
Amount: $20,000.
Number of awards: 7.
Deadline: June 30.
How to apply: Applications are available online.
Exclusive: Visit www.UltimateScholarshipBook.com and enter code HU55220 for updates on this award.

(553) • IACI/NUI Visiting Fellowship in Irish Studies

Irish-American Cultural Institute (IACI)
An Foras Cultuir Gael-Mheircheanach, 1 Lackawanna Place, Morristown, NJ 07960
Phone: 973-605-1991
http://www.iaci-usa.org
Purpose: To award fellowships to Irish studies scholars to spend one semester at the University of Ireland-Galway.
Eligibility: Applicants must provide a description of how the fellowship will be used and a curriculum vitae with a list of publications.
Target applicant(s): Graduate school students. Adult students.
Amount: $4,000.
Number of awards: Varies.
Deadline: February 28.
How to apply: Application is available online.
Exclusive: Visit www.UltimateScholarshipBook.com and enter code IR55320 for updates on this award.

(554) • iCanvas Art Scholarship

iCanvas
8280 Austin Avenue, Morton Grove, IL 60053
Phone: 800-980-1089
Email: adam.reinertsen@icanvas.com
https://www.icanvas.com/scholarship-form
Purpose: To support art students pursuing higher education.
Eligibility: Applicants must be currently enrolled in college or graduate program in the U.S. Students must submit photo of an original work of art and describe their inspiration and medium.
Target applicant(s): College students. Graduate school students.
Amount: $1,000.
Number of awards: 1.
Deadline: December 7.
How to apply: Applications are available online.
Exclusive: Visit www.UltimateScholarshipBook.com and enter code IC55420 for updates on this award.

(555) • IDSA Undergraduate Scholarships

Industrial Designers Society of America
555 Grove Street, Suite 200, Herndon, VA 20170
Phone: 703-707-6000
Email: idsa@idsa.org
http://www.idsa.org
Purpose: To help industrial design students in their final year of schooling.
Eligibility: Applicants must be full-time students enrolled in an IDSA-listed program in their next-to-last year of the program, have a minimum 3.0 GPA, be members of an IDSA Student Chapter and be U.S. citizens or residents. Applicants must submit a letter of intent, 20 visual examples of their work and a transcript. Awards are based solely on the excellence of the submitted works.
Target applicant(s): College students. Adult students.
Minimum GPA: 3.0
Amount: $1,500.
Number of awards: 1.
Deadline: May 31.
How to apply: Applications are available online.

Exclusive: Visit www.UltimateScholarshipBook.com and enter code IN55520 for updates on this award.

(556) • IFDA Leaders Commemorative Scholarship

International Furnishings and Design Association (IFDA)
36 Bay View Road, Wellesley, MA 02482
Phone: 781-894-3240
Email: linda@westonstudiodesign.com
http://www.ifdaef.org/

Purpose: To aid interior design students.

Eligibility: Applicants must be full-time undergraduate students at an accredited U.S. postsecondary institution. They must be majoring in interior design or a closely-related design subject and have completed four design courses at the time of application. Preference will be given to students who demonstrate leadership and volunteer experience. Selection is based on the overall strength of the application.

Target applicant(s): College students. Adult students.

Amount: $1,500.

Number of awards: 1.

Deadline: March 31.

How to apply: Applications are available online. An application form, personal essay, one recommendation letter and design work examples are required.

Exclusive: Visit www.UltimateScholarshipBook.com and enter code IN55620 for updates on this award.

(557) • IFDA Student Member Scholarship

International Furnishings and Design Association (IFDA)
36 Bay View Road, Wellesley, MA 02482
Phone: 781-894-3240
Email: linda@westonstudiodesign.com
http://www.ifdaef.org/

Purpose: To aid interior design students who are members of the International Furnishings and Design Association (IFDA).

Eligibility: Applicants must be full-time undergraduate students who are attending an accredited U.S. postsecondary institution. They must be majoring in interior design or a closely-related design subject and have completed a minimum of four design courses. Selection is based on the overall strength of the application.

Target applicant(s): College students. Adult students.

Amount: $2,000.

Number of awards: 1.

Deadline: March 31.

How to apply: Applications are available online. An application form, personal statement, two recommendation letters and design work examples are required.

Exclusive: Visit www.UltimateScholarshipBook.com and enter code IN55720 for updates on this award.

(558) • ILA Jeanne S. Chall Research Fellowship

International Literacy Association
The Jeanne S. Chall Research Fellowship, Division of Research and Policy, P.O. Box 8139, Newark, DE 19714-8139
Phone: 302-731-1600
Email: research@reading.org
https://www.literacyworldwide.org/about-us/awards-grants

Purpose: To support dissertation research in reading.

Eligibility: Applicants must be doctoral students planning or beginning their dissertation on one of the following topics in the field of reading: beginning reading, readability, reading difficulty, stages of reading development, the relation of vocabulary to reading and diagnosing and teaching adults with limited reading ability. Applicants must also be members of the International Literacy Association.

Target applicant(s): Graduate school students. Adult students.

Amount: $5,000.

Number of awards: 1.

Deadline: January 15.

How to apply: Applications are available online.

Exclusive: Visit www.UltimateScholarshipBook.com and enter code IN55820 for updates on this award.

(559) • Illustrators of the Future

L. Ron Hubbard's Writers of the Future Contest
7051 Hollywood Boulevard, Los Angeles, CA 90028
Phone: 323-466-3310
Email: contests@authorservicesinc.com
http://www.writersofthefuture.com

Purpose: To discover deserving amateur aspiring illustrators.

Eligibility: Applicants must not have published more than three black-and-white story illustrations or more than one color painting in national media. Applicants must also submit three original illustrations done in either color or black-and-white medium in three different themes.

Target applicant(s): High school students. College students. Graduate school students. Adult students.

Amount: $1,500-$5,000.

Number of awards: 3 each quarter and a grand prize awarded annually.

Deadline: December 31, March 31, June 30, September 30.

How to apply: There is no application form.

Exclusive: Visit www.UltimateScholarshipBook.com and enter code L.55920 for updates on this award.

(560) • International Junior Competition

Gina Bachauer International Piano Foundation
138 W. 300 S, Salt Lake City, UT 84101
Phone: 801-297-4250
Email: info@bachauer.com
http://www.bachauer.com

Purpose: To reward top piano prodigies, ages 11 to 18.

Eligibility: Applicants must perform at this competition in Salt Lake City, Utah. Students are provided with housing but must provide own transportation to and from Salt Lake City. Applicants must perform a 20-minute program of solo music and a 30-minute program of solo music. Two competition categories available: ages 11 to 14 and ages 15 to 18.

Target applicant(s): Junior high students or younger. High school students.

Amount: Up to $7,000.

Number of awards: 6.

Deadline: June.

How to apply: Applications are available online.

Exclusive: Visit www.UltimateScholarshipBook.com and enter code GI56020 for updates on this award.

(561) • International Scholarships

American Institute for Foreign Study
College Division, 1 High Ridge Park, Stamford, CT 06905
Phone: 800-727-2437
Email: studyabroad@aifs.com
https://www.aifsabroad.com/scholarships.asp

Purpose: To promote international understanding through study abroad.
Eligibility: Applicants must be currently enrolled college undergraduates with a minimum 3.0 GPA who show leadership potential and are involved in extra-curricular activities centered on multicultural or international issues. Applicants must submit a 1,000-word essay on how study abroad will change their lives.
Target applicant(s): College students. Adult students.
Minimum GPA: 3.0
Amount: $500-$1,000.
Number of awards: Varies.
Deadline: April 15 for fall semester, October 1 for spring semester and March 1 for summer.
How to apply: Applications are available online.
Exclusive: Visit www.UltimateScholarshipBook.com and enter code AM56120 for updates on this award.

(562) • International Trumpet Guild Conference Scholarship

International Trumpet Guild
P.O. Box 2688, Davenport, IA 52809-2688
Email: confscholarships@trumpetguild.org
http://www.trumpetguild.org
Purpose: To improve the artistic level of trumpet players.
Eligibility: Applicants must be students and record audition songs onto a tape or CD. There are different age group categories, and each category has its own performance requirements. Applicants must be ITG members.
Target applicant(s): Junior high students or younger. High school students. College students. Graduate school students.
Amount: Varies.
Number of awards: Varies.
Deadline: February 1.
How to apply: Applications are available online.
Exclusive: Visit www.UltimateScholarshipBook.com and enter code IN56220 for updates on this award.

(563) • Irish Cultural and Educational Grant

Irish Festivals Inc.
1532 Wauwatosa Avenue, Milwaukee, WI 53213
Phone: 414-476-3378
Email: culturalgrant@celticmke.com
http://www.irishfest.com
Purpose: To support students wishing to study Irish culture.
Eligibility: Applicants can be of any age and do not have to be residents of the Milwaukee area. Selection is based on the proposed project to study some aspect of Irish culture.
Target applicant(s): Junior high students or younger. High school students. College students. Graduate school students. Adult students.
Amount: Varies.
Number of awards: Varies.
Deadline: October 31.
How to apply: Applications are available online and by mail.
Exclusive: Visit www.UltimateScholarshipBook.com and enter code IR56320 for updates on this award.

(564) • ItaliaRail Study Abroad in Italy Scholarship

ItaliaRail
201 Somerville Avenue, 2nd Floor, Somerville, MA 02143
Phone: 877-375-7245
https://www.italiarail.com/scholarship
Purpose: To support undergraduate students in studying abroad in Italy.
Eligibility: Applicants must have enrolled in their college or university's study abroad program in Italy. Students must submit college transcripts, FAFSA Student Aid Report, a resume and an essay explaining why they want to study abroad in Italy. Selection is based on the overall strength of the application.
Target applicant(s): College students. Adult students.
Amount: $1,000.
Number of awards: 2.
Deadline: December 15.
How to apply: Applications are available online.
Exclusive: Visit www.UltimateScholarshipBook.com and enter code IT56420 for updates on this award.

(565) • Jack Kent Cooke Young Artist Award

From the Top
295 Huntington Avenue, Suite 201, Boston, MA 02115
Phone: 617-437-0707
https://www.fromthetop.org/apply/
Purpose: To reward classical instrumentalists, vocalists and composers who have not yet entered college for extraordinary musical accomplishment.
Eligibility: Applicants must have interest in performing on NPR's From the Top. Selection is primarily based on demonstration of strong musical ability, unmet financial need and strength of character.
Target applicant(s): High school students.
Amount: Up to $10,000.
Number of awards: 20.
Deadline: January 8, March 5, October 2.
How to apply: Applications are available online.
Exclusive: Visit www.UltimateScholarshipBook.com and enter code FR56520 for updates on this award.

(566) • Joel Polsky Academic Achievement Award

American Society of Interior Designers (ASID) Educational Foundation Inc.
608 Massachusetts Avenue NE, Washington, DC 20002-6006
Phone: 202-546-3480
https://www.asid.org/resources/awards/scholarships-and-grants
Purpose: To recognize an interior design student's project.
Eligibility: Applicants must be undergraduate or graduate students in interior design and should submit entry forms and projects such as research papers or doctoral and master's theses that focus on interior design topics. The projects are judged on content, breadth of material, coverage of the topic, innovative subject matter, bibliography and references. The society may exhibit any entry for two years.
Target applicant(s): High school students. College students. Graduate school students. Adult students.
Amount: $5,000.
Number of awards: 1.
Deadline: April 26.
How to apply: Applications are available online.
Exclusive: Visit www.UltimateScholarshipBook.com and enter code AM56620 for updates on this award.

(567) • John F. and Anna Lee Stacey Scholarship Fund for Art Education

John F. and Anna Lee Stacey Scholarship Fund
1700 NE 63rd Street, Oklahoma City, OK 73111
Phone: 405-478-2250
Email: info@nationalcowboymuseum.org
http://www.nationalcowboymuseum.org/education/staceyfund/

Purpose: To educate young men and women who aim to enter the art profession.

Eligibility: Applicants must be between the ages of 18 and 35 and must submit no more than 10 of their paintings or drawing work for judging along with a letter outlining the applicant's ambitions and plans. Submissions should be in the form of digital images on a disk with a dpi of 150. Letters of recommendation will also be taken into account during selection.

Target applicant(s): High school students. College students. Graduate school students. Adult students.

Amount: $5,000.

Number of awards: Varies.

Deadline: February 1.

How to apply: Applications are available online.

Exclusive: Visit www.UltimateScholarshipBook.com and enter code JO56720 for updates on this award.

(568) • John Lennon Scholarship Competition

BMI Foundation Inc.
7 World Trade Center, 250 Greenwich Street, New York, NY 10007
Phone: 212-586-2000
Email: info@bmifoundation.org
http://www.bmifoundation.org

Purpose: Established in 1997 by Yoko Ono in conjunction with the BMI Foundation, the John Lennon Scholarship recognizes the talent of young songwriters.

Eligibility: Applicants must be age 17 to 24 and write an original song to be reviewed by a prestigious panel of judges. Entries are to be submitted by music schools, universities, youth orchestras and the Music Educators National Conference (MENC).

Target applicant(s): College students. Graduate school students.

Amount: Up to $20,000.

Number of awards: 3.

Deadline: April 5.

How to apply: Please see the website for a full list of eligible organizations that may submit entries.

Exclusive: Visit www.UltimateScholarshipBook.com and enter code BM56820 for updates on this award.

(569) • John O. Crane Memorial Fellowship

Institute of Current World Affairs
1779 Massachusetts Avenue NW, Suite 605, Washington, DC 20036
Phone: 202-364-4068
Email: apply@icwa.org
http://www.icwa.org

Purpose: To promote independent study abroad in Eastern Europe and the Middle East.

Eligibility: Applicants must be under the age of 36 and must have strong, credible ties to American society. They must propose an independent research project that would be conducted in Eastern Europe or the Middle East and be proficient in a native language that is commonly spoken in the proposed research site. Selection is based on the overall strength of the application.

Target applicant(s): Graduate school students. Adult students.

Amount: Full financial support.

Number of awards: Varies.

Deadline: Varies.

How to apply: Application instructions are available online. A letter of interest and resume are required for the initial phase of the application process by August 1.

Exclusive: Visit www.UltimateScholarshipBook.com and enter code IN56920 for updates on this award.

(570) • Julius and Esther Stulberg International String Competition

Julius and Esther Stulberg Competition Inc.
359 South Kalamazoo Mall, Suite 14, Kalamazoo, MI 49007
Phone: 269-343-2776
Email: stulbergcomp@yahoo.com
http://www.stulberg.org

Purpose: To support young instrumentalists.

Eligibility: Applicants must be students of violin, viola, cello or double bass, be 19 years of age or younger as of January 1 of the year of competition and perform a Bach piece and a solo for the competition, which is typically held in May.

Target applicant(s): Junior high students or younger. High school students.

Amount: Up to $6,000.

Number of awards: 5.

Deadline: February 1.

How to apply: Applications are available online. An application form, proof of age and audition CD are required.

Exclusive: Visit www.UltimateScholarshipBook.com and enter code JU57020 for updates on this award.

(571) • Junior Fellowships

Dumbarton Oaks
1703 32nd Street NW , Washington, DC 20007
Phone: 202-339-6413
Email: FellowshipPrograms@doaks.org
http://www.doaks.org

Purpose: To provide fellowships to scholars engaged in Byzantine studies, Pre-Columbian studies and garden and landscape studies.

Eligibility: Applicants at the time of application should have fulfilled all preliminary requirements for a Ph.D. and be willing to work on a dissertation or final project at Dumbarton Oaks under the direction of a faculty member at their own university. The fellowships are in the following areas: Byzantine Studies (including related aspects of late Roman, early Christian, western medieval, Slavic and Near Eastern Studies), Pre-Columbian Studies (of Mexico, Central America and Andean South America) and garden and landscape studies. Fellowships are based on demonstrated scholarly ability and preparation of the candidate (including knowledge of the required languages) and value of the study or project and its relevance to Dumbarton Oaks.

Target applicant(s): Graduate school students. Adult students.

Amount: Up to $21,000.

Number of awards: Varies.

Deadline: November 1.

How to apply: Applicants must submit ten complete, collated sets of: application letter, proposal and personal and professional data. They must also submit an official transcript and three recommendation letters, with one from the faculty advisor.

Exclusive: Visit www.UltimateScholarshipBook.com and enter code DU57120 for updates on this award.

(572) • Kerope Zildjian Concert Percussion Scholarship

Avedis Zildjian Company
22 Longwater Drive, Norwell, MA 02061
Phone: 800-229-1623
Email: keitha@zildjian.com
http://www.zildjian.com

Purpose: To support a high-achieving student percussionist who is currently enrolled in an undergraduate program in the music arena.
Eligibility: Applicants must be full-time undergraduate music students who are also outstanding percussionists. The CD submission of a percussion solo is required. Selection is based on the overall quality of the application and submission.
Target applicant(s): College students. Adult students.
Amount: $5,000 plus free cymbals.
Number of awards: 1.
Deadline: June 9.
How to apply: Entry forms are available online. Entry form, CD contents form, one-page resume and two copies of CD recording are required and should be mailed to the attention of Kerope Zildjian.
Exclusive: Visit www.UltimateScholarshipBook.com and enter code AV57220 for updates on this award.

(573) • KidGuard for Education Essay Scholarship Program

KidGuard
117 W. 9th Street, Suite 1009, Los Angeles, CA 90015
Email: apply@kidguard.com
https://www.kidguard.com/nonprofits/scholarship/

Purpose: To reward students who have ideas on how to bring awareness and ideas to the problem of online safety.
Eligibility: Applicants must be undergraduate or graduate students already enrolled full-time in a college or university. Students must write an essay with their ideas on the topic given on the scholarship page.
Target applicant(s): College students. Graduate school students. Adult students.
Amount: $500-$1,500.
Number of awards: Varies.
Deadline: October 31.
How to apply: Applications are available online.
Exclusive: Visit www.UltimateScholarshipBook.com and enter code KI57320 for updates on this award.

(574) • Language Grants

Blakemore Foundation
1201 Third Avenue, Suite 4900, Seattle, WA 98101
Phone: 206-359-8778
Email: contactus@blakemorefoundation.org
http://www.blakemorefoundation.org

Purpose: To support students pursuing a professional, business, technical or academic career that involves the regular use of Chinese, Japanese, Korean, Thai, Vietnamese, Indonesian, Khmer or Burmese.
Eligibility: Applicants must be at or near an advanced level in one of the languages listed above, having completed (at minimum) the equivalent of third-year college-level language classes.
Target applicant(s): College students. Graduate school students. Adult students.
Amount: Varies.
Number of awards: Varies.
Deadline: December 30.
How to apply: Applications are available online.
Exclusive: Visit www.UltimateScholarshipBook.com and enter code BL57420 for updates on this award.

(575) • Legacy Scholarship for Undergraduates

American Society of Interior Designers (ASID) Educational Foundation Inc.
608 Massachusetts Avenue NE, Washington, DC 20002-6006
Phone: 202-546-3480
https://www.asid.org/resources/awards/scholarships-and-grants

Purpose: To support undergraduate students who are pursuing a degree in interior design.
Eligibility: Applicants must be enrolled in their junior or senior year of undergraduate study. Selection is primarily based on demonstration of academic performance and creative achievement. Students must submit a design portfolio, official transcripts, a letter of recommendation and a personal statement.
Target applicant(s): College students. Adult students.
Amount: $4,000.
Number of awards: 1.
Deadline: April 18.
How to apply: Applications are available online.
Exclusive: Visit www.UltimateScholarshipBook.com and enter code AM57520 for updates on this award.

(576) • Leif and Inger Sjoberg Award

American-Scandinavian Foundation
58 Park Avenue, New York, NY 10016
Phone: 212-779-3587
Email: info@amscan.org
http://www.amscan.org

Purpose: To encourage the English translation of Scandinavian literature.
Eligibility: The award is given to the best English translation of poetry, fiction, drama or literary prose written by a Scandinavian author in Danish, Finnish, Icelandic, Norwegian or Swedish after 1800. Translations may not previously have been published in the English language.
Target applicant(s): Junior high students or younger. High school students. College students. Graduate school students. Adult students.
Amount: $2,000.
Number of awards: 1.
Scholarship may be renewable.
Deadline: June 15.
How to apply: There is no application form. Please see website for submission details.
Exclusive: Visit www.UltimateScholarshipBook.com and enter code AM57620 for updates on this award.

(577) • Lions International Peace Poster Contest

Lions Club International
300 W. 22nd Street, Oak Brook, IL 60523-8842
Phone: 630-571-5466
Email: pr@lionsclubs.org
http://www.lionsclubs.org

Purpose: To award creative youngsters cash prizes for outstanding poster designs.
Eligibility: Students must be 11, 12 or 13 years old as of the deadline and must be sponsored by their local Lions club. Entries will be judged at the local, district, multiple district and international levels. Posters

will be evaluated on originality, artistic merit and expression of the assigned theme.
Target applicant(s): Junior high students or younger.
Amount: $500-$5,000.
Number of awards: 24.
Deadline: November 15.
How to apply: Applications are available from your local Lion's Club.
Exclusive: Visit www.UltimateScholarshipBook.com and enter code LI57720 for updates on this award.

---

(578) • Lotte Lenya Competition

Kurt Weill Foundation for Music
7 East 20th Street, 3rd Floor, New York, NY 10003
Phone: 212-505-5240
Email: kwfinfo@kwf.org
http://www.kwf.org
Purpose: To recognize excellence in music theater performance.
Eligibility: Applicants must be between 19 and 32 years old and attend a regional competition, performing four selections. If contestants are unable to participate in any of the scheduled regional auditions, they may instead submit a DVD, which must contain all four of the required repertoire selections. Finalists will be chosen, based on vocal beauty and technique, interpretation, acting, repertoire variety and presence.
Target applicant(s): High school students. College students. Graduate school students. Adult students.
Amount: $500-$20,000 plus travel stipend.
Number of awards: Varies.
Deadline: January 22.
How to apply: Applications are available online.
Exclusive: Visit www.UltimateScholarshipBook.com and enter code KU57820 for updates on this award.

---

(579) • Love Your Body Poster Contest

National Organization for Women Foundation
LYB Poster Contest, 1100 H Street, NW, Suite 300, Washington, DC 20005
http://now.org/now-foundation/
Purpose: To reward poster artists who effectively encourage women to love their bodies.
Eligibility: Applicants may be non-students or may be students of any grade level at a primary, secondary or postsecondary school. They can be residents of any country. They must design and submit an original poster that challenges limiting, stereotypical or negative portrayals of women in the media. Selection is based on poster message and graphical attractiveness.
Target applicant(s): Junior high students or younger. High school students. College students. Graduate school students. Adult students.
Amount: Up to $350.
Number of awards: 4.
Deadline: March 1.
How to apply: Entry instructions are available online. A poster is required.
Exclusive: Visit www.UltimateScholarshipBook.com and enter code NA57920 for updates on this award.

---

(580) • Malala Yousafzai Scholarship

Online Logo Maker
http://www.onlinelogomaker.com/scholarships-for-women
Purpose: To encourage adult women to pursue education.
Eligibility: Applicants must be women age 30 or older who are starting post-secondary education or returning to school to continue interrupted studies. Students must be pursuing education in the arts and design field.
Target applicant(s): Adult students.
Amount: $1,000.
Number of awards: 1.
Deadline: December 1.
How to apply: Applications are available online.
Exclusive: Visit www.UltimateScholarshipBook.com and enter code ON58020 for updates on this award.

---

(581) • Marian A. Smith Costume Award

Southeastern Theatre Conference Inc.
1175 Revolution Mill Drive, Studio 14, Greensboro, NC 27405
Phone: 336-272-3645
Email: emilystrickland@sjrstate.edu
http://www.setc.org/
Purpose: To support graduate students majoring in costume design and/or technology.
Eligibility: Applicants must be finished with their undergraduate degrees at an SETC region institution by the August prior to application. They must also be first-time as well as full-time attendees of a regionally accredited graduate school specializing in costume design and/or costume technology. Selection is based on the overall strength of the application and interview.
Target applicant(s): College students. Graduate school students. Adult students.
Amount: $1,500.
Number of awards: 1.
Deadline: January 21.
How to apply: Applications are available online. An application, personal letter, resume, ten samples of completed work, five references, transcripts and interview are required.
Exclusive: Visit www.UltimateScholarshipBook.com and enter code SO58120 for updates on this award.

---

(582) • Minted Design Grant

Minted
222 Grant Avenue, San Francisco, CA 94108
Phone: 888-828-6468
http://www.minted.com
Purpose: To support undergraduate or graduate art students.
Eligibility: Applicants must be currently enrolled full-time in an undergraduate or graduate art or design program.
Target applicant(s): College students. Graduate school students. Adult students.
Amount: $4,000.
Number of awards: 3.
Deadline: July 21.
How to apply: Applications are available online.
Exclusive: Visit www.UltimateScholarshipBook.com and enter code MI58220 for updates on this award.

---

(583) • Most Promising Logo Design Scholar

Free Logo Services
36 Bromfield Street, Suite 302, Boston, MA 02108
Email: scholarships@freelogoservices.com
https://www.freelogoservices.com/
Purpose: To reward students engaged in studies related to graphic arts and graphic design.

Eligibility: Applicants must have completed at least one year of coursework in graphic design, product design or branding and have at least a 2.5 GPA. Students must submit three original logo designs for the following three industries: automotive, construction and beauty and massage.
Target applicant(s): High school students. College students. Graduate school students. Adult students.
Minimum GPA: 2.5
Amount: $1,500.
Number of awards: 1.
Deadline: December 31.
How to apply: To apply, email an official transcript, two letters of recommendation and logo designs.
Exclusive: Visit www.UltimateScholarshipBook.com and enter code FR58320 for updates on this award.

(584) • MVP Visuals Design Scholarship

MVP Visuals Design Scholarship
215 Mood Road, Enfield, CT 06082
Phone: 800-980-6871
Email: hello@mvpvisuals.com
http://mvpvisuals.com/pages/mvp-scholarships
Purpose: To assist students who are aspiring artists.
Eligibility: Applicants must be planning to attend or be current undergraduate students at a U.S. university and must major in graphic arts and design or applied arts. Students must create a digital visual design based on the university they are or will be attending.
Target applicant(s): High school students. College students. Adult students.
Amount: $500.
Number of awards: 2.
Deadline: January 1, June 1.
How to apply: The design and 200- to 300-word description of the design must be emailed.
Exclusive: Visit www.UltimateScholarshipBook.com and enter code MV58420 for updates on this award.

(585) • Nadia Christensen Prize

American-Scandinavian Foundation
58 Park Avenue, New York, NY 10016
Phone: 212-779-3587
Email: info@amscan.org
http://www.amscan.org
Purpose: To recognize individuals who translate Scandinavian writings.
Eligibility: Selection is based on the overall strength of the application.
Target applicant(s): Junior high students or younger. High school students. College students. Graduate school students. Adult students.
Amount: $2,500.
Number of awards: 1.
Deadline: June 15.
How to apply: Applications are available online. Applications must include one copy of the work that was translated in its original language, one copy of the English translation of the work, a CV containing contact information for the translator and a letter granting the translation to be entered in the competition and published.
Exclusive: Visit www.UltimateScholarshipBook.com and enter code AM58520 for updates on this award.

(586) • Nancy and Harry Koenigsberg Student Award

Textile Study Group of New York
P.O. Box 3592, Grand Central Station, New York, NY 10163
http://www.tsgny.org/awards
Purpose: To support students creating fiber artwork.
Eligibility: Applicants must be current undergraduate or graduate students in a college, school, or university in CT, DC, MA, MD, ME, NH, NJ, NY, PA, RI, VA or VT who create fiber artwork. Students must submit images of their original artwork, artist statement and resume along with their application. This award is available once every three years.
Target applicant(s): College students. Graduate school students. Adult students.
Amount: $1,500.
Number of awards: 1.
Deadline: April 1.
How to apply: Applications are available online.
Exclusive: Visit www.UltimateScholarshipBook.com and enter code TE58620 for updates on this award.

(587) • National High School Poetry Contest/ Easterday Poetry Award

Live Poets Society
P.O. Box 8841, Turnersville, NJ 08012
Email: lpsnj@comcast.net
http://www.highschoolpoetrycontest.com
Purpose: To provide a venue for young poets to be recognized.
Eligibility: Applicants must be U.S. high school students. Submitted poems must be 20 lines or less, in English, unpublished and not simultaneously submitted to any other competition. Applicants may only submit one poem during any 90-day span and must include a self-addressed, stamped envelope with each mailed entry, or applicants may submit their poems online. Submissions are accepted year-round.
Target applicant(s): High school students.
Amount: Up to $2,500.
Number of awards: Varies.
Deadline: March 31, June 30, September 30, December 31.
How to apply: There is no application form.
Exclusive: Visit www.UltimateScholarshipBook.com and enter code LI58720 for updates on this award.

(588) • National Junior Classical League (NJCL) Scholarships

National Junior Classical League
1122 Oak Street North, Fargo, ND 58102
Phone: 513-529-7741
Email: administrator@njcl.org
http://www.njcl.org
Purpose: To support students studying the classics.
Eligibility: Applicants must be NJCL members in good standing, entering college the upcoming year and studying the classics. Special consideration is given to those planning to teach Latin, Greek or classical humanities. Selection is based on financial need, JCL service, academics and recommendations.
Target applicant(s): High school students.
Amount: $1,200-$2,500.
Number of awards: Varies.
Deadline: June 15.
How to apply: Applications are available online or by written request.

Exclusive: Visit www.UltimateScholarshipBook.com and enter code NA58820 for updates on this award.

(589) · National Latin Exam Scholarship

National Latin Exam
University of Mary Washington, 1301 College Avenue,
Fredericksburg, VA 22401
Phone: 888-378-7721
Email: nle@umw.edu
http://www.nle.org

Purpose: To reward students for their Latin proficiency.
Eligibility: Applicants must be gold medal winners in Latin III-IV Prose, III-IV Poetry or Latin V-VI on the National Latin Exam. Applicants must be high school seniors who agree to take at least one Latin or classical Greek each semester during their first year of college. A classics in translation course does not count.
Target applicant(s): High school students.
Amount: $2,000.
Number of awards: Varies.
Scholarship may be renewable.
Deadline: Varies.
How to apply: Applications are mailed to eligible students. Renewal applications are available online.
Exclusive: Visit www.UltimateScholarshipBook.com and enter code NA58920 for updates on this award.

(590) · National Peace Essay Contest

United States Institute of Peace
2301 Constitution Avenue NW, Washington, DC 20036
Phone: 202-457-1700
Email: essay_contest@usip.org
https://www.usip.org/public-education/AFSAEssayContest

Purpose: To expand educational opportunities for young Americans.
Eligibility: Applicants must be in grades 9 through 12 in the U.S. Home schooled students or students who are U.S. citizens attending high schools overseas are eligible. Applicants need the sponsorship of any school, school club, youth group, community group or religious organization. Selection is based on the quality of the research, analysis, form, style and mechanics of the essay.
Target applicant(s): High school students.
Amount: $1,250-$2,500.
Number of awards: 2.
Deadline: March 15.
How to apply: Applications are available online.
Exclusive: Visit www.UltimateScholarshipBook.com and enter code UN59020 for updates on this award.

(591) · National Sculpture Society Scholarship

National Sculpture Society
75 Varick Street, 11th Floor, New York, NY 10013
Phone: 212-764-5645
Email: nss1893@aol.com
http://www.nationalsculpture.org

Purpose: To award scholarships to students of figurative or representative sculpture.
Eligibility: Applicants must provide brief biographies and an explanation of their background in sculpture, two recommendation letters and photographs of their sculpture work. Students must also demonstrate financial need.
Target applicant(s): College students. Graduate school students. Adult students.
Amount: $2,000.
Number of awards: 4.
Deadline: May 30.
How to apply: Follow the application guidelines listed on the website.
Exclusive: Visit www.UltimateScholarshipBook.com and enter code NA59120 for updates on this award.

(592) · National Security Education Program David L. Boren Undergraduate Scholarships

Institute of International Education
1400 K Street NW, Washington, DC 20005
Phone: 202-326-7672
Email: boren@iie.org
http://www.iie.org

Purpose: To provide an opportunity for undergraduate students to study abroad in certain countries that are vital to U.S. security interests.
Eligibility: Applicants must be U.S. undergraduate students who have a strong interest in working for the U.S. federal government after graduation. They must intend to study abroad in one of several countries that have been overlooked traditionally by students wishing to travel overseas for academic purposes. They must be able to demonstrate how their studies abroad would contribute to U.S. national security interests. Preference will be given to students who can commit to a full academic year of study abroad. Selection is based on the overall strength of the application.
Target applicant(s): High school students. College students. Adult students.
Amount: Up to $20,000.
Number of awards: Varies.
Deadline: February 8.
How to apply: Applications are available online. An application form and supporting materials are required.
Exclusive: Visit www.UltimateScholarshipBook.com and enter code IN59220 for updates on this award.

(593) · National Vocal Competition for Young Opera Singers

Loren L. Zachary Society for the Performing Arts
2250 Gloaming Way, Beverly Hills, CA 90210
Phone: 310-276-2731
http://www.zacharysociety.org

Purpose: To support students pursuing a professional operatic stage career.
Eligibility: Applicants must be 21-35 years old, reside in the U.S. or Canada and must be available for all phases of the competition.
Target applicant(s): College students. Graduate school students. Adult students.
Amount: Varies.
Number of awards: Varies.
Deadline: January 19 (New York), February 7 (Los Angeles).
How to apply: Applications are available online.
Exclusive: Visit www.UltimateScholarshipBook.com and enter code LO59320 for updates on this award.

(594) • NFMC Lynn Freeman Olson Composition Awards

National Federation of Music Clubs Olson Awards
James Schnars, 331 Cleveland Street, Apartment 804, Clearwater, FL 33755
Phone: 317-882-4003
Email: info@nfmc-music.org
http://www.nfmc-music.org/competitions-awards/
Purpose: To support student composers.
Eligibility: Applicants must be at least in grade 7 and no older than age 25. Applicants must be members of the National Federation of Music Clubs and must submit an original piano composition to be judged. This biennial award is given in odd-numbered years.
Target applicant(s): Junior high students or younger. High school students.
Amount: $500-$1,000.
Number of awards: Varies.
Deadline: March 1.
How to apply: Applications are available online.
Exclusive: Visit www.UltimateScholarshipBook.com and enter code NA59420 for updates on this award.

(595) • NFMC Wendell Irish Viola Award

National Federation of Music Clubs (AR)
Dr. George Keck, 2112 Hinson Road, Suite 23, Little Rock, AR 72212
Phone: 317-882-4003
Email: keckg@att.net
http://www.nfmc-music.org
Purpose: To recognize musically talented students.
Eligibility: Applicants must be between the ages of 12 and 18 and must be Individual Junior Special members or Active Junior Club members of the National Federation of Music Clubs. Applicants must enter in their state of residence by submitting a taped performance.
Target applicant(s): Junior high students or younger. High school students.
Amount: $250-$1,000.
Number of awards: 7.
Deadline: February 1.
How to apply: Applications are available online.
Exclusive: Visit www.UltimateScholarshipBook.com and enter code NA59520 for updates on this award.

(596) • Odenza Vacations Review My Video Scholarship

Odenza Vacations Review My Video Scholarship
4445 Eastgate Mall, Suite 200, San Diego, CA 92121
Phone: 866-339-6006
https://www.odenzavacations.com/scholarshipcontest/
Purpose: To assist students who submit a video review.
Eligibility: Applicants must be ages 16 to 25, be U.S. or Canadian citizens and have a minimum 2.5 GPA. Students must also have at least one full year remaining in post-secondary studies. The student who has the best video critique will win the scholarship.
Target applicant(s): High school students. College students.
Minimum GPA: 2.5
Amount: $500.
Number of awards: 1.
Deadline: September 30.
How to apply: Application information is available online.
Exclusive: Visit www.UltimateScholarshipBook.com and enter code OD59620 for updates on this award.

(597) • Office Supply Scholarship

BulkOfficeSupply.com
1614 Hereford Road, Hewlett, NY 11557
Phone: 800-658-1488
Email: service@bulkofficesupply.com
http://www.bulkofficesupply.com/scholarships-in-new-york
Purpose: To support students pursuing teaching or art or who plan on owning their own business.
Eligibility: Applicants must be high school students or college freshmen or sophomores. Students must be pursing degree programs in teaching or art or must wish to own their own business. Applicants will need to submit a 500- to 600-word essay describing where they plan to or are currently attending school, their desired major, how the student developed an interest in teaching, art or owning their own business and how the scholarship would help them to reach their goals.
Target applicant(s): High school students. College students. Adult students.
Amount: $1,000.
Number of awards: 1.
Deadline: February 1.
How to apply: Applications are available online and must include the essay.
Exclusive: Visit www.UltimateScholarshipBook.com and enter code BU59720 for updates on this award.

(598) • Optimist International Essay Contest

Optimist International
4494 Lindell Boulevard, St. Louis, MO 63108
Phone: 314-371-6000
Email: programs@optimist.org
http://www.optimist.org
Purpose: To reward students based on their essay-writing skills.
Eligibility: Applicants must be under 18 years of age as of December 31 of the current school year and application must be made through a local Optimist Club. The essay topic changes each year. Applicants compete at the club, district and international level. District winners receive a $2,500 scholarship. Scoring is based on organization, vocabulary and style, grammar and punctuation, neatness and adherence to the contest rules. The club-level contests are held in early February but vary by club. The deadline for clubs to submit their winning essay to the district competition is February 28.
Target applicant(s): High school students.
Amount: $2,500.
Number of awards: Varies.
Deadline: Early February.
How to apply: Contact your local Optimist Club.
Exclusive: Visit www.UltimateScholarshipBook.com and enter code OP59820 for updates on this award.

(599) • Part-Time Student Scholarship

International Furnishings and Design Association (IFDA)
36 Bay View Road, Wellesley, MA 02482
Phone: 781-894-3240
Email: linda@westonstudiodesign.com
http://www.ifdaef.org/
Purpose: To aid part-time students who are majoring in interior design.

Eligibility: Applicants must be undergraduate students at an accredited U.S. postsecondary institution. They must be majoring in interior design or a related design subject, have completed four design courses at the time of application and be attending school on a part-time basis. Selection is based on the overall strength of the application.
Target applicant(s): College students. Adult students.
Amount: $1,500.
Number of awards: 1.
Deadline: March 31.
How to apply: Applications are available online. An application form, one letter of recommendation, personal essay and design work examples are required.
Exclusive: Visit www.UltimateScholarshipBook.com and enter code IN59920 for updates on this award.

(600) • Patriot's Pen Youth Essay Contest

Veterans of Foreign Wars
406 W. 34th Street, Kansas City, MO 64111
Phone: 816-968-1117
Email: kharmer@vfw.org
https://www.vfw.org/community/youth-and-education
Purpose: To give students in grades 6 through 8 an opportunity to write essays that express their views on democracy.
Eligibility: Applicants must be enrolled as a 6th, 7th or 8th grader in a public, private or parochial school in the U.S., its territories or possessions. Home-schooled students and dependents of U.S. military or civilian personnel in overseas schools may also apply. Foreign exchange students and former applicants who placed in the national finals are ineligible. Students must submit essays based on an annual theme to their local VFW posts. If an essay is picked to advance, the entry is judged at the District (regional) level, then the Department (state) level and finally at the National level. Essays are judged 30 percent on knowledge of the theme, 35 percent on development of the theme and 35 percent on clarity.
Target applicant(s): Junior high students or younger.
Amount: Up to $5,000.
Number of awards: 54.
Deadline: October 31.
How to apply: Applications are available online or by contacting the local VFW office. Entries must be turned into the local VFW office. Contact information for these offices can be found online or by calling the VFW National Programs headquarters at 816-968-1117.
Exclusive: Visit www.UltimateScholarshipBook.com and enter code VE60020 for updates on this award.

(601) • Preply Essay Competition

Preply Inc.
1371 Beacon Street, Suite 301, Brookline, MA 02446
https://preply.com/en/scholarships
Purpose: To encourage multilingualism among students.
Eligibility: Applicants must be current high school, undergraduate or graduate students age 16-35 years old. Students must write an essay pertaining to the subjects of online education, professionalism and multilingualism.
Target applicant(s): High school students. College students. Adult students.
Amount: $2,000.
Number of awards: 3.
Deadline: June 29.
How to apply: Applications are available online.
Exclusive: Visit www.UltimateScholarshipBook.com and enter code PR60120 for updates on this award.

(602) • Platt Family Scholarship Prize Essay Contest

Lincoln Forum
c/o Don McCue, Curator of the Lincoln Memorial Shrine, 125 West Vine Street, Redlands, CA 92373
Phone: 909-798-7632
Email: archives@akspl.org
http://www.thelincolnforum.org
Purpose: To reward students who have written the best essays on a topic related to Abraham Lincoln.
Eligibility: Applicants must be full-time undergraduate students who are enrolled at a U.S. college or university during the spring term of the contest entry year. They must submit an essay on a sponsor-determined topic that is related to Abraham Lincoln. Selection is based on the overall strength of the essay.
Target applicant(s): College students. Adult students.
Amount: $500-$1,500.
Number of awards: 3.
Deadline: July 31.
How to apply: Entry instructions are available online. An essay is required.
Exclusive: Visit www.UltimateScholarshipBook.com and enter code LI60220 for updates on this award.

(603) • Playwright Discovery Award

John F. Kennedy Center for the Performing Arts
2700 F Street NW, Washington, DC 20566
Phone: 800-444-1324
Email: vsainfo@kennedy-center.org
http://education.kennedy-center.org/education/vsa/programs/
Purpose: To award promising young writers scholarship funds and a chance to have one of their scripts professionally produced at the John F. Kennedy Center for the Performing Arts.
Eligibility: Applicants must be students in grades 6-12. Applicants are to create an original one-act script of less than 40 pages that documents the experience of living with a disability. Applicants themselves need not be disabled, but the script must address the issue. Selected scripts will be performed for middle school, high school and adult audiences. First and second place winners will have their plays performed at the JFK Performing Arts Center.
Target applicant(s): Junior high students or younger. High school students.
Amount: Varies.
Number of awards: Varies.
Deadline: February 1.
How to apply: Applications are available online.
Exclusive: Visit www.UltimateScholarshipBook.com and enter code JO60320 for updates on this award.

(604) • Poster Contest for High School Students

Christophers
5 Hanover Square, 22nd Floor, New York, NY 10004
Phone: 212-759-4050
Email: youth@christophers.org
http://www.christophers.org
Purpose: To reward students for interpreting a given theme through poster art.

Eligibility: Entrants must be high school students. Students must work individually to create posters of original content. Posters are judged by a panel based on overall impact, expression of the year's theme, artistic merit and originality.
Target applicant(s): High school students.
Amount: $100-$1,000.
Number of awards: Up to 8.
Deadline: February 19.
How to apply: Applications are available online.
Exclusive: Visit www.UltimateScholarshipBook.com and enter code CH60420 for updates on this award.

(605) • Princess Grace Awards

Princess Grace Awards
150 E. 58th Street, 25th Floor, New York, NY 10155
Phone: 212-317-1470
Email: grants@pgfusa.org
http://www.pgfusa.com
Purpose: To assist emerging young artists in theater, dance and film to realize their career goals.
Eligibility: Applicants must submit an example of their work in the category in which they apply: theatre, dance, choreography, film or playwriting. Theatre and dance applicants require the sponsorship of a professional company or school, one nominee per institution. Awards are based on the artistic quality of the artist's work, potential for future excellence and activities. Applicants must be U.S. citizens and (except playwrights) must be nominated by a school department chair/dean or company artistic director. Awards must be completed in the United States.
Target applicant(s): High school students. College students. Adult students.
Amount: Up to $30,000.
Number of awards: Varies.
Deadline: Varies.
How to apply: Applications are available online.
Exclusive: Visit www.UltimateScholarshipBook.com and enter code PR60520 for updates on this award.

(606) • Print and Graphics Scholarship

Print and Graphics Scholarship Foundation
301 Brush Creek Rd, Warrendale, PA 15086
Phone: 412-259-1740
Email: pgsf@printing.org
https://pgsf.org/
Purpose: To provide financial assistance for postsecondary education to students interested in graphic communications careers.
Eligibility: Applicants must be high school seniors, high school graduates or college students enrolled in a two- or four-year college printing or graphics program. Applicants must be full-time students, be interested in a career in printing technology, printing management, publishing or graphic communications and able to maintain a 3.0 GPA.
Target applicant(s): High school students. College students. Adult students.
Minimum GPA: 3.0
Amount: $1,000-$5,000.
Number of awards: Varies.
Scholarship may be renewable.
Deadline: March 1.
How to apply: Applications are available online.
Exclusive: Visit www.UltimateScholarshipBook.com and enter code PR60620 for updates on this award.

(607) • Prize in Ethics Essay Contest

Elie Wiesel Foundation for Humanity
555 Madison Avenue, 20th Floor, New York, NY 10022
Phone: 212-490-7788
Email: info@eliewieselfoundation.org
http://www.eliewieselfoundation.org
Purpose: To promote the thought and discussion of ethics and their place in education.
Eligibility: Applicants must be registered full-time juniors and seniors at accredited colleges and universities in the U.S. Students must write an essay dealing with ethics and have a faculty sponsor review their essay and sign the entry form.
Target applicant(s): College students. Adult students.
Amount: $500-$5,000.
Number of awards: 5.
Deadline: February 10.
How to apply: Applications are available online.
Exclusive: Visit www.UltimateScholarshipBook.com and enter code EL60720 for updates on this award.

(608) • Ruth Clark Furniture Design Scholarship

International Furnishings and Design Association (IFDA)
36 Bay View Road, Wellesley, MA 02482
Phone: 781-894-3240
Email: linda@westonstudiodesign.com
http://www.ifdaef.org/
Purpose: To aid interior design students who have an interest in residential furniture design.
Eligibility: Applicants must be full-time undergraduate or graduate students who are majoring in interior design or a closely related subject. They must have a concentration in residential upholstered and/or wood furniture design. Selection is based on the overall strength of the application.
Target applicant(s): College students. Graduate school students. Adult students.
Amount: $3,000.
Number of awards: 1.
Deadline: March 31.
How to apply: Applications are available online. An application form, transcript, personal essay, five original furniture designs and one recommendation letter are required.
Exclusive: Visit www.UltimateScholarshipBook.com and enter code IN60820 for updates on this award.

(609) • Ruth Lilly and Dorothy Sargent Rosenberg Poetry Fellowship Program

Poetry Magazine
444 N. Michigan Avenue, Suite 1850, Chicago, IL 60611-4034
Phone: 312-787-7070
Email: mail@poetryfoundation.org
https://www.poetryfoundation.org/programs/foundation/awards
Purpose: To encourage the study of writing and poetry.
Eligibility: Applicants must be U.S. residents between the ages of 21 and 31. They must be currently enrolled undergraduate or graduate students majoring in English or creative writing.
Target applicant(s): College students. Graduate school students. Adult students.
Amount: $25,800.
Number of awards: 5.
Deadline: April 30.

How to apply: Applications are available online. An essay and a poetry submission are required.
Exclusive: Visit www.UltimateScholarshipBook.com and enter code PO60920 for updates on this award.

(610) • Sara Tucker Study Grant

Richard Tucker Music Foundation
1790 Broadway, Suite 715, New York, NY 10019
Phone: 212-757-2218
http://www.richardtucker.org
Purpose: To support students who are transitioning from school to a professional career in music.
Eligibility: Applicants must have recently completed a graduate degree program or work in a young artist or apprentice program at a regional company and be generally under 30 years of age. Students must have had various performing opportunities but not in major roles.
Target applicant(s): College students. Adult students.
Amount: $5,000.
Number of awards: 4.
Deadline: July 1.
How to apply: Applications are available online.
Exclusive: Visit www.UltimateScholarshipBook.com and enter code RI61020 for updates on this award.

(611) • Scholastic Art and Writing Awards

Scholastic Art and Writing Awards
557 Broadway, New York, NY 10012
Phone: 212-343-6100
Email: info@artandwriting.org
http://www.artandwriting.org/scholarships/
Purpose: To reward creative young writers and artists.
Eligibility: Applicants must be in grades 7 through 12 in U.S. or Canadian schools and must submit writing pieces or portfolios in one of the following categories: dramatic script, general writing portfolio, humor, journalism, nonfiction portfolio, novel, personal essay/memoir, poetry, science fiction/fantasy, short story and short short story.
Target applicant(s): Junior high students or younger. High school students.
Amount: Up to $10,000.
Number of awards: Varies.
Deadline: Varies.
How to apply: Applications are available online.
Exclusive: Visit www.UltimateScholarshipBook.com and enter code SC61120 for updates on this award.

(612) • Senior Fellowship Program

National Gallery of Art
2000B South Club Drive, Landover, MD 20785
Phone: 202-842-6482
http://www.nga.gov
Purpose: To award fellowships to scholars in the visual arts.
Eligibility: Applicants should have held the Ph.D. for five years or more or possess an equivalent record of professional accomplishment at the time of application. They must submit application forms, proposals, copies of publications and three letters of recommendation. Fellowships are for full-time research, and scholars are expected to reside in Washington and to participate in the activities of the Center. One Paul Mellon Fellowship, one Frese Senior Fellowship and four to six Ailsa Mellon Bruce and Samuel H. Kress Senior Fellowships will be awarded for the academic year. The Paul Mellon and Ailsa Mellon Bruce Senior Fellowships support research in the history, theory and criticism of the visual arts of any geographical area and of any period. The Samuel H. Kress Senior Fellowships support research on European art before the early nineteenth century. The Frese Senior Fellowship is for study in the history, theory and criticism of sculpture, prints and drawings or decorative arts of any geographical area and of any period. Applications are also accepted from scholars in other disciplines whose work is related.
Target applicant(s): Graduate school students. Adult students.
Amount: Up to $50,000.
Number of awards: 4-8.
Deadline: October 15.
How to apply: Applications are available online.
Exclusive: Visit www.UltimateScholarshipBook.com and enter code NA61220 for updates on this award.

(613) • Signet Classic Student Scholarship Essay Contest

Penguin Group (USA)
Academic Marketing Department, Signet Classic Student Scholarship, 375 Hudson Street, New York, NY 10014
http://www.penguin.com
Purpose: To reward high school students for their essays on literature.
Eligibility: Applicants must be high school juniors or seniors or equivalent home schooled students and write an essay on one of five selected topics based on a piece of literature. Each English teacher may only submit one junior and one senior essay. Selection is based on style, content, grammar and originality.
Target applicant(s): High school students.
Amount: $1,000.
Number of awards: 5.
Deadline: April 14.
How to apply: English teachers submit entries. Essays from home-schooled students may be submitted by a parent or guardian.
Exclusive: Visit www.UltimateScholarshipBook.com and enter code PE61320 for updates on this award.

(614) • Sinfonia Foundation Scholarship

Sinfonia Foundation
Scholarship Committee, 10600 Old State Road, Evansville, IN 47711-1399
Phone: 800-473-2649 x110
Email: sef@sinfonia.org
http://www.sinfonia.org/SEF/
Purpose: To assist the collegiate members and chapters of Sinfonia.
Eligibility: Applicants must be in college for at least two semesters with good academic standing and submit references and an essay.
Target applicant(s): College students. Adult students.
Amount: $2,500-$7,500.
Number of awards: 3.
Deadline: May 20.
How to apply: Applications are available online.
Exclusive: Visit www.UltimateScholarshipBook.com and enter code SI61420 for updates on this award.

(615) • Stella Blum Research Grant

Costume Society of America (CSA)
Ann Wass, 5903 60th Avenue, Riverdale, MD 20737
Phone: 800-272-9447
Email: national.office@costumesocietyamerica.com

http://www.costumesocietyamerica.com
Purpose: To support a CSA student member working in the field of North American costume.
Eligibility: Applicants must be accepted into an undergraduate or graduate degree program at an accredited university for the time during which the grant would apply, conduct a research project in the area of North American costume and be members of the Costume Society of America (CSA) in good standing. Applications are judged according to significance of topic, feasibility, time frame, methodology, bibliography, budget, applicants' qualifications and how the research might further the field of costumes.
Target applicant(s): High school students. College students. Graduate school students. Adult students.
Amount: $2,000 plus a travel component of up to $500 to attend National Symposium.
Number of awards: 1.
Deadline: May 1.
How to apply: Applications are available by email or phone.
Exclusive: Visit www.UltimateScholarshipBook.com and enter code CO61520 for updates on this award.

---

(616) • Stillman Kelley National Instrumental Awards

National Federation of Music Clubs Stillman-Kelley Award
Nathalie Steinbach, 15 Mount Vernon Avenue, Fredericksburg, VA 22405
Phone: 512-892-5633
http://www.nfmc-music.org
Purpose: To support young musicians and composers.
Eligibility: Applicants must be instrumentalists, must not reach their 19th birthday by March 1 and be members of the National Federation of Music Clubs. This award rotates by region with the Northeastern and Southeastern regions in even years and Central and Western regions in odd years.
Target applicant(s): High school students.
Amount: $200-$1,000.
Number of awards: 8.
Deadline: February 1.
How to apply: Applications are available online.
Exclusive: Visit www.UltimateScholarshipBook.com and enter code NA61620 for updates on this award.

---

(617) • Student Academy Awards Competition

Academy of Motion Picture Arts and Sciences
8949 Wilshire Boulevard, Beverly Hills, CA 90211
Phone: 310-247-3031
Email: sguthrie@oscars.org
http://www.oscars.org
Purpose: To support filmmakers with no previous professional experience.
Eligibility: Applicants must be full-time students at an accredited U.S. college, university, film school or art school. Films must be made as a part of a school curriculum in the categories of alternative, animation, documentary or narrative. Selection is based on originality, entertainment, production quality and resourcefulness. A film under 40 minutes is required.
Target applicant(s): College students. Graduate school students. Adult students.
Amount: Varies.
Number of awards: Varies.
Deadline: June 1.
How to apply: Applications are available online.
Exclusive: Visit www.UltimateScholarshipBook.com and enter code AC61720 for updates on this award.

---

(618) • Student Design Competition

International Housewares Association
6400 Shafer Court, Suite 650, Rosemont, IL 60018
Phone: 847-292-4200
http://www.housewares.org
Purpose: To honor and encourage young, up-and-coming designers to enter careers in the housewares industry.
Eligibility: Applicants must be enrolled as an undergraduate or graduate student at an IDSA-affiliated college or university.
Target applicant(s): College students. Graduate school students. Adult students.
Amount: Varies.
Number of awards: Varies.
Deadline: December 22.
How to apply: Applications are available online.
Exclusive: Visit www.UltimateScholarshipBook.com and enter code IN61820 for updates on this award.

---

(619) • Student Translation Award

American Translators Association
225 Reinekers Lane, Suite 590, Alexandria, VA 22314
Phone: 703-683-6100
Email: ata@atanet.org
http://www.atanet.org
Purpose: To encourage translation projects by students.
Eligibility: Applicants must be graduate or undergraduate students or a group of students attending an accredited U.S. college or university. The project should have post-grant results such as a publication, conference presentation or teaching material. Computer-assisted translations, dissertations and theses are not eligible, and students who are already published translators are not eligible. Translations must be from a foreign language into English. Preference is given to students who have been or are currently enrolled in translator training programs. There is a limit of one entry per student. Applicants should submit entry forms, statements of purpose, letter of recommendation, translation sample with corresponding source-language text, proof of permission to publish from copyright holder and sample outline or other material demonstrating the nature of the work (if the project is not a translation).
Target applicant(s): High school students. College students. Graduate school students. Adult students.
Amount: $500 plus $500 for conference.
Number of awards: 1.
Deadline: June 8.
How to apply: Applications are available online.
Exclusive: Visit www.UltimateScholarshipBook.com and enter code AM61920 for updates on this award.

---

(620) • Study Abroad Europe Scholarship

Study Aboard Europe
111 East Mosholu Parkway Suite 3F, New York, NY 10467
Phone: 718-710-0498
Email: info@studyabroadineurope.com
http://www.studyabroadineurope.com
Purpose: To assist students who wish to study abroad in one of Study Abroad Europe's programs.
Eligibility: Applicants must be U.S. college students with a minimum 3.0 GPA.

Target applicant(s): College students. Adult students.
Minimum GPA: 3.0
Amount: $250-$1,000.
Number of awards: 3.
Deadline: April 1, June 1, October 1.
How to apply: Applications are available online. An application form, a one-page essay and a letter of recommendation from a professor or an assistant professor are required.
Exclusive: Visit www.UltimateScholarshipBook.com and enter code ST62020 for updates on this award.

---

(621) · Swackhamer Disarmament Video Contest

Nuclear Age Peace Foundation
1187 Coast Village Road, PMB 121, Suite 1, Santa Barbara, CA 93108-2794
Phone: 805-965-3443
http://www.peacecontests.org
Purpose: To encourage high school students to create a video on world peace.
Eligibility: Students must be in any high school in the world and submit a video on the provided topic. Selection is based on analysis of the subject matter, originality, development of point of view, insight, clarity of expression, organization and grammar. Video submissions should not exceed 90 seconds in length on the topic of the "The Imperative of Reaching Nuclear Zero: The Marshall Islands Stands Up for All Humanity."
Target applicant(s): High school students.
Amount: Up to $500.
Number of awards: 5.
Deadline: April 1.
How to apply: Applications are available online.
Exclusive: Visit www.UltimateScholarshipBook.com and enter code NU62120 for updates on this award.

---

(622) · Taylor/Blakeslee University Fellowships

Council for the Advancement of Science Writing (CASW)
P.O. Box 910, Hedgesville, WV 25427
Phone: 304-754-6786
Email: diane@casw.edu
http://www.casw.org
Purpose: To help graduate students in science writing.
Eligibility: Applicants must be U.S. citizens who are enrolled in U.S. graduate-level science writing programs.
Target applicant(s): Graduate school students. Adult students.
Amount: $5,000.
Number of awards: Varies.
Deadline: March 18.
How to apply: Contact the organization for more information.
Exclusive: Visit www.UltimateScholarshipBook.com and enter code CO62220 for updates on this award.

---

(623) · Thelma A. Robinson Award in Ballet

National Federation of Music Clubs (Coral Gables, FL)
Gay Dill, National Chairman, 814 South Second Street, Atwood, KS 67730
Phone: 330-638-4003
Email: gaydill@att.net
http://www.nfmc-music.org
Purpose: To support students who are ballet dancers.
Eligibility: Applicants must be between the ages of 13 and 19. There is no entry fee, but applicants must be members of the NFMC.
Target applicant(s): Junior high students or younger. High school students.
Amount: $2,500.
Number of awards: 1.
Deadline: October 1.
How to apply: Applications are available online. Award is only open in even-numbered years.
Exclusive: Visit www.UltimateScholarshipBook.com and enter code NA62320 for updates on this award.

---

(624) · Thespian Scholarships

Educational Theatre Association
2343 Auburn Avenue, Cincinnati, OH 45219-2815
Phone: 513-421-3900
Email: awards@schooltheatre.org
https://www.schooltheatre.org/programs/ags
Purpose: To support student thespians.
Eligibility: Applicants must be seniors in high school, active members of the International Thespian Society and planning to major or minor in communicative arts. Most of the scholarships require an audition or tech portfolio.
Target applicant(s): High school students.
Amount: Varies.
Number of awards: Varies.
Deadline: May 1.
How to apply: Applications are available online.
Exclusive: Visit www.UltimateScholarshipBook.com and enter code ED62420 for updates on this award.

---

(625) · Tombow's Create Your Best Work Art Scholarship

Tombow
355 Satellite Boulevard NE, Suite 300, Suwanee, GA 30024
Phone: 800-835-3232
Email: marketing@tombowusa.org
https://www.tombowusa.com/art-scholarship
Purpose: To support students pursuing visual arts degrees.
Eligibility: Applicants must be graduating high school seniors or college freshmen or sophomore students in the U.S. Students must be enrolled or accepted into a U.S. university, college or art school and pursuing a visual arts degree. Applicants must submit a portfolio along with their application materials.
Target applicant(s): High school students. College students. Adult students.
Amount: $5,000.
Number of awards: 3.
Deadline: March 1.
How to apply: Applications are available online.
Exclusive: Visit www.UltimateScholarshipBook.com and enter code TO62520 for updates on this award.

---

(626) · Tricia LeVangie Green/Sustainable Design Scholarship

International Furnishings and Design Association (IFDA)
36 Bay View Road, Wellesley, MA 02482
Phone: 781-894-3240
Email: linda@westonstudiodesign.com

http://www.ifdaef.org/
Purpose: To aid interior design students who have a demonstrated interest in the green movement.
Eligibility: Applicants must be undergraduate students who are enrolled in an interior design or related furnishings design degree program at a U.S. postsecondary institution and have completed four design courses at the time of application. They must have a demonstrated interest in the green movement as it pertains to eco-friendly design and sustainability. Selection is based on the overall strength of the application.
Target applicant(s): College students. Adult students.
Amount: $1,500.
Number of awards: 1.
Deadline: March 31.
How to apply: Applications are available online. An application form, transcript, personal essay, two design work examples and one recommendation letter are required.
Exclusive: Visit www.UltimateScholarshipBook.com and enter code IN62620 for updates on this award.

---

(627) • TurboSquid Spring Scholarship

TurboSquid
935 Gravier Street, Suite 1600, New Orleans, LA 70112
Email: sales@turbosquid.com
https://www.turbosquid.com/scholarships
Purpose: To support students interested in the 3D industry.
Eligibility: Applicants must be graduating high school seniors or currently enrolled full-time undergraduate or graduate college students. Students must have a minimum grade point average of 3.0. Applicants must submit application and essay.
Target applicant(s): High school students. College students. Graduate school students. Adult students.
Minimum GPA: 3.0
Amount: $5,000.
Number of awards: 1.
Deadline: July 31.
How to apply: Applications are available online.
Exclusive: Visit www.UltimateScholarshipBook.com and enter code TU62720 for updates on this award.

---

(628) • Two Ten Footwear Design Scholarship

Two Ten Footwear Foundation
1466 Main Street, Waltham, MA 02451
Phone: 800-346-3210
http://www.twoten.org
Purpose: To support students who are completing footwear design studies.
Eligibility: Applicants must be citizens of the United States and accepted or enrolled at accredited colleges or vocational institutions. Students must provide a portfolio that includes three design drawings. Applicants must also include their most recent transcripts and keep a 2.5 grade point average while studying in the field of design. Selection is based on financial need and design talent.
Target applicant(s): High school students. College students. Graduate school students. Adult students.
Minimum GPA: 2.5
Amount: Up to $5,000.
Number of awards: Varies.
Scholarship may be renewable.
Deadline: April 14.
How to apply: Applications are available online.
Exclusive: Visit www.UltimateScholarshipBook.com and enter code TW62820 for updates on this award.

---

(629) • Ukulele Festival Hawaii's College Scholarship Program

Ukulele Festival Hawaii
c/o Roy Sakuma Productions, Inc., 3555 Harding Avenue, Suite 1, Honolulu, HI 96816
Phone: 808-732-3739
Email: info@ukulelefestivalhawaii.org
http://www.roysakuma.net/
Purpose: To support students who play the ukulele.
Eligibility: Applicants must be Hawaii high school seniors in good standing. They must plan to attend a four-year college or university in the fall following graduation.
Target applicant(s): High school students.
Amount: $2,000.
Number of awards: Varies.
Deadline: April 30.
How to apply: Applications are available from Roy Sakuma Productions. An application form is required.
Exclusive: Visit www.UltimateScholarshipBook.com and enter code UK62920 for updates on this award.

---

(630) • Undergraduate Scholarships

Sigma Alpha Iota Philanthropies
Director, Undergraduate Scholarships, One Tunnel Road, Asheville, NC 28805
Phone: 828-251-0606
Email: jkpete@cox.net
http://www.sai-national.org
Purpose: To assist members of the Sigma Alpha Iota organization who have demonstrated outstanding leadership abilities, musical talent and scholastic achievement.
Eligibility: Applicants must be active members for at least one year in the Sigma Alpha Iota organization, be in good standing and demonstrate financial need.
Target applicant(s): College students. Adult students.
Amount: $1,000-$2,400.
Number of awards: 13.
Deadline: March 15.
How to apply: Applications are available online.
Exclusive: Visit www.UltimateScholarshipBook.com and enter code SI63020 for updates on this award.

---

(631) • Vectorworks Design Scholarship

Nemetschek Vectorworks
7150 Riverwood Drive, Columbia, MD 21046
Phone: 410-290-5114
http://www.vectorworks.net
Purpose: To reward students for excellent design work.
Eligibility: Applicants must be pursuing an undergraduate or graduate degree in a design-related field at an accredited educational institution. Students must submit a design project. Submissions may be made by individual students or by groups of up to six students. Selection is primarily based on design quality, technology, originality and explanation of the design.
Target applicant(s): College students. Graduate school students. Adult students.
Amount: $10,000.

Number of awards: 10.
Deadline: July 15.
How to apply: Applications are available online.
Exclusive: Visit www.UltimateScholarshipBook.com and enter code NE63120 for updates on this award.

---

(632) • Vercille Voss IFDA Graduate Student Scholarship

International Furnishings and Design Association (IFDA)
36 Bay View Road, Wellesley, MA 02482
Phone: 781-894-3240
Email: linda@westonstudiodesign.com
http://www.ifdaef.org/
Purpose: To aid interior design graduate students.
Eligibility: Applicants must be graduate students who are majoring in interior design or a closely related subject at a U.S. postsecondary institution. Selection is based on the overall strength of the application.
Target applicant(s): College students. Graduate school students. Adult students.
Amount: $2,000.
Number of awards: 1.
Deadline: March 31.
How to apply: Applications are available online. An application form, transcript, personal essay, two original design work examples, one recommendation letter and proof of graduate school acceptance (for entering students only) are required.
Exclusive: Visit www.UltimateScholarshipBook.com and enter code IN63220 for updates on this award.

---

(633) • Visiting Senior Fellowship Program

National Gallery of Art
2000B South Club Drive, Landover, MD 20785
Phone: 202-842-6482
http://www.nga.gov
Purpose: To award fellowships to scholars in visual arts.
Eligibility: Applicants must have held their Ph.D. for five years or possess an equivalent record of professional accomplishment at the time of application. Applications are considered for research in the history, theory and criticism of the visual arts of any geographical area and of any period. Applicants must submit application forms, proposals, copies of a publication and two letters of recommendation. Fellowships are for full-time research, and scholars are expected to reside in Washington and to participate in the activities of the Center. Applications are also accepted from scholars in other disciplines whose work is related. The Center awards up to twelve short-term Paul Mellon and Ailsa Mellon Bruce Visiting Senior Fellowships. The deadlines are March 21 for the fellowship from September to February and September 21 for March through August.
Target applicant(s): Graduate school students. Adult students.
Amount: $6,000-$8,000.
Number of awards: Up to 12.
Scholarship may be renewable.
Deadline: March 21, September 21.
How to apply: Applications are available online.
Exclusive: Visit www.UltimateScholarshipBook.com and enter code NA63320 for updates on this award.

---

(634) • Werner B. Thiele Memorial Scholarship

Gravure Education Foundation
P.O. Box 25617, Rochester, NY 14625
Phone: 315-589-8879
Email: lwshatch@gaa.org
http://www.gaa.org/gravure-education-foundation
Purpose: To award scholarships to students majoring in printing, graphic arts or graphic communications.
Eligibility: Applicants must be enrolled full-time at one of the GEF Learning Resource Centers: Arizona State University, California Polytechnic State University, Clemson University, Murray State, Rochester Institute of Technology, University of Wisconsin - Stout or Western Michigan University. Applicants must have a minimum 3.0 GPA.
Target applicant(s): College students. Graduate school students. Adult students.
Minimum GPA: 3.0
Amount: $1,000.
Number of awards: 1.
Deadline: April 28.
How to apply: Applications are available online or by mail.
Exclusive: Visit www.UltimateScholarshipBook.com and enter code GR63420 for updates on this award.

---

(635) • Women Band Directors International College Scholarships

Women Band Directors International
Karen Williams, WBDI Scholarship Chair, 3994 White Oak Road, Waynesville, NC 28785
Email: agreen@lamar.k12.ga.us
http://www.womenbanddirectors.org/awards.html
Purpose: To support future female band directors.
Eligibility: Applicants must be studying music education with the intention of becoming a band director.
Target applicant(s): College students. Graduate school students. Adult students.
Amount: Varies.
Number of awards: 11.
Deadline: December 1.
How to apply: Applications are available online.
Exclusive: Visit www.UltimateScholarshipBook.com and enter code WO63520 for updates on this award.

---

(636) • Worldstudio AIGA Scholarships

Worldstudio/AIGA
233 Broadway, 17th Floor, New York, NY 10279
Email: scholarships@aiga.org
http://www.aiga.org/worldstudio-scholarship/
Purpose: To support art and design students who need financial assistance.
Eligibility: Applicants must be full-time undergraduate or graduate students in fine arts, graphic design, illustration, interactive design/ motion graphics or photography. They must have a GPA of at least 2.0 and demonstrate financial need. Applicants must be U.S. citizens or permanent residents. Minority and economically disadvantaged students will be given special consideration.
Target applicant(s): High school students. College students. Graduate school students. Adult students.
Minimum GPA: 2.0
Amount: $500-$5,000.
Number of awards: Varies.
Deadline: May 1.
How to apply: Applications are available online.

Exclusive: Visit www.UltimateScholarshipBook.com and enter code WO63620 for updates on this award.

(637) • Writer's Square Scholarship Program

Writer's Square
2450 Mission Street #2, San Marino, CA 91108
Email: marketing@writerssquare.org
http://www.writerssquare.org
Purpose: To promote creativity and help students develop their writing skills.
Eligibility: Applicants must be enrolled students from first grade up to graduate school. Students must submit an essay pertaining to a given topic. Applicants may submit only one entry.
Target applicant(s): Junior high students or younger. High school students. College students. Graduate school students. Adult students.
Amount: $100-$1,000.
Number of awards: 3.
Deadline: September 30.
How to apply: Applications are available online.
Exclusive: Visit www.UltimateScholarshipBook.com and enter code WR63720 for updates on this award.

(638) • Wyland National Art Challenge

Wyland Foundation
6 Mason, Irvine, CA 92618
Phone: 949-643-7070
Email: artchallenge@wylandfoundation.org
http://www.wylandfoundation.org/artchallenge
Purpose: To encourage students with an interest in conservation and art.
Eligibility: Applicants must be students in grades kindergarten through twelve in a U.S. school. Students must participate in the painting of a 4x8 foot mural that addresses the theme of conservation.
Target applicant(s): Junior high students or younger. High school students.
Amount: $1,500.
Number of awards: 3.
Deadline: December 1.
How to apply: Applications are available online.
Exclusive: Visit www.UltimateScholarshipBook.com and enter code WY63820 for updates on this award.

(639) • Young American Creative Patriotic Art Contest

Ladies Auxiliary VFW
406 West 34th Street, 10th Floor, Kansas City, MO 64111
Phone: 816-561-8655
Email: info@vfwauxiliary.org
https://vfwauxiliary.org/scholarships/
Purpose: To encourage patriotic art.
Eligibility: Applicants must be high school students in the same state as the sponsoring Ladies Auxiliary. They must submit one piece of patriotic art on paper or canvas. Art must have been completed during the current school year and must be accompanied by a teacher's signature. Applicants must participate in a local Auxiliary competition before advancing to the national level.
Target applicant(s): High school students.
Amount: Up to $21,000.
Number of awards: Varies.
Deadline: March 31.
How to apply: Applications are available online.
Exclusive: Visit www.UltimateScholarshipBook.com and enter code LA63920 for updates on this award.

(640) • Youth Free Expression Network Film Contest

National Coalition Against Censorship (NCAC)
19 Fulton Street, Suite 407, New York, NY 10038
Phone: 212-807-6222
Email: ncac@ncac.org
http://ncac.org
Purpose: To reward students who create films on a given topic related to censorship.
Eligibility: Students must be 19 years or younger. Films must be four minutes or less in a variety of genres including documentary, music video and experimental. Top three winners receive cash stipends.
Target applicant(s): Junior high students or younger. High school students. College students.
Amount: Up to $1,000.
Number of awards: 3.
Deadline: March 15.
How to apply: Applications are available online.
Exclusive: Visit www.UltimateScholarshipBook.com and enter code NA64020 for updates on this award.

SOCIAL SCIENCES

(641) • A. Harry Passow Classroom Teacher Scholarship

National Association for Gifted Children
1331 H Street NW, Suite 1001, Chair, Awards Committee,
Washington, DC 20005
Phone: 202-785-4268
Email: nagc@nagc.org
http://www.nagc.org

Purpose: To reward excellent teachers of gifted students of grades K-12.
Eligibility: Applicants must be teachers of gifted students of grades K-12 and be continuing their education. Applicants must also have been members of NAGC for at least one year. Selection is based on commitment to teaching as shown by reviews from students, parents, principal and peers and admission into a graduate or certification program in gifted education.
Target applicant(s): Graduate school students. Adult students.
Amount: $2,000.
Number of awards: Up to 2.
Deadline: May 4.
How to apply: Applications are available online.
Exclusive: Visit www.UltimateScholarshipBook.com and enter code NA64120 for updates on this award.

(642) • AALL Educational Scholarships

American Association of Law Libraries
105 W. Adams, Suite 3300, Chicago, IL 60603
Phone: 312-939-4764
Email: scholarships@aall.org
https://www.aallnet.org/mm/Member-Resources

Purpose: To encourage students to pursue careers as law librarians.
Eligibility: There are five levels of awards: 1. Library Degree for Law School Graduates, awarded to a law school graduate with law library experience pursuing a degree at an accredited library school. 2. Library School Graduates Attending Law School, awarded to a library school graduate pursuing a degree at an accredited law school who has law library experience and no more than 36 semester credit hours left before obtaining the law degree. 3. Library Degree for Non-Law School Graduates, awarded to a college graduate with law library experience who is seeking a degree involving law librarianship courses at an accredited library school. 4. Library School Graduates Seeking A Non-Law Degree, awarded to library school graduates who are seeking degrees in fields other than law. 5. Law Librarians in Continuing Education Courses, awarded to law librarians with a degree from an accredited library or law school who are continuing their education. 6. Dual JD/MLIS Degree, awarded to college graduates working toward a dual degree in an accredited law school and library school. Preference is given to AALL members, but a non-member can apply. All applicants must intend to have careers as law librarians. There must be financial need for awards 1-4.
Target applicant(s): Graduate school students. Adult students.
Amount: Varies.
Number of awards: Varies.
Scholarship may be renewable.
Deadline: April 1.
How to apply: Applications are available online, by mail with a self-addressed, stamped envelope, by fax, by phone or by email.
Exclusive: Visit www.UltimateScholarshipBook.com and enter code AM64220 for updates on this award.

(643) • ABO Capital Scholarship

ABO Capital
641 Lexington Avenue, 15th Floor, New York, NY 10022
Phone: 212-634-6353
Email: scholarship@abocapital.net
http://www.abocapital.net/scholarship/

Purpose: To encourage students who have great ideas on ways to change the world by boosting economic opportunities in Africa.
Eligibility: Applicants must write an essay with their ideas as part of the application process. Students must be at least 18 years of age who are currently enrolled in an undergraduate, graduate or university program to enter.
Target applicant(s): High school students. College students. Graduate school students. Adult students.
Amount: Up to $30,000 including semester in Africa.
Number of awards: 4.
Deadline: December 31.
How to apply: Applications are available online.
Exclusive: Visit www.UltimateScholarshipBook.com and enter code AB64320 for updates on this award.

(644) • Accounting Student Scholarship Program

Wiley Efficient Learning
P.O. Box 4223, Sedona, AZ 86340
Phone: 888-884-5669
Email: info@efficientlearning.com
http://www.efficientlearning.com

Purpose: To assist students who are taking accounting courses.
Eligibility: Applicants must be full-time or part-time college student taking at least one accounting course. Selection is based on a random drawing.
Target applicant(s): College students. Graduate school students. Adult students.
Amount: $500.
Number of awards: 1.
Deadline: April 30.
How to apply: Applications are available online.
Exclusive: Visit www.UltimateScholarshipBook.com and enter code WI64420 for updates on this award.

(645) • ACLS Fellowships

American Council of Learned Societies (ACLS)
633 Third Avenue, New York, NY 10017-6795
Phone: 212-697-1505
Email: mgoldfeder@acls.org
https://www.acls.org/

Purpose: To support a scholar in the study of humanities.
Eligibility: Applicants must have a Ph.D. degree and at least a three year period since their last supported research. An application, a proposal, bibliography, publications list and two reference letters are required. The award levels are based on the position of the applicant: professor and equivalent, associate professor and equivalent and assistant professor and equivalent. The ACLS fellowships include ACLS/SSRC/NEH International and Area Studies Fellowships and ACLS/New York Public Library Fellowships.
Target applicant(s): Graduate school students. Adult students.
Amount: Up to $70,000.
Number of awards: Varies.
Deadline: September 28.
How to apply: Applications are available online.

Exclusive: Visit www.UltimateScholarshipBook.com and enter code AM64520 for updates on this award.

(646) • ACOR-CAORC Fellowships

American Center of Oriental Research (ACOR)
656 Beacon Street, 5th Floor, Boston, MA 02215-2010
Phone: 617-353-6571
Email: acor@bu.edu
http://www.acorjordan.org
Purpose: To assist master's and pre-doctoral students conducting research in Jordan.
Eligibility: Applicants must be U.S. citizen graduate students researching topics involving scholarship in Near Eastern studies. Recipients are required to engage in scholarly and cultural activities while residing at the American Center of Oriental Research (ACOR) in Jordan. The fellowships last from two to six months. The award includes room and board at ACOR, transportation, a stipend and research funds.
Target applicant(s): Graduate school students. Adult students.
Amount: Varies.
Number of awards: Varies.
Deadline: February 1.
How to apply: Applications are available online.
Exclusive: Visit www.UltimateScholarshipBook.com and enter code AM64620 for updates on this award.

(647) • Adelle and Erwin Tomash Fellowship in the History of Information Processing

Charles Babbage Institute
Center for the History of Information Processing, 211 Andersen Library, University of Minnesota, 222 - 21st Avenue South, Minneapolis, MN 55455
Phone: 612-624-5050
Email: yostx003@tc.umn.edu
http://www.cbi.umn.edu
Purpose: To support a graduate student who is researching the history of computing.
Eligibility: Applicants must be graduate students who have completed all doctoral degree requirements except the research and writing of the dissertation. Students must submit a curriculum vitae and a five-page statement and justification of the research program.
Target applicant(s): Graduate school students. Adult students.
Amount: $14,000.
Number of awards: 1.
Deadline: January 15.
How to apply: Visit the website for more information.
Exclusive: Visit www.UltimateScholarshipBook.com and enter code CH64720 for updates on this award.

(648) • Adult Students in Scholastic Transition (ASIST)

Executive Women International (EWI)
3860 South 2300 East, Suite 211, Salt Lake City, UT 84109
Phone: 801-355-2800
Email: ewi@ewiconnect.com
http://ewiconnect.com/scholarships/
Purpose: To assist adult students who face major life transitions.
Eligibility: Applicants may be single parents, individuals just entering the workforce or displaced workers.
Target applicant(s): College students. Adult students.
Amount: $2,000-$10,000.
Number of awards: 13.
Deadline: Varies by chapter.
How to apply: Contact your local EWI chapter.
Exclusive: Visit www.UltimateScholarshipBook.com and enter code EX64820 for updates on this award.

(649) • AICPA/Accountemps Student Scholarship

American Institute of Certified Public Accountants
220 Leigh Farm Road, Durham, NC 27707
Phone: 919-402-4500
Email: service@aicpa.org
http://www.aicpa.org
Purpose: To aid AICPA Student Affiliate members who are pursuing higher education in information systems, accounting or finance.
Eligibility: Applicants must be U.S. citizens or permanent residents who are full-time students at an accredited U.S. college or university. They must be majoring in accounting, finance or information systems and must have completed at least 30 semester or 45 quarter hours of study, including six or more semester hours in accounting. They must have a GPA of 3.0 or higher. Current Certified Public Accountants (CPAs) are ineligible. Selection is based on academic merit, leadership skills and professional potential.
Target applicant(s): College students. Graduate school students. Adult students.
Minimum GPA: 3.0
Amount: $10,000.
Number of awards: 4.
Deadline: April 1.
How to apply: Applications are available online. An application form, official transcript, course schedule, standardized test score report (graduate students only), personal essay and two letters of recommendation are required.
Exclusive: Visit www.UltimateScholarshipBook.com and enter code AM64920 for updates on this award.

(650) • AIET Graduate Scholarship

Appraisal Institute Education Trust
200 W. Madison, Suite 1500, Chicago, IL 60606
Phone: 312-335-4133
Email: wwoodburn@appraisalinstitute.org
http://www.appraisalinstitute.org
Purpose: To support students who are working on a college degree concentrating on real estate appraisal, land economics, real estate or allied fields.
Eligibility: Applicants must be students majoring in real estate appraisal, land economics, real estate or allied fields. Students must be masters or doctoral candidates. Applicants must be full- or part-time students at a U.S. degree granting college or university with a strong academic record.
Target applicant(s): Graduate school students. Adult students.
Amount: $2,000.
Number of awards: Varies.
Deadline: April 15.
How to apply: Applications are available online.
Exclusive: Visit www.UltimateScholarshipBook.com and enter code AP65020 for updates on this award.

(651) • AIET Undergraduate Scholarship

Appraisal Institute Education Trust
200 W. Madison, Suite 1500, Chicago, IL 60606
Phone: 312-335-4133
Email: wwoodburn@appraisalinstitute.org

http://www.appraisalinstitute.org
Purpose: To support students concentrating in real estate appraisal, land economics, real estate or allied fields.
Eligibility: Applicants must be students majoring in real estate appraisal, land economics, real estate or allied fields. Students must have a strong academic record.
Target applicant(s): College students. Adult students.
Amount: $1,000.
Number of awards: Varies.
Deadline: April 15.
How to apply: Applications are available online.
Exclusive: Visit www.UltimateScholarshipBook.com and enter code AP65120 for updates on this award.

---

(652) • Airport Rentals United States Student Scholarship

Airport Rentals
Excelsior Building, Level 4, 6 Commerce Street, Auckland City, New Zealand 1143
Phone: 800-311-1512
https://www.airportrentals.com/scholarship/united-states
Purpose: To support entrepreneurial students.
Eligibility: Applicants must be U.S. citizens. Students must be currently enrolled with a grade point average of 3.25 or higher. Applicants must submit an essay along with application.
Target applicant(s): College students. Adult students.
Minimum GPA: 3.25
Amount: $4,000.
Number of awards: 1.
Deadline: May 1.
How to apply: Applications are available online.
Exclusive: Visit www.UltimateScholarshipBook.com and enter code AI65220 for updates on this award.

---

(653) • Alice L. Haltom Educational Fund Scholarship

Alice L. Haltom Educational Fund
P.O. Box 70530, Houston, TX 77270
http://www.alhef.org/scholarship/
Purpose: To support students pursuing information and records management.
Eligibility: Applicants must be U.S. or Canadian citizens pursuing an education for a career in information and records management. Students must submit an essay, three letters of recommendation and transcripts along with their application.
Target applicant(s): College students. Graduate school students. Adult students.
Amount: $2,000.
Number of awards: Varies.
Deadline: May 1.
How to apply: Applications are available online.
Exclusive: Visit www.UltimateScholarshipBook.com and enter code AL65320 for updates on this award.

---

(654) • Allied Van Lines Scholarship

Allied Van Lines
Phone: 800-689-8684
https://www.allied.com/scholarship
Purpose: To support students pursuing logistics and moving-related fields.
Eligibility: Applicants must be U.S. citizens or permanent residents enrolling as full-time students pursuing an undergraduate degree in logistics or related field. Students must provide transcripts, enrollment verification and an essay.
Target applicant(s): College students. Adult students.
Amount: $1,000.
Number of awards: 3.
Deadline: December 15.
How to apply: Applications are available online.
Exclusive: Visit www.UltimateScholarshipBook.com and enter code AL65420 for updates on this award.

---

(655) • Alpha Kappa Psi Scholarships

Alpha Kappa Psi Foundation
7801 E. 88th Street, Indianapolis, IN 46256
Phone: 317-872-1553
Email: foundation@akpsi.org
https://akpsifoundation.org/grants-and-scholarships/
Purpose: To support students who are members of the Alpha Kappa Psi society.
Eligibility: Applicants must be initiated Alpha Kappa Psi students who are currently undergraduate or graduate students with at least a 2.75 GPA. Students must have a strong record of chapter or campus leadership.
Target applicant(s): College students. Graduate school students. Adult students.
Minimum GPA: 2.75
Amount: $500-$1,500.
Number of awards: Varies.
Deadline: March 15.
How to apply: Applications are available online.
Exclusive: Visit www.UltimateScholarshipBook.com and enter code AL65520 for updates on this award.

---

(656) • American Bar Association Law Student Writing Competition

American Bar Association
321 North Clark Street, Chicago, IL 60654
Phone: 312-988-5624
Email: abalsd@americanbar.org
http://abaforlawstudents.com/events/
Purpose: To support and recognize achievement among law students.
Eligibility: The American Bar Association (ABA) sponsors a variety of essay and writing competitions for ABA student members. Applicants must write an article about antitrust and have it published in an ABA-accredited school's law review or journal. Law students currently enrolled or graduating can write eligible articles of general interest to the antitrust law community, such as Civil and Criminal Antitrust Law, Competition Policy, Consumer Protection and International Competition Law. Selection is based on the strength of the essay.
Target applicant(s): Graduate school students. Adult students.
Amount: Varies.
Number of awards: Varies.
Deadline: Varies.
How to apply: Applications are available online. Application requirements vary by competition.
Exclusive: Visit www.UltimateScholarshipBook.com and enter code AM65620 for updates on this award.

(657) • American Culinary Federation Scholarships

American Culinary Federation
180 Center Place Way, St. Augustine, FL 32095
Phone: 904-824-4468
Email: acf@acfchefs.net
http://www.acfchefs.org

Purpose: To support high school and college students looking to further their education or compete in student culinary teams at ACF conferences.

Eligibility: Applicants must have a minimum GPA of 2.5, be graduating high school seniors and be accepted into an accredited college or university or be currently enrolled students in an accredited college or university. Applicants must also be planning to major in culinary or pastry arts or be ACF registered apprentices and have career aspirations of being a chef or pastry chef. Selection is based on GPA, participation in culinary competitions, volunteer activities, involvement in the ACF, essay and references.

Target applicant(s): High school students. College students. Adult students.

Minimum GPA: 2.5

Amount: Varies.

Number of awards: Varies.

Deadline: Varies.

How to apply: Applications are available online. An application form, essay and references are required.

Exclusive: Visit www.UltimateScholarshipBook.com and enter code AM65720 for updates on this award.

(658) • American Express Scholarship Competition

American Hotel and Lodging Educational Foundation (AHLEF)
1250 I Street NW, Suite 1100, Washington, DC 20005-3931
Phone: 202-289-3180
Email: foundation@ahlef.org
https://www.ahlef.org/Scholarships/Academic_Scholarships/

Purpose: To provide financial assistance to students pursuing a degree in hospitality management.

Eligibility: Applicants must be enrolled in an accredited undergraduate program resulting in a degree in hospitality management. Students or their parents must be employed in the lodging industry by an American Hotel and Lodging Association member facility.

Target applicant(s): College students. Adult students.

Amount: $500-$2,000.

Number of awards: Varies.

Deadline: May 1.

How to apply: Applications are available online.

Exclusive: Visit www.UltimateScholarshipBook.com and enter code AM65820 for updates on this award.

(659) • American Society of Travel Agents (ASTA) Holland America Line Graduate Research Scholarship

Tourism Cares
275 Turnpike Street, Suite 307, Canton, MA 02021
Phone: 781-821-5990
Email: scholarships@tourismcares.org
http://www.tourismcares.org/academic-scholarships/

Purpose: To aid graduate students who are conducting tourism-related research.

Eligibility: Applicants may be permanent residents of any country but must be accepted or enrolled as graduate students at an accredited U.S. or Canadian four-year postsecondary institution. They must be conducting tourism-related research and must have a GPA of 3.0 or higher on a four-point scale. Selection is based on the overall strength of the research project.

Target applicant(s): College students. Graduate school students. Adult students.

Minimum GPA: 3.0

Amount: $4,000.

Number of awards: 1.

Deadline: April 3.

How to apply: Applications are available online. An application form, one letter of recommendation, a resume, a research proposal, a personal essay and an official transcript are required.

Exclusive: Visit www.UltimateScholarshipBook.com and enter code TO65920 for updates on this award.

(660) • American Society of Travel Agents (ASTA) Joseph R. Stone Graduate Scholarship

Tourism Cares
275 Turnpike Street, Suite 307, Canton, MA 02021
Phone: 781-821-5990
Email: scholarships@tourismcares.org
http://www.tourismcares.org/academic-scholarships/

Purpose: To aid those who are studying travel, tourism and hospitality at the graduate level.

Eligibility: Applicants must be permanent residents of the U.S. or Canada and be entering or returning graduate students at an accredited U.S. or Canadian four-year institution. They must be studying travel, tourism or hospitality and must have a GPA of 3.0 or higher on a four-point scale. Selection is based on the overall strength of the application.

Target applicant(s): College students. Graduate school students. Adult students.

Minimum GPA: 3.0

Amount: $2,000.

Number of awards: 1.

Deadline: April 3.

How to apply: Applications are available online. An application form, proof of residency, a resume, an official transcript, two letters of recommendation and a personal essay are required.

Exclusive: Visit www.UltimateScholarshipBook.com and enter code TO66020 for updates on this award.

(661) • Ankin Law Office College Scholarship

Ankin Law Office
10 N Dearborn, Suite 500, Chicago, IL 60602
Phone: 844-600-0000
http://ankinlaw.com/aaaa_scholarship/

Purpose: To support students pursuing post-secondary education.

Eligibility: Applicants must be enrolling as full-time students in an accredited post-secondary institution in the fall. Students must write an essay on the given topic listed on the website pertaining to personal injury law. Applicants must verify need and proof of enrollment.

Target applicant(s): High school students. College students. Graduate school students. Adult students.

Amount: $1,500.

Number of awards: 1.

Deadline: July 15.

How to apply: Applications are available online.

Exclusive: Visit www.UltimateScholarshipBook.com and enter code AN66120 for updates on this award.

(662) • APF/COGDOP Graduate Research Scholarships

American Psychological Foundation
750 First Street NE, Washington, DC 20002-4242
Phone: 202-336-5843
Email: foundation@apa.org
http://www.apa.org/apf/funding/index.aspx
Purpose: To assist graduate psychology students.
Eligibility: Applicants must attend a school whose psychology department is a member in good standing of Council of Graduate Departments of Psychology (COGDOP). Applicants are nominated by their schools' departments with no more than three nominees at each school.
Target applicant(s): Graduate school students. Adult students.
Amount: $1,000-$5,000.
Number of awards: 22.
Deadline: June 30.
How to apply: Applicants must be nominated.
Exclusive: Visit www.UltimateScholarshipBook.com and enter code AM66220 for updates on this award.

(663) • ARIT Fellowships for Research in Turkey

American Research Institute in Turkey (ARIT)
3260 South Street, Philadelphia, PA 19104-6324
Phone: 215-898-3474
Email: leinwand@sas.upenn.edu
http://ccat.sas.upenn.edu/ARIT
Purpose: To support scholars in their research in Turkey.
Eligibility: Applicants must be scholars or advanced graduate students involved in research on ancient, medieval or modern times in Turkey, in any field of the humanities and social sciences. Student applicants must have completed all requirements for the doctorate except the dissertation before beginning any ARIT-sponsored research. Non-U.S. applicants must be connected to an educational institution in the U.S. or Canada. Applicants should submit applications, three letters of recommendation and graduate transcripts.
Target applicant(s): Graduate school students. Adult students.
Amount: Varies.
Number of awards: Varies.
Deadline: November 1.
How to apply: Applications are available online.
Exclusive: Visit www.UltimateScholarshipBook.com and enter code AM66320 for updates on this award.

(664) • ARRL Foundation General Fund Scholarship

American Radio Relay League Foundation
225 Main Street, Newington, CT 06111-1494
Phone: 860-594-0348
Email: foundation@arrl.org
http://www.arrl.org/scholarship-program
Purpose: To assist ham radio operators in furthering their educations.
Eligibility: Applicants must have any level of ham radio license.
Target applicant(s): High school students. College students. Graduate school students. Adult students.
Amount: $2,000.
Number of awards: Varies.
Deadline: January 31.
How to apply: Applications are available online. Completed applications must be submitted by mail.
Exclusive: Visit www.UltimateScholarshipBook.com and enter code AM66420 for updates on this award.

(665) • Asparagus Club, Thomas K. Zaucha Scholarship

National Grocers Association
1005 N. Glebe Road, Suite 250, Arlington, VA 22201
Phone: 225-387-6126
http://www.nationalgrocers.org
Purpose: To support students pursuing degrees related to the grocery field.
Eligibility: Applicants must be rising sophomores through postgraduate students, have a minimum 2.5 GPA and be enrolled in a two- or four-year degree-granting institution. Students must major in business, food management, IT or another field related to a career in the grocery industry. Experience in the grocery industry is preferred but not required.
Target applicant(s): College students. Graduate school students. Adult students.
Minimum GPA: 2.5
Amount: $1,000-$7,000.
Number of awards: 1.
Deadline: April 15.
How to apply: Applications are available online.
Exclusive: Visit www.UltimateScholarshipBook.com and enter code NA66520 for updates on this award.

(666) • Association of Equipment Management Professionals Foundation Scholarships

Association of Equipment Management Professionals (AEMP)
P.O. Box 1368, Glenwood Springs, CO 81602
Phone: 970-384-0510
Email: stan@aemp.org
http://www.aemp.org/page/Scholarships
Purpose: To support students interested in the field of heavy equipment management.
Eligibility: Applicants must have a GPA of 2.0 or higher and plan to attend a school that offers a diesel technology program. Scholarship recipients must maintain a 3.0 or higher GPA in their studies. Preference is given to students who are motivated, responsible and have the potential for great achievement.
Target applicant(s): High school students. College students. Adult students.
Minimum GPA: 2.0
Amount: Up to $2,000.
Number of awards: Varies.
Deadline: May 10.
How to apply: Applications are available online. An application form, transcript and two letters of recommendation are required.
Exclusive: Visit www.UltimateScholarshipBook.com and enter code AS66620 for updates on this award.

(667) • Association William S. Bullinger Scholarship

Federal Circuit Bar Association
1620 I Street NW, Suite 801, Washington, DC 20006
Phone: 202-466-3923
Email: fcbascholarships@fedcirbar.org
http://www.fedcirbar.org
Purpose: To support financially needy but academically promising law students.

Eligibility: Applicants must be undergraduate or graduate law students who demonstrate financial need and academic promise. They must submit a one-page statement describing their financial circumstances, their interest in law and their qualifications for the scholarship along with transcripts and a curriculum vitae.
Target applicant(s): College students. Graduate school students. Adult students.
Amount: $5,000.
Number of awards: 1.
Deadline: April 15.
How to apply: There is no application form.
Exclusive: Visit www.UltimateScholarshipBook.com and enter code FE66720 for updates on this award.

(668) · BEA National Scholarships in Broadcasting

Broadcast Education Association
1771 N Street NW, Washington, DC 20036
Phone: 888-380-7222
Email: beainfo@beaweb.org
http://www.beaweb.org
Purpose: To honor broadcasters and the broadcast industry.
Eligibility: Applicants must be college juniors or seniors or graduate students at BEA member universities, students pursuing freshman and sophomore instruction only or students who have already completed BEA two-year programs at a four-year college.
Target applicant(s): High school students. College students. Graduate school students. Adult students.
Amount: $1,500 to $4,000.
Number of awards: 10.
Deadline: October 11.
How to apply: Applications are available online.
Exclusive: Visit www.UltimateScholarshipBook.com and enter code BR66820 for updates on this award.

(669) · Begun Scholarship

California Library Association
248 E. Foothill Boulevard, Suite 101, Monrovia, CA 91016
Phone: 916-779-4573
Email: info@cla-net.org
http://www.cla-net.org
Purpose: To assist California library or information sciences graduate students at California schools.
Eligibility: Applicants must be California graduate students attending an American Library Association accredited school and have completed core coursework toward a master's of library and science or information studies degree. Recipients must also plan to become a children's or young adult librarian in a California public library and to join the California Library Association if not already a member.
Target applicant(s): Graduate school students. Adult students.
Minimum GPA: 3.0
Amount: $3,000.
Number of awards: 1.
Deadline: Varies.
How to apply: Applications are available online.
Exclusive: Visit www.UltimateScholarshipBook.com and enter code CA66920 for updates on this award.

(670) · Benson & Bingham

Benson & Bingham
11441 Allerton Park Drive, Suite 100, Las Vegas, NV 89135
Phone: 702-684-6900
Email: scholarship@bensonbingham.com
https://www.bensonbingham.com/benson-bingham-annual-scholarship
Purpose: To support students pursuing an education in law.
Eligibility: Applicants must be U.S. citizens or permanent residents currently enrolled in or recently accepted to an accredited law school. Students must have a grade point average of 3.0 or higher. Applicants must provide an essay, college transcripts and proof of law school attendance.
Target applicant(s): College students. Graduate school students. Adult students.
Minimum GPA: 3.0
Amount: $2,000.
Number of awards: 3.
Deadline: August 31.
How to apply: Applications are available online.
Exclusive: Visit www.UltimateScholarshipBook.com and enter code BE67020 for updates on this award.

(671) · Betsy Plank/PRSSA Scholarship

Public Relations Student Society of America
33 Maiden Lane, 11th Floor, New York, NY 10038
Phone: 212-460-1474
Email: prssa@prsa.org
http://prssa.prsa.org/scholarships-and-awards/
Purpose: To assist public relations students.
Eligibility: Applicants must be PRSSA members enrolled in an undergraduate public relations program and be college juniors or seniors. Eligible students may be nominated from each PRSSA chapter. Selection is based on academic achievement, leadership, experience and commitment to public relations. Applicants need to include a 300-word statement of commitment to public relations.
Target applicant(s): College students. Adult students.
Amount: $1,000-$5,000.
Number of awards: 3.
Deadline: May 26.
How to apply: Applications are available online.
Exclusive: Visit www.UltimateScholarshipBook.com and enter code PU67120 for updates on this award.

(672) · Betty Rendel Scholarships

National Federation of Republican Women
124 North Alfred Street, Alexandria, VA 22314
Phone: 703-548-9688
Email: mail@nfrw.org
http://www.nfrw.org
Purpose: To aid female government, economics and political science majors.
Eligibility: Applicants must be U.S. citizens. They must be female undergraduates who have completed at least two years of their program of study. They must be majoring in economics, political science or government. Selection is based on the overall strength of the application.
Target applicant(s): College students. Adult students.
Amount: $1,000.
Number of awards: 3.
Deadline: June 1.
How to apply: Applications are available online. An application form, official transcript, three recommendation letters and two personal essays are required.

Exclusive: Visit www.UltimateScholarshipBook.com and enter code NA67220 for updates on this award.

(673) • Bill, W2ONV and Ann Salerno Memorial Scholarship

American Radio Relay League Foundation
225 Main Street, Newington, CT 06111-1494
Phone: 860-594-0348
Email: foundation@arrl.org
http://www.arrl.org/scholarship-program

Purpose: To provide financial assistance to amateur radio operators with high academic achievement.

Eligibility: Applicants must hold an active Amateur Radio License of any class and attend an accredited four-year college or university. They must have a GPA of 3.7 or higher, and their household income may not exceed $100,000 per year. They must not have previously received the Salerno Scholarship.

Target applicant(s): High school students. College students. Adult students.

Minimum GPA: 3.7

Amount: $1,000.

Number of awards: 2.

Deadline: February 16.

How to apply: Applications are available online.

Exclusive: Visit www.UltimateScholarshipBook.com and enter code AM67320 for updates on this award.

(674) • Bob East Scholarship

National Press Photographers Foundation Bob East Scholarship
Chuck Fadely, The Miami Herald, One Herald Plaza, Miami, FL 33132
Phone: 305-376-2015
http://www.nppf.org

Purpose: To encourage newcomers in photojournalism.

Eligibility: Applicants must either be an undergraduate in the first three and one half years of college or be planning to pursue postgraduate work.

Target applicant(s): High school students. College students. Graduate school students. Adult students.

Amount: $2,000.

Number of awards: 1.

Deadline: January 6.

How to apply: Applications are available online.

Exclusive: Visit www.UltimateScholarshipBook.com and enter code NA67420 for updates on this award.

(675) • Bob Richardson Legacy Scholarship

National Grocers Association
1005 N. Glebe Road, Suite 250, Arlington, VA 22201
Phone: 225-387-6126
http://www.nationalgrocers.org

Purpose: To support students pursuing a degree related to the grocery field.

Eligibility: Applicants must be rising sophomores through postgraduate students, have a minimum 2.5 GPA and be enrolled in a two- or four-year degree-granting institution. Students must major in business, food management, IT or another field related to a career in the grocery industry. Experience in the grocery industry is preferred but not required.

Target applicant(s): College students. Graduate school students. Adult students.

Minimum GPA: 2.5

Amount: Varies.

Number of awards: 1.

Deadline: April 15.

How to apply: Applications are available online.

Exclusive: Visit www.UltimateScholarshipBook.com and enter code NA67520 for updates on this award.

(676) • Bodie McDowell Scholarship

Outdoor Writers Association of America
121 Hickory Street, Suite 1, Missoula, MT 59801
Phone: 406-728-7434
Email: krhoades@owaa.org
http://www.owaa.org

Purpose: To support students in outdoor communications fields.

Eligibility: Applicants must be students of outdoor communications fields including print, film, art or broadcasting and must be either undergraduate students entering their junior or senior year or graduate students.

Target applicant(s): College students. Graduate school students. Adult students.

Amount: $1,000-$5,000.

Number of awards: 3 or more.

Deadline: March 1.

How to apply: Applicants are available online.

Exclusive: Visit www.UltimateScholarshipBook.com and enter code OU67620 for updates on this award.

(677) • Bonnie Tiegel Memorial Scholarship Program

Scholarship America Bonnie Tiegel
Phone: 507-931-1682
Email: tiegelmemorial@scholarshipamerica.org
https://www.scholarsapply.org/tiegelmemorial/

Purpose: To support students pursuing an education in journalism, broadcast journalism or communications.

Eligibility: Applicants must be high school seniors, graduates or current post-secondary undergraduates who plan to enroll full-time at an accredited college or university. Students must seek a degree in broadcast journalism, communications or journalism. Applicants must submit application, complete transcripts, applicant appraisal form and letter of recommendation.

Target applicant(s): High school students. College students. Adult students.

Amount: $2,500.

Number of awards: 1.

Deadline: May 31.

How to apply: Applications are available online.

Exclusive: Visit www.UltimateScholarshipBook.com and enter code SC67720 for updates on this award.

(678) • Boren Scholarships

National Security Education Program Initiative, Administered by Institute of International Education
1400 K Street, NW, 7th Floor, Washington, DC 20005
Phone: 800-618-6737
https://www.nsep.gov/

Purpose: To reward students who desire to study abroad in preparation for a career in U.S. national security.

Eligibility: Applicants must be U.S. citizens and undergraduate matriculated students at an accredited U.S. institution who have chosen a proposed country of study.

Target applicant(s): College students. Adult students.
Amount: $8,000-$20,000.
Number of awards: Varies.
Deadline: February 7.
How to apply: Applications are available online.
Exclusive: Visit www.UltimateScholarshipBook.com and enter code NA67820 for updates on this award.

---

(679) • Bound to Stay Bound Books Scholarship

Association for Library Service to Children
50 E. Huron Street, Chicago, IL 60611
Phone: 800-545-2433
Email: cjewell@ala.org
http://www.ala.org/alsc/awardsgrants
Purpose: To support students pursuing their MLS degrees.
Eligibility: Applicants must intend to pursue an MLS or advanced degree, plan to work in children's librarianship and be U.S. or Canadian citizens. Selection is based on academic excellence, leadership and a desire to work with children in any type of library.
Target applicant(s): College students. Graduate school students. Adult students.
Amount: $7,500.
Number of awards: 4.
Deadline: March 1.
How to apply: Applications are available online.
Exclusive: Visit www.UltimateScholarshipBook.com and enter code AS67920 for updates on this award.

---

(680) • Brenda Renee Horn Memorial Scholarship

Funeral Service Foundation
13625 Bishop's Drive, Brookfield, WI 53005-6607
Phone: 877-402-5900
Email: info@funeralservicefoundation.org
http://www.funeralservicefoundation.org
Purpose: To help a promising mortuary science student with tuition costs.
Eligibility: Applicants must be enrolled or plan to be enrolled in an accredited mortuary science program at the time of the scholarship deadline. Students must have a GPA of 2.0 or higher. Selection is based on the overall strength of the application.
Target applicant(s): College students. Graduate school students. Adult students.
Minimum GPA: 2.0
Amount: $3,000.
Number of awards: 1.
Deadline: December 31.
How to apply: Applications are available online. An application form, essay, academic transcript and video submissions are required.
Exclusive: Visit www.UltimateScholarshipBook.com and enter code FU68020 for updates on this award.

---

(681) • BSA Research Fellowship

Bibliographical Society of America
P.O. Box 1537, Lenox Hill Station, New York, NY 10021
Phone: 212-452-2710
Email: bsafellowships@bibsocamer.org
http://www.bibsocamer.org
Purpose: To provide financial assistance to those pursuing bibliographical studies.
Eligibility: Applicants must submit proposals for studying books as historical evidence or an examination of the history of book trades or publishing history.
Target applicant(s): College students. Graduate school students. Adult students.
Amount: $3,000-$6,000.
Number of awards: Varies.
Deadline: December 1.
How to apply: Applications are available online.
Exclusive: Visit www.UltimateScholarshipBook.com and enter code BI68120 for updates on this award.

---

(682) • Buckfire & Buckfire PC Law School Diversity Scholarship

Buckfire & Buckfire PC
25800 Northwestern Highway, Suite 890, Southfield, MI 48075
Phone: 248-569-4646
Email: info@buckfirelaw.com
http://www.buckfirelaw.com
Purpose: To assist law school students who are minorities or who demonstrate a commitment to issues of diversity.
Eligibility: Applicants must be a member of an ethnic or racial minority or an individual who demonstrates a commitment to issues of diversity. Students must also be U.S. citizens attending an accredited U.S. law school, have a minimum 3.0 GPA and have completed at least one semester of classes at law school.
Target applicant(s): Graduate school students. Adult students.
Minimum GPA: 3.0
Amount: $2,000.
Number of awards: 1.
Deadline: April 1.
How to apply: Applications are available online.
Exclusive: Visit www.UltimateScholarshipBook.com and enter code BU68220 for updates on this award.

---

(683) • Byron Hanke Fellowship

Foundation for Community Association Research
6402 Arlington Boulevard, Suite 500, Falls Church, VA 22042
Phone: 703-970-9220
http://www.cairf.org
Purpose: To support graduate students who are working on topics related to community associations.
Eligibility: Applicants must be currently enrolled in an accredited master's, doctoral or law program in the U.S. or Canada. Students must submit a research paper on community associations. Selection is primarily based on demonstration of research and writing abilities, academic achievement and faculty recommendations.
Target applicant(s): Graduate school students. Adult students.
Amount: $5,000.
Number of awards: 1.
Deadline: May 1.
How to apply: Applications are available online.
Exclusive: Visit www.UltimateScholarshipBook.com and enter code FO68320 for updates on this award.

---

(684) • CaGIS Scholarships

National Society of Professional Surveyors (NSPS/AAGS)
Attn: Scholarships, 5119 Pegasus Court, Suite Q, Frederick, MD 21704

Phone: 240-439-4615x105
Email: trisha.milburn@nsps.us.com
http://www.nsps.us.com/?page=Scholarships
Purpose: To support excellence in cartography or GIScience.
Eligibility: Applicants must be enrolled full-time in a four-year undergraduate or graduate degree program in cartography or geographic information science. Prior scholarship winners may apply. Applicants are judged on their records, statements, letters of recommendation and professional activities.
Target applicant(s): College students. Graduate school students. Adult students.
Amount: $750-$1,500.
Number of awards: 3.
Scholarship may be renewable.
Deadline: January 20.
How to apply: Applications are available online.
Exclusive: Visit www.UltimateScholarshipBook.com and enter code NA68420 for updates on this award.

(685) • California - Hawaii Elks Association Vocational Grants

California-Hawaii Elks Association
5450 E. Lamona Avenue, Fresno, CA 93727-2224
Phone: 559-255-4531
Email: chea@chea-elks.org
https://chea-elks.org/youth-activities/scholarships
Purpose: To provide assistance to those pursuing vocational/technical education.
Eligibility: Applicants must be U.S. citizens and California or Hawaii residents. They must plan to pursue a vocational or technical course of study above and supplemental to high school or preparatory school. A high school diploma or equivalent is not required. Students planning to transfer into a bachelor's degree program upon completion of vocational studies are not eligible.
Target applicant(s): High school students. College students. Adult students.
Amount: $500-$2,000.
Number of awards: Varies.
Scholarship may be renewable.
Deadline: Varies.
How to apply: Applications are available online.
Exclusive: Visit www.UltimateScholarshipBook.com and enter code CA68520 for updates on this award.

(686) • Caples Student Campaign of the Year Award

ASL Marketing
2 Dubon Court, Farmingdale, NY 11735
Phone: 516-248-6100
http://www.caples.org
Purpose: To support students who are interested in direct marketing.
Eligibility: Applicants can be from anywhere in the world and the award is based on the boldness of the concept, the logic of the execution and the overall strength of the outcome.
Target applicant(s): College students. Adult students.
Amount: Varies.
Number of awards: Varies.
Deadline: Varies.
How to apply: Applications are available online.
Exclusive: Visit www.UltimateScholarshipBook.com and enter code AS68620 for updates on this award.

(687) • CardRates.com Financial Futures Scholarship

CardRates.com
15 SE 1st Avenue, Suite B, Gainesville, FL 32601
http://www.cardrates.com/scholarship/
Purpose: To support students pursuing a career in the personal finance industry.
Eligibility: Applicants must be U.S. residents and current college students or graduating high school seniors enrolling in college. Students must be majoring in a field related to personal finance such as business, accounting, finance, mathematics or management and hold a minimum 3.5 GPA.
Target applicant(s): High school students. College students. Adult students.
Minimum GPA: 3.5
Amount: $1,000.
Number of awards: 1.
Deadline: July 31.
How to apply: Applications are available online.
Exclusive: Visit www.UltimateScholarshipBook.com and enter code CA68720 for updates on this award.

(688) • Carl Marks Advisors Student Case Competition

Turnaround Management Association
150 N. Wacker Drive, Suite 1900, Chicago, IL 60606
Phone: 312-578-2028
https://turnaround.org/about/tma-awards
Purpose: To reward students for outstanding company or industry case analyses.
Eligibility: Applicants must be enrolled in an undergraduate, MBA or law school program. Students must submit an in-depth analysis of a company or industry. Applicants may submit presentations individually or as a team with up to three other students. Selection is based on the overall strength of the analysis.
Target applicant(s): College students. Graduate school students. Adult students.
Amount: $3,000.
Number of awards: 2.
Deadline: June 6.
How to apply: Applications are available online.
Exclusive: Visit www.UltimateScholarshipBook.com and enter code TU68820 for updates on this award.

(689) • Carole J. Streeter, KB9JBR Scholarship

American Radio Relay League Foundation
225 Main Street, Newington, CT 06111-1494
Phone: 860-594-0348
Email: foundation@arrl.org
http://www.arrl.org/scholarship-program
Purpose: To support students who are involved in amateur radio.
Eligibility: Applicants must have an amateur radio license of Technician Class or higher. Preference will be given to applicants with Morse Code proficiency and those studying health and healing arts.
Target applicant(s): High school students. College students. Adult students.
Amount: $1,000.
Number of awards: 1.
Deadline: January 31.
How to apply: Applications are available online.

Exclusive: Visit www.UltimateScholarshipBook.com and enter code AM68920 for updates on this award.

(690) • Carole Simpson Scholarship

Radio Television Digital News Association
529 14th Street NW, Suite 1240, Washington, DC 20045
Phone: 202-659-6510
Email: karenh@rtdna.org
http://www.rtdna.org
Purpose: To honor professional achievements in electronic journalism.
Eligibility: Applicants must be full-time college sophomores or higher with at least one full academic year remaining. Applicants may be enrolled in any major as long as their career intent is television or radio news. Applicants may only apply for one RTNDA scholarship. Preference is given to students of color.
Target applicant(s): College students. Adult students.
Amount: $2,000.
Number of awards: 1.
Deadline: January 15.
How to apply: Applications are available online.
Exclusive: Visit www.UltimateScholarshipBook.com and enter code RA69020 for updates on this award.

(691) • Chaine des Rotiseurs Scholarship

American Culinary Federation
180 Center Place Way, St. Augustine, FL 32095
Phone: 904-824-4468
Email: acf@acfchefs.net
http://www.acfchefs.org
Purpose: To assist students attending culinary programs.
Eligibility: Applicants must be enrolled in an accredited post-secondary school of culinary arts or AAC-approved post-secondary culinary training program, be excellent students and have completed at least one grading period. Applicants should submit applications, two recommendation letters, financial aid release forms, transcripts and signed photo releases. Selection is based on application, financial need, references and transcript.
Target applicant(s): College students. Adult students.
Amount: Varies.
Number of awards: Varies.
Deadline: May 1 and September 1.
How to apply: Applications are available online.
Exclusive: Visit www.UltimateScholarshipBook.com and enter code AM69120 for updates on this award.

(692) • Charles and Lucille Family Foundation Undergraduate Scholarships

Charles and Lucille King Family Foundation
366 Madison Avenue, 10th Floor, New York, NY 10017
Phone: 212-682-2913
Email: info@kingfoundation.org
http://www.kingfoundation.org
Purpose: To assist film and television students.
Eligibility: Applicants must be undergraduate juniors or seniors and demonstrate academic ability, financial need and professional potential. Applicants must also major in film and television. Applicants must submit applications, personal statements, three recommendation letters and transcripts.
Target applicant(s): College students. Adult students.
Amount: Up to $3,500.
Number of awards: Varies.
Scholarship may be renewable.
Deadline: April 1.
How to apply: Applications are available online or by written request between September 1 and April 1.
Exclusive: Visit www.UltimateScholarshipBook.com and enter code CH69220 for updates on this award.

(693) • Charles Clarke Cordle Memorial Scholarship

American Radio Relay League Foundation
225 Main Street, Newington, CT 06111-1494
Phone: 860-594-0348
Email: foundation@arrl.org
http://www.arrl.org/scholarship-program
Purpose: To assist ham radio operators in furthering their educations.
Eligibility: Applicants must have any class of ham radio license, have a minimum 2.5 GPA and be residents of and attend school in Georgia or Alabama.
Target applicant(s): High school students. College students. Graduate school students. Adult students.
Minimum GPA: 2.5
Amount: $1,000.
Number of awards: 1.
Deadline: January 31.
How to apply: Applications are available online but may not be completed electronically. All completed applications must be mailed.
Exclusive: Visit www.UltimateScholarshipBook.com and enter code AM69320 for updates on this award.

(694) • Charles N. Fisher Memorial Scholarship

American Radio Relay League Foundation
225 Main Street, Newington, CT 06111-1494
Phone: 860-594-0348
Email: foundation@arrl.org
http://www.arrl.org/scholarship-program
Purpose: To assist ham radio operators in furthering their educations.
Eligibility: Applicants must have any class of ham radio license, be residents of the ARRL Southwestern Division (Arizona, Los Angeles, Orange County, San Diego or Santa Barbara), attend a regionally-accredited college or university and study electronics, communications or a related field.
Target applicant(s): High school students. College students. Graduate school students. Adult students.
Amount: $1,000.
Number of awards: 1.
Deadline: January 31.
How to apply: Applications are available online. Completed applications must be submitted by mail, not electronically.
Exclusive: Visit www.UltimateScholarshipBook.com and enter code AM69420 for updates on this award.

(695) • Charlie and Becky Bray Legacy Scholarship

National Grocers Association
1005 N. Glebe Road, Suite 250, Arlington, VA 22201
Phone: 225-387-6126
http://www.nationalgrocers.org
Purpose: To support students pursuing degrees related to the grocery field.
Eligibility: Applicants must be rising sophomores through postgraduate students, have a minimum 2.5 GPA and be enrolled in a two- or four-

year degree-granting institution. Students must major in business, food management, IT or another field related to a career in the grocery industry. Experience in the grocery industry is preferred but not required.
Target applicant(s): College students. Graduate school students. Adult students.
Minimum GPA: 2.5
Amount: Varies.
Number of awards: 1.
Deadline: April 15.
How to apply: Applications are available online.
Exclusive: Visit www.UltimateScholarshipBook.com and enter code NA69520 for updates on this award.

(696) • Chester Burger Scholarship for Excellence in Public Relations

Public Relations Student Society of America
33 Maiden Lane, 11th Floor, New York, NY 10038
Phone: 212-460-1474
Email: prssa@prsa.org
http://prssa.prsa.org/scholarships-and-awards/
Purpose: To encourage public relations and journalism graduate students to pursue careers in corporate public relations.
Eligibility: Applicants must be entering or current graduate students at a U.S. college or university. They must be majoring in journalism, public relations or a related field. They must have an undergraduate GPA of 3.0 or higher on a four-point scale and be interested in pursuing a career in corporate public relations. Selection is based on the overall strength of the application.
Target applicant(s): College students. Graduate school students. Adult students.
Minimum GPA: 3.0
Amount: $1,000.
Number of awards: 1.
Deadline: May 9.
How to apply: Applications are available online. An application form, resume, essay and two recommendation letters are required.
Exclusive: Visit www.UltimateScholarshipBook.com and enter code PU69620 for updates on this award.

(697) • Chicago FM Club Scholarships

American Radio Relay League Foundation
225 Main Street, Newington, CT 06111-1494
Phone: 860-594-0348
Email: foundation@arrl.org
http://www.arrl.org/scholarship-program
Purpose: To assist ham radio operators in furthering their educations.
Eligibility: Applicants must have at least a technician ham radio license, be residents of the FCC Ninth Call District (Illinois, Indiana or Wisconsin) and be students at an accredited post-secondary two- or four-year college or trade school.
Target applicant(s): High school students. College students. Adult students.
Amount: $500.
Number of awards: Varies.
Deadline: January 31.
How to apply: Applications are available online but must be sent in by mail.
Exclusive: Visit www.UltimateScholarshipBook.com and enter code AM69720 for updates on this award.

(698) • Chips Quinn Scholars Program for Diversity in Journalism

Freedom Forum Institute
555 Pennsylvania Avenue NW, Washington, DC 20001
Phone: 202-292-6271
https://www.freedomforuminstitute.org
Purpose: To support minority students pursuing a career in the journalism field.
Eligibility: Applicants must be able to attend a seven-day training in Nashville, Tennessee (May). In most cases, applicants must have a car for the internship. Students must be college juniors or seniors, graduate students or recent graduates who are majoring in journalism.
Target applicant(s): College students. Graduate school students. Adult students.
Amount: Varies.
Number of awards: Varies.
Deadline: October.
How to apply: Applications are available online.
Exclusive: Visit www.UltimateScholarshipBook.com and enter code FR69820 for updates on this award.

(699) • CLA Scholarship for Minority Students in Memory of Edna Yelland

California Library Association
248 E. Foothill Boulevard, Suite 101, Monrovia, CA 91016
Phone: 916-779-4573
Email: info@cla-net.org
http://www.cla-net.org
Purpose: To assist minority California graduate students who are pursuing degrees in library or information science.
Eligibility: Applicants must be California residents, be American Indian, African American, Mexican American, Latino, Asian American, Pacific Islander or Filipino and be accepted into or enrolled in an American Library Association accredited state library school. The award is based on financial need, and an interview is required.
Target applicant(s): College students. Graduate school students. Adult students.
Amount: $2,500.
Number of awards: up to 3.
Deadline: Varies.
How to apply: Applications are available online.
Exclusive: Visit www.UltimateScholarshipBook.com and enter code CA69920 for updates on this award.

(700) • Clifford H. "Ted" Rees, Jr. Scholarship

Air-Conditioning, Heating and Refrigeration Institute
Clifford H. "Ted" Rees, Jr. Scholarship Foundation, 2111 Wilson Boulevard, Suite 500, Arlington, VA 22201
Phone: 703-524-8800
Email: ReesApplications@ahrinet.org
http://careersinhvacr.org/site/293/Careers/Scholarships
Purpose: To support students preparing for careers in heating, ventilation, air-conditioning and refrigeration (HVACR) technology.
Eligibility: Applicants must be U.S. citizens, nationals or resident aliens intending to become U.S. citizens. They must be enrolled in an accredited HVACR technician training program and have plans to become entry-level commercial refrigeration technicians, residential air-conditioning and heating technicians or light commercial air-conditioning and heating technicians after graduation. Selection is

based on stated career goals and commitment to pursuing entry-level work in the HVACR field.
Target applicant(s): College students. Adult students.
Amount: Up to $2,000.
Number of awards: 15.
Deadline: June 1 (fall), October 1 (spring).
How to apply: Applications are available online. An application form, two recommendation letters, personal statement and copy of alien registration card (if applicable) are required.
Exclusive: Visit www.UltimateScholarshipBook.com and enter code AI70020 for updates on this award.

(701) • Cogburn Law Offices Scholarship

Cogburn Law Offices
2879 St. Rose Parkway, Suite 200, Henderson, NV 89052
Phone: 702-748-7777
http://cogburnlaw.com/cogburn-law-offices-scholarship/
Purpose: To support students who are seeking a college education.
Eligibility: Applicants must be U.S. citizens or permanent residents enrolling as full-time students in an accredited college or university, community college or law school in the fall. Students must complete the application and an essay or video addressing the topic presented on the website.
Target applicant(s): High school students. College students. Graduate school students. Adult students.
Amount: $5,000.
Number of awards: 1.
Deadline: July 15.
How to apply: Applications are available online.
Exclusive: Visit www.UltimateScholarshipBook.com and enter code CO70120 for updates on this award.

(702) • College Photographer of the Year

National Press Photographers Foundation College Photographer of the Year
David Rees, CPOY Director, School of Journalism, The University of Missouri, 106 Lee Hills Hall, Columbus, MO 65211
Phone: 573-882-4442
Email: jourdlr@showme.missouri.edu
http://nppf.org/nppf-scholarships-grants-and-awards/
Purpose: To reward outstanding student work in photojournalism and provide a forum for student photographers to gauge their skills.
Eligibility: Applicants must be currently enrolled in a full-time four-year college or university, provide a portfolio and demonstrate financial need. Applicants can apply to as many NPPA scholarships as desired, but only one award will be granted to each winner.
Target applicant(s): High school students. College students. Graduate school students. Adult students.
Amount: Varies.
Number of awards: Varies.
Deadline: January 6.
How to apply: Applications are available by written or email request.
Exclusive: Visit www.UltimateScholarshipBook.com and enter code NA70220 for updates on this award.

(703) • College/University Excellence of Scholarship Awards

National Council for Geographic Education
1101 14th Street NW, Suite 350, Washington, DC 20005-5647
Phone: 256-782-5293
Email: ncge@jsu.edu
http://www.ncge.org/awards
Purpose: To recognize senior geography majors.
Eligibility: Every college or university geography department in North America may submit the name of its outstanding graduating senior geography majors. The students receive certificates. The nominating faculty must be AAG or NCGE members.
Target applicant(s): College students. Adult students.
Amount: Varies.
Number of awards: Varies.
Deadline: May 15.
How to apply: Nomination materials are described online.
Exclusive: Visit www.UltimateScholarshipBook.com and enter code NA70320 for updates on this award.

(704) • Collegiate Journalism Award

Fund for American Studies
1621 New Hampshire Avenue NW, Washington, DC 20009
Phone: 800-741-6964
Email: admissions@tfas.org
https://tfas.org/awards/
Purpose: To reward collegiate reporters for excellent journalism.
Eligibility: Applicants must be undergraduate students enrolled at a four-year educational institution. Students must submit news stories they have written within the past academic year that have been published in a college newspaper/publication. Selection is based on the overall strength of the submission.
Target applicant(s): College students. Adult students.
Amount: $500-$2,500.
Number of awards: 2.
Deadline: April 4.
How to apply: Applications are available online.
Exclusive: Visit www.UltimateScholarshipBook.com and enter code FU70420 for updates on this award.

(705) • Connecticut Broadcasters Association Scholarship

Connecticut Broadcasters Association
P.O. Box 1785, Avon, CT 06001
Phone: 860-305-2038
Email: mryan@ctba.org
http://www.ctba.org
Purpose: To support students pursuing a broadcasting-related degree program.
Eligibility: Applicants must be Connecticut residents and be pursuing a degree in a broadcast related field such as: journalism, marketing, production, broadcast engineering or communications. Selection is based on financial need and/or merit.
Target applicant(s): College students. Adult students.
Amount: Up to $5,000.
Number of awards: 10.
Deadline: March 16.
How to apply: Applications are available online.
Exclusive: Visit www.UltimateScholarshipBook.com and enter code CO70520 for updates on this award.

(706) • Consolidated Foodservice Scholarship

Consolidated Foodservice
11206 Ampere Court, Louisville, KY 40299

Phone: 800-550-0706
https://www.consolidatedfoodservice.com/scholarship
Purpose: To support the next generation of chefs and restaurant managers.
Eligibility: Applicants must be graduating high school seniors enrolling in post-secondary education or students already enrolled in a college or accredited institution. Students must be majoring in culinary arts or hospitality management and must submit an essay along with the application.
Target applicant(s): High school students. College students. Adult students.
Amount: $500.
Number of awards: 1.
Deadline: June 15.
How to apply: Applications are available online.
Exclusive: Visit www.UltimateScholarshipBook.com and enter code CO70620 for updates on this award.

(707) · Cosmetology Scholarship

Salon Supply Store
350 Hiatt Drive, Palm Beach Gardens, FL 33418
Phone: 800-617-0525
Email: scholarship@salonsupplystore.com
https://www.salonsupplystore.com/
Purpose: To assist cosmetology students.
Eligibility: Applicants must be legal residents in the U.S. or District of Columbia who are 18 years of age or older. Students should be currently enrolled (or have been accepted to enroll) in an accredited post-secondary institution of higher learning (e.g. trade school, college or university) studying cosmetology. Applicants must submit a brief video of their best looks, skills or beauty tips.
Target applicant(s): College students. Adult students.
Amount: $1,000.
Number of awards: 1.
Deadline: October 1.
How to apply: Applications are available online.
Exclusive: Visit www.UltimateScholarshipBook.com and enter code SA70720 for updates on this award.

(708) · Costa Rican Vacations Scholarship Program

Costa Rica Vacations
Costa Rican Vacations - Travel Agency, Calle 70, San José Province, San Jose, Costa Rica
Phone: 800-606-1860
http://www.vacationscostarica.com/about-us/scholarships
Purpose: To support students in pursuing post-secondary studies in the fields of tourism, hospitality and sustainable development.
Eligibility: Applicants must be enrolled at a U.S.-based university. A minimum GPA of 2.8 is required. Students must submit an essay explaining their career goals in the areas of tourism, hospitality or sustainable development.
Target applicant(s): College students. Graduate school students. Adult students.
Minimum GPA: 2.8
Amount: $1,000.
Number of awards: 2.
Deadline: February 15.
How to apply: Applications are available online.
Exclusive: Visit www.UltimateScholarshipBook.com and enter code CO70820 for updates on this award.

(709) · Criminal Lawyer Scholarship

DM Cantor
40 N. Central Avenue, Suite 2300, Phoenix, AZ 85004
Phone: 602-307-0808
https://dmcantor.com/criminal-defense-lawyer-scholarship-fund
Purpose: To assist students pursuing law education.
Eligibility: Applicants must be 18 years of age and enrolling in or currently enrolled in an accredited college or university in the U.S. Students must write an essay discussing the necessity and value of presumption of innocence and reasonable doubt in the criminal justice system.
Target applicant(s): High school students. College students. Graduate school students. Adult students.
Amount: $2,500.
Number of awards: 1.
Deadline: July 31.
How to apply: Applications are available online.
Exclusive: Visit www.UltimateScholarshipBook.com and enter code DM70920 for updates on this award.

(710) · Daniel Burrus Scholarship Fund

Burrus Research
Phone: 262-533-0010
Email: scholarship@burrus.com
http://www.burrus.com/scholarship/
Purpose: To help students achieve higher education.
Eligibility: Applicants must be high school students enrolling in a college or university the following semester or a full-time college student in good academic standing. Students must demonstrate a desire to continue their education and positively impact their community. Applicants must submit an essay and student bio.
Target applicant(s): High school students. College students. Adult students.
Amount: $1,000.
Number of awards: 3.
Deadline: May 15.
How to apply: Applications are available online.
Exclusive: Visit www.UltimateScholarshipBook.com and enter code BU71020 for updates on this award.

(711) · Darrel Hess Community College Geography Scholarship

Association of American Geographers (AAG) Hess Scholarship
1710 Sixteenth Street NW, Washington, DC 20009-3198
Phone: 202-234-1450
Email: grantsawards@aag.org
http://www.aag.org
Purpose: To support geography majors.
Eligibility: Applicants must be currently enrolled at a U.S. community college, junior college, city college or similar two-year educational institution, have completed at least two transfer courses in geography and plan to transfer to a four-year institution as a geography major. The award is based on academic excellence and promise. Applications, personal statements, two recommendation letters and transcripts are required.
Target applicant(s): College students. Adult students.
Amount: $1,500.
Number of awards: 2.
Deadline: December 31.
How to apply: Applications are available online.

Exclusive: Visit www.UltimateScholarshipBook.com and enter code AS71120 for updates on this award.

(712) • Dating and Relationship Psychology Scholarship

DatingAdvice.com
c/o Digital Brands Inc., 15 SE 1st Avenue, Suite B, Gainesville, FL 32601
http://www.datingadvice.com
Purpose: To assist psychology students who are planning careers in relationship counseling or a related field.
Eligibility: Applicants must be U.S. undergraduate or graduate students majoring in psychology and must have a minimum 3.5 GPA. Students must write a 500- to 900-word essay on the topic of "The Psychology of Online Dating."
Target applicant(s): College students. Graduate school students. Adult students.
Minimum GPA: 3.5
Amount: $1,000.
Number of awards: 1.
Deadline: June 30.
How to apply: An official transcript and essay must be submitted by mail.
Exclusive: Visit www.UltimateScholarshipBook.com and enter code DA71220 for updates on this award.

(713) • David S. Barr Awards

Newspaper Guild - CWA
David S. Barr Award, 501 Third Street NW, Washington, DC 20001-2797
Phone: 202-434-7177
Email: guild@cwa-union.org
http://www.newsguild.org
Purpose: To support student journalists.
Eligibility: Applicants must be high school or post-secondary students at any type of institution and have published or broadcast a work in the previous year that helped to correct an injustice or promote justice and fairness. Students who have worked or are working as professional journalists not including internships are not eligible to enter. No more than one entry per applicant may be submitted.
Target applicant(s): High school students. College students. Graduate school students. Adult students.
Amount: $1,000-$1,500.
Number of awards: 2.
Deadline: January 31.
How to apply: Applications are available online. An application form, five copies of submitted work and brief summary of work are required.
Exclusive: Visit www.UltimateScholarshipBook.com and enter code NE71320 for updates on this award.

(714) • Daymond John's Success Formula Entrepreneurial Scholarship Success Formula

Daymond John's Success Formula
1810 East Sahara Avenue #100, Las Vegas, NV 89104
Phone: 800-206-0429
Email: scholarship@djsuccessformula.com
https://daymondjohnssuccessformula.com/scholarships/
Purpose: To encourage students who are pursuing a career as an entrepreneur.
Eligibility: Applicants must be in good standing at an accredited college, university or trade school and must create a video as part of the application process.
Target applicant(s): High school students. College students. Adult students.
Amount: $1,500.
Number of awards: 2.
Scholarship may be renewable.
Deadline: August 18, November 30.
How to apply: Applications are available online.
Exclusive: Visit www.UltimateScholarshipBook.com and enter code DA71420 for updates on this award.

(715) • Dayton Amateur Radio Association Scholarship

American Radio Relay League Foundation
225 Main Street, Newington, CT 06111-1494
Phone: 860-594-0348
Email: foundation@arrl.org
http://www.arrl.org/scholarship-program
Purpose: To provide financial assistance to students who are amateur radio operators.
Eligibility: Applicants must be accepted or enrolled at an accredited four-year institution of higher learning. They must possess an Amateur Radio License of any class.
Target applicant(s): High school students. College students. Adult students.
Amount: $1,000.
Number of awards: 4.
Deadline: January 31.
How to apply: Applications are available online.
Exclusive: Visit www.UltimateScholarshipBook.com and enter code AM71520 for updates on this award.

(716) • Distinguished Service Award for Students

Society for Technical Communication
Manager of the Distinguished Community Awards Committee, 9401 Lee Highway, Suite 300, Fairfax, VA 22031
Phone: 703-522-4114
Email: stc@stc.org
http://www.stc.org
Purpose: To assist students who are pursuing degrees in an area of technical communication.
Eligibility: Applicants must be full-time undergraduate or graduate students who have completed at least one year of post-secondary education and who have at least one full year of academic work remaining to complete their degree programs. Students must also be in the field of communication of information about technical subjects and be student members of the STC. Applicants must be nominated by student chapters.
Target applicant(s): College students. Graduate school students. Adult students.
Amount: Varies.
Number of awards: Varies.
Deadline: October 28.
How to apply: Applications are available online.
Exclusive: Visit www.UltimateScholarshipBook.com and enter code SO71620 for updates on this award.

(717) • DMC Digital Marketing Essay Scholarship

M is Good
8216 Creedmoor Road, Suite 201, Raleigh, NC 27613
Phone: 984-212-5716
https://misgood.com/scholarship/
Purpose: To support students interested in marketing.
Eligibility: Applicants must have declared a marketing-related major or minor at a U.S. university, college, technical or online school and demonstrate a desire for marketing and digital marketing. Students must be U.S. citizens or legal residents. Applicants must submit an essay discussing small business marketing principles.
Target applicant(s): High school students. College students. Adult students.
Amount: $500.
Number of awards: 2.
Deadline: July 30.
How to apply: Applications are available online.
Exclusive: Visit www.UltimateScholarshipBook.com and enter code M 71720 for updates on this award.

(718) • Donald Riebhoff Memorial Scholarship

American Radio Relay League Foundation
225 Main Street, Newington, CT 06111-1494
Phone: 860-594-0348
Email: foundation@arrl.org
http://www.arrl.org/scholarship-program
Purpose: To assist ham radio operators in furthering their educations.
Eligibility: Applicants must have at least a technician ham radio license, be undergraduate or graduate students in international studies at an accredited post-secondary institution and be members of ARRL.
Target applicant(s): High school students. College students. Graduate school students. Adult students.
Amount: $1,000.
Number of awards: 1.
Deadline: January 31.
How to apply: Applications are available online. Completed applications must be mailed in. They cannot be completed electronically.
Exclusive: Visit www.UltimateScholarshipBook.com and enter code AM71820 for updates on this award.

(719) • Dr. Harold Kerzner Scholarships

Project Management Institute Educational Foundation
14 Campus Boulevard, Newtown Square, PA 19073
Phone: 610-356-4600
Email: pmief@pmi.org
https://pmief.org/scholarships/academic-scholarships
Purpose: To aid project management students.
Eligibility: Applicants must be current or entering undergraduate or graduate students who are studying or planning to study project management at a degree-granting college or university. Selection is based on academic achievement and extracurricular activities.
Target applicant(s): College students. Graduate school students. Adult students.
Amount: Up to $7,500.
Number of awards: 4.
Deadline: May 1.
How to apply: Applications are available online. An application form, official transcript, resume, three reference letters and two essays are required.
Exclusive: Visit www.UltimateScholarshipBook.com and enter code PR71920 for updates on this award.

(720) • Dr. James L. Lawson Memorial Scholarship

American Radio Relay League Foundation
225 Main Street, Newington, CT 06111-1494
Phone: 860-594-0348
Email: foundation@arrl.org
http://www.arrl.org/scholarship-program
Purpose: To assist ham radio operators in furthering their educations.
Eligibility: Applicants must have at least a general ham radio license, be residents of and attend post-secondary institutions in the New England states (Connecticut, Maine, Massachusetts, New Hampshire, Rhode Island or Vermont) or New York state and be pursuing a bachelor's or graduate degree in electronics, communications or a related field.
Target applicant(s): High school students. College students. Graduate school students. Adult students.
Amount: $500.
Number of awards: 1.
Deadline: January 31.
How to apply: Applications are available online but cannot be completed electronically. All applications must be mailed.
Exclusive: Visit www.UltimateScholarshipBook.com and enter code AM72020 for updates on this award.

(721) • Earl Warren Scholarship

NAACP Legal Defense and Educational Fund
99 Hudson Street, Suite 1600, New York, NY 10013
Phone: 212-965-2200
http://www.naacpldf.org/
Purpose: To reward promising law students who have potential for training as civil rights and public interest attorneys.
Eligibility: Applicants must be law students entering their first or second year of full-time legal study at an accredited law school. Students must show a strong commitment to racial justice and civil rights. Applicants must be U.S. citizens. Students must either be college graduates, enrolled in their final year of college or university or be a first-year law student. Applicants must have a strong record of academic achievement.
Target applicant(s): College students. Graduate school students. Adult students.
Amount: $30,000.
Number of awards: Varies.
Scholarship may be renewable.
Deadline: May 1.
How to apply: Applications are available online.
Exclusive: Visit www.UltimateScholarshipBook.com and enter code NA72120 for updates on this award.

(722) • Ecolab Scholarship Competition

American Hotel and Lodging Educational Foundation (AHLEF)
1250 I Street NW, Suite 1100, Washington, DC 20005-3931
Phone: 202-289-3180
Email: foundation@ahlef.org
https://www.ahlef.org/Scholarships/Academic_Scholarships/
Purpose: To provide scholarships for students who intend to earn a degree in hospitality management.
Eligibility: Applicants must be enrolled or intend to enroll full-time in a two- or four-year U.S. college or university.
Target applicant(s): High school students. College students. Adult students.

Amount: $1,000-$2,000.
Number of awards: Varies.
Deadline: May 1.
How to apply: Applications are available online.
Exclusive: Visit www.UltimateScholarshipBook.com and enter code AM72220 for updates on this award.

---

(723) · Ed Bradley Scholarship

Radio Television Digital News Association
529 14th Street NW, Suite 1240, Washington, DC 20045
Phone: 202-659-6510
Email: karenh@rtdna.org
http://www.rtdna.org
Purpose: To honor professional achievements in electronic journalism.
Eligibility: Applicants must be full-time college sophomores or higher with at least one full academic year remaining. Applicants may be enrolled in any major as long as their career intent is television or radio news. Applicants may only apply for one RTNDA scholarship.
Target applicant(s): College students. Adult students.
Amount: $10,000.
Number of awards: 1.
Deadline: January 15.
How to apply: Applications are available online.
Exclusive: Visit www.UltimateScholarshipBook.com and enter code RA72320 for updates on this award.

---

(724) · Edmond A. Metzger Scholarship

American Radio Relay League Foundation
225 Main Street, Newington, CT 06111-1494
Phone: 860-594-0348
Email: foundation@arrl.org
http://www.arrl.org/scholarship-program
Purpose: To assist ham radio operators in furthering their educations.
Eligibility: Applicants must have at least a novice ham radio license, be undergraduate or graduate students in electrical engineering, be residents of and attend schools in the ARRL Central Division (Illinois, Indiana or Wisconsin) and be members of ARRL.
Target applicant(s): College students. Graduate school students. Adult students.
Amount: $500.
Number of awards: 1.
Deadline: January 31.
How to apply: Applications are available online. Completed applications must be mailed in. They cannot be completed electronically.
Exclusive: Visit www.UltimateScholarshipBook.com and enter code AM72420 for updates on this award.

---

(725) · Educational Foundation Scholarship

International Society of Automation
67 T.W. Alexander Drive, P.O. Box 12277, Research Triangle Park, NC 27709
Phone: 919-549-8411
Email: info@isa.org
https://www.isa.org/students/scholarships/
Purpose: To support students interested in the fields of automation and control.
Eligibility: Applicants must be full-time students in a graduate, undergraduate or two-year degree program. Students must have a minimum GPA of 2.5 and be enrolled in a program in automation and control or another closely related field.
Target applicant(s): College students. Graduate school students. Adult students.
Minimum GPA: 2.5
Amount: Varies.
Number of awards: Varies.
Deadline: March 15.
How to apply: Applications are available online.
Exclusive: Visit www.UltimateScholarshipBook.com and enter code IN72520 for updates on this award.

---

(726) · Edward J. Nell Memorial Scholarships in Journalism

Quill and Scroll Society
University of Iowa School of Journalism and Mass Communications, 100 Adler Journalism Building, Iowa City, IA 52242
Phone: 319-335-3457
Email: quill-scroll@uiowa.edu
http://www.quillandscroll.org
Purpose: To aid high school journalists seeking to improve their skills and techniques.
Eligibility: Applicants to the Nell Scholarship must have been national winners in the Yearbook Excellence Contest or the International Writing/Photography Contest.
Target applicant(s): High school students.
Amount: Varies.
Number of awards: Varies.
Deadline: May 10.
How to apply: Applications are available online.
Exclusive: Visit www.UltimateScholarshipBook.com and enter code QU72620 for updates on this award.

---

(727) · EGIA Foundation Scholarship Program

EGIA Foundation
3800 Watt Avenue, Suite 105, Sacramento, CA 95821
Phone: 507-931-1682
Email: egiafoundation@scholarshipamerica.org
https://egiafoundation.org/what-we-do/scholarship
Purpose: To support students wishing to pursue a career in the HVACR industry.
Eligibility: Applicants must be a high school senior, high school graduate or GED equivalent who is enrolled or planning to enroll at an accredited two-year college, vocational or technical school or other approved technical institute to pursue studies in HVACR. A minimum 2.0 GPA or higher is required.
Target applicant(s): High school students.
Minimum GPA: 2.0
Amount: $2,500.
Number of awards: 20.
Deadline: April 1.
How to apply: Applications are available online
Exclusive: Visit www.UltimateScholarshipBook.com and enter code EG72720 for updates on this award.

---

(728) · Emerging Entrepreneur Scholarship Grant

LegalZoom
101 N. Brand Avenue, Glendale, CA 91203
Phone: 800-773-0888
https://www.legalzoom.com/scholarship-grant.html
Purpose: To support entrepreneurial students.

Eligibility: Applicants must be U.S. citizens or permanent legal residents of at least 18 years of age. Students must submit their idea for a business startup.
Target applicant(s): High school students. College students. Adult students.
Amount: $5,000.
Number of awards: 1.
Deadline: September 10.
How to apply: Applications are available online.
Exclusive: Visit www.UltimateScholarshipBook.com and enter code LE72820 for updates on this award.

---

(729) • Enid Hall Griswold Memorial Scholarship

National Society Daughters of the American Revolution
Committee Services Office, Attn.: Scholarships, 1776 D Street NW, Washington, DC 20006-5303
Phone: 202-628-1776
Email: scholarships@dar.org
http://www.dar.org/national-society/scholarships
Purpose: To assist college students pursuing studies in political science, history, government or economics.
Eligibility: Applicants must be college juniors or seniors majoring in political science, history, government or economics. All applicants must obtain a letter of sponsorship from their local DAR chapter. However, affiliation with DAR is not required.
Target applicant(s): College students. Adult students.
Amount: $5,000.
Number of awards: 2.
Deadline: February 10.
How to apply: Applications are available by written request with a self-addressed, stamped envelope.
Exclusive: Visit www.UltimateScholarshipBook.com and enter code NA72920 for updates on this award.

---

(730) • Esther R. Sawyer Research Award

Institute of Internal Auditors Research Foundation
247 Maitland Avenue, Altamonte Springs, FL 32701-4201
Phone: 407-937-1100
Email: research@theiia.org
http://www.theiia.org
Purpose: To reward internal auditing students.
Eligibility: Applicants should be accepted to or currently enrolled in a graduate program in internal auditing at an IIA-endorsed school or have taken internal auditing undergraduate courses at an IIA-endorsed school and be enrolled in any graduate program in internal auditing or business. An original manuscript on a topic related to modern internal auditing is required. The award is based on the topic, value to the audit profession, originality and the quality of writing.
Target applicant(s): High school students. College students. Graduate school students. Adult students.
Amount: Up to $5,000.
Number of awards: 1.
Deadline: March 1.
How to apply: Application materials are described online.
Exclusive: Visit www.UltimateScholarshipBook.com and enter code IN73020 for updates on this award.

---

(731) • Excellence of Scholarship Awards

National Council for Geographic Education
1101 14th Street NW, Suite 350, Washington, DC 20005-5647
Phone: 256-782-5293
Email: ncge@jsu.edu
http://www.ncge.org/awards
Purpose: To recognize outstanding geography students.
Eligibility: Applicants must be high school seniors who plan to major in geography. Nominators must be NCGE members who nominate students in their classes.
Target applicant(s): High school students.
Amount: Varies.
Number of awards: Varies.
Deadline: May 15.
How to apply: Nominating materials are described online.
Exclusive: Visit www.UltimateScholarshipBook.com and enter code NA73120 for updates on this award.

---

(732) • Executive Women International Scholarship Program

Executive Women International (EWI)
3860 South 2300 East, Suite 211, Salt Lake City, UT 84109
Phone: 801-355-2800
Email: ewi@ewiconnect.com
http://ewiconnect.com/scholarships/
Purpose: To assist high school students in achieving their higher education goals.
Eligibility: Applicants must be high school seniors who plan to pursue four-year degrees at accredited colleges or universities. Selection is based on application materials, communication skills, academic record, extracurricular activities and leadership.
Target applicant(s): High school students.
Amount: $1,000-$5,000.
Number of awards: Varies.
Deadline: April 30.
How to apply: Applications are available by request from the applicant's local Executive Women International chapter. An application form and supporting documents are required.
Exclusive: Visit www.UltimateScholarshipBook.com and enter code EX73220 for updates on this award.

---

(733) • Expert Institute Legal Blog Post Writing Contest

Expert Institute
75 Maiden Lane, Suite 704, New York, NY 10038
Phone: 888-858-9511
http://www.theexpertinstitute.com/writing-contest
Purpose: To support law students interested in entering a contest by writing a blog-style article on the use of expert witnesses in litigation.
Eligibility: Applicants must be current J.D. students within the U.S and must submit a 1,000- to 2,500-word article on the use of expert witnesses in litigation. The article must be written in blog post format to "entertain and engage as well as to inform and educate." Specific case references and examples are required as are in-line citations. Selection is based on quality of writing and writing style, originality and depth of research and analysis.
Target applicant(s): Graduate school students. Adult students.
Amount: $2,000.
Number of awards: 3.
Deadline: December 31.
How to apply: Articles must be submitted online. A blog-style article in .doc or .docx, full name, contact information, photo, school name and address and valid .edu email address are required.

Exclusive: Visit www.UltimateScholarshipBook.com and enter code EX73320 for updates on this award.

(734) • First Data Technology Legacy Scholarship

National Grocers Association
1005 N. Glebe Road, Suite 250, Arlington, VA 22201
Phone: 225-387-6126
http://www.nationalgrocers.org
Purpose: To support students pursuing degrees related to the grocery field.
Eligibility: Applicants must be rising sophomores through postgraduate students, have a minimum 2.5 GPA and be enrolled in a two- or four-year degree-granting institution. Students must major in business, food management, IT or another field related to a career in the grocery industry. Experience in the grocery industry is preferred but not required.
Target applicant(s): College students. Graduate school students. Adult students.
Minimum GPA: 2.5
Amount: Varies.
Number of awards: 2.
Deadline: April 15.
How to apply: Applications are available online.
Exclusive: Visit www.UltimateScholarshipBook.com and enter code NA73420 for updates on this award.

(735) • Florence C. and Robert H. Lister Fellowship

Crow Canyon Archeological Center
23390 Road K, Cortez, CO 81321-9908
Phone: 800-422-8975
Email: schoolprograms@crowcanyon.org
http://www.crowcanyon.org
Purpose: To assist graduate students in the archeology of American Indian cultures of the Southwest.
Eligibility: Applicants must be enrolled in a North American Ph.D. program and have projects based on archaeological, ethnoarchaeological or paleoenvironmental research in the southwestern United States and northern Mexico. The award is offered every other year.
Target applicant(s): Graduate school students. Adult students.
Amount: $7,000.
Number of awards: 1.
Deadline: Varies.
How to apply: Applications are available online.
Exclusive: Visit www.UltimateScholarshipBook.com and enter code CR73520 for updates on this award.

(736) • FMS Solutions Holdings, LLC Legacy Scholarship

National Grocers Association
1005 N. Glebe Road, Suite 250, Arlington, VA 22201
Phone: 225-387-6126
http://www.nationalgrocers.org
Purpose: To support students pursuing education related to the grocery field.
Eligibility: Applicants must be rising sophomores through postgraduate students, have a minimum 2.5 GPA and be enrolled in a two- or four-year degree-granting institution. Students must major in business, food management, IT or another field related to a career in the grocery industry. Experience in the grocery industry is preferred but not required. Preference given to children of state or local law enforcement officers.
Target applicant(s): College students. Graduate school students. Adult students.
Minimum GPA: 2.5
Amount: Varies.
Number of awards: 1.
Deadline: April 15.
How to apply: Applications are available online.
Exclusive: Visit www.UltimateScholarshipBook.com and enter code NA73620 for updates on this award.

(737) • FOARE Scholarship Program

Foundation for Outdoor Advertising Research and Education (FOARE)
The Family Scholarship Endowment, c/o Thomas M. Smith & Associates, 4601 Tilden Street NW, Washington, DC 20016
http://oaaa.org/AboutOAAA/FOARE/FOAREScholarshipProgram.aspx
Purpose: To support undergraduate and graduate students in pursuing a career in the outdoor advertising industry.
Eligibility: Applicants must be graduating seniors, undergraduate students or graduate students. Selection is primarily based on demonstration of financial need, career goals, academic achievement, community service and extracurricular involvement.
Target applicant(s): High school students. College students. Graduate school students. Adult students.
Amount: $3,000-$5,000.
Number of awards: 10.
Deadline: June 12.
How to apply: Applications are available online.
Exclusive: Visit www.UltimateScholarshipBook.com and enter code FO73720 for updates on this award.

(738) • FOWA Scholarship for Outdoor Communicators

Florida Outdoor Writers Association
24 NW 33 Court, Suite A, Gainesville, FL 32607
Phone: 352-284-1763
Email: dozimmer@ufl.edu
http://www.fowa.org/fowa-scholarship-program/
Purpose: To aid students who plan to enter the field of outdoor communications.
Eligibility: Applicants must be students at Florida colleges or universities or students from any school whose applications are endorsed by a FOWA member or faculty advisor. They must have a career goal that entails communicating love and appreciation of hunting, fishing and other outdoor activities. Selection is based on essay, faculty advisor or FOWA member endorsement, scholastic merit and extracurricular activities. Preference is given to journalism and communications majors.
Target applicant(s): College students. Adult students.
Amount: $1,000.
Number of awards: Varies.
Deadline: May 19.
How to apply: Applications are available online. A cover page, essay, resume and letter of endorsement are required. Other supporting materials will be considered.
Exclusive: Visit www.UltimateScholarshipBook.com and enter code FL73820 for updates on this award.

(739) • Francis X. Crowley Scholarship

New England Water Works Association
125 Hopping Brook Road, Holliston, MA 01746
Phone: 508-893-7979
Email: tmacelhaney@preloadinc.com
http://www.newwa.org

Purpose: To support civil engineering, environmental engineering and business management students.

Eligibility: Applicants must be New England Water Works Association student members. They must be enrolled in a postsecondary degree program in civil engineering, environmental engineering or business management. Selection is based on the overall strength of the application.

Target applicant(s): High school students. College students. Graduate school students. Adult students.

Amount: $3,000.

Number of awards: 1.

Deadline: April 1.

How to apply: Applications are available online. An application form, a personal essay, an official transcript and one recommendation letter are required.

Exclusive: Visit www.UltimateScholarshipBook.com and enter code NE73920 for updates on this award.

(740) • Frank Blau, Jr. Award

Nexstar Legacy Foundation
125 Little Canada Road West, Suite 200, Little Canada, MN 55117
Phone: (651) 789-8518
http://www.nexstarfoundation.org

Purpose: To support students who are seeking a four-year degree related to running an HVAC, plumbing or electrical business.

Eligibility: Applicants must be seeking a four-year university degree. Students must be seeking a degree in either business management, mechanical engineering, marketing or another business function related to running an HVAC, plumbing or electrical business.

Target applicant(s): High school students. College students. Adult students.

Amount: $6,000.

Number of awards: 1.

Deadline: November 1.

How to apply: Applications are available online.

Exclusive: Visit www.UltimateScholarshipBook.com and enter code NE74020 for updates on this award.

(741) • Frank J. Richter Scholarship

American Association of Railroad Superintendents
P.O. Box 200, LaFox, IL 60147
Phone: 331-643-3369
http://www.supt.org/Scholarships

Purpose: To support undergraduate and graduate students in pursuing a degree in a transportation-related field.

Eligibility: Applicants must be enrolled full-time at an accredited educational institution. A minimum GPA of 2.75 is required. Students must submit official grade transcripts and two letters of recommendation. Selection is based on the overall strength of the application.

Target applicant(s): College students. Graduate school students. Adult students.

Minimum GPA: 2.75

Amount: $1,000.

Number of awards: 1.

Deadline: July 1.

How to apply: Applications are available online.

Exclusive: Visit www.UltimateScholarshipBook.com and enter code AM74120 for updates on this award.

(742) • Frank M. Coda Scholarship

American Society of Heating, Refrigerating and Air-Conditioning Engineers (ASHRAE)
1791 Tullie Circle, NE, Atlanta, GA 30329
Phone: 404-636-8400
Email: lbenedict@ashrae.org
http://www.ashrae.org

Purpose: To support undergraduate students who are preparing for careers in the heating, ventilation, air-conditioning and refrigeration industry.

Eligibility: Applicants must be current or entering full-time undergraduates enrolled in a bachelor's of science, bachelor's of engineering or pre-engineering degree program in preparation for a career in HVACR. They must attend a school that has an ASHRAE student branch, is accredited by ABET or is accredited by a non-USA agency that has signed a Memorandum of Understanding with ABET or the Washington Accord. They must be in the top 30 percent of their class and must have a GPA of 3.0 or higher on a four-point scale. Selection is based on the overall strength of the application.

Target applicant(s): High school students. College students. Adult students.

Minimum GPA: 3.0

Amount: $5,000.

Number of awards: 1.

Scholarship may be renewable.

Deadline: December 1.

How to apply: Applications are available online. An application form, official college transcript (or proof of enrollment for rising freshmen) and two letters of reference are required.

Exclusive: Visit www.UltimateScholarshipBook.com and enter code AM74220 for updates on this award.

(743) • Frank Sarli Memorial Scholarship

National Court Reporters Association
8224 Old Courthouse Road, Vienna, VA 22182-3808
Phone: 800-272-6272
Email: dgaede@ncrahq.org
http://www.ncraonline.org

Purpose: To support the court reporting profession.

Eligibility: Applicants must be in good academic standing at an approved court-reporting program, be members of the NCRA and have a minimum 3.5 GPA.

Target applicant(s): College students. Adult students.

Minimum GPA: 3.5

Amount: $2,000.

Number of awards: 1.

Deadline: Varies.

How to apply: Applications are available online.

Exclusive: Visit www.UltimateScholarshipBook.com and enter code NA74320 for updates on this award.

(744) • Fred R. McDaniel Memorial Scholarship

American Radio Relay League Foundation
225 Main Street, Newington, CT 06111-1494
Phone: 860-594-0348
Email: foundation@arrl.org

http://www.arrl.org/scholarship-program
Purpose: To assist ham radio operators in furthering their educations.
Eligibility: Applicants must have at least a general ham radio license, be residents of and attend a post-secondary institution in the FCC Fifth Call District (Texas, Oklahoma, Arkansas, Louisiana, Mississippi or New Mexico) and be studying for a bachelor's or graduate degree in electronics, communications or a related field. Preference is given to applicants with a 3.0 GPA or higher.
Target applicant(s): High school students. College students. Graduate school students. Adult students.
Minimum GPA: 3.0
Amount: $500.
Number of awards: 1.
Deadline: January 31.
How to apply: Applications are available online but must be sent in by mail.
Exclusive: Visit www.UltimateScholarshipBook.com and enter code AM74420 for updates on this award.

(745) • Frederic G. Melcher Scholarship

Association for Library Service to Children
50 E. Huron Street, Chicago, IL 60611
Phone: 800-545-2433
Email: cjewell@ala.org
http://www.ala.org/alsc/awardsgrants
Purpose: To support students who want to become children's librarians.
Eligibility: Applicants must intend to pursue an MLS degree, plan to work in children's librarianship and be U.S. or Canadian citizens. Selection is based on academic excellence, leadership and desire to work with children in any type of library.
Target applicant(s): College students. Graduate school students. Adult students.
Amount: $7,500.
Number of awards: 2.
Deadline: March 1.
How to apply: Applications are available online.
Exclusive: Visit www.UltimateScholarshipBook.com and enter code AS74520 for updates on this award.

(746) • Frederick Burkhardt Residential Fellowships for Recently Tenured Scholars

American Council of Learned Societies (ACLS)
633 Third Avenue, New York, NY 10017-6795
Phone: 212-697-1505
Email: mgoldfeder@acls.org
https://www.acls.org/
Purpose: To support scholars researching in the humanities field.
Eligibility: Applicants must be recently tenured humanists and must be employed in tenured positions at U.S. degree-granting institutions during the fellowship. An application, a proposal, a bibliography, a publications list, three reference letters and one institutional statement are required. Previous supported research leaves do not affect eligibility.
Target applicant(s): Graduate school students. Adult students.
Amount: $95,000.
Number of awards: Varies.
Deadline: September 28.
How to apply: Applications are available online.
Exclusive: Visit www.UltimateScholarshipBook.com and enter code AM74620 for updates on this award.

(747) • Fredrikson & Byron Foundation Minority Scholarship Program

Fredrikson and Byron, P.A.
200 S. Sixth Street, Suite 4000, Minneapolis, MN 55402-1425
Phone: 612-492-7000
Email: market@fredlaw.com
http://www.fredlaw.com
Purpose: To provide opportunities for law students from diverse backgrounds.
Eligibility: In addition to the financial award, scholarship winners are also invited to serve as summer associates at the firm. An application form, two recommendations, a writing sample, a current law school transcript, an undergraduate transcript and a resume are required.
Target applicant(s): Graduate school students. Adult students.
Amount: $15,000.
Number of awards: 1.
Deadline: March 31.
How to apply: Applications are available online.
Exclusive: Visit www.UltimateScholarshipBook.com and enter code FR74720 for updates on this award.

(748) • FTEE Scholarship: Undergraduate Major in Technology and Engineering Education

International Technology and Engineering Educators Association
Foundation for Technology and Engineering Educators, 1914 Association Drive, Suite 201, Reston, VA 20191-1539
Phone: 703-860-2100
Email: iteea@iteea.org
https://www.iteea.org/Activities/AwardsScholarships.aspx
Purpose: To support undergraduate students majoring in technology education teacher preparation.
Eligibility: Applicants must be members of ITEEA, be full-time undergraduate students and have a minimum 2.5 GPA.
Target applicant(s): College students. Adult students.
Minimum GPA: 2.5
Amount: $1,000.
Number of awards: 1.
Deadline: December 1.
How to apply: Application information is available online.
Exclusive: Visit www.UltimateScholarshipBook.com and enter code IN74820 for updates on this award.

(749) • Fund for American Studies Internships

Fund for American Studies
1621 New Hampshire Avenue NW, Washington, DC 20009
Phone: 800-741-6964
Email: admissions@tfas.org
https://tfas.org/awards/
Purpose: To provide scholarships for students attending one of the Fund's internship programs.
Eligibility: There are programs in comparative political and economic systems, political journalism, business and government, philanthropy and international institutes. Each program includes classes, an internship and special events. Students live in on-campus housing at George Washington University or in furnished apartments in the Capitol Hill neighborhood. Each student takes 3-9 credit hours in courses at George Mason University in addition to interning 30-35 hours per week. Summer and school-year programs are available.
Target applicant(s): College students. Adult students.
Amount: Varies.

Number of awards: Varies.
Deadline: Varies.
How to apply: Applications are available online.
Exclusive: Visit www.UltimateScholarshipBook.com and enter code FU74920 for updates on this award.

(750) • Fundera College Scholarship

Fundera
123 William Street, 21st Floor, New York, NY 10038
Phone: 800-386-3372
https://www.fundera.com/resources/fundera-scholarship
Purpose: To assist aspiring entrepreneurs with the cost of education.
Eligibility: Applicants must be enrolling or currently enrolled at a university or college in the U.S. Students must create a short video pertaining to small business and technology and publish it on social media channels.
Target applicant(s): High school students. College students. Graduate school students. Adult students.
Amount: $2,000.
Number of awards: 1.
Deadline: June 1.
How to apply: Applications are available online.
Exclusive: Visit www.UltimateScholarshipBook.com and enter code FU75020 for updates on this award.

(751) • Future Teacher Scholarship

Journalism Education Association Future Teacher Scholarship
828 Mid-Campus Drive South, 105 Kedzie Hall, Manhattan, KS 66506-1505
Phone: 785-532-5532
Email: cbowen@kent.edu
http://www.jea.org
Purpose: To support education majors who intend to teach scholastic journalism.
Eligibility: Applicants must be a college junior, senior or graduate student in a program designed to prepare him/her for teaching at the secondary level. Current secondary-school journalism teachers who are in a degree program to improve their journalism teaching skills are also eligible.
Target applicant(s): College students. Graduate school students. Adult students.
Amount: $1,000.
Number of awards: 5.
Deadline: July 15.
How to apply: Applications are available online.
Exclusive: Visit www.UltimateScholarshipBook.com and enter code JO75120 for updates on this award.

(752) • Gamma Theta Upsilon-Geographical Honor Society Scholarships

Gamma Theta Upsilon
Dr. Michael Longan, Geography and Meteorology Department, Kallay-Christopher Hall , 201C Valparaiso University, Valparaiso, IN 46383
Phone: 219-464-6874
Email: Mike.Longan@valpo.edu
http://gammathetaupsilon.org/scholarships.html
Purpose: To support geography knowledge and awareness by awarding monetary assistance to college and graduate students.
Eligibility: Applicants must be initiated through a Gamma Theta Upsilon chapter.
Target applicant(s): College students. Graduate school students. Adult students.
Amount: Varies.
Number of awards: 5.
Deadline: June 1.
How to apply: Applications are available online.
Exclusive: Visit www.UltimateScholarshipBook.com and enter code GA75220 for updates on this award.

(753) • Gary Yoshimura Scholarship

Public Relations Student Society of America
33 Maiden Lane, 11th Floor, New York, NY 10038
Phone: 212-460-1474
Email: prssa@prsa.org
http://prssa.prsa.org/scholarships-and-awards/
Purpose: To assist public relations students.
Eligibility: Applicants must be PRSSA members with a minimum 3.0 GPA in the pursuit of higher education in the public relations field. Applicants must submit an essay on personal or professional challenges and a statement on financial need.
Target applicant(s): High school students. College students. Graduate school students. Adult students.
Minimum GPA: 3.0
Amount: $2,400.
Number of awards: 1.
Deadline: May 26.
How to apply: Applications are available online.
Exclusive: Visit www.UltimateScholarshipBook.com and enter code PU75320 for updates on this award.

(754) • George A. Strait Minority Scholarship

American Association of Law Libraries
105 W. Adams, Suite 3300, Chicago, IL 60603
Phone: 312-939-4764
Email: scholarships@aall.org
https://www.aallnet.org/mm/Member-Resources
Purpose: To encourage minorities to enter careers as law librarians.
Eligibility: Applicants must be a member of a minority group as defined by U.S. government rules, degree candidates in an accredited library or law school and intend to pursue a career as law librarians. Law library experience is preferred. Applicants must also have financial need and have at least one quarter or semester left after the scholarship is given.
Target applicant(s): Graduate school students. Adult students.
Amount: Varies.
Number of awards: Varies.
Scholarship may be renewable.
Deadline: April 1.
How to apply: Applications are available online, by mail with a self-addressed, stamped envelope, by fax, by phone or by email.
Exclusive: Visit www.UltimateScholarshipBook.com and enter code AM75420 for updates on this award.

(755) • Giles Sutherland Rich Memorial Scholarship

Federal Circuit Bar Association
1620 I Street NW, Suite 801, Washington, DC 20006
Phone: 202-466-3923
Email: fcbascholarships@fedcirbar.org
http://www.fedcirbar.org

Purpose: To support promising law students who demonstrate financial need.
Eligibility: Applicants must be undergraduate or graduate law students who demonstrate academic ability and financial need. They must submit a one-page statement describing their financial need, their interest in law and their qualifications for the award. Applicants must also submit a transcript and curriculum vitae.
Target applicant(s): College students. Graduate school students. Adult students.
Amount: $10,000.
Number of awards: 1.
Deadline: April 15.
How to apply: There is no application form.
Exclusive: Visit www.UltimateScholarshipBook.com and enter code FE75520 for updates on this award.

---

(756) • Goldberg-Miller Public Finance Scholarship

Government Finance Officers Association
203 N. LaSalle Street, Suite 2700, Chicago, IL 60601
Phone: 312-977-9700
http://www.gfoa.org
Purpose: To support graduate students pursuing a career in state/provincial or local government finance.
Eligibility: Applicants must be permanent residents of the U.S. or Canada. Students may not be previous winners of a Government Finance Officers Association (GFOA) scholarship.
Target applicant(s): Graduate school students. Adult students.
Amount: $15,000.
Number of awards: 1.
Deadline: January.
How to apply: Applications available online.
Exclusive: Visit www.UltimateScholarshipBook.com and enter code GO75620 for updates on this award.

---

(757) • Golden Gate Restaurant Association Scholarship Foundation

Golden Gate Restaurant Association
Scholarship Foundation, 220 Montgomery Street, Suite 990, San Francisco, CA 94104
Phone: 415-781-5348
Email: ggra@ggra.org
http://www.ggra.org
Purpose: To provide scholarships for college students who wish to pursue a career in the restaurant/food service industry.
Eligibility: Applicants must be California residents at time of application submission and pursue a major in food service.
Target applicant(s): High school students. College students. Adult students.
Amount: Varies.
Number of awards: Varies.
Deadline: April 30.
How to apply: Applications are available online or by mail.
Exclusive: Visit www.UltimateScholarshipBook.com and enter code GO75720 for updates on this award.

---

(758) • Gorilla 76 Women in Marketing Scholarship

Gorilla 76
408 N. Euclid Avenue, St. Louis, MO 63108
Email: scholarship@gorilla76.com
https://www.gorilla76.com/the-gorilla-76-women-in-marketing-scholarship/
Purpose: To support female students pursuing a career in digital marketing.
Eligibility: Applicants must be female students at the sophomore or upperclassmen level of an accredited college or university. Students must provide a resume, GPA and two essays.
Target applicant(s): College students. Adult students.
Amount: $750.
Number of awards: 1.
Deadline: August 6.
How to apply: Applications are available online.
Exclusive: Visit www.UltimateScholarshipBook.com and enter code GO75820 for updates on this award.

---

(759) • Great Scholarship Program

Great Clips
4400 W. 78th Street, Suite 700, Minneapolis, MN 55435
Phone: 800-999-5959
http://jobs.greatclips.com/page/show/schools-scholarships
Purpose: To support students who are pursuing a career in cosmetology.
Eligibility: Selection is based on the overall strength of the application.
Target applicant(s): High school students.
Amount: $250-$1,500.
Number of awards: Varies.
Deadline: March 31.
How to apply: Applications are available online.
Exclusive: Visit www.UltimateScholarshipBook.com and enter code GR75920 for updates on this award.

---

(760) • GreenPal Business Scholarship

GreenPal
1312 5th Avenue North, Nashville, TN 37208
http://www.yourgreenpal.com/scholarship
Purpose: To assist students who are running a small business or who have a small business idea.
Eligibility: Applicants must be high school seniors or college freshmen or sophomores who own and operate a small business or who have a business plan to begin a small business while in college. Students must also be business majors and have a minimum 3.0 GPA. Applicants must also attend full-time a two- or four-year college, university or vocational or technical school in the U.S.
Target applicant(s): High school students. College students. Adult students.
Minimum GPA: 3.0
Amount: $2,000.
Number of awards: 1.
Scholarship may be renewable.
Deadline: February 28.
How to apply: Applications are available online.
Exclusive: Visit www.UltimateScholarshipBook.com and enter code GR76020 for updates on this award.

---

(761) • Harrell Family Fellowship

American Center of Oriental Research (ACOR)
656 Beacon Street, 5th Floor, Boston, MA 02215-2010
Phone: 617-353-6571
Email: acor@bu.edu
http://www.acorjordan.org

Purpose: To assist a graduate student with expenses on an archaeological project in Jordan.
Eligibility: Applicants must be graduate students in a program approved by a recognized academic review body. The funds must be used for archaeological or related research.
Target applicant(s): Graduate school students. Adult students.
Amount: $2,000.
Number of awards: 1.
Deadline: February 1.
How to apply: Applications are available online.
Exclusive: Visit www.UltimateScholarshipBook.com and enter code AM76120 for updates on this award.

(762) • Harry A. Applegate Scholarship

DECA Inc.
1908 Association Drive, Reston, VA 20191
Phone: 703-860-5000
Email: kathy_onion@deca.org
http://www.deca.org
Purpose: To reward current active members of DECA, the high school division or Delta Epsilon Chi, the college division of DECA.
Eligibility: Applicants must plan to be full-time students at a two-year or four-year program in marketing, entrepreneurship or management. This award is based on merit, not financial need, but applicants may include financial need statements for review. Applicants should submit transcripts, test scores, a statement of club participation, proof of leadership outside DECA, three recommendation letters and proof of membership.
Target applicant(s): High school students. College students. Adult students.
Amount: Varies.
Number of awards: Varies.
Deadline: January 13.
How to apply: Applications are available online and should be submitted to state/provincial DECA advisors.
Exclusive: Visit www.UltimateScholarshipBook.com and enter code DE76220 for updates on this award.

(763) • Harry S. Truman Research Grant

Harry S. Truman Library Institute for National and International Affairs
Grants Administrator, 500 W. U.S. Highway 24, Independence, MO 64050
Phone: 816-268-8248
Email: sullivan.hstli@gmail.com
http://www.trumanlibraryinstitute.org/research-grants/
Purpose: To promote the Truman Library as a center for research.
Eligibility: Graduate students and post-doctoral scholars are most encouraged to apply, but others completing advanced research will be considered. Preference is given to research that has a high chance of being published or otherwise shared publicly. Applicants can receive up to two research grants in a five-year period. Grant winners must submit a report at the end of their studies.
Target applicant(s): Graduate school students. Adult students.
Amount: Up to $2,500.
Number of awards: Varies.
Deadline: April 1 and October 1.
How to apply: Applications are available online.
Exclusive: Visit www.UltimateScholarshipBook.com and enter code HA76320 for updates on this award.

(764) • Hawaii Association of Broadcasters Scholarship

Hawaii Association of Broadcasters Inc.
P.O. Box 61562, Honolulu, HI 96839
Phone: 808-599-1455
Email: jamie@hawaiibroadcasters.com
http://hawaiibroadcasters.com/wp/index.php/scholarships/
Purpose: To support students pursuing careers in broadcasting.
Eligibility: Applicants must be high school seniors or undergraduate students and attend an accredited two- or four-year college, university or broadcast school in the U.S. full-time. Students must also have a 2.5 GPA or higher and intend to work in the broadcast industry in Hawaii upon completion of their education.
Target applicant(s): High school students. College students. Adult students.
Minimum GPA: 2.5
Amount: Varies.
Number of awards: 1.
Deadline: Varies.
How to apply: Applications are available online. An application form, letter of recommendation and a personal interview are required.
Exclusive: Visit www.UltimateScholarshipBook.com and enter code HA76420 for updates on this award.

(765) • Helen Lansdowne Resor Scholarship

J. Walter Thompson
466 Lexington Avenue, New York, NY 10017
Phone: 212-210-7000
https://www.jwt.com/hlrscholarship/
Purpose: To support female creative advertising students pursue a higher education.
Eligibility: Applicants must be female undergraduate, graduate or portfolio students with at least twelve months remaining until graduation. Students must show creative talent and promise in a course of study such as art direction, design or copywriting.
Target applicant(s): High school students. College students. Graduate school students. Adult students.
Amount: $10,000.
Number of awards: 5.
Deadline: May 14.
How to apply: Applications are available online.
Exclusive: Visit www.UltimateScholarshipBook.com and enter code J.76520 for updates on this award.

(766) • Henry Belin du Pont Dissertation Fellowship

Hagley Museum and Library
Center for the History of Business, Technology and Society, 298 Buck Road, Wilmington, DE 19807
Phone: 302-658-2400
Email: clockman@Hagley.org
http://www.hagley.org
Purpose: To provide four-month fellowships for doctoral students performing dissertation research.
Eligibility: Applicants must be doctoral students who have completed all course work and are performing dissertation research. Research topics should involve historical questions and should relate to the collections in the Hagley Library. Fellows will receive housing, office space, a computer and Internet access. A presentation is required at the end of the residence period.
Target applicant(s): Graduate school students. Adult students.

Amount: $6,500 plus housing.
Number of awards: Varies.
Deadline: November 15.
How to apply: Applications are available online. For more information contact Dr. Roger Horowitz at rhorowitz@hagley.org.
Exclusive: Visit www.UltimateScholarshipBook.com and enter code HA76620 for updates on this award.

---

(767) · Herbert Hoover Presidential Library Association Travel Grant Program

Hoover Presidential Foundation
P.O. Box 696, West Branch, IA 52358
Phone: 800-828-0475
Email: info@hooverpf.org
http://www.hooverpresidentialfoundation.org
Purpose: To provide financial aid to individuals to research at the Herbert Hoover Presidential Library in West Branch, Iowa.
Eligibility: Applicants must be current graduate students, post-doctoral scholars or independent researchers. Applicants must also ensure that the library's contents will meet their research needs before applying.
Target applicant(s): Graduate school students. Adult students.
Amount: $500-$1,500.
Number of awards: Varies.
Deadline: March 1.
How to apply: Applications are available online.
Exclusive: Visit www.UltimateScholarshipBook.com and enter code HO76720 for updates on this award.

---

(768) · Horatio Alger Career & Technical Scholarship

Horatio Alger Association
Attn.: Scholarship Department, 99 Canal Center Plaza, Suite 320, Alexandria, VA 22314
Phone: 703-684-9444
Email: association@horatioalger.org
https://scholars.horatioalger.org/
Purpose: To support students who have overcome great obstacles.
Eligibility: Applicants must be U.S. citizens under the age of 30 who are enrolling in a career or technical program at an accredited non-profit institution. Students must demonstrate financial need and perseverance in overcoming adversity.
Target applicant(s): High school students. College students. Adult students.
Amount: $2,500.
Number of awards: 2,061.
Deadline: June 15.
How to apply: Applications are available online.
Exclusive: Visit www.UltimateScholarshipBook.com and enter code HO76820 for updates on this award.

---

(769) · HORIZONS Foundation Scholarship

Women In Defense
HORIZONS Foundation, c/o National Defense Industrial Association, 2111 Wilson Boulevard, Suite 400, Arlington, VA 22201
Phone: 703-247-2552
Email: jcasey@ndia.org
http://wid.ndia.org
Purpose: To encourage women to pursue careers related to the national security interests of the United States and to provide development opportunities to women already working in national security fields.
Eligibility: Applicants must be full- or part-time female students at an accredited Michigan university or college and must have reached at least junior level status. Students must be residents of Michigan. Applicants must also demonstrate an interest in a career related to national security and defense, have a minimum GPA of 3.25 and demonstrate financial need. Preference is given to students in security studies, military history, government relations, engineering, computer science, physics, mathematics, business, law, international relations, political science or economics.
Target applicant(s): College students. Graduate school students. Adult students.
Minimum GPA: 3.25
Amount: Varies.
Number of awards: Varies.
Deadline: May 12.
How to apply: Applications are available online.
Exclusive: Visit www.UltimateScholarshipBook.com and enter code WO76920 for updates on this award.

---

(770) · HSMAI Foundation Scholarship

Hospitality Sales and Marketing Association International (HSMAI)
7918 Jones Branch Drive, Suite 300, McLean, VA 22102
Phone: 703-506-2010
Email: info@hsmai.org
http://www.hsmai.org/trends/content.cfm?ItemNumber=4856&navItemNumber=526
Purpose: To assist students pursuing a career in hospitality sales and marketing.
Eligibility: Applicants must be full-time or part-time undergraduate or graduate students pursuing a career in hospitality sales and marketing. Amounts of scholarships vary from year to year.
Target applicant(s): College students. Graduate school students. Adult students.
Amount: Varies.
Number of awards: Varies.
Deadline: Varies.
How to apply: Applications are available online.
Exclusive: Visit www.UltimateScholarshipBook.com and enter code HO77020 for updates on this award.

---

(771) · Huntington Fellowships

Huntington Library, Art Collections and Botanical Gardens
1151 Oxford Road, San Marino, CA 91108
Phone: 626-405-2194
Email: cpowell@huntington.org
http://www.huntington.org
Purpose: To provide fellowships to doctoral students and recipients in British and American history, literature, art history and the history of science and medicine.
Eligibility: Applicants must have a Ph.D. or equivalent or be doctoral candidates at the dissertation stage. Cover sheets, project descriptions, curriculum vitae and three letters of recommendation are required.
Target applicant(s): Graduate school students. Adult students.
Amount: $3,000.
Number of awards: More than 150.
Deadline: November 15.
How to apply: Application materials are described online.
Exclusive: Visit www.UltimateScholarshipBook.com and enter code HU77120 for updates on this award.

(772) • Huntington-British Academy Fellowships for Study in Great Britain

Huntington Library, Art Collections and Botanical Gardens
1151 Oxford Road, San Marino, CA 91108
Phone: 626-405-2194
Email: cpowell@huntington.org
http://www.huntington.org

Purpose: To offer scholars exchange fellowships to research British and American history, literature, art history and the history of science and medicine.
Eligibility: Applicants must have a Ph.D. or equivalent. Applicants must submit cover sheets, project descriptions, curriculum vitae and three letters of recommendation.
Target applicant(s): Graduate school students. Adult students.
Amount: Varies.
Number of awards: Varies.
Deadline: November 15.
How to apply: There is no application form, and application materials are described online.
Exclusive: Visit www.UltimateScholarshipBook.com and enter code HU77220 for updates on this award.

(773) • IEHA Scholarship

International Executive Housekeepers Association (IEHA) Education Foundation
1001 Eastwind Drive, Suite 301, Westerville, OH 43081-3361
Phone: 800-200-6342
Email: excel@ieha.org
http://www.ieha.org

Purpose: To support IEHA members who are pursuing undergraduate or associate's degrees or IEHA certification.
Eligibility: Applicants must submit a 2,000-word manuscript about an issue in the housekeeping industry. The winning manuscript will be selected by a panel of judges and published.
Target applicant(s): High school students. College students. Adult students.
Amount: Varies.
Number of awards: Varies.
Deadline: January 10.
How to apply: Applications are available online.
Exclusive: Visit www.UltimateScholarshipBook.com and enter code IN77320 for updates on this award.

(774) • IFEC Scholarships Award

International Foodservice Editorial Council (IFEC)
P.O. Box 491, Hyde Park, NY 12538
Phone: 845-229-6973
Email: ifec@ifeconline.com
http://www.ifeconline.com

Purpose: To assist students interested in foodservice combined with communication arts.
Eligibility: Applicants must be enrolled at a post-secondary, degree-granting educational institution and must demonstrate training, skill and interest in the foodservice industry and communication arts. Eligible majors from foodservice and communications areas include culinary arts, hotel/restaurant/hospitality management, dietetics, nutrition, food science/technology, journalism, public relations, mass communication, English, broadcast journalism, marketing, photography, graphic arts and related studies.
Target applicant(s): College students. Graduate school students. Adult students.
Amount: $1,500-$6,000.
Number of awards: 6.
Deadline: March 15.
How to apply: Applications are available online.
Exclusive: Visit www.UltimateScholarshipBook.com and enter code IN77420 for updates on this award.

(775) • IFSEA Worthy Goal Scholarship

International Food Service Executives Association
4955 Miller Street, Suite 107, Wheat Ridge, CO 80033
Phone: 502-589-3602
https://www.ifsea.org

Purpose: To help students receive food service management training beyond the high school level.
Eligibility: Applicants must be enrolled or accepted at a college as a full-time student in a food service related major. Students must provide a financial statement, personal statement, list of work experience and professional activities, transcripts, recommendations and a statement describing how the scholarship would help them reach their goals.
Target applicant(s): High school students. College students. Graduate school students. Adult students.
Amount: $250-$1,500.
Number of awards: Varies.
Deadline: February 1.
How to apply: Applications are available online.
Exclusive: Visit www.UltimateScholarshipBook.com and enter code IN77520 for updates on this award.

(776) • IMA Memorial Education Fund Scholarship

Institute of Management Accountants (IMA)
10 Paragon Drive, Montvale, NJ 07645-1760
Phone: 800-638-4427
Email: students@imanet.org
http://www.imanet.org

Purpose: To support students in fields related to management accounting.
Eligibility: Applicants must be full- and part-time undergraduate and graduate students, be IMA student members and declare which four- or five-year management accounting, financial management or information technology related program they plan to pursue as a career or list a related field. Candidates should submit applications, resumes, transcripts, two recommendations and statements. Advanced degree students must pass one part of the CMA/CFM certification.
Target applicant(s): College students. Graduate school students. Adult students.
Minimum GPA: 3.0
Amount: $1,000-$2,500.
Number of awards: Varies.
Deadline: March 20.
How to apply: Applications are available online.
Exclusive: Visit www.UltimateScholarshipBook.com and enter code IN77620 for updates on this award.

(777) • Imagine America High School Scholarship Program

Imagine America Foundation
12001 Sunrise Valley Drive, Suite 203, Reston, VA 20191

Phone: 571-267-3010
Email: Leed@imagine-america.org
https://www.imagine-america.org/students/scholarships-education/
Purpose: To help high school seniors pursue a postsecondary career education.
Eligibility: Applicants must have a minimum 2.5 high school GPA, demonstrate financial need and have demonstrated community service during their senior year.
Target applicant(s): High school students.
Minimum GPA: 2.5
Amount: $1,000.
Number of awards: 5.
Deadline: December 31.
How to apply: Applications are available online.
Exclusive: Visit www.UltimateScholarshipBook.com and enter code IM77720 for updates on this award.

(778) · Incoming Freshman Scholarship

American Hotel and Lodging Educational Foundation (AHLEF)
1250 I Street NW, Suite 1100, Washington, DC 20005-3931
Phone: 202-289-3180
Email: foundation@ahlef.org
https://www.ahlef.org/Scholarships/Academic_Scholarships/
Purpose: To recognize high school students who are interested in hospitality-related programs.
Eligibility: Applicants must be graduating seniors with preference given to those who have completed the two-year Lodging Management Program (LMP) high school program. Students must be planning to attend a post-secondary institution, be U.S. citizens or permanent residents and have a minimum 2.0 GPA.
Target applicant(s): High school students.
Minimum GPA: 2.0
Amount: $2,000-$4,000.
Number of awards: Varies.
Deadline: May 1.
How to apply: Applications are available online.
Exclusive: Visit www.UltimateScholarshipBook.com and enter code AM77820 for updates on this award.

(779) · International Facility Management Association Foundation Scholarship Program

International Facility Management Association
800 Gessner Road, Suite 900, Houston, TX 77024-4257
Phone: 713-623-4362
Email: amy.arnold@ifma.org
http://foundation.ifma.org
Purpose: To support students currently enrolled in facility management or facility management-related programs.
Eligibility: Applicants must be college or graduate students and include a letter of professional intent, resume and letter of recommendation with application.
Target applicant(s): College students. Graduate school students. Adult students.
Minimum GPA: 3.2
Amount: Varies.
Number of awards: Varies.
Deadline: April 20.
How to apply: Applications are available online.
Exclusive: Visit www.UltimateScholarshipBook.com and enter code IN77920 for updates on this award.

(780) · International Technology Engineering Educators Association Scholarship - FTEE/ Undergraduate

International Technology and Engineering Educators Association Foundation for Technology and Engineering Educators, 1914 Association Drive, Suite 201, Reston, VA 20191-1539
Phone: 703-860-2100
Email: iteea@iteea.org
https://www.iteea.org/Activities/AwardsScholarships.aspx
Purpose: To encourage students majoring in technology and engineering education teacher preparation.
Eligibility: Applicants must be members of the International Technology Education Association. Students must not be a senior by the application deadline. Applicants must be full-time undergraduate students majoring in technology and engineering education teacher preparation.
Target applicant(s): College students. Adult students.
Minimum GPA: 2.5
Amount: $1,000.
Number of awards: 1.
Deadline: December 1.
How to apply: Applications are available online.
Exclusive: Visit www.UltimateScholarshipBook.com and enter code IN78020 for updates on this award.

(781) · IRARC Memorial Joseph P. Rubino WA4MMD Scholarship

American Radio Relay League Foundation
225 Main Street, Newington, CT 06111-1494
Phone: 860-594-0348
Email: foundation@arrl.org
http://www.arrl.org/scholarship-program
Purpose: To provide financial assistance to amateur radio operators who are seeking an undergraduate degree or electronic technician certification.
Eligibility: Applicants must hold an active Amateur Radio License in any class and be studying at an accredited institution. They must have a minimum GPA of 2.5. Preference is given to Florida residents, particularly those from Brevard County and those with need and lower GPAs.
Target applicant(s): High school students. College students. Adult students.
Minimum GPA: 2.5
Amount: $750.
Number of awards: Varies.
Deadline: January 31.
How to apply: Applications are available online.
Exclusive: Visit www.UltimateScholarshipBook.com and enter code AM78120 for updates on this award.

(782) · J. Franklin Jameson Fellowship in American History

American Historical Association
400 A Street SE, Washington, DC 20003
Phone: 202-544-2422
Email: info@historians.org
http://www.historians.org
Purpose: To support one semester of scholarly research in the Library of Congress collections.

Eligibility: Applicants must hold a Ph.D. or equivalent, must have earned the degree within the past seven years and may not have published a book-length historical work. Projects should focus on American history.
Target applicant(s): Graduate school students. Adult students.
Amount: $5,000.
Number of awards: Varies.
Deadline: April 1.
How to apply: Application instructions are available online.
Exclusive: Visit www.UltimateScholarshipBook.com and enter code AM78220 for updates on this award.

---

(783) • Jack G Shaheen Mass Communications Scholarship

American-Arab Anti-Discrimination Committee
1705 DeSales Street NW, Suite 500, Washington, DC 20036
Phone: 202-244-2990
http://www.adc.org/adcri/jack-g-shaheen-mass-communications-scholarships/
Purpose: To reward Arab-American students who excel in media studies.
Eligibility: Applicants must be U.S. citizens of Arab heritage currently enrolled in college as an undergraduate junior or senior or as a graduate student. Students must be majoring in journalism, radio television or film. Applicants must have a minimum GPA of 3.0 and provide academic transcripts, a one-page statement, two letters of recommendation and copies of your work.
Target applicant(s): College students. Graduate school students. Adult students.
Minimum GPA: 3.0
Amount: $2,500.
Number of awards: 1.
Deadline: June 8.
How to apply: Applications are available online.
Exclusive: Visit www.UltimateScholarshipBook.com and enter code AM78320 for updates on this award.

---

(784) • JAM Paper Teacher Scholarship

Jam Paper and Envelope
185 Legrand Avenue, Northvale, NJ 07647
Phone: 201-567-6666
Email: scholarship@jampaper.com
http://www.jampaper.com/scholarships.asp
Purpose: To assist students who plan to pursue a career in education.
Eligibility: Applicants must be pursuing a degree in education or a related field and be enrolled at an accredited U.S. college or university.
Target applicant(s): High school students. College students. Adult students.
Amount: $500.
Number of awards: 1.
Deadline: July 14.
How to apply: A 400- to 500-word essay must be emailed.
Exclusive: Visit www.UltimateScholarshipBook.com and enter code JA78420 for updates on this award.

---

(785) • James A. Turner, Jr. Memorial Scholarship

American Welding Society Foundation
550 NW LeJeune Road, Miami, FL 33126
Phone: 800-443-9353
Email: info@aws.org
http://www.aws.org
Purpose: To aid those interested in a management career in welding store operations or distributorship.
Eligibility: Applicants must be full-time students pursuing a four-year bachelor's of business degree, plan to enter management careers in welding store operations or distributorship, be high school graduates at least 18 years of age and be employed a minimum of 10 hours per week at a welding distributorship. Preference is given to members of the American Welding Society.
Target applicant(s): High school students. College students. Graduate school students. Adult students.
Amount: $3,500.
Number of awards: 1.
Deadline: February 15.
How to apply: Applications are available online.
Exclusive: Visit www.UltimateScholarshipBook.com and enter code AM78520 for updates on this award.

---

(786) • James Beard Foundation Scholarship

James Beard Foundation Scholarship Program/Scholarship America
One Scholarship Way, Saint Peter, MN 56082
https://www.scholarsapply.org/jamesbeard/
Purpose: To support students pursuing a culinary education.
Eligibility: Applicants must be graduating high school seniors or graduates pursuing a culinary or food-focused program at an accredited institution.
Target applicant(s): High school students. College students. Adult students.
Amount: Up to $20,000.
Number of awards: 100.
Deadline: May 15.
How to apply: Applications are available online.
Exclusive: Visit www.UltimateScholarshipBook.com and enter code JA78620 for updates on this award.

---

(787) • Jane M. Klausman Women in Business Scholarship Fund

Zonta International
1211 West 22nd Street, Suite 900, Oak Brook, IL 60523
Phone: 630-928-1400
Email: zontaintl@zonta.org
http://www.zonta.org
Purpose: To help female business management majors overcome gender barriers.
Eligibility: Applicants must be women of any age pursuing a business or business-related program who demonstrate outstanding potential. Applicants must also have an outstanding academic record in their college career, and they must show intent to complete a business program.
Target applicant(s): College students. Graduate school students. Adult students.
Amount: $1,000-$7,000.
Number of awards: 44.
Deadline: July 1.
How to apply: Applications are available online or from your local Zonta Club.
Exclusive: Visit www.UltimateScholarshipBook.com and enter code ZO78720 for updates on this award.

(788) • Jennifer C. Groot Fellowship

American Center of Oriental Research (ACOR)
656 Beacon Street, 5th Floor, Boston, MA 02215-2010
Phone: 617-353-6571
Email: acor@bu.edu
http://www.acorjordan.org
Purpose: To assist students with expenses on an archaeological project.
Eligibility: Applicants must be undergraduate or graduate students with little or no archaeological field experience and be U.S. or Canadian citizens. Recipients will travel to Jordan for the project.
Target applicant(s): High school students. College students. Graduate school students. Adult students.
Amount: $1,500.
Number of awards: up to 3.
Deadline: February 1.
How to apply: Applications are available online but must be submitted by mail.
Exclusive: Visit www.UltimateScholarshipBook.com and enter code AM78820 for updates on this award.

(789) • JFLF Awards Programs

James F. Lincoln Arc Welding Foundation
Secretary, P.O. Box 17188, Cleveland, OH 44117-9949
http://www.jflf.org
Purpose: To award prizes for arc welding projects made by the applicant or a group of applicants.
Eligibility: Projects may fit into one of the following categories: home, recreational or artistic equipment; shop tool, machine or mechanical device; a structure; agricultural equipment or a repair. Applicants must submit a paper about the creation of the project and be enrolled in a shop class. Applicants must also be enrolled in high school, adult evening classes, two-year/community college, vocational school, apprentice program, trade school, in-plant training or technical school and may not be college students enrolled in a bachelor's or master's program.
Target applicant(s): High school students. College students. Adult students.
Amount: Up to $1,000.
Number of awards: 95.
Deadline: February 1.
How to apply: Applications are available online.
Exclusive: Visit www.UltimateScholarshipBook.com and enter code JA78920 for updates on this award.

(790) • Joe Francis Haircare Scholarship Program

Joe Francis Haircare Scholarship Foundation
P.O. Box 50625, Minneapolis, MN 55405
Phone: 651-769-1757
http://www.joefrancis.com
Purpose: To provide barber and cosmetology students with financial aid.
Eligibility: Applicants must be sponsored by one of the following: a fully accredited, recognized barber or cosmetology school, a licensed salon owner or manager, a full-service distributor or a member of the International Chain Association, Beauty and Barber Supply Institute, Cosmetology Advancement Foundation or National Cosmetology Association. Applicants must be actively enrolled in cosmetology school or planning to enroll during or after the award month of August. Judging is based on financial need, motivation and character.
Target applicant(s): High school students. College students. Adult students.
Amount: $1,200.
Number of awards: Varies.
Deadline: June 1.
How to apply: Applications are available online.
Exclusive: Visit www.UltimateScholarshipBook.com and enter code JO79020 for updates on this award.

(791) • Joe Perdue Scholarship

Club Foundation
1733 King Street, Alexandria, VA 22314
Phone: 703-739-9500
Email: schaverr@clubfoundation.org
http://www.clubfoundation.org
Purpose: To support students pursuing careers in private club management.
Eligibility: Applicants must be pursuing managerial careers in the private club industry, have completed their freshman year of college, have a minimum 2.5 GPA and be enrolled full-time for the following year. An essay and letters of recommendation are also required.
Target applicant(s): College students. Adult students.
Minimum GPA: 2.5
Amount: $2,500.
Number of awards: Varies.
Deadline: May 1.
How to apply: Applications are available online.
Exclusive: Visit www.UltimateScholarshipBook.com and enter code CL79120 for updates on this award.

(792) • John Bayliss Radio Scholarship

John Bayliss Broadcast Foundation
171 17th Street, Pacific Grove, CA 93950
Phone: 212-424-6410
Email: cbutrum@baylissfoundation.org
http://www.beaweb.org/bayliss/radio.html
Purpose: This scholarship helps students who are pursuing careers in radio.
Eligibility: Applicants must be attending an institution of higher learning in the U.S., be entering their junior or senior year and have a GPA of 3.0 or higher. Students must be working toward a career in the radio industry. Preference is given to students with a history of radio-related activities and those pursuing careers in commercial radio.
Target applicant(s): College students. Adult students.
Minimum GPA: 3.0
Amount: $5,000.
Number of awards: Varies.
Deadline: Varies.
How to apply: Applications are available online. An application form, resume, transcript, essay and three letters of recommendation are required.
Exclusive: Visit www.UltimateScholarshipBook.com and enter code JO79220 for updates on this award.

(793) • John D. Graham Scholarship

Public Relations Student Society of America
33 Maiden Lane, 11th Floor, New York, NY 10038
Phone: 212-460-1474
Email: prssa@prsa.org
http://prssa.prsa.org/scholarships-and-awards/
Purpose: To aid journalism and public relations students.
Eligibility: Applicants must be rising undergraduate seniors who are enrolled in a journalism or public relations degree program. Selection

is based on academic merit, leadership, writing ability, relevant work experience and stated career goals.
Target applicant(s): College students. Adult students.
Amount: $1,000-$3,000.
Number of awards: 3.
Deadline: May 9.
How to apply: Applications are available online. An application form, resume and one recommendation letter are required.
Exclusive: Visit www.UltimateScholarshipBook.com and enter code PU79320 for updates on this award.

(794) • John F. Kennedy Profile in Courage Essay Contest

John F. Kennedy Library Foundation
Columbia Point, Boston, MA 02125
Phone: 617-514-1649
Email: profiles@nara.gov
http://www.jfklibrary.org/Education/Profile-in-Courage-Essay-Contest.aspx
Purpose: To encourage students to research and write about politics and John F. Kennedy.
Eligibility: Applicants must be in grades 9 through 12 in public or private schools or be home-schooled and write an essay about the political courage of a U.S. elected official who served during or after 1956. Essays must have source citations. Applicants must register online before sending essays and have a nominating teacher review the essay. The winner and teacher will be invited to the Kennedy Library to accept the award, and the winner's teacher will receive a grant. Essays are judged on content (55 percent) and presentation (45 percent).
Target applicant(s): High school students.
Amount: $100-$20,000.
Number of awards: Up to 25.
Deadline: January 18.
How to apply: Applications are available online. A registration form and essay are required.
Exclusive: Visit www.UltimateScholarshipBook.com and enter code JO79420 for updates on this award.

(795) • Joseph S. Rumbaugh Historical Oration Contest

National Society, Sons of the American Revolution
1000 South Fourth Street, Louisville, KY 40203
Phone: 502-589-1776
Email: sdelong1@san.rr.com
http://www.sar.org
Purpose: To encourage students to learn more about the Revolutionary War and its impact on modern America.
Eligibility: Applicants must prepare a speech of five to six minutes on some aspect of the Revolutionary War. The contest is open to high school students at public, private and parochial high schools, as well as home-schooled students. Eligibility for the national contest is determined by contests on the state and local level.
Target applicant(s): High school students.
Amount: $200-$5,000.
Number of awards: Varies.
Deadline: Varies.
How to apply: Applications are available from local chapters of Sons of the American Revolution.
Exclusive: Visit www.UltimateScholarshipBook.com and enter code NA79520 for updates on this award.

(796) • Jungle Scholar

Jungle Scout
98 San Jacinto Boulevard, Austin, TX 78701
Phone: 512-664-2014
Email: scholar@junglescout.com
https://www.junglescout.com/jungle-scholar/
Purpose: To support students pursuing business and computer science.
Eligibility: Applicants must be students in a U.S. institution pursuing a degree in business- or computer science-related fields with a passion for entrepreneurship. Students must submit an e-commerce or SaaS concept with their application materials.
Target applicant(s): High school students. College students. Graduate school students. Adult students.
Amount: $2,000.
Number of awards: 1.
Deadline: November 15.
How to apply: Applications are available online.
Exclusive: Visit www.UltimateScholarshipBook.com and enter code JU79620 for updates on this award.

(797) • Junior Fellowships

American Institute of Indian Studies
1130 E. 59th Street, Chicago, IL 60637
Phone: 773-702-8638
Email: aiis@uchicago.edu
http://www.indiastudies.org
Purpose: To support doctoral candidates at U.S. universities who wish to travel to India to conduct dissertation research on Indian aspects of their academic discipline.
Eligibility: Applicants must be doctoral candidates at a U.S. university. Junior fellows are affiliated with Indian universities and research mentors. Awards may last up to 11 months.
Target applicant(s): Graduate school students. Adult students.
Amount: Varies.
Number of awards: Varies.
Deadline: July 1.
How to apply: Applications are available by mail or email.
Exclusive: Visit www.UltimateScholarshipBook.com and enter code AM79720 for updates on this award.

(798) • K2TEO Martin J. Green, Sr. Memorial Scholarship

American Radio Relay League Foundation
225 Main Street, Newington, CT 06111-1494
Phone: 860-594-0348
Email: foundation@arrl.org
http://www.arrl.org/scholarship-program
Purpose: To provide financial assistance to students who are amateur radio operators.
Eligibility: Applicants must hold a general class or higher amateur radio license. Preference is given to students from ham families.
Target applicant(s): High school students. College students. Graduate school students. Adult students.
Amount: $1,000.
Number of awards: 1.
Deadline: January 31.
How to apply: Applications are available online.
Exclusive: Visit www.UltimateScholarshipBook.com and enter code AM79820 for updates on this award.

(799) • Kapitall Joes vs. Pros

New Kapitall Holdings
1460 Broadway, 4th Floor, New York, NY 10036
https://kapitall.com/JVP
Purpose: To support students interested in the stock market.
Eligibility: Applicants must compete in a stock market tournament using virtual dollars. Students must sign up for a free account with the sponsor.
Target applicant(s): Junior high students or younger.
Amount: $10,000.
Number of awards: 1.
Deadline: August 31.
How to apply: Applications are available online.
Exclusive: Visit www.UltimateScholarshipBook.com and enter code NE79920 for updates on this award.

(800) • Kimberly-Clark Corporation Legacy Scholarship

National Grocers Association
1005 N. Glebe Road, Suite 250, Arlington, VA 22201
Phone: 225-387-6126
http://www.nationalgrocers.org
Purpose: To support students pursuing a degree related to the grocery field.
Eligibility: Applicants must be rising sophomores through postgraduate students, have a minimum 2.5 GPA and be enrolled in a two- or four-year degree-granting institution. Students must major in business, food management, IT or another field related to a career in the grocery industry. Experience in the grocery industry is preferred but not required.
Target applicant(s): College students. Graduate school students. Adult students.
Minimum GPA: 2.5
Amount: Varies.
Number of awards: 1.
Deadline: April 15.
How to apply: Applications are available online.
Exclusive: Visit www.UltimateScholarshipBook.com and enter code NA80020 for updates on this award.

(801) • Kit C. King Graduate Scholarship Fund

National Press Photographers Association Kit C. King Graduate Scholarship Fund
Kit C. King Graduate Scholarship Fund, 120 Hooper Street, Athens, GA 30602-3018
Phone: 706-542-2506
Email: jwbrown@nppf.org
http://nppf.org/nppf-scholarships-grants-and-awards/
Purpose: To support photojournalism students.
Eligibility: Applicants must provide a portfolio, be pursuing an advanced degree in journalism with an emphasis in photojournalism and demonstrate financial need. Applicants can apply to as many NPPA scholarships as desired, but only one award will be granted per winner.
Target applicant(s): Graduate school students. Adult students.
Amount: $2,000.
Number of awards: 1.
Deadline: January 6.
How to apply: Applications are available online.
Exclusive: Visit www.UltimateScholarshipBook.com and enter code NA80120 for updates on this award.

(802) • L. B. Cebik, W4RNL and Jean Cebik, N4TZP Memorial Scholarship

American Radio Relay League Foundation
225 Main Street, Newington, CT 06111-1494
Phone: 860-594-0348
Email: foundation@arrl.org
http://www.arrl.org/scholarship-program
Purpose: To provide scholarship assistance to amateur radio operators.
Eligibility: Applicants must hold a Technician Class Amateur Radio License or higher, and they must be attending a four-year college or university.
Target applicant(s): High school students. College students. Adult students.
Amount: $1,000.
Number of awards: 1.
Deadline: January 31.
How to apply: Applications are available online.
Exclusive: Visit www.UltimateScholarshipBook.com and enter code AM80220 for updates on this award.

(803) • L. Phil and Alice J. Wicker Scholarship

American Radio Relay League Foundation
225 Main Street, Newington, CT 06111-1494
Phone: 860-594-0348
Email: foundation@arrl.org
http://www.arrl.org/scholarship-program
Purpose: To assist ham radio operators in furthering their educations.
Eligibility: Applicants must have at least a general ham radio license, be residents of and attending school in the ARRL Roanoke Division (North Carolina, South Carolina, Virginia, West Virginia) and be undergraduate or graduate students in electronics, communications or another related field.
Target applicant(s): College students. Graduate school students. Adult students.
Amount: $500.
Number of awards: 1.
Deadline: January 31.
How to apply: Applications are available online. Completed applications must be submitted by mail.
Exclusive: Visit www.UltimateScholarshipBook.com and enter code AM80320 for updates on this award.

(804) • Laurels Fund Scholarship

Educational Foundation for Women in Accounting
136 South Keowee Street, Dayton, OH 45402-2241
Phone: 610-407-9229
Email: info@efwa.org
http://www.efwa.org
Purpose: To provide scholarships to women pursuing advanced degrees in accounting.
Eligibility: This award is available to women pursuing a Ph.D. in accounting. The awardees are selected based on scholarship, service and financial need. Applicants must have completed their comprehensive exams before the previous fall semester.
Target applicant(s): Graduate school students. Adult students.
Amount: Up to $5,000.
Number of awards: Varies.
Deadline: May 15.
How to apply: Applications are available online.

Exclusive: Visit www.UltimateScholarshipBook.com and enter code ED80420 for updates on this award.

(805) • Lawrence G. Foster Award for Excellence in Public Relations

Public Relations Student Society of America
33 Maiden Lane, 11th Floor, New York, NY 10038
Phone: 212-460-1474
Email: prssa@prsa.org
http://prssa.prsa.org/scholarships-and-awards/
Purpose: To assist public relations students.
Eligibility: Applicants must be undergraduate students majoring in public relations who are committed to careers in public relations and must be PRSSA members. Applicants must submit an essay on what excellence in public relations is and how they plan to achieve excellence in their own careers.
Target applicant(s): High school students. College students. Adult students.
Amount: $1,500.
Number of awards: 1.
Deadline: June 9.
How to apply: Applications are available online.
Exclusive: Visit www.UltimateScholarshipBook.com and enter code PU80520 for updates on this award.

(806) • Learning and Leadership Grants

NEA Foundation
1201 16th Street NW, Washington, DC 20036
Phone: 202-822-7840
Email: NEAFoundation@nea.org
http://www.neafoundation.org/pages/grants-to-educators/
Purpose: To support public school teachers, public education support professionals and faculty or staff in public institutions of higher education in professional development experiences such as summer institutes or action research.
Eligibility: Applicants must be current public school teachers in grades K-12, public school education support professionals or faculty and staff at public higher education institutions. The professional development must improve practice, curriculum and student achievement. Funds may be used for fees, travel expenses, books or materials. There is also a grant for groups for $5,000.
Target applicant(s): Graduate school students. Adult students.
Amount: $2,000-$5,000.
Number of awards: Varies.
Deadline: February 1, June 1, October 15.
How to apply: Applications are available online. Applications may be submitted at any time and are reviewed three times each year on February 1, June 1 and October 15.
Exclusive: Visit www.UltimateScholarshipBook.com and enter code NE80620 for updates on this award.

(807) • Lee Thornton Scholarship

Radio Television Digital News Association
529 14th Street NW, Suite 1240, Washington, DC 20045
Phone: 202-659-6510
Email: karenh@rtdna.org
http://www.rtdna.org
Purpose: To support students pursuing careers in radio, television or digital journalism.
Eligibility: Applicants must be a sophomore, junior or senior at a college or university with preference given to students of the University of Maryland and Howard University. Students should be pursuing a degree in journalism, broadcasting or communications. Applicants must include URL links to three to five work samples.
Target applicant(s): College students. Adult students.
Amount: $2,000.
Number of awards: 1.
Deadline: January 15.
How to apply: Applications are available online.
Exclusive: Visit www.UltimateScholarshipBook.com and enter code RA80720 for updates on this award.

(808) • Legal Leaders Scholarship

Console & Hollawell
525 Route 73 North, Suite 117, Marlton, NJ 08053
Phone: 856-778-5500
Email: jlister@consoleandhollawell.com
http://www.consoleandhollawell.com
Purpose: To assist students who are pursuing careers in law.
Eligibility: Applicants must be pursuing a degree in pre-law or paralegal studies or working towards their juris doctorate in any concentration of the law. Applicants must also be U.S. citizens and full-time students attending or planning to attend an accredited institution of higher education and must have a minimum 3.0 GPA.
Target applicant(s): High school students. College students. Graduate students. Adult students.
Minimum GPA: 3.0
Amount: $1,000.
Number of awards: 1.
Deadline: July 15.
How to apply: Applications are available online. An application form and 500-word essay on how the student will "make the world a better place through their work in the law" are required. In addition, students must also provide a transcript and proof of acceptance and enrollment.
Exclusive: Visit www.UltimateScholarshipBook.com and enter code CO80820 for updates on this award.

(809) • Legal Opportunity Scholarship Fund

American Bar Association
321 North Clark Street, Chicago, IL 60654
Phone: 312-988-5624
Email: abalsd@americanbar.org
http://abaforlawstudents.com/events/
Purpose: To assist first-year law school students.
Eligibility: Applicants must be U.S. citizens or permanent residents. They must be entering the first year of law school during the year of application. They must have a cumulative undergraduate GPA of 2.5 or higher. Selection is based on the overall strength of the application.
Target applicant(s): College students. Graduate school students. Adult students.
Minimum GPA: 2.5
Amount: $15,000.
Number of awards: 20.
Scholarship may be renewable.
Deadline: March 2.
How to apply: Applications are available online. An application form, personal statement, two recommendation letters and a transcript are required.
Exclusive: Visit www.UltimateScholarshipBook.com and enter code AM80920 for updates on this award.

(810) • LexisNexis / John R. Johnson Memorial Scholarship Endowment

American Association of Law Libraries
105 W. Adams, Suite 3300, Chicago, IL 60603
Phone: 312-939-4764
Email: scholarships@aall.org
https://www.aallnet.org/mm/Member-Resources
Purpose: To encourage current and future law librarians in memory of John Johnson, a prominent law librarian.
Eligibility: Applicants who apply for any of the AALL Educational Scholarships become automatically eligible to receive this award. No separate application is necessary. Applicants must intend to have careers as law librarians. Preference is given to AALL members, but a non-member may apply.
Target applicant(s): Graduate school students. Adult students.
Amount: Varies.
Number of awards: Varies.
Scholarship may be renewable.
Deadline: Varies.
How to apply: Applications are available online, by mail with a self-addressed, stamped envelope, by fax, by phone or by email.
Exclusive: Visit www.UltimateScholarshipBook.com and enter code AM81020 for updates on this award.

(811) • LimNexus Scholarship

National Asian Pacific American Bar Association Law Foundation
P.O. Box 65081, Washington, DC 20035
https://www.napabalawfoundation.org/foundation-scholarships
Purpose: To support students who demonstrate a commitment to serving the Asian Pacific American community.
Eligibility: Applicants must be U.S. citizens or permanent residents who are enrolled in an accredited U.S. law school. Students must demonstrate academic achievement, leadership potential and commitment in serving or contributing to the Asian Pacific American community. Applicants must include an essay emphasizing experiences that illustrate their commitment to the APA community.
Target applicant(s): Graduate school students. Adult students.
Amount: $2,500.
Number of awards: 1.
Deadline: September 3.
How to apply: Applications are available online.
Exclusive: Visit www.UltimateScholarshipBook.com and enter code NA81120 for updates on this award.

(812) • Litherland/FTEE Scholarship

International Technology and Engineering Educators Association
Foundation for Technology and Engineering Educators, 1914 Association Drive, Suite 201, Reston, VA 20191-1539
Phone: 703-860-2100
Email: iteea@iteea.org
https://www.iteea.org/Activities/AwardsScholarships.aspx
Purpose: To provide scholarships for undergraduate students pursuing a career in teaching technology.
Eligibility: Applicants must be members of ITEEA, be full-time undergraduate students majoring in technology and engineering education teacher preparation. Students must also have a minimum 2.5 GPA.
Target applicant(s): College students. Adult students.
Minimum GPA: 2.5
Amount: $1,000.
Number of awards: 1.
Deadline: December 1.
How to apply: Application information is available online.
Exclusive: Visit www.UltimateScholarshipBook.com and enter code IN81220 for updates on this award.

(813) • LivSecure Scholarship

LivSecure
3803 West Chester Pike, Suite 100, Newtown Square, PA 19073
Phone: 484-420-0314
Email: megan.nonemacher@myalarmcenter.com
https://www.livsecure.com/student-scholarships/
Purpose: To support students who are studying to make our neighborhoods a safer place.
Eligibility: Applicants must be a high school senior or a freshman or sophomore in college. Students should be currently studying law enforcement, law, criminal justice or a related field. Applicants must submit a 500- to 1,000-word essay on why they chose a law enforcement-related career and what they hope to achieve from their chosen career.
Target applicant(s): High school students. College students. Adult students.
Amount: $1,000.
Number of awards: 1.
Deadline: July 1.
How to apply: Applications must be emailed to scholarships@livesecure.com and include a cover page with name, address, phone, email, year in school, school, school address and school phone number. The email should also include the essay in a word document file.
Exclusive: Visit www.UltimateScholarshipBook.com and enter code LI81320 for updates on this award.

(814) • Lou and Carole Prato Sports Reporting Scholarship

Radio Television Digital News Association
529 14th Street NW, Suite 1240, Washington, DC 20045
Phone: 202-659-6510
Email: karenh@rtdna.org
http://www.rtdna.org
Purpose: To provide monetary assistance to a student pursuing a career as a sports reporter for radio or television.
Eligibility: Applicants must be full-time college sophomores or higher with at least one full academic year remaining. Applicants may be enrolled in any major but must have a career goal of becoming a sports reporter for television or radio. Applicants may only apply for one RTNDA scholarship.
Target applicant(s): College students. Adult students.
Amount: $1,000.
Number of awards: 1.
Deadline: January 15.
How to apply: Applications are available online.
Exclusive: Visit www.UltimateScholarshipBook.com and enter code RA81420 for updates on this award.

(815) • Lou Hochberg Awards

Orgone Biophysical Research Laboratory
P.O. Box 1148, Ashland, OR 97520
Phone: 541-522-0118
Email: info@orgonelab.org
http://www.orgonelab.org/hochberg.htm

Purpose: The Orgone Biophysical Research Lab offers a number of awards to students, scholars and journalists through a program set up by Louis Hochberg, a social worker who was dedicated to the sociological discoveries of Wilhelm Reich.
Eligibility: The Lou Hochberg Awards are given to winning theses and dissertations, university and college essays, high school essays and published articles that focus on Reich's sociological work. There are categories for students, scholars or journalists beginning at high school age through adulthood. A suggested list of topics and a bibliography is available online.
Target applicant(s): High school students. College students. Graduate school students. Adult students.
Amount: $500-$1,500.
Number of awards: Varies.
Deadline: Varies.
How to apply: Each award has a specific set of instructions for submitting a package for consideration. Guidelines are listed online.
Exclusive: Visit www.UltimateScholarshipBook.com and enter code OR81520 for updates on this award.

(816) · Luci S. Williams Houston Memorial Scholarship

Bay Area Black Journalists Association
1714 Franklin Street #100-260, Oakland, CA 94612
Phone: 510-740-8012
Email: info@babja.org
http://babja.org
Purpose: To support aspiring photojournalists.
Eligibility: Applicants must be enrolled in a Bay Area college or university. Those students attending college out of state must have graduated from a Bay Area high school. Applicants must be studying photojournalism in one of the following: television, radio, print or multimedia.
Target applicant(s): College students. Adult students.
Amount: $2,500.
Number of awards: 1.
Deadline: October 17.
How to apply: Applications are available online. An application form, transcript, resume, work samples, three letters of recommendation and an essay are required.
Exclusive: Visit www.UltimateScholarshipBook.com and enter code BA81620 for updates on this award.

(817) · Lydia Donaldson Tutt-Jones Memorial Research Grant

African American Success Foundation Inc.
7027 West Broward Boulevard, #313, Fort Lauderdale, FL 33317
Phone: 954-792-1117
https://blacksuccessfoundation.org/grant-rules/
Purpose: To support the research of African American success in education.
Eligibility: Applicants must be graduate students or professionals pursuing research study pertaining to the educational success of African American students. Students must provide a letter of recommendation from a faculty member who will provide oversight for their research. Applicants must submit a proposal clearly outlining their research.
Target applicant(s): Graduate school students. Adult students.
Amount: $5,000.
Number of awards: 1.
Deadline: June 7.
How to apply: Applications are available online.
Exclusive: Visit www.UltimateScholarshipBook.com and enter code AF81720 for updates on this award.

(818) · Maley/FTEE Teacher Professional Development Scholarship

International Technology and Engineering Educators Association Foundation for Technology and Engineering Educators, 1914 Association Drive, Suite 201, Reston, VA 20191-1539
Phone: 703-860-2100
Email: iteea@iteea.org
https://www.iteea.org/Activities/AwardsScholarships.aspx
Purpose: To support technology education teachers.
Eligibility: Applicants must be members of ITEEA and plan to pursue or continue graduate study. Candidates must provide their plans for graduate study, description of need, college transcript and three recommendation letters.
Target applicant(s): College students. Graduate school students. Adult students.
Amount: $1,000.
Number of awards: Varies.
Deadline: December 1.
How to apply: Application information is available online.
Exclusive: Visit www.UltimateScholarshipBook.com and enter code IN81820 for updates on this award.

(819) · Maple Flooring Manufacturers Association Scholarship

Maple Flooring Manufacturers Association
One Parkview Plaza Suite 800, Oakbrook Terrace, IL 60181
Phone: 888-480-9138
Email: mfma@maplefloor.org
http://www.maplefloor.org/Programs-Services/Scholarship-Program.aspx
Purpose: To support students pursuing a higher education at a secondary, advanced or trade school.
Eligibility: Applicants must be legal residents of the U.S. attending college in the United States. Students must write a 500-word essay and be studying in one of the following fields: architecture, athletic administration, athletics, boiler inspection training, biological conservation, bio-mechanical sciences, building construction, civil engineering, coaching, commercial driving schools, construction sciences or management, dance education, forest science, forestry studies, engineering technology, environmental resource management, exercise science, industrial technology schools, kinesiology, LEED training or certification, mechanic schools, mechanical drafting, machine technologies, natural resources / conservation, physical administration, physical education, physical rehabilitation or therapy, recreation and park administration, small engine repair schools, sports and fitness management, survey schools, trucking schools or wood sciences.
Target applicant(s): High school students. College students. Adult students.
Amount: $1,000.
Number of awards: 5.
Deadline: July 9.
How to apply: Applications are available online.
Exclusive: Visit www.UltimateScholarshipBook.com and enter code MA81920 for updates on this award.

(820) • Mary Lou Brown Scholarship

American Radio Relay League Foundation
225 Main Street, Newington, CT 06111-1494
Phone: 860-594-0348
Email: foundation@arrl.org
http://www.arrl.org/scholarship-program
Purpose: To assist ham radio operators with furthering their educations.
Eligibility: Applicants must have at least a general ham radio license, be residents of the ARRL Northwest Division (Alaska, Idaho, Montana, Oregon or Washington), be working for a bachelor's or graduate degree, have a minimum 3.0 GPA and have demonstrated interest in promoting the Amateur Radio Service.
Target applicant(s): High school students. College students. Graduate school students. Adult students.
Minimum GPA: 3.0
Amount: $2,500.
Number of awards: Varies.
Deadline: January 31.
How to apply: Applications are available online. Completed applications must be submitted by mail.
Exclusive: Visit www.UltimateScholarshipBook.com and enter code AM82020 for updates on this award.

(821) • Matthew H. Parry Memorial Scholarship

Project Management Institute Educational Foundation
14 Campus Boulevard, Newtown Square, PA 19073
Phone: 610-356-4600
Email: pmief@pmi.org
https://pmief.org/scholarships/academic-scholarships
Purpose: To aid students who are interested in pursuing a career in project management.
Eligibility: Applicants must be undergraduate students who are enrolled in a degree-granting program. They must have an interest in pursuing a career in project management. Selection is based on the overall strength of the application.
Target applicant(s): College students. Adult students.
Amount: $2,000.
Number of awards: Varies.
Deadline: May 1.
How to apply: Applications are available online. An application form, transcript, resume, two essays and three recommendation letters are required.
Exclusive: Visit www.UltimateScholarshipBook.com and enter code PR82120 for updates on this award.

(822) • MBA Fellowship

Goldman Sachs
200 West Street, New York, NY 10282
http://www.goldmansachs.com/careers/students/programs/americas/mba-fellowship.html
Purpose: To recognize outstanding students.
Eligibility: Applicants must be first-year MBA students. Students must be seeking a summer associate position at Goldman Sachs. Applicants must be Black, Hispanic/Latino, Native American or women.
Target applicant(s): Graduate school students. Adult students.
Amount: $35,000.
Number of awards: Varies.
Deadline: Varies.
How to apply: Applications are available online.
Exclusive: Visit www.UltimateScholarshipBook.com and enter code GO82220 for updates on this award.

(823) • Media Fellows Program

Washington Media Scholars Foundation
815 Slaters Lane, Suite 201, Alexandria, VA 22314
Phone: 703-299-4399
Email: kara.watt@mediascholars.org
http://www.mediascholars.org
Purpose: To aid students who plan to pursue careers in the field of public policy advertising.
Eligibility: Applicants must be rising undergraduate juniors and seniors who are attending school full time. They must be degree-seeking students who are majoring in subjects that provide preparation for a career in strategic public policy research, planning, advertising or buying. Eligible majors include but are not limited to political science, mass communication, marketing and journalism. They must have a demonstrated interest in pursuing a career in the field of strategic media planning. They must have a major GPA of 3.0 or higher and must demonstrate financial need. Selection is based on the overall strength of the application.
Target applicant(s): College students. Adult students.
Minimum GPA: 3.0
Amount: Varies.
Number of awards: Varies.
Deadline: July 14.
How to apply: Applications are available online. An application form, essay and one recommendation letter are required.
Exclusive: Visit www.UltimateScholarshipBook.com and enter code WA82320 for updates on this award.

(824) • Memorial Classic Golf Tournament Scholarship

Funeral Service Foundation
13625 Bishop's Drive, Brookfield, WI 53005-6607
Phone: 877-402-5900
Email: info@funeralservicefoundation.org
http://www.funeralservicefoundation.org
Purpose: To help students continue their education in funeral service and mortuary science education.
Eligibility: Applicants must be enrolled full- or part-time in an American Board of Funeral Service Education accredited program. Selection is based on the overall strength of the application.
Target applicant(s): College students. Graduate school students. Adult students.
Minimum GPA: 2.0
Amount: $1,000.
Number of awards: Varies.
Deadline: March 30.
How to apply: Applications are available online. An application form, essay, academic transcript and video submissions are required.
Exclusive: Visit www.UltimateScholarshipBook.com and enter code FU82420 for updates on this award.

(825) • Merchants Exchange of Portland Scholarship

Merchants Exchange of Portland Scholarship Fund
200 SW Market Street, Suite 190, Portland, OR 97201
Phone: 503-804-0633
http://www.pdxmex.com/scholarship
Purpose: To support students seeking a maritime field career.

Eligibility: Applicants must be current juniors or seniors at a four-year college or university, freshmen or sophomores in a two-year degree program, students in a U.S. Coast Guard-approved training program or graduate students in Maritime affairs or international trade. Students must have a minimum GPA of 2.5 and provide transcripts, essays and a letter of recommendation.
Target applicant(s): College students. Graduate school students. Adult students.
Minimum GPA: 2.5
Amount: $2,000.
Number of awards: 5.
Deadline: May 31.
How to apply: Applications are available online.
Exclusive: Visit www.UltimateScholarshipBook.com and enter code ME82520 for updates on this award.

(826) • Minorities and Women Educational Scholarship

Appraisal Institute Education Trust
200 W. Madison, Suite 1500, Chicago, IL 60606
Phone: 312-335-4133
Email: wwoodburn@appraisalinstitute.org
http://www.appraisalinstitute.org
Purpose: To assist minority and women college students in pursuing degrees in real estate appraisal or related fields.
Eligibility: Applicants must be women or American Indians, Alaska Natives, Asians, African Americans, Hispanics or Latinos, Native Hawaiians or other Pacific Islanders. Applicants must be full- or part-time students enrolled in real estate courses and working toward a degree, have a minimum 2.5 GPA and demonstrate financial need.
Target applicant(s): High school students. College students. Adult students.
Minimum GPA: 2.5
Amount: $1,000.
Number of awards: Varies.
Deadline: April 15.
How to apply: Applications are available online.
Exclusive: Visit www.UltimateScholarshipBook.com and enter code AP82620 for updates on this award.

(827) • Minority Fellowship Program

American Sociological Association Minority Fellowship Program
1430 K Street NW, Suite 600, Washington, DC 20005
Phone: 202-383-9005
Email: minority.affairs@asanet.org
http://www.asanet.org/career-center/grants-and-fellowships
Purpose: To provide pre-doctoral graduate education for sociology students.
Eligibility: Applicants must be enrolled in and have completed one full year in a Ph.D. program in Sociology. Students must be members of an underrepresented minority group in the U.S.: African American, Latino, Asian/Pacific Islander or American Indians/Alaska Natives. Applicants must also be U.S. citizens, non-citizen nationals of the U.S. or have been lawfully admitted to the U.S. for permanent residence. The fellowship is awarded for 12 months and typically renewable for up to three years in total. Tuition and fees are arranged with the home department. MFP Fellows are selected each year by the MFP Advisory Panel, a rotating, appointed group of senior scholars in sociology. Fellows can be involved in any area of sociological research, though particular MFP award lines devoted to drug abuse research may be possible contingent on funding.
Target applicant(s): Graduate school students. Adult students.
Amount: $18,000.
Number of awards: Varies.
Deadline: January 31.
How to apply: Applications are available online.
Exclusive: Visit www.UltimateScholarshipBook.com and enter code AM82720 for updates on this award.

(828) • Mister Rogers Memorial Scholarship

Television Academy Foundation
5220 Lankershim Boulevard, North Hollywood, CA 91601
http://www.emmys.com/foundation/programs/mister-rogers
Purpose: To encourage careers in children's media.
Eligibility: Applicants must be graduating seniors continuing on to graduate school or current graduate students pursuing a degree relevant to children's media. Students must submit a project proposal supporting the values and principles of Fred Rogers' work.
Target applicant(s): College students. Graduate school students. Adult students.
Amount: $5,000.
Number of awards: 2.
Deadline: Varies.
How to apply: Applications are available online.
Exclusive: Visit www.UltimateScholarshipBook.com and enter code TE82820 for updates on this award.

(829) • MLA Scholarship

Medical Library Association
65 East Wacker Place, Suite 1900, Chicago, IL 60601-7246
Phone: 312-419-9094
Email: lopez@mail.mlahq.org
http://www.mlanet.org
Purpose: To aid a student with finishing their education at an ALA-accredited library school.
Eligibility: Applicants must be either entering or less than half-way through an accredited graduate school program in a field relevant to library science and be U.S. or Canadian citizens or permanent residents.
Target applicant(s): Graduate school students. Adult students.
Amount: Up to $5,000.
Number of awards: 1.
Deadline: December 1.
How to apply: Applications are available online.
Exclusive: Visit www.UltimateScholarshipBook.com and enter code ME82920 for updates on this award.

(830) • MLA Scholarship for Minority Students

Medical Library Association
65 East Wacker Place, Suite 1900, Chicago, IL 60601-7246
Phone: 312-419-9094
Email: lopez@mail.mlahq.org
http://www.mlanet.org
Purpose: To aid minority students entering or currently attending graduate library school.
Eligibility: Applicants must be African-American, Hispanic, Asian, Native American or Pacific Islander and entering or currently attending an ALA-accredited library school and be no more than halfway through the program. Applicants must also be citizens or permanent residents of the United States or Canada.
Target applicant(s): Graduate school students. Adult students.
Amount: Up to $5,000.
Number of awards: 1.

Deadline: December 1.
How to apply: Applications are available online.
Exclusive: Visit www.UltimateScholarshipBook.com and enter code ME83020 for updates on this award.

(831) • MLA/NLM Spectrum Scholarship

Medical Library Association
65 East Wacker Place, Suite 1900, Chicago, IL 60601-7246
Phone: 312-419-9094
Email: lopez@mail.mlahq.org
http://www.mlanet.org
Purpose: To aid minority students in becoming health sciences information professionals.
Eligibility: Applicants must be American Indian/Alaska Native, Asian, Black/African American, Hispanic/Latino or Native Hawaiian/Other Pacific Islander students attending accredited library schools who are studying fields relevant to library science and who plan to enter the health sciences information field.
Target applicant(s): College students. Graduate school students. Adult students.
Amount: Varies.
Number of awards: Varies.
Deadline: March 1.
How to apply: Applications are available online.
Exclusive: Visit www.UltimateScholarshipBook.com and enter code ME83120 for updates on this award.

(832) • Mondelez International Legacy Scholarship

National Grocers Association
1005 N. Glebe Road, Suite 250, Arlington, VA 22201
Phone: 225-387-6126
http://www.nationalgrocers.org
Purpose: To support students pursuing education related to the grocery field.
Eligibility: Applicants must be rising sophomores through postgraduate students, have a minimum 2.5 GPA and be enrolled in a two- or four-year degree-granting institution. Students must major in business, food management, IT or another field related to a career in the grocery industry. Experience in the grocery industry is preferred but not required.
Target applicant(s): College students. Graduate school students. Adult students.
Minimum GPA: 2.5
Amount: Varies.
Number of awards: 1.
Deadline: April 15.
How to apply: Applications are available online.
Exclusive: Visit www.UltimateScholarshipBook.com and enter code NA83220 for updates on this award.

(833) • Moody Research Grant

Lyndon B. Johnson Foundation
2313 Red River Street, Austin, TX 78705
Phone: 512-721-0263
Email: samantha@lbjfoundation.org
http://www.lbjlibrary.org
Purpose: To assist with the travel and room-and-board expenses of those wishing to conduct research at the Lyndon B. Johnson Foundation Library.
Eligibility: Applicants must first contact the library to determine if their topic is appropriate for study at the facility. Applicants must also calculate the estimated amount of the grant before making a request.
Target applicant(s): College students. Adult students.
Amount: $600-$3,000.
Number of awards: Varies.
Deadline: March 15 and September 15.
How to apply: Applications are available online.
Exclusive: Visit www.UltimateScholarshipBook.com and enter code LY83320 for updates on this award.

(834) • My Alarm Center Student Scholarship

My Alarm Center
3803 West Chester Pike, Suite 100, Newtown Square, PA 19073
Phone: (855) 334-6562
https://www.myalarmcenter.com
Purpose: To support students in pursuing a degree in law enforcement, law, criminal justice or a related field.
Eligibility: Applicants must be graduating high school seniors or college freshmen/sophomores. Students must submit an essay outlining their professional goals. Selection is based on the overall strength of the submission.
Target applicant(s): High school students. College students. Adult students.
Amount: $1,000.
Number of awards: 3.
Deadline: July 1.
How to apply: Applications are available online.
Exclusive: Visit www.UltimateScholarshipBook.com and enter code MY83420 for updates on this award.

(835) • NACA Mid Atlantic Graduate Student Scholarship

National Association for Campus Activities
13 Harbison Way, Columbia, SC 29212
Phone: 803-732-6222
Email: info@naca.org
https://www.naca.org/FOUNDATION/Pages/Scholarships.aspx
Purpose: To provide assistance to graduate students who are attending a college or university on the East Coast.
Eligibility: Applicants must be enrolled in master's or doctorate degree programs in student personnel services or a related area. Applicants must be attending a graduate school in Washington, DC, Delaware, Maryland, New Jersey, New York or eastern Pennsylvania, be involved in campus activities and plan to pursue a career in campus activities.
Target applicant(s): Graduate school students. Adult students.
Amount: Varies.
Number of awards: Varies.
Deadline: June 30.
How to apply: Applications are available online.
Exclusive: Visit www.UltimateScholarshipBook.com and enter code NA83520 for updates on this award.

(836) • Nancy Curry Scholarship

School Nutrition Association
120 Waterfront Street, Suite 300, National Harbor, MD 20745
Phone: 301-686-3100
Email: servicecenter@schoolnutrition.org
https://schoolnutrition.org/Membership/AwardsScholarships/

Purpose: To support students wishing to enter the school foodservice industry.
Eligibility: Applicants or the parents of applicants must be School Nutrition Association members for at least one year and be enrolled in a school foodservice-related program at an educational institution. Children of SNA members are not eligible to apply. Applicants must be currently employed in school food service.
Target applicant(s): High school students. College students. Graduate school students. Adult students.
Amount: $500.
Number of awards: 1.
Deadline: April 4.
How to apply: Applications are available online.
Exclusive: Visit www.UltimateScholarshipBook.com and enter code SC83620 for updates on this award.

(837) • Nancy McManus Washington Internship Scholarships

Pi Sigma Alpha
The Washington Center, 2301 M Street NW, Fifth Floor, Washington, DC 20037-1427
Email: info@twc.edu
http://www.apsanet.org/~psa/
Purpose: To provide Pi Sigma Alpha members with scholarships to participate in summer or fall term internships in Washington, DC.
Eligibility: Applicants must belong to Pi Sigma Alpha and be nominated by their local chapter. The award is for a political science internship is based on academic achievement and service to the organization.
Target applicant(s): College students. Graduate school students. Adult students.
Amount: $2,000.
Number of awards: 4.
Deadline: May 1.
How to apply: Applications are available online.
Exclusive: Visit www.UltimateScholarshipBook.com and enter code PI83720 for updates on this award.

(838) • Naomi Berber Memorial Scholarship

Print and Graphics Scholarship Foundation
Attn.: Kristina Iorio, 301 Brush Creek Road, Warrendale, PA 15086-7529
Phone: 412-259-1721
Email: kiorio@printing.org
https://www.printing.org/programs/awards/naomi-berber-memorial-award
Purpose: To support students interested in careers in printing and graphic communication.
Eligibility: Applicants must be high school seniors, graduates or students at two- or four-year colleges. They must be full-time students and maintain a GPA of 3.0 or higher.
Target applicant(s): High school students. College students. Adult students.
Minimum GPA: 3.0
Amount: Varies.
Number of awards: Varies.
Deadline: July 31.
How to apply: Applications are available online. An application form, transcript, two letters of recommendation, course of study and self-addressed stamped envelope are required.
Exclusive: Visit www.UltimateScholarshipBook.com and enter code PR83820 for updates on this award.

(839) • National Academic Scholarships

Association of Government Accountants (AGA)
2208 Mount Vernon Avenue, Alexandria, VA 22301-1314
Phone: 800-242-7211x309
Email: rortiz@agacgfm.org
http://www.agacgfm.org
Purpose: To support public financial management students.
Eligibility: Applicants for full-time or part-time scholarships must be an AGA member or family member (spouse, child or grandchild), and scholarships must be used for full-time or part-time undergraduate study in a financial management academic area such as accounting, auditing, budgeting, economics, finance, electronic data processing, information resources management or public administration. Essays and transcripts are required. There are two categories for high school students/graduates and undergraduates/graduates. The Academic Scholarships are based on academic achievement and the student's potential for making a contribution to public financial management. A reference letter from an AGA member and from another professional such as a professor, guidance counselor or employer is required. Applicants to the Community Service Scholarships do not have to be AGA members, must be pursuing a degree in a financial management academic discipline and must be actively involved in community service projects. The awards are based on community service and accomplishments. A letter of recommendation from a community service organization and from another professional are required.
Target applicant(s): High school students. College students. Graduate school students. Adult students.
Minimum GPA: 2.5
Amount: $1,500-$3,000.
Number of awards: Varies.
Deadline: April 14.
How to apply: Applications are available online.
Exclusive: Visit www.UltimateScholarshipBook.com and enter code AS83920 for updates on this award.

(840) • National D-Day Museum Online Essay Contest

National D-Day Museum Foundation
945 Magazine Street, New Orleans, LA 70130
Phone: 504-528-1944
Email: collin.makamson@nationalww2museum.org
https://www.nationalww2museum.org/students-teachers/school-programs
Purpose: To increase awareness of World War II by giving students the opportunity to compete in an essay contest.
Eligibility: Applicants must be high school or middle school students in the United States, its territories or its military bases. They must prepare an essay of up to 1,000 words based on a topic specified by the sponsor and related to World War II. Only the first 500 valid essays will be accepted.
Target applicant(s): Junior high students or younger. High school students.
Amount: Varies.
Number of awards: Varies.
Deadline: December 29.
How to apply: Applications are available online. An essay and contact information are required.
Exclusive: Visit www.UltimateScholarshipBook.com and enter code NA84020 for updates on this award.

(841) • National Foundation Scholarships

Institute of Scrap Recycling Industries
1615 L Street, Suite 600, Washington, DC 20036
Phone: 202-662-8500
http://www.isri.org/about-isri/recycling-research-foundation
Purpose: To support students seeking a graduate degree in scrap processing or recycling.
Eligibility: Applicants must be pursuing a graduate level degree, be a U.S. citizen and have a minimum 2.5 GPA. The program is open to those seeking a graduate degree in a program that supports the scrap processing and recycling industry as a whole.
Target applicant(s): Graduate school students. Adult students.
Minimum GPA: 2.5
Amount: $5,000.
Number of awards: 1.
Deadline: June 15.
How to apply: Applications are available online.
Exclusive: Visit www.UltimateScholarshipBook.com and enter code IN84120 for updates on this award.

(842) • National History Day Contest

National History Day
4511 Knox Road, Suite 205, College Park, MD 20740
Phone: 301-314-9739
Email: info@nhd.org
http://www.nhd.org
Purpose: To reward students for their scholarship, initiative and cooperation.
Eligibility: Applicants must be in grades 6-12 and prepare throughout the school year history presentations based on an annual theme. Around February or March students compete in district History Day contests. District winners then prepare for the state contests, held usually in April or May. Those winners advance to the national contest held in June at the University of Maryland.
Target applicant(s): Junior high students or younger. High school students.
Amount: Varies.
Number of awards: Varies.
Deadline: Varies.
How to apply: Applications are available online.
Exclusive: Visit www.UltimateScholarshipBook.com and enter code NA84220 for updates on this award.

(843) • National Press Club Scholarship for Journalism Diversity

National Press Club
529 14th Street NW, 13th Floor, Washington, DC 20045
Phone: 202-662-7500
http://www.press.org
Purpose: To support promising future journalists.
Eligibility: Applicants must be high school seniors, have a GPA of 3.0 or higher and plan to enter college the year after graduation. Students must intend to become a journalist and bring diversity to U.S. journalism.
Target applicant(s): High school students.
Minimum GPA: 3.0
Amount: $2,000 plus $500 book stipend.
Number of awards: 1.
Deadline: March 1.
How to apply: Applications are available online. An application form, essay, transcript, copy of FAFSA, letter of acceptance or proof of college application, three letters of recommendation and up to five work samples are required.
Exclusive: Visit www.UltimateScholarshipBook.com and enter code NA84320 for updates on this award.

(844) • National Scholarship Program

American Board of Funeral Service Education
Scholarship Committee, 3414 Ashland Avenue, Suite G, St. Joseph, MO 64506
Phone: 816-233-3747
http://www.abfse.org
Purpose: To assist students enrolled in funeral service or mortuary science programs.
Eligibility: Applicants must be undergraduate students who have completed at least one semester or quarter of study in funeral service or mortuary science education at an accredited school and have at least one term remaining in their study. Applicants must be U.S. citizens.
Target applicant(s): College students. Adult students.
Amount: $500-$2,500.
Number of awards: Varies.
Deadline: March 1 and September 1.
How to apply: Applications are available online.
Exclusive: Visit www.UltimateScholarshipBook.com and enter code AM84420 for updates on this award.

(845) • National Tour Association (NTA) Eric Friedheim Graduate Scholarship

Tourism Cares
275 Turnpike Street, Suite 307, Canton, MA 02021
Phone: 781-821-5990
Email: scholarships@tourismcares.org
http://www.tourismcares.org/academic-scholarships/
Purpose: To assist graduate students who are studying hospitality, travel and tourism.
Eligibility: Applicants must be U.S. permanent residents who are entering or returning full-time graduate students at an accredited U.S. four-year college or university. They must be studying hospitality, travel or tourism and must have a GPA of 3.0 or higher on a four-point scale. Selection is based on the overall strength of the application.
Target applicant(s): College students. Graduate school students. Adult students.
Minimum GPA: 3.0
Amount: $2,000.
Number of awards: 2.
Deadline: April 3.
How to apply: Applications are available online. An application form, a personal essay, a resume, proof of residency, two recommendation letters and an official transcript are required.
Exclusive: Visit www.UltimateScholarshipBook.com and enter code TO84520 for updates on this award.

(846) • National Tour Association (NTA) Luray Caverns Graduate Research Scholarship

Tourism Cares
275 Turnpike Street, Suite 307, Canton, MA 02021
Phone: 781-821-5990
Email: scholarships@tourismcares.org
http://www.tourismcares.org/academic-scholarships/
Purpose: To aid graduate students who are conducting tourism-related research.

Eligibility: Applicants can be permanent residents of any country but must be enrolled at an accredited U.S. or Canadian four-year postsecondary institution. They must be entering or returning graduate students who are conducting research that focuses on tourism. They must have a proven commitment to the tourism industry, and must have a GPA of 3.0 or higher on a four-point scale. Selection is based on the strength of the research project.
Target applicant(s): College students. Graduate school students. Adult students.
Minimum GPA: 3.0
Amount: $3,000.
Number of awards: 1.
Deadline: April 3.
How to apply: Applications are available online. An application form, proof of residency, a personal essay, a resume, a research proposal, an official transcript and one letter of recommendation are required.
Exclusive: Visit www.UltimateScholarshipBook.com and enter code TO84620 for updates on this award.

(847) · National Tour Association (NTA) New Horizons-Kathy LeTarte Undergraduate Scholarship

Tourism Cares
275 Turnpike Street, Suite 307, Canton, MA 02021
Phone: 781-821-5990
Email: scholarships@tourismcares.org
http://www.tourismcares.org/academic-scholarships/
Purpose: To aid Michigan residents who are studying travel, tourism and hospitality at the undergraduate level.
Eligibility: Applicants must be permanent residents of Michigan and must be enrolled at an accredited U.S. or Canadian four-year postsecondary institution. They must be rising undergraduate juniors or seniors who are studying travel, tourism or hospitality. They must have 60 or more credits completed by May of the application year and must have a GPA of 3.0 or higher on a four-point scale. Selection is based on the overall strength of the application.
Target applicant(s): College students. Adult students.
Minimum GPA: 3.0
Amount: $2,000.
Number of awards: 1.
Deadline: April 3.
How to apply: Applications are available online. An application form, personal essay, official transcript, proof of Michigan residency, resume and two letters of recommendation are required.
Exclusive: Visit www.UltimateScholarshipBook.com and enter code TO84720 for updates on this award.

(848) · National Tour Association (NTA) Travel Leaders Graduate Scholarship

Tourism Cares
275 Turnpike Street, Suite 307, Canton, MA 02021
Phone: 781-821-5990
Email: scholarships@tourismcares.org
http://www.tourismcares.org/academic-scholarships/
Purpose: To assist graduate students who are studying hospitality, travel and tourism.
Eligibility: Applicants may be permanent residents of any country but must be entering or returning graduate students at an accredited U.S. or Canadian four-year college or university. They must be full-time students who are studying hospitality, travel or tourism and must have a GPA of 3.0 or higher on a four-point scale. Selection is based on the overall strength of the application.
Target applicant(s): College students. Graduate school students. Adult students.
Minimum GPA: 3.0
Amount: $2,000.
Number of awards: 3.
Deadline: April 3.
How to apply: Applications are available online. An application form, proof of residency, a personal essay, two letters of recommendation, an official transcript and a resume are required.
Exclusive: Visit www.UltimateScholarshipBook.com and enter code TO84820 for updates on this award.

(849) · National Washington Crossing Foundation Scholarship

Washington Crossing Foundation
P.O. Box 503, Levittown, PA 19058
Phone: 215-949-8841
Email: info@gwcf.org
http://www.gwcf.org
Purpose: To support students who are planning careers in government service.
Eligibility: Students must be in their senior year of high school. Applicants must submit an essay and a letter of recommendation.
Target applicant(s): High school students.
Amount: $500-$5,000.
Number of awards: Varies.
Scholarship may be renewable.
Deadline: January 15.
How to apply: Applications are available online.
Exclusive: Visit www.UltimateScholarshipBook.com and enter code WA84920 for updates on this award.

(850) · NEA-Retired Jack Kinnaman Memorial Scholarship

National Education Association
Center for Governance, Attn: The NEA-Retired Jack Kinnaman Memorial Scholarship, 1201 16th Street NW, 8th Floor, Washington, DC 20036
Phone: 202-822-7132
http://www.nea.org
Purpose: To honor the memory of NEA-retired vice president and former advisory council member Jack Kinnaman.
Eligibility: Applicants must be NEA student members, major in education and have a minimum 2.5 GPA. An essay describing activities in NEA, a brief paragraph describing financial need, two letters of recommendation and a copy of the most recent transcript are required.
Target applicant(s): College students. Adult students.
Minimum GPA: 2.5
Amount: $2,500.
Number of awards: Varies.
Deadline: April 15.
How to apply: Applications are available online.
Exclusive: Visit www.UltimateScholarshipBook.com and enter code NA85020 for updates on this award.

(851) · Nell Bryant Robinson Scholarship

Phi Upsilon Omicron Inc.
National Office , P.O. Box 50970, Bowling Green, KY 42102-4270
Phone: 270-904-1340

Email: national@phiu.org
http://www.phiu.org
Purpose: To aid Phi Upsilon Omicron members who are pursuing bachelor's degrees in family and consumer sciences.
Eligibility: Preference is given to applicants who are majoring in food and nutrition or dietetics. Selection is based on the overall strength of the application.
Target applicant(s): College students. Adult students.
Amount: Varies.
Number of awards: Varies.
Deadline: February 1.
How to apply: Applications are available online. An application form, official transcript, personal statement and three recommendation letters are required.
Exclusive: Visit www.UltimateScholarshipBook.com and enter code PH85120 for updates on this award.

---

(852) • Nettie Dracup Memorial Scholarship

National Society of Professional Surveyors (NSPS/AAGS)
Attn: Scholarships, 5119 Pegasus Court, Suite Q, Frederick, MD 21704
Phone: 240-439-4615x105
Email: trisha.milburn@nsps.us.com
http://www.nsps.us.com/?page=Scholarships
Purpose: To aid geodetic surveying students.
Eligibility: Applicants must be U.S. citizens who are undergraduate students enrolled in an accredited degree program in geodetic surveying. They must be members of the National Society of Professional Surveyors (NSPS). Selection is based on the applicant's academic achievement, personal statement, recommendations and professional activities.
Target applicant(s): High school students. College students. Adult students.
Amount: $2,000.
Number of awards: 1.
Deadline: March 31.
How to apply: Applications are available online. An application form, official transcript, personal statement, three recommendation letters and proof of ACSM membership are required.
Exclusive: Visit www.UltimateScholarshipBook.com and enter code NA85220 for updates on this award.

---

(853) • New England FEMARA Scholarships

American Radio Relay League Foundation
225 Main Street, Newington, CT 06111-1494
Phone: 860-594-0348
Email: foundation@arrl.org
http://www.arrl.org/scholarship-program
Purpose: To assist ham radio operators in furthering their educations.
Eligibility: Applicants must have at least a technician ham radio license and be residents of the New England States (Connecticut, Maine, Massachusetts, New Hampshire, Rhode Island or Vermont).
Target applicant(s): High school students. College students. Graduate school students. Adult students.
Amount: $2,000.
Number of awards: Varies.
Deadline: January 31.
How to apply: Applications are available online. Completed applications must be mailed in. They cannot be completed electronically.
Exclusive: Visit www.UltimateScholarshipBook.com and enter code AM85320 for updates on this award.

---

(854) • NFMC Gretchen E. Van Roy Music Education Scholarship

National Federation of Music Clubs (FL)
NFMC Gretchen E. Van Roy Music Education Scholarship, Cheryl Schmidt, Chairman, 1100 SW 4th Street, Willmar, MN 56201
Phone: 317-882-4003
Email: cschmidt@en-tel.net
http://www.nfmc-music.org/competitions-awards/
Purpose: To support students majoring in music education.
Eligibility: Applicants must be college juniors majoring in music education and must be affiliated with the National Federation of Music Clubs.
Target applicant(s): College students. Adult students.
Amount: $1,200.
Number of awards: 1.
Deadline: April 1.
How to apply: Applications are available online.
Exclusive: Visit www.UltimateScholarshipBook.com and enter code NA85420 for updates on this award.

---

(855) • North American Van Lines Logistics Scholarship

North American Van Lines
Phone: 800-369-9115
http://www.northamerican.com/scholarship
Purpose: To support students pursuing a degree in logistics or supply chain management.
Eligibility: Applicants must be U.S. citizens and enrolled full-time as an undergraduate at an eligible educational institution. Funds must be used for qualified educational expenses. Students should be pursuing a degree in logistics or supply chain management. Applicants will need to submit a 400-800 word essay on why they selected a career in logistics/supply chain management. The essay should convey a sincere, personalized tone.
Target applicant(s): High school students. College students. Adult students.
Amount: $1,000.
Number of awards: 5.
Deadline: December 15.
How to apply: Applications are available online and must be submitted along with an official transcript, a verification of enrollment and the essay.
Exclusive: Visit www.UltimateScholarshipBook.com and enter code NO85520 for updates on this award.

---

(856) • NPPF Television News Scholarship

National Press Photographers Foundation Television News Scholarship
120 Hooper Street, Athens, GA 30602-3018
Phone: 706-542-2506
Email: jwbrown@nppf.org
http://www.nppa.org
Purpose: To support students with television news photojournalism potential but with little opportunity and great need.
Eligibility: Applicants must be full-time juniors or seniors at a four-year college or university, provide a portfolio and demonstrate financial need. Applicants must also have courses in TV news photojournalism and continue in this program towards a bachelor's degree. Applicants can apply to as many NPPA scholarships as desired, but only one award will be granted per winner.
Target applicant(s): College students. Adult students.

Amount: $2,000.
Number of awards: 1.
Deadline: January 6.
How to apply: Applications are available online.
Exclusive: Visit www.UltimateScholarshipBook.com and enter code NA85620 for updates on this award.

(857) · NSA Scholarship Foundation

National Society of Accountants Scholarship Program
1330 Braddock Place, Suite 540, Alexandria, VA 22314
Phone: 800-966-6679
http://www.nsacct.org
Purpose: To support students entering the accounting profession.
Eligibility: Applicants must be undergraduate students majoring in accounting with a minimum 3.0 GPA and be U.S. or Canadian citizens.
Target applicant(s): High school students. College students. Adult students.
Minimum GPA: 3.0
Amount: $500-$2,200.
Number of awards: 39.
Deadline: April 3.
How to apply: Applications are available online.
Exclusive: Visit www.UltimateScholarshipBook.com and enter code NA85720 for updates on this award.

(858) · Optimist International Oratorical Contest

Optimist International
4494 Lindell Boulevard, St. Louis, MO 63108
Phone: 314-371-6000
Email: programs@optimist.org
http://www.optimist.org
Purpose: To reward students based on their oratorical performance.
Eligibility: Applicants must be students in the U.S., Canada or Caribbean under the age of 16 as of December 31st of the entry year. Selection is based on an oratorical contest.
Target applicant(s): Junior high students or younger. High school students.
Amount: $1,000-$2,500.
Number of awards: 2-3.
Deadline: Varies.
How to apply: Contact your local Optimist Club.
Exclusive: Visit www.UltimateScholarshipBook.com and enter code OP85820 for updates on this award.

(859) · Otto M. Stanfield Legal Scholarship

Unitarian Universalist Association
24 Farnsworth Street, Boston, MA 02210
Phone: 617-742-2100
Email: uufp@uua.org
http://www.uua.org/giving/awards
Purpose: To help Unitarian Universalist students entering or attending law school.
Eligibility: Applicants should be planning to attend or currently attending law school at the graduate level. The award is based on activity with Unitarian Universalism and financial need. Applicants should submit transcripts and recommendations.
Target applicant(s): Graduate school students. Adult students.
Amount: Varies.
Number of awards: Varies.
Deadline: February 15.
How to apply: Applications are available online.
Exclusive: Visit www.UltimateScholarshipBook.com and enter code UN85920 for updates on this award.

(860) · Overseas Press Club Foundation Scholarships/Internships

Overseas Press Club Foundation
40 West 45 Street, New York, NY 10036
Phone: 201-493-9087
Email: foundation@opcofamerica.org
http://www.overseaspressclubfoundation.org
Purpose: To encourage undergraduate and graduate students attending American colleges and universities to pursue careers as foreign correspondents.
Eligibility: Scholarships are open to undergraduate and graduate students with an interest in a career as a foreign correspondent. Eligible students must be attending American colleges or universities.
Target applicant(s): College students. Graduate school students. Adult students.
Amount: $2,000-$3,000.
Number of awards: 15.
Deadline: December 1.
How to apply: Applications are available online.
Exclusive: Visit www.UltimateScholarshipBook.com and enter code OV86020 for updates on this award.

(861) · Paul and Helen L. Grauer Scholarship

American Radio Relay League Foundation
225 Main Street, Newington, CT 06111-1494
Phone: 860-594-0348
Email: foundation@arrl.org
http://www.arrl.org/scholarship-program
Purpose: To assist ham radio operators in furthering their educations.
Eligibility: Applicants must have at least a novice ham radio license, be residents and attend school in the ARRL Midwest Division (Iowa, Kansas, Missouri or Nebraska) and be undergraduate or graduate students in electronics, communications or another related field.
Target applicant(s): High school students. College students. Graduate school students. Adult students.
Amount: $1,000.
Number of awards: 1.
Deadline: January 31.
How to apply: Applications are available online. Completed applications must be submitted by mail.
Exclusive: Visit www.UltimateScholarshipBook.com and enter code AM86120 for updates on this award.

(862) · PAVE Student Design Competition

Planning and Visual Education Partnership (PAVE) c/o Kroger Company
PAVE Entries Attn.: Ken Pray, 1014 Vine Street, Cincinnati, OH 45202
Email: info@paveglobal.org
http://paveglobal.org/Competitions.aspx?typeid=26
Purpose: To provide undergraduate students with an opportunity to obtain real-life retail design experience.
Eligibility: Applicants must be college undergraduate students in the area of retail design and planning, visual merchandising, interior design

or branding. Students will create a design project based on the given information relating to Kroger stores.
Target applicant(s): College students. Adult students.
Amount: Varies.
Number of awards: Varies.
Deadline: November 1.
How to apply: Application and project details are available online.
Exclusive: Visit www.UltimateScholarshipBook.com and enter code PL86220 for updates on this award.

(863) • Peter and Jody Larkin Legacy Scholarship

National Grocers Association
1005 N. Glebe Road, Suite 250, Arlington, VA 22201
Phone: 225-387-6126
http://www.nationalgrocers.org
Purpose: To support students pursuing a degree related to the grocery field.
Eligibility: Applicants must be rising sophomores through postgraduate students, have a minimum 2.5 GPA and be enrolled in a two- or four-year degree-granting institution. Students must major in business, food management, IT or another field related to a career in the grocery industry. Experience in the grocery industry is preferred but not required.
Target applicant(s): College students. Graduate school students. Adult students.
Minimum GPA: 2.5
Amount: Varies.
Number of awards: 1.
Deadline: April 15.
How to apply: Applications are available online.
Exclusive: Visit www.UltimateScholarshipBook.com and enter code NA86320 for updates on this award.

(864) • PHD Scholarship

American Radio Relay League Foundation
225 Main Street, Newington, CT 06111-1494
Phone: 860-594-0348
Email: foundation@arrl.org
http://www.arrl.org/scholarship-program
Purpose: To assist ham radio operators in furthering their educations.
Eligibility: Applicants must have any class of ham radio license, be residents of the ARRL Midwest Division (Iowa, Kansas, Missouri, Nebraska) and be studying journalism, computer science or electronic engineering. Applicants may also be the children of deceased amateur radio operators.
Target applicant(s): College students. Graduate school students. Adult students.
Amount: $1,000.
Number of awards: 1.
Deadline: January 31.
How to apply: Applications are available online but may not be completed electronically. All completed applications must be mailed.
Exclusive: Visit www.UltimateScholarshipBook.com and enter code AM86420 for updates on this award.

(865) • Phi Delta Kappa Scholarship Grant for Prospective Educators

Phi Delta Kappa International
P.O. Box 7888, Bloomington, IN 47407
Phone: 812-339-1156
Email: scholarships@pdkintl.org
http://www.pdkintl.org
Purpose: To support prospective educators who have a connection to Phi Delta Kappa or are members of Educators Rising.
Eligibility: Applicants must meet at least one of the following criteria: a high school senior who plans on majoring in education and is a good standing member of Educators Rising, a high school senior who is going to major in education and is the child or grandchild of a Kappan in good standing, a high school senior majoring in education who has obtained at least one reference letter from a Kappan in good standing, an undergraduate member of PDK who is currently enrolled in an education program or an undergraduate member of Educators Rising who is currently enrolled in an education program.
Target applicant(s): High school students. College students. Adult students.
Amount: Varies.
Number of awards: Varies.
Deadline: April 2.
How to apply: Applications are available online.
Exclusive: Visit www.UltimateScholarshipBook.com and enter code PH86520 for updates on this award.

(866) • Pierre and Patricia Bikai Fellowship

American Center of Oriental Research (ACOR)
656 Beacon Street, 5th Floor, Boston, MA 02215-2010
Phone: 617-353-6571
Email: acor@bu.edu
http://www.acorjordan.org
Purpose: To help graduate students in an archaeological project at the American Center of Oriental Research.
Eligibility: Applicants must be graduate students. The fellowship includes room and board at ACOR and $600 a month and may be combined with the Harrell and Groot fellowships. The fellowship does not support field work or travel. Recipients must live at the ACOR center in Jordan from June of one year to May of the next.
Target applicant(s): Graduate school students. Adult students.
Amount: $600 monthly plus room and board.
Number of awards: 2.
Deadline: February 1.
How to apply: Applications are available online.
Exclusive: Visit www.UltimateScholarshipBook.com and enter code AM86620 for updates on this award.

(867) • PMI Eric Jenett Founders Scholarship

Project Management Institute Educational Foundation
14 Campus Boulevard, Newtown Square, PA 19073
Phone: 610-356-4600
Email: pmief@pmi.org
https://pmief.org/scholarships/academic-scholarships
Purpose: To aid project management students.
Eligibility: Applicants must be undergraduate students who are enrolled in a bachelor's degree program in project management or a related subject at an accredited post-secondary institution. Selection is based on the overall strength of the application.
Target applicant(s): College students. Adult students.
Amount: $2,000.
Number of awards: Varies.
Deadline: May 1.
How to apply: Applications are available online. An application form, resume, two essays and three recommendation letters are required.
Exclusive: Visit www.UltimateScholarshipBook.com and enter code PR86720 for updates on this award.

(868) · PPN Scholarship for Book and Cover Design

Publishing Professionals Network
c/o Postal Annex, 274 Redwood Shores Parkway, Box 129, Redwood City, CA 94065-1173
Phone: 916-320-0638
Email: operations@pubpronetwork.org
https://pubpronetwork.org/

Purpose: To support students pursuing careers in book design.
Eligibility: Applicants must be enrolled in a college, university or technical school in Alaska, Arizona, California, Colorado, Hawaii, Idaho, Montana, Nevada, New Mexico, Oregon, Utah, Washington or Wyoming and have a GPA of 2.0 or higher. Selection is based on book and cover design projects.
Target applicant(s): College students. Adult students.
Minimum GPA: 2.0
Amount: $1,000.
Number of awards: Varies.
Deadline: February 19.
How to apply: Applications are available from your school's publishing department. An application form, letter from faculty member and student book project are required.
Exclusive: Visit www.UltimateScholarshipBook.com and enter code PU86820 for updates on this award.

(869) · Predoctoral Fellowships for Historians of American Art to Travel Abroad

National Gallery of Art
2000B South Club Drive, Landover, MD 20785
Phone: 202-842-6482
http://www.nga.gov

Purpose: To award fellowships to doctoral students in art history who are studying aspects of art and architecture of the United States, including native and pre-Revolutionary America.
Eligibility: Applicants must be nominated by the chair of a graduate department of art history or other appropriate department. Each department may support two candidates. Applicants should submit proposals, itineraries, a curriculum vitae, two letters of support from professors and an additional letter of nomination from the chair. The fellowship is for a period of six to eight weeks of continuous travel abroad in areas such as Africa, Asia, South America or Europe to sites of historical and cultural interest. The travel fellowship is intended to encourage art-historical experience beyond the applicant's major field not for the advancement of a dissertation. Preference is given to those who have had little opportunity for professional travel abroad.
Target applicant(s): Graduate school students. Adult students.
Amount: Up to $6,000.
Number of awards: Up to 4.
Deadline: November 15.
How to apply: Application materials are described online.
Exclusive: Visit www.UltimateScholarshipBook.com and enter code NA86920 for updates on this award.

(870) · Presidential Scholarships

National Asian Pacific American Bar Association Law Foundation
P.O. Box 65081, Washington, DC 20035
https://www.napabalawfoundation.org/foundation-scholarships/

Purpose: To support students who demonstrate a commitment to contribute to the Asian Pacific American community.
Eligibility: Applicants must be U.S. citizens or permanent residents and enrolled in an accredited U.S. law school. Students must demonstrate academic achievement, leadership potential and commitment to serving the Asian Pacific American community. Applicants must provide letters of recommendation along with an essay as part of their application.
Target applicant(s): Graduate school students. Adult students.
Amount: $7,500.
Number of awards: 2.
Deadline: September 3.
How to apply: Applications are available online.
Exclusive: Visit www.UltimateScholarshipBook.com and enter code NA87020 for updates on this award.

(871) · PricewaterhouseCoopers Ascend Scholarship

Ascend: Pan-Asian Leaders in Finance and Accounting
247 West 30th Street, 12th Floor, New York, NY 10001
Phone: 212-248-4888
Email: scholarships@ascendleadership.org
http://www.ascendleadership.org/

Purpose: To aid Ascend student members who are studying accounting.
Eligibility: Applicants must be active student members of Ascend. They must be undergraduate freshmen, sophomores or juniors who are studying accounting at an accredited U.S. college or university. They must have a GPA of 3.5 or higher. Students who have worked for a Big 4 accounting firm are ineligible. Selection is based on the overall strength of the application.
Target applicant(s): College students. Adult students.
Minimum GPA: 3.5
Amount: $1,000.
Number of awards: 2.
Deadline: May 1.
How to apply: Applications are available online. An application form, transcript, personal essay, resume and talent profile are required.
Exclusive: Visit www.UltimateScholarshipBook.com and enter code AS87120 for updates on this award.

(872) · Prize in International Insolvency Studies

International Insolvency Institute
10332 Main Street, PMB 112, Fairfax, VA 22030
Phone: 416-595-2965
Email: ftibando@millerthomson.com
http://www.iiiglobal.org

Purpose: To recognize outstanding international insolvency researchers, commentators and analysts.
Eligibility: Applicants must be undergraduate students, graduate students or practitioners of international insolvency studies who have less than nine years of experience. They must submit original analysis, commentary or legal research on the subject of international insolvency. Selection is based on the overall strength of the submission.
Target applicant(s): College students. Graduate school students. Adult students.
Amount: $2,000-$3,000.
Number of awards: Up to 9.
Deadline: March 31.
How to apply: Application instructions are available online. A scholarly paper is required.
Exclusive: Visit www.UltimateScholarshipBook.com and enter code IN87220 for updates on this award.

(873) • Project Vote Smart National Internship Program

Project Vote Smart
Internship Coordinator, 1 Common Ground, Philipsburg, MT 59858
Phone: 406-859-8683
Email: intern@votesmart.org
http://votesmart.org/
Purpose: To encourage students and recent college graduates to develop an interest in voter education.
Eligibility: Applicants must be current college students in good standing or recent college graduates. They must be able to approach voter education work with a non-partisan attitude and be willing to commit to a ten-week internship. Selection is based on the overall strength of the application.
Target applicant(s): College students. Adult students.
Amount: All living costs (including room and board).
Number of awards: Varies.
Deadline: Rolling.
How to apply: Applications are available online. An application form, resume, cover letter and three references are required.
Exclusive: Visit www.UltimateScholarshipBook.com and enter code PR87320 for updates on this award.

(874) • Prospective Educator Scholarships

Pi Lambda Theta Scholarships
P.O. Box 7888, Bloomington, IN 47407-7888
Phone: 812-339-1156
Email: scholarships@pdkintl.org
https://pilambda.org/scholarships/
Purpose: To recognize education majors with leadership potential and a dedication to education.
Eligibility: Applicants must be members of Educators Rising, PDK International or Pi Lambda Theta and must be current undergraduate students.
Target applicant(s): College students. Adult students.
Minimum GPA: 3.5
Amount: Up to $2,500.
Number of awards: Varies.
Deadline: April 2.
How to apply: Applications are available online. Transcripts, letters of recommendation and essays are required.
Exclusive: Visit www.UltimateScholarshipBook.com and enter code PI87420 for updates on this award.

(875) • Ray and Gertrude Marshall Scholarship

American Culinary Federation
180 Center Place Way, St. Augustine, FL 32095
Phone: 904-824-4468
Email: acf@acfchefs.net
http://www.acfchefs.org
Purpose: To assist students in culinary programs.
Eligibility: Applicants must be ACF junior members enrolled in a post-secondary culinary arts program or an ACF apprenticeship program and must have completed at least one grading period. Selection is based on financial need, GPA, recommendations and work experience.
Target applicant(s): College students. Adult students.
Amount: Varies.
Number of awards: Varies.
Deadline: May 1 and September 1.
How to apply: Applications are available online or by written request.
Exclusive: Visit www.UltimateScholarshipBook.com and enter code AM87520 for updates on this award.

(876) • Ray M. Greenly Scholarship

National Retail Federation
1101 New York Avenue NW, Washington, DC 20005
Phone: 800-673-4692
Email: scholarships@nrf.com
http://www.nrf.com
Purpose: To support students interested in retail careers in any field. Possible career arenas include marketing, operations, merchandising, logistics, information technology and analytics.
Eligibility: Applicants must be nominated by a university or college with a current NRF Student Association group and have high academic achievements as well as a strong interest in retail. Students must be current sophomores or juniors with a minimum 3.0 GPA and enrolled as full-time students at NRF Foundation University Partner Schools. Selection is based on demonstrating leadership ability within the retail industry, an intense work ethic and the ability to embrace change and innovation, work as a team player and exemplification of the highest moral character.
Target applicant(s): College students. Adult students.
Minimum GPA: 3.0
Amount: $5,000.
Number of awards: Varies.
Deadline: April 3.
How to apply: Applications are available online. An application form, three essays, one letter of recommendation and a photograph of the applicant are required.
Exclusive: Visit www.UltimateScholarshipBook.com and enter code NA87620 for updates on this award.

(877) • Ray, NRP and Katie, WKTE Pautz Scholarship

American Radio Relay League Foundation
225 Main Street, Newington, CT 06111-1494
Phone: 860-594-0348
Email: foundation@arrl.org
http://www.arrl.org/scholarship-program
Purpose: To provide financial assistance to amateur radio operators from the ARRL Midwest Division.
Eligibility: Applicants must be ARRL members with a General Class or higher Amateur Radio License. They must be residents of Iowa, Kansas, Missouri or Nebraska and should major in electronics, computer science or a related field at a four-year institution.
Target applicant(s): High school students. College students. Adult students.
Amount: $500-$1,000.
Number of awards: 1.
Deadline: January 31.
How to apply: Applications are available online.
Exclusive: Visit www.UltimateScholarshipBook.com and enter code AM87720 for updates on this award.

(878) • Rehabmart.com Scholarship

Rehabmart.com
1353 Athens Highway, Elberton, GA 30635
Phone: 800-827 8283
Email: assistance@rehabmart.com
http://www.rehabmart.com/scholarship/

Purpose: To support students with disabilities, health science students or students majoring in special needs education.
Eligibility: Applicants must be a student with a disability, a student enrolling as a health sciences major or any special education student who is currently attending a secondary school or has been accepted to attend a secondary school, technical college, junior college or four-year college or university. Students will need to submit an essay on medical devices or technology that affects the disabled.
Target applicant(s): High school students. College students. Adult students.
Amount: $250-$2,500.
Number of awards: Varies.
Deadline: May 31.
How to apply: Applications are available online.
Exclusive: Visit www.UltimateScholarshipBook.com and enter code RE87820 for updates on this award.

---

(879) • Reid Blackburn Scholarship

National Press Photographers Foundation
Blackburn Scholarship, 120 Hooper Street, Athens, GA 30602-3018
Phone: 360-759-8027
Email: fay.blackburn@columbian.com
http://www.nppa.org
Purpose: To support photojournalism students.
Eligibility: Applicants must have completed one year at a full-time four-year college or university, provide a portfolio, demonstrate financial need and must have courses in photojournalism and have at least half a year of undergraduate study left. Applicants can apply to as many NPPA scholarships as desired, but only one award will be granted per winner.
Target applicant(s): College students. Adult students.
Amount: $2,000.
Number of awards: Varies.
Deadline: January 6.
How to apply: Applications are available online.
Exclusive: Visit www.UltimateScholarshipBook.com and enter code NA87920 for updates on this award.

---

(880) • Richard C. Maguire Scholarship

Rock Island Arsenal Museum
Richard C. Maguire Scholarship Committee, Attn: SIORI-CFM, Rock Island Arsenal, Rock Island, IL 61299
http://www.arsenalhistoricalsociety.org/maguire.html
Purpose: To support students who are enrolled in a master's degree or doctoral program in history or a related field.
Eligibility: Applicants must be a citizen of the United States, have been accepted into an accredited college or university postgraduate course of study in history or a related field and intend to complete and earn a master's degree or doctorate.
Target applicant(s): Graduate school students. Adult students.
Amount: $1,000.
Number of awards: 1.
Deadline: May 1.
How to apply: Applications are available online.
Exclusive: Visit www.UltimateScholarshipBook.com and enter code RO88020 for updates on this award.

---

(881) • Richard W. Bendicksen Memorial Scholarship

American Radio Relay League Foundation
225 Main Street, Newington, CT 06111-1494
Phone: 860-594-0348
Email: foundation@arrl.org
http://www.arrl.org/scholarship-program
Purpose: To provide financial assistance to amateur radio operators.
Eligibility: Applicants must hold an active amateur radio license of any class, and they must be attending a four-year institution of higher learning.
Target applicant(s): High school students. College students. Adult students.
Amount: $2,000.
Number of awards: 1.
Deadline: January 31.
How to apply: Applications are available online.
Exclusive: Visit www.UltimateScholarshipBook.com and enter code AM88120 for updates on this award.

---

(882) • Risk Management Association Foundation Scholarship

Risk Management Association Foundation Scholarship Program
One Scholarship Way, Saint Peter, MN 56082
Phone: 800-537-4180
Email: rma@scholarshipamerica.org
https://www.scholarsapply.org/rma/
Purpose: To support students who have already completed two years of college.
Eligibility: Applicants must be a U.S. or Canadian citizen who is a current undergraduate student interested in pursuing a career in the banking industry and has completed a minimum of two years of college majoring in accounting, business, finance, economics, banking or related fields of study. Students must be attending full-time and have a minimum 3.0 GPA.
Target applicant(s): College students. Adult students.
Minimum GPA: 3.0
Amount: $2,000-$8,000.
Number of awards: 40.
Scholarship may be renewable.
Deadline: October 21.
How to apply: Application available online.
Exclusive: Visit www.UltimateScholarshipBook.com and enter code RI88220 for updates on this award.

---

(883) • Ritchie-Jennings Memorial Scholarship

Association of Certified Fraud Examiners
Scholarships Program Coordinator, The Gregor Building, 716 West Avenue, Austin, TX 78701
Phone: 512-478-9000
Email: memberservices@acfe.com
http://www.acfe.com
Purpose: To support the college education of accounting, business, finance and criminal justice students who may become Certified Fraud Examiners in the future.
Eligibility: Applicants must be full-time undergraduate or graduate students with a declared major or minor in criminal justice, accounting, business or finance. Students must submit three letters of recommendation, with at least one from a Certified Fraud Examiner or local CFE Chapter and must write an essay on why they deserve the scholarship and how fraud awareness will help their career.
Target applicant(s): College students. Graduate school students. Adult students.
Amount: $1,000-$10,000.
Number of awards: Varies.

Deadline: January 27.
How to apply: Applications are available online.
Exclusive: Visit www.UltimateScholarshipBook.com and enter code AS88320 for updates on this award.

(884) • Robert Yourzak Scholarship Award

Project Management Institute Educational Foundation
14 Campus Boulevard, Newtown Square, PA 19073
Phone: 610-356-4600
Email: pmief@pmi.org
https://pmief.org/scholarships/academic-scholarships
Purpose: This scholarship helps project management students.
Eligibility: Applicants must be project management students who are enrolled in a degree-granting program at a post-secondary institution. Selection is based on the overall strength of the application.
Target applicant(s): College students. Adult students.
Amount: $2,000.
Number of awards: Varies.
Deadline: May 1.
How to apply: Applications are available online. An application form, official transcript, two personal essays, three recommendation letters and a resume are required.
Exclusive: Visit www.UltimateScholarshipBook.com and enter code PR88420 for updates on this award.

(885) • Roger Collins Leadership Scholarship

National Grocers Association
1005 N. Glebe Road, Suite 250, Arlington, VA 22201
Phone: 225-387-6126
http://www.nationalgrocers.org
Purpose: To support students pursuing degrees related to the grocery field.
Eligibility: Applicants must be rising sophomores through postgraduate students, have a minimum 2.5 GPA and be enrolled in a two- or four-year degree-granting institution. Students must major in business, food management, IT or another field related to a career in the grocery industry. Experience in the grocery industry is preferred but not required.
Target applicant(s): College students. Graduate school students. Adult students.
Minimum GPA: 2.5
Amount: Varies.
Number of awards: 1.
Deadline: April 15.
How to apply: Applications are available online.
Exclusive: Visit www.UltimateScholarshipBook.com and enter code NA88520 for updates on this award.

(886) • Roller Skating Foundation Scholarship, Current College Student Category

Roller Skating Foundation
6905 Corporate Drive, Indianapolis, IN 46278
Phone: 317-347-2626
Email: foundation@rollerskating.com
http://www.rollerskating.org
Purpose: To aid sports, hotel and food and beverage management students.
Eligibility: Applicants must be rising undergraduate seniors who are majoring in sports, hotel or food and beverage management. They must have a cumulative GPA of 3.4 or higher on a four-point scale and must demonstrate leadership ability. Selection is based on the overall strength of the application.
Target applicant(s): College students. Adult students.
Minimum GPA: 3.4
Amount: $1,000.
Number of awards: 1.
Deadline: April 1.
How to apply: Applications are available online. An application form, transcript, personal essay, three recommendation letters and income tax information are required.
Exclusive: Visit www.UltimateScholarshipBook.com and enter code RO88620 for updates on this award.

(887) • Ron Culp Scholarship for Mentorship

Public Relations Student Society of America
33 Maiden Lane, 11th Floor, New York, NY 10038
Phone: 212-460-1474
Email: prssa@prsa.org
http://prssa.prsa.org/scholarships-and-awards/
Purpose: To aid public relations and journalism students who have mentored others wishing to pursue careers in public relations.
Eligibility: Applicants must be members of the Public Relations Student Society of America (PRSSA) who are in good standing. They must be rising undergraduate seniors who are majoring in journalism, public relations or a related subject at an accredited, four-year postsecondary institution. They must be preparing for careers in public relations and must have mentored others who intend to pursue careers in the field of public relations. Selection is based on the overall strength of the application.
Target applicant(s): College students. Adult students.
Amount: $1,000.
Number of awards: 1.
Deadline: May 9.
How to apply: Applications are available online. Nomination from someone who is familiar with the applicant's mentoring activities is required.
Exclusive: Visit www.UltimateScholarshipBook.com and enter code PU88720 for updates on this award.

(888) • RTNDA President's Scholarship

Radio Television Digital News Association
529 14th Street NW, Suite 1240, Washington, DC 20045
Phone: 202-659-6510
Email: karenh@rtdna.org
http://www.rtdna.org
Purpose: To honor students pursuing careers in radio, television or digital journalism.
Eligibility: Applicants must be full-time college sophomores, juniors or seniors with at least one full academic year remaining. Applicants may be enrolled in any major as long as their career intent is to pursue a career in radio, television or digital journalism. Applicants may only apply for one RTNDA scholarship.
Target applicant(s): College students. Adult students.
Amount: $1,000.
Number of awards: 1.
Deadline: January 15.
How to apply: Applications are available online.
Exclusive: Visit www.UltimateScholarshipBook.com and enter code RA88820 for updates on this award.

(889) • Ruth Segal Scholarship

Foundation for Outdoor Advertising Research and Education (FOARE)
The Family Scholarship Endowment, c/o Thomas M. Smith & Associates, 4601 Tilden Street NW, Washington, DC 20016
http://oaaa.org/AboutOAAA/FOARE/FOAREScholarshipProgram.aspx
Purpose: To support students who are pursuing a degree in government affairs, urban affairs, public affairs, political science or a related discipline.
Eligibility: Applicants must be graduating seniors, undergraduate students or graduate students. Selection is primarily based on demonstration of financial need, academic achievement, employment history, community service and extracurricular involvement.
Target applicant(s): High school students. College students. Graduate school students. Adult students.
Amount: $4,500.
Number of awards: 1.
Deadline: June 12.
How to apply: Applications are available online.
Exclusive: Visit www.UltimateScholarshipBook.com and enter code FO88920 for updates on this award.

(890) • Sarah Rebecca Reed Scholarship

Beta Phi Mu
Beta Phi Mu Headquarters, P.O. Box 42139, Philadelphia, PA 19101
Phone: 850-644-3907
https://www.betaphimu.org/
Purpose: To encourage scholastic achievement and excellence in graduate level library of information studies at an ALA accredited school.
Eligibility: Applicants must be pursuing graduate level studies in library of information at an ALA accredited school. Beta Phi Mu exists to recognize and encourage scholastic achievement among library and information studies students.
Target applicant(s): College students. Graduate school students. Adult students.
Amount: $2,250.
Number of awards: 2.
Deadline: March 15.
How to apply: Applications are available online.
Exclusive: Visit www.UltimateScholarshipBook.com and enter code BE89020 for updates on this award.

(891) • Scholarship for Start-Up Entrepreneurs

Bob's Watches
15176 Goldenwest Street, Huntington Beach, CA 92683
Phone: 800-494-3708
Email: scholarship@bobswatches.com
https://www.bobswatches.com/entrepreneurs-and-scholarships
Purpose: To support student entrepreneurship.
Eligibility: Applicants must submit a business proposal for an online start-up company. Students must describe their concept, values and mission statement along with an analysis of their business' originality, competition, marketing and budget disbursement.
Target applicant(s): High school students. College students. Adult students.
Amount: $1,000.
Number of awards: 1.
Deadline: June 30.
How to apply: Applications are available online.
Exclusive: Visit www.UltimateScholarshipBook.com and enter code BO89120 for updates on this award.

(892) • Schwan's Food Service Scholarship

School Nutrition Association
120 Waterfront Street, Suite 300, National Harbor, MD 20745
Phone: 301-686-3100
Email: servicecenter@schoolnutrition.org
https://schoolnutrition.org/Membership/AwardsScholarships/
Purpose: To support those entering the school foodservice industry.
Eligibility: Applicants must be School Nutrition Association members for at least one year and be pursuing a field of study related to school foodservice. Applicants must also be employed in school foodservice.
Target applicant(s): High school students. College students. Graduate school students. Adult students.
Amount: Up to $2,500.
Number of awards: Varies.
Scholarship may be renewable.
Deadline: April 4.
How to apply: Applications are available online.
Exclusive: Visit www.UltimateScholarshipBook.com and enter code SC89220 for updates on this award.

(893) • Scott Alan Turner Personal Finance Scholarship

Turner Solutions, LLC
2560 King Arthur Boulevard, Suite 124-107, Lewisville, TX 75056
Phone: 817-719-8040
Email: scholarship@scottalanturner.com
https://scottalanturner.com/personal-finance-scholarship/
Purpose: To encourage students who are interested in learning about personal finance and money management.
Eligibility: Applicants must be U.S. citizens or legal residents of the United States graduating high school students or current undergraduate students in good standing at their college or university. Students must be between 16 and 21 years of age, have a 3.0 GPA and either plan to enroll or already be enrolled part- or full-time at a two or four year college or university.
Target applicant(s): High school students. College students.
Minimum GPA: 3.0
Amount: $500-$1,000.
Number of awards: 2.
Deadline: July 1.
How to apply: Applications are available online.
Exclusive: Visit www.UltimateScholarshipBook.com and enter code TU89320 for updates on this award.

(894) • SE Ranking

SE Ranking
228 Hamilton Avenue, Palo Alto, CA 94301
Phone: 415-704-4387
Email: scholarship@seranking.com
https://seranking.com/scholarship.html
Purpose: To support students with marketing skills.
Eligibility: Applicants must be currently enrolled or admitted at an accredited university or college and write an essay on pertaining to one of the given marketing prompts.
Target applicant(s): High school students. College students. Graduate school students. Adult students.
Amount: $1,000.
Number of awards: 1.
Deadline: June 30.
How to apply: Applications are available online.

Exclusive: Visit www.UltimateScholarshipBook.com and enter code SE89420 for updates on this award.

(895) · Seasons in Malibu Scholarship

Seasons in Malibu Scholarship
32223 Pacific Coast Highway, Malibu, CA 90265
https://seasonsmalibu.com/general-education-and-mental-health-education-scholarship/
Purpose: To support students pursuing a degree in mental health.
Eligibility: Applicants must be enrolled at or accepted to enroll at a university or college with the intent to pursue a major in the mental health field. Applicants must complete an essay along with the application.
Target applicant(s): High school students. College students. Adult students.
Amount: $1,500.
Number of awards: 1.
Deadline: March 31.
How to apply: Applications are available online.
Exclusive: Visit www.UltimateScholarshipBook.com and enter code SE89520 for updates on this award.

(896) · Shawn Carter Foundation Scholarship

Shawn Carter Foundation
Email: scsfapplicant@shawncartersf.com
http://www.shawncartersf.com
Purpose: To assist students at vocational or trade schools.
Eligibility: Applicants must be high school seniors or college students and be between the ages of 18 and 25. Applicants must also be U.S. citizens and have a minimum 2.5 GPA.
Target applicant(s): High school students. College students.
Minimum GPA: 2.5
Amount: $1,500-$2,500.
Number of awards: Varies.
Deadline: April 30.
How to apply: Applications are available online.
Exclusive: Visit www.UltimateScholarshipBook.com and enter code SH89620 for updates on this award.

(897) · Shields-Gillespie Scholarship

American Orff-Schulwerk Association (AOSA)
P.O. Box 391089, Cleveland, OH 44139-8089
Phone: 440-543-5366
Email: info@aosa.org
http://aosa.org
Purpose: To assist pre-K and kindergarten teachers with program funding, including instruments and training.
Eligibility: Applicants must be a member of AOSA. Applicants must be U.S. citizens or have lived in the United States for the past five years. Programs should focus on music/movement learning.
Target applicant(s): High school students. College students. Graduate school students. Adult students.
Amount: Varies.
Number of awards: Varies.
Deadline: January 15.
How to apply: Applications are available online for AOSA members.
Exclusive: Visit www.UltimateScholarshipBook.com and enter code AM89720 for updates on this award.

(898) · Small Business Invention Scholarship

Swiftpage
621 17th Street, Suite 500, Denver, CO 80293
Phone: 877-228-8377
Email: actmarketing@swiftpage.com
https://www.act.com/scholarship
Purpose: To encourage the pursuit of small business.
Eligibility: Applicants must be current high school, undergraduate or graduate students at an accredited institution. Students must submit both a video presentation and an essay about their small business growth idea.
Target applicant(s): High school students. College students. Graduate school students. Adult students.
Amount: $2,500.
Number of awards: 1.
Deadline: December 7.
How to apply: Applications are available online.
Exclusive: Visit www.UltimateScholarshipBook.com and enter code SW89820 for updates on this award.

(899) · SNF Professional Growth Scholarship

School Nutrition Association
120 Waterfront Street, Suite 300, National Harbor, MD 20745
Phone: 301-686-3100
Email: servicecenter@schoolnutrition.org
https://schoolnutrition.org/Membership/AwardsScholarships/
Purpose: To support the continuing education of School Nutrition Association members.
Eligibility: Applicants must be members of the School Nutrition Association for at least one year who are enrolled in an undergraduate or graduate program in a school foodservice related field. Applicants must be currently employed in school foodservice.
Target applicant(s): High school students. College students. Graduate school students. Adult students.
Amount: Up to $2,500.
Number of awards: Varies.
Scholarship may be renewable.
Deadline: April 4.
How to apply: Applications are available online.
Exclusive: Visit www.UltimateScholarshipBook.com and enter code SC89920 for updates on this award.

(900) · Special Education Scholarship

Disability Care Center
2875 South Orange Avenue #500, Orlando, FL 32806
Phone: 888-504-0035
Email: scholarship@disabilitycarecenter.org
http://www.disabilitycarecenter.org
Purpose: To assist students who are majoring in a special education field.
Eligibility: Applicants must be majoring in special education and must be taking at least one major-required class in the upcoming fall semester. Applicants must also be U.S. citizens and have a minimum GPA of 2.5 or greater. Students will need to submit an essay describing why they are pursuing career in special education and how they plan to make a difference in the lives of the disabled. Selection is based on the essay.
Target applicant(s): High school students. College students. Adult students.
Minimum GPA: 2.5
Amount: $500.
Number of awards: 1.

Deadline: August 1.
How to apply: Applications are available online and must include proof of college acceptance or college ID, proof of registration for fall classes, a copy of most recent transcript, documentation confirming U.S. citizenship and the essay.
Exclusive: Visit www.UltimateScholarshipBook.com and enter code DI90020 for updates on this award.

(901) • Specialty Equipment Market Association (SEMA) Memorial Scholarship

Specialty Equipment Market Association
1575 S. Valley Vista Drive, Diamond Bar, CA 91765
Phone: 909-396-0289
Email: education@sema.org
http://www.sema.org/scholarships
Purpose: To support the education of students pursuing careers in the automotive aftermarket.
Eligibility: Applicants must show financial need, have a minimum 2.5 GPA and pursue a career in the automotive aftermarket or related field.
Target applicant(s): College students. Graduate school students. Adult students.
Minimum GPA: 2.5
Amount: $2,000-$5,000.
Number of awards: Varies.
Deadline: March 1.
How to apply: Applications are available online.
Exclusive: Visit www.UltimateScholarshipBook.com and enter code SP90120 for updates on this award.

(902) • SPS Future Teacher Scholarship

Society of Physics Students
One Physics Ellipse , College Park, MD 20740
Phone: 301-209-3007
Email: SPS-Programs@aip.org
https://www.spsnational.org/
Purpose: To provide scholarships to physics majors who are participating in a teacher education program and who intend to pursue a career in physics education.
Eligibility: Applicants must be members of SPS and intend to pursue a career in teaching physics. Students must be undergraduate physics majors at least in their junior year of study at the time of application.
Target applicant(s): College students. Adult students.
Amount: $2,000.
Number of awards: 1.
Deadline: March 22.
How to apply: Applications are available online or from chapter advisors.
Exclusive: Visit www.UltimateScholarshipBook.com and enter code SO90220 for updates on this award.

(903) • SquareFoot Scholarship

SquareFoot
48 W 21st Street, New York, NY 10010
Phone: 917-909-2953
Email: contact@squarefoot.com
https://www.squarefoot.com/scholarship/
Purpose: To support students pursuing real estate, technology and entrepreneurship.
Eligibility: Applicants must be current college or university-level juniors with a GPA of 3.0 or higher. Students must submit an essay on a given topic.
Target applicant(s): College students. Adult students.
Minimum GPA: 3.0
Amount: $3,000.
Number of awards: 3.
Deadline: October 30.
How to apply: Applications are available online.
Exclusive: Visit www.UltimateScholarshipBook.com and enter code SQ90320 for updates on this award.

(904) • SSPI Scholarship Program

Society of Satellite Professionals International (SSPI)
Tamara Bond, 55 Broad Street, 14th Floor, New York, NY 10004
Phone: 212-809-5199
Email: rbell@sspi.org
http://www.sspi.org
Purpose: To help high school and university graduates with undergraduate and post-graduate study in satellite-related disciplines.
Eligibility: Applicants must be high school seniors, undergraduate or graduate students who are members of SSPI (membership is free) studying satellite-related technologies, policies or applications. Some scholarships have requirements such as interests, financial need, residency, gender, race or GPA. The award is based on commitment to education and careers in the satellite fields, academic and leadership achievement, potential for contribution to the satellite communications industry and a scientific, engineering, research, business or creative submission.
Target applicant(s): High school students. College students. Graduate school students. Adult students.
Amount: $2,500-$3,500.
Number of awards: Varies.
Deadline: April 14.
How to apply: Applications are available online.
Exclusive: Visit www.UltimateScholarshipBook.com and enter code SO90420 for updates on this award.

(905) • Stephen D. Pisinski Memorial Scholarship

Public Relations Student Society of America
33 Maiden Lane, 11th Floor, New York, NY 10038
Phone: 212-460-1474
Email: prssa@prsa.org
http://prssa.prsa.org/scholarships-and-awards/
Purpose: To aid journalism, public relations and communications students.
Eligibility: Applicants must be members of the Public Relations Student Society of America (PRSSA). They must be rising undergraduate juniors or seniors who are majoring in journalism, public relations or communications. They must have a cumulative GPA of 3.3 or higher on a four-point scale. Selection is based on the overall strength of the application.
Target applicant(s): College students. Adult students.
Minimum GPA: 3.3
Amount: $1,500.
Number of awards: 1.
Deadline: May 9.
How to apply: Applications are available online. An application form, official transcript, resume, two writing samples, an essay and two recommendation letters are required.

Exclusive: Visit www.UltimateScholarshipBook.com and enter code PU90520 for updates on this award.

(906) • Steven J. Finkel Service Excellence Scholarship

House of Blues Music Forward Foundation
7060 Hollywood Boulevard, Floor 2, Los Angeles, CA 90028
Phone: 323-769-4645
Email: info@hobmusicforward.org
https://hobmusicforward.org/program/scholarships/

Purpose: To encourage students who are passionate about the live music customer experience for fans, artists and employees.
Eligibility: Applicants must be full-time juniors or seniors enrolled at an accredited college or university pursuing a career in live entertainment such as: music business management, customer service, hospitality or other related fields. A minimum 3.0 GPA or higher is required. Students must submit a 500-word essay explaining their career goals within the entertainment industry.
Target applicant(s): College students. Adult students.
Minimum GPA: 3.0
Amount: $10,000.
Number of awards: 1.
Deadline: March 31.
How to apply: Applications are available online.
Exclusive: Visit www.UltimateScholarshipBook.com and enter code HO90620 for updates on this award.

(907) • Still Photographer Scholarship

National Press Photographers Association
Still Photographer Scholarship, 120 Hooper Street, Athens, GA 30602-3018
Phone: 706-542-2506
Email: tkenniff@nppa.org
http://www.nppa.org

Purpose: To honor the profession of photojournalism.
Eligibility: Applicants must have completed one year in a full-time four-year college or university with courses in photojournalism, provide a portfolio and demonstrate financial need. Applicants can apply to as many NPPA scholarships as desired, but only one award will be granted per winner.
Target applicant(s): College students. Adult students.
Amount: $2,000.
Number of awards: Varies.
Deadline: January 6.
How to apply: Applications are available online.
Exclusive: Visit www.UltimateScholarshipBook.com and enter code NA90720 for updates on this award.

(908) • Stuart Cameron and Margaret McLeod Memorial Scholarship

Institute of Management Accountants (IMA)
10 Paragon Drive, Montvale, NJ 07645-1760
Phone: 800-638-4427
Email: students@imanet.org
http://www.imanet.org

Purpose: To help management accounting students.
Eligibility: Applicants must be full- and part-time undergraduate and graduate students, be IMA student members and declare which four- or five-year management accounting, financial management or information technology related program they plan to pursue as a career or list a related field. Candidates should submit applications, resumes, transcripts, two recommendations and statements. Advanced degree students must pass one part of the CMA/CFM certification.
Target applicant(s): College students. Graduate school students. Adult students.
Minimum GPA: 3.0
Amount: $5,000.
Number of awards: 1.
Deadline: March 20.
How to apply: Applications are available online.
Exclusive: Visit www.UltimateScholarshipBook.com and enter code IN90820 for updates on this award.

(909) • Student Achievement Grants

NEA Foundation
1201 16th Street NW, Washington, DC 20036
Phone: 202-822-7840
Email: NEAFoundation@nea.org
http://www.neafoundation.org/pages/grants-to-educators/

Purpose: To promote the academic achievement of students in U.S. public schools and public higher education institutions by providing funds for teachers.
Eligibility: Applicants must be current public school teachers in PreK-12, public school education support professionals or faculty or staff at public higher education institutions. Preference is given to those who work with economically disadvantaged students and NEA members. The grants may be used for materials, supplies, equipment, transportation, software or scholars-in-residence and in some cases professional development. The work should "engage students in critical thinking and problem solving that deepens their knowledge of standards-based subject matter."
Target applicant(s): Graduate school students. Adult students.
Amount: $2,000-$5,000.
Number of awards: Varies.
Deadline: February 1, June 1, October 15.
How to apply: Applications are available online and may be submitted at any time. Applications are reviewed three times each year on February 1, June 1 and October 15.
Exclusive: Visit www.UltimateScholarshipBook.com and enter code NE90920 for updates on this award.

(910) • Student with a Disability Scholarship

American Speech-Language-Hearing Foundation
2200 Research Boulevard, Rockville, MD 20850
Phone: 301-296-8700
Email: foundation@asha.org
http://www.ashfoundation.org

Purpose: To support a graduate student with a disability studying communication sciences and disorders.
Eligibility: Master's degree candidates must be in programs accredited by the Council on Academic Accreditation for Audiology and Speech Pathology, but doctoral programs do not have to be accredited. The applicants should submit a transcript, essay, reference form and statement of good standing; be recommended by a faculty or workplace committee and have not received scholarships from the ASHA Foundation. Students must attend their programs full-time.
Target applicant(s): Graduate school students. Adult students.
Amount: $5,000.
Number of awards: 1.
Deadline: May 22.

How to apply: Applications are available online.
Exclusive: Visit www.UltimateScholarshipBook.com and enter code AM91020 for updates on this award.

(911) • Summer Fellowship Program

American Institute for Economic Research
P.O. Box 1000, Attn.: Susan Gillette, Assistant to the President, Great Barrington, MA 01230
Phone: 413-528-1216
Email: fellowship@aier.org
https://www.aier.org/summer-fellowship-program
Purpose: To provide summer fellowships for college seniors entering a doctoral program in economics or economics-related studies.
Eligibility: Applicants must be college seniors who will enter a doctoral program in economics or an affiliated program.
Target applicant(s): College students. Adult students.
Amount: Room and board plus $500 stipend.
Number of awards: Varies.
Deadline: February 15.
How to apply: Applications are available online.
Exclusive: Visit www.UltimateScholarshipBook.com and enter code AM91120 for updates on this award.

(912) • TACTYC Accounting Scholarship

Teachers of Accounting at Two-Year Colleges
Lori Hatchell - TACTYC Treasurer, P.O. Box 69, Greeley, CO 80632-0069
Email: scholarship@tactyc.org
http://www.tactyc.org
Purpose: To aid accounting students who either are pursuing a two-year undergraduate degree or who are moving to a four-year institution after having completed a two-year accounting degree.
Eligibility: Applicants must be undergraduate accounting students. They must be pursuing a two-year degree or must be pursuing a bachelor's degree in accounting after having completed a two-year accounting degree program. Selection is based on recommendations, GPA and stated career goals.
Target applicant(s): College students. Adult students.
Amount: $1,000.
Number of awards: Varies.
Deadline: March 1.
How to apply: Applications are available online. An application form and supporting materials are required.
Exclusive: Visit www.UltimateScholarshipBook.com and enter code TE91220 for updates on this award.

(913) • Teacher Education Scholarship Fund

American Montessori Society
Attn.: Abbie Kelly, Director of Teacher Education, Affiliation and Services, 116 East 16th Street, New York, NY 10003
Phone: 212-358-1250
Email: abbie@amshq.org
http://www.amshq.org
Purpose: To support future Montessori teachers.
Eligibility: Applicants must be accepted, are in the process of being accepted or are already enrolled in an AMS-affiliated teacher education program. Financial need, the applicant's personal statement and letters of recommendation are considered.
Target applicant(s): High school students. College students. Adult students.
Amount: Varies.
Number of awards: Varies.
Scholarship may be renewable.
Deadline: May 1.
How to apply: Applications are available online.
Exclusive: Visit www.UltimateScholarshipBook.com and enter code AM91320 for updates on this award.

(914) • Teacher of the Year Award

Veterans of Foreign Wars Teacher of the Year Award
406 W. 34th Street, Kansas City, MO 64111
Phone: 816-968-1117
Email: tbeauchamp@vfw.org
http://www.vfw.org
Purpose: To salute the nation's top elementary, junior high and high school teachers who educate their students about citizenship and American history and traditions.
Eligibility: Applicants must be current classroom teachers who teach at least half of the school day in a classroom environment, grades K-12. Previous winners from the state or national levels are not eligible. Fellow teachers, supervisors or other interested individuals who are not related to the nominee may send in nominations; no self-nominations will be accepted.
Target applicant(s): Graduate school students. Adult students.
Amount: $1,000.
Number of awards: 3.
Deadline: October 31.
How to apply: Applications are available online but initial nominations must be sent to the local VFW office. Visit the website for more information.
Exclusive: Visit www.UltimateScholarshipBook.com and enter code VE91420 for updates on this award.

(915) • TechChecks Business Leadership Scholarship

TechChecks
138 Daniel Drive, Lakewood, NJ 08701
Phone: 866-527 3758
Email: sales@techchecks.net
https://www.techchecks.net/
Purpose: To reward students who have strong academic credentials and are pursuing a degree that emphasizes business or marketing.
Eligibility: Applicants must be high school seniors or current college students pursuing a degree in business administration or another business-related field. A minimum 3.5 GPA is required. Students must be U.S. citizens and preference will be given to those who are female, have a disability or belong to one of the following minority groups: African American, Hispanic/Latino, Asian American/Pacific Islander or Native American/American Indian (must provide proof of membership to a tribe). Students must submit an essay on the topic provided. Essay selection will be based on the quality of research, originality and presentation.
Target applicant(s): High school students. College students. Graduate school students. Adult students.
Minimum GPA: 3.5
Amount: $1,000.
Number of awards: 4.
Deadline: June 15.
How to apply: Applications are available online and must include an official transcript as well as the required essay.
Exclusive: Visit www.UltimateScholarshipBook.com and enter code TE91520 for updates on this award.

(916) • Timothy S.Y. Lam Foundation Education Scholarships

Timothy S.Y. Lam Foundation
P.O. Box 98141, Las Vegas, NV 89193-8141
Phone: 702-900-7584
Email: info@timothysylam.org
http://www.timothysylam.org/education_scholarships.aspx

Purpose: To support students pursuing a career in the hospitality industry.

Eligibility: Applicants must be at least 18 years of age and pursuing a degree or certification in the hospitality industry. An essay is required with the application. There are two deadlines each year: May 15 and November 15.

Target applicant(s): College students. Adult students.

Amount: Up to $2,000.

Number of awards: 7.

Deadline: May 15 and November 15.

How to apply: Applications are available online, and must include a resume, an essay, one letter of reference, a photo and an official transcript.

Exclusive: Visit www.UltimateScholarshipBook.com and enter code TI91620 for updates on this award.

(917) • TLMI Four Year College Degree Scholarship Program

Tag and Label Manufacturers Institute Inc.
TLMI Scholarship Committee, 1 Blackburn Center, Gloucester, MA 01930
Phone: 978-282-1400
Email: office@tlmi.com
http://www.tlmi.com

Purpose: To assist upper-level students planning to pursue a career in tag and label manufacturing.

Eligibility: Applicants must demonstrate an interest in the tag and label manufacturing industry while taking appropriate courses at an accredited four-year college. They must be full-time sophomores or juniors with a GPA of at least 3.0. Applicants must submit a personal statement and three letters of recommendation attesting to their character.

Target applicant(s): College students. Adult students.

Minimum GPA: 3.0

Amount: $5,000.

Number of awards: Up to 6.

Deadline: March 31.

How to apply: Applications are available online and by phone.

Exclusive: Visit www.UltimateScholarshipBook.com and enter code TA91720 for updates on this award.

(918) • TLMI Two-Year College or Technical Degree Program Scholarship

Tag and Label Manufacturers Institute Inc.
TLMI Scholarship Committee, 1 Blackburn Center, Gloucester, MA 01930
Phone: 978-282-1400
Email: office@tlmi.com
http://www.tlmi.com

Purpose: To aid students who are enrolled in a flexographic printing program of study.

Eligibility: Applicants must be enrolled full-time in a flexographic printing program at a two-year college or degree-granting technical school. They must have a GPA of 3.0 or higher and have a demonstrated interest in pursuing a career in the tag and label industry. Selection is based on the overall strength of the application.

Target applicant(s): College students. Adult students.

Minimum GPA: 3.0

Amount: $1,000.

Number of awards: Up to 4.

Deadline: March 31.

How to apply: Applications are available online. An application form, official transcript and personal statement are required.

Exclusive: Visit www.UltimateScholarshipBook.com and enter code TA91820 for updates on this award.

(919) • Tom and Judith Comstock Scholarship

American Radio Relay League Foundation
225 Main Street, Newington, CT 06111-1494
Phone: 860-594-0348
Email: foundation@arrl.org
http://www.arrl.org/scholarship-program

Purpose: To assist ham radio operators in furthering their educations.

Eligibility: Applicants must have any class of ham radio license, be residents of Texas or Oklahoma and be high school seniors accepted at a two- or four-year college or university.

Target applicant(s): High school students.

Amount: $2,000.

Number of awards: 1.

Deadline: January 31.

How to apply: Applications are available online but may not be completed electronically. All completed applications must be mailed.

Exclusive: Visit www.UltimateScholarshipBook.com and enter code AM91920 for updates on this award.

(920) • Tom Steel Post-Graduate Fellowship

Pride Law Fund
P.O. Box 2602, San Francisco, CA 94126-2602
Email: Steel@pridelawfund.org
http://www.pridelawfund.org

Purpose: To support law students with a project that serves the lesbian, gay, bisexual and transgendered community.

Eligibility: Applicants must be students in their last year of law school or lawyers within three years of graduating from law school. The award is based on the quality and scope of the project, proposal, public service activities and relation to the LGBT community. Applicants should submit applications, resumes, project descriptions, two reference letters, budget, timetable and law school transcript.

Target applicant(s): Graduate school students. Adult students.

Amount: $30,000.

Number of awards: 1.

Deadline: January 13.

How to apply: Applications are available online.

Exclusive: Visit www.UltimateScholarshipBook.com and enter code PR92020 for updates on this award.

(921) • TOPSS Competition for High School Psychology Students

American Psychological Foundation
750 First Street NE, Washington, DC 20002-4242
Phone: 202-336-5843
Email: foundation@apa.org
http://www.apa.org/apf/funding/index.aspx

Purpose: To assist students who are studying psychology.
Eligibility: Applicants must be high school students who have been or are presently enrolled in a psychology course and must write an essay answering a question from the APA. A Teachers of Psychology in Secondary Schools (TOPSS) member must sponsor all candidates, and each school may submit no more than five papers.
Target applicant(s): High school students.
Amount: $250.
Number of awards: 4.
Deadline: March 15.
How to apply: Submission information is available online.
Exclusive: Visit www.UltimateScholarshipBook.com and enter code AM92120 for updates on this award.

(922) • Tourism Cares Academic Scholarship Program

Tourism Cares
275 Turnpike Street, Suite 307, Canton, MA 02021
Phone: 781-821-5990
Email: scholarships@tourismcares.org
http://www.tourismcares.org/academic-scholarships/
Purpose: To support undergraduate and graduate students studying in programs related to the areas of hospitality, tourism or travel at accredited educational institutions.
Eligibility: Applicants must be United States citizens enrolled full-time or part-time at accredited schools for the upcoming fall semester. Multiple individual scholarship awards are included in this program. Specific eligibility criteria vary for each award. Selection is based upon motivation, volunteer service, involvement in extracurricular activities, academic success and leadership ability.
Target applicant(s): College students. Adult students.
Amount: $1,000-$4,000.
Number of awards: Varies.
Deadline: April 3.
How to apply: Applications are available online. An application and transcripts are required for all awards. Other requirements vary with individual awards.
Exclusive: Visit www.UltimateScholarshipBook.com and enter code TO92220 for updates on this award.

(923) • Tourism Cares Sustainable Tourism Scholarships

Tourism Cares
275 Turnpike Street, Suite 307, Canton, MA 02021
Phone: 781-821-5990
Email: scholarships@tourismcares.org
http://www.tourismcares.org/academic-scholarships/
Purpose: To promote sustainable tourism and to assist graduate students who are studying tourism.
Eligibility: Applicants must be enrolled in a tourism program at the graduate level at an accredited college or university in any country and have a GPA of 3.0 or higher. Students in developing countries are encouraged to apply.
Target applicant(s): Graduate school students. Adult students.
Minimum GPA: 3.0
Amount: Varies.
Number of awards: Varies.
Deadline: April 3.
How to apply: Applications are available online.
Exclusive: Visit www.UltimateScholarshipBook.com and enter code TO92320 for updates on this award.

(924) • Tri State Surveying and Photogrammetry Kris M. Kunze Memorial Scholarship

National Society of Professional Surveyors (NSPS/AAGS)
Attn: Scholarships, 5119 Pegasus Court, Suite Q, Frederick, MD 21704
Phone: 240-439-4615x105
Email: trisha.milburn@nsps.us.com
http://www.nsps.us.com/?page=Scholarships
Purpose: To aid current and future land surveying professionals who are taking courses in business.
Eligibility: Applicants must be National Society of Professional Surveyors (NSPS) members. They must be licensed professional land surveyors, certified photogrammetrists, land surveying interns or current full-time land surveying students who are taking courses in business administration or management. Selection is based on academic merit, personal statement, recommendations, professional involvement and financial need. Scholarship is offered in odd years only.
Target applicant(s): College students. Adult students.
Amount: $2,000.
Number of awards: 1.
Deadline: March 31.
How to apply: Applications are available online. An application form, official transcript, personal statement, three letters of recommendation and proof of NSPS membership are required.
Exclusive: Visit www.UltimateScholarshipBook.com and enter code NA92420 for updates on this award.

(925) • Two-Year Associate and Technology Scholarship

Shell
P.O. Box 162, 2501 AN, The Hague, NE
Phone: 713-718-6379
Email: shellscholarships@hccsfoundation.org
https://www.shell.us/
Purpose: To support students who are seeking a degree in a technology field.
Eligibility: Applicants must be U.S. citizens and be taking at least six credit hours in the fall and spring. A minimum 2.5 GPA or higher is required. Students should be pursuing a degree in process/production technology, petroleum technology, compressor technology, electrical technology, industrial maintenance technology, instrumentation technology or machinist technology.
Target applicant(s): College students. Adult students.
Minimum GPA: 2.5
Amount: $2,200.
Deadline: March 31.
How to apply: Applications are available online.
Exclusive: Visit www.UltimateScholarshipBook.com and enter code SH92520 for updates on this award.

(926) • Ultimate Promotion Scholarship

Slant Marketing
150 N. Wacker Drive, Suite 1220, Chicago, IL 60606
Phone: 312-929 3789
Email: slantscholarship@gmail.com
http://www.slantmarketing.com
Purpose: To reward students for creating an ultimate promotional experience for a product.
Eligibility: Applicants must be at least 18 years of age and a college undergraduate to apply. Students must be pursuing a degree in

marketing, advertising, public relations and/or business administration. Applicants must be U.S. citizens. Students will need to imagine and submit an essay describing a promotion to be put on by one of their favorite brands explaining the underlying strategic value of their idea. A minimum 3.0 GPA required.
Target applicant(s): College students. Adult students.
Minimum GPA: 3.0
Amount: $1,500.
Number of awards: Varies.
Deadline: August 1.
How to apply: Applications must be emailed and include a full cover page with name, full contact details and the name of your college or university.
Exclusive: Visit www.UltimateScholarshipBook.com and enter code SL92620 for updates on this award.

(927) • Undergraduate Scholarship

National Restaurant Association Educational Foundation
2055 L Street NW Suite 700, Washington, DC 20036
Phone: 800-765-2122
Email: scholars@naref.org
http://www.nraef.org
Purpose: To assist restaurant and food service students.
Eligibility: Applicants must be U.S. citizens or permanent residents, plan to use the award at a food service-related program at an accredited college or university and plan to take a minimum of nine credit hours per term.
Target applicant(s): High school students. College students. Adult students.
Minimum GPA: 2.75
Amount: $2,500 to $10,000.
Number of awards: Varies.
Deadline: April 1.
How to apply: Applications are available online.
Exclusive: Visit www.UltimateScholarshipBook.com and enter code NA92720 for updates on this award.

(928) • United Commercial Travelers of America (UCT) Scholarship Program

Order of United Commercial Travelers of America
1801 Watermark Drive, Suite 100, P.O. Box 159019, Columbus, OH 43215-8619
Phone: 614-487-9680
http://www.uct.org
Purpose: To support students or teachers who work primarily with students who have intellectual disabilities.
Eligibility: Applicants must be a current teacher or current undergraduate student who is pursuing course work to enhance their work with individuals who have intellectual disabilities. Students must work in North America.
Target applicant(s): College students. Adult students.
Amount: Up to $2,500.
Number of awards: 1.
Scholarship may be renewable.
Deadline: November 15.
How to apply: Applications are available online.
Exclusive: Visit www.UltimateScholarshipBook.com and enter code OR92820 for updates on this award.

(929) • United States Senate Youth Program

William Randolph Hearst Foundation
90 New Montgomery Street, Suite 1212, San Francisco, CA 94105
Phone: 800-841-7048 x 4540
Email: ussyp@hearstfdn.org
http://ussenateyouth.org
Purpose: To expose students to their government in action.
Eligibility: Applicants must be high school juniors or seniors in an elected position at school or in civic or educational offices. USSYP brings the highest level officials from each branch of government together with a group of 104 high school student delegates for an intensive week-long educational program held in Washington, DC.
Target applicant(s): High school students.
Amount: $10,000.
Number of awards: 104.
Deadline: Varies by state.
How to apply: To apply, contact your high school principal, counselor or state selection contact. State selection contact information is located on the home page of the website.
Exclusive: Visit www.UltimateScholarshipBook.com and enter code WI92920 for updates on this award.

(930) • University of California Public Policy and International Affairs Law Fellowship

University of California at Berkeley
UCPPIA Summer Institute, Goldman School of Public Policy, 2607 Hearst Avenue, Berkeley, CA 94720-7320
Phone: 510-642-4670
Email: noah.romero@berkeley.edu
http://gspp.berkeley.edu/ppia
Purpose: To encourage prospective graduate students to pursue a joint degree in law and public policy.
Eligibility: Applicants must be U.S. citizens or legal permanent residents. They must be rising undergraduate seniors who have at least one more semester (or two more quarters) of coursework remaining before graduation. They must be interested in law and public service careers, and must have a demonstrated interest in policy issues that affect underserved populations. They must have overcome obstacles in their pursuit of higher education. Selection is based on the overall strength of the application.
Target applicant(s): College students. Adult students.
Amount: At least $5,000.
Number of awards: 10.
Deadline: Varies.
How to apply: Applications are available online. An application form and personal statement are required.
Exclusive: Visit www.UltimateScholarshipBook.com and enter code UN93020 for updates on this award.

(931) • University of California Public Policy and International Affairs Summer Institute

University of California at Berkeley
UCPPIA Summer Institute, Goldman School of Public Policy, 2607 Hearst Avenue, Berkeley, CA 94720-7320
Phone: 510-642-4670
Email: noah.romero@berkeley.edu
http://gspp.berkeley.edu/ppia
Purpose: To aid students who are interested in pursuing graduate studies in public policy.

Eligibility: Applicants must be U.S. citizens or legal permanent residents who are rising undergraduate seniors who have at least one more semester (or two more quarters) of coursework remaining before graduation. They must be interested in public service careers and must have a demonstrated interest in policy issues that affect underserved populations. They must have overcome obstacles in their pursuit of higher education. Selection is based on the overall strength of the application.
Target applicant(s): College students. Adult students.
Amount: Varies.
Number of awards: 30.
Deadline: Varies.
How to apply: Applications are available online. An application form and personal statement are required.
Exclusive: Visit www.UltimateScholarshipBook.com and enter code UN93120 for updates on this award.

(932) • University of the Aftermarket Foundation Scholarship

Global Automotive Aftermarket Symposium, Inc.
c/o Auto Care Association, 7101 Wisconsin Avenue, Suite 1300, Bethesda, MD 20814
Phone: 312-768-7379
http://www.automotivescholarships.com
Purpose: To support students who intend to have a career in the automotive industry.
Eligibility: Applicants must have graduated from high school or acquired their GED. Students must be enrolled or planning to enroll as a full-time student in a two- or four- year college or an ASE/NATEF certified post-secondary automotive, collision repair or heavy duty program.
Target applicant(s): High school students. College students. Adult students.
Amount: Varies.
Number of awards: Varies.
Deadline: March 31.
How to apply: Applications are available online.
Exclusive: Visit www.UltimateScholarshipBook.com and enter code GL93220 for updates on this award.

(933) • USGIF Scholarship Program

United States Geospatial Intelligence Foundation (USGIF)
2325 Dulles Corner Boulevard, Suite 450, Herndon, VA 20171
Phone: 888-698-7443
Email: scholarships@usgif.org
http://usgif.org/
Purpose: To assist those who are studying geospatial sciences.
Eligibility: Applicants must be high school seniors or college or graduate students. Selection is based on academic and professional achievement in a field related to geospatial intelligence tradecraft.
Target applicant(s): High school students. College students. Graduate school students. Adult students.
Amount: Varies.
Number of awards: Varies.
Deadline: May 15.
Exclusive: Visit www.UltimateScholarshipBook.com and enter code UN93320 for updates on this award.

(934) • Vern and Elaine Clark Outdoor Advertising Industry "Champion" Scholarship Endowment

Foundation for Outdoor Advertising Research and Education (FOARE)
The Family Scholarship Endowment, c/o Thomas M. Smith & Associates, 4601 Tilden Street NW, Washington, DC 20016
http://oaaa.org/AboutOAAA/FOARE/FOAREScholarshipProgram.aspx
Purpose: To support undergraduate and graduate students who are pursuing a career in the outdoor advertising industry.
Eligibility: Selection is primarily based on academic achievement, career goals and community involvement. Applicants must submit a letter of recommendation from someone in the outdoor advertising industry and a letter of recommendation addressing the applicant's community service.
Target applicant(s): High school students. College students. Graduate school students. Adult students.
Amount: $4,000.
Number of awards: 1.
Deadline: June 12.
How to apply: Applications are available online.
Exclusive: Visit www.UltimateScholarshipBook.com and enter code FO93420 for updates on this award.

(935) • Vidal Sassoon Professional Beauty Education Scholarship Program

Beauty Changes Lives
9927 E. Bell Road, Suite 110, Scottsdale, AZ 85260
Phone: 800-831-1086
http://www.beautychangeslives.org
Purpose: To support licensed hairstylists in attending a North American Sassoon Academy program.
Eligibility: Applicants must be attending a member school of the American Association of Cosmetology Schools. Selection is based on the overall strength of the application.
Target applicant(s): College students. Adult students.
Amount: $5,000.
Number of awards: 10.
Deadline: March 13, August 28.
How to apply: Applications are available online.
Exclusive: Visit www.UltimateScholarshipBook.com and enter code BE93520 for updates on this award.

(936) • Vincent Chin Scholarship

Asian American Journalists Association
5 Third Street, Suite 1108, San Francisco, CA 94103
Phone: 415-346-2051
Email: naov@aaja.org
http://www.aaja.org
Purpose: To support college students interested in pursuing careers in journalism.
Eligibility: Applicants must be undergraduate students enrolled full-time and must be currently taking or planning to take journalism courses and/or pursuing a career in journalism. Applicants are not required to be Asian Americans but must support the mission of the AAJA and be committed to work within the community. Selection is based on the applicant's promise to support the field of journalism and issues faced by Pacific Islanders and Asian Americans. In addition, selection is based on financial need, academic achievement and demonstrated

ability in journalism as well as the applicant's resume, two letters of recommendation, essay and work samples.
Target applicant(s): College students. Adult students.
Amount: $500.
Number of awards: 1.
Deadline: April 16.
How to apply: Applications are available online.
Exclusive: Visit www.UltimateScholarshipBook.com and enter code AS93620 for updates on this award.

---

(937) • Virtual Business Scholarship

Knowledge Matters
1 Roundhouse Plaza, Suite 304, Northampton, MA 01060
Phone: 877-965-3276
http://www.knowledgematters.com
Purpose: To support high school juniors and seniors in pursuing a degree in business, marketing or personal finance.
Eligibility: Applicants must be nominated by a high school teacher. Students must demonstrate excellence in business, marketing or personal finance courses. Selection is based on the overall strength of the application.
Target applicant(s): High school students.
Amount: $2,000.
Number of awards: 1.
Deadline: April 1.
How to apply: Applications are available online.
Exclusive: Visit www.UltimateScholarshipBook.com and enter code KN93720 for updates on this award.

---

(938) • Wesley-Logan Prize

American Historical Association
400 A Street SE, Washington, DC 20003
Phone: 202-544-2422
Email: info@historians.org
http://www.historians.org
Purpose: To award a prize to a scholarly/literary book focusing on the history of dispersion, relocation, settlement or adjustment of people from Africa or on their return to that continent.
Eligibility: Books must have been published between May 1 of the previous year and April 30 of the entry year. Entries are mailed directly to committee members.
Target applicant(s): Junior high students or younger. High school students. College students. Graduate school students. Adult students.
Amount: Varies.
Number of awards: Varies.
Deadline: May 15.
How to apply: Application information is available on approximately March 30.
Exclusive: Visit www.UltimateScholarshipBook.com and enter code AM93820 for updates on this award.

---

(939) • WIIT Charitable Trust Scholarship

Women in International Trade Charitable Trust
c/o Affinity Strategies, 100 M Street S.E., Suite 600, Washington, DC 20003
Phone: 202-293-2948
http://www.wiittrust.org
Purpose: To support female undergraduate and graduate students who are pursuing a degree in international trade.
Eligibility: Applicants must submit an essay that analyzes a U.S. free trade agreement. Selection is based on the overall strength of the submission. Students must be enrolled at an accredited U.S. educational institution.
Target applicant(s): College students. Graduate school students. Adult students.
Amount: Up to $1,500.
Number of awards: 2.
Deadline: July 31.
How to apply: Applications are available online.
Exclusive: Visit www.UltimateScholarshipBook.com and enter code WO93920 for updates on this award.

---

(940) • Wikibuy eCommerce and Online Retail Scholarship

Wikibuy
3939 Bee Cave Road, Austin, TX 78746
Email: scholarshipsubmissions@wikibuy.com
https://wikibuy.com/scholarship
Purpose: To encourage students who pursue academic excellence and have a strong entrepreneurial spirit.
Eligibility: Applicants must be currently enrolled or planning to be enrolled in the fall in a business program at an accredited post-secondary school in the United States. Applicants must submit a 500-word essay on the prompt found on the website highlighting their entrepreneurial and innovative spirit. Special consideration given to those seeking a career in online retail and eCommerce. A minimum 3.4 GPA or higher is required.
Target applicant(s): High school students. College students. Graduate school students. Adult students.
Minimum GPA: 3.4
Amount: $2,500.
Number of awards: 1.
Deadline: August 21.
How to apply: Applications are available online.
Exclusive: Visit www.UltimateScholarshipBook.com and enter code WI94020 for updates on this award.

---

(941) • William B. Ruggles Right to Work Scholarship

National Institute for Labor Relations Research (NILRR)
William B. Ruggles Scholarship Selection Committee, 5211 Port Royal Road, Suite 510, Springfield, VA 22151
Phone: 703-321-9606
Email: research@nilrr.org
http://www.nilrr.org
Purpose: To support students who are dedicated to high journalistic standards.
Eligibility: Applicants must be undergraduate or graduate students majoring in journalism and demonstrate an understanding of the principles of voluntary unionism and the economic and social problems of compulsory unionism.
Target applicant(s): High school students. College students. Graduate school students. Adult students.
Amount: $2,000.
Number of awards: 1.
Deadline: December 31.
How to apply: Applications are available online.
Exclusive: Visit www.UltimateScholarshipBook.com and enter code NA94120 for updates on this award.

(942) • Women Grocers of America (WGA) Mary Macey Scholarship(s)

National Grocers Association
1005 N. Glebe Road, Suite 250, Arlington, VA 22201
Phone: 225-387-6126
http://www.nationalgrocers.org
Purpose: To support students pursuing a degree related to the grocery field.
Eligibility: Applicants must be rising sophomores through postgraduate students, have a minimum 2.5 GPA and be enrolled in a two- or four-year degree-granting institution. Students must major in business, food management, IT or another field related to a career in the grocery industry. Experience in the grocery industry is preferred but not required.
Target applicant(s): College students. Graduate school students. Adult students.
Minimum GPA: 2.5
Amount: Varies.
Number of awards: Varies.
Deadline: April 15.
How to apply: Applications are available online.
Exclusive: Visit www.UltimateScholarshipBook.com and enter code NA94220 for updates on this award.

(943) • Women in Geographic Education Scholarship

National Council for Geographic Education
1101 14th Street NW, Suite 350, Washington, DC 20005-5647
Phone: 256-782-5293
Email: ncge@jsu.edu
http://www.ncge.org/awards
Purpose: To aid undergraduate or graduate women planning careers in geographic education.
Eligibility: Applicants must be enrolled in a program leading to a career in geographic education, submit an essay on the provided topic and have an overall GPA of 3.0 and a geography GPA of 3.5. Applicants must have a minimum of 15 undergraduate or 9 graduate credits in geography. The winner receives an additional $300 travel stipend if she attends the NCGE Annual Meeting.
Target applicant(s): College students. Graduate school students. Adult students.
Minimum GPA: 3.0
Amount: $500.
Number of awards: 1.
Deadline: February 1.
How to apply: Applications are available online.
Exclusive: Visit www.UltimateScholarshipBook.com and enter code NA94320 for updates on this award.

(944) • YASME Foundation Scholarship

American Radio Relay League Foundation
225 Main Street, Newington, CT 06111-1494
Phone: 860-594-0348
Email: foundation@arrl.org
http://www.arrl.org/scholarship-program
Purpose: To support science and engineering students who are involved in amateur radio.
Eligibility: Applicants must have an active amateur radio license. Students must be enrolled in a four-year college or university. Preference will be given to students in the top 10 percent of their class and those who have participated in community service and local amateur radio clubs.
Target applicant(s): High school students. College students. Adult students.
Amount: $3,000.
Number of awards: Varies.
Scholarship may be renewable.
Deadline: January 31.
How to apply: Applications are available online.
Exclusive: Visit www.UltimateScholarshipBook.com and enter code AM94420 for updates on this award.

(945) • Youth Scholarship

Society of Broadcast Engineers
9102 N. Meridian Street, Suite 150, Indianapolis, IN 46260
Phone: 317-846-9000
Email: mclappe@sbe.org
http://www.sbe.org
Purpose: To help students who plan to pursue a career in the technical aspects of broadcasting.
Eligibility: Applicants must be graduating high school seniors who plan to enroll in a technical school, college or university and should pursue studies leading to a career in broadcasting engineering or a related field. Preference is given to members of SBE, but any student may apply. Applicants should submit applications, transcripts, biographies and statements. Recipients must write a paper about broadcast engineering.
Target applicant(s): High school students.
Amount: $1,000-$1,500.
Number of awards: Up to 3.
Deadline: July 1.
How to apply: Applications are available online.
Exclusive: Visit www.UltimateScholarshipBook.com and enter code SO94520 for updates on this award.

(946) • Zachary Taylor Stevens Memorial Scholarship

American Radio Relay League Foundation
225 Main Street, Newington, CT 06111-1494
Phone: 860-594-0348
Email: foundation@arrl.org
http://www.arrl.org/scholarship-program
Purpose: To support students who are involved in amateur radio.
Eligibility: Applicants must have an amateur radio license of Technician Class or higher. Preference will be given to students residing in call areas in Michigan, Ohio and West Virginia. Students may be enrolled in a two-year or four-year college or technical school.
Target applicant(s): High school students. College students. Adult students.
Amount: $750.
Number of awards: 1.
Deadline: January 31.
How to apply: Applications are available online.
Exclusive: Visit www.UltimateScholarshipBook.com and enter code AM94620 for updates on this award.

SCIENCES

(947) • A Place for Mom Senior Wisdom Video Scholarship

A Place for Mom
701 5th Avenue, Suite 3200, Seattle, WA 98104
Phone: 866-333-7935
Email: scholarship@aplaceformom.com
https://www.aplaceformom.com/scholarship
Purpose: To assist students enrolled in programs in gerontology, long term care administration, social work, medicine, nursing or sociology.
Eligibility: Applicants must be enrolled in an associate's degree, bachelor's degree or graduate level program at a two- or four-year university. Students must write an essay as part of the application process.
Target applicant(s): College students. Graduate school students. Adult students.
Amount: $1,000.
Number of awards: 5.
Deadline: Varies.
How to apply: Applications are available online.
Exclusive: Visit www.UltimateScholarshipBook.com and enter code A 94720 for updates on this award.

(948) • A.O. Putnam Memorial Scholarship

Institute of Industrial and Systems Engineers
3577 Parkway Lane, Suite 200, Norcross, GA 30092
Phone: 800-494-0460
Email: bcameron@iienet.org
http://www.iise.org/
Purpose: To help undergraduate Institute members who plan to pursue careers in management consulting.
Eligibility: Applicants must be undergraduate students enrolled in a college in the United States, Canada or Mexico with an accredited industrial engineering program, major in industrial engineering and be active members. Preference is given to students who plan to work in management consulting. Students may not apply directly for this scholarship and must be nominated. The award is based on academic ability, character, leadership, potential service to the industrial engineering profession and financial need. Minimum 3.4 GPA required.
Target applicant(s): High school students. College students. Adult students.
Minimum GPA: 3.4
Amount: $1,000.
Number of awards: 2.
Deadline: November 15.
How to apply: Nomination forms are available online.
Exclusive: Visit www.UltimateScholarshipBook.com and enter code IN94820 for updates on this award.

(949) • AAAE Foundation Scholarship

American Association of Airport Executives
601 Madison Street, Ste. 400, Alexandria, VA 22314
Phone: 703-824-0500
Email: member.services@aaae.org
http://www.aaae.org
Purpose: To support students of aviation.
Eligibility: Applicants must be enrolled in an aviation program with at least junior standing and at least a 3.0 GPA. Eligibility is unrelated to membership in AAAE. Winners are selected based on academic records, financial need, participation in school and community activities, work experience and a personal statement. Applicants must recommended by their school.
Target applicant(s): College students. Graduate school students. Adult students.
Minimum GPA: 3.0
Amount: $500-$1,500.
Number of awards: 8.
Deadline: March 31.
How to apply: To obtain an application, contact the scholarship or financial aid office at the college you attend. Scholarship information is usually mailed to universities and colleges in early January.
Exclusive: Visit www.UltimateScholarshipBook.com and enter code AM94920 for updates on this award.

(950) • AACE International Competitive Scholarships

Association for the Advancement of Cost Engineering
Attn: Staff Director - Education, 1265 Suncrest Towne Centre Drive, Morgantown, WV 26505-1876
http://www.aacei.org
Purpose: To aid students enrolled in programs related to cost engineering and cost management.
Eligibility: Applicants must be full-time students enrolled in one of the following programs: agricultural engineering, architectural engineering, building construction, business administration, chemical engineering, civil engineering, industrial engineering, manufacturing engineering, mechanical engineering, mining engineering, electrical engineering or quantity surveying. Minimum 3.0 GPA required. Those who are in their final year of undergraduate study must be accepted to attend a graduate program full-time in the next academic year. Selection is based on academic performance (35 percent), extracurricular activities (35 percent) and essay (30 percent).
Target applicant(s): College students. Graduate school students. Adult students.
Minimum GPA: 3.0
Amount: $2,500.
Number of awards: Varies.
Deadline: February 28.
How to apply: Applications are available online. An application form and essay are required.
Exclusive: Visit www.UltimateScholarshipBook.com and enter code AS95020 for updates on this award.

(951) • AACT National Candy Technologists John Kitt Memorial Scholarship Program

Warrell Corp
Attn: Kevin Silva, 1250 Slate Hill Road, Camp Hill, PA 17011
Phone: 201-652-2655
Email: aactinfo@gomc.com
http://www.aactcandy.org
Purpose: To aid students with a demonstrated interested in confectionery technology.
Eligibility: Applicants must be rising college sophomores, juniors or seniors at an accredited four-year college or university in North America. They must major in food science, chemical science, biological science or a related area. A GPA of 3.0 or higher is required.
Target applicant(s): College students. Adult students.
Minimum GPA: 3.0
Amount: $5,000.
Number of awards: 1.
Deadline: April 4.

How to apply: Applications are available online. An application form, list of academic, work and other activities, list of honors and awards, statement of goals and transcript are required.
Exclusive: Visit www.UltimateScholarshipBook.com and enter code WA95120 for updates on this award.

(952) • AAGS - NSPS Scholarships

National Society of Professional Surveyors (NSPS/AAGS)
Attn: Scholarships, 5119 Pegasus Court, Suite Q, Frederick, MD 21704
Phone: 240-439-4615x105
Email: trisha.milburn@nsps.us.com
http://www.nsps.us.com/?page=Scholarships
Purpose: To reward excellent surveying and mapping students.
Eligibility: There are several different types of awards. The first is for students enrolled in two-year degree programs in surveying technology. The second is for students enrolled in or accepted to a graduate program in geodetic surveying or geodesy. The third is for students enrolled in four-year degree programs in surveying (or in related areas such as geomatics or surveying engineering). The last type is for students enrolled in a two-year or four-year surveying (or closely related) degree program, either full or part-time. All awards are based on academic record, statement, recommendation letters and professional activities.
Target applicant(s): High school students. College students. Graduate school students. Adult students.
Amount: $2,000-$3,000.
Number of awards: Varies.
Deadline: March 31.
How to apply: Applications are available online.
Exclusive: Visit www.UltimateScholarshipBook.com and enter code NA95220 for updates on this award.

(953) • AAGS Joseph F. Dracup Scholarship Award

National Society of Professional Surveyors (NSPS/AAGS)
Attn: Scholarships, 5119 Pegasus Court, Suite Q, Frederick, MD 21704
Phone: 240-439-4615x105
Email: trisha.milburn@nsps.us.com
http://www.nsps.us.com/?page=Scholarships
Purpose: To aid ACSM members who are enrolled in a four-year degree program in surveying or a closely related subject.
Eligibility: Applicants must be members of AAGS (American Association for Geodetic Surveying). Preference will be given to students whose coursework is significantly focused on geodetic surveying. Students who will be graduating before December of the award disbursement year are ineligible. Selection is based on academic merit, personal statement, recommendations, professional involvement and financial need.
Target applicant(s): High school students. College students. Adult students.
Amount: $2,000.
Number of awards: 1.
Scholarship may be renewable.
Deadline: March 31.
How to apply: Applications are available online. An application form, personal statement, official transcript, three recommendation letters and proof of ACSM membership are required.
Exclusive: Visit www.UltimateScholarshipBook.com and enter code NA95320 for updates on this award.

(954) • Abel Wolman Fellowship

American Water Works Association
6666 W. Quincy Avenue, Denver, CO 80235-3098
Phone: 800-926-7337
Email: scholarships@awwa.org
http://www.awwa.org
Purpose: To support doctoral students pursuing advanced training and research in the field of water supply and treatment.
Eligibility: Applicants must obtain a Ph.D. within two years of the award, must be citizens of the U.S., Canada or Mexico and should submit applications, transcripts, GRE scores, three recommendation letters, course of study and description of the dissertation research study and how it pertains to water supply and treatment. The award is based on academics, the connection between the research and water supply and treatment and the applicant's research skills.
Target applicant(s): Graduate school students. Adult students.
Amount: Varies.
Number of awards: Varies.
Scholarship may be renewable.
Deadline: January 12.
How to apply: Applications are available online.
Exclusive: Visit www.UltimateScholarshipBook.com and enter code AM95420 for updates on this award.

(955) • Academic Achievement Award

American Water Works Association
6666 W. Quincy Avenue, Denver, CO 80235-3098
Phone: 800-926-7337
Email: scholarships@awwa.org
http://www.awwa.org
Purpose: To recognize contributions to the field of public water supply.
Eligibility: Master's theses and doctoral dissertations that are relevant to the water supply industry are eligible. Unbound manuscripts must be the work of a single author and be submitted during the competition year in which they were submitted for the degree. Students may major in any area as long as the research is directly related to the drinking water supply industry. In addition to the application, students must submit a one-page abstract of the manuscript and a letter of endorsement from the major professor or department chair. The doctoral dissertation awards are $3,000 and $1,500. The master's thesis awards are $3,000 and $1,500.
Target applicant(s): Graduate school students. Adult students.
Amount: $1,500-$3,000.
Number of awards: 4.
Deadline: October 1.
How to apply: Applications are available online.
Exclusive: Visit www.UltimateScholarshipBook.com and enter code AM95520 for updates on this award.

(956) • Academic Study Award

American Association of Occupational Health Nurses (AAOHN) Foundation
330 N. Wabash Avenue, Suite 2000, Chicago, IL 60611
Phone: 312-321-5173
Email: info@aaohn.org
http://aaohn.org/page/foundation
Purpose: To provide further education for occupational and environmental health professionals.
Eligibility: Applicants must be registered nurses enrolled full- or part-time in a nationally accredited school of nursing baccalaureate program with an interest in occupational and environmental health or

be registered nurses enrolled full- or part-time in a graduate program that has application to occupational and environmental health. Applicants should submit a narrative and letters of recommendation.
Target applicant(s): College students. Graduate school students. Adult students.
Amount: $2,500.
Number of awards: 4.
Scholarship may be renewable.
Deadline: December 1.
How to apply: Applications are available online.
Exclusive: Visit www.UltimateScholarshipBook.com and enter code AM95620 for updates on this award.

(957) · Academy of Nutrition and Dietetics Foundation Student Scholarship

Academy of Nutrition and Dietetics
120 South Riverside Plaza, Suite 2000, Chicago, IL 60606-6995
Phone: 800-877-1600
Email: scholarship@eatright.org
http://www.eatright.org
Purpose: To encourage students in a dietetic program.
Eligibility: Applicants should be American Dietetic Association members and enrolled in their junior or senior year of a baccalaureate or coordinated program in dietetics or the second year of study in a dietetic technician program, a dietetic internship program or a graduate program. One application form is used for all ADAF scholarships.
Target applicant(s): College students. Graduate school students. Adult students.
Amount: $500-$3,000.
Number of awards: Varies.
Deadline: April 17.
How to apply: Applications are available online.
Exclusive: Visit www.UltimateScholarshipBook.com and enter code AC95720 for updates on this award.

(958) · ACEC New York Scholarship Program

American Council of Engineering Companies of New York
6 Airline Drive, Albany, NY 12205
Phone: 518-452-8611
Email: amanda@acecny.org
http://www.acecny.org
Purpose: To support students who plan to become consulting engineers.
Eligibility: Applicants must be in their third year of study in a four-year program or their fourth year of study in a five-year program at an engineering school in New York State. They must major in mechanical engineering, electrical engineering, structural engineering, civil engineering, environmental engineering, chemical engineering, engineering technology or surveying. They must plan to make New York State their home and/or career area. Selection is based on work experience (25 percent), college activities and recommendations (15 percent), essay (30 percent) and GPA (30 percent).
Target applicant(s): College students. Adult students.
Amount: $2,500-$5,000.
Number of awards: Varies.
Deadline: January 13.
How to apply: Applications are available online. An application form, essay, transcript and two recommendations are required.
Exclusive: Visit www.UltimateScholarshipBook.com and enter code AM95820 for updates on this award.

(959) · ACI Scholarship

American Concrete Institute
Attn.: ACI Foundation, Scholarship Coordinator, 38800 Country Club Drive, Farmington Hills, MI 48331
Phone: 248-848-3700
Email: scholarships@concrete.org
https://www.scholarshipcouncil.org/
Purpose: To support students who are interested in studying concrete.
Eligibility: Applicants must be nominated by a faculty member who is also a member of ACI in order to receive an application. Students must be full-time undergraduate or graduate students during the award year who plan to study in the U.S. or Canada. Applicants must be proficient in the English language. Students should submit applications via email.
Target applicant(s): College students. Graduate school students. Adult students.
Amount: $3,000-$5,000.
Number of awards: Varies.
Deadline: October.
How to apply: Applications are available online.
Exclusive: Visit www.UltimateScholarshipBook.com and enter code AM95920 for updates on this award.

(960) · ACI Student Fellowship Program

American Concrete Institute
Attn.: ACI Foundation, Scholarship Coordinator, 38800 Country Club Drive, Farmington Hills, MI 48331
Phone: 248-848-3700
Email: scholarships@concrete.org
https://www.scholarshipcouncil.org/
Purpose: To encourage careers in the concrete field.
Eligibility: Applicants must be full-time undergraduate or graduate students nominated by a faculty member who is also a member of the ACI. Students must be studying engineering, construction management or another relevant field. Applicants may live anywhere in the world, but actual study must take place in the U.S. or Canada. Finalists for a fellowship must attend an ACI convention for an interview. In addition to the monetary award, the scholarship also includes conference fees, mentoring and a potential internship.
Target applicant(s): College students. Graduate school students. Adult students.
Amount: Up to $15,000.
Number of awards: Varies.
Scholarship may be renewable.
Deadline: October 15.
How to apply: Applicants must be nominated by ACI-member faculty in order to receive an application.
Exclusive: Visit www.UltimateScholarshipBook.com and enter code AM96020 for updates on this award.

(961) · ACI-NA Airport Commissioner's Scholarships

Airports Council International-North America
University Aviation Association, Attn: ACI-NA Commissioners School Fund, 2415 Moore's Mill Road, Suite 265-216, Auburn, AL 36830
Phone: 334-844-2434
Email: npick@aci-na.org
http://www.aci-na.org/content/aci-na-scholarships
Purpose: To assist students who plan careers in airport management or administration.

Eligibility: Applicants must be enrolled in an undergraduate or graduate program in airport management or airport operations. Applicants must attend an accredited school in the U.S. or Canada and have a GPA of at least 3.0.
Target applicant(s): High school students. College students. Graduate school students. Adult students.
Minimum GPA: 3.0
Amount: Up to $2,500.
Number of awards: Up to 3.
Deadline: April 15.
How to apply: Applications are available online.
Exclusive: Visit www.UltimateScholarshipBook.com and enter code AI96120 for updates on this award.

---

(962) • ADEA/Sigma Phi Alpha Linda Devore Scholarship

American Dental Education Association
655 K Street NW, Suite 800, Washington, DC 20001
Phone: 202-289-7201
Email: lunde@adea.org
http://www.adea.org/awards/
Purpose: To aid allied dental education students.
Eligibility: Applicants must be members of the American Dental Education Association (ADEA) and be enrolled in a dental hygiene, dental education or public health degree program. They must be in good academic standing and demonstrate leadership in dental education or health care. Selection is based on the overall strength of the application.
Target applicant(s): College students. Graduate school students. Adult students.
Amount: $1,000.
Number of awards: 1.
Deadline: November 1.
How to apply: Applications are available online. An application form, an official transcript, a personal statement and two reference letters are required.
Exclusive: Visit www.UltimateScholarshipBook.com and enter code AM96220 for updates on this award.

---

(963) • ADHA Institute Scholarship Program

American Dental Hygienists' Association (ADHA) Institute for Oral Health
Scholarship Award Program, 444 North Michigan Avenue, Suite 3400, Chicago, IL 60611
Phone: 312-440-8900
Email: institute@adha.net
http://www.adha.org
Purpose: To assist students pursuing a career in dental hygiene.
Eligibility: Applicants should be enrolled full-time (unless applying for a part-time scholarship) in an accredited dental hygiene program in the U.S., be finishing their first year and have a minimum 3.0 GPA. Undergraduate students should be active members of the Student American Dental Hygienists' Association or the American Dental Hygienists Association. Graduate students should be active members of the Student American Dental Hygienists' Association or the American Dental Hygienists Association, have a valid dental hygiene license and a bachelor's degree. There should be financial need of at least $1,500, with the exception of the merit-based scholarships.
Target applicant(s): College students. Graduate school students. Adult students.
Minimum GPA: 3.0
Amount: Varies.
Number of awards: Varies.
Deadline: February 1.
How to apply: Applications are available online.
Exclusive: Visit www.UltimateScholarshipBook.com and enter code AM96320 for updates on this award.

---

(964) • AFCEA Ralph W. Shrader Diversity Scholarships

Armed Forces Communications and Electronics Association (AFCEA)
4400 Fair Lakes Court, Fairfax, VA 22033
Phone: 703-631-6149
http://www.afcea.org
Purpose: Monetary assistance is awarded to graduate students studying electrical, computer, chemical or aerospace engineering, mathematics, physics, computer science, computer technology, electronics, communications technology or engineering or information management systems.
Eligibility: Applicants must be U.S. citizens, full-time postgraduate students working toward a master's degree in electrical, computer, chemical or aerospace engineering, mathematics, physics, computer science, computer technology, electronics, communications technology, communications engineering or information management at an accredited U.S. university. Distance learning or online programs will not qualify. Primary consideration will be given for demonstrated excellence. Applicants do not need to be affiliated with the U.S. military.
Target applicant(s): Graduate school students. Adult students.
Amount: Varies.
Number of awards: Varies.
Deadline: April 15.
How to apply: Applications are available online.
Exclusive: Visit www.UltimateScholarshipBook.com and enter code AR96420 for updates on this award.

---

(965) • AfterCollege / AACN Nursing Scholarship Fund

American Association of Colleges of Nursing
One Dupont Circle NW, Suite 530, Washington, DC 20036
Phone: 202-463-6930
Email: scholarships@aftercollege.com
http://www.aacnnursing.org/Students/Financial-Aid
Purpose: To assist students pursuing careers in nursing.
Eligibility: Applicants must be enrolled in a bachelor's, master's or doctoral program in nursing at an AACN member institution and have a minimum 3.25 GPA.
Target applicant(s): College students. Graduate school students. Adult students.
Minimum GPA: 3.25
Amount: $2,500.
Number of awards: 4.
Deadline: June 30, September 30, December 31, March 31.
How to apply: Applications are available online. Winners are announced within 60 days of each deadline.
Exclusive: Visit www.UltimateScholarshipBook.com and enter code AM96520 for updates on this award.

---

(966) • AGC Education and Research Foundation Undergraduate Scholarship

Associated General Contractors (AGC) Education and Research Foundation

2300 Wilson Boulevard, Suite 400, Arlington, VA 22201
Phone: (703) 837-5342
http://www.agcfoundation.org
Purpose: To support rising undergraduate construction and construction-related engineering students pursue their ABET and ACCE-accredited construction and construction-related engineering degrees.
Eligibility: Applicants must be second-year students at a two-year college planning to transfer to a four-year program for the fall, rising college sophomores or juniors in a four-year program or seniors in a five-year program. Juniors and seniors must have one full academic year of study remaining at the time of application submission and be pursuing a B.S. degree in construction or construction-related engineering program.
Target applicant(s): College students. Adult students.
Minimum GPA: 2.0
Amount: $2,500.
Number of awards: 100.
Scholarship may be renewable.
Deadline: November 1.
How to apply: Applications are available online.
Exclusive: Visit www.UltimateScholarshipBook.com and enter code AS96620 for updates on this award.

(967) • AGC Graduate Scholarships

Associated General Contractors of America
2300 Wilson Boulevard, Suite 300, Arlington, VA 22201
Phone: 703-837-5342
Email: patricianm@agc.org
http://www.agc.org
Purpose: Monetary assistance is awarded to college seniors pursuing graduate degrees that will lead to careers in construction or civil engineering.
Eligibility: Applicants must be college seniors enrolled in an undergraduate construction or civil engineering degree program or college graduates with a degree in construction or civil engineering. Applicants must also be enrolled or planning to enroll full-time in a graduate level construction or civil engineering degree program.
Target applicant(s): College students. Graduate school students. Adult students.
Amount: $7,500.
Number of awards: Varies.
Deadline: November 1.
How to apply: Applications are available online.
Exclusive: Visit www.UltimateScholarshipBook.com and enter code AS96720 for updates on this award.

(968) • AGC Undergraduate Scholarships

Associated General Contractors of America
2300 Wilson Boulevard, Suite 300, Arlington, VA 22201
Phone: 703-837-5342
Email: patricianm@agc.org
http://www.agc.org
Purpose: To assist students pursuing studies that lead to a career in construction or civil engineering.
Eligibility: Applicants must be a second-year student at a two-year school planning to transfer to a four-year program, or a rising college sophomore or junior in a four-year program or rising senior in a five-year program enrolled in or planning to enroll in ABET- or ACCE-accredited construction or civil engineering programs pursuing a B.S. degree in construction or construction-related engineering.
Target applicant(s): College students. Adult students.
Amount: $2,500.
Number of awards: Varies.
Scholarship may be renewable.
Deadline: November 1.
How to apply: Applications are available online.
Exclusive: Visit www.UltimateScholarshipBook.com and enter code AS96820 for updates on this award.

(969) • AHIMA Foundation Merit Scholarships

American Health Information Management Association (AHIMA) Foundation
233 N. Michigan Avenue, 21st Floor, Chicago, IL 60601-5809
Phone: 312-233-1131
Email: info@ahimafoundation.org
http://www.ahimafoundation.org
Purpose: To provide merit scholarships to those enrolled in degree programs pursuing health information technology or health information administration.
Eligibility: Applicants must be members of AHIMA, have a minimum 3.0 GPA on a 4.0 scale, have completed 24 credit hours in health information management (HIM) or health information technology (HIT), have at least six credit hours remaining in their course of study and be taking at least six hours per semester in pursuit of the degree. The degrees eligible are AA degrees, BA/BS degrees and those who are credentialed and pursing a master's degree. Scholarships are also available for HIM professionals pursuing graduate degrees in the health information field.
Target applicant(s): College students. Graduate school students. Adult students.
Minimum GPA: 3.0
Amount: $1,000-$2,500.
Number of awards: Varies.
Deadline: September 30.
How to apply: Applications are available online.
Exclusive: Visit www.UltimateScholarshipBook.com and enter code AM96920 for updates on this award.

(970) • AIA/Architects Foundation Diversity Advancement Scholarship

American Institute of Architects
1735 New York Ave NW, Washington, DC 20006-5292
Phone: 800-242-3837
Email: divscholarship@aia.org
https://www.aia.org/pages/2736-scholarships
Purpose: To provide scholarships for students who intend to study architecture and who could not otherwise afford to enter a degree-seeking program.
Eligibility: Applicants must be students from a minority race or ethnicity who intend to study architecture in an NAAB-accredited program. Students who are U.S. residents entering, attending or transferring to an NAAB-accredited program are also eligible.
Target applicant(s): High school students. College students. Adult students.
Amount: $4,000.
Number of awards: Varies.
Scholarship may be renewable.
Deadline: Varies.
How to apply: Applications are available by email. An application form and a recommendation letter are required.
Exclusive: Visit www.UltimateScholarshipBook.com and enter code AM97020 for updates on this award.

(971) • AIAA Foundation Undergraduate Scholarship Program

American Institute of Aeronautics and Astronautics
12700 Sunrise Valley Drive, Suite 200, Reston, VA 20191-5807
Phone: 800-639-AIAA
Email: stephenb@aiaa.org
http://www.aiaa.org
Purpose: AIAA advances the arts, sciences and technology of aeronautics and astronautics.
Eligibility: Applicants must be enrolled in an accredited college or university and have completed at least one semester or quarter of college work with a minimum 3.3 GPA. Applicants must plan to enter a career in science or engineering related to the technical activities of the AIAA. Applicants must be AIAA student members in good standing to apply. Selection is based on scholarship, career goals, recommendations and extracurricular activities.
Target applicant(s): College students. Adult students.
Minimum GPA: 3.3
Amount: $500-$5,000.
Number of awards: Varies.
Scholarship may be renewable.
Deadline: January 31.
How to apply: Applications are available online.
Exclusive: Visit www.UltimateScholarshipBook.com and enter code AM97120 for updates on this award.

(972) • AISI/AIST Foundation Premier Scholarship

Association for Iron and Steel Technology (AIST)
186 Thorn Hill Road, Warrendale, PA 15086-7528
Phone: 724-814-3000
Email: lwharrey@aist.org
https://www.aist.org
Purpose: To encourage engineering students to pursue careers in the iron and steel industry.
Eligibility: Applicants must be undergraduate sophomores who are enrolled full-time at an accredited college or university and be majoring in engineering. They must have a GPA of 3.0 or higher on a four-point scale and must have a demonstrated career interest in the iron and steel industry. Selection is based on the overall strength of the application.
Target applicant(s): College students. Adult students.
Minimum GPA: 3.0
Amount: $12,000.
Number of awards: 1.
Scholarship may be renewable.
Deadline: October 31.
How to apply: Applications are available online. An application form, transcript, personal essay and two letters of recommendation are required.
Exclusive: Visit www.UltimateScholarshipBook.com and enter code AS97220 for updates on this award.

(973) • AIST Benjamin F. Fairless Scholarship (AIME)

Association for Iron and Steel Technology (AIST)
186 Thorn Hill Road, Warrendale, PA 15086-7528
Phone: 724-814-3000
Email: lwharrey@aist.org
https://www.aist.org
Purpose: To honor the memory of Benjamin F. Fairless, former Chairman of the Board of U.S. Steel Corporation.
Eligibility: Applicants must be enrolled full-time in an accredited university in North America and majoring in engineering, metallurgy or materials science. Applicants must also have a GPA of 2.5 or higher and plan to pursue a career in the iron and steel industry.
Target applicant(s): College students. Adult students.
Minimum GPA: 2.5
Amount: $3,000.
Number of awards: 2.
Deadline: October 31.
How to apply: Applications are available online.
Exclusive: Visit www.UltimateScholarshipBook.com and enter code AS97320 for updates on this award.

(974) • AIST Foundation Steel Research and Applications Grant

Association for Iron and Steel Technology (AIST)
186 Thorn Hill Road, Warrendale, PA 15086-7528
Phone: 724-814-3000
Email: lwharrey@aist.org
https://www.aist.org
Purpose: To increase the number of students interested in employment in the steel industry.
Eligibility: Applicants are teams consisting of a qualified professor and undergraduate and graduate students. Teams will submit proposals for grant funding for research to benefit the steel industry and must be assisted by a steel industry representative currently employed with a steel producing company.
Target applicant(s): College students. Graduate school students. Adult students.
Minimum GPA: 2.5
Amount: $50,000.
Number of awards: 1.
Scholarship may be renewable.
Deadline: June 30.
How to apply: Applications are available online.
Exclusive: Visit www.UltimateScholarshipBook.com and enter code AS97420 for updates on this award.

(975) • AIST Ronald E. Lincoln Memorial Scholarship

Association for Iron and Steel Technology (AIST)
186 Thorn Hill Road, Warrendale, PA 15086-7528
Phone: 724-814-3000
Email: lwharrey@aist.org
https://www.aist.org
Purpose: To honor the memory of Ronald Lincoln and to reward students who demonstrate leadership and innovation.
Eligibility: Applicants must be enrolled full-time in an accredited university in North America and majoring in engineering, metallurgy or materials science. Applicants must also have a GPA of 2.5 or higher and plan to pursue a career in the iron and steel industry.
Target applicant(s): College students. Adult students.
Minimum GPA: 2.5
Amount: $3,000.
Number of awards: 3.
Deadline: October 31.
How to apply: Applications are available online.
Exclusive: Visit www.UltimateScholarshipBook.com and enter code AS97520 for updates on this award.

(976) • AIST Smith Graduate Scholarship

Association for Iron and Steel Technology (AIST)
186 Thorn Hill Road, Warrendale, PA 15086-7528
Phone: 724-814-3000
Email: lwharrey@aist.org
https://www.aist.org

Purpose: To aid graduate engineering students who are interested in careers in metallurgy.

Eligibility: Applicants must be full-time graduate students who are enrolled in an engineering degree program at an accredited college or university in the U.S. or Canada. They must have a demonstrated interest in pursuing a career in metallurgy within the iron and steel industry. Selection is based on the overall strength of the application.

Target applicant(s): Graduate school students. Adult students.

Amount: Up to $6,000.

Number of awards: Varies.

Deadline: October 31.

How to apply: Applications are available online. An application form and supporting materials are required.

Exclusive: Visit www.UltimateScholarshipBook.com and enter code AS97620 for updates on this award.

(977) • AIST William E. Schwabe Memorial Scholarship

Association for Iron and Steel Technology (AIST)
186 Thorn Hill Road, Warrendale, PA 15086-7528
Phone: 724-814-3000
Email: lwharrey@aist.org
https://www.aist.org

Purpose: To honor the memory of William E. Schwabe, steelmaking pioneer.

Eligibility: Applicants must be enrolled full-time in an accredited university in North America and majoring in engineering, metallurgy or materials science. Applicants must also have a GPA of 2.5 or higher and plan to pursue a career in the iron and steel industry.

Target applicant(s): College students. Adult students.

Minimum GPA: 2.5

Amount: $3,000.

Number of awards: 1.

Deadline: October 31.

How to apply: Applications are available online.

Exclusive: Visit www.UltimateScholarshipBook.com and enter code AS97720 for updates on this award.

(978) • AIST Willy Korf Memorial Fund

Association for Iron and Steel Technology (AIST)
186 Thorn Hill Road, Warrendale, PA 15086-7528
Phone: 724-814-3000
Email: lwharrey@aist.org
https://www.aist.org

Purpose: To honor the memory of the late Willy Korf, the founder of the Korf Group, and to assist students who plan to enter the fields of engineering, metallurgy or materials science in the iron and steel industry.

Eligibility: Applicants must be enrolled full-time in an accredited university in North America, and majoring in engineering, metallurgy or materials science. Applicants must also have a GPA of 3.0 or higher and plan to pursue a career in the iron and steel industry.

Target applicant(s): High school students. College students. Adult students.

Minimum GPA: 3.0

Amount: $3,000.

Number of awards: 4.

Deadline: October 31.

How to apply: Applications are available online.

Exclusive: Visit www.UltimateScholarshipBook.com and enter code AS97820 for updates on this award.

(979) • Alice T. Schafer Mathematics Prize

Association for Women in Mathematics
11240 Waples Mill Road, Suite 200, Fairfax, VA 22030
Phone: 703-934-0163
Email: awm@awm-math.org
http://www.awm-math.org

Purpose: To support female students who are studying mathematics.

Eligibility: Nominees must be female college undergraduates and either be U.S. citizens or have a school address in the U.S. Selection is based on performance in advanced mathematics courses and special programs, interest in mathematics, ability to conduct independent work and performance in mathematical competitions at the local or national level.

Target applicant(s): College students. Adult students.

Amount: Varies.

Number of awards: Varies.

Deadline: October 1.

How to apply: Applicants must be nominated.

Exclusive: Visit www.UltimateScholarshipBook.com and enter code AS97920 for updates on this award.

(980) • Alice W. Rooke Scholarship

National Society Daughters of the American Revolution
Committee Services Office, Attn.: Scholarships, 1776 D Street NW, Washington, DC 20006-5303
Phone: 202-628-1776
Email: scholarships@dar.org
http://www.dar.org/national-society/scholarships

Purpose: To assist students in becoming medical doctors.

Eligibility: Applicants must be accepted into or enrolled in a graduate course of study to become a medical doctor. All applicants must obtain a letter of sponsorship from their local DAR chapter. However, affiliation with DAR is not required.

Target applicant(s): Graduate school students. Adult students.

Amount: Up to $5,000.

Number of awards: 1.

Scholarship may be renewable.

Deadline: February 10.

How to apply: Applications are available by written request with a self-addressed, stamped envelope.

Exclusive: Visit www.UltimateScholarshipBook.com and enter code NA98020 for updates on this award.

(981) • Allied Dental Health Scholarships

American Dental Association Foundation
211 East Chicago Avenue, Chicago, IL 60611
Phone: 312-440-2763
Email: famularor@ada.org
http://www.ada.org

Purpose: To encourage students to pursue careers in dental hygiene, dental assisting, dentistry and dental laboratory technology.

Eligibility: Applicants must be either in their final year of study in an accredited dental hygiene program, entering students in an accredited dental assisting program or in their final year of study in an accredited

dental laboratory technician program. Selection is based on minimum financial need of $1,000, academic achievement, a biographical sketch and references. A minimum 3.0 GPA is required. Only two scholarship applications per school are allowed, so schools may set their own in-school application deadlines that are earlier.
Target applicant(s): College students. Graduate school students. Adult students.
Minimum GPA: 3.0
Amount: $1,000.
Number of awards: Varies.
Deadline: Second Friday in March.
How to apply: Applications are available from dental school officials.
Exclusive: Visit www.UltimateScholarshipBook.com and enter code AM98120 for updates on this award.

(982) · Alpha Mu Tau Fraternity Undergraduate Scholarships

American Society for Clinical Laboratory Science
Alpha Mu Tau Scholarship, Attn: Joe Briden, AMTF Scholarship Coordinator, 7809 S. 21st Drive, Phoenix, AZ 85041-7736
Phone: 571-748-3770
Email: awards@ascls.org
http://www.ascls.org
Purpose: To support new professionals in the clinical laboratory sciences.
Eligibility: Applicants must be undergraduate students entering or in their last year of study in an NAACLS-accredited program in Clinical Laboratory Science/Medical Technology or Clinical Laboratory Technician/Medical Laboratory Technician. Applicants must be a U.S. citizen or a permanent resident of the U.S.
Target applicant(s): College students. Adult students.
Amount: Varies.
Number of awards: Varies.
Deadline: March 15.
How to apply: Applications are available online.
Exclusive: Visit www.UltimateScholarshipBook.com and enter code AM98220 for updates on this award.

(983) · AMBUCS Scholars

AMBUCS
P.O. Box 5127, High Point, NC 27262
Phone: 800-838-1845
Email: janiceb@ambucs.org
http://www.ambucs.org
Purpose: To provide more opportunities for the disabled by encouraging students to become therapists.
Eligibility: Applicants must be undergraduate juniors or seniors or graduate students pursuing their master's or doctoral degrees and must have been accepted into an accredited program in physical therapy, occupational therapy, speech language pathology or hearing audiology. Assistant programs are ineligible. Selection is based on financial need, U.S. citizenship, community service, academic achievement, character and career plans.
Target applicant(s): College students. Graduate school students. Adult students.
Amount: $500-$6,000.
Number of awards: Varies.
Deadline: May 15.
How to apply: Applications are available online.
Exclusive: Visit www.UltimateScholarshipBook.com and enter code AM98320 for updates on this award.

(984) · Amelia Earhart Fellowships

Zonta International
1211 West 22nd Street, Suite 900, Oak Brook, IL 60523
Phone: 630-928-1400
Email: zontaintl@zonta.org
http://www.zonta.org
Purpose: To support women in science and engineering.
Eligibility: Applicants must be pursuing graduate PhD/doctoral degrees in aerospace-related sciences and aerospace-related engineering.
Target applicant(s): Graduate school students. Adult students.
Amount: $10,000.
Number of awards: 35.
Deadline: November 15.
Exclusive: Visit www.UltimateScholarshipBook.com and enter code ZO98420 for updates on this award.

(985) · American Architectural Foundation and Sir John Soane's Museum Foundation Traveling Fellowship

American Institute of Architects
1735 New York Ave NW, Washington, DC 20006-5292
Phone: 800-242-3837
Email: divscholarship@aia.org
https://www.aia.org/pages/2736-scholarships
Purpose: To provide scholarships enabling graduate students to travel to England and to study the work of Sir John Soane (or Sir John Soane's Museum and its collections).
Eligibility: Applicants must be enrolled in graduate programs focusing on the history of art, architecture, decorative arts or interior design.
Target applicant(s): Graduate school students. Adult students.
Amount: $5,000.
Number of awards: 2.
Deadline: March 1.
How to apply: Applications are available online.
Exclusive: Visit www.UltimateScholarshipBook.com and enter code AM98520 for updates on this award.

(986) · American Quarter Horse Foundation (AQHF) General Scholarship

American Quarter Horse Foundation
Scholarship Program, 2601 East Interstate 40, Amarillo, TX 79104
Phone: 806-378-5029
Email: foundation@aqha.org
http://www.aqha.com
Purpose: To encourage future Quarter Horse industry professionals.
Eligibility: Applicants must be current members of AQHA and have a minimum 2.5 GPA. Students must be current college students. Selection is based on financial need, academic achievement, equine involvement, references and career plans. A transcript and three references are required for all scholarships.
Target applicant(s): College students. Graduate school students. Adult students.
Minimum GPA: 2.5
Amount: Varies.
Number of awards: Varies.
Scholarship may be renewable.
Deadline: December 1.
How to apply: Applications are available online.
Exclusive: Visit www.UltimateScholarshipBook.com and enter code AM98620 for updates on this award.

(987) • American Water Scholarship

American Water Works Association
6666 W. Quincy Avenue, Denver, CO 80235-3098
Phone: 800-926-7337
Email: scholarships@awwa.org
http://www.awwa.org
Purpose: To support graduate-level students interested in giving service to the water industry.
Eligibility: Applicants must be graduate students working towards a masters or doctoral degree. Students must be planning a career related to the service of the water industry. Selection is based upon the overall strength of the application.
Target applicant(s): College students. Graduate school students. Adult students.
Amount: $5,000.
Number of awards: Varies.
Deadline: January 12.
How to apply: Applications are available online.
Exclusive: Visit www.UltimateScholarshipBook.com and enter code AM98720 for updates on this award.

(988) • AMS Graduate Fellowship in the History of Science

American Meteorological Society
Fellowship and Scholarship Department, 45 Beacon Street, Boston, MA 02108-3693
Phone: 617-227-2426 x246
Email: dsampson@ametsoc.org
http://www.ametsoc.org/AMS/
Purpose: To support students writing dissertations on the history of atmospheric or related oceanic or hydrologic sciences.
Eligibility: Applicants must be graduate students who plan to write dissertations on the history of atmospheric or related oceanic or hydrologic sciences. Students must submit a cover letter with vitae, official transcripts, a typed description of the dissertation topic and three letters of recommendation.
Target applicant(s): Graduate school students. Adult students.
Amount: $15,000.
Number of awards: Varies.
Deadline: February 3.
How to apply: Submit materials to address listed.
Exclusive: Visit www.UltimateScholarshipBook.com and enter code AM98820 for updates on this award.

(989) • AMS Graduate Fellowships

American Meteorological Society
Fellowship and Scholarship Department, 45 Beacon Street, Boston, MA 02108-3693
Phone: 617-227-2426 x246
Email: dsampson@ametsoc.org
http://www.ametsoc.org/AMS/
Purpose: To attract students to prepare for careers in the meteorological, oceanic and hydrologic fields.
Eligibility: Applicants must be entering their first year of graduate study the following year and plan to pursue advanced degrees in the atmospheric and related oceanic and hydrologic sciences and have a minimum 3.25 GPA. Awards are based on undergraduate performance. References, transcripts and GRE scores may be sent under separate cover. References can be sent to dfernand@ametsoc.org.
Target applicant(s): College students. Adult students.
Minimum GPA: 3.25
Amount: $25,000.
Number of awards: Varies.
Deadline: January 13.
How to apply: Applications are available online.
Exclusive: Visit www.UltimateScholarshipBook.com and enter code AM98920 for updates on this award.

(990) • AMS Minority Scholarship

American Meteorological Society
Fellowship and Scholarship Department, 45 Beacon Street, Boston, MA 02108-3693
Phone: 617-227-2426 x246
Email: dsampson@ametsoc.org
http://www.ametsoc.org/AMS/
Purpose: To support minority students who have been traditionally underrepresented in the sciences, especially Hispanic, Native American and African American students.
Eligibility: Applicants must be minority students who will be entering their freshman year of college in the following fall and must plan to pursue degrees in the atmospheric or related oceanic and hydrologic sciences. Applicants must submit applications, transcripts, recommendation letters and SAT or equivalent scores. Original materials should be mailed to the closest AMS Local Chapter listed at the bottom of the application, and copies should be mailed to headquarters.
Target applicant(s): High school students.
Amount: $6,000.
Number of awards: Varies.
Scholarship may be renewable.
Deadline: February 3.
How to apply: Applications are available online.
Exclusive: Visit www.UltimateScholarshipBook.com and enter code AM99020 for updates on this award.

(991) • AMS Senior Named Scholarships

American Meteorological Society
Fellowship and Scholarship Department, 45 Beacon Street, Boston, MA 02108-3693
Phone: 617-227-2426 x246
Email: dsampson@ametsoc.org
http://www.ametsoc.org/AMS/
Purpose: To encourage undergraduate students to pursue careers in the atmospheric and related oceanic and hydrologic sciences.
Eligibility: Applicants must be full-time students majoring in the atmospheric or related oceanic or hydrologic science and entering their final undergraduate year, show intent to make the atmospheric or related sciences their career and have a minimum 3.25 GPA. For the Schroeder scholarship, applicants must demonstrate financial need. For the Murphy scholarship, applicants must demonstrate interest in weather forecasting through curricular or extracurricular activities and for the Crow scholarship, applicants must demonstrate interest in applied meteorology. The Glahn scholarship will be awarded to a student with a strong interest in statistical meteorology.
Target applicant(s): College students. Adult students.
Minimum GPA: 3.25
Amount: Up to $10,000.
Number of awards: Varies.
Deadline: February 3.
How to apply: Applications are available online.
Exclusive: Visit www.UltimateScholarshipBook.com and enter code AM99120 for updates on this award.

(992) · AMT Student Scholarship

American Medical Technologists
10700 W. Higgins Road, Suite 150, Rosemont, IL 60018
Phone: 800-275-1268
https://www.americanmedtech.org

Purpose: To provide financial assistance to students interested in medical technology careers.

Eligibility: Applicants must be high school graduates or current seniors planning to attend an accredited institution to pursue an American Medical Technologists-certified career, which includes medical laboratory technology, medical assisting, dental assisting, phlebotomy and office laboratory technician. Applicants must provide evidence of financial need.

Target applicant(s): High school students.
Amount: $500.
Number of awards: 5.
Deadline: April 1.
How to apply: Applications are available online.
Exclusive: Visit www.UltimateScholarshipBook.com and enter code AM99220 for updates on this award.

(993) · Amtrol Inc. Scholarship

American Ground Water Trust
50 Pleasant Street, Concord, NH 03301
Phone: 603-228-5444
https://agwt.org/content/scholarships

Purpose: To provide scholarships for high school seniors to pursue a career in a ground water-related field.

Eligibility: Applicants must be high school seniors with intentions to pursue a career in ground water management or a related field. Students must be entering their freshman year at a four-year accredited institution. Prior research or experience with the field is required.

Target applicant(s): High school students.
Minimum GPA: 3.0
Amount: Varies.
Number of awards: Varies.
Deadline: June 1.
How to apply: Applications are available online.
Exclusive: Visit www.UltimateScholarshipBook.com and enter code AM99320 for updates on this award.

(994) · Analytical Chemistry Scholarship

Jordi Labs
200 Gilbert Street, Mansfield, MA 02048
Phone: 508-966-1301
Email: tperez@jordilabs.com
https://jordilabs.com/blog/analytical-chemistry-scholarship/

Purpose: To support the pursuit of a science degree.

Eligibility: Applicants must be enrolling as or currently enrolled undergraduate or graduate students pursuing a career in analytical chemistry.

Target applicant(s): High school students. College students. Graduate school students. Adult students.
Amount: $1,000.
Number of awards: 5.
Deadline: July 31.
How to apply: Applications are available online.
Exclusive: Visit www.UltimateScholarshipBook.com and enter code JO99420 for updates on this award.

(995) · Angus Foundation Scholarships

American Foundation
3201 Frederick Avenue, St. Joseph, MO 64506
Phone: 816-383-5100
Email: angus@angus.org
http://www.angusfoundation.org/fdn/

Purpose: To provide scholarships to youth active with the Angus breed.

Eligibility: Applicants must have been members of the National Junior Angus Association and must be junior, regular or life members of the American Angus Association at the time of application. Applicants must be high school seniors or enrolled in a junior college, four-year college or other accredited institution of post-secondary education in an undergraduate program and have a minimum 2.0 GPA. Students may not have reached their 25th birthday by January 1 of the year of application.

Target applicant(s): High school students. College students.
Minimum GPA: 2.0
Amount: $1,000-$5,000.
Number of awards: Varies.
Deadline: May 1.
How to apply: Applications are available online or by written request.
Exclusive: Visit www.UltimateScholarshipBook.com and enter code AM99520 for updates on this award.

(996) · Annie's Sustainable Agriculture Scholarships

Annie's Homegrown Inc.
Attn: Annie's Scholarship Committee, 1610 5th Street, Berkeley, CA 94710
Phone: 800-288-1089
Email: scholarships@annies.com
http://www.annies.com

Purpose: To aid undergraduate and graduate students preparing for careers in sustainable foods and organic agriculture.

Eligibility: Applicants must be full-time undergraduate or graduate students attending an institution of higher learning located in the United States. They must be in the process of completing a significant amount of coursework in sustainable agriculture. Selection is based on the overall strength of the application.

Target applicant(s): High school students. College students. Graduate school students. Adult students.
Amount: Varies.
Number of awards: Varies.
Deadline: January 6.
How to apply: Applications are available online. An application form, personal statement, transcript and two letters of recommendation are required.
Exclusive: Visit www.UltimateScholarshipBook.com and enter code AN99620 for updates on this award.

(997) · Annual NBNA Scholarships

National Black Nurses Association
8630 Fenton Street, Suite 330, Silver Spring, MD 20910-3803
Phone: 301-589-3200
Email: Info@nbna.org
http://www.nbna.org

Purpose: To promote excellence in education and in continuing education programs for African American nurses and allied health professionals.

Eligibility: Applicants must be African Americans currently enrolled in a nursing program and be in good academic standing, be members of

the NBNA, be members of a local chapter and have at least a full year of school remaining. Applicants must submit with their application an essay, references, an official transcript and evidence of participation in student nurse activities and involvement in the African American community.
Target applicant(s): College students. Adult students.
Amount: $1,000-$6,000.
Number of awards: Varies.
Deadline: April 15.
How to apply: Applications are available online.
Exclusive: Visit www.UltimateScholarshipBook.com and enter code NA99720 for updates on this award.

(998) • ANS Graduate Scholarship

American Nuclear Society
555 North Kensington Avenue, La Grange Park, IL 60526
Phone: 800-323-3044
Email: hr@ans.org
http://www.ans.org
Purpose: To assist full-time graduate students who are pursuing advanced degrees in a nuclear-related field.
Eligibility: Applicants must be full-time students at an accredited graduate school in a program leading to an advanced degree in nuclear science, nuclear engineering or a nuclear-related field. There are also individual graduate scholarships. Applicants should submit applications, transcripts, recommendation letter and three reference forms.
Target applicant(s): Graduate school students. Adult students.
Amount: Varies.
Number of awards: Up to 29.
Deadline: February 1.
How to apply: Applications are available online.
Exclusive: Visit www.UltimateScholarshipBook.com and enter code AM99820 for updates on this award.

(999) • ANS Incoming Freshman Scholarships

American Nuclear Society
555 North Kensington Avenue, La Grange Park, IL 60526
Phone: 800-323-3044
Email: hr@ans.org
http://www.ans.org
Purpose: To aid high school seniors who are planning to major in nuclear engineering at the undergraduate level.
Eligibility: Applicants must be graduating high school seniors who have been accepted at an accredited postsecondary institution. They must have plans to major in nuclear engineering. Selection is based on academic merit, personal essay and recommendations.
Target applicant(s): High school students.
Amount: $1,000.
Number of awards: Up to 4.
Deadline: April 1.
How to apply: Applications are available online. An application form, personal essay, two letters of recommendation and an official transcript are required.
Exclusive: Visit www.UltimateScholarshipBook.com and enter code AM99920 for updates on this award.

(1000) • ANS Undergraduate Scholarship

American Nuclear Society
555 North Kensington Avenue, La Grange Park, IL 60526
Phone: 800-323-3044
Email: hr@ans.org
http://www.ans.org
Purpose: To assist undergraduate students who are pursuing careers in the field of nuclear science.
Eligibility: Applicants must be at least sophomores or students who have completed two or more years and will be entering as juniors or seniors in an accredited university and must be enrolled in a program leading to a degree in nuclear science, nuclear engineering or a nuclear-related field. Applicants should submit applications, transcripts, recommendation letter and three reference forms. There are individual undergraduate scholarships for students who have completed two or more years in a course of study leading to a degree in nuclear science, nuclear engineering or a nuclear-related field.
Target applicant(s): College students. Adult students.
Amount: Varies.
Number of awards: Up to 38.
Deadline: February 1.
How to apply: Applications are available online.
Exclusive: Visit www.UltimateScholarshipBook.com and enter code AM100020 for updates on this award.

(1001) • AOC Scholarships

Association of Old Crows
1000 N. Payne Street, Suite 200, Alexandria, VA 22314-1652
Phone: 703-549-1600
Email: stourangeau@warriorss.com
http://www.crows.org
Purpose: To encourage students interested in strong defense capability emphasizing electronic warfare and information operations.
Eligibility: Applicants must be U.S. citizens enrolled full-time at an accredited college or university in an undergraduate degree program as a junior or senior. Students should be studying engineering or technology with a minimum cumulative GPA of 3.0. Selection is based on interest and potential future contribution to national defense and academic excellence in the STEM area of study.
Target applicant(s): College students. Adult students.
Minimum GPA: 3.0
Amount: $12,500.
Number of awards: 2.
Deadline: March 31.
How to apply: Applications are available online.
Exclusive: Visit www.UltimateScholarshipBook.com and enter code AS100120 for updates on this award.

(1002) • AORN Foundation Scholarship Program

Association of Perioperative Registered Nurses
2170 S. Parker Road, Suite 400, Denver, CO 80231
Phone: 800-755-2676
Email: sstokes@aorn.org
http://www.aorn.org/aorn-foundation/scholarships-available
Purpose: To encourage the education of nurses and future nurses.
Eligibility: Applicants must be current nursing students or AORN members accepted to an accredited program and have a minimum 3.0 GPA. Applicants must also demonstrate financial need.
Target applicant(s): College students. Graduate school students. Adult students.
Minimum GPA: 3.0
Amount: Varies.
Number of awards: Varies.
Deadline: June 15.
How to apply: Applications are available online.

Exclusive: Visit www.UltimateScholarshipBook.com and enter code AS100220 for updates on this award.

(1003) • AOS Student and Postdoctoral Research Awards

American Ornithologists' Union
Avian Ecology Lab, Archbold Biological Station, 123 Main Drive, Venus, FL 33960
Phone: 863-465-2571
Email: rbowman@archbold-station.org
http://www.aou.org
Purpose: To provide research funding for members of the American Ornithologists Union.
Eligibility: Applicants must be members of the AOU and must submit proposals for research projects on avian biology, avian systematics, paleo-ornithology, biogeography, neotropical biology or ornithology.
Target applicant(s): High school students. College students. Graduate school students. Adult students.
Amount: Up to $2,500.
Number of awards: Varies.
Deadline: January 27.
How to apply: The submission procedure and tips for writing a proposal are described on the website.
Exclusive: Visit www.UltimateScholarshipBook.com and enter code AM100320 for updates on this award.

(1004) • Appaloosa Youth Association Art Contest

Appaloosa Horse Club
Appaloosa Youth Association, 2720 West Pullman Road, Moscow, ID 83843
Phone: 208-882-5578
Email: youth@appaloosa.com
http://www.appaloosayouth.com/
Purpose: To allow students to showcase their artistic talents with Appaloosa-themed projects.
Eligibility: Applicants age 18 and under should submit drawings, paintings and hand-built ceramics or sculptures with the Appaloosa theme. There are three age divisions: 10 and under and 11 to 13 and 14 to 18. Awards are based on originality, creativity and the theme.
Target applicant(s): Junior high students or younger. High school students.
Amount: $50-$100.
Number of awards: 9.
Deadline: May 1.
How to apply: Applications are available online.
Exclusive: Visit www.UltimateScholarshipBook.com and enter code AP100420 for updates on this award.

(1005) • Appaloosa Youth Association Essay Contest

Appaloosa Horse Club
Appaloosa Youth Association, 2720 West Pullman Road, Moscow, ID 83843
Phone: 208-882-5578
Email: youth@appaloosa.com
http://www.appaloosayouth.com/
Purpose: To reward students for essays that demonstrate their love of the Appaloosa breed.
Eligibility: Applicants must be 18 and under and should submit entry forms and essays on the provided themes. There are two age divisions: 13 and under and 14 to 18. Awards are based on originality and accuracy.
Target applicant(s): Junior high students or younger. High school students.
Amount: $50-$100.
Number of awards: 6.
Deadline: May 1.
How to apply: Applications are available online.
Exclusive: Visit www.UltimateScholarshipBook.com and enter code AP100520 for updates on this award.

(1006) • Appaloosa Youth Association Speech Contest

Appaloosa Horse Club
Appaloosa Youth Association, 2720 West Pullman Road, Moscow, ID 83843
Phone: 208-882-5578
Email: youth@appaloosa.com
http://www.appaloosayouth.com/
Purpose: To reward students for their speeches on Appaloosa.
Eligibility: Applicants should be 18 and under and can enter two divisions: a speech on a pre-determined topic or an impromptu speech. Age groups are 13 and under and 14 to 18. The speech is given at the World Championship Appaloosa Youth World Show.
Target applicant(s): Junior high students or younger. High school students.
Amount: $100.
Number of awards: 4.
Deadline: May 15.
How to apply: Applications are available online.
Exclusive: Visit www.UltimateScholarshipBook.com and enter code AP100620 for updates on this award.

(1007) • Apprentice Ecologist Initiative Youth Scholarship Program

Nicodemus Wilderness Project
P.O. Box 40712, Albuquerque, NM 87196-0712
Email: mail@wildernessproject.org
http://www.wildernessproject.org
Purpose: To aid ecologically-minded youth.
Eligibility: Applicants must be students who are between the ages of 13 and 21. They must devise and complete an environmental conservation project then write an essay describing the experience. Selection is based on the quality of the project and essay.
Target applicant(s): Junior high students or younger. High school students. College students.
Amount: $1,750.
Number of awards: 3.
Deadline: December 31.
How to apply: Application instructions are available online. An essay and a project photo are required.
Exclusive: Visit www.UltimateScholarshipBook.com and enter code NI100720 for updates on this award.

(1008) • ASABE Foundation Engineering Scholarship

American Society of Agricultural and Biological Engineers Foundation
Administrator, Scholarship Fund, 2950 Niles Road, St. Joseph, MI 49085
Phone: 269-429-0300
http://www.asabe.org

Purpose: To assist student members of ASABE.
Eligibility: Applicants must have completed at least one year of undergraduate study and have at least one year of undergraduate study remaining, major in agricultural or biological engineering at an eligible accredited degree program in the U.S. or Canada, have a minimum 2.5 GPA and demonstrate financial need. Students must also be members of ASABE.
Target applicant(s): College students. Adult students.
Minimum GPA: 2.5
Amount: $1,200.
Number of awards: 1.
Deadline: March 15.
How to apply: Application is available online.
Exclusive: Visit www.UltimateScholarshipBook.com and enter code AM100820 for updates on this award.

(1009) • ASCA/AISC Student Design Competition

Association of Collegiate Schools of Architecture
1735 New York Avenue NW, Washington, DC 20006
Phone: 202-785-2324
Email: eellis@acsa-arch.org
http://www.acsa-arch.org
Purpose: To encourage innovation in architecture.
Eligibility: Applicants must be architecture students at ACSA member schools in the United States, Canada or Mexico and be college juniors, seniors or graduate students. Students must submit a design project on one of the association's featured themes, and they must work under the direction of a faculty sponsor.
Target applicant(s): College students. Graduate school students. Adult students.
Amount: $300-$2,000.
Number of awards: 6.
Deadline: March 29.
How to apply: Applications are available online.
Exclusive: Visit www.UltimateScholarshipBook.com and enter code AS100920 for updates on this award.

(1010) • ASCO Numatics Industrial Automation Engineering Scholarship

ASCO Numatics
160 Park Avenue, Florham Park, NJ 07932
Phone: 973-966-2000
https://www.asco.com/en-us/Pages/scholarship.aspx
Purpose: To support students pursuing careers in industrial automation and related disciplines.
Eligibility: Applicants must have completed their sophomore year in a bachelor's degree program or be enrolled in a graduate program. ASCO employees and their relatives are not eligible. Winners are not eligible to apply for future scholarships.
Target applicant(s): College students. Graduate school students. Adult students.
Amount: $5,000.
Number of awards: 2.
Deadline: April 10.
How to apply: Applications are available online.
Exclusive: Visit www.UltimateScholarshipBook.com and enter code AS101020 for updates on this award.

(1011) • ASDSO Senior Undergraduate Scholarship

Association of State Dam Safety Officials
239 S. Limestone Street, Lexington, KY 40508
Phone: 859-550-2788 x 6
Email: info@damsafety.org
https://damsafety.org/
Purpose: To increase awareness of careers in dam safety.
Eligibility: Applicants must be U.S. citizens who will be full-time seniors in the following school year in an accredited civil engineering program or a related field and show an interest in a career related to dam design, construction or operation. Students must have a minimum 2.5 GPA for the first three years of college, be recommended by their academic advisor and write an essay on what ASDSO is and why dam safety is important. Selection is based on academic achievement, financial need, work experience and activities and essay.
Target applicant(s): College students. Adult students.
Minimum GPA: 2.5
Amount: $5,000-$10,000.
Number of awards: Varies.
Deadline: March 31.
How to apply: Applications are available online.
Exclusive: Visit www.UltimateScholarshipBook.com and enter code AS101120 for updates on this award.

(1012) • ASEV Scholarships

American Society for Enology and Viticulture
P.O. Box 1855, Davis, CA 95617-1855
Phone: 530-753-3142
Email: society@asev.org
http://www.asev.org
Purpose: To support those seeking a degree in enology, viticulture or in a curriculum focusing on a science basic to the wine and grape industry.
Eligibility: Applicants must be undergraduate or graduate students enrolled in or accepted into a full-time accredited four-year university program and must reside in North America (Canada, Mexico or the U.S.). Undergraduate students must be at least juniors for the upcoming academic year and have a minimum 3.0 GPA. Graduate students must have a minimum 3.2 GPA. Applicants must be enrolled in a major or in a graduate group concentrating on enology or viticulture or in a curriculum with a focus on a science basic to the wine and grape industry. The application, transcripts and two letters of recommendation are required.
Target applicant(s): College students. Graduate school students. Adult students.
Minimum GPA: 3.0 for undergraduate students, 3.2 for graduate students
Amount: Varies.
Number of awards: Varies.
Deadline: March 1.
How to apply: Applications are available online, by phone or by email.
Exclusive: Visit www.UltimateScholarshipBook.com and enter code AM101220 for updates on this award.

(1013) • ASF Olin Fellowships

Atlantic Salmon Federation
P.O. Box 807, Calais, ME 04619-0807
Phone: 506-529-1033
Email: asfweb@nbnet.nb.ca
http://www.asf.ca

Purpose: To help fund projects that focus on solving problems in Atlantic salmon biology, management and conservation.
Eligibility: Applicants must be studying or actively engaged in salmon management or research. The award is open to U.S. and Canadian applicants.
Target applicant(s): College students. Adult students.
Amount: $1,000-$3,000.
Number of awards: Varies.
Deadline: March 15.
How to apply: Applications are available by mail.
Exclusive: Visit www.UltimateScholarshipBook.com and enter code AT101320 for updates on this award.

(1014) • ASHA Youth Scholarships

American Saddlebred Horse Association Foundation
4083 Iron Works Parkway, Lexington, KY 40511
Phone: 859-259-2742
Email: b.newell@asha.net
https://www.asha.net/clubs/youthscholarships/
Purpose: To help youths involved with Saddlebreds.
Eligibility: This award is based on academic excellence, financial need, extracurricular activities, community service, involvement with American Saddlebred horses and personal references. An interview may be part of the selection process. Applicants should write an essay about school experiences, special interests, hobbies and American Saddlebred Horse Association activities. Scholarships are given only to high school seniors or recent graduates.
Target applicant(s): High school students.
Amount: Varies.
Number of awards: Varies.
Deadline: April 30.
How to apply: Applications are available online.
Exclusive: Visit www.UltimateScholarshipBook.com and enter code AM101420 for updates on this award.

(1015) • ASHRAE Engineering Technology Scholarships

American Society of Heating, Refrigerating and Air-Conditioning Engineers (ASHRAE)
1791 Tullie Circle, NE, Atlanta, GA 30329
Phone: 404-636-8400
Email: lbenedict@ashrae.org
http://www.ashrae.org
Purpose: To support students who are interested in pursuing a career in engineering or technology.
Eligibility: Applicants must be full-time undergraduate students pursuing a bachelor's or associate's degree in an engineering or engineering technology program, have a cumulative GPA of 3.0 and be a student member of ASHRAE. Selection is based on the overall strength of the application.
Target applicant(s): College students. Adult students.
Minimum GPA: 3.0
Amount: $5,000.
Number of awards: 4.
Scholarship may be renewable.
Deadline: November 15.
How to apply: Applications are available online.
Exclusive: Visit www.UltimateScholarshipBook.com and enter code AM101520 for updates on this award.

(1016) • ASHRAE Memorial Scholarship

American Society of Heating, Refrigerating and Air-Conditioning Engineers (ASHRAE)
1791 Tullie Circle, NE, Atlanta, GA 30329
Phone: 404-636-8400
Email: lbenedict@ashrae.org
http://www.ashrae.org
Purpose: To support undergraduate students enrolled in an engineering or engineering technology program recognized by ASHRAE.
Eligibility: Applicants must be enrolled full-time in an accredited undergraduate engineering or engineering technology program recognized by ASHRAE. Students must maintain a GPA of no less than 3.0, demonstrate financial need and show a potential service to the HVAC&R profession. Applicants must also meet at least one of three criteria: undergraduate institution hosts a recognized ASHRAE student branch, program of study is accredited by the Accreditation Board for Engineering and Technology (ABET), program of study is accredited by an agency outside the USA that is a signatory of the Washington Accord or has a signed Memorandum of Understanding with ABET.
Target applicant(s): High school students. College students. Adult students.
Minimum GPA: 3.0
Amount: $5,000.
Number of awards: 1.
Scholarship may be renewable.
Deadline: December 1.
How to apply: Applications are available online.
Exclusive: Visit www.UltimateScholarshipBook.com and enter code AM101620 for updates on this award.

(1017) • ASLA Council of Fellows Scholarships

Landscape Architecture Foundation
1129 20th Street NW, Suite 202, Washington, DC 20036
Phone: 202-331-7070
Email: scholarships@lafoundation.org
https://lafoundation.org/scholarship/
Purpose: To encourage students who are financially needy or who are from underrepresented groups to pursue careers in landscape architecture.
Eligibility: Applicants must be U.S. citizens or permanent residents. They must be in the third, fourth or fifth year of a Landscape Architecture Accreditation Board (LAAB)-accredited undergraduate degree program in landscape architecture. Selection is based on the overall strength of the application.
Target applicant(s): College students. Adult students.
Amount: $5,000.
Number of awards: Up to 3.
Deadline: February 15.
How to apply: Applications are available online. An application form, personal essay, two recommendation letters, financial aid information and an applicant photo are required.
Exclusive: Visit www.UltimateScholarshipBook.com and enter code LA101720 for updates on this award.

(1018) • ASME Auxiliary Lucy and Charles W. E. Clarke Scholarship

American Society of Mechanical Engineers (ASME)
Two Park Avenue, New York, NY 10016-5990
Phone: 800-843-2763
Email: lefeverb@asme.org
http://www.asme.org

Purpose: To help FIRST Robotics team members who are interested in pursuing a career in mechanical engineering or mechanical engineering technology.
Eligibility: Applicants must be high school seniors who are FIRST Robotics team members. They must be nominated for the award by an ASME member, an ASME Auxiliary member or a student ASME member who is also involved with FIRST. Students must plan to enroll in an ABET-accredited or similarly accredited mechanical engineering or mechanical engineering technology degree program. They must be able to begin undergraduate studies no later than the fall following graduation from high school. Selection is based on the overall strength of the application.
Target applicant(s): High school students.
Amount: $5,000.
Number of awards: Varies.
Deadline: March 15.
How to apply: Applications are available online. An application form, nomination letter, resume or transcript and financial data worksheet are required.
Exclusive: Visit www.UltimateScholarshipBook.com and enter code AM101820 for updates on this award.

(1019) • ASME Foundation Scholarships

American Society of Mechanical Engineers (ASME)
Two Park Avenue, New York, NY 10016-5990
Phone: 800-843-2763
Email: lefeverb@asme.org
http://www.asme.org
Purpose: To aid ASME student members who are enrolled in an undergraduate mechanical engineering, mechanical engineering technology or related degree program.
Eligibility: Applicants must be current ASME student members who are currently enrolled in (or have been accepted into) an ABET-accredited (or similarly accredited) undergraduate degree program in mechanical engineering, mechanical engineering technology or a subject related to one of these. They must be rising or current sophomores, juniors or seniors with a minimum 3.5 GPA. Selection is based on academic achievement and professional potential in engineering.
Target applicant(s): College students. Adult students.
Minimum GPA: 3.5
Amount: $11,000.
Number of awards: 1.
Deadline: March 1.
How to apply: Applications are available online through an electronic application system. Current ASME membership, submittal of application through the online system, a transcript and recommendation letters are required.
Exclusive: Visit www.UltimateScholarshipBook.com and enter code AM101920 for updates on this award.

(1020) • ASNE Scholarship Program

American Society of Naval Engineers
1452 Duke Street, Alexandria, VA 22314-3458
Phone: 703-836-6727
Email: dwoodbury@navalengineers.org
http://www.navalengineers.org/Students
Purpose: To encourage college students to enter the field of naval engineering and to provide support to naval engineers pursuing advanced education.
Eligibility: Applications must be for the last year of a full-time or co-op undergraduate program or for one year of full-time graduate study for a designated engineering or physical science degree at an accredited school. Applicants must be U.S. citizens pursuing careers in naval engineering. Graduate student applicants must be members of ASNE. An applicant's academic record, work history, professional promise and interest, extracurricular activities and recommendations are considered. Financial need may be considered.
Target applicant(s): College students. Graduate school students. Adult students.
Amount: $3,000-$4,000.
Number of awards: Varies.
Deadline: Varies.
How to apply: Applications are available online or by written request.
Exclusive: Visit www.UltimateScholarshipBook.com and enter code AM102020 for updates on this award.

(1021) • ASNT Fellowship

American Society for Nondestructive Testing
Awards and Honors Program, 1711 Arlingate Lane, P.O. Box 28518, Columbus, OH 43228-0518
Phone: 614-274-6003 x 233
Email: awards@asnt.org
http://www.asnt.org
Purpose: To fund research in nondestructive testing.
Eligibility: The award is given to an educational institution accredited by ABET to fund research in nondestructive testing (NDT) at the postgraduate level. One proposal per faculty member will be considered annually. Applicants should submit research proposal, program of study, description of facilities, budget, background on faculty advisor and background on graduate student.
Target applicant(s): Graduate school students. Adult students.
Amount: $20,000.
Number of awards: Up to 5.
Deadline: October 15.
How to apply: Applications are available online.
Exclusive: Visit www.UltimateScholarshipBook.com and enter code AM102120 for updates on this award.

(1022) • Association of Federal Communications Consulting Engineers Scholarships

Association of Federal Communications Consulting Engineers
P.O. Box 19333, Washington, DC 20036-0333
Phone: 703-780-4824
Email: scholarships@afcce.org
http://www.afcce.org
Purpose: To aid full-time undergraduate students attending an accredited college or university in pursuit of a degree in a telecommunications-related subject.
Eligibility: Applicants must be full-time (12+ units per semester) undergraduate or graduate students at an accredited postsecondary institution. They must be rising juniors or above and must be enrolled in a subject that is related to the radio communications consulting engineering field. They must have or acquire an AFCCE member who will act as a sponsor. Selection is based on the overall strength of the application.
Target applicant(s): College students. Graduate school students. Adult students.
Amount: Up to $2,500.
Number of awards: Varies.
Deadline: October 31 (spring), May 31 (fall).

How to apply: Applications are available online. An application form, transcript, personal statement and sponsorship by an AFCCE member are required.
Exclusive: Visit www.UltimateScholarshipBook.com and enter code AS102220 for updates on this award.

(1023) · Association of Food and Drug Officials Scholarship Award

Association of Food and Drug Officials
2550 Kingston Road, Suite 311, York, PA 17402
Phone: 717-757-2888
Email: afdo@afdo.org
http://www.afdo.org
Purpose: To support college students who are studying food, drug or consumer product safety.
Eligibility: Applicants must be in their third or fourth year of college at an accredited institution and demonstrate a desire to work in a career of research, regulatory work, quality control or teaching in an area related to food, drug or consumer product safety. Applicants must also have demonstrated leadership capabilities, a minimum 3.0 GPA and submit two letters of recommendation from faculty.
Target applicant(s): College students. Adult students.
Minimum GPA: 3.0
Amount: $1,500.
Number of awards: 3.
Deadline: February 1.
How to apply: Applications are available online.
Exclusive: Visit www.UltimateScholarshipBook.com and enter code AS102320 for updates on this award.

(1024) · Association of Information Technology Professionals (AITP) Scholarships

Association of Information Technology Professionals (AITP) Scholarships
P.O. Box 583, Omaha, NE 68101
Email: omahaAITP@gmail.com
http://www.aitpomaha.com/scholarship-information.html
Purpose: To support students pursuing information systems and technology education.
Eligibility: Applicants must be enrolling in or currently enrolled in an accredited two- or four-year program in Nebraska, Iowa, Missouri, Kansas, North Dakota or South Dakota with the intent of earning a degree in information systems, computer science or related field.
Target applicant(s): High school students. College students. Adult students.
Amount: $1,000.
Number of awards: Varies.
Deadline: June 1.
How to apply: Applications are available online.
Exclusive: Visit www.UltimateScholarshipBook.com and enter code AS102420 for updates on this award.

(1025) · ASTM International Katherine and Bryant Mather Scholarship

ASTM International
100 Barr Harbor Drive, P.O. Box C700, West Conshohocken, PA 19428-2959
Phone: 610-832-9585
Email: awards@astm.org
https://www.astm.org/studentmember/Student_Awards.html
Purpose: To aid students who are enrolled in degree programs that are related to the cement and concrete technology industry.
Eligibility: Applicants must be full-time undergraduate sophomores, undergraduate juniors, undergraduate seniors or graduate students. They must be enrolled in a degree program that is related to cement construction or concrete materials technology at an accredited institution of higher learning. Selection is based on the overall strength of the application.
Target applicant(s): College students. Graduate school students. Adult students.
Amount: Up to $7,500.
Number of awards: Varies.
Scholarship may be renewable.
Deadline: April 30.
How to apply: Applications are available online. An application form, one reference letter, an official transcript and a personal statement are required.
Exclusive: Visit www.UltimateScholarshipBook.com and enter code AS102520 for updates on this award.

(1026) · Astronaut Scholarship

Astronaut Scholarship Foundation
Kennedy Space Center, SR 405, Titusville, FL 32899
Phone: 321-449-4876
Email: info@astronautscholarship.org
http://www.astronautscholarship.org
Purpose: To ensure the United States' continued leadership in science by assisting promising physical science and engineering students.
Eligibility: Applicants must be sophomore, junior or senior undergraduate or graduate students in natural or applied science, engineering or mathematics at Brown University, Colorado School of Mines, Clemson University, Florida Institute of Technology, Georgia Institute of Technology, Harvey Mudd College, Johns Hopkins University, Louisiana State University, Massachusetts Institute of Technology, Miami University, North Carolina State University, North Dakota State University, Ohio State, Pennsylvania State University, Purdue University, Syracuse University, Texas A&M University, Tufts University, University of Arizona, University of Central Florida, University of Chicago, University of Colorado, University of Kansas, University of Kentucky, University of Minnesota, University of Michigan, University of Oklahoma, University of Rochester, University of Southern California, University of Texas at Austin, University of Virginia, University of Washington, University of Wisconsin or Washington University and must be nominated by faculty or staff. Applicants may not directly apply for the scholarship. Students must have excellent grades and performed research or lab work in their field.
Target applicant(s): College students. Graduate school students. Adult students.
Amount: $10,000.
Number of awards: 32.
Deadline: Varies.
How to apply: Applicants must be nominated.
Exclusive: Visit www.UltimateScholarshipBook.com and enter code AS102620 for updates on this award.

(1027) · AUA Foundation Research Scholars Program

American Foundation for Urologic Disease Inc.
1000 Corporate Boulevard, Linthicum, MD 21090
Phone: 410-689-3750
Email: grants@auafoundation.org
http://www.urologyhealth.org

Purpose: To help young men and women who intend to pursue careers in urologic research.
Eligibility: Applicants must be researchers who conduct their research in the U.S. or Canada. Funding is provided for post-doctoral research only.
Target applicant(s): Graduate school students. Adult students.
Amount: Varies.
Number of awards: Varies.
Deadline: September 8.
How to apply: Applications are available online.
Exclusive: Visit www.UltimateScholarshipBook.com and enter code AM102720 for updates on this award.

(1028) · Automotive Hall of Fame Scholarships

Automotive Hall of Fame
Award and Scholarship Programs, 21400 Oakwood Boulevard, Dearborn, MI 48124
Phone: 313-240-4000
http://www.automotivehalloffame.org/scholarships/
Purpose: To assist students interested in automotive careers.
Eligibility: Applicants must be interested in automotive careers. Other requirements vary depending on the specific scholarship. Minimum GPA of 3.0 required.
Target applicant(s): High school students. College students. Adult students.
Minimum GPA: 3.0
Amount: Varies.
Number of awards: Varies.
Deadline: June 30.
How to apply: Applications are available online or by sending a self-addressed, stamped envelope.
Exclusive: Visit www.UltimateScholarshipBook.com and enter code AU102820 for updates on this award.

(1029) · Auxiliary Legacy Scholarship

National Society of Professional Engineers
1420 King Street, Alexandria, VA 22314-2794
Phone: 703-684-2885
Email: students@nspe.org
https://www.nspe.org/resources/students/scholarships
Purpose: To aid female students who want to major in engineering.
Eligibility: Applicants must be female college sophomores majoring in engineering. Applicants must be U.S. citizens. Selection is based only on achievement.
Target applicant(s): College students. Adult students.
Amount: $1,000.
Number of awards: 1.
Scholarship may be renewable.
Deadline: March 1.
How to apply: Applications are available online.
Exclusive: Visit www.UltimateScholarshipBook.com and enter code NA102920 for updates on this award.

(1030) · Avacare Medical Scholarship

Avacare Medical
1665 Corporate Road West, Lakewood, NJ 08701
Phone: 877-813-7799
Email: scholarships@avacaremedical.com
https://www.avacaremedical.com/scholarship
Purpose: To reward students who participate in inspiring acts of kindness.
Eligibility: Applicants must be at least 13 years of age, have a minimum 3.0 GPA and be a U.S. citizen. Students must be studying or planning on studying a medicine-related field. Students must be at least a high school senior. Selection is based on judge scores as well as public votes. Submissions may be a blog post, an image or a short video clip. Finalists are selected based on content, creativity and quality of work.
Target applicant(s): High school students. College students. Graduate school students. Adult students.
Minimum GPA: 3.0
Amount: $1,000.
Number of awards: 1.
Deadline: December 15.
How to apply: A completed project must be mailed or emailed along with a transcript, full name, email address, phone number and which medical field pursuing.
Exclusive: Visit www.UltimateScholarshipBook.com and enter code AV103020 for updates on this award.

(1031) · Aviation Distributors and Manufacturers Association Scholarship Program

Aviation Distributors and Manufacturers Association
100 North 20th Street, Suite 400, Philadelphia, PA 19103-1462
Phone: 215-320-3872
Email: adma@fernley.com
http://members.adma.org/adma
Purpose: To help students who are planning to pursue careers in aviation.
Eligibility: Applicants must be third- or fourth-year students enrolled at an accredited four-year institution of higher learning and working towards the Bachelor of Science (BS) in aviation management or professional piloting, or must be second-year A&P mechanic students enrolled in an accredited two-year program. They must have a minimum GPA of 3.0. Selection is based on academic achievement, recommendation letters, extracurricular activities, leadership skills and financial need.
Target applicant(s): College students. Adult students.
Minimum GPA: 3.0
Amount: Varies.
Number of awards: Varies.
Deadline: March 31.
How to apply: Applications are available online. An application form, two recommendation letters, a transcript and a personal statement are required.
Exclusive: Visit www.UltimateScholarshipBook.com and enter code AV103120 for updates on this award.

(1032) · Aviation Insurance Association Education Foundation Scholarship

Aviation Insurance Association
7200 W. 75th Street, Overland Park, KS 66204
Phone: 913-627-9632
Email: mandie@aiaweb.org
http://www.aiaweb.org/Scholarships.aspx
Purpose: To help upper division undergraduate aviation students and graduate aviation students.
Eligibility: Applicants must be enrolled in an undergraduate or graduate program in aviation at a school that is a member of the University Aviation Association (UAA). They must have completed at least 45 units of coursework in their degree program, 15 or more of which

must be for aviation courses. They must have a GPA of 2.5 or higher. Students must also currently be an intern or recently have completed an internship program within the aviation insurance industry in one of the following areas: agent/broker, underwriter, claims professional or attorney. Awards are given in the spring and fall.
Target applicant(s): College students. Graduate school students. Adult students.
Minimum GPA: 2.5
Amount: $2,500.
Number of awards: 4.
Deadline: Varies.
How to apply: Applications are available online. Five sets of the following items are required: application form, personal statement, transcript, one letter of recommendation and any FAA certificates (if applicable).
Exclusive: Visit www.UltimateScholarshipBook.com and enter code AV103220 for updates on this award.

(1033) • Baroid Scholarship

American Ground Water Trust
50 Pleasant Street, Concord, NH 03301
Phone: 603-228-5444
https://agwt.org/content/scholarships
Purpose: To support high school seniors intending to pursue a career in a ground water-related field.
Eligibility: Applicants must be high school seniors entering an accredited four-year college or university and intending to pursue a career in a ground water-related field.
Target applicant(s): High school students.
Minimum GPA: 3.0
Amount: $2,000.
Number of awards: Varies.
Deadline: June 1.
How to apply: Applications are available online.
Exclusive: Visit www.UltimateScholarshipBook.com and enter code AM103320 for updates on this award.

(1034) • Barry M. Goldwater Scholarship and Excellence in Education Program

Barry M. Goldwater Scholarship and Excellence in Education Foundation
6225 Brandon Avenue, Suite 315, Springfield, VA 22150
Phone: 703-756-6012
Email: goldwater@act.org
http://goldwater.scholarsapply.org
Purpose: To assist college students who pursue studies that lead to careers as scientists, mathematicians and engineers.
Eligibility: Applicants must be full-time college sophomores or juniors, U.S. citizens or resident aliens, have a minimum "B" GPA and be in the upper fourth of their class. Award must be used during the junior or senior year of college. Selection is based on potential and intent to pursue careers in mathematics, the natural sciences or engineering.
Target applicant(s): College students. Adult students.
Minimum GPA: 3.0
Amount: Up to $7,500.
Number of awards: Up to 300.
Deadline: January.
How to apply: Institutions nominate college sophomores or juniors. Applicants may not apply directly to the foundation.
Exclusive: Visit www.UltimateScholarshipBook.com and enter code BA103420 for updates on this award.

(1035) • Bart Kamen Memorial FIRST Scholarship

FIRST
200 Bedford Street, Manchester, NH 03101
Email: scholarships@firstinspires.org
https://www.firstinspires.org/bart-kamen-scholarship
Purpose: To support undergraduate students pursuing medical education.
Eligibility: Applicants must be a high school senior or graduate enrolling in an undergraduate program as a full-time student at a college or university in the U.S. Students must be applying for or accepted to a program in biomedical engineering or pre-med studies. Applicants must have participated for a minimum of one year as a team member on a FIRST LEGO league, FIRST Tech Challenge or FIRST Robotics competition team.
Target applicant(s): High school students.
Amount: $10,000.
Number of awards: 4.
Scholarship may be renewable.
Deadline: February 1.
How to apply: Applications are available online.
Exclusive: Visit www.UltimateScholarshipBook.com and enter code FI103520 for updates on this award.

(1036) • Battery Division Student Research Award

Electrochemical Society
65 South Main Street, Building D, Pennington, NJ 08534-2839
Phone: 609-737-1902
Email: awards@electrochem.org
http://www.electrochem.org/programs/
Purpose: To recognize young engineers and scientists in the field of electrochemical power sources.
Eligibility: Applicants must be accepted or enrolled in a college or university and must submit transcripts, an outline of the proposed research project, a description of how the project is related to the field of electrochemical power sources, a record of achievements in industrial work and a letter of recommendation from the research supervisor. Awards are based on academic performance, past research, proposed research and the recommendation.
Target applicant(s): High school students. College students. Graduate school students. Adult students.
Amount: $1,000.
Number of awards: Varies.
Deadline: March 15.
How to apply: Application materials are described online.
Exclusive: Visit www.UltimateScholarshipBook.com and enter code EL103620 for updates on this award.

(1037) • Beef Industry Scholarship

National Cattlemen's Foundation
9110 East Nichols Avenue, Suite 300 , Centennial, CO 80112
Phone: 303-694-0305
Email: ncf@beef.org
http://www.nationalcattlemensfoundation.org
Purpose: To aid students who are preparing for careers in the beef industry.
Eligibility: Applicants must be graduating high school seniors or college undergraduates, and they must have plans to be enrolled full-time in

a two-year or four-year undergraduate program during the upcoming academic year. They must be enrolled in a beef industry-related program of study and have a demonstrated interest in pursuing a career in the beef industry through previous coursework taken, internships completed or other life experiences. They or their families must be members of the National Cattlemen's Beef Association. Selection is based on the strength of the essay, letter of intent and reference letters.
Target applicant(s): High school students. College students. Adult students.
Amount: $1,500.
Number of awards: 10.
Scholarship may be renewable.
Deadline: December 19.
How to apply: Applications are available online. An application form, letter of intent, personal essay and two reference letters are required.
Exclusive: Visit www.UltimateScholarshipBook.com and enter code NA103720 for updates on this award.

(1038) • Behavioral Sciences Student Fellowship

Epilepsy Foundation
8301 Professional Place East, Suite 200, Landover, MD 20785-2353
Phone: 800-332-1000
Email: ContactUs@efa.org
http://www.epilepsy.com/
Purpose: To encourage students to pursue careers in epilepsy research or practice settings.
Eligibility: Applicants must be undergraduate or graduate students in the behavioral sciences, have an epilepsy-related study, have a qualified mentor who can supervise the project and have an interest in careers in epilepsy research or practice settings. The project must be in the U.S. and should not be for dissertation research. The award is based on the quality of the project, relevance to epilepsy, interest in epilepsy and the quality of the proposed lab or facility. Applicants must submit three recommendation letters, statement of intent, biographical sketch and research plan.
Target applicant(s): High school students. College students. Graduate school students. Adult students.
Amount: Varies.
Number of awards: Varies.
Deadline: Varies.
How to apply: Application materials are described online.
Exclusive: Visit www.UltimateScholarshipBook.com and enter code EP103820 for updates on this award.

(1039) • Benjamin J. Keiser Memorial Coastal Engineering Scholarship

Surfers' Environmental Alliance
P.O. Box 3154, Long Branch, NJ 07740-3154
Email: rlee@seasurfer.org
http://www.seasurfer.org/sea-scholarships
Purpose: To support students who have a passion for environmental awareness and marine conservation.
Eligibility: Applicants must be in high school through graduate level studies, have at least a 3.2 GPA, be a U.S. citizen and be pursuing or plan on pursuing a degree in coastal engineering. Selection is based on goals, community service and involvement and academic excellence.
Target applicant(s): High school students. College students. Graduate school students. Adult students.
Minimum GPA: 3.2
Amount: Up to $3,500.
Number of awards: Varies.
Deadline: May 15.
How to apply: Applications are available online and include an essay.
Exclusive: Visit www.UltimateScholarshipBook.com and enter code SU103920 for updates on this award.

(1040) • Benton-Meier Scholarships

American Psychological Foundation
750 First Street NE, Washington, DC 20002-4242
Phone: 202-336-5843
Email: foundation@apa.org
http://www.apa.org/apf/funding/index.aspx
Purpose: To assist neuropsychology graduate students.
Eligibility: Applicants must demonstrate need and demonstrate potential for a promising career in the field of neuropsychology. Applicants should also submit a letter that documents their scholarly and research accomplishments, financial need and how the award will be used.
Target applicant(s): Graduate school students. Adult students.
Amount: $2,500.
Number of awards: 2.
Deadline: June 1.
How to apply: A request for proposal form is available online.
Exclusive: Visit www.UltimateScholarshipBook.com and enter code AM104020 for updates on this award.

(1041) • Bergmeyer Scholarship

Planning and Visual Education Partnership (PAVE) c/o Kroger Company
PAVE Entries Attn.: Ken Pray, 1014 Vine Street, Cincinnati, OH 45202
Email: info@paveglobal.org
http://paveglobal.org/Competitions.aspx?typeid=26
Purpose: To support students who have potential in the fields of interior design and architecture.
Eligibility: Applicants must be currently enrolled in a program working toward a degree in interior design or architecture specifically for the retail industry. Students must have at least a 3.0 GPA. Applicants must currently be taking at least 12 credit hours. Students must be in their second year or higher enrolled in an advanced degree program or an advanced specialty program.
Target applicant(s): College students. Graduate school students. Adult students.
Minimum GPA: 3.0
Amount: $2,500.
Number of awards: Varies.
Deadline: February 3.
How to apply: Applications are available online.
Exclusive: Visit www.UltimateScholarshipBook.com and enter code PL104120 for updates on this award.

(1042) • Berna Lou Cartwright Scholarship

American Society of Mechanical Engineers (ASME)
Two Park Avenue, New York, NY 10016-5990
Phone: 800-843-2763
Email: lefeverb@asme.org
http://www.asme.org
Purpose: To aid U.S. mechanical engineering majors.
Eligibility: Applicants must be U.S. citizens who are entering the final year of an ABET-accredited undergraduate degree program in mechanical engineering. Selection is based on academic achievement,

character, participation in the American Society of Mechanical Engineers (if applicable) and financial need.
Target applicant(s): College students. Adult students.
Amount: $3,000.
Number of awards: Up to 2.
Deadline: March 1.
How to apply: Applications are available online. An application form, official transcript and three recommendation letters are required.
Exclusive: Visit www.UltimateScholarshipBook.com and enter code AM104220 for updates on this award.

(1043) • Bill Kane Scholarship, Undergraduate

Shape America
1900 Association Drive, Reston, VA 20191
Phone: 800-213-7193
http://www.shapeamerica.org
Purpose: To support health education students.
Eligibility: Applicants must be full-time undergraduate health majors in their sophomore, junior or senior years. They must have a GPA of at least 3.25 and write an essay about what they hope to accomplish as a health educator.
Target applicant(s): College students. Adult students.
Minimum GPA: 3.25
Amount: $1,000.
Number of awards: 1.
Deadline: October 15.
How to apply: Applications are available online.
Exclusive: Visit www.UltimateScholarshipBook.com and enter code SH104320 for updates on this award.

(1044) • Bill Kirk Scholarship Endowment

National FFA Organization
P.O. Box 68960, 6060 FFA Drive, Indianapolis, IN 46268-0960
Phone: 888-332-2668
Email: scholarships@ffa.org
https://www.ffa.org/participate/scholarships
Purpose: To support FFA leaders working toward a four-year degree in agricultural sciences or agricultural education.
Eligibility: Applicants must be FFA members with a minimum 3.5 GPA pursuing a degree in agricultural education or sciences. Those with leadership experience on the local, state or national level are preferred. Selection is based on the overall strength of the application.
Target applicant(s): High school students. College students.
Minimum GPA: 3.5
Amount: $1,000.
Number of awards: 1.
Deadline: February 8.
How to apply: Applications are available online.
Exclusive: Visit www.UltimateScholarshipBook.com and enter code NA104420 for updates on this award.

(1045) • Biographies of Contemporary Women in Mathematics Essay Contest

Association for Women in Mathematics
11240 Waples Mill Road, Suite 200, Fairfax, VA 22030
Phone: 703-934-0163
Email: awm@awm-math.org
http://www.awm-math.org
Purpose: To increase awareness of women's contributions to the mathematical sciences.
Eligibility: Applicants must interview a woman working in a mathematical career and write an essay based on the interview. Applicants may be from the sixth grade to graduate school students.
Target applicant(s): Junior high students or younger. High school students. College students. Adult students.
Amount: Varies.
Number of awards: At least 3.
Deadline: January 31.
How to apply: Applications are available online and must be submitted online.
Exclusive: Visit www.UltimateScholarshipBook.com and enter code AS104520 for updates on this award.

(1046) • BluePay STEM Scholarship

BluePay
184 Shuman Boulevard, Suite 350, Naperville, IL 60563
Phone: 866-444-6216
https://www.bluepay.com/company/scholarship/
Purpose: To assist students who are majoring in a STEM field of study.
Eligibility: Applicants must be undergraduate or graduate students attending an accredited college or university and majoring in a STEM field. An essay of 500 to 1,000 words is required on the topic provided.
Target applicant(s): College students. Graduate school students. Adult students.
Amount: Up to $1,000.
Number of awards: 3.
Deadline: August 17.
How to apply: Applications are available online.
Exclusive: Visit www.UltimateScholarshipBook.com and enter code BL104620 for updates on this award.

(1047) • BMW/SAE Engineering Scholarship

Society of Automotive Engineers International
Scholarships Program, 400 Commonwealth Drive, Warrendale, PA 15096
Phone: 724-776-4841
Email: scholarships@sae.org
http://students.sae.org/scholarships/
Purpose: To support engineering students with high potential.
Eligibility: Applicants must be U.S. citizens with a GPA of 3.75 or higher. They must rank in the 90th percentile in math and critical reading on the SAT or ACT and must pursue an engineering or related degree through an ABET-accredited program.
Target applicant(s): College students. Adult students.
Minimum GPA: 3.75
Amount: $1,500.
Number of awards: 1.
Scholarship may be renewable.
Deadline: March 15.
How to apply: Applications are available online. An application form, transcript and SAT/ACT scores are required.
Exclusive: Visit www.UltimateScholarshipBook.com and enter code SO104720 for updates on this award.

(1048) • Brian Jenneman Memorial Scholarship

Community Foundation of Louisville
Waterfront Plaza, West Tower, 325 West Main Street, Suite 1110, Louisville, KY 40202
Phone: 502-585-4649
Email: ebonyo@cflouisville.org

https://www.cflouisville.org/scholarships/
Purpose: To help U.S. students who are training to become paramedics.
Eligibility: Applicants must be 18 years of age or older and must be accepted into a certified paramedic training program. They must be U.S. residents and must be in a training program based in the U.S. Selection is based on commitment to the paramedic profession and to public service.
Target applicant(s): High school students.
Amount: Varies.
Number of awards: Varies.
Scholarship may be renewable.
Deadline: March 15.
How to apply: Applications are available online. An application form, official transcript and three recommendation forms are required.
Exclusive: Visit www.UltimateScholarshipBook.com and enter code CO104820 for updates on this award.

(1049) • BrightLife Direct Physical Therapy Scholarship

BrightLife Direct
6925 Willow Street NW, Suite D, Washington, DC 20012
Phone: 877-545-8585
Email: scholarship@brightlifedirect.com
http://www.brightlifedirect.com/brightlife-physical-therapist-scholarship.asp
Purpose: To assist students who are seeking to become certified occupational and physical therapists.
Eligibility: Applicants must be U.S. citizens, in good academic standing with a minimum 3.0 GPA, currently enrolled in a CAPTE or ACOTE accredited program and have completed at least one year of their program. Students will need to complete a short essay on why they decided to pursue a career in physical/occupational therapy.
Target applicant(s): College students. Adult students.
Minimum GPA: 3.0
Amount: $1,000.
Number of awards: 1.
Deadline: July 14.
How to apply: Applications are available online.
Exclusive: Visit www.UltimateScholarshipBook.com and enter code BR104920 for updates on this award.

(1050) • Brill Family Scholarship

Society of Women Engineers
130 East Randolph Street, Suite 3500, Chicago, IL 60601
Phone: 877-793-4636
Email: scholarships@swe.org
http://societyofwomenengineers.swe.org/scholarships
Purpose: To encourage women advancing in the field of engineering through a college education.
Eligibility: Applicants must have a minimum 3.0 GPA and be a full time student. Students must be U.S. citizens and must be planning to study at an ABET-accredited program in aeronautical/aerospace engineering or biomedical engineering.
Target applicant(s): College students. Adult students.
Minimum GPA: 3.0
Amount: $1,500.
Number of awards: 1.
Deadline: February 15.
How to apply: Applications are available online.
Exclusive: Visit www.UltimateScholarshipBook.com and enter code SO105020 for updates on this award.

(1051) • Bryant L. Bench Carollo Engineers Inc. Scholarship

American Water Works Association
6666 W. Quincy Avenue, Denver, CO 80235-3098
Phone: 800-926-7337
Email: scholarships@awwa.org
http://www.awwa.org
Purpose: To support masters-level students interested in water-energy nexus within the water industry.
Eligibility: Applicants must be pursuing a masters degree. They must also have an interest in water-energy nexus issues in relation to water, water reuse or wastewater. This is a one-time award. Selection is based upon the overall strength of the application.
Target applicant(s): College students. Graduate school students. Adult students.
Amount: $10,000.
Number of awards: 1.
Deadline: January 10.
How to apply: Applications are available online.
Exclusive: Visit www.UltimateScholarshipBook.com and enter code AM105120 for updates on this award.

(1052) • BSN Scholarship

Association of Rehabilitation Nurses
8735 W. Higgins Road, Suite 300, Chicago, IL 60631-2738
Phone: 800-229-7530
Email: gelliott@connect2amc.com
http://www.rehabnurse.org/awards/content/Scholarships.html
Purpose: To help nurses pursuing a bachelor's of science in nursing.
Eligibility: Applicants must be members of and involved in ARN, enrolled in a bachelor's of science in nursing (BSN) program, have completed at least one course, be currently practicing rehabilitation nursing and have a minimum of two years' experience in rehabilitation nursing. Applications, transcripts, a summary of professional and educational goals and achievements and two recommendation letters are required. Applications should be submitted by fax or email.
Target applicant(s): College students. Adult students.
Amount: $1,500.
Number of awards: Varies.
Deadline: July 1.
How to apply: Applications are available online.
Exclusive: Visit www.UltimateScholarshipBook.com and enter code AS105220 for updates on this award.

(1053) • Buffered Scholarship for Women in STEM

Buffered
Email: scholarships@buffered.com
https://bufferedscholarship.com/
Purpose: To support women studying STEM fields.
Eligibility: Applicants must be female students with a GPA of 3.0 or higher who are enrolled in or will be enrolling in an undergraduate or graduate degree program in a STEM field in the U.S. or Canada. Students must write an original essay pertaining to NET Neutrality.
Target applicant(s): High school students. College students. Graduate school students. Adult students.
Minimum GPA: 3.0
Amount: $5,000.
Number of awards: 1.
Deadline: July 1.
How to apply: Applications are available online.

Exclusive: Visit www.UltimateScholarshipBook.com and enter code BU105320 for updates on this award.

(1054) · Build U. Scholarship

Buildium
38 Chauncy Street, 12th Floor, Boston, MA 02111
Phone: 888-414-1933
http://www.buildium.com/buildiums-build-u-scholarship
Purpose: To support students who are committed to pursing a major in Science, Technology, Engineering or Mathematics (STEM).
Eligibility: Applicants must be at least 18 years old, enrolled in an accredited U.S. or Canadian undergraduate or graduate program and demonstrate a good post-secondary academic performance. Students must submit a personal essay using no more than 1,000 words and submit a copy of an unofficial transcript or acceptance letter for proof of enrollment.
Target applicant(s): College students. Graduate school students. Adult students.
Amount: $2,500.
Number of awards: 2.
Deadline: April 15, November 1.
How to apply: Applications are available online.
Exclusive: Visit www.UltimateScholarshipBook.com and enter code BU105420 for updates on this award.

(1055) · Bunge North America FFA Scholarship

National FFA Organization
P.O. Box 68960, 6060 FFA Drive, Indianapolis, IN 46268-0960
Phone: 888-332-2668
Email: scholarships@ffa.org
https://www.ffa.org/participate/scholarships
Purpose: To support FFA members working toward undergraduate degrees in select areas.
Eligibility: Applicants must be current FFA members under 23 years of age working toward two-year or four-year degrees at U.S. institutions in the areas of agricultural production, communication, education, management, finance, sales, marketing, science, engineering or public service in agriculture. Applicants must live in one of the 48 continental states and must possess a minimum 2.5 GPA. Selection is based on leadership ability and the overall strength of the application.
Target applicant(s): High school students. College students.
Minimum GPA: 2.5
Amount: $1,000.
Number of awards: 8.
Deadline: February 1.
How to apply: Applications are available online.
Exclusive: Visit www.UltimateScholarshipBook.com and enter code NA105520 for updates on this award.

(1056) · BurialInsurancePlan.org Mortuary Science Scholarship

Burial Insurance Plan
503 Ballarat Avenue N., P.O. Box 358, North Bend, WA 98045
Phone: 425-677-4297
Email: admin@burialinsuranceplan.org
http://burialinsuranceplan.org/
Purpose: To support the goals of students in the mortuary sciences field.
Eligibility: Applicants must be at least 17 years of age and be accepted into a mortuary or actuarial sciences program, not yet started or currently enrolled at the undergraduate or graduate level, at an accredited institution of learning. Students will need to submit an ID for proof of age, an application, proof of enrollment or acceptance letter and an essay of 500-1,000 words explaining why they are choosing the mortuary services field and what they hope to accomplish in their career.
Target applicant(s): High school students. College students. Graduate school students. Adult students.
Amount: $500.
Number of awards: 1.
Deadline: February 10.
How to apply: Applications are available online. An application, birth date verification, proof of enrollment or acceptance and an essay are required.
Exclusive: Visit www.UltimateScholarshipBook.com and enter code BU105620 for updates on this award.

(1057) · C.B. Gambrell Undergraduate Scholarship

Institute of Industrial and Systems Engineers
3577 Parkway Lane, Suite 200, Norcross, GA 30092
Phone: 800-494-0460
Email: bcameron@iienet.org
http://www.iise.org/
Purpose: To help undergraduate industrial engineering students from the U.S.
Eligibility: Applicants must be full-time undergraduate students who have completed their freshman year in an accredited industrial engineering program, have a minimum 3.4 GPA, major in industrial engineering and be active members. Students may not apply directly for this scholarship and must be nominated. The award is based on academic ability, character, leadership, potential service to the industrial engineering profession and financial need.
Target applicant(s): College students. Adult students.
Minimum GPA: 3.4
Amount: $1,000.
Number of awards: 2.
Deadline: November 15.
How to apply: Nomination forms are available online.
Exclusive: Visit www.UltimateScholarshipBook.com and enter code IN105720 for updates on this award.

(1058) · Campus Safety Health and Environmental Management Association Scholarship

National Safety Council
CSHEMA, Scholarship Committee, CSHEMA Division, National Safety Council, 12100 Sunset Hills Road ,Suite 130, Reston, VA 20190-3221
Phone: 703-234-4141
Email: info@cshema.org
http://www.nsc.org/pages/home.aspx
Purpose: To encourage the study of safety.
Eligibility: Applicants must be full-time undergraduate or graduate students with at least one year left in their degree program. Applicants must also write an essay about health, safety or environmental issues relevant to the university or college campus.
Target applicant(s): High school students. College students. Adult students.
Amount: $3,000.
Number of awards: 1.
Deadline: March 31.
How to apply: Applications are available online.
Exclusive: Visit www.UltimateScholarshipBook.com and enter code NA105820 for updates on this award.

(1059) • CampusRN Scholarship Fund

CampusRN
2464 Massachusetts Avenue, Suite 210, Cambridge, MA 02140
Phone: 617-661-2613
Email: scholarships@campusrn.com
http://www.campusrn.com
Purpose: To provide financial assistance for nursing students from all 50 states.
Eligibility: Applicants must be nursing students at schools that have registered in the scholarship program by linking to the CampusRN website. An essay is required. Finalists may be asked to submit awards, letters of recommendation and other materials upon selection. One award is given for each of the six geographical regions.
Target applicant(s): College students. Graduate school students. Adult students.
Amount: $2,500.
Number of awards: 6.
Deadline: May 1.
How to apply: Applications are available online.
Exclusive: Visit www.UltimateScholarshipBook.com and enter code CA105920 for updates on this award.

(1060) • Careers in Agriculture Scholarship Program

Winfield Solutions LLC
Careers in Agriculture - MS 5735, P.O. Box 64281, St. Paul, MN 55164-0281
Phone: 855-494-6343
Email: info@winfieldsolutionsllc.com
http://www.winfield.com/default.aspx
Purpose: To aid high school seniors and college freshmen and sophomores who are interested in pursuing a career in agriculture.
Eligibility: Applicants must be high school seniors who plan to enroll in a two-year or four-year degree program related to agriculture in the fall following graduation or first- or second-year college students pursuing degrees in agronomy, crop production or related fields. Dependents of employees of Winfield Solutions LLC or Land O' Lakes Inc. are ineligible. Selection is based on academic achievement, proven leadership in agriculture and professional interest in the field of agriculture.
Target applicant(s): High school students. College students. Adult students.
Amount: $1,000.
Number of awards: 20.
Deadline: February 10.
How to apply: Applications are available online. An application form, two character evaluations, a transcript and a personal essay are required.
Exclusive: Visit www.UltimateScholarshipBook.com and enter code WI106020 for updates on this award.

(1061) • Carville M. Akehurst Memorial Scholarship

Horticultural Research Institute
525 9th Street NW, Suite 800, Washington, DC 20004
Phone: 202-789-2900
http://www.hriresearch.org
Purpose: To provide scholarships for undergraduate and graduate students who plan to pursue careers in horticulture.
Eligibility: Applicants must be enrolled full-time in a landscaping or horticultural program at a two- or four-year accredited institution and be residents of Maryland, Virginia or West Virginia.
Target applicant(s): College students. Graduate school students. Adult students.
Minimum GPA: 2.7
Amount: $1,000.
Number of awards: 1.
Scholarship may be renewable.
Deadline: September 8.
How to apply: Applications are available online.
Exclusive: Visit www.UltimateScholarshipBook.com and enter code HO106120 for updates on this award.

(1062) • Cedarcrest Farms Scholarship

American Jersey Cattle Association
6486 East Main Street, Reynoldsburg, OH 43068-2362
Phone: 614-861-3636
Email: info@usjersey.com
http://www.usjersey.com
Purpose: To aid American Jersey Cattle Association members studying dairy product marketing, large animal veterinary practice, dairy manufacturing or dairy production.
Eligibility: Applicants must be AJCA members studying dairy manufacturing, dairy product marketing, dairy production or large animal veterinary practice at the undergraduate or graduate level. They must have a GPA of 2.5 or above and must plan to pursue a career in agriculture. Selection is based on the overall strength of the application.
Target applicant(s): College students. Graduate school students. Adult students.
Minimum GPA: 2.5
Amount: $1,750.
Number of awards: Varies.
Deadline: July 1.
How to apply: Applications are available online. An application form, transcript and up to two letters of recommendation are required.
Exclusive: Visit www.UltimateScholarshipBook.com and enter code AM106220 for updates on this award.

(1063) • Chairish Design Your Future Scholarship

Chairish
465 California Street, Suite 1250, San Francisco, CA 94104
https://www.chairish.com/pages/scholarship
Purpose: To support students pursuing design-related fields.
Eligibility: Applicants must be currently enrolled or enrolling at an accredited two-year, four-year or technical institution in the United States and pursuing a degree in the design and engineering-related fields. Students must be from an underrepresented or disadvantaged background such as a racial minority or have a disability, have a minimum 2.0 GPA and must submit an essay along with the application.
Target applicant(s): High school students. College students. Graduate school students. Adult students.
Minimum GPA: 2.0
Amount: $2,500.
Number of awards: 2.
Deadline: June 30.
How to apply: Applications are available online.
Exclusive: Visit www.UltimateScholarshipBook.com and enter code CH106320 for updates on this award.

(1064) • Charles H. Bussmann Undergraduate Scholarship

Marine Technology Society
1100 H Street NW, Suite LL-100, Washington, DC 20005
Phone: 202-717-8705

https://www.mtsociety.org/education/scholarships.aspx
Purpose: To support Marine Technology Society members who are pursuing an undergraduate degree in a marine-related field.
Eligibility: Applicants must be MTS student members who are accepted for enrollment or enrolled full-time at an educational institution. Selection is based on the overall strength of the application.
Target applicant(s): High school students. College students. Adult students.
Amount: $2,500.
Number of awards: 1.
Deadline: April 19.
How to apply: Applications are available online.
Exclusive: Visit www.UltimateScholarshipBook.com and enter code MA106420 for updates on this award.

(1065) • Charlotte McGuire Scholarship

American Holistic Nurses Association
AHNA Office Manager, 2900 SW Plass Court, Topeka, KS 66611-1980
Phone: 800-278-2462 x10
Email: info@ahna.org
http://www.ahna.org
Purpose: To provide scholarships to nurses in undergraduate or graduate nursing programs or other graduate programs related to holistic nursing.
Eligibility: Applicants must be pursuing an education in holistic nursing and be members of the AHNA. Applicants must have a minimum 3.0 GPA.
Target applicant(s): College students. Graduate school students. Adult students.
Minimum GPA: 3.0
Amount: Varies.
Number of awards: Varies.
Deadline: April 15.
How to apply: Applications are available online or from AHNA Headquarters.
Exclusive: Visit www.UltimateScholarshipBook.com and enter code AM106520 for updates on this award.

(1066) • Charlotte Woods Memorial Scholarship

Logistics and Transportation Association of North America (LTNA)
P.O. Box 426, Union, WA 98592
http://www.ltna.org/scholarship-application.html
Purpose: To support students who want to enter the transportation industry.
Eligibility: Applicants must be graduating high school seniors or college undergraduate students enrolled in an accredited institution of higher learning in a vocational or degree program in the fields of transportation logistics, supply-chain management, traffic management, transportation safety and/or related transportation industry operations and services and must be LTNA members or dependents of members. The awards are based upon scholastic ability, potential, professional interest and character. Financial need is also considered. Applicants must have a minimum 3.0 GPA.
Target applicant(s): High school students. College students. Adult students.
Minimum GPA: 3.0
Amount: Varies.
Number of awards: Varies.
Deadline: July 25.
How to apply: Applications are available online.
Exclusive: Visit www.UltimateScholarshipBook.com and enter code LO106620 for updates on this award.

(1067) • ChiroHealthUSA Foxworth Family Scholarship

ChiroHealthUSA
120 Stone Creek Boulevard, Suite 100, Flowood, MS 39232
https://app.smarterselect.com/programs/42257-Chiro-Health-Usa
Purpose: To support students studying chiropractic health.
Eligibility: Applicants must be full-time students enrolled in a doctorate of chiropractic program at an accredited U.S. institution and hold a minimum 2.7 GPA. Students must provide two recommendations along with their application.
Target applicant(s): Graduate school students. Adult students.
Minimum GPA: 2.7
Amount: $15,000.
Number of awards: 1.
Deadline: May 31.
How to apply: Applications are available online.
Exclusive: Visit www.UltimateScholarshipBook.com and enter code CH106720 for updates on this award.

(1068) • Chuck Reville, K3FT Memorial Scholarship

Foundation for Amateur Radio, Inc.
FAR Scholarships, P.O. Box 911, Columbia, MD 21044
Phone: 410-552-2652
Email: farscholarships@gmail.com
http://www.farweb.org
Purpose: To support licensed amateur radio enthusiasts who are pursuing bachelor's degrees in engineering or any of the physical sciences.
Eligibility: Applicants must be licensed amateur radio enthusiasts who are enrolled full-time in a bachelor's degree program in engineering or physical science. Selection is based on the overall strength of the application.
Target applicant(s): College students. Adult students.
Amount: $1,000.
Number of awards: 1.
Deadline: April 30.
How to apply: Applications are available online. An application form is required.
Exclusive: Visit www.UltimateScholarshipBook.com and enter code FO106820 for updates on this award.

(1069) • Clutch Prep STEM Scholarship

Clutch Prep
2125 Biscayne Boulevard, Miami, FL 33137
https://www.clutchprep.com/scholarships
Purpose: To support students pursuing STEM education.
Eligibility: Applicants must be currently enrolled in a two- or four-year program at an accredited college or university pursuing a degree in a STEM field.
Target applicant(s): High school students. College students. Adult students.
Amount: $1,500.
Number of awards: 1.
Deadline: April 30.
How to apply: Applications are available online.
Exclusive: Visit www.UltimateScholarshipBook.com and enter code CL106920 for updates on this award.

(1070) • Colgate "Bright Smiles, Bright Futures" Minority Scholarships

American Dental Hygienists' Association (ADHA) Institute for Oral Health
Scholarship Award Program, 444 North Michigan Avenue, Suite 3400, Chicago, IL 60611
Phone: 312-440-8900
Email: institute@adha.net
http://www.adha.org
Purpose: To support members of groups underrepresented in dental hygiene programs.
Eligibility: Applicants must have completed one year of an accredited dental hygiene curriculum and be a member of a group that is underrepresented in the field of dental hygiene. Examples of eligible groups include African-American, Hispanic, Asian, Native American and male students. Applicants must also demonstrate financial need of at least $1,500, be active members of SADHA or ADHA and submit a goals statement.
Target applicant(s): College students. Adult students.
Amount: $1,250.
Number of awards: 2.
Deadline: February 1.
How to apply: Applications are available online.
Exclusive: Visit www.UltimateScholarshipBook.com and enter code AM107020 for updates on this award.

(1071) • Collegiate Inventors Competition

National Inventors Hall of Fame
3701 Highland Park NW, North Canton, OH 44720
Phone: 330-849-6887
Email: collegiate@invent.org
http://www.invent.org
Purpose: To encourage college students in science, engineering, mathematics, technology and creative invention and to stimulate interest in technology and economic leadership.
Eligibility: Applicants must have been full-time college or university students during part of the 12-month period prior to the entry date. Up to four students may work as a team, and at least one student must meet the full-time criteria. Judging is based on originality and inventiveness, as well as the invention's potential value to society.
Target applicant(s): College students. Graduate school students. Adult students.
Amount: Varies.
Number of awards: Varies.
Deadline: June 5.
How to apply: Applications are available online.
Exclusive: Visit www.UltimateScholarshipBook.com and enter code NA107120 for updates on this award.

(1072) • CompHealth Medical Scholarship

CompHealth
7259 S. Bingham Junction Boulevard, Midvale, UT 84047
Phone: 866-615-5536
http://www.comphealth.com/resources/scholarship/
Purpose: To support students pursuing a medical degree.
Eligibility: Applicants must be U.S. citizens enrolled or planning to enroll as a full-time student at an accredited post-secondary institution. Students must have a minimum grade point average of 3.0. Applicants must submit application and a video response to one of the application questions.
Target applicant(s): High school students. College students. Adult students.
Minimum GPA: 3.0
Amount: $5,000.
Number of awards: 1.
Deadline: August 1.
How to apply: Applications are available online.
Exclusive: Visit www.UltimateScholarshipBook.com and enter code CO107220 for updates on this award.

(1073) • Composites Division/Harold Giles Scholarship

Society of Plastics Engineers
6 Berkshire Boulevard, Suite 306, Bethel, CT 06801
Phone: 203-775-0471
Email: info@4spe.org
http://www.4spe.org/spe-foundation
Purpose: To aid undergraduate and graduate students who have an interest in the plastics industry.
Eligibility: Applicants must have an interest in the plastics industry, major in or take courses leading to a career in the plastics industry and be in good academic standing. Financial need is considered.
Target applicant(s): College students. Graduate school students. Adult students.
Amount: Varies.
Number of awards: 2.
Deadline: April 1.
How to apply: Applications are available online.
Exclusive: Visit www.UltimateScholarshipBook.com and enter code SO107320 for updates on this award.

(1074) • Computational Science Graduate Fellowship

Department of Energy
Krell Institute, 1609 Golden Aspen Drive, Suite 101, Ames, IA 50010
Phone: 515-956-3696
https://www.krellinst.org
Purpose: To support students pursuing a Ph.D. in engineering and the physical, computer, mathematical or life sciences.
Eligibility: Applicants must be enrolled at an accredited U.S. college or university during the fellowship period.
Target applicant(s): College students. Adult students.
Amount: Varies.
Number of awards: Varies.
Scholarship may be renewable.
Deadline: January 17.
How to apply: Applications are available online.
Exclusive: Visit www.UltimateScholarshipBook.com and enter code DE107420 for updates on this award.

(1075) • Corrosion Division Morris Cohen Graduate Student Award

Electrochemical Society
65 South Main Street, Building D, Pennington, NJ 08534-2839
Phone: 609-737-1902
Email: awards@electrochem.org
http://www.electrochem.org/programs/
Purpose: To recognize graduate research in corrosion science and/or engineering.

Eligibility: Applicants must be graduate students who have completed all the requirements for their degrees within two years prior to the nomination deadline. Nomination may be made by the applicant's research supervisor or someone familiar with the applicant's research work. A summary of the applicant's master's or Ph.D. research work, reports, memberships and involvement with scientific societies, awards, an academic record and reprints of publications are required.
Target applicant(s): College students. Graduate school students. Adult students.
Amount: $1,000 plus travel expenses.
Number of awards: 1.
Deadline: December 15.
How to apply: Application materials are listed online.
Exclusive: Visit www.UltimateScholarshipBook.com and enter code EL107520 for updates on this award.

(1076) • Creative Biolabs

Creative Biolabs
45 Ramsey Road, Shirley, NY 11967
Phone: 631-871-5806
Email: info@creative-biolabs.com
http://www.creative-biolabs.com/scholarship-program.html
Purpose: To support students pursuing medical and science-related education.
Eligibility: Applicants must be enrolled as a freshman, undergraduate, graduate or doctoral student at an accredited college or university. Students must be pursuing a major in a science related field. Applicants must have a cumulative grade point average of 3.0 or higher. Students must submit, application, transcripts and essay.
Target applicant(s): College students. Graduate school students. Adult students.
Minimum GPA: 3.0
Amount: $1,000.
Number of awards: 2.
Deadline: August 15.
How to apply: Applications are available online.
Exclusive: Visit www.UltimateScholarshipBook.com and enter code CR107620 for updates on this award.

(1077) • Crest Oral-B Laboratories Dental Hygiene Scholarships

American Dental Hygienists' Association (ADHA) Institute for Oral Health
Scholarship Award Program, 444 North Michigan Avenue, Suite 3400, Chicago, IL 60611
Phone: 312-440-8900
Email: institute@adha.net
http://www.adha.org
Purpose: To support students pursuing a baccalaureate degree with an interest in research in dental hygiene as well as private and public dental hygiene education.
Eligibility: Applicants must be full-time students at an accredited college or university in the United States pursuing a baccalaureate degree in dental hygiene or a related field and must have completed at least one year of a dental hygiene curriculum. Applicants must also have a strong interest in pursuing research in dental hygiene and promoting private and public dental hygiene education, be active members of the ADHA, have a minimum dental hygiene GPA of 3.5 and have a minimum demonstrated financial need of $1,500. Selection is based upon professional and academic excellence and the overall strength of the application.
Target applicant(s): College students. Adult students.
Minimum GPA: 3.5
Amount: $1,000.
Number of awards: 2.
Deadline: February 1.
How to apply: Applications are available online after October 1.
Exclusive: Visit www.UltimateScholarshipBook.com and enter code AM107720 for updates on this award.

(1078) • Cummin's Inc. Scholarship

Society of Women Engineers
130 East Randolph Street, Suite 3500, Chicago, IL 60601
Phone: 877-793-4636
Email: scholarships@swe.org
http://societyofwomenengineers.swe.org/scholarships
Purpose: To support African-American female college engineering students.
Eligibility: Applicants must be U.S. citizens with a 3.0 GPA, be from an under-represented group and be willing to intern. Students must major in automotive engineering, chemical engineering, computer engineering, computer science, electrical engineering, industrial engineering, mechanical engineering, manufacturing engineering, materials science and engineering, industrial systems, metrology or metallurgy.
Target applicant(s): College students. Adult students.
Minimum GPA: 3.0
Amount: $2,500.
Number of awards: 2.
Deadline: February 15.
How to apply: Applications are available online.
Exclusive: Visit www.UltimateScholarshipBook.com and enter code SO107820 for updates on this award.

(1079) • Curtis E. Huntington Memorial Scholarship

Actuarial Foundation
475 North Martingale Road, Suite 600, Schaumburg, IL 60173
Phone: 847-706-3535
Email: scholarships@actfnd.org
http://www.actuarialfoundation.org
Purpose: To assist students who plan to become actuaries.
Eligibility: Applicants must be undergraduate students who will receive their degrees by August 31 of the year following the application deadline. Students must be in the top quartile of their class and have completed a minimum of one actuarial examination. A recommendation from a professor is required. Only one applicant per school is permitted. Preference is given to applicants who have demonstrated leadership ability in extracurricular activities.
Target applicant(s): College students. Adult students.
Amount: $2,000.
Number of awards: Varies.
Deadline: June 16.
How to apply: Applications are available online.
Exclusive: Visit www.UltimateScholarshipBook.com and enter code AC107920 for updates on this award.

(1080) • D.W. Simpson Actuarial Science Scholarship

D.W. Simpson and Company
4121 N. Ravenswood Avenue, Chicago, IL 60613
Phone: 312-867-2300
Email: actuaries@dwsimpson.com
https://www.dwsimpson.com/scholarships

Purpose: To assist college students interested in an actuarial science career.
Eligibility: Eligible students must be college seniors majoring in actuarial science who are eligible to work in the U.S. and have taken and passed a minimum of one actuarial examination. Applicants must have maintained a minimum GPA of 3.2 in their major and an overall minimum GPA of 3.0.
Target applicant(s): College students. Adult students.
Minimum GPA: 3.0
Amount: $1,000.
Number of awards: 2.
Deadline: April 30 and October 31.
How to apply: Applications are available online.
Exclusive: Visit www.UltimateScholarshipBook.com and enter code D.108020 for updates on this award.

(1081) • Dairy Student Recognition Program

National Dairy Shrine
P.O. Box 725, Denmark, WI 54208
Phone: 920-863-6333
Email: info@dairyshrine.org
http://www.dairyshrine.org
Purpose: To recognize graduating college seniors planning careers related to dairy.
Eligibility: Applicants must be U.S. citizens planning to enter the fields such as dairy production agriculture, marketing, agricultural law, business, veterinary medicine or environmental science. Selection is based on leadership skills, academic achievement and interest in dairy cattle.
Target applicant(s): High school students. College students. Adult students.
Amount: Varies.
Number of awards: Varies.
Deadline: April 15.
How to apply: Applications are available online, and two applicants per college or university are accepted each year.
Exclusive: Visit www.UltimateScholarshipBook.com and enter code NA108120 for updates on this award.

(1082) • Dan L. Meisinger Sr. Memorial Learn to Fly Scholarship

National Air Transportation Foundation Meisinger Scholarship
818 Connecticut Avenue NW, Suite 900, Washington, DC 20006
Phone: 202-774-1535
Email: safety1st@nata.aero
http://www.nata.aero
Purpose: To provide an annual flight training scholarship.
Eligibility: Applicants must be enrolled in an aviation program with a B or better GPA and be a resident of Kansas, Missouri or Illinois. Students should be recommended by an aviation professional; independent applications are also considered.
Target applicant(s): College students. Graduate school students. Adult students.
Minimum GPA: 3.0
Amount: $2,500.
Number of awards: Varies.
Deadline: Last Friday in November.
How to apply: Applications are available online.
Exclusive: Visit www.UltimateScholarshipBook.com and enter code NA108220 for updates on this award.

(1083) • David Alan Quick Scholarship

EAA Aviation Center
3000 Poberezny Road, Oshkosh, WI 54902
Phone: 920-426-4800
Email: scholarships@eaa.org
http://www.eaa.org/en/eaa
Purpose: To support students in aerospace or aeronautical engineering.
Eligibility: Applicants must be in their junior or senior year at an accredited college or university pursuing a degree in aerospace or aeronautical engineering. Applicants must be involved in school and community activities as well as aviation and be EAA members or be recommended by an EAA member.
Target applicant(s): College students. Adult students.
Amount: $500.
Number of awards: 1.
Scholarship may be renewable.
Deadline: February 28.
How to apply: Applications are available online.
Exclusive: Visit www.UltimateScholarshipBook.com and enter code EA108320 for updates on this award.

(1084) • David Arver Memorial Scholarship

Aircraft Electronics Association
3570 NE Ralph Powell Road, Lee's Summit, MO 64064
Phone: 816-347-8400
Email: info@aea.net
http://www.aea.net
Purpose: To support students who wish to pursue a career in avionics or aircraft repair.
Eligibility: Applicants must be high school seniors or college students who plan to or are attending an accredited school in an avionics or aircraft repair program.
Target applicant(s): High school students. College students. Adult students.
Amount: $1,000.
Number of awards: 1.
Deadline: February 15.
How to apply: Applications are available by contacting the organization for more information.
Exclusive: Visit www.UltimateScholarshipBook.com and enter code AI108420 for updates on this award.

(1085) • David R. Jones IV Scholarship

Association of Modified Asphalt Producers
AMAP Headquarters, P.O. Box 305, Avon, OH 44011
Phone: 314-843-2627
http://modifiedasphalt.org
Purpose: To support graduate and undergraduate students in asphalt technology.
Eligibility: Applicants must be college graduate or undergraduate students who are currently enrolled at an accredited college and have completed their sophomore year. Students must be majoring in a field that is related to asphalt technology such as chemical engineering, civil engineering, chemistry or any related major. Applicants with experience and interest in the field of asphalt technology will be given preference.
Target applicant(s): College students. Graduate school students. Adult students.
Amount: $2,000.
Number of awards: 3.
Deadline: January 20.

How to apply: Applications are available online.
Exclusive: Visit www.UltimateScholarshipBook.com and enter code AS108520 for updates on this award.

(1086) • David S. Bruce Awards for Excellence in Undergraduate Research

American Physiological Society
Education Office, 9650 Rockville Pike, Bethesda, MD 20814-3991
Phone: 301-634-7787
Email: education@the-aps.org
http://www.the-aps.org
Purpose: To reward undergraduate students for excellence in experimental biology research.
Eligibility: Applicants must be enrolled as an undergraduate at time of application and at time of meeting. Students must be first authors of the abstract and must be working with an APS member who will confirm the authorship. Applicants must submit a one-page paper discussing research and career plans and an abstract to be reviewed by a committee at the annual Experimental Biology meeting.
Target applicant(s): College students. Adult students.
Amount: $400.
Number of awards: Varies.
Deadline: January 12.
How to apply: Applications are available online.
Exclusive: Visit www.UltimateScholarshipBook.com and enter code AM108620 for updates on this award.

(1087) • Dean Foods Company FFA Scholarship

National FFA Organization
P.O. Box 68960, 6060 FFA Drive, Indianapolis, IN 46268-0960
Phone: 888-332-2668
Email: scholarships@ffa.org
https://www.ffa.org/participate/scholarships
Purpose: To support FFA members and non-members in the pursuit of four-year degrees in select major areas.
Eligibility: Applicants must be under the age of 23 and pursuing four-year degrees at U.S. institutions in the following major areas: dairy science, livestock management, sustainable agriculture, food science and technology or pre-vet/veterinary sciences. Selection is based on exceptional leadership ability, demonstrated service to the community and financial need.
Target applicant(s): High school students. College students.
Amount: $1,000-$5,000.
Number of awards: 10.
Deadline: February 8.
How to apply: Applications are available online.
Exclusive: Visit www.UltimateScholarshipBook.com and enter code NA108720 for updates on this award.

(1088) • DEED Funding Opportunities

Demonstration of Energy & Efficiency Developments (DEED)
1875 Connecticut Avenue, NW, Suite 1200, Washington, DC 20009
Phone: 202-467-2960
http://www.publicpower.org
Purpose: To support engineering students interested in technical careers.
Eligibility: Applicants must be U.S. citizens attending an accredited college, university or vocational institution full-time and must not be graduating within a year of the application deadline. Selection is based on the overall strength of the application.
Target applicant(s): College students. Graduate school students. Adult students.
Amount: $5,000.
Number of awards: Varies.
Deadline: February 15, October 15.
How to apply: Applications are available online.
Exclusive: Visit www.UltimateScholarshipBook.com and enter code DE108820 for updates on this award.

(1089) • Delta Faucet Company Scholarships

Plumbing-Heating-Cooling Contractors National Association
180 South Washington Street, Suite 100, Falls Church, VA 22046
Phone: 800-533-7694
Email: scholarships@naphcc.org
http://www.phccweb.org
Purpose: To elevate the technical and business competence of the plumbing-heating-cooling (p-h-c) industry by awarding scholarships to students who are enrolled in a p-h-c-related major.
Eligibility: Applicants must be students who are currently enrolled or plan to be enrolled in a p-h-c-related major at an accredited four-year college or university or two-year technical college, community college or trade school. Apprentice program students must also be working full-time for a licensed plumbing or HVAC contractor who is a member of the PHCC. Two $2,500 scholarships are awarded to students who are enrolled in either a PHCC-approved apprentice program or a full-time certificate or degree program at an accredited two-year community college, technical college or trade school. Four $2,500 scholarships are awarded to students who are enrolled in an undergraduate degree program at an accredited four-year college or university.
Target applicant(s): High school students. College students. Adult students.
Amount: $2,500.
Number of awards: Up to 6.
Deadline: May 1.
How to apply: Applications are available online, by email or by phone.
Exclusive: Visit www.UltimateScholarshipBook.com and enter code PL108920 for updates on this award.

(1090) • Dennis Raveling Scholarship

California Waterfowl Association
1346 Blue Oaks Boulevard, Roseville, CA 95678
Phone: 916-648-1406
Email: nchavez@calwaterfowl.org
http://www.calwaterfowl.org/scholarships
Purpose: To support students pursuing an advanced degree in a field that supports waterfowl or wetlands ecology.
Eligibility: Applicant must be pursuing an advanced degree in wildlife, zoology, botany, ecology or other biological sciences that are related to wetlands ecology. Selection is based on dedication to wetland preservation, high academic achievement and the merit of the project submitted.
Target applicant(s): College students. Graduate school students. Adult students.
Amount: $1,000-$2,000.
Number of awards: 2.
Deadline: October 31.
How to apply: Applicants must send a one-page proposal summary of original research or a management project, a resume, a statement of interest, a letter of support from a faculty member and a list of at least two references to the California Waterfowl Association. There is no formal application form.

Exclusive: Visit www.UltimateScholarshipBook.com and enter code CA109020 for updates on this award.

(1091) • Denny Lydic Scholarship

Logistics and Transportation Association of North America (LTNA)
P.O. Box 426, Union, WA 98592
http://www.ltna.org/scholarship-application.html

Purpose: To support students in the field of transportation.

Eligibility: Applicants must be graduating high school seniors or college undergraduate students enrolled in an accredited institution of higher learning in a vocational or degree program in the fields of transportation logistics, supply-chain management, traffic management, transportation safety and/or related transportation industry operations and services. The awards are based upon scholastic ability, potential, professional interest and character. Financial need is also considered. Minimum GPA of 3.0 required.

Target applicant(s): High school students. College students. Adult students.

Minimum GPA: 3.0

Amount: Varies.

Number of awards: Varies.

Deadline: July 25.

How to apply: Applications are available online.

Exclusive: Visit www.UltimateScholarshipBook.com and enter code LO109120 for updates on this award.

(1092) • Dental Student Scholarship

American Dental Association Foundation
211 East Chicago Avenue, Chicago, IL 60611
Phone: 312-440-2763
Email: famularor@ada.org
http://www.ada.org

Purpose: To encourage students to pursue careers in dental hygiene, dental assisting, dentistry and dental laboratory technology.

Eligibility: Applicants must be full-time entering second-year students in an accredited dental program and demonstrate a minimum financial need of $2,500. Applicants must submit applications, two reference forms and biographies. Selection is based on financial need, academic achievement, biographical sketch and references. Only two scholarship applications are allowed per school, so schools may set their own in-school application deadlines that are earlier.

Target applicant(s): College students. Graduate school students. Adult students.

Minimum GPA: 3.0

Amount: Up to $2,500.

Number of awards: 25.

Deadline: Second Friday in November.

How to apply: Applications are available from dental school officials.

Exclusive: Visit www.UltimateScholarshipBook.com and enter code AM109220 for updates on this award.

(1093) • Desk and Derrick Educational Trust

Desk and Derrick Educational Trust
c/o Shirley Bridwell, Burk Royalty, P.O. Box 94903, Wichita Falls, TX 76308
Phone: 281-392-7181
Email: info@theeducationaltrust.org
http://www.theeducationaltrust.org

Purpose: To promote studies in the energy industry.

Eligibility: Applicants must be U.S. or Canadian citizens, have completed two years of undergraduate study, have a minimum 3.2 GPA and demonstrate financial need. Students must be pursuing a degree in a field related to the petroleum, energy or allied industries and plan to work full-time in the petroleum, energy or allied industry or research alternative fuels such as coal, electric, solar, wind hydroelectric, nuclear or ethanol.

Target applicant(s): College students. Adult students.

Minimum GPA: 3.2

Amount: Varies.

Number of awards: Varies.

Deadline: April 1.

How to apply: Applications are available online.

Exclusive: Visit www.UltimateScholarshipBook.com and enter code DE109320 for updates on this award.

(1094) • Discovery Scholarship

Beneath the Sea
495 New Rochelle Road, Suite 2A, Bronxville, NY 10708
Phone: 914-664-4310
Email: scholarships@beneaththesea.org
http://www.beneaththesea.org/862

Purpose: To aid young students who have an interest in pursuing a career in marine sciences.

Eligibility: Applicants must be 12 to 18 years of age. The design of this scholarship is to help motivate young students to consider a marine career. Selection is based on an essay in which the applicants describe future goals and why they are interested in a career in the marine sciences.

Target applicant(s): Junior high students or younger. High school students.

Amount: $1,500.

Number of awards: Varies.

Deadline: December 15.

How to apply: Applications are available online and must include two letters of recommendation.

Exclusive: Visit www.UltimateScholarshipBook.com and enter code BE109420 for updates on this award.

(1095) • Distillery Scholarship Program

Distillery
301 Arizona Avenue, Suite 250, Santa Monica, CA 90401
Email: mail@distillery.com
https://distillery.com/scholarship-program/

Purpose: To support students pursuing software design and development.

Eligibility: Applicants must be currently enrolled as an undergraduate or graduate student at an accredited U.S. four-year college or university with a declared major in computer science, computer engineering, software engineering, IT or related field. Students must provide an essay and transcript along with their application.

Target applicant(s): College students. Graduate school students. Adult students.

Amount: $1,000.

Number of awards: 1.

Deadline: January 15.

How to apply: Applications are available online.

Exclusive: Visit www.UltimateScholarshipBook.com and enter code DI109520 for updates on this award.

(1096) · Diversity in STEAM Magazine Scholarship

Diversity in STEAM Magazine
18 Technology Drive, Suite 170, Irvine, CA 92618
Phone: 800-592-7832
https://www.diversityinsteam.com/scholarship-opportunity/

Purpose: To support students who are pursuing a field in science, technology, engineering, art or mathematics.

Eligibility: Applicants must be U.S. legal residents and be currently enrolled or planning to enroll in a degree program in a science, technology, engineering, art or mathematics field. Students must submit an essay, graphic or creative presentation on their college experience and future goals within their STEAM field. Selection is based upon the applicant's genuine desire and goal of using the scholarship to help advance in their field and an overall passion for knowledge.

Target applicant(s): High school students. College students. Graduate school students. Adult students.

Amount: $500.

Number of awards: 1.

Deadline: August 15.

How to apply: Applications are available online.

Exclusive: Visit www.UltimateScholarshipBook.com and enter code DI109620 for updates on this award.

(1097) · DMI Milk Marketing Scholarship

National Dairy Shrine
P.O. Box 725, Denmark, WI 54208
Phone: 920-863-6333
Email: info@dairyshrine.org
http://www.dairyshrine.org

Purpose: To encourage students to pursue careers in the marketing of dairy foods.

Eligibility: Applicants must be second, third or fourth year college students at two- or four-year universities, have a minimum 2.5 GPA and major in dairy science, animal science, agricultural communications, agricultural education, general agriculture or food and nutrition.

Target applicant(s): College students. Adult students.

Minimum GPA: 2.5

Amount: $1,000-$1,500.

Number of awards: Up to 5.

Deadline: April 15.

How to apply: Applications are available online.

Exclusive: Visit www.UltimateScholarshipBook.com and enter code NA109720 for updates on this award.

(1098) · DNA Day Essay Contest

American Society of Human Genetics
6120 Executive Boulevard, Suite 500, Rockville, MD 20852
Phone: 301-634-7300
http://www.ashg.org

Purpose: To support high school students who are interested in genetics.

Eligibility: Applicants must be in grades 9-12 and submit an essay in which they discuss the application of gene therapy in curing or repairing a particular disease or condition. Selection favors presentations that offer well-reasoned arguments, thus exemplifying a student's deep understanding of all concepts related to the essay question.

Target applicant(s): High school students.

Amount: $1,000.

Number of awards: 13.

Deadline: March 8.

How to apply: Applications are available online.

Exclusive: Visit www.UltimateScholarshipBook.com and enter code AM109820 for updates on this award.

(1099) · Don Reynolds Memorial Scholarship

Beneath the Sea
495 New Rochelle Road, Suite 2A, Bronxville, NY 10708
Phone: 914-664-4310
Email: scholarships@beneaththesea.org
http://www.beneaththesea.org/862

Purpose: To aid young people with an interest in exploring and protecting the ocean environment.

Eligibility: Applicants must be 17 to 25 years of age and pursuing a marine career. Students must be able to explain how a scuba diving certification will help to further their career and educational goals. Selection will be based on the essay as well as academic achievement, extracurricular activities, community service and work experience.

Target applicant(s): High school students. College students. Graduate school students.

Amount: $1,000.

Number of awards: 1.

Deadline: December 15.

How to apply: Applications are available online and must include two letters of recommendation.

Exclusive: Visit www.UltimateScholarshipBook.com and enter code BE109920 for updates on this award.

(1100) · Donald F. and Mildred Topp Othmer Scholarships

American Institute of Chemical Engineers - (AIChE)
120 Wall Street, Floor 23, New York, NY 10005-4020
Phone: 800-242-4363
Email: awards@aiche.org
https://www.aiche.org/community/awards

Purpose: To support AIChE student members.

Eligibility: Applicants must be members of an AIChE Student Chapter or Chemical Engineering Club. Applicants must be nominated by their student chapter advisors. Awards are presented on the basis of academic achievement and involvement in student chapter activities.

Target applicant(s): College students. Graduate school students. Adult students.

Amount: $1,000.

Number of awards: 15.

Deadline: June 15.

How to apply: Applications are available online.

Exclusive: Visit www.UltimateScholarshipBook.com and enter code AM110020 for updates on this award.

(1101) · Dorothy Budnek Memorial Scholarship

Association for Radiologic and Imaging Nursing
2201 Cooperative Way, Suite 600, Herndon, VA 20171
Phone: 866-486-2762
Email: info@arinursing.org
http://www.arinursing.org

Purpose: To help ARNA members continue their nursing education.

Eligibility: Applicants must be active members of the American Radiological Nurses Association for three years, have a current nursing license and be enrolled in an approved academic program. Students should submit the application, a statement of purpose, two recommendation letters, a transcript which shows a minimum 2.5 GPA, a statement of financial support and a copy of the nursing license.

Target applicant(s): Graduate school students. Adult students.
Minimum GPA: 2.5
Amount: $600.
Number of awards: 1.
Deadline: September 15.
How to apply: Applications are available online.
Exclusive: Visit www.UltimateScholarshipBook.com and enter code AS110120 for updates on this award.

(1102) • Dorothy M. and Earl S. Hoffman Award

American Vacuum Society
125 Maiden Lane, 15th Floor, New York, NY 10038
Phone: 212-248-0200
Email: angela@avs.org
http://www.avs.org
Purpose: To recognize excellence in continuing graduate studies in the sciences and technologies related to AVS.
Eligibility: Applicants must be graduate students in an accredited academic institution. An application, summary of research, letters of recommendation and transcript are required. The award is based on achievement in research and academic record. The top five student nominees are invited to present talks on their research to the trustees at the international symposium. The trustees then select one recipient for the Dorothy M. and Earl S. Hoffman Award. The award covers travel expenses to the symposium.
Target applicant(s): Graduate school students. Adult students.
Amount: Varies.
Number of awards: 1.
Deadline: May 1.
How to apply: Applications are available online.
Exclusive: Visit www.UltimateScholarshipBook.com and enter code AM110220 for updates on this award.

(1103) • Douglas Dockery Thomas Fellowship in Garden History and Design

Landscape Architecture Foundation
1129 20th Street NW, Suite 202, Washington, DC 20036
Phone: 202-331-7070
Email: scholarships@lafoundation.org
https://lafoundation.org/scholarship/
Purpose: To aid graduate students who are working on research projects related to garden design.
Eligibility: Applicants must be graduate students who are enrolled at a U.S. college or university. They must be researching some aspect of garden design. Selection is based on academic merit and applicability of proposed research to the aims of the Garden Club of America.
Target applicant(s): Graduate school students. Adult students.
Amount: $4,000.
Number of awards: 1.
Deadline: February 1.
How to apply: Application instructions are available online. A cover letter, research proposal, budget proposal, resume and three recommendation letters are required.
Exclusive: Visit www.UltimateScholarshipBook.com and enter code LA110320 for updates on this award.

(1104) • Dr. Esther Wilkins Scholarship

American Dental Hygienists' Association (ADHA) Institute for Oral Health
Scholarship Award Program, 444 North Michigan Avenue, Suite 3400, Chicago, IL 60611
Phone: 312-440-8900
Email: institute@adha.net
http://www.adha.org
Purpose: To support students who have completed an entry-level program in dental hygiene and are pursuing additional degrees in order to obtain a career in dental hygiene education.
Eligibility: Applicants must be full-time students at an accredited college or university in the United States pursuing a degree in dental hygiene education or a related field and must have completed at least one year of a dental hygiene curriculum. Applicants must also have completed an entry-level program in dental hygiene and be active members of the ADHA. They must have a minimum 3.0 GPA and have a minimum demonstrated financial need of $1,500. Selection is based upon the overall strength of the application.
Target applicant(s): College students. Graduate school students. Adult students.
Minimum GPA: 3.0
Amount: $1,000.
Number of awards: Varies.
Deadline: February 1.
How to apply: Applications are available online after October 1. An application form and essay are required.
Exclusive: Visit www.UltimateScholarshipBook.com and enter code AM110420 for updates on this award.

(1105) • Dr. Robert H. Goddard Scholarship

National Space Club
204 E Street NE, Washington, DC 20002
Phone: 202-547-0060
Email: info@spaceclub.org
http://www.spaceclub.org/youth-education.html
Purpose: To support students interested in increasing scientific knowledge through space research and exploration.
Eligibility: Applicants must be at least a junior attending an accredited university and also a U.S. citizen. Selection is based on the interest and aptitude of the student to utilize engineering and science to advance scientific knowledge through space research and exploration.
Target applicant(s): College students. Graduate school students. Adult students.
Amount: $10,000.
Number of awards: 1.
Deadline: December 2.
How to apply: Applications are available online.
Exclusive: Visit www.UltimateScholarshipBook.com and enter code NA110520 for updates on this award.

(1106) • Duane M. Hanson Scholarship

American Society of Heating, Refrigerating and Air-Conditioning Engineers (ASHRAE)
1791 Tullie Circle, NE, Atlanta, GA 30329
Phone: 404-636-8400
Email: lbenedict@ashrae.org
http://www.ashrae.org
Purpose: To support engineering students pursuing a degree that will prepare them for an HVAC&R profession.
Eligibility: Applicants must be enrolled in a full-time undergraduate engineering program of study traditionally designed to prepare student for a career in HVAC&R profession. Students must have GPA of at least 3.0. Applicants must also meet at least one of three criteria:

undergraduate institution hosts a recognized ASHRAE student branch, program of study is accredited by the Accreditation Board for Engineering and Technology (ABET), program of study is accredited by an agency outside the U.S. that is a signatory of the Washington Accord or has a signed Memorandum of Understanding with ABET.
Target applicant(s): High school students. College students. Adult students.
Minimum GPA: 3.0
Amount: $5,000.
Number of awards: 1.
Scholarship may be renewable.
Deadline: December 1.
How to apply: Applications are available online.
Exclusive: Visit www.UltimateScholarshipBook.com and enter code AM110620 for updates on this award.

(1107) · Dutch and Ginger Arver Scholarship

Aircraft Electronics Association
3570 NE Ralph Powell Road, Lee's Summit, MO 64064
Phone: 816-347-8400
Email: info@aea.net
http://www.aea.net
Purpose: To support students who wish to pursue a career in avionics or aircraft repair.
Eligibility: Applicants must be high school seniors or college students who plan to or are attending an accredited school in avionics or aircraft repair.
Target applicant(s): High school students. College students. Adult students.
Amount: $1,000.
Number of awards: 1.
Deadline: February 15.
How to apply: Applications are available by contacting the organization for more information.
Exclusive: Visit www.UltimateScholarshipBook.com and enter code AI110720 for updates on this award.

(1108) · Dwight D. Gardner Scholarship

Institute of Industrial and Systems Engineers
3577 Parkway Lane, Suite 200, Norcross, GA 30092
Phone: 800-494-0460
Email: bcameron@iienet.org
http://www.iise.org/
Purpose: To reward undergraduate members.
Eligibility: Applicants must be undergraduate students enrolled in a college in the United States, Canada or Mexico with an accredited industrial engineering program, major in industrial engineering and be active members. Students may not apply directly for this scholarship and must be nominated. The award is based on academic ability, character, leadership, potential service to the industrial engineering profession and financial need.
Target applicant(s): High school students. College students. Adult students.
Minimum GPA: 3.4
Amount: $2,500-$3,500.
Number of awards: 3.
Deadline: November 15.
How to apply: Nomination forms are available online.
Exclusive: Visit www.UltimateScholarshipBook.com and enter code IN110820 for updates on this award.

(1109) · E. Noel Luddy Scholarship

Association of Federal Communications Consulting Engineers
P.O. Box 19333, Washington, DC 20036-0333
Phone: 703-780-4824
Email: scholarships@afcce.org
http://www.afcce.org
Purpose: To support students majoring in engineering, broadcasting, telecommunications or related fields.
Eligibility: Applicants must be full-time students working toward an undergraduate degree at an accredited four-year educational institution or a graduate degree through an accredited program in engineering or a field related to broadcasting or telecommunications. Applicants must also have an AFCCE sponsor. Selection is based on the overall strength of the application.
Target applicant(s): College students. Graduate school students. Adult students.
Amount: Up to $2,500.
Number of awards: Varies.
Deadline: October 31, May 31.
How to apply: Applications are available online. An application form, AFCCE sponsor, personal statement and transcript are required.
Exclusive: Visit www.UltimateScholarshipBook.com and enter code AS110920 for updates on this award.

(1110) · E.J. Sierieja Memorial Fellowship

Institute of Industrial and Systems Engineers
3577 Parkway Lane, Suite 200, Norcross, GA 30092
Phone: 800-494-0460
Email: bcameron@iienet.org
http://www.iise.org/
Purpose: To reward graduate students pursuing advanced studies in the area of transportation.
Eligibility: Applicants must be full-time graduate students, majoring in transportation and active members. Students may not apply directly for this scholarship and must be nominated. The award is based on academic ability, character, leadership, potential service to the industrial engineering profession and financial need. Preference is given to students focusing on rail transportation.
Target applicant(s): Graduate school students. Adult students.
Minimum GPA: 3.4
Amount: $2,000.
Number of awards: 1.
Deadline: November 15.
How to apply: Nomination forms are available online.
Exclusive: Visit www.UltimateScholarshipBook.com and enter code IN111020 for updates on this award.

(1111) · East Asia and Pacific Summer Institutes

National Science Foundation East Asia and Pacific Summer Institutes
4201 Wilson Boulevard, Arlington, VA 22230
Phone: 703-292-5111
Email: eapsi@nsf.gov
https://www.nsf.gov/
Purpose: To develop globally-engaged U.S. scientists and engineers knowledgeable about the Asian and Pacific regions.
Eligibility: Applicants must be U.S. graduate students enrolled in a research-oriented master's or Ph.D. program or college graduates enrolled in a joint bachelor's/master's program at a U.S. institution. Students must pursue studies in science, engineering and education research. The award provides summer research experience in Australia, China,

Japan, Korea, New Zealand, Singapore or Taiwan, a $5,000 stipend, round-trip airfare, living expenses and orientation in Washington, DC.
Target applicant(s): Graduate school students. Adult students.
Amount: $5,000 stipend plus airfare and living expenses.
Number of awards: Varies.
Deadline: November 9.
How to apply: Applications are available online. A cover sheet, application form, project summary, project description, biographical sketch, two letters of recommendation and supplementary documents listed on the website are required.
Exclusive: Visit www.UltimateScholarshipBook.com and enter code NA111120 for updates on this award.

(1112) • Eckenfelder Scholarship

Brown and Caldwell
Attn.: HR/Scholarships Program, 1527 Cole Boulevard, Suite 300, Lakewood, CO 80401
Phone: 800-727-2224
Email: scholarships@brwncald.com
http://www.brownandcaldwell.com
Purpose: To support students majoring in civil, mechanical, electrical or environmental engineering or one of the environmental sciences.
Eligibility: Applicants must be enrolled full-time in an accredited college or university at time of application and must be college juniors or seniors or graduate students. Students must submit a personal essay, two letters of recommendation and official transcripts of academic record.
Target applicant(s): College students. Graduate school students. Adult students.
Minimum GPA: 3.0
Amount: $5,000.
Number of awards: Varies.
Deadline: April 15.
How to apply: Applications are available online.
Exclusive: Visit www.UltimateScholarshipBook.com and enter code BR111220 for updates on this award.

(1113) • Edward D. Hendrickson/SAE Engineering Scholarship

Society of Automotive Engineers International
Scholarships Program, 400 Commonwealth Drive, Warrendale, PA 15096
Phone: 724-776-4841
Email: scholarships@sae.org
http://students.sae.org/scholarships/
Purpose: To reward students pursuing an engineering or related science degree.
Eligibility: Students must maintain a 3.75 GPA. Applicants must rank in the 90th percentile in both math and critical reading on either the SAT or the ACT. Scholarship may be renewed for an additional three years. Students must be pursuing their degree through an ABET accredited program.
Target applicant(s): High school students. College students. Adult students.
Minimum GPA: 3.75
Amount: $5,000.
Number of awards: 1.
Scholarship may be renewable.
Deadline: March 15.
How to apply: Applications are available online.
Exclusive: Visit www.UltimateScholarshipBook.com and enter code SO111320 for updates on this award.

(1114) • Eight and Forty Lung and Respiratory Nursing Scholarship Fund

American Legion
Attn.: Americanism and Children and Youth Division, P.O. Box 1055, Indianapolis, IN 46206
Phone: 317-630-1249
Email: acy@legion.org
http://www.legion.org
Purpose: To assist registered nurses.
Eligibility: Applicants must plan to be employed full-time in hospitals, clinics or health departments in a position related to lung and respiratory control.
Target applicant(s): College students. Graduate school students. Adult students.
Minimum GPA: 3.0
Amount: $3,000.
Number of awards: Varies.
Deadline: May 15.
How to apply: Applications are available by written request.
Exclusive: Visit www.UltimateScholarshipBook.com and enter code AM111420 for updates on this award.

(1115) • Elekta Radiation Therapy Scholarship

American Society of Radiologic Technologists Foundation (ASRT)
ASRT Foundation, 15000 Central Avenue South East, Albuquerque, NM 87123
Phone: 800-444-2778
https://foundation.asrt.org/what-we-do/scholarships
Purpose: To encourage the best radiation therapy students to pursue a higher education.
Eligibility: Applicants must be members of the American Society of Radiologic Technologists (ASRT) and must be U.S. citizens, national or permanent residents. Students must finish their certificate or program degree by September 1 of the year in which scholarship applications are due. Applicants must be enrolled in an accredited radiologic science programs with at least one semester of radiologic studies completed with a 3.0 GPA and be in good standing with ASRT.
Target applicant(s): College students. Adult students.
Minimum GPA: 3.0
Amount: $5,000.
Number of awards: 4.
Scholarship may be renewable.
Deadline: Varies.
How to apply: Applications are available online.
Exclusive: Visit www.UltimateScholarshipBook.com and enter code AM111520 for updates on this award.

(1116) • Elizabeth McLean Memorial Scholarship

Society of Women Engineers
130 East Randolph Street, Suite 3500, Chicago, IL 60601
Phone: 877-793-4636
Email: scholarships@swe.org
http://societyofwomenengineers.swe.org/scholarships
Purpose: To support female students working towards a career in civil engineering.
Eligibility: Applicants must be women majoring in civil engineering with a 3.0 GPA. Students must be in school full-time.

Target applicant(s): College students. Adult students.
Minimum GPA: 3.0
Amount: $1,500.
Number of awards: 1.
Deadline: February 15.
How to apply: Applications are available online.
Exclusive: Visit www.UltimateScholarshipBook.com and enter code SO111620 for updates on this award.

(1117) • Elmer J. and Hester Jane Johnson Memorial FFA Scholarship

National FFA Organization
P.O. Box 68960, 6060 FFA Drive, Indianapolis, IN 46268-0960
Phone: 888-332-2668
Email: scholarships@ffa.org
https://www.ffa.org/participate/scholarships
Purpose: To support FFA members working toward a four-year degree in agricultural education.
Eligibility: Applicants must complete the financial portion of the application and be pursuing a four-year degree in agricultural education. Selection is based upon financial need, leadership ability and academic ability.
Target applicant(s): High school students. College students.
Amount: $1,000.
Number of awards: 1.
Deadline: February 8.
How to apply: Applications are available online.
Exclusive: Visit www.UltimateScholarshipBook.com and enter code NA111720 for updates on this award.

(1118) • Elson T. Killam Memorial Scholarship

New England Water Works Association
125 Hopping Brook Road, Holliston, MA 01746
Phone: 508-893-7979
Email: tmacelhaney@preloadinc.com
http://www.newwa.org
Purpose: To support civil and environmental engineering students who are members of the New England Water Works Association.
Eligibility: Applicants must be enrolled in a civil or environmental engineering degree program and must be members of NEWWA. Students must reside in New England or attend a college/university in New England. Selection is based on the overall strength of the application.
Target applicant(s): High school students. College students. Graduate school students. Adult students.
Amount: $1,500.
Number of awards: 1.
Deadline: April 1.
How to apply: Applications are available online. An application form, official transcript and one recommendation letter are required.
Exclusive: Visit www.UltimateScholarshipBook.com and enter code NE111820 for updates on this award.

(1119) • ENA Foundation Undergraduate Scholarship

Emergency Nurses Association
915 Lee Street, Des Plaines, IL 60016
Phone: 847-460-4100
Email: foundation@ena.org
http://www.ena.org
Purpose: To promote research and education in emergency care.
Eligibility: Applicants must be nurses pursuing baccalaureate degrees in nursing and must have been ENA members for at least 12 months before applying. Selection is based on application, statement of goals, references and transcript.
Target applicant(s): College students. Adult students.
Amount: $2,500.
Number of awards: 1.
Deadline: April 28.
How to apply: Applications are available online.
Exclusive: Visit www.UltimateScholarshipBook.com and enter code EM111920 for updates on this award.

(1120) • EngineerGirl Essay Contest

National Academy of Engineering
500 Fifth Street NW, Room 1047, Washington, DC 20001
http://www.engineergirl.org
Purpose: To support engineering-minded elementary, middle and high school students.
Eligibility: Applicants must be a student in the third through twelfth grades who submit an essay positing how engineering might positively impact a vulnerable species' life. One submission only; also, employees or those related to or living with employees of the National Academies of Sciences, Engineering and Medicine are prohibited from applying, as are prior winners who wish to reapply within the same category.
Target applicant(s): Junior high students or younger. High school students.
Amount: $500.
Number of awards: 1.
Deadline: February 1.
How to apply: Applications are available online.
Exclusive: Visit www.UltimateScholarshipBook.com and enter code NA112020 for updates on this award.

(1121) • Engineering Undergraduate Scholarship

American Society for Nondestructive Testing
Awards and Honors Program, 1711 Arlingate Lane, P.O. Box 28518, Columbus, OH 43228-0518
Phone: 614-274-6003 x 233
Email: awards@asnt.org
http://www.asnt.org
Purpose: To support students studying nondestructive testing.
Eligibility: Applicants must be undergraduate students enrolled in an engineering program of an accredited university and specialize in nondestructive testing (NDT). A nominating letter, transcript, three letters of recommendation and an essay describing the role of NDT/NDE in their career are required.
Target applicant(s): College students. Adult students.
Amount: $3,000.
Number of awards: Up to 3.
Deadline: December 15.
How to apply: Applications are available online.
Exclusive: Visit www.UltimateScholarshipBook.com and enter code AM112120 for updates on this award.

(1122) • Eugene S. Kropf Scholarship

University Aviation Association - Eugene S. Kropf Scholarship
Kevin R. Kuhlmann, Professor of Aviation and Aerospace Science, Metropolitan State College of Denver, Campus Box 30, P.O. Box 173362, Denver, CO 80217-3362

Phone: 334-844-2434
Email: uaamail@uaa.aero
http://www.uaa.aero/
Purpose: To support students studying an aviation-related curriculum.
Eligibility: Applicants must be U.S. citizens enrolled in an aviation-related curriculum of a two-year or a four-year degree at a UAA member college or university. Students must have a 3.0 GPA and write a 250-word paper on how they can improve aviation education.
Target applicant(s): College students. Adult students.
Minimum GPA: 3.0
Amount: $500.
Number of awards: Varies.
Deadline: June 15.
How to apply: Applications are available online.
Exclusive: Visit www.UltimateScholarshipBook.com and enter code UN112220 for updates on this award.

(1123) • Evolve IP Scholarship

Evolve IP
989 Old Eagle School Road, Suite 815, Wayne, PA 19087
Phone: 610-964 8000
Email: info@evolveip.net
http://www.evolveip.net/about/scholarship
Purpose: To support students who are pursuing a degree in technology or computer sciences.
Eligibility: Applicants must be a high school or college student who plans on a career in technology or computer sciences. Scholarships will be awarded based on need in addition to the strength of the student's academic background and demonstrated leadership.
Target applicant(s): High school students. College students. Adult students.
Amount: $500-$1,000.
Number of awards: 2.
Deadline: June 30.
How to apply: Applications are available online
Exclusive: Visit www.UltimateScholarshipBook.com and enter code EV112320 for updates on this award.

(1124) • ExploraVision Science Competition

ExploraVision
Toshiba/NSTA ExploraVision Awards, 1840 Wilson Boulevard, Arlington, VA 22201
Phone: (800) 397-5679
http://www.exploravision.org
Purpose: To encourage students to contemplate the technology of the future through working together and researching the technology and science of today.
Eligibility: Applicants must be citizens or legal residents of the United States or Canada who are no older than 21. Students must enter in teams of two to four. Teams must submit an entry form, an abstract, a description of their project, a bibliography and five sample web pages. Twenty-four teams will be selected as winners based on scientific accuracy, communication, feasibility of vision and creativity of their projects.
Target applicant(s): Junior high students or younger. High school students.
Amount: $10,000.
Number of awards: 1.
Deadline: February 8.
How to apply: Applications are available online.
Exclusive: Visit www.UltimateScholarshipBook.com and enter code EX112420 for updates on this award.

(1125) • Explorers Club Student Grants

Explorers Club
46 E. 70th Street, New York, NY 10021
Phone: 212-628-8383
Email: youth@explorers.org
http://www.explorers.org
Purpose: To provide grants for high school and college students to research the natural sciences through field research.
Eligibility: Applicants must provide a three-page explanation of their project, be high school or college students and be U.S. residents. The grants allow students to conduct field research in the natural sciences under the supervision of a qualified scientist or institution.
Target applicant(s): High school students. College students. Graduate school students. Adult students.
Amount: $500-$5,000.
Number of awards: Varies.
Deadline: October 10.
How to apply: Applications are available online.
Exclusive: Visit www.UltimateScholarshipBook.com and enter code EX112520 for updates on this award.

(1126) • Ezoe Memorial Foundation Academic Scholarship

Ezoe Memorial Foundation
208, Toranomon Hoso Building, I-20-3, Nishi-Shinbashi, Minato-ku, Tokyo, Ja 105-0003
Email: info@ezoe-mf.or.jp
http://ezoe-mf.or.jp/en/
Purpose: To support students interested in being globally active in their field.
Eligibility: Applicants must be under 24 years old on April 1 and be currently enrolled or planning to enroll in a college outside of Japan that meets the criteria of being in the top 30 schools, being a top 30 school for the applicant's field of study or ranking as a number one school. Students must be pursuing a science-related program and be interested in becoming globally active. The application process and interviews will be held in Japanese.
Target applicant(s): High school students. College students. Adult students.
Amount: Varies.
Number of awards: 10.
Deadline: October 9.
How to apply: Applications are available online.
Exclusive: Visit www.UltimateScholarshipBook.com and enter code EZ112620 for updates on this award.

(1127) • F.W. "Beich" Beichley Scholarship

American Society of Mechanical Engineers (ASME)
Two Park Avenue, New York, NY 10016-5990
Phone: 800-843-2763
Email: lefeverb@asme.org
http://www.asme.org
Purpose: To support mechanical engineering students.
Eligibility: Applicants must be ASME student members enrolled in an eligible accredited mechanical engineering baccalaureate program. Selection is based on leadership, scholastic ability, potential contribution

to the mechanical engineering profession and financial need. The scholarship is only applicable for study in the junior or senior year.
Target applicant(s): College students. Adult students.
Amount: $3,000.
Number of awards: 1.
Deadline: March 1.
How to apply: Applications are available online.
Exclusive: Visit www.UltimateScholarshipBook.com and enter code AM112720 for updates on this award.

(1128) • FA Davis Student Award

American Association of Medical Assistants' Endowment
20 North Wacker Drive, Suite 1575, Chicago, IL 60606
Phone: 800-228-2262
Email: info@aama-ntl.org
http://www.aama-ntl.org
Purpose: To reward aspiring medical assistants for ad design.
Eligibility: Applicants must be enrolled in and have finished a quarter or a semester at an accredited postsecondary medical assisting program. Students must create one ad that supports the medical assisting profession, the CMA credential and the AAMA. The ad must have a slogan, body copy and a call to action and can be designed using any medium.
Target applicant(s): High school students. College students. Graduate school students. Adult students.
Amount: $1,500.
Number of awards: 2.
Deadline: July 15.
How to apply: Applications are available online.
Exclusive: Visit www.UltimateScholarshipBook.com and enter code AM112820 for updates on this award.

(1129) • FarmAid FFA Scholarship

National FFA Organization
P.O. Box 68960, 6060 FFA Drive, Indianapolis, IN 46268-0960
Phone: 888-332-2668
Email: scholarships@ffa.org
https://www.ffa.org/participate/scholarships
Purpose: To support students who are FFA members, come from family farms and are pursuing four-year degrees in agriculture.
Eligibility: Applicants must complete the financial analysis part of the application. A minimum GPA of 2.0 is required. Selection is based on the overall strength of the application.
Target applicant(s): High school students. College students.
Minimum GPA: 2.0
Amount: $3,000 over three years.
Number of awards: 4.
Deadline: February 8.
How to apply: A complete application form is required.
Exclusive: Visit www.UltimateScholarshipBook.com and enter code NA112920 for updates on this award.

(1130) • Father James B. Macelwane Annual Award in Meteorology

American Meteorological Society
Fellowship and Scholarship Department, 45 Beacon Street, Boston, MA 02108-3693
Phone: 617-227-2426 x246
Email: dsampson@ametsoc.org
http://www.ametsoc.org/AMS/
Purpose: To encourage interest in meteorology among college students.
Eligibility: Applicants must be enrolled as undergraduates and submit an original student paper on an aspect of atmospheric science. No more than two students from any one institution may enter papers in any one contest, and there is no application form needed.
Target applicant(s): College students. Adult students.
Amount: $1,000.
Number of awards: 1.
Deadline: June 9.
How to apply: Submit materials to address listed.
Exclusive: Visit www.UltimateScholarshipBook.com and enter code AM113020 for updates on this award.

(1131) • Feeding Tomorrow General Education Scholarships/Freshman Scholarships

Institute of Food Technologists (IFT)
525 W. Van Buren, Suite 1000, Chicago, IL 60607
Phone: 312-782-8424
Email: ejplummer@ift.org
http://www.ift.org/community/students/competitions.aspx
Purpose: To help young food scientists who plan to work in industry, government and academia.
Eligibility: Applicants for the freshman scholarships must be academically outstanding high school graduates or seniors who will enter college for the first time in an approved program in food science/technology and must have a minimum 3.0 GPA. All candidates must submit applications, transcripts and a recommendation.
Target applicant(s): High school students.
Minimum GPA: 3.0
Amount: Varies.
Number of awards: Varies.
Deadline: April 15.
How to apply: Applications are available online.
Exclusive: Visit www.UltimateScholarshipBook.com and enter code IN113120 for updates on this award.

(1132) • Fellowship Award

Damon Runyon Cancer Research Foundation
One Exchange Plaza, 55 Broadway, Suite 302, New York, NY 10006
Phone: 212-455-0520
Email: awards@damonrunyon.org
http://www.damonrunyon.org
Purpose: To support the training of postdoctoral scientists as they start their research careers.
Eligibility: Applicants must have completed one or more of the following degrees or its equivalent: M.D., Ph.D., M.D./Ph.D., D.D.S. or D.V.M. Applicants should submit an application cover sheet, sponsor's biographical sketch, CV, degree certificate, letter, research proposal, summary of research form, up to three reprints of work and four letters of reference. This is a three-year award with various deadlines and funding. The research must be conducted at a university, hospital or research institution. International candidates may apply to do their research only in the United States.
Target applicant(s): Graduate school students. Adult students.
Amount: $52,000-$60,000 plus expenses.
Number of awards: Varies.
Deadline: March 15 and August 15.
How to apply: Applications are available online.
Exclusive: Visit www.UltimateScholarshipBook.com and enter code DA113220 for updates on this award.

(1133) · Fellowship in Aerospace History

American Historical Association
400 A Street SE, Washington, DC 20003
Phone: 202-544-2422
Email: info@historians.org
http://www.historians.org

Purpose: To provide funding for an academic research project related to aerospace history.

Eligibility: Applicants must possess a doctorate degree in history or a related field or be enrolled in a doctorate program (all coursework completed). One fellow will be appointed for one academic year. The fellow will be expected to write a report and present a paper or lecture on the research at the end of the term.

Target applicant(s): Graduate school students. Adult students.
Amount: $21,250.
Number of awards: At least 1.
Deadline: April 1.
How to apply: Applications are available online.
Exclusive: Visit www.UltimateScholarshipBook.com and enter code AM113320 for updates on this award.

(1134) · Foundation for Neonatal Research and Education Scholarships

Foundation for Neonatal Research and Education
c/o Anthony J. Jannetti, Inc., East Holly Avenue, Box 56, Pitman, NJ 08071-0056
Phone: 856-256-2343
Email: contact@fnre.com
http://www.ajj.com/fnre

Purpose: To aid practicing neonatal nurses who are pursuing additional education through an undergraduate or graduate degree program in nursing.

Eligibility: Applicants must be accepted into a Bachelor of Science in Nursing (BSN) program (current Registered Nurses), a Master of Science in Nursing (MSN) program for advanced practice in neonatal nursing, a doctoral degree program in nursing or a Master's or post-Master's nursing degree program in Business Management or Nursing Administration. They must have a GPA of 3.0 or higher and must be actively involved in neonatal nursing at the professional level. They cannot have received a grant or scholarship from the FNRE within the past five years, and they cannot be current members of the FNRE Scholarship Committee or Board. Selection is based on the overall strength of the application.

Target applicant(s): College students. Graduate school students. Adult students.
Minimum GPA: 3.0
Amount: Varies.
Number of awards: Varies.
Deadline: May 1.
How to apply: Applications are available online. An application form, resume, enrollment verification letter, personal statement, three evaluation letters and a transcript are required.
Exclusive: Visit www.UltimateScholarshipBook.com and enter code FO113420 for updates on this award.

(1135) · Foundation for Surgical Technology Medical Mission Scholarship

Association of Surgical Technologists
6 W. Dry Creek Circle, Littleton, CO 80120
Phone: 800-637-7433
Email: scholarships@ast.org
http://www.ast.org

Purpose: To help practitioners with continuing education or medical missionary work.

Eligibility: Applicants must be active AST members, document the educational program or mission program and provide two recommendation letters.

Target applicant(s): Adult students.
Amount: Varies.
Number of awards: Varies.
Deadline: December 31.
How to apply: Applications are available online.
Exclusive: Visit www.UltimateScholarshipBook.com and enter code AS113520 for updates on this award.

(1136) · Foundation for Surgical Technology Scholarships

Association of Surgical Technologists
6 W. Dry Creek Circle, Littleton, CO 80120
Phone: 800-637-7433
Email: scholarships@ast.org
http://www.ast.org

Purpose: To support the continuing education of surgical technology students.

Eligibility: Applicants should be enrolled in accredited surgical technology programs and be eligible to sit for the Certified Surgical Technologist examination sponsored by the National Board of Surgical Technology and Surgical Assisting. Applications, transcripts, a minimum 3.0 GPA, essays and recommendation letters are required.

Target applicant(s): College students. Adult students.
Minimum GPA: 3.0
Amount: Varies.
Number of awards: Varies.
Deadline: March 15.
How to apply: Applications are available online.
Exclusive: Visit www.UltimateScholarshipBook.com and enter code AS113620 for updates on this award.

(1137) · Foundation of the National Student Nurses' Association Career Mobility Scholarships

National Student Nurses' Association
45 Main Street, Suite 606, Brooklyn, NY 11201
Phone: 718-210-0705
Email: nsna@nsna.org
http://www.nsna.org

Purpose: To aid nursing and pre-nursing students who are enrolled in LPN to RN, RN to BSN and RN to MSN programs.

Eligibility: Applicants must be nursing or pre-nursing students who are pursuing LPN to RN, RN to BSN or RN to MSN degrees. Selection is based on the overall strength of the application.

Target applicant(s): College students. Graduate school students. Adult students.
Amount: $1,000-$7,500.
Number of awards: Varies.
Deadline: January.
How to apply: Applications are available online. An application form and supporting documents are required.
Exclusive: Visit www.UltimateScholarshipBook.com and enter code NA113720 for updates on this award.

(1138) · Foundation of the National Student Nurses' Association Specialty Scholarship

National Student Nurses' Association
45 Main Street, Suite 606, Brooklyn, NY 11201
Phone: 718-210-0705
Email: nsna@nsna.org
http://www.nsna.org

Purpose: To aid nursing students who are planning to pursue careers in specialized areas.
Eligibility: Applicants must be nursing students who are interested in a specialized area of nursing practice. Selection is based on the overall strength of the application.
Target applicant(s): College students. Adult students.
Amount: $1,000-$7,500.
Number of awards: Varies.
Deadline: January.
How to apply: Applications are available online. An application form and supporting materials are required.
Exclusive: Visit www.UltimateScholarshipBook.com and enter code NA113820 for updates on this award.

(1139) · Fran O'Sullivan Women in Lenovo Leadership (WILL) Scholarship

Society of Women Engineers
130 East Randolph Street, Suite 3500, Chicago, IL 60601
Phone: 877-793-4636
Email: scholarships@swe.org
http://societyofwomenengineers.swe.org/scholarships

Purpose: To support female students who are pursuing a college degree in the field of engineering.
Eligibility: Applicants must be female college freshmen, sophomores, juniors, seniors or graduate students. Students with financial need must have a 3.0 GPA and be attending school full-time.
Target applicant(s): College students. Graduate school students. Adult students.
Minimum GPA: 3.0
Amount: $5,000.
Number of awards: 1.
Deadline: February 15.
How to apply: Applications are available online.
Exclusive: Visit www.UltimateScholarshipBook.com and enter code SO113920 for updates on this award.

(1140) · Frank and Brennie Morgan Prize for Outstanding Research in Mathematics by an Undergraduate Student

American Mathematical Society and Mathematical Association of America
Professor Carla Savage, MAA Secretary, Computer Science Department, North Carolina State University, Box 8206, Raleigh, NC 27695
Phone: 410-704-2980
Email: siegel@towson.edu
http://www.ams.org

Purpose: Awarded to an undergraduate student (or students who have collaborated) for research in the field of mathematics.
Eligibility: Applicants must be undergraduate students at colleges or universities in the United States or its possessions, Canada and Mexico. Students must be nominated.
Target applicant(s): High school students. College students. Adult students.
Amount: $1,200.
Number of awards: 1.
Deadline: June 30.
How to apply: Nomination information is available by email. Questions should be directed to Dr. Martha J. Siegel at the address above. Nominations and submissions should be sent to: Morgan Prize Committee, c/o Robert J. Daverman, American Mathematical Society, 312D Ayres Hall, University of Tennessee, Knoxville, TN 37996.
Exclusive: Visit www.UltimateScholarshipBook.com and enter code AM114020 for updates on this award.

(1141) · Frank and Dorothy Miller ASME Auxiliary Scholarships

American Society of Mechanical Engineers (ASME)
Two Park Avenue, New York, NY 10016-5990
Phone: 800-843-2763
Email: lefeverb@asme.org
http://www.asme.org

Purpose: To support U.S. mechanical engineering and mechanical engineering technology undergraduates.
Eligibility: Applicants must be U.S. citizens and residents of North America. They must be rising undergraduate sophomores, juniors or seniors who are enrolled in an ABET-accredited (or equivalent) mechanical engineering, mechanical engineering technology or related program at a U.S. postsecondary institution. They must be ASME student members who are in good standing. Selection is based on leadership, integrity and potential contribution to the field of mechanical engineering.
Target applicant(s): College students. Adult students.
Amount: $2,000.
Number of awards: 2.
Deadline: March 1.
How to apply: The application form is available through ASME's online scholarship application system. This form, an official transcript, a personal statement and up to two recommendation letters are required.
Exclusive: Visit www.UltimateScholarshipBook.com and enter code AM114120 for updates on this award.

(1142) · Fred M. Young, Sr./SAE Engineering Scholarship

Society of Automotive Engineers International
Scholarships Program, 400 Commonwealth Drive, Warrendale, PA 15096
Phone: 724-776-4841
Email: scholarships@sae.org
http://students.sae.org/scholarships/

Purpose: To support high school seniors who are planning to study engineering at the undergraduate level.
Eligibility: Applicants must be U.S. citizens and must be high school seniors. They must have SAT or ACT scores that rank in the 90th percentile and must have a GPA of 3.75 or higher on a four-point scale. They must plan to enroll in an ABET-accredited undergraduate engineering program. Selection is based on the overall strength of the application.
Target applicant(s): High school students.
Minimum GPA: 3.75
Amount: $1,000.
Number of awards: 1.
Scholarship may be renewable.

Deadline: March 15.
How to apply: Applications are available online. An application form, official transcript and standardized test scores are required.
Exclusive: Visit www.UltimateScholarshipBook.com and enter code SO114220 for updates on this award.

(1143) · Freshman Undergraduate Scholarship

American Meteorological Society
Fellowship and Scholarship Department, 45 Beacon Street, Boston, MA 02108-3693
Phone: 617-227-2426 x246
Email: dsampson@ametsoc.org
http://www.ametsoc.org/AMS/
Purpose: To encourage high school students to pursue careers in the atmospheric and related oceanic and hydrologic sciences.
Eligibility: Applicants must enter as full-time freshmen the following fall and major in the atmospheric or related oceanic and hydrologic sciences. Applicants should submit applications, transcripts, recommendation letter and SAT or equivalent scores.
Target applicant(s): High school students.
Amount: $5,000.
Number of awards: Varies.
Scholarship may be renewable.
Deadline: February 3.
How to apply: Applications are available online.
Exclusive: Visit www.UltimateScholarshipBook.com and enter code AM114320 for updates on this award.

(1144) · Full-Time Employee Student Scholarship

Air Traffic Control Association
1101 King Street, Suite 300, Alexandria, VA 22314
Phone: 703-299-2430
Email: info@atca.org
http://www.atca.org
Purpose: To help students in advanced study programs in air traffic control and other aviation disciplines.
Eligibility: Applicants must be enrolled half- to full-time in an accredited college or university in coursework to enhance skills in air traffic control or other aviation disciplines which leads to a bachelor's degree or higher. Students must plan to continue their education the following year and be employed full-time in an aviation-related field. Applicants must have a minimum of 30 semester or 45 quarter hours still to be finished before graduation.
Target applicant(s): College students. Graduate school students. Adult students.
Amount: Varies.
Number of awards: Varies.
Deadline: May 1.
How to apply: Applications are available online. An application form, two letters of reference, academic transcripts, an essay and answers to career and leadership questions are required.
Exclusive: Visit www.UltimateScholarshipBook.com and enter code AI114420 for updates on this award.

(1145) · Future of Video Surveillance Scholarship

Eyewitness Surveillance
7521 Connelley Drive, Suite A, Hanover, MD 21076
Phone: 800-270-9014
Email: scholarship@eyewitnessmail.com
http://www.eyewitnesssurveillance.com/
Purpose: To support students seeking a degree in criminal justice or information technology.
Eligibility: Applicants must be an undergraduate enrolled in a two-year or four-year college or university studying or planning to study criminal justice or information technology. Students must be enrolled full-time in the fall semester. A minimum 3.0 GPA is required. Applicants must submit via email a 1,000-word essay on one of the given prompts.
Target applicant(s): College students. Adult students.
Minimum GPA: 3.0
Amount: $1,000.
Number of awards: 1.
Deadline: September 1.
How to apply: Essays must be submitted by email.
Exclusive: Visit www.UltimateScholarshipBook.com and enter code EY114520 for updates on this award.

(1146) · Future U.S. Nurse Scholarship

Travel Nurse Source
Phone: 877-696-7482
Email: info@travelnursesource.com
https://www.travelnursesource.com/resources/scholarship/
Purpose: To support the education of future nurses.
Eligibility: Applicants must be legal U.S. residents. Students must be either currently enrolled baccalaureate or higher students at an accredited U.S. nursing school with a grade point average of 2.5 or better or accepted into a baccalaureate or higher nursing program for the upcoming semester.
Target applicant(s): High school students. College students. Adult students.
Minimum GPA: 2.5
Amount: $2,000.
Number of awards: 1.
Deadline: October 13.
How to apply: Applications are available online.
Exclusive: Visit www.UltimateScholarshipBook.com and enter code TR114620 for updates on this award.

(1147) · Gabe A. Hartl Scholarship

Air Traffic Control Association
1101 King Street, Suite 300, Alexandria, VA 22314
Phone: 703-299-2430
Email: info@atca.org
http://www.atca.org
Purpose: To support air traffic control students.
Eligibility: Applicants must be enrolled in or plan to be enrolled in a two- to four-year postsecondary program in air traffic control as a part-time or full-time student. The program must be approved by the Federal Aviation Administration as a college training initiative supporter. They must have 30 or more semester hours (or 45 or more quarter hours) remaining in their program of study at the time of submitting the application. Selection is based on the overall strength of the application.
Target applicant(s): High school students. College students. Adult students.
Amount: Varies.
Number of awards: Varies.
Deadline: May 1.
How to apply: Applications are available online. An application form, official transcript, two letters of recommendation and essay response are required.
Exclusive: Visit www.UltimateScholarshipBook.com and enter code AI114720 for updates on this award.

(1148) • Gaige Fund Award

American Society of Ichthyologists and Herpetologists
P.O. Box 1897, Lawrence, KS 66044-8897
Phone: 785-843-1235
Email: asih@allenpress.com
http://www.asih.org/membership/student-awards
Purpose: To support young herpetologists.
Eligibility: Applicants must be members of ASIH and studying for an advanced degree. The award may be used for museum or laboratory study, travel, fieldwork or other activities that will enhance their careers and their contributions to the science of herpetology. Both merit and need will be considered.
Target applicant(s): College students. Graduate school students. Adult students.
Amount: $400-$1,000.
Number of awards: Varies.
Deadline: March 1.
How to apply: Applications are available by email or written request.
Exclusive: Visit www.UltimateScholarshipBook.com and enter code AM114820 for updates on this award.

(1149) • Garland Duncan Scholarships

American Society of Mechanical Engineers (ASME)
Two Park Avenue, New York, NY 10016-5990
Phone: 800-843-2763
Email: lefeverb@asme.org
http://www.asme.org
Purpose: To support mechanical engineering students.
Eligibility: Applicants must be ASME student members, be enrolled in an eligible accredited mechanical engineering baccalaureate program, have strong academic performance and be college sophomores, juniors or seniors. Selection is based on character, integrity, leadership, scholastic ability, potential contribution to the mechanical engineering profession and financial need.
Target applicant(s): College students. Adult students.
Amount: $5,000.
Number of awards: 2.
Deadline: March 1.
How to apply: Applications are available online.
Exclusive: Visit www.UltimateScholarshipBook.com and enter code AM114920 for updates on this award.

(1150) • Garmin Scholarship

Aircraft Electronics Association
3570 NE Ralph Powell Road, Lee's Summit, MO 64064
Phone: 816-347-8400
Email: info@aea.net
http://www.aea.net
Purpose: To support students who wish to pursue a career in avionics and aircraft repair.
Eligibility: Applicants must be high school seniors or college students who plan to or are attending an accredited school in an avionics or aircraft repair program.
Target applicant(s): High school students. College students. Adult students.
Amount: $2,000.
Number of awards: Varies.
Deadline: February 15.
How to apply: Applications are available online.
Exclusive: Visit www.UltimateScholarshipBook.com and enter code AI115020 for updates on this award.

(1151) • Gary Wagner, K3OMI Scholarship

American Radio Relay League Foundation
225 Main Street, Newington, CT 06111-1494
Phone: 860-594-0348
Email: foundation@arrl.org
http://www.arrl.org/scholarship-program
Purpose: To support engineering students who are involved in amateur radio.
Eligibility: Applicants must have an amateur radio license of Novice Class or higher. Students may be pursuing a bachelor's degree in any field of engineering. They must be residents of one of the following states: North Carolina, Virginia, West Virginia, Maryland or Tennessee. Preference will be given to students with financial need.
Target applicant(s): High school students. College students. Adult students.
Amount: $1,000.
Number of awards: 1.
Deadline: February 16.
How to apply: Applications are available online.
Exclusive: Visit www.UltimateScholarshipBook.com and enter code AM115120 for updates on this award.

(1152) • GBT Student Support Program

National Radio Astronomy Observatory (NRAO)
NRAO Headquarters, 520 Edgemont Road, Charlottesville, VA 22903
Phone: 434-296-0211
Email: info@nrao.edu
http://www.nrao.edu
Purpose: To support student research at the Robert C. Byrd Green Bank Telescope (GBT).
Eligibility: GBT is the largest fully steerable single aperture antenna. Students begin the application process by completing a preliminary funding proposal form. If the proposal is accepted, they will be informed of further requirements.
Target applicant(s): College students. Graduate school students. Adult students.
Amount: Up to $35,000.
Number of awards: Varies.
Deadline: June 9.
How to apply: Applications are available online.
Exclusive: Visit www.UltimateScholarshipBook.com and enter code NA115220 for updates on this award.

(1153) • GCSAA Scholars Competition

Golf Course Superintendents Association of America
1421 Research Park Drive, Lawrence, KS 66049
Phone: 800-472-7878
Email: mwright@gcsaa.org
http://www.gcsaa.org
Purpose: To support students preparing for careers in golf course management.
Eligibility: Applicants must be GCSAA members who are undergraduate students enrolled in an accredited degree program in turf management or a closely related subject. They must have completed at least 24 semester credits or one year of full-time study in their degree program. Selection

is based on academic excellence, career potential, recommendations, work history and extracurricular activities.
Target applicant(s): College students. Adult students.
Amount: $500-$6,000.
Number of awards: Varies.
Deadline: June 1.
How to apply: Applications are available online. An application form, personal essay, transcripts and reports from the applicant's academic advisor and golf course superintendent are required.
Exclusive: Visit www.UltimateScholarshipBook.com and enter code GO115320 for updates on this award.

(1154) • General James H. Doolittle Scholarship

Communities Foundation of Texas
5500 Caruth Haven Lane, Dallas, TX 75225
Phone: 214-750-4222
Email: info@cftexas.org
https://www.cftexas.org/cft-scholarships
Purpose: To support aeronautical engineering and aerospace science students.
Eligibility: Applicants must be undergraduate juniors, undergraduate seniors or graduate students enrolled in a degree program in aerospace science or aeronautical engineering. Students do not need to be Texas residents. Selection is based on the overall strength of the application.
Target applicant(s): College students. Graduate school students. Adult students.
Minimum GPA: 2.75
Amount: Up to $5,000.
Number of awards: Varies.
Deadline: March 1.
How to apply: Applications are available online. An application form and supporting documents are required.
Exclusive: Visit www.UltimateScholarshipBook.com and enter code CO115420 for updates on this award.

(1155) • GeneTex Scholarship Program

GeneTex Inc.
2456 Alton Parkway, Irvine, CA 92606
Phone: 949-553-1900
Email: scholarship@genetex.com
http://www.genetex.com/scholarship
Purpose: To support students pursuing STEM degrees.
Eligibility: Applicants must be enrolled at an accredited college or university and be in good standing. Students must be majoring in a STEM (science, technology, engineering or math) area.
Target applicant(s): High school students. College students. Adult students.
Amount: $2,000.
Number of awards: 1.
Deadline: August 31.
How to apply: Applications are available online.
Exclusive: Visit www.UltimateScholarshipBook.com and enter code GE115520 for updates on this award.

(1156) • George A. Hall / Harold F. Mayfield Grant

Wilson Ornithological Society
Department of Biology and Biomedical Science, Dr. James Chace, Associate Professor, 100 Ochre Point Avenue, Newport, RI 02840-4192
Email: rbpayne@umich.edu
http://www.wilsonsociety.org
Purpose: To assist those who are conducting avian research.
Eligibility: Applicants must be independent researchers without access to funds available at colleges, universities or government agencies and must be non-professionals currently conducting avian research. Applicants must also be willing to present their research results at an annual meeting of the Wilson Ornithological Society.
Target applicant(s): Graduate school students. Adult students.
Amount: $1,000.
Number of awards: 1.
Deadline: February 1.
How to apply: Applications are available online.
Exclusive: Visit www.UltimateScholarshipBook.com and enter code WI115620 for updates on this award.

(1157) • Gertrude Cox Scholarship For Women In Statistics

American Statistical Association
Attn: Awards Nominations, 732 N. Washington Street, Alexandria, VA 22314
Phone: 703-684-1221
Email: awards@amstat.org
http://www.amstat.org
Purpose: To encourage women to pursue education for careers in statistics.
Eligibility: Applicants must be women who are full-time students in a graduate-level statistics programs.
Target applicant(s): Graduate school students. Adult students.
Amount: $1,000.
Number of awards: 2.
Deadline: February 23.
How to apply: Applications are available online.
Exclusive: Visit www.UltimateScholarshipBook.com and enter code AM115720 for updates on this award.

(1158) • Gilbreth Memorial Fellowship

Institute of Industrial and Systems Engineers
3577 Parkway Lane, Suite 200, Norcross, GA 30092
Phone: 800-494-0460
Email: bcameron@iienet.org
http://www.iise.org/
Purpose: To support graduate student Institute members.
Eligibility: Applicants must be graduate students at an institution in the United States, Canada or Mexico, majoring in industrial engineering or its equivalent and active members. Students may not apply directly for this scholarship and must be nominated. The award is based on academic ability, character, leadership, potential service to the industrial engineering profession and financial need.
Target applicant(s): Graduate school students. Adult students.
Minimum GPA: 3.4
Amount: $1,250-$2,000.
Number of awards: 4.
Deadline: November 15.
How to apply: Nomination forms are available online.
Exclusive: Visit www.UltimateScholarshipBook.com and enter code IN115820 for updates on this award.

(1159) • Giuliano Mazzetti Scholarship

Society of Manufacturing Engineers Education Foundation
One SME Drive, P.O. Box 930, Dearborn, MI 48121
Phone: 313-425-3300
Email: foundation@sme.org
http://www.smeef.org

Purpose: To support undergraduate students of manufacturing engineering and technology.

Eligibility: Applicants must be full-time undergraduate students who have completed 30 or more credit hours at a postsecondary institution located in the United States or Canada. They must be studying manufacturing engineering, technology or a related subject and must have plans to pursue a career in one of these same fields. Students must have a GPA of 3.0 or more on a four-point scale. Selection is based on the overall strength of the application.

Target applicant(s): College students. Adult students.

Minimum GPA: 3.0

Amount: Varies.

Number of awards: Varies.

Deadline: February 1.

How to apply: Applications are available online. An application form, personal statement, resume, transcript and two recommendation letters are required.

Exclusive: Visit www.UltimateScholarshipBook.com and enter code SO115920 for updates on this award.

(1160) • Gladys Anderson Emerson Scholarship

Iota Sigma Pi (ISP) ND
Professor Kathryn A. Thomasson, Iota Sigma Pi Director for Student Awards, University of North Dakota, Department of Chemistry, P.O. Box 9024, Grand Forks, ND 58202-9024
Phone: 701-777-3199
Email: kthomasson@chem.und.edu
http://www.iotasigmapi.info

Purpose: To reward achievement in the fields of chemistry and biochemistry by women.

Eligibility: Applicants must have attained junior status at an accredited college or university, be female and be nominated by a member of Iota Sigma Pi.

Target applicant(s): College students. Adult students.

Amount: $2,000.

Number of awards: Up to 2.

Deadline: February 15.

How to apply: Applications are available online.

Exclusive: Visit www.UltimateScholarshipBook.com and enter code IO116020 for updates on this award.

(1161) • Gloria Barron Wilderness Society Scholarship

Wilderness Society
1615 M Street NW, Washington, DC 20036
Phone: 800-843-9453
Email: https://wilderness.org
https://wilderness.org

Purpose: To support graduate students pursuing a career in long-term protection of wilderness in the U.S.

Eligibility: Applicants must provide a cover letter, proposal, current resume and letters of recommendation along with the application.

Target applicant(s): Graduate school students. Adult students.

Amount: Varies.

Number of awards: Varies.

Deadline: April 20.

How to apply: Applications are available online.

Exclusive: Visit www.UltimateScholarshipBook.com and enter code WI116120 for updates on this award.

(1162) • Gordon Rankin Corrosion Engineering Scholarship

National Association of Corrosion Engineers (NACE) International Foundation
15835 Park Ten Place, Houston, TX 77084-5145
Phone: 281-228-6205
Email: nace.foundation@nace.org
http://nace-foundation.org/programs/students/scholarships/

Purpose: To aid students in their continued studies in corrosion.

Eligibility: Applicants must be U.S. citizens enrolled full-time as an undergraduate at an accredited two or four-year U.S. college or university. Applicants must be enrolled in the study of corrosion or corrosion control and must have a GPA of 3.0 or higher.

Target applicant(s): College students. Adult students.

Minimum GPA: 3.0

Amount: $1,000.

Number of awards: Up to 2.

Deadline: January 5.

How to apply: Applications are available online. An application form, two recommendation forms, an academic transcript and scholarship essay questions are required.

Exclusive: Visit www.UltimateScholarshipBook.com and enter code NA116220 for updates on this award.

(1163) • Graduate Research Award (GRA)

American Vacuum Society
125 Maiden Lane, 15th Floor, New York, NY 10038
Phone: 212-248-0200
Email: angela@avs.org
http://www.avs.org

Purpose: To support graduate studies in the sciences and technologies related to the AVS.

Eligibility: Applicants must be graduate students in an accredited academic institution. Awards are based on research and academic record. The awards cover travel expenses to the international symposium. Applicants should submit applications, recommendation letters, research summaries and transcripts.

Target applicant(s): Graduate school students. Adult students.

Amount: Varies.

Number of awards: 10.

Deadline: May 1.

How to apply: Applications are available online.

Exclusive: Visit www.UltimateScholarshipBook.com and enter code AM116320 for updates on this award.

(1164) • Graduate Research Fellowship Program

National Science Foundation
GRF Operations Center, 1818 N Street NW, Suite 600, Washington, DC 20036
Phone: 866-NSF-GRFP
Email: info@nsfgrfp.org
https://www.fastlane.nsf.gov/

Purpose: To assist science and engineering graduate students.

Eligibility: Applicants must be full-time students who have completed no more than 12 months of graduate study and be U.S. citizens,

U.S. nationals or permanent residents. The fields of study are interdisciplinary, computer and information science and engineering, mathematical sciences, geosciences, psychology, social sciences, life sciences, chemistry, physics and astronomy and engineering.
Target applicant(s): Graduate school students. Adult students.
Amount: Up to $44,000.
Number of awards: 2,700.
Deadline: November 4.
How to apply: Applications are available online. An online application form, official transcript and three letters of reference submitted electronically are required.
Exclusive: Visit www.UltimateScholarshipBook.com and enter code NA116420 for updates on this award.

(1165) · Graduate Scholarships

Institute of Food Technologists (IFT)
525 W. Van Buren, Suite 1000, Chicago, IL 60607
Phone: 312-782-8424
Email: ejplummer@ift.org
http://www.ift.org/community/students/competitions.aspx
Purpose: To reward graduate students researching food science or technology.
Eligibility: Applicants should be graduate students pursuing an M.S. and/or Ph.D. at the time the fellowship becomes effective and should research an area of food science or technology. Applications, transcripts and three recommendation letters are required.
Target applicant(s): Graduate school students. Adult students.
Amount: $1,000-$5,000.
Number of awards: Varies.
Deadline: April 1.
How to apply: Applications are available online.
Exclusive: Visit www.UltimateScholarshipBook.com and enter code IN116520 for updates on this award.

(1166) · Graduate Scholarships Program

Society of Naval Architects and Marine Engineers
99 Canal Center Plaza, Suite 310, Alexandria, VA 22314
Phone: 201-798-4800
Email: efaustino@sname.org
http://www.sname.org/educationoptions/scholarships
Purpose: To aid students who are pursuing a master's degree in a subject that is related to the marine industry.
Eligibility: Applicants must be members of the Society of Naval Architects and Marine Engineers (SNAME). They must be working towards a master's degree in ocean engineering, marine engineering, naval architecture or another marine-related subject. Students who will be receiving their degree before October 1 of the application year are ineligible. Selection is based on the overall strength of the application.
Target applicant(s): College students. Graduate school students. Adult students.
Amount: Up to $20,000.
Number of awards: Varies.
Deadline: February 1.
How to apply: Applications are available online. An application form, transcript, standardized test scores and three recommendation letters are required.
Exclusive: Visit www.UltimateScholarshipBook.com and enter code SO116620 for updates on this award.

(1167) · Graduate Student Research Grants

Geological Society of America Graduate Student Research Grants
Matt Dawson, P.O. Box 9140, Boulder, CO 80301-9140
Phone: 303-357-1018
Email: mdawson@geosociety.org
http://www.geosociety.org/grants/gradgrants.htm
Purpose: To support thesis and dissertation research for graduate students in geological science.
Eligibility: Applicants must currently be enrolled in a geological science graduate program at an institution in the United States, Canada, Mexico or Central America. Applicants must also be members of the Geological Society of America (GSA).
Target applicant(s): Graduate school students. Adult students.
Amount: Varies.
Number of awards: Varies.
Deadline: February 1.
How to apply: Applications are available online.
Exclusive: Visit www.UltimateScholarshipBook.com and enter code GE116720 for updates on this award.

(1168) · Graduate Student Scholarship

American Speech-Language-Hearing Foundation
2200 Research Boulevard, Rockville, MD 20850
Phone: 301-296-8700
Email: foundation@asha.org
http://www.ashfoundation.org
Purpose: To support graduate students in communication sciences and disorders.
Eligibility: Applicants must be full-time graduate students in U.S. communication sciences and disorders programs. Master's degree candidates must be in programs accredited by the Council on Academic Accreditation for Audiology and Speech Pathology, but doctoral programs do not have to be accredited. Transcripts, an essay, a reference form and a statement of good standing are required.
Target applicant(s): College students. Graduate school students. Adult students.
Amount: $5,000.
Number of awards: Up to 21.
Deadline: May 22.
How to apply: Applications are available online.
Exclusive: Visit www.UltimateScholarshipBook.com and enter code AM116820 for updates on this award.

(1169) · Graduate Summer Student Research Assistantship

National Radio Astronomy Observatory (NRAO)
NRAO Headquarters, 520 Edgemont Road, Charlottesville, VA 22903
Phone: 434-296-0211
Email: info@nrao.edu
http://www.nrao.edu
Purpose: To allow graduate students to perform astronomical research at National Radio Astronomy Observatory (NRAO) sites.
Eligibility: Applicants must be first- or second-year graduate students interested in astronomical research. Recipients work on-site for 10 to 12 weeks, beginning in late May or early June.
Target applicant(s): Graduate school students. Adult students.
Amount: Varies.
Number of awards: Varies.
Deadline: February 1.

How to apply: Applications are available online.
Exclusive: Visit www.UltimateScholarshipBook.com and enter code NA116920 for updates on this award.

(1170) • H.P. "Bud" Milligan Aviation Scholarship

EAA Aviation Center
3000 Poberezny Road, Oshkosh, WI 54902
Phone: 920-426-4800
Email: scholarships@eaa.org
http://www.eaa.org/en/eaa
Purpose: To support excellence among individuals studying aviation.
Eligibility: Applicants must be enrolled in an accredited college, aviation academy or technical school pursuing a course of study focusing on aviation. Applicants must also be involved in school and community activities as well as aviation and be an EAA member or be recommended by an EAA member.
Target applicant(s): High school students. College students. Adult students.
Amount: $500.
Number of awards: 1.
Scholarship may be renewable.
Deadline: February 28.
How to apply: Applications are available online.
Exclusive: Visit www.UltimateScholarshipBook.com and enter code EA117020 for updates on this award.

(1171) • Hansen Scholarship

EAA Aviation Center
3000 Poberezny Road, Oshkosh, WI 54902
Phone: 920-426-4800
Email: scholarships@eaa.org
http://www.eaa.org/en/eaa
Purpose: To support excellence among individuals studying the technologies and the skills needed in the field of aviation.
Eligibility: Applicants must be enrolled in an accredited college or university pursuing a degree in aerospace engineering or aeronautical engineering and must be involved in school and community activities as well as aviation. Applicants must be in good academic standing. Financial need will be considered. Applicants must also be EAA members or be recommended by an EAA member.
Target applicant(s): College students. Graduate school students. Adult students.
Amount: $1,000.
Number of awards: 1.
Scholarship may be renewable.
Deadline: February 28.
How to apply: Applications are available online.
Exclusive: Visit www.UltimateScholarshipBook.com and enter code EA117120 for updates on this award.

(1172) • Harness Tracks of America Scholarship Fund

Harness Tracks of America
4640 E. Sunrise, Suite 200, Tucson, AZ 85718
Phone: 520-529-2525
Email: info@harnesstracks.com
http://www.harnesstracks.com
Purpose: To provide assistance to students who are involved in the harness racing industry.
Eligibility: Applicants must have a parent or parents involved in harness racing or must be active in the business. Applicants must also demonstrate active merit or financial need.
Target applicant(s): High school students. College students. Adult students.
Amount: $5,000.
Number of awards: 3.
Deadline: June 26.
How to apply: Applications are available by telephone.
Exclusive: Visit www.UltimateScholarshipBook.com and enter code HA117220 for updates on this award.

(1173) • Harold and Inge Marcus Scholarship

Institute of Industrial and Systems Engineers
3577 Parkway Lane, Suite 200, Norcross, GA 30092
Phone: 800-494-0460
Email: bcameron@iienet.org
http://www.iise.org/
Purpose: To aid industrial engineering students who are members of the Institute of Industrial Engineers (IIE).
Eligibility: Applicants must be undergraduate industrial engineering students who have been formally nominated for the award by their industrial engineering department heads. They must be full-time students who are active IIE members in good standing and must have an undergraduate GPA of 3.4 or higher on a four-point scale. Selection is based on academic achievement, integrity, financial need and potential contribution to the industrial engineering field.
Target applicant(s): College students. Adult students.
Minimum GPA: 3.4
Amount: $1,000.
Number of awards: 5.
Deadline: November 15.
How to apply: Applications will be mailed to those who have been formally nominated by their department heads. A formal nomination, an application packet and supporting documents are required.
Exclusive: Visit www.UltimateScholarshipBook.com and enter code IN117320 for updates on this award.

(1174) • Harold Bettinger Scholarship

American Floral Endowment
1001 North Fairfax Street, Suite 201, Alexandria, VA 22314
Phone: 703-838-5211
Email: dchedester@afeendowment.org
http://endowment.org/scholarships/
Purpose: To aid current horticulture students who are planning to pursue careers in a horticulture-related business.
Eligibility: Applicants must be U.S. or Canadian citizens or residents. They must be graduate students or rising undergraduate sophomores, juniors or seniors. They must have a GPA of 2.0 or higher. They must be horticulture students who are pursuing a major or minor in business or marketing, and must have plans to pursue a career in the horticulture business field. Selection is based on the overall strength of the application.
Target applicant(s): College students. Graduate school students. Adult students.
Minimum GPA: 2.0
Amount: Varies.
Number of awards: Varies.
Deadline: May 1.
How to apply: Applications are available online. An application form, two letters of recommendation, a personal statement and a transcript are required.

Exclusive: Visit www.UltimateScholarshipBook.com and enter code AM117420 for updates on this award.

(1175) • Harry J. Harwick Scholarship

Medical Group Management Association
104 Inverness Terrace East, Englewood, CO 80112
Phone: 877-275-6462
Email: acmpe@mgma.com
http://www.mgma.com

Purpose: To aid undergraduate and graduate students of public health, health care management, health care administration and related areas of medical practice management.

Eligibility: Applicants must be enrolled in an undergraduate or graduate degree program in public health, health care management, health care administration or a related medical practice management subject. Undergraduates must be enrolled in a program that is a member of the Association of University Programs in Health Administration (AUPHA), and graduate students must be enrolled in a program that has been accredited by the Commission on Accreditation of Healthcare Management Education (CAHME). Selection is based on the overall strength of the application.

Target applicant(s): High school students. College students. Graduate school students. Adult students.

Amount: $3,500.

Number of awards: Varies.

Deadline: May 1.

How to apply: Applications are available online. An application form and supporting documents are required.

Exclusive: Visit www.UltimateScholarshipBook.com and enter code ME117520 for updates on this award.

(1176) • Hazen and Sawyer Scholarship

American Water Works Association
6666 W. Quincy Avenue, Denver, CO 80235-3098
Phone: 800-926-7337
Email: scholarships@awwa.org
http://www.awwa.org

Purpose: To support students pursuing masters degrees in the water science industry.

Eligibility: Selection is based upon the applicant's ability to become a leader in research and consulting in the drinking water arena. Award is presented at the AWWA conference.

Target applicant(s): College students. Graduate school students. Adult students.

Amount: $5,000 plus travel money to AWWA conference.

Number of awards: Varies.

Deadline: January 12.

How to apply: Applications are available online.

Exclusive: Visit www.UltimateScholarshipBook.com and enter code AM117620 for updates on this award.

(1177) • HDR/Hendry "Bud" Benjes Scholarship

American Water Works Association
6666 W. Quincy Avenue, Denver, CO 80235-3098
Phone: 800-926-7337
Email: scholarships@awwa.org
http://www.awwa.org

Purpose: To support students pursuing master's degrees in the water science industry.

Eligibility: Applicants must be graduate students working towards master's degrees in the water science industry. Selection is based upon the overall strength of the application. Award is presented at the AWWA conference.

Target applicant(s): College students. Graduate school students. Adult students.

Amount: $5,000 plus travel money to AWWA conference.

Number of awards: 1.

Deadline: January 12.

How to apply: Applications are available online.

Exclusive: Visit www.UltimateScholarshipBook.com and enter code AM117720 for updates on this award.

(1178) • Health Careers Scholarship

International Order of the King's Daughters and Sons
Director, P.O. Box 1040, Chautauqua, NY 14722
http://www.iokds.org

Purpose: To assist students interested in pursuing health careers.

Eligibility: Applicants must be full-time students pursuing a career in medicine, dentistry, nursing, pharmacy, physical or occupational therapy or medical technologies. R.N. students and those pursuing an M.D. or D.D.S must have completed at least one year of schooling at an accredited institution. All others must be entering at least their third year of school. Pre-med students are not eligible. Applicants must be U.S. or Canadian citizens.

Target applicant(s): College students. Graduate school students. Adult students.

Amount: Varies.

Number of awards: Varies.

Deadline: April 1.

How to apply: Applications are available by sending a self-addressed, stamped legal size envelope.

Exclusive: Visit www.UltimateScholarshipBook.com and enter code IN117820 for updates on this award.

(1179) • Healthline Stronger

Healthline
660 Third Street, San Francisco, CA 94107
Phone: 415-281-3100
http://www.healthline.com/health/scholarship-program

Purpose: To support emerging future health leaders.

Eligibility: Applicants must be enrolling in or currently enrolled in a U.S. graduate program. Students must be U.S. residents. Applicants must have a minimum 3.0 grade point average and demonstrate leadership and a connection to a rare or chronic disease.

Target applicant(s): College students. Adult students.

Minimum GPA: 3.0

Amount: $5,000.

Number of awards: 4.

Deadline: May 1.

How to apply: Applications are available online.

Exclusive: Visit www.UltimateScholarshipBook.com and enter code HE117920 for updates on this award.

(1180) • Hedy Lamarr Achievement Award for Emerging Leaders in Entertainment Technology

DEG: The Digital Entertainment Group
Attn.: Hedy Lamarr Achievement Award Judging Panel, 10635 Santa Monica Boulevard, Suite 160, Los Angeles, CA 90025

Email: thedegonline@gmail.com
http://degonline.org/
Purpose: To support female college juniors who have shown exceptional promise in the fields of entertainment and technology.
Eligibility: Applicants must be female students in their junior year at an accredited institution in the United States who are pursuing a career in entertainment and technology. Students must be citizens of the United States and have a minimum 3.0 GPA.
Target applicant(s): College students. Adult students.
Minimum GPA: 3.0
Amount: $5,000-$10,000.
Number of awards: 3.
Deadline: February 15.
How to apply: Applications are available online.
Exclusive: Visit www.UltimateScholarshipBook.com and enter code DE118020 for updates on this award.

(1181) · Henry Adams Scholarship

American Society of Heating, Refrigerating and Air-Conditioning Engineers (ASHRAE)
1791 Tullie Circle, NE, Atlanta, GA 30329
Phone: 404-636-8400
Email: lbenedict@ashrae.org
http://www.ashrae.org
Purpose: To aid undergraduate engineering students who are preparing for careers in the heating, ventilation, air-conditioning and refrigeration (HVACR) industry.
Eligibility: Applicants must be undergraduate engineering or pre-engineering students. They must be enrolled in or accepted into an ABET-accredited school, a school that is accredited by a non-U.S. agency that has entered into a Memorandum of Understanding agreement with ABET or a school that hosts a recognized student branch of the American Society of Heating, Refrigerating and Air-Conditioning Engineers (ASHRAE). The applicant's program of study must offer adequate preparation for a career in the HVACR industry. Applicants must have a GPA of 3.0 or higher and must be ranked in the top 30 percent of their class. Selection is based on the overall strength of the application.
Target applicant(s): High school students. College students. Adult students.
Minimum GPA: 3.0
Amount: $3,000.
Number of awards: 1.
Scholarship may be renewable.
Deadline: December 1.
How to apply: Applications are available online. An application form, official transcript and one recommendation letter are required.
Exclusive: Visit www.UltimateScholarshipBook.com and enter code AM118120 for updates on this award.

(1182) · Herbert Levy Memorial Scholarship

Society of Physics Students
One Physics Ellipse , College Park, MD 20740
Phone: 301-209-3007
Email: SPS-Programs@aip.org
https://www.spsnational.org/
Purpose: To provide financial assistance for physics students in any year of undergraduate study.
Eligibility: Applicants must be physics majors, be members of SPS and demonstrate scholarly achievement and financial need.
Target applicant(s): College students. Adult students.
Amount: $2,000.
Number of awards: 1.
Deadline: March 22.
How to apply: Applications are available online or from SPS Chapter Advisors.
Exclusive: Visit www.UltimateScholarshipBook.com and enter code SO118220 for updates on this award.

(1183) · Hertz Foundation's Graduate Fellowship Award

Fannie and John Hertz Foundation
Attn: Applications, 2300 First Street , Suite 250, Livermore, CA 94550
Phone: 925-373-1642
Email: askhertz@hertzfoundation.org
http://www.hertzfoundation.org
Purpose: To help graduate students in the applied physical and engineering sciences.
Eligibility: Applicants must be college seniors planning to pursue or graduate students currently pursuing a Ph.D. in the applied physical and engineering sciences or modern biology which applies the physical sciences. Successful applicants must attend one of the foundation's approved schools. The award is based on merit, creativity and potential for research.
Target applicant(s): College students. Graduate school students. Adult students.
Amount: Up to full tuition plus stipend.
Number of awards: Varies.
Scholarship may be renewable.
Deadline: October 28.
How to apply: Applications are available online, by phone or by email.
Exclusive: Visit www.UltimateScholarshipBook.com and enter code FA118320 for updates on this award.

(1184) · HIMSS Foundation Scholarship

Healthcare Information and Management Systems Society
230 E. Ohio Street, Suite 500, Chicago, IL 60611-3269
Phone: 312-664-4467
http://www.himss.org
Purpose: To provide scholarships based on academic achievement and leadership in the field of healthcare information and management systems.
Eligibility: Applicants must be members of HIMSS and study healthcare information and management systems. Scholarships are also available from individual chapters listed on the HIMSS website.
Target applicant(s): College students. Graduate school students. Adult students.
Amount: $5,000.
Number of awards: 4.
Deadline: October 15.
How to apply: Application details are available online.
Exclusive: Visit www.UltimateScholarshipBook.com and enter code HE118420 for updates on this award.

(1185) · Holly Cornell Scholarship

American Water Works Association
6666 W. Quincy Avenue, Denver, CO 80235-3098
Phone: 800-926-7337
Email: scholarships@awwa.org
http://www.awwa.org

Purpose: To support female and/or minority master's students pursuing advanced training in the field of water supply and treatment.
Eligibility: Applicants must be females and/or minorities who have been accepted to or are current master's degree students in engineering. Applications, transcripts, GRE scores, three recommendation letters, statements and course of study are required. The award is based on academics and leadership.
Target applicant(s): Graduate school students. Adult students.
Amount: $7,500.
Number of awards: 1.
Deadline: January 12.
How to apply: Applications are available online.
Exclusive: Visit www.UltimateScholarshipBook.com and enter code AM118520 for updates on this award.

(1186) • Hooper Memorial Scholarship

Logistics and Transportation Association of North America (LTNA)
P.O. Box 426, Union, WA 98592
http://www.ltna.org/scholarship-application.html
Purpose: To support students who want to enter the transportation industry.
Eligibility: Applicants must be graduating high school seniors or college undergraduate students enrolled in an accredited institution of higher learning in a vocational or degree program in the fields of transportation logistics, supply-chain management, traffic management, transportation safety and/or related transportation industry operations and services. The awards are based upon scholastic ability, potential, professional interest and character. Financial need is also considered. Applicants must have a minimum 3.0 GPA.
Target applicant(s): High school students. College students. Adult students.
Minimum GPA: 3.0
Amount: Varies.
Number of awards: Varies.
Deadline: July 25.
How to apply: Applications are available online.
Exclusive: Visit www.UltimateScholarshipBook.com and enter code LO118620 for updates on this award.

(1187) • Horkheimer/Smith Youth Service Award

Astronomical League
9201 Ward Parkway, Suite 100, Kansas City, MO 64114
Phone: 816-333-7759
Email: horkheimerservice@astroleague.org
http://www.astroleague.org
Purpose: To assist young Astronomical League members.
Eligibility: Applicants must be Astronomical League members under the age of 19 on the date of the application. The award is based on astronomical service and service to the league.
Target applicant(s): Junior high students or younger. High school students.
Amount: $1,750 plus travel expenses.
Number of awards: 3.
Deadline: February 15.
How to apply: Applications are available online.
Exclusive: Visit www.UltimateScholarshipBook.com and enter code AS118720 for updates on this award.

(1188) • Houzz Women in Architecture

Houzz Inc.
285 Hamilton Avenue, Palo Alto, CA 94301
Email: scholarships@houz.com
http://houzz.com/scholarships
Purpose: To support women architecture students.
Eligibility: Applicants must be female students enrolled at an U.S. university as an undergraduate or graduate student. Students must be majoring in architecture.
Target applicant(s): College students. Graduate school students. Adult students.
Amount: $2,500.
Number of awards: 2.
Deadline: June 30.
How to apply: Applications are available online.
Exclusive: Visit www.UltimateScholarshipBook.com and enter code HO118820 for updates on this award.

(1189) • HSA Research Grants

Herb Society of America
Attn.: Research Grant, 9019 Kirtland Chardon Road, Kirtland, OH 44094
Phone: 440-256-0514
Email: herbs@herbsociety.org
http://www.herbsociety.org
Purpose: To educate about herbs and contribute to the fields of horticulture, science, literature, history, art and/or economics.
Eligibility: Applicants must have a proposed program of scientific, academic or artistic investigation of herbal plants. Applicants must describe their research needs in 500 words or less and include a proposed budget with specific budget items listed. This grant may not be used in combination with funding from another source and may not be used to pay for salaries, tuition or private garden development.
Target applicant(s): High school students. College students. Adult students.
Amount: Up to $5,000.
Number of awards: Varies by year.
Deadline: January 31.
How to apply: Applications are available online or by written request.
Exclusive: Visit www.UltimateScholarshipBook.com and enter code HE118920 for updates on this award.

(1190) • Hutton Junior Fisheries Biology Program

American Fisheries Society (AFS)
425 Barlow Place, Suite 110, Bethesda, MD 20814
Phone: 301-897-8616
https://hutton.fisheries.org/
Purpose: To stimulate interest in pursuing fisheries science and aquatic resources among high school students.
Eligibility: Applicants must be a junior or senior in high school. Students must provide official copies of student transcripts. Preference will be given to qualified women and minority applicants.
Target applicant(s): High school students.
Amount: $4,000.
Number of awards: Varies.
Deadline: January 31.
How to apply: Applications are available online.
Exclusive: Visit www.UltimateScholarshipBook.com and enter code AM119020 for updates on this award.

(1191) • IEEE Presidents' Scholarship

Institute of Electrical and Electronics Engineers (IEEE)
445 Hoes Lane, Piscataway, NJ 08854
Phone: 732-562-3860
Email: supportieee@ieee.org
http://www.ieee.org/scholarships
Purpose: To reward a student for a project relevant to electrical engineering, electronics engineering, computer science or other IEEE fields of interest.
Eligibility: Applicants must be student members who use engineering, science and computing to solve a problem. Students may compete individually or as a team.
Target applicant(s): High school students.
Amount: $10,000.
Number of awards: Varies.
Scholarship may be renewable.
Deadline: May 12.
How to apply: Contact the organization for more information.
Exclusive: Visit www.UltimateScholarshipBook.com and enter code IN119120 for updates on this award.

(1192) • IIE Council of Fellows Undergraduate Scholarship

Institute of Industrial and Systems Engineers
3577 Parkway Lane, Suite 200, Norcross, GA 30092
Phone: 800-494-0460
Email: bcameron@iienet.org
http://www.iise.org/
Purpose: To support undergraduate student members.
Eligibility: Applicants must be full-time undergraduate students enrolled in a college in the United States, Canada or Mexico with an accredited industrial engineering program, major in industrial engineering and be active members. Students may not apply directly for this scholarship and must be nominated. The award is based on academic ability, character, leadership, potential service to the industrial engineering profession and financial need. Applicant must have a minimum 3.4 GPA.
Target applicant(s): College students. Adult students.
Minimum GPA: 3.4
Amount: $1,500.
Number of awards: 2.
Deadline: November 15.
How to apply: Nomination forms are available online.
Exclusive: Visit www.UltimateScholarshipBook.com and enter code IN119220 for updates on this award.

(1193) • Industrial Electrolysis and Electrochemical Engineering Division H.H. Dow Memorial Student Award

Electrochemical Society
65 South Main Street, Building D, Pennington, NJ 08534-2839
Phone: 609-737-1902
Email: awards@electrochem.org
http://www.electrochem.org/programs/
Purpose: To recognize young engineers and scientists in the fields of electrochemical engineering and applied electrochemistry.
Eligibility: Applicants must be accepted to or enrolled in a graduate program. The application requires transcripts, a description of the research project, a description of how the project relates to electrochemical engineering or applied electrochemistry, a biography, a resume or curriculum vitae and a letter of recommendation from the research supervisor. The award is based on academic performance, research and the recommendation.
Target applicant(s): Graduate school students. Adult students.
Amount: $1,000.
Number of awards: Varies.
Deadline: September 15.
How to apply: Application materials are described online.
Exclusive: Visit www.UltimateScholarshipBook.com and enter code EL119320 for updates on this award.

(1194) • Industrial Electrolysis and Electrochemical Engineering Division Student Achievement Awards

Electrochemical Society
65 South Main Street, Building D, Pennington, NJ 08534-2839
Phone: 609-737-1902
Email: awards@electrochem.org
http://www.electrochem.org/programs/
Purpose: To recognize young engineers and scientists in electrochemical engineering and to encourage the recipients to enter careers in the field.
Eligibility: Applicants must be accepted by or enrolled in a college or university and propose a research project. The application must include transcripts, research outline, statement describing how the project relates to electrochemical engineering, record of industrial work and letter of recommendation from the research supervisor. The award is based on academic performance, research and the recommendation.
Target applicant(s): High school students. College students. Graduate school students. Adult students.
Amount: $1,000.
Number of awards: Varies.
Deadline: September 15.
How to apply: Application materials are described online.
Exclusive: Visit www.UltimateScholarshipBook.com and enter code EL119420 for updates on this award.

(1195) • Injection Molding Division Scholarship

Society of Plastics Engineers
6 Berkshire Boulevard, Suite 306, Bethel, CT 06801
Phone: 203-775-0471
Email: info@4spe.org
http://www.4spe.org/spe-foundation
Purpose: To aid students who have employment or academic experience in injection molding.
Eligibility: Applicants must be full-time undergraduate or graduate students who are in good academic standing. They must have experience in injection molding through courses taken, research conducted or formal employment. They must have an interest in the plastics/polymer industry and must have taken courses that would prepare them for a career in this field. Selection is based on academic merit and financial need.
Target applicant(s): High school students. College students. Graduate school students. Adult students.
Amount: $3,000.
Number of awards: 1.
Deadline: April 1.
How to apply: Applications are available online. An application form, three recommendation letters, transcripts, a personal statement, a list of extracurricular activities and honors and employment history are required.
Exclusive: Visit www.UltimateScholarshipBook.com and enter code SO119520 for updates on this award.

(1196) • Inspiring Girls Engineering Award

Charles Stark Draper Laboratory
555 Technology Square, Cambridge, MA 02139
Email: engineeringpossibilites@draper.com
http://www.draper.com

Purpose: To encourage female high school students in Massachusetts to pursue engineering education.
Eligibility: Applicants must be female high school students in grades 9-12 enrolled in a Massachusetts-based school and residents of the state. Students must submit answers to technical questions along with an essay.
Target applicant(s): High school students.
Amount: $500.
Number of awards: 1.
Deadline: March 16.
How to apply: Applications are available online.
Exclusive: Visit www.UltimateScholarshipBook.com and enter code CH119620 for updates on this award.

(1197) • Institute of Electrical and Electronics Engineers Life Members' Fellowship in Electrical History

Institute of Electrical and Electronics Engineers (IEEE)
445 Hoes Lane, Piscataway, NJ 08854
Phone: 732-562-3860
Email: supportieee@ieee.org
http://www.ieee.org/scholarships

Purpose: To support students in engineering and technology-related fields.
Eligibility: Applicants must be studying engineering, computer science and information technology, physical sciences, biological and medical sciences, mathematics, technical communications, education, management or law and policy. The award may be used during one year of full-time graduate work or one year of post-doctoral research. Students must provide a detailed 15-page description of the proposed research, along with three letters of recommendation.
Target applicant(s): Graduate school students. Adult students.
Deadline: February 1.
How to apply: Applications are available online.
Exclusive: Visit www.UltimateScholarshipBook.com and enter code IN119720 for updates on this award.

(1198) • International Gas Turbine Institute Scholarship

American Society of Mechanical Engineers (ASME)
Two Park Avenue, New York, NY 10016-5990
Phone: 800-843-2763
Email: lefeverb@asme.org
http://www.asme.org

Purpose: To aid American Society of Mechanical Engineers (ASME) student members who are interested in the gas turbine industry.
Eligibility: Applicants must be student members of ASME who are in good standing. They must be enrolled in an accredited undergraduate or graduate degree program in mechanical engineering or aerospace engineering. They must be interested in the turbomachinery, gas turbine or propulsion industry. Preference will be given to those who have employment or research experience in one of the aforementioned industries. Selection is based on academic achievement and demonstrated interest in the gas turbine industry.
Target applicant(s): High school students. College students. Graduate school students. Adult students.
Amount: $2,000.
Number of awards: 1.
Deadline: June 15.
How to apply: Applications may be completed online. An electronic application form, official transcript, personal statement and one to two recommendation letters are required.
Exclusive: Visit www.UltimateScholarshipBook.com and enter code AM119820 for updates on this award.

(1199) • International Student Scholarship

American Speech-Language-Hearing Foundation
2200 Research Boulevard, Rockville, MD 20850
Phone: 301-296-8700
Email: foundation@asha.org
http://www.ashfoundation.org

Purpose: To support an international graduate student in communication sciences and disorders.
Eligibility: Applicants must be full-time students in the U.S. Master's degree candidates must be in programs accredited by the Council on Academic Accreditation for Audiology and Speech Pathology, but doctoral programs do not have to be accredited. The applicants should submit transcripts, an essay and a reference form.
Target applicant(s): College students. Graduate school students. Adult students.
Amount: $5,000.
Number of awards: Up to 2.
Deadline: May 22.
How to apply: Applications are available online.
Exclusive: Visit www.UltimateScholarshipBook.com and enter code AM119920 for updates on this award.

(1200) • International Women's Fishing Association Scholarship

International Women's Fishing Association
P.O. Box 31507, Palm Beach Gardens, FL 33420
Email: kelleykeys@aol.com
https://iwfa.memberclicks.net

Purpose: To help students in graduate programs in the marine sciences.
Eligibility: Applicants must have graduated or have been approved for graduation from an accredited college or university and plan on pursuing a graduate degree in the marine sciences. Selection is based on academic success, personal character, aptitude in the student's area of study and financial need.
Target applicant(s): Graduate school students. Adult students.
Amount: Up to $2,000.
Number of awards: Varies.
Deadline: March 1.
How to apply: Applications are available online. Students must include an official transcript, a photo, a letter describing career goals and a list of three people who will be sending letters of recommendation.
Exclusive: Visit www.UltimateScholarshipBook.com and enter code IN120020 for updates on this award.

(1201) • Intertech Foundation STEM Scholarship

Intertech Foundation
1575 Thomas Center Drive, Eagan, MN 55122
Phone: 651-288-7000
https://www.intertech.com/

Purpose: To assist college-bound students who have excelled at math and science.

Eligibility: Applicants must be college-bound high school seniors or current college students who are U.S. citizens and have at least a 3.3 GPA. Students must plan to major in computer science in college.
Target applicant(s): High school students. College students. Adult students.
Minimum GPA: 3.3
Amount: $2,500.
Number of awards: 1.
Deadline: March 15.
How to apply: There is no application form. A high school transcript, a resume, two letters of recommendation, a copy of a college acceptance letter and a one-page essay about how the student plans to participate in the professional software development industry are required.
Exclusive: Visit www.UltimateScholarshipBook.com and enter code IN120120 for updates on this award.

(1202) • Irene and Daisy MacGregor Memorial Scholarship

National Society Daughters of the American Revolution
Committee Services Office, Attn.: Scholarships, 1776 D Street NW, Washington, DC 20006-5303
Phone: 202-628-1776
Email: scholarships@dar.org
http://www.dar.org/national-society/scholarships
Purpose: To assist students in becoming medical doctors.
Eligibility: Applicants must be accepted into or enrolled in a graduate course of study to become a medical doctor. Those pursuing study in psychiatric nursing at the graduate level at a medical school may also apply, and preference is given to females. All applicants must obtain a letter of sponsorship from their local DAR chapter. However, affiliation with DAR is not required.
Target applicant(s): Graduate school students. Adult students.
Amount: Up to $5,000.
Number of awards: Varies.
Scholarship may be renewable.
Deadline: February 10.
How to apply: Applications are available by written request with a self-addressed, stamped envelope.
Exclusive: Visit www.UltimateScholarshipBook.com and enter code NA120220 for updates on this award.

(1203) • Irene Woodall Graduate Scholarship

American Dental Hygienists' Association (ADHA) Institute for Oral Health
Scholarship Award Program, 444 North Michigan Avenue, Suite 3400, Chicago, IL 60611
Phone: 312-440-8900
Email: institute@adha.net
http://www.adha.org
Purpose: To support students pursuing a master's degree in dental hygiene.
Eligibility: Applicants must be full-time students at an accredited college or university in the United States pursuing a master's degree in dental hygiene or a related field and must have completed at least one year of a dental hygiene curriculum. Applicants must also be active members of the ADHA, have a minimum 3.5 GPA and have a minimum demonstrated financial need of $1,500. Selection is based upon the overall strength of the application.
Target applicant(s): College students. Graduate school students. Adult students.
Minimum GPA: 3.5
Amount: $1,000.
Number of awards: 1.
Deadline: February 1.
How to apply: Applications are available online after October 1.
Exclusive: Visit www.UltimateScholarshipBook.com and enter code AM120320 for updates on this award.

(1204) • IRF Fellowship Program

International Road Federation
Madison Place, 500 Montgomery Street, 5th Floor, Alexandria, VA 22314
Phone: 703-535-1001
Email: info@irfnews.org
http://www.irfnet.org
Purpose: To provide fellowships in support of graduate study in a transportation-related field.
Eligibility: Applicants must demonstrate potential leadership in the highway industry in financing, administration, planning, design, construction, operations or maintenance. They must also have two years of work experience in transportation, a bachelor's of science degree (or equivalent) in a transportation-related discipline and a commitment to full-time study for a minimum of one year.
Target applicant(s): Graduate school students. Adult students.
Amount: Varies.
Number of awards: Varies.
Deadline: September 30.
How to apply: More information is available online.
Exclusive: Visit www.UltimateScholarshipBook.com and enter code IN120420 for updates on this award.

(1205) • IWSH Essay Scholarship

International Water, Sanitation and Hygiene Foundation
4755 E. Philadelphia Street, Ontario, CA 91761
Phone: 909-472-4100
Email: essay@iwsh.org
http://www.iwsh.org
Purpose: To encourage students who have an awareness of the importance of the plumbing industry.
Eligibility: Applicants must be a high school senior or enrolled in an accredited technical school, community college, trade school or four-year accredited college/university. Students must submit an essay between 880 to 1,600 words on the topic listed on the website.
Target applicant(s): High school students. College students. Adult students.
Amount: $500-$1,000.
Number of awards: 1-3.
Deadline: April 30.
How to apply: Applications are available online.
Exclusive: Visit www.UltimateScholarshipBook.com and enter code IN120520 for updates on this award.

(1206) • Jack Horkheimer Service Award/Parker Award

Astronomical League
9201 Ward Parkway, Suite 100, Kansas City, MO 64114
Phone: 816-333-7759
Email: horkheimerservice@astroleague.org
http://www.astroleague.org
Purpose: To recognize exceptional service by high school League astronomers.

Eligibility: Applicants must be a League member under 19 years of age. Selection is based upon service to the League.
Target applicant(s): High school students.
Amount: $1,000.
Number of awards: 1.
Deadline: March 31.
How to apply: Applications are available online. An application form, photo, details of public service, documentation of Astronomy Club duties or officer positions held, documentation of League Observing Awards earned, documentation of general observing achievements and documentation of other Astronomical Service are required.
Exclusive: Visit www.UltimateScholarshipBook.com and enter code AS120620 for updates on this award.

(1207) • Jackson Laboratory Scholarship

Jackson Laboratory
Training & Education Office, 600 Main Street, Bar Harbor, ME 04609
Phone: 207-288-6250
Email: scholarship@jax.org
https://www.jax.org/scholarship
Purpose: To reward students pursuing a college education in research or medical fields.
Eligibility: Applicants must reside in Connecticut, Maine or in Sacramento County, California and must be pursuing a degree in biomedicine. Students must receive a nomination from a teacher and have financial need or be first-generation college students. Students must also have a 3.5 GPA and be graduating high school seniors.
Target applicant(s): High school students.
Minimum GPA: 3.5
Amount: $10,000.
Number of awards: 3.
Deadline: February 1.
How to apply: Applications are available online.
Exclusive: Visit www.UltimateScholarshipBook.com and enter code JA120720 for updates on this award.

(1208) • Jane Delano Student Nurse Scholarship

American Red Cross
National Headquarters, 431 18th Street NW, Washington, DC 20006
Phone: 202-303-5000
Email: NationalAwards@redcross.org
http://www.redcross.org
Purpose: To aid Red Cross volunteers who are attending nursing school.
Eligibility: Applicants must be enrolled in an accredited nursing school and be in good academic standing. They must have volunteered with a Red Cross unit at least once within the past five years and have completed at least one academic year of college at the time of application. Selection is based on the overall strength of the application.
Target applicant(s): College students. Graduate school students. Adult students.
Amount: Varies.
Number of awards: Varies.
Deadline: May.
How to apply: Applications are available online. An application form, a personal essay, an endorsement from a Red Cross unit and an endorsement from the student's nursing school dean or chair are required.
Exclusive: Visit www.UltimateScholarshipBook.com and enter code AM120820 for updates on this award.

(1209) • Jean Theodore Lacordaire Prize

Coleopterists Society
Dr. Darren A. Pollock, Chair, Department of Biology , Eastern New Mexico University, Portales, NM 88130
Phone: 575-562-2862
Email: Darren.Pollock@enmu.edu
http://www.coleopsoc.org/
Purpose: To recognize the work of coleopterists.
Eligibility: Applicants must be graduate students whose papers are nominated for the competition. The papers must be based on the applicant's dissertation research about coleoptera (beetle) systematics or biology published in the preceding calendar year. Self-nominations are not accepted.
Target applicant(s): Graduate school students. Adult students.
Amount: $300.
Number of awards: 1.
Deadline: March 1.
How to apply: Application materials are described online.
Exclusive: Visit www.UltimateScholarshipBook.com and enter code CO120920 for updates on this award.

(1210) • Jill S. Tietjen P.E. Scholarship

Society of Women Engineers
130 East Randolph Street, Suite 3500, Chicago, IL 60601
Phone: 877-793-4636
Email: scholarships@swe.org
http://societyofwomenengineers.swe.org/scholarships
Purpose: To support female engineering students pursuing a higher education.
Eligibility: Applicants must be currently enrolled in an accredited engineering or engineering technology program with a minimum of a 3.0 GPA. The award is to be used during the sophomore, junior or senior year of college.
Target applicant(s): College students. Adult students.
Minimum GPA: 3.0
Amount: $1,750.
Number of awards: 1.
Deadline: February 15.
How to apply: Applications are available online.
Exclusive: Visit www.UltimateScholarshipBook.com and enter code SO121020 for updates on this award.

(1211) • Jimmy A. Young Memorial Education Recognition Award

American Association for Respiratory Care
9425 North MacArthur Boulevard, Suite 100, Irving, TX 75063-4706
Phone: 972-243-2272
Email: info@aarc.org
http://www.aarc.org/education/educator-resources/scholarships/
Purpose: To recognize outstanding minority students in respiratory care education programs.
Eligibility: Applicants must be enrolled in an accredited respiratory care education program and have a minimum 3.0 GPA. Students must submit an original paper on respiratory care. Preference is given to minority students.
Target applicant(s): College students. Graduate school students. Adult students.
Minimum GPA: 3.0
Amount: Up to $1,000.

Number of awards: 1.
Deadline: June 1.
How to apply: Applications are available online.
Exclusive: Visit www.UltimateScholarshipBook.com and enter code AM121120 for updates on this award.

(1212) • John and Elsa Gracik Scholarships

American Society of Mechanical Engineers (ASME)
Two Park Avenue, New York, NY 10016-5990
Phone: 800-843-2763
Email: lefeverb@asme.org
http://www.asme.org
Purpose: To support mechanical engineering students.
Eligibility: Applicants must be ASME student members, enrolled in an eligible accredited mechanical engineering baccalaureate program and be U.S. citizens. Selection is based on scholastic ability, financial need, character, leadership and potential contribution to the mechanical engineering profession.
Target applicant(s): College students. Adult students.
Amount: $2,500.
Number of awards: 10.
Deadline: March 1.
How to apply: Applications are available online.
Exclusive: Visit www.UltimateScholarshipBook.com and enter code AM121220 for updates on this award.

(1213) • John and Muriel Landis Scholarship

American Nuclear Society
555 North Kensington Avenue, La Grange Park, IL 60526
Phone: 800-323-3044
Email: hr@ans.org
http://www.ans.org
Purpose: To assist disadvantaged students to seek careers in a nuclear-related field.
Eligibility: Applicants must be undergraduate or graduate students enrolled or planning to enroll in a U.S. college or university who are also planning a career in nuclear science, nuclear engineering or another nuclear-related field. High school seniors may apply. Students must have greater than average financial need. Applicants must submit applications, transcripts, sponsor forms and three reference forms.
Target applicant(s): High school students. College students. Graduate school students. Adult students.
Amount: $5,000.
Number of awards: Up to 9.
Deadline: February 1.
How to apply: Applications are available online.
Exclusive: Visit www.UltimateScholarshipBook.com and enter code AM121320 for updates on this award.

(1214) • John C. Bajus Scholarship

Marine Technology Society
1100 H Street NW, Suite LL-100, Washington, DC 20005
Phone: 202-717-8705
https://www.mtsociety.org/education/scholarships.aspx
Purpose: To support Marine Technology Society members who are pursuing a degree in a marine-related field.
Eligibility: Applicants must be MTS student members who are accepted for enrollment or enrolled full-time in an undergraduate or graduate program. Selection is primarily based on demonstration of commitment to community service and volunteer work.
Target applicant(s): College students. Graduate school students. Adult students.
Amount: $1,000.
Number of awards: 1.
Deadline: April 19.
How to apply: Applications are available online.
Exclusive: Visit www.UltimateScholarshipBook.com and enter code MA121420 for updates on this award.

(1215) • John Henry Comstock Graduate Student Awards

Entomological Society of America
3 Park Place, Suite 307, Annapolis, MD 21401-3722
Phone: 301-731-4535
Email: esa@entsoc.org
http://www.entsoc.org
Purpose: To encourage graduate students interested in entomology to attend the Annual Meeting of the Entomological Society of America.
Eligibility: Applicants must be graduate students and members of the ESA. Each ESA branch has its own eligibility requirements, so an interested student must contact their Branch Secretary-Treasurer for more information.
Target applicant(s): Graduate school students. Adult students.
Amount: Travel expenses plus $100.
Number of awards: 6.
Deadline: Varies.
How to apply: Applications are available online.
Exclusive: Visit www.UltimateScholarshipBook.com and enter code EN121520 for updates on this award.

(1216) • John J. McKetta Scholarship

American Institute of Chemical Engineers - (AIChE)
120 Wall Street, Floor 23, New York, NY 10005-4020
Phone: 800-242-4363
Email: awards@aiche.org
https://www.aiche.org/community/awards
Purpose: To support chemical engineering students.
Eligibility: Applicants must be chemical engineering incoming undergraduate juniors or seniors and be planning a career in the chemical engineering process industries. Applicants must also have a minimum 3.0 GPA and be attending an ABET accredited school in the U.S., Canada or Mexico. Selection is based on an essay outlining career goals, leadership in an AIChE student chapter or other university sponsored activity and letters of recommendation. Preference is given to members of AIChE.
Target applicant(s): College students. Adult students.
Minimum GPA: 3.0
Amount: $5,000.
Number of awards: 1.
Deadline: June 15.
How to apply: Applications are available online.
Exclusive: Visit www.UltimateScholarshipBook.com and enter code AM121620 for updates on this award.

(1217) • John L. Imhoff Scholarship

Institute of Industrial and Systems Engineers
3577 Parkway Lane, Suite 200, Norcross, GA 30092
Phone: 800-494-0460
Email: bcameron@iienet.org
http://www.iise.org/

Purpose: To reward a student who has contributed to the development of the industrial engineering profession through international understanding.
Eligibility: Applicants must be pursuing a B.S., master's or doctorate degree in an accredited IE program, have a minimum 3.4 GPA and have at least two years of school remaining. Students may not apply directly for this scholarship and must be nominated. An essay describing the candidate's international contributions to industrial engineering and three references are required. IIE membership is not required.
Target applicant(s): High school students. College students. Adult students.
Minimum GPA: 3.4
Amount: $1,000.
Number of awards: At least 1.
Deadline: November 15.
How to apply: More information is available online.
Exclusive: Visit www.UltimateScholarshipBook.com and enter code IN121720 for updates on this award.

(1218) • John Mabry Forestry Scholarship

Railway Tie Association
115 Commerce Drive, Suite C, Fayetteville, GA 30214
Phone: 770-460-5553
Email: ties@rta.org
http://www.rta.org
Purpose: To aid forestry school students.
Eligibility: Applicants must be enrolled in an accredited forestry program at an postsecondary institution. They must be in the second year of a two-year technical school program or in the third or fourth year of a four-year college or university program. Students who are in the final year of their program must remain enrolled for the entirety of the academic year. Selection is based on academic merit, leadership ability, stated career goals and financial need.
Target applicant(s): College students. Adult students.
Amount: $2,000.
Number of awards: 2.
Deadline: June 30.
How to apply: Applications are available online. An application form and supporting documents are required.
Exclusive: Visit www.UltimateScholarshipBook.com and enter code RA121820 for updates on this award.

(1219) • John S. Marshall Memorial Scholarship

American Institute of Mining, Metallurgical and Petroleum Engineers (AIME)
12999 East Adam Aircraft Circle, Englewood, CO 80112
Phone: 303-325-5185
Email: aime@aimehq.org
http://www.aimehq.org/programs/scholarships
Purpose: To aid mining engineering students.
Eligibility: Applicants must be rising undergraduate juniors or seniors who are enrolled in an ABET-accredited mining engineering degree program on a full-time basis. They must be student members of the Society for Mining, Metallurgy and Exploration (SME). They must have plans to pursue a career in the mining industry and must demonstrate financial need. Selection is based on the overall strength of the application.
Target applicant(s): College students. Adult students.
Amount: Varies.
Number of awards: Varies.
Deadline: October 15.
How to apply: Applications are available online. An application form and two letters of recommendation are required.
Exclusive: Visit www.UltimateScholarshipBook.com and enter code AM121920 for updates on this award.

(1220) • John S.W. Fargher, Jr. Scholarship

Institute of Industrial and Systems Engineers
3577 Parkway Lane, Suite 200, Norcross, GA 30092
Phone: 800-494-0460
Email: bcameron@iienet.org
http://www.iise.org/
Purpose: To reward graduate students in industrial engineering who have demonstrated leadership.
Eligibility: Applicants must be full-time graduate students with at least one full year left who are enrolled in a college in the United States with an accredited industrial engineering program. Candidates must also major in industrial engineering or engineering management and be active members who have demonstrated leadership in industrial engineering-related activities. Students may not apply directly for this scholarship and must be nominated.
Target applicant(s): Graduate school students. Adult students.
Minimum GPA: 3.0
Amount: Varies.
Number of awards: 1.
Deadline: September 1.
How to apply: More information is available online.
Exclusive: Visit www.UltimateScholarshipBook.com and enter code IN122020 for updates on this award.

(1221) • John V. Wehausen Graduate Scholarship

Society of Naval Architects and Marine Engineers
99 Canal Center Plaza, Suite 310, Alexandria, VA 22314
Phone: 201-798-4800
Email: efaustino@sname.org
http://www.sname.org/educationoptions/scholarships
Purpose: To aid students who are seeking a master's degree in a marine-related subject.
Eligibility: Applicants must be members of the Society of Naval Architects and Marine Engineers (SNAME) or another respected marine society. They must be pursuing a master's degree in naval architecture, ocean engineering, marine engineering or another marine-related subject. Students who will be completing their degree before April 15 of the award disbursement year are ineligible. Selection is based on the overall strength of the application.
Target applicant(s): College students. Graduate school students. Adult students.
Amount: Up to $20,000.
Number of awards: 1.
Deadline: February 1.
How to apply: Applications are available online. An application form, transcript and three reference letters are required.
Exclusive: Visit www.UltimateScholarshipBook.com and enter code SO122120 for updates on this award.

(1222) • John Wright Memorial Scholarship

Tree Research and Education Endowment Fund
552 S. Washington Street, Suite 109, Naperville, IL 60540
Phone: 630-369-8300
Email: treefund@treefund.org
http://www.treefund.org

Purpose: To help undergraduate and technical college students pursuing careers in commercial arboriculture.
Eligibility: Applicants must be high school seniors entering college or community college or returning college students seeking a first bachelor's degree or associate's degree while attending an accredited U.S. college or university. All applicants must plan to enter the arboriculture industry and have a minimum 3.0 GPA. Consideration will be given for honorably discharged veterans and present members of the U.S. Armed Forces, Reserves and National Guard.
Target applicant(s): High school students. College students. Adult students.
Minimum GPA: 3.0
Amount: $2,000.
Number of awards: 1.
Deadline: May 15.
How to apply: Applications are available online.
Exclusive: Visit www.UltimateScholarshipBook.com and enter code TR122220 for updates on this award.

(1223) · Johnny Davis Memorial Scholarship

Aircraft Electronics Association
3570 NE Ralph Powell Road, Lee's Summit, MO 64064
Phone: 816-347-8400
Email: info@aea.net
http://www.aea.net
Purpose: To support students of avionics and aircraft repair.
Eligibility: Applicants must be high school seniors or college students who plan to or are attending an accredited school in an avionics or aircraft repair program.
Target applicant(s): High school students. College students. Adult students.
Amount: $1,000.
Number of awards: 1.
Deadline: February 15.
How to apply: Applications are available by contacting the organization for more information.
Exclusive: Visit www.UltimateScholarshipBook.com and enter code AI122320 for updates on this award.

(1224) · Jordan Viders Spirit of the Sea Award and Scholarship

Beneath the Sea
495 New Rochelle Road, Suite 2A, Bronxville, NY 10708
Phone: 914-664-4310
Email: scholarships@beneaththesea.org
http://www.beneaththesea.org/862
Purpose: To support young people with a passion for exploring and protecting the ocean environment.
Eligibility: Applicants must be 30 years of age or younger and on a career path to use electronics to help expand our underwater knowledge. Students should be able to explain the impact of using electronics to explore the ocean environment and their future goals within this field.
Target applicant(s): High school students. College students. Graduate school students. Adult students.
Amount: $1,000.
Number of awards: 10.
Deadline: December 15.
How to apply: Applications are available online and must include two letters of recommendation.
Exclusive: Visit www.UltimateScholarshipBook.com and enter code BE122420 for updates on this award.

(1225) · Joseph C. Johnson Memorial Grant

American Society of Certified Engineering Technicians (ASCET)
P.O. Box 95, Cape May Court House, NJ 08210
Phone: 773-242-7238
Email: general-manager@ascet.org
http://www.ascet.org/FinancialAid
Purpose: To support engineering technology students.
Eligibility: Applicants must have a minimum 3.0 GPA, be U.S. citizens or legal residents of the country in which they are currently living, be either a student, certified, regular, registered or associate member of the American Society of Certified Engineering Technicians (ASCET) and be full- or part-time students in an engineering technology program. Students in a two-year program should apply in the first year to receive the grant for their second year. Students in a four-year program who apply in the third year may receive the grant for their fourth year. Applicants must show financial need and submit three letters of recommendation.
Target applicant(s): College students. Adult students.
Minimum GPA: 3.0
Amount: $750.
Number of awards: 1.
Deadline: April 1.
How to apply: Must contact office for application.
Exclusive: Visit www.UltimateScholarshipBook.com and enter code AM122520 for updates on this award.

(1226) · Joseph Frasca Excellence in Aviation Scholarship

University Aviation Association (UAA)
Dr. David NewMyer, College of Applied Sciences and Arts, Southern Illinois University Carbondale, 1365 Douglas Drive, MC 6623, Carbondale, IL 62901-6623
Phone: 618-453-8898
Email: newmyer@siu.edu
https://www.uaa.aero/scholarships.php
Purpose: To encourage students to reach the highest level of achievement in their aviation studies.
Eligibility: Applicants must be juniors or seniors enrolled at a UAA member college or university with at least a 3.0 GPA. Students must demonstrate excellence in all areas related to aviation and have FAA certification in either aviation maintenance or flight. Applicants must be a member of at least one aviation organization and be involved in aviation activities that demonstrate interest in and enthusiasm for aviation.
Target applicant(s): College students. Adult students.
Minimum GPA: 3.0
Amount: $1,000.
Number of awards: 2.
Deadline: April 21.
How to apply: Applications are available online.
Exclusive: Visit www.UltimateScholarshipBook.com and enter code UN122620 for updates on this award.

(1227) · Joseph M. Parish Memorial Grant

American Society of Certified Engineering Technicians (ASCET)
P.O. Box 95, Cape May Court House, NJ 08210
Phone: 773-242-7238
Email: general-manager@ascet.org
http://www.ascet.org/FinancialAid
Purpose: To help engineering technology students.
Eligibility: Applicants must have a minimum 3.0 GPA, be U.S. citizens or legal residents of the country in which they are currently living, be

student members of the American Society of Certified Engineering Technicians (ASCET) and be full-time students in an engineering technology program. Applicants in a two-year program should apply in the first year to receive the grant for their second year. Students in a four-year program who apply in the third year may receive the grant for their fourth year. Applicants must show financial need. Students pursuing a BS degree in engineering are not eligible for this grant.
Target applicant(s): College students. Adult students.
Minimum GPA: 3.0
Amount: $500.
Number of awards: 1.
Scholarship may be renewable.
Deadline: April 1.
How to apply: Applications are available online.
Exclusive: Visit www.UltimateScholarshipBook.com and enter code AM122720 for updates on this award.

(1228) • Junior Showmanship Scholarship Program

American Kennel Club
260 Madison Avenue, New York, NY 10016
Phone: 212-696-8200
http://www.akc.org
Purpose: To assist students who are involved with AKC purebred dogs.
Eligibility: Applicants must be under age 18 with an AKC registered purebred dog. Selection is based on involvement with AKC registered dogs, academic achievement and financial need. The scholarship program awards a total of $150,000 annually.
Target applicant(s): Junior high students or younger. High school students.
Amount: Varies.
Number of awards: Varies.
Deadline: March 1.
How to apply: Applications are available online.
Exclusive: Visit www.UltimateScholarshipBook.com and enter code AM122820 for updates on this award.

(1229) • Kappa Delta Phi

American Occupational Therapy Foundation
Attn: Jeanne Cooper, 4720 Montgomery Lane, Suite 202, Bethesda, MD 20814
Phone: 240-292-1034
Email: jcooper@aotf.org
http://www.aotf.org/scholarshipsgrants
Purpose: To encourage students who are pursuing post-baccalaureate degrees in occupational therapy.
Eligibility: Applicants must be currently enrolled full-time in an AOTA accredited occupational therapy program. Students must have completed at least one year of occupational therapy specific course work. Priority is given to students of Arizona, California, Florida, Iowa, Indiana, Kentucky, Missouri and Ohio.
Target applicant(s): College students. Graduate school students. Adult students.
Amount: $2,000.
Number of awards: Varies.
Deadline: Varies.
How to apply: Applications are available online.
Exclusive: Visit www.UltimateScholarshipBook.com and enter code AM122920 for updates on this award.

(1230) • Karen O'Neil Memorial Scholarship

Emergency Nurses Association
915 Lee Street, Des Plaines, IL 60016
Phone: 847-460-4100
Email: foundation@ena.org
http://www.ena.org
Purpose: To promote advanced degrees in emergency nursing.
Eligibility: Applicants must be nurses pursuing an advanced degree and must have been ENA members for at least 12 months before applying.
Target applicant(s): Graduate school students. Adult students.
Amount: $3,000.
Number of awards: 1.
Deadline: April 28.
How to apply: Applications are available online.
Exclusive: Visit www.UltimateScholarshipBook.com and enter code EM123020 for updates on this award.

(1231) • Karla Girts Memorial Community Outreach Scholarship

American Dental Hygienists' Association (ADHA) Institute for Oral Health
Scholarship Award Program, 444 North Michigan Avenue, Suite 3400, Chicago, IL 60611
Phone: 312-440-8900
Email: institute@adha.net
http://www.adha.org
Purpose: To support undergraduate students and those working towards degree completion within the dental hygiene arena who are also committed to work within the geriatric population in an effort to improve the oral health of this population.
Eligibility: Applicants must be full-time students at an accredited college or university in the United States pursuing an associate, baccalaureate or degree completion program in dental hygiene or a related field and must commit to working towards improvement of oral health within the geriatric population. Applicants must have completed at least one year of a dental hygiene curriculum, be active members of the ADHA, have a minimum 3.0 GPA and have a minimum demonstrated financial need of $1,500. Selection is based upon the overall strength of the application.
Target applicant(s): College students. Graduate school students. Adult students.
Minimum GPA: 3.0
Amount: $2,000.
Number of awards: 2.
Deadline: February 1.
How to apply: Applications are available online after October 1. An application form and essay are required.
Exclusive: Visit www.UltimateScholarshipBook.com and enter code AM123120 for updates on this award.

(1232) • Kenneth Andrew Roe Scholarship

American Society of Mechanical Engineers (ASME)
Two Park Avenue, New York, NY 10016-5990
Phone: 800-843-2763
Email: lefeverb@asme.org
http://www.asme.org
Purpose: To support students who are studying mechanical engineering.
Eligibility: Applicants must be ASME student members, be enrolled in an ABET accredited mechanical engineering baccalaureate program, be North American residents and be U.S. citizens. Applicants must also

have strong academic performance, character and integrity. The award is to be used during the junior or senior undergraduate years.
Target applicant(s): College students. Adult students.
Amount: $13,000.
Number of awards: 1.
Deadline: March 1.
How to apply: Applications are available online.
Exclusive: Visit www.UltimateScholarshipBook.com and enter code AM123220 for updates on this award.

(1233) · LabRoots Scholarship

Labroots
18340 Yorba Linda Boulevard, Suite 107 PMB 427, Yorba Linda, CA 92886
https://www.labroots.com/scholarships/details/4
Purpose: To support students in STEM studies.
Eligibility: Applicants must be enrolled in or accepted for an undergraduate or graduate degree at a recognized university. Students must be seeking a degree in a STEM field.
Target applicant(s): High school students. College students. Graduate school students. Adult students.
Amount: $3,000.
Number of awards: 1.
Deadline: April 30.
How to apply: Applications are available online.
Exclusive: Visit www.UltimateScholarshipBook.com and enter code LA123320 for updates on this award.

(1234) · Landscape Forms Design for People Scholarship

Landscape Architecture Foundation
1129 20th Street NW, Suite 202, Washington, DC 20036
Phone: 202-331-7070
Email: scholarships@lafoundation.org
https://lafoundation.org/scholarship/
Purpose: To aid landscape architecture students.
Eligibility: Applicants must be full-time undergraduate students who are enrolled in a landscape architecture degree program at a school that has been accredited by the Landscape Architectural Accreditation Board (LAAB). They must be in the final year of their degree program. Selection is based on academic merit and creativity.
Target applicant(s): College students. Adult students.
Amount: $3,000.
Number of awards: 1.
Deadline: February 15.
How to apply: Applications are available online. An application form, essay, work samples and two recommendation letters are required.
Exclusive: Visit www.UltimateScholarshipBook.com and enter code LA123420 for updates on this award.

(1235) · Larry Williams Photography and AYA Photo Contest

Appaloosa Horse Club
Appaloosa Youth Association, 2720 West Pullman Road, Moscow, ID 83843
Phone: 208-882-5578
Email: youth@appaloosa.com
http://www.appaloosayouth.com/
Purpose: To support students who express their love of the Appaloosa through photography.
Eligibility: Applicants must submit multiple photographs in two divisions: 13 and under and 14 to 18.
Target applicant(s): Junior high students or younger. High school students.
Amount: Up to $100.
Number of awards: 6.
Deadline: May 1.
How to apply: Applications are available online.
Exclusive: Visit www.UltimateScholarshipBook.com and enter code AP123520 for updates on this award.

(1236) · Larson Aquatic Research Support (LARS)

American Water Works Association
6666 W. Quincy Avenue, Denver, CO 80235-3098
Phone: 800-926-7337
Email: scholarships@awwa.org
http://www.awwa.org
Purpose: To support doctoral and master's students interested in careers in the fields of corrosion control, treatment and distribution of domestic and industrial water supplies, aquatic chemistry and/or environmental chemistry.
Eligibility: Applicants must pursue an advanced (master's or doctoral) degree at an institution of higher education located in Canada, Guam, Puerto Rico, Mexico or the U.S. Applications, resumes, transcripts, GRE scores, three recommendation letters and a course of study are required. Master's students also must submit a statement of educational plans and career objectives or a research plan. Ph.D. students must submit research plans. The master's grant is $5,000, and the doctoral grant is $7,000. The award is based on academics and leadership.
Target applicant(s): Graduate school students. Adult students.
Amount: $5,000-$7,000.
Number of awards: 2.
Deadline: January 12.
How to apply: Applications are available online.
Exclusive: Visit www.UltimateScholarshipBook.com and enter code AM123620 for updates on this award.

(1237) · Lawrence C. Fortier Memorial Scholarship

Air Traffic Control Association
1101 King Street, Suite 300, Alexandria, VA 22314
Phone: 703-299-2430
Email: info@atca.org
http://www.atca.org
Purpose: To help students seeking higher education in air traffic control and other aviation disciplines.
Eligibility: Applicants must be accepted or enrolled half- to full-time at an accredited university or college with the intention of continuing studies the following year. Applicants must complete coursework towards a bachelor's degree or higher and have a minimum of 30 semester hours or 45 quarter hours left to complete before graduation. Students must pursue aviation-related courses of study.
Target applicant(s): High school students. College students. Graduate school students. Adult students.
Amount: Varies.
Number of awards: Varies.
Deadline: May 1.
How to apply: Applications are available online. An application form, two letters of reference, academic transcripts, an essay and answers to leadership and career questions are required.

Exclusive: Visit www.UltimateScholarshipBook.com and enter code AI123720 for updates on this award.

(1238) • Lawrence Ginocchio Aviation Scholarship

UAA/Barden Aviation Scholarship
1200 G Street NW, Suite 1100, Washington, DC 20005
Phone: 202-783-9250
Email: info@nbaa.org
https://www.nbaa.org/prodev/scholarships/

Purpose: To aid undergraduate aviation students of integrity.

Eligibility: Applicants must be undergraduate sophomores, juniors or seniors who are enrolled at a school that is a National Business Aviation Association (NBAA)/University Aviation Association (UAA) member institution. They must have a GPA of 3.0 or higher on a four-point scale. Applicants must demonstrate personal qualities of honor, selflessness and helping others through business aviation activities. Selection is based on the overall strength of the application.

Target applicant(s): College students. Adult students.
Minimum GPA: 3.0
Amount: $4,500.
Number of awards: 5.
Deadline: July 31.

How to apply: Applications are available online. An application form, resume, official transcript, personal essay and two recommendation letters are required.

Exclusive: Visit www.UltimateScholarshipBook.com and enter code UA123820 for updates on this award.

(1239) • Leaders Scholarship

Medical Group Management Association
104 Inverness Terrace East, Englewood, CO 80112
Phone: 877-275-6462
Email: acmpe@mgma.com
http://www.mgma.com

Purpose: To support students pursuing advanced degrees in the medical field.

Eligibility: Applicants must be enrolled in a graduate degree program pertaining to medical practice management at a university located in the U.S. Students must include transcripts, two letters of reference, curriculum and resume along with the application.

Target applicant(s): Graduate school students. Adult students.
Amount: $5,000.
Number of awards: 1.
Deadline: May 4.
How to apply: Applications are available online.

Exclusive: Visit www.UltimateScholarshipBook.com and enter code ME123920 for updates on this award.

(1240) • Lee Magnon Memorial Scholarship

National Association of Corrosion Engineers (NACE) International Foundation
15835 Park Ten Place, Houston, TX 77084-5145
Phone: 281-228-6205
Email: nace.foundation@nace.org
http://nace-foundation.org/programs/students/scholarships/

Purpose: To help outstanding students pursue a career in the field of engineering and/or science.

Eligibility: Applicants must be enrolled full-time as an undergraduate at an accredited two- or four-year college or university. Applicants must be studying engineering and/or science at their chosen school. Applicants must have permanent residence in the NACE Central Area which includes the following states: Arkansas, Colorado, Illinois, Iowa, Kansas, Louisiana, Minnesota, Missouri, Montana, Nebraska, New Mexico, North Dakota, Oklahoma, South Dakota, Texas, Wisconsin and Wyoming.

Target applicant(s): College students. Adult students.
Amount: $2,500.
Number of awards: 1.
Deadline: January 1.

How to apply: Applications are available online. An application form, two recommendation forms, an academic transcript and scholarship essay questions are required.

Exclusive: Visit www.UltimateScholarshipBook.com and enter code NA124020 for updates on this award.

(1241) • Lee S. Evans Scholarship

National Housing Endowment
1201 15th Street NW, Washington, DC 20005
Phone: 202-266-8069
Email: Scholarships@nahb.org
http://www.nationalhousingendowment.org

Purpose: To aid students who are preparing for careers in residential construction management.

Eligibility: Applicants must be full-time undergraduate or graduate students. They must have completed at least one semester of college coursework at the time of applying for the scholarship and must have at least one year remaining in their programs of study at the time of award disbursement; fifth-year seniors are ineligible. Applicants must have a demonstrated interest in pursuing a career in the residential construction industry. Preference will be given to current student members of the National Association of Home Builders (NAHB) and to applicants who are enrolled in a four-year degree program that focuses on construction management. Selection is based on academic merit, recommendations, extracurricular activities, work experience and financial need.

Target applicant(s): College students. Graduate school students. Adult students.
Amount: Varies.
Number of awards: Varies.
Scholarship may be renewable.
Deadline: March 28.

How to apply: Applications are available online. An application form, an official transcript, a degree program outline and two letters of recommendation are required.

Exclusive: Visit www.UltimateScholarshipBook.com and enter code NA124120 for updates on this award.

(1242) • Lee Tarbox Memorial Scholarship

Aircraft Electronics Association
3570 NE Ralph Powell Road, Lee's Summit, MO 64064
Phone: 816-347-8400
Email: info@aea.net
http://www.aea.net

Purpose: To support students of avionics and aircraft repair.

Eligibility: Applicants must be high school seniors or college students who plan to or are attending an accredited school in an avionics or aircraft repair program.

Target applicant(s): High school students. College students. Adult students.
Amount: $2,500.
Number of awards: 1.
Deadline: April 1.

How to apply: Applications are available by contacting the organization for more information.
Exclusive: Visit www.UltimateScholarshipBook.com and enter code AI124220 for updates on this award.

(1243) • Len Assante Scholarship Fund

National Ground Water Association
601 Dempsey Road, Westerville, OH 43081-8978
Phone: 800-551-7379
Email: ngwa@ngwa.org
http://www.ngwa.org
Purpose: To support students in fields related to the ground water industry.
Eligibility: Applicants must be high school graduates or college students with a minimum 2.5 GPA who are studying fields related to the ground water industry including geology, hydrology, hydrogeology, environmental sciences or microbiology or well drilling two-year associate degree programs.
Target applicant(s): High school students. College students. Adult students.
Minimum GPA: 2.5
Amount: Up to $5,000.
Number of awards: Varies.
Deadline: January 15.
How to apply: Applications are available by mail or e-mail.
Exclusive: Visit www.UltimateScholarshipBook.com and enter code NA124320 for updates on this award.

(1244) • Lewis C. Hoffman Scholarship

American Ceramic Society
600 North Cleveland Avenue, Suite 210, Westerville, OH 43082
Phone: 866-721-3322
Email: mstout@ceramics.org
http://www.ceramics.org
Purpose: To support undergraduate ceramics and materials science and engineering students.
Eligibility: Applicants must be full-time undergraduates who will have completed 70 or more semester credits (or quarter credit equivalent) at the time of award disbursement. Selection is based on essay response, GPA, recommendation letter, extracurricular involvements and standardized test scores (if available).
Target applicant(s): College students. Adult students.
Amount: $2,000.
Number of awards: 1.
Deadline: May 15.
How to apply: This scholarship does not require an application form. The applicant's essay response, a recommendation letter and a list of extracurricular activities is required.
Exclusive: Visit www.UltimateScholarshipBook.com and enter code AM124420 for updates on this award.

(1245) • Lewis W. Newlan Award

RCI Foundation
Phone: 507-931-1682
Email: rcif@scholarshipamerica.org
http://www.rcifoundation.org
Purpose: To support students pursuing a career in the construction or building envelope industry.
Eligibility: Applicants must be current undergraduate or graduate level students who have completed a minimum of 24 credit hours. Students must enroll full-time at an accredited college, university, vocational or technical school for the entire academic year in an architecture, engineering, construction or building science program. A minimum 2.75 GPA is required. Applicants must be U.S. or Canadian citizens.
Target applicant(s): College students. Graduate school students. Adult students.
Minimum GPA: 2.75
Amount: $2,500.
Number of awards: 10.
Deadline: February 28.
How to apply: Applications are available online.
Exclusive: Visit www.UltimateScholarshipBook.com and enter code RC124520 for updates on this award.

(1246) • Libbie H Hyman Memorial Scholarship

Society for Integrative and Comparative Biology
1313 Dolley Madison Boulevard, Suite 402, McLean, VA 22101
Phone: 703-790-1745
http://www.sicb.org/grants/hyman/
Purpose: To support students seeking field station experience to study invertebrates.
Eligibility: Applicants must be first- or second-year graduate students or advanced undergraduates seeking to carry on invertebrate research at a marine, freshwater or terrestrial field station. Students must complete the application including a proposal, two letters of reference and transcripts.
Target applicant(s): College students. Graduate school students. Adult students.
Amount: Varies.
Number of awards: Varies.
Deadline: February 5.
How to apply: Applications are available online.
Exclusive: Visit www.UltimateScholarshipBook.com and enter code SO124620 for updates on this award.

(1247) • Liberty Mutual Safety Research Fellowship Program

American Society of Safety Engineers
520 N. Northwest Highway, Park Ridge, IL 60068
Phone: 847-699-2929
Email: tshaunnessey@asse.org
http://foundation.asse.org/
Purpose: To award research fellowships to promote safety research.
Eligibility: Applicants must be U.S. citizens and either have their Ph.D. or be working toward a masters or Ph.D. Preference is given to applicants working within an ABET-accredited safety program. The selection committee prefers applied safety/health research with a broad appeal and gives special consideration to ASSE members. Recipients must spend four to six weeks during the summer at the Liberty Mutual Research Center, in Hopkinton, MA, and write an article on their research or an outline for a grant proposal to continue the research.
Target applicant(s): Graduate school students. Adult students.
Amount: Up to $15,000 stipend.
Number of awards: Varies.
Deadline: December 1.
How to apply: Applications are available online.
Exclusive: Visit www.UltimateScholarshipBook.com and enter code AM124720 for updates on this award.

(1248) • Light Metals Division Scholarship

Minerals, Metals and Materials Society
184 Thorn Hill Road, Warrendale, PA 15086
Phone: 724-776-9000
Email: students@tms.org
http://www.tms.org

Purpose: To aid undergraduate students who are majoring in metallurgical engineering or materials science and engineering.

Eligibility: Applicants must be full-time undergraduate sophomores or juniors who are enrolled in a degree program in metallurgical engineering or materials science and engineering. They must be student members of TMS, The Minerals, Metals and Materials Society. Selection is based on academic merit, extracurricular activities, recommendations and personal statement.

Target applicant(s): College students. Adult students.
Amount: $4,000.
Number of awards: 3.
Deadline: March 15.
How to apply: Applications are available online. An application form, transcript, personal statement and three recommendation letters are required.
Exclusive: Visit www.UltimateScholarshipBook.com and enter code MI124820 for updates on this award.

(1249) • Lisa Zaken Award For Excellence

Institute of Industrial and Systems Engineers
3577 Parkway Lane, Suite 200, Norcross, GA 30092
Phone: 800-494-0460
Email: bcameron@iienet.org
http://www.iise.org/

Purpose: To reward excellence in scholarly activities and leadership related to the industrial engineering profession on campus.

Eligibility: Applicants must be undergraduate or graduate students with at least one year remaining, have a 3.0 or higher GPA, major in industrial engineering and be active members who have been leaders in IIE. Students may not apply directly for this scholarship and must be nominated. The award is based on academic ability and leadership related to industrial engineering.

Target applicant(s): College students. Graduate school students. Adult students.
Minimum GPA: 3.0
Amount: $2,500.
Number of awards: 1.
Deadline: November 15.
How to apply: Nomination forms are available online.
Exclusive: Visit www.UltimateScholarshipBook.com and enter code IN124920 for updates on this award.

(1250) • Lockheed Martin/HENAAC Scholars Program

Great Minds in STEM (HENAAC)
602 Monterey Pass Road, Monterey Park, CA 91754
Phone: 323-262-0997
Email: jcano@greatmindsinstem.org
http://www.greatmindsinstem.org

Purpose: To aid computer science and engineering students.

Eligibility: Applicants must be U.S. citizens or permanent residents and full-time students who are majoring in computer science or aerospace, electrical, mechanical, software or systems engineering. They must have a GPA of 3.0 or higher. Applicants are not required to be Hispanic but must demonstrate strong leadership and involvement in the Hispanic community. Selection is based on the overall strength of the application.

Target applicant(s): High school students. College students. Adult students.
Minimum GPA: 3.0
Amount: $500-$10,000.
Number of awards: Varies.
Scholarship may be renewable.
Deadline: April 30.
How to apply: Applications are available online. An application form, official transcript, recommendation letters, personal essay and resume are required.
Exclusive: Visit www.UltimateScholarshipBook.com and enter code GR125020 for updates on this award.

(1251) • Lois Britt Pork Industry Memorial Scholarship Program

National Pork Producers Council
122 C Street, NW, Suite 875, Washington, DC 20001
Phone: 202-347-3600
Email: Boellingc@nppc.org
http://www.nppc.org

Purpose: To support students who are preparing for careers in the pork industry.

Eligibility: Applicants must be undergraduates enrolled in either a two-year swine program or a four-year college of agriculture. They must be interested in pursuing a career in the pork industry. Selection is based on the strength of the personal essay.

Target applicant(s): College students. Adult students.
Amount: Varies.
Number of awards: Varies.
Deadline: January 6.
How to apply: Applications are available online. An information sheet, cover letter, personal essay and two reference letters are required.
Exclusive: Visit www.UltimateScholarshipBook.com and enter code NA125120 for updates on this award.

(1252) • Long-Term Member Sponsored Scholarship

Society of Automotive Engineers International
Scholarships Program, 400 Commonwealth Drive, Warrendale, PA 15096
Phone: 724-776-4841
Email: scholarships@sae.org
http://students.sae.org/scholarships/

Purpose: This scholarship recognizes outstanding SAE student members who actively support SAE and its activities.

Eligibility: Applicants must be college juniors and student members of SAE, major in engineering and actively support SAE and its programs. The scholarship will be awarded purely on the basis of the student's support for SAE and its programs.

Target applicant(s): College students. Adult students.
Amount: $1,000.
Number of awards: Varies.
Deadline: March 15.
How to apply: Applications are available online.
Exclusive: Visit www.UltimateScholarshipBook.com and enter code SO125220 for updates on this award.

(1253) • Louis Agassiz Fuertes Award

Wilson Ornithological Society
Department of Biology and Biomedical Science, Dr. James Chace, Associate Professor, 100 Ochre Point Avenue, Newport, RI 02840-4192
Email: rbpayne@umich.edu
http://www.wilsonsociety.org
Purpose: To support ornithologists' research.
Eligibility: Applicants must be students or young professionals doing avian research. Applicants must be willing to report their research results at an annual meeting of the Wilson Ornithological Society.
Target applicant(s): High school students. College students. Graduate school students. Adult students.
Amount: $2,500.
Number of awards: Up to 2.
Deadline: February 1.
How to apply: Applications are available online.
Exclusive: Visit www.UltimateScholarshipBook.com and enter code WI125320 for updates on this award.

(1254) • Lowell Gaylor Memorial Scholarship

Aircraft Electronics Association
3570 NE Ralph Powell Road, Lee's Summit, MO 64064
Phone: 816-347-8400
Email: info@aea.net
http://www.aea.net
Purpose: To support students of avionics and aircraft repair.
Eligibility: Applicants must be high school seniors or college students who plan to or are attending an accredited school in an avionics or aircraft repair program.
Target applicant(s): High school students. College students. Adult students.
Amount: $1,000.
Number of awards: 1.
Deadline: February 15.
How to apply: Applications are available by contacting the organization for more information.
Exclusive: Visit www.UltimateScholarshipBook.com and enter code AI125420 for updates on this award.

(1255) • Lowell H. and Dorothy Loving Undergraduate Scholarship

National Society of Professional Surveyors (NSPS/AAGS)
Attn: Scholarships, 5119 Pegasus Court, Suite Q, Frederick, MD 21704
Phone: 240-439-4615x105
Email: trisha.milburn@nsps.us.com
http://www.nsps.us.com/?page=Scholarships
Purpose: To aid undergraduate surveying and mapping students.
Eligibility: Applicants must be members of the National Society of Professional Surveyors (NSPS). They must be undergraduate juniors or seniors who are enrolled in a surveying and mapping degree program at a four-year institution located in the U.S. They must have a plan of study that includes coursework in two or more of the following areas: spatial measurement system analysis and design, land surveying, photogrammetry and remote sensing or geometric geodesy. Selection is based on academic merit, personal statement, recommendation letters, professional involvement and financial need.
Target applicant(s): College students. Adult students.
Amount: $2,000.
Number of awards: 1.
Scholarship may be renewable.
Deadline: Varies.
How to apply: Applications are available online. An application form, personal statement, proof of ACSM membership, three letters of recommendation and an official transcript are required.
Exclusive: Visit www.UltimateScholarshipBook.com and enter code NA125520 for updates on this award.

(1256) • Loy McCandless Marks Scholarship in Tropical Horticulture

Garden Club of America
14 East 60th Street, New York, NY 10022
Phone: 212-753-8287
Email: scholarshipapplications@gcamerica.org
https://www.gcamerica.org/index.cfm/scholarships/details/id/19
Purpose: To promote the study of tropical plants in horticulture and landscape architecture.
Eligibility: Applicants must be U.S. citizens or permanent residents enrolled in a U.S. institution as a graduate or advanced undergraduate. Students must use the award to study abroad within one year.
Target applicant(s): College students. Graduate school students. Adult students.
Amount: $5,000.
Number of awards: 1.
Deadline: February 1.
How to apply: Applications are available online.
Exclusive: Visit www.UltimateScholarshipBook.com and enter code GA125620 for updates on this award.

(1257) • LTK Engineering Services Scholarship

Conference of Minority Transportation Officials
100 M Street SE, Suite 917, Washington, DC 20003
Phone: 202-857-8065
Email: info@comto.org
http://www.comto.org/page/Scholarships
Purpose: To support students who are majoring in engineering or other technical fields related to transportation.
Eligibility: Applicants must either be current COMTO members or be willing to join within 30 days of receiving the scholarship. Students must be at least in their junior year of college or in graduate school, and they must have at least a 3.0 GPA. Applicants must be enrolled in at least twelve credits per semester. Students must submit a short essay and two letters of recommendation.
Target applicant(s): College students. Graduate school students. Adult students.
Minimum GPA: 3.0
Amount: $6,000.
Number of awards: 1.
Deadline: March 10.
How to apply: Applications are available online.
Exclusive: Visit www.UltimateScholarshipBook.com and enter code CO125720 for updates on this award.

(1258) • Ludo Frevel Crystallography Scholarships

International Centre for Diffraction Data
12 Campus Boulevard, Newtown Square, PA 19073
http://www.icdd.com
Purpose: To support graduate students in crystallography-related fields.

Eligibility: Applicants must be graduate students enrolled in a degree program relating to crystallography. Students must submit a proposed research project along with their application.
Target applicant(s): Graduate school students. Adult students.
Amount: $2,500.
Number of awards: Varies.
Deadline: October 17.
How to apply: Applications are available online.
Exclusive: Visit www.UltimateScholarshipBook.com and enter code IN125820 for updates on this award.

(1259) • Making the Future Scholarship

Cognizant
125 Jeffrey Avenue, Holliston, MA 01746
Phone: 508-429-0700
http://www.cognizant.com
Purpose: To support undergraduate students who are pursuing a degree in science, technology, engineering or mathematics.
Eligibility: Applicants must submit documentation of a STEM project that demonstrates creativity and innovation. A minimum GPA of 2.5 is required. Selection is primarily based on project design, presentation and mastery of skills.
Target applicant(s): High school students. College students. Adult students.
Minimum GPA: 2.5
Amount: $5,000.
Number of awards: Varies.
Deadline: March 31.
How to apply: Applications are available online.
Exclusive: Visit www.UltimateScholarshipBook.com and enter code CO125920 for updates on this award.

(1260) • Mandell and Lester Rosenblatt Undergraduate Scholarship

Society of Naval Architects and Marine Engineers
99 Canal Center Plaza, Suite 310, Alexandria, VA 22314
Phone: 201-798-4800
Email: efaustino@sname.org
http://www.sname.org/educationoptions/scholarships
Purpose: To assist college undergraduates who are studying marine industry fields.
Eligibility: Applicants must be U.S., Canadian or international college students who are members of the SNAME and are working towards degrees in naval architecture, marine engineering, ocean engineering or marine industry related areas fields. An application form, three recommendation letters and an essay are required.
Target applicant(s): High school students. College students. Adult students.
Amount: Up to $6,000.
Number of awards: 1.
Scholarship may be renewable.
Deadline: June 1.
How to apply: Applications are available online.
Exclusive: Visit www.UltimateScholarshipBook.com and enter code SO126020 for updates on this award.

(1261) • Marliave Fund

Association of Engineering Geologists Foundation Marliave Fund
P.O. Box 161683, Boiling Springs, SC 29316
Email: staff@aegfoundation.org
http://www.aegfoundation.org
Purpose: To reward outstanding students in engineering geology and geological engineering.
Eligibility: Applicants must be seniors or graduate students in a college or university program directly applicable to geological engineering and be members of the Association of Engineering Geologists.
Target applicant(s): College students. Graduate school students. Adult students.
Amount: Varies.
Number of awards: 1.
Deadline: February 1.
How to apply: Applications are available online or by written request.
Exclusive: Visit www.UltimateScholarshipBook.com and enter code AS126120 for updates on this award.

(1262) • Marshall E. McCullough Scholarship

National Dairy Shrine
P.O. Box 725, Denmark, WI 54208
Phone: 920-863-6333
Email: info@dairyshrine.org
http://www.dairyshrine.org
Purpose: To support students who plan careers in agricultural-related communications.
Eligibility: Applicants must be high school seniors planning to enter a four-year university with intent to major in the dairy or animal sciences with a communications emphasis or agricultural journalism with a dairy or animal science emphasis, and they must intend to work in the dairy industry following graduation.
Target applicant(s): High school students.
Amount: $1,500-$2,000.
Number of awards: 2.
Deadline: April 15.
How to apply: Applications are available online.
Exclusive: Visit www.UltimateScholarshipBook.com and enter code NA126220 for updates on this award.

(1263) • Marvin Mundel Memorial Scholarship

Institute of Industrial and Systems Engineers
3577 Parkway Lane, Suite 200, Norcross, GA 30092
Phone: 800-494-0460
Email: bcameron@iienet.org
http://www.iise.org/
Purpose: To assist undergraduate engineering students with an interest in work measurement and methods engineering.
Eligibility: Applicants must be full-time undergraduate students enrolled in a college in the United States, Canada or Mexico with an accredited industrial engineering program, major in industrial engineering and be active members. Students may not apply directly for this scholarship and must be nominated. The award is based on academic ability, character, leadership, potential service to the industrial engineering profession and financial need. Preference is given to students with a demonstrated interest in work measurement and methods engineering.
Target applicant(s): High school students. College students. Adult students.
Minimum GPA: 3.4
Amount: $1,250.
Number of awards: 2.
Deadline: November 15.
How to apply: Nomination forms are available online.

Exclusive: Visit www.UltimateScholarshipBook.com and enter code IN126320 for updates on this award.

(1264) • Mary Rhein Memorial Scholarship

Mu Alpha Theta Scholarship Committee
c/o University of Oklahoma , 3200 Marshall Avenue, Suite 190, Norman, OK 73019
Phone: 405-325-4489
Email: matheta@ou.edu
http://www.mualphatheta.org

Purpose: To aid graduating high school seniors who are active Mu Alpha Theta members.

Eligibility: Applicants must be graduating high school seniors who are outstanding mathematics students. They must be active Mu Alpha Theta members who have been of service in the area of mathematics and who have participated in local, regional or national mathematics competitions. Applicants must have plans to pursue a mathematics-related career. Selection is based on the overall strength of the application.

Target applicant(s): High school students. College students. Adult students.

Amount: $5,000.

Number of awards: 1.

Deadline: March 1.

How to apply: Applications are available online. An application form, student essay, official transcript and three recommendation letters are required.

Exclusive: Visit www.UltimateScholarshipBook.com and enter code MU126420 for updates on this award.

(1265) • Mary V. Munger Scholarship

Society of Women Engineers
130 East Randolph Street, Suite 3500, Chicago, IL 60601
Phone: 877-793-4636
Email: scholarships@swe.org
http://societyofwomenengineers.swe.org/scholarships

Purpose: To support female students working towards a major in engineering.

Eligibility: Applicants must be planning to study at an ABET-accredited program in engineering, technology or computing and have a minimum 3.0 GPA. The award may be used during the junior or senior year of college and is open to re-entry or adult students.

Target applicant(s): College students. Adult students.

Minimum GPA: 3.0

Amount: $2,750.

Number of awards: 2.

Deadline: February 15.

How to apply: Applications are available online.

Exclusive: Visit www.UltimateScholarshipBook.com and enter code SO126520 for updates on this award.

(1266) • Masonic-Range Science Scholarship

Society for Range Management (SRM)
10030 W. 27th Avenue, Wheat Ridge, CO 80215-6601
Phone: 303-986-3309
Email: vtrujillo@rangelands.org
http://www.rangelands.org

Purpose: To help a high school senior, college freshman or college sophomore majoring in range science or a closely related field.

Eligibility: Applicants must be sponsored by a member of the Society for Range Management (SRM), the National Association of Conservation Districts (NACD) or the Soil and Water Conservation Society (SWCS). Applicants must also submit an application form, transcript, SAT or ACT scores and two letters of reference.

Target applicant(s): High school students. College students. Adult students.

Amount: Varies.

Number of awards: Varies.

Deadline: January 6.

How to apply: Applications are available online.

Exclusive: Visit www.UltimateScholarshipBook.com and enter code SO126620 for updates on this award.

(1267) • Materials Processing and Manufacturing Division Scholarship

Minerals, Metals and Materials Society
184 Thorn Hill Road, Warrendale, PA 15086
Phone: 724-776-9000
Email: students@tms.org
http://www.tms.org

Purpose: To aid undergraduate student members of TMS who are majoring in metallurgical engineering or materials science and engineering.

Eligibility: Applicants must be full-time undergraduate sophomores or juniors whose studies must be focused on the integration of process control technology into manufacturing, materials technology research or the manufacturing process. Selection is based on academic merit, personal statement, recommendations, leadership skills, extracurricular activities and coursework relevance.

Target applicant(s): College students. Adult students.

Amount: $2,500.

Number of awards: 2.

Deadline: March 15.

How to apply: Applications are available online. An application form, personal statement, three recommendation letters and a transcript are required.

Exclusive: Visit www.UltimateScholarshipBook.com and enter code MI126720 for updates on this award.

(1268) • Medical Scrubs Collection

Medical Scrubs Collection
1665 Corporate Road West, Lakewood, NJ 08701
Phone: 888-567-2782
Email: scholarships@medicalscrubscollection.com
https://medicalscrubscollection.com/scholarship-program

Purpose: To reward students pursuing medical education.

Eligibility: Applicants must be U.S. citizens or registered aliens. Students must be high school seniors or currently enrolled in an accredited U.S. post-secondary institution. Applicants must have a minimum grade point average of 3.0 and intend to pursue a degree in a medical field.

Target applicant(s): High school students. College students. Adult students.

Minimum GPA: 3.0

Amount: $1,000.

Number of awards: 1.

Deadline: December 15.

How to apply: Applications are available online.

Exclusive: Visit www.UltimateScholarshipBook.com and enter code ME126820 for updates on this award.

(1269) · Medical Student Training in Aging Research (MSTAR) Program

American Federation for Aging Research (AFAR)
55 West 39th Street, 16th Floor, New York, NY 10018
Phone: 212-703-9977
Email: grants@afar.org
http://www.afar.org
Purpose: To support early medical students who demonstrate an interest in geriatric medicine or age-related research with an opportunity to serve under top experts in the field.
Eligibility: Applicants must be osteopathic or allopathic students who have completed at least one year of medical school at a U.S. institution. Students must have a faculty sponsor from their home institution. The program lasts 8 to 12 weeks, and monthly stipends are provided.
Target applicant(s): Graduate school students. Adult students.
Amount: $1,980 per month.
Number of awards: Up to 100.
Deadline: January 27.
How to apply: Applications are available online.
Exclusive: Visit www.UltimateScholarshipBook.com and enter code AM126920 for updates on this award.

(1270) · Melvin J. Schiff Fellowship Fund

National Association of Corrosion Engineers (NACE) International Foundation
15835 Park Ten Place, Houston, TX 77084-5145
Phone: 281-228-6205
Email: nace.foundation@nace.org
http://nace-foundation.org/programs/students/scholarships/
Purpose: To help an outstanding student, professional or technician interested in furthering their knowledge of corrosion and corrosion control.
Eligibility: Applicants must be a permanent resident of the U.S. and be professionals, technicians or full- or part-time students enrolled in an accredited U.S. college or university. Selection is based on the overall strength of the application.
Target applicant(s): College students. Graduate school students. Adult students.
Amount: $1,000.
Number of awards: 1.
Deadline: January 5.
How to apply: Applications are available online. An application form, two recommendation forms, an academic transcript and essay scholarship questions are required.
Exclusive: Visit www.UltimateScholarshipBook.com and enter code NA127020 for updates on this award.

(1271) · Melvin R. Green Scholarships

American Society of Mechanical Engineers (ASME)
Two Park Avenue, New York, NY 10016-5990
Phone: 800-843-2763
Email: lefeverb@asme.org
http://www.asme.org
Purpose: To support mechanical engineering students.
Eligibility: Applicants must have outstanding character and integrity, be ASME student members, be enrolled in an eligible accredited mechanical engineering baccalaureate program, be college sophomores, juniors, seniors or graduate students and have strong academic performance. Selection is based on scholastic ability, leadership, financial need and potential contribution to mechanical engineering profession.
Target applicant(s): College students. Graduate school students. Adult students.
Amount: $4,000.
Number of awards: Up to 2.
Deadline: March 1.
How to apply: Applications are available online.
Exclusive: Visit www.UltimateScholarshipBook.com and enter code AM127120 for updates on this award.

(1272) · Members-at-Large Reentry Award

Iota Sigma Pi (ISP)
Dr. Joanne Bedlek-Anslow, MAL Coordinator, Camden High School, Science, 1022 Ehrenclou Drive, Camden, SC 29020
http://www.iotasigmapi.info
Purpose: To recognize potential achievement in chemistry and related fields for a woman undergraduate or graduate student who has been absent from academia for at least three years.
Eligibility: Applicants must be female undergraduate or graduate students at an accredited four-year institution and be nominated by a faculty member or an Iota Sigma Pi member.
Target applicant(s): College students. Graduate school students. Adult students.
Amount: $1,500.
Number of awards: 1.
Deadline: February 15.
How to apply: Application information is available online.
Exclusive: Visit www.UltimateScholarshipBook.com and enter code IO127220 for updates on this award.

(1273) · Meredith Thoms Memorial Scholarship

Society of Women Engineers
130 East Randolph Street, Suite 3500, Chicago, IL 60601
Phone: 877-793-4636
Email: scholarships@swe.org
http://societyofwomenengineers.swe.org/scholarships
Purpose: To support female students pursuing a college degree in engineering.
Eligibility: Applicants must be enrolled in an accredited engineering or engineering technology program with a 3.0 GPA. The award may be used during the sophomore, junior or senior year of college.
Target applicant(s): College students. Adult students.
Minimum GPA: 3.0
Amount: $2,700.
Number of awards: 5.
Deadline: February 15.
How to apply: Applications are available online.
Exclusive: Visit www.UltimateScholarshipBook.com and enter code SO127320 for updates on this award.

(1274) · MG2 Scholarship

Planning and Visual Education Partnership (PAVE) c/o Kroger Company
PAVE Entries Attn.: Ken Pray, 1014 Vine Street, Cincinnati, OH 45202
Email: info@paveglobal.org
http://paveglobal.org/Competitions.aspx?typeid=26
Purpose: To support students with potential in the fields of interior design and architecture.
Eligibility: Applicants must be currently enrolled in a program working toward a degree in interior design or architecture specifically for the

retail industry. Students must have at least a 3.0 GPA. Applicants must currently be taking at least 12 credit hours. Students must be U.S. citizens studying within the United States.
Target applicant(s): College students. Adult students.
Minimum GPA: 3.0
Amount: $2,500.
Number of awards: Varies.
Deadline: March 1.
How to apply: Applications are available online.
Exclusive: Visit www.UltimateScholarshipBook.com and enter code PL127420 for updates on this award.

(1275) • MGMA Midwest Section Scholarship

Medical Group Management Association
104 Inverness Terrace East, Englewood, CO 80112
Phone: 877-275-6462
Email: acmpe@mgma.com
http://www.mgma.com
Purpose: To aid MGMA Midwest Section members who are pursuing higher education in a subject that is related to medical practice management.
Eligibility: Applicants must be members of the Medical Group Management Association (MGMA). They must be residents of one of the MGMA Midwest Section states, namely Illinois, Indiana, Iowa, Michigan, Minnesota, Nebraska, North Dakota, Ohio, South Dakota or Wisconsin. They must be undergraduate or graduate students who are enrolled in a degree program that is related to medical practice management (such as public health, business administration or health care administration). Selection is based on the overall strength of the application.
Target applicant(s): High school students. College students. Graduate school students. Adult students.
Amount: $2,500.
Number of awards: Varies.
Deadline: May 1.
How to apply: Applications are available online. An application form and supporting materials are required.
Exclusive: Visit www.UltimateScholarshipBook.com and enter code ME127520 for updates on this award.

(1276) • MGMA Western Section Scholarship

Medical Group Management Association
104 Inverness Terrace East, Englewood, CO 80112
Phone: 877-275-6462
Email: acmpe@mgma.com
http://www.mgma.com
Purpose: To aid MGMA Western Section members who are pursuing higher education in subjects that are related to medical practice management.
Eligibility: Applicants must be residents of one of the MGMA Western Section states, namely Alaska, Arizona, California, Colorado, Hawaii, Idaho, Montana, Nevada, New Mexico, Oregon, Utah, Washington or Wyoming. They must be undergraduate or graduate students who are enrolled in a degree program relating to medical practice management (such as public health, business administration or health care administration). Selection is based on the overall strength of the application.
Target applicant(s): High school students. College students. Graduate school students. Adult students.
Amount: $2,500.
Number of awards: Varies.
Deadline: May 1.
How to apply: Applications are available online. An application form and supporting materials are required.
Exclusive: Visit www.UltimateScholarshipBook.com and enter code ME127620 for updates on this award.

(1277) • Michael Kidger Memorial Scholarship

International Society for Optical Engineering
P.O. Box 10, Bellingham, WA 98227-0010
Phone: 360-676-3290
Email: scholarships@spie.org
http://www.spie.org
Purpose: To support students in the optical design field.
Eligibility: Applicants must be in the optical design field and must have one year remaining of their studies. Students must submit a summary of their academic background and interest in optical design and two letters of recommendation.
Target applicant(s): College students. Adult students.
Amount: $5,000.
Number of awards: 1.
Deadline: March 31.
How to apply: Applications are available online.
Exclusive: Visit www.UltimateScholarshipBook.com and enter code IN127720 for updates on this award.

(1278) • Michael Moody Fitness Scholarship

Michael Moody Fitness
900 N. North Branch Street, Chicago, IL 60642
Phone: 773-484-8094
Email: michael@michaelmoodyfitness.com
http://www.michaelmoodyfitness.com/student-scholarship-chicago/
Purpose: To support students seeking a career in health and fitness related fields.
Eligibility: Applicants must be U.S. citizens or legal residents and be a current high school senior, undergraduate or graduate level student planning on enrolling in an accredited college or university full-time in the upcoming school year. Students should be able to demonstrate that they have outstanding achievement in school, as well as participation and leadership in school activities and work experience. Applicants should be pursuing a degree in one of the following: athletic training, personal training, physical education teaching and coaching, health and physical fitness, exercise science, sports and recreation management, health sciences or another related field.
Target applicant(s): High school students. College students. Graduate school students. Adult students.
Amount: $1,500.
Number of awards: 1.
Deadline: July 15.
How to apply: Applications are available online and must include details of outstanding achievement in school, list of school and community activities, work experience and current high school or university cumulative GPA on a 4.0 scale. Only electronic applications will be considered. Only the first 1,000 applications will be considered.
Exclusive: Visit www.UltimateScholarshipBook.com and enter code MI127820 for updates on this award.

(1279) • Microsoft Tuition Scholarships

Microsoft Corporation
One Microsoft Way, Redmond, WA 98052-8303
Phone: 800-642-7676

Email: scholars@microsoft.com
https://careers.microsoft.com
Purpose: Offering more than a half-million dollars in scholarships, Microsoft is looking for undergraduates who display an interest in the software industry and are committed to leadership.
Eligibility: Applicants must be in a full-time undergraduate program in computer science and related STEM (Science, Technology, Engineering and Math) disciplines. Recipients will have to complete salaried internships in Redmond, Washington. There are special scholarships for women, minorities and disabled students.
Target applicant(s): College students. Adult students.
Minimum GPA: 3.0
Amount: Varies.
Number of awards: Varies.
Deadline: February 9.
How to apply: Application requirements are online.
Exclusive: Visit www.UltimateScholarshipBook.com and enter code MI127920 for updates on this award.

(1280) • Mid-Continent Instruments and Avionics Scholarship

Aircraft Electronics Association
3570 NE Ralph Powell Road, Lee's Summit, MO 64064
Phone: 816-347-8400
Email: info@aea.net
http://www.aea.net
Purpose: To support students who wish to pursue a career in avionics or aircraft repair.
Eligibility: Applicants must be high school seniors or college students who plan to or are attending an accredited school in an avionics or aircraft repair program.
Target applicant(s): High school students. College students. Adult students.
Amount: $1,000.
Number of awards: 1.
Deadline: April 1.
How to apply: Applications are available by contacting the organization for more information.
Exclusive: Visit www.UltimateScholarshipBook.com and enter code AI128020 for updates on this award.

(1281) • MIE Solutions

MIE Solutions
13252 Garden Grove Boulevard, Suite 215, Garden Grove, CA 92843
Phone: 714-786-6230
Email: support@mie-solutions.com
https://www.mie-solutions.com/scholarship-opportunity/
Purpose: To support students pursuing computer science and engineering studies.
Eligibility: Applicants must be legal U.S. residents currently attending an accredited U.S. college or university or a graduating senior enrolling in an accredited post-secondary institution. Students must provide an essay or presentation regarding their interest in computer science.
Target applicant(s): High school students. College students. Adult students.
Amount: $500.
Number of awards: 1.
Deadline: August 15.
How to apply: Applications are available online.
Exclusive: Visit www.UltimateScholarshipBook.com and enter code MI128120 for updates on this award.

(1282) • Migrant Health Scholarships

National Center for Farmworker Health Inc.
Migrant Health Scholarship, 1770 FM 967, Buda, TX 78610
Phone: 512-312-2700
Email: favre@ncfh.org
http://www.ncfh.org/scholarships.html
Purpose: To aid migrant health center staff who wish to pursue higher education in health care.
Eligibility: Applicants must be employees at a migrant/community health center. They must be interested in seeking further training in health care. Special consideration will be given to applicants who have a family background in farm working. Selection is based on demonstrated professional commitment to migrant health, stated career goals and personal experiences.
Target applicant(s): High school students. College students. Graduate school students. Adult students.
Amount: Varies.
Number of awards: Varies.
Deadline: Varies.
How to apply: Applications are available online. An application form and supporting materials are required.
Exclusive: Visit www.UltimateScholarshipBook.com and enter code NA128220 for updates on this award.

(1283) • Minority Dental Student Scholarship

American Dental Association Foundation
211 East Chicago Avenue, Chicago, IL 60611
Phone: 312-440-2763
Email: famularor@ada.org
http://www.ada.org
Purpose: To encourage minority students to pursue careers in dental hygiene, dental assisting, dentistry and dental laboratory technology.
Eligibility: Applicants must be African American, Hispanic or Native American full-time students in their second year in an accredited dental program and must demonstrate a minimum financial need of $2,500. Applicants must submit applications, two reference forms, enrollment letters and biographies. Selection is based on financial need, academic achievement, biographical sketch and references. A minimum 3.25 GPA is required. Only two scholarship applications per school are allowed, so schools may set their own in-school application deadlines that are earlier.
Target applicant(s): College students. Adult students.
Minimum GPA: 3.25
Amount: Up to $2,500.
Number of awards: Up to 25.
Deadline: Second Friday in November.
How to apply: Applications are available from dental school officials.
Exclusive: Visit www.UltimateScholarshipBook.com and enter code AM128320 for updates on this award.

(1284) • Minority Fellowship Program

American Nurses Association (ANA)
8515 Georgia Avenue, Suite 400, Silver Spring, MD 20910-3492
Phone: 301-628-5247
Email: mfp@ana.org
http://www.nursingworld.org
Purpose: To provide stipends and tuition assistance to nurses studying minority psychiatric-mental health and substance abuse.

Eligibility: Applicants must be members of the ANA, have their master's degree and plan to pursue doctoral degrees. Eligible applicants must be registered nurses and members of a ethnic/racial minority group.
Target applicant(s): Graduate school students. Adult students.
Amount: Varies.
Number of awards: Varies.
Deadline: April 30.
How to apply: Applications available online.
Exclusive: Visit www.UltimateScholarshipBook.com and enter code AM128420 for updates on this award.

(1285) · Minority Student Scholarship

American Speech-Language-Hearing Foundation
2200 Research Boulevard, Rockville, MD 20850
Phone: 301-296-8700
Email: foundation@asha.org
http://www.ashfoundation.org
Purpose: To support a minority graduate student in communication sciences and disorders.
Eligibility: Applicants should be full-time minority graduate students. Master's degree candidates must be in programs accredited by the Council on Academic Accreditation for Audiology and Speech Pathology, but doctoral programs do not have to be accredited. Transcripts, an essay and a reference form are required.
Target applicant(s): College students. Graduate school students. Adult students.
Amount: $5,000.
Number of awards: Up to 2.
Deadline: May 22.
How to apply: Applications are available online.
Exclusive: Visit www.UltimateScholarshipBook.com and enter code AM128520 for updates on this award.

(1286) · Mollie Butler Memorial Scholarship

Welsh Pony and Cob Society
720 Green Street, Stephens City, VA 22655
Phone: 540-868-7669
http://www.welshpony.org
Purpose: To support students pursuing education and research in equine-related fields.
Eligibility: Applicants must be graduating high school or attending college, graduate school or professional training in equine fields of study.
Target applicant(s): College students. Graduate school students. Adult students.
Amount: $500-$1,000.
Number of awards: 2.
Deadline: July 1.
How to apply: Applications are available online.
Exclusive: Visit www.UltimateScholarshipBook.com and enter code WE128620 for updates on this award.

(1287) · Moody's Mega Math Challenge

Society for Industrial and Applied Mathematics/SIAM
3600 Market Street, 6th Floor, Philadelphia, PA 19104
Phone: 215-382-9800
https://www.siam.org/
Purpose: To support students who complete a math challenge.
Eligibility: Applicants must be from high schools in the United States. Students on the team must be juniors and seniors from the same high school.
Target applicant(s): High school students.
Amount: $5,000-$20,000.
Number of awards: Varies.
Deadline: February 22.
How to apply: Applications are available online.
Exclusive: Visit www.UltimateScholarshipBook.com and enter code SO128720 for updates on this award.

(1288) · Morphisec's Women in Cybersecurity Scholarships

Morphisec
275 Grove Street, Suite 2-400, Newton, MA 02466
Phone: 617-209-2552
Email: scholarships@morphisec.com
https://www.morphisec.com/about-us/cybersecurity-scholarships/
Purpose: To support students who intend to pursue a career in the field of cybersecurity.
Eligibility: Applicants must be female students enrolled at an accredited college or university for the upcoming school year pursuing a degree in either cybersecurity, information assurance, information security or information systems security. An essay must be completed as part of the application process. Students must be citizens of the United States.
Target applicant(s): High school students. College students. Graduate school students. Adult students.
Amount: $1,000-$2,500.
Number of awards: 3.
Deadline: May 15.
How to apply: Applications are available online.
Exclusive: Visit www.UltimateScholarshipBook.com and enter code MO128820 for updates on this award.

(1289) · MTI Bert Krisher Memorial Scholarship

National Association of Corrosion Engineers (NACE) International Foundation
15835 Park Ten Place, Houston, TX 77084-5145
Phone: 281-228-6205
Email: nace.foundation@nace.org
http://nace-foundation.org/programs/students/scholarships/
Purpose: To help students pursue careers in materials engineering in the process industries.
Eligibility: Applicants must be enrolled full-time as an undergraduate at an accredited college or university in North America, Europe or Asia. Selection is based on experience, academic achievement, personal and professional activities and overall strength of the application.
Target applicant(s): College students. Adult students.
Amount: $5,000.
Number of awards: Up to 2.
Deadline: January 15.
How to apply: Applications are available online. An application form, three recommendation forms, an academic transcript, a work experience form and essay scholarship questions are required.
Exclusive: Visit www.UltimateScholarshipBook.com and enter code NA128920 for updates on this award.

(1290) · MTS Student Scholarship for Graduating High School Seniors

Marine Technology Society
1100 H Street NW, Suite LL-100, Washington, DC 20005
Phone: 202-717-8705

https://www.mtsociety.org/education/scholarships.aspx
Purpose: To support Marine Technology Society members who are pursuing an undergraduate degree in a marine-related field.
Eligibility: Applicants must be MTS student members who are accepted for enrollment or enrolled full-time at an educational institution. Selection is based on the overall strength of the application.
Target applicant(s): High school students.
Amount: $2,000.
Number of awards: 1.
Deadline: April 19.
How to apply: Applications are available online.
Exclusive: Visit www.UltimateScholarshipBook.com and enter code MA129020 for updates on this award.

(1291) • MTS Student Scholarship for Two-Year, Technical, Engineering and Community College Students

Marine Technology Society
1100 H Street NW, Suite LL-100, Washington, DC 20005
Phone: 202-717-8705
https://www.mtsociety.org/education/scholarships.aspx
Purpose: To support students who are enrolled at a two-year, technical, engineering or community college in a marine-related field
Eligibility: Applicants must be MTS student members who are accepted for enrollment or enrolled full-time at an educational institution.
Target applicant(s): High school students. College students. Adult students.
Amount: $2,000.
Number of awards: 1.
Deadline: April 19.
How to apply: Applications are available online.
Exclusive: Visit www.UltimateScholarshipBook.com and enter code MA129120 for updates on this award.

(1292) • MTS Student Scholarship for Undergraduate Students

Marine Technology Society
1100 H Street NW, Suite LL-100, Washington, DC 20005
Phone: 202-717-8705
https://www.mtsociety.org/education/scholarships.aspx
Purpose: To support Marine Technology Society members who are pursuing an undergraduate degree in a marine-related field.
Eligibility: Applicants must be MTS student members who are accepted for enrollment or enrolled full-time at an educational institution.
Target applicant(s): College students. Graduate school students. Adult students.
Amount: $2,000.
Number of awards: 1.
Deadline: April 19.
How to apply: Applications are available online.
Exclusive: Visit www.UltimateScholarshipBook.com and enter code MA129220 for updates on this award.

(1293) • Murse World Scholarship

Murse World
1665 Corporate Road West, Lakewood, NJ 08701
Phone: 732-719-8600
Email: scholarships@murseworld.com
https://www.murseworld.com/scholarship
Purpose: To assist students pursuing medical education.
Eligibility: Applicants must be graduating high school seniors or currently enrolled in an accredited U.S. college or university with the intent of pursuing a degree in a medical field including therapy, nursing, dentistry and nutrition. Students must be U.S. citizens or legal residents with a minimum GPA of 3.0 and must write an original essay.
Target applicant(s): High school students. College students. Graduate school students. Adult students.
Minimum GPA: 3.0
Amount: $1,000.
Number of awards: 1.
Deadline: December 15.
How to apply: Applications are available online.
Exclusive: Visit www.UltimateScholarshipBook.com and enter code MU129320 for updates on this award.

(1294) • Myrtle and Earl Walker Scholarship

Society of Manufacturing Engineers Education Foundation
One SME Drive, P.O. Box 930, Dearborn, MI 48121
Phone: 313-425-3300
Email: foundation@sme.org
http://www.smeef.org
Purpose: To help manufacturing engineering and technology undergraduates.
Eligibility: Applicants must be full-time undergraduate students who are studying manufacturing engineering or technology at an accredited postsecondary institution located in the U.S. or Canada. They must have a GPA of 3.0 or higher on a four-point scale and must have completed 15 or more credit hours. They must have plans to pursue a career in manufacturing engineering or technology. Selection is based on the overall strength of the application.
Target applicant(s): College students. Adult students.
Minimum GPA: 3.0
Amount: Varies.
Number of awards: Varies.
Deadline: February 1.
How to apply: Applications are available online. An application form, personal statement, resume, transcript and two recommendation letters are required.
Exclusive: Visit www.UltimateScholarshipBook.com and enter code SO129420 for updates on this award.

(1295) • N.G. Kaul Memorial Scholarship

New York Water Environment Association Inc.
525 Plum Street, Suite 102, Syracuse, NY 13204
Phone: 877-556-9932
Email: theresa@nywea.org
http://www.nywea.org
Purpose: To support students pursuing advanced degrees in environmental engineering and science.
Eligibility: Applicants must be graduate students pursuing degrees in environmental or civil engineering or environmental science with a concentration on water quality. Students must provide two letters of recommendations, a transcript, a resume and two essays along with their application.
Target applicant(s): Graduate school students. Adult students.
Amount: $5,000.
Number of awards: Varies.
Deadline: February 28.
How to apply: Applications are available online.

Exclusive: Visit www.UltimateScholarshipBook.com and enter code NE129520 for updates on this award.

(1296) • NACE Eastern Area Scholarship

National Association of Corrosion Engineers (NACE) International Foundation
15835 Park Ten Place, Houston, TX 77084-5145
Phone: 281-228-6205
Email: nace.foundation@nace.org
http://nace-foundation.org/programs/students/scholarships/

Purpose: To help students interested in their pursuit of a career in the field of engineering and/or science.

Eligibility: Applicants must be a permanent resident of the United States and be enrolled full-time as an undergraduate in an accredited engineering or physical science degree program at a two or four-year college or university. Students must have a GPA of 3.0 or higher and have a permanent address within the NACE Eastern Area which includes the following states and/or U.S. Territories: Alabama, Connecticut, Delaware, Florida, Georgia, Indiana (excluding Lake, Porter La Porte, Newton and Jasper counties), Kentucky, Maine, Maryland, Massachusetts, Michigan, Mississippi, New Hampshire, New Jersey, New York, North Carolina, Ohio, Pennsylvania, Puerto Rico, Rhode Island, South Carolina, Tennessee, Vermont, Virginia and West Virginia.

Target applicant(s): College students. Adult students.

Minimum GPA: 3.0

Amount: $3,000.

Number of awards: 1.

Deadline: January 5.

How to apply: Applications are available online. An application form, two recommendation forms, an academic transcript and essay scholarship questions are required.

Exclusive: Visit www.UltimateScholarshipBook.com and enter code NA129620 for updates on this award.

(1297) • NACE Foundation Academic Scholarship

National Association of Corrosion Engineers (NACE) International Foundation
15835 Park Ten Place, Houston, TX 77084-5145
Phone: 281-228-6205
Email: nace.foundation@nace.org
http://nace-foundation.org/programs/students/scholarships/

Purpose: To aid students in the study of corrosion or corrosion control.

Eligibility: Applicants must be enrolled full-time as an undergraduate student at a two or four-year accredited college or university. Applicants must be pursuing a science or engineering degree. Selection is based on the overall strength of the application.

Target applicant(s): College students. Adult students.

Amount: $5,000.

Number of awards: Up to 5.

Deadline: January 5.

How to apply: Applications are available online. An application form, two recommendation forms, an academic transcript and essay scholarship questions are required.

Exclusive: Visit www.UltimateScholarshipBook.com and enter code NA129720 for updates on this award.

(1298) • NACE Past Presidents Scholarship

National Association of Corrosion Engineers (NACE) International Foundation
15835 Park Ten Place, Houston, TX 77084-5145
Phone: 281-228-6205
Email: nace.foundation@nace.org
http://nace-foundation.org/programs/students/scholarships/

Purpose: To aid students in their pursuit of study in science or engineering related to corrosion or corrosion control.

Eligibility: Applicants must be enrolled full-time as an undergraduate at a two- or four-year accredited college or university and must be pursuing a degree in the field of science and/or engineering. Selection is based on the overall strength of the application.

Target applicant(s): College students. Adult students.

Amount: $2,500.

Number of awards: 2.

Deadline: January 5.

How to apply: Applications are available online. An application form, two recommendation forms, an academic transcript and essay scholarship questions are required.

Exclusive: Visit www.UltimateScholarshipBook.com and enter code NA129820 for updates on this award.

(1299) • Naomi Brack Student Scholarship

Organization for Associate Degree Nursing National Office
7794 Grow Drive , Pensacola, FL 32514-7072
Phone: 877-966-6236
Email: harriet.mcclung@oadn.org
http://www.oadn.org

Purpose: To aid associate's degree nursing (ADN) students.

Eligibility: Applicants must be currently enrolled in an associate's degree program in nursing at a state-approved institution. They must have a GPA of 3.0 or more on a four-point scale and must be active in their school's student nursing association. Selection is based on the overall strength of the application.

Target applicant(s): College students. Adult students.

Minimum GPA: 3.0

Amount: $1,000.

Number of awards: Varies.

Deadline: September 30.

How to apply: Applications are available online. An application form, personal statement, transcript, nomination form and two letters of recommendation are required.

Exclusive: Visit www.UltimateScholarshipBook.com and enter code OR129920 for updates on this award.

(1300) • NAPA Research and Education Foundation Scholarship

National Asphalt Pavement Association
5100 Forbes Boulevard, Lanham, MD 20706-4407
Phone: 888-468-6499
http://www.asphaltpavement.org/

Purpose: To aid engineering and construction students who are interested in hot mix asphalt technology.

Eligibility: Applicants must be U.S. citizens who are enrolled full-time at an accredited postsecondary institution. They must be majoring in construction management, civil engineering or construction engineering. The applicant's school must offer at least one course on hot mix asphalt (HMA) technology. Selection is based on academic achievement, leadership potential, extracurricular involvements and stated career goals.

Target applicant(s): College students. Graduate school students. Adult students.
Amount: Varies.
Number of awards: Varies.
Scholarship may be renewable.
Deadline: Varies.
How to apply: Applications may be requested from the student's state National Asphalt Pavement Association representative. An application form and supporting materials are required.
Exclusive: Visit www.UltimateScholarshipBook.com and enter code NA130020 for updates on this award.

(1301) · National Association for Surface Finishing Scholarships

National Association for Surface Finishing
1155 Fifteenth Street NW, Washington, DC 20005
Phone: 202-457-8401
http://www.nasf.org
Purpose: To support students pursuing the study of surface science.
Eligibility: Applicants must be undergraduate juniors or seniors or graduate students studying chemical engineering, material science, mechanical, metallurgical or environmental engineering or chemistry. Students must have a minimum 3.0 GPA if an undergraduate or 3.3 if a graduate-level student.
Target applicant(s): College students. Graduate school students. Adult students.
Minimum GPA: 3.0 for undergraduate students, 3.3 for graduate students
Amount: $1,500.
Number of awards: 1.
Deadline: February 23.
How to apply: Applications are available online.
Exclusive: Visit www.UltimateScholarshipBook.com and enter code NA130120 for updates on this award.

(1302) · National Aviation Explorer Scholarships

Explorers Learning for Life
1325 West Walnut Hill Lane, P.O. Box 152225, Irving, TX 75015-2225
Phone: 855-806-9992
Email: exploring@lflmail.org
http://www.exploring.org/scholarships/
Purpose: To support students who are pursuing careers in the aviation industry.
Eligibility: Students must be active members of an Aviation Explorer post. Applicants must submit an essay and three letters of recommendation.
Target applicant(s): Junior high students or younger. High school students. College students. Adult students.
Amount: $3,000-$10,000.
Number of awards: Varies.
Deadline: May 1.
How to apply: Applications are available online.
Exclusive: Visit www.UltimateScholarshipBook.com and enter code EX130220 for updates on this award.

(1303) · National Dairy Shrine/lager Dairy Scholarship

National Dairy Shrine
P.O. Box 725, Denmark, WI 54208
Phone: 920-863-6333
Email: info@dairyshrine.org
http://www.dairyshrine.org
Purpose: To aid dairy and animal science students who are planning for careers in the dairy industry.
Eligibility: Applicants must be entering the second year of a two-year agricultural college program in dairy or animal science. They must have a GPA of 2.5 or higher on a four-point scale. Selection is based on academic merit, leadership skills and professional commitment to the dairy industry.
Target applicant(s): College students. Adult students.
Minimum GPA: 2.5
Amount: $1,000.
Number of awards: 1.
Deadline: April 15.
How to apply: Applications are available online. An application form, official transcript, personal essay and two recommendation letters are required.
Exclusive: Visit www.UltimateScholarshipBook.com and enter code NA130320 for updates on this award.

(1304) · National Environmental Health Association Graduate Scholarship

National Environmental Health Association and the American Academy of Sanitarians
NEHA/AAS Scholarship, 720 South Colorado Boulevard, Suite 1000-N, Denver, CO 80246-1926
Phone: 303-756-9090
Email: cdimmitt@neha.org
http://www.neha.org
Purpose: To encourage commitment to environmental health studies.
Eligibility: Applicants must be enrolled in a graduate program at an accredited institution with a declared curriculum in environmental health sciences and have at least one semester of coursework remaining.
Target applicant(s): Graduate school students. Adult students.
Amount: $2,000.
Number of awards: 1.
Deadline: March 15.
How to apply: Applications are available online.
Exclusive: Visit www.UltimateScholarshipBook.com and enter code NA130420 for updates on this award.

(1305) · National Foliage Foundation General Scholarships

National Foliage Foundation
1533 Park Center Drive, Orlando, FL 32835
Phone: 800-375-3642
Email: info@nationalfoliagefoundation.org
http://www.nationalfoliagefoundation.org
Purpose: To aid horticulture students who are interested in pursuing careers in foliage growing and marketing.
Eligibility: Applicants must be graduating high school seniors or full-time undergraduate or graduate students. They must be enrolled in or planning to enroll in a horticulture or related degree program and must have a GPA of 2.5 or higher. They must be interested in pursuing a career in foliage marketing or growing. Selection is based on the overall strength of the application.
Target applicant(s): High school students. College students. Graduate school students. Adult students.
Minimum GPA: 2.5

Amount: Varies.
Number of awards: Varies.
Scholarship may be renewable.
Deadline: January 15.
How to apply: Applications are available online. An application form, transcript, two recommendation letters and a personal essay are required.
Exclusive: Visit www.UltimateScholarshipBook.com and enter code NA130520 for updates on this award.

(1306) · National Garden Clubs Scholarship

National Garden Clubs Inc.
4401 Magnolia Avenue, St. Louis, MO 63110
Phone: 314-776-7574
Email: headquarters@gardenclub.org
http://www.gardenclub.org
Purpose: To promote the study of horticulture and related fields.
Eligibility: Applicants must be full-time juniors, seniors, graduate students or sophomores applying for their junior year and major in one of the following fields: agriculture education, horticulture, floriculture, landscape design, botany, biology, plant pathology/science, forestry, agronomy, environmental concerns, economics, environmental conservation, city planning, wildlife science, habitat or forest/systems ecology, land management or related areas. Students must have a minimum 3.25 cumulative GPA and be a U.S. citizen.
Target applicant(s): College students. Graduate school students. Adult students.
Minimum GPA: 3.25
Amount: $4,000.
Number of awards: Up to 41.
Deadline: February 1.
How to apply: Applications are available online and must be mailed to the applicants' state Garden Club scholarship chairman.
Exclusive: Visit www.UltimateScholarshipBook.com and enter code NA130620 for updates on this award.

(1307) · National Potato Council Scholarship

National Potato Council
1300 L Street NW #910, Washington, DC 20005
Phone: 202-682-9456
http://www.nationalpotatocouncil.org
Purpose: To aid students pursuing studies that support the potato industry.
Eligibility: Applicants must be graduate agribusiness students. Selection is based on academic achievement, leadership abilities and potato-related areas of graduate study (such as agricultural engineering, agronomy, crop and soil sciences, entomology, food sciences, horticulture and plant pathology).
Target applicant(s): Graduate school students. Adult students.
Amount: $10,000.
Number of awards: 1.
Deadline: June 16.
How to apply: Applications are available online. An application form, essay, transcripts, list of activities and two references are required.
Exclusive: Visit www.UltimateScholarshipBook.com and enter code NA130720 for updates on this award.

(1308) · National Space Club Keynote Scholar

National Space Club
204 E Street NE, Washington, DC 20002
Phone: 202-547-0060.
Email: info@spaceclub.org
http://www.spaceclub.org/youth-education.html
Purpose: To aid STEM students.
Eligibility: Applicants must be U.S. citizens and must be high school seniors, undergraduates or graduate students planning to attend or attending an accredited college or university with the intention to follow a course of study related to a career in a science, technology, engineering or math field with a preference for space-related interests. Selection is based on the overall strength of the application.
Target applicant(s): High school students. College students. Graduate school students. Adult students.
Amount: $10,000.
Number of awards: 1.
Deadline: December 2.
How to apply: Applications are available online. An application form, transcripts, two letters of recommendation, statement of intent and video audition are required.
Exclusive: Visit www.UltimateScholarshipBook.com and enter code NA130820 for updates on this award.

(1309) · National Student Design Competition

American Institute of Chemical Engineers - (AIChE)
120 Wall Street, Floor 23, New York, NY 10005-4020
Phone: 800-242-4363
Email: awards@aiche.org
https://www.aiche.org/community/awards
Purpose: To test chemical engineering students' skills in calculation and evaluation of technical data and economic factors.
Eligibility: Applicants must be members of an AIChE student chapter and enter a contest to solve a chemical engineering design problem.
Target applicant(s): College students. Graduate school students. Adult students.
Amount: $200-$500.
Number of awards: 3.
Deadline: June 10.
How to apply: Applications are available online.
Exclusive: Visit www.UltimateScholarshipBook.com and enter code AM130920 for updates on this award.

(1310) · National Student Nurses' Association Scholarship

National Student Nurses' Association
45 Main Street, Suite 606, Brooklyn, NY 11201
Phone: 718-210-0705
Email: nsna@nsna.org
http://www.nsna.org
Purpose: To promote interest in the nursing field.
Eligibility: Applicants must be currently enrolled in a state-approved school of nursing or pre-nursing in associate degree, baccalaureate, diploma, doctorate or master's programs.
Target applicant(s): College students. Graduate school students. Adult students.
Amount: $1,000-$5,000.
Number of awards: Varies.
Deadline: January 16.
How to apply: Applications are available online.
Exclusive: Visit www.UltimateScholarshipBook.com and enter code NA131020 for updates on this award.

(1311) • National Wildlife Federation EcoLeaders Fellowship Program

National Wildlife Federation
P.O. Box 1583, Merrifield, VA 22116-1583
Phone: 800-822-9919
Email: Fellows@nwf.org
http://www.nwf.org
Purpose: The fellowship program provides funding for campus ecology projects.
Eligibility: Applicants must create a plan for a campus ecology program, working with a project advisor and verifier. All Campus Ecology fellows are required to attend a training program.
Target applicant(s): Graduate school students. Adult students.
Amount: Varies.
Number of awards: Varies.
Deadline: May 21.
How to apply: Applications are available online.
Exclusive: Visit www.UltimateScholarshipBook.com and enter code NA131120 for updates on this award.

(1312) • National Young Astronomer Award

Astronomical League
9201 Ward Parkway, Suite 100, Kansas City, MO 64114
Phone: 816-333-7759
Email: horkheimerservice@astroleague.org
http://www.astroleague.org
Purpose: To support young astronomers.
Eligibility: Applicants must be 14 to 19 years old, not yet enrolled in college at the award deadline and do not have to be members of an astronomy club or of the Astronomical League. International students of the same age are eligible if they are enrolled in a U.S. secondary school on the application deadline. The application consists of the application form, summary of astronomy-related activities and optional exhibits.
Target applicant(s): Junior high students or younger. High school students.
Amount: Varies.
Number of awards: 3.
Deadline: January 31.
How to apply: Applications are available online.
Exclusive: Visit www.UltimateScholarshipBook.com and enter code AS131220 for updates on this award.

(1313) • NAWIC Founders' Undergraduate Scholarship

National Association of Women in Construction
327 South Adams Street, Fort Worth, TX 76104
Phone: 800-552-3506
Email: nawic@nawic.org
http://www.nawic.org
Purpose: To aid undergraduates who are preparing for careers in construction.
Eligibility: Applicants must be full-time, degree-seeking undergraduates who are studying a construction-related subject at a postsecondary institution located in the U.S. or Canada. Students do not need to be female. They must have a cumulative GPA of 3.0 or higher and have plans to pursue a career in a construction-related field. Selection is based on stated career goals, extracurricular activities, work experience, academic achievement and financial need.
Target applicant(s): College students. Adult students.
Minimum GPA: 3.0
Amount: Varies.
Number of awards: Varies.
Scholarship may be renewable.
Deadline: February 28.
How to apply: Applications are available online. An application form, transcript, employment history, extracurricular activities list and personal statement are required.
Exclusive: Visit www.UltimateScholarshipBook.com and enter code NA131320 for updates on this award.

(1314) • NBRC/AMP Gareth B. Gish, MS, RRT Memorial and William F. Miller, MD Postgraduate Education Recognition Awards

American Association for Respiratory Care
9425 North MacArthur Boulevard, Suite 100, Irving, TX 75063-4706
Phone: 972-243-2272
Email: info@aarc.org
http://www.aarc.org/education/educator-resources/scholarships/
Purpose: To aid qualified respiratory therapists in pursuing advanced degrees.
Eligibility: Applicants must be respiratory therapists who have been accepted into an advanced degree program of a fully accredited school. Application must be accompanied by an original essay describing how the award will aid in achieving an advanced degree and future goals in health care. A minimum 3.0 GPA is required.
Target applicant(s): College students. Graduate school students. Adult students.
Minimum GPA: 3.0
Amount: $2,500.
Number of awards: 2.
Deadline: June 1.
How to apply: Applications are available online.
Exclusive: Visit www.UltimateScholarshipBook.com and enter code AM131420 for updates on this award.

(1315) • NBRC/AMP William W. Burgin, Jr. MD and Robert M. Lawrence, MD Education Recognition Award

American Association for Respiratory Care
9425 North MacArthur Boulevard, Suite 100, Irving, TX 75063-4706
Phone: 972-243-2272
Email: info@aarc.org
http://www.aarc.org/education/educator-resources/scholarships/
Purpose: To recognize outstanding students in respiratory care education programs.
Eligibility: Applicants must be third or fourth-year students enrolled in an accredited respiratory therapy program leading to a bachelor's degree and must have a minimum 3.0 GPA. In addition to an original paper dealing with respiratory care, applicants must submit an original essay describing how this award will help them reach their degrees and their future goals in the field of health care.
Target applicant(s): College students. Adult students.
Minimum GPA: 3.0
Amount: Up to $7,500.
Number of awards: 1.
Deadline: June 1.
How to apply: Applications are available online.

Exclusive: Visit www.UltimateScholarshipBook.com and enter code AM131520 for updates on this award.

(1316) • NCAPA Endowment Grant

North Carolina Academy of Physician Assistants
Attn: Kat Nicholas, 1121 Slater Road, Durham, NC 27703
Phone: 800-352-2271
Email: ncapa@ncapa.org
http://ncapa.org/students/scholarships/
Purpose: To aid physician assistant school students.
Eligibility: Applicants must be current student members of the North Carolina Academy of Physician Assistants (NCAPA). They must be rising second- or third-year students in an accredited physician assistant degree program. Selection is based on the overall strength of the application.
Target applicant(s): College students. Graduate school students. Adult students.
Amount: Varies.
Number of awards: Varies.
Deadline: June 11.
How to apply: Applications are available online. An application form, financial aid statement, personal essay and official transcript are required.
Exclusive: Visit www.UltimateScholarshipBook.com and enter code NO131620 for updates on this award.

(1317) • NCGA William C. Berg Academic Excellence in Agriculture Scholarship

National Corn Growers Association
632 Cepi Drive, Chesterfield, MO 63005
Phone: 636-733-9004
Email: corninfo@ncga.com
http://www.ncga.com/topics/education/college-scholarships
Purpose: To support students pursuing degrees in agriculture-related fields.
Eligibility: Applicants must be pursuing an undergraduate or graduate degree in an agricultural field and be a member or child of a member of the NCGA.
Target applicant(s): College students. Graduate school students. Adult students.
Amount: $1,000.
Number of awards: 5.
Deadline: December 1.
How to apply: Applications are available online.
Exclusive: Visit www.UltimateScholarshipBook.com and enter code NA131720 for updates on this award.

(1318) • NCPA Foundation Presidential Scholarship

National Community Pharmacists Association
NCPA Foundation, 100 Daingerfield Road, Alexandria, VA 22314
Phone: 703-683-8200
Email: info@ncpanet.org
http://www.ncpanet.org
Purpose: To support students who plan to enter the pharmaceutical field.
Eligibility: Applicants must be student members of NCPA and enrolled in a U.S. school or college of pharmacy full-time. Selection is based on academic achievement and leadership.
Target applicant(s): College students. Graduate school students. Adult students.
Amount: $2,000.
Number of awards: Varies.
Deadline: March 15.
How to apply: Applications are available online.
Exclusive: Visit www.UltimateScholarshipBook.com and enter code NA131820 for updates on this award.

(1319) • NDPRB Undergraduate Scholarship Program

National Dairy Promotion and Research Board
c/o Nate Janssen, Dairy Management Inc., 10255 West Higgins Road, Suite 900, Rosemont, IL 60018-5615
Phone: 847-627-3335
Email: nate.janssen@rosedmi.com
http://www.dairy.org
Purpose: To aid undergraduates who are studying a dairy-related subject.
Eligibility: Applicants must be rising undergraduate sophomores, juniors or seniors. They must be majoring in a subject that emphasizes dairy (such as agriculture education, business, communications, economics, food science, journalism, marketing or public relations). Applicants must plan to pursue a career in the dairy industry. Selection is based on stated career goals, academic excellence, dairy-related coursework completed, leadership and integrity.
Target applicant(s): College students. Adult students.
Amount: $3,500.
Number of awards: Up to 11.
Scholarship may be renewable.
Deadline: April 21.
How to apply: Applications are available online. An application form, personal statement, one recommendation letter and an official transcript are required.
Exclusive: Visit www.UltimateScholarshipBook.com and enter code NA131920 for updates on this award.

(1320) • NDS / Klussendorf / McKown Scholarships

National Dairy Shrine
P.O. Box 725, Denmark, WI 54208
Phone: 920-863-6333
Email: info@dairyshrine.org
http://www.dairyshrine.org
Purpose: To honor students in dairy husbandry fields.
Eligibility: Applicants must be first, second or third year college students at two- or four-year universities, must major in a dairy husbandry field and plan to enter the dairy field.
Target applicant(s): College students. Adult students.
Amount: $1,500.
Number of awards: 7.
Deadline: April 15.
How to apply: Applications are available online.
Exclusive: Visit www.UltimateScholarshipBook.com and enter code NA132020 for updates on this award.

(1321) • NDSEG Fellowship Program

Department of Defense, American Society for Engineering Education
1818 N Street NW, Suite 600, Washington, DC 20036
Phone: 202-331-3546
Email: ndseg@asee.org
http://www.ndsegfellowships.org/
Purpose: To award fellowships to those in science and engineering.
Eligibility: Applicants must pursue a doctoral degree in an area of Department of Defense interest: aeronautical and astronautical engineering, biosciences, chemical engineering, chemistry, civil

engineering, cognitive, neural and behavioral sciences, computer and computational sciences, electrical engineering, geosciences, materials science and engineering, mathematics, mechanical engineering, naval architecture and ocean engineering, oceanography and physics. Applicants must have completed no more than one academic year of graduate study as a part-time or full-time student or be in their final year of undergraduate studies. The award is based on academic achievement, personal statements, recommendations and Graduate Record Examination scores. Fellowships may be used only at U.S. institutions of higher education offering doctoral degrees.
Target applicant(s): College students. Graduate school students. Adult students.
Amount: Full tuition plus fees, stipend and medical insurance.
Number of awards: Varies.
Scholarship may be renewable.
Deadline: December 31.
How to apply: Applications are available online.
Exclusive: Visit www.UltimateScholarshipBook.com and enter code DE132120 for updates on this award.

(1322) • NEHA/AAS/APU Scholarship Awards

National Environmental Health Association and the American Academy of Sanitarians
NEHA/AAS Scholarship, 720 South Colorado Boulevard, Suite 1000-N, Denver, CO 80246-1926
Phone: 303-756-9090
Email: cdimmitt@neha.org
http://www.neha.org
Purpose: To support students planning careers in environmental health.
Eligibility: Applicants must be either undergraduate or graduate students. The undergraduate scholarships are to be used during the junior or senior year at an Environmental Health Accreditation Council (EHAC) or NEHA member school. The graduate scholarship is available to applicants who are enrolled in a graduate program of study in environmental health sciences and/or public health and have at least one semester of coursework remaining.
Target applicant(s): College students. Graduate school students. Adult students.
Amount: $1,000-$2,000.
Number of awards: 4.
Scholarship may be renewable.
Deadline: March 15.
How to apply: Applications are available online.
Exclusive: Visit www.UltimateScholarshipBook.com and enter code NA132220 for updates on this award.

(1323) • Nellie Yeoh Whetten Award

American Vacuum Society
125 Maiden Lane, 15th Floor, New York, NY 10038
Phone: 212-248-0200
Email: angela@avs.org
http://www.avs.org
Purpose: To support women in graduate studies in the sciences and technologies related to AVS.
Eligibility: Applicants must be female graduate students in an accredited academic institution and must send an application, report on candidate form, two letters of recommendation and college and graduate school transcripts.
Target applicant(s): Graduate school students. Adult students.
Amount: Varies.
Number of awards: Varies.
Deadline: May 1.
How to apply: Applications are available online.
Exclusive: Visit www.UltimateScholarshipBook.com and enter code AM132320 for updates on this award.

(1324) • Neuroscience Research Prize

American Academy of Neurology
201 Chicago Avenue, Minneapolis, MN 55415
Phone: 651-695-2704
Email: ejackson@aan.com
http://www.aan.com
Purpose: To encourage high school students of scientific aptitude to explore the field of neuroscience.
Eligibility: Applicants must be U.S. high school students. They must have completed an original, independent laboratory research project on a subject that is related to the brain or nervous system. Selection is based on creativity, the strength of the applicant's research report and relevance of the research project to neuroscience.
Target applicant(s): High school students.
Amount: $1,000.
Number of awards: 4.
Deadline: Varies.
How to apply: Applications are available online. An application form and research report are required.
Exclusive: Visit www.UltimateScholarshipBook.com and enter code AM132420 for updates on this award.

(1325) • New Century Scholars Doctoral Scholarship

American Speech-Language-Hearing Foundation
2200 Research Boulevard, Rockville, MD 20850
Phone: 301-296-8700
Email: foundation@asha.org
http://www.ashfoundation.org
Purpose: To support graduate students and researchers who are studying communication sciences and disorders.
Eligibility: Students applying for the scholarship must be enrolled in a research or teaching doctoral program to obtain a Ph.D. or its equivalent. Researchers applying for the grant must have teacher-investigator careers, either in an academic environment or in external research institutions.
Target applicant(s): Graduate school students. Adult students.
Amount: $10,000.
Number of awards: Up to 15.
Deadline: May 8.
How to apply: Applications are available online.
Exclusive: Visit www.UltimateScholarshipBook.com and enter code AM132520 for updates on this award.

(1326) • NFMC Dorothy Dann Bullock Music Therapy Award and the NFMC Ruth B. Robertson Music Therapy Award

National Federation of Music Clubs Bullock and Robertson Awards
Margaret Smith, 2501 Maple Ridge Drive, Tuscaloosa, AL 35406
Phone: 317-882-4003
Email: Margbill1956@att.net
http://www.nfmc-music.org/competitions-awards/
Purpose: To assist students who plan to enter careers in music therapy.
Eligibility: Applicants must be college students majoring in music therapy in schools approved by the National Association of Music Therapists and AMTA. Selection is based on musical talent, skills and

training with an emphasis on piano ability in accompanying and sight reading. Other selection criteria are self-reliance, leadership, ability to work with groups and dedication to music therapy as a career. Applicants must be members of the National Federation of Music Clubs.
Target applicant(s): College students. Adult students.
Amount: $1,400.
Number of awards: Varies.
Deadline: March 1.
How to apply: Applications are available online.
Exclusive: Visit www.UltimateScholarshipBook.com and enter code NA132620 for updates on this award.

(1327) • NHSC Scholarship

U.S. Department of Health and Human Services
Health Resources and Services Administration, Bureau of Health Workforce, 5600 Fishers Lane, Rockville, MD 20857
Phone: 800-221-9393
Email: callcenter@hrsa.gov
http://nhsc.hrsa.gov/scholarships/index.html
Purpose: To aid students committed to providing health care in communities of great need.
Eligibility: Applicants must be enrolled or accepted into allopathic or osteopathic medical schools, family nurse practitioner programs, nurse-midwifery programs, physician assistant programs or dental school. Upon completion of training, scholars must choose practice sites in federally designated health professional shortage areas for one year for each year of support received.
Target applicant(s): College students. Graduate school students. Adult students.
Amount: Full tuition and fees plus stipend.
Number of awards: Varies.
Scholarship may be renewable.
Deadline: April 27.
How to apply: Applications are available by telephone request.
Exclusive: Visit www.UltimateScholarshipBook.com and enter code U.132720 for updates on this award.

(1328) • NIH Undergraduate Scholarship Program

Office of Intramural Training and Education
National Institute of Health - DHHS, 2 Center Drive, Building 2, Room 2E24, Bethesda, MD 20892-0230
Phone: 800-528-7689
Email: ugsp@nih.gov
http://www.training.nih.gov/programs/ugsp
Purpose: To offer competitive scholarships to students who are committed to careers in biomedical, behavioral and social science health-related research.
Eligibility: Applicants must be enrolled or accepted for enrollment as full-time students at an accredited undergraduate institution, have an underprivileged background and have a minimum 3.3 GPA or be within the top 5 percent of their class. Applicants must also show a commitment to pursuing careers in biomedical, behavioral and social science research at the NIH.
Target applicant(s): College students. Adult students.
Minimum GPA: 3.3
Amount: Up to $20,000.
Number of awards: Varies.
Scholarship may be renewable.
Deadline: March 14.
How to apply: Applications are available online.
Exclusive: Visit www.UltimateScholarshipBook.com and enter code OF132820 for updates on this award.

(1329) • Noodle Pros MCAT Scholarship

StudySoup
1381 9th Avenue, San Francisco, CA 94122
Phone: 415-658-9115
https://studysoup.com/scholarships/
Purpose: To offset the cost of the MCAT exam.
Eligibility: Applicants must be members of a pre-med organization and enrolled at a college or university at the sophomore level or higher. Students must have a minimum GPA of 3.0 and plan on taking the MCAT exam to pursue further studies.
Target applicant(s): College students. Adult students.
Minimum GPA: 3.0
Amount: $500.
Number of awards: 1.
Deadline: October 1.
How to apply: Applications are available online.
Exclusive: Visit www.UltimateScholarshipBook.com and enter code ST132920 for updates on this award.

(1330) • North American Network Operators Group Scholarship

North American Network Operators' Group
2864 Carpenter Road, Suite 100, Ann Arbor, MI 48108
Phone: 507-931-1682
Email: nanog@scholarshipamerica.org
https://www.scholarsapply.org/nanog/
Purpose: To assist students pursuing engineering degrees.
Eligibility: Applicants must be current undergraduate or graduate students pursuing a degree in one of the following fields: computer engineering, computer science, electrical engineering, network engineering or telecommunications (graduate-level only). Students must have a grade point average of 3.0 or higher and be enrolled either part- or full-time in an accredited institution for the coming academic year.
Target applicant(s): College students. Graduate school students. Adult students.
Minimum GPA: 3.0
Amount: $10,000.
Number of awards: 4.
Deadline: June 2.
How to apply: Applications are available online.
Exclusive: Visit www.UltimateScholarshipBook.com and enter code NO133020 for updates on this award.

(1331) • NorthCoast Medical

American Occupational Therapy Foundation
Attn: Jeanne Cooper, 4720 Montgomery Lane, Suite 202, Bethesda, MD 20814
Phone: 240-292-1034
Email: jcooper@aotf.org
http://www.aotf.org/scholarshipsgrants
Purpose: To encourage students who are pursuing post-baccalaureate degrees in occupational therapy.
Eligibility: Applicants must be currently enrolled full-time in an AOTA accredited occupational therapy program. Students must have completed at least one year of occupational therapy specific course work.
Target applicant(s): College students. Graduate school students. Adult students.

Amount: $5,000.
Number of awards: Varies.
Deadline: Varies.
How to apply: Applications are available online.
Exclusive: Visit www.UltimateScholarshipBook.com and enter code AM133120 for updates on this award.

(1332) • Novus Biologicals Scholarship Program

Novus Biologicals
8100 Southpark Way, A-8, Littleton, CO 80120
Phone: 303-730-1950
Email: scholarship@novusbio.com
http://www.novusbio.com/scholarship-program.html
Purpose: To reward students who plan to pursue a career in science.
Eligibility: Students must provide a personal statement and a character statement. Applicants must be accepted to or enrolled in a science-related program. Scholarship awarded twice each year.
Target applicant(s): High school students. College students. Graduate school students. Adult students.
Amount: $1,500.
Number of awards: 2.
Deadline: July 20.
How to apply: Applications are available online.
Exclusive: Visit www.UltimateScholarshipBook.com and enter code NO133220 for updates on this award.

(1333) • NPCA Educational Foundation Scholarships

National Precast Concrete Association (NPCA)
1320 City Center Drive, Suite 200, Carmel, IN 46032
Phone: 800-366-7731
Email: mharrell@precast.org
http://www.precast.org
Purpose: To aid students who are preparing for careers in the precast concrete industry.
Eligibility: Applicants must be high school seniors or undergraduate students who are enrolled in or planning to enroll in a program of study that is related to the building, construction or precast concrete industries. Selection is based on the overall strength of the application.
Target applicant(s): High school students. College students. Adult students.
Amount: Up to $2,500.
Number of awards: Varies.
Scholarship may be renewable.
Deadline: March 20.
How to apply: Applications are available online. An application form, transcript and two letters of recommendation are required.
Exclusive: Visit www.UltimateScholarshipBook.com and enter code NA133320 for updates on this award.

(1334) • NPFDA Scholarships

National Poultry and Food Distributors Association
2014 Osborne Road, St. Marys, GA 31558
Phone: 770-535-9901
Email: info@npfda.org
http://www.npfda.org/npfda-scholarships
Purpose: To aid undergraduates who are enrolled in poultry- or agriculture-related degree programs.
Eligibility: Applicants must be rising undergraduate juniors or seniors who are full-time students at a U.S. postsecondary institution. They must be pursuing a poultry- or agriculture-related program of study. Selection is based on the overall strength of the application.
Target applicant(s): College students. Adult students.
Amount: $2,500.
Number of awards: 5.
Deadline: May 31.
How to apply: Applications are available online. An application form, official transcript, personal statement and one letter of recommendation are required.
Exclusive: Visit www.UltimateScholarshipBook.com and enter code NA133420 for updates on this award.

(1335) • Nurse Candidate Program

Navy Medicine Professional Development Center
8955 Wood Road, Bethesda, MD 20889-5611
Phone: 301-295-2333
Email: usn.ohstudent@mail.mil
https://www.navy.com/joining/college-options/ncp
Purpose: To aid students who are pursuing the bachelor of science in nursing (BSN).
Eligibility: Applicants must be U.S. citizens and be full-time students who have completed two or more years of a four-year bachelor of science in nursing (BSN) degree program at an accredited college or university. They must meet the Navy's physical fitness requirements. Recipients of this award will be required to fulfill an active duty service obligation of up to five years as an officer in the Navy Nurse Corps. Selection is based on the overall strength of the application.
Target applicant(s): College students. Adult students.
Amount: Up to $34,000.
Number of awards: Varies.
Scholarship may be renewable.
Deadline: Varies.
How to apply: Applications may be obtained by contacting a Navy recruiting officer. An application form and supporting materials are required.
Exclusive: Visit www.UltimateScholarshipBook.com and enter code NA133520 for updates on this award.

(1336) • Nurse Corps Scholarship Program

Health Resources and Services Administration (HRSA)
5600 Fishers Lane, Rockville, MD 20857
Phone: 800-221-9393
Email: gethelp@hrsa.org
http://www.hrsa.gov
Purpose: To aid needy students in obtaining nursing training and education in order to specifically decrease the major shortage of nurses in given health care facilities.
Eligibility: Applicants must be U.S. citizens accepted by or enrolled in a nursing program at an accredited nursing school within the U.S. leading to an associate, baccalaureate or graduate nursing degree or diploma. Applicants must have no federal judgment liens and not be delinquent on a federal debt or have current service commitments. They must begin their nursing program no later than September 30. Selection is based on financial need, academic success, essay answers, resume and letters of recommendation. Preference is given to applicants enrolled full-time in undergraduate or master's nurse practitioner programs. Financial support is provided in exchange for a commitment to serve at least 2 years in a qualifying Nurse Corps site.
Target applicant(s): High school students. College students. Graduate school students. Adult students.
Amount: Full tuition, fees and monthly stipend.

Number of awards: Varies.
Deadline: May 21.
How to apply: Applications are available online. An application form, proof of U.S. citizenship, verification of acceptance report, student aid report, essay answers, resume/curriculum vitae, transcripts and two letters of recommendation are required.
Exclusive: Visit www.UltimateScholarshipBook.com and enter code HE133620 for updates on this award.

(1337) · Nurseries Foundation Award

Oregon Association of Nurseries
29751 SW Town Center Loop West, Wilsonville, OR 97070
Phone: 503-682-5089
Email: onf@oan.org
http://www.oan.org
Purpose: To aid horticulture students.
Eligibility: Applicants must be majoring in horticulture. Selection is based on the overall strength of the application.
Target applicant(s): College students. Adult students.
Amount: $1,000.
Number of awards: 1.
Deadline: March 1.
How to apply: Applications are available online. An application form, official transcript and three recommendation letters are required.
Exclusive: Visit www.UltimateScholarshipBook.com and enter code OR133720 for updates on this award.

(1338) · Odebrecht Award for Sustainable Development

Odebrecht
201 Alhambra Circle #1400, Coral Gables, FL 33134
http://www.odebrechtaward.com
Purpose: To support students enrolled in building and construction management, engineering, architecture or chemistry programs in developing sustainable technology.
Eligibility: Applicants must be enrolled full-time at an accredited university during the academic term in which the competition takes place. Students may submit projects individually or in a group of up to three students enrolled at the same university. Applicants must submit a project on engineering contributions to sustainable development. Selection is based on the project's applicability, technical contribution, content, reasoning and clarity.
Target applicant(s): College students. Graduate school students. Adult students.
Amount: $10,000-$45,000.
Number of awards: 3.
Deadline: May 31.
How to apply: Applications are available online.
Exclusive: Visit www.UltimateScholarshipBook.com and enter code OD133820 for updates on this award.

(1339) · Old Guard Oral Presentation Competition

American Society of Mechanical Engineers (ASME)
Two Park Avenue, New York, NY 10016-5990
Phone: 800-843-2763
Email: lefeverb@asme.org
http://www.asme.org
Purpose: To support the professional development of student members of the American Society of Mechanical Engineers (ASME).
Eligibility: Applicants must be certified as ASME student members in good standing. They must be undergraduate engineering students who have been chosen by their student section or academic department head to participate. Applicants must do a 20-minute oral presentation on a relevant engineering topic. Selection is based on presentation content, organization, delivery, effectiveness and discussion.
Target applicant(s): College students. Adult students.
Amount: Varies.
Number of awards: Varies.
Deadline: Varies.
How to apply: Entry forms are available online. An entry form and oral presentation are required.
Exclusive: Visit www.UltimateScholarshipBook.com and enter code AM133920 for updates on this award.

(1340) · Olin E. Teague Scholarship

National Space Club
204 E Street NE, Washington, DC 20002
Phone: 202-547-0060
Email: info@spaceclub.org
http://www.spaceclub.org/youth-education.html
Purpose: To aid students pursuing a degree in the aerospace fields.
Eligibility: Applicants must be a high school senior attending an accredited U.S. high school and also be a U.S. citizen. Students should plan on pursuing a degree that will lead to a career in an aerospace field.
Target applicant(s): High school students.
Amount: $4,000.
Number of awards: 1.
Deadline: October 15.
How to apply: Applications are available online.
Exclusive: Visit www.UltimateScholarshipBook.com and enter code NA134020 for updates on this award.

(1341) · Operations and Power Division Scholarship

American Nuclear Society
555 North Kensington Avenue, La Grange Park, IL 60526
Phone: 800-323-3044
Email: hr@ans.org
http://www.ans.org
Purpose: To aid nuclear science and nuclear engineering students.
Eligibility: Applicants must be U.S. citizens or permanent residents and be student members of the American Nuclear Society (ANS). They must be undergraduate or graduate students who have completed two or more years of study toward a four-year degree in nuclear science or nuclear engineering. Students must be enrolled at an accredited U.S. postsecondary institution. Selection is based on academic merit.
Target applicant(s): College students. Adult students.
Amount: Varies.
Number of awards: Varies.
Deadline: February 1.
How to apply: Applications are available online. An application form, transcript and three references are required.
Exclusive: Visit www.UltimateScholarshipBook.com and enter code AM134120 for updates on this award.

(1342) · Organic Aromas Scholarship Program

Organic Aromas
One Commerce Center, 1201 Orange Street #600, Wilmington, DE 19899
Phone: 650-989-5013

Email: info@organicaromas.com
https://organicaromas.com/pages/the-organic-aromas-aromatherapy-scholarship
Purpose: To support students who are advocates of essential oils and aromatherapy as they pursue a higher education.
Eligibility: Applicants must be enrolled in any field at the undergraduate or graduate level although special consideration is given to those pursuing careers in health care and life sciences. Students must write an essay of 500 to 1000 words on incorporating essential oils to improve mental and physical well-being which should be well documented and may be published and/or used for marketing purposes.
Target applicant(s): High school students. College students. Graduate school students. Adult students.
Amount: $1,000.
Number of awards: Varies.
Deadline: June 30.
How to apply: Applications are available online.
Exclusive: Visit www.UltimateScholarshipBook.com and enter code OR134220 for updates on this award.

(1343) · Outstanding Undergraduate Researchers Award Program

Computing Research Association
1828 L Street NW, Suite 800, Washington, DC 20036-4632
Phone: 202-234-2111
Email: info@cra.org
http://www.cra.org
Purpose: To support undergraduates who have completed outstanding research in the field of computing.
Eligibility: Applicants must be undergraduates at a North American college or university and must have conducted some type of computing research. Nominations from two faculty members and a recommendation from the chair of the applicant's home department are also required. Preference is given to undergraduate seniors. Selection is based on the quality of computing research, academic achievement and community involvement.
Target applicant(s): College students. Adult students.
Amount: Up to $1,500.
Number of awards: 4.
Deadline: October 24.
How to apply: The nomination form is available online. A recommendation from the chair of the applicant's home department and nominations from two faculty members are required.
Exclusive: Visit www.UltimateScholarshipBook.com and enter code CO134320 for updates on this award.

(1344) · Paradigm Challenge

Project Paradigm
P.O. Box 27729, Los Angeles, CA 90027
http://www.projectparadigm.org
Purpose: To encourage youth to use STEM plus kindness, creativity and collaboration to make a difference in the world.
Eligibility: Applicants must be 18 years of age or younger. Students will need to submit a description of 140 characters or less of their idea to reduce waste in their homes, schools, community or around the world.
Target applicant(s): Junior high students or younger. High school students.
Amount: $500-$25,000.
Number of awards: 100.
Deadline: May 1.
How to apply: Applications available online.
Exclusive: Visit www.UltimateScholarshipBook.com and enter code PR134420 for updates on this award.

(1345) · Paros-Digiquartz Scholarship

Marine Technology Society
1100 H Street NW, Suite LL-100, Washington, DC 20005
Phone: 202-717-8705
https://www.mtsociety.org/education/scholarships.aspx
Purpose: To support Marine Technology Society members with an interest in marine instrumentation in pursuing post-secondary education.
Eligibility: Applicants must be MTS student members who are accepted for enrollment or enrolled full-time in an undergraduate or graduate program.
Target applicant(s): College students. Graduate school students. Adult students.
Amount: $2,000.
Number of awards: 1.
Deadline: April 19.
How to apply: Applications are available online.
Exclusive: Visit www.UltimateScholarshipBook.com and enter code MA134520 for updates on this award.

(1346) · Paul A. Stewart Awards

Wilson Ornithological Society
Department of Biology and Biomedical Science, Dr. James Chace, Associate Professor, 100 Ochre Point Avenue, Newport, RI 02840-4192
Email: rbpayne@umich.edu
http://www.wilsonsociety.org
Purpose: To promote bird research.
Eligibility: Applicants' proposals should, but are not required to, cover the area of the study of bird movements based on banding, using the analysis and recovery of banded birds, with an emphasis on economic ornithology. Applicants must be willing to present their research results at an annual meeting of the Wilson Ornithological Society.
Target applicant(s): Junior high students or younger. High school students. College students. Graduate school students. Adult students.
Amount: $1,000.
Number of awards: Up to 4.
Deadline: February 1.
How to apply: Applications are available online.
Exclusive: Visit www.UltimateScholarshipBook.com and enter code WI134620 for updates on this award.

(1347) · Payette Sho-Ping Chin Memorial Academic Scholarship

American Institute of Architects
740 15th Street NW, Washington, DC 20005
Phone: 202-787-1001
http://www.archfoundation.org/aaf/aaf/Programs.Fellowships.htm
Purpose: To support women seeking an architectural degree.
Eligibility: Applicants must be female students in their third year of undergraduate or any level of graduate study in an accredited architecture program. Students must have a grade point average of 3.0 or better and be a U.S. citizen.
Target applicant(s): College students. Graduate school students. Adult students.
Minimum GPA: 3.0
Amount: $10,000.

Number of awards: 1.
Deadline: January 25.
How to apply: Applications are available online
Exclusive: Visit www.UltimateScholarshipBook.com and enter code AM134720 for updates on this award.

(1348) · Payzer Scholarship

EAA Aviation Center
3000 Poberezny Road, Oshkosh, WI 54902
Phone: 920-426-4800
Email: scholarships@eaa.org
http://www.eaa.org/en/eaa
Purpose: To support students interested in technical careers.
Eligibility: Applicants must be accepted or enrolled in an accredited college or university with an emphasis on technical information and must intend to pursue a career in engineering, mathematics or the physical or biological sciences. Applicants must also be involved in school and community activities as well as aviation and be members of EAA.
Target applicant(s): High school students. College students. Graduate school students. Adult students.
Amount: $5,000.
Number of awards: 1.
Deadline: February 28.
How to apply: Applications are available online.
Exclusive: Visit www.UltimateScholarshipBook.com and enter code EA134820 for updates on this award.

(1349) · PEG Management Fellowship

National Society of Professional Engineers
1420 King Street, Alexandria, VA 22314-2794
Phone: 703-684-2885
Email: students@nspe.org
https://www.nspe.org/resources/students/scholarships
Purpose: To aid students in engineering.
Eligibility: Applicants must be graduate students pursuing an MBA, master's degree in public administration or master's degree in engineering management and must also be engineering interns or licensed professional engineers. Selection is based on undergraduate GPA, GRE or GMAT score, professional activities, community activities, two recommendation letters, essay and membership. Preference is given to government employees.
Target applicant(s): Graduate school students. Adult students.
Amount: $2,500.
Number of awards: 1.
Deadline: March 15.
How to apply: Applications are available online.
Exclusive: Visit www.UltimateScholarshipBook.com and enter code NA134920 for updates on this award.

(1350) · Peggy Dixon Two-Year Scholarship

Society of Physics Students
One Physics Ellipse , College Park, MD 20740
Phone: 301-209-3007
Email: SPS-Programs@aip.org
https://www.spsnational.org/
Purpose: To help students seeking a bachelor's degree in physics to transition from a two-year to a four-year program.
Eligibility: Applicants must be members of SPS. Students must have finished at least one semester or quarter of the introductory physics sequence and must be registered in the appropriate subsequent physics classes.
Target applicant(s): College students. Adult students.
Amount: $2,000.
Number of awards: 1.
Deadline: March 22.
How to apply: Applications are available online or from chapter advisors.
Exclusive: Visit www.UltimateScholarshipBook.com and enter code SO135020 for updates on this award.

(1351) · Perennial Plant Association Scholarship

Perennial Plant Association
3383 Schirtzinger Road, Hilliard, OH 43026
Phone: 614-771-8431
Email: ppa@perennialplant.org
http://www.perennialplant.org
Purpose: To aid undergraduates who are studying horticulture or a related subject.
Eligibility: Applicants must be enrolled in a two- or four-year degree program while majoring or minoring in horticulture or a related subject. They must have a GPA of 3.0 or higher on a four-point scale. Previous recipients of this scholarship are not eligible. Preference will be given to applicants who are planning to pursue careers in perennials. Selection is based on the overall strength of the application.
Target applicant(s): College students. Adult students.
Minimum GPA: 3.0
Amount: $1,000.
Number of awards: Varies.
Deadline: February 1.
How to apply: Applications are available online. An application form, official transcript, personal statement and three recommendation letters are required.
Exclusive: Visit www.UltimateScholarshipBook.com and enter code PE135120 for updates on this award.

(1352) · Perfect Plants

Perfect Plants
P.O. Box 442, Lloyd, FL 32337
Email: contact@myperfectplants.com
https://myperfectplants.com/scholarship-application/
Purpose: To support students pursuing horticultural education.
Eligibility: Applicants must be current or enrolling undergraduate students with a minimum GPA of 3.0 who are pursuing a course of study leading to a career in the horticultural industry. Students must submit an essay and letters of recommendation along with their application and transcripts.
Target applicant(s): High school students. College students. Adult students.
Minimum GPA: 3.0
Amount: $1,000.
Number of awards: 1.
Deadline: August 20.
How to apply: Applications are available online.
Exclusive: Visit www.UltimateScholarshipBook.com and enter code PE135220 for updates on this award.

(1353) · Petroleum Division College Scholarships

ASME International Petroleum Technology Institute
Collegiate Council, 11757 Katy Freeway, Houston, TX 77079

Phone: 281-493-3491
http://www.asme-ipti-cc.org/
Purpose: To aid undergraduate engineering students who are members of the American Society of Mechanical Engineers (ASME).
Eligibility: Applicants must be ASME student members who are enrolled in an ABET-accredited undergraduate degree program in engineering. They must have an overall GPA of 2.5 or higher on a four-point scale. Selection is based on the overall strength of the application.
Target applicant(s): High school students. College students. Adult students.
Minimum GPA: 2.5
Amount: $2,000.
Number of awards: 20.
Deadline: September 1.
How to apply: Applications are available online. An application form, official transcript, personal statement and one recommendation letter are required.
Exclusive: Visit www.UltimateScholarshipBook.com and enter code AS135320 for updates on this award.

(1354) • Petroleum Division High School Scholarships

ASME International Petroleum Technology Institute
Collegiate Council, 11757 Katy Freeway, Houston, TX 77079
Phone: 281-493-3491
http://www.asme-ipti-cc.org/
Purpose: To aid high school seniors who are planning to major in engineering.
Eligibility: Applicants must have a pre-declared major of engineering listed on their college applications and a GPA of 3.0 or higher on a four-point scale. Selection is based on the overall strength of the application.
Target applicant(s): High school students.
Minimum GPA: 3.0
Amount: $1,000.
Number of awards: 8.
Deadline: September 1.
How to apply: Applications are available online. An application form, personal essay, official transcript and one letter of recommendation are required.
Exclusive: Visit www.UltimateScholarshipBook.com and enter code AS135420 for updates on this award.

(1355) • PHCC Educational Foundation Scholarship

Plumbing-Heating-Cooling Contractors National Association
180 South Washington Street, Suite 100, Falls Church, VA 22046
Phone: 800-533-7694
Email: scholarships@naphcc.org
http://www.phccweb.org
Purpose: To elevate the technical and business competence of the plumbing-heating-cooling (p-h-c) industry by awarding scholarships to students who are enrolled in a p-h-c-related major.
Eligibility: Applicants must be currently enrolled or plan to enroll in a p-h-c-related major at an accredited four-year college or university or two-year technical college, community college or trade school. Students enrolled in an approved apprentice program must also be working full-time for a licensed plumbing or HVACR contractor who is a member of the PHCC. Two scholarships will be awarded to students who are enrolled in either a PHCC-approved apprentice program or a full-time certificate or degree program at an accredited two-year community college, technical college or trade school. Three scholarships are awarded to students who are enrolled in an undergraduate degree program at an accredited four-year college or university.
Target applicant(s): High school students. College students. Adult students.
Amount: $1,000-$5,000.
Number of awards: Up to 39.
Deadline: May 1.
How to apply: Applications are available online or by email.
Exclusive: Visit www.UltimateScholarshipBook.com and enter code PL135520 for updates on this award.

(1356) • Phoebe Pember Memorial Scholarship

United Daughters of the Confederacy
328 North Boulevard, Richmond, VA 23220
Phone: 804-355-1636
Email: hqudc@rcn.com
http://www.hqudc.org
Purpose: To aid Confederate descendants who are undergraduate nursing students.
Eligibility: Applicants must be the direct descendant of an eligible Confederate. They must be enrolled in an undergraduate degree program in nursing at an accredited U.S. college or university and have a GPA of 3.0 or higher on a four-point scale. Selection is based on the overall strength of the application.
Target applicant(s): College students. Adult students.
Minimum GPA: 3.0
Amount: Varies.
Number of awards: Varies.
Scholarship may be renewable.
Deadline: Varies.
How to apply: Applications are available online. An application form, personal statement, official transcript, one letter of recommendation, endorsement from sponsoring UDC Chapter, applicant photo and proof of Confederate ancestry are required.
Exclusive: Visit www.UltimateScholarshipBook.com and enter code UN135620 for updates on this award.

(1357) • Physician Assistant Foundation Scholarship

Physician Assistant Foundation
PA Foundation Scholarship Committee, 950 North Washington Street, Alexandria, VA 22314-1552
Phone: 703-519-5686
Email: aapa@aapa.org
http://www.aapa.org
Purpose: To support physician assistants.
Eligibility: Applicants must be American Academy of Physician Assistants (AAPA) members and currently enrolled in the professional phase of a PA training program at an ARC-PA-accredited physician assistant program. Students are judged on the basis of financial need, community and professional involvement, goals and academic performance.
Target applicant(s): College students. Adult students.
Amount: $1,000.
Number of awards: 26.
Deadline: May 31.
How to apply: Applications are available online.
Exclusive: Visit www.UltimateScholarshipBook.com and enter code PH135720 for updates on this award.

(1358) • Physio-Control Advanced Nursing Practice Scholarship

Emergency Nurses Association
915 Lee Street, Des Plaines, IL 60016
Phone: 847-460-4100
Email: foundation@ena.org
http://www.ena.org

Purpose: Monetary assistance for an advanced degree is awarded to an emergency nurse. Priority is given to those pursuing careers in cardiac nursing.
Eligibility: Applicants must be nurses pursuing advanced clinical practice degrees to become clinical nurse specialists or nurse practitioners. Preference is given to applicants focusing on cardiac nursing. Applicants must have been ENA members for at least 12 months before applying.
Target applicant(s): College students. Adult students.
Minimum GPA: 3.0
Amount: $2,000.
Number of awards: 1.
Deadline: April 28.
How to apply: Applications are available online.
Exclusive: Visit www.UltimateScholarshipBook.com and enter code EM135820 for updates on this award.

(1359) • Pioneers of Flight

National Air Transportation Foundation
Pioneers of Flight Scholarship Program, Attn.: Professor Gregory Schwab, Chair, Department of Aerospace Technology, TC 216, Indiana State University, Terre Haute, IN 47809
Email: aeschwab@isugw.indstate.edu
http://www.nata.aero

Purpose: To assist students pursuing general aviation as a career.
Eligibility: Applicants must be full-time students at an accredited four-year institution, be sophomores or juniors at the time of application and plan to pursue a career in aviation. Students must have a minimum 3.0 GPA.
Target applicant(s): College students. Adult students.
Minimum GPA: 3.0
Amount: $1,000.
Number of awards: 2.
Deadline: Last Friday in December.
How to apply: Applications are available online.
Exclusive: Visit www.UltimateScholarshipBook.com and enter code NA135920 for updates on this award.

(1360) • Plastics Pioneers Association Scholarships

Society of Plastics Engineers
6 Berkshire Boulevard, Suite 306, Bethel, CT 06801
Phone: 203-775-0471
Email: info@4spe.org
http://www.4spe.org/spe-foundation

Purpose: To aid students who are planning for careers in plastics technology and engineering.
Eligibility: Applicants must be full-time undergraduate students who intend to pursue careers as plastics technicians or engineers. Selection is based on the overall strength of the application.
Target applicant(s): High school students. College students. Adult students.
Amount: $3,000.
Number of awards: Varies.
Deadline: April 1.
How to apply: Applications are available online. An application form, three recommendation letters, a transcript and personal statement are required.
Exclusive: Visit www.UltimateScholarshipBook.com and enter code SO136020 for updates on this award.

(1361) • Polymer Modifiers and Additives Division Scholarships

Society of Plastics Engineers
6 Berkshire Boulevard, Suite 306, Bethel, CT 06801
Phone: 203-775-0471
Email: info@4spe.org
http://www.4spe.org/spe-foundation

Purpose: To aid students who have an interest in the plastics industry.
Eligibility: Applicants must have an interest in the plastics industry, major in or take courses leading to a career in the plastics industry and be in good academic standing. Financial need is considered.
Target applicant(s): High school students. College students. Adult students.
Amount: Varies.
Number of awards: Varies.
Deadline: April 1.
How to apply: Applications are available online.
Exclusive: Visit www.UltimateScholarshipBook.com and enter code SO136120 for updates on this award.

(1362) • Powerline Prodigies Student Scholarship

Powerline Group
1201 Route 112 Suite 800, Port Jefferson Station, NY 11776
Phone: 914-720-2031
Email: scholarships@thepowerlinegroup.com
http://thepowerlinegroup.com/company/community-outreach/powerline-prodigies-college-scholarships/

Purpose: To support students who have a passion for technology.
Eligibility: Applicants must be full-time undergraduate students who are enrolled full-time at an accredited college or university in the upcoming school year. One scholarship will go to a student attending college in Long Island, NY and another to any student nationwide. Students must have a strong academic record and be pursuing a degree in one of these fields: computer science, technology or software development. An essay is required as part of the application process.
Target applicant(s): High school students. College students. Adult students.
Amount: $5,000.
Number of awards: 2.
Deadline: May 1.
How to apply: Applications are available online.
Exclusive: Visit www.UltimateScholarshipBook.com and enter code PO136220 for updates on this award.

(1363) • PPG Protective and Marine Coatings Academic Scholarship

National Association of Corrosion Engineers (NACE) International Foundation
15835 Park Ten Place, Houston, TX 77084-5145
Phone: 281-228-6205
Email: nace.foundation@nace.org
http://nace-foundation.org/programs/students/scholarships/

Purpose: To help students interested in pursuing science and/or engineering degrees.

Eligibility: Applicants must be an undergraduate enrolled full-time at an accredited two- or four-year college or university and must be pursuing a degree with an emphasis on corrosion or coatings. Applicants must have a GPA of 3.0 or higher in their chosen field of study.
Target applicant(s): College students. Adult students.
Minimum GPA: 3.0
Amount: $5,000.
Number of awards: Up to 2.
Deadline: January 5.
How to apply: Applications are available online. An application form, three recommendation forms, an academic transcript and essay scholarship questions are required.
Exclusive: Visit www.UltimateScholarshipBook.com and enter code NA136320 for updates on this award.

(1364) • Predoctoral Fellowship Program

National Gallery of Art
2000B South Club Drive, Landover, MD 20785
Phone: 202-842-6482
http://www.nga.gov
Purpose: To support advanced graduate research in the history, theory and criticism of art, architecture and urbanism.
Eligibility: Applicants for predoctoral fellowships must be nominated by the chair of the graduate department of art history or other appropriate departments. Applicants must have completed all departmental requirements, including course work, residency and general and preliminary examinations. Certification in two languages other than English is required. Applicants should submit nomination forms, supporting letters from two individuals and writing samples. There are various fellowships. The David E. Finley Fellowship requires applicants have a significant interest in curatorial work. The Paul Mellon Fellowship is for the completion of a doctoral dissertation in Western art. The Samuel H. Kress Fellowship is for the completion of a doctoral dissertation in European art on a topic before the early nineteenth century. The Wyeth Fellowship is for the completion of a doctoral dissertation that concerns aspects of art of the United States, including native and pre-Revolutionary America. The Ittleson Fellowship is for the completion of a doctoral dissertation in the visual arts in a field other than Western art. The Andrew W. Mellon Fellowship is for the completion of a doctoral dissertation in cross-cultural studies or in a field other than Western art through the twentieth century. The Robert H. and Clarice Smith Fellowship is for research on Northern European art between 1400 and 1700, intended for the advancement or completion of either a doctoral dissertation or a resulting publication. The Chester Dale Fellowships are for the advancement or completion of a doctoral dissertation in any area of Western art, with a preference for modern and contemporary topics. The Center offers a Paul Mellon Postdoctoral Fellowship for recipients of the David E. Finley, Paul Mellon, Samuel H. Kress, Wyeth, Ittleson, Andrew W. Mellon and two-year Chester Dale fellowships if the dissertation has been accepted by June 1 of the residence year. Several candidates for each fellowship will be invited to Washington for interviews.
Target applicant(s): Graduate school students. Adult students.
Amount: $30,000 plus allowances.
Number of awards: 9.
Deadline: November 15.
How to apply: Application materials are described online. Contact your dissertation advisor and departmental chair to obtain nomination forms.
Exclusive: Visit www.UltimateScholarshipBook.com and enter code NA136420 for updates on this award.

(1365) • Predoctoral Research Training Fellowship

Epilepsy Foundation
8301 Professional Place East, Suite 200, Landover, MD 20785-2353
Phone: 800-332-1000
Email: ContactUs@efa.org
http://www.epilepsy.com/
Purpose: To support pre-doctoral students with dissertation research relating to epilepsy.
Eligibility: Applicants must be full-time graduate students pursuing a Ph.D. degree in neuroscience, physiology, pharmacology, psychology, biochemistry, genetics, nursing, pharmacy or other related areas; have a dissertation research project; have a qualified mentor who can supervise the project and have access to resources to conduct the project. The project must be in the U.S. and its territories. The award is based on the quality of the dissertation project, relevance to epilepsy, the applicant's qualifications, the mentor's qualifications and the quality of the proposed environment.
Target applicant(s): Graduate school students. Adult students.
Amount: Varies.
Number of awards: Varies.
Deadline: Varies.
How to apply: Applicants must submit three recommendation letters including one from the mentor, a statement of intent, a biographical sketch, a cover sheet form, a lay summary, transcripts and a research plan.
Exclusive: Visit www.UltimateScholarshipBook.com and enter code EP136520 for updates on this award.

(1366) • Presidents Scholarship of the Institute of Industrial Engineers

Institute of Industrial and Systems Engineers
3577 Parkway Lane, Suite 200, Norcross, GA 30092
Phone: 800-494-0460
Email: bcameron@iienet.org
http://www.iise.org/
Purpose: To support undergraduate industrial engineering students.
Eligibility: Applicants must be active student members of the Institute of Industrial Engineers (IIE). They must be full-time undergraduates enrolled in an industrial engineering degree program and have a GPA of 3.4 or higher on a four-point scale. They must have demonstrated leadership skills. Applicants must be nominated by their academic department heads. Selection is based on professional leadership potential, character, financial need and academic merit.
Target applicant(s): College students. Adult students.
Minimum GPA: 3.4
Amount: $1,000.
Number of awards: 1.
Deadline: November 15.
How to apply: Nomination forms are available online. A nomination form completed by the applicant's academic department head is required.
Exclusive: Visit www.UltimateScholarshipBook.com and enter code IN136620 for updates on this award.

(1367) • Pretty Photoshop Actions Bi-annual Scholarship

Pretty Photoshop Actions
Email: scholarship@photoshopactions.com
https://www.photoshopactions.com/pages/pretty-photoshop-actions-scholarship-program
Purpose: To help offset the cost of higher education.

Eligibility: Applicants must be graduating high school seniors or enrolled at a college or university in the U.S. or Canada. Students must create an Adobe Photoshop tutorial essay.
Target applicant(s): High school students. College students. Adult students.
Amount: $500.
Deadline: April 15, October 15.
How to apply: Applications are available online.
Exclusive: Visit www.UltimateScholarshipBook.com and enter code PR136720 for updates on this award.

(1368) • Pulte Group Build Your Future Scholarship Program

National Housing Endowment
1201 15th Street NW, Washington, DC 20005
Phone: 202-266-8069
Email: Scholarships@nahb.org
http://www.nationalhousingendowment.org
Purpose: To aid U.S. students who plan to pursue careers in the building industry.
Eligibility: Applicants must be U.S. undergraduate freshmen, sophomores or juniors who are enrolled full-time in a housing-related degree program (construction, civil engineering, architecture, building trades or management, etc.). They must have at least one full academic year remaining in their course of study and maintain an overall GPA of at least 2.5 and major GPA of at least 3.0. Preference will be given to applicants who demonstrate financial need or who are members of a building industry-related service or professional organization, especially the National Association of Home Builders. Selection is based on financial need, academic achievement, GPA, work experience, extracurricular activities and professional goals.
Target applicant(s): College students. Adult students.
Minimum GPA: 2.5
Amount: Varies.
Number of awards: Varies.
Scholarship may be renewable.
Deadline: March 27.
How to apply: Applications are available online. An application form, a transcript, two recommendation letters, a list of degree requirements, a personal essay and a statement of financial status are required.
Exclusive: Visit www.UltimateScholarshipBook.com and enter code NA136820 for updates on this award.

(1369) • Quanta Picosecond Laser Annual Scholarship

Quanta
611 Corporate Circle, Suites A-B, Golden, CO 80401
Phone: 844-694-1064
Email: scholarship@quantausa.com
https://quantausa.com/quanta-picosecond-laser-annual-scholarship/
Purpose: To support future innovators.
Eligibility: Applicants must enrolled in an accredited college or university for the upcoming year. Students must have a GPA of 3.0 and plan to pursue education in engineering, physics, medicine, biology or natural or applied sciences.
Target applicant(s): High school students. College students. Adult students.
Minimum GPA: 3.0
Amount: $1,000.
Number of awards: 1.
Deadline: July 31.
How to apply: Applications are available online.
Exclusive: Visit www.UltimateScholarshipBook.com and enter code QU136920 for updates on this award.

(1370) • R&D Systems Scholarship Program

R&D Systems, Inc.
614 McKinley Place NE, Minneapolis, MN 55413
Phone: 800-343-7475
Email: scholarship@novusbio.com
https://www.rndsystems.com/grants-scholarships/scholarship-application
Purpose: To support students who are pursuing a degree in a science related field.
Eligibility: Applicants must be enrolled, or plan to be enrolled, in a undergraduate or graduate level science program.
Target applicant(s): High school students. College students. Graduate school students. Adult students.
Amount: $1,500.
Number of awards: 1.
Deadline: July 20.
How to apply: Applications are available online.
Exclusive: Visit www.UltimateScholarshipBook.com and enter code R&137020 for updates on this award.

(1371) • Rain Bird Intelligent Use of Water Scholarship

Landscape Architecture Foundation
1129 20th Street NW, Suite 202, Washington, DC 20036
Phone: 202-331-7070
Email: scholarships@lafoundation.org
https://lafoundation.org/scholarship/
Purpose: To recognize outstanding landscape architecture students.
Eligibility: Applicants must be college juniors or fourth- or fifth-year seniors who are landscape architecture, horticulture or irrigation science students who have a demonstrated commitment to the landscape architecture profession and exhibit financial need. Applications can only be sent by email.
Target applicant(s): College students. Adult students.
Amount: $2,500.
Number of awards: 1.
Deadline: February 15.
How to apply: Applicants should follow the guidelines.
Exclusive: Visit www.UltimateScholarshipBook.com and enter code LA137120 for updates on this award.

(1372) • Ralph K. Hillquist Honorary SAE Scholarship

Society of Automotive Engineers International
Scholarships Program, 400 Commonwealth Drive, Warrendale, PA 15096
Phone: 724-776-4841
Email: scholarships@sae.org
http://students.sae.org/scholarships/
Purpose: To aid mechanical and automotive engineering students.
Eligibility: Applicants must be U.S. citizens and full-time undergraduate juniors who are enrolled in an ABET-accredited mechanical or automotive engineering degree program at a U.S. college or university. They must have a GPA of 3.0 or higher. Preference will be given to applicants who have completed coursework in noise and vibration (e.g. physics, statics, vibration or dynamics). Selection is based on academic merit, leadership and special studies in noise and vibration.

Target applicant(s): College students. Adult students.
Minimum GPA: 3.0
Amount: $1,000.
Number of awards: 1.
Deadline: March 15.
How to apply: Applications are available online. An application form, official transcript and standardized test scores are required.
Exclusive: Visit www.UltimateScholarshipBook.com and enter code SO137220 for updates on this award.

(1373) • Raney Fund Award

American Society of Ichthyologists and Herpetologists
P.O. Box 1897, Lawrence, KS 66044-8897
Phone: 785-843-1235
Email: asih@allenpress.com
http://www.asih.org/membership/student-awards
Purpose: To support young ichthyologists.
Eligibility: Applicants should be members of ASIH and should be enrolled for an advanced degree, although those with developing careers may receive the award under exceptional circumstances. Awards may be used for museums or laboratory study, travel, fieldwork or other activities that will enhance their professional careers and their contributions to the science of ichthyology. Scholarships are awarded on the basis of merit and need.
Target applicant(s): Graduate school students. Adult students.
Amount: $400-$1,000.
Number of awards: Varies.
Deadline: March 1.
How to apply: Applications are available by email or written request.
Exclusive: Visit www.UltimateScholarshipBook.com and enter code AM137320 for updates on this award.

(1374) • Raymond Davis Scholarship

Society for Imaging Science and Technology
7003 Kilworth Lane, Springfield, VA 22151
Phone: 703-642-9090
Email: info@imaging.org
http://www.imaging.org
Purpose: To support students who are studying imaging science and technology.
Eligibility: Applicants must be full-time graduate or undergraduate students studying photographic or imaging engineering or science who have completed or will complete two academic years of college before the term of the scholarship.
Target applicant(s): College students. Graduate school students. Adult students.
Amount: At least $1,000.
Number of awards: Varies.
Deadline: October 1.
How to apply: Applications are available online.
Exclusive: Visit www.UltimateScholarshipBook.com and enter code SO137420 for updates on this award.

(1375) • Regeneron Science Talent Search

Regeneron Science Talent Search
Society for Science and the Public, 1719 North Street NW, Washington, DC 20036
Phone: 202-785-2255
Email: ssp@societyforscience.org
https://student.societyforscience.org/regeneron-sts
Purpose: To recognize excellence in science among the nation's youth and encourage the exploration of science.
Eligibility: Applicants must be high school seniors in the U.S., Puerto Rico, Guam, Virgin Islands, American Samoa, Wake or Midway Islands or the Marianas. U.S. citizens attending foreign schools are also eligible. Applicants must complete college entrance exams and complete individual research projects and provide a report on the research.
Target applicant(s): High school students.
Amount: $7,500-$150,000.
Number of awards: 40.
Deadline: November 14.
How to apply: Applications are available by request.
Exclusive: Visit www.UltimateScholarshipBook.com and enter code RE137520 for updates on this award.

(1376) • Research Training Fellowships for Medical Students (Medical Fellows Program)

Howard Hughes Medical Institute
4000 Jones Bridge Road, Chevy Chase, MD 20815-6789
Phone: 301-951-6708
Email: medfellows@hhmi.org
http://www.hhmi.org
Purpose: To support a year of full-time biomedical research training for medical and dental students.
Eligibility: Applicants must be enrolled in a U.S. medical, dental or veterinary school, and the fellowship research may be conducted at an academic or nonprofit institution in the United States or abroad if the fellow's mentor is affiliated with a U.S. institution. The research should focus on biological processes or disease mechanisms. The fellowship is based on the applicant's ability, potential research career as a physician/scientist and training. Applicants must submit research plans, personal statements, letters of reference, transcripts and MCAT or DAT scores.
Target applicant(s): Graduate school students. Adult students.
Amount: $43,000.
Number of awards: Varies.
Deadline: January 11.
How to apply: Applications are available online.
Exclusive: Visit www.UltimateScholarshipBook.com and enter code HO137620 for updates on this award.

(1377) • Reuben Trane Scholarship

American Society of Heating, Refrigerating and Air-Conditioning Engineers (ASHRAE)
1791 Tullie Circle, NE, Atlanta, GA 30329
Phone: 404-636-8400
Email: lbenedict@ashrae.org
http://www.ashrae.org
Purpose: To support engineering undergraduates who are preparing for careers in the heating, ventilation, air-conditioning and refrigeration (HVACR) industry.
Eligibility: Applicants must be attending a school that houses a student branch of the American Society of Heating, Refrigerating and Air-Conditioning Engineers (ASHRAE), is ABET-accredited (U.S. institutions) or is ABET-affiliated (international institutions). Applicants must be undergraduate students who are enrolled in an engineering or pre-engineering curriculum that provides adequate preparation for a career in the HVACR industry. They must have a GPA of 3.0 or higher on a four-point scale or must be in the top 30 percent of their class. Selection is based on the overall strength of the application.
Target applicant(s): High school students. College students. Adult students.

Minimum GPA: 3.0
Amount: $10,000.
Number of awards: 3.
Scholarship may be renewable.
Deadline: December 1.
How to apply: Applications are available online. The application form, official transcript, one letter of recommendation and the evaluation form from an ASHRAE student branch interview (if applicable) are required.
Exclusive: Visit www.UltimateScholarshipBook.com and enter code AM137720 for updates on this award.

(1378) • RevPart STEM Scholarship

RevPart
129 Bethea Road, Suite 402, Fayetteville, GA 30214
Phone: 844-738-7278
Email: info@revpart.com
https://revpart.com/scholarship/
Purpose: To encourage students pursuing a higher education in their chosen study of area of study in a STEM related field.
Eligibility: Applicants must be a current undergraduate or graduate student majoring in a STEM related field at an accredited college or institution.
Target applicant(s): High school students. College students. Graduate school students. Adult students.
Amount: $250-$1,000.
Number of awards: 3.
Deadline: August 1.
How to apply: Applications are available online.
Exclusive: Visit www.UltimateScholarshipBook.com and enter code RE137820 for updates on this award.

(1379) • Richard J. Stull Student Essay Competition in Healthcare Management

American College of Healthcare Executives
One North Franklin Street, Suite 1700, Chicago, IL 60606
Phone: 312-424-9316
Email: sbrown@ache.org
http://www.ache.org
Purpose: To support future healthcare executives.
Eligibility: Applicants must be undergraduate or graduate students enrolled in a healthcare administration degree program at a U.S. or Canadian postsecondary institution that is an American College of Healthcare Executives (ACHE) Higher Education network participant. They must be ACHE student associates or active affiliates. Submitted essays cannot have been published before and must be the sole creation of the applicant. Residents and other postgraduate students are ineligible. Selection is based on relevance of subject matter, creativity, practical applicability of subject matter and clarity.
Target applicant(s): High school students. College students. Graduate school students. Adult students.
Amount: Up to $3,000.
Number of awards: 6.
Deadline: December 5.
How to apply: Essay submission guidelines are available online. An essay is required.
Exclusive: Visit www.UltimateScholarshipBook.com and enter code AM137920 for updates on this award.

(1380) • Richard Jensen Scholarship

National Alliance of Independent Crop Consultants
P.O. Box 209, Vonore, TN 37885
Phone: 901-861-0511
Email: AllisonJones@NAICC.org
http://naicc.org/foundations/scholarship/
Purpose: To aid undergraduate students of crop production.
Eligibility: Applicants must be undergraduate juniors who are majoring in an agricultural subject that is related to crop production (such as agronomy, horticulture, weed science, soil sciences, entomology or plant pathology). Selection is based on the overall strength of the application.
Target applicant(s): College students. Adult students.
Amount: $3,000.
Number of awards: 1.
Deadline: November 1.
How to apply: Applications are available online. An application form, transcript, proof of enrollment and two reference letters are required.
Exclusive: Visit www.UltimateScholarshipBook.com and enter code NA138020 for updates on this award.

(1381) • Richard L. Davis, FACMPE - Managers Scholarship

Medical Group Management Association
104 Inverness Terrace East, Englewood, CO 80112
Phone: 877-275-6462
Email: acmpe@mgma.com
http://www.mgma.com
Purpose: To aid medical practice management professionals who are college students.
Eligibility: Applicants must be current medical practice management professionals who are enrolled in an undergraduate or graduate degree program that is related to medical practice management. Selection is based on the overall strength of the application.
Target applicant(s): College students. Graduate school students. Adult students.
Amount: $2,500.
Number of awards: Varies.
Deadline: May 1.
How to apply: Applications are available online. An application form and supporting materials are required.
Exclusive: Visit www.UltimateScholarshipBook.com and enter code ME138120 for updates on this award.

(1382) • Richard L. Davis, FACMPE/Barbara B. Watson, FACMPE - National Scholarship

Medical Group Management Association
104 Inverness Terrace East, Englewood, CO 80112
Phone: 877-275-6462
Email: acmpe@mgma.com
http://www.mgma.com
Purpose: To aid medical practice management students.
Eligibility: Applicants must be undergraduate or graduate students who are enrolled in a degree program that is related to medical practice management (such as healthcare administration, public health or business administration). Selection is based on the overall strength of the application.
Target applicant(s): High school students. College students. Graduate school students. Adult students.
Amount: $2,500.
Number of awards: Varies.

Deadline: May 1.
How to apply: Applications are available online. An application form and supporting materials are required.
Exclusive: Visit www.UltimateScholarshipBook.com and enter code ME138220 for updates on this award.

(1383) • Richard Lee Vernon Aviation Scholarship

EAA Aviation Center
3000 Poberezny Road, Oshkosh, WI 54902
Phone: 920-426-4800
Email: scholarships@eaa.org
http://www.eaa.org/en/eaa
Purpose: To support students pursuing training leading to a professional aviation occupations.
Eligibility: Applicants must be accepted to an accredited college, university or aviation technical school pursuing a course of study focusing on aviation. Applicants must also be involved in school and community activities as well as aviation. Recipient must show need for financial support.
Target applicant(s): High school students. College students. Adult students.
Amount: $500.
Number of awards: 1.
Deadline: February 28.
How to apply: Applications are available online.
Exclusive: Visit www.UltimateScholarshipBook.com and enter code EA138320 for updates on this award.

(1384) • RMEL Foundation Scholarships

Rocky Mountain Electrical League
6855 South Havana Street, Suite 430, Centennial, CO 80112
Phone: 303-865-5544
Email: jamessakamoto@rmel.org
http://www.rmel.org
Purpose: To support students pursuing certificate or degree-seeking programs related to the electric energy industry.
Eligibility: Applicants must be U.S. citizens and full-time students pursuing either a certificate, associate or baccalaureate degree in the electric energy arena including: power plant technology, electric line working, power line technology, electrical power technology, electrical line worker technology, electrical distribution systems, utility line technician and traditional or alternative power generation technology. Selection is based on future goals in the electric energy arena, motivation, service and academic performance.
Target applicant(s): High school students. College students. Graduate school students. Adult students.
Amount: Up to $3,000.
Number of awards: Varies.
Deadline: February 9.
How to apply: Applications are available online. An application form and transcripts are required.
Exclusive: Visit www.UltimateScholarshipBook.com and enter code RO138420 for updates on this award.

(1385) • Robert B. Oliver ASNT Scholarship

American Society for Nondestructive Testing
Awards and Honors Program, 1711 Arlingate Lane, P.O. Box 28518, Columbus, OH 43228-0518
Phone: 614-274-6003 x 233
Email: awards@asnt.org
http://www.asnt.org
Purpose: To support students in nondestructive testing.
Eligibility: Applicants must be undergraduate students enrolled in an engineering program of an accredited university and specialize in nondestructive testing (NDT). A nominating letter, transcript and an essay describing the role of NDT/NDE in their career are required. The award is based on creativity, content, format and readability and the student's involvement in a research project.
Target applicant(s): College students. Adult students.
Amount: $2,500.
Number of awards: Up to 3.
Deadline: February 15.
How to apply: Applications are available online.
Exclusive: Visit www.UltimateScholarshipBook.com and enter code AM138520 for updates on this award.

(1386) • Robert E. Altenhofen Memorial Scholarship

American Society for Photogrammetry and Remote Sensing (ASPRS)
The Imaging and Geospatial Information Society
5410 Grosvenor Lane, Suite 210, Bethesda, MD 20814
Phone: 301-493-0290 x101
Email: scholarships@asprs.org
http://www.asprs.org
Purpose: To encourage and commend college students who display ability in the theoretical aspects of photogrammetry.
Eligibility: Applicants must be undergraduate or graduate students and submit several pieces with their applications including: a two-page statement regarding plans for continuing studies in theoretical photogrammetry, papers, research reports or other items written by the applicants and academic transcripts. Recipients are required to submit a report on the work they accomplish during the award period.
Target applicant(s): High school students. College students. Graduate school students. Adult students.
Amount: $2,000.
Number of awards: 1.
Deadline: November 15.
How to apply: Applications are available online.
Exclusive: Visit www.UltimateScholarshipBook.com and enter code AM138620 for updates on this award.

(1387) • Robert E. Dougherty Educational Foundation Scholarship Award

Composite Panel Association
Robert E. Dougherty Educational Foundation, 19465 Deerfield Avenue, Suite 306, Leesburg, VA 20176
Phone: 703-724-1128
Email: gheroux@cpamail.org
http://www.pbmdf.com
Purpose: To aid students who are preparing for careers in the composite panel field.
Eligibility: Applicants must be nominated for this award by a Robert E. Dougherty Educational Foundation member company or member institution. They must be North American citizens and be graduate or undergraduate students who are studying industrial engineering, mechanical engineering, chemistry, forest products, wood science or wood technology. Selection is based on the overall strength of the application.
Target applicant(s): College students. Graduate school students. Adult students.
Amount: Up to $5,000.
Number of awards: 5.

Scholarship may be renewable.
Deadline: March 10.
How to apply: Applications are available online. An application form, official transcript and academic adviser appraisal are required.
Exclusive: Visit www.UltimateScholarshipBook.com and enter code CO138720 for updates on this award.

(1388) • Robert E. Thunen Memorial Scholarships

Thunen Scholarship Committee
IES San Francisco Section, Mary-Jane Lawless, 1201 Park Avenue, Suite 100, Emeryville, CA 94608
Phone: 510-864-0204
Email: mrcatisbac@aol.com
https://www.ies.org/membership/society-awards/
Purpose: To help students who plan to pursue illumination as a career.
Eligibility: Applicants must be full-time junior, senior or graduate students in an accredited four-year college in Northern California, Nevada, Oregon or Washington who plan to pursue illumination as a career. The application, statement of purpose and at least three letters of recommendation are required. Students should review the IES Lighting Handbook to see the available fields of study.
Target applicant(s): College students. Graduate school students. Adult students.
Amount: $2,500.
Number of awards: At least 2.
Deadline: April 1.
How to apply: Applications are available by mail and email.
Exclusive: Visit www.UltimateScholarshipBook.com and enter code TH138820 for updates on this award.

(1389) • Robert Eggert Memorial FFA Scholarship

National FFA Organization
P.O. Box 68960, 6060 FFA Drive, Indianapolis, IN 46268-0960
Phone: 888-332-2668
Email: scholarships@ffa.org
https://www.ffa.org/participate/scholarships
Purpose: To support FFA members working toward a four-year degree in agribusiness.
Eligibility: Applicants must have a minimum 3.2 GPA and a proven history of public service and excellence in academics. Selection is based on the overall strength of the application.
Target applicant(s): High school students. College students.
Minimum GPA: 3.2
Amount: $1,000.
Number of awards: 1.
Deadline: February 8.
How to apply: Applications are available online.
Exclusive: Visit www.UltimateScholarshipBook.com and enter code NA138920 for updates on this award.

(1390) • Robert H. Herbert Undergraduate Scholarship

Society of Naval Architects and Marine Engineers
99 Canal Center Plaza, Suite 310, Alexandria, VA 22314
Phone: 201-798-4800
Email: efaustino@sname.org
http://www.sname.org/educationoptions/scholarships
Purpose: To assist college undergraduates who are studying marine industry fields.
Eligibility: Applicants must be U.S., Canadian or international college students who are members of the SNAME and are working towards degrees in naval architecture, marine engineering, ocean engineering or marine industry related areas fields. An application form, three recommendation letters and an essay are required.
Target applicant(s): College students. Adult students.
Amount: Up to $6,000.
Number of awards: 1.
Deadline: June 1.
How to apply: Applications are available online.
Exclusive: Visit www.UltimateScholarshipBook.com and enter code SO139020 for updates on this award.

(1391) • Robert W. Lyons Award

RCI Foundation
Phone: 507-931-1682
Email: rcif@scholarshipamerica.org
http://www.rcifoundation.org
Purpose: To support students pursuing a degree in engineering, architecture or construction sciences.
Eligibility: Applicants must be current undergraduate or graduate level students who have completed a minimum of 24 credit hours. Students must plan to enroll full-time at an accredited college, university, vocational or technical school for the entire academic year in an architecture, engineering, construction or building sciences program. A minimum 2.75 GPA is required. Applicants must be U.S. or Canadian citizens.
Target applicant(s): College students. Graduate school students. Adult students.
Minimum GPA: 2.75
Amount: $5,000.
Number of awards: 2.
Deadline: February 28.
How to apply: Applications available online.
Exclusive: Visit www.UltimateScholarshipBook.com and enter code RC139120 for updates on this award.

(1392) • Roofing Industry Scholarship - Melvin Kruger Endowed Scholarship

National Roofing Foundation (NRF)
10255 West Higgins Road, Suite 600, Rosemont, IL 60018
Phone: (847) 299-9070
http://www.nrca.net
Purpose: To support members of the National Roofing Contractors Association (NRCA).
Eligibility: Applicants must be full-time employees of NRCA member companies or their immediate family members. Students must be high school seniors or graduates or full-time undergraduate students at an accredited two- or four-year post-secondary institution. Applicants must major in a roofing or building construction course of study for a full academic year.
Target applicant(s): High school students. College students. Adult students.
Amount: $5,000.
Number of awards: 3.
Scholarship may be renewable.
Deadline: January 31.
How to apply: Applications are available online.
Exclusive: Visit www.UltimateScholarshipBook.com and enter code NA139220 for updates on this award.

(1393) • Roy J. Shlemon Awards

Geological Society of America Foundation (GSAF)
P.O. Box 9140, Boulder, CO 80301
Phone: 800-472-1988 x1054
Email: info@gsafweb.org
https://gsafweb.org/funds-and-awards/
Purpose: To assist graduate students in conducting research in environmental and engineering geology.
Eligibility: Applicants must be members of the Geological Society of America's Engineering Geology Division, and they must be conducting research at the master's or doctoral level.
Target applicant(s): Graduate school students. Adult students.
Amount: Up to $3,000.
Number of awards: At least 2.
Deadline: March 31.
How to apply: Applications are available online.
Exclusive: Visit www.UltimateScholarshipBook.com and enter code GE139320 for updates on this award.

(1394) • Rubber Division Undergraduate Scholarship

American Chemical Society
Christie Robinson, Training and Development Director, Rubber Division, ACS, 411 Wolf Ledges Parkway, Suite 201, Akron, OH 44311
Phone: 800-227-5558
Email: crobinson@rubber.org
http://www.acs.org
Purpose: To aid undergraduate students who are majoring in subjects related to the rubber industry.
Eligibility: Applicants must be rising undergraduate juniors or seniors. They must be majoring in chemistry, chemical engineering, polymer science, mechanical engineering, physics or any other subject that is related to the rubber industry. Selection is based on the overall strength of the application.
Target applicant(s): College students. Adult students.
Amount: $5,000.
Number of awards: 2.
Deadline: March 1.
How to apply: Applications are available online. An application form and supporting materials are required.
Exclusive: Visit www.UltimateScholarshipBook.com and enter code AM139420 for updates on this award.

(1395) • Russell and Sigurd Varian Award

American Vacuum Society
125 Maiden Lane, 15th Floor, New York, NY 10038
Phone: 212-248-0200
Email: angela@avs.org
http://www.avs.org
Purpose: To support continuing graduate studies in the sciences and technologies related to AVS.
Eligibility: Applicants must be graduate students in an accredited academic institution. Five finalists are invited to present talks on their research to the trustees at the international symposium. The trustees then select one student to receive the award, which also covers travel expenses. Applicants should submit applications, research summaries, letters of recommendations and transcripts.
Target applicant(s): Graduate school students. Adult students.
Amount: Varies.
Number of awards: 1.
Deadline: May 1.
How to apply: Applications are available online.
Exclusive: Visit www.UltimateScholarshipBook.com and enter code AM139520 for updates on this award.

(1396) • Ruth Abernathy Presidential Scholarship

Shape America
1900 Association Drive, Reston, VA 20191
Phone: 800-213-7193
http://www.shapeamerica.org
Purpose: To honor deserving students in the areas of health, physical education, recreation and dance.
Eligibility: Applicants must be members of the American Alliance for Health, Physical Education, Recreation and Dance (AAHPERD), but they may join when applying and must major in health, physical education, recreation or dance. Undergraduate applicants must have a minimum 3.5 GPA and have junior or senior status when applying. Graduate applicants must have a minimum 3.5 GPA and have completed one semester of full-time study. Selection is based on scholastic achievement, leadership, community service and character.
Target applicant(s): College students. Graduate school students. Adult students.
Minimum GPA: 3.5
Amount: $1,250-$1,750.
Number of awards: 5.
Deadline: October 15.
How to apply: Applications are available online.
Exclusive: Visit www.UltimateScholarshipBook.com and enter code SH139620 for updates on this award.

(1397) • Samuel Fletcher Tapman ASCE Student Chapter/Club Scholarship

American Society of Civil Engineers (ASCE)
Attn.: Honors and Awards Program, 1801 Alexander Bell Drive, Reston, VA 20191-4400
Phone: (800) 548-2723
http://www.asce.org
Purpose: To support worthy civil engineering undergraduate students further their education.
Eligibility: Applicants must be enrolled in an ABET-accredited civil engineering program or related field. Students must be members in good standing of their local ASCE Student Chapters at the time of application submission and award acceptance. Scholarships must be used by sophomore, junior or senior engineering students.
Target applicant(s): College students. Adult students.
Amount: $3,000.
Number of awards: 12.
Scholarship may be renewable.
Deadline: February 10.
How to apply: Applications are available online.
Exclusive: Visit www.UltimateScholarshipBook.com and enter code AM139720 for updates on this award.

(1398) • Savvy Scholarship

Savvy Apps
1850 Centennial Park Drive, Suite 100, Reston, VA 20191
Phone: 703-544-9191
https://savvyapps.com/scholarship
Purpose: To support students passionate about creating mobile apps.

Eligibility: Applicants must be graduating high school seniors or currently enrolled undergraduates in their freshman or sophomore year pursuing a degree in design or development at an accredited university in the U.S. Students must write an essay describing how they exemplify the Savvy guiding principles in their lives.
Target applicant(s): High school students. College students. Adult students.
Amount: $1,000.
Number of awards: 1.
Deadline: December 31.
How to apply: Applications are available online.
Exclusive: Visit www.UltimateScholarshipBook.com and enter code SA139820 for updates on this award.

(1399) • Scholarships for Disadvantaged Students

Department of Health and Human Services
Health Resources and Services Administration, Bureau of Health Workforce, 5600 Fishers Lane, Rockville, MD 20857
Phone: 800-221-9393
Email: kross@hrsa.gov
https://bhw.hrsa.gov/loansscholarships
Purpose: To support students from disadvantaged backgrounds who are pursuing health-related careers.
Eligibility: Applicants must be full-time students, be from a disadvantaged background, demonstrate financial need and be studying in a health field, including medicine, nursing, veterinary medicine, dentistry, pharmacy and others. They must be U.S. citizens, nationals or permanent residents. All other criteria are set by individual schools.
Target applicant(s): High school students. College students. Graduate school students. Adult students.
Amount: Up to $30,000.
Number of awards: Varies.
Deadline: Varies.
How to apply: Applications are available from participating schools.
Exclusive: Visit www.UltimateScholarshipBook.com and enter code DE139920 for updates on this award.

(1400) • Schonstedt Scholarship in Surveying

National Society of Professional Surveyors (NSPS/AAGS)
Attn: Scholarships, 5119 Pegasus Court, Suite Q, Frederick, MD 21704
Phone: 240-439-4615x105
Email: trisha.milburn@nsps.us.com
http://www.nsps.us.com/?page=Scholarships
Purpose: To aid surveying students.
Eligibility: Applicants must be members of the American Congress on Surveying and Mapping (ACSM). They must be enrolled in a four-year surveying degree program. Preference will be given to applicants with junior or senior standing. Selection is based on academic merit, personal statement, references and extracurricular activities.
Target applicant(s): College students. Adult students.
Amount: $2,000.
Number of awards: 1.
Scholarship may be renewable.
Deadline: March 31.
How to apply: Applications are available online. An application form, proof of ASCM membership, official transcript, personal statement and three reference letters are required.
Exclusive: Visit www.UltimateScholarshipBook.com and enter code NA140020 for updates on this award.

(1401) • Science Ambassador Scholarship

Cards Against Humanity
1917 N. Elston Avenue, Chicago, IL 60642-1219
Email: sas@cardsagainsthumanity.com
http://www.scienceambassadorscholarship.org
Purpose: To support women pursuing STEM education.
Eligibility: Applicants must self-identify as female and be graduating high school seniors or currently enrolled full-time undergraduate students. Students must be majoring in a STEM-related field. Applicants must create a video for their application submission.
Target applicant(s): Junior high students or younger.
Amount: Varies.
Number of awards: 1.
Deadline: December 11.
How to apply: Applications are available online.
Exclusive: Visit www.UltimateScholarshipBook.com and enter code CA140120 for updates on this award.

(1402) • SEA Environmental Studies Scholarship

Surfers' Environmental Alliance
P.O. Box 3154, Long Branch, NJ 07740-3154
Email: rlee@seasurfer.org
http://www.seasurfer.org/sea-scholarships
Purpose: To aid students who seek to promote environmental awareness and marine conservation.
Eligibility: Students must be in high school through graduate level studies, have at least a 3.2 GPA, be a U.S. citizen and be pursuing environmental studies/sciences. Selection is based on goals, community service and involvement and academic excellence.
Target applicant(s): High school students. College students. Graduate school students. Adult students.
Minimum GPA: 3.2
Amount: Up to $3,500.
Number of awards: Varies.
Deadline: May 15.
How to apply: Applications are available online and include an essay.
Exclusive: Visit www.UltimateScholarshipBook.com and enter code SU140220 for updates on this award.

(1403) • SEE Education Foundation Scholarships

International Society of Explosives Engineers
30325 Bainbridge Road , Cleveland, OH 44139
Phone: 440-349-4400
Email: isee@isee.org
https://www.isee.org/students
Purpose: To aid students who are preparing for careers in the commercial explosives industry.
Eligibility: Applicants must be pursuing a degree from a technical, undergraduate, graduate or doctoral program in fields of education related to the commercial explosives industry. Students should demonstrate financial need. Selection is based on the overall strength of the application.
Target applicant(s): College students. Graduate school students. Adult students.
Amount: Varies.
Number of awards: Varies.
Deadline: May 5.
How to apply: Applications are available online. An application form, goal statement, income information, two letters of reference and an official transcript are required.

Exclusive: Visit www.UltimateScholarshipBook.com and enter code IN140320 for updates on this award.

(1404) • Sertoma Communicative Disorders Scholarship

Sertoma International
1912 E. Meyer Boulevard, Kansas City, MO 64132
Phone: 816-333-8300
Email: infosertoma@sertomahq.org
http://www.sertoma.org
Purpose: To fund graduate students of audiology and speech-language pathology.
Eligibility: Applicants must be citizens of the U.S. Applicants must also be accepted into a graduate level program in speech language pathology and/or audiology at a college in the U.S. recognized by ASHA's Council and have a minimum 3.2 overall GPA in all undergraduate and graduate-level courses.
Target applicant(s): College students. Graduate school students. Adult students.
Minimum GPA: 3.2
Amount: $1,000.
Number of awards: Varies.
Deadline: March 30.
How to apply: Applications are available online.
Exclusive: Visit www.UltimateScholarshipBook.com and enter code SE140420 for updates on this award.

(1405) • Sharps Scholarship Program

Sharps Compliance Inc.
9220 Kirby Drive, Suite 500, Houston, TX 77054
Phone: 800-772-5657
Email: scholarship@sharpsinc.com
http://www.sharpsinc.com
Purpose: To reward health care students who have written the best essays on the topic of accidental needle-stick injuries.
Eligibility: Applicants must be U.S. or Canadian citizens. They must be enrolled or planning to enroll at an accredited college or university during the fall or spring term following the application deadline. They must be studying or planning to study a health care-related subject and must submit a 1,250- to 1,500-word essay on the topic of how to prevent accidental needle-stick injuries. Selection is based on the overall strength of the essay.
Target applicant(s): High school students. College students. Adult students.
Amount: $750-$1,500.
Number of awards: 3.
Deadline: June 16.
How to apply: Application instructions are available online. An entry form and essay are required.
Exclusive: Visit www.UltimateScholarshipBook.com and enter code SH140520 for updates on this award.

(1406) • Siemens Competition in Math, Science and Technology

Siemens Foundation
170 Wood Avenue South, Iselin, NJ 08830
Phone: 877-822-5233
Email: foundation.us@siemens.com
http://www.siemens-foundation.org
Purpose: To provide high school students with an opportunity to meet other students interested in math, science and technology and to provide monetary assistance with college expenses.
Eligibility: Students must submit research reports either individually or in teams of two or three members. Individual applicants must be high school seniors. Team project applicants must be high school students but do not need to be seniors. Projects may be scientific research, technological inventions or mathematical theories.
Target applicant(s): High school students.
Amount: $1,000-$100,000.
Number of awards: Varies.
Deadline: September 20.
How to apply: Applications are available online.
Exclusive: Visit www.UltimateScholarshipBook.com and enter code SI140620 for updates on this award.

(1407) • Sigma Phi Alpha Undergraduate Scholarship

American Dental Hygienists' Association (ADHA) Institute for Oral Health
Scholarship Award Program, 444 North Michigan Avenue, Suite 3400, Chicago, IL 60611
Phone: 312-440-8900
Email: institute@adha.net
http://www.adha.org
Purpose: To aid outstanding Sigma Phi Alpha Dental Hygiene Honor Society students.
Eligibility: Applicants must be members of the Sigma Phi Alpha Dental Hygiene Honor Society who are enrolled in a certificate, associate's degree or bachelor's degree program in dental hygiene at a school that has an active chapter of Sigma Phi Alpha. They must have a major GPA of 3.5 or higher. Selection is based on the overall strength of the application.
Target applicant(s): High school students. College students. Adult students.
Minimum GPA: 3.5
Amount: $1,000.
Number of awards: 1.
Deadline: February 1.
How to apply: Applications are available online. An application form and supporting materials are required.
Exclusive: Visit www.UltimateScholarshipBook.com and enter code AM140720 for updates on this award.

(1408) • SimpliSafe STEM Scholarship

SimpliSafe
294 Washington Street, Boston, MA 02108
Email: scholars@simplisafe.com
https://simplisafescholars.org/
Purpose: To support students pursuing STEM education.
Eligibility: Applicants must be U.S. citizens enrolled in an accredited post-secondary institution in the U.S. as undergraduate or graduate students. Students must be pursuing a degree in a science, technology, engineering or mathematics field with a GPA of 3.0 or higher.
Target applicant(s): College students. Graduate school students. Adult students.
Minimum GPA: 3.0
Amount: Varies.
Number of awards: Varies.
Deadline: November 30.
How to apply: Applications are available online.
Exclusive: Visit www.UltimateScholarshipBook.com and enter code SI140820 for updates on this award.

(1409) · Small Cash Grant Program

American Society of Certified Engineering Technicians (ASCET)
P.O. Box 95, Cape May Court House, NJ 08210
Phone: 773-242-7238
Email: general-manager@ascet.org
http://www.ascet.org/FinancialAid
Purpose: To help engineering technology students.
Eligibility: Applicants must be a student, certified, regular, registered or associate member of the American Society of Certified Engineering Technicians (ASCET) or be high school seniors in the last five months of the academic year who will be enrolled in an engineering technology curriculum no later than six months following the selection for the award. Students must have passing grades in their present curriculum and submit transcripts and a recommendation letter.
Target applicant(s): High school students. College students. Adult students.
Amount: $400.
Number of awards: Varies.
Deadline: Varies.
How to apply: Applications are available online.
Exclusive: Visit www.UltimateScholarshipBook.com and enter code AM140920 for updates on this award.

(1410) · SMART Scholarship

American Society for Engineering Education
1818 N. Street, NW, Suite 600, Washington, DC 20036-2479
Phone: 202-331-3500
Email: smart@asee.org
https://smart.asee.org/
Purpose: To support undergraduate and graduate students pursuing degrees in Science, Technology, Engineering and Mathematics (STEM) fields.
Eligibility: Applicants must be a U.S. citizen, 18 or older, have a minimum GPA of 3.0, be able to participate in summer internships at the Department of Defense (DoD) and be willing to accept post-graduate work at the DoD. The award includes payment of full tuition, a stipend, a book allowance and room and board.
Target applicant(s): College students. Graduate school students. Adult students.
Minimum GPA: 3.0
Amount: Varies.
Number of awards: Varies.
Scholarship may be renewable.
Deadline: December 1.
How to apply: Applications are available online.
Exclusive: Visit www.UltimateScholarshipBook.com and enter code AM141020 for updates on this award.

(1411) · SNMTS Paul Cole Scholarship

Society of Nuclear Medicine and Molecular Imaging
Development Office, 1850 Samuel Morse Drive, Reston, VA 20190
Phone: 703-708-9000
Email: tellmer@snmmi.org
http://www.snmmi.org/
Purpose: To promote excellence in healthcare through the support of education and research in nuclear medicine technology.
Eligibility: Applicants must have a minimum 2.5 GPA and be high school seniors or college undergraduates enrolled in or accepted by accredited institutions and be in the nuclear medicine technology field. Applicant must prove financial need.
Target applicant(s): High school students. College students. Graduate school students. Adult students.
Minimum GPA: 2.5
Amount: $500-$1,000.
Number of awards: 18.
How to apply: Applications are available online.
Exclusive: Visit www.UltimateScholarshipBook.com and enter code SO141120 for updates on this award.

(1412) · Society of American Registered Architects Student Scholarship

Society of American Registered Architects
P.O. Box 280, Newport, TN 37822
Phone: 888-385-7272
Email: cathiemoscato@sara-national.org
https://www.saraeducationfund.org/student-scholarship
Purpose: To support students pursuing architectural degrees.
Eligibility: Applicants must be enrolled as full-time students in an architectural program at a college or university in the U.S. Students must be in the top 25 percent of their class and demonstrate strong character and integrity. Applicants must include examples of work, recommendations, transcripts and essay along with application.
Target applicant(s): College students. Adult students.
Amount: $3,000.
Number of awards: 1.
Deadline: August 3.
How to apply: Applications are available online.
Exclusive: Visit www.UltimateScholarshipBook.com and enter code SO141220 for updates on this award.

(1413) · Society of Exploration Geophysicists (SEG) Scholarship

Society of Exploration Geophysicists
Scholarship Committee, SEG Foundation, P.O. Box 702740, Tulsa, OK 74170-2740
Phone: 918-497-5500
Email: scholarships@seg.org
http://www.seg.org
Purpose: To fund individuals who are involved or interested in the field of geophysics.
Eligibility: Applicants must intend to pursue a career in exploration geophysics. Applicants must also be one of the following: A high school student with above average grades planning to enter college the next fall term, an undergraduate whose grades are above average or a graduate student pursuing a career in exploration geophysics in operations, teaching or research.
Target applicant(s): High school students. College students. Graduate school students. Adult students.
Amount: $500-$14,000.
Number of awards: Varies.
Scholarship may be renewable.
Deadline: March 1.
How to apply: Applications are available online or by written request.
Exclusive: Visit www.UltimateScholarshipBook.com and enter code SO141320 for updates on this award.

(1414) • Society of Manufacturing Engineers Directors Scholarship

Society of Manufacturing Engineers Education Foundation
One SME Drive, P.O. Box 930, Dearborn, MI 48121
Phone: 313-425-3300
Email: foundation@sme.org
http://www.smeef.org

Purpose: To aid undergraduate manufacturing engineering students.
Eligibility: Applicants must be full-time undergraduates who are enrolled at an accredited U.S. or Canadian postsecondary institution. They must be majoring in manufacturing engineering or a related subject and have completed at least 30 college credit hours. They must have a GPA of 3.5 or higher on a four-point scale and must have plans to pursue a career in manufacturing. Preference will be given to those with proven leadership skills. Selection is based on the overall strength of the application.
Target applicant(s): College students. Adult students.
Minimum GPA: 3.5
Amount: Varies.
Number of awards: Varies.
Deadline: February 1.
How to apply: Applications are available online. An application form and supporting materials are required.
Exclusive: Visit www.UltimateScholarshipBook.com and enter code SO141420 for updates on this award.

(1415) • Society of Plastics Engineers (SPE) Foundation Scholarships

Society of Plastics Engineers
6 Berkshire Boulevard, Suite 306, Bethel, CT 06801
Phone: 203-775-0471
Email: info@4spe.org
http://www.4spe.org/spe-foundation

Purpose: To aid students who have demonstrated or expressed an interest in the plastics industry.
Eligibility: Applicants must have a demonstrated or expressed interest in the plastics industry and be majoring in or taking courses that would lead to a career in the plastics industry. Applicants must be in good academic standing. Financial need is considered for most scholarships.
Target applicant(s): College students. Graduate school students. Adult students.
Amount: Varies.
Number of awards: Varies.
Scholarship may be renewable.
Deadline: April 1.
How to apply: Applications are available online.
Exclusive: Visit www.UltimateScholarshipBook.com and enter code SO141520 for updates on this award.

(1416) • Society of Vacuum Coaters Foundation Scholarship

Society of Vacuum Coaters Foundation
Attn.: Nicol Campana, 9639 Kinsman Road, Materials Park, OH 44073-0002
Email: svcfoundation@svc.org
http://www.svcfoundation.org

Purpose: To promote the study of vacuum coating technology.
Eligibility: Applicants must be entering or currently enrolled in studies related to vacuum coating technology at an accredited technical, vocational, two-year, undergraduate or graduate program. Preference is given to those majoring in engineering, physics, materials science or other fields related to vacuum coating. Selection is based on the applicant's field of study, academic achievement, personal qualities and financial need.
Target applicant(s): High school students. College students. Graduate school students. Adult students.
Amount: Varies.
Number of awards: Varies.
Deadline: December 1.
How to apply: Applications are available online. Two copies of scholarship materials must be submitted including the application form, transcript and two recommendation forms.
Exclusive: Visit www.UltimateScholarshipBook.com and enter code SO141620 for updates on this award.

(1417) • Southwest Park and Recreation Training Institute Student Scholarships

Southwest Park and Recreation Training Institute
Sally Rodriguez, Executive Director, 9660 Audelia Road, Suite 123-74, Dallas, TX 75238
Phone: 214-538-3344
Email: sallyr@swprti.org
http://www.swprti.org

Purpose: To aid students who are preparing for careers in parks and recreation.
Eligibility: Applicants must be graduate students or undergraduate sophomores, juniors or seniors. They must be majoring in recreation, recreation administration, park administration, landscape architecture or a related subject and have a GPA of 2.0 or higher on a four-point scale. Selection is based on the overall strength of the application.
Target applicant(s): College students. Graduate school students. Adult students.
Minimum GPA: 2.0
Amount: $1,000.
Number of awards: 3.
Deadline: Varies.
How to apply: Applications are available online. An application form and supporting materials are required.
Exclusive: Visit www.UltimateScholarshipBook.com and enter code SO141720 for updates on this award.

(1418) • SPIE Scholarships in Optics and Photonics

International Society for Optical Engineering
P.O. Box 10, Bellingham, WA 98227-0010
Phone: 360-676-3290
Email: scholarships@spie.org
http://www.spie.org

Purpose: To promote students who have the potential to contribute to the field of optics.
Eligibility: Applicants must be high school, undergraduate or graduate students enrolled part-time or full-time in programs in the field of optics, photonics, imaging, optoelectronics program or related discipline (e.g., physics or electrical engineering). Students must be members of SPIE, although they may submit a membership application along with the scholarship application, and high school applicants receive a one-year complimentary membership. Applicants must also submit two sealed letters of reference.
Target applicant(s): High school students. College students. Graduate school students. Adult students.
Amount: Up to $11,000.
Number of awards: Varies.
Deadline: February 15.

How to apply: Applications are available online.
Exclusive: Visit www.UltimateScholarshipBook.com and enter code IN141820 for updates on this award.

(1419) • SPIE Travel Scholarship

International Society for Optical Engineering
P.O. Box 10, Bellingham, WA 98227-0010
Phone: 360-676-3290
Email: scholarships@spie.org
http://www.spie.org
Purpose: To assist students who need support to travel to SPIE organized conferences and exhibitions.
Eligibility: Applicants must be high school, college or graduate students who are planning to attend conferences and exhibitions organized by SPIE. Applicants must be full-time or part-time students who are enrolled in an optics or photonics program at an accredited school. The students must also submit two letters of recommendation. Selection is based on the merit of the application, based on the experience and education level of the individual student.
Target applicant(s): College students. Graduate school students. Adult students.
Amount: $2,000.
Number of awards: Varies.
Deadline: September 15.
How to apply: Applications are available online.
Exclusive: Visit www.UltimateScholarshipBook.com and enter code IN141920 for updates on this award.

(1420) • Spring Meadow Nursery Scholarship

Horticultural Research Institute
525 9th Street NW, Suite 800, Washington, DC 20004
Phone: 202-789-2900
http://www.hriresearch.org
Purpose: To help students obtain a degree in horticulture.
Eligibility: Applicants must be enrolled full-time in an undergraduate or graduate landscape horticultural or related program at a two- or four-year accredited institution. Preference is given to those who plan to pursue a career in horticulture. Students must have a 2.25 overall GPA and a 2.7 GPA in their major.
Target applicant(s): College students. Graduate school students. Adult students.
Minimum GPA: 2.25
Amount: $3,500.
Number of awards: 3.
Scholarship may be renewable.
Deadline: September 8.
How to apply: Applications are available online.
Exclusive: Visit www.UltimateScholarshipBook.com and enter code HO142020 for updates on this award.

(1421) • SPS Leadership Scholarships

Society of Physics Students
One Physics Ellipse , College Park, MD 20740
Phone: 301-209-3007
Email: SPS-Programs@aip.org
https://www.spsnational.org/
Purpose: To further the study of physics.
Eligibility: Applicants must be undergraduates at least in their junior year, physics majors and active members of SPS.
Target applicant(s): College students. Adult students.
Amount: $2,000-$5,000.
Number of awards: Varies.
Deadline: March 22.
How to apply: Applications are available online and from SPS Chapter Advisors.
Exclusive: Visit www.UltimateScholarshipBook.com and enter code SO142120 for updates on this award.

(1422) • STEEL Engineering Education Link Initiative

Association for Iron and Steel Technology (AIST)
186 Thorn Hill Road, Warrendale, PA 15086-7528
Phone: 724-814-3000
Email: lwharrey@aist.org
https://www.aist.org
Purpose: To increase the number of students studying engineering and pursuing careers in the iron and steel industry.
Eligibility: Applicants must commit to a paid summer internship at a North American steel company or industry supplier and must be a citizen of the United States, Canada or Mexico. Students must be enrolled full-time in a four-year undergraduate program at an accredited North American university. Applicants must maintain a minimum GPA of 2.5 and demonstrate interest in the iron and steel industry.
Target applicant(s): College students. Adult students.
Minimum GPA: 2.5
Amount: $6,000.
Number of awards: Up to 20.
Scholarship may be renewable.
Deadline: October 31.
How to apply: Applications are available online. Questions about this specific scholarship may be directed to blakshmi@steel.org or 202-452-7143.
Exclusive: Visit www.UltimateScholarshipBook.com and enter code AS142220 for updates on this award.

(1423) • Steinman Scholarship

National Society of Professional Engineers
1420 King Street, Alexandria, VA 22314-2794
Phone: 703-684-2885
Email: students@nspe.org
https://www.nspe.org/resources/students/scholarships
Purpose: To aid talented students studying engineering.
Eligibility: Applicants must be undergraduate engineering majors who will enter the junior year and be U.S. citizens. Selection is based on GPA, internship experience, recommendations and ethics essay.
Target applicant(s): College students. Adult students.
Amount: $10,000.
Number of awards: 1.
Deadline: March 1.
How to apply: Applications are available online.
Exclusive: Visit www.UltimateScholarshipBook.com and enter code NA142320 for updates on this award.

(1424) • STEM Scholarship Program

Widespread Electrical Sales
11925 I-70 Frontage Road N., Suite 300, Wheat Ridge, CO 80033
Phone: 877-999-7077
Email: scholarship@widespread.com
https://www.widespreadsales.com/Scholarship
Purpose: To support students pursuing STEM related degrees.

Eligibility: Applicants must be full-time students in a college, university or vocational school program pursuing a degree in a STEM (science, technology, engineering, mathematics) related field. Students will submit a 500- to 1,500-word essay on one of the following: how technology affects the future, how electricity has changed the world or how technology has impacted your life.
Target applicant(s): College students. Graduate school students. Adult students.
Amount: $500.
Number of awards: 1.
Deadline: January 1.
How to apply: To apply email the essay to scholarship@widespread.com.
Exclusive: Visit www.UltimateScholarshipBook.com and enter code WI142420 for updates on this award.

(1425) • Stephanie Carroll Memorial Scholarship

NADONA/LTC
1329 E. Kemper Road, Suite 4100A, Springdale, OH 45246
Phone: 800-222-0539
http://www.nadona.org
Purpose: To support students who are interested in pursuing studies in long-term care or geriatrics.
Eligibility: Applicants must be undergraduate or graduate students enrolled in an accredited nursing program who will make a commitment to practice in long-term care or geriatrics for two years following graduation. Students may submit applications electronically at info@nadona.org. Selection is based on the overall strength of the application.
Target applicant(s): College students. Graduate school students. Adult students.
Amount: Varies.
Number of awards: 1.
Deadline: June 30.
How to apply: Applications are available online.
Exclusive: Visit www.UltimateScholarshipBook.com and enter code NA142520 for updates on this award.

(1426) • Steven G. King Play Environments Scholarship

Landscape Architecture Foundation
1129 20th Street NW, Suite 202, Washington, DC 20036
Phone: 202-331-7070
Email: scholarships@lafoundation.org
https://lafoundation.org/scholarship/
Purpose: To aid landscape architecture students who are interested in designing play environments.
Eligibility: Applicants must be landscape architecture graduate students or upperclass undergraduate students. They must be enrolled at a college or university that has been accredited by the Landscape Architectural Accreditation Board (LAAB). They must have a demonstrated interest in designing play environments. Selection is based on the overall strength of the application.
Target applicant(s): College students. Graduate school students. Adult students.
Amount: $5,000.
Number of awards: 1.
Deadline: February 1.
How to apply: Applications are available online. An application form, essay, play environment plan and two recommendation letters are required.
Exclusive: Visit www.UltimateScholarshipBook.com and enter code LA142620 for updates on this award.

(1427) • Stoye and Storer Awards

American Society of Ichthyologists and Herpetologists
P.O. Box 1897, Lawrence, KS 66044-8897
Phone: 785-843-1235
Email: asih@allenpress.com
http://www.asih.org/membership/student-awards
Purpose: To recognize the best oral and poster presentations in categories related to ichthyology and herpetology.
Eligibility: Applicants must be the sole authors and presenters of their projects, be members of ASIH, be full-time students or have completed a thesis or dissertation defense during the previous 12 months. Presentations are judged by introduction, methods, data analysis and interpretation, conclusions, presentation and visual aids.
Target applicant(s): College students. Graduate school students. Adult students.
Amount: Varies.
Number of awards: Varies.
Deadline: Varies.
How to apply: Applications are available by request.
Exclusive: Visit www.UltimateScholarshipBook.com and enter code AM142720 for updates on this award.

(1428) • Structural Materials Division Scholarship

Minerals, Metals and Materials Society
184 Thorn Hill Road, Warrendale, PA 15086
Phone: 724-776-9000
Email: students@tms.org
http://www.tms.org
Purpose: To aid metallurgical and materials science engineering students.
Eligibility: Applicants must be student members of The Minerals, Metals and Materials Society (TMS), be full-time undergraduate sophomores or juniors and be majoring in metallurgical or materials science engineering. Their studies must concentrate on the science and engineering of load-bearing materials. Selection is based on the overall strength of the application.
Target applicant(s): College students. Adult students.
Amount: $2,500.
Number of awards: 1.
Deadline: March 15.
How to apply: Applications are available online. An application form, personal statement, transcript and three recommendation letters are required.
Exclusive: Visit www.UltimateScholarshipBook.com and enter code MI142820 for updates on this award.

(1429) • Student Poster Session Awards

Electrochemical Society
65 South Main Street, Building D, Pennington, NJ 08534-2839
Phone: 609-737-1902
Email: awards@electrochem.org
http://www.electrochem.org/programs/
Purpose: To reward students for work related to fields of interest to ECS.
Eligibility: Applicants must be pursuing degrees at any college or university and prepare an abstract on work performed. The applicants must also prepare a poster to present at the society meeting where they

will be judged. Two awards are in the categories of electrochemical science and technology and solid-state science and technology.
Target applicant(s): College students. Graduate school students. Adult students.
Amount: Varies.
Number of awards: Varies.
Deadline: Varies.
How to apply: Application materials are described online.
Exclusive: Visit www.UltimateScholarshipBook.com and enter code EL142920 for updates on this award.

(1430) · Student Research Awards

Crohn's and Colitis Foundation of America Inc.
733 Third Avenue, Suite 510, New York, NY 10017
Phone: 800-932-2423
Email: info@ccfa.org
http://www.ccfa.org
Purpose: To stimulate interest in research careers in inflammatory bowel disease by providing salary support for research projects.
Eligibility: Applicants must be undergraduate, graduate or medical students not yet engaged in thesis research. Students must attend an accredited North American school and conduct their research with a mentor. The planned research project must last at least 10 weeks and must be relevant to IBD.
Target applicant(s): College students. Graduate school students. Adult students.
Amount: Up to $2,500.
Number of awards: Up to 16.
Deadline: March 15.
How to apply: Applications are available online.
Exclusive: Visit www.UltimateScholarshipBook.com and enter code CR143020 for updates on this award.

(1431) · Student Research Scholarships

Bat Conservation International
Scholarship Program, P.O. Box 162603, Austin, TX 78716
Phone: 512-327-9721
Email: grants@batcon.org
http://www.batcon.org
Purpose: To support students who will contribute to our knowledge about bats.
Eligibility: Applicants must be graduate students and submit a research proposal that addresses a specific area of bat conservation. The application form provides several potential research topics.
Target applicant(s): College students. Graduate school students. Adult students.
Amount: Up to $5,000.
Number of awards: Varies.
Deadline: Varies.
How to apply: Applications are available online.
Exclusive: Visit www.UltimateScholarshipBook.com and enter code BA143120 for updates on this award.

(1432) · StudyPug Math Help Scholarship

StudyPug
1200 - 3779 Sexsmith Road, Richmond, BC V6X 3Z9
Phone: 604-343-1104
https://www.studypug.com/scholarship.html
Purpose: To support students pursuing post-secondary education.
Eligibility: Applicants must be currently enrolled in high school or college in the United States or Canada. Students must write an essay on the given topic pertaining to mathematics.
Target applicant(s): High school students. College students. Adult students.
Amount: $1,000.
Number of awards: 1.
Deadline: December 15.
How to apply: Applications are available online.
Exclusive: Visit www.UltimateScholarshipBook.com and enter code ST143220 for updates on this award.

(1433) · Supporting STEM Scholarship

Hoshizaki Ice Maker
3230 Kline Road, Jacksonville, FL 32246
Phone: 800-965-0081
Email: info@hoshizkiicemaker.com
https://hoshizakiicemaker.com/stem-scholarship
Purpose: To support students in STEM related fields.
Eligibility: Applicants must be a high-school senior or college level student, be enrolled full-time and maintain a 3.0 or higher GPA. Students must be studying a STEM-related field. Selection is based on passion for the STEM field of study, strong moral character and leadership ability.
Target applicant(s): High school students. College students. Adult students.
Minimum GPA: 3.0
Amount: $1,000.
Number of awards: 1.
Deadline: June 30.
How to apply: Applications are available online.
Exclusive: Visit www.UltimateScholarshipBook.com and enter code HO143320 for updates on this award.

(1434) · Susan Miszkowicz Memorial Scholarship

Society of Women Engineers
130 East Randolph Street, Suite 3500, Chicago, IL 60601
Phone: 877-793-4636
Email: scholarships@swe.org
http://societyofwomenengineers.swe.org/scholarships
Purpose: To support female students working towards a college degree in engineering.
Eligibility: Applicants must be currently enrolled in an accredited engineering, technology or computing program with a minimum of a 3.0 GPA. The award is to be used during the sophomore, junior or senior year of college.
Target applicant(s): College students. Adult students.
Minimum GPA: 3.0
Amount: $1,500.
Number of awards: 1.
Deadline: February 15.
How to apply: Applications are available online.
Exclusive: Visit www.UltimateScholarshipBook.com and enter code SO143420 for updates on this award.

(1435) · Tau Beta Pi/Society of Automotive Engineers Engineering Scholarship

Society of Automotive Engineers International
Scholarships Program, 400 Commonwealth Drive, Warrendale, PA 15096

Phone: 724-776-4841
Email: scholarships@sae.org
http://students.sae.org/scholarships/
Purpose: To aid future college students who are planning to major in engineering.
Eligibility: Applicants must be U.S. citizens, be graduating high school seniors and have plans to major in engineering at an ABET-accredited institution. They must have a GPA of 3.75 or higher and must have SAT or ACT scores that rank in the 90th percentile. Selection is based on the overall strength of the application.
Target applicant(s): High school students.
Minimum GPA: 3.75
Amount: $1,000.
Number of awards: 6.
Deadline: March 15.
How to apply: Applications are available online. An application form, official transcript and standardized test scores are required.
Exclusive: Visit www.UltimateScholarshipBook.com and enter code SO143520 for updates on this award.

(1436) • Ted and Ruth Neward Scholarship

Society of Plastics Engineers
6 Berkshire Boulevard, Suite 306, Bethel, CT 06801
Phone: 203-775-0471
Email: info@4spe.org
http://www.4spe.org/spe-foundation
Purpose: To aid students who have an interest in the plastics industry.
Eligibility: Applicants must be U.S. citizens, have an interest in the plastics industry, major in or take courses leading to a career in the plastics industry and be in good academic standing. Financial need is considered.
Target applicant(s): College students. Graduate school students. Adult students.
Amount: Varies.
Number of awards: Varies.
Deadline: April 1.
How to apply: Applications are available online.
Exclusive: Visit www.UltimateScholarshipBook.com and enter code SO143620 for updates on this award.

(1437) • Ted Rollins ECO Scholarship

Ted Rollins
1000 West Morehead Street, Suite 150, Charlotte, NC 28208
Email: scholarship@tedrollinsecoscholars.com
http://www.tedrollinsecoscholars.com
Purpose: To support students pursuing a major related to sustainability.
Eligibility: Applicants must be either high school seniors or current undergraduate students planning to major in sustainability. Students must plan to take at least 10 credit hours during the upcoming fall semester. Applicants must write an essay on a topic assigned on the website.
Target applicant(s): High school students. College students. Adult students.
Amount: $1,000.
Number of awards: 1.
Deadline: June 15.
How to apply: Applications are available online.
Exclusive: Visit www.UltimateScholarshipBook.com and enter code TE143720 for updates on this award.

(1438) • Theodore D. Harrington Scholarship

National Association of Corrosion Engineers (NACE) International Foundation
15835 Park Ten Place, Houston, TX 77084-5145
Phone: 281-228-6205
Email: nace.foundation@nace.org
http://nace-foundation.org/programs/students/scholarships/
Purpose: To support an individual with an interest in furthering their knowledge of corrosion control.
Eligibility: Applicants must have a permanent residence in the NACE Western Area which includes the following states: Arizona, California, Idaho, Nevada, Oregon, Utah and Washington. Applicants must take courses offered by an accredited college or university or programs approved by the area upon application. Selection is based on the overall strength of information provided by the applicant.
Target applicant(s): College students. Graduate school students. Adult students.
Amount: $1,200.
Number of awards: 1.
Deadline: January 5.
How to apply: Applications are available online. An academic transcript, two nomination forms, one recommendation form and essay scholarship questions are required.
Exclusive: Visit www.UltimateScholarshipBook.com and enter code NA143820 for updates on this award.

(1439) • Thermo Fisher Scientific Antibody Scholarship

Thermo Fisher Scientific
3747 N. Meridian Road, Rockford, IL 61101
Phone: 815-968-0747
Email: antibodyscholarship@thermofisher.com
http://www.thermofisher.com
Purpose: To help students with the expenses related to their pursuit of higher education.
Eligibility: Applicants must be enrolled or accepted for enrollment as an undergraduate or graduate student at an accredited college or university. Students must have a cumulative grade point average of 3.0 and declared a major of one of the following: chemistry, biology, biochemistry or a related life science field. Applicants must be United States citizens or students possessing the appropriate visa status to study in the U.S. Selection is based on the overall strength of the application and any submitted materials.
Target applicant(s): High school students. College students. Graduate school students. Adult students.
Minimum GPA: 3.0
Amount: $5,000-$10,000.
Number of awards: 6.
Deadline: May 31.
How to apply: Applications are available online.
Exclusive: Visit www.UltimateScholarshipBook.com and enter code TH143920 for updates on this award.

(1440) • Thermoforming Division Memorial Scholarships

Society of Plastics Engineers
6 Berkshire Boulevard, Suite 306, Bethel, CT 06801
Phone: 203-775-0471
Email: info@4spe.org
http://www.4spe.org/spe-foundation
Purpose: To aid students who have an interest in the plastics industry.

Eligibility: Applicants must have an interest in the plastics industry, major in or take courses leading to a career in the plastics industry and be in good academic standing. Applicants must have experience in the thermoforming industry, such as courses taken, research conducted or jobs held.
Target applicant(s): College students. Graduate school students. Adult students.
Amount: Varies.
Number of awards: Varies.
Deadline: April 1.
How to apply: Applications are available online.
Exclusive: Visit www.UltimateScholarshipBook.com and enter code SO144020 for updates on this award.

(1441) · Thermoplastic Elastomers Special Interest Group Scholarship

Society of Plastics Engineers
6 Berkshire Boulevard, Suite 306, Bethel, CT 06801
Phone: 203-775-0471
Email: info@4spe.org
http://www.4spe.org/spe-foundation
Purpose: To aid students who have a demonstrated interest in thermoplastic elastomers.
Eligibility: Applicants must be full-time undergraduate or graduate students who have a proven interest in thermoplastic elastomers. This interest must be shown by relevant jobs held, internships completed, coursework completed or research undertaken. Selection is based on the overall strength of the application.
Target applicant(s): College students. Graduate school students. Adult students.
Amount: $2,500.
Number of awards: 1.
Deadline: April 1.
How to apply: Applications are available online. An application form, official transcript, three references and a personal statement are required.
Exclusive: Visit www.UltimateScholarshipBook.com and enter code SO144120 for updates on this award.

(1442) · Thermoplastic Materials and Foams Division Scholarship

Society of Plastics Engineers
6 Berkshire Boulevard, Suite 306, Bethel, CT 06801
Phone: 203-775-0471
Email: info@4spe.org
http://www.4spe.org/spe-foundation
Purpose: To aid undergraduate students who have a demonstrated interest in thermoplastic materials and foams.
Eligibility: Applicants must be full-time undergraduate students who are interested in thermoplastic materials and foams. This interest must be shown by relevant internship experiences, jobs held, coursework completed or research undertaken. Selection is based on the overall strength of the application.
Target applicant(s): High school students. College students. Adult students.
Amount: $2,500.
Number of awards: 1.
Deadline: April 1.
How to apply: Applications are available online. An application form, three references, transcript and personal statement are required.
Exclusive: Visit www.UltimateScholarshipBook.com and enter code SO144220 for updates on this award.

(1443) · Thermoset Division/James I. Mackenzie and James H. Cunningham Scholarships

Society of Plastics Engineers
6 Berkshire Boulevard, Suite 306, Bethel, CT 06801
Phone: 203-775-0471
Email: info@4spe.org
http://www.4spe.org/spe-foundation
Purpose: To aid students who have an interest in the plastics industry and have experience in the thermoset industry.
Eligibility: Applicants must have an interest in the plastics industry and major in or take courses leading to a career in the plastics industry. Applicants must also have experience in the thermoset industry, such as courses taken, research conducted or jobs held. One award is given for undergraduate students and one for graduate students.
Target applicant(s): College students. Graduate school students. Adult students.
Amount: Varies.
Number of awards: Varies.
Deadline: April 1.
How to apply: Applications are available online.
Exclusive: Visit www.UltimateScholarshipBook.com and enter code SO144320 for updates on this award.

(1444) · Thomas E. Powers/Detroit Section Scholarship

Society of Plastics Engineers
6 Berkshire Boulevard, Suite 306, Bethel, CT 06801
Phone: 203-775-0471
Email: info@4spe.org
http://www.4spe.org/spe-foundation
Purpose: To aid undergraduate students who are interested in the plastics industry.
Eligibility: Applicants must be full-time undergraduate students in good academic standing who have completed coursework in or are majoring in a subject that relates to the plastics industry (such as engineering, polymer science, physics or chemistry). Selection is based on the overall strength of the application.
Target applicant(s): College students. Adult students.
Amount: $4,000.
Number of awards: 1.
Deadline: April 1.
How to apply: Applications are available online. An application form, personal statement, transcript and three recommendation letters are required.
Exclusive: Visit www.UltimateScholarshipBook.com and enter code SO144420 for updates on this award.

(1445) · Thomas M. Stetson Scholarship

American Ground Water Trust
50 Pleasant Street, Concord, NH 03301
Phone: 603-228-5444
https://agwt.org/content/scholarships
Purpose: To provide scholarships for high school seniors pursuing careers in a ground water-related field.
Eligibility: Applicants must be high school seniors with intentions to pursue a career in ground water-related field. Applicants must attend a college or university located west of the Mississippi River. A minimum GPA of 3.0 is required.
Target applicant(s): High school students.
Minimum GPA: 3.0
Amount: $2,000.

Number of awards: 1.
Deadline: June 1.
How to apply: Applications are available online.
Exclusive: Visit www.UltimateScholarshipBook.com and enter code AM144520 for updates on this award.

(1446) • Thomas R. Camp Scholarship

American Water Works Association
6666 W. Quincy Avenue, Denver, CO 80235-3098
Phone: 800-926-7337
Email: scholarships@awwa.org
http://www.awwa.org
Purpose: To support students conducting applied research in the drinking water field.
Eligibility: Applicants must pursue graduate degrees at an institution of higher education in Canada, Guam, Puerto Rico, Mexico or the U.S. This is awarded to doctoral students in even years and master's students in odd years. Applicants must submit applications, resumes, transcripts, GRE scores, three recommendation letters, statements and research plans. The award is based on academics and leadership.
Target applicant(s): Graduate school students. Adult students.
Amount: $5,000.
Number of awards: 1.
Deadline: January 12.
How to apply: Applications are available online.
Exclusive: Visit www.UltimateScholarshipBook.com and enter code AM144620 for updates on this award.

(1447) • Tilford Fund

Association of Engineering Geologists Foundation
Tilford Fund, 4123 Broadway, Suite 817, Oakland, CA 94611
Phone: 510-990-0059
Email: staff@aegfoundation.org
https://www.aegfoundation.org
Purpose: To provide financial assistance for field studies in engineering geology.
Eligibility: Applicants must be members of the Association of Engineering Geologists who are college or graduate students. Applicants are chosen on the basis of scholarship, ability, participation and potential for contributions to the profession.
Target applicant(s): College students. Graduate school students. Adult students.
Amount: Varies.
Number of awards: Varies.
Deadline: February 1.
How to apply: Applications are available online.
Exclusive: Visit www.UltimateScholarshipBook.com and enter code AS144720 for updates on this award.

(1448) • Timothy S. and Palmer W. Bigelow, Jr. Scholarship

Horticultural Research Institute
525 9th Street NW, Suite 800, Washington, DC 20004
Phone: 202-789-2900
http://www.hriresearch.org
Purpose: To help students from New England who want to pursue a career in horticulture.
Eligibility: Applicants must be seniors in a two-year course and have finished the first year, juniors in a four-year course and have finished the first two years or be graduate students. Undergraduates must have a minimum 2.25 GPA and graduate students a minimum 3.0 GPA. Students must be from Connecticut, Maine, Massachusetts, New Hampshire, Rhode Island or Vermont. Preference will be given to applicants who have financial need and who plan to work in the nursery industry after graduation, including starting a business.
Target applicant(s): College students. Graduate school students. Adult students.
Minimum GPA: 2.25 for undergraduate students, 3.0 for graduate students
Amount: $3,000.
Number of awards: 1.
Deadline: September 8.
How to apply: Applications are available online or by mail.
Exclusive: Visit www.UltimateScholarshipBook.com and enter code HO144820 for updates on this award.

(1449) • TiMOTION Engineering and Excellence Scholarship

TiMOTION
921 Matthews Mint Hill Road, Suite F, Matthews, NC 28105
Phone: 704-708-6924
Email: samantha.r@timotion.com
http://www.timotion.com/job.php?JobID=10
Purpose: To support students who are aspiring engineers, ergonomists or technology students.
Eligibility: Applicants must be full-time students enrolled in an engineering, ergonomics or technology program at an accredited undergraduate secondary program. Students must have a 3.0 GPA and be able to provide evidence of strong involvement in community service. Applicants must write an essay as part of their application.
Target applicant(s): High school students. College students. Adult students.
Minimum GPA: 3.0
Amount: $2,000.
Number of awards: 5.
Deadline: December 1.
How to apply: Applications are available online.
Exclusive: Visit www.UltimateScholarshipBook.com and enter code TI144920 for updates on this award.

(1450) • TMC/SAE Donald D. Dawson Technical Scholarship

Society of Automotive Engineers International
Scholarships Program, 400 Commonwealth Drive, Warrendale, PA 15096
Phone: 724-776-4841
Email: scholarships@sae.org
http://students.sae.org/scholarships/
Purpose: To aid current and future engineering students.
Eligibility: Applicants must be U.S. citizens, be high school seniors or current undergraduate students and be enrolled in or planning to enroll in an ABET-accredited engineering degree program. They must have a GPA of 3.25 or higher and an SAT math score of 600 or higher and a critical reading score of 550 or higher or must have an ACT composite score of 27 or higher. Selection is based on the overall strength of the application.
Target applicant(s): High school students. College students. Adult students.
Minimum GPA: 3.25
Amount: $1,500.

Number of awards: 1.
Scholarship may be renewable.
Deadline: March 15.
How to apply: Applications are available online. An application form, personal essay, official transcript and standardized test scores are required.
Exclusive: Visit www.UltimateScholarshipBook.com and enter code SO145020 for updates on this award.

(1451) · TMS Best Paper Contest

Minerals, Metals and Materials Society
184 Thorn Hill Road, Warrendale, PA 15086
Phone: 724-776-9000
Email: students@tms.org
http://www.tms.org
Purpose: To support the professional development of metallurgy and materials science students.
Eligibility: Applicants must be student members of The Minerals, Metals and Materials Society (TMS). They must prepare and submit a technical essay on a topic that is related to metallurgy or materials science. Selection is based on originality and the quality of research.
Target applicant(s): High school students. College students. Graduate school students. Adult students.
Amount: $250.
Number of awards: 4.
Deadline: May 1.
How to apply: Submission guidelines are available online. A technical essay, cover sheet and faculty endorsement are required.
Exclusive: Visit www.UltimateScholarshipBook.com and enter code MI145120 for updates on this award.

(1452) · TMS Technical Division Student Poster Contest

Minerals, Metals and Materials Society
184 Thorn Hill Road, Warrendale, PA 15086
Phone: 724-776-9000
Email: students@tms.org
http://www.tms.org
Purpose: To aid student members of the Minerals, Metals and Materials Society.
Eligibility: Applicants must be student members of the Minerals, Metals and Materials Society (TMS), be full-time undergraduate or graduate students and create a poster that addresses a topic that would be of interest for one of the five technical divisions of TMS. Selection is based on the overall strength of the poster.
Target applicant(s): College students. Graduate school students. Adult students.
Amount: Up to $1,000.
Number of awards: 10.
Deadline: Varies.
How to apply: Applications are available online. An application form and poster are required.
Exclusive: Visit www.UltimateScholarshipBook.com and enter code MI145220 for updates on this award.

(1453) · TMS/International Symposium of Superalloys Scholarships

Minerals, Metals and Materials Society
184 Thorn Hill Road, Warrendale, PA 15086
Phone: 724-776-9000
Email: students@tms.org
http://www.tms.org
Purpose: To aid metallurgical engineering and materials science and engineering students.
Eligibility: Applicants must be student members of the Minerals, Metals and Materials Society (TMS) and be full-time undergraduate or graduate students majoring in metallurgical engineering or materials science and engineering. They must have a demonstrated interest in the high-temperature, high-performance materials used in the gas turbine industry. Selection is based on academic merit, extracurricular activities, relevant coursework completed and recommendation letters.
Target applicant(s): College students. Graduate school students. Adult students.
Amount: $2,000.
Number of awards: 2.
Deadline: March 15.
How to apply: Applications are available online. An application form, transcript, personal essay and three recommendation letters are required.
Exclusive: Visit www.UltimateScholarshipBook.com and enter code MI145320 for updates on this award.

(1454) · Trent R. Dames & William W. Moore Fellowship

American Society of Civil Engineers (ASCE)
Attn.: Honors and Awards Program, 1801 Alexander Bell Drive, Reston, VA 20191-4400
Phone: (800) 548-2723
http://www.asce.org
Purpose: To support engineers, earth scientists, professors and graduate students pursuing graduate studies researching new applications and advancements in geotechnical engineering or earth sciences in relation to social, economic, environmental and political issues.
Eligibility: Applicants must be members of ASCE at the time of application submission. Prior fellowship recipients can apply for any additional fellowships provided they meet the current fellowship's eligibility requirements. Completed applications and all supporting material as outlined in the application process must be submitted.
Target applicant(s): Graduate school students. Adult students.
Amount: $6,000.
Number of awards: 2.
Deadline: February 10.
How to apply: Applications are available online.
Exclusive: Visit www.UltimateScholarshipBook.com and enter code AM145420 for updates on this award.

(1455) · Tuskegee Airmen Scholarship Foundation Scholarships

Tuskegee Airmen Scholarship Foundation
1816 S. Figueroa Street, Suite 4.13, Los Angeles, CA 90015
Phone: 213-742-9541
Email: info@taisf.org
http://www.taisf.org
Purpose: To aid students who intend to pursue careers in aviation, aerospace engineering, aerospace research or engineering technology.
Eligibility: Applicants must be high school seniors who have a GPA of 3.0 or higher on a four-point scale. They must have a demonstrated interest in pursuing a career in aerospace research, aerospace engineering, aviation or engineering technology. Selection is based on academic merit, extracurricular activities, character and financial need.
Target applicant(s): High school students.

Minimum GPA: 3.0
Amount: $1,500.
Number of awards: 40.
Scholarship may be renewable.
Deadline: January 26.
How to apply: Applications are available by request from the student's local Tuskegee Airmen chapter. An application form, two essays and family income verification are required.
Exclusive: Visit www.UltimateScholarshipBook.com and enter code TU145520 for updates on this award.

(1456) • Tutor the People Pre-Med Scholarship

Tutor the People LLC
87 Lafayette Street, New York, NY 10013
http://tutorthepeople.com
Purpose: To support undergraduate students in pursuing a pre-medical education.
Eligibility: Applicants must submit an essay explaining their professional and educational goals in the field of medicine. Selection is based on the overall strength of the submission.
Target applicant(s): High school students. College students. Adult students.
Amount: $1,000.
Number of awards: 1.
Deadline: August 1.
How to apply: Applications are available online.
Exclusive: Visit www.UltimateScholarshipBook.com and enter code TU145620 for updates on this award.

(1457) • UAA Janice K. Barden Aviation Scholarship

UAA/Barden Aviation Scholarship
1200 G Street NW, Suite 1100, Washington, DC 20005
Phone: 202-783-9250
Email: info@nbaa.org
https://www.nbaa.org/prodev/scholarships/
Purpose: To aid aviation students attending a University Aviation Association (UAA) or National Business Aviation Association (NBAA) member school.
Eligibility: Applicants must be U.S. citizens who are studying a subject that is related to aviation. Selection is based on the overall strength of the application. Applicants must have a minimum 3.0 GPA.
Target applicant(s): College students. Adult students.
Minimum GPA: 3.0
Amount: $1,000.
Number of awards: 5.
Deadline: November 30.
How to apply: Applications are available online. An application form, personal essay, transcript, resume and one recommendation letter are required.
Exclusive: Visit www.UltimateScholarshipBook.com and enter code UA145720 for updates on this award.

(1458) • Undergraduate Award for Excellence in Chemistry

Iota Sigma Pi (ISP) ND
Professor Kathryn A. Thomasson, Iota Sigma Pi Director for Student Awards, University of North Dakota, Department of Chemistry, P.O. Box 9024, Grand Forks, ND 58202-9024
Phone: 701-777-3199
Email: kthomasson@chem.und.edu
http://www.iotasigmapi.info
Purpose: To reward female undergraduate students for excellence in the field of chemistry study.
Eligibility: Applicants must be female senior chemistry students at an accredited four-year college or university and be nominated by a member of the faculty.
Target applicant(s): College students. Adult students.
Amount: $500.
Number of awards: 1.
Deadline: February 15.
How to apply: Applications are available online.
Exclusive: Visit www.UltimateScholarshipBook.com and enter code IO145820 for updates on this award.

(1459) • Undergraduate Engineering Scholarships

American Society of Heating, Refrigerating and Air-Conditioning Engineers (ASHRAE)
1791 Tullie Circle, NE, Atlanta, GA 30329
Phone: 404-636-8400
Email: lbenedict@ashrae.org
http://www.ashrae.org
Purpose: To encourage heating, ventilating, air conditioning and refrigeration education.
Eligibility: Applicants must be full-time undergraduates majoring in engineering or pre-engineering in a related course of study approved by the Accreditation Board for Engineering and Technology (ABET) or another accrediting agency recognized by ASHRAE with a minimum 3.0 GPA. Selection is based on leadership, character and potential contribution to the heating, ventilating, air conditioning or refrigeration profession. Applicants must also submit three recommendations from instructors and an official transcript.
Target applicant(s): High school students. College students. Adult students.
Minimum GPA: 3.0
Amount: $5,000.
Number of awards: Varies.
Deadline: December 1.
How to apply: Applications are available online.
Exclusive: Visit www.UltimateScholarshipBook.com and enter code AM145920 for updates on this award.

(1460) • Undergraduate Scholarship and Construction Trades Scholarship

National Association of Women in Construction
327 South Adams Street, Fort Worth, TX 76104
Phone: 800-552-3506
Email: nawic@nawic.org
http://www.nawic.org
Purpose: To offer financial aid to students pursuing construction-related degrees.
Eligibility: Applicants must be currently enrolled in a construction-related degree program as full-time students, have at least one term of study remaining in a course of study leading to a degree or an associate degree in a construction-related field, desire a career in a construction-related field and have a minimum 3.0 GPA. Awards are given to male and female students.
Target applicant(s): College students. Adult students.
Minimum GPA: 3.0
Amount: $500-$2,500.
Number of awards: Varies.

Deadline: February 28.
How to apply: Applications are available online.
Exclusive: Visit www.UltimateScholarshipBook.com and enter code NA146020 for updates on this award.

(1461) • Undergraduate Scholarships

Institute of Food Technologists (IFT)
525 W. Van Buren, Suite 1000, Chicago, IL 60607
Phone: 312-782-8424
Email: ejplummer@ift.org
http://www.ift.org/community/students/competitions.aspx
Purpose: To encourage undergraduate students in food science or technology.
Eligibility: Applicants must be college sophomores, juniors or seniors pursuing an approved program in food science or food technology. Applications, transcripts and a recommendation letter are required.
Target applicant(s): College students. Adult students.
Amount: $1,000-$3,000.
Number of awards: 9.
Deadline: April 2.
How to apply: Applications are available online.
Exclusive: Visit www.UltimateScholarshipBook.com and enter code IN146120 for updates on this award.

(1462) • Undergraduate Student Research Grants: South-Central Section

Geological Society of America South-Central Section
Wm. Jay Sims, Earth Science Department, University of Arkansas at Little Rock, 2801 S. University, Little Rock, AR 72204-1099
Phone: 303-357-1000
Email: programs@geosociety.org
http://www.geosociety.org
Purpose: To provide research grants to undergraduate students studying geology who are members of GSA.
Eligibility: Applicants must be members of GSA, attend school in the South-Central section and present research at a section meeting or the GSA annual meeting.
Target applicant(s): High school students. College students. Adult students.
Amount: $500.
Number of awards: Varies.
Deadline: April 1.
How to apply: Applications are available online.
Exclusive: Visit www.UltimateScholarshipBook.com and enter code GE146220 for updates on this award.

(1463) • Undergraduate Student Summer Research Fellowships

American Physiological Society
Education Office, 9650 Rockville Pike, Bethesda, MD 20814-3991
Phone: 301-634-7787
Email: education@the-aps.org
http://www.the-aps.org
Purpose: To support full-time summer study for undergraduate students in the laboratory of an established researcher.
Eligibility: Applicants must be enrolled in an undergraduate program, and faculty sponsor must be an active member of APS. Students must have a minimum 3.0 GPA. Fellowships are awarded to students pursuing a career as a basic research scientist.
Target applicant(s): High school students. College students. Adult students.
Minimum GPA: 3.0
Amount: $4,000 stipend plus up to $1,300 travel expenses.
Number of awards: Varies.
Deadline: February 1.
How to apply: Applications are available online.
Exclusive: Visit www.UltimateScholarshipBook.com and enter code AM146320 for updates on this award.

(1464) • Undergraduate Summer Student Research Assistantship

National Radio Astronomy Observatory (NRAO)
NRAO Headquarters, 520 Edgemont Road, Charlottesville, VA 22903
Phone: 434-296-0211
Email: info@nrao.edu
http://www.nrao.edu
Purpose: To allow students to perform astronomical research at National Radio Astronomy Observatory (NRAO) sites.
Eligibility: Depending on the specific program, applicants must be either undergraduates or graduating college seniors. Recipients work on-site for 10 to 12 weeks, beginning in late May or early June.
Target applicant(s): College students. Adult students.
Amount: Varies.
Number of awards: Varies.
Deadline: February 1.
How to apply: Applications are available online.
Exclusive: Visit www.UltimateScholarshipBook.com and enter code NA146420 for updates on this award.

(1465) • United Parcel Service Scholarship for Female Students

Institute of Industrial and Systems Engineers
3577 Parkway Lane, Suite 200, Norcross, GA 30092
Phone: 800-494-0460
Email: bcameron@iienet.org
http://www.iise.org/
Purpose: To help female undergraduate engineering students.
Eligibility: Applicants must be full-time female students at an institution in the United States, Canada or Mexico with an accredited industrial engineering program, majoring in industrial engineering or its equivalent and active members. Students may not apply directly for this scholarship and must be nominated. The award is based on academic ability, character, leadership, potential service to the industrial engineering profession and financial need. Applicants must have a minimum 3.4 GPA.
Target applicant(s): College students. Adult students.
Minimum GPA: 3.4
Amount: $4,000.
Number of awards: 1.
Deadline: November 15.
How to apply: Nomination forms are available online.
Exclusive: Visit www.UltimateScholarshipBook.com and enter code IN146520 for updates on this award.

(1466) • USDA/1890 National Scholars Program

U.S. Department of Agriculture
c/o Juanita Whiting, 1400 Independence Avenue SW, Washington, DC 20250

Phone: 301-851-2062
Email: Juanita.L.Whiting@aphis.usda.gov
https://www.aphis.usda.gov/aphis/home
Purpose: To aid students who are planning to study agriculture or a related subject in college.
Eligibility: Applicants must be U.S. citizens and be rising undergraduate freshmen, sophomores or juniors who have a high school diploma or a GED. They must have a GPA of 3.0 or higher. They must plan to enroll or be enrolled at an 1890 Land Grant institution and have plans to major in agriculture; agriculture business/management; agriculture economics; agricultural engineering/mechanics; agricultural productions and technology; agronomy or crop science; animal science; botany; farm and range management; fish, game or wildlife management; food services/technology; forestry and related services; home economics/nutrition/human development; horticulture; natural resources management; soil conservation/soil science or other related disciplines (e.g., biological sciences, pre-veterinary medicine or computer science). They must also have proven leadership skills and must have experience with community service. Selection is based on the overall strength of the application.
Target applicant(s): High school students. College students. Adult students.
Minimum GPA: 3.0
Amount: Varies.
Number of awards: Varies.
Deadline: December 31.
How to apply: Applications are available by request from the Civil Rights Enforcement and Compliance section of the Animal and Plant Health Inspection Service branch of the USDA. An application form and supporting materials are required.
Exclusive: Visit www.UltimateScholarshipBook.com and enter code U.146620 for updates on this award.

(1467) • Usrey Family Scholarship

Horticultural Research Institute
525 9th Street NW, Suite 800, Washington, DC 20004
Phone: 202-789-2900
http://www.hriresearch.org
Purpose: To help students who are seeking careers in horticulture.
Eligibility: Applicants must be in an undergraduate or graduate landscape horticulture program or related field at a two or four-year California state university or college. Applicants must also be current, full-time students, academically competitive and have a minimum 2.25 GPA and a minimum 2.7 GPA in the major. Preference is given to applicants who plan to work in the nursery industry after graduation. Applicants must submit applications, cover letters, resumes, transcripts and two recommendation letters.
Target applicant(s): College students. Graduate school students. Adult students.
Minimum GPA: 2.25
Amount: $1,000.
Number of awards: 1.
Deadline: September 8.
How to apply: Applications are available online.
Exclusive: Visit www.UltimateScholarshipBook.com and enter code HO146720 for updates on this award.

(1468) • Vertical Flight Foundation Technical Scholarships

Vertical Flight Foundation
217 N. Washington Street, Alexandria, VA 22314
Phone: 703-684-6777
Email: staff@vtol.org
http://www.vtol.org
Purpose: The Vertical Flight Foundation was founded to support the education in rotorcraft and vertical-takeoff-and-landing aircraft engineering.
Eligibility: Applicants must be full-time students at accredited schools of engineering and submit a transcript with an academic endorsement from a professor or dean. Applicants need not be members of AHS.
Target applicant(s): High school students. College students. Graduate school students. Adult students.
Amount: Up to $6,000.
Number of awards: Varies.
Deadline: February 1.
How to apply: Applications are available online.
Exclusive: Visit www.UltimateScholarshipBook.com and enter code VE146820 for updates on this award.

(1469) • VIP Women in Technology Scholarship

Visionary Integration Professionals
80 Iron Point Circle, Suite 100, Folsom, CA 95630
Phone: 916-985-9625
Email: wits@trustvip.com
http://www.trustvip.com
Purpose: To aid female students who are preparing for careers in information technology or a related subject.
Eligibility: Applicants must be attending or accepted at a two- or four-year postsecondary institution located in the U.S. They must be planning to pursue a career in information technology or a related field. Selection is based on academic merit, a personal essay and extracurricular activities.
Target applicant(s): High school students. College students. Adult students.
Minimum GPA: 3.0
Amount: Up to $2,500.
Number of awards: Varies.
Deadline: March 1.
How to apply: Applications are available online. An application form, official transcript, personal essay and list of extracurricular activities are required.
Exclusive: Visit www.UltimateScholarshipBook.com and enter code VI146920 for updates on this award.

(1470) • Walter B. Sinnott Scholarship

American Water Works Association - New York Section
Submit To: Jenny Ingrao, Executive Director, New York Section
American Water Works Association, 614 Seventh North Street, Liverpool, NY 13088
Phone: 315-455-2614
https://nysawwa.org/
Purpose: To reward students who are enrolled in a program to study in the water supply field.
Eligibility: Students must be at least a freshman enrolled full-time at an accredited college or university in the United States.
Target applicant(s): College students. Adult students.
Amount: $2,500.
Number of awards: 1.
Deadline: February 28.
How to apply: Applications are available online.
Exclusive: Visit www.UltimateScholarshipBook.com and enter code AM147020 for updates on this award.

(1471) • Welch Scholars Grant

American Osteopathic Foundation (AOF)
142 East Ontario Street, Suite 1450, Chicago, IL 60611
Phone: 312-202-8234
https://aof.org/grants-awards
Purpose: To support osteopathic medical students.
Eligibility: Applicants must be osteopathic medical students who have successfully completed their first year of studies. Students must be in good academic standing at an accredited College of Osteopathic Medicine. Applicants are chosen based on academic achievement, participation in extracurricular activities and financial need.
Target applicant(s): Graduate school students. Adult students.
Amount: $1,500.
Number of awards: Varies.
Deadline: Varies.
How to apply: Applications are available online.
Exclusive: Visit www.UltimateScholarshipBook.com and enter code AM147120 for updates on this award.

(1472) • William A. Fischer Memorial Scholarship

American Society for Photogrammetry and Remote Sensing (ASPRS)
The Imaging and Geospatial Information Society
5410 Grosvenor Lane, Suite 210, Bethesda, MD 20814
Phone: 301-493-0290 x101
Email: scholarships@asprs.org
http://www.asprs.org
Purpose: To support graduate study in new uses of remote sensing data or techniques that relate to the natural, cultural or agricultural resources of the Earth.
Eligibility: Applicants must be prospective or current graduate students and submit letters of recommendation, a two-page statement detailing educational and career plans for continuing studies in remote sensing applications and transcripts. It is also recommended that applicants submit technical papers, research reports or other items that indicate their capabilities. Recipients must submit a report of their work during the award period.
Target applicant(s): Graduate school students. Adult students.
Amount: $2,000.
Number of awards: 1.
Deadline: November 15.
How to apply: Applications are available online.
Exclusive: Visit www.UltimateScholarshipBook.com and enter code AM147220 for updates on this award.

(1473) • William F. Helms Internship Program

U.S. Department of Agriculture
c/o Juanita Whiting, 1400 Independence Avenue SW, Washington, DC 20250
Phone: 301-851-2062
Email: Juanita.L.Whiting@aphis.usda.gov
https://www.aphis.usda.gov/aphis/home
Purpose: To support students who are pursuing higher education studies in agriculture or the biological sciences.
Eligibility: Applicants must be U.S. citizens who are undergraduate sophomores or juniors at an accredited U.S. college or university. They must be studying a subject in agriculture or the biological sciences and have a GPA of 2.5 or higher. Applicants must agree to work for the Agency during school breaks (both summer and holiday breaks) a minimum of 640 hours prior to completion of studies. Selection is based on the overall strength of the application.
Target applicant(s): College students. Adult students.
Minimum GPA: 2.5
Amount: Up to $5,000.
Number of awards: Varies.
Scholarship may be renewable.
Deadline: Varies.
How to apply: Applications are available by request from the U.S. Department of Agriculture. An application form, personal statement, transcript, three recommendation letters and documentation of U.S. military service (if applicable) are required.
Exclusive: Visit www.UltimateScholarshipBook.com and enter code U.147320 for updates on this award.

(1474) • William J. Adams, Jr. and Marijane E. Adams Scholarship

American Society of Agricultural and Biological Engineers Foundation
Administrator, Scholarship Fund, 2950 Niles Road, St. Joseph, MI 49085
Phone: 269-429-0300
http://www.asabe.org
Purpose: To aid undergraduate students with an interest in agricultural machinery product design and development.
Eligibility: Applicants must be biological or agricultural engineering majors in eligible accredited programs in the U.S. or Canada. Applicants must also have completed at least one year of undergraduate study and have at least one year of undergraduate study remaining, have a minimum 2.5 GPA, have an interest in agricultural machinery product design and development and demonstrate financial need.
Target applicant(s): College students. Adult students.
Minimum GPA: 2.5
Amount: $1,200.
Number of awards: 1.
Deadline: March 15.
How to apply: Application is by formal letter.
Exclusive: Visit www.UltimateScholarshipBook.com and enter code AM147420 for updates on this award.

(1475) • William J. McHenry Scholarship

Planning and Visual Education Partnership (PAVE) c/o Kroger Company
PAVE Entries Attn.: Ken Pray, 1014 Vine Street, Cincinnati, OH 45202
Email: info@paveglobal.org
http://paveglobal.org/Competitions.aspx?typeid=26
Purpose: To support students who show potential in the field of visual merchandising.
Eligibility: Students must have at least a 3.0 GPA. Applicants must currently be taking at least 12 credit hours. Students must be U.S. citizens enrolled in a visual merchandising program within the state of California. Applicants must be in one of the first three years of their program.
Target applicant(s): College students. Adult students.
Minimum GPA: 3.0
Amount: $1,250.
Number of awards: Varies.
Deadline: March 1.
How to apply: Applications are available online.
Exclusive: Visit www.UltimateScholarshipBook.com and enter code PL147520 for updates on this award.

(1476) • Wire Reinforcement Institute Education Foundation Graduate Student Scholarship

Wire Reinforcement Institute
942 Main Street, Hartford, CT 06103
Phone: 860-240-9545
http://wirereinforcementinstitute.org/scholarship_career/

Purpose: To support students who are pursuing a graduate degree in civil or structural engineering.
Eligibility: Applicants must be enrolled full-time in a graduate program at an accredited educational institution in the U.S. or Canada. Selection is primarily based on academic achievement, career goals and extracurricular involvement. Applicants must maintain at least twelve credit hours per semester.
Target applicant(s): Graduate school students. Adult students.
Amount: $4,000.
Number of awards: Varies.
Deadline: April 15.
How to apply: Applications are available online.
Exclusive: Visit www.UltimateScholarshipBook.com and enter code WI147620 for updates on this award.

(1477) • Wire Reinforcement Institute Education Foundation Undergraduate Scholarship

Wire Reinforcement Institute
942 Main Street, Hartford, CT 06103
Phone: 860-240-9545
http://wirereinforcementinstitute.org/scholarship_career/

Purpose: To support students who are pursuing an undergraduate degree in civil or structural engineering.
Eligibility: Applicants must be entering their sophomore year or higher and have declared a major in civil or structural engineering. Students must be enrolled for at least 12 credits per semester at a four-year educational institution. Selection is primarily based on academic achievement, career goals and extracurricular involvement.
Target applicant(s): College students. Adult students.
Amount: $4,000.
Number of awards: Varies.
Deadline: April 15.
How to apply: Applications are available online.
Exclusive: Visit www.UltimateScholarshipBook.com and enter code WI147720 for updates on this award.

(1478) • Women Forward in Technology Scholarship Program

Distil Networks
115 Sansome Street, Suite 600, San Francisco, CA 94104
Phone: 703-997-9674
Email: scholarship@distilnetworks.com
https://www.distilnetworks.com/women-forward-in-technology-scholarship/

Purpose: To support female students pursuing STEM education.
Eligibility: Applicants must be enrolling in or currently enrolled at an accredited U.S. university majoring in a science, technology, engineering or math field. Students must be female with a minimum grade point average of 3.5.
Target applicant(s): High school students. College students. Graduate school students. Adult students.
Minimum GPA: 3.5
Amount: $3,000.
Number of awards: Varies.
Deadline: June 15.
How to apply: Applications are available online.
Exclusive: Visit www.UltimateScholarshipBook.com and enter code DI147820 for updates on this award.

(1479) • Women in STEM Scholarship/BHW Scholarship

BHW Group
6011 W. Courtyard Drive, Suite 410, Austin, TX 78730
Phone: 512-220-0035
https://thebhwgroup.com/scholarship

Purpose: To support female students pursuing a degree in a science or mathematics field.
Eligibility: Applicants must be incoming freshman or currently enrolled female students pursuing an undergraduate or master's degree. Students must be majoring in science, technology, engineering or mathematics. Applicants must be enrolled in a U.S. school and submit an essay along with their completed application.
Target applicant(s): High school students. College students. Graduate school students. Adult students.
Amount: $3,000.
Number of awards: 1.
Deadline: April 15.
How to apply: Applications are available online.
Exclusive: Visit www.UltimateScholarshipBook.com and enter code BH147920 for updates on this award.

(1480) • Women in Technology Scholarship

StudySoup
1381 9th Avenue, San Francisco, CA 94122
Phone: 415-658-9115
https://studysoup.com/scholarships/

Purpose: To support women in computer science and technology.
Eligibility: Applicants must be female students planning to pursue post-secondary education in computer science or computer programming. Students may be high school seniors enrolling within a year, current undergraduates or graduate students or currently enrolled in a certified computer programming program. Applicants must be U.S. or Canadian students.
Target applicant(s): High school students. College students. Adult students.
Amount: $1,000.
Number of awards: 1.
Deadline: May 5.
How to apply: Applications are available online.
Exclusive: Visit www.UltimateScholarshipBook.com and enter code ST148020 for updates on this award.

(1481) • Women Techmakers Scholars Program

Google Inc. Women Techmakers
1600 Amphitheatre Parkway, Mountain View, CA 94043
Email: WTMScholars@google.com
https://www.womentechmakers.com/scholars

Purpose: To encourage female students to excel in computing and technology to become active leaders and role models in their field.
Eligibility: Applicants must be female students who are currently enrolled at an accredited university for the upcoming school year studying computer science or computer engineering. Students must intend to be enrolled or accepted as full-time students in a bachelor's, master's or Ph.D. program at a university and have a strong academic

record. Applicants must show leadership and have a passion for increasing the involvement of women in the field of computer science.
Target applicant(s): College students. Graduate school students. Adult students.
Amount: $10,000.
Number of awards: Varies.
Deadline: December 11.
How to apply: Applications are available online.
Exclusive: Visit www.UltimateScholarshipBook.com and enter code GO148120 for updates on this award.

(1482) • Women's Scholarship

National Strength and Conditioning Association (NSCA) Foundation
1885 Bob Johnson Drive, Colorado Springs, CO 80906
Phone: 800-815-6826
http://www.nsca.com/foundation/
Purpose: To encourage women to enter the field of strength and conditioning.
Eligibility: Applicants should be women age 17 and older who have been accepted by an accredited institution for a graduate degree in strength and conditioning. Applicants must be NSCA members and plan to pursue careers in strength and conditioning. A cover letter of application, application form, resume, transcript, three letters of recommendation and essay are required. The award is based on grades, strength and conditioning experience, NSCA involvement, awards, community involvement, essay and recommendations.
Target applicant(s): High school students. College students. Graduate school students. Adult students.
Amount: $1,500.
Number of awards: Varies.
Deadline: October 15.
How to apply: Application materials are described online.
Exclusive: Visit www.UltimateScholarshipBook.com and enter code NA148220 for updates on this award.

(1483) • Women's Wildlife Management/ Conservation Scholarship

National Rifle Association
11250 Waples Mill Road, Fairfax, VA 22030
Phone: 800-672-3888
Email: grantprogram@nrahq.org
https://awards.nra.org/awards/
Purpose: To support women who are seeking a career in the wildlife management and conservation field.
Eligibility: Applicants must be a female college junior or senior, have a 3.0 or higher GPA and be majoring in wildlife management/ conservation. Selection is based on extracurricular activities, community service, work experience, a required essay and the letter of reference.
Target applicant(s): College students. Adult students.
Minimum GPA: 3.0
Amount: $1,000.
Number of awards: Varies.
Scholarship may be renewable.
Deadline: November 1.
How to apply: Applications are submitted online and include a 200-300 word essay and at least one letter of recommendation.
Exclusive: Visit www.UltimateScholarshipBook.com and enter code NA148320 for updates on this award.

(1484) • Yanmar/SAE Scholarship

Society of Automotive Engineers International
Scholarships Program, 400 Commonwealth Drive, Warrendale, PA 15096
Phone: 724-776-4841
Email: scholarships@sae.org
http://students.sae.org/scholarships/
Purpose: This scholarship is sponsored by the SAE Foundation and the Yanmar Diesel America Corporation.
Eligibility: Applicants must be full-time college juniors pursuing an engineering or related science degree or enrolled in a postgraduate engineering or related science program. Applicants must also pursue a course of study or research related to the conservation of energy in transportation, agriculture and construction and power generation.
Target applicant(s): College students. Graduate school students. Adult students.
Amount: $1,000.
Number of awards: 1.
Scholarship may be renewable.
Deadline: March 15.
How to apply: Applications are available online.
Exclusive: Visit www.UltimateScholarshipBook.com and enter code SO148420 for updates on this award.

(1485) • Youth Incentive Award

Coleopterists Society
Dr. David G. Furth, Entomology, NHB, MRC 165, P.O. Box 37012, Smithsonian institution, Washington, DC 20013-7012
Phone: 202-633-0990
Email: furthd@si.edu
http://www.coleopsoc.org
Purpose: To recognize young people studying beetles.
Eligibility: Applicants should be coleopterists in grades 7-12 and submit individual proposals such as field collecting trips to conduct beetle species inventories or diversity studies, attending workshops or visiting entomology or natural history museums for training and projects on beetles, studying beetle biology, etc. Students are strongly encouraged to find an adult advisor (i.e., teacher, youth group leader, parent) to provide guidance in the proposal development, but the proposal must be written by the applicant. The Coleopterists Society can help establish contacts between applicants and professional coleopterists. The award is based on creativity, educational benefit to the applicant, scientific merit, feasibility and budget. There are two winners: one for grades 7-9 and one for grades 10-12.
Target applicant(s): Junior high students or younger. High school students.
Amount: $200 to $400.
Number of awards: 2.
Deadline: November 1.
How to apply: Applications are available online.
Exclusive: Visit www.UltimateScholarshipBook.com and enter code CO148520 for updates on this award.

(1486) • Youth Program

Appaloosa Horse Club
Appaloosa Youth Association, 2720 West Pullman Road, Moscow, ID 83843
Phone: 208-882-5578
Email: youth@appaloosa.com
http://www.appaloosayouth.com/

Purpose: To reward student members of the Appaloosa Youth Association or the Appaloosa Horse Club who are pursuing higher education.
Eligibility: Applicants must be members of the Appaloosa Youth Association or the Appaloosa Horse Club and must attend or plan to attend an institute of higher learning. Students may also be the son or daughter of Appaloosa Horse Club members.
Target applicant(s): High school students. College students. Graduate school students. Adult students.
Minimum GPA: 2.5
Amount: $1,000-$2,000.
Number of awards: Up to 9.
Scholarship may be renewable.
Deadline: March 20.
How to apply: Applications are available online.
Exclusive: Visit www.UltimateScholarshipBook.com and enter code AP148620 for updates on this award.

(1487) • Zach Sullivan Geneva Rock Scholarship

Geneva Rock
302 West 5400 South, Suite 200, Murray, UT 84107
https://genevarock.com/scholarship/
Purpose: To support students dedicated to building the future.
Eligibility: Applicants must be currently enrolled or enrolling in an accredited university, college, trade or vocational school pursuing a career in a construction-related field. Students must include a written essay along with their application.
Target applicant(s): College students. Adult students.
Amount: $2000.
Number of awards: 2.
Deadline: July 1, November 15.
How to apply: Applications are available online.
Exclusive: Visit www.UltimateScholarshipBook.com and enter code GE148720 for updates on this award.

STATE OF RESIDENCE

(1488) • A.D. Osherman Scholarship Fund

Greater Houston Community Foundation
5120 Woodway Drive, Suite 6000, Houston, TX 77056
Phone: 713-333-2200
https://www.ghcfscholar.org
Purpose: To support students of Texas in pursuing post-secondary education.
Eligibility: Applicants must demonstrate financial need. A minimum GPA of 2.75 is required. Students must take a minimum of 12 credits in both the fall and spring semesters. Preference is given to minority students, veterans and/or first-generation college students.
Target applicant(s): High school students. College students. Adult students.
Minimum GPA: 2.75
Amount: $3,000.
Number of awards: 3.
Deadline: February 1.
How to apply: Applications are available online.
Exclusive: Visit www.UltimateScholarshipBook.com and enter code GR148820 for updates on this award.

(1489) • Aaron Michael Powell Youth Shooting Memorial Scholarship

Aaron Michael Powell Youth Shooting Memorial
P.O. Box 62, Lowndesville, SC 29659
Phone: 864-940-1063
Email: bpowell@wctel.net
http://www.sc-sportingclays.com
Purpose: To help young students achieve their higher education goals.
Eligibility: Applicants must be high school seniors and be involved in a shooting sport discipline in Georgia or South Carolina. Selection is based on letters of recommendation, an essay explaining what shooting sports have meant to you and a letter explaining future goals and financial need.
Target applicant(s): High school students.
Amount: Varies.
Number of awards: Varies.
Deadline: Varies.
How to apply: Applications are available online and must include three letters of recommendation, an essay and a letter to the committee.
Exclusive: Visit www.UltimateScholarshipBook.com and enter code AA148920 for updates on this award.

(1490) • Academic Challenge Scholarship

Arkansas Department of Higher Education
423 Main Street, Suite 400, Little Rock, AR 72201
Phone: 501-371-2050
Email: finaid@adhe.arknet.edu
http://www.adhe.edu/Pages/home.aspx
Purpose: To encourage Arkansas high school graduates to enroll in Arkansas colleges and universities.
Eligibility: Applicants must be graduating Arkansas high school seniors who meet academic minimum standards and income requirements. Must submit FAFSA.
Target applicant(s): High school students.
Minimum GPA: 2.25
Amount: $2,000-$5,000.
Number of awards: Varies.

Scholarship may be renewable.
Deadline: June 1.
How to apply: Applications are available through your high school counselor. FAFSA required.
Exclusive: Visit www.UltimateScholarshipBook.com and enter code AR149020 for updates on this award.

(1491) • Academic Excellence Scholarship

State of Wisconsin Higher Educational Aids Board
P.O. Box 7885, Madison, WI 53707
Phone: 608-267-2206
Email: heabmail@wisconsin.gov
http://heab.state.wi.us
Purpose: To assist outstanding Wisconsin students who are planning to attend college in Wisconsin.
Eligibility: Applicants must be high school seniors who plan to enroll full-time at an eligible Wisconsin college or university. The award is given to the student with the highest GPA in each public and private Wisconsin high school.
Target applicant(s): High school students.
Amount: Up to $2,250.
Number of awards: Varies.
Deadline: March 1.
How to apply: No application is required. Each high school designates the student who has the highest GPA of the graduating high school class.
Exclusive: Visit www.UltimateScholarshipBook.com and enter code ST149120 for updates on this award.

(1492) • Academic Rodeo Scholarships

East Texas State Fair
2112 West Front Street, Tyler, TX 75702
Phone: 903-597-2501
Email: dnewman@etstatefair.com
http://www.etstatefair.com/
Purpose: To support those students who participate in the Park of East Texas Academic Rodeo.
Eligibility: Applicants must be in grades 6 through 8 or 9 through 12 and must place in the top three in a contest at the Academic Rodeo in the current year. Selection is based on academic achievement, extracurricular activities, community service and goals.
Target applicant(s): Junior high students or younger. High school students.
Amount: Varies.
Number of awards: Varies.
Deadline: February 14.
How to apply: Applications are available online and are to include an official transcript, four letters of recommendation and an essay.
Exclusive: Visit www.UltimateScholarshipBook.com and enter code EA149220 for updates on this award.

(1493) • Academic Scholars Program

Oklahoma State Regents for Higher Education/Academic Scholars Program
655 Research Parkway, Suite 200, Oklahoma City, OK 73104
Phone: 800-858-1840
Email: studentinfo@osrhe.edu
https://secure.okcollegestart.org/Financial_Aid_Planning/Scholarships/Academic_Scholarships/Academic_Scholars_Program.aspx
Purpose: To assist students in attending Oklahoma colleges and universities.
Eligibility: Applicants can qualify for the program by being Oklahoma or out-of-state students who are named National Merit Scholars, National Merit Finalists or U.S. Presidential Scholars; by being Oklahoma residents who score above the 99.5 percentile on the SAT or ACT or by being nominated by an Oklahoma public college or institution. Applicants must attend an Oklahoma college or university. Selection is based on academic merit.
Target applicant(s): High school students.
Amount: Up to $5,500.
Number of awards: Varies.
Scholarship may be renewable.
Deadline: Varies.
How to apply: Applications are available from the applicant's high school guidance counselor, by telephone request and online. An application form and supporting documents are required.
Exclusive: Visit www.UltimateScholarshipBook.com and enter code OK149320 for updates on this award.

(1494) • Access College Early Scholarship

Nebraska Coordinating Commission for Postsecondary Education
P.O. Box 95005, Lincoln, NE 68509-5005
Phone: 402-471-2847
Email: ritchie.morrow@nebraska.gov
https://ccpe.nebraska.gov/
Purpose: To support Nebraska high school students who are enrolled in early college courses.
Eligibility: Applicants must demonstrate financial need through proof of participation in government aid programs or documentation of recent family hardships. They may be in any year of high school.
Target applicant(s): High school students.
Amount: Full tuition and fees.
Number of awards: Varies.
Scholarship may be renewable.
Deadline: Varies.
How to apply: Applications are available online.
Exclusive: Visit www.UltimateScholarshipBook.com and enter code NE149420 for updates on this award.

(1495) • Access to Better Learning and Education Grant Program

Florida Department of Education
Office of Student Financial Assistance, State Scholarship and Grant Programs, 325 West Gaines Street, Suite 1314, Tallahassee, FL 32399-0400
Phone: 888-827-2004
Email: osfa@fldoe.org
http://www.floridastudentfinancialaid.org
Purpose: To help undergraduate students from Florida who want to attend Florida private colleges or universities.
Eligibility: Applicants must be Florida residents for at least a year and first-time undergraduate students enrolled in degree programs (except theology or divinity degrees). Applicants must meet Florida's general state aid eligibility requirements and enroll in at least 12 credit hours per semester. Award renewable for up to nine semesters. Participating institutions determine application procedures, deadlines and student eligibility. Award amount determined by the Legislature in the General Appropriation Act each year.
Target applicant(s): High school students. College students. Adult students.

Amount: Varies.
Number of awards: Varies.
Scholarship may be renewable.
Deadline: Varies.
How to apply: Contact the financial aid office at eligible Florida colleges and universities.
Exclusive: Visit www.UltimateScholarshipBook.com and enter code FL149520 for updates on this award.

(1496) • ACEC Colorado Scholarship Program

American Council of Engineering Companies of Colorado
800 Grant Street, Suite 100, Denver, CO 80203
Phone: 303-832-2200
Email: acec@acec-co.org
http://www.acec-co.org
Purpose: To support engineering students.
Eligibility: Applicants must be full-time students pursuing a bachelor's degree in engineering or surveying at an accredited college or university in Colorado. They must be entering their junior, senior or fifth year. Selection is based on GPA (24 points), essay (25 points), work experience (24 points), recommendation (17 points) and extracurricular activities (10 points).
Target applicant(s): College students. Adult students.
Amount: Varies.
Number of awards: Varies.
Deadline: January 20.
How to apply: Applications are available online. An application form, transcript, essay and recommendation are required.
Exclusive: Visit www.UltimateScholarshipBook.com and enter code AM149620 for updates on this award.

(1497) • ACEC Scholarship

American Council of Engineering Companies California (ACEC)
1303 J Street, Suite 450, Sacramento, CA 95814
Phone: 916-441-7991
http://www.acec-ca.org/?page=ScholarshipApp
Purpose: To support students interested in pursuing a degree in engineering or land surveying.
Eligibility: Applicants must be U.S. citizens, undergraduate students enrolled full-time in an engineering or land surveying program or graduate students enrolled at least half-time. Students must have a minimum GPA of 3.5 in completed engineering/land surveying courses and a minimum overall GPA of 3.2. Selection is made based on the overall strength of the application.
Target applicant(s): College students. Graduate school students. Adult students.
Minimum GPA: 3.2
Amount: $7,500.
Number of awards: Varies.
Deadline: January 3.
How to apply: Applications are available online.
Exclusive: Visit www.UltimateScholarshipBook.com and enter code AM149720 for updates on this award.

(1498) • ACLU of Utah Youth Activist Scholarship

American Civil Liberties Union of Utah
355 North 300 West, Salt Lake City, UT 84102
Phone: 801-521-9862
Email: scholarship@acluutah.org
http://www.acluutah.org
Purpose: To support Utah students who have demonstrated a strong commitment to civil liberties.
Eligibility: Applicants must be high school seniors who plan to attend college full-time. Applicants must have demonstrated their commitment to civil liberties through activism. Previous winners have been involved in programs related to racial diversity, rights of disabled students, women's equality, freedom of religion, freedom of expression and equality for all. Students with GPAs of less than 3.0 must submit an explanation of their grades.
Target applicant(s): High school students.
Amount: $1,000.
Number of awards: 3.
Deadline: January 12.
How to apply: Applications are available online.
Exclusive: Visit www.UltimateScholarshipBook.com and enter code AM149820 for updates on this award.

(1499) • Adult Student Grant

State Student Assistance Commission of Indiana
W462 Indiana Government Center South, 402 West Washington Street, Indianapolis, IN 46204
Phone: 888-528-4719
Email: grants@ssaci.state.in.us
http://www.in.gov/che/
Purpose: To help part-time Indiana students pursue higher education.
Eligibility: Applicants must be Indiana residents and a U.S. citizen or eligible non-citizen. Students must be undergraduates taking at least six but not more than 12 credit hours per term at eligible institutions. This is a need-based award.
Target applicant(s): College students. Adult students.
Amount: $1,000.
Number of awards: Varies.
Scholarship may be renewable.
Deadline: July 1.
How to apply: Applications are available online.
Exclusive: Visit www.UltimateScholarshipBook.com and enter code ST149920 for updates on this award.

(1500) • Advanced Practice Healthcare Scholarship Program

Office of Statewide Health Planning and Development
Health Professions Education Foundation, 400 R Street, Suite 460, Sacramento, CA 95811-6213
Phone: 916-326-3640
Email: hpef-email@oshpd.ca.gov
http://www.oshpd.ca.gov/HPEF/
Purpose: To increase medical care to underserved areas of California by assisting residents who are studying to become dentists, dental hygienists, nurse practitioners, certified midwives and physician assistants.
Eligibility: Applicants must be California residents who have been accepted by or are enrolled in an accredited California program. Financial need, work experience and career goals are considered, and preference is given to applicants who plan to remain in a medically underserved area past the service time. Those selected must sign a two-year service agreement to work in a medically underserved area of California.
Target applicant(s): College students. Graduate school students. Adult students.
Amount: Up to $50,000.
Number of awards: Varies.
Scholarship may be renewable.

Deadline: February 28.
How to apply: Applications are available online.
Exclusive: Visit www.UltimateScholarshipBook.com and enter code OF150020 for updates on this award.

(1501) • AFS Twin City Memorial Scholarship

Foundry Educational Foundation
1695 North Penny Lane, Schaumburg, IL 60173
Phone: 847-490-9200
Email: info@fefinc.org
http://www.fefinc.org/scholarships.html
Purpose: To aid students from Minnesota, western Wisconsin and northern Iowa who are attending a Foundry Education Foundation (FEF) member school.
Eligibility: Applicants must be residents of Minnesota, western Wisconsin or northern Iowa. Preference will be given to students who are completing coursework in a foundry-related subject. Selection is based on the overall strength of the application.
Target applicant(s): College students. Adult students.
Amount: Varies.
Number of awards: Varies.
Deadline: October 6.
How to apply: Applications are available online. An application form and supporting materials are required.
Exclusive: Visit www.UltimateScholarshipBook.com and enter code FO150120 for updates on this award.

(1502) • AFS Wisconsin Past President Scholarship

Foundry Educational Foundation
1695 North Penny Lane, Schaumburg, IL 60173
Phone: 847-490-9200
Email: info@fefinc.org
http://www.fefinc.org/scholarships.html
Purpose: To aid Wisconsin-area students who wish to pursue careers in the cast metal industry.
Eligibility: Students must be enrolled at an Foundry Educational Foundation (FEF) member school, a school located in Wisconsin or a school located in a state that is adjacent to Wisconsin. They also must have previous work experience, preferably in the cast metal industry. Selection is based on the student's academic record, his or her residential proximity to the AFS Wisconsin Chapter area, the proximity of the student's school to the AFS Wisconsin Chapter area, relevance of the student's degree program to the cast metal industry and relevant work experience.
Target applicant(s): High school students. College students. Adult students.
Amount: Varies.
Number of awards: Varies.
Deadline: December 15.
How to apply: Applications are available online. A completed FEF profile and supporting documents are required.
Exclusive: Visit www.UltimateScholarshipBook.com and enter code FO150220 for updates on this award.

(1503) • AGC of Massachusetts Scholarships

Associated General Contractors of Massachusetts
888 Worcester Street, Suite 40, Wellesley, MA 02482
Phone: 781-786-8917
Email: canoni@agcmass.org
http://www.agcmass.org/scholarships
Purpose: To aid Massachusetts residents who are college sophomores, juniors or seniors and who are enrolled in degree programs related to construction or civil engineering.
Eligibility: Applicants must be undergraduate sophomores or above at an accredited college or university. They must be legal residents of Massachusetts (though they may attend school outside of the state) and must be enrolled in a degree program related to construction or civil engineering. Selection is based on financial need and the overall strength of the application.
Target applicant(s): College students. Adult students.
Amount: Varies.
Number of awards: Varies.
Scholarship may be renewable.
Deadline: June 1.
How to apply: Applications are available online. An application form and an official transcript are required.
Exclusive: Visit www.UltimateScholarshipBook.com and enter code AS150320 for updates on this award.

(1504) • AGC of Ohio Scholarships

Associated General Contractors of Ohio
1755 Northwest Boulevard , Columbus, OH 43212
Phone: 614-486-6446
Email: parker@agcohio.com
https://agcohio.com/scholarships
Purpose: To support undergraduate students who are residents of Ohio and interested in pursuing careers in construction-related fields.
Eligibility: Applicants must be a U.S. citizens and undergraduate students in at least the second year of a two-year, four-year or five-year degree seeking program. The minimum GPA requirement is 2.5. Selection is based on the overall strength of the application.
Target applicant(s): College students. Adult students.
Minimum GPA: 2.5
Amount: $1,000.
Number of awards: 7.
Deadline: February 3.
How to apply: Applications are available online. An application form, official college transcripts and essay are required and must be mailed.
Exclusive: Visit www.UltimateScholarshipBook.com and enter code AS150420 for updates on this award.

(1505) • Agnes M. Lindsay Scholarship

Massachusetts Department of Higher Education
Office of Student Financial Assistance, 454 Broadway, Suite 200, Revere, MA 02151
Phone: 617-727-9420
Email: osfa@osfa.mass.edu
http://www.mass.edu/osfa/students/forstudents.asp
Purpose: To provide assistance to Massachusetts students who are from rural parts of the state, demonstrate financial need and attend a Massachusetts public institution of higher education.
Eligibility: Applicants must be permanent Massachusetts residents for at least one year before the beginning of the academic year. Applicants must also be enrolled full-time in an undergraduate program and maintain satisfactory academic progress.
Target applicant(s): High school students. College students. Adult students.
Amount: Varies.
Number of awards: Varies.
Deadline: Varies.
How to apply: Applications are available by phone.

Exclusive: Visit www.UltimateScholarshipBook.com and enter code MA150520 for updates on this award.

(1506) • Aid for Part-Time Study

New York State Higher Education Services Corporation (HESC)
99 Washington Avenue, Albany, NY 12255
Phone: 888-697-4372
Email: scholarships@hesc.ny.gov
http://www.hesc.ny.gov

Purpose: To assist part-time undergraduate students at New York State institutions.
Eligibility: Applicants must meet income eligibility requirements, be enrolled for at least 3 but less than 12 semester hours per semester or at least 4 but less than 8 semester hours per quarter in an eligible undergraduate program, be New York State residents and be U.S. citizens or eligible noncitizens. Tuition charges must exceed $100 per year, and once payments begin, students must maintain a C average.
Target applicant(s): High school students. College students. Adult students.
Amount: Up to $2,000.
Number of awards: Varies.
Scholarship may be renewable.
Deadline: Varies.
How to apply: Contact the financial aid office to receive an APTS application.
Exclusive: Visit www.UltimateScholarshipBook.com and enter code NE150620 for updates on this award.

(1507) • Alabama Concrete Industries Association Scholarships

Alabama Concrete Industries Association
1745 Platt Place, Montgomery, AL 36117
Phone: 334-265-0501
Email: rlindsay@alconcrete.org
http://www.alconcrete.org

Purpose: To support students studying fields related to the concrete industry.
Eligibility: Applicants must be college seniors majoring in architecture, engineering or building sciences at universities in Alabama. They must be Alabama residents with a 2.5 or higher GPA.
Target applicant(s): College students. Adult students.
Minimum GPA: 2.5
Amount: $8,000.
Number of awards: 2.
Scholarship may be renewable.
Deadline: November 30.
How to apply: Applications are available from your school's guidance office. An application form, letter of recommendation and essay are required.
Exclusive: Visit www.UltimateScholarshipBook.com and enter code AL150720 for updates on this award.

(1508) • Alaska World Affair Council

Alaska World Affairs Council
406 G Street, Suite 207, Anchorage, Alaska 99501
Phone: 907-276-8038
Email: info@alaskaworldaffairs.org
http://www.alaskaworldaffairs.org/students/scholarships/

Purpose: To support Alaskan students.
Eligibility: Applicants must be current Alaskan high school seniors planning to attend a post-secondary institution in Alaska in the fall. Students must demonstrate community involvement, leadership, character, academic ability and financial need.
Target applicant(s): High school students.
Amount: $2,500.
Number of awards: 2.
Deadline: April 1.
How to apply: Applications are available online.
Exclusive: Visit www.UltimateScholarshipBook.com and enter code AL150820 for updates on this award.

(1509) • Albert E. and Florence W. Newton Nursing Scholarship

Rhode Island Foundation
One Union Station, Providence, RI 02903
Phone: 401-274-4564
Email: rbogert@rifoundation.org
http://www.rifoundation.org

Purpose: To aid undergraduate nursing students.
Eligibility: Applicants must be undergraduate students seeking a diploma or degree in nursing. They must demonstrate financial need. Preference will be given to Rhode Island residents. Selection is based on academic merit and financial need.
Target applicant(s): High school students. College students. Adult students.
Amount: $500-$2,000.
Number of awards: Varies.
Scholarship may be renewable.
Deadline: April 14.
How to apply: Applications are available online. An application form and supporting materials are required.
Exclusive: Visit www.UltimateScholarshipBook.com and enter code RH150920 for updates on this award.

(1510) • Albert H. Hix. W8AH Memorial Scholarship

American Radio Relay League Foundation
225 Main Street, Newington, CT 06111-1494
Phone: 860-594-0348
Email: foundation@arrl.org
http://www.arrl.org/scholarship-program

Purpose: To provide scholarship assistance to amateur radio operators who are from the West Virginia Section or Roanoke Division or who are attending school in the West Virginia section.
Eligibility: Applicants must hold a General Class or higher Amateur Radio License and have a GPA of 3.0 or higher.
Target applicant(s): High school students. College students. Adult students.
Minimum GPA: 3.0
Amount: $500.
Number of awards: 1.
Deadline: January 31.
How to apply: Applications are available online.
Exclusive: Visit www.UltimateScholarshipBook.com and enter code AM151020 for updates on this award.

(1511) • Albert M. Lappin Scholarship

American Legion, Department of Kansas
1314 SW Topeka Boulevard, Topeka, KS 66612

Phone: 785-232-9315
http://www.ksamlegion.org
Purpose: To assist the education of needy and worthy children of American Legion and American Legion Auxiliary members.
Eligibility: Applicants must be high school seniors or college freshmen or sophomores who are average or better students. They must be the son or daughter of a veteran and enrolling or enrolled in a post-secondary school in Kansas. A parent must have been a member of the Kansas American Legion or American Legion Auxiliary for the previous three years. In addition, the children of deceased parents are eligible if the parent was a paid member at the time of death. Applicants must submit a 1040 income statement, documentation of parent's veteran status, three letters of recommendation with only one from a teacher, an essay on the topic of "Why I Want to Go to College" and a high school transcript. Applicants must maintain a C average in college and verify enrollment at the start of each semester.
Target applicant(s): High school students. College students. Adult students.
Amount: $1,000.
Number of awards: 1.
Deadline: February 15.
How to apply: Applications are available online.
Exclusive: Visit www.UltimateScholarshipBook.com and enter code AM151120 for updates on this award.

(1512) · Alert Scholarship

Alert Magazine
P.O. Box 4833, Boise, ID 83711
Phone: 208-375-7911
http://www.alertmagazine.org
Purpose: To promote the prevention of drug and alcohol abuse.
Eligibility: Scholarships are awarded for the best editorials on the prevention of drug and alcohol abuse. Winning editorials will be published in "Alert Magazine". Applicants must be high school students between the ages of 18 and 19 and residents of Alaska, Colorado, Idaho, Minnesota, Montana, North Dakota, Oregon, South Dakota, Washington or Wyoming. Applicants must have a minimum 2.5 GPA.
Target applicant(s): High school students.
Minimum GPA: 2.5
Amount: $500.
Number of awards: 1.
Deadline: Ongoing.
How to apply: No application necessary. To apply, submit a 650-800 word essay along with official transcript and personal photograph.
Exclusive: Visit www.UltimateScholarshipBook.com and enter code AL151220 for updates on this award.

(1513) · Alisa's Angels Scholarship

Alisa's Angels Foundation
3404 N. Soldier Trail, Tucson, AZ 85749
http://alisasangels.org
Purpose: To support graduating seniors of Arizona in pursuing post-secondary education.
Eligibility: A minimum GPA of 2.75 is required. Selection is primarily based on demonstration of service to others. Students must submit high school transcripts, an essay describing their service work and a letter of recommendation from a teacher, counselor or faith leader.
Target applicant(s): High school students.
Minimum GPA: 2.75
Amount: $5,000.
Number of awards: Varies.
Scholarship may be renewable.
Deadline: February 1.
How to apply: Applications are available online.
Exclusive: Visit www.UltimateScholarshipBook.com and enter code AL151320 for updates on this award.

(1514) · All Iowa Opportunity Scholarship

Iowa College Student Aid Commission
430 East Grand Avenue, Floor 3, Des Moines, IA 50309-1920
Phone: 515-725-3400
Email: info@iowacollegeaid.org
https://www.iowacollegeaid.gov
Purpose: To recognize Iowa's top students.
Eligibility: Applicants must be Iowa residents who have a minimum 2.5 GPA and demonstrate financial need. Awards may only be used at eligible Iowa institutions. Selection is based on class rank and standardized test scores.
Target applicant(s): High school students.
Minimum GPA: 2.5
Amount: Up to $8,368.
Number of awards: Varies.
Deadline: March 1.
How to apply: Applications are available online.
Exclusive: Visit www.UltimateScholarshipBook.com and enter code IO151420 for updates on this award.

(1515) · Allan Eldin and Agnes Sutorik Geiger Scholarship Fund

Hawaii Community Foundation - Scholarships
827 Fort Street Mall, Honolulu, HI 96813
Phone: 888-731-3863
Email: scholarships@hcf-hawaii.org
https://www.hawaiicommunityfoundation.org
Purpose: To support Hawaii students who are pursuing degrees in veterinary science.
Eligibility: Students must have at least a 3.0 GPA, be full-time students and demonstrate financial need.
Target applicant(s): College students. Graduate school students. Adult students.
Minimum GPA: 3.0
Amount: Varies.
Number of awards: Varies.
Deadline: January 31.
How to apply: To apply, register online, complete the online application and select the scholarships to which you wish to apply. In addition, mail the supporting materials: printed confirmation page from the online application, personal statement, copy of Student Aid Report (SAR) available at www.fafsa.ed.gov and official transcript.
Exclusive: Visit www.UltimateScholarshipBook.com and enter code HA151520 for updates on this award.

(1516) · Allan Johnston Memorial Scholarship

Los Alamos National Laboratory Foundation
1112 Plaza del Norte, Espanola, NM 87532
Phone: 505-753-8890
Email: tony@lanlfoundation.org
http://www.lanlfoundation.org
Purpose: To support undergraduate students from northern New Mexico.

Eligibility: Students must have at least a 3.25 cumulative unweighted GPA, and they must have either an SAT score (combined Math plus Critical Reading only) of at least 930 or an ACT score of at least 19. Applicants must submit an essay and two letters of recommendation.
Target applicant(s): High school students. College students. Adult students.
Minimum GPA: 3.25
Amount: $1,000.
Number of awards: Varies.
Deadline: January 16.
How to apply: Applications are available online.
Exclusive: Visit www.UltimateScholarshipBook.com and enter code LO151620 for updates on this award.

(1517) • Allied Healthcare Scholarship Program

Office of Statewide Health Planning and Development
Health Professions Education Foundation, 400 R Street, Suite 460, Sacramento, CA 95811-6213
Phone: 916-326-3640
Email: hpef-email@oshpd.ca.gov
http://www.oshpd.ca.gov/HPEF/
Purpose: To increase the number of allied healthcare professionals working in medically underserved areas of California.
Eligibility: Applicants must be enrolled in a California community college or university and be studying one of the following programs: medical imaging, occupational therapy, physical therapy, respiratory care, social work, pharmacy and diagnostic medical sonography, pharmacy technician, medical laboratory technologist, surgical technician or ultrasound technician. Those selected will complete a one-year service contract or work volunteer hours in a medically underserved area of California. Financial need, work experience, academic achievement and community involvement are considered. Preference is given to those who expect to graduate within two years of application.
Target applicant(s): High school students. College students. Graduate school students. Adult students.
Minimum GPA: 2.0
Amount: Up to $8,000.
Number of awards: Varies.
Scholarship may be renewable.
Deadline: February 28.
How to apply: Applications are available online.
Exclusive: Visit www.UltimateScholarshipBook.com and enter code OF151720 for updates on this award.

(1518) • Alma White - Delta Kappa Gamma Scholarship

Hawaii Community Foundation - Scholarships
827 Fort Street Mall, Honolulu, HI 96813
Phone: 888-731-3863
Email: scholarships@hcf-hawaii.org
https://www.hawaiicommunityfoundation.org
Purpose: To support students in Hawaii who are planning careers in teaching.
Eligibility: Applicants must be majoring in education. Students must be a college junior, college senior or graduate student. Minimum 2.7 GPA required.
Target applicant(s): College students. Graduate school students. Adult students.
Minimum GPA: 2.7
Amount: Varies.
Number of awards: Varies.
Deadline: January 31.
How to apply: To apply, register online, complete the online application and select the scholarships to which you wish to apply. In addition, mail the supporting materials: printed confirmation page from the online application, personal statement, copy of Student Aid Report (SAR) available at www.fafsa.ed.gov and official transcript.
Exclusive: Visit www.UltimateScholarshipBook.com and enter code HA151820 for updates on this award.

(1519) • Alyssa McCroskey Memorial Scholarship

California Association on Postsecondary Education and Disability (CAPED)
10073 Valley View Street, #242, Cypress, CA 90630
Phone: 562-397-2810
Email: capedscholarships2018@gmail.com
http://www.caped.io/scholarships/
Purpose: To support students with a learning disability who are pursuing higher education.
Eligibility: Applicants must have a verifiable learning disability and be making a positive difference in the lives of other students who are struggling to maintain or regain their mental health. Students must be currently enrolled as a student at a four-year California college or university with a GPA of 2.5 for undergraduates or 3.0 for graduate students. Applicants must have completed at least six semester or eight quarter units as an undergraduate student or three semester or four quarter units as a graduate student.
Target applicant(s): College students. Graduate school students. Adult students.
Minimum GPA: 2.5 for undergraduate students, 3.0 for graduate students
Amount: $1,000.
Number of awards: 1.
Deadline: August 31.
How to apply: Applications are available online.
Exclusive: Visit www.UltimateScholarshipBook.com and enter code CA151920 for updates on this award.

(1520) • Ambassador Minerva Jean Falcon Hawaii Scholarship

Hawaii Community Foundation - Scholarships
827 Fort Street Mall, Honolulu, HI 96813
Phone: 888-731-3863
Email: scholarships@hcf-hawaii.org
https://www.hawaiicommunityfoundation.org
Purpose: To support students of Filipino ancestry.
Eligibility: Students must be starting their freshman year of college, must attend school in Hawaii and must have a minimum 2.7 GPA.
Target applicant(s): High school students. College students. Adult students.
Minimum GPA: 2.7
Amount: Varies.
Number of awards: Varies.
Deadline: January 31.
How to apply: To apply, register online, complete the online application and select the scholarships to which you wish to apply. In addition, mail the supporting materials: printed confirmation page from the online application, personal statement, copy of Student Aid Report (SAR) available at www.fafsa.ed.gov and official transcript.
Exclusive: Visit www.UltimateScholarshipBook.com and enter code HA152020 for updates on this award.

(1521) • American Association of Japanese University Women Scholarship Program

American Association of Japanese University Women
Scholarship Committee, 3543 West Boulevard, Los Angeles, CA 90016
Phone: 310-230-7860
Email: aajuwscholar@gmail.com
http://www.aajuw.org

Purpose: To support female students who demonstrate leadership and facilitate cultural relationships.

Eligibility: Applicants must be starting their junior or senior year in college or be in graduate school at a California school. They must be able to attend the awards ceremony in Los Angeles at their own expense. Applicants must demonstrate a desire to fulfill a leadership role in their chosen field of study and be a contributor to U.S.-Japan relations and cultural exchanges. Students must also submit an essay showing how their studies will contribute to leadership or to the relationship between the United States and Japan.

Target applicant(s): College students. Graduate school students. Adult students.

Amount: $2,000.

Number of awards: Varies.

Deadline: September 30.

How to apply: Applications are available online. Application form, transcripts, resume, an essay and two letters of recommendation are required.

Exclusive: Visit www.UltimateScholarshipBook.com and enter code AM152120 for updates on this award.

(1522) • American Council of Engineering Companies of New Jersey Member Organization Scholarship

American Council of Engineering Companies of New Jersey
310 West State Street, Trenton, NJ 08618
Phone: 609-571-9958
Email: info@acecnj.org
http://www.acecnj.org/scholarship.php

Purpose: To help students who are enrolled in engineering or accredited land surveying degree programs.

Eligibility: Applicants must be rising undergraduate juniors or above enrolled in an ABET-accredited bachelor's degree program in engineering, a master's degree program in engineering, a doctoral degree program in engineering or an accredited land surveying program. Master's students must either be enrolled in an ABET-accredited program or must hold a bachelor's degree in engineering from an ABET-accredited school. Doctoral students must hold either an ABET-accredited bachelor's degree or an ABET-accredited master's degree in engineering. They must be U.S. citizens. Selection is based on GPA, personal essay, recommendation letter, work experience and extracurricular involvement.

Target applicant(s): College students. Graduate school students. Adult students.

Amount: Up to $5,000.

Number of awards: Up to 6.

Deadline: February 3.

How to apply: Applications are available online. An application form, a personal essay, an official transcript and one recommendation form are required.

Exclusive: Visit www.UltimateScholarshipBook.com and enter code AM152220 for updates on this award.

(1523) • American Indian Endowed Scholarship

Washington Student Achievement Council
917 Lakeridge Way SW, Olympia, WA 98502
Phone: 360-753-7850
http://www.wsac.wa.gov/financial-aid

Purpose: To help students who have ties to the Native American community and have financial need pay for higher education.

Eligibility: Applicants must have financial need according to a completed Free Application for Federal Student Aid (FAFSA), be residents of Washington state and enroll full-time as an undergraduate or graduate in an eligible program.

Target applicant(s): High school students. College students. Graduate school students. Adult students.

Amount: $500-$2,000.

Number of awards: Varies.

Scholarship may be renewable.

Deadline: February 1.

How to apply: Applications are available online.

Exclusive: Visit www.UltimateScholarshipBook.com and enter code WA152320 for updates on this award.

(1524) • American Institute of Graphic Arts (AIGA) Honolulu Chapter Scholarship Fund

Hawaii Community Foundation - Scholarships
827 Fort Street Mall, Honolulu, HI 96813
Phone: 888-731-3863
Email: scholarships@hcf-hawaii.org
https://www.hawaiicommunityfoundation.org

Purpose: To support students who are majoring in graphic design, visual communication or commercial arts.

Eligibility: Students must be residents of Hawaii.

Target applicant(s): High school students. College students. Adult students.

Minimum GPA: 2.7

Amount: Varies.

Number of awards: Varies.

Deadline: January 31.

How to apply: To apply, register online, complete the online application and select the scholarships to which you wish to apply. In addition, mail the supporting materials: printed confirmation page from the online application, personal statement, copy of Student Aid Report (SAR) available at www.fafsa.ed.gov and official transcript.

Exclusive: Visit www.UltimateScholarshipBook.com and enter code HA152420 for updates on this award.

(1525) • American Justice Video and Essay Scholarship

Washington State Association for Justice
1809 7th Avenue #1500, Seattle, WA 98101-1328
Phone: 206-464-1011
Email: anita@washingtonjustice.org
https://www.washingtonjustice.org

Purpose: To promote awareness of the role that the civil justice system plays in society through an essay contest.

Eligibility: Applicants must be attending high school in the state of Washington and must subsequently attend college in order to receive the scholarship. Students must submit a video up to 60 seconds or a 700- to 800-word essay on the given topic on advocacy in the American justice system.

Target applicant(s): High school students.

Amount: $3,500.
Number of awards: 2.
Deadline: March 17.
How to apply: Applications are available online.
Exclusive: Visit www.UltimateScholarshipBook.com and enter code WA152520 for updates on this award.

(1526) · American Legion - Connecticut Oratorical Contest

American Legion - Connecticut
287 West Street, Rocky Hill, CT 06067
Phone: 860-436-9986
http://www.ctlegion.org
Purpose: Scholarship awards are given to high school students who win an oratorical contest on the understanding of the U.S. Constitution.
Eligibility: Applicants must prepare an oration on an assigned topic with specific time constraints. Students will explore the substance and meaning of the Constitution.
Target applicant(s): High school students.
Amount: Varies.
Number of awards: Varies.
Deadline: March 3.
How to apply: Applications are available online.
Exclusive: Visit www.UltimateScholarshipBook.com and enter code AM152620 for updates on this award.

(1527) · American Legion Auxiliary, Department of California $1,000 Scholarships

American Legion Auxiliary, Department of California
401 Van Ness Avenue, Suite 319, San Francisco, CA 94102-4570
Phone: 415-861-5092
Email: calegionaux@calegionaux.org
http://calegionaux.org/scholarships.htm
Purpose: To provide support to the children of U.S. Armed Forces members.
Eligibility: One of the applicant's parents must have served in the U.S. Armed Forces during an eligible period. Applicants must be California resident high school seniors or graduates who have had to postpone school due to health or financial reasons and plan to attend a California college or university. Applicants must also demonstrate financial need.
Target applicant(s): High school students.
Amount: $1,000.
Number of awards: 4.
Deadline: March 16.
How to apply: Applications are available online.
Exclusive: Visit www.UltimateScholarshipBook.com and enter code AM152720 for updates on this award.

(1528) · American Legion Auxiliary, Department of California $2,000 Scholarships

American Legion Auxiliary, Department of California
401 Van Ness Avenue, Suite 319, San Francisco, CA 94102-4570
Phone: 415-861-5092
Email: calegionaux@calegionaux.org
http://calegionaux.org/scholarships.htm
Purpose: To provide support to children of U.S. Armed Forces members.
Eligibility: One of the applicant's parents must have served in the U.S. Armed Forces during an eligible period. Applicants must attend a California college or university, be California resident high school seniors or graduates who have not begun college because of illness or need and demonstrate need.
Target applicant(s): High school students.
Amount: $2,000.
Number of awards: 1.
Deadline: March 16.
How to apply: Applications are available online.
Exclusive: Visit www.UltimateScholarshipBook.com and enter code AM152820 for updates on this award.

(1529) · American Legion Auxiliary, Department of California $500 Scholarships

American Legion Auxiliary, Department of California
401 Van Ness Avenue, Suite 319, San Francisco, CA 94102-4570
Phone: 415-861-5092
Email: calegionaux@calegionaux.org
http://calegionaux.org/scholarships.htm
Purpose: To provide support to the children of U.S. Armed Forces members.
Eligibility: One of applicant's parents must have served in the U.S. Armed Forces during an eligible period. Applicants must be California resident high school seniors or graduates who have had to postpone school due to health or financial reasons and plan to attend a California college or university. Applicants must also demonstrate financial need.
Target applicant(s): High school students. College students. Adult students.
Amount: $500.
Number of awards: 3.
Deadline: March 15.
How to apply: Applications are available online.
Exclusive: Visit www.UltimateScholarshipBook.com and enter code AM152920 for updates on this award.

(1530) · American Legion Department of Arkansas High School Oratorical Scholarship Program

American Legion, Department of Arkansas
Department Oratorical Chairman, Roger Lacy, P.O. Box 3280, Little Rock, AR 72203
Phone: 501-375-1104
Email: alegion@swbell.net
http://www.arlegion.org
Purpose: To enhance high school students' experience with and understanding of the U.S. Constitution. The contest will help develop students' leadership skills and civic appreciation, as well as the ability to deliver thoughtful, insightful orations regarding U.S. citizenship and its inherent responsibilities.
Eligibility: Applicants must be high school students under the age of 20 who are U.S. citizens or legal residents and residents of the state. Students first give an oration within their state and winners compete at the national level. The oration must be related to the Constitution of the United States focusing on the duties and obligations citizens have to the government. It must be in English and be between eight and ten minutes. There is also an assigned topic which is posted on the website, and it should be between three and five minutes.
Target applicant(s): High school students.
Amount: $1,000-$2,000.
Number of awards: 3.
Deadline: December 31.
How to apply: Applications are available online.

Exclusive: Visit www.UltimateScholarshipBook.com and enter code AM153020 for updates on this award.

(1531) • American Legion Department of Florida General Scholarship

American Legion, Department of Florida
Elizabeth Douglas, Programs Director, 1912A Lee Road, Orlando, FL 32810
Phone: 800-393-3378
Email: mail@floridalegion.org
http://www.floridalegion.org
Purpose: To support descendants of American Legion members and deceased veterans.
Eligibility: Applicants must be direct descendants of American Legion members in good standing or deceased U.S. veterans who would have been eligible for membership. They must be seniors at accredited Florida high schools who plan to pursue undergraduate study upon graduation. Funds must be used within four years of graduation, excluding active military service.
Target applicant(s): High school students.
Amount: $500-$2,500.
Number of awards: 7.
Deadline: March 1.
How to apply: Applications are available online. An application form and copy of documentation of veteran's service are required.
Exclusive: Visit www.UltimateScholarshipBook.com and enter code AM153120 for updates on this award.

(1532) • American Legion Scholarship Award

American Legion - Department of Illinois
2720 East Lincoln Street, Bloomington, IL 61704
Phone: 309-663-0361
Email: hdqs@illegion.org
http://www.illegion.org/scholarships/
Purpose: To award scholarships to graduating students enrolled in Illinois high schools.
Eligibility: Applicants must be children or grandchildren of American Legion Illinois members and must be in their senior year of high school. Awards may be used to further education at an accredited college, university or technical school.
Target applicant(s): High school students.
Amount: Varies.
Number of awards: Varies.
Deadline: March 15.
How to apply: Application information is available by contacting the American Legion, Department of Illinois.
Exclusive: Visit www.UltimateScholarshipBook.com and enter code AM153220 for updates on this award.

(1533) • Americanism and Government Scholarship Program

American Legion, Department of Wisconsin
2930 American Legion Drive, P.O. Box 388, Portage, WI 53901-0388
Phone: 608-745-1090
Email: info@wilegion.org
http://www.wilegion.org
Purpose: To reward outstanding performance on the Americanism and Government Test, a 50-question examination based on state and federal government and history.
Eligibility: Participants must be enrolled in a Wisconsin high school and in their sophomore, junior or senior year.
Target applicant(s): High school students.
Amount: $250-$500.
Number of awards: 45.
Deadline: April 17.
How to apply: Application information is available by contacting your local principal, teacher or guidance counselor.
Exclusive: Visit www.UltimateScholarshipBook.com and enter code AM153320 for updates on this award.

(1534) • Americanism Essay Scholarship

American Legion - Department of Illinois
2720 East Lincoln Street, Bloomington, IL 61704
Phone: 309-663-0361
Email: hdqs@illegion.org
http://www.illegion.org/scholarships/
Purpose: To reward outstanding 500-word essays written on assigned topics.
Eligibility: Applicants must be enrolled in an Illinois school in grades seven to twelve.
Target applicant(s): Junior high students or younger. High school students.
Amount: $100-$1,200.
Number of awards: 15.
Deadline: February 2.
How to apply: Application information is available by contacting the local American Legion Unit or Auxiliary.
Exclusive: Visit www.UltimateScholarshipBook.com and enter code AM153420 for updates on this award.

(1535) • Angie M. Houtz Memorial Fund Scholarship

Angie M. Houtz Memorial Fund
414 Bottsford Avenue, Upper Marlboro, MD 20774
Email: angiefund@yahoo.com
http://www.theangiefund.com
Purpose: To honor the memory of Angie Houtz, victim of the September 11, 2001 attack on the Pentagon.
Eligibility: Applicants must attend or be accepted to attend a public college in Maryland full-time. They must have an unweighted GPA of 3.0 or higher and have participated in at least 200 hours of community service. They cannot be related to a member of the scholarship fund's board of directors.
Target applicant(s): High school students. College students. Adult students.
Minimum GPA: 3.0
Amount: $3,000.
Number of awards: At least 1.
Deadline: April 30.
How to apply: Applications are available online.
Exclusive: Visit www.UltimateScholarshipBook.com and enter code AN153520 for updates on this award.

(1536) • Ann Griffel Scholarship

Iowa Golf Association
Attn: Ann Griffel Scholarship Committee, 1605 North Ankeny Boulevard, Suite 210, Ankeny, IA 50023
Phone: 888-388-4442
http://www.iowagolf.org
Purpose: To support girls who have played golf in the state of Iowa.

Eligibility: Applicants must plan to attend an Iowa college, university or trade school. Selection is based on academic performance, extracurricular activities and leadership qualities.
Target applicant(s): High school students.
Amount: $2,000.
Number of awards: Varies.
Deadline: March 17.
How to apply: Applications are sent to all high school girls golf coaches in the state of Iowa at the beginning of the year. The application should be mailed in, along with two letters of recommendation, a high school transcript, a photo and a personal essay.
Exclusive: Visit www.UltimateScholarshipBook.com and enter code IO153620 for updates on this award.

(1537) • Anthony Muñoz Scholarship Fund

Anthony Muñoz Foundation
8919 Rossash Road, Cincinnati, OH 45236
Phone: 513-772-4900
Email: cwillis@munozfoundation.org
http://www.munozfoundation.org
Purpose: To assist Kentucky, Indiana and Ohio students.
Eligibility: Applicants must be high school seniors who reside in the counties specified by the foundation and plan to attend college in Kentucky, Indiana or Ohio. Students must have a minimum ACT composite score of 18 or at least a 2.5 GPA and must demonstrate academic achievement, leadership and financial need.
Target applicant(s): High school students.
Minimum GPA: 2.5
Amount: $20,000.
Number of awards: Up to 7.
Deadline: May 1.
How to apply: Applications are available online and must be mailed or faxed.
Exclusive: Visit www.UltimateScholarshipBook.com and enter code AN153720 for updates on this award.

(1538) • Antonio Cirino Memorial Award

Rhode Island Foundation
One Union Station, Providence, RI 02903
Phone: 401-274-4564
Email: rbogert@rifoundation.org
http://www.rifoundation.org
Purpose: To support Rhode Island students who are pursuing careers in art education.
Eligibility: Applicants must demonstrate an interest in learning about and practicing art. Preference will be given to visual artists. Students must be enrolled or planning to enroll in a master's or doctoral program that will lead to a career in art education.
Target applicant(s): College students. Graduate school students. Adult students.
Amount: $2,000-$12,000.
Number of awards: Varies.
Scholarship may be renewable.
Deadline: April 28.
How to apply: Applications are available online.
Exclusive: Visit www.UltimateScholarshipBook.com and enter code RH153820 for updates on this award.

(1539) • Arc of Washington State Trust Fund Stipend Award

Arc of Washington State
Attn: Diana Stadden, 2638 State Avenue NE, Olympia, WA 98506
Phone: 360-357-5596
Email: info@arctrustfund.org
http://www.arcwa.org
Purpose: To help students attending school in Alaska, Idaho, Oregon and Washington state who wish to pursue careers working with the developmentally disabled.
Eligibility: Applicants must be undergraduate juniors or above (including graduate-level students) and must be enrolled in a college or university located in Idaho, Washington state, Alaska or Oregon. They must be interested in working with the developmentally disabled. Selection is based on the overall strength of the application.
Target applicant(s): College students. Graduate school students. Adult students.
Amount: Varies.
Number of awards: Varies.
Deadline: Varies.
How to apply: Applications are available online. An application form, official transcripts, personal statement and two letters of recommendation are required.
Exclusive: Visit www.UltimateScholarshipBook.com and enter code AR153920 for updates on this award.

(1540) • Archibald Rutledge Scholarship Program

South Carolina State Department of Education
1429 Senate Street, Columbia, SC 29201
Phone: 803-734-0323
Email: cpower@ed.sc.gov
http://ed.sc.gov
Purpose: To support students who exhibit academic and artistic excellence.
Eligibility: Applicants must be high school seniors in South Carolina public schools, have attended South Carolina public schools for the past two consecutive years and be U.S. citizens. There are five categories: creative writing, dance, music, theater and visual arts. For the creative writing category, a sonnet, lyric or narrative poem no longer than one page must be submitted. For the dance category, an original, short dance composition of three to ten minutes. For the music category, an original composition of three to ten minutes must be submitted. For the theater category, an original one-act play with a performing time of eight to fifteen minutes. For the visual arts category, an original visual composition must be submitted. Compositions are judged on creativity, originality and quality of expression and content.
Target applicant(s): High school students.
Amount: $2,000.
Number of awards: 5.
Deadline: February 6.
How to apply: Applications are available online. An application form, composition and process folio are required.
Exclusive: Visit www.UltimateScholarshipBook.com and enter code SO154020 for updates on this award.

(1541) • Arizona BPW Foundation Annual Scholarships

Arizona Business and Professional Women's Foundation
P.O. Box 32596, Phoenix, AZ 85064
http://www.arizonabpwfoundation.com/scholarships.html
Purpose: To provide education assistance to women.

Eligibility: Applicants must be women who are returning to school to broaden their job prospects at a community college or trade school in Arizona. They must provide a career goal statement, financial need statement, most recent transcript, most recent income tax return and two letters of recommendation.
Target applicant(s): High school students. College students. Adult students.
Amount: Varies.
Number of awards: Varies.
Deadline: May 1.
How to apply: Applications are available online.
Exclusive: Visit www.UltimateScholarshipBook.com and enter code AR154120 for updates on this award.

(1542) • Arizona Chapter MOAA ROTC Scholarships

Military Officers Association of American-Arizona Chapter
41122 N. Majesty Way, Anthem, AZ 85086
Phone: 602-943-0028
Email: charles.bitner@gmail.com
http://azmoaa.org/operations/jrtc-scholarships/
Purpose: To provide educational assistance to ROTC students.
Eligibility: Applicants must be non-contracted ROTC students in the last half of their junior year. They must be in good academic standing and demonstrate loyalty and potential for military leadership.
Target applicant(s): College students. Adult students.
Amount: Varies.
Number of awards: Varies.
Deadline: Varies.
How to apply: Applications are available online.
Exclusive: Visit www.UltimateScholarshipBook.com and enter code MI154220 for updates on this award.

(1543) • Arizona National Livestock Show Scholarship

Arizona National Livestock Show
1826 W. McDowell Road, Phoenix, AZ 85007
Phone: 602-258-8568
Email: information@anls.org
https://anls.org/
Purpose: To assist students who participate in the Arizona National Livestock Show.
Eligibility: Applicants must be currently taking at least 12 hours and have completed at least 12 semester hours at a college or university and have a minimum 2.5 GPA.
Target applicant(s): College students. Adult students.
Minimum GPA: 2.5
Amount: $40,000 total for all awards.
Number of awards: Up to 20.
Deadline: March 15.
How to apply: Applications are available online.
Exclusive: Visit www.UltimateScholarshipBook.com and enter code AR154320 for updates on this award.

(1544) • Arizona Network of Executive Women in Hospitality Scholarship Awards

Network of Executive Women in Hospitality, Arizona
c/o Kristin Wolfe, 5122 E. Shea Boulevard, Suite 1050, Scottsdale, AZ 85254
Phone: 800-593-6394
Email: Kristin@daisycake.com
http://newh.org/chapters/arizona/
Purpose: To support Arizona students wishing to enter the hospitality industry.
Eligibility: Applicants must be enrolled in a degree or certification program for which they have completed half of the requirements. They must plan to pursue a career in the hospitality industry including hotel/restaurant management, culinary/foodservice, architecture or interior design. Financial need and a 3.0 or higher GPA are required.
Target applicant(s): College students. Adult students.
Minimum GPA: 3.0
Amount: $2,500.
Number of awards: 2.
Deadline: October 15.
How to apply: Applications are available online. An application form, essay, transcript and letters of recommendation are required.
Exclusive: Visit www.UltimateScholarshipBook.com and enter code NE154420 for updates on this award.

(1545) • Arkansas Cheer Coaches Association Cheer Classics Team of Excellence

Arkansas Cheer Coaches Association
Attn.: Connie Moody, P.O. Box 1654, Heber Springs, AR 72543
http://www.arkansascheercoaches.com
Purpose: To support Arkansas senior cheerleaders who promote a high level of school spirit in the community as they further their education beyond high school.
Eligibility: Applicants must be senior cheerleaders who will be competing in the Cheer Classics put on by the Arkansas Cheer Coaches Association. Selection is based on the two-page essay, community service and three letters of recommendation.
Target applicant(s): High school students.
Amount: Varies.
Number of awards: Varies.
Deadline: March 17.
How to apply: Applications are available online. In addition to the online form, applicants must submit a two-page essay and three letters of recommendation.
Exclusive: Visit www.UltimateScholarshipBook.com and enter code AR154520 for updates on this award.

(1546) • Arkansas Game and Fish Commission Conservation Scholarship

Arkansas Game and Fish Commission
2 Natural Resources Drive, Little Rock, AR 72205
Phone: 800-364-4263
Email: Shawna.Hitchcock@agfc.ar.gov
http://www.agfc.com
Purpose: To aid Arkansas students preparing for careers in natural resources conservation.
Eligibility: Applicants must be Arkansas residents who are high school seniors or undergraduate or graduate-level college students. They must have a GPA of 2.5 or above and must be planning to pursue a career in natural resources conservation. They cannot have received full scholarship or grant funding from another source. Selection is based on the standardized scoring of each application as a whole.
Target applicant(s): High school students. College students. Graduate school students. Adult students.
Minimum GPA: 2.5
Amount: Up to $2,000 per semester.
Number of awards: Varies.

Scholarship may be renewable.
Deadline: Mid-June.
How to apply: Applications are available online. An application form, personal statement, essay, official transcript, three personal references, one recommendation letter, photograph and statement of intent to pursue a four-year degree (for those currently attending a two-year institution) are required.
Exclusive: Visit www.UltimateScholarshipBook.com and enter code AR154620 for updates on this award.

(1547) • Arkansas Service Memorial Scholarship Endowment

Arkansas Community Foundation
1400 W. Markham, Suite 206, Little Rock, AR 72201
Phone: 888-220-2723
Email: arcf@arcf.org
http://www.arcf.org
Purpose: To provide financial assistance for students with a parent who died in service to his or her community, state or nation.
Eligibility: Applicants must be Arkansas residents who plan to attend an institution of higher learning in the state. Scholarships are awarded by local Arkansas Community Foundation chapters.
Target applicant(s): High school students. College students. Graduate school students. Adult students.
Amount: $2,500.
Number of awards: Varies.
Deadline: March 1.
How to apply: Applications are available online.
Exclusive: Visit www.UltimateScholarshipBook.com and enter code AR154720 for updates on this award.

(1548) • Art Scholarship

Liberty Graphics
P.O. Box 5, 44 Main Street, Liberty, ME 04949
Phone: 207-589-4596
Email: sales@lgtees.com
http://www.lgtees.com
Purpose: To encourage exploration and expression through traditional visual mediums.
Eligibility: Applicants must be seniors at a Maine high school and be legal residents of Maine. Students must submit artwork, usually with a theme of Maine and the outdoors.
Target applicant(s): High school students.
Amount: $1,000.
Number of awards: 1.
Deadline: March 20.
How to apply: Applications are available from your high school guidance counselor or on the Liberty Graphics website beginning in late February or early March of each year.
Exclusive: Visit www.UltimateScholarshipBook.com and enter code LI154820 for updates on this award.

(1549) • Aspire Award

Tennessee Student Assistance Corporation
404 James Robertson Parkway, Suite 1510, Parkway Towers, Nashville, TN 37243
Phone: 800-342-1663
Email: tsac.aidinfo@tn.gov
http://www.tn.gov/collegepays/section/money-for-college
Purpose: To provide supplemental support to recipients of the Tennessee HOPE Scholarship.
Eligibility: Applicants must be entering freshmen with a minimum ACT score of 21, minimum SAT score of 980 or minimum 3.0 GPA. Home-schooled applicants must have a minimum ACT score of 21 or SAT score of 980. GED applicants must have a minimum GED score of 525 and minimum ACT score of 21 or SAT score of 980. Independent students or the parents of dependent students must have an adjusted gross income under $36,000.
Target applicant(s): High school students.
Minimum GPA: 3.0
Amount: Up to $750 per semester.
Number of awards: Varies.
Deadline: Varies.
How to apply: Applications are available through completion of the FAFSA.
Exclusive: Visit www.UltimateScholarshipBook.com and enter code TE154920 for updates on this award.

(1550) • Associate Degree Nursing Scholarship Program

Office of Statewide Health Planning and Development
Health Professions Education Foundation, 400 R Street, Suite 460, Sacramento, CA 95811-6213
Phone: 916-326-3640
Email: hpef-email@oshpd.ca.gov
http://www.oshpd.ca.gov/HPEF/
Purpose: To increase the number of registered nurses working in medically underserved areas of California.
Eligibility: Applicants must be California residents enrolled in an associate degree nursing program at a California school, have a minimum 2.0 GPA and be fluent in a language other than English. Financial need, work experience, community involvement and academic achievement are considered. Preference is given to those who will graduate within two years and to those who plan to remain in a medically underserved area past the service time required. Recipients must sign a two-year service contract to work in a medically underserved area as an RN.
Target applicant(s): High school students. College students. Adult students.
Minimum GPA: 2.0
Amount: Up to $10,000.
Number of awards: Varies.
Scholarship may be renewable.
Deadline: February 28.
How to apply: Applications are available online.
Exclusive: Visit www.UltimateScholarshipBook.com and enter code OF155020 for updates on this award.

(1551) • Associated General Contractors of Connecticut Scholarships

Connecticut Construction Industries Association
912 Silas Deane Highway, Suite 112, Wethersfield, CT 06109
Phone: 860-529-6855
Email: ccia-info@ctconstruction.org
http://www.ctconstruction.org
Purpose: To aid students planning to pursue careers in civil engineering or building and construction technology.
Eligibility: Applicants must be high school seniors who intend to enroll in a four-year civil engineering or construction technology program or who plan to complete a construction program at a two-year institution before entering a four-year institution. They must be U.S. citizens

or legal residents and must be interested in a career in construction. Selection is based on academic achievement, level of interest in a construction career, work experience, evaluation forms, extracurricular activities and financial need. The award is for two years.
Target applicant(s): High school students.
Amount: $2,500.
Number of awards: Varies.
Deadline: March 31.
How to apply: Applications are available online. An application form, two personal evaluation forms, one faculty evaluation form and an official transcript are required.
Exclusive: Visit www.UltimateScholarshipBook.com and enter code CO155120 for updates on this award.

(1552) • Associated General Contractors of Minnesota Scholarships

Associated General Contractors of Minnesota
Capitol Office Building, 525 Park Street, Suite 110, St. Paul, MN 55103-2186
Phone: 651-632-8929
Email: mbeckmann@agcmn.org
http://www.agcmn.org
Purpose: To support outstanding students in Minnesota.
Eligibility: Applicants must attend a Minnesota institution of higher learning with a concentration in construction or construction-related courses. Applications are judged equally on academic performance, career objectives, financial need, personal information and application clarity.
Target applicant(s): College students. Adult students.
Amount: $500-$2,500.
Number of awards: 5-8.
Deadline: May 26.
How to apply: Applications are available online. An application form, personal statement, academic core plan, career objectives and recent color photo are required.
Exclusive: Visit www.UltimateScholarshipBook.com and enter code AS155220 for updates on this award.

(1553) • ASWA Seattle Chapter Scholarship

American Society of Women Accountants - Seattle Chapter
800 Fifth Avenue, Suite 101, PMB 237, Seattle, WA 98104-3191
Phone: 206-467-8645
Email: scholarship@aswaseattle.org
http://seattleafwa.org/
Purpose: To aid accounting students in Washington state.
Eligibility: Applicants must be part-time or full-time accounting students at an accredited postsecondary institution located in Washington state. Students must have finished at least 30 semester hours (or 45 quarter hours) within four weeks of the application deadline. They must have an overall GPA of 2.0 or higher. The scholarship is open to both male and female students. Selection is based on GPA, stated career goals and financial need.
Target applicant(s): College students. Graduate school students. Adult students.
Minimum GPA: 2.0
Amount: Varies.
Number of awards: Varies.
Deadline: May 31.
How to apply: Applications are available online. An application form, an official transcript, two recommendation letters and financial aid transcripts are required.
Exclusive: Visit www.UltimateScholarshipBook.com and enter code AM155320 for updates on this award.

(1554) • Atsuhiko Tateuchi Memorial Scholarship

Seattle Foundation
1200 Fifth Avenue, Suite 1300, Seattle, WA 98101-3151
Phone: 206-515-2119
Email: scholarships@seattlefoundation.org
http://www.seattlefoundation.org
Purpose: To provide financial assistance for hard-working students from the Pacific Rim states.
Eligibility: Applicants must be high school seniors or undergraduate students from Washington, Oregon, California, Hawaii or Alaska with demonstrated financial need. They must have a GPA of 3.0 or higher. Preference is given to students with Japanese or other Asian ancestry.
Target applicant(s): High school students. College students. Adult students.
Minimum GPA: 3.0
Amount: $5,000.
Number of awards: 10.
Scholarship may be renewable.
Deadline: March 1.
How to apply: Applications are available online.
Exclusive: Visit www.UltimateScholarshipBook.com and enter code SE155420 for updates on this award.

(1555) • AWAF Scholarships

Association for Women in Architecture Foundation
1315 Storm Parkway, Torrance, CA 90501
Phone: 310-534-8466
Email: scholarships@awaplusd.org
http://awaplusd.org/scholarships/
Purpose: To support women studying architecture.
Eligibility: Applicants must be female residents of California or attend a California school and must be enrolled in one of the following majors: architecture, landscape architecture, urban and/or land planning, interior design or environmental design. Applicants must also have completed a minimum of 18 units in their major by the application due date. The award is based on grades, personal statement, financial need, recommendations and submitted materials.
Target applicant(s): College students. Graduate school students. Adult students.
Amount: Varies.
Number of awards: Varies.
Deadline: March 23.
How to apply: Applications are available online.
Exclusive: Visit www.UltimateScholarshipBook.com and enter code AS155520 for updates on this award.

(1556) • AWC Seattle Professional Chapter Scholarships

Association for Women in Communications - Scholarships
P.O. Box 60262, Shoreline, WA 98160
Phone: 206-654-2929
Email: tina@writeasrain.com
http://www.seattleawc.org
Purpose: To support students of communications.
Eligibility: Applicants must be Washington State residents who are college juniors, seniors or graduate students at Washington State four-year colleges. Students must major in print and broadcast journalism,

television and radio production, film advertising, public relations, marketing, graphic design, multimedia design, photography or technical communication. Selection is based on demonstrated excellence in communications, contributions toward communications, scholastic achievement, financial need and work samples.
Target applicant(s): College students. Adult students.
Amount: $2,000.
Number of awards: 2.
Deadline: March 31.
How to apply: Applications are available online. An application form, cover letter, transcript, resume and two work samples are required.
Exclusive: Visit www.UltimateScholarshipBook.com and enter code AS155620 for updates on this award.

(1557) • Bach Organ Scholarship

Rhode Island Foundation
One Union Station, Providence, RI 02903
Phone: 401-274-4564
Email: rbogert@rifoundation.org
http://www.rifoundation.org
Purpose: To support organ music majors.
Eligibility: Applicants must be residents of the state of Rhode Island. Students must be currently enrolled in a college music program, majoring in organ music and they must show financial need.
Target applicant(s): High school students. College students. Graduate school students. Adult students.
Amount: $800-$1,000.
Number of awards: Varies.
Deadline: April 21.
How to apply: Applications are available online.
Exclusive: Visit www.UltimateScholarshipBook.com and enter code RH155720 for updates on this award.

(1558) • Bachelor of Science Nursing Scholarship Program

Office of Statewide Health Planning and Development
Health Professions Education Foundation, 400 R Street, Suite 460, Sacramento, CA 95811-6213
Phone: 916-326-3640
Email: hpef-email@oshpd.ca.gov
http://www.oshpd.ca.gov/HPEF/
Purpose: To increase the number of professional nurses practicing in medically underserved areas of California by assisting nursing students attending California schools.
Eligibility: Applicants must be attending a California undergraduate nursing program and be fluent in a language other than English. Financial need, work experience, academic achievement and community involvement are considered. A two-year service agreement to work in a medically underserved area of California is required. Preference is given to those who expect to graduate within two years and to those who plan to remain in a medically underserved area after the service agreement has expired. Applicant must have minimum 2.0 GPA.
Target applicant(s): College students. Adult students.
Minimum GPA: 2.0
Amount: Up to $13,000.
Number of awards: Varies.
Scholarship may be renewable.
Deadline: February 28.
How to apply: Applications are available online.
Exclusive: Visit www.UltimateScholarshipBook.com and enter code OF155820 for updates on this award.

(1559) • BAFTX Graduate Scholarship

British American Foundation of Texas
Email: info@baftx.org
https://www.baftx.org
Purpose: To support graduate students from Texas or the UK pursuing STEM education.
Eligibility: Applicants must be residents of Texas or the U.K. enrolled as full-time graduate students within the Texas or U.K. education system with demonstrated financial need. Students must be 21 years or older majoring in STEM or business with a GPA of 3.25 or higher.
Target applicant(s): College students. Graduate school students. Adult students.
Minimum GPA: 3.25
Amount: Varies.
Number of awards: 1.
Deadline: March 31.
How to apply: Applications are available online.
Exclusive: Visit www.UltimateScholarshipBook.com and enter code BR155920 for updates on this award.

(1560) • BAFTX Undergraduate Award

British American Foundation of Texas
Email: info@baftx.org
https://www.baftx.org
Purpose: To help offset the cost of higher education for Texas or United Kingdom residents.
Eligibility: Applicants must be residents of Texas or the United Kingdom enrolled as full-time students within Texas or the U.K. and demonstrate financial need. Students must be pursuing a major in science, technology, engineering, math or business and have a minimum GPA of 3.25. Applicants must be able to interview and attend an awards dinner.
Target applicant(s): High school students. College students. Adult students.
Minimum GPA: 3.25
Amount: Varies.
Number of awards: 1.
Deadline: March 31.
How to apply: Applications are available online.
Exclusive: Visit www.UltimateScholarshipBook.com and enter code BR156020 for updates on this award.

(1561) • Beginning Teacher Scholarships

Texas Retired Teachers Foundation
Attn: Scholarship Committee, 313 E. 12th Street, Suite 220, Austin, TX 78701
Phone: 512-476-1622
Email: info@trtf.org
https://trtf.org/category/initiatives/
Purpose: To assist Texas students whose relatives are members of the Texas Retired Teachers Association.
Eligibility: Applicants must be relatives of an active member of the Texas Retired Teachers Association (TRTA), earning or earned a bachelor's or master's degree in education and pursuing or have pursued their teaching certification exam.
Target applicant(s): High school students. College students. Graduate school students. Adult students.

Amount: $750.
Number of awards: 10.
Deadline: March 16.
How to apply: Applications are available online.
Exclusive: Visit www.UltimateScholarshipBook.com and enter code TE156120 for updates on this award.

(1562) • Ben W. Fortson, Jr., Scholarship

Surveying and Mapping Society of Georgia
P.O. Box 778 , Douglasville, GA 30133-0778
Phone: 770-947-1767
Email: ginger_samsog@att.net
http://www.samsog.org
Purpose: To help Georgia undergraduate land surveying students.
Eligibility: Applicants must be Georgia residents enrolled in an undergraduate land surveying program of study at an accredited institution of higher learning. They must have completed at least 20 percent of their program requirements before receiving any scholarship monies awarded. Students must also maintain a 2.4 overall GPA and 2.7 GPA in surveying courses. Preference is given to full-time students seeking a bachelor's degree. Selection is based on the overall strength of the application.
Target applicant(s): College students. Adult students.
Minimum GPA: 2.4
Amount: Varies.
Number of awards: Varies.
Deadline: Varies.
How to apply: Applications are available online. An application form and transcript are required.
Exclusive: Visit www.UltimateScholarshipBook.com and enter code SU156220 for updates on this award.

(1563) • Benjamin C. Blackburn Scholarship

Friends of the Frelinghuysen Arboretum
The Benjamin C. Blackburn Scholarship Committee, 353 East Hanover Avenue, P.O. Box 1295, Morristown, NJ 07962-1295
Phone: 973-326-7601
Email: webmaster@arboretumfriends.org
http://www.arboretumfriends.org
Purpose: To help New Jersey students who are planning for careers in agronomy, botany, environmental science, floriculture, horticulture, landscape design or plant science.
Eligibility: Applicants must be New Jersey residents. They must be enrolled in the Landscape and Horticultural Technology Program at County College of Morris and have a GPA of 3.0 or higher. If awarded the scholarship, the recipient will be expected to give a 10-minute speech on his or her horticultural interests and goals at the Arboretum's annual meeting. Selection is based on the overall strength of the application.
Target applicant(s): College students. Adult students.
Minimum GPA: 3.0
Amount: Up to $3,000.
Number of awards: At least 1.
Deadline: April 7.
How to apply: Applications are available online. An application form, personal essay, transcript, a list of the courses that currently are being taken and four letters of recommendation are required.
Exclusive: Visit www.UltimateScholarshipBook.com and enter code FR156320 for updates on this award.

(1564) • Benjamin Franklin/Edith Green Scholarship

Oregon Office of Student Access and Completion
1500 Valley River Drive, Suite 100, Eugene, OR 97401
Phone: 541-687-7422
Email: cheryl.a.connolly@state.or.us
https://oregonstudentaid.gov/
Purpose: To assist Oregon high school students who are planning to attend a public four-year postsecondary institution in Oregon.
Eligibility: Applicants must be U.S. citizens or legal residents. They must be Oregon residents, be graduating high school seniors and have a GPA of 3.45 to 3.55. Applicants who owe a refund on an educational grant or who have defaulted on an educational loan are ineligible. Selection is based on financial need.
Target applicant(s): High school students.
Minimum GPA: 3.45
Amount: Varies.
Number of awards: Varies.
Deadline: March 1.
How to apply: Applications are available online. An application form, supporting materials and FAFSA completion are required.
Exclusive: Visit www.UltimateScholarshipBook.com and enter code OR156420 for updates on this award.

(1565) • Better Business Bureau of Delaware Education Foundation Video Scholarship

Better Business Bureau (BBB) of Delaware Education Foundation
Attn.: Scholarship Committee, 60 Reads Way, New Castle, DE 19720
Phone: 302-221-5259
Email: csauers@delaware.bbb.org
http://www.bbb.org/delaware/
Purpose: To assist Delaware high school seniors.
Eligibility: Applicants must submit a short 30- to 60-second video on the annual theme provided. Selection is based on communication of the theme, creativity and production value.
Target applicant(s): High school students.
Amount: $2,500.
Number of awards: 1.
Deadline: January 10.
Exclusive: Visit www.UltimateScholarshipBook.com and enter code BE156520 for updates on this award.

(1566) • Better Business Bureau of Delaware Foundation Student Ethics Scholarship

Better Business Bureau (BBB) of Delaware Education Foundation
Attn.: Scholarship Committee, 60 Reads Way, New Castle, DE 19720
Phone: 302-221-5259
Email: csauers@delaware.bbb.org
http://www.bbb.org/delaware/
Purpose: To assist Delaware high school seniors who exemplify high ethics.
Eligibility: Applicants must demonstrate leadership, community service, personal integrity and academic strength and must plan to attend an accredited college or university. A minimum GPA of 3.0 is required of applicants. Applicants must be nominated/sponsored by an employee, owner or company principal representing a BBB Accredited Business.
Target applicant(s): High school students.
Minimum GPA: 3.0
Amount: $2,500.

Number of awards: 2.
Deadline: January 10.
How to apply: Applicants must be nominated by an employee or owner of a company that is accredited by the BBB. An application form, two letters of recommendation, an essay, supporting documentation, a copy of the transcript and certification by sponsor to the BBB are required.
Exclusive: Visit www.UltimateScholarshipBook.com and enter code BE156620 for updates on this award.

(1567) • Betty Bacon Memorial Scholarship

California Association on Postsecondary Education and Disability (CAPED)
10073 Valley View Street, #242, Cypress, CA 90630
Phone: 562-397-2810
Email: capedscholarships2018@gmail.com
http://www.caped.io/scholarships/
Purpose: To support students with a learning disability who are pursuing higher education.
Eligibility: Applicants must have a verifiable learning disability and be currently enrolled as a student at a four-year California college or university with a GPA of 2.5 for undergraduates or 3.0 for graduate students. Students must have completed at least six semester or eight quarter units as an undergraduate student or three semester or four quarter units as a graduate student.
Target applicant(s): College students. Graduate school students. Adult students.
Minimum GPA: 2.5 for undergraduate students, 3.0 for graduate students
Amount: $1,000.
Number of awards: 1.
Deadline: August 31.
How to apply: Applications are available online.
Exclusive: Visit www.UltimateScholarshipBook.com and enter code CA156720 for updates on this award.

(1568) • BI-LO/SpiritFest Scholarship

ERay Promotions
Attention: Scholarship Committee, 342 Crepe Myrtle Drive, Greer, SC 29651
Phone: 864-420-7973
http://www.eraypromotions.com
Purpose: To recognize academic excellence and leadership qualities of minority students.
Eligibility: Applicants must be minority high school seniors with a minimum 3.0 GPA. Applicants must complete an application which including a 300-word autobiography which highlights volunteer activities, leadership experience, extracurricular activities, work experience, honors and special awards. Three letters of recommendation and an official transcript must also be submitted.
Target applicant(s): High school students.
Minimum GPA: 3.0
Amount: $1,000.
Number of awards: 1.
Deadline: July 25.
How to apply: Applications are available online.
Exclusive: Visit www.UltimateScholarshipBook.com and enter code ER156820 for updates on this award.

(1569) • Bick Bickson Scholarship Fund

Hawaii Community Foundation - Scholarships
827 Fort Street Mall, Honolulu, HI 96813
Phone: 888-731-3863
Email: scholarships@hcf-hawaii.org
https://www.hawaiicommunityfoundation.org
Purpose: To support students pursuing studies in marketing, law or travel.
Eligibility: Applicants must be residents of Hawaii who have need of financial assistance and plan to attend an accredited college or university full-time within the United States as an undergraduate or graduate student. Students must have a 3.0 GPA and plan to major in one of the following areas: marketing, law or travel industry management.
Target applicant(s): High school students. College students. Graduate school students. Adult students.
Minimum GPA: 3.0
Amount: Varies.
Number of awards: Varies.
Deadline: January 31.
How to apply: Applications are available online.
Exclusive: Visit www.UltimateScholarshipBook.com and enter code HA156920 for updates on this award.

(1570) • Big Y Scholarship Programs

Big Y
Scholarship Committee, P.O. Box 7840, Springfield, MA 01102-7840
Phone: 413-504-4047
http://www.bigy.com
Purpose: To reward students in the Big Y market area and those affiliated with Big Y.
Eligibility: Applicants must either be Big Y employees or their dependents or must reside or attend school in western or central Massachusetts, Norfolk County, Massachusetts or Connecticut. The scholarships are available to high school seniors, undergraduates, graduates, community college students and adult students. Applicants should submit transcripts, college entrance exams scores and two recommendation letters. Big Y employees must submit one recommendation from their supervisor. Selection is based on achievements, awards, community involvement, leadership positions and class rank. Eight scholarships are available specifically for dependents of law enforcement officers and firefighters.
Target applicant(s): High school students. College students. Graduate school students. Adult students.
Amount: Varies.
Number of awards: 300.
Deadline: February 1.
How to apply: Applications are available at any Big Y location from October through January each year. Applications are also available at guidance offices of schools within Big Y's market area.
Exclusive: Visit www.UltimateScholarshipBook.com and enter code BI157020 for updates on this award.

(1571) • Bill Teegins Memorial Scholarship

Oklahoma Association of Broadcasters
6520 N. Western, Suite 104, Oklahoma City, OK 73116
Phone: 405-848-0771
Email: struby@oabok.org
https://oabok.org/careerseducation/scholarships/
Purpose: To support students majoring in broadcasting at Oklahoma colleges and universities.

Eligibility: Applicants must be enrolled in an Oklahoma college or university broadcasting program, be majoring in broadcasting and have an intent to enter the broadcasting career upon graduation. Students must be a junior or senior for the upcoming school year and must maintain a "B" average.
Target applicant(s): College students. Adult students.
Minimum GPA: 3.0
Amount: $2,000.
Number of awards: 1.
Deadline: February 9.
How to apply: Applications are available online.
Exclusive: Visit www.UltimateScholarshipBook.com and enter code OK157120 for updates on this award.

(1572) • Bird Dog Foundation's College Scholarship Essay Contest

Bird Dog Foundation Inc.
505 West Highway 57, P.O. Box 774, Grand Junction, TN 38039
Phone: 731-764-2058
http://www.birddogfoundation.com
Purpose: To promote interest in wildlife conservation and related subjects.
Eligibility: Applicants must be high school seniors who are preparing to enter freshman year of college or university. Entrants must reside in Tennessee, Mississippi or Arkansas. Applicants may not be related to any employee or sitting board member of the Bird Dog Foundation. Students who are residents of any of the 50 states and who are affiliated with a bird hunting or sporting dog club are eligible to apply.
Target applicant(s): High school students.
Amount: $2,000.
Number of awards: 3.
Deadline: April 15.
How to apply: Applications are available online.
Exclusive: Visit www.UltimateScholarshipBook.com and enter code BI157220 for updates on this award.

(1573) • Blossom Kalama Evans Memorial Scholarship Fund

Hawaii Community Foundation - Scholarships
827 Fort Street Mall, Honolulu, HI 96813
Phone: 888-731-3863
Email: scholarships@hcf-hawaii.org
https://www.hawaiicommunityfoundation.org
Purpose: To support students who are dedicated to serving the native Hawaiian community.
Eligibility: Applicants must be of Hawaiian ancestry, have at least a 2.7 GPA and must be a college junior, college senior or graduate student.
Target applicant(s): College students. Graduate school students. Adult students.
Minimum GPA: 2.7
Amount: Varies.
Number of awards: Varies.
Deadline: January 31.
How to apply: To apply, register online, complete the online application and select the scholarships to which you wish to apply. In addition, mail the supporting materials: printed confirmation page from the online application, personal statement, copy of Student Aid Report (SAR) available at www.fafsa.ed.gov and official transcript.
Exclusive: Visit www.UltimateScholarshipBook.com and enter code HA157320 for updates on this award.

(1574) • Bob C. Powers Scholarship

North Texas Fair and Rodeo
2217 N. Carroll Boulevard, Denton, TX 76201
Phone: 940-387-2632
Email: nkimmey@ntfair.com
http://www.ntfair.com/p/get-involved/195
Purpose: To support graduating high school seniors by investing in their future.
Eligibility: Applicants must be a high school senior and involved in school, their community and FFA, FHA or 4-H activities. Selection is based on academic achievement, extracurricular activities and financial need.
Target applicant(s): High school students.
Amount: $2,000.
Number of awards: 1.
Deadline: April 1.
How to apply: Applications are available online and must include two letters of recommendation and two photos.
Exclusive: Visit www.UltimateScholarshipBook.com and enter code NO157420 for updates on this award.

(1575) • Bob Eddy Scholarship Program

Connecticut Society of Professional Journalists
Attn: Paul Singley, P.O. Box 5071, Woodbridge, CT 06525
Phone: 212-683-5700 x364
Email: psingley@ctspj.org
http://connecticutspj.org/
Purpose: To support students interested in journalism careers.
Eligibility: Applicants must be rising college juniors or seniors at a four-year college and Connecticut residents or students of Connecticut schools. They should be able to submit samples of work that shows interest and competency in journalism.
Target applicant(s): College students. Adult students.
Amount: $500-$2,500.
Number of awards: 4.
Deadline: April 12.
How to apply: Applications are available online. An application form, transcript, essay and writing samples, tapes or related work in any media are required.
Exclusive: Visit www.UltimateScholarshipBook.com and enter code CO157520 for updates on this award.

(1576) • Bob Stevens Memorial Scholarship

Garden State Scholastic Press Foundation
New Jersey Press Foundation, 840 Bear Tavern Road, Suite 305, West Trenton, NJ 08628-1019
Email: scholarship@gsspa.org
http://www.gsspa.org
Purpose: To support high school journalism students.
Eligibility: Applicants must be graduating New Jersey high school seniors who are nominated by a GSSPA member, have a GPA of 3.0 or higher and have participated in high school journalism for at least two years.
Target applicant(s): High school students.
Minimum GPA: 3.0
Amount: $1,500.
Number of awards: 1.
Deadline: February 15.

How to apply: Applications are available online. An application form, transcript, three or four letters of recommendation and portfolio with work samples are required.
Exclusive: Visit www.UltimateScholarshipBook.com and enter code GA157620 for updates on this award.

(1577) • Boeing Company STEM Scholarship

Independent Colleges of Washington
600 Stewart Street, Suite 600, Seattle, WA 98101
Phone: 206-623-4494
Email: info@icwashington.org
http://www.icwashington.org/scholarships/
Purpose: To assist students attending independent Washington colleges.
Eligibility: Applicants must be a junior or senior enrolled at an ICW member institution at the time of the award and be involved with community service. A GPA of 3.25 is required and applicants must be majoring in science, technology, engineering, mathematics, a health care field or be preparing to teach in a STEM field.
Target applicant(s): College students. Adult students.
Minimum GPA: 3.25
Amount: $2,500.
Number of awards: 1.
Deadline: March 17.
How to apply: Applications are available online. An application form, resume, essay, letter of recommendation and transcript are required.
Exclusive: Visit www.UltimateScholarshipBook.com and enter code IN157720 for updates on this award.

(1578) • Boettcher Foundation Scholarship

Boettcher Foundation
600 Seventeenth Street, Suite 2210 South, Denver, CO 80202-5422
Phone: 800-323-9640
Email: scholarships@boettcherfoundation.org
http://boettcherfoundation.org/
Purpose: To recognize high school seniors who plan to make contributions to the people in the state of Colorado.
Eligibility: Applicants must be high school seniors and current, legal residents of the state of Colorado who will graduate in the top 5 percent of their class. Applicants must have a composite score of 27 on the ACT or 1200 on the SAT. They should submit applications, essays, transcripts and standardized test scores. Selection is based on academic merit, demonstration of leadership skills, community service and character.
Target applicant(s): High school students.
Amount: Full tuition plus $2,800 stipend.
Number of awards: 40.
Scholarship may be renewable.
Deadline: November 1.
How to apply: Contact high school counselors for more information.
Exclusive: Visit www.UltimateScholarshipBook.com and enter code BO157820 for updates on this award.

(1579) • Bohdan Kolinsky Memorial Sports Journalism Scholarship

Connecticut Sports Writers Alliance
P.O. Box 70, Unionville, CT 06085-0070
Phone: 860-677-0087
Email: rbrtbarton@aol.com
http://www.ctsportswriters.com/
Purpose: To aid aspiring sports journalists.
Eligibility: Applicants must be Connecticut high school seniors, be admitted to an accredited four-year college and plan to pursue studies leading to a career in sports journalism. Students who meet academic standards can receive additional aid.
Target applicant(s): High school students.
Amount: $2,000.
Number of awards: 1.
Scholarship may be renewable.
Deadline: February 9.
How to apply: Applications are available online. An application form, essay, summary of academic and employment history, evidence of good academic standing, letter of recommendation and three samples of published work are required.
Exclusive: Visit www.UltimateScholarshipBook.com and enter code CO157920 for updates on this award.

(1580) • Booz Allen Hawaii Scholarship Fund

Hawaii Community Foundation - Scholarships
827 Fort Street Mall, Honolulu, HI 96813
Phone: 888-731-3863
Email: scholarships@hcf-hawaii.org
https://www.hawaiicommunityfoundation.org
Purpose: To support undergraduate students in Hawaii.
Eligibility: Students must be residents of Hawaii or dependents of military members stationed there. Applicants must be attending or planning to attend a four-year college or university. Students must have at least a 3.0 GPA.
Target applicant(s): High school students. College students. Adult students.
Minimum GPA: 3.0
Amount: Varies.
Number of awards: Varies.
Deadline: January 31.
How to apply: To apply, register online, complete the online application and select the scholarships to which you wish to apply. In addition, mail the supporting materials: printed confirmation page from the online application, personal statement, copy of Student Aid Report (SAR) available at www.fafsa.ed.gov and official transcript.
Exclusive: Visit www.UltimateScholarshipBook.com and enter code HA158020 for updates on this award.

(1581) • Boy Scout and Eagle Scout Scholarship

American Legion, Department of Illinois
P.O. Box 2910, Bloomington, IL 61702-2910
Phone: 309-663-0361
http://www.illegion.org/scholarships/
Purpose: To reward a member of the Boy Scouts with a one-year scholarship.
Eligibility: Applicants must be graduating seniors in high school, Senior Boy Scouts or Explorers and residents of Illinois. Students must write an essay on Americanism and/or Boy Scout programs.
Target applicant(s): High school students.
Amount: $1,000.
Number of awards: 3.
Deadline: April 15.
How to apply: Application information is available by contacting your local Boy Scout office or American Legion Scout Chairman.
Exclusive: Visit www.UltimateScholarshipBook.com and enter code AM158120 for updates on this award.

(1582) • Business and Professional Women of Kentucky Foundation Grant

Kentucky Federation of Business and Professional Women
c/o Joanne Story, BPW/KY Foundation Scholarship Chair, 380 Beauchamp Boulevard, Somerset, KY 42503
Phone: 606-875-3200
Email: joanne.story@kctcs.edu
http://bpw-ky.org/
Purpose: To promote economic self-sufficiency for Kentucky women.
Eligibility: Applicants must be Kentucky residents who are at least 18 years of age. They must be employed or planning a career in the Kentucky workforce and attending an institution of higher learning. Individuals may receive a grant no more than once every 24 months.
Target applicant(s): High school students. College students. Adult students.
Amount: Varies.
Number of awards: Varies.
Deadline: April 30 and October 15.
How to apply: Applications are available online.
Exclusive: Visit www.UltimateScholarshipBook.com and enter code KE158220 for updates on this award.

(1583) • Business and Professional Women/Maine Continuing Education Scholarship

Futurama Foundation
c/o Marilyn Ladd, Office Manager, 103 County Road, Oakland, ME 04963
Email: mvladd@colby.edu
http://bpwmefoundation.org/scholarship-program/
Purpose: To provide financial assistance to female students.
Eligibility: Applicants must be Maine residents who have completed at least one year of college or will have done so by the end of the spring semester following application. They must be in good standing or on an approved leave of absence of one year or less at their educational institution. Financial need is required, and the student must have a definite plan to complete the program in which she is enrolled.
Target applicant(s): College students. Adult students.
Amount: $1,200.
Number of awards: 1.
Deadline: April 13.
How to apply: Applications are available online.
Exclusive: Visit www.UltimateScholarshipBook.com and enter code FU158320 for updates on this award.

(1584) • Byers Scholarship

Keep Iowa Beautiful
300 E. Locust Street, Suite 100, Des Moines, IA 50309
Phone: 515-323-6507
https://keepiowabeautiful.com/grants-awards/byers-scholarship/
Purpose: To support Iowa high school seniors.
Eligibility: Applicants must be graduating high school seniors in Iowa who plan to enroll in an Iowa college or university to study environmental science, community development, landscape architecture, architecture, community planning or marketing and communications.
Target applicant(s): High school students.
Amount: $1,000.
Number of awards: 5.
Deadline: January 4.
How to apply: Applications are available online.
Exclusive: Visit www.UltimateScholarshipBook.com and enter code KE158420 for updates on this award.

(1585) • C. Bertrand and Marian Othmer Schultz Collegiate Scholarship

Nebraska Academy of Sciences, Inc.
302 Morrill Hall, 14th and U Streets, Lincoln, NE 68588-0339
Phone: 402-472-2644
Email: nebacad@unl.edu
https://nebraskaacademyofsciences.wildapricot.org/GrantsandScholarships
Purpose: To assist Nebraska college students who are majoring in a natural science.
Eligibility: Applicants must be sophomores or juniors who attend a four-year, accredited college or university in Nebraska and major in a natural science including chemistry, physics, biology or geology. Students must plan to enter a career in a science-related industry, science teaching or scientific research.
Target applicant(s): College students. Adult students.
Amount: $3,000.
Number of awards: Varies.
Deadline: February 1.
How to apply: Applications are available online. A letter of nomination, transcript and letter describing the applicant's career plans are available.
Exclusive: Visit www.UltimateScholarshipBook.com and enter code NE158520 for updates on this award.

(1586) • Cal Grant A

California Student Aid Commission
Specialized Programs Operations Branch - Chafee, P.O. Box 419029, Rancho Cordova, CA 95741-9029
Phone: 888-224-7268
Email: studentsupport@csac.ca.gov
http://www.csac.ca.gov/
Purpose: To assist California students in obtaining higher education.
Eligibility: Applicants must be California residents who are attending or plan to attend an eligible California college or university pursuing at least two years of coursework. They must enroll for no less than half time and meet program income requirements. They may not have already earned a bachelor's degree or higher, and they must not be in default on a student loan or owe a grant repayment without having made satisfactory arrangements for repayment. Students with a GPA of 3.0 or higher who meet all requirements will receive an entitlement award, and students with a GPA of at least 2.4 may apply for a competitive award.
Target applicant(s): High school students. College students. Adult students.
Minimum GPA: 2.4
Amount: Varies.
Number of awards: Varies.
Scholarship may be renewable.
Deadline: March 2.
How to apply: Application materials are available online. A FAFSA and a GPA verification form are required.
Exclusive: Visit www.UltimateScholarshipBook.com and enter code CA158620 for updates on this award.

(1587) • Cal Grant B

California Student Aid Commission
Specialized Programs Operations Branch - Chafee, P.O. Box 419029, Rancho Cordova, CA 95741-9029

Phone: 888-224-7268
Email: studentsupport@csac.ca.gov
http://www.csac.ca.gov/
Purpose: To provide living expense, tuition and fee assistance for low income students.
Eligibility: Applicants must be California residents with financial need for attendance at an eligible California college or university. They must enroll for at least half time. A minimum GPA of 2.0 is required. Students who meet financial and eligibility requirements will receive a Cal Grant B entitlement award. Other eligible students can apply for a Cal Grant B competitive award. Competitive award selection is based on family income, education level of parents, GPA, time out of high school and special considerations.
Target applicant(s): High school students. College students. Adult students.
Minimum GPA: 2.0
Amount: Varies.
Number of awards: Varies.
Scholarship may be renewable.
Deadline: March 2.
How to apply: Application materials are available online. A FAFSA and a GPA verification form are required.
Exclusive: Visit www.UltimateScholarshipBook.com and enter code CA158720 for updates on this award.

(1588) • Cal Grant C

California Student Aid Commission
Specialized Programs Operations Branch - Chafee, P.O. Box 419029, Rancho Cordova, CA 95741-9029
Phone: 888-224-7268
Email: studentsupport@csac.ca.gov
http://www.csac.ca.gov/
Purpose: To aid students participating in occupational and vocational programs.
Eligibility: Applicants must be California residents. They must enroll in a vocational program at a California community college, independent college or vocational school that is at least four months long. Funds may be received for up to two years. Eligible students will receive an application by mail from the California Student Aid Commission.
Target applicant(s): High school students. College students. Adult students.
Amount: Varies.
Number of awards: Varies.
Scholarship may be renewable.
Deadline: March 2.
How to apply: Applications are available by mail. A FAFSA and an application form are required.
Exclusive: Visit www.UltimateScholarshipBook.com and enter code CA158820 for updates on this award.

(1589) • Cal Grant Entitlement Award

California Student Aid Commission
Specialized Programs Operations Branch - Chafee, P.O. Box 419029, Rancho Cordova, CA 95741-9029
Phone: 888-224-7268
Email: studentsupport@csac.ca.gov
http://www.csac.ca.gov/
Purpose: To support California resident students.
Eligibility: Applicants must complete the Free Application for Federal Student Aid (FAFSA) and file a verified grade point average with the California Student Aid Commission. Students must be California residents, be U.S. citizens or eligible noncitizens, meet U.S. Selective Service requirements, attend an eligible California postsecondary institution, be enrolled at least half-time, maintain satisfactory academic progress and not be in default on any student loan. Cal Grant A Entitlement Awards are for undergraduate institutions of not less than two academic years. Cal Grant B Entitlement Awards are for low-income students for living and transportation expenses, supplies and books at institutions of not less than one year. Cal Grant C Awards are for occupational or vocational programs. Cal Grant T Awards are for teacher credential candidates.
Target applicant(s): High school students. College students. Adult students.
Amount: Varies.
Number of awards: Varies.
Deadline: March 2.
How to apply: Applications are available by request.
Exclusive: Visit www.UltimateScholarshipBook.com and enter code CA158920 for updates on this award.

(1590) • California - Hawaii Elks Major Project Undergraduate Scholarship Program for Students with Disabilities

California-Hawaii Elks Association
5450 E. Lamona Avenue, Fresno, CA 93727-2224
Phone: 559-255-4531
Email: chea@chea-elks.org
https://chea-elks.org/youth-activities/scholarships
Purpose: To provide education assistance for students with disabilities.
Eligibility: Applicants must be U.S. citizens and California or Hawaii residents who have a physical, neurological, visual or hearing impairment or a speech/language disorder. They must be high school seniors or graduates or have passed the GED or California High School Proficiency Examination.
Target applicant(s): High school students.
Amount: $1,000-$3,000.
Number of awards: 20-30.
Scholarship may be renewable.
Deadline: March 15.
How to apply: Applications are available online.
Exclusive: Visit www.UltimateScholarshipBook.com and enter code CA159020 for updates on this award.

(1591) • California Council of the Blind Scholarships

California Council of the Blind
1303 J Street, Sacramento, CA 95814-2900
Phone: 510-537-7877
Email: ccotb@ccbnet.org
http://www.ccbnet.org/scholar_intro.htm
Purpose: To assist blind California residents for college, graduate or vocational studies.
Eligibility: Applicants must be legally blind residents of California attending an accredited college, university or vocational school full-time or with at least 12 units per term. The school does not have to be in California. Proof of blindness is required. A letter from the local chapter's president or member recommending the applicant is helpful. Award money can't be spent on food, clothing or shelter.
Target applicant(s): College students. Graduate school students. Adult students.
Amount: Varies.
Number of awards: Varies.

Scholarship may be renewable.
Deadline: May 15.
How to apply: Applications are available online.
Exclusive: Visit www.UltimateScholarshipBook.com and enter code CA159120 for updates on this award.

(1592) · California Fee Waiver Program for Children of Veterans

California Department of Veterans Affairs
1227 O Street, Sacramento, CA 95814
Phone: 800-952-5626
https://www.calvet.ca.gov
Purpose: To provide educational assistance for dependents of veterans.
Eligibility: Applicants must be the children, spouses, unmarried surviving spouses or registered domestic partners of veterans who are deceased or totally disabled due to service-related causes. The veteran must have served during a qualifying war period, and the child must be under 27 years of age (30 if the child is a veteran). There is no age limit for spouses or domestic partners. Children of veterans who have a service-connected disability, had one at the time of death or died of service-related causes may qualify if their income is at or below the national poverty level. In this case, there is no age limit.
Target applicant(s): High school students. College students. Adult students.
Amount: Full tuition.
Number of awards: Varies.
Scholarship may be renewable.
Deadline: Varies.
How to apply: Applications are available online.
Exclusive: Visit www.UltimateScholarshipBook.com and enter code CA159220 for updates on this award.

(1593) · California Fee Waiver Program for Dependents of Deceased or Disabled National Guard Members

California Department of Veterans Affairs
1227 O Street, Sacramento, CA 95814
Phone: 800-952-5626
https://www.calvet.ca.gov
Purpose: To provide education assistance to dependents of deceased or disabled National Guard members.
Eligibility: Applicants must be dependents or surviving spouses or domestic partners of California National Guard members who were killed or permanently disabled during active duty in service to the state. Spouses or domestic partners must not have remarried or terminated the relationship.
Target applicant(s): High school students. College students. Adult students.
Amount: Full tuition.
Number of awards: Varies.
Scholarship may be renewable.
Deadline: Varies.
How to apply: Applications are available online.
Exclusive: Visit www.UltimateScholarshipBook.com and enter code CA159320 for updates on this award.

(1594) · California Fee Waiver Program for Recipients of the Medal of Honor and Their Children

California Department of Veterans Affairs
1227 O Street, Sacramento, CA 95814
Phone: 800-952-5626
https://www.calvet.ca.gov
Purpose: To provide financial assistance for Medal of Honor recipients and their families.
Eligibility: Applicants must be Medal of Honor recipients, their children or dependents of a Registered Domestic Partner. Children must meet age, income and residency requirements. This award is only applicable toward undergraduate studies.
Target applicant(s): High school students. College students. Adult students.
Amount: Full tuition.
Number of awards: Varies.
Scholarship may be renewable.
Deadline: Varies.
How to apply: Applications are available online.
Exclusive: Visit www.UltimateScholarshipBook.com and enter code CA159420 for updates on this award.

(1595) · California Law Enforcement Personnel Dependents Grant Program

California Student Aid Commission
Specialized Programs Operations Branch - Chafee, P.O. Box 419029, Rancho Cordova, CA 95741-9029
Phone: 888-224-7268
Email: studentsupport@csac.ca.gov
http://www.csac.ca.gov/
Purpose: To provide assistance for the families of deceased or disabled law enforcement personnel.
Eligibility: Applicants must be spouses or children of California peace officers, Department of Corrections or Youth Authority employees or full-time firefighters who were killed or totally disabled due to accident or injury in the line of duty. They must enroll at an accredited California community college, college or university for a minimum of six units. Financial need is required. Awards match the amount of a Cal Grant award.
Target applicant(s): High school students. College students. Adult students.
Amount: $100-$12,192.
Number of awards: Varies.
Scholarship may be renewable.
Deadline: Rolling.
How to apply: Applications are available by mail or phone. An application form, copy of FAFSA Student Aid Report and documentation of the law enforcement personnel's death or injury are required.
Exclusive: Visit www.UltimateScholarshipBook.com and enter code CA159520 for updates on this award.

(1596) · California Masonic Foundation Scholarship

California Masonic Foundation
1111 California Street, San Francisco, CA 94108-2284
Phone: 415-776-7000
Email: foundation@californiamasons.org
http://www.freemason.org
Purpose: To aid students in pursuit of a higher education.
Eligibility: Applicants must be U.S. citizens, be California residents for at least one year, be current high school seniors with a minimum 3.0

GPA, plan to attend an accredited two- or four-year college or university full-time and demonstrate financial need. There are a number of awards based on residence, career goals and general selection criteria.
Target applicant(s): High school students.
Minimum GPA: 3.0
Amount: Varies.
Number of awards: Varies.
Scholarship may be renewable.
Deadline: Varies.
How to apply: Applications are available online.
Exclusive: Visit www.UltimateScholarshipBook.com and enter code CA159620 for updates on this award.

(1597) · California Oratorical Contest

American Legion, Department of California
1601 7th Street, Sanger, CA 93657
Phone: 415-431-2400
Email: calegion@pacific.net
http://www.calegion.org
Purpose: To enhance high school students' experience with and understanding of the U.S. Constitution. The contest will help develop students' leadership skills and civic appreciation, as well as the ability to deliver thoughtful, insightful orations regarding U.S. citizenship and its inherent responsibilities.
Eligibility: Applicants must be high school students under the age of 20 who are U.S. citizens or legal residents and residents of the state. Students first give an oration within their state and winners compete at the national level. The oration must be related to the Constitution of the United States focusing on the duties and obligations citizens have to the government. It must be in English and be between eight and ten minutes. There is also an assigned topic which is posted on the website, and it should be between three and five minutes.
Target applicant(s): Junior high students or younger. High school students.
Amount: $1,500-$18,000.
Number of awards: Varies.
Deadline: March.
How to apply: Applications are available by email.
Exclusive: Visit www.UltimateScholarshipBook.com and enter code AM159720 for updates on this award.

(1598) · California Restaurant Association Educational Foundation Scholarship for High School Seniors

California Restaurant Association
621 Capitol Mall, Suite 2000, Sacramento, CA 95814
Phone: 800-765-4842
Email: craef@calrest.org
http://www.calrestfoundation.org/scholarships/
Purpose: To aid students with restaurant work experience.
Eligibility: Applicants must be high school seniors who are California residents and U.S. citizens or permanent residents and be enrolled in at least nine credit hours at an accredited institution of higher learning and have a GPA of 2.5 or higher. Students must plan to enroll in two consecutive semesters and have at least 250 hours of work experience in the restaurant industry.
Target applicant(s): High school students.
Minimum GPA: 2.5
Amount: Varies.
Number of awards: Varies.
Deadline: May 12.
How to apply: Applications are available online. An application form, essay, copy of curriculum, transcript, proof of work experience and one to three letters of recommendation are required.
Exclusive: Visit www.UltimateScholarshipBook.com and enter code CA159820 for updates on this award.

(1599) · California Restaurant Association Educational Foundation Scholarships for Undergraduate Students

California Restaurant Association
621 Capitol Mall, Suite 2000, Sacramento, CA 95814
Phone: 800-765-4842
Email: craef@calrest.org
http://www.calrestfoundation.org/scholarships/
Purpose: To support students with restaurant work experience.
Eligibility: Applicants must be California residents, U.S. citizens or permanent residents and undergraduate students who are enrolled in at least nine credit hours at an accredited institution of higher learning. A GPA of 2.5 or higher is required. Applicants must enroll in two consecutive semesters and have completed at least one grading term of a postsecondary program. High school students going into their freshman year must have 250 hours of restaurant work experience, rising sophomores must have 400 hours and those beyond the sophomore year must have 550 hours of experience.
Target applicant(s): High school students. College students. Adult students.
Minimum GPA: 2.5
Amount: Varies.
Number of awards: Varies.
Deadline: May 12.
How to apply: Applications are available online. An application form, essay, copy of curriculum, transcript, proof of work experience and one to three letters of recommendation are required.
Exclusive: Visit www.UltimateScholarshipBook.com and enter code CA159920 for updates on this award.

(1600) · California State PTA Scholarship

California State PTA
2327 L Street, Sacramento, CA 95816-5014
Phone: 916-440-1985
Email: grants@capta.org
http://capta.org/programs-events/scholarships/
Purpose: To support high school seniors who have contributed to the community.
Eligibility: Applicants must attend a public California high school, be high school seniors who have served their school and community and be members of the PTA.
Target applicant(s): High school students.
Amount: $500-$750.
Number of awards: 2.
Deadline: February 1.
How to apply: Applications are available online.
Exclusive: Visit www.UltimateScholarshipBook.com and enter code CA160020 for updates on this award.

(1601) · Candon, Todd and Seabolt Scholarship Fund

Hawaii Community Foundation - Scholarships
827 Fort Street Mall, Honolulu, HI 96813

Phone: 888-731-3863
Email: scholarships@hcf-hawaii.org
https://www.hawaiicommunityfoundation.org
Purpose: To support Hawaii students who are majoring in accounting or finance.
Eligibility: Students must be in their junior or senior year of college with at least a 3.2 GPA.
Target applicant(s): College students. Adult students.
Minimum GPA: 3.2
Amount: Varies.
Number of awards: Varies.
Deadline: January 31.
How to apply: To apply, register online, complete the online application and select the scholarships to which you wish to apply. In addition, mail the supporting materials: printed confirmation page from the online application, personal statement, copy of Student Aid Report (SAR) available at www.fafsa.ed.gov and official transcript.
Exclusive: Visit www.UltimateScholarshipBook.com and enter code HA160120 for updates on this award.

(1602) · CAPED Excellence Scholarship

California Association for Postsecondary Education and Disability
Disabled Student Programs and Services, San Bernardino Valley College, 701 South Mt. Vernon Avenue, San Bernardino, CA 92410
Phone: 909-384-8663
Email: capedscholarships@gmail.com
http://www.caped.io/
Purpose: To provide financial assistance to high achievers in academics, community and campus life.
Eligibility: Applicants must have a verifiable disability and demonstrate financial need. A minimum GPA of 2.5 is required for undergraduates and a minimum GPA of 3.0 for graduate students. Applicants must be taking at least six semester units or four quarter units at a public or private California institution of higher learning.
Target applicant(s): High school students. College students. Graduate school students. Adult students.
Minimum GPA: 2.5 for undergraduate students, 3.0 for graduate students
Amount: $1,500.
Number of awards: 1.
Deadline: August 31.
How to apply: Applications are available online.
Exclusive: Visit www.UltimateScholarshipBook.com and enter code CA160220 for updates on this award.

(1603) · CAPPS Scholarship Program

California Association of Private Postsecondary Schools
2520 Venture Oaks Way, Suite 170, Sacramento, CA 95833
Phone: 916-447-5500
Email: info@cappsonline.org
http://www.cappsonline.org
Purpose: To allow private postsecondary schools to offer tuition scholarships to students.
Eligibility: Applicants must be legal California residents who have fulfilled the admission requirements for the school that is pledging their CAPPS scholarship. Application is restricted to high school and adult students only. Recipients are chosen on the basis of application date and each individual school's judging standards.
Target applicant(s): High school students. Adult students.
Amount: Varies.
Number of awards: 5.
Deadline: August 5.
How to apply: Applications are available online.
Exclusive: Visit www.UltimateScholarshipBook.com and enter code CA160320 for updates on this award.

(1604) · Career Aid for Technical Students Program

New Hampshire Charitable Foundation
37 Pleasant Street, Concord, NH 03301-4005
Phone: 603-225-6641
Email: info@nhcf.org
https://www.nhcf.org/how-can-we-help-you/
Purpose: To aid students who need training beyond high school to meet their career goals.
Eligibility: Applicants must be New Hampshire residents who are dependent students between the ages of 17 and 24. They must plan to enroll at least half-time in an accredited vocational or technical program that does not lead to a bachelor's degree. They must apply for federal financial aid and demonstrate financial need.
Target applicant(s): High school students. College students.
Amount: Varies.
Number of awards: Varies.
Deadline: Rolling.
How to apply: Applications are available online. Application form, transcript, evaluation form and financial statement are required.
Exclusive: Visit www.UltimateScholarshipBook.com and enter code NE160420 for updates on this award.

(1605) · Career Colleges and Schools of Texas Scholarship Program

Career Colleges and Schools of Texas
Lisa Tomsio, 823 Congress Avenue, Suite 230, Austin, TX 78701
Phone: 512-402-7797
Email: scholars@careerscholarships.org
http://ccst.org/
Purpose: To help Texas high school seniors who want to attend trade or technical schools in the state.
Eligibility: Participating institutions, which are listed on the website, provide scholarships to students who choose to enroll at their schools. Since each school has its own guidelines, applicants should contact a particular school for more information.
Target applicant(s): High school students.
Amount: $1,000.
Number of awards: Varies.
Deadline: Varies.
How to apply: Applicants should contact their high school counselors or participating schools.
Exclusive: Visit www.UltimateScholarshipBook.com and enter code CA160520 for updates on this award.

(1606) · Career Cruising and Method Test Prep Award

Wisconsin School Counselor Association
2820 Walton Commons, Suite 103, Madison, WI 53718
Phone: 608-204-9825
Email: nechodomk@gmail.com
http://www.wscaweb.com
Purpose: To support Wisconsin students.
Eligibility: Applicants must be seniors at a public or private Wisconsin high school. They must plan to attend an institution of higher learning in the school year following graduation.
Target applicant(s): High school students.

Amount: $1,000.
Number of awards: 4.
Deadline: November 1.
How to apply: Applications are available online. An application form and essay are required.
Exclusive: Visit www.UltimateScholarshipBook.com and enter code WI160620 for updates on this award.

(1607) • Carl C. Smith Memorial Scholarship

Oklahoma Association of Broadcasters
6520 N. Western, Suite 104, Oklahoma City, OK 73116
Phone: 405-848-0771
Email: struby@oabok.org
https://oabok.org/careerseducation/scholarships/
Purpose: To support students majoring in broadcasting at Oklahoma colleges and universities.
Eligibility: Applicants must be enrolled in an Oklahoma college or university broadcasting program, be majoring in broadcasting and have an intent to enter the broadcasting career upon graduation. Students must be a junior or senior for the upcoming school year and must maintain a "B" average.
Target applicant(s): College students. Adult students.
Minimum GPA: 3.0
Amount: $2,000.
Number of awards: 1.
Deadline: February 9.
How to apply: Applications are available online.
Exclusive: Visit www.UltimateScholarshipBook.com and enter code OK160720 for updates on this award.

(1608) • Carl W. Christiansen Scholarship

Rhode Island Society of Certified Public Accountants
40 Sharpe Drive, Unit 5, Cranston, RI 02920
Phone: 401-331-5720
Email: djacobson@riscpa.org
http://www.rifoundation.org/WorkingTogether/ForScholarshipSeekers.aspx
Purpose: To support Rhode Island students who are pursuing careers in public accounting.
Eligibility: Students must have at least a 3.0 GPA. Applicants must submit a short essay and a letter of recommendation.
Target applicant(s): College students. Adult students.
Minimum GPA: 3.0
Amount: Varies.
Number of awards: Varies.
Deadline: Varies.
How to apply: Applications are available online.
Exclusive: Visit www.UltimateScholarshipBook.com and enter code RH160820 for updates on this award.

(1609) • Cash Grant Program

Massachusetts Department of Higher Education
Office of Student Financial Assistance, 454 Broadway, Suite 200, Revere, MA 02151
Phone: 617-727-9420
Email: osfa@osfa.mass.edu
http://www.mass.edu/osfa/students/forstudents.asp
Purpose: To help needy students pay college or university fees and non-state-supported tuition.
Eligibility: Students must be permanent residents of Massachusetts for at least one year before the academic year for which the grant is awarded. Students must also demonstrate financial need, be enrolled in at least three credits per semester in an eligible undergraduate program and not have previously earned a bachelor's degree or higher.
Target applicant(s): High school students. College students. Adult students.
Amount: Up to full tuition.
Number of awards: Varies.
Scholarship may be renewable.
Deadline: Varies.
How to apply: Applications are available from your financial aid office.
Exclusive: Visit www.UltimateScholarshipBook.com and enter code MA160920 for updates on this award.

(1610) • Categorical Tuition Waiver

Massachusetts Department of Higher Education
Office of Student Financial Assistance, 454 Broadway, Suite 200, Revere, MA 02151
Phone: 617-727-9420
Email: osfa@osfa.mass.edu
http://www.mass.edu/osfa/students/forstudents.asp
Purpose: To provide financial support to Massachusetts students who would otherwise not be able to afford higher education.
Eligibility: Applicants must be residents of the state of Massachusetts for at least one year prior to the beginning of the academic year in which the scholarship is used. They also must be members of one of the following groups of people: veterans or active members of the armed forces, Native Americans, senior citizens or clients of either the Massachusetts Rehabilitation Commission or Commission for the Blind. Students must be enrolled in at least three credits per semester in a state undergraduate or certificate program, and they must remain in satisfactory academic standing.
Target applicant(s): High school students. College students. Adult students.
Amount: Up to full tuition.
Number of awards: Varies.
Deadline: Varies.
How to apply: Applications are available at college financial aid offices.
Exclusive: Visit www.UltimateScholarshipBook.com and enter code MA161020 for updates on this award.

(1611) • Cathay Bank Foundation Scholarship

Asian Pacific Community Fund
1145 Wilshire Boulevard, Suite 105, Los Angeles, CA 90017
Phone: 213-624-6400
Email: scholarships@apcf.org
http://www.apcf.org
Purpose: To assist low-income students to pursue higher education.
Eligibility: Applicants must be high school seniors residing in California, Illinois, Maryland, Massachusetts, Nevada, New Jersey, New York, Texas or Washington who are enrolling as first-year students in an accredited four-year college in one of the listed states of residency. Students must have a minimum GPA of 3.0 and have a household income that falls at or below the low-income level. There is no ethnicity requirement.
Target applicant(s): High school students.
Minimum GPA: 3.0
Amount: $1,000.
Number of awards: 20.
Deadline: May 27.
How to apply: Applications are available online.

Exclusive: Visit www.UltimateScholarshipBook.com and enter code AS161120 for updates on this award.

(1612) • Cayetano Foundation Scholarships

Hawaii Community Foundation - Scholarships
827 Fort Street Mall, Honolulu, HI 96813
Phone: 888-731-3863
Email: scholarships@hcf-hawaii.org
https://www.hawaiicommunityfoundation.org
Purpose: To support exceptional Hawaii students.
Eligibility: Applicants must be upcoming high school graduates in Hawaii. They must have a GPA of 3.5 or higher. Preference is given to students who have overcome financial and social obstacles and to the students with the greatest financial need.
Target applicant(s): High school students.
Minimum GPA: 3.5
Amount: Varies.
Number of awards: Varies.
Deadline: January 31.
How to apply: Applications are available online. An application form, personal statement, copy of FAFSA Student Aid Report, transcript, two letters of recommendation and an essay are required.
Exclusive: Visit www.UltimateScholarshipBook.com and enter code HA161220 for updates on this award.

(1613) • CCCAM Scholarships

Competitive Cheer Coaches Association of Michigan
5675 N. Division, Comstock Park, MI 49321
Email: cccamexecutiveboard@gmail.com
http://www.cccam.org/
Purpose: To support the pursuit of higher education by competitive cheer athletes.
Eligibility: Applicants must be a graduating senior, be a current member of a Michigan High School Athletic Association (MHSAA) competitive cheer team and have a minimum GPA of 3.5 through their junior year. The applicant's cheer team must compete in the annual Scholarship Invitational and the team coach must be a current CCCAM member.
Target applicant(s): High school students.
Minimum GPA: 3.5
Amount: Varies.
Number of awards: Varies.
Deadline: February 6.
How to apply: Applications are available online and must be completed and mailed in with the applicant's short essay, a sealed copy of the high school transcript and two letters of recommendation.
Exclusive: Visit www.UltimateScholarshipBook.com and enter code CO161320 for updates on this award.

(1614) • CCNMA Scholarships

CCNMA: Latino Journalists of California
ASU Cronkite School of Journalism, 725 Arizona Avenue, Suite 404, Santa Monica, CA 90401-1734
Phone: 424-229-9482
Email: ccnmainfo@ccnma.org
http://ccnma.org/scholarships-and-awards/
Purpose: To support Latino students with career goals in journalism.
Eligibility: Applicants must be Latino and either California residents or be attending California schools. While the student's degree does not have to be in journalism, they must demonstrate plans to pursue a career in journalism. An interview and autobiographical essay are required. Awards are based also on financial need, academic achievement and civic responsibility.
Target applicant(s): High school students. College students. Graduate school students. Adult students.
Amount: $500-$1,000.
Number of awards: Varies.
Deadline: June 15.
How to apply: Applications are available online.
Exclusive: Visit www.UltimateScholarshipBook.com and enter code CC161420 for updates on this award.

(1615) • Celgene's Sol J. Barer Scholarship In Life Sciences

Independent College Fund of New Jersey
797 Springfield Avenue, Summit, NJ 07901
Phone: 908-277-3424
Email: scholarships@njcolleges.org
http://www.njcolleges.org
Purpose: To aid life sciences students who are attending a New Jersey independent college or university.
Eligibility: Applicants must be rising undergraduate juniors or seniors at a New Jersey independent college or university. They must be majoring in one of the life sciences and have a GPA of 3.25 or higher on a four-point scale. Selection is based on academic merit and career potential.
Target applicant(s): College students. Adult students.
Minimum GPA: 3.25
Amount: $2,500.
Number of awards: 5.
Deadline: December 21.
How to apply: Applications are available online. An application form, transcript, resume, one recommendation letter and personal statement are required.
Exclusive: Visit www.UltimateScholarshipBook.com and enter code IN161520 for updates on this award.

(1616) • Central Arizona DX Association Scholarship

American Radio Relay League Foundation
225 Main Street, Newington, CT 06111-1494
Phone: 860-594-0348
Email: foundation@arrl.org
http://www.arrl.org/scholarship-program
Purpose: To provide scholarship assistance to amateur radio operators from Arizona.
Eligibility: Applicants must be Arizona residents with a Technician Class or higher Amateur Radio License. They must have a GPA of 3.2 or higher. Graduating high school seniors receive preference over current college students.
Target applicant(s): High school students. College students. Adult students.
Minimum GPA: 3.2
Amount: $1,000.
Number of awards: 1.
Deadline: January 31.
How to apply: Applications are available online.
Exclusive: Visit www.UltimateScholarshipBook.com and enter code AM161620 for updates on this award.

(1617) • Certificate, License or Other Industry-Recognized Credential

New Hampshire Charitable Foundation
37 Pleasant Street, Concord, NH 03301-4005
Phone: 603-225-6641
Email: info@nhcf.org
https://www.nhcf.org/how-can-we-help-you/

Purpose: To support students who are pursuing short-term vocational or technical studies.

Eligibility: Applicants must be residents of New Hampshire and be pursuing a certificate, license or other credential in vocational or technical fields such as: automotive technology, plumbing, construction, heating, advanced manufacturing, computer repair, licensed nursing, etc. Preference is given to students whose fields are in the traditional manufacturing trade sector, who have a clear vision of how their education will improve their career goals and who have had little or no other educational training opportunities.

Target applicant(s): College students. Adult students.
Amount: Varies.
Number of awards: Varies.
Deadline: Rolling.
How to apply: Applications are available online.
Exclusive: Visit www.UltimateScholarshipBook.com and enter code NE161720 for updates on this award.

(1618) • CESDA Diversity Scholarship

Colorado Educational Services and Development Association
P.O. Box 40214, Denver, CO 80204
Phone: 303-352-3231
Email: melissa.quinteros@ccd.edu
http://www.cesda.org

Purpose: To provide financial assistance for disadvantaged students.

Eligibility: Applicants must be either first generation college students, members of underrepresented ethnic or racial minorities or show financial need. They must be Colorado residents who are high school seniors at the time of application. Students must have a GPA of 2.8 or higher and enroll in a two- or four-year Colorado college or university in the fall following graduation. They must take at least six credit hours to qualify.

Target applicant(s): High school students.
Minimum GPA: 2.8
Amount: $1,000.
Number of awards: 6.
Deadline: January 1.
How to apply: Applications are available online.
Exclusive: Visit www.UltimateScholarshipBook.com and enter code CO161820 for updates on this award.

(1619) • CEW Scholarships

Center for the Education of Women
330 E. Liberty, Ann Arbor, MI 48104-2274
Phone: 734-998-7080
http://www.umich.edu/~cew

Purpose: To support women who are returning to college after an interruption.

Eligibility: Applicants must be women who are returning to school. For undergraduates, a minimum 2 year (24 month) consecutive interruption in education anytime since high school. For graduate students, a minimum 5 year (60 month) consecutive interruption in education anytime since high school. Candidates must be working toward a clear educational goal at any University of Michigan campus. Preference is given to women wishing to study in non-traditional fields such as mathematics, physical sciences and engineering.

Target applicant(s): Graduate school students. Adult students.
Amount: $1,000-$10,000.
Number of awards: Approximately 40.
Deadline: February 15.
How to apply: Applications are available online.
Exclusive: Visit www.UltimateScholarshipBook.com and enter code CE161920 for updates on this award.

(1620) • CHAHRM Scholarship

Colorado Healthcare Association for Human Resource Management
c/o Michelle Pollart, Scholarship Chair, Prowers Medical Center, 401 Kendall Drive, Lamar, CO 81052
Phone: 719-336-7119
Email: chahrm@hotmail.com
http://www.chahrm.org

Purpose: To aid students enrolled in a healthcare or human resources degree program.

Eligibility: Applicants must be in the final year of study for a degree in a healthcare- or human resources-related subject at an accredited technical college or university. They must have a GPA of 3.0 or higher. Selection is based on academic merit, stated career goals, work history, extracurricular activities and references.

Target applicant(s): College students. Adult students.
Minimum GPA: 3.0
Amount: $1,000.
Number of awards: 2.
Deadline: September 15.
How to apply: Applications are available online. An application form, a transcript, a personal essay and a faculty advisor reference are required.
Exclusive: Visit www.UltimateScholarshipBook.com and enter code CO162020 for updates on this award.

(1621) • Charles Dubose Scholarship

Connecticut Architecture Foundation
370 James Street, Suite 402, New Haven, CT 06513
Phone: 203-865-2195
Email: aiainfo@aiact.org
http://www.aiact.org

Purpose: To assist architecture students.

Eligibility: Applicants must have completed two years of an NAAB accredited architecture program leading to a bachelor's degree as of June 30 of the year of application. Students enrolled in non-accredited programs who have been accepted to an NAAB accredited master's degree program, as well as those currently enrolled in such a program, are also eligible. Applicants must be full-time students. Preference is given to students at the University of Pennsylvania, Georgia Institute of Technology and Fontainebleau summer program and to Connecticut residents.

Target applicant(s): College students. Graduate school students. Adult students.
Amount: $1,200-$5,000.
Number of awards: Varies.
Deadline: April 29.
How to apply: Applications are available online. An application form, statement of goals, resume, financial aid information sheet, two letters of reference and submission of a favorite project are required.
Exclusive: Visit www.UltimateScholarshipBook.com and enter code CO162120 for updates on this award.

(1622) · Charles McDaniel Teacher Scholarship

Georgia Student Finance Commission
2082 East Exchange Place, Tucker, GA 30084
Phone: 800-505-4732
Email: gsfcinfo@gsfc.org
https://www.gafutures.org/
Purpose: To support students in Georgia pursuing a degree in teaching.
Eligibility: Applicants must be full-time juniors or seniors at a public Georgia college or university. They must be admitted to their school's college or department of education and have a GPA of 3.25 or higher. Applicants must be legal residents of Georgia, have graduated from a Georgia high school, be U.S. citizens or permanent resident aliens, be in compliance with Selective Service requirements and not be in default on student financial aid. Eligible colleges and universities can nominate one student each year.
Target applicant(s): College students. Adult students.
Minimum GPA: 3.25
Amount: $1,000.
Number of awards: 3.
Deadline: July 15.
How to apply: Applications are available online and from college education departments.
Exclusive: Visit www.UltimateScholarshipBook.com and enter code GE162220 for updates on this award.

(1623) · Charles W. and Annette Hill Scholarship

American Legion, Department of Kansas
1314 SW Topeka Boulevard, Topeka, KS 66612
Phone: 785-232-9315
http://www.ksamlegion.org
Purpose: To provide financial assistance to needy and worthy children of members of the American Legion.
Eligibility: Applicants must be descendants of an American Legion member with a GPA of at least 3.0. Special consideration will be given to students studying science, engineering or business administration. Applicants must submit three letters of recommendation with only one from a teacher, an essay on "Why I Want to Go to College," a high school transcript, documentation of parent's veteran status and a 1040 income statement. Applicants must maintain a 3.0 GPA in college and verify enrollment at the start of each semester.
Target applicant(s): High school students. College students. Adult students.
Minimum GPA: 3.0
Amount: $1,000.
Number of awards: 1.
Scholarship may be renewable.
Deadline: February 15.
How to apply: Applications are available online.
Exclusive: Visit www.UltimateScholarshipBook.com and enter code AM162320 for updates on this award.

(1624) · Charles W. Riley Fire and Emergency Medical Services Scholarship Program

Maryland Higher Education Commission
Office of Student Financial Assistance, 6 North Liberty Street, Baltimore, MD 21201
Phone: 800-974-1024
Email: osfamail@mhec.state.md.us
http://www.maryland.gov
Purpose: To support Maryland students who are majoring and working in firefighting or emergency medical services fields.
Eligibility: Applicants must be active firefighters, ambulance or rescue squad members living and serving in the state of Maryland. Students must attend a Maryland college majoring in fire service technology or emergency medical technology. They must continue to serve throughout college and for one year after graduating.
Target applicant(s): College students. Adult students.
Minimum GPA: 2.5
Amount: At least 1/2 tuition and fees.
Number of awards: Varies.
Scholarship may be renewable.
Deadline: March 1.
How to apply: Applications are available online.
Exclusive: Visit www.UltimateScholarshipBook.com and enter code MA162420 for updates on this award.

(1625) · Chen Foundation Scholarship Program

Taiwanese American Scholarship Fund
1145 Wilshire Boulevard, Suite 105, First floor, Los Angeles, CA 90017
Phone: 213-624-6400 x 6
Email: scholarships@apcf.org
http://tascholarshipfund.org
Purpose: To assist economically-challenged youth to pursue higher education.
Eligibility: Applicants must be high school seniors, reside in California and plan to attend a California state university or California community college as a freshman in the fall of the upcoming academic year. Students must have a minimum 3.0 GPA and must provide proof that their household income is below the California State Low Income Level. There is no ethnicity requirement for the award.
Target applicant(s): High school students.
Minimum GPA: 3.0
Amount: $2,000.
Number of awards: 10.
Scholarship may be renewable.
Deadline: March 29.
How to apply: Applications are available online and must be accompanied by one recommendation form and an official high school transcript.
Exclusive: Visit www.UltimateScholarshipBook.com and enter code TA162520 for updates on this award.

(1626) · Cheryl A. Ruggiero Scholarship

Rhode Island Society of Certified Public Accountants
40 Sharpe Drive, Unit 5, Cranston, RI 02920
Phone: 401-331-5720
Email: djacobson@riscpa.org
http://www.rifoundation.org/WorkingTogether/ForScholarshipSeekers.aspx
Purpose: To support female students who are pursuing careers in public accounting.
Eligibility: Students must be residents of the state of Rhode Island, and they must have at least a 3.0 GPA. Applicants must submit a short essay and a letter of recommendation.
Target applicant(s): College students. Adult students.
Minimum GPA: 3.0
Amount: $1,300.
Number of awards: Varies.
Deadline: January 9.

How to apply: Applications are available online.
Exclusive: Visit www.UltimateScholarshipBook.com and enter code RH162620 for updates on this award.

(1627) • CHI Health Scholarship Program

CHI Health
https://www.chihealth.com
Purpose: To support Nebraska and Iowa students pursuing medical education.
Eligibility: Applicants must be graduating high school seniors from Nebraska or Iowa who are pursuing a post-secondary degree in a health care field or acquiring a license or certification in a health care field. Students must be accepted into an accredited college, university or health care program and have a minimum GPA of 3.0.
Target applicant(s): High school students.
Minimum GPA: 3.0
Amount: $1,500.
Number of awards: 12.
Deadline: April 2.
How to apply: Applications are available online.
Exclusive: Visit www.UltimateScholarshipBook.com and enter code CH162720 for updates on this award.

(1628) • Chick and Sophie Major Memorial Duck Calling Contest

Stuttgart Arkansas Chamber of Commerce
P.O. Box 1500, 507 S. Main, Stuttgart, AR 72160
Phone: 870-673-1602
Email: stuttgartchamber@centurytel.net
http://www.stuttgartarkansas.org
Purpose: To assist students who win the duck calling contest.
Eligibility: Applicants must be graduating high school seniors and participate in the annual competition that occurs in Stuttgart, Arkansas.
Target applicant(s): High school students.
Amount: $500-$2,000.
Number of awards: 4.
Deadline: November 25.
How to apply: Details on the competition are available online.
Exclusive: Visit www.UltimateScholarshipBook.com and enter code ST162820 for updates on this award.

(1629) • Children and Youth Scholarships

American Legion, Department of Maine
5 Verti Drive, Winslow, ME 04901-0727
Phone: 207-873-3229
Email: legionme@mainelegion.org
http://www.mainelegion.org
Purpose: To provide financial support to Maine students.
Eligibility: Applicants must be high school seniors or college students attending or planning to attend an accredited college or vocational school. Applicants must also demonstrate financial need and include two letters of recommendation and a personal statement.
Target applicant(s): High school students. College students. Adult students.
Amount: $500.
Number of awards: 7.
Deadline: May 1.
How to apply: Applications are available online.
Exclusive: Visit www.UltimateScholarshipBook.com and enter code AM162920 for updates on this award.

(1630) • Chiropractic Education Assistance Scholarship

Oklahoma State Regents for Higher Education/Chiropractic Education Assistance Scholarship
655 Research Parkway, Suite 200, Oklahoma City, OK 73104
Phone: 800-858-1840
Email: studentinfo@osrhe.edu
https://secure.okcollegestart.org/Financial_Aid_Planning/Scholarships/Career_Scholarships/Chiropractic_Education_Assistance_Scholarship.aspx
Purpose: To support Oklahoma state residents pursuing chiropractic studies at accredited out-of-state schools.
Eligibility: Applicants must be residents of the state of Oklahoma who have lived in Oklahoma for at least the past five years who are either enrolled or accepted at an accredited school for chiropractic study. Students must have a 3.0 GPA.
Target applicant(s): High school students. College students. Adult students.
Minimum GPA: 3.0
Amount: Up to $6,000.
Number of awards: Varies.
Scholarship may be renewable.
Deadline: July 31.
How to apply: Applications are available online.
Exclusive: Visit www.UltimateScholarshipBook.com and enter code OK163020 for updates on this award.

(1631) • Christa McAuliffe Scholarship

Tennessee Student Assistance Corporation
404 James Robertson Parkway, Suite 1510, Parkway Towers, Nashville, TN 37243
Phone: 800-342-1663
Email: tsac.aidinfo@tn.gov
http://www.tn.gov/collegepays/section/money-for-college
Purpose: To support Tennessee students who are pursuing careers in teaching.
Eligibility: Applicants must be in the second semester of their junior year in a teaching program at a Tennessee college, and they must be enrolled full-time. Students must have at least a 3.5 GPA and an SAT or ACT score that is at least as high as the national average. They must not have any defaulted state or federal student loans. Recipients must agree to teach in a Tennessee elementary or secondary school for a period of time upon graduation.
Target applicant(s): College students. Adult students.
Minimum GPA: 3.5
Amount: $500.
Number of awards: 1.
Deadline: April 1.
How to apply: Applications are available online.
Exclusive: Visit www.UltimateScholarshipBook.com and enter code TE163120 for updates on this award.

(1632) • Christian A. Herter Memorial Scholarship Program

Massachusetts Department of Higher Education
Office of Student Financial Assistance, 454 Broadway, Suite 200, Revere, MA 02151

Phone: 617-727-9420
Email: osfa@osfa.mass.edu
http://www.mass.edu/osfa/students/forstudents.asp
Purpose: To provide educational opportunities to Massachusetts students who demonstrate academic promise and a desire to attend post-secondary institutions.
Eligibility: Applicants must be enrolled in a public or private secondary school in the Commonwealth of Massachusetts and be legal residents of the state. Applicants must have a cumulative grade point average of 2.5 and exhibit difficult personal circumstances, high financial need and strong academic promise to continue education beyond the secondary level.
Target applicant(s): High school students.
Minimum GPA: 2.5
Amount: Varies.
Number of awards: Varies.
Scholarship may be renewable.
Deadline: February 3.
How to apply: Applications are available online.
Exclusive: Visit www.UltimateScholarshipBook.com and enter code MA163220 for updates on this award.

(1633) • CIF Scholar-Athlete of the Year

California Interscholastic Federation (CIF)
CIF State Office, Attn.: CIF Scholar-Athlete of the Year, 4658 Duckhorn Drive, Sacramento, CA 95834
Phone: 916-239-4477
Email: info@cifstate.org
http://www.cifstate.org/parents-students/awards_and_scholarships/index
Purpose: To recognize high school student-athletes with exemplary academic and athletic careers and personal standards.
Eligibility: Applicants must be high school seniors with a minimum 3.5 GPA, demonstrate outstanding athletic performance in a minimum of two years of varsity play in California and exhibit character, trustworthiness, respect, responsibility, fairness, caring and citizenship.
Target applicant(s): High school students.
Minimum GPA: 3.5
Amount: $5,000.
Number of awards: 2.
Deadline: February 10.
How to apply: Applications are available by request.
Exclusive: Visit www.UltimateScholarshipBook.com and enter code CA163320 for updates on this award.

(1634) • Cindy Luberto Scholarship for Women Athletes

CT RollerGirls, Inc
P.O. Box 1774, Naugatuck, CT 06770
Email: scholarship@ctrollerderby.com
http://www.ctrollerderby.com/
Purpose: To support Connecticut women athletes who participate in recreational, community or school athletics.
Eligibility: Applicants must be female high school seniors and participate in a sport that is organized, recreational or intramural. Selection is based on a 250-word essay describing the passion for the sport that is played and how that sport or your participation is unique.
Target applicant(s): High school students.
Amount: $500.
Number of awards: 1.
Deadline: April 10.
How to apply: Applications are available online and include an essay and a photo of the applicant playing the sport.
Exclusive: Visit www.UltimateScholarshipBook.com and enter code CT163420 for updates on this award.

(1635) • Clair A. Hill Scholarship

Association of California Water Agencies
910 K Street, Suite 100, Sacramento, CA 95814
Phone: 916-441-4545
Email: awards@acwa.com
http://www.acwa.com
Purpose: To support California undergraduates pursuing degrees in a water resources-related subject.
Eligibility: Applicants must be California residents who are rising juniors or seniors at a participating postsecondary institution located in California. They must be pursuing an undergraduate degree in a water resources-related subject and be full-time students enrolled for the entirety of the upcoming school year. Selection is based on professional commitment to the water resources field, academic achievement and financial need.
Target applicant(s): College students. Adult students.
Amount: $5,000.
Number of awards: 1.
Deadline: February 1.
How to apply: Applications are available online. An application form, personal essay, transcript and two to three letters of recommendation are required.
Exclusive: Visit www.UltimateScholarshipBook.com and enter code AS163520 for updates on this award.

(1636) • Clanseer and Anna Johnson Scholarships

Community Foundation of New Jersey
P.O. Box 338, Morristown, NJ 07963-0338
Phone: 973-267-5533
Email: csmith@cfnj.org
http://cfnj.org/current-funds/student-scholarships/
Purpose: To provide education assistance for disadvantaged African American students.
Eligibility: Applicants must have been born in the United States and be New Jersey residents. They must have an A or B average in science and math-related subjects and maintain above average grades overall. Financial need and merit are considered. Scholarship winners are asked to perform at least ten hours of community service each week for a year following graduation.
Target applicant(s): High school students.
Amount: $6,000.
Number of awards: 4.
Deadline: June 30.
How to apply: Applications are available online.
Exclusive: Visit www.UltimateScholarshipBook.com and enter code CO163620 for updates on this award.

(1637) • Clean Air Choice Biodiesel Scholarship

American Lung Association in Minnesota
490 Concordia Avenue, Saint Paul, MN 55103
Phone: 651-268-7603
http://www.cleanairchoice.org
Purpose: To support students with an interest in raising awareness of biodiesel and emerging alternative fuel.

Eligibility: Applicants must be graduating high school seniors in Minnesota with plans to attend post-secondary education. Students must either write an essay or create a video as part of the application process.
Target applicant(s): High school students.
Amount: $1,000.
Number of awards: 2.
Deadline: March 30.
How to apply: Applications are available online.
Exclusive: Visit www.UltimateScholarshipBook.com and enter code AM163720 for updates on this award.

(1638) • Clem Judd, Jr., Memorial Scholarship

Hawaii Lodging and Tourism Association
2270 Kalakaua Avenue, Suite 1702, Honolulu, HI 96815
Phone: 808-923-0407
Email: info@hawaiilodging.org
http://www.hawaiilodging.org/scholarship-opportunities.html
Purpose: To help Hawaiian residents majoring in hotel management.
Eligibility: Applicants must have a minimum 3.0 GPA, be a resident of Hawaii, be able to prove Hawaiian ancestry and be a junior or senior enrolled full-time at a U.S. university or college.
Target applicant(s): College students. Adult students.
Minimum GPA: 3.0
Amount: $1,000-$2,500.
Number of awards: Up to 2.
Deadline: July 31.
How to apply: Applications are available by written request beginning February 1.
Exclusive: Visit www.UltimateScholarshipBook.com and enter code HA163820 for updates on this award.

(1639) • Collaborative Teachers Tuition Waiver

Massachusetts Department of Higher Education
Office of Student Financial Assistance, 454 Broadway, Suite 200, Revere, MA 02151
Phone: 617-727-9420
Email: osfa@osfa.mass.edu
http://www.mass.edu/osfa/students/forstudents.asp
Purpose: To provide graduate school tuition waivers for Massachusetts teachers who become student teacher mentors.
Eligibility: Applicants must be public school teachers living and working in the state of Massachusetts. They must also agree to mentor a student teacher from a state college or university in their own classroom, and they must be planning to attend graduate school at one of the nine campuses of Massachusetts State College or the University of Massachusetts.
Target applicant(s): Graduate school students. Adult students.
Amount: Varies.
Number of awards: Varies.
Scholarship may be renewable.
Deadline: Varies.
How to apply: Applications are available at college financial aid offices.
Exclusive: Visit www.UltimateScholarshipBook.com and enter code MA163920 for updates on this award.

(1640) • College Access Program

Kentucky Higher Education Assistance Authority
P.O. Box 798, Frankfort, KY 40602
Phone: 800-928-8926
Email: blane@kheaa.com
http://www.kheaa.com
Purpose: To aid Kentucky students with financial need.
Eligibility: Applicants must be Kentucky residents, be enrolled at least half-time in undergraduate academic programs and have an Expected Family Contribution (EFC) based on the FAFSA of lower than approximately $3,850.
Target applicant(s): High school students. College students. Adult students.
Amount: Up to $1,900.
Number of awards: Varies.
Deadline: Varies.
How to apply: Complete the Free Application for Federal Student Aid (FAFSA).
Exclusive: Visit www.UltimateScholarshipBook.com and enter code KE164020 for updates on this award.

(1641) • College Affordability Grant

New Mexico Higher Education Department
2044 Galisteo Street, Suite 4, Santa Fe, NM 87505-2100
Phone: 505-476-8400
Email: cesaria.tapia1@state.nm.us
http://www.hed.state.nm.us/students/
Purpose: To support New Mexico residents who are attending public colleges in the state.
Eligibility: Applicants must demonstrate financial need, and they cannot have any other state grants or scholarships. Students must be enrolled in at least six credit hours per semester.
Target applicant(s): High school students. College students. Adult students.
Amount: Up to $1,000.
Number of awards: Varies.
Scholarship may be renewable.
Deadline: Varies.
How to apply: Applications are available at college financial aid offices.
Exclusive: Visit www.UltimateScholarshipBook.com and enter code NE164120 for updates on this award.

(1642) • Collegiate Scholarship

Texas 4-H Youth Development Foundation
4180 Highway 6, College Station, TX 77845
Phone: 979-845-1211
Email: texas4h@ag.tamu.edu
https://texas4-h.tamu.edu/scholarships/
Purpose: To support undergraduate students in Texas.
Eligibility: Applicants must have actively participated in a 4-H program during their high school years. They must be currently enrolled full-time with at least a 2.7 GPA. Recipients must have completed at least 30 credit hours by the time scholarship payments begin. Awards are based on financial need, academic achievement and 4-H experience.
Target applicant(s): College students. Adult students.
Minimum GPA: 2.7
Amount: Varies.
Number of awards: Varies.
Deadline: Varies.
How to apply: Applications are available online.
Exclusive: Visit www.UltimateScholarshipBook.com and enter code TE164220 for updates on this award.

(1643) • Collegiate Shooting Scholarship Program

National Rifle Association
11250 Waples Mill Road, Fairfax, VA 22030
Phone: 800-672-3888
Email: grantprogram@nrahq.org
https://awards.nra.org/awards/

Purpose: To support students who have a strong interest in shooting sports as they continue their education beyond high school.
Eligibility: Applicants must live in Pennsylvania or Virginia, be a high school senior, have at least a 3.0 GPA and have a strong interest in shooting sports and the Second Amendment. Selection is based on the application, essay and letter of reference.
Target applicant(s): High school students.
Minimum GPA: 3.0
Amount: $5,000.
Number of awards: Varies.
Deadline: June 1.
How to apply: Applications are available online. A copy of a letter of acceptance to the college or university of choice must be sent with the application.
Exclusive: Visit www.UltimateScholarshipBook.com and enter code NA164320 for updates on this award.

(1644) • Colorado Council Volunteerism and Community Service Scholarship

Colorado Council Volunteerism & Community Service
P.O. Box 3383, Pagosa Springs, CO 81147
Phone: 970-264-2231
Email: mthompson@pagosa.k12.co.us
http://www.coloradocouncil.org/scholarship

Purpose: To support Colorado students interested in community service who are pursuing higher education.
Eligibility: Applicants must be graduating high school seniors who have been residents of Colorado for their final two years of high school. Students must be accepted at a Colorado Council Member Institution and be enrolled as a full-time student within six months after graduation from high school.
Target applicant(s): High school students.
Minimum GPA: 2.5
Amount: $1,500.
Number of awards: 14.
Deadline: January 31.
How to apply: Applications are available online.
Exclusive: Visit www.UltimateScholarshipBook.com and enter code CO164420 for updates on this award.

(1645) • Colorado Masons Benevolent Fund Scholarships

Colorado Masons Benevolent Fund Association
P.O. Box 703, Westminster, CO 80036-0703
Phone: 719-623-5349
Email: education@cmbfa.org
http://www.cmbfa.org

Purpose: To help Colorado students.
Eligibility: Applicants must be graduating seniors from a Colorado public high school planning to attend a Colorado postsecondary institution. Selection is based on leadership, maturity, need and scholastic ability without reference to race, creed, color, sex or Masonic relationship.
Target applicant(s): High school students.
Amount: Up to $10,000.
Number of awards: Varies.
Scholarship may be renewable.
Deadline: March 31.
How to apply: Applications are available online.
Exclusive: Visit www.UltimateScholarshipBook.com and enter code CO164520 for updates on this award.

(1646) • Colorado Nurses Association Nightingale Scholarship

Colorado Nurses Foundation
2851 S. Parker Road, Suite 1210, Aurora, CO 80014
Phone: 720-457-1191
Email: sonja.hix-cortina@civicamanagement.com
https://www.coloradonursesfoundation.com/scholarships/

Purpose: To aid Colorado nursing students who are Colorado Nurses Association or Colorado Student Nurse Association members.
Eligibility: Students must be Colorado residents who are Colorado Nurses Association or Colorado Student Nurses Association members. They must be second-year ASN students; third- or fourth-year BSN students; RNs enrolled at a school of nursing at any postsecondary level; currently practicing RNs enrolled in a doctoral nursing program or Doctor of Nursing Practice (DNP) students. Undergraduates must have a GPA of 3.25 or above, and graduate students must have a GPA of 3.5 or above. Applicants must have plans to practice nursing in the state of Colorado after graduation. Selection is based on stated career goals, GPA, financial need, participation in community and professional organizations and commitment to practicing nursing in Colorado.
Target applicant(s): High school students. College students. Graduate school students. Adult students.
Minimum GPA: 3.25 for undergraduate students, 3.5 for graduate students
Amount: Varies.
Number of awards: Varies.
Deadline: October 31.
How to apply: Applications are available online. An application form, statement of financial need, personal essay, two recommendations, resume, transcript and copy of CNA or CSNA membership card are required.
Exclusive: Visit www.UltimateScholarshipBook.com and enter code CO164620 for updates on this award.

(1647) • Colorado Oratorical Contest

American Legion, Department of Colorado
7465 E. 1st Avenue, Suite D, Denver, CO 80230
Phone: 303-366-5201
Email: drivercoach69@yahoo.com
http://www.coloradolegion.org

Purpose: To enhance high school students' experience with and understanding of the U.S. Constitution. The contest will help develop students' leadership skills and civic appreciation, as well as the ability to deliver thoughtful, insightful orations regarding U.S. citizenship and its inherent responsibilities.
Eligibility: Applicants must be high school students under the age of 20 who are U.S. citizens or legal residents and residents of the state. Students first give an oration within their state and winners compete at the national level. The oration must be related to the Constitution of the United States focusing on the duties and obligations citizens have to the government. It must be in English and be between eight and ten minutes. There is also an assigned topic which is posted on the website, and it should be between three and five minutes.

Target applicant(s): Junior high students or younger. High school students.
Amount: $1,000-$18,000.
Number of awards: Varies.
Deadline: January 29.
How to apply: Applications are available online.
Exclusive: Visit www.UltimateScholarshipBook.com and enter code AM164720 for updates on this award.

(1648) • Colorado Press Association High School Scholarship

Denver Foundation
55 Madison, 8th Floor, Denver, CO 80206
Phone: 303-300-1790
Email: information@denverfoundation.org
http://www.denverfoundation.org/grants/page/scholarships
Purpose: To reward high school seniors who have been active and held a leadership position in their high school journalism programs.
Eligibility: Applicants must be current high school seniors who are graduating from a Colorado high school. Students must have held at least one leadership position in their journalism organization such as the high school newspaper, yearbook or media club during their senior year. Applicants must attend an accredited four-year college or university in Colorado for the upcoming fall.
Target applicant(s): High school students.
Amount: $1,500.
Number of awards: 3.
Deadline: March 5.
How to apply: Applications are available online.
Exclusive: Visit www.UltimateScholarshipBook.com and enter code DE164820 for updates on this award.

(1649) • Colorado Student Grant

Colorado Department of Higher Education
1560 Broadway, Suite 1600, Denver, CO 80202
Phone: 303-862-3001
http://highered.colorado.gov/
Purpose: To assist Colorado student residents.
Eligibility: Applicants must be Colorado residents who plan to enroll or are enrolled in eligible programs at eligible Colorado postsecondary institutions. Applicants must make satisfactory academic progress and have not defaulted in educational loans or grants. Awards are need-based and merit-based and are made by institutions to students.
Target applicant(s): High school students. College students. Adult students.
Amount: Varies.
Number of awards: Varies.
Deadline: Varies.
How to apply: Contact your financial aid office.
Exclusive: Visit www.UltimateScholarshipBook.com and enter code CO164920 for updates on this award.

(1650) • Colorado Women's Education Foundation

Colorado Women's Education Foundation
P.O. Box 1189, Boulder, CO 80306-1189
Phone: 303-443-2573
Email: office@cwef.org
http://cwef.org/scholarships/
Purpose: To provide education assistance for adult women.
Eligibility: Applicants must be women who are 25 years of age or older, United States citizens and Colorado residents for at least 12 months prior to the application deadline. They must be enrolled in or attending an accredited Colorado college, university or vocational training institution.
Target applicant(s): College students. Adult students.
Amount: Varies.
Number of awards: Varies.
Deadline: May 31.
How to apply: Applications are available online.
Exclusive: Visit www.UltimateScholarshipBook.com and enter code CO165020 for updates on this award.

(1651) • Commonwealth "Good Citizen" Scholarships

Association of Independent Colleges and Universities of Pennsylvania
101 North Front Street, Harrisburg, PA 17101-1404
Phone: 717-232-8649
Email: klinger@aicup.org
http://www.aicup.org/Foundation-Scholarships
Purpose: To provide financial assistance for students who have demonstrated good citizenship.
Eligibility: Applicants must have demonstrated a commitment to community service and creativity in shaping volunteer activities. They must be full-time current or upcoming undergraduate students at an AICUP member college or university. A two-page essay is required.
Target applicant(s): High school students. College students. Adult students.
Amount: Varies.
Number of awards: Varies.
Deadline: Mid-April.
How to apply: Applications are available from financial aid offices of qualifying institutions.
Exclusive: Visit www.UltimateScholarshipBook.com and enter code AS165120 for updates on this award.

(1652) • Community Banker Association of Illinois Annual Essay Scholarship Program

Community Banker Association of Illinois
901 Community Drive, Springfield, IL 62703-5184
Phone: 800-736-2224
Email: bobbiw@cbai.com
http://www.cbai.com
Purpose: To assist Illinois high school seniors.
Eligibility: Applicants must write essays and be sponsored by a participating CBAI member bank. There is an essay topic related to community banking, and the short essays are judged on understanding of community banking philosophy, accurate information, clear and concise sentences, logical organization, proper grammar, correct punctuation and spelling and conclusion/summary.
Target applicant(s): High school students.
Amount: Up to $4,000.
Number of awards: 16.
Deadline: February 1.
How to apply: A list of participating banks and more information is available by email.
Exclusive: Visit www.UltimateScholarshipBook.com and enter code CO165220 for updates on this award.

(1653) · Community Scholarship Fund

Hawaii Community Foundation - Scholarships
827 Fort Street Mall, Honolulu, HI 96813
Phone: 888-731-3863
Email: scholarships@hcf-hawaii.org
https://www.hawaiicommunityfoundation.org

Purpose: To assist college and graduate students majoring in arts, education, humanities or social science.

Eligibility: Applicants must demonstrate accomplishment, motivation, initiative, vision and intention to work in Hawaii and major in the arts, architecture, education, humanities or social science.

Target applicant(s): High school students. College students. Graduate school students. Adult students.

Minimum GPA: 3.3

Amount: Varies.

Number of awards: Varies.

Deadline: January 31.

How to apply: To apply, register online, complete the online application and select the scholarships to which you wish to apply. In addition, mail the supporting materials: printed confirmation page from the online application, personal statement, copy of Student Aid Report (SAR) available at www.fafsa.ed.gov and official transcript.

Exclusive: Visit www.UltimateScholarshipBook.com and enter code HA165320 for updates on this award.

(1654) · Competitive Scholarships

New Mexico Higher Education Department
2044 Galisteo Street, Suite 4, Santa Fe, NM 87505-2100
Phone: 505-476-8400
Email: cesaria.tapia1@state.nm.us
http://www.hed.state.nm.us/students/

Purpose: To provide a financial incentive for exceptional out-of-state students to attend college in New Mexico.

Eligibility: Applicants must be non-residents of the state of New Mexico, and they must be willing to enroll full-time in a public four-year university in New Mexico. Students applying to Eastern New Mexico University, New Mexico Highlands University, New Mexico Institute of Mining and Technology or Western New Mexico University must have one of the following combinations: a GPA of at least 3.0 and an ACT score of at least 23, or a GPA of at least 3.5 and an ACT of at least 20. Students applying to the University of New Mexico or New Mexico State University must have either an ACT score of 26 and a GPA of 3.0 or an ACT score of 23 and a GPA of 3.5.

Target applicant(s): High school students. College students. Adult students.

Minimum GPA: 3.0

Amount: $100.

Number of awards: Varies.

Scholarship may be renewable.

Deadline: Varies.

How to apply: Applications are available at college financial aid offices.

Exclusive: Visit www.UltimateScholarshipBook.com and enter code NE165420 for updates on this award.

(1655) · Confederation of Oregon School Administrators Scholarships

Confederation of Oregon School Administrators
707 13th Street SE, Suite 100, Salem, OR 97301
Phone: 503-581-3141
Email: sara@oasc.org
https://www.cosa.k12.or.us/

Purpose: To provide financial assistance to Oregon students who plan to attend Oregon colleges or universities.

Eligibility: Applicants must be graduating seniors at an Oregon public high school who plan to attend a public or private institution of higher learning in the state. They must have a 3.5 or higher GPA, be active in school and community activities and be endorsed by a COSA member.

Target applicant(s): High school students.

Minimum GPA: 3.5

Amount: $1,000.

Number of awards: 10.

Deadline: February 20.

How to apply: Applications are available online.

Exclusive: Visit www.UltimateScholarshipBook.com and enter code CO165520 for updates on this award.

(1656) · Connecticut Aid for Public College Students

Connecticut Office of Higher Education
39 Woodland Street, Hartford, CT 06105-2326
Phone: 860-947-1855
Email: sfa@ctohe.org
http://www.ctohe.org

Purpose: To assist Connecticut student residents.

Eligibility: Applicants must be Connecticut residents attending a public Connecticut college or university. The award is based on financial need.

Target applicant(s): High school students. College students. Adult students.

Amount: Up to amount of unmet financial need.

Number of awards: Varies.

Deadline: Varies.

How to apply: Apply through your college financial aid office.

Exclusive: Visit www.UltimateScholarshipBook.com and enter code CO165620 for updates on this award.

(1657) · Connecticut Association of Land Surveyors Memorial Scholarship Fund

Connecticut Association of Land Surveyors Inc.
78 Beaver Road, Wethersfield, CT 06109
Phone: 860-563-1990
Email: kathy@ctsurveyors.com
http://ctsurveyors.org

Purpose: To support Connecticut students who are preparing for careers in land surveying.

Eligibility: Applicants must be Connecticut residents who are enrolled in or who have been accepted into a postsecondary academic program in surveying or a related subject (geography, engineering or science). They must have plans to pursue a career in land surveying and must demonstrate interest in the field through previous work experience or other activities. Selection is based on the overall strength of the application.

Target applicant(s): College students. Adult students.

Amount: Varies.

Number of awards: Varies.

Deadline: June 1.

How to apply: Applications are available online. A resume, transcript and statement of qualifications are required.

Exclusive: Visit www.UltimateScholarshipBook.com and enter code CO165720 for updates on this award.

(1658) • Connecticut Building Congress Scholarships

Connecticut Building Congress Scholarship Fund, Inc.
c/o DiBlasi Associates, P.C., 500 Purdy Hill Road, Monroe, CT 06468
Phone: 203-452-1331
Email: TomD@DiBlasi-Engrs.com
http://www.cbc-ct.org/CBC_Scholarship
Purpose: To aid students pursuing degrees in construction fields.
Eligibility: Applicants must be graduating seniors at Connecticut high schools and Connecticut residents. Students must be entering associate, bachelor's or master's degree programs in architecture, engineering, construction management, surveying, planning or another construction-related course of study.
Target applicant(s): High school students.
Amount: $500-$2,000.
Number of awards: Varies.
Scholarship may be renewable.
Deadline: March 10.
How to apply: Applications are available online. An application form, essay, transcript and FAFSA Student Aid Report are required.
Exclusive: Visit www.UltimateScholarshipBook.com and enter code CO165820 for updates on this award.

(1659) • Connecticut Chapter Air and Waste Management Association Scholarship

Air and Waste Management Association-Connecticut Chapter
c/o Dana Lowes-Hobson, TRC, 21 Griffin Road North, Windsor, CT 06095
Phone: 860-298-6203
Email: Dlowes-hobson@trcsolutions.com
http://www.awmanewengland.org
Purpose: To aid Connecticut students who are preparing for careers in air and waste management or other environmental areas.
Eligibility: Applicants must be Connecticut residents who have been accepted at or are enrolled at a postsecondary institution full-time. They must be studying or have plans to study a science or engineering subject that is related to air and waste management or a related environmental subject, and they must intend to pursue careers in one of these areas. Selection is based on academic achievement, stated career goals, extracurricular involvements and letters of recommendation.
Target applicant(s): High school students. College students. Adult students.
Amount: $1,000.
Number of awards: 1.
Scholarship may be renewable.
Deadline: First weekday in April.
How to apply: Applications are available online. An application form, transcript, resume, two letters of recommendation and plan of study statement are required.
Exclusive: Visit www.UltimateScholarshipBook.com and enter code AI165920 for updates on this award.

(1660) • Continuing/Re-entry Students Scholarship

American Legion Auxiliary, Department of California
401 Van Ness Avenue, Suite 319, San Francisco, CA 94102-4570
Phone: 415-861-5092
Email: calegionaux@calegionaux.org
http://calegionaux.org/scholarships.htm
Purpose: To provide support to children of U.S. Armed Forces members.
Eligibility: One of the applicant's parents must have served in the U.S. Armed Forces during an eligible period. Applicants must be California residents planning to attend a California college or university and must be continuing or re-entry college students.
Target applicant(s): College students. Adult students.
Amount: $500-$1,000.
Number of awards: 5.
Deadline: March 16, September 1.
How to apply: Applications are available online.
Exclusive: Visit www.UltimateScholarshipBook.com and enter code AM166020 for updates on this award.

(1661) • Cora Aguda Manayan Fund

Hawaii Community Foundation - Scholarships
827 Fort Street Mall, Honolulu, HI 96813
Phone: 888-731-3863
Email: scholarships@hcf-hawaii.org
https://www.hawaiicommunityfoundation.org
Purpose: To support Hawaii students of Filipino ancestry who are dedicated to helping others.
Eligibility: Students must be majoring in a health-related field. Preference may be given to students who are attending school in Hawaii. Applicants must have a minimum 3.0 GPA and have financial need.
Target applicant(s): High school students. College students. Adult students.
Minimum GPA: 3.0
Amount: Varies.
Number of awards: Varies.
Deadline: January 31.
How to apply: To apply, register online, complete the online application and select the scholarships to which you wish to apply. In addition, mail the supporting materials: printed confirmation page from the online application, personal statement, copy of Student Aid Report (SAR) available at www.fafsa.ed.gov and official transcript.
Exclusive: Visit www.UltimateScholarshipBook.com and enter code HA166120 for updates on this award.

(1662) • COSA Youth Development Program Scholarships

Confederation of Oregon School Administrators
707 13th Street SE, Suite 100, Salem, OR 97301
Phone: 503-581-3141
Email: sara@oasc.org
https://www.cosa.k12.or.us/
Purpose: To provide financial assistance for Oregon students.
Eligibility: Applicants must be students at an Oregon public high school who are active in their communities and schools. They must have a GPA of 3.5 or higher and plan to attend an Oregon college or university. A field of study must be chosen. An endorsement from a COSA member is required, and the student must enroll in college the fall after high school graduation.
Target applicant(s): High school students.
Minimum GPA: 3.5
Amount: $1,000.
Number of awards: 10.
Deadline: March 1.
How to apply: Applications are available online, from your high school guidance counselor and the COSA office. An application form, one-page autobiography, letter of recommendation from a COSA member and transcript are required.

Exclusive: Visit www.UltimateScholarshipBook.com and enter code CO166220 for updates on this award.

(1663) • Courageous Heart Scholarship

Texas 4-H Youth Development Foundation
4180 Highway 6, College Station, TX 77845
Phone: 979-845-1211
Email: texas4h@ag.tamu.edu
https://texas4-h.tamu.edu/scholarships/
Purpose: To support Texas high school students who have overcome serious obstacles related to health, family or education.
Eligibility: Applicants must be current active members and have actively participated in a 4-H program for two of the past three years. They must have formally applied to a Texas college or university, and they must meet all requirements for admission. Students must provide documentation of the obstacles they have faced.
Target applicant(s): High school students.
Amount: $5,000.
Number of awards: Varies.
Deadline: February 7.
How to apply: Applications are available online.
Exclusive: Visit www.UltimateScholarshipBook.com and enter code TE166320 for updates on this award.

(1664) • Critical Care Scholarship Program

Critical Care Training Center
6426 Bellingham Avenue, North Hollywood, CA 91606
Phone: 818-766-1111
Email: scholarship@acls123.com
http://www.acls123.com/interactive-scholarship-program/
Purpose: To assist future healthcare providers throughout California.
Eligibility: Applicants must be California residents pursuing a degree in healthcare/nursing. Students are required to submit an essay on the designated topic found on the website. After applicants are narrowed down, the essays will then need to be shared on Facebook, Twitter, LinkedIn or other social networking pages and receive votes. The contest runs quarterly.
Target applicant(s): College students. Adult students.
Amount: $2,500.
Number of awards: 4.
Deadline: Quarterly.
How to apply: Applications are available online.
Exclusive: Visit www.UltimateScholarshipBook.com and enter code CR166420 for updates on this award.

(1665) • Crumley Roberts Founder's Scholarship

Crumley Roberts, Attorneys at Law
2400 Freeman Mill Road, Greensboro, NC 27406
Phone: 866-336-4547
Email: scholarship@crumleyroberts.com
http://www.crumleyroberts.com/community/scholarships/
Purpose: To help North Carolina high school seniors who have performed community service.
Eligibility: Applicants must plan to attend four-year colleges or universities. Transcripts, three recommendation letters, applications and essays are required. No phone calls, please.
Target applicant(s): High school students.
Minimum GPA: 3.0
Amount: $2,500.
Number of awards: 5.
Deadline: January 31.
How to apply: Applications are available online.
Exclusive: Visit www.UltimateScholarshipBook.com and enter code CR166520 for updates on this award.

(1666) • Crumley Roberts Next Step Scholarship

Crumley Roberts, Attorneys at Law
2400 Freeman Mill Road, Greensboro, NC 27406
Phone: 866-336-4547
Email: scholarship@crumleyroberts.com
http://www.crumleyroberts.com/community/scholarships/
Purpose: To support North Carolina community college students who plan to transfer to accredited four-year institutions of higher learning.
Eligibility: Applicants must be a minimum of 18 years of age and have a minimum GPA of 3.2. Selection is based on the quality of the essay alone.
Target applicant(s): College students. Adult students.
Minimum GPA: 3.2
Amount: $2,500.
Number of awards: 1.
Deadline: February 19.
How to apply: Applications are available to be printed online but must then be mailed. An application form, two letters of recommendation, a transcript and an essay are required.
Exclusive: Visit www.UltimateScholarshipBook.com and enter code CR166620 for updates on this award.

(1667) • CSCA Scholarship

Colorado Spirit Coaches Association
P.O. Box 248, Parker, CO 80134
Phone: 303-840-4287
Email: csca@comcast.net
http://cscaonline.org/
Purpose: To honor spirit leaders based on their contributions to the sport of spirit.
Eligibility: Applicants must apply to and audition for the CSCA All Colorado Spirit Team. One spirit leader will be selected as a scholarship recipient based on community involvement, number of years in a spirit program, academic achievement and letters of recommendation. Applicants must have a minimum 3.0 GPA.
Target applicant(s): High school students.
Minimum GPA: 3.0
Amount: Varies.
Number of awards: 1.
Deadline: October 30.
How to apply: Applications for CSCA All Colorado Spirit Team are available online. Applicants must also audition in person at the annual College Fair.
Exclusive: Visit www.UltimateScholarshipBook.com and enter code CO166720 for updates on this award.

(1668) • CTA César E. Chávez Memorial Education Awards Program

California Teachers Association (CTA)
CTA Human Rights Department, P.O. Box 921, Burlingame, CA 94011-0921
Phone: 650-697-1400
http://www.cta.org/scholarships
Purpose: To honor César Chávez by rewarding students and teachers who follow his vision and guiding principles.

Eligibility: A student or group of up to five students must submit an essay or visual piece under the supervision of a teacher or professor who is a member of the CTA. Students may be in kindergarten through high school or in community college. All works must focus on topics such as non-violence and their relationship to Chávez's legacy. Visit the website for a complete list of topics and specific essay and visual arts submission requirements.
Target applicant(s): Junior high students or younger. High school students. College students. Adult students.
Amount: Up to $550.
Number of awards: Varies.
Deadline: December 2.
How to apply: Applications are available online.
Exclusive: Visit www.UltimateScholarshipBook.com and enter code CA166820 for updates on this award.

(1669) • CTAHPERD Gibson-Laemel Scholarship

Connecticut Association of Health, Physical Education, Recreation and Dance
c/o Janice Skene, CTAHPERD Scholarship Chair, Buttonball Lane School, 376 Buttonball Lane, Glastonbury, CT 06033
Phone: 860-652-7276
Email: skenej@glastonburyus.org
http://www.ctahperd.org
Purpose: To support students majoring in areas related to physical education.
Eligibility: Applicants must be Connecticut students who have declared a major in health, physical education, recreation or dance. Students must be college juniors or seniors, maintain a GPA of 2.7 or higher and be CTAHPERD members.
Target applicant(s): College students. Adult students.
Minimum GPA: 2.7
Amount: $1,000.
Number of awards: Varies.
Deadline: June 15.
How to apply: Applications are available online. An application form, personal statement, transcript and two letters of recommendation are required.
Exclusive: Visit www.UltimateScholarshipBook.com and enter code CO166920 for updates on this award.

(1670) • Curtis/Hunt Memorial Scholarship

New York State Women's 500 Club
Mike Pettinella, 55 Edgewood Drive, Batavia, NY 14020
Phone: 585-343-3736
Email: bowlny300@yahoo.com
http://www.bowlny.com/
Purpose: To support New York State female USBC Youth bowlers in pursuit of a college education.
Eligibility: Applicants must be a New York State female USBC Youth certified bowler who has bowled at least 30 games. Applicants must also be a high school senior or college freshman. Selection is based on bowling achievements, academic success and active participation in school, civic and community activities.
Target applicant(s): High school students. College students. Adult students.
Amount: $500.
Number of awards: 1.
Deadline: February 1.
How to apply: Applications are available online. The form consists of the student application and essay, a form to be completed by a league official, a form to be completed by a school official and an official high school transcript.
Exclusive: Visit www.UltimateScholarshipBook.com and enter code NE167020 for updates on this award.

(1671) • Cynthia and Alan Baran Fine Arts and Music Scholarship Fund

Community Foundation of Middle Tennessee
3833 Cleghorn Avenue, Suite 400, Nashville, TN 37215-2519
Phone: 888-540-5200
Email: pcole@cfmt.org
https://www.cfmt.org/grants-scholarships/
Purpose: To aid students in pursuing careers in visual arts and music.
Eligibility: Applicants must be current students at an accredited college or university, take at least six credit hours and be enrolled in a bachelor's of fine art, bachelor's of studio art, master's of fine art or bachelor's or master's in music program. Art students must major in painting, drawing, sculpture, ceramics, photography or printmaking. Preference for music scholarships is given to those studying acoustic mandolin or acoustic guitar. A minimum GPA of 3.0 is required.
Target applicant(s): College students. Graduate school students. Adult students.
Minimum GPA: 3.0
Amount: Varies.
Number of awards: Varies.
Deadline: March 15.
How to apply: Applications are available online. An application form, transcript, essay, Student Aid Report and two appraisal forms are required.
Exclusive: Visit www.UltimateScholarshipBook.com and enter code CO167120 for updates on this award.

(1672) • Czech Center Museum Houston Academic Scholarship

Czech Cultural Center
4920 San Jacinto, Houston, TX 77004
Phone: 713-528-2060
Email: czech@czechcenter.org
http://www.czechcenter.org
Purpose: To provide financial assistance to children of Czech descent.
Eligibility: Applicants must have at least one Czech parent and be full-time undergraduate degree candidates to a four-year college or university. They must either be Texas residents or sons or daughters of members of the Czech Cultural Center Houston. Financial need is considered.
Target applicant(s): High school students. College students. Adult students.
Amount: $1,000.
Number of awards: 3.
Scholarship may be renewable.
Deadline: June 1.
How to apply: Applications are available online.
Exclusive: Visit www.UltimateScholarshipBook.com and enter code CZ167220 for updates on this award.

(1673) • Daniel Cardillo Charitable Fund

Maine Community Foundation
245 Main Street, Ellsworth, ME 04605
Phone: 207-667-9735
Email: jwarren@mainecf.org
http://www.mainecf.org

Purpose: To provide financial support for young people to pursue their extracurricular interests.
Eligibility: Students must be passionately committed to an activity outside of school, and they must show financial need for further pursuit of that activity. Applicants should also be able to show that they care deeply about other people.
Target applicant(s): High school students.
Amount: Varies.
Number of awards: Varies.
Deadline: May 1.
How to apply: Applications are available online.
Exclusive: Visit www.UltimateScholarshipBook.com and enter code MA167320 for updates on this award.

(1674) • Daniel E. Lambert Memorial Scholarship

American Legion, Department of Maine
5 Verti Drive, Winslow, ME 04901-0727
Phone: 207-873-3229
Email: legionme@mainelegion.org
http://www.mainelegion.org
Purpose: To support the descendants of veterans who demonstrate financial need and who are residents of Maine.
Eligibility: Applicants must be enrolled in an accredited college or vocational technical school and be U.S. citizens. A parent or grandparent must be a veteran, verified by a copy of military discharge papers with the application. Applicants must have good character and believe in the American way of life.
Target applicant(s): College students. Adult students.
Amount: $1,000.
Number of awards: Up to 2.
Deadline: May 1.
How to apply: Applications are available online.
Exclusive: Visit www.UltimateScholarshipBook.com and enter code AM167420 for updates on this award.

(1675) • Daniels Scholarship Program

Daniels Fund
101 Monroe Street, Denver, CO 80206
Phone: 303-393-7220
http://www.danielsfund.org
Purpose: To support students who have a proven record of character strength, leadership and a commitment to their communities in accomplishing their goal of obtaining a post-secondary education.
Eligibility: Applicants must be graduating high school seniors enrolling in any nonprofit accredited college or university and be a resident of Colorado, New Mexico, Utah or Wyoming. Students must submit a FAFSA to demonstrate financial need, have a minimum 2.0 GPA and earn an ACT score of 17 and minimum SAT Math score of 470 along with a minimum SAT Critical Reading score of 450.
Target applicant(s): High school students.
Minimum GPA: 2.0
Amount: Varies.
Number of awards: Varies.
Scholarship may be renewable.
Deadline: November 30.
How to apply: Applications are available online.
Exclusive: Visit www.UltimateScholarshipBook.com and enter code DA167520 for updates on this award.

(1676) • David E. Simon Scholarship

Indiana Golf Association
P.O. Box 516, Franklin, IN 46131
Phone: 317-738-9696
Email: astrong@indianagolf.org
http://www.indianagolf.org
Purpose: To aid those students who have worked at an Indiana golf facility in their pursuit of a college education.
Eligibility: Applicants must be a senior in high school, have worked in an Indiana golf facility in the previous 12 months, have a 3.0 GPA, display strong character and prove financial need. Selection is based on financial need, personal essay and academic achievement.
Target applicant(s): High school students.
Minimum GPA: 3.0
Amount: $5,000.
Number of awards: Varies.
Deadline: March 3.
How to apply: Applications are available online and must include an IRS 1040 form, high school transcript, personal essay and at least one letter of reference. In addition to the main application form, students should submit the academic evaluation form and employment evaluation form.
Exclusive: Visit www.UltimateScholarshipBook.com and enter code IN167620 for updates on this award.

(1677) • DC Tuition Assistance Grant Program

Government of the District of Columbia
DC Tuition Assistance Grant Program, 810 First Street NE, Third Floor, Washington, DC 20002
Phone: 877-485-6751
Email: osse@dc.gov
http://osse.dc.gov
Purpose: To provide financial assistance to students in the District of Columbia who wish to attend either a public university in a different state or a historically black college or university.
Eligibility: Applicants must be residents who have lived in the District of Columbia for at least 12 months prior to the beginning of their freshman year of college. Applicants must also either plan to or be currently enrolled at least half-time in an undergraduate or certificate program.
Target applicant(s): High school students. College students.
Amount: Up to $10,000.
Number of awards: Varies.
Scholarship may be renewable.
Deadline: June 30.
How to apply: Applications are available online.
Exclusive: Visit www.UltimateScholarshipBook.com and enter code GO167720 for updates on this award.

(1678) • Delaware Diamond State Scholarship

Department of Education - School Supports
The Townsend Building, 401 Federal Street, Suite 2, Dover, DE 19901-3639
Phone: 800-292-7935
Email: dhec@doe.k12.de.us
http://www.doe.k12.de.us/page/316
Purpose: To support academically-talented Delaware student residents.
Eligibility: Applicants must be residents of Delaware, U.S. citizens or eligible non-citizens, high school seniors who rank in the upper quarter of their class and score a minimum of 1200 on the SAT and enroll as full-time students in a degree program at a regionally accredited college.
Target applicant(s): High school students.

Amount: $1,250.
Number of awards: 50.
Scholarship may be renewable.
Deadline: March 6.
How to apply: Applications are available online.
Exclusive: Visit www.UltimateScholarshipBook.com and enter code DE167820 for updates on this award.

(1679) • Delaware Educational Benefits for Children of Deceased Veterans and Others

Department of Education - School Supports
The Townsend Building, 401 Federal Street, Suite 2, Dover, DE 19901-3639
Phone: 800-292-7935
Email: dhec@doe.k12.de.us
http://www.doe.k12.de.us/page/316
Purpose: To assist children of deceased veterans.
Eligibility: Applicants must be U.S. citizens or eligible non-citizens who have been Delaware residents for at least three years prior to application. They must be the child of an armed forces member who died from a service-related cause, is/was a prisoner of war or has been declared missing in action; a state police officer whose death was service-related or a Department of Transportation employee who worked on the state highway system whose death was job-related. Applicants must be 16 to 24 years of age. Priority is given to students attending a Delaware public college, followed by students attending Delaware private colleges and those attending out-of-state institutions. Those attending private or out-of-state colleges must pursue majors that are not offered by Delaware public colleges.
Target applicant(s): High school students. College students.
Amount: Full tuition and fees.
Number of awards: Varies.
Scholarship may be renewable.
Deadline: 6-8 weeks prior to the start of classes.
How to apply: Applications are available online. An application form is required.
Exclusive: Visit www.UltimateScholarshipBook.com and enter code DE167920 for updates on this award.

(1680) • Delaware Scholarship Incentive Program

Department of Education - School Supports
The Townsend Building, 401 Federal Street, Suite 2, Dover, DE 19901-3639
Phone: 800-292-7935
Email: dhec@doe.k12.de.us
http://www.doe.k12.de.us/page/316
Purpose: To assist Delaware student residents.
Eligibility: Applicants must be legal residents of Delaware and U.S. citizens or eligible non-citizens who are enrolled full-time at a regionally-accredited undergraduate institution in Delaware or Pennsylvania. Other undergraduate and graduate students will be considered if their major is not available at a public college in Delaware. Students must demonstrate substantial financial need and have a minimum 2.5 GPA. Applicants must also submit the Free Application for Federal Student Aid (FAFSA).
Target applicant(s): High school students. College students. Graduate school students. Adult students.
Minimum GPA: 2.5
Amount: $1,000 a year.
Number of awards: Varies.
Scholarship may be renewable.
Deadline: April 15.
How to apply: Delaware residents are automatically considered for the scholarship when their FAFSA form is received.
Exclusive: Visit www.UltimateScholarshipBook.com and enter code DE168020 for updates on this award.

(1681) • Delaware Solid Waste Authority John P. "Pat" Healy Scholarship

Department of Education - School Supports
The Townsend Building, 401 Federal Street, Suite 2, Dover, DE 19901-3639
Phone: 800-292-7935
Email: dhec@doe.k12.de.us
http://www.doe.k12.de.us/page/316
Purpose: To aid Delaware students who are preparing for careers in environmental engineering or environmental science.
Eligibility: Applicants must be Delaware residents, U.S. citizens or eligible non-citizens and full-time students. They must be high school seniors, undergraduate freshmen or undergraduate sophomores majoring in or planning to major in environmental sciences or environmental engineering at a Delaware college or university. They also must complete a Free Application for Federal Student Aid (FAFSA) form for the upcoming school year. Selection is based on academic achievement, leadership skills, extracurricular involvement and financial need.
Target applicant(s): High school students. College students. Adult students.
Amount: $1,500-$2,500.
Number of awards: Varies.
Scholarship may be renewable.
Deadline: March 6.
How to apply: Applications are available online. An application form, personal essay, transcript and FAFSA are required.
Exclusive: Visit www.UltimateScholarshipBook.com and enter code DE168120 for updates on this award.

(1682) • Delegate Scholarship

Maryland Higher Education Commission
Office of Student Financial Assistance, 6 North Liberty Street, Baltimore, MD 21201
Phone: 800-974-1024
Email: osfamail@mhec.state.md.us
http://www.maryland.gov
Purpose: To assist Maryland undergraduate and graduate students who can demonstrate financial need.
Eligibility: Applicants must be legal residents of the state of Maryland and complete the Free Application for Federal Student Aid (FAFSA). They must show financial need if the Office of Student Financial Assistance (OFSA) makes the award for the applicant's delegate. Applicants must be or must plan to be degree-seeking students at a Maryland institution. Selection is based on the overall strength of the application.
Target applicant(s): High school students. College students. Graduate school students. Adult students.
Amount: Up to $19,000.
Number of awards: Varies.
Scholarship may be renewable.
Deadline: March 1.
How to apply: Complete and file the Free Application for Federal Student Aid (FAFSA). Contact delegate's office for specific application forms. The Office of Student Financial Assistance (OSFA) can provide a list of all state legislators. An application form and supporting documents are required.

Exclusive: Visit www.UltimateScholarshipBook.com and enter code MA168220 for updates on this award.

(1683) · Dennis Schoepp Memorial Scholarship

Funeral Service Foundation
13625 Bishop's Drive, Brookfield, WI 53005-6607
Phone: 877-402-5900
Email: info@funeralservicefoundation.org
http://www.funeralservicefoundation.org
Purpose: To aid students with tuition costs associated with mortuary science education.
Eligibility: Applicants must be a student of funeral service from Montana and be enrolled full- or part-time in an American Board of Funeral Service Education accredited program. Selection is based on the overall strength of the application.
Target applicant(s): College students. Graduate school students. Adult students.
Minimum GPA: 2.0
Amount: Varies.
Number of awards: Varies.
Deadline: March 30.
How to apply: Applications are available online. An application form, essay, academic transcript and video submissions are required.
Exclusive: Visit www.UltimateScholarshipBook.com and enter code FU168320 for updates on this award.

(1684) · Department of Children and Families (DCF) Foster Child Tuition Waiver and Fee Assistance Program

Massachusetts Department of Higher Education
Office of Student Financial Assistance, 454 Broadway, Suite 200, Revere, MA 02151
Phone: 617-727-9420
Email: osfa@osfa.mass.edu
http://www.mass.edu/osfa/students/forstudents.asp
Purpose: To provide financial support to Massachusetts foster children who are pursuing higher education.
Eligibility: Applicants must be current or former foster children who were placed in Massachusetts state custody for at least 12 months due to a Care and Protection Petition. They must not have been adopted or returned home, and they must be 24 years old or younger. Students must be enrolled as full-time undergraduates at a state-supported school.
Target applicant(s): High school students. College students. Adult students.
Amount: Full tuition.
Number of awards: Varies.
Deadline: Varies.
How to apply: Applications are available at college financial aid offices.
Exclusive: Visit www.UltimateScholarshipBook.com and enter code MA168420 for updates on this award.

(1685) · Dick Griffiths Memorial Scholarship

California Association on Postsecondary Education and Disability (CAPED)
10073 Valley View Street, #242, Cypress, CA 90630
Phone: 562-397-2810
Email: capedscholarships2018@gmail.com
http://www.caped.io/scholarships/
Purpose: To support students with a learning disability in math who are pursuing higher education.
Eligibility: Applicants must have a verifiable learning disability in math and be currently enrolled as a student at a California college or university with a GPA of 2.5 for undergraduates or 3.0 for graduate students. Students must have completed at least six semester or eight quarter units as an undergraduate student or three semester or four quarter units as a graduate student.
Target applicant(s): College students. Graduate school students. Adult students.
Minimum GPA: 2.5 for undergraduate students, 3.0 for graduate students
Amount: $1,000.
Number of awards: 1.
Deadline: August 31.
How to apply: Applications are available online.
Exclusive: Visit www.UltimateScholarshipBook.com and enter code CA168520 for updates on this award.

(1686) · Direct Energy Live Brighter Scholarship

Direct Energy
12 Greenway Plaza #250, Houston, TX 77046
Phone: 713-904-4687
Email: descholarship@directengergy.com
https://www.directenergy.com/scholarship
Purpose: To support students who promote energy efficiency.
Eligibility: Applicants must be at least 18 years of age and enrolled at an accredited college in the U.S. Students must be residents of a state where Direct Energy offers services: Connecticut, Delaware, Illinois, Indiana, Maryland, Massachusetts, Michigan, New Jersey, New York, Ohio, Pennsylvania, Texas, New Hampshire, Rhode Island and Washington, DC. Applicants must have a minimum 3.0 grade point average and complete both an essay and a short video.
Target applicant(s): College students. Graduate school students. Adult students.
Minimum GPA: 3.0
Amount: $2,500.
Number of awards: 3.
Deadline: December 15.
How to apply: Applications are available online.
Exclusive: Visit www.UltimateScholarshipBook.com and enter code DI168620 for updates on this award.

(1687) · District of Columbia Tuition Assistance Grant

DC Tuition Assistance Grant Office
810 First Street NE, Third Floor, Washington, DC 20002
Phone: 202-727-2824
Email: osse@dc.gov
http://osse.dc.gov
Purpose: To make attending out-of-state, private and Historically Black schools more affordable for DC residents.
Eligibility: Applicants must be residents of Washington, DC for at least 12 months before the start of their freshman year of college, high school graduates or GED recipients, enrolled at least half-time at an eligible institution and be 24 years of age or younger. Applicants must maintain satisfactory academic progress, not have defaulted on student loans, have registered with the Selective Service, be U.S. citizens or permanent residents, have not already received a B.A. or B.S. and have not been incarcerated. The award provides up to $10,000 a year for the difference between in-state and out-of-state tuition at public four year institutions in the U.S. and up to $2,500 per year for private colleges in DC, private Historically Black Colleges and Universities or two-year colleges nationwide.

Target applicant(s): High school students. College students.
Amount: $2,500-$10,000.
Number of awards: Varies.
Scholarship may be renewable.
Deadline: June 30.
How to apply: Applications are available online.
Exclusive: Visit www.UltimateScholarshipBook.com and enter code DC168720 for updates on this award.

(1688) • Dominique Lisa Pandolfo Scholarship

Community Foundation of New Jersey
P.O. Box 338, Morristown, NJ 07963-0338
Phone: 973-267-5533
Email: csmith@cfnj.org
http://cfnj.org/current-funds/student-scholarships/
Purpose: To help young women achieve their goals and be successful.
Eligibility: Applicants must be females who have been nominated by the Dominique Lisa Pandolfo Scholarship Committee. They must exhibit outstanding character, potential, merit, personality and leadership qualities, and they must demonstrate financial need. Applicants must be New Jersey residents.
Target applicant(s): High school students.
Amount: $5,000.
Number of awards: 1.
Deadline: June 30.
How to apply: Applications are available online.
Exclusive: Visit www.UltimateScholarshipBook.com and enter code CO168820 for updates on this award.

(1689) • Don't Mess with Texas Scholarship

Don't Mess with Texas
Sherry Matthews Advocacy, 200 South Congress Avenue, Austin, TX 78704
Phone: 512-476-4368
Email: scholarship@dontmesswithtexas.org
http://www.dontmesswithtexas.org/education-overview/scholarships/
Purpose: To support students concerned about litter.
Eligibility: Student must be a Texas high school senior who wants to attend a two- or four-year college or university in Texas. To apply for the scholarship, students must complete the application and one or two essays and submit two letters of recommendation (one from a school-related source and the other from a non-school related source).
Target applicant(s): High school students.
Amount: Varies.
Number of awards: Varies.
Deadline: March 26.
How to apply: Applications are available online.
Exclusive: Visit www.UltimateScholarshipBook.com and enter code DO168920 for updates on this award.

(1690) • Don't Wait to Reach Your Potential Scholarship for Alabama Teens

Potential Magazine
61 Market Place, Montgomery, AL 36117
Phone: 334-518-7810
http://potentialmagazine.com
Purpose: To help Alabama students pursue post-secondary education.
Eligibility: Applicants must be Alabama residents in grades 9-12. Students are required to sign up for the weekly eNewsletter.
Target applicant(s): High school students.
Amount: $500.
Number of awards: 1.
Deadline: May 4.
How to apply: Applications are available online.
Exclusive: Visit www.UltimateScholarshipBook.com and enter code PO169020 for updates on this award.

(1691) • Dorian De Long Arts and Music Scholarship

Jefferson County Education Association
1447 Nelson Street, Lakewood, CO 80215
Email: ddamscholarship@gmail.com
https://www.ddamscholarship.com
Purpose: To support students who are pursuing a degree in the arts.
Eligibility: Applicants must be graduating Colorado high school seniors who are pursuing the study of arts.
Target applicant(s): High school students.
Amount: $1,500.
Number of awards: 1.
Scholarship may be renewable.
Deadline: March 15.
How to apply: Applications are available online.
Exclusive: Visit www.UltimateScholarshipBook.com and enter code JE169120 for updates on this award.

(1692) • Doris and Clarence Glick Classical Music Scholarship

Hawaii Community Foundation - Scholarships
827 Fort Street Mall, Honolulu, HI 96813
Phone: 888-731-3863
Email: scholarships@hcf-hawaii.org
https://www.hawaiicommunityfoundation.org
Purpose: To provide financial assistance for Hawaii students of classical music.
Eligibility: Applicants must be majoring in music with an emphasis on classical music. They must have a GPA of 2.7 or higher, and they must describe their program of study as it relates to classical music in their personal statement.
Target applicant(s): High school students. College students. Graduate school students. Adult students.
Minimum GPA: 2.7
Amount: Varies.
Number of awards: Varies.
Deadline: January 31.
How to apply: To apply, register online, complete the online application and select the scholarships to which you wish to apply. In addition, mail the supporting materials: printed confirmation page from the online application, personal statement, copy of Student Aid Report (SAR) available at www.fafsa.ed.gov and official transcript.
Exclusive: Visit www.UltimateScholarshipBook.com and enter code HA169220 for updates on this award.

(1693) • Dorothy Campbell Memorial Scholarship

Oregon Office of Student Access and Completion
1500 Valley River Drive, Suite 100, Eugene, OR 97401
Phone: 541-687-7422
Email: cheryl.a.connolly@state.or.us
https://oregonstudentaid.gov/

Purpose: To assist female Oregon high school students who have an interest in golf.
Eligibility: Applicants must be U.S. citizens or legal residents, Oregon residents and graduating high school seniors. They must have a GPA of 2.75 or higher and must have plans to attend a four-year Oregon college or university. Applicants must not owe a refund on an educational grant and must not be in default of an educational loan. Preference is given to applicants who are members of a high school golf team (if available). Selection is based on financial need.
Target applicant(s): High school students.
Minimum GPA: 2.75
Amount: Varies.
Number of awards: Varies.
Scholarship may be renewable.
Deadline: March 1.
How to apply: Applications are available online. An application form, personal essay, supporting materials and completion of the FAFSA are required.
Exclusive: Visit www.UltimateScholarshipBook.com and enter code OR169320 for updates on this award.

(1694) · Dorothy D. Greer Journalist of the Year Scholarship Competition

Colorado Student Media Association
Jack Kennedy, CSMA Executive Director, 9253 Sori Lane, Highlands Ranch, CO 80126
Phone: 303-550-4755
Email: jpkjournalism@gmail.com
http://colostudentmedia.com/
Purpose: To support outstanding young journalists.
Eligibility: Applicants must be Colorado high school seniors whose schools are members of the Colorado Student Media Association. Students must have worked on their yearbook or newspaper for at least two years. A GPA of 3.0 or higher is required. Selection criteria include neatness (10 percent), quality of work (40 percent), personal statement (20 percent), letters of recommendation (20 percent) and grades (10 percent).
Target applicant(s): High school students.
Minimum GPA: 3.0
Amount: Up to $2,000.
Number of awards: 1.
Deadline: February 15.
How to apply: Applications are available online. An application form, personal statement, transcript, three to four letters of recommendation, samples of published work and action photo are required.
Exclusive: Visit www.UltimateScholarshipBook.com and enter code CO169420 for updates on this award.

(1695) · Douvas Memorial Scholarship

Wyoming Department of Education
2300 Capitol Avenue, Hathaway Building, 2nd Floor, Cheyenne, WY 82002-0050
Phone: 307-777-3469
Email: laurie.hernandez@wyo.gov
http://edu.wyoming.gov
Purpose: To assist first generation Americans in obtaining higher education.
Eligibility: Applicants must have been born in the United States but have parents who were born outside the country. They must be high school seniors or between the ages of 18 and 22, and they must be Wyoming residents. They must attend a Wyoming community college or the University of Wyoming.
Target applicant(s): High school students. College students.
Amount: $500.
Number of awards: 1.
Deadline: May 5.
How to apply: Applications are available online.
Exclusive: Visit www.UltimateScholarshipBook.com and enter code WY169520 for updates on this award.

(1696) · Downeast Feline Fund

Maine Community Foundation
245 Main Street, Ellsworth, ME 04605
Phone: 207-667-9735
Email: jwarren@mainecf.org
http://www.mainecf.org
Purpose: To provide support to students from Maine who are pursuing veterinary education.
Eligibility: Applicants must be graduates of Maine high schools. They must be currently enrolled in a school of veterinary medicine. Preference will be given to students who are in their third or fourth year of school.
Target applicant(s): College students. Adult students.
Amount: Varies.
Number of awards: Varies.
Deadline: June 15.
How to apply: Applications are available online.
Exclusive: Visit www.UltimateScholarshipBook.com and enter code MA169620 for updates on this award.

(1697) · Dr. Alvin and Monica Saake Foundation Scholarship

Hawaii Community Foundation - Scholarships
827 Fort Street Mall, Honolulu, HI 96813
Phone: 888-731-3863
Email: scholarships@hcf-hawaii.org
https://www.hawaiicommunityfoundation.org
Purpose: To provide assistance for Hawaii students who are majoring in sports medicine and related fields.
Eligibility: Applicants must plan to attend an accredited college or university full-time, major in kinesiology, sports medicine, physical therapy, occupational therapy or a related field. They must have a minimum GPA of 2.7 and be college juniors, college seniors or graduate students.
Target applicant(s): College students. Graduate school students. Adult students.
Minimum GPA: 2.7
Amount: Varies.
Number of awards: Varies.
Deadline: January 31.
How to apply: To apply, register online, complete the online application and select the scholarships to which you wish to apply. In addition, mail the supporting materials: printed confirmation page from the online application, personal statement, copy of Student Aid Report (SAR) available at www.fafsa.ed.gov and official transcript.
Exclusive: Visit www.UltimateScholarshipBook.com and enter code HA169720 for updates on this award.

(1698) • Dr. and Mrs. Arthur F. Sullivan Fund

Connecticut Community Foundation Center for Philanthropy
43 Field Street, Waterbury, CT 06702
Phone: 203-753-1315
Email: scholarships@conncf.org
http://www.conncf.org
Purpose: To provide financial assistance to students who are entering or enrolled in medical school.
Eligibility: Applicants must be accepted to or enrolled in medical school. They must reside in the Connecticut Community Foundation's service area and demonstrate exemplary academic achievement.
Target applicant(s): College students. Graduate school students. Adult students.
Amount: Varies.
Number of awards: Varies.
Deadline: March 15.
How to apply: Applications are available online.
Exclusive: Visit www.UltimateScholarshipBook.com and enter code CO169820 for updates on this award.

(1699) • Dr. Edison and Sallie Miyawaki Scholarship Fund

Hawaii Community Foundation - Scholarships
827 Fort Street Mall, Honolulu, HI 96813
Phone: 888-731-3863
Email: scholarships@hcf-hawaii.org
https://www.hawaiicommunityfoundation.org
Purpose: To reward students with outstanding achievement in extracurricular activities.
Eligibility: Applicants must be Hawaii residents who plan to attend an accredited institution of higher learning. They must have a GPA between 2.5 and 3.0, demonstrate financial need and participate in an extracurricular sports program.
Target applicant(s): High school students. College students. Graduate school students. Adult students.
Minimum GPA: 2.5
Amount: Varies.
Number of awards: Varies.
Deadline: January 31.
How to apply: To apply, register online, complete the online application and select the scholarships to which you wish to apply. In addition, mail the supporting materials: printed confirmation page from the online application, personal statement, copy of Student Aid Report (SAR) available at www.fafsa.ed.gov and official transcript.
Exclusive: Visit www.UltimateScholarshipBook.com and enter code HA169920 for updates on this award.

(1700) • Dr. Hans and Clara Zimmerman Foundation Education Scholarship

Hawaii Community Foundation - Scholarships
827 Fort Street Mall, Honolulu, HI 96813
Phone: 888-731-3863
Email: scholarships@hcf-hawaii.org
https://www.hawaiicommunityfoundation.org
Purpose: To provide financial assistance to Hawaii students who want to study education.
Eligibility: Applicants major in education with an emphasis in teaching. They must have a GPA of 2.8 or higher, demonstrate good character and be full-time students. Preference is given to students of Hawaiian ethnicity and to students with at least two years of teaching experience. Applicants must discuss their teaching philosophies in their personal statement.
Target applicant(s): High school students. College students. Graduate school students. Adult students.
Minimum GPA: 2.8
Amount: Varies.
Number of awards: Varies.
Deadline: January 31.
How to apply: To apply, register online, complete the online application and select the scholarships to which you wish to apply. In addition, mail the supporting materials: printed confirmation page from the online application, personal statement, copy of Student Aid Report (SAR) available at www.fafsa.ed.gov and official transcript.
Exclusive: Visit www.UltimateScholarshipBook.com and enter code HA170020 for updates on this award.

(1701) • Dr. Hans and Clara Zimmerman Foundation Health Scholarships

Hawaii Community Foundation - Scholarships
827 Fort Street Mall, Honolulu, HI 96813
Phone: 888-731-3863
Email: scholarships@hcf-hawaii.org
https://www.hawaiicommunityfoundation.org
Purpose: To provide financial assistance to Hawaii students who want to study in health fields.
Eligibility: Applicants must plan to major in a health-related field other than sports medicine, non-clinical psychology or social work at a U.S. college or university. They must be full-time college juniors, college seniors or graduate students, and they must have a GPA of 3.0 or higher.
Target applicant(s): College students. Graduate school students. Adult students.
Minimum GPA: 3.0
Amount: Varies.
Number of awards: Varies.
Deadline: January 31.
How to apply: To apply, register online, complete the online application and select the scholarships to which you wish to apply. In addition, mail the supporting materials: printed confirmation page from the online application, personal statement, copy of Student Aid Report (SAR) available at www.fafsa.ed.gov and official transcript.
Exclusive: Visit www.UltimateScholarshipBook.com and enter code HA170120 for updates on this award.

(1702) • Dr. William S. Boyd Scholarship

Chiropractic Association of Louisiana
10636 Timberlake Drive, Baton Rouge, LA 70810
Phone: 225-769-5560
Email: lachiro@premier.net
http://www.cal-online.org
Purpose: To aid Louisiana chiropractic students.
Eligibility: Applicants must be Louisiana residents who are juniors or seniors at a CCE-accredited chiropractic college located in Louisiana. They must have a GPA of 2.75 or higher and must intend to work in Louisiana after graduation. Selection is based on the overall strength of the application.
Target applicant(s): College students. Adult students.
Minimum GPA: 2.75
Amount: Varies.
Number of awards: At least 1.
Deadline: June 30.

How to apply: Applications are available by request from the CAL. An application form, three letters of recommendation and an endorsement from a current member of the CAL are required.
Exclusive: Visit www.UltimateScholarshipBook.com and enter code CH170220 for updates on this award.

(1703) • Dunkin' Donuts Connecticut Scholarship

Dunkin' Donuts Connecticut Scholarship
Email: dunkindonuts@scholarshipamerica.org
https://www.dunkindonuts.com/scholarship/
Purpose: To provide financial assistance for well-rounded students.
Eligibility: Applicants must be high school seniors and Connecticut residents who excel in academics, demonstrate leadership and participate in school and community activities. They must plan to enroll at least half-time in a bachelor's degree, associate degree or certificate program at an accredited institution of higher learning.
Target applicant(s): High school students.
Amount: $1,000.
Number of awards: Varies.
Deadline: March 15.
How to apply: Applications are available from Dunkin' Donuts stores and high school guidance offices beginning March 1 of each year.
Exclusive: Visit www.UltimateScholarshipBook.com and enter code DU170320 for updates on this award.

(1704) • Dunkin' Donuts New Hampshire Scholarship

Dunkin' Donuts New Hampshire Scholarship
Email: studentdocs@nhcf.org
https://www.dunkindonuts.com/scholarship/
Purpose: To provide financial assistance for well-rounded students.
Eligibility: Applicants must be high school seniors and New Hampshire residents who excel in academics, demonstrate leadership and participate in school and community activities. They must plan to enroll at least half-time in a bachelor's degree, associate degree or certificate program at an accredited institution of higher learning.
Target applicant(s): High school students.
Amount: $1,000.
Number of awards: Varies.
Deadline: April 15.
How to apply: Applications are available from Dunkin' Donuts stores and high school guidance offices beginning March 1 of each year.
Exclusive: Visit www.UltimateScholarshipBook.com and enter code DU170420 for updates on this award.

(1705) • Dunkin' Donuts Rhode Island Scholarship

Dunkin' Donuts Rhode Island Scholarship
Email: dunkindonuts@scholarshipamerica.org
https://www.dunkindonuts.com/scholarship/
Purpose: To provide financial assistance for well-rounded students.
Eligibility: Applicants must be high school seniors and Rhode Island residents who excel in academics, demonstrate leadership and participate in school and community activities. They must plan to enroll at least half-time in a bachelor's degree, associate degree or certificate program at an accredited institution of higher learning.
Target applicant(s): High school students.
Amount: $1,000.
Number of awards: Varies.
Deadline: March 15.
How to apply: Applications are available from Dunkin' Donuts stores and high school guidance offices beginning March 1 of each year.
Exclusive: Visit www.UltimateScholarshipBook.com and enter code DU170520 for updates on this award.

(1706) • E.H. Marth Food Protection and Food Science Scholarship

WAFP Scholarship Committee
c/o Tera Montgomery, 1 University Plaza, Platteville, WI 53818
Phone: 608-342-6027
Email: montgomeryt@uwplatt.edu
http://www.wifoodprotection.org/scholarships.php
Purpose: To support students who are preparing for careers that are related to food or environmental sanitation.
Eligibility: Applicants must be Wisconsin residents who are enrolled at or have been accepted into a postsecondary institution that is either located in the state of Wisconsin or that has a reciprocal enrollment agreement with Wisconsin. They must be or plan to be enrolled full-time in an undergraduate academic program that is related to food science, environmental sanitation or dairy science. Selection is based on the overall strength of the application.
Target applicant(s): College students. Adult students.
Amount: $3,000.
Number of awards: 1.
Scholarship may be renewable.
Deadline: July 1.
How to apply: Applications are available online. An application form, official transcript and letter of recommendation are required.
Exclusive: Visit www.UltimateScholarshipBook.com and enter code WA170620 for updates on this award.

(1707) • Eagle Scout of the Year

American Legion, Department of Wisconsin
2930 American Legion Drive, P.O. Box 388, Portage, WI 53901-0388
Phone: 608-745-1090
Email: info@wilegion.org
http://www.wilegion.org
Purpose: To reward outstanding service as an Eagle Scout at the state level.
Eligibility: Applicants must demonstrate outstanding service in community, church and school and must be at least 15 years of age, in high school and either members of a troop chartered by the American Legion/Auxiliary or sons or grandsons of members of the American Legion/Auxiliary. Students must have received the Eagle Scout Award as well as the Boy Scout religious emblem. Scholarships may be used to attend a state-accredited college, university or other school above the high school level.
Target applicant(s): High school students.
Amount: $2,500-$10,000.
Number of awards: 4.
Deadline: Varies.
How to apply: Applications are available from the local Legion Post or from the Wisconsin American Legion Headquarters.
Exclusive: Visit www.UltimateScholarshipBook.com and enter code AM170720 for updates on this award.

(1708) • Early Bird Scholarship

Oregon Office of Student Access and Completion
1500 Valley River Drive, Suite 100, Eugene, OR 97401
Phone: 541-687-7422
Email: cheryl.a.connolly@state.or.us

https://oregonstudentaid.gov/
Purpose: To support students who submit their scholarship applications early.
Eligibility: Applicants must submit a completed scholarship application package by the early bird deadline. Students must enroll at least half-time in college. Applicants with error-free applications are entered in this drawing and chosen at random for the award.
Target applicant(s): College students. Adult students.
Amount: $1,000.
Number of awards: Varies.
Deadline: February 15.
How to apply: Applications are available online.
Exclusive: Visit www.UltimateScholarshipBook.com and enter code OR170820 for updates on this award.

(1709) • Early Childhood Educators Scholarship

Massachusetts Department of Higher Education
Office of Student Financial Assistance, 454 Broadway, Suite 200, Revere, MA 02151
Phone: 617-727-9420
Email: osfa@osfa.mass.edu
http://www.mass.edu/osfa/students/forstudents.asp
Purpose: To support the education of Massachusetts teachers employed in early childhood settings.
Eligibility: Applicants must be legal residents of Massachusetts who have worked as early childhood educators in the state for at least one year prior to receiving the scholarship. They must continue working in the profession while enrolled in school and upon completion of the degree. Students must be enrolled in Early Childhood Education or a related undergraduate program, and they cannot have any previously earned bachelor's degrees.
Target applicant(s): College students. Graduate school students. Adult students.
Amount: Varies.
Number of awards: Varies.
Scholarship may be renewable.
Deadline: June 1.
How to apply: Applications are available online.
Exclusive: Visit www.UltimateScholarshipBook.com and enter code MA170920 for updates on this award.

(1710) • Early College for ME

Early College for ME
Maine Community College System, 323 State Street, Augusta, ME 04330-7131
Phone: 207-629-4000
Email: mpour@mccs.me.edu
https://www.mccs.me.edu/
Purpose: To help high school students who are undecided about college.
Eligibility: Applicants must be in their junior year at one of the 74 Maine high schools participating in the program. The list of schools is online at http://www.earlycollege.me.edu/participating.html. Students must be Maine residents for at least one year prior to entering the first year of college and must have not yet made plans for college and yet be capable of succeeding at a community college. High schools may also take financial need into consideration when selecting students for the program as well as whether or not the student is the first one to attend college in their family. The program provides community college courses in the senior year of high school, as available, as well as financial aid for a one-year or two-year degree program at a Maine community college.
Target applicant(s): High school students.
Amount: Up to $2,000.
Number of awards: Varies.
Deadline: Varies, set by each school.
How to apply: Speak with your guidance counselor at your high school about entering the program.
Exclusive: Visit www.UltimateScholarshipBook.com and enter code EA171020 for updates on this award.

(1711) • Early Starters Award

British American Foundation of Texas
Email: info@baftx.org
https://www.baftx.org
Purpose: To set Texas students on the track of saving for college.
Eligibility: Applicants must be residents of Texas and attend middle school within the Texas education system. Students must have an "A" grade average and demonstrate financial need.
Target applicant(s): Junior high students or younger.
Minimum GPA: 3.4
Amount: $1,000.
Number of awards: 1.
Deadline: March 31.
How to apply: Applications are available online.
Exclusive: Visit www.UltimateScholarshipBook.com and enter code BR171120 for updates on this award.

(1712) • Ed and Charlotte Rodgers Scholarships

Alabama Road Builders Association Inc.
630 Adams Avenue, Montgomery, AL 36104
Phone: 334-832-4331
Email: hayley@alrba.org
http://www.alrba.org
Purpose: To support financially needy civil engineering students.
Eligibility: Applicants must be full-time civil engineering students who have completed their sophomore year of college. They must be in good standing academically, have a good GPA and demonstrate financial need. Selection is based on leadership skills, awards received and extracurricular involvements.
Target applicant(s): College students. Adult students.
Amount: Varies.
Number of awards: Varies.
Deadline: August 1.
How to apply: Applications are available online. An application form, a recent photo and a personal essay are required.
Exclusive: Visit www.UltimateScholarshipBook.com and enter code AL171220 for updates on this award.

(1713) • Edmund F. Maxwell Foundation Scholarship

Edmund F. Maxwell Foundation
P.O. Box 55548, Seattle, WA 98155-0548
Email: admin@maxwell.org
http://www.maxwell.org
Purpose: The scholarship is intended to assist high-achieving students who follow the ideals of Edmund F. Maxwell: ability, aptitude and citizenship.
Eligibility: Applicants must be from western Washington, plan to attend an accredited independent school that is primarily not tax-funded and have a minimum SAT score of 1200. Students must submit a FAFSA form and demonstrate financial need.
Target applicant(s): High school students.
Amount: Up to $5,000.

Number of awards: Varies.
Scholarship may be renewable.
Deadline: April 28.
How to apply: Applications are available online.
Exclusive: Visit www.UltimateScholarshipBook.com and enter code ED171320 for updates on this award.

(1714) • Educational Award/Graduating High School Female

New York State Women's 600 Club
Connie Canfield, Chairman, 1288 Scribner Hollow Road, East Jewett, NY 12424-5538
Phone: 518-589-5319
Email: cmc600ed@gmail.com
http://www.bowlny.com/
Purpose: To support New York graduating high school senior female bowlers as they embark on their college careers.
Eligibility: Applicant must be a member of a league or high school bowling team certified by USBC. Applicants must also have bowled at least 39 games in the current season or 18 games during the current high school season. Each applicant must also be sponsored by a current member of the New York State Women's 600 Bowling Club.
Target applicant(s): High school students.
Amount: Varies.
Number of awards: Varies.
Deadline: March 1.
How to apply: Applications are available online and consist of forms to be completed by the applicant, a league official, a school official and the NYSW 600 member sponsor.
Exclusive: Visit www.UltimateScholarshipBook.com and enter code NE171420 for updates on this award.

(1715) • Educational Excellence Scholarship

Kentucky Higher Education Assistance Authority
P.O. Box 798, Frankfort, KY 40602
Phone: 800-928-8926
Email: blane@kheaa.com
http://www.kheaa.com
Purpose: To reward outstanding Kentucky high school students.
Eligibility: Applicants must have a minimum 2.5 GPA, be graduating from eligible Kentucky high schools and meet high school graduation requirements. The scholarship amount is based on high school GPA and ACT composite score.
Target applicant(s): High school students.
Minimum GPA: 2.5
Amount: Up to $500.
Number of awards: Varies.
Scholarship may be renewable.
Deadline: Varies.
How to apply: High schools send eligible students' GPAs to the Kentucky Department of Education. There is no application for this award.
Exclusive: Visit www.UltimateScholarshipBook.com and enter code KE171520 for updates on this award.

(1716) • Educational Opportunity Fund (EOF) Grant

New Jersey Commission on Higher Education
P.O. Box 542, Trenton, NJ 08625
Phone: 609-292-4310
Email: meverett@che.state.nj.us
http://www.state.nj.us/highereducation
Purpose: To support underprivileged students in New Jersey.
Eligibility: Applicants must be able to show financial need and a background of family poverty, and they cannot exceed the established maximum income. They must be enrolled full-time in one of the participating public or private colleges in New Jersey, and they must have been residents of the state for at least 12 months prior to enrollment. Students pursuing a bachelor's degree cannot have any prior baccalaureate degrees, and students pursuing a two-year degree cannot have any previous associate's degrees. Applicants must not major in theology or divinity.
Target applicant(s): High school students. College students. Graduate school students. Adult students.
Amount: $200-$2,500.
Number of awards: Varies.
Scholarship may be renewable.
Deadline: Varies.
How to apply: Applications are available from campus EOF directors.
Exclusive: Visit www.UltimateScholarshipBook.com and enter code NE171620 for updates on this award.

(1717) • Educational Training Voucher Programs for Foster Youth

Foster Care to Success
21351 Gentry Drive, Suite 130, Sterling, VA 20166
Phone: 800-585-6188
Email: support@statevoucher.org
http://www.fc2success.org/programs/scholarships-and-grants/
Purpose: To support foster care students pursuing a higher education.
Eligibility: Applicants must have been in foster care for their 18th birthday and have aged out at that time, been adopted from foster care with the adoption finalized after their 16th birthday, or have their foster care case closed between the ages of 18 and 21. Students must be residents of Alabama, Arizona, Colorado, Maryland, Missouri, New York, North Carolina, Ohio or the District of Columbia. Students must be a U.S. citizen with assets worth less than $10,000. Applicants must be at least 17 but younger than 21 to apply for the first time. Students must have been accepted into a degree, certificate or other accredited program at a college, university, technical or vocational school.
Target applicant(s): High school students. College students. Adult students.
Amount: $5,000.
Number of awards: Varies.
Scholarship may be renewable.
Deadline: January 1.
How to apply: Applications are available online.
Exclusive: Visit www.UltimateScholarshipBook.com and enter code FO171720 for updates on this award.

(1718) • Edward L. Simeth Scholarships

Tool, Die and Machining Association of Wisconsin
W175 N11117 Stonewood Drive, Suite 204, Germantown, WI 53022
Phone: 262-532-2440
Email: toolmaker@TDMAW.org
https://tdmaw.org/education-careers/scholarships/
Purpose: To support Wisconsin students who are enrolled in a machine tool operations or tool and die training program at an accredited technical school.

Eligibility: Applicants must be Wisconsin residents, and they must have a high school diploma or GED. They must have completed at least one semester at an accredited technical school located in Wisconsin and be enrolled in a machine tool operations or tool and die program. Selection is based on the overall strength of the application.
Target applicant(s): College students. Adult students.
Minimum GPA: 3.0
Amount: Up to $500 per semester.
Number of awards: Varies.
Scholarship may be renewable.
Deadline: January 15, June 15.
How to apply: Applications are available online. An application form, an official transcript and two references are required.
Exclusive: Visit www.UltimateScholarshipBook.com and enter code TO171820 for updates on this award.

(1719) • Edward Payson and Bernice Piilani Irwin Scholarship

Hawaii Community Foundation - Scholarships
827 Fort Street Mall, Honolulu, HI 96813
Phone: 888-731-3863
Email: scholarships@hcf-hawaii.org
https://www.hawaiicommunityfoundation.org
Purpose: To provide financial assistance to Hawaii students who are pursuing careers in journalism.
Eligibility: Applicants must be college juniors, college seniors or graduate students majoring in journalism or communications. They must have a GPA of 2.75 or higher.
Target applicant(s): College students. Graduate school students. Adult students.
Minimum GPA: 2.75
Amount: Varies.
Number of awards: Varies.
Deadline: January 31.
How to apply: To apply, register online, complete the online application and select the scholarships to which you wish to apply. In addition, mail the supporting materials: printed confirmation page from the online application, personal statement, copy of Student Aid Report (SAR) available at www.fafsa.ed.gov and official transcript.
Exclusive: Visit www.UltimateScholarshipBook.com and enter code HA171920 for updates on this award.

(1720) • Eizo and Toyo Sakumoto Trust Scholarship

Hawaii Community Foundation - Scholarships
827 Fort Street Mall, Honolulu, HI 96813
Phone: 888-731-3863
Email: scholarships@hcf-hawaii.org
https://www.hawaiicommunityfoundation.org
Purpose: To assist Hawaiian students of Japanese ancestry.
Eligibility: Applicants must be Hawaii residents of primarily Japanese ancestry who were born in the state and who are a graduate level student at a college or university in Hawaii. They must have a GPA of 3.5 or higher and prove financial need.
Target applicant(s): Graduate school students. Adult students.
Minimum GPA: 3.5
Amount: Varies.
Number of awards: Varies.
Deadline: January 31.
How to apply: To apply, register online, complete the online application and select the scholarships to which you wish to apply. In addition, mail the supporting materials: printed confirmation page from the online application, personal statement, copy of Student Aid Report (SAR) available at www.fafsa.ed.gov and official transcript.
Exclusive: Visit www.UltimateScholarshipBook.com and enter code HA172020 for updates on this award.

(1721) • Eldon Roesler Scholarship

Wisconsin Agri-Business Association
2801 International Lane, Suite 105, Madison, WI 53704
Phone: 608-223-1111
Email: info@wiagribusiness.org
http://www.wiagribusiness.org
Purpose: To aid Wisconsin students who are preparing for careers in agriculture.
Eligibility: Applicants must be Wisconsin residents who have completed at least one year of undergraduate study at a Wisconsin postsecondary institution. They must be enrolled in or plan to pursue a career in an agriculture-related subject and must have a GPA of 2.75 or higher. Preference is given to the children of WASA members and the children of WASA company employees. Selection is based on academic achievement, leadership skills and financial need.
Target applicant(s): College students. Adult students.
Minimum GPA: 2.75
Amount: $1,000.
Number of awards: 4.
Deadline: April 30.
How to apply: Applications are available online. An application form, two letters of reference, a transcript and a personal essay are required.
Exclusive: Visit www.UltimateScholarshipBook.com and enter code WI172120 for updates on this award.

(1722) • Ellison Onizuka Memorial Scholarship Fund

Hawaii Community Foundation - Scholarships
827 Fort Street Mall, Honolulu, HI 96813
Phone: 888-731-3863
Email: scholarships@hcf-hawaii.org
https://www.hawaiicommunityfoundation.org
Purpose: To provide financial assistance to Hawaii students who plan to major in aerospace engineering.
Eligibility: Applicants must be graduating high school in the year of application and plan to pursue a degree in aerospace engineering or a related field. Students must have a GPA of 3.0, and their transcripts must list their SAT scores.
Target applicant(s): High school students.
Minimum GPA: 3.0
Amount: Varies.
Number of awards: Varies.
Deadline: January 31.
How to apply: To apply, register online, complete the online application and select the scholarships to which you wish to apply. In addition, mail the supporting materials: printed confirmation page from the online application, two letters of recommendation, personal statement, copy of Student Aid Report (SAR) available at www.fafsa.ed.gov and official transcript. The personal statement must describe participation in extracurricular activities, clubs and community service.
Exclusive: Visit www.UltimateScholarshipBook.com and enter code HA172220 for updates on this award.

(1723) • Emily M. Hewitt Memorial Scholarship

Calaveras Big Trees Association
P.O. Box 1196, Arnold, CA 95223
Phone: 209-795-3840
Email: info@bigtrees.org
http://www.bigtrees.org

Purpose: To support students who are committed to communicate a love of nature and an understanding of need to practice conservation.

Eligibility: Applicants must be enrolled full-time in an accredited California post-secondary educational institution and must have career goals that are related to communicating and interpreting nature's wonder. Students pursuing degrees in environmental protection, forestry, wildlife and fisheries biology, parks and recreation, park management, environmental law and public policy, environmental art and California history are encouraged to apply. Selection is based on dedication to the ideals of the scholarship and financial need.

Target applicant(s): High school students. College students. Graduate school students. Adult students.

Amount: $1,500.

Number of awards: 1.

Deadline: April 15.

How to apply: Student must submit a statement of personal and career goals, a resume (and portfolio if applicable) and transcripts of all college work completed to date. On the cover page, include your name, address, phone number and college major.

Exclusive: Visit www.UltimateScholarshipBook.com and enter code CA172320 for updates on this award.

(1724) • Engineering Foundation of Wisconsin Scholarship

Wisconsin Society of Professional Engineers
7044 South 13th Street, Oak Creek, WI 53154
Phone: 414-908-4950
Email: customercare@wspe.org
http://www.wspe.org

Purpose: To aid Wisconsin high school seniors who are planning to pursue education and careers in engineering.

Eligibility: Applicants must be current high school seniors who are U.S. citizens and Wisconsin residents. They must plan to enroll in an undergraduate engineering program at an ABET-accredited school and must intend to pursue careers in engineering after graduating. They must have a GPA of 3.0 or more and an ACT composite score of at least 24. Selection is based on GPA, ACT score, class rank, extracurricular involvement, honors, personal essay and any AP or college-level courses taken.

Target applicant(s): High school students.

Minimum GPA: 3.0

Amount: $2,000.

Number of awards: 2.

Deadline: Varies.

How to apply: Applications are available online. An application form, transcript and personal essay are required.

Exclusive: Visit www.UltimateScholarshipBook.com and enter code WI172420 for updates on this award.

(1725) • Engineers Foundation of Ohio General Fund Scholarship

Engineers Foundation of Ohio
400 South Fifth Street, Suite 300, Columbus, OH 43215-5430
Phone: 614-223-1177
Email: efo@ohioengineer.com
http://www.ohioengineer.com

Purpose: To aid Ohio engineering students.

Eligibility: Applicants must be U.S. citizens and residents of Ohio. They must be rising juniors or seniors enrolled full-time in an ABET-accredited engineering program that leads to the bachelor of science or its equivalent. They must have a GPA of 3.0 or higher on a 4-point scale. Selection is based on academic achievement, extracurricular involvements and financial need.

Target applicant(s): College students. Adult students.

Minimum GPA: 3.0

Amount: $1,000.

Number of awards: 1.

Deadline: January 15.

How to apply: Applications are available online. An application form, personal essay, faculty evaluation and transcript are required.

Exclusive: Visit www.UltimateScholarshipBook.com and enter code EN172520 for updates on this award.

(1726) • Epsilon Sigma Alpha

North Carolina Division of Vocational Rehabilitation Services
2801 Mail Service Center, Raleigh, NC 27699-2801
Phone: 888-234-6400
Email: jterrell@ncbar.org
http://www.cfnc.org

Purpose: To provide financial assistance to students who want to work with exceptional children.

Eligibility: Applicants must be enrolled in an accredited college or university, either at the undergraduate level or as a North Carolina teacher seeking training, and must be training to work with special needs children up to the age of 21 in an educational setting. They must agree to teach at a North Carolina public school for at least one year after graduation.

Target applicant(s): College students. Graduate school students. Adult students.

Amount: $500-$2,500.

Number of awards: Varies.

Deadline: Varies.

How to apply: Applications are available online.

Exclusive: Visit www.UltimateScholarshipBook.com and enter code NO172620 for updates on this award.

(1727) • ERC Eco Scholarship Fund

Environmental Research Center
3111 Camino Del Rio North, Suite 400, San Diego, CA 92108
Phone: 619-500-3090
http://www.erc501c3.org

Purpose: To support graduating high school seniors residing in California who intend to major in an environmental studies program.

Eligibility: Applicants must be U.S. citizens and residents of California who are graduating high school seniors. Students must be accepted to a California college or university and intend to pursue a degree in environmental studies. A minimum high school GPA of 3.25 is required and applicants must have completed at least one high school science class in addition to the minimum amount required for graduation.

Target applicant(s): High school students.

Minimum GPA: 3.25

Amount: $1,000.

Number of awards: Varies.

Deadline: Ongoing.

How to apply: Applications are available online.

Exclusive: Visit www.UltimateScholarshipBook.com and enter code EN172720 for updates on this award.

(1728) • Eskridge Auto Group Free Ride

Eskridge Auto Group
5307 South Division, Guthrie, OK 73044
http://www.eskridgechevy.com/free_ride
Purpose: To reward hard working Oklahoma students.
Eligibility: Applicants must be nominated for the award. Students must be high school seniors with a minimum 3.25 grade point average. Applicants must complete an interview if chosen as a finalist.
Target applicant(s): High school students.
Minimum GPA: 3.25
Amount: $25,000.
Number of awards: Varies.
Deadline: January 7.
How to apply: Applications are available online.
Exclusive: Visit www.UltimateScholarshipBook.com and enter code ES172820 for updates on this award.

(1729) • Esther Kanagawa Memorial Art Scholarship

Hawaii Community Foundation - Scholarships
827 Fort Street Mall, Honolulu, HI 96813
Phone: 888-731-3863
Email: scholarships@hcf-hawaii.org
https://www.hawaiicommunityfoundation.org
Purpose: To provide financial assistance to Hawaii students who are majoring in fine arts.
Eligibility: Applicants must be current high schools seniors who plan to major in fine arts at an accredited college or university. They must have a GPA of 2.7 or higher and demonstrate financial need and good character.
Target applicant(s): High school students.
Minimum GPA: 2.7
Amount: Varies.
Number of awards: Varies.
Deadline: January 31.
How to apply: To apply, register online, complete the online application and select the scholarships to which you wish to apply. In addition, mail the supporting materials: printed confirmation page from the online application, personal statement, copy of Student Aid Report (SAR) available at www.fafsa.ed.gov and official transcript.
Exclusive: Visit www.UltimateScholarshipBook.com and enter code HA172920 for updates on this award.

(1730) • Excellence in Service Award

Florida's Office of Campus Volunteers
Florida Campus Compact, 1801 Miccosukee Commons Drive, Suite 200, Tallahassee, FL 32308
Phone: 850-488-7782
Email: info@floridacompact.org
http://www.floridacompact.org/awards/
Purpose: To reward students who perform outstanding acts of service in their communities.
Eligibility: Applicants must be full-time undergraduate students at an accredited public or private institution of higher education within the state of Florida.
Target applicant(s): College students. Adult students.
Amount: Varies.
Number of awards: Varies.
Deadline: July 21.
How to apply: Applications are available online.
Exclusive: Visit www.UltimateScholarshipBook.com and enter code FL173020 for updates on this award.

(1731) • Exemption for Highest Ranking High School Graduate

Texas Higher Education Coordinating Board
1200 East Anderson Lane, Austin, TX 78752
Phone: 512-427-6101
Email: pamela.harris@thecb.state.tx.us
http://www.collegeforalltexans.com/
Purpose: To support students who are the top graduate of their high school class.
Eligibility: Applicant must be a resident, nonresident or foreign student of Texas and intending on attending a Texas public college or university. Students must provide documentation of their high school ranking. Applicants will receive full tuition for their first year of college.
Target applicant(s): High school students.
Amount: Varies.
Number of awards: Varies.
Deadline: Varies.
How to apply: Applications are available online.
Exclusive: Visit www.UltimateScholarshipBook.com and enter code TE173120 for updates on this award.

(1732) • Exemption for Texas Veterans (Hazelwood Exemption)

Texas Higher Education Coordinating Board
1200 East Anderson Lane, Austin, TX 78752
Phone: 512-427-6101
Email: pamela.harris@thecb.state.tx.us
http://www.collegeforalltexans.com/
Purpose: To support qualified veterans with educational benefits at public institutions of higher education in Texas.
Eligibility: Applicants must be a qualified veteran, spouse or dependent child to qualify for this exemption. Students must have been accepted to a Texas public college or university. Applicants must provide proof of GI Bill benefits. Students must enroll in the Hazlewood On-Line database as part of the exemption process.
Target applicant(s): College students. Adult students.
Amount: Up to 150 semester hours.
Number of awards: 1.
Scholarship may be renewable.
Deadline: Varies.
How to apply: Applications are available online.
Exclusive: Visit www.UltimateScholarshipBook.com and enter code TE173220 for updates on this award.

(1733) • Exemption from Tuition Fees for Dependents of Kentucky Veterans

Kentucky Department of Veterans Affairs
Attn.: Tuition Waiver Coordinator, 321 West Main Street, Suite 390, Louisville, KY 40202
Phone: 502-595-4447
Email: barbaraa.hale@ky.gov
https://veterans.ky.gov/Benefits/Pages/education.aspx
Purpose: To support the families of Kentucky veterans.
Eligibility: Applicants must be children, stepchildren, adopted children, spouses or unremarried widows or widowers of qualifying Kentucky

veterans. The veteran must have died on active duty or as a result of a service-connected disability, be 100 percent disabled from service, be totally disabled with wartime service or be deceased and have served during wartime. Children of veterans must be 26 years of age or younger.
Target applicant(s): High school students. College students. Adult students.
Amount: Full tuition.
Number of awards: Varies.
Deadline: Varies.
How to apply: Applications are available online. An application form, birth or marriage certificate, veteran's discharge certificate, death certificate or disability award letter and evidence of Kentucky residency are required.
Exclusive: Visit www.UltimateScholarshipBook.com and enter code KE173320 for updates on this award.

(1734) • F. Koehnen Ltd. Scholarship Fund

Hawaii Community Foundation - Scholarships
827 Fort Street Mall, Honolulu, HI 96813
Phone: 888-731-3863
Email: scholarships@hcf-hawaii.org
https://www.hawaiicommunityfoundation.org
Purpose: To provide financial assistance to students whose parents or grandparents are employed in Hawaiian retail establishments.
Eligibility: Applicants must be Hawaii high school graduates with a GPA of 2.0 or higher. They must be children or grandchildren of retail employees on the island of Hawaii.
Target applicant(s): High school students. College students. Graduate school students. Adult students.
Minimum GPA: 2.0
Amount: Varies.
Number of awards: Varies.
Deadline: January 31.
How to apply: To apply, register online, complete the online application and select the scholarships to which you wish to apply. In addition, mail the supporting materials: printed confirmation page from the online application, personal statement, copy of Student Aid Report (SAR) available at www.fafsa.ed.gov and official transcript.
Exclusive: Visit www.UltimateScholarshipBook.com and enter code HA173420 for updates on this award.

(1735) • Family District 1 Scholarships

American Hellenic Education Progressive Association
1909 Q Street NW, Suite 500, Washington, DC 20009
Phone: 202-232-6300
Email: ahepa@ahepa.org
https://ahepa.org/Education-Scholarships.htm
Purpose: To provide financial assistance for those pursuing higher education.
Eligibility: Applicants must be graduating seniors, high school graduates or current undergraduate or graduate students who plan to attend a college or university full-time during the calendar year of application. They must be residents of Alabama, Georgia, Mississippi, South Carolina, Tennessee or Florida.
Target applicant(s): High school students. College students. Graduate school students. Adult students.
Amount: Varies.
Number of awards: Varies.
Deadline: April 15.
How to apply: Applications are available online. The current application must be used and must be sent by certified mail and return receipt requested.
Exclusive: Visit www.UltimateScholarshipBook.com and enter code AM173520 for updates on this award.

(1736) • Federal Chafee Educational and Training Grant

Oregon Office of Student Access and Completion
1500 Valley River Drive, Suite 100, Eugene, OR 97401
Phone: 541-687-7422
Email: cheryl.a.connolly@state.or.us
https://oregonstudentaid.gov/
Purpose: To provide financial assistance to students who have been in foster care.
Eligibility: Applicants must be in foster care or have been in foster care for at least six months after their 14th birthday or be adopted from the foster care system after age 16. Funding is provided on a first come, first served basis. The deadlines are: August 1 for the fall term, November 1 for the winter term, February 1 for the spring term and May 1 for the summer term.
Target applicant(s): High school students. College students. Graduate school students.
Amount: Up to $5,000.
Number of awards: Varies.
Scholarship may be renewable.
Deadline: August 1, November 1, February 1, May 1.
How to apply: Applications are available online.
Exclusive: Visit www.UltimateScholarshipBook.com and enter code OR173620 for updates on this award.

(1737) • Fellowship on Women and Public Policy

Center for Women in Government and Civil Society
University at Albany, SUNY, 135 Western Avenue, Draper Hall 302, Albany, NY 12222
Phone: 518-442-3900
http://www.cwig.albany.edu
Purpose: To encourage New York state graduate students to pursue jobs in public policy.
Eligibility: Students must be enrolled in a graduate program at an accredited college or university in New York and have completed at least 12 credits before applying but not be scheduled to graduate before the internship, and must have minimum 3-5 years work/internship experience and minimum 3.0 GPA. Applicants must demonstrate an interest in improving the status of women and underrepresented populations.
Target applicant(s): Graduate school students. Adult students.
Minimum GPA: 3.0
Amount: $10,000 stipend and tuition assistance.
Number of awards: Varies.
Deadline: Varies.
How to apply: Applications are available online.
Exclusive: Visit www.UltimateScholarshipBook.com and enter code CE173720 for updates on this award.

(1738) • Fields of Learning Scholarship

Fields of Learning
9357 Sperry Road, Kirtland Hills, OH 44060
Phone: 440-256-3757
http://www.fieldsoflearning.org

Purpose: To encourage students who wish to pursue education following high school and have an interest in high school football.
Eligibility: Applicants must write an essay of 700 to 1,500 words based on a true story about what the student has learned related to high school football. Students must intend to use the funds for post high school education within one year of graduating high school. Applicants can be in grades nine through twelve. Students do not have to be on the football team to apply.
Target applicant(s): High school students.
Amount: Varies.
Number of awards: Varies.
Deadline: March 31.
How to apply: Applications are available online.
Exclusive: Visit www.UltimateScholarshipBook.com and enter code FI173820 for updates on this award.

(1739) • First Generation Matching Grant Program

Florida Department of Education
Office of Student Financial Assistance, State Scholarship and Grant Programs, 325 West Gaines Street, Suite 1314, Tallahassee, FL 32399-0400
Phone: 888-827-2004
Email: osfa@fldoe.org
http://www.floridastudentfinancialaid.org
Purpose: To help Florida undergraduate students with financial need who are enrolled in state universities and whose parents have not earned bachelor's degrees.
Eligibility: Applicants must submit applications and the Free Application for Federal Student Aid (FAFSA). Each university determines its own deadline.
Target applicant(s): High school students. College students. Adult students.
Amount: Varies.
Number of awards: Varies.
Deadline: Varies.
How to apply: Applications are at the financial aid offices of state universities.
Exclusive: Visit www.UltimateScholarshipBook.com and enter code FL173920 for updates on this award.

(1740) • First State Manufactured Housing Association Scholarship

Department of Education - School Supports
The Townsend Building, 401 Federal Street, Suite 2, Dover, DE 19901-3639
Phone: 800-292-7935
Email: dhec@doe.k12.de.us
http://www.doe.k12.de.us/page/316
Purpose: To provide assistance to residents of manufactured homes.
Eligibility: Applicants must be legal residents of Delaware. They may be high school seniors or former graduates seeking higher education. They must have lived in a manufactured home for at least one year prior to application. They may enroll in any accredited program full- or part-time. Selection criteria include scholastic achievement, financial need, essay and recommendations.
Target applicant(s): High school students. College students. Adult students.
Amount: Up to $1,000.
Number of awards: Up to 4.
Deadline: March 6.
How to apply: Applications are available online. An application form, essay, FAFSA and transcript are required.
Exclusive: Visit www.UltimateScholarshipBook.com and enter code DE174020 for updates on this award.

(1741) • Florida Bright Futures Scholarship Program

Florida Department of Education
Office of Student Financial Assistance, State Scholarship and Grant Programs, 325 West Gaines Street, Suite 1314, Tallahassee, FL 32399-0400
Phone: 888-827-2004
Email: osfa@fldoe.org
http://www.floridastudentfinancialaid.org
Purpose: Lottery-funded scholarships are awarded to Florida high school seniors as reward for academic achievements and to assist with postsecondary education.
Eligibility: Applicants must earn a Florida high school diploma or equivalent, have not been found guilty or pled no contest to a felony charge and meet the award's academic requirements. Applicants must also be Florida residents, U.S. citizens or eligible noncitizens and be accepted by and enrolled in an eligible Florida public or private college or vocational school at least quarter time. Application must be completed during the senior year of high school.
Target applicant(s): High school students.
Amount: Varies.
Number of awards: Varies.
Deadline: High school graduation.
How to apply: Apply by completing the Florida Financial Aid Application. The application is available online at www.floridastudentfinancialaid.org or from your high school guidance counselor.
Exclusive: Visit www.UltimateScholarshipBook.com and enter code FL174120 for updates on this award.

(1742) • Florida Engineers in Construction Scholarship

Florida Engineering Society
125 South Gadsden Street, Tallahassee, FL 32301
Phone: 850-224-7121
Email: allen@fleng.org
http://www.fleng.org
Purpose: To aid Florida engineering majors who are interested in careers in construction.
Eligibility: Applicants must be undergraduate juniors or seniors enrolled in an accredited degree program in engineering at a Florida university. They must have a GPA of at least 3.0 on a 4.0 scale and must have plans to pursue a career in construction. Selection is based on the overall strength of the application.
Target applicant(s): College students. Adult students.
Minimum GPA: 3.0
Amount: $1,000.
Number of awards: 1.
Deadline: February 11.
How to apply: Applications are available online. An application form, a transcript and one letter of recommendation are required.
Exclusive: Visit www.UltimateScholarshipBook.com and enter code FL174220 for updates on this award.

(1743) • Florida Governor's Black History Month Essay Contest

Volunteer Florida
Black History Month Committee, 3800 Esplanade Way, Suite 180, Tallahassee, FL 32311
Phone: 850-414-7400
Email: jovita@volunteerflorida.org
http://www.floridablackhistory.com
Purpose: To promote Black History Month.
Eligibility: Applicants must be Florida students in grades 4-12 and compose an essay on the given topic. Winners receive a four-year full scholarship to a Florida state college or university and a trip to the Governor's Black History Month celebration.
Target applicant(s): Junior high students or younger. High school students.
Amount: Full tuition.
Number of awards: 3.
Scholarship may be renewable.
Deadline: March 2.
How to apply: Applications are available online. A parental waiver, essay and student's contact information are required.
Exclusive: Visit www.UltimateScholarshipBook.com and enter code VO174320 for updates on this award.

(1744) • Florida Oratorical Contest

American Legion, Department of Florida
Elizabeth Douglas, Programs Director, 1912A Lee Road, Orlando, FL 32810
Phone: 800-393-3378
Email: mail@floridalegion.org
http://www.floridalegion.org
Purpose: To enhance high school students' experience with and understanding of the U.S. Constitution. The contest will help develop students' leadership skills and civic appreciation, as well as the ability to deliver thoughtful, insightful orations regarding U.S. citizenship and its inherent responsibilities.
Eligibility: Applicants must be high school students under the age of 20 who are U.S. citizens or legal residents and residents of the state. Students first give an oration within their state and winners compete at the national level. The oration must be related to the Constitution of the United States focusing on the duties and obligations citizens have to the government. It must be in English and be between eight and ten minutes. There is also an assigned topic which is posted on the website, and it should be between three and five minutes.
Target applicant(s): Junior high students or younger. High school students.
Amount: $500-$18,000.
Number of awards: Varies.
Deadline: Varies.
How to apply: Applications are available by contacting the local American Legion Post.
Exclusive: Visit www.UltimateScholarshipBook.com and enter code AM174420 for updates on this award.

(1745) • Florida Student Assistance Grant Program

Florida Department of Education
Office of Student Financial Assistance, State Scholarship and Grant Programs, 325 West Gaines Street, Suite 1314, Tallahassee, FL 32399-0400
Phone: 888-827-2004
Email: osfa@fldoe.org
http://www.floridastudentfinancialaid.org
Purpose: To help degree-seeking, Florida resident, undergraduate students who have financial need and who are enrolled in participating postsecondary institutions.
Eligibility: There are three student financial aid programs: The Florida Public Student Assistance Grant is for students who attend state universities and public community colleges. The Florida Private Student Assistance Grant is for students who attend eligible private, non-profit, four-year colleges and universities. The Florida Postsecondary Student Assistance Grant is for students who attend eligible degree-granting private colleges and universities that are ineligible under the Florida Private Student Assistance Grant. High school students in the top 20 percent of their classes receive priority funding.
Target applicant(s): High school students. College students. Adult students.
Amount: At least $200.
Number of awards: Varies.
Scholarship may be renewable.
Deadline: Varies.
How to apply: Applicants must submit the Free Application for Federal Student Aid (FAFSA).
Exclusive: Visit www.UltimateScholarshipBook.com and enter code FL174520 for updates on this award.

(1746) • Ford Opportunity Scholarship

Oregon Office of Student Access and Completion
1500 Valley River Drive, Suite 100, Eugene, OR 97401
Phone: 541-687-7422
Email: cheryl.a.connolly@state.or.us
https://oregonstudentaid.gov/
Purpose: To assist Oregon undergraduate students who are single parents.
Eligibility: Applicants must be U.S. citizens or legal residents, high school graduates or GED recipients and Oregon residents who are single heads of household with custody of one or more dependent children. They must be supporting their child(ren) without the aid of a domestic partner. Applicants must have a minimum 3.0 GPA or 2650 GED score and must be attending or planning to attend a non-profit Oregon college or community college on a full-time basis by fall of the application year. Applicants who owe an educational loan grant or who have defaulted student loans are ineligible, as are those who already hold a bachelor's degree. Selection is based on financial need.
Target applicant(s): High school students. College students. Adult students.
Minimum GPA: 3.0
Amount: Varies.
Number of awards: Varies.
Deadline: March 1.
How to apply: Applications are available online. An application form, proof of GPA or GED score and completion of the FAFSA are required.
Exclusive: Visit www.UltimateScholarshipBook.com and enter code OR174620 for updates on this award.

(1747) • Ford Scholars Scholarship

Oregon Office of Student Access and Completion
1500 Valley River Drive, Suite 100, Eugene, OR 97401
Phone: 541-687-7422
Email: cheryl.a.connolly@state.or.us
https://oregonstudentaid.gov/

Purpose: To assist Oregon students who plan to pursue a bachelor's degree.
Eligibility: Applicants must be U.S. citizens or legal residents. They must be Oregon or Siskiyou County, California residents who are high school graduates, GED recipients or community college students who will be transferring to an Oregon or California four-year college with junior standing during the fall of the application year. They must have a GPA of 3.0 or higher or a GED score of 2650 or higher, have plans to earn a bachelor's degree at a non-profit Oregon or California institution and be enrolled as a full-time student no later than the fall of the application year. They must owe no educational grant refund money and must have no defaulted student loans. Applicants who have earned a bachelor's degree previously are ineligible. Selection is based on financial need.
Target applicant(s): High school students. College students. Adult students.
Minimum GPA: 3.0
Amount: Varies.
Number of awards: Varies.
Scholarship may be renewable.
Deadline: March 1.
How to apply: Applications are available online. An application form, proof of GPA or GED score and completion of the FAFSA are required.
Exclusive: Visit www.UltimateScholarshipBook.com and enter code OR174720 for updates on this award.

(1748) • Foster Child Grant Program

Massachusetts Department of Higher Education
Office of Student Financial Assistance, 454 Broadway, Suite 200, Revere, MA 02151
Phone: 617-727-9420
Email: osfa@osfa.mass.edu
http://www.mass.edu/osfa/students/forstudents.asp
Purpose: To assist children who have lived in foster homes in obtaining higher education.
Eligibility: Applicants must be placed in the custody of the Department of Social Services and be permanent residents of the state of Massachusetts. Students must be younger than 25 years of age at the start of the academic year and apply for financial aid.
Target applicant(s): High school students. College students. Graduate school students.
Amount: Up to $6,000.
Number of awards: Varies.
Scholarship may be renewable.
Deadline: Varies.
How to apply: Applications are available by phone from the Massachusetts Office of Student Financial Assistance or from your social worker.
Exclusive: Visit www.UltimateScholarshipBook.com and enter code MA174820 for updates on this award.

(1749) • Four-year or Bachelor's Degree Program

New Hampshire Charitable Foundation
37 Pleasant Street, Concord, NH 03301-4005
Phone: 603-225-6641
Email: info@nhcf.org
https://www.nhcf.org/how-can-we-help-you/
Purpose: To support New Hampshire students who are seeking a four-year degree program.
Eligibility: Applicants must be New Hampshire residents who are enrolling in a four-year degree program. Students must prove financial need. Selection is based on need, academic merit, community service, extracurricular activities and work experience.
Target applicant(s): College students. Adult students.
Amount: $250-$7,500.
Deadline: April 13.
How to apply: Applications are available online.
Exclusive: Visit www.UltimateScholarshipBook.com and enter code NE174920 for updates on this award.

(1750) • Frances A. Mays Scholarship Award

Virginia Association for Health, Physical Education, Recreation and Dance
7812 Falling Hill Terrace, Chesterfield, VA 23832
Phone: 804-304-1768
Email: Toni.BrownBerry@lcps.org
http://www.vahperd.org
Purpose: To aid students majoring in fields related to physical education.
Eligibility: Applicants must be seniors at Virginia colleges or universities pursuing a degree in health, physical education, recreation or dance and be members of VAHPERD and AAHPERD. Students must demonstrate high ideals, good scholarship and professional ethics. Applicants must be nominated by their schools.
Target applicant(s): College students. Adult students.
Minimum GPA: 2.8
Amount: Varies.
Number of awards: 1.
Deadline: October 1.
How to apply: Applications are available from your university's VAHPERD representative. An application form and letter of reference are required.
Exclusive: Visit www.UltimateScholarshipBook.com and enter code VI175020 for updates on this award.

(1751) • Frances Lansbury Memorial Award/Adult Female Learner

New York State Women's 600 Club
Connie Canfield, Chairman, 1288 Scribner Hollow Road, East Jewett, NY 12424-5538
Phone: 518-589-5319
Email: cmc600ed@gmail.com
http://www.bowlny.com/
Purpose: To promote the continuing education of a New York woman.
Eligibility: Applicant must be 20 years old by March 1 and be continuing her education in a school of higher education. She must also be sponsored by a current New York State Women's 600 Bowling Club member.
Target applicant(s): College students. Graduate school students. Adult students.
Amount: Varies.
Number of awards: 1.
Deadline: March 1.
How to apply: Applications are available online and consist of forms to be completed by the applicant, the sponsor and the employer or school official.
Exclusive: Visit www.UltimateScholarshipBook.com and enter code NE175120 for updates on this award.

(1752) · Frank del Olmo Memorial Scholarship

CCNMA: Latino Journalists of California
ASU Cronkite School of Journalism, 725 Arizona Avenue, Suite 404, Santa Monica, CA 90401-1734
Phone: 424-229-9482
Email: ccnmainfo@ccnma.org
http://ccnma.org/scholarships-and-awards/
Purpose: To assist California Latino college students who demonstrate a desire to pursue a career in journalism.
Eligibility: Applicants must be Latino, be either California residents or attending California schools and have an interest in pursuing a journalism career. An interview is required. Financial need, academic achievement and community involvement are also considered.
Target applicant(s): High school students. College students. Adult students.
Amount: $500-$1,000.
Number of awards: Varies.
Deadline: June 15.
How to apply: Applications are available online.
Exclusive: Visit www.UltimateScholarshipBook.com and enter code CC175220 for updates on this award.

(1753) · Frank McHenry Memorial Scholarship

Eastern Region USA Roller Skating
30 Wyndham Road, Voorhees, NJ 08043
Phone: 610-328-1314
Email: dwalsh999@comcast.net
http://www.erusars.org/
Purpose: To support Eastern Regional artistic roller skaters who plan to continue their education beyond high school.
Eligibility: Applicants must be high school seniors who are involved with competitive artistic roller skating in the New Jersey, Pennsylvania or Delaware. Students must be members of a USA Roller Skating club and be registered to compete in the Eastern Regional Championships. Selection is based on skating participation and success, academic achievement and financial need.
Target applicant(s): High school students.
Amount: $1,000.
Number of awards: 1.
Deadline: June 14.
How to apply: Applications are available online.
Exclusive: Visit www.UltimateScholarshipBook.com and enter code EA175320 for updates on this award.

(1754) · Frank O'Bannon Grant Program

State Student Assistance Commission of Indiana
W462 Indiana Government Center South, 402 West Washington Street, Indianapolis, IN 46204
Phone: 888-528-4719
Email: grants@ssaci.state.in.us
http://www.in.gov/che/
Purpose: To aid Indiana students in attending eligible postsecondary schools.
Eligibility: Applicants must be high school graduates and attend or plan to attend eligible Indiana colleges or universities full-time.
Target applicant(s): High school students. College students. Adult students.
Amount: Varies.
Number of awards: Varies.
Deadline: March 10.
How to apply: Complete the Free Application for Federal Student Aid (FAFSA).
Exclusive: Visit www.UltimateScholarshipBook.com and enter code ST175420 for updates on this award.

(1755) · Fresh Start Scholarship

Fresh Start Scholarship Foundation, Inc.
P.O. Box 7784, Wilmington, DE 19803
Phone: 302-397-3440
Email: FSSF@freshstartscholarship.org
http://www.freshstartscholarship.org
Purpose: To help women who are returning to school.
Eligibility: Applicants should be women at least 20 years old with financial need who have a high school diploma or G.E.D., have had at least a two year break in education either after finishing high school or during college studies and are enrolled in a Delaware college in a two- or four-year degree program at the undergraduate level. Applicants should have at least a C average if already in college.
Target applicant(s): College students. Adult students.
Minimum GPA: 2.0
Amount: Varies.
Number of awards: Varies.
Deadline: Varies.
How to apply: Applications are available online or by mail and include a personal statement. A social service agency or college representative should recommend applicants.
Exclusive: Visit www.UltimateScholarshipBook.com and enter code FR175520 for updates on this award.

(1756) · Friends of the California State Fair Scholarship Program

California State Fair
1600 Exposition Boulevard, Sacramento, CA 95815
Phone: 916-263-3247
Email: scholarship@calexpo.com
http://www.castatefair.org/scholarship/
Purpose: To reward and motivate well-rounded, high-achieving California students.
Eligibility: Applicants must be enrolled or plan to enroll in a four-year accredited California institution of higher learning. They must have a GPA of 3.0 or higher and have a valid California ID.
Target applicant(s): High school students. College students. Graduate school students. Adult students.
Minimum GPA: 3.0
Amount: Up to $5,000.
Number of awards: Varies.
Deadline: February 28.
How to apply: Applications are available online.
Exclusive: Visit www.UltimateScholarshipBook.com and enter code CA175620 for updates on this award.

(1757) · Future Teachers Scholarship

Oklahoma State Regents for Higher Education/Future Teachers Scholarship
655 Research Parkway, Suite 200, Oklahoma City, OK 73104
Phone: 800-858-1840
Email: studentinfo@osrhe.edu
https://secure.okcollegestart.org/Financial_Aid_Planning/Scholarships/Career_Scholarships/Future_Teachers_Scholarship_Program.aspx

Purpose: To encourage students to become teachers in critical teacher shortage areas in Oklahoma public schools.
Eligibility: Applicants must be residents of Oklahoma who have been nominated by their institution on the basis of rank in the top 15 percent of high school class, rank in the top 15 percent of students in SAT or ACT scores, admission to an education program at an accredited Oklahoma institution or high academic achievement in undergraduate coursework. Applicants must maintain a GPA of 2.5 or higher and agree to teach in a shortage area in an Oklahoma public school for at least three years after graduation and licensure.
Target applicant(s): High school students. College students. Adult students.
Minimum GPA: 2.5
Amount: Up to $1,500.
Number of awards: 125.
Deadline: Varies.
How to apply: Applications are submitted by the nominating institution.
Exclusive: Visit www.UltimateScholarshipBook.com and enter code OK175720 for updates on this award.

(1758) · Garden Club of Ohio Inc. Scholarships

Garden Club of Ohio Inc.
Aggie Goss, GCO Scholarship Chairman, 8677 Hollis Lane, Brecksville, OH 44141
Phone: 440-526-6313
Email: aggiegoss@yahoo.com
http://www.gardenclubofohio.org
Purpose: To support Ohio students pursuing higher education in subjects related to plant science, environmental science, horticulture, floriculture, city planning and wildlife.
Eligibility: Applicants must be residents of Ohio and must be enrolled in a postsecondary degree program related to environmental science, plant science, horticulture, floriculture, city planning or wildlife. They must be rising undergraduate juniors, undergraduate seniors or graduate students and have a GPA of 3.25 or higher. Selection is based on the overall strength of the application.
Target applicant(s): College students. Graduate school students. Adult students.
Minimum GPA: 3.25
Amount: Varies.
Number of awards: Varies.
Deadline: February 1.
How to apply: Applications are available online. An application form, transcript, personal statement, financial aid statement and three letters of recommendation are required.
Exclusive: Visit www.UltimateScholarshipBook.com and enter code GA175820 for updates on this award.

(1759) · GEAR UP Idaho Scholarship 2

Idaho State Board of Education
P.O. Box 83720 , Boise, ID 83720-0037
Phone: 208-334-2270
Email: Joy.Miller@osbe.idaho.gov
https://boardofed.idaho.gov/scholarships/
Purpose: Monetary assistance is provided to Idaho resident high school students for freshman expenses at Idaho colleges or universities.
Eligibility: Applicants must have graduated from an Idaho high school, be entering freshmen at an eligible Idaho college or university, be residents of Idaho and have a minimum 3.0 GPA or minimum ACT score of 20. Applicants must also be younger than 22 years old and complete at least 12 credits per semester with a minimum 2.5 GPA to remain eligible for renewal.
Target applicant(s): High school students.
Minimum GPA: 3.0
Amount: Varies.
Number of awards: Varies.
Scholarship may be renewable.
Deadline: March 1.
How to apply: Contact eligible college or university financial aid office.
Exclusive: Visit www.UltimateScholarshipBook.com and enter code ID175920 for updates on this award.

(1760) · General Assembly Merit Scholarship

Tennessee Student Assistance Corporation
404 James Robertson Parkway, Suite 1510, Parkway Towers, Nashville, TN 37243
Phone: 800-342-1663
Email: tsac.aidinfo@tn.gov
http://www.tn.gov/collegepays/section/money-for-college
Purpose: To provide supplemental support to recipients of the Tennessee HOPE Scholarship.
Eligibility: Students graduating from public schools or category 1, 2 and 3 private schools must have at least a 3.75 GPA and either a 29 on the ACT or a 1280 on the SAT. Home-schooled or non-category 1, 2 or 3 private school students must complete at least 12 college credit hours while in high school, and they must have at least a 3.0 GPA in those courses. Recipients of the Aspire Award are not eligible.
Target applicant(s): High school students. College students. Adult students.
Minimum GPA: 3.75
Amount: Up to $1,500.
Number of awards: Varies.
Deadline: Varies.
How to apply: Applications are available through completion of the FAFSA.
Exclusive: Visit www.UltimateScholarshipBook.com and enter code TE176020 for updates on this award.

(1761) · George and Donna Nigh Public Service Scholarship

Oklahoma State Regents for Higher Education/George and Donna Nigh Public Service Scholarship
655 Research Parkway, Suite 200, Oklahoma City, OK 73104
Phone: 800-858-1840
Email: studentinfo@osrhe.edu
https://secure.okcollegestart.org/Financial_Aid_Planning/Scholarships/Career_Scholarships/Nigh_Public_Service_Scholarship.aspx
Purpose: To support Oklahoma students who are pursuing a career in public service.
Eligibility: Applicants must be residents of the state of Oklahoma who are enrolled full-time in an undergraduate program at an Oklahoma college or university. Students must be enrolled in a program leading to a career in public service and must demonstrate exceptional academic achievement.
Target applicant(s): College students. Adult students.
Amount: $1,000.
Number of awards: Varies.
Deadline: Varies.
How to apply: Applications are available online.

Exclusive: Visit www.UltimateScholarshipBook.com and enter code OK176120 for updates on this award.

(1762) · George Mason Business Scholarship Fund

Hawaii Community Foundation - Scholarships
827 Fort Street Mall, Honolulu, HI 96813
Phone: 888-731-3863
Email: scholarships@hcf-hawaii.org
https://www.hawaiicommunityfoundation.org

Purpose: To assist Hawaii students who are majoring in business administration.

Eligibility: Applicants must be seniors at a Hawaiian college or university and have a GPA of 3.0 or higher. They must discuss why they have chosen to pursue a business career and how they expect to make a difference in the business world in their personal statement.

Target applicant(s): College students. Adult students.

Minimum GPA: 3.0

Amount: Varies.

Number of awards: Varies.

Deadline: January 31.

How to apply: To apply, register online, complete the online application and select the scholarships to which you wish to apply. In addition, mail the supporting materials: printed confirmation page from the online application, personal statement, copy of Student Aid Report (SAR) available at www.fafsa.ed.gov and official transcript.

Exclusive: Visit www.UltimateScholarshipBook.com and enter code HA176220 for updates on this award.

(1763) · Georgia Oratorical Contest

American Legion, Department of Georgia
3035 Mt. Zion Road, Stockbridge, GA 30281
Phone: 678-289-8883
Email: amerlegga@bellsouth.net
http://www.galegion.org

Purpose: To enhance high school students' experience with and understanding of the U.S. Constitution. The contest will help develop students' leadership skills and civic appreciation, as well as the ability to deliver thoughtful, insightful orations regarding U.S. citizenship and its inherent responsibilities.

Eligibility: Applicants must be high school students under the age of 20 who are U.S. citizens or legal residents and residents of the state. Students first give an oration within their state and winners compete at the national level. The oration must be related to the Constitution of the United States focusing on the duties and obligations citizens have to the government. It must be in English and be between eight and ten minutes. There is also an assigned topic which is posted on the website, and it should be between three and five minutes.

Target applicant(s): Junior high students or younger. High school students.

Amount: Up to $1,300.

Number of awards: Varies.

Deadline: Varies.

How to apply: Applications are available by contacting the local American Legion Post.

Exclusive: Visit www.UltimateScholarshipBook.com and enter code AM176320 for updates on this award.

(1764) · Georgia Press Educational Foundation Scholarships

Georgia Press Educational Foundation, Inc.
Georgia Press Building, 30266 Mercer University Drive, Suite 200, Atlanta, GA 30343-4137
Phone: 770-454-6776
Email: mail@gapress.org
http://www.gapress.org

Purpose: To aid students interested in newspaper journalism.

Eligibility: Applicants must be high school seniors or undergraduate students who have been Georgia residents for three years, or their parents must have been Georgia residents for two years. Students must attend a Georgia college or university, demonstrate financial need and be recommended by a counselor, principal, professor or Georgia Press Association member.

Target applicant(s): High school students. College students. Adult students.

Amount: $1,500-$2,000.

Number of awards: Varies.

Deadline: March 1.

How to apply: Applications are available online. An application form, transcript, copy of SAT scores, copy of tax return, anticipated budget, school photograph and letter of recommendation are required.

Exclusive: Visit www.UltimateScholarshipBook.com and enter code GE176420 for updates on this award.

(1765) · Georgia Thespians Achievement Scholarships

Georgia Thespians
2897 North Druid Hills Road, Box 225, Atlanta, GA 30329
Phone: 678-910-4487
Email: gathespiansscholarships@gmail.com
http://www.gathespians.org

Purpose: To support outstanding thespians.

Eligibility: Applicants must be Georgia high school juniors or seniors and perform an audition in one of the following categories: acting, technical theatre, singing or theatre education.

Target applicant(s): High school students.

Amount: $2,000.

Number of awards: 5.

Deadline: January 7.

How to apply: Applications are available online. An application form and resume of thespian troupe experience are required.

Exclusive: Visit www.UltimateScholarshipBook.com and enter code GE176520 for updates on this award.

(1766) · Georgia Tuition Equalization Grant

Georgia Student Finance Commission
2082 East Exchange Place, Tucker, GA 30084
Phone: 800-505-4732
Email: gsfcinfo@gsfc.org
https://www.gafutures.org/

Purpose: To support Georgia resident students.

Eligibility: Applicants must be full-time students at eligible private colleges or universities in Georgia and be U.S. citizens and legal residents of the state of Georgia.

Target applicant(s): College students. Adult students.

Amount: $300 per quarter or $450 per semester.

Number of awards: Varies.

Scholarship may be renewable.

Deadline: Varies.
How to apply: Applications are available online.
Exclusive: Visit www.UltimateScholarshipBook.com and enter code GE176620 for updates on this award.

(1767) • GET-IT Student Scholarship

Michigan Council of Women in Technology Foundation
Attn.: Scholarship Committee, 6 Parklane Boulevard, Suite 615, Dearborn, MI 48126
Phone: 248-218-2578
Email: scholarships@mcwt.org
https://mcwt.org/University_Programs_195.html
Purpose: To aid female information technology students.
Eligibility: Applicants must be high school seniors, Michigan residents and U.S. citizens who are involved in the GET-IT program and have a GPA of 3.0 or higher. There is more information about starting a GET-IT program at your school on the MCWTF website. Students must enroll in a degree program in information systems, business applications, computer science, instructional technology, health technology, computer engineering, software engineering, information security, graphics design, or music technology.
Target applicant(s): High school students.
Minimum GPA: 3.0
Amount: $5,000.
Number of awards: Varies.
Scholarship may be renewable.
Deadline: Varies.
How to apply: Applications are available online. An application form, transcript and two letters of recommendation are required.
Exclusive: Visit www.UltimateScholarshipBook.com and enter code MI176720 for updates on this award.

(1768) • Gilbert Matching Student Grant

Massachusetts Department of Higher Education
Office of Student Financial Assistance, 454 Broadway, Suite 200, Revere, MA 02151
Phone: 617-727-9420
Email: osfa@osfa.mass.edu
http://www.mass.edu/osfa/students/forstudents.asp
Purpose: To assist needy students in attending private institutions of higher education or nursing schools.
Eligibility: Students must be permanent residents of Massachusetts, demonstrate financial need, maintain satisfactory academic progress and attend an eligible Massachusetts institution. Applicants must not have earned a bachelor's or professional degree, nor a first diploma from a hospital or professional nursing program.
Target applicant(s): High school students. College students. Adult students.
Amount: $200-$2,500.
Number of awards: Varies.
Scholarship may be renewable.
Deadline: Varies.
How to apply: Applications are available from your school's financial aid office.
Exclusive: Visit www.UltimateScholarshipBook.com and enter code MA176820 for updates on this award.

(1769) • Golden Apple Scholars of Illinois (Illinois Scholars Program)

Golden Apple Foundation
8 South Michigan Avenue, Chicago, IL 60603
Phone: 312-407-0006
http://www.goldenapple.org
Purpose: To offer scholarships to promising students pursuing teaching degrees.
Eligibility: Applicants must be Illinois high school seniors or college sophomores at one of the 53 partner universities in Illinois who are interested in teaching. There are a limited number of spots for college sophomores, and all college students must be nominated by a university liaison. A minimum GPA of 2.5 is required. Students must commit to teaching in an Illinois school of need for five years after graduation.
Target applicant(s): High school students. College students. Adult students.
Minimum GPA: 2.5
Amount: Up to $23,000.
Number of awards: Varies.
Scholarship may be renewable.
Deadline: February 15.
How to apply: Applications are available by calling 312-407-0433, extension 105.
Exclusive: Visit www.UltimateScholarshipBook.com and enter code GO176920 for updates on this award.

(1770) • Golden LEAF Scholars Program - Two-Year Colleges

North Carolina Division of Vocational Rehabilitation Services
2801 Mail Service Center, Raleigh, NC 27699-2801
Phone: 888-234-6400
Email: jterrell@ncbar.org
http://www.cfnc.org
Purpose: To provide need-based financial assistance to North Carolina community college students.
Eligibility: Applicants must be residents of one of the 73 eligible counties and meet specific income requirements as evidenced by FAFSA information (for curriculum students) or the federal TRIO formula (for occupational education students). Degree-seeking students must be enrolled at least half-time.
Target applicant(s): High school students. College students. Adult students.
Amount: $3,000 per year.
Number of awards: Varies.
Scholarship may be renewable.
Deadline: March 1.
How to apply: Applications are available online.
Exclusive: Visit www.UltimateScholarshipBook.com and enter code NO177020 for updates on this award.

(1771) • Good Eats Scholarship Fund

Hawaii Community Foundation - Scholarships
827 Fort Street Mall, Honolulu, HI 96813
Phone: 888-731-3863
Email: scholarships@hcf-hawaii.org
https://www.hawaiicommunityfoundation.org
Purpose: To provide financial assistance to Hawaii students pursuing degrees in agriculture and culinary arts, and to encourage them to return to Hawaii upon graduation.

Eligibility: Applicants must be Hawaii residents who plan to study culinary arts or agriculture at a college or university in the continental United States. They must have a GPA of 2.7 or higher and demonstrate interest in food production and preparation through their school or community activities.
Target applicant(s): High school students. College students. Adult students.
Minimum GPA: 2.7
Amount: Varies.
Number of awards: Varies.
Deadline: January 31.
How to apply: To apply, register online, complete the online application and select the scholarships to which you wish to apply. In addition, mail the supporting materials: printed confirmation page from the online application, personal statement, copy of Student Aid Report (SAR) available at www.fafsa.ed.gov and official transcript.
Exclusive: Visit www.UltimateScholarshipBook.com and enter code HA177120 for updates on this award.

(1772) · Gorgas Scholarship Competition

Alabama Junior Academy of Science
c/o Dr. Ellen Buckner, CHS 1506, Samford University, 800 Lakeshore Drive, Birmingham, AL 35229
Phone: 251-445-9449
Email: ebbuckner@gmail.com
http://alabamajunioracademyofscience.org/
Purpose: To aid Alabama residents who are planning to pursue higher education in science.
Eligibility: Applicants must be Alabama residents who are high school seniors and have completed a scientific research project and an accompanying report of no more than 20 pages. They must have completed all college entrance requirements by October 1 of the year of application submission. Selection is based on the quality of the scientific research paper that is submitted as part of the application.
Target applicant(s): High school students.
Amount: Up to $10,000.
Number of awards: Varies.
Deadline: December 21.
How to apply: Applications are available online. An entry form, research paper, official transcript, one letter of recommendation and additional research-related documentation are required.
Exclusive: Visit www.UltimateScholarshipBook.com and enter code AL177220 for updates on this award.

(1773) · Governor Guinn Millennium Scholarship Program

Nevada Office of the State Treasurer
101 N. Carson Street, Suite 4, Carson City, NV 89701
Phone: 702-486-3383
Email: MillenniumScholars@nevadatreasurer.gov
http://www.nevadatreasurer.gov/Programs/Programs/
Purpose: To assist students who have attained high academic achievement in a Nevada high school.
Eligibility: Applicants must graduate from a Nevada public or private high school with a GPA of 3.25 or higher, pass all areas of the Nevada High School Proficiency Exam and have been a resident of Nevada for at least two years in high school.
Target applicant(s): College students. Adult students.
Minimum GPA: 3.25
Amount: Varies.
Number of awards: 2.
Scholarship may be renewable.
Deadline: April 3.
How to apply: Applications are not required. Your school district will submit your name to the State Treasurer's office if you are eligible.
Exclusive: Visit www.UltimateScholarshipBook.com and enter code NE177320 for updates on this award.

(1774) · Governor's "Best and Brightest" Scholarship Program: Merit-At-Large Scholarships

Montana University System
Student Financial Services (SFS), Scholarship Department, P.O. Box 203101, Helena, MT 59620-3201
Phone: 800-537-7508
Email: mtscholarships@montana.edu
https://mus.edu/Prepare/Pay/Scholarships/
Purpose: To assist students in obtaining higher education. Home schooled and other non-traditional students are encouraged to apply.
Eligibility: Applicants must be residents of Montana who are entering college as freshmen and seeking their first certificate or undergraduate degree. Students must be accepted by an eligible Montana campus and must take the ACT/SAT by December 31 of the student's senior year of high school. Applicants must obtain a cumulative high school GPA of at least 3.0 or score at least 20 on the ACT or 1440 on the SAT.
Target applicant(s): High school students.
Minimum GPA: 3.0
Amount: $2,000.
Number of awards: Varies.
Scholarship may be renewable.
Deadline: March 15.
How to apply: Applications are available online.
Exclusive: Visit www.UltimateScholarshipBook.com and enter code MO177420 for updates on this award.

(1775) · Governor's Cup Scholarship

Idaho State Board of Education
P.O. Box 83720 , Boise, ID 83720-0037
Phone: 208-334-2270
Email: Joy.Miller@osbe.idaho.gov
https://boardofed.idaho.gov/scholarships/
Purpose: Monetary assistance is provided to Idaho resident high school seniors planning to attend state colleges.
Eligibility: Applicants must be Idaho high school seniors planning to attend Idaho colleges or universities full-time and have a minimum 2.8 GPA. Public service is a significant factor.
Target applicant(s): High school students.
Minimum GPA: 2.8
Amount: $3,000.
Number of awards: 25.
Scholarship may be renewable.
Deadline: February 15.
How to apply: Applications are available online.
Exclusive: Visit www.UltimateScholarshipBook.com and enter code ID177520 for updates on this award.

(1776) · Governor's Distinguished Scholarship

Arkansas Department of Higher Education
423 Main Street, Suite 400, Little Rock, AR 72201
Phone: 501-371-2050
Email: finaid@adhe.arknet.edu

http://www.adhe.edu/Pages/home.aspx
Purpose: To assist outstanding Arkansas high school graduates to encourage them to attend postsecondary schools in Arkansas.
Eligibility: Applicants must be Arkansas graduating high school seniors who will attend an Arkansas college or university. Selection is based on academic achievement, test scores and leadership. A minimum ACT score of 32, SAT score of 1410 or 3.5 GPA in academic courses is required.
Target applicant(s): High school students.
Minimum GPA: 3.5
Amount: $4,000.
Number of awards: Varies.
Scholarship may be renewable.
Deadline: February 1.
How to apply: Applications are available through your high school counselor and online.
Exclusive: Visit www.UltimateScholarshipBook.com and enter code AR177620 for updates on this award.

(1777) • GPB Art Harris Scholarship

Great Plains Bank
5909 NW Expressway, Suite 400, Oklahoma City, OK 73132
Phone: 405-720-4813
Email: lhopkins@gpbankok.net
https://www.gpbankok.com/about
Purpose: To support students pursuing a higher education who live in the Great Plains Bank service area.
Eligibility: Applicants must be graduating high school seniors within the Great Plains Bank service area who have at least a 2.0 GPA. Students must have need of financial assistance and be residents of Oklahoma state and citizens of the United States. An essay is required as part of the application process.
Target applicant(s): High school students.
Minimum GPA: 2.0
Amount: $5,000.
Number of awards: 1.
Deadline: March 31.
How to apply: Applications are available online.
Exclusive: Visit www.UltimateScholarshipBook.com and enter code GR177720 for updates on this award.

(1778) • Grace Moore Scholarship

New Jersey Council of Figure Skating Clubs
73 Sam Bonnell Drive, Clinton, NJ 08809
Email: smwelsh126@comcast.net
http://icehousenjfsc.org/
Purpose: To honor the memory of Grace Moore, a member of the New Jersey skating community and national figure skating judge.
Eligibility: Applicants must maintain a New Jersey U.S. Figure Skating club as their home club and have competed in U.S. Figure Skating qualifying competitions for two years for a senior scholarship and one year for a junior scholarship. Selection is based on skating achievement in the disciplines of freestyle, pairs and dance in relation to the skater's age, progress and attitude.
Target applicant(s): Junior high students or younger. High school students. College students. Adult students.
Amount: Varies.
Number of awards: Varies.
Deadline: March 15.
How to apply: Applications are available online. An application form, essay and certification are required.
Exclusive: Visit www.UltimateScholarshipBook.com and enter code NE177820 for updates on this award.

(1779) • Graduate Tuition Waiver

Massachusetts Department of Higher Education
Office of Student Financial Assistance, 454 Broadway, Suite 200, Revere, MA 02151
Phone: 617-727-9420
Email: osfa@osfa.mass.edu
http://www.mass.edu/osfa/students/forstudents.asp
Purpose: To provide financial support to Massachusetts graduate students.
Eligibility: Students must be enrolled in graduate level courses at a Massachusetts public school that is not a community college. Applicants must not owe any refunds on previously received financial aid, and they must not have defaulted on any government loans.
Target applicant(s): Graduate school students. Adult students.
Amount: Varies.
Number of awards: Varies.
Deadline: Varies.
How to apply: Applications are available at college financial aid offices.
Exclusive: Visit www.UltimateScholarshipBook.com and enter code MA177920 for updates on this award.

(1780) • Granville P. Meade Scholarship

Virginia Department of Education
P.O. Box 2120, Richmond, VA 23218
Phone: 804-225-3349
Email: joseph.wharff@doe.virginia.gov
http://www.doe.virginia.gov/
Purpose: To support graduating high school seniors in Virginia.
Eligibility: Students must have been born in Virginia, and they must plan to attend a public or private Virginia school. They must demonstrate financial need, academic achievement, extracurricular activities and good character. Recipients must maintain a 2.5 GPA.
Target applicant(s): High school students.
Minimum GPA: 2.5
Amount: $2,000.
Number of awards: Varies.
Scholarship may be renewable.
Deadline: March 10.
How to apply: Applications are available online.
Exclusive: Visit www.UltimateScholarshipBook.com and enter code VI178020 for updates on this award.

(1781) • Greater Kanawha Valley Foundation Scholarship Program

Greater Kanawha Valley Foundation
1600 Huntington Square, 900 Lee Street, East, Charleston, WV 25301
Phone: 304-346-3620
Email: shoover@tgkvf.org
http://www.tgkvf.org
Purpose: To provide financial assistance to prospective college students from the state of West Virginia.
Eligibility: Applicants must be residents of West Virginia, be full-time students (12 hours) and demonstrate good moral character. Many awards are available, and each individual award may have additional eligibility requirements. Applicants must have a minimum 2.5 GPA and an ACT score of at least 20.

Target applicant(s): High school students. College students. Adult students.
Minimum GPA: 2.5
Amount: Varies.
Number of awards: Varies.
Scholarship may be renewable.
Deadline: January 15.
How to apply: Applications are available online.
Exclusive: Visit www.UltimateScholarshipBook.com and enter code GR178120 for updates on this award.

(1782) • Greenhouse Scholars Scholarship

Greenhouse Scholars
1881 9th Street, Suite 200, Boulder, CO 80302
Phone: 303-469-5473
Email: info@greenhousescholars.org
http://www.greenhousescholars.org
Purpose: To provide financial assistance to high-performing, under-resourced students who are leaders and contributors to their communities.
Eligibility: Applicants must be high school seniors who plan to attend a four-year college or university. They must be U.S. citizens or permanent residents who reside and attend school in Colorado, Georgia or Illinois. They must have an unweighted GPA of 3.5 or higher, and they must demonstrate leadership, perseverance and financial need. Their household income must be $70,000 a year or less. Winners participate in an internship and summer symposium.
Target applicant(s): High school students.
Minimum GPA: 3.5
Amount: Up to $5,000.
Number of awards: Varies.
Scholarship may be renewable.
Deadline: December 1.
How to apply: Applications are available online.
Exclusive: Visit www.UltimateScholarshipBook.com and enter code GR178220 for updates on this award.

(1783) • Gregory A. Chaille Public Service Scholarship

Oregon Office of Student Access and Completion
1500 Valley River Drive, Suite 100, Eugene, OR 97401
Phone: 541-687-7422
Email: cheryl.a.connolly@state.or.us
https://oregonstudentaid.gov/
Purpose: To support students who are planning to become public servants in their graduate studies.
Eligibility: Applicants must be accepted to a graduate program at a public or nonprofit college or university and attend at least half-time. Students must fill out the FAFSA. Applicants must also submit an essay about how they plan to make a positive impact on their community and the world. Selection is based on financial need and the overall strength of the application.
Target applicant(s): College students. Graduate school students. Adult students.
Amount: Varies.
Number of awards: Varies.
Scholarship may be renewable.
Deadline: March 1.
How to apply: Applications are available online.
Exclusive: Visit www.UltimateScholarshipBook.com and enter code OR178320 for updates on this award.

(1784) • Grimm-Koch-Lockhart Scholarship Fund

ConCarolinas Inc.
2505 Derita Avenue #26336, P.O. Box 680803, Charlotte, NC 28269
Phone: 704-906-6072
Email: conchair@concarolinas.org
http://www.concarolinas.org
Purpose: To support Carolinas students pursuing higher education.
Eligibility: Applicants must be high school seniors or college students attending or planning on attending a college or university in North Carolina or South Carolina.
Target applicant(s): High school students. College students. Graduate school students. Adult students.
Amount: $500.
Number of awards: 1.
Deadline: May 7.
How to apply: Applications are available online.
Exclusive: Visit www.UltimateScholarshipBook.com and enter code CO178420 for updates on this award.

(1785) • Guy M. Wilson Scholarship

American Legion, Department of Michigan
212 N. Verlinden Avenue, Ste. A, Lansing, MI 48915
Phone: 517-371-4720 x11
Email: programs@michiganlegion.org
http://www.michiganlegion.org
Purpose: To aid students who are the sons or daughters or grandchildren of veterans who plan to attend a Michigan college.
Eligibility: Applicants must be residents of Michigan who are planning to attend a Michigan college or university and who are the sons or daughters or grandchildren of veterans. Students must have a minimum GPA of 2.5 and must have demonstrated financial need. Applicants must provide proof of a parent's military service record and an indication of their abilities to fulfill their goals and intentions. They should send scholarship information to their county district committee person.
Target applicant(s): High school students.
Minimum GPA: 2.5
Amount: $500.
Number of awards: Varies.
Deadline: January 9.
How to apply: Applications are available online.
Exclusive: Visit www.UltimateScholarshipBook.com and enter code AM178520 for updates on this award.

(1786) • Guy P. Gannett Scholarship

Maine Community Foundation
245 Main Street, Ellsworth, ME 04605
Phone: 207-667-9735
Email: jwarren@mainecf.org
http://www.mainecf.org
Purpose: To provide renewable financial support to students in Maine who are majoring in journalism or a related field.
Eligibility: Students must be graduates of Maine high schools or home-schooled in Maine. Applicants are considered for the award based on their interest in journalism, financial need and academic achievement. They must also continue to demonstrate an interest in journalism in college.

Target applicant(s): High school students. College students. Graduate school students. Adult students.
Amount: Varies.
Number of awards: Varies.
Scholarship may be renewable.
Deadline: May 1.
How to apply: Applications are available online in January or by contacting the Maine Community Foundation.
Exclusive: Visit www.UltimateScholarshipBook.com and enter code MA178620 for updates on this award.

(1787) • H.L. Taylor Scholarship Program

Iowa PTA
P.O. Box 10634, Cedar Rapids, IA 52410
Phone: 319-573-0049
Email: execdir@iowapta.org
http://iowapta.org/index.php/programs/scholarships
Purpose: To support Iowa students pursuing post-secondary education.
Eligibility: Applicants must be graduating high school seniors in Iowa whose school district has an active PTA at any level of education. Students must be residents of Iowa and plan to enroll at an accredited Iowa post-secondary institution.
Target applicant(s): High school students.
Amount: $500.
Number of awards: Varies.
Deadline: February 15.
How to apply: Applications are available online.
Exclusive: Visit www.UltimateScholarshipBook.com and enter code IO178720 for updates on this award.

(1788) • H.M. Muffly Memorial Scholarship

Colorado Nurses Foundation
2851 S. Parker Road, Suite 1210, Aurora, CO 80014
Phone: 720-457-1191
Email: sonja.hix-cortina@civicamanagement.com
https://www.coloradonursesfoundation.com/scholarships/
Purpose: To aid nursing students working towards bachelor's, master's or doctoral degrees.
Eligibility: Applicants must be Colorado residents who are planning to practice nursing in Colorado. They must be juniors or seniors working towards the Bachelor of Science in Nursing (BSN); Registered Nurses (RNs) pursuing the bachelor's degree or higher in a school of nursing; practicing RNs pursuing a doctoral degree in nursing or second- or third-year Doctor of Nursing Practice (DNP) students. Undergraduates must have a GPA of 3.25 or higher, and graduate students must have a GPA of 3.5 or higher. Selection is based on GPA, financial need, recommendations, community involvement and commitment to professional practice in Colorado.
Target applicant(s): College students. Graduate school students. Adult students.
Minimum GPA: 3.25 for undergraduate students, 3.5 for graduate students
Amount: $2,500.
Number of awards: 2.
Deadline: October 31.
How to apply: Applications are available online. An application form, schedule of classes, two recommendation letters, financial need statement, transcript and personal essay are required.
Exclusive: Visit www.UltimateScholarshipBook.com and enter code CO178820 for updates on this award.

(1789) • Hal W. Almen/West OKC Rotary Scholarship

Oklahoma City Community Foundation
1000 North Broadway, Oklahoma City, OK 73102
Phone: 405-606-2917
Email: scholarships@occf.org
https://occf.org/
Purpose: To support students from the state of Oklahoma with furthering their education.
Eligibility: Applicants must be a graduating senior from a Oklahoma high school. Students must have a 2.75 GPA or higher to be considered for this award. Financial need is considered and applicant's family income cannot exceed $100,000. Students must provide a written statement that focuses on how their local Rotary club supports their local community.
Target applicant(s): High school students.
Minimum GPA: 2.75
Amount: $4,000.
Number of awards: 3.
Deadline: March 1.
How to apply: Applications are available online.
Exclusive: Visit www.UltimateScholarshipBook.com and enter code OK178920 for updates on this award.

(1790) • Harold C. & Frances L. Stuart Scholarship

Oklahoma Association of Broadcasters
6520 N. Western, Suite 104, Oklahoma City, OK 73116
Phone: 405-848-0771
Email: struby@oabok.org
https://oabok.org/careerseducation/scholarships/
Purpose: To support students majoring in broadcasting at Oklahoma colleges and universities.
Eligibility: Applicants must be enrolled in an Oklahoma college or university broadcasting program, be majoring in broadcasting and have an intent to enter the broadcasting career upon graduation. Students must be a junior or senior for the upcoming school year and must maintain a "B" average.
Target applicant(s): College students. Adult students.
Minimum GPA: 3.0
Amount: $2,000.
Number of awards: 1.
Deadline: February 9.
How to apply: Applications are available online.
Exclusive: Visit www.UltimateScholarshipBook.com and enter code OK179020 for updates on this award.

(1791) • Harold K. Douthit Scholarship

Ohio News Media Foundation
1335 Dublin Road, Suite 216-B, Columbus, OH 43215
Phone: 614-486-6677
Email: ariggs@ohionews.org
https://www.ohionews.org/aws/ONA/pt/sp/foundation_scholarships
Purpose: To support students pursuing a major in a journalism-related field at an Ohio college or university.
Eligibility: Applicants must be enrolled in an Ohio college or university and be majoring in a journalism-related field such as journalism, advertising or marketing. Students must have at least a 3.0 GPA and write an essay as part of their application showcasing their writing skill along with including work samples related to degree.
Target applicant(s): College students. Adult students.
Minimum GPA: 3.0

Amount: $1,500.
Number of awards: 1.
Deadline: March 31.
How to apply: Applications are available online.
Exclusive: Visit www.UltimateScholarshipBook.com and enter code OH179120 for updates on this award.

(1792) · Harriet Hayes Austin Memorial Scholarship for Nursing

Topeka Community Foundation
5431 SW 29th Street, Suite 300 , Topeka, KS 66614
Phone: 785-272-4804
Email: matalone@topekacommunityfoundation.org
http://www.topekacommunityfoundation.org
Purpose: To aid students who are pursuing the Bachelor of Science in Nursing (BSN) degree at an accredited postsecondary institution located in Kansas.
Eligibility: Applicants must be U.S. citizens who are enrolled in or who plan to enroll in a BSN program at an accredited school located in Kansas. They must demonstrate financial need. Preference is given to Kansas residents. Selection is based on the overall strength of the application.
Target applicant(s): High school students. College students. Adult students.
Amount: $1,000.
Number of awards: 5.
Deadline: February 6.
How to apply: Applications are available online. An application form, official transcript, one letter of recommendation, personal statements, financial analysis form and proof of U.S. citizenship are required.
Exclusive: Visit www.UltimateScholarshipBook.com and enter code TO179220 for updates on this award.

(1793) · Harry Alan Gregg Foundation Grants

Harry Alan Gregg Foundation Grants
1 Verney Drive, Greenfield, NH 03047
Phone: 603-547-3311
Email: hgf@crotchedmountain.org
http://www.crotchedmountain.org
Purpose: To provide financial assistance for the disabled.
Eligibility: Applicants must be New Hampshire residents with physical, intellectual or emotional disabilities or their families. Funds may be used for a variety of purposes but must benefit the person with a disability. Selection is based on need. Applications are reviewed four times a year, with deadlines in March, June, September and December.
Target applicant(s): High school students. College students. Graduate school students. Adult students.
Amount: Up to $1,200.
Number of awards: Varies.
Deadline: Varies.
How to apply: Applications are available online. Documentation of the expense must be provided before payment will be made.
Exclusive: Visit www.UltimateScholarshipBook.com and enter code HA179320 for updates on this award.

(1794) · Harry Barfield KBA Scholarship Program

Kentucky Broadcasters Association
101 Enterprise Drive, Frankfort, KY 40601
Phone: 888-843-5221
Email: kba@kba.org
http://www.kba.org
Purpose: To aid aspiring young broadcasters.
Eligibility: Applicants must be attending a college or university in Kentucky and major or plan to major in broadcasting or telecommunications. Preference is given to second semester sophomores, and funds are awarded in the junior year and renewable for the senior year. Applicants should have a minimum 3.0 GPA, although some consideration will be given to those with lower GPAs who have exceptional credentials otherwise.
Target applicant(s): College students. Adult students.
Minimum GPA: 3.0
Amount: $2,500.
Number of awards: Varies.
Scholarship may be renewable.
Deadline: April 24.
How to apply: Applications are available online. An application form, transcript, essay, list of extracurricular activities and letter of recommendation are required.
Exclusive: Visit www.UltimateScholarshipBook.com and enter code KE179420 for updates on this award.

(1795) · Harry S. Chandler Scholarship

Oregon Office of Student Access and Completion
1500 Valley River Drive, Suite 100, Eugene, OR 97401
Phone: 541-687-7422
Email: cheryl.a.connolly@state.or.us
https://oregonstudentaid.gov/
Purpose: To support students who are planning to become attorneys in their graduate studies.
Eligibility: Applicants must be intending to enter an accredited, public or nonprofit law school in the United States for the fall semester. Students must fill out the FAFSA. Selection is based on financial need and the overall strength of the application, with preference for applicants who are planning to focus on dispute/mediation resolution, problem-solving, employment/labor law or business ethics.
Target applicant(s): College students. Adult students.
Amount: Varies.
Number of awards: Varies.
Scholarship may be renewable.
Deadline: March 1.
How to apply: Applications are available online.
Exclusive: Visit www.UltimateScholarshipBook.com and enter code OR179520 for updates on this award.

(1796) · Hattie Tedrow Memorial Fund Scholarship

American Legion, Department of North Dakota
405 W. Maine Avenue, Suite 4A, P.O. Box 5057, West Fargo, ND 58078
Phone: 701-293-3120
Email: LegionEd@legion.org
http://ndala.org/
Purpose: To support descendants of veterans.
Eligibility: Applicants must be high school seniors, North Dakota residents and U.S. citizens. They must be direct descendants of veterans with honorable service in the U.S. military.
Target applicant(s): High school students.
Amount: Up to $2,000.
Number of awards: Varies.
Deadline: April 1.
How to apply: Applications are available by mail. An application form, essay and proof of veteran's military service are required.

Exclusive: Visit www.UltimateScholarshipBook.com and enter code AM179620 for updates on this award.

(1797) • Hawaii Community Foundation Scholarships

Hawaii Community Foundation - Scholarships
827 Fort Street Mall, Honolulu, HI 96813
Phone: 888-731-3863
Email: scholarships@hcf-hawaii.org
https://www.hawaiicommunityfoundation.org
Purpose: To help Hawaii residents who show financial need.
Eligibility: The Hawaii Community Foundation Scholarship Program has over 200 different scholarship funds covering areas such as vocational education, those in foster care, ethnicity, religion and major. Applicants must be Hawaii residents who plan to attend nonprofit two- or four-year colleges as either full-time undergraduate or graduate students. Applicants must also have academic achievement and good moral character. A personal statement, Student Aid Report, transcript, recommendation letter and essay may be required depending on the specific scholarship.
Target applicant(s): High school students. College students. Graduate school students. Adult students.
Amount: Varies.
Number of awards: Varies.
Deadline: January 31.
How to apply: Applications are available online.
Exclusive: Visit www.UltimateScholarshipBook.com and enter code HA179720 for updates on this award.

(1798) • Hawaii High School Athletic Association Hall of Honor

Hawaii High School Athletic Association
P.O. Box 62029, Honolulu, HI 96839
Phone: 808-800-4092
Email: info@hhsaa.org
http://www.sportshigh.com
Purpose: To support Hawaii high school seniors who are athletes.
Eligibility: Applicants must be graduating high school seniors and athletes in any organized sport in Hawaii. Selection is based primarily on sports achievements. Factors considered include contributions to the team, sportsmanship, character, participation in school activities and community involvement.
Target applicant(s): High school students.
Amount: $2,000.
Number of awards: 12.
Deadline: May 6.
How to apply: Applications are available by written request.
Exclusive: Visit www.UltimateScholarshipBook.com and enter code HA179820 for updates on this award.

(1799) • Hawaii Pizza Hut Scholarship Fund

Hawaii Community Foundation - Scholarships
827 Fort Street Mall, Honolulu, HI 96813
Phone: 888-731-3863
Email: scholarships@hcf-hawaii.org
https://www.hawaiicommunityfoundation.org
Purpose: To support students in Hawaii with financial need.
Eligibility: Applicants must be Hawaii residents, attend a two- or four-year college or university and have a GPA between 3.0 and 3.5.
Target applicant(s): High school students. College students. Adult students.
Minimum GPA: 3.0
Amount: Varies.
Number of awards: Varies.
Deadline: January 31.
How to apply: To apply, register online, complete the online application and select the scholarships to which you wish to apply. In addition, mail the supporting materials: printed confirmation page from the online application, personal statement, copy of Student Aid Report (SAR) available at www.fafsa.ed.gov and official transcript.
Exclusive: Visit www.UltimateScholarshipBook.com and enter code HA179920 for updates on this award.

(1800) • Hawaii Rotary Youth Foundation Scholarship

Hawaii Rotary Youth Foundation
3536 Harding Avenue, Honolulu, HI 96816
Phone: (808) 735-1073
http://www.hawaiirotaryyouthfoundation.org
Purpose: To encourage graduating high school seniors from Hawaii to pursue a higher education.
Eligibility: Applicants must be graduating high school seniors sponsored by a District 5000 Rotary Club in the state of Hawaii. Students must plan to enroll full-time at a four-year college or university in the United States. Applicants must be U.S. citizens and residents of Hawaii.
Target applicant(s): High school students.
Amount: $5,000.
Number of awards: Varies.
Deadline: January 31.
How to apply: Applications are available online.
Exclusive: Visit www.UltimateScholarshipBook.com and enter code HA180020 for updates on this award.

(1801) • Hawaii Society of Certified Public Accountants Scholarship Fund

Hawaii Community Foundation - Scholarships
827 Fort Street Mall, Honolulu, HI 96813
Phone: 888-731-3863
Email: scholarships@hcf-hawaii.org
https://www.hawaiicommunityfoundation.org
Purpose: To provide financial assistance for those pursuing degrees in accounting.
Eligibility: Applicants must be college juniors, college seniors or graduate students attending an accredited four-year Hawaii institution of higher learning with a major or concentration in accounting. They must have a minimum GPA of 3.0.
Target applicant(s): College students. Graduate school students. Adult students.
Minimum GPA: 3.0
Amount: Varies.
Number of awards: Varies.
Deadline: January 31.
How to apply: To apply, register online, complete the online application and select the scholarships to which you wish to apply. In addition, mail the supporting materials: printed confirmation page from the online application, personal statement, copy of Student Aid Report (SAR) available at www.fafsa.ed.gov and official transcript.
Exclusive: Visit www.UltimateScholarshipBook.com and enter code HA180120 for updates on this award.

(1802) • Hawaii Veterans Memorial Fund Scholarship

Hawaii Community Foundation - Scholarships
827 Fort Street Mall, Honolulu, HI 96813
Phone: 888-731-3863
Email: scholarships@hcf-hawaii.org
https://www.hawaiicommunityfoundation.org

Purpose: To provide financial assistance for Hawaii graduate students.
Eligibility: Applicants must be pursuing graduate studies at a U.S. college or university. They must have a GPA of 3.5 or higher. An additional award is available for students with high academic achievement, excellent character and an interest in contributing to professional and community service activities in Hawaii. Applicants do not need to be veterans or the children of veterans.
Target applicant(s): College students. Graduate school students. Adult students.
Minimum GPA: 3.5
Amount: Varies.
Number of awards: Varies.
Deadline: January 31.
How to apply: To apply, register online, complete the online application and select the scholarships to which you wish to apply. In addition, mail the supporting materials: printed confirmation page from the online application, personal statement, copy of Student Aid Report (SAR) available at www.fafsa.ed.gov and official transcript.
Exclusive: Visit www.UltimateScholarshipBook.com and enter code HA180220 for updates on this award.

(1803) • Headwaters Essay Contest

Headwaters Magazine
153 South Prospect Street, Burlington, VT 05401
Email: headwaters@uvm.edu
http://uvmheadwaters.org

Purpose: To support students who have an interest in the clean energy campus of the future.
Eligibility: Applicants must be undergraduate students at New England universities from one of the following states: Connecticut, Maine, Massachusetts, New Hampshire, Rhode Island or Vermont. Students must write an essay as part of the application process.
Target applicant(s): College students. Adult students.
Amount: $500-$1,000.
Number of awards: 3.
Deadline: February 2.
How to apply: Applications are available online.
Exclusive: Visit www.UltimateScholarshipBook.com and enter code HE180320 for updates on this award.

(1804) • Health Professional Loan Repayment

Washington Student Achievement Council
917 Lakeridge Way SW, Olympia, WA 98502
Phone: 360-753-7850
http://www.wsac.wa.gov/financial-aid

Purpose: To attract health professionals to work in shortage areas in Washington state.
Eligibility: Applicants must be employed, or be under contract to be employed, at an eligible site, provide proof of eligible student debt, provide primary care and sign a contract to serve for at least three years. Applicants may apply for a fourth and fifth year award of up to $25,000 per year based on debt remaining. Eligible professions are physician, physician assistant or nurse practitioner, licensed nurse, midwife, pharmacist, dentist or dental hygienist.
Target applicant(s): College students. Adult students.
Amount: Up to $75,000.
Number of awards: Varies.
Scholarship may be renewable.
Deadline: April 14.
How to apply: Applications are available online.
Exclusive: Visit www.UltimateScholarshipBook.com and enter code WA180420 for updates on this award.

(1805) • Health Research and Educational Trust Health Career Scholarships

New Jersey Hospital Association
760 Alexander Road, P.O. Box 1, Princeton, NJ 08543-0001
Phone: 609-275-4000
Email: jhritz@njha.com
http://www.njha.com

Purpose: To aid New Jersey students enrolled in certain healthcare-related degree programs.
Eligibility: Applicants must be New Jersey residents. They must be undergraduate juniors, undergraduate seniors or graduate students enrolled in a nursing, allied health professions, healthcare administration or hospital administration degree program. Applicants must have a GPA of 3.0 or higher and must demonstrate financial need. Selection is based on the quality of the personal essay submitted as part of the application.
Target applicant(s): College students. Graduate school students. Adult students.
Minimum GPA: 3.0
Amount: At least $2,000.
Number of awards: Varies.
Deadline: September 18.
How to apply: Application instructions are available online. Applicant contact information, a personal essay, an official transcript and proof of financial need are required.
Exclusive: Visit www.UltimateScholarshipBook.com and enter code NE180520 for updates on this award.

(1806) • Henry A. Zuberano Scholarship

Hawaii Community Foundation - Scholarships
827 Fort Street Mall, Honolulu, HI 96813
Phone: 888-731-3863
Email: scholarships@hcf-hawaii.org
https://www.hawaiicommunityfoundation.org

Purpose: To assist Hawaii students who are majoring in political science, international relations, international business or public administration.
Eligibility: Applicants must have a GPA of 2.7 or higher.
Target applicant(s): High school students. College students. Adult students.
Minimum GPA: 2.7
Amount: Varies.
Number of awards: Varies.
Deadline: January 31.
How to apply: To apply, register online, complete the online application and select the scholarships to which you wish to apply. In addition, mail the supporting materials: printed confirmation page from the online application, personal statement, copy of Student Aid Report (SAR) available at www.fafsa.ed.gov and official transcript.
Exclusive: Visit www.UltimateScholarshipBook.com and enter code HA180620 for updates on this award.

(1807) • Henry Sachs Foundation Scholarship

Henry Sachs Foundation
90 S. Cascade Avenue, Suite 1410, Colorado Springs, CO 80903
Phone: 719-633-2353
Email: info@sachsfoundation.org
http://www.sachsfoundation.org/scholarships
Purpose: To aid African-American high school students in Colorado to obtain a college education.
Eligibility: Applicants must be African-American residents of Colorado for at least five years. Applicants must be either seniors in high school or have graduated in the last three years but are not currently attending college. Awards are based on high school grade point average and financial need. If selected, applicants must attend a personal interview in order to receive the grant money.
Target applicant(s): High school students.
Minimum GPA: 3.0
Amount: $6,000.
Number of awards: Varies.
Scholarship may be renewable.
Deadline: March 15.
How to apply: Applications are available online.
Exclusive: Visit www.UltimateScholarshipBook.com and enter code HE180720 for updates on this award.

(1808) • Herbert Hoover Uncommon Student Award

Hoover Presidential Foundation
P.O. Box 696, West Branch, IA 52358
Phone: 800-828-0475
Email: info@hooverpf.org
http://www.hooverpresidentialfoundation.org
Purpose: To honor Herbert Hoover by rewarding students who live up to his ideal of the "uncommon man."
Eligibility: Applicants must be juniors in an Iowa high school or be homeschooled. Students must submit a project proposal and two letters of recommendation. Recipients must attend a weekend program during the summer and are expected to complete the proposed project. Grades, essays and test scores are not considered.
Target applicant(s): High school students.
Amount: $5,000.
Number of awards: Up to 15.
Deadline: March 15.
How to apply: Applications are available online.
Exclusive: Visit www.UltimateScholarshipBook.com and enter code HO180820 for updates on this award.

(1809) • Herff Jones Scholarship

University Interscholastic League
1701 Manor Road, Austin, TX 78722
Phone: 512-471-5883
Email: jacton@uiltexas.org
http://www.tilfoundation.org/scholarships/list/
Purpose: To support high school yearbook staff.
Eligibility: Applicants must be graduating high school seniors in Texas, have a 3.0 or higher GPA and plan to major or minor in a communications-related field. Students must also have been involved in journalism during high school.
Target applicant(s): High school students.
Minimum GPA: 3.0
Amount: Varies.
Number of awards: Varies.
Deadline: March 28.
How to apply: Applications are available online. An application form, letter of recommendation and three to five samples of student journalism work are required.
Exclusive: Visit www.UltimateScholarshipBook.com and enter code UN180920 for updates on this award.

(1810) • Herman J. Smith Scholarship

National Housing Endowment
1201 15th Street NW, Washington, DC 20005
Phone: 202-266-8069
Email: Scholarships@nahb.org
http://www.nationalhousingendowment.org
Purpose: To aid students who are planning for careers in mortgage finance or the construction industry.
Eligibility: Applicants must be full-time undergraduate or graduate students attending an accredited four-year institution. They must have at least one more year of study to complete after the date of award disbursement; fifth-year seniors are ineligible for this award. They must be majoring in and planning to pursue a career in mortgage finance, construction management or another construction-related subject. Preference is given to Texas residents, students who attend school in Texas and current members of their school's National Association of Home Builders student chapter. Selection is based on academic merit, recommendations, work experience, extracurricular activities, career goals and financial need.
Target applicant(s): College students. Graduate school students. Adult students.
Amount: Varies.
Number of awards: Varies.
Scholarship may be renewable.
Deadline: March 26.
How to apply: Applications are available online. An application form, course schedule, official transcripts and three recommendation letters are required.
Exclusive: Visit www.UltimateScholarshipBook.com and enter code NA181020 for updates on this award.

(1811) • Herman Sani Scholarship

Iowa Golf Association
Attn: Ann Griffel Scholarship Committee, 1605 North Ankeny Boulevard, Suite 210, Ankeny, IA 50023
Phone: 888-388-4442
http://www.iowagolf.org
Purpose: To assist Iowa college-bound students as they further their education.
Eligibility: Applicant must be a high school senior with a background in golf. Selection is based on academic achievement, extracurricular activities and leadership qualities. Selection is not based on golf accomplishments or abilities.
Target applicant(s): High school students.
Amount: $2,000.
Number of awards: Varies.
Scholarship may be renewable.
Deadline: March 17.
How to apply: Applications are available online and include a personal essay, two letters of recommendation and an official transcript.
Exclusive: Visit www.UltimateScholarshipBook.com and enter code IO181120 for updates on this award.

(1812) • Hermine Solt Student Scholarship

Pennsylvania Association of Educational Office Professionals (PAEOP)
Lenore Filipovic, Phoenixville Area School District, 386 City Line Avenue, Phoenixville, PA 19460
Email: herminsoltstudentscholarship@gmail.com
https://www.paeop.com/page/76

Purpose: To support students in Pennsylvania who are pursuing a higher education in a business-related field.
Eligibility: Applicants must be graduating high school seniors from either a Pennsylvania high school or Pennsylvania cyber charter school who have a 3.0 GPA. Students must attending an approved post-secondary institution, college, or university majoring in the business field.
Target applicant(s): High school students.
Minimum GPA: 3.0
Amount: $500.
Number of awards: Varies.
Deadline: March 1.
How to apply: Applications are available online.
Exclusive: Visit www.UltimateScholarshipBook.com and enter code PE181220 for updates on this award.

(1813) • Hideko and Zenzo Matsuyama Scholarship Fund

Hawaii Community Foundation - Scholarships
827 Fort Street Mall, Honolulu, HI 96813
Phone: 888-731-3863
Email: scholarships@hcf-hawaii.org
https://www.hawaiicommunityfoundation.org

Purpose: To provide financial assistance for high school graduates who are seeking higher education.
Eligibility: Applicants must be graduates of Hawaiian high schools or GED recipients who plan to attend a college or university in Hawaii or the continental U.S. full-time. They must have a GPA of 3.0 or higher. Applicants must be of Japanese ancestry.
Target applicant(s): High school students. College students. Adult students.
Minimum GPA: 3.0
Amount: Varies.
Number of awards: Varies.
Deadline: January 31.
How to apply: To apply, register online, complete the online application and select the scholarships to which you wish to apply. In addition, mail the supporting materials: printed confirmation page from the online application, personal statement, copy of Student Aid Report (SAR) available at www.fafsa.ed.gov and official transcript.
Exclusive: Visit www.UltimateScholarshipBook.com and enter code HA181320 for updates on this award.

(1814) • High Technology Scholar/Intern Tuition Waiver

Massachusetts Department of Higher Education
Office of Student Financial Assistance, 454 Broadway, Suite 200, Revere, MA 02151
Phone: 617-727-9420
Email: osfa@osfa.mass.edu
http://www.mass.edu/osfa/students/forstudents.asp

Purpose: To provide financial aid and internship connections to computer technology and engineering students in Massachusetts.
Eligibility: Students must be enrolled in an undergraduate program at a Massachusetts public college and must not have previously earned a bachelor's degree. Applicants must have approval from the company or organization that is funding the scholarship. Students must not owe refunds on any previous financial aid or have any defaulted government loans.
Target applicant(s): High school students. College students. Adult students.
Amount: Up to full tuition.
Number of awards: Varies.
Deadline: Varies.
How to apply: Applications are available at college financial aid offices.
Exclusive: Visit www.UltimateScholarshipBook.com and enter code MA181420 for updates on this award.

(1815) • Higher Education Academic Scholarship Program (Bright Flight)

Missouri Student Assistance Resource Services (MOSTARS)
Missouri Department of Higher Education, Attn: Bright Flight, P.O. Box 1469, Jefferson City, MO 65102
Phone: 800-473-6757
http://dhe.mo.gov/ppc/grants/

Purpose: This merit-based program encourages top-ranked high school seniors to attend approved Missouri postsecondary schools.
Eligibility: Applicants must be U.S. citizens or eligible noncitizens, Missouri residents and have an ACT or SAT score within the top 3 percent of all Missouri students taking those tests. Applicants must be high school seniors who enroll as first-time, full-time students at an approved Missouri postsecondary school.
Target applicant(s): High school students.
Amount: Up to $3,000.
Number of awards: Varies.
Scholarship may be renewable.
Deadline: None.
How to apply: For an application contact your high school counselor or MOSTARS.
Exclusive: Visit www.UltimateScholarshipBook.com and enter code MI181520 for updates on this award.

(1816) • Higher Education Adult Part-Time Student (HEAPS) Grant Program

West Virginia Higher Education Policy Commission
1018 Kanawha Boulevard, East, Suite 700, Charleston, WV 25301
Phone: 304-558-2101
Email: Jacob.Abrams@wvhepc.edu
http://www.wvhepc.edu/

Purpose: To assist adult West Virginia students.
Eligibility: Applicants must be West Virginia residents, be U.S. citizens or permanent residents, be enrolled or accepted for enrollment in an undergraduate institution on a part-time basis and demonstrate financial need.
Target applicant(s): High school students. College students. Adult students.
Amount: $2,000.
Number of awards: Varies.
Scholarship may be renewable.
Deadline: Varies.
How to apply: Complete the Free Application for Federal Student Aid (FAFSA).

Exclusive: Visit www.UltimateScholarshipBook.com and enter code WE181620 for updates on this award.

(1817) • Higher Education Legislative Plan (HELP)

Mississippi Office of Student Financial Aid
3825 Ridgewood Road, Jackson, MS 39211
Phone: 800-327-2980
Email: sfa@ihl.state.ms.us
http://www.ihl.state.ms.us

Purpose: To assist financially needy Mississippi students to afford tuition.

Eligibility: Applicants must be U.S. citizens or eligible noncitizens, Mississippi residents and have a minimum college GPA of 2.5 and have graduated from high school within the past two years. Applicants must be attending an eligible Mississippi institution, must have a minimum ACT score of 20 and must document an average gross income of $39,500 or less over the prior two years, and must have the results of a processed Student Aid Report (SAR). Students who file the Free Application for Federal Student Aid (FAFSA) will receive a SAR report.

Target applicant(s): High school students. College students. Adult students.

Minimum GPA: 2.5

Amount: Full tuition.

Number of awards: Varies.

Scholarship may be renewable.

Deadline: March 31.

How to apply: Contact the Mississippi Office of Student Financial Aid for an application.

Exclusive: Visit www.UltimateScholarshipBook.com and enter code MI181720 for updates on this award.

(1818) • Hispanic Annual Salute

Hispanic Annual Salute
P.O. Box 40720, Denver, CO 80204
Phone: 303-577-8111
Email: rhurtado@denver.bbb.org
http://www.hispanicannualsalute.org/scholarships

Purpose: To support Colorado high school students pursuing a college education.

Eligibility: Applicants must be high school seniors residing in Colorado with unpaid notable volunteer contributions in the Hispanic community.

Target applicant(s): High school students.

Minimum GPA: 2.5

Amount: $2,000.

Number of awards: Varies.

Deadline: April 28.

How to apply: Applications are available online.

Exclusive: Visit www.UltimateScholarshipBook.com and enter code HI181820 for updates on this award.

(1819) • Ho'omaka Hou - A New Beginning Fund

Hawaii Community Foundation - Scholarships
827 Fort Street Mall, Honolulu, HI 96813
Phone: 888-731-3863
Email: scholarships@hcf-hawaii.org
https://www.hawaiicommunityfoundation.org

Purpose: To support students who have overcome substance abuse or other difficulties in their lives.

Eligibility: Applicants must show financial need. Students must attend college or technical school in Hawaii. Minimum 2.7 GPA required.

Target applicant(s): High school students. College students. Adult students.

Minimum GPA: 2.7

Amount: Varies.

Number of awards: Varies.

Deadline: January 31.

How to apply: Applications are available online. In addition, mail the supporting materials: personal statement, one letter of recommendation, copy of Student Aid Report (SAR) available at www.fafsa.ed.gov and official transcript.

Exclusive: Visit www.UltimateScholarshipBook.com and enter code HA181920 for updates on this award.

(1820) • Honors Award

Louisiana Office of Student Financial Assistance
605 N. Fifth Street, Baton Rouge, LA 70802
Phone: 800-259-5626 x1012
Email: custserv@la.gov
http://www.osfa.la.gov/

Purpose: To aid Louisiana student residents.

Eligibility: Applicants must be Louisiana residents and U.S. citizens, apply during their senior year in high school, use the award at a Louisiana college or university, have a minimum 3.0 GPA and have a minimum ACT score of 27 or equivalent SAT score.

Target applicant(s): High school students.

Minimum GPA: 3.0

Amount: Full tuition plus $800 stipend.

Number of awards: Varies.

Scholarship may be renewable.

Deadline: July 1.

How to apply: The application is the Free Application for Federal Student Aid (FAFSA). ACT or SAT scores must also be reported.

Exclusive: Visit www.UltimateScholarshipBook.com and enter code LO182020 for updates on this award.

(1821) • HOPE Scholarship Program

Georgia Student Finance Commission
2082 East Exchange Place, Tucker, GA 30084
Phone: 800-505-4732
Email: gsfcinfo@gsfc.org
https://www.gafutures.org/

Purpose: To support students attending Georgia institutions.

Eligibility: Applicants must have graduated from high school and be attending or planning to attend college in Georgia. Students must be U.S. citizens or eligible non-citizens, be a legal resident of the state of Georgia and have a minimum 3.0 GPA. Students should submit applications as early as possible.

Target applicant(s): High school students. College students. Adult students.

Minimum GPA: 3.0

Amount: Varies.

Number of awards: Varies.

Scholarship may be renewable.

Deadline: Last day of classes.

How to apply: Applications are available online.

Exclusive: Visit www.UltimateScholarshipBook.com and enter code GE182120 for updates on this award.

(1822) · Houston Livestock Show and Rodeo Scholarships

Houston Livestock Show and Rodeo
Educational Programs Department, P.O. Box 20070, Houston, TX 77225-0070
Phone: 832-667-1285
Email: scholarship@rodeohouston.com
http://www.rodeohouston.com
Purpose: To support graduating high school students who are Texas residents.
Eligibility: Applicants must be U.S. citizens and be graduating high school seniors from public schools who have completed a current FAFSA. Applicants must also plan to attend and have applied to an accredited, not-for-profit university in Texas after graduation. SAT or ACT scores are required. Selection is based on financial need, academic performance and demonstrated leadership. Multiple types of scholarship are available. Specific eligibility criteria and deadlines differ for each scholarship.
Target applicant(s): High school students.
Amount: Varies.
Number of awards: Varies.
Deadline: Varies.
How to apply: Applications are available online. A copy of the application and other required documentation (varies for each scholarship) must be mailed to the Office of Educational Programs.
Exclusive: Visit www.UltimateScholarshipBook.com and enter code HO182220 for updates on this award.

(1823) · Howard P. Rawlings Educational Assistance (EA) Grant

Maryland Higher Education Commission
Office of Student Financial Assistance, 6 North Liberty Street, Baltimore, MD 21201
Phone: 800-974-1024
Email: osfamail@mhec.state.md.us
http://www.maryland.gov
Purpose: To help Maryland students who demonstrate financial need.
Eligibility: Applicants (and their parents, if applicants are dependents) must be residents of the state of Maryland. They must be high school seniors or undergraduate students and must be or plan to become full-time, degree-seeking students. They must complete the Free Application for Federal Student Aid (FAFSA) and must demonstrate financial need. Selection is based on financial need.
Target applicant(s): High school students. College students. Adult students.
Amount: $400-$3,000.
Number of awards: Varies.
Scholarship may be renewable.
Deadline: March 1.
How to apply: To apply, applicants must fill out and submit the FAFSA.
Exclusive: Visit www.UltimateScholarshipBook.com and enter code MA182320 for updates on this award.

(1824) · Howard P. Rawlings Guaranteed Access (GA) Grant

Maryland Higher Education Commission
Office of Student Financial Assistance, 6 North Liberty Street, Baltimore, MD 21201
Phone: 800-974-1024
Email: osfamail@mhec.state.md.us
http://www.maryland.gov
Purpose: To help Maryland students with financial need afford college.
Eligibility: Applicants and their parents must both be legal residents of the state of Maryland. Applicants must be U.S. citizens or eligible noncitizens, complete the Free Application for Federal Student Aid (FAFSA) and the Guaranteed Access (GA) Grant application. Applicants and families must also meet the established income limits to qualify.
Target applicant(s): High school students.
Amount: Up to $18,400.
Number of awards: Varies.
Scholarship may be renewable.
Deadline: March 1.
How to apply: Complete the FAFSA.
Exclusive: Visit www.UltimateScholarshipBook.com and enter code MA182420 for updates on this award.

(1825) · Hugh A. Smith Scholarship Fund

American Legion, Department of Kansas
1314 SW Topeka Boulevard, Topeka, KS 66612
Phone: 785-232-9315
http://www.ksamlegion.org
Purpose: To provide assistance to needy and worthy children of American Legion and American Legion Auxiliary members.
Eligibility: Applicants must be average or better students who are high school seniors or college freshmen or sophomores enrolling or enrolled in a post-secondary school in Kansas. They must be the son or daughter of a veteran, and a parent must have been a member of the Kansas American Legion or American Legion Auxiliary for the past three years. The children of deceased parents are also eligible if the parent was a paid member at the time of death. Applicants must submit three letters of recommendation, including one from a teacher, an essay on "Why I Want to Go to College," high school transcript, a 1040 income statement and documentation of parent's veteran status.
Target applicant(s): High school students. College students. Adult students.
Amount: $500.
Number of awards: 1.
Deadline: February 15.
How to apply: Applications are available online.
Exclusive: Visit www.UltimateScholarshipBook.com and enter code AM182520 for updates on this award.

(1826) · IAD Foundation Scholarships

Iowa Automobile Dealers Foundation for Education
1111 Office Park Road, West Des Moines, IA 50265
Phone: 515-440-7625
Email: mcason@iada.com
http://www.iada.com/foundationforeducation.aspx
Purpose: To support Iowa students pursuing automotive-related studies.
Eligibility: Applicants must be Iowa high school graduates enrolling in a two- or four-year post-secondary institution to pursue automotive-related studies.
Target applicant(s): High school students.
Amount: Varies.
Number of awards: 9.
Deadline: March 1.
How to apply: Applications are available online.
Exclusive: Visit www.UltimateScholarshipBook.com and enter code IO182620 for updates on this award.

(1827) • ICAN Outstanding Student Scholarship

Iowa College Access Network
St. Ambrose University, North Davenport Education Center, 1950 E. 54th Street, Davenport, IA 52807
Phone: 877-272-4692
Email: ican@icansucceed.org
http://www.icansucceed.org

Purpose: To support Iowa students preparing to enter post-secondary education.
Eligibility: Applicants must be graduating high school seniors who are enrolling in a two- or four-year institution in Iowa. Students must write an essay as part of their application materials.
Target applicant(s): High school students.
Amount: $250.
Number of awards: 2.
Deadline: March 1.
How to apply: Applications are available online.
Exclusive: Visit www.UltimateScholarshipBook.com and enter code IO182720 for updates on this award.

(1828) • ICCA Scholarships

Iowa Cheerleading Coaches' Association
Attn.: JoEllen Wesselmann, P.O. Box 207, Huxley, IA 50124
Phone: 515-494-3541
Email: iccajo@hotmail.com
http://iowacheercoaches.org/

Purpose: To aid graduating Iowa cheerleaders who display outstanding scholastic achievement in their pursuit of higher education.
Eligibility: Applicants must be a high school senior and have a coach who is a current member of the Iowa Cheerleading Coaches' Association. Students must also have a 3.5 GPA or higher. Selection is based on academic achievement, leadership and community involvement.
Target applicant(s): High school students.
Minimum GPA: 3.5
Amount: $500.
Number of awards: Varies.
Deadline: February 1.
How to apply: Applications are available online and include the basic application, the one page essay, activity listing, cheerleading coach letter of recommendation, additional letter of recommendation and letter from high school counselor verifying grade point average.
Exclusive: Visit www.UltimateScholarshipBook.com and enter code IO182820 for updates on this award.

(1829) • Ichiro and Masako Hirata Scholarship

Hawaii Community Foundation - Scholarships
827 Fort Street Mall, Honolulu, HI 96813
Phone: 888-731-3863
Email: scholarships@hcf-hawaii.org
https://www.hawaiicommunityfoundation.org

Purpose: To provide financial assistance to Hawaii students who are pursuing degrees in education.
Eligibility: Applicants must be majoring or concentrating in education. They must be college juniors, college seniors or graduate students and have a GPA of 3.0 or higher.
Target applicant(s): College students. Graduate school students. Adult students.
Minimum GPA: 3.0
Amount: Varies.
Number of awards: Varies.
Deadline: January 31.
How to apply: To apply, register online, complete the online application and select the scholarships to which you wish to apply. In addition, mail the supporting materials: printed confirmation page from the online application, personal statement, copy of Student Aid Report (SAR) available at www.fafsa.ed.gov and official transcript.
Exclusive: Visit www.UltimateScholarshipBook.com and enter code HA182920 for updates on this award.

(1830) • Idaho State Broadcasters Association Scholarships

Idaho State Broadcasters Association
1674 Hill Road, Suite 3, Boise, ID 83702
Phone: 208-345-3072
Email: isba@qwestoffice.net
http://www.idahobroadcasters.org

Purpose: To aid students planning careers in broadcasting.
Eligibility: Applicants must be enrolled full-time in an Idaho college or university, have exhibited superior potential in activities or courses related to broadcasting and be respected among their peer groups. Students must have a GPA of 2.0 or higher in the first two years of college and a GPA of 2.5 in the last two years.
Target applicant(s): College students. Adult students.
Minimum GPA: 2.0
Amount: $1,000.
Number of awards: At least 2.
Deadline: March 15.
How to apply: Applications are available online. An application form, letter of recommendation, transcript and essay are required.
Exclusive: Visit www.UltimateScholarshipBook.com and enter code ID183020 for updates on this award.

(1831) • Illinois AMVETS Junior ROTC Scholarship

Illinois AMVETS Service Foundation
AMVETS Department of Illinois, 2200 South Sixth Street, Springfield, IL 62703
Phone: 217-528-4713
Email: crystal@ilamvets.org
http://www.ilamvets.org

Purpose: To provide financial assistance for college to high school ROTC members.
Eligibility: Applicants must be Illinois high school seniors who are participating in a Junior ROTC program and have taken the SAT or ACT.
Target applicant(s): High school students.
Amount: $1,000.
Number of awards: Varies.
Deadline: March 1.
How to apply: Applications are available online.
Exclusive: Visit www.UltimateScholarshipBook.com and enter code IL183120 for updates on this award.

(1832) • Illinois AMVETS Ladies Auxiliary Memorial Scholarship

Illinois AMVETS Service Foundation
AMVETS Department of Illinois, 2200 South Sixth Street, Springfield, IL 62703
Phone: 217-528-4713
Email: crystal@ilamvets.org
http://www.ilamvets.org

Purpose: To provide financial assistance to children and grandchildren of U.S. veterans and members of the military.
Eligibility: Applicants must be Illinois high school seniors who have taken the SAT or ACT, and they must be the children or grandchildren of veterans who were honorably discharged after September 15, 1940 or who are currently serving in the military.
Target applicant(s): High school students.
Amount: Varies.
Number of awards: Varies.
Deadline: March 1.
How to apply: Applications are available online.
Exclusive: Visit www.UltimateScholarshipBook.com and enter code IL183220 for updates on this award.

(1833) • Illinois AMVETS Ladies Auxiliary Worchid Scholarship

Illinois AMVETS Service Foundation
AMVETS Department of Illinois, 2200 South Sixth Street,
Springfield, IL 62703
Phone: 217-528-4713
Email: crystal@ilamvets.org
http://www.ilamvets.org
Purpose: To provide financial assistance for students whose parents are U.S. veterans.
Eligibility: Applicants must be Illinois high school seniors whose mother or father is now deceased but had served after September 15, 1940, and was Honorably Discharged. Death of the parent does not have to be from military action or as a result of a service-related disability. Applicants must also have taken the SAT or ACT.
Target applicant(s): High school students.
Amount: Varies.
Number of awards: Varies.
Deadline: July 15.
How to apply: Applications are available online.
Exclusive: Visit www.UltimateScholarshipBook.com and enter code IL183320 for updates on this award.

(1834) • Illinois AMVETS Sad Sacks Nursing Scholarship

Illinois AMVETS Service Foundation
AMVETS Department of Illinois, 2200 South Sixth Street,
Springfield, IL 62703
Phone: 217-528-4713
Email: crystal@ilamvets.org
http://www.ilamvets.org
Purpose: To assist Illinois students who are pursuing a career in nursing.
Eligibility: Applicants must be Illinois high school seniors who have been accepted into a nursing program or students who are already attending nursing school in Illinois. They must have financial need and a satisfactory academic record, character and activity record. Dependents of deceased or disabled veterans receive priority.
Target applicant(s): High school students. College students. Adult students.
Amount: Varies.
Number of awards: Varies.
Deadline: March 1.
How to apply: Applications are available online.
Exclusive: Visit www.UltimateScholarshipBook.com and enter code IL183420 for updates on this award.

(1835) • Illinois AMVETS Service Foundation Scholarship

Illinois AMVETS Service Foundation
AMVETS Department of Illinois, 2200 South Sixth Street,
Springfield, IL 62703
Phone: 217-528-4713
Email: crystal@ilamvets.org
http://www.ilamvets.org
Purpose: To help Illinois students pay for college.
Eligibility: Applicants musts be Illinois high school seniors who have taken the SAT or ACT. Preference is given to students who are the children or grandchildren of Illinois veterans.
Target applicant(s): High school students.
Amount: $1,000.
Number of awards: Varies.
Deadline: March 1.
How to apply: Applications are available online.
Exclusive: Visit www.UltimateScholarshipBook.com and enter code IL183520 for updates on this award.

(1836) • Illinois AMVETS Trade School Scholarship

Illinois AMVETS Service Foundation
AMVETS Department of Illinois, 2200 South Sixth Street,
Springfield, IL 62703
Phone: 217-528-4713
Email: crystal@ilamvets.org
http://www.ilamvets.org
Purpose: To provide financial assistance to Illinois students who plan to attend a trade school.
Eligibility: Applicants must be seniors at an Illinois high school who have been accepted into a trade school program. Students must submit a copy of their acceptance letter with the application form. Preference is given to students who are the children or grandchildren of veterans.
Target applicant(s): High school students.
Amount: $1,000.
Number of awards: Varies.
Deadline: March 1.
How to apply: Applications are available online.
Exclusive: Visit www.UltimateScholarshipBook.com and enter code IL183620 for updates on this award.

(1837) • Illinois Association for Health, Physical Education, Recreation and Dance Scholarships

Illinois Association for Health, Physical Education, Recreation and Dance
P.O. Box 1326, Jacksonville, IL 62651
Phone: 217-245-6413
Email: iahperd@gmail.com
http://www.iahperd.org/grants/scholarships
Purpose: To support physical education students.
Eligibility: Applicants must be full-time junior or senior level undergraduate students at colleges or universities in Illinois and must major in health, physical education, recreation or dance. Students must have been members of IAHPERD since December 1 of the previous year and may receive this award no more than twice.
Target applicant(s): College students. Adult students.
Amount: $1,500-$2,000.
Number of awards: 6.
Scholarship may be renewable.
Deadline: June 2.

How to apply: Applications are available online. An application form, cover letter, resume, essay, transcript and two letters of recommendation are required.
Exclusive: Visit www.UltimateScholarshipBook.com and enter code IL183720 for updates on this award.

(1838) • Illinois Department of Children and Family Services Scholarship Program

Illinois Department of Children and Family Services
406 E. Monroe Street, Springfield, IL 62701
Phone: 217-557-5805
https://www.illinois.gov/dcfs/Pages/default.aspx
Purpose: To support students who have been under the guardianship of the Department of Children and Family Services.
Eligibility: Applicants must be between 16 and 21 years of age as of the application deadline and have a diploma from an accredited high school or a GED by the end of the current school year. Students must be in the Subsidized Guardianship Program, or the department must have court-ordered legal guardianship or have had legal guardianship for the applicant before adoption was finalized. Recipients must attend an Illinois state community college or university.
Target applicant(s): High school students. College students.
Amount: Up to full tuition plus $511 monthly stipend.
Number of awards: 53.
Scholarship may be renewable.
Deadline: March 31.
How to apply: Applications are available online. An application form, transcript or copy of GED, SAT or ACT scores, three letters of recommendation and a college transcript (if applicable) are required.
Exclusive: Visit www.UltimateScholarshipBook.com and enter code IL183820 for updates on this award.

(1839) • Illinois Hospital Research and Educational Foundation Scholarship

Illinois Hospital Research and Educational Foundation
1151 East Warrenville Road, Naperville, IL 60563
Phone: 630-276-5400
Email: webmaster@team-iha.org
http://www.ihatoday.org
Purpose: To aid Illinois students enrolled in hospital-related healthcare certificate and degree programs.
Eligibility: Applicants must be Illinois residents. They must be either enrolled in or accepted into a hospital-related healthcare degree or certificate program, excluding any programs having a general education curriculum (such as pre-medicine programs). Applicants must have at least one year remaining in their program of study. They should have a GPA of 3.5 on a four-point scale in order to be competitive for this award. Selection is based on academic merit and financial need.
Target applicant(s): High school students. College students. Adult students.
Amount: $1,000.
Number of awards: Varies.
Deadline: April 15.
How to apply: Applications are available online. An application form, official transcript, two letters of recommendation, personal statement and proof of acceptance into a qualifying degree program (for rising freshmen only) are required.
Exclusive: Visit www.UltimateScholarshipBook.com and enter code IL183920 for updates on this award.

(1840) • Illinois Oratorical Program Scholarships

American Legion - Department of Illinois
2720 East Lincoln Street, Bloomington, IL 61704
Phone: 309-663-0361
Email: hdqs@illegion.org
http://www.illegion.org/scholarships/
Purpose: To enhance high school students' experience with and understanding of the U.S. Constitution. The contest will help develop students' leadership skills and civic appreciation, as well as the ability to deliver thoughtful, insightful orations regarding U.S. citizenship and its inherent responsibilities.
Eligibility: Applicants must be high school students under the age of 20 who are U.S. citizens or legal residents and residents of the state. Students first give an oration within their state and winners compete at the national level. The oration must be related to the Constitution of the United States focusing on the duties and obligations citizens have to the government. It must be in English and be between eight and ten minutes. There is also an assigned topic which is posted on the website, and it should be between three and five minutes.
Target applicant(s): High school students.
Amount: $100-$2,000.
Number of awards: 11.
Deadline: January 26.
How to apply: Application information is available by contacting the local American Legion Post or Illinois Department Headquarters.
Exclusive: Visit www.UltimateScholarshipBook.com and enter code AM184020 for updates on this award.

(1841) • Incentive Program for Aspiring Teachers

Massachusetts Department of Higher Education
Office of Student Financial Assistance, 454 Broadway, Suite 200, Revere, MA 02151
Phone: 617-727-9420
Email: osfa@osfa.mass.edu
http://www.mass.edu/osfa/students/forstudents.asp
Purpose: To provide financial support for Massachusetts college students who are studying to become teachers.
Eligibility: Applicants must be in their third or fourth year at a public college in the state of Massachusetts, and they must be enrolled in a field with teacher shortages. They must have a 3.0 GPA in general education courses, and they must remain in satisfactory academic standing while receiving the scholarship. Students must agree to work in a public school in Massachusetts for two years after earning a bachelor's degree.
Target applicant(s): College students. Adult students.
Minimum GPA: 3.0
Amount: Full tuition.
Number of awards: Varies.
Scholarship may be renewable.
Deadline: Varies.
How to apply: Applications are available at college financial aid offices.
Exclusive: Visit www.UltimateScholarshipBook.com and enter code MA184120 for updates on this award.

(1842) • Independence Excavating, A DiGeronimo Company Scholarship

Associated General Contractors of Ohio
1755 Northwest Boulevard , Columbus, OH 43212
Phone: 614-486-6446
Email: parker@agcohio.com
https://agcohio.com/scholarships

Purpose: To aid students who are preparing for construction-related careers at postsecondary institutions located in Ohio, Pennsylvania and West Virginia.
Eligibility: Applicants must be U.S. citizens. They must be in at least the second year of study in a two-year, four-year or five-year undergraduate degree program that is related to construction. They must be enrolled at a postsecondary institution located in West Virginia, Pennsylvania or Ohio and have a GPA of 2.5 or higher. Applicants must have plans to work in the construction industry. Selection is based on the overall strength of the application.
Target applicant(s): College students. Adult students.
Minimum GPA: 2.5
Amount: Varies.
Number of awards: Varies.
Deadline: Varies.
How to apply: Applications are available online. An application form, transcript and personal essay are required.
Exclusive: Visit www.UltimateScholarshipBook.com and enter code AS184220 for updates on this award.

(1843) • Indiana Broadcasters Association College Scholarships

Indiana Broadcasters Association
P.O. Box 902, Carmel, IN 46082
Phone: 317-770-0970
Email: sam@indianabroadcasters.org
https://www.indianabroadcasters.org/scholarships/
Purpose: To support student broadcasters.
Eligibility: Applicants must be Indiana residents and current college students with a 3.0 or higher GPA. Students must be actively participating in a college broadcast facility or working for a commercial broadcast facility and be attending an IBA member institution that has a radio/TV facility on campus and/or offers majors in telecommunications or broadcast journalism.
Target applicant(s): College students. Adult students.
Minimum GPA: 3.0
Amount: Varies.
Number of awards: 6.
Deadline: Varies.
How to apply: Applications are available online. An application form, essay and transcript request form are required.
Exclusive: Visit www.UltimateScholarshipBook.com and enter code IN184320 for updates on this award.

(1844) • Indiana Golf Foundation Scholarship

Indiana Golf Association
P.O. Box 516, Franklin, IN 46131
Phone: 317-738-9696
Email: astrong@indianagolf.org
http://www.indianagolf.org
Purpose: To support youth who have participated in the Indiana Junior Golf Program.
Eligibility: Applicants must be high school seniors who have participated in the Indiana Junior Golf Program for at least two years, have a 3.0 GPA or higher, display strong character and have financial need. Selection is based on these criteria as well as a personal essay.
Target applicant(s): High school students.
Minimum GPA: 3.0
Amount: $2,500.
Number of awards: 4.
Deadline: March 3.
How to apply: Applications are available online and must also include the personal essay, high school transcript, IRS Form 1040 and at least one letter of recommendation.
Exclusive: Visit www.UltimateScholarshipBook.com and enter code IN184420 for updates on this award.

(1845) • Indiana Oratorical Contest

American Legion, Department of Indiana
5440 Herbert Lord Road, Indianapolis, IN 46216
Phone: 317-630-1300
Email: programs@indlegion.org
http://www.indianalegion.org
Purpose: To enhance high school students' experience with and understanding of the U.S. Constitution. The contest will help develop students' leadership skills and civic appreciation, as well as the ability to deliver thoughtful, insightful orations regarding U.S. citizenship and its inherent responsibilities.
Eligibility: Applicants must be high school students under the age of 20 who are U.S. citizens or legal residents and residents of the state. Students first give an oration within their state and winners compete at the national level. The oration must be related to the Constitution of the United States focusing on the duties and obligations citizens have to the government. It must be in English and be between eight and ten minutes. There is also an assigned topic which is posted on the website, and it should be between three and five minutes.
Target applicant(s): High school students.
Amount: $200-$3,400.
Number of awards: Varies.
Deadline: March 5.
How to apply: Application information is available from the local American Legion Post and online.
Exclusive: Visit www.UltimateScholarshipBook.com and enter code AM184520 for updates on this award.

(1846) • Iowa 4-H College Scholarships

Iowa 4-H Foundation
Extension 4-H Youth Building, 1259 Stange Road, Ames, IA 50011-1002
Phone: 515-294-4443
https://www.iowa4hfoundation.org
Purpose: To assist Iowa 4-H participants to pursue higher education.
Eligibility: Applicants must be Iowa residents and 4-H members who are enrolling in or currently enrolled in an Iowa post-secondary institution. Students must submit two letters of recommendation along with their materials.
Target applicant(s): High school students. College students. Adult students.
Amount: Varies.
Number of awards: Varies.
Deadline: February 1.
How to apply: Applications are available online.
Exclusive: Visit www.UltimateScholarshipBook.com and enter code IO184620 for updates on this award.

(1847) • Iowa Financial Know-How Challenge: Senior Scholarship

Iowa Student Loan
6775 Vista Drive, West Des Moines, IA 50266-9305
Phone: 515-273-7656

Email: scholarship@studentloan.org
http://www.IowaStudentLoan.org/Come2Iowa
Purpose: To reward Iowa students interested in financial literacy.
Eligibility: Applicants must be legal U.S. residents who reside in Iowa. Students must be graduating seniors at an Iowa high school and plan to attend college. Applicants must complete online financial literacy tutorials and assessments as well as write an essay.
Target applicant(s): High school students.
Amount: $2,000.
Number of awards: 30.
Deadline: February 22.
How to apply: Applications are available online.
Exclusive: Visit www.UltimateScholarshipBook.com and enter code IO184720 for updates on this award.

(1848) • Iowa Newspaper Association Scholarships

Iowa Newspaper Association
319 E 5th Street, Des Moines, IA 50309
Phone: 515-244-2145
Email: ina@inanews.com
http://www.inanews.com
Purpose: To support students preparing for careers in the newspaper industry.
Eligibility: Applicants must be Iowa residents who are high school seniors or current college students and must attend an in-state college or university. Students must plan to work in the newspaper industry in Iowa upon completion of their degrees.
Target applicant(s): High school students. College students. Adult students.
Amount: $500-$1,000.
Number of awards: Varies.
Deadline: February 17.
How to apply: Applications are available online. An application form, two letters of reference, personal statement and two writing samples are required.
Exclusive: Visit www.UltimateScholarshipBook.com and enter code IO184820 for updates on this award.

(1849) • Iowa Oratorical Contest

American Legion, Department of Iowa
720 Lyon Street, Des Moines, IA 50309
Phone: 800-365-8387
Email: programs@ialegion.org
http://www.ialegion.org
Purpose: To enhance high school students' experience with and understanding of the U.S. Constitution. The contest will help develop students' leadership skills and civic appreciation, as well as the ability to deliver thoughtful, insightful orations regarding U.S. citizenship and its inherent responsibilities.
Eligibility: Applicants must be high school students under the age of 20 who are U.S. citizens or legal residents and residents of the state. Students first give an oration within their state and winners compete at the national level. The oration must be related to the Constitution of the United States focusing on the duties and obligations citizens have to the government. It must be in English and be between eight and ten minutes. There is also an assigned topic which is posted on the website, and it should be between three and five minutes.
Target applicant(s): High school students.
Amount: Up to $18,000.
Number of awards: Varies.
Deadline: Varies.
How to apply: Applications are available online.
Exclusive: Visit www.UltimateScholarshipBook.com and enter code AM184920 for updates on this award.

(1850) • Iowa PGA Foundation Charlie Burkart Scholarship

Iowa PGA Foundation
3184 HWY 22 Riverside, Riverside, IA 52327
https://www.iowapgajuniorgolf.com/charlie-burkart/
Purpose: To assist Iowa student golf athletes to pursue post-secondary education.
Eligibility: Applicants must reside within the boundaries of the Iowa PGA section, including the cities of Monmouth, Macomb, Galesburg, Moline, Rock Island, Kewanee and Galena. Students must demonstrate an interest in golf, community involvement and financial need.
Target applicant(s): High school students. College students. Adult students.
Amount: $1,500.
Number of awards: 1.
Scholarship may be renewable.
Deadline: June 14.
How to apply: Applications are available online.
Exclusive: Visit www.UltimateScholarshipBook.com and enter code IO185020 for updates on this award.

(1851) • Iowa Physician Assistant Society Scholarship

Iowa Physician Assistant Society
6919 Vista Drive, West Des Moines, IA 50266
Phone: 515-282-8192
Email: info@iapasociety.org
http://www.iapasociety.org
Purpose: To aid Iowa students who are enrolled in a physician assistant degree program.
Eligibility: Applicants must be enrolled in an approved Physician Assistant (PA) degree program at a postsecondary institution located in Iowa. They must have had an outstanding undergraduate academic record, strong leadership skills and a well-developed knowledge of the role of the professional physician assistant. Selection is based on academic merit, demonstrated leadership ability, commitment to the field of physician assisting, extracurricular activities and professional awareness.
Target applicant(s): College students. Adult students.
Amount: $1,000.
Number of awards: 3.
Deadline: September 5.
How to apply: Applications are available online. An application form, transcript and personal statement are required.
Exclusive: Visit www.UltimateScholarshipBook.com and enter code IO185120 for updates on this award.

(1852) • Iowa Pork Foundation Scholarship

Iowa Pork Producers Association
1636 NW 114th Street, P.O. Box 71009, Clive, IA 50325
Phone: 800-372-7675
Email: info@iowapork.org
http://www.iowapork.org
Purpose: To aid Iowa agriculture students who are interested in the pork industry.
Eligibility: Applicants must be Iowa residents who are enrolled at or who plan to enroll at a two-year or four-year postsecondary institution

located in Iowa. They must be majoring in or have plans to major in an agriculture-related undergraduate program that focuses on swine production. They must maintain a GPA of 2.5 or higher. Selection is based on the overall strength of the application.
Target applicant(s): High school students. College students. Adult students.
Minimum GPA: 2.5
Amount: $1,000-$1,500.
Number of awards: 16.
Scholarship may be renewable.
Deadline: April 1.
How to apply: Applications are available online. An application form, two recommendation letters and a transcript are required.
Exclusive: Visit www.UltimateScholarshipBook.com and enter code IO185220 for updates on this award.

(1853) • Iowa Scholarship for the Arts

Iowa Arts Council
600 E. Locust, Des Moines, IA 50319-0290
Phone: 515-281-6412
https://iowaculture.gov/arts
Purpose: To aid outstanding young artists.
Eligibility: Applicants must be Iowa residents and graduating high school seniors and show proven artistic ability in dance, literature, music, theatre, traditional arts or visual arts. Students must be accepted full-time to an accredited Iowa college or university and must major in one of the aforementioned areas.
Target applicant(s): High school students.
Amount: $1,500.
Number of awards: Varies.
Deadline: February 2.
How to apply: Applications are available online. An application form, two letters of recommendation and an essay are required.
Exclusive: Visit www.UltimateScholarshipBook.com and enter code IO185320 for updates on this award.

(1854) • Iowa Thespian Chapter Board Senior Scholarships

Iowa Thespian Chapter
Leslie LaCorte, Iowa Thespian Treasurer, Davenport North High School, 626 West 53rd Street, Davenport, IA 52806
Phone: 563-332-5151
Email: myattw@pleasval.k12.ia.us
http://www.iowathespians.org
Purpose: To aid promising young thespians.
Eligibility: Applicants must be Iowa high school seniors and have an overall GPA of 2.0 or higher with a GPA of 3.0 or higher in arts-related classes. Students must be members of the International Thespian Society in good standing. Applicants must plan to major or minor in theatre, film, radio and television, broadcasting, music or dance. Applicants must also perform an audition at the Iowa Thespian Festival in the performance, technical or theatre educator category.
Target applicant(s): High school students.
Minimum GPA: 2.0
Amount: $1,000.
Number of awards: Varies.
Deadline: October 19.
How to apply: Applications are available from the Iowa Thespian Society. An application form and resume are required.
Exclusive: Visit www.UltimateScholarshipBook.com and enter code IO185420 for updates on this award.

(1855) • Iowa Tuition Grants

Iowa College Student Aid Commission
430 East Grand Avenue, Floor 3, Des Moines, IA 50309-1920
Phone: 515-725-3400
Email: info@iowacollegeaid.org
https://www.iowacollegeaid.gov
Purpose: To help students attend Iowa's independent colleges and universities.
Eligibility: Applicants must be enrolled in or planning to enroll at least part-time in an eligible Iowa college or university and demonstrate financial need. Priority is given to the neediest applicants.
Target applicant(s): High school students. College students. Adult students.
Amount: Varies.
Number of awards: Varies.
Scholarship may be renewable.
Deadline: July 1.
How to apply: Complete the Free Application for Federal Student Aid (FAFSA).
Exclusive: Visit www.UltimateScholarshipBook.com and enter code IO185520 for updates on this award.

(1856) • Iowa Vocational-Technical Tuition Grants

Iowa College Student Aid Commission
430 East Grand Avenue, Floor 3, Des Moines, IA 50309-1920
Phone: 515-725-3400
Email: info@iowacollegeaid.org
https://www.iowacollegeaid.gov
Purpose: To aid those Iowa residents enrolled in vocational-technical programs at community colleges.
Eligibility: Applicants must be enrolled in or planning to enroll in a career education or option course for 3 credit hours consisting of at least 15 weeks duration at an Iowa area community college and be U.S. citizens or permanent residents. Applicants must prove financial need.
Target applicant(s): High school students. College students. Adult students.
Amount: Up to $900.
Number of awards: Varies.
Scholarship may be renewable.
Deadline: July 1.
How to apply: Complete the Free Application for Federal Student Aid (FAFSA).
Exclusive: Visit www.UltimateScholarshipBook.com and enter code IO185620 for updates on this award.

(1857) • Irvine W. Cook WA0CGS Scholarship

American Radio Relay League Foundation
225 Main Street, Newington, CT 06111-1494
Phone: 860-594-0348
Email: foundation@arrl.org
http://www.arrl.org/scholarship-program
Purpose: To provide scholarship assistance to Kansas residents who are amateur radio operators.
Eligibility: Applicants must be residents of Kansas and holders of an active amateur radio license of any class. Preference is given to students who are studying electronics, communications or a related subject at the baccalaureate level or higher.

Target applicant(s): College students. Graduate school students. Adult students.
Amount: $1,000.
Number of awards: 1.
Deadline: January 31.
How to apply: Applications are available online.
Exclusive: Visit www.UltimateScholarshipBook.com and enter code AM185720 for updates on this award.

(1858) • ISAA Scholarship Program

Iowa State Archery Association
ISAA Scholarship Program, Jan Kostka, Chair, 1425 Plymouth Road, Mason City, IA 50401
Email: jankostka@mac.com
http://www.isaaproam.com
Purpose: To aid students who have participated in the Iowa State Archery Association as they continue their education beyond high school.
Eligibility: Applicants must be a high school senior, have obtained a GED or be a full-time college student. The student must have been an active member of ISAA for at least two years. Selection is based on participation in ISAA activities, academic achievement, financial need, community involvement and the reference letters.
Target applicant(s): High school students. College students. Graduate school students. Adult students.
Amount: Up to $1,000.
Number of awards: Varies.
Deadline: December 31.
How to apply: Applications are available online.
Exclusive: Visit www.UltimateScholarshipBook.com and enter code IO185820 for updates on this award.

(1859) • Ivomec Generations of Excellence Internship and Scholarship Program

Texas CattleWomen
Erin Worrell, 657 Blue Oak Trail, Harper, TX 78631
Phone: 512-413-1616
Email: worrellerin@gmail.com
http://txcattlewomen.org/
Purpose: To aid Texas students who are preparing for careers in the beef industry.
Eligibility: Applicants must be permanent residents of Texas and be graduate students or rising undergraduate juniors or seniors who are enrolled at a Texas college or university. They must be majoring in agriculture or a related subject, must have a background in beef cattle and have a GPA of 2.5 or higher. Selection is based on the overall strength of the application.
Target applicant(s): College students. Graduate school students. Adult students.
Minimum GPA: 2.5
Amount: $1,000.
Number of awards: 1.
Deadline: May 1.
How to apply: Applications are available online. An application form and supporting materials are required.
Exclusive: Visit www.UltimateScholarshipBook.com and enter code TE185920 for updates on this award.

(1860) • J.D. Edsal Scholarship

Rhode Island Foundation
One Union Station, Providence, RI 02903
Phone: 401-274-4564
Email: rbogert@rifoundation.org
http://www.rifoundation.org
Purpose: To support undergraduate students who are planning to work in advertising, film or television.
Eligibility: Applicants must be residents of Rhode Island. They must be majoring in advertising, film-making or television production. Students must be attending school full-time.
Target applicant(s): High school students. College students. Adult students.
Amount: Varies.
Number of awards: Varies.
Deadline: Varies.
How to apply: Applications are available online.
Exclusive: Visit www.UltimateScholarshipBook.com and enter code RH186020 for updates on this award.

(1861) • J.R. Popalisky Scholarship

American Water Works Association - Missouri Section
Chester A. Bender, P.E., Scholarship Committee Chair, c/o Ponzer Youngquist, P.A., 227 East Dennis Avenue, Olathe, KS 66061
Phone: 913-782-0541
Email: cbender@pyengineers.com
http://www.awwa-mo.org
Purpose: To aid Missouri students whose coursework is related to the water supply industry.
Eligibility: Applicants must be U.S. citizens who are enrolled at an accredited college or university located in Missouri. They must have completed coursework in subjects relating to the water supply industry (such as environmental engineering, civil engineering or environmental science). Students who are receiving funding from an employer are ineligible. Selection is based on coursework relevance, GPA, financial need, recommendations, personal essay and extracurricular activities.
Target applicant(s): College students. Adult students.
Amount: $1,000.
Number of awards: At least 1.
Deadline: March 23.
How to apply: Applications are available online. An application form, personal essay and a financial analysis form are required.
Exclusive: Visit www.UltimateScholarshipBook.com and enter code AM186120 for updates on this award.

(1862) • Jack E. Barger, Sr. Memorial Nursing Scholarship

Nursing Foundation of Pennsylvania
3605 Vartan Way, Suite 204, Harrisburg, PA 17110
Phone: 717-827-4369
Email: info@thenfp.org
http://www.thenfp.org/scholarships/
Purpose: To aid Pennsylvania nursing undergraduates who are serving in the military, are veterans, are military spouses, are veterans' spouses or who are the children of active duty military or veterans.
Eligibility: Candidates must be residents of Pennsylvania and must be enrolled in an undergraduate nursing program at an institution located in Pennsylvania. They must be active duty military, veterans, military spouses, veterans' spouses or the children of active duty military or veterans. Candidates are nominated for this award by the deans and

department heads in the school of nursing at their institutions. Selection of award recipients will be determined by lottery.
Target applicant(s): High school students. College students. Adult students.
Amount: Varies.
Number of awards: Varies.
Deadline: April 30.
How to apply: Candidates are not required to submit an application for this award. Instead, the dean or department head of the candidate's school must submit a formal nomination to the scholarship committee.
Exclusive: Visit www.UltimateScholarshipBook.com and enter code NU186220 for updates on this award.

(1863) · Jack F. Tolbert Memorial Student Grant Program

Maryland Higher Education Commission
Office of Student Financial Assistance, 6 North Liberty Street, Baltimore, MD 21201
Phone: 800-974-1024
Email: osfamail@mhec.state.md.us
http://www.maryland.gov
Purpose: To assist students who are attending or planning to attend a private career school.
Eligibility: Students and their parents if they are dependents must be residents of Maryland. Applicants must also enroll at an approved private career school in the state for at least 18 hours per week.
Target applicant(s): High school students. College students. Adult students.
Amount: Up to $500.
Number of awards: Varies.
Scholarship may be renewable.
Deadline: Rolling.
How to apply: Students apply by completing the Free Application for Federal Student Aid (FAFSA) and turning it in to the financial aid office of the career school they will attend.
Exclusive: Visit www.UltimateScholarshipBook.com and enter code MA186320 for updates on this award.

(1864) · Jack Hughes Education Scholarship

California Nevada Racquetball Association
Terry Rogers, CNRA Scholarship Chairperson, 8317 Divernon Avenue, Las Vegas, NV 89149
Email: info@californianevadaracquetball.org
http://www.californiaracquetball.org
Purpose: To help graduating seniors and college undergraduates who are USA Racquetball (USAR) members expand racquetball.
Eligibility: Applicants must be high school seniors who will be graduating or college undergraduates. Students must reside in California or Nevada and demonstrate a desire to expand racquetball. Applicants must also be current USAR members.
Target applicant(s): High school students. College students. Adult students.
Amount: Varies.
Number of awards: Varies.
Deadline: August 15.
How to apply: Applications are available online.
Exclusive: Visit www.UltimateScholarshipBook.com and enter code CA186420 for updates on this award.

(1865) · Jackson Family Scholarship

Orange County Community Foundation
4041 MacArthur Boulevard, Suite 510, Newport Beach, CA 92660
Phone: 949-553-4202
Email: cmontesano@oc-cf.org
http://www.oc-cf.org
Purpose: To support students of California who are pursuing a degree in nursing.
Eligibility: Applicants must be accepted to an accredited nursing program and must have completed a minimum of two semesters. A minimum GPA of 3.0 is required. Students must intend on enrolling full-time.
Target applicant(s): College students. Adult students.
Minimum GPA: 3.0
Amount: $1,000.
Number of awards: Varies.
Deadline: March 15.
How to apply: Applications are available online.
Exclusive: Visit www.UltimateScholarshipBook.com and enter code OR186520 for updates on this award.

(1866) · James B. Morris Scholarship

James B. Morris Scholarship Fund
P.O. Box 12145, Des Moines, IA 50312
http://www.morrisscholarship.org
Purpose: To support Iowa minority students pursuing post-secondary education.
Eligibility: Applicants must be U.S. citizens of a minority ethnic status who are either Iowa high school graduates attending any U.S. college or university or non-Iowa residents who are attending an Iowa college or university. Students must have a minimum GPA of 2.5.
Target applicant(s): High school students. College students. Graduate school students. Adult students.
Minimum GPA: 2.5
Amount: Varies.
Number of awards: Varies.
Deadline: February 28.
How to apply: Applications are available online.
Exclusive: Visit www.UltimateScholarshipBook.com and enter code JA186620 for updates on this award.

(1867) · James F. and Doris M. Barton Scholarship

American Quarter Horse Foundation
Scholarship Program, 2601 East Interstate 40, Amarillo, TX 79104
Phone: 806-378-5029
Email: foundation@aqha.org
http://www.aqha.com
Purpose: To aid New York students who are current members of the Empire State Youth Quarter Horse Association and either the American Quarter Horse Association or the American Quarter Horse Youth Association.
Eligibility: Applicants must be New York residents who are members of the Empire State Youth Quarter Horse Association (ESYQHA). They also must be members of either the American Quarter Horse Association (AQHA) or the American Quarter Horse Youth Association (AQHYA). They must be enrolled in or planning to enroll in a two- or four-year degree program at an accredited postsecondary institution. Applicants must have a GPA of 3.0 or higher. Selection is based on the overall strength of the application.

Target applicant(s): High school students. College students. Adult students.
Minimum GPA: 3.0
Amount: $5,000.
Number of awards: Varies.
Deadline: December 1.
How to apply: Applications are available online. An application form, Student Aid Report (SAR), transcript, two recommendations, proof of residency and proof of association membership are required.
Exclusive: Visit www.UltimateScholarshipBook.com and enter code AM186720 for updates on this award.

(1868) • James F. Davis Memorial Scholarship

National Foliage Foundation
1533 Park Center Drive, Orlando, FL 32835
Phone: 800-375-3642
Email: info@nationalfoliagefoundation.org
http://www.nationalfoliagefoundation.org
Purpose: To aid students pursuing higher education in horticulture or a related discipline in Florida.
Eligibility: Applicants must be rising freshmen or undergraduates at an accredited postsecondary institution located in Florida. They must be full-time students who are enrolled in or who are planning to enroll in a degree program in horticulture or a related subject. They must have a GPA of 2.0 or higher. Selection is based on the overall strength of the application.
Target applicant(s): High school students. College students. Adult students.
Minimum GPA: 2.0
Amount: Varies.
Number of awards: Varies.
Scholarship may be renewable.
Deadline: January 15.
How to apply: Applications are available online. An application form, transcript, personal essay and two letters of recommendation are required.
Exclusive: Visit www.UltimateScholarshipBook.com and enter code NA186820 for updates on this award.

(1869) • James H. Dunn, Jr. Memorial Fellowship

Governor's Office of the State of Illinois
Dunn Fellowship Program, 207 State House, Springfield, IL 62706
Phone: 217-782-0244
Email: GOV.DunnFellowshipApp@illinois.gov
http://www.illinois.gov/gov/
Purpose: To provide college graduates with an opportunity to experience daily operations in state government for one year.
Eligibility: Fellows must possess a bachelor's degree. Fellows will be assigned to various posts in the Governor's office or in an office under the Governor's jurisdiction.
Target applicant(s): College students. Adult students.
Amount: $31,332 plus benefits.
Number of awards: Varies.
Deadline: March 17.
How to apply: Applications are available online or by mail.
Exclusive: Visit www.UltimateScholarshipBook.com and enter code GO186920 for updates on this award.

(1870) • James J. Burns and C.A. Haynes Textile Scholarship

Rhode Island Foundation
One Union Station, Providence, RI 02903
Phone: 401-274-4564
Email: rbogert@rifoundation.org
http://www.rifoundation.org
Purpose: To support students who are planning to work in the textile industry.
Eligibility: Students must be currently enrolled in a textile program. They must demonstrate financial need or academic excellence. Preference will be given to students whose parents are members of the National Association of Textile Supervisors.
Target applicant(s): High school students. College students. Graduate school students. Adult students.
Amount: $1,000.
Number of awards: Varies.
Deadline: May 5.
How to apply: Applications are available online.
Exclusive: Visit www.UltimateScholarshipBook.com and enter code RH187020 for updates on this award.

(1871) • James V. Day Scholarship

American Legion, Department of Maine
5 Verti Drive, Winslow, ME 04901-0727
Phone: 207-873-3229
Email: legionme@mainelegion.org
http://www.mainelegion.org
Purpose: To provide financial assistance to the children or grandchildren of American Legion, Department of Maine members.
Eligibility: Applicants must be U.S. citizens, residents of Maine and graduating high school seniors. They must be enrolled in an accredited college or vocational technical school and provide evidence of financial need. Applicants must demonstrate good character and a belief in the American way of life.
Target applicant(s): High school students.
Amount: $500.
Number of awards: Up to 2.
Deadline: May 1.
How to apply: Applications are available online.
Exclusive: Visit www.UltimateScholarshipBook.com and enter code AM187120 for updates on this award.

(1872) • Janelle Downing Memorial 4-H Scholarship

Missouri 4-H Foundation
1110 S. College Avenue, Room 152, Columbia, MO 65211
Phone: 573-882-2680
Email: 4hfoundation@missouri.edu
http://4h.missouri.edu/foundation/scholarships.aspx
Purpose: To aid present and former Missouri 4-H members who are preparing for careers in veterinary medicine and animal science.
Eligibility: Applicants must be Missouri residents who are present or former members of 4-H and who are rising undergraduate freshmen who are planning to major in veterinary medicine, pre-veterinary medicine or animal science. They must have a GPA of 3.0 or higher on a four-point scale. Preference will be given to those who will be enrolling at the University of Missouri College of Agriculture as freshmen. Selection is based on 4-H achievements, stated career goals and financial need.
Target applicant(s): High school students.
Minimum GPA: 3.0

Amount: $1,000.
Number of awards: 1.
Deadline: March 1.
How to apply: Applications are available online. An application form, transcript, financial information and essay are required.
Exclusive: Visit www.UltimateScholarshipBook.com and enter code MI187220 for updates on this award.

(1873) • Jean Lee/Jeff Marvin Collegiate Scholarships

Indiana Association for Health, Physical Education, Recreation and Dance
2007 Wilno Drive, Marion, IN 46952
Phone: 765-664-8319
Email: hatch@cometck.com
http://www.inahperd.org
Purpose: To aid students pursuing degrees in physical education-related fields.
Eligibility: Applicants must be attending an Indiana college or university and be upcoming juniors or seniors who are majoring in health education, physical education, recreation, dance education or allied areas.
Target applicant(s): College students. Adult students.
Amount: $1,000.
Number of awards: 6.
Deadline: January 15.
How to apply: Applications are available online. An application form, goals statement, statement of need, list of activities during college attendance, philosophy statement and two letters of recommendation are required.
Exclusive: Visit www.UltimateScholarshipBook.com and enter code IN187320 for updates on this award.

(1874) • Jeff Krosnoff Scholarship

Jeff Krosnoff Scholarship Fund
P.O. Box 8585, La Crescenta, CA 91214-0585
Email: Tracy@jeffkrosnoffscholarship.com
http://www.jeffkrosnoffscholarship.com
Purpose: To support California high school seniors who plan to enter four-year colleges.
Eligibility: Applicants must have an excellent academic record with a cumulative high school GPA of at least 3.0. Students must submit a transcript and a two- to four-page essay. The essay is given the greatest weight in the selection process.
Target applicant(s): High school students.
Minimum GPA: 3.0
Amount: $10,000.
Number of awards: 1.
Deadline: January 18.
How to apply: Applications are available online.
Exclusive: Visit www.UltimateScholarshipBook.com and enter code JE187420 for updates on this award.

(1875) • Jere W. Thompson, Jr. Scholarship

Dallas Foundation
Reagan Place at Old Parkland, 3963 Maple Avenue, Suite 390, Dallas, TX 75219
Phone: 214-741-9898
Email: rlasseter@dallasfoundation.org
https://www.dallasfoundation.org/scholarships.aspx
Purpose: To aid Texas civil engineering and construction engineering undergraduates.
Eligibility: Applicants must be rising undergraduate juniors enrolled full-time at a Texas postsecondary institution. They must be majoring in civil engineering or construction engineering and must demonstrate financial need. Selection is based on the overall strength of the application. Special consideration may go to those living in Collin, Dallas, Denton and Tarrant counties. Applicants must have a minimum 3.0 GPA.
Target applicant(s): College students. Adult students.
Minimum GPA: 3.0
Amount: Up to $8,000.
Number of awards: Varies.
Scholarship may be renewable.
Deadline: May 1.
How to apply: Applications are available online. An application form, financial information survey, a copy of the applicant's FAFSA form, an official transcript, personal statement and one to three recommendation letters are required.
Exclusive: Visit www.UltimateScholarshipBook.com and enter code DA187520 for updates on this award.

(1876) • Jerome B. Steinbach Scholarship

Oregon Office of Student Access and Completion
1500 Valley River Drive, Suite 100, Eugene, OR 97401
Phone: 541-687-7422
Email: cheryl.a.connolly@state.or.us
https://oregonstudentaid.gov/
Purpose: To assist Oregon undergraduate students.
Eligibility: Applicants must be natural-born U.S. citizens and Oregon residents. They must be rising undergraduate sophomores, juniors or seniors at an accredited U.S. postsecondary institution and have a GPA of 3.5 or higher. U.S. Bank employees and their relatives are ineligible. Selection is based on financial need.
Target applicant(s): College students. Adult students.
Minimum GPA: 3.5
Amount: Varies.
Number of awards: Varies.
Scholarship may be renewable.
Deadline: Varies.
How to apply: Applications are available online. A completed FAFSA, application form and supporting documents are required.
Exclusive: Visit www.UltimateScholarshipBook.com and enter code OR187620 for updates on this award.

(1877) • Jimmie L. Dean Scholarship

Jimmie L. Dean Scholarship Foundation, Inc.
20 East 5th Street, Suite 1200G, Tulsa, OK 74103
Email: info@jimmiedeanfoundation.org
https://jimmiedeanfoundation.org
Purpose: To encourage Oklahoma students to pursue education.
Eligibility: Applicants must be legal residents and have lived in Oklahoma for the past six years. Students must be graduating from an Oklahoma high school or have completed graduation requirements through homeschooling. Applicants must be attending an Oklahoma college, university or technical school as a full-time, first-time student.
Target applicant(s): High school students.
Amount: Up to $10,000.
Number of awards: Varies.
Scholarship may be renewable.
Deadline: April 15.
How to apply: Applications are available online.

Exclusive: Visit www.UltimateScholarshipBook.com and enter code JI187720 for updates on this award.

(1878) • Jimmy Rane Foundation Scholarships

Jimmy Rane Foundation
P.O. Box 40, Abbeville, AL 36310
Phone: 800-310-4053
Email: contactus@applyists.com
http://www.jimmyranefoundation.org
Purpose: To support students who are planning to pursue undergraduate degrees.
Eligibility: Applicants must be high school seniors or college freshmen or sophomores who are residents of Alabama, Arkansas, Delaware, Florida, Georgia, Iowa, Kansas, Kentucky, Louisiana, Maryland, Mississippi, Missouri, Nebraska, New Jersey, New York, North Carolina, Ohio, Oklahoma, Pennsylvania, South Carolina, Tennessee, Texas, Virginia, West Virginia or the District of Columbia. Students must have a minimum GPA of 3.0 for high school seniors or 2.75 for college students. Selection is based on academic excellence, community involvement, leadership skills, awards and honors and financial need.
Target applicant(s): High school students. College students.
Minimum GPA: 3.0 for high school students, 2.75 for college students
Amount: $500-$5,000.
Number of awards: Varies.
Deadline: February 8.
How to apply: Applications are available online.
Exclusive: Visit www.UltimateScholarshipBook.com and enter code JI187820 for updates on this award.

(1879) • Joe Foss, An American Hero Scholarship

Sioux Falls Area Community Foundation
The Depot at Cherapa Place, 200 N. Cherapa Place, Sioux Falls, SD 57103-2205
Phone: 605-336-7055
Email: pgale@sfacf.org
http://www.sfacf.org/scholarships/
Purpose: To support high school seniors who have strong values, courage and patriotism.
Eligibility: Applicants must have at least a 3.5 GPA and an ACT score of 21 or above. Students must reside in South Dakota.
Target applicant(s): High school students.
Minimum GPA: 3.5
Amount: $1,000.
Number of awards: 6.
Deadline: March 15.
How to apply: Applications are available online.
Exclusive: Visit www.UltimateScholarshipBook.com and enter code SI187920 for updates on this award.

(1880) • Joel Abromson Memorial Scholarship

Equality Maine Foundation
550 Forest Avenue, P.O. Box 1951, Portland, ME 04101
Phone: 207-761-3732
Email: info@equalitymaine.org
http://www.equalitymaine.org
Purpose: To promote equality for students regardless of their sexual orientation and gender expression through an essay contest.
Eligibility: Applicants must be Maine high school seniors, and they must be accepted to an institution of higher learning.
Target applicant(s): High school students.
Amount: $1,000.
Number of awards: Varies.
Deadline: April 15.
How to apply: Students may apply by sending a cover letter, essay, two letters of recommendation and a copy of their college acceptance letter to EqualityMaine.
Exclusive: Visit www.UltimateScholarshipBook.com and enter code EQ188020 for updates on this award.

(1881) • Joel Garcia Memorial Scholarship

CCNMA: Latino Journalists of California
ASU Cronkite School of Journalism, 725 Arizona Avenue, Suite 404, Santa Monica, CA 90401-1734
Phone: 424-229-9482
Email: ccnmainfo@ccnma.org
http://ccnma.org/scholarships-and-awards/
Purpose: To support Latino students studying journalism who are California residents or are attending California schools.
Eligibility: Applicants must be Latino and either attending California schools or be California residents attending out-of-state schools. Students must show an interest in journalism (broadcast, print, photo or online) and demonstrate financial need and academic achievement.
Target applicant(s): High school students. College students. Adult students.
Amount: $500-$1,000.
Number of awards: Varies.
Deadline: June 15.
How to apply: Applications are available online, by email, by mail or by phone.
Exclusive: Visit www.UltimateScholarshipBook.com and enter code CC188120 for updates on this award.

(1882) • Johanna Drew Cluney Fund

Hawaii Community Foundation - Scholarships
827 Fort Street Mall, Honolulu, HI 96813
Phone: 888-731-3863
Email: scholarships@hcf-hawaii.org
https://www.hawaiicommunityfoundation.org
Purpose: To aid students pursuing vocational education.
Eligibility: Applicants must be Hawaii residents who are enrolled full-time in vocational degree programs at a University of Hawaii school and who have a minimum 2.0 GPA. They must be first-time degree seekers who plan to enter the workforce upon graduation.
Target applicant(s): College students. Adult students.
Minimum GPA: 2.0
Amount: Varies.
Number of awards: Varies.
Deadline: January 31.
How to apply: Applications are available online. An application form, personal statement and letter of recommendation are required.
Exclusive: Visit www.UltimateScholarshipBook.com and enter code HA188220 for updates on this award.

(1883) • John and Abigail Adams Scholarship

Massachusetts Department of Higher Education
Office of Student Financial Assistance, 454 Broadway, Suite 200, Revere, MA 02151
Phone: 617-727-9420
Email: osfa@osfa.mass.edu
http://www.mass.edu/osfa/students/forstudents.asp

Purpose: To attract high-performing high school seniors to Massachusetts public institutions of higher education and to reward previous achievements.
Eligibility: Applicants must be permanent residents of Massachusetts, score in the Advanced category in one category of the 10th grade MCAS test and in the Proficient or Advanced category in the other and have a combined MCAS score in the top 25 percent of their school district. Scholarship winners must maintain a 3.0 or higher GPA for continued eligibility.
Target applicant(s): High school students.
Minimum GPA: 3.0
Amount: Up to full tuition.
Number of awards: Varies.
Scholarship may be renewable.
Deadline: Varies.
How to apply: No application is necessary, but students must complete the Free Application for Federal Student Aid.
Exclusive: Visit www.UltimateScholarshipBook.com and enter code MA188320 for updates on this award.

(1884) • John and Anne Clifton Scholarship

Hawaii Community Foundation - Scholarships
827 Fort Street Mall, Honolulu, HI 96813
Phone: 888-731-3863
Email: scholarships@hcf-hawaii.org
https://www.hawaiicommunityfoundation.org
Purpose: To assist students pursuing vocational degrees.
Eligibility: Applicants must be enrolled in a vocational program at a University of Hawaii school and have at least a 2.0 GPA.
Target applicant(s): High school students. College students. Adult students.
Minimum GPA: 2.0
Amount: Varies.
Number of awards: Varies.
Deadline: January 31.
How to apply: Applications are available online.
Exclusive: Visit www.UltimateScholarshipBook.com and enter code HA188420 for updates on this award.

(1885) • John B. White, JR. Memorial Scholarship

Georgia's Own Foundation
1155 Peachtree Street NE, Suite 600, Atlanta, GA 30309
Phone: 800-533-2062
http://georgiasownfoundation.org
Purpose: To support students dedicated to community service.
Eligibility: Applicants must be high school seniors graduating from an accredited Georgia high school and accepted to a public university in Georgia. Students must be the first generation in their family to attend college. Applicants must demonstrate financial need and community involvement.
Target applicant(s): High school students.
Amount: $5,000.
Number of awards: 1.
Deadline: May 26.
How to apply: Applications are available online.
Exclusive: Visit www.UltimateScholarshipBook.com and enter code GE188520 for updates on this award.

(1886) • John D. and Virginia Riesch Scholarship

Wisconsin Medical Society Foundation
330 East Lakeside Street, Madison, WI 53715
Phone: 866-442-3800
Email: elizabeth.ringle@wismed.org
http://www.wisconsinmedicalsociety.org
Purpose: To aid students who are training to become physicians or nurses.
Eligibility: Applicants must be U.S. citizens. They must be full-time students enrolled in a medical school or nursing degree program at an accredited Wisconsin college or university. Rising undergraduate freshmen, undergraduate medical students and nursing students enrolled in a less than two-year program are ineligible. Preference will be given to Wisconsin residents and to applicants who are planning to practice in Wisconsin. Selection is based on academic merit, personal qualities, recommendations and financial need.
Target applicant(s): College students. Graduate school students. Adult students.
Amount: Varies.
Number of awards: 2.
Deadline: February 1.
How to apply: Applications are available online. An application form, personal statement, transcript and two recommendation letters are required.
Exclusive: Visit www.UltimateScholarshipBook.com and enter code WI188620 for updates on this award.

(1887) • John Dawe Dental Education Fund

Hawaii Community Foundation - Scholarships
827 Fort Street Mall, Honolulu, HI 96813
Phone: 888-731-3863
Email: scholarships@hcf-hawaii.org
https://www.hawaiicommunityfoundation.org
Purpose: To provide financial assistance to Hawaii students pursuing careers in dental professions.
Eligibility: Applicants must be enrolled full-time in a school of dentistry, dental hygiene or dental assisting. They must have a GPA of 2.7 or higher. Two letters of recommendation and a letter from the applicant's school confirming enrollment in the dentistry or dental hygiene program are required.
Target applicant(s): High school students. College students. Adult students.
Minimum GPA: 2.7
Amount: Varies.
Number of awards: Varies.
Deadline: January 31.
How to apply: To apply, register online, complete the online application and select the scholarships to which you wish to apply. In addition, mail the supporting materials: printed confirmation page from the online application, personal statement, copy of Student Aid Report (SAR) available at www.fafsa.ed.gov and official transcript.
Exclusive: Visit www.UltimateScholarshipBook.com and enter code HA188720 for updates on this award.

(1888) • John R. Lillard VAOC Scholarship

Virginia Department of Aviation
VAOC Scholarship, Attn: Betty Wilson, 5702 Gulfstream Road, Richmond, VA 23250-2422
Phone: 804-236-3624
Email: director@doav.virginia.gov

http://www.doav.virginia.gov
Purpose: To aid Virginia high school seniors who are planning for careers in aviation.
Eligibility: Applicants must be Virginia high school seniors who have an unweighted GPA of 3.5 or higher. They must be accepted into or enrolled in an aviation-related program at an accredited postsecondary institution and must have plans to pursue a career in aviation. Selection is based on academic merit, personal essay, leadership skills and financial need.
Target applicant(s): High school students.
Minimum GPA: 3.5
Amount: $3,000.
Number of awards: Varies.
Deadline: March 9.
How to apply: Applications are available online. An application form, personal essay, official transcript, verification of college acceptance or enrollment, list of extracurricular activities and up to three recommendation letters are required.
Exclusive: Visit www.UltimateScholarshipBook.com and enter code VI188820 for updates on this award.

(1889) • John Schwartz Scholarship

American Institute of Wine and Food - Pacific Northwest Chapter
213-37 39th Avenue, Box 216, Bayside, NY 11361
Phone: 800-274-2493
Email: bsteinmetz100@hotmail.com
http://www.aiwf.org
Purpose: To aid students pursuing culinary degrees.
Eligibility: Applicants must have been Washington State residents for at least two years, be enrolled in a Washington State accredited culinary or winemaking arts program and have a GPA of 3.0 or higher.
Target applicant(s): College students. Adult students.
Minimum GPA: 3.0
Amount: $2,000.
Number of awards: 4.
Deadline: Varies.
How to apply: Applications are available from your school's culinary or winemaking arts department. An application form, resume and references are required.
Exclusive: Visit www.UltimateScholarshipBook.com and enter code AM188920 for updates on this award.

(1890) • John W. Rogers Memorial Scholarship

Missouri Bankers Foundation
P.O. Box 57 , 207 East Capitol Avenue , Jefferson City, MO 65101
Phone: 573-636-8151
Email: rpreston@mobankers.com
https://www.mobankers.com/
Purpose: To aid high school seniors who are planning to pursue higher education in agriculture or a banking-related subject.
Eligibility: Applicants must be graduating high school seniors who have plans to major in agriculture or a banking-related subject at the postsecondary level. Preference will be given to applicants who are planning to attend the University of Missouri-Columbia. Selection is based on the overall strength of the application.
Target applicant(s): High school students.
Amount: $1,000.
Number of awards: 2.
Deadline: March 10.
How to apply: Applications are available online. An application form, official transcript, ACT scores, a list of extracurricular activities and two recommendation letters are required.
Exclusive: Visit www.UltimateScholarshipBook.com and enter code MI189020 for updates on this award.

(1891) • Jose Marti Scholarship Challenge Grant

Florida Department of Education
Office of Student Financial Assistance, State Scholarship and Grant Programs, 325 West Gaines Street, Suite 1314, Tallahassee, FL 32399-0400
Phone: 888-827-2004
Email: osfa@fldoe.org
http://www.floridastudentfinancialaid.org
Purpose: To help Florida students in need who are of Hispanic origin.
Eligibility: Applicants must have been born in or have a natural parent who was born in either Mexico or Spain, or a Hispanic country of the Caribbean, Central or South America, regardless of race. Students must plan to attend Florida public or eligible private institutions as undergraduate or graduate students, but graduating high school seniors get preference.
Target applicant(s): High school students. College students. Graduate school students. Adult students.
Minimum GPA: 3.0
Amount: $2,000.
Number of awards: Varies.
Scholarship may be renewable.
Deadline: April 1.
How to apply: Applicants must submit the initial student Florida Financial Aid Application by April 1 and the Free Application for Federal Student Aid (FAFSA) by May 15.
Exclusive: Visit www.UltimateScholarshipBook.com and enter code FL189120 for updates on this award.

(1892) • Joseph Shinoda Memorial Scholarship

Joseph Shinoda Memorial Scholarship Foundation Inc.
c/o Barbara A. McCaleb, Executive Secretary, 234 Via La Paz, San Luis Obispo, CA 93401
http://www.shinodascholarship.org
Purpose: To aid students who are preparing for careers in commercial floriculture.
Eligibility: Applicants must be enrolled at an accredited four-year institution in the U.S. or at a community college located in California and be rising undergraduate sophomores, juniors or seniors. They must be majoring in a floriculture-related subject and be planning to pursue a career in domestic floriculture in the U.S. after graduation. Selection is based on academic merit, character, work experience and financial need.
Target applicant(s): College students. Adult students.
Amount: $1,000-$5,000.
Number of awards: Varies.
Deadline: March 30.
How to apply: Applications are available online. An application form, an official transcript and two letters of recommendation are required.
Exclusive: Visit www.UltimateScholarshipBook.com and enter code JO189220 for updates on this award.

(1893) • Judge William F. Cooper Scholarship

Center for Scholarship Administration
4320 Wade Hampton Boulevard, Suite G, Taylors, SC 29687-0031
Phone: 864-268-3363

Email: allisonleewagoner@bellsouth.net
https://www.csascholars.org/index.php
Purpose: To provide financial assistance to female students from Georgia who plan to attend college.
Eligibility: Applicants must be high school seniors who have financial need. Students must have an acceptable GPA and plan to study in any field except law, theology or medicine. Nursing is acceptable.
Target applicant(s): High school students.
Amount: Varies.
Number of awards: Varies.
Scholarship may be renewable.
Deadline: January 2.
How to apply: Applications are available online.
Exclusive: Visit www.UltimateScholarshipBook.com and enter code CE189320 for updates on this award.

(1894) • Juliette M. Atherton Scholarship - Seminary Studies

Hawaii Community Foundation - Scholarships
827 Fort Street Mall, Honolulu, HI 96813
Phone: 888-731-3863
Email: scholarships@hcf-hawaii.org
https://www.hawaiicommunityfoundation.org
Purpose: To support Hawaii students who plan to be ordained in the Protestant faith.
Eligibility: Students must be attending a graduate school of theology.
Target applicant(s): Graduate school students. Adult students.
Minimum GPA: 2.7
Amount: Varies.
Number of awards: Varies.
Deadline: January 31.
How to apply: To apply, register online, complete the online application and select the scholarships to which you wish to apply. In addition, mail the supporting materials: printed confirmation page from the online application, personal statement, copy of Student Aid Report (SAR) available at www.fafsa.ed.gov and official transcript.
Exclusive: Visit www.UltimateScholarshipBook.com and enter code HA189420 for updates on this award.

(1895) • KAB Broadcast Scholarship Program

Kansas Association of Broadcasters
Scholarship Committee, 214 SW 6th Avenue, Suite 300, Topeka, KS 66603
Phone: 785-235-1307
Email: kent@kab.net
http://www.kab.net/Programs/StudentServices/
Purpose: To support future broadcasters.
Eligibility: Applicants must be Kansas residents and be attending a Kansas college or university the fall semester after application. Those attending four-year institutions must be entering the junior or senior year, and those attending two-year institutions must be entering their sophomore year. Students must enroll in a broadcast or related curriculum for at least 12 hours. A GPA of 2.5 or greater is required.
Target applicant(s): College students. Adult students.
Minimum GPA: 2.5
Amount: Up to $16,000.
Number of awards: Varies.
Deadline: May 1.
How to apply: Applications are available online. An application form, essay and up to three letters of recommendation are required.
Exclusive: Visit www.UltimateScholarshipBook.com and enter code KA189520 for updates on this award.

(1896) • Kaiser Permanente Health Care Career Scholarship

Kaiser Permanente
Phone: 503-813-3992
Email: kpnw-scholarsihps@kp.org
http://www.kp.org/communitybenefit/scholarship/nw
Purpose: To empower students to enter the healthcare profession.
Eligibility: Applicants must be from Oregon or southwest Washington and be graduating high school seniors from approved schools in the Kaiser Permanente Northwest service area, which spans from north of Longview, Washington to Eugene, Oregon. Applicants must have a 2.5 GPA and plan to enroll full-time at a college or university for the upcoming fall semester.
Target applicant(s): High school students.
Minimum GPA: 2.5
Amount: $2,000-$10,000.
Number of awards: 139.
Deadline: December 13.
How to apply: Applications are available online.
Exclusive: Visit www.UltimateScholarshipBook.com and enter code KA189620 for updates on this award.

(1897) • Kansas Agricultural Aviation Association Scholarship

Kansas Agricultural Aviation Association
P.O. Box 585, Colwich, KS 67030
Phone: 316-796-1180
Email: grossflying@hotmail.com
http://www.ksagaviation.org
Purpose: To aid Kansas students who are pursuing higher education in Kansas.
Eligibility: Applicants must be Kansas residents and high school graduates who are planning to enroll at a Kansas postsecondary institution. They must be recommended for the award by a member of the Kansas Agricultural Aviation Association (KAAA) and must demonstrate financial need. Preference will be given to students who are majoring in or planning to major in agriculture, agricultural business, aviation or engineering. Selection is based on academic merit and financial need.
Target applicant(s): High school students.
Amount: $2,500.
Number of awards: 1.
Deadline: March 15.
How to apply: Applications are available online. An application form, transcript, financial need statement and two recommendation letters are required.
Exclusive: Visit www.UltimateScholarshipBook.com and enter code KA189720 for updates on this award.

(1898) • Kansas Career Technical Workforce Grant

Kansas Board of Regents
Curtis State Office Building, Suite 520, 1000 SW Jackson Street, Topeka, KS 66612
Phone: 785-430-4255
Email: dlindeman@ksbor.org
http://www.kansasregents.org/students/student_financial_aid
Purpose: To assist Kansas students to attend vocational colleges.

Eligibility: Applicants must be enrolled in approved vocational programs and take the vocational exam. Selection is based on exam scores. Students must register for the vocational exam by the scholarship deadline.
Target applicant(s): High school students. College students. Adult students.
Amount: Up to $1,000.
Number of awards: Varies.
Scholarship may be renewable.
Deadline: May 1.
How to apply: Applications are available online.
Exclusive: Visit www.UltimateScholarshipBook.com and enter code KA189820 for updates on this award.

(1899) • Kansas City IFMA Scholarship

International Facility Management Association - Kansas City Chapter
P.O. Box 412591, Kansas City, MO 64141
Phone: 816-329-5009
Email: scholarship@kcifma.com
http://ifmakc.org/
Purpose: To aid Kansas and Missouri students who are planning for careers in facility management.
Eligibility: Applicants must be full-time undergraduates, full-time graduate students or part-time graduate students enrolled at a postsecondary institution located in Kansas or Missouri. They must be majoring in a subject that is related to facility management (such as business operations, construction science, interior design, environmental design, architecture or engineering). Selection is based on stated career goals, GPA, recommendations, extracurricular activities and applicant interview.
Target applicant(s): College students. Graduate school students. Adult students.
Amount: At least $500.
Number of awards: Varies.
Deadline: April 30.
How to apply: Applications are available online. An application form, letter of professional intent, two letters of recommendation and an official transcript are required.
Exclusive: Visit www.UltimateScholarshipBook.com and enter code IN189920 for updates on this award.

(1900) • Kansas Comprehensive Grants

Kansas Board of Regents
Curtis State Office Building, Suite 520, 1000 SW Jackson Street, Topeka, KS 66612
Phone: 785-430-4255
Email: dlindeman@ksbor.org
http://www.kansasregents.org/students/student_financial_aid
Purpose: To help needy Kansas students attend Kansas colleges and universities.
Eligibility: Applicants must be enrolled full-time at an eligible Kansas institution. Selection is based on financial need.
Target applicant(s): College students. Adult students.
Amount: $100-$3,500.
Number of awards: Varies.
Deadline: April 1.
How to apply: Complete the Free Application for Federal Student Aid (FAFSA).
Exclusive: Visit www.UltimateScholarshipBook.com and enter code KA190020 for updates on this award.

(1901) • Kansas Ethnic Minority Scholarship

Kansas Board of Regents
Curtis State Office Building, Suite 520, 1000 SW Jackson Street, Topeka, KS 66612
Phone: 785-430-4255
Email: dlindeman@ksbor.org
http://www.kansasregents.org/students/student_financial_aid
Purpose: To aid outstanding Kansas minority students with financial need.
Eligibility: Applicants must be African American, Native Indian or Alaskan Native, Asian or Pacific Islander or Hispanic. Priority is given to graduating high school seniors. Applicants must have one of the following: a minimum ACT score of 21 or SAT score of 990, a minimum 3.0 GPA, a top 33 percent ranking in their high school class, completion of Kansas Scholars Curriculum, selection by National Merit Corporation or selection by College Board as a Hispanic Scholar.
Target applicant(s): High school students.
Minimum GPA: 3.0
Amount: Up to $1,850.
Number of awards: Varies.
Scholarship may be renewable.
Deadline: May 1.
How to apply: Applications are available online.
Exclusive: Visit www.UltimateScholarshipBook.com and enter code KA190120 for updates on this award.

(1902) • Kansas Nutrition Council Scholarship

Kansas Nutrition Council
Donna Keyser, Chair, KNC Awards and Scholarship Committee, 1434 Givens Road, Manhattan, KS 66503
Phone: 785-776-0212
Email: mdtreeh@cox.net
https://www.sneb.org/kansas-nutrition-council/
Purpose: To aid Kansas students who are pursuing higher education in nutrition, family and consumer sciences or a related subject.
Eligibility: Applicants must be Kansas residents who are rising undergraduate juniors, rising undergraduate seniors or graduate students enrolled at a college or university located in Kansas. They must be majoring in nutrition, dietetics, family and consumer sciences or a related subject. Selection is based on the overall strength of the application.
Target applicant(s): College students. Graduate school students. Adult students.
Amount: $1,000.
Number of awards: 1.
Deadline: February 1.
How to apply: Applications are available online. An application form, personal essay, two recommendation letters and an official transcript are required.
Exclusive: Visit www.UltimateScholarshipBook.com and enter code KA190220 for updates on this award.

(1903) • Kansas Oratorical Contest

American Legion, Department of Kansas
1314 SW Topeka Boulevard, Topeka, KS 66612
Phone: 785-232-9315
http://www.ksamlegion.org
Purpose: To enhance high school students' experience with and understanding of the U.S. Constitution. The contest will help develop students' leadership skills and civic appreciation, as well as the ability

to deliver thoughtful, insightful orations regarding U.S. citizenship and its inherent responsibilities.
Eligibility: Applicants must be high school students under the age of 20 who are U.S. citizens or legal residents and residents of the state. Students first give an oration within their state and winners compete at the national level. The oration must be related to the Constitution of the United States focusing on the duties and obligations citizens have to the government. It must be in English and be between eight and ten minutes. There is also an assigned topic which is posted on the website, and it should be between three and five minutes.
Target applicant(s): High school students.
Amount: $150-$750.
Number of awards: Varies.
Deadline: March 18.
How to apply: Applications are available from schools and local American Legion Posts.
Exclusive: Visit www.UltimateScholarshipBook.com and enter code AM190320 for updates on this award.

(1904) • Kansas State Scholarship

Kansas Board of Regents
Curtis State Office Building, Suite 520, 1000 SW Jackson Street, Topeka, KS 66612
Phone: 785-430-4255
Email: dlindeman@ksbor.org
http://www.kansasregents.org/students/student_financial_aid
Purpose: To aid needy Kansas students designated as state scholars.
Eligibility: Applicants must have taken the ACT, completed the Regents Scholars Curriculum and be graduating seniors. Applicants are ranked by an index combining ACT score and GPA. The top students are chosen.
Target applicant(s): High school students.
Amount: Varies.
Number of awards: Varies.
Scholarship may be renewable.
Deadline: May 1.
How to apply: Complete the Free Application for Federal Student Aid (FAFSA).
Exclusive: Visit www.UltimateScholarshipBook.com and enter code KA190420 for updates on this award.

(1905) • Karen Ann Shopis-Fox Memorial Scholarship

American Society of Landscape Architects
370 James Street, 4th Floor, New Haven, CT 06513
Phone: 800-878-1474
Email: executivedirector@ctasla.org
http://www.ctasla.org
Purpose: To support students who are studying landscape architecture or environmental education.
Eligibility: Applicants must be Connecticut residents and be enrolled in an accredited post-secondary landscape architecture or environmental education program. Both undergraduate and graduate students may apply.
Target applicant(s): College students. Graduate school students. Adult students.
Amount: $1,500-$2,500.
Number of awards: Varies.
Deadline: March 15.
How to apply: Applications are available online. An application form, transcript, personal statement and letter of recommendation are required.
Exclusive: Visit www.UltimateScholarshipBook.com and enter code AM190520 for updates on this award.

(1906) • Kathryn D. Sullivan Earth and Marine Science Fellowship

South Carolina Space Grant Consortium
Department of Geology and Environmental Sciences, College of Charleston, 66 George Street, Charleston, SC 29424
Phone: 843-953-5463
Email: scozzarot@cofc.edu
http://scspacegrant.cofc.edu/scholarships-and-fellowships
Purpose: To aid graduate students who are studying the natural sciences, technology or engineering.
Eligibility: Applicants must be U.S. citizens and be either full-time graduate students enrolled in an accredited consortium member institution or a successful applicant for full time admission to a Masters or Doctorate program in an accredited consortium member institution. Selection is based on recommendation letters, academic merit, faculty sponsorship and stated academic goals and interests in science, technology and engineering.
Target applicant(s): Graduate school students. Adult students.
Amount: $12,000.
Number of awards: 1.
Deadline: January 23.
How to apply: Applications are available online. An application form, personal essay, two recommendation letters, a transcript and a resume are required.
Exclusive: Visit www.UltimateScholarshipBook.com and enter code SO190620 for updates on this award.

(1907) • Kathy Larson/Laurel Zechlinski Memorial Scholarships

Michigan Llama Association Scholarship Awards
MLA Kathy Larson/Laurel Zechlinski Memorial Scholarships, c/o Ken Frambes, Chairman, 14775 Peckham Road, Albion, MI 49224
Phone: 517-857-3787
Email: frambes@springcom.com
http://www.michiganllama.org
Purpose: To assist members of MLA and the children of members.
Eligibility: Applicants must be current members or the children of members and be currently attending high school or an accredited trade or technical school, junior college or university. Students must be taking a minimum of 12 semester hours or 10 term hours and have a minimum 2.7 high school GPA or a minimum 3.0 college GPA. Applicants must also demonstrate good citizenship in their school and community.
Target applicant(s): High school students. College students. Adult students.
Minimum GPA: 2.7 for high school students, 3.0 for college students
Amount: $1,000.
Number of awards: 2.
Deadline: May 1.
How to apply: Applications are available online.
Exclusive: Visit www.UltimateScholarshipBook.com and enter code MI190720 for updates on this award.

(1908) • Kentucky Tuition Grant

Kentucky Higher Education Assistance Authority
P.O. Box 798, Frankfort, KY 40602
Phone: 800-928-8926
Email: blane@kheaa.com
http://www.kheaa.com
Purpose: To provide grants to Kentucky residents to attend the Commonwealth's independent colleges.

Eligibility: Applicants must be full-time students enrolled at eligible private institutions. Students must not be enrolled in divinity, theology or religious education degree programs. This is a need-based program.
Target applicant(s): High school students. College students. Adult students.
Amount: Up to $2,920.
Number of awards: Varies.
Deadline: Varies.
How to apply: Complete the Free Application for Federal Student Aid (FAFSA).
Exclusive: Visit www.UltimateScholarshipBook.com and enter code KE190820 for updates on this award.

(1909) • Kentucky Veterans Tuition Waiver Program

Kentucky Department of Veterans Affairs
Attn.: Tuition Waiver Coordinator, 321 West Main Street, Suite 390, Louisville, KY 40202
Phone: 502-595-4447
Email: barbaraa.hale@ky.gov
https://veterans.ky.gov/Benefits/Pages/education.aspx
Purpose: To assist the families of Kentucky veterans in obtaining higher education.
Eligibility: Applicants must be Kentucky residents and be children, stepchildren, adopted children, spouses or unremarried widows/widowers of Kentucky veterans and must be age 26 or younger. The veteran must have died in active duty or as a result of a service-connected disability, have a service-connected 100 percent disability, have served during wartime and be totally disabled or have died for any reason.
Target applicant(s): High school students. College students. Adult students.
Amount: Full tuition waiver.
Number of awards: Varies.
Scholarship may be renewable.
Deadline: Varies.
How to apply: Applications are available online.
Exclusive: Visit www.UltimateScholarshipBook.com and enter code KE190920 for updates on this award.

(1910) • Kilbourn-Sawyer Memorial Scholarship

Vermont Student Assistance Corporation
Scholarships, P.O. Box 2000, Winooski, VT 05404
Phone: 888-253-4819
Email: info@vsac.org
http://www.vsac.org
Purpose: To aid Vermont students who are planning to pursue higher education in a construction-related field.
Eligibility: Applicants must be Vermont residents, U.S. citizens or eligible non-citizens and graduating high school seniors. They must demonstrate academic achievement and financial need and plan to pursue higher education in construction or engineering at an institution that has been approved for federal Title IV funding. Selection is based on personal essays, academic merit, recommendation letter and financial need.
Target applicant(s): High school students.
Amount: $2,500.
Number of awards: 1.
Deadline: March 3.
How to apply: Applications are available online. An application form, official transcript, academic certification form, two personal essays and one recommendation letter are required.
Exclusive: Visit www.UltimateScholarshipBook.com and enter code VE191020 for updates on this award.

(1911) • Kittie M. Fairey Educational Fund Scholarships

Center for Scholarship Administration, Inc.
Kittie M. Fairey Educational Fund Scholarship Program, 4320 Wade Hampton Boulevard, Suite G, Taylors, SC 29687-0031
Phone: 864-268-3363
Email: allisonleewagoner@bellsouth.net
https://www.csascholars.org/index.php
Purpose: To help South Carolina high school seniors who want to attend colleges or universities in the state.
Eligibility: Applicants must be South Carolina high school seniors with a combined SAT score of 1800 or composite ACT score of 26 who plan to be full-time students at an accredited college or university in South Carolina. Selection is based on academic merit and financial need, and the applicant's parents' adjusted gross income must not exceed $40,000. A transcript, recommendation letter, essay and parents' tax documents are required.
Target applicant(s): High school students.
Minimum GPA: 3.0
Amount: Varies.
Number of awards: Varies.
Scholarship may be renewable.
Deadline: January 15.
How to apply: Applications are available online.
Exclusive: Visit www.UltimateScholarshipBook.com and enter code CE191120 for updates on this award.

(1912) • Kohl Excellence Scholarships

Herb Kohl Educational Foundation Inc.
Kim Marggraf, P.O. Box 877, Sheboygan, WI 53082-0877
Phone: 920-457-1727
Email: marggraf@excel.net
http://www.kohleducation.org
Purpose: To assist Wisconsin students in obtaining higher education.
Eligibility: Applicants must be Wisconsin residents who are graduating high school in the year of application. They must be in good standing with their schools and demonstrate the potential for success in postsecondary education. Deadlines vary by school but are generally the second week of November.
Target applicant(s): High school students.
Amount: $5,000.
Number of awards: 100.
Deadline: Second week of November.
How to apply: Applications are available online starting in October of each year and from Wisconsin high schools in mid-September. Three letters of recommendation are required.
Exclusive: Visit www.UltimateScholarshipBook.com and enter code HE191220 for updates on this award.

(1913) • Kokosing Construction Co. Scholarship

Associated General Contractors of Ohio
1755 Northwest Boulevard , Columbus, OH 43212
Phone: 614-486-6446
Email: parker@agcohio.com
https://agcohio.com/scholarships
Purpose: To support undergraduate students who are residents of Ohio and interested in pursuing careers in construction-related fields.

Eligibility: Applicants must be a U.S. citizens and undergraduate students in at least the second year of a two-year, four-year or five-year degree seeking program. The minimum GPA requirement is 2.5. Selection is based on the overall strength of the application.
Target applicant(s): College students. Adult students.
Minimum GPA: 2.5
Amount: $1,000.
Number of awards: 1.
Deadline: February 5.
How to apply: Applications are available online. An application form, official college transcripts and essay are required and must be mailed.
Exclusive: Visit www.UltimateScholarshipBook.com and enter code AS191320 for updates on this award.

(1914) • L.G. Wells Scholarship

Confederation of Oregon School Administrators
707 13th Street SE, Suite 100, Salem, OR 97301
Phone: 503-581-3141
Email: sara@oasc.org
https://www.cosa.k12.or.us/
Purpose: To aid Oregon students who are planning to pursue undergraduate studies at an Oregon college or university.
Eligibility: Applicants must be graduating seniors at an Oregon public high school, have a GPA of 3.5 or higher and be active participants in extracurricular and community-related activities. They must have plans to attend an Oregon institution of higher learning and must plan to begin postsecondary studies during the fall following high school graduation. They must demonstrate financial need or must have plans to major in education or engineering. Applicants must be formally endorsed by a member of the Confederation of Oregon School Administrators (COSA). Selection is based on the overall strength of the application.
Target applicant(s): High school students.
Minimum GPA: 3.5
Amount: $1,000.
Number of awards: 3.
Deadline: March 1.
How to apply: Applications are available online. An application form, endorsement from a COSA member, personal statement and transcript are required.
Exclusive: Visit www.UltimateScholarshipBook.com and enter code CO191420 for updates on this award.

(1915) • Lambeth Family Scholarship

Seattle Foundation
1200 Fifth Avenue, Suite 1300, Seattle, WA 98101-3151
Phone: 206-515-2119
Email: scholarships@seattlefoundation.org
http://www.seattlefoundation.org
Purpose: To aid students who are pursuing higher education in computer science, the natural sciences, business, mathematics or engineering.
Eligibility: Applicants must be enrolled in a degree-granting program in business, computer science, engineering, mathematics or the natural sciences. Selection is based on the overall strength of the application.
Target applicant(s): High school students. College students. Adult students.
Amount: $3,000.
Number of awards: 8.
Deadline: March 1.
How to apply: Applications are available online. An application form and supporting documents are required.
Exclusive: Visit www.UltimateScholarshipBook.com and enter code SE191520 for updates on this award.

(1916) • Lance Corporal Phillip E. Frank ~ Fifth Third Bank Memorial Scholarship

Heart of a Marine Foundation
P.O. Box 1732, Elk Grove Village, IL 60007
Phone: 847-621-7324
Email: info@heartofamarine.org
http://www.heartofamarine.org
Purpose: To support high school seniors, discharged military personnel and veterans who have outstanding character.
Eligibility: Applicants must be graduating high school seniors or discharged military personnel. Students must demonstrate loyalty, patriotism, honor, respect and compassion for others.
Target applicant(s): High school students.
Amount: $2,000.
Number of awards: 3.
Deadline: March 31.
How to apply: Applications are available online.
Exclusive: Visit www.UltimateScholarshipBook.com and enter code HE191620 for updates on this award.

(1917) • Laptop/Printer Grant

Michigan Council of Women in Technology Foundation
Attn.: Scholarship Committee, 6 Parklane Boulevard, Suite 615, Dearborn, MI 48126
Phone: 248-218-2578
Email: scholarships@mcwt.org
https://mcwt.org/University_Programs_195.html
Purpose: To help female students who need computers.
Eligibility: Applicants must be Michigan residents who are pursuing degrees in information systems, computer science, computer engineering, software engineering or information security and need a laptop to achieve their goals. Students must have a GPA of 3.0 or higher. Selection criteria include GPA, essay, technology-related activities, letters of recommendation, community service and completeness of application.
Target applicant(s): High school students. College students. Graduate school students. Adult students.
Minimum GPA: 3.0
Amount: Varies.
Number of awards: Varies.
Deadline: Varies.
How to apply: Applications are available online. An application form, transcript and letter of recommendation are required.
Exclusive: Visit www.UltimateScholarshipBook.com and enter code MI191720 for updates on this award.

(1918) • Laura N. Dowsett Fund

Hawaii Community Foundation - Scholarships
827 Fort Street Mall, Honolulu, HI 96813
Phone: 888-731-3863
Email: scholarships@hcf-hawaii.org
https://www.hawaiicommunityfoundation.org
Purpose: To support Hawaii students who are majoring in occupational therapy.
Eligibility: Applicants must be college juniors, college seniors or graduate students. Minimum 2.7 GPA required.
Target applicant(s): College students. Graduate school students. Adult students.

Minimum GPA: 2.7
Amount: Varies.
Number of awards: Varies.
Deadline: January 31.
How to apply: To apply, register online, complete the online application and select the scholarships to which you wish to apply. In addition, mail the supporting materials: printed confirmation page from the online application, personal statement, copy of Student Aid Report (SAR) available at www.fafsa.ed.gov and official transcript.
Exclusive: Visit www.UltimateScholarshipBook.com and enter code HA191820 for updates on this award.

(1919) • Leadership for Diversity Scholarship

California School Library Association
6444 E. Spring Street #247, Long Beach, CA 90815-1553
Phone: 888-655-8480
Email: info@csla.net
http://www.csla.net
Purpose: To encourage diversity in the library media teacher profession.
Eligibility: Applicants must be members of a traditionally underrepresented group attending or planning to attend an accredited library media teacher credential program and plan to work in California for three years after completing the program. Applicants must provide a 250-word statement about their qualifications, career goals, financial situation and commitment to supporting multicultural students and two letters of reference.
Target applicant(s): High school students. College students. Graduate school students. Adult students.
Amount: $1,500.
Number of awards: 1.
Deadline: October 15.
How to apply: Applications are available online.
Exclusive: Visit www.UltimateScholarshipBook.com and enter code CA191920 for updates on this award.

(1920) • Leadership Scholarship

Los Alamos National Laboratory Foundation
1112 Plaza del Norte, Espanola, NM 87532
Phone: 505-753-8890
Email: tony@lanlfoundation.org
http://www.lanlfoundation.org
Purpose: To support students from northern New Mexico who have demonstrated leadership skills in their homes, schools and communities.
Eligibility: Students must have at least a 3.25 cumulative unweighted GPA, and they must have either an SAT score (combined Math plus Critical Reading only) of at least 930 or an ACT score of at least 19. Applicants must submit an essay and two letters of recommendation.
Target applicant(s): High school students. College students. Adult students.
Minimum GPA: 3.25
Amount: $2,500.
Number of awards: Varies.
Scholarship may be renewable.
Deadline: January.
How to apply: Applications are available online.
Exclusive: Visit www.UltimateScholarshipBook.com and enter code LO192020 for updates on this award.

(1921) • LEAF Scholarships

California Landscape Contractors Association
1491 River Park Drive, Suite 100, Sacramento, CA 95815
Phone: 916-830-2780
Email: leaf@clca.org
http://www.clca.org
Purpose: To support ornamental horticulture students.
Eligibility: Applicants must attend an accredited California community college or state university and take a minimum of six credits.
Target applicant(s): College students. Adult students.
Amount: Varies.
Number of awards: Varies.
Deadline: April 15.
How to apply: Applications are available online. An application form, transcript and three letters of reference are required.
Exclusive: Visit www.UltimateScholarshipBook.com and enter code CA192120 for updates on this award.

(1922) • Learning Disabilities Association of Iowa Scholarship

Learning Disabilities Association of Iowa
5665 Greendale Road, Suite D, Johnston, IA 50131
Phone: 515-280-8558
http://iowa.ldaamerica.net/announcement/
Purpose: To support Iowa students pursuing post-secondary education.
Eligibility: Applicants must be graduating high school seniors in Iowa enrolling in post-secondary education who have learning disabilities.
Target applicant(s): High school students.
Amount: Varies.
Number of awards: 2.
Deadline: March 31.
How to apply: Applications are available online.
Exclusive: Visit www.UltimateScholarshipBook.com and enter code LE192220 for updates on this award.

(1923) • Lebanese American Heritage Club Scholarships

Lebanese American Heritage Club
835 Mason Street, Suite A-160, Dearborn, MI 48124
Phone: 888-315-5242
Email: info@lahc.org
https://lahc.org/scholarship-program/
Purpose: To encourage members of the Lebanese American community to become involved with regional and national media.
Eligibility: Applicants must U.S. citizens and Michigan residents and have a GPA of 3.0 or higher (3.5 for graduate students). They must maintain full-time status. Special consideration is given to students majoring in mass communications, political science and related fields, those enrolled or planning to attend institutions that contribute to the Arab American Scholarship Fund and those who did not receive the scholarship in the preceding year.
Target applicant(s): High school students. College students. Graduate school students. Adult students.
Minimum GPA: 3.0
Amount: Varies.
Number of awards: Varies.
Deadline: March 17.
How to apply: Applications are available online.
Exclusive: Visit www.UltimateScholarshipBook.com and enter code LE192320 for updates on this award.

(1924) • Lee-Jackson Foundation Scholarship

Lee-Jackson Foundation
P.O. Box 8121, Charlottesville, VA 22906
Phone: 434-977-1861
http://www.lee-jackson.org

Purpose: To honor the memories of Robert E. Lee and Thomas J. "Stonewall" Jackson and provide scholarships to Virginia students.

Eligibility: Applicants must be juniors, seniors or the equivalent in a Virginia public high school, private high school or homeschooling program and be residents of Virginia who plan to attend an accredited four-year college or university in the U.S. as full-time students. Financial need is not a basis for selection. Applicants must write an essay that demonstrates an appreciation for the character and virtues of Generals Robert E. Lee and Thomas "Stonewall" Jackson.

Target applicant(s): High school students.

Amount: $1,000-$10,000.

Number of awards: 18.

Deadline: February 3.

How to apply: Applications are available online and must be submitted to your school principal or guidance counselor by your school's deadline. Your school must then submit the application by the foundation's deadline.

Exclusive: Visit www.UltimateScholarshipBook.com and enter code LE192420 for updates on this award.

(1925) • Legislative for Future Excellence (LIFE) Scholarship Program

South Carolina Commission on Higher Education
1122 Lady Street, Suite 300, Columbia, SC 29201
Phone: 803-737-2262
Email: cbrown@che.sc.gov
http://www.che.sc.gov

Purpose: Monetary assistance is provided to South Carolina resident students pursuing higher education.

Eligibility: Applicants must graduate from a high school in South Carolina or outside of South Carolina if parent is a legal resident of South Carolina, attend an eligible South Carolina public or private college full-time and be a resident of South Carolina. Entering freshmen must meet two of the following: have a minimum 3.0 GPA, a minimum SAT score of 1100 or ACT score of 24 or graduate in the top 30 percent of their class.

Target applicant(s): High school students. College students. Adult students.

Minimum GPA: 3.0

Amount: Up to full tuition.

Number of awards: Varies.

Scholarship may be renewable.

Deadline: Varies.

How to apply: Your college will determine your eligibility based on your high school transcript. There is no application form.

Exclusive: Visit www.UltimateScholarshipBook.com and enter code SO192520 for updates on this award.

(1926) • Legislative Lottery Scholarships

New Mexico Higher Education Department
2044 Galisteo Street, Suite 4, Santa Fe, NM 87505-2100
Phone: 505-476-8400
Email: cesaria.tapia1@state.nm.us
http://www.hed.state.nm.us/students/

Purpose: To support graduating New Mexico high school seniors with financial need.

Eligibility: Applicants must be graduating high school seniors in New Mexico, enroll full-time at an eligible New Mexico public college or university and maintain a minimum 2.5 GPA during the first college semester.

Target applicant(s): High school students.

Amount: Varies.

Number of awards: Varies.

Scholarship may be renewable.

Deadline: Varies.

How to apply: Contact your financial aid office.

Exclusive: Visit www.UltimateScholarshipBook.com and enter code NE192620 for updates on this award.

(1927) • Lemieux-Lovejoy Youth Scholarship

Futurama Foundation
c/o Marilyn Ladd, Office Manager, 103 County Road, Oakland, ME 04963
Email: mvladd@colby.edu
http://bpwmefoundation.org/scholarship-program/

Purpose: To honor the memory of Rachel E. Lemieux and to provide financial assistance to Maine high school seniors and recent graduates.

Eligibility: Applicants must be female Maine residents who are high school seniors or who have recently graduated from high school.

Target applicant(s): High school students.

Amount: $1,200.

Number of awards: 1.

Deadline: April 13.

How to apply: Applications are available from your local BPW chapter.

Exclusive: Visit www.UltimateScholarshipBook.com and enter code FU192720 for updates on this award.

(1928) • Leo Bourassa Scholarship

Virginia Lakes and Watersheds Association
VLWA Scholarship Committee, CH2M HILL, 5701 Cleveland Street, Suite 200, Virginia Beach, VA 23462
Phone: 757-671-6222
Email: scholarship@vlwa.org
http://www.vlwa.org

Purpose: To acknowledge students for their accomplishments in the field of water resources.

Eligibility: Applicants must be Virginia residents and students in good standing at an accredited college or university in the state. They must complete at least two semesters of undergraduate study by the award date. They must also be full-time undergraduate or full- or part-time graduate students enrolled in curriculum related to water resources.

Target applicant(s): College students. Graduate school students. Adult students.

Amount: $1,000-$3,000.

Number of awards: 2-4.

Deadline: April 1.

How to apply: Applications are available online.

Exclusive: Visit www.UltimateScholarshipBook.com and enter code VI192820 for updates on this award.

(1929) • Leo H. Grether Memorial Scholarship

Iowa High School Music Association
P.O. Box 10, Boone, IA 50036
http://www.ihsma.org

Purpose: To support Iowa students pursuing vocal music education.
Eligibility: Applicants must be Iowa citizens and graduating high school seniors enrolling in college to pursue a vocal music education major. Students must submit a recording of two selections and essay along with their application materials.
Target applicant(s): High school students.
Amount: $2,500.
Number of awards: 1.
Deadline: April 15.
How to apply: Applications are available online.
Exclusive: Visit www.UltimateScholarshipBook.com and enter code IO192920 for updates on this award.

(1930) • Licensed Vocational Nurse to Associate Degree Nursing Scholarship

Health Professions Education Foundation
400 R Street, Suite 460, Sacramento, CA 95811
Phone: 916-326-3640
Email: stran@oshpd.ca.gov
http://www.oshpd.ca.gov
Purpose: To aid licensed vocational nurses in California who are pursuing an associate's degree in nursing.
Eligibility: Applicants must be licensed vocational nurses (LVNs) who are enrolled in or have been accepted into an accredited associate's degree in nursing (ADN) program in the state of California. They must be attending or planning to attend school at least part-time (six or more credits per semester) and must commit to two years of nursing practice in an underserved area of California after graduation. Selection is based on the overall strength of the application.
Target applicant(s): College students. Adult students.
Amount: Up to $8,000.
Number of awards: Varies.
Deadline: February 28.
How to apply: Applications are available online. An application form, official transcript, personal statement, financial information, two recommendation letters and proof of vocational nurse licensure are required.
Exclusive: Visit www.UltimateScholarshipBook.com and enter code HE193020 for updates on this award.

(1931) • Lila M. Van Sweringen Student Scholarship

Educational Office Professionals of Ohio
Mrs. Carla Huntsinger, Scholarship Chairperson, 100 Scarlet Oaks Drive, Cincinnati, OH 45241
http://www.eopo-oh.org/sscholar.html
Purpose: To support high school seniors and college students from Ohio who are pursuing a higher education in an office-related career.
Eligibility: Applicants must be residents of Ohio who are either current college students or high school seniors who will be attending a post-secondary institution in the fall of the next school year. Students must be pursuing an office-related career.
Target applicant(s): High school students. College students. Adult students.
Amount: $1,000.
Number of awards: Varies.
Deadline: February 17.
How to apply: Applications are available online.
Exclusive: Visit www.UltimateScholarshipBook.com and enter code ED193120 for updates on this award.

(1932) • Lilly Endowment Community Scholarship Program

Independent Colleges of Indiana
30 South Meridian Street, Suite 800, Indianapolis, IN 46204
Phone: 317-236-6090
Email: smartchoice@icindiana.org
http://www.icindiana.org
Purpose: To raise the level of education in Indiana.
Eligibility: Applicants must be Indiana high school seniors who have been accepted into a full-time bachelor's degree program at an accredited public or private institution of higher learning in Indiana.
Target applicant(s): High school students.
Amount: Full tuition plus fees and $900 book stipend.
Number of awards: 142.
Scholarship may be renewable.
Deadline: Varies.
How to apply: Applications are available online and from local Indiana Community Foundations.
Exclusive: Visit www.UltimateScholarshipBook.com and enter code IN193220 for updates on this award.

(1933) • Lily and Catello Sorrentino Memorial Scholarship

Rhode Island Foundation
One Union Station, Providence, RI 02903
Phone: 401-274-4564
Email: rbogert@rifoundation.org
http://www.rifoundation.org
Purpose: To assist adult students who are continuing their undergraduate studies at colleges or universities in Rhode Island.
Eligibility: Applicants must be residents of Rhode Island, be over 25 years of age and attend a non-parochial college or university in the state.
Target applicant(s): College students. Adult students.
Amount: Varies.
Number of awards: Varies.
Deadline: April 28.
How to apply: Applications are available online.
Exclusive: Visit www.UltimateScholarshipBook.com and enter code RH193320 for updates on this award.

(1934) • Linda Craig Memorial Scholarship Presented by St. Vincent Sports Performance

Pacers Foundation
Linda Craig Memorial Scholarship Committee, 125 S. Pennsylvania Street, Indianapolis, IN 46204
Phone: 317-917-2500
Email: bill.benner@pacers.com
http://www.pacersfoundation.org/
Purpose: To support Indiana students interested in sports medicine, physical therapy and related fields.
Eligibility: Applicants must U.S. citizens who have completed at least one full year of an undergraduate program majoring in medicine, sports medicine, physical therapy or a related area. They must have a GPA of at least 3.0 and demonstrate outstanding character, integrity and leadership. Applicants may not have received a full scholarship from any other organization.
Target applicant(s): College students. Adult students.
Minimum GPA: 3.0
Amount: $2,500.
Number of awards: 3.

Deadline: April 15.
How to apply: Applications are available online.
Exclusive: Visit www.UltimateScholarshipBook.com and enter code PA193420 for updates on this award.

(1935) · Lisa Sechrist Memorial Foundation Scholarship

Lisa Sechrist Memorial Foundation Scholarship Selection Committee
c/o Brookfield Residential, Attn: Kim Mackmin, 3201 Jermantown Road, Suite 300, Fairfax, VA 22030
Email: Kim.Mackmin@Brookfieldhomes.com
http://www.lisasechrist.com/scholarship.html
Purpose: To honor the memory of Lisa Sechrist by assisting young women in obtaining a college education.
Eligibility: Applicants must be Virginia high school seniors in the process of applying to an accredited college, university or technical school or who have already been accepted. Members of honor societies and those who participate in sports or other extracurricular activities will receive special consideration. Selection is based on need, integrity, merit and academic potential.
Target applicant(s): High school students.
Amount: $10,000.
Number of awards: 1.
Scholarship may be renewable.
Deadline: March 31.
How to apply: Applications are available online.
Exclusive: Visit www.UltimateScholarshipBook.com and enter code LI193520 for updates on this award.

(1936) · Loan Assistance Repayment Program Primary Care Services

Maryland Higher Education Commission
Office of Student Financial Assistance, 6 North Liberty Street, Baltimore, MD 21201
Phone: 800-974-1024
Email: osfamail@mhec.state.md.us
http://www.maryland.gov
Purpose: To support primary care physicians and medical residents.
Eligibility: Medical resident applicants must be graduates of a Maryland college, and they must have at least one year remaining in a primary care residency program. Physician applicants must have a valid primary care license and currently work in an underserved area of Maryland. All applicants must have outstanding loans on which they have not defaulted. Specialization in one of the following fields is required: general internal medicine, family practice medicine, general pediatrics, obstetrics/gynecology or gynecology. Applicants must agree to work in an underserved area of Maryland for two to four years after winning the scholarship and completing their residency.
Target applicant(s): Graduate school students. Adult students.
Amount: Up to $25,000.
Number of awards: Varies.
Scholarship may be renewable.
Deadline: April 15, October 15.
How to apply: Applications are available from the Department of Health and Mental Hygiene.
Exclusive: Visit www.UltimateScholarshipBook.com and enter code MA193620 for updates on this award.

(1937) · Lois Livingston McMillen Memorial Fund

Connecticut Community Foundation Center for Philanthropy
43 Field Street, Waterbury, CT 06702
Phone: 203-753-1315
Email: scholarships@conncf.org
http://www.conncf.org
Purpose: To provide financial assistance to women who are studying or plan to study art, especially painting or design.
Eligibility: Applicants must be women who plan to study art at an accredited college or university, or in an artist-in-residence program. They must also live in the Connecticut Community Foundation's service area.
Target applicant(s): High school students. College students. Adult students.
Amount: Varies.
Number of awards: Varies.
Deadline: March 15.
How to apply: Applications are available online.
Exclusive: Visit www.UltimateScholarshipBook.com and enter code CO193720 for updates on this award.

(1938) · Lori Rhett Memorial Scholarship

National Association for Campus Activities
13 Harbison Way, Columbia, SC 29212
Phone: 803-732-6222
Email: info@naca.org
https://www.naca.org/FOUNDATION/Pages/Scholarships.aspx
Purpose: The scholarship recognizes the achievements of student leaders who are undergraduate or graduate students.
Eligibility: Applicants must be U.S. citizens and have a minimum GPA of 2.5. Students must hold a significant campus leadership position and demonstrate significant leadership skills and abilities. Applicants must also be making significant contributions through on- or off-campus volunteering and must attend school in Alaska, Idaho, Montana, Oregon or Washington.
Target applicant(s): College students. Graduate school students. Adult students.
Minimum GPA: 2.5
Amount: Varies.
Number of awards: 1.
Deadline: September 30.
How to apply: Applications are available online.
Exclusive: Visit www.UltimateScholarshipBook.com and enter code NA193820 for updates on this award.

(1939) · Los Alamos Employees' Scholarship

Los Alamos National Laboratory Foundation
1112 Plaza del Norte, Espanola, NM 87532
Phone: 505-753-8890
Email: tony@lanlfoundation.org
http://www.lanlfoundation.org
Purpose: To provide financial assistance for students in northern New Mexico who plan to pursue undergraduate degrees in fields of study that will benefit the community.
Eligibility: Selection is based on academic performance, including the pursuit in high school of a rigorous course of study, GPA and standardized test scores, varied extracurricular and community service activities, strong critical thinking skills and career goals that are relevant to the needs of the northern New Mexico community. Some consideration is also given to financial need, ethnic diversity and equally

representing all the regions of northern New Mexico. Applicants must have a minimum 3.25 GPA and either minimum score of 19 on the ACT or 930 on the SAT (Math and Critical Reading).
Target applicant(s): College students. Adult students.
Minimum GPA: 3.25
Amount: Varies.
Number of awards: Varies.
Scholarship may be renewable.
Deadline: January 22.
How to apply: Applications are available online.
Exclusive: Visit www.UltimateScholarshipBook.com and enter code LO193920 for updates on this award.

(1940) • Lottery Tuition Assistance Program

South Carolina Commission on Higher Education
Mr. Gerrick Hampton, Lottery Tuition Assistance Program Manager, 1122 Lady Street, Suite 300, Columbia, SC 29201
Phone: 803-734-4397
Email: ghampton@che.sc.gov
http://www.che.sc.gov
Purpose: To assist South Carolina residents attending a two-year public or independent institution of higher learning.
Eligibility: Applicants must complete the Free Application for Federal Student Aid (FAFSA), be residents of South Carolina and be enrolled as a degree-seeking student in a minimum of six credit hours at an eligible two-year technical institution, a USC two-year regional campus or Spartanburg Methodist College.
Target applicant(s): High school students. College students. Adult students.
Amount: Up to $1,200 per term.
Number of awards: Varies.
Deadline: Varies.
How to apply: Applications are available by telephone request.
Exclusive: Visit www.UltimateScholarshipBook.com and enter code SO194020 for updates on this award.

(1941) • Louis B. Russell Scholarship

Indiana State Teachers Association
150 W. Market Street, Suite 900, Indianapolis, IN 46204
Phone: 844-275-4782
Email: ccherry@ista-in.org
https://www.ista-in.org/our-profession/scholarships-awards
Purpose: To provide financial assistance to ethnic minorities who are seeking vocational or technical education.
Eligibility: Applicants must be ethnic minority high school seniors who plan to pursue education in the area of industrial arts, vocational education or technical education at an accredited college or university.
Target applicant(s): High school students.
Amount: $1,000.
Number of awards: 1.
Scholarship may be renewable.
Deadline: March 1.
How to apply: Applications are available online.
Exclusive: Visit www.UltimateScholarshipBook.com and enter code IN194120 for updates on this award.

(1942) • Louisiana Go Grant

Louisiana Office of Student Financial Assistance
605 N. Fifth Street, Baton Rouge, LA 70802
Phone: 800-259-5626 x1012
Email: custserv@la.gov
http://www.osfa.la.gov/
Purpose: To help students from moderate and low income families afford a college education.
Eligibility: Applicants must be Louisiana residents who have been admitted and enrolled in an undergraduate program at a Louisiana public or private college or university. They must be first-time freshmen or adult students who have not been enrolled in credit-bearing courses for at least one academic year. Financial need is required.
Target applicant(s): High school students. College students. Adult students.
Amount: Up to $3,000.
Number of awards: Varies.
Deadline: Varies.
How to apply: All eligible students who have filed a Free Application for Federal Student Aid are considered for this grant.
Exclusive: Visit www.UltimateScholarshipBook.com and enter code LO194220 for updates on this award.

(1943) • Louisiana Memorial Scholarship

American Radio Relay League Foundation
225 Main Street, Newington, CT 06111-1494
Phone: 860-594-0348
Email: foundation@arrl.org
http://www.arrl.org/scholarship-program
Purpose: To provide financial assistance to Louisiana students who are amateur radio operators.
Eligibility: Applicants must hold a Technician Class or higher Amateur Radio License and either be Louisiana residents or attend school in Louisiana. They must have a GPA of 3.0 or higher. Only students who are accepted to or enrolled in a four-year college or university are eligible.
Target applicant(s): High school students. College students. Adult students.
Minimum GPA: 3.0
Amount: $750.
Number of awards: 1.
Deadline: January 31.
How to apply: Applications are available online.
Exclusive: Visit www.UltimateScholarshipBook.com and enter code AM194320 for updates on this award.

(1944) • Luso-American Education Foundation General Youth Scholarship

Luso-American Education Foundation
P.O. Box 2967, Dublin, CA 94568
Phone: 925-828-3883
Email: odom@luso-american.org
https://www.luso-american.org/laef
Purpose: To provide educational opportunities for Portuguese students.
Eligibility: Applicants must be residents of California and high school students who are of Portuguese descent with a GPA of 3.5 or higher, or who are taking classes in the Portuguese language with a GPA of 3.0 or higher. They must be enrolled in a college, university, trade or business school and have taken the SAT or ACT. Two letters of recommendation are required.
Target applicant(s): High school students.
Minimum GPA: 3.0
Amount: $500-$1,500.
Number of awards: Varies.
Deadline: February 15.

How to apply: Applications are available by phone, fax, mail or email.
Exclusive: Visit www.UltimateScholarshipBook.com and enter code LU194420 for updates on this award.

(1945) • M. Josephine O'Neil Arts Award

Delta Kappa Gamma Society International Lambda State Organization
c/o Athena Columbus, 8127 North Oketo Avenue, Niles, IL 60714-2941
Phone: 847-983-8326
Email: athenac13@comcast.net
http://www.deltakappagamma.org/IL
Purpose: To support outstanding female artists.
Eligibility: Applicants must be Illinois residents and be sophomores at an accredited community college or current or upcoming juniors at an accredited four-year college or university. Students must demonstrate outstanding accomplishment in music, visual arts, dance, theater or the literary arts.
Target applicant(s): College students. Adult students.
Amount: Up to $6,000.
Number of awards: Varies.
Deadline: February 1.
How to apply: Applications are available online. An application form, transcript, evidence of accomplishment in the arts (such as reviews, awards, etc.) and an artwork sample are required.
Exclusive: Visit www.UltimateScholarshipBook.com and enter code DE194520 for updates on this award.

(1946) • Mabel Mayforth Scholarship

Federated Garden Clubs of Vermont Inc.
c/o Marybeth Tevis, Scholarship Chair, 973 Stock Farm Road, Randolph, VT 05060
Phone: 802-728-6083
Email: marybeth@eravt.com
http://www.vermontfgcv.com
Purpose: To support students who are studying in fields related to plants.
Eligibility: Applicants must be Vermont residents who are college juniors, seniors or graduate students and must major horticulture, landscape, design, conservation, forestry, agronomy, plant pathology or biology with a special interest in plants, ecology and allied subjects. They must be full-time students at an accredited institution with a GPA of 3.0 or higher. Previous winners may reapply.
Target applicant(s): College students. Graduate school students. Adult students.
Minimum GPA: 3.0
Amount: Varies.
Number of awards: 1.
Deadline: March 1.
How to apply: Applications are available online. An application form, list of extracurricular activities, letter of application, transcript and three letters of recommendation are required.
Exclusive: Visit www.UltimateScholarshipBook.com and enter code FE194620 for updates on this award.

(1947) • Mackinac Scholarship

American Society of Civil Engineers-Michigan Section
ASCE Scholarships, 215 N. Walnut Street, Lansing, MI 48933
Phone: 517-332-2066
Email: cschmitz@acecmi.org
http://sections.asce.org/michigan
Purpose: To aid Michigan civil engineering students.
Eligibility: Applicants must be U.S. citizens and Michigan residents. They must be rising undergraduate juniors or seniors who are enrolled full-time in an ABET-accredited civil engineering degree program. They must have a GPA of 2.5 or higher on a four-point scale. Selection is based on academic achievement, personal qualities and financial need.
Target applicant(s): College students. Adult students.
Minimum GPA: 2.5
Amount: $10,000.
Number of awards: 1.
Deadline: May (Memorial Day).
How to apply: Applications are available online. An application form and an official transcript are required.
Exclusive: Visit www.UltimateScholarshipBook.com and enter code AM194720 for updates on this award.

(1948) • Maine BPW Continuing Education Scholarship

Futurama Foundation
c/o Marilyn Ladd, Office Manager, 103 County Road, Oakland, ME 04963
Email: mvladd@colby.edu
http://bpwmefoundation.org/scholarship-program/
Purpose: To provide financial assistance to Maine women who are already attending an institution of higher learning.
Eligibility: Applicants must be female Maine residents who are currently attending a college or training program.
Target applicant(s): College students. Graduate school students. Adult students.
Amount: $1,200.
Number of awards: Varies.
Deadline: April 13.
How to apply: Applications are available from your local BPW chapter.
Exclusive: Visit www.UltimateScholarshipBook.com and enter code FU194820 for updates on this award.

(1949) • Maine Demolay and Pine Tree Youth Foundation Scholarships

Maine Demolay and Pine Tree Youth Foundation
Benjamin Weisner, 288 Rowe Station Road, New Gloucester, ME 04402
Phone: 207-773-5184
Email: grandlodge@mainemason.org
http://www.pinetreeyouth.org
Purpose: To support Maine high school seniors.
Eligibility: Applicants must submit a short essay. Students must demonstrate educational and civic achievement.
Target applicant(s): High school students.
Amount: Varies.
Number of awards: Varies.
Deadline: March 23.
How to apply: Applications are available online.
Exclusive: Visit www.UltimateScholarshipBook.com and enter code MA194920 for updates on this award.

(1950) • Maine Innkeepers Association Hospitality Scholarships

Maine Innkeepers Association
45 Melville Street, Augusta, ME 04330

Phone: 207-213-2060
Email: info@maineinns.com
http://www.maineinns.com/education-foundation/
Purpose: To support students enrolled in hospitality-related programs.
Eligibility: Applicants must be Maine residents and accepted to an accredited institution of higher learning with specialties in hotel administration or culinary sciences. Students must plan to begin a career in hospitality upon completion of their degrees.
Target applicant(s): High school students. College students. Adult students.
Amount: Varies.
Number of awards: Varies.
Deadline: April 7.
How to apply: Applications are available from the Maine Innkeepers Association.
Exclusive: Visit www.UltimateScholarshipBook.com and enter code MA195020 for updates on this award.

(1951) · Maine Oratorical Contest

American Legion, Department of Maine
5 Verti Drive, Winslow, ME 04901-0727
Phone: 207-873-3229
Email: legionme@mainelegion.org
http://www.mainelegion.org
Purpose: To enhance high school students' experience with and understanding of the U.S. Constitution. The contest will help develop students' leadership skills and civic appreciation, as well as the ability to deliver thoughtful, insightful orations regarding U.S. citizenship and its inherent responsibilities.
Eligibility: Applicants must be high school students under the age of 20 who are U.S. citizens or legal residents and residents of the state. Students first give an oration within their state and winners compete at the national level. The oration must be related to the Constitution of the United States focusing on the duties and obligations citizens have to the government. It must be in English and be between eight and ten minutes. There is also an assigned topic which is posted on the website, and it should be between three and five minutes.
Target applicant(s): High school students.
Amount: $125 to $1,500.
Number of awards: 4.
Deadline: December 1.
How to apply: Application information is available by contacting the local American Legion Post.
Exclusive: Visit www.UltimateScholarshipBook.com and enter code AM195120 for updates on this award.

(1952) · Maine State Society Foundation Scholarship

Maine State Society Foundation of Washington, DC
6508 Bowie Drive, Springfield, VA 22150
Email: mssfscholarship@gmail.com
http://mainestatesociety.org/foundation/
Purpose: To provide financial assistance to Maine students.
Eligibility: Applicants or their parent must have been born in or have been a legal resident of the state of Maine for at least four years. Applicants must be full-time students who are at least sophomores and must attend an accredited, non-profit college or university located in Maine.
Target applicant(s): College students.
Minimum GPA: 3.0
Amount: At least $1,000.
Number of awards: Varies.
Deadline: March 15.
How to apply: Applications are available by mail and online.
Exclusive: Visit www.UltimateScholarshipBook.com and enter code MA195220 for updates on this award.

(1953) · Maine Veterans Dependents Educational Benefits

Bureau of Veterans' Services
117 State House Station, Augusta, ME 04333-0117
Phone: 207-430-6035
Email: mainebvs@maine.gov
http://www.maine.gov/veterans/
Purpose: To provide the opportunity for dependents of veterans to obtain higher education.
Eligibility: Applicants must be children whose mother or father is or was a veteran in the state of Maine. They must be at least 16 years old and be high school graduates. They must be pursuing a college degree. Benefits must be awarded prior to the dependent's 22nd birthday, unless he is serving in the U.S. Armed Forces, in which case they may be awarded until his 26th birthday.
Target applicant(s): High school students. College students. Adult students.
Amount: Varies.
Number of awards: Varies.
Scholarship may be renewable.
Deadline: Varies.
How to apply: Applications are available online.
Exclusive: Visit www.UltimateScholarshipBook.com and enter code BU195320 for updates on this award.

(1954) · Maine Vietnam Veterans Scholarship

Maine Community Foundation
245 Main Street, Ellsworth, ME 04605
Phone: 207-667-9735
Email: jwarren@mainecf.org
http://www.mainecf.org
Purpose: To support Vietnam veterans from Maine and their descendants.
Eligibility: Applicants must either have served in the United States Armed Forces in Vietnam or be descendants of someone who served in Vietnam. In some cases, children of U.S. Armed Forces veterans in general may qualify.
Target applicant(s): High school students. College students. Graduate school students. Adult students.
Amount: Varies.
Number of awards: Varies.
Deadline: May 1.
How to apply: Applications are available at high school guidance offices or online.
Exclusive: Visit www.UltimateScholarshipBook.com and enter code MA195420 for updates on this award.

(1955) · Malcolm Baldrige Scholarship

Connecticut Community Foundation Center for Philanthropy
43 Field Street, Waterbury, CT 06702
Phone: 203-753-1315
Email: scholarships@conncf.org
http://www.conncf.org
Purpose: To provide financial assistance to students in international business, trade or manufacturing.

Eligibility: Applicants must be Connecticut students who are entering or currently attending a Connecticut college or university, and they must demonstrate exemplary academic achievement. International business students must be fluent in or be formally studying a foreign language.
Target applicant(s): High school students. College students. Adult students.
Amount: Varies.
Number of awards: Varies.
Deadline: March 15.
How to apply: Applications are available online.
Exclusive: Visit www.UltimateScholarshipBook.com and enter code CO195520 for updates on this award.

(1956) · Mamoru and Aiko Takitani Foundation Scholarship

Mamoru and Aiko Takitani Foundation
P.O. Box 10687, Honolulu, HI 96816-0687
Phone: 808-228-0209
Email: info@takitanifoundation.org
http://www.takitani.org
Purpose: To assist Hawaii resident students with business school, technical school, community college or four-year college expenses.
Eligibility: Applicants must be graduating high school seniors and Hawaii residents. Applicants must also demonstrate scholastic achievement, participation in activities and have been accepted into an accredited institution. Community service and financial need are also considered.
Target applicant(s): High school students.
Amount: $1,000-$10,000.
Number of awards: Varies.
Deadline: February 1.
How to apply: Contact your high school guidance counselor.
Exclusive: Visit www.UltimateScholarshipBook.com and enter code MA195620 for updates on this award.

(1957) · Margaret A. Pemberton Scholarship

Black Nurses Association of Greater Washington, DC Area Inc.
P.O. Box 55285 , Washington, DC 20040
Phone: 202-291-8866
Email: contactus@bnaofgwdca.org
http://www.bnaofgwdca.org
Purpose: To aid Washington, DC students who are planning to pursue higher education in nursing.
Eligibility: Applicants must be U.S. citizens, be graduating seniors who are students at a Washington, DC high school and be accepted into a National League for Nursing bachelor's degree program at a U.S. postsecondary institution. They must have a GPA of 2.8 or higher and must demonstrate financial need. Selection is based on the overall strength of the application.
Target applicant(s): High school students.
Minimum GPA: 2.8
Amount: Varies.
Number of awards: 1.
Deadline: April 15.
How to apply: Applications are available online. An application form, personal statement, official transcript, copy of college acceptance letter and two recommendation letters are required.
Exclusive: Visit www.UltimateScholarshipBook.com and enter code BL195720 for updates on this award.

(1958) · Margaret A. Stafford Nursing Scholarship

Delaware Community Foundation
P.O. Box 1636, Wilmington, DE 19899
Phone: 302-571-8004
Email: rgentsch@delcf.org
http://www.delcf.org
Purpose: To aid Delaware students who are pursuing higher education in nursing.
Eligibility: Applicants must be Delaware residents who are enrolled in or who have been accepted into a nursing degree program at an accredited college or university. Selection is based on the overall strength of the application.
Target applicant(s): High school students. College students. Adult students.
Amount: Varies.
Number of awards: Varies.
Deadline: March 15.
How to apply: Applications are available online. An application form, transcript, personal statement and two recommendation letters are required.
Exclusive: Visit www.UltimateScholarshipBook.com and enter code DE195820 for updates on this award.

(1959) · Margaret Raley New York State Migrant Scholarship

Geneseo Migrant Center
3 Mt. Morris-Leicester Road, Leicester, NY 14481
Phone: 800-245-5681
Email: info@migrant.net
http://www.migrant.net
Purpose: To recognize the educational achievement of migrant farmworker students with a history of migration to and/or within New York State.
Eligibility: Applicants must be migrants who are high school seniors and have plans to attend a post-secondary institution or other advanced training. Applicants must also have a history of migration to and/ or within New York State. Recipients are selected on the basis of demonstrated commitment to educational goals, participation in school/MEOP-related activities, participation in community-related activities, demonstration of good citizenship qualities, presentation of high mobility and the overcoming of unusual odds or need.
Target applicant(s): High school students.
Amount: Up to $500.
Number of awards: Varies.
Deadline: April 1.
How to apply: Applications are available online.
Exclusive: Visit www.UltimateScholarshipBook.com and enter code GE195920 for updates on this award.

(1960) · Marguerite Ross Barnett Memorial Scholarship

Missouri Student Assistance Resource Services (MOSTARS)
Missouri Department of Higher Education, Attn: Bright Flight, P.O. Box 1469, Jefferson City, MO 65102
Phone: 800-473-6757
http://dhe.mo.gov/ppc/grants/
Purpose: This scholarship was established for students who are employed while attending school part-time.
Eligibility: Applicants must be U.S. citizens or eligible noncitizens, Missouri residents and enrolled at least half-time but less than full-time

at a participating Missouri college or university. Applicants must also be employed for at least 20 hours per week and be able to demonstrate financial need.
Target applicant(s): High school students. College students. Adult students.
Minimum GPA: 2.5
Amount: Tuition for 6-9 credit hours.
Number of awards: Varies.
Scholarship may be renewable.
Deadline: August 1.
How to apply: Applications are available online.
Exclusive: Visit www.UltimateScholarshipBook.com and enter code MI196020 for updates on this award.

(1961) • Maria C. Jackson/General George A. White Scholarship

Oregon Office of Student Access and Completion
1500 Valley River Drive, Suite 100, Eugene, OR 97401
Phone: 541-687-7422
Email: cheryl.a.connolly@state.or.us
https://oregonstudentaid.gov/
Purpose: To support students who served, or whose parents serve or have served, in U.S. armed forces and resided in Oregon at time of enlistment.
Eligibility: Applicants must submit a FAFSA form. Students must be attending a college in Oregon. There is no GPA requirement for graduate-level students and students attending a technical school. U.S. Bank employees, their children and near relatives are not eligible for this scholarship.
Target applicant(s): High school students. College students. Graduate school students. Adult students.
Minimum GPA: 3.75
Amount: Varies.
Number of awards: Varies.
Deadline: March 1.
How to apply: Applications are available online.
Exclusive: Visit www.UltimateScholarshipBook.com and enter code OR196120 for updates on this award.

(1962) • MARILN Professional Scholarship Award

Massachusetts/Rhode Island League for Nursing
Award Committee, P.O. Box 407, Westwood, MA 02090
Phone: 781-366-0722
Email: nursing.mariln@gmail.com
http://www.nln.org
Purpose: To aid Massachusetts and Rhode Island practical nursing students.
Eligibility: Applicants must be Massachusetts or Rhode Island residents and have lived in Massachusetts or Rhode Island for at least four years before having entered that practical nursing program. They must be full-time students who have completed two consecutive semesters of their program of study. Selection is based on stated career goals and professional potential.
Target applicant(s): College students. Adult students.
Amount: Varies.
Number of awards: Varies.
Deadline: July 31.
How to apply: Applications are available online. An application form, official transcript, personal essay and two recommendation letters are required.
Exclusive: Visit www.UltimateScholarshipBook.com and enter code MA196220 for updates on this award.

(1963) • Marion Maccarrell Scott Scholarship

Hawaii Community Foundation - Scholarships
827 Fort Street Mall, Honolulu, HI 96813
Phone: 888-731-3863
Email: scholarships@hcf-hawaii.org
https://www.hawaiicommunityfoundation.org
Purpose: To support graduating high school students in Hawaii who are committed to world peace.
Eligibility: Applicants must have attended a public high school in Hawaii, and they must plan to attend college on the U.S. mainland. Students must have at least a 2.8 GPA.
Target applicant(s): High school students.
Minimum GPA: 2.8
Amount: Varies.
Number of awards: Varies.
Deadline: January 31.
How to apply: To apply, register online, complete the online application and select the scholarships to which you wish to apply. In addition, mail the supporting materials: printed confirmation page from the online application, personal statement, essay, copy of Student Aid Report (SAR) available at www.fafsa.ed.gov and official transcript.
Exclusive: Visit www.UltimateScholarshipBook.com and enter code HA196320 for updates on this award.

(1964) • Mark Rawlings Memorial Scholarship

Oklahoma Association of Broadcasters
6520 N. Western, Suite 104, Oklahoma City, OK 73116
Phone: 405-848-0771
Email: struby@oabok.org
https://oabok.org/careerseducation/scholarships/
Purpose: To support students majoring in broadcasting at Oklahoma colleges and universities.
Eligibility: Applicants must be enrolled in an Oklahoma college or university broadcasting program, be majoring in broadcasting and have an intent to enter the broadcasting career upon graduation. Students must be a junior or senior for the upcoming school year and must maintain a "B" average.
Target applicant(s): College students. Adult students.
Minimum GPA: 3.0
Amount: $2,000.
Number of awards: 1.
Deadline: February 9.
How to apply: Applications are available online.
Exclusive: Visit www.UltimateScholarshipBook.com and enter code OK196420 for updates on this award.

(1965) • Marlin R. Scarborough Memorial Scholarship

South Dakota Board of Regents
306 East Capitol Ave, Suite 200, Pierre, SD 57501-2545
Phone: 605-773-3455
Email: info@sdbor.edu
http://www.sdbor.edu
Purpose: To support undergraduate students in South Dakota.
Eligibility: Applicants must submit an essay detailing their leadership qualities, academic achievements and community service. Students must attend a public South Dakota university with at least a 3.5 GPA, and

they must be in their junior year at the time they receive the scholarship funding.
Target applicant(s): College students. Adult students.
Minimum GPA: 3.5
Amount: Varies.
Number of awards: 1.
Deadline: Varies.
How to apply: Applications are available online.
Exclusive: Visit www.UltimateScholarshipBook.com and enter code SO196520 for updates on this award.

(1966) • Martin Devlin Scholarship

Physician Assistant Academy of Vermont
45 Lyme Road, Suite 304, Hanover, NH 03755
Phone: 603-643-2325
Email: paav@conmx.net
http://www.paav.org
Purpose: To aid current and recent Vermont physician assistant students.
Eligibility: Applicants must be Vermont residents and must be currently enrolled in a physician assistant program in Vermont or must be recent graduates of such a program who have outstanding student loans and are working or intending to work in Vermont. Previous winners of this scholarship are ineligible. Selection is based on the overall strength of the application.
Target applicant(s): College students. Graduate school students. Adult students.
Amount: $1,000.
Number of awards: 1.
Deadline: June 30.
How to apply: Applications are available online. An application form, personal statement, school enrollment verification (if applicable) and employment verification (if applicable) are required.
Exclusive: Visit www.UltimateScholarshipBook.com and enter code PH196620 for updates on this award.

(1967) • Marvin L. Zuidema Scholarship Award

American Society of Civil Engineers-Michigan Section
ASCE Scholarships, 215 N. Walnut Street, Lansing, MI 48933
Phone: 517-332-2066
Email: cschmitz@acecmi.org
http://sections.asce.org/michigan
Purpose: To aid American Society of Civil Engineers (ASCE) student members in Michigan who have contributed meaningfully to student civil engineering activities.
Eligibility: Applicants must be U.S. citizens, Michigan residents and rising juniors or seniors who are enrolled full-time in an ABET-accredited civil engineering degree program. They must have a GPA of 2.5 or higher on a four-point scale and have made a notable contribution to civil engineering student activities. Selection is based on academic merit.
Target applicant(s): College students. Adult students.
Minimum GPA: 2.5
Amount: $1,500.
Number of awards: 1.
Deadline: Memorial Day.
How to apply: Applications are available online. An application form and an official transcript are required.
Exclusive: Visit www.UltimateScholarshipBook.com and enter code AM196720 for updates on this award.

(1968) • Mary Ann K. Murtha Memorial Scholarship

American Legion Auxiliary, Department of New York
112 State Street, Suite 1310, Albany, NY 12207
Phone: 518-463-1162
Email: nyalaeducation@gmail.com
http://www.deptny.org/?page_id=2128
Purpose: To provide financial assistance to students whose parents, grandparents or great-grandparents served in the Armed Forces during wartime.
Eligibility: Applicants must be children, grandchildren or great-grandchildren of Armed Forces veterans who served during World War I, World War II, the Korean Conflict, the Vietnam War, Grenada/Lebanon, Panama, the Persian Gulf and War on Terrorism. Students must be high school seniors, U.S. citizens and New York State residents.
Target applicant(s): High school students.
Amount: $1,000.
Number of awards: 1.
Deadline: March 15.
How to apply: Applications are available online.
Exclusive: Visit www.UltimateScholarshipBook.com and enter code AM196820 for updates on this award.

(1969) • Mary Benevento/CTAHPERD Scholarship

Connecticut Association of Health, Physical Education, Recreation and Dance
c/o Janice Skene, CTAHPERD Scholarship Chair, Buttonball Lane School, 376 Buttonball Lane, Glastonbury, CT 06033
Phone: 860-652-7276
Email: skenej@glastonburyus.org
http://www.ctahperd.org
Purpose: To aid Connecticut students who are planning to pursue higher education in school health teaching, physical education, recreation or dance.
Eligibility: Applicants must be U.S. citizens and Connecticut residents. They must be high school seniors who are planning to pursue a bachelor's degree in school health teaching, physical education, recreation or dance at an accredited Connecticut postsecondary institution. Selection is based on academic merit, professional potential and character.
Target applicant(s): High school students.
Amount: $1,000.
Number of awards: Varies.
Deadline: June 15.
How to apply: Applications are available online. An application form, transcript, personal statement and one letter of recommendation are required.
Exclusive: Visit www.UltimateScholarshipBook.com and enter code CO196920 for updates on this award.

(1970) • Mary Eileen Dixey Scholarship

American Occupational Therapy Foundation
Attn: Jeanne Cooper, 4720 Montgomery Lane, Suite 202, Bethesda, MD 20814
Phone: 240-292-1034
Email: jcooper@aotf.org
http://www.aotf.org/scholarshipsgrants
Purpose: To aid New Hampshire occupational therapy students.
Eligibility: Applicants must be New Hampshire residents who are members of the American Occupational Therapy Association (AOTA). They must be enrolled full-time in an accredited occupational therapy program at the associate's or master's degree level in the state of New

Hampshire. Master's level students must be enrolled in a first professional degree program and must have completed at least one year of study to be eligible. Selection is based on the overall strength of the application.
Target applicant(s): College students. Graduate school students. Adult students.
Amount: Varies.
Number of awards: Varies.
Deadline: October 27.
How to apply: Applications are available online. An application form, two personal references and a program director statement are required.
Exclusive: Visit www.UltimateScholarshipBook.com and enter code AM197020 for updates on this award.

(1971) • Mary Keith Duff Memorial Scholarship

Travis Credit Union
P.O. Box 2069, Vacaville, CA 95696
Phone: 707-449-4000
https://www.traviscu.org/community/events-seminars-community-education/scholarships/
Purpose: To assist members of the Travis Credit Union.
Eligibility: Applicants must be graduating high school seniors and have a minimum 3.0 GPA. Selection is based on GPA, honors and awards, employment and community service, leadership and extracurricular activities, essay and financial need. Students must plan to enroll in a two-year or four-year college or university full-time or with 12 or more credits or units.
Target applicant(s): High school students.
Minimum GPA: 3.0
Amount: $2,000.
Number of awards: 22.
Deadline: March 5.
How to apply: Applications are available online between January 1 and March 5 of each year.
Exclusive: Visit www.UltimateScholarshipBook.com and enter code TR197120 for updates on this award.

(1972) • Mary Macon McGuire Scholarship

General Federation of Women's Clubs of Virginia
P.O. Box 8750, Richmond, VA 23226
Phone: 804-288-3724
Email: scholarships@gfwcvirginia.org
http://www.gfwcvirginia.org/forms.htm
Purpose: To support Virginia women who are returning to school in order to better support their families.
Eligibility: Applicants must be a female head of household and a resident of Virginia. Students must be currently enrolled in a course of study at an accredited Virginia school. Students must submit an essay and three letters of recommendation. Applicants must show financial need.
Target applicant(s): College students. Adult students.
Amount: $2,500.
Number of awards: 2.
Deadline: March 15.
How to apply: Applications are available online.
Exclusive: Visit www.UltimateScholarshipBook.com and enter code GE197220 for updates on this award.

(1973) • Maschhoffs Inc. Pork Industry Scholarship

Iowa Foundation for Agricultural Advancement
Winner's Circle Scholarships, c/o SGI, 30805 595th Avenue, Cambridge, IA 50046
Phone: 515-291-3941
Email: linda@slweldon.net
http://www.iowastatefair.org/participate/competition/
Purpose: To aid college-bound Iowa students.
Eligibility: Applicants must be Iowa residents who are active in 4-H or Future Farmers of America (FFA). They must be planning to attend an Iowa postsecondary institution full-time at the undergraduate level beginning in the fall of the application year. They must have experience in swine projects and activities. Preference will be given to applicants who plan to work in the pork industry after graduation. Selection is based on academic merit, awards and recognitions, agricultural projects and professional plans.
Target applicant(s): High school students.
Amount: Varies.
Number of awards: Varies.
Deadline: Varies.
How to apply: Applications are available online. An application form and personal essay are required.
Exclusive: Visit www.UltimateScholarshipBook.com and enter code IO197320 for updates on this award.

(1974) • Masonic Scholarship Program

Grand Lodge of Iowa, A.F. and A.M.
Scholarship Selection Committee, P.O. Box 279, Cedar Rapids, IA 52406-0279
Phone: 319-365-1438
Email: scholarships@gl-iowa.org
https://grandlodgeofiowa.org/grand-lodge/awards/
Purpose: To reward high school seniors from Iowa public high schools for academics and leadership skills.
Eligibility: Applicants must be pursuing a post-secondary education in any state at an institution which provides a two-year or four-year college program or vocational training. They do not need to have a Masonic connection. Selection is based on academic record, communication skills and financial need, but the most important is service to school and community with an emphasis on leadership roles. Finalists will be asked to appear before the committee for personal interviews.
Target applicant(s): High school students.
Amount: $2,000.
Number of awards: 60.
Deadline: February 1.
How to apply: Applications are available online or from guidance departments at Iowa public high schools.
Exclusive: Visit www.UltimateScholarshipBook.com and enter code GR197420 for updates on this award.

(1975) • Masonry Institute of Iowa Foundation Scholarship Program

Masonry Institute of Iowa
6919 Vista Drive, West Des Moines, IA 50266
Email: admin@masonryinstituteofiowa.org
https://masonryinstituteofiowa.wildapricot.org/Scholarships
Purpose: To support students pursuing construction, architecture and engineering.
Eligibility: Applicants must be current Iowa high school or college students attending an Iowa institution and pursuing a program related to construction, engineering, masonry or architecture.
Target applicant(s): High school students. College students. Adult students.
Amount: Varies.
Number of awards: Varies.

Deadline: March 10.
How to apply: Applications are available online.
Exclusive: Visit www.UltimateScholarshipBook.com and enter code MA197520 for updates on this award.

(1976) • Massachusetts Community Colleges Access Grant

Massachusetts Community Colleges
85 Devonshire Street, 7th Floor, Boston, MA 02109
Phone: 617-542-2911
Email: info@masscc.org
http://www.masscc.org/student-resources/financial-aid-resources
Purpose: To make a Massachusetts community college education accessible for all.
Eligibility: Applicants must be pursuing an associate degree at a Massachusetts community college. Students whose household income is $36,000 per year or less are eligible to receive funds to cover full tuition and fees.
Target applicant(s): High school students. College students. Adult students.
Amount: Up to full tuition.
Number of awards: Varies.
Deadline: Varies.
How to apply: Applications are available from Massachusetts community college financial aid offices.
Exclusive: Visit www.UltimateScholarshipBook.com and enter code MA197620 for updates on this award.

(1977) • Massachusetts Part-Time Grant

Massachusetts Department of Higher Education
Office of Student Financial Assistance, 454 Broadway, Suite 200, Revere, MA 02151
Phone: 617-727-9420
Email: osfa@osfa.mass.edu
http://www.mass.edu/osfa/students/forstudents.asp
Purpose: To aid Massachusetts part-time undergraduate students.
Eligibility: Applicants must U.S. citizens or eligible non-citizens who have been Massachusetts residents for at least one year. They must be enrolled in an undergraduate degree or certificate program on a part-time basis (6 to 11 credits per semester) at a Massachusetts postsecondary institution. They must not owe refund money on an educational grant or have any defaulted student loans. Applicants who have earned a bachelor's or professional degree previously are ineligible.
Target applicant(s): High school students. College students. Adult students.
Amount: At least $200.
Number of awards: Varies.
Scholarship may be renewable.
Deadline: Varies.
How to apply: Application is made by completing the FAFSA and then contacting your financial aid office.
Exclusive: Visit www.UltimateScholarshipBook.com and enter code MA197720 for updates on this award.

(1978) • Massachusetts Student Broadcaster Scholarship

Massachusetts Broadcasters Association
43 Riverside Avenue, PMB 401, Medford, MA 02155
Phone: 800-471-1875
Email: jordan@massbroadcasters.org
http://www.massbroadcasters.org
Purpose: To support student broadcasters.
Eligibility: Applicants must be Massachusetts residents who are enrolled or plan to enroll in an accredited institution of higher learning that offers degrees in television and radio broadcasting. Students must meet their school's definition of a full-time student. Selection is based on financial need, academic merit, community service, extracurricular activities and work experience.
Target applicant(s): High school students. College students. Adult students.
Amount: $2,000-$3,000.
Number of awards: 11.
Deadline: April 3.
How to apply: Applications are available online. An application form, transcript and financial statement are required.
Exclusive: Visit www.UltimateScholarshipBook.com and enter code MA197820 for updates on this award.

(1979) • MASSGrant

Massachusetts Department of Higher Education
Office of Student Financial Assistance, 454 Broadway, Suite 200, Revere, MA 02151
Phone: 617-727-9420
Email: osfa@osfa.mass.edu
http://www.mass.edu/osfa/students/forstudents.asp
Purpose: To provide need-based financial assistance to undergraduate students who reside in Massachusetts and who are enrolled in and pursuing a program of higher education.
Eligibility: Applicants must be permanent legal residents of Massachusetts and have an Expected Family Contribution (EFC) between $0 and $5,198. Applicants must be enrolled as full-time students in a certificate, associate or bachelor's degree program and not have received a prior bachelor's degree or its equivalent.
Target applicant(s): High school students. College students. Adult students.
Amount: Varies.
Number of awards: Varies.
Scholarship may be renewable.
Deadline: Varies.
How to apply: Complete and submit the Free Application for Federal Student Aid (FAFSA).
Exclusive: Visit www.UltimateScholarshipBook.com and enter code MA197920 for updates on this award.

(1980) • Master's, Ph.D. or Other Advanced Degree Program

New Hampshire Charitable Foundation
37 Pleasant Street, Concord, NH 03301-4005
Phone: 603-225-6641
Email: info@nhcf.org
https://www.nhcf.org/how-can-we-help-you/
Purpose: To support New Hampshire students who are seeking graduate level studies.
Eligibility: Applicants must be New Hampshire residents who are enrolling in graduate level studies, including master's, Ph.D. or another advanced degree program. Selection is based on financial need, academic merit, community service, school activities and work experience. Students must file a FAFSA and submit a copy of the SAR with the application.
Target applicant(s): Graduate school students. Adult students.

Amount: Varies.
Number of awards: Varies.
Deadline: April 13.
How to apply: Applications are available online.
Exclusive: Visit www.UltimateScholarshipBook.com and enter code NE198020 for updates on this award.

(1981) • Math and Science Teaching Incentive Scholarships

New York State Higher Education Services Corporation (HESC)
99 Washington Avenue, Albany, NY 12255
Phone: 888-697-4372
Email: scholarships@hesc.ny.gov
http://www.hesc.ny.gov
Purpose: To support students in New York who are planning careers in math or science secondary education.
Eligibility: Applicants must have at least a 2.5 GPA. Recipients must agree to work for at least five years after graduation as a secondary school science or math teacher in the state of New York.
Target applicant(s): College students. Graduate school students. Adult students.
Minimum GPA: 2.5
Amount: Up to full tuition.
Number of awards: Varies.
Scholarship may be renewable.
Deadline: Varies.
How to apply: Applications are available online.
Exclusive: Visit www.UltimateScholarshipBook.com and enter code NE198120 for updates on this award.

(1982) • MCEC Technical Scholarship

Grand Lodge of Iowa, A.F. and A.M.
Scholarship Selection Committee, P.O. Box 279, Cedar Rapids, IA 52406-0279
Phone: 319-365-1438
Email: scholarships@gl-iowa.org
https://grandlodgeofiowa.org/grand-lodge/awards/
Purpose: To support Iowa students pursuing trade education.
Eligibility: Applicants must be graduating high school seniors in Iowa who plan to enroll in a mechanical or trade course of study at an accredited Iowa community college.
Target applicant(s): High school students.
Amount: Varies.
Number of awards: Varies.
Deadline: March 1.
How to apply: Applications are available online.
Exclusive: Visit www.UltimateScholarshipBook.com and enter code GR198220 for updates on this award.

(1983) • McGraw Foundation and Fifth Third Bank Emergency Financial Aid Award

Associated Colleges of Illinois
70 East Lake Street, Suite 1418, Chicago, IL 60601
Phone: 312-263-2391
Email: cwilloughby@acifund.org
http://acifund.org/
Purpose: To aid undergraduates students who are in need of emergency financial assistance.
Eligibility: Applicants must be full-time undergraduate students at one of ACI's 23 member institutions who are from middle-income families. They must be experiencing a personal financial emergency, must be ineligible for other sources of emergency aid and cannot be receiving any such aid from any other source. Applicants must have tried to secure part-time employment. Selection is based on financial need.
Target applicant(s): College students. Adult students.
Amount: Varies.
Number of awards: Varies.
Deadline: Varies.
How to apply: Applications are available online. An application form and a personal essay are required.
Exclusive: Visit www.UltimateScholarshipBook.com and enter code AS198320 for updates on this award.

(1984) • McLean Scholarship for Nursing and Physician Assistant Majors

Association of Independent Colleges and Universities of Pennsylvania
101 North Front Street, Harrisburg, PA 17101-1404
Phone: 717-232-8649
Email: klinger@aicup.org
http://www.aicup.org/Foundation-Scholarships
Purpose: To aid undergraduates who are studying to become nurses and physician assistants.
Eligibility: Applicants must be full-time undergraduates who are majoring in nursing or physician assisting at an Association of Independent Colleges and Universities of Pennsylvania (AICUP) member school. They must have a GPA of 3.0 or higher and must have proven leadership skills. Selection is based on the overall strength of the application.
Target applicant(s): College students. Adult students.
Minimum GPA: 3.0
Amount: $2,500.
Number of awards: 7.
Deadline: April 15.
How to apply: Applications are available online. An application form and personal essay are required.
Exclusive: Visit www.UltimateScholarshipBook.com and enter code AS198420 for updates on this award.

(1985) • Medallion Fund

New Hampshire Charitable Foundation
37 Pleasant Street, Concord, NH 03301-4005
Phone: 603-225-6641
Email: info@nhcf.org
https://www.nhcf.org/how-can-we-help-you/
Purpose: To improve the skilled workforce in areas of need in New Hampshire.
Eligibility: Applicants must be enrolling in an accredited vocational or technical program that does not lead to a bachelor's or advanced degree. They must be legal residents of New Hampshire and intend to work in a vocational or technical career when their schooling is complete. Preference is given to those who plan to go into the manufacturing trade sector or have little or no other opportunities for training or education.
Target applicant(s): High school students. College students. Adult students.
Amount: Varies.
Number of awards: Varies.
Deadline: Rolling.
How to apply: Applications are available online.

Exclusive: Visit www.UltimateScholarshipBook.com and enter code NE198520 for updates on this award.

(1986) • MEFA UPlan Prepaid Tuition Waiver Program

Massachusetts Educational Financing Authority
160 Federal Street, 4th Floor, Boston, MA 02110
Phone: 800-449-6332
Email: info@mefa.org
http://www.mefa.org
Purpose: To provide financial aid in the form of tuition waivers to Massachusetts students who prepay their tuition at lower rates.
Eligibility: Applicants must be planning to attend a school in the state of Massachusetts which participates in the UPlan program.
Target applicant(s): Junior high students or younger. High school students. College students. Adult students.
Amount: Varies.
Number of awards: Varies.
Scholarship may be renewable.
Deadline: Varies.
How to apply: Applications are available online.
Exclusive: Visit www.UltimateScholarshipBook.com and enter code MA198620 for updates on this award.

(1987) • Mellinger Scholarships

Edward Arthur Mellinger Educational Foundation Inc.
1025 E. Broadway, P.O. Box 770, Monmouth, IL 61462
Phone: 309-734-2419
Email: info@mellinger.org
http://www.mellinger.org
Purpose: The E. A. Mellinger Foundation supports education as a memorial to its namesake.
Eligibility: Applicants must live in western Illinois or eastern Iowa, submit the FAFSA form and demonstrate financial need and attend an accredited university. Awards are based on academic achievement. Part-time students are also eligible for scholarships, and loans are also available to graduate students.
Target applicant(s): High school students. College students. Adult students.
Amount: Varies.
Number of awards: Varies.
Scholarship may be renewable.
Deadline: May 1.
How to apply: Applications are available by mail or online. Application forms are only available from February 1 to May 1 each year.
Exclusive: Visit www.UltimateScholarshipBook.com and enter code ED198720 for updates on this award.

(1988) • Mexican Scholarship Fund

Central Indiana Community Foundation
615 North Alabama Street, Suite 119, Indianapolis, IN 46204-1498
Phone: 317-634-2423
Email: scholarships@cicf.org
http://www.cicf.org
Purpose: To provide financial assistance to Indiana residents of Mexican descent.
Eligibility: Applicants must have a minimum GPA of 3.0, demonstrate academic promise and demonstrate financial need. Preference is given to students of Mexican descent. Awards may be used for tuition, required fees or room and board.
Target applicant(s): High school students.
Minimum GPA: 3.0
Amount: Varies.
Number of awards: Varies.
Deadline: February 7.
How to apply: Applications are available online.
Exclusive: Visit www.UltimateScholarshipBook.com and enter code CE198820 for updates on this award.

(1989) • MFA Foundation Scholarships

MFA Incorporated
201 Ray Young Drive, Columbia, MO 65201
Phone: 573-874-5111
http://www.mfa-inc.com
Purpose: To aid Midwest college-bound high school seniors.
Eligibility: Applicants must be high school seniors who live in an area where a sponsoring MFA agency is located. They must have plans to enroll full-time at an accredited college or university no later than September 1 of the application year. Selection is based on character, extracurricular activities and financial need.
Target applicant(s): High school students.
Amount: $2,000.
Number of awards: About 300.
Deadline: March 15.
How to apply: Applications are available by request from the applicant's high school counselor. An application form and supporting materials are required.
Exclusive: Visit www.UltimateScholarshipBook.com and enter code MF198920 for updates on this award.

(1990) • Michael Curry Summer Internship Program

Governor's Office of the State of Illinois Michael Curry Summer Internship Program
207 State House, Springfield, IL 62706
Phone: 217-782-0244
Email: GOV.CurryInternship@illinois.gov
http://www.illinois.gov/gov/
Purpose: To provide internships for college juniors, seniors or graduate students.
Eligibility: Applicants must be Illinois residents. Recipients work full-time in an agency under the jurisdiction of the Governor for 10 weeks during the summer.
Target applicant(s): College students. Graduate school students. Adult students.
Amount: $1,346 stipend.
Number of awards: Varies.
Deadline: March 17.
How to apply: Applications are available online or by mail.
Exclusive: Visit www.UltimateScholarshipBook.com and enter code GO199020 for updates on this award.

(1991) • Michigan Competitive Scholarship

Michigan Student Aid
Student Scholarships and Grants, P.O. Box 30462, Lansing, MI 48909-7962
Phone: 888-447-2687
Email: ssg@michigan.gov
http://www.michigan.gov/mistudentaid/
Purpose: To assist students who plan to attend a Michigan public or private college.

Eligibility: Applicants must be Michigan residents since July 1 of the previous calendar year and have received a qualifying score on the ACT and a minimum 2.0 GPA. Applicants must also demonstrate financial need and be enrolled in an approved Michigan college or university. Applicants cannot be pursuing a degree in theology, divinity or religious education. This award is based on both financial need and academic merit.
Target applicant(s): High school students. College students. Adult students.
Minimum GPA: 2.0
Amount: Varies.
Number of awards: Varies.
Scholarship may be renewable.
Deadline: March 1.
How to apply: File a Free Application for Federal Student Aid (FAFSA).
Exclusive: Visit www.UltimateScholarshipBook.com and enter code MI199120 for updates on this award.

(1992) • Michigan Engineering Scholarships

Michigan Society of Professional Engineers
P.O. Box 15276, Lansing, MI 48901-5276
Phone: 517-487-9388
Email: Scholarship@MichiganSPE.org
https://www.michiganspe.org/scholarships/
Purpose: To aid Michigan students who are planning to pursue an undergraduate degree in engineering.
Eligibility: Applicants must be U.S. citizens, residents of Michigan and high school seniors. They must be accepted at an ABET-accredited college or university in Michigan and must have plans to pursue a degree in engineering. Students must have a GPA of 3.0 or higher for both the 10th and 11th grade years and a minimum composite ACT score of 26 or higher. Selection is based on GPA, ACT score, personal essay, extracurricular activities, any college-level coursework completed and honors received.
Target applicant(s): High school students.
Minimum GPA: 3.0
Amount: Varies.
Number of awards: Varies.
Deadline: February 3.
How to apply: Applications are available online. An application form, personal essay and official transcript are required.
Exclusive: Visit www.UltimateScholarshipBook.com and enter code MI199220 for updates on this award.

(1993) • Michigan Oratorical Contest

American Legion, Department of Michigan
212 N. Verlinden Avenue, Ste. A, Lansing, MI 48915
Phone: 517-371-4720 x11
Email: programs@michiganlegion.org
http://www.michiganlegion.org
Purpose: To enhance high school students' experience with and understanding of the U.S. Constitution. The contest will help develop students' leadership skills and civic appreciation, as well as the ability to deliver thoughtful, insightful orations regarding U.S. citizenship and its inherent responsibilities.
Eligibility: Applicants must be high school students under the age of 20 who are U.S. citizens or legal residents and residents of the state. Students first give an oration within their state and winners compete at the national level. The oration must be related to the Constitution of the United States focusing on the duties and obligations citizens have to the government. It must be in English and be between eight and ten minutes. There is also an assigned topic which is posted on the website, and it should be between three and five minutes.
Target applicant(s): High school students.
Amount: Up to $1,500.
Number of awards: Varies.
Deadline: November 19.
How to apply: Application information is available online under the link "Forms and Applications."
Exclusive: Visit www.UltimateScholarshipBook.com and enter code AM199320 for updates on this award.

(1994) • Michigan PA Foundation Annual Scholarship Award

Michigan Physician Assistant Foundation
759 Grand Marais, Grosse Pointe Park, MI 48230
Email: deuben@att.net
http://mipaf.org/scholarship/
Purpose: To aid Michigan physician assistant students.
Eligibility: Applicants must be in the final year of clinical study in a physician assistant degree program at a school located in Michigan. They must be involved in community service or professional activities and be outstanding academically or demonstrate financial need. Selection is based on professional involvement, community service, academic merit and financial need.
Target applicant(s): College students. Graduate school students. Adult students.
Amount: Varies.
Number of awards: Varies.
Deadline: August 30.
How to apply: Applications are available online. An application form, personal essay and verification of student status are required.
Exclusive: Visit www.UltimateScholarshipBook.com and enter code MI199420 for updates on this award.

(1995) • Michigan Tuition Grant

Michigan Student Aid
Student Scholarships and Grants, P.O. Box 30462, Lansing, MI 48909-7962
Phone: 888-447-2687
Email: ssg@michigan.gov
http://www.michigan.gov/mistudentaid/
Purpose: To assist Michigan students who are pursuing higher education in Michigan.
Eligibility: Applicants must be U.S. citizens, permanent residents or approved refugees. They must be Michigan residents who have lived there since at least July 1 of the previous calendar year and must be undergraduate students who are attending an approved Michigan college or university at least part-time. They must demonstrate financial need and not be in default on a federal student loan. Applicants who are pursuing degrees in divinity, theology or religious education are ineligible. Selection is based on financial need.
Target applicant(s): College students. Adult students.
Amount: Up to full tuition.
Number of awards: Varies.
Scholarship may be renewable.
Deadline: March 1.
How to apply: Application is made by filing the FAFSA.
Exclusive: Visit www.UltimateScholarshipBook.com and enter code MI199520 for updates on this award.

(1996) • Michigan Tuition Incentive Program

Michigan Department of Treasury
P.O. Box 30462, Lansing, MI 48909
Phone: 888-447-2687
Email: osg@michigan.gov
http://www.michigan.gov/

Purpose: To encourage Michigan students to complete high school and seek higher education.
Eligibility: Applicants must be upcoming high school graduates or GED recipients under the age of 20 and also must have received Medicaid for 24 months in a 36 month period after their 12th birthday. Qualifying students will receive an acceptance form, which must be returned to the Office of Scholarships and Grants to become eligible. The program covers tuition and mandatory fees for students pursuing an associate degree and up to $2,000 for studies in pursuit of a four-year degree.
Target applicant(s): High school students.
Amount: Up to full tuition.
Number of awards: Varies.
Scholarship may be renewable.
Deadline: Varies.
How to apply: Applications are available from the Michigan Department of Human Services.
Exclusive: Visit www.UltimateScholarshipBook.com and enter code MI199620 for updates on this award.

(1997) • Mid-Atlantic Chapter CMAA Scholarships

Construction Management Association of America-Mid Atlantic Chapter
Richard A. Bernardini, PE, CCM, LEED-AP, c/o Envision Consultants, P.O. Box 536, Mullica Hill, NJ 08062
Phone: 609-377-0333
Email: rbernardini@tnward-ac.com
http://www.cmaamidatlantic.org/scholarship-program/

Purpose: To assist students who plan careers in the construction industry.
Eligibility: Applicants must be current full-time or part-time undergraduate or graduate level college students who are pursuing a curriculum related to the construction industry and reside or attend college in Pennsylvania, New Jersey or Delaware. Students must have completed one full year of academic studies and have a minimum of one full year of studies remaining.
Target applicant(s): College students. Graduate school students. Adult students.
Amount: $3,000.
Number of awards: Varies.
Deadline: April 25.
How to apply: Applications are available online and must be submitted by email. An application form, an essay and a transcript are required.
Exclusive: Visit www.UltimateScholarshipBook.com and enter code CO199720 for updates on this award.

(1998) • Middle School Essay Contest

American Legion, Department of Virginia
1708 Commonwealth Avenue, Richmond, VA 23230
Phone: 804-353-6606
http://www.valegion.org

Purpose: To promote citizenship in young Virginia students.
Eligibility: Applicants must be middle school students and write an essay on an assigned topic. The essay should be written at the student's desk during school time and will be evaluated based on originality, sincerity and the student's ability to communicate meaning.
Target applicant(s): Junior high students or younger.
Amount: Up to $500.
Number of awards: Varies.
Deadline: March 1.
How to apply: Applications are available online and from sponsoring Posts.
Exclusive: Visit www.UltimateScholarshipBook.com and enter code AM199820 for updates on this award.

(1999) • Midwest Student Exchange Program

Midwestern Higher Education Compact
105 Fifth Avenue South, Suite 450, Minneapolis, MN 55401
Phone: 612-677-2777
Email: msep@mhec.org
http://msep.mhec.org

Purpose: The program aims to make attending out-of-state schools more affordable for students in member states.
Eligibility: Applicants must currently live in Illinois, Indiana, Kansas, Michigan, Minnesota, Missouri, Nebraska, North Dakota or Wisconsin and wish to attend a participating school in one of these states outside their own. Other eligibility requirements vary depending on the state and school. Awards are tuition reduction for out-of-state schools in the participating region.
Target applicant(s): High school students. College students. Graduate school students. Adult students.
Amount: Varies.
Number of awards: Varies.
Scholarship may be renewable.
Deadline: Varies.
How to apply: Students must clearly mark that they are an MSEP student when applying to the school of their choice.
Exclusive: Visit www.UltimateScholarshipBook.com and enter code MI199920 for updates on this award.

(2000) • Mikkelson Foundation Scholarship

Mikkelson Foundation
P.O. Box 768, Monument, CO 80132
http://mikkelsonfoundation.org

Purpose: To support graduating seniors of Colorado in pursuing a degree in engineering, physical or biological sciences or mathematics.
Eligibility: Applicants must have a minimum GPA of 3.7 and a minimum SAT score of 1200 or a minimum ACT score of 28. Students must submit three letters of recommendation, official transcripts and a personal essay.
Target applicant(s): High school students.
Minimum GPA: 3.7
Amount: $3,000.
Number of awards: 2.
Deadline: April 12.
How to apply: Applications are available online.
Exclusive: Visit www.UltimateScholarshipBook.com and enter code MI200020 for updates on this award.

(2001) • Mildred Towle Scholarship - Study Abroad

Hawaii Community Foundation - Scholarships
827 Fort Street Mall, Honolulu, HI 96813
Phone: 888-731-3863
Email: scholarships@hcf-hawaii.org

https://www.hawaiicommunityfoundation.org
Purpose: To support Hawaii students who plan to study abroad.
Eligibility: Applicants must study abroad as a junior, senior or graduate student. Students must have at least a 3.0 GPA. Preference will be given to applicants pursuing studies in the social sciences regarding international understanding and interracial fellowship. Applicants must prove financial need.
Target applicant(s): College students. Graduate school students. Adult students.
Minimum GPA: 3.0
Amount: Varies.
Number of awards: Varies.
Deadline: January 31.
How to apply: To apply, register online, complete the online application and select the scholarships to which you wish to apply. In addition, mail the supporting materials: printed confirmation page from the online application, personal statement, copy of Student Aid Report (SAR) available at www.fafsa.ed.gov and official transcript.
Exclusive: Visit www.UltimateScholarshipBook.com and enter code HA200120 for updates on this award.

(2002) · Mildred Towle Scholarship for African-Americans

Hawaii Community Foundation - Scholarships
827 Fort Street Mall, Honolulu, HI 96813
Phone: 888-731-3863
Email: scholarships@hcf-hawaii.org
https://www.hawaiicommunityfoundation.org
Purpose: To support African American students who are attending colleges in Hawaii.
Eligibility: Students must have at least a 3.0 GPA.
Target applicant(s): High school students. College students. Adult students.
Minimum GPA: 3.0
Amount: Varies.
Number of awards: Varies.
Deadline: January 31.
How to apply: To apply, register online, complete the online application and select the scholarships to which you wish to apply. In addition, mail the supporting materials: printed confirmation page from the online application, personal statement, copy of Student Aid Report (SAR) available at www.fafsa.ed.gov and official transcript.
Exclusive: Visit www.UltimateScholarshipBook.com and enter code HA200220 for updates on this award.

(2003) · Milton Fisher Scholarship for Innovation and Creativity

Milton Fisher Scholarship for Innovation and Creativity
Community Foundation for Greater New Haven, 70 Audubon Street, New Haven, CT 06510-9755
Phone: 203-777-2386
Email: mfscholarship@gmail.com
http://www.rbffoundation.org/scholarship.html
Purpose: To reward and encourage innovative problem solving.
Eligibility: Applicants must be high school juniors or seniors or must be entering or in the first year of an undergraduate degree program. Students must be Connecticut or New York City residents who attend or plan to attend an institution in the U.S. or students who attend or plan to attend a Connecticut or New York City institution of higher learning. Students must have come up with a solution to a problem faced by their school, community or family; solve an artistic, scientific or technical problem or develop a new group that serves an important need.
Target applicant(s): High school students. College students. Adult students.
Amount: Up to $5,000.
Number of awards: 6.
Scholarship may be renewable.
Deadline: May 1.
How to apply: Applications are only submitted online at www.rbffoundation.org.
Exclusive: Visit www.UltimateScholarshipBook.com and enter code MI200320 for updates on this award.

(2004) · Minnesota Academic Excellence Scholarship

Minnesota Office of Higher Education Services
1450 Energy Park Drive, Suite 350, Saint Paul, MN 55108-5227
Phone: 651-642-0567
Email: meghan.flores@state.mn.us
http://www.ohe.state.mn.us/
Purpose: To help students who have demonstrated outstanding ability, achievement and potential in selected areas of study.
Eligibility: Applicants must be Minnesota residents who have been admitted to a full-time program in an approved Minnesota college or university. Applicants must have demonstrated achievement in one of the following subjects: English or creative writing, fine arts, foreign language, math, science or social science.
Target applicant(s): High school students. College students. Adult students.
Amount: Up to full tuition.
Number of awards: Varies.
Scholarship may be renewable.
Deadline: Varies.
How to apply: For information about the status of this program, applicants should contact the schools they wish to attend.
Exclusive: Visit www.UltimateScholarshipBook.com and enter code MI200420 for updates on this award.

(2005) · Minnesota Division Izaak Walton League Scholarship

Izaak Walton League of America-Minnesota Division
2233 University Avenue West, Suite 339, St. Paul, MN 55114
Phone: 651-221-0215
Email: ikes@minnesotaikes.org
http://www.minnesotaikes.org
Purpose: To aid Minnesota residents who are studying environmental or conservation subjects in college.
Eligibility: Applicants must be U.S. citizens and Minnesota residents. They must be in the second year or higher of a college degree program in environmental science, environmental education, conservation, environmental law, wildlife management or a related subject. Selection is based on academic merit and financial need.
Target applicant(s): College students. Adult students.
Amount: Up to $1,000.
Number of awards: Varies.
Deadline: Varies.
How to apply: Applications are available online. An application form, transcript, personal essay, resume and two letters of recommendation are required.

Exclusive: Visit www.UltimateScholarshipBook.com and enter code IZ200520 for updates on this award.

(2006) • Minnesota Hockey Scholarship

Minnesota Hockey
Executive Director, Minnesota Hockey Scholarship Committee, 317 Washington Street, St. Paul, MN 55102
Phone: 651-602-5727
Email: info@minnesotahockey.org
http://www.minnesotahockey.org
Purpose: To support hockey students who wish to further their education beyond high school.
Eligibility: Applicants must be a resident of Minnesota, a high school senior, participate on a youth Junior Gold team or a girl's 19 and under team of an affiliate association of Minnesota Hockey and have a minimum GPA of 2.0. Selection is based on academic achievement, a personal essay and the letters of recommendation.
Target applicant(s): High school students.
Minimum GPA: 2.0
Amount: $1,000.
Number of awards: Varies.
Deadline: March 7.
How to apply: Applications are available online.
Exclusive: Visit www.UltimateScholarshipBook.com and enter code MI200620 for updates on this award.

(2007) • Minnesota Indian Scholarship Program

Minnesota Office of Higher Education Services
1450 Energy Park Drive, Suite 350, Saint Paul, MN 55108-5227
Phone: 651-642-0567
Email: meghan.flores@state.mn.us
http://www.ohe.state.mn.us/
Purpose: To provide money to help Native American students pay for higher education.
Eligibility: Applicants must be at least one-fourth Native American, Minnesota residents and members of a federally recognized Indian tribe. Applicants must be a high school graduate or possess a GED and have been accepted by an approved college, university or vocational school in Minnesota.
Target applicant(s): High school students. College students. Graduate school students. Adult students.
Amount: Up to $6,000.
Number of awards: Varies.
Scholarship may be renewable.
Deadline: July 1.
How to apply: This award is administered by the Minnesota Department of Children, Families, and Learning (CFL), and must be approved by the Minnesota Indian Scholarship Committee. To receive an application, contact your local tribal education office.
Exclusive: Visit www.UltimateScholarshipBook.com and enter code MI200720 for updates on this award.

(2008) • Minnesota Oratorical Contest

American Legion, Department of Minnesota
Third Floor, Veterans Service Building, 20 W. 12th Street, Room 300A, St. Paul, MN 55155
Phone: 651-291-1800
Email: department@mnlegion.org
http://www.mnlegion.org
Purpose: To enhance high school students' experience with and understanding of the U.S. Constitution. The contest will help develop students' leadership skills and civic appreciation, as well as the ability to deliver thoughtful, insightful orations regarding U.S. citizenship and its inherent responsibilities.
Eligibility: Applicants must be high school students under the age of 20 who are U.S. citizens or legal residents and residents of the state. Students first give an oration within their state and winners compete at the national level. The oration must be related to the Constitution of the United States focusing on the duties and obligations citizens have to the government. It must be in English and be between eight and ten minutes. There is also an assigned topic which is posted on the website, and it should be between three and five minutes.
Target applicant(s): High school students.
Amount: Up to $1,500.
Number of awards: 4.
Deadline: February 12.
How to apply: Application information is available by email.
Exclusive: Visit www.UltimateScholarshipBook.com and enter code AM200820 for updates on this award.

(2009) • Minnesota State Grant

Minnesota Office of Higher Education Services
1450 Energy Park Drive, Suite 350, Saint Paul, MN 55108-5227
Phone: 651-642-0567
Email: meghan.flores@state.mn.us
http://www.ohe.state.mn.us/
Purpose: To aid Minnesota students who are pursuing higher education in Minnesota.
Eligibility: Applicants must be U.S. citizens or permanent residents who are Minnesota residents. They must be high school graduates, GED recipients or at least 17 years old by the end of the academic year. They must be enrolled in a diploma, certificate or degree program for at least three credits at an eligible Minnesota school. Applicants who are in default of a federal or state SELF student loan are ineligible, as are those who owe the Office of Higher Education for the overpayment of a state grant. They cannot have earned a baccalaureate degree previously or be more than 30 days past due on child support payments. Selection is based on financial need.
Target applicant(s): High school students. College students. Adult students.
Amount: Up to $11,753.
Number of awards: Varies.
Scholarship may be renewable.
Deadline: Varies.
How to apply: Application is made by filing the FAFSA.
Exclusive: Visit www.UltimateScholarshipBook.com and enter code MI200920 for updates on this award.

(2010) • Minority Scholarship

Ohio News Media Foundation
1335 Dublin Road, Suite 216-B, Columbus, OH 43215
Phone: 614-486-6677
Email: ariggs@ohionews.org
https://www.ohionews.org/aws/ONA/pt/sp/foundation_scholarships
Purpose: To support minority graduating high school seniors from Ohio who are pursuing a degree in a journalism-related field at an Ohio college or university.
Eligibility: Applicants must be African American, Hispanic, Asian American or American Indian high school students graduating from an Ohio high school and must be enrolled at an Ohio college or university

for the upcoming fall. Students must have at least a 2.5 GPA and be majoring in a journalism-related field such as journalism, advertising or marketing. Applicants must write an autobiography as part of their essay, must get recommendations and may submit work samples.
Target applicant(s): High school students.
Minimum GPA: 2.5
Amount: $1,500.
Number of awards: 1.
Deadline: March 31.
How to apply: Applications are available online.
Exclusive: Visit www.UltimateScholarshipBook.com and enter code OH201020 for updates on this award.

(2011) • Minority Teacher Scholarship

State Student Assistance Commission of Indiana
W462 Indiana Government Center South, 402 West Washington Street, Indianapolis, IN 46204
Phone: 888-528-4719
Email: grants@ssaci.state.in.us
http://www.in.gov/che/
Purpose: To support students in Indiana who are pursuing degrees in teaching, special education, physical therapy or occupational therapy.
Eligibility: Applicants must be enrolled or planning to enroll in college full-time. Students must have at least a 2.0 GPA, and financial need may be considered. Preference will be given to black and Hispanic students. Students must agree to work in the state of Indiana for a period of time after graduation.
Target applicant(s): High school students. College students. Adult students.
Minimum GPA: 2.0
Amount: Varies.
Number of awards: Varies.
Scholarship may be renewable.
Deadline: September 4.
How to apply: Applications are available at the financial aid office of attending institution.
Exclusive: Visit www.UltimateScholarshipBook.com and enter code ST201120 for updates on this award.

(2012) • Mississippi Association of Broadcasters Scholarship Program

Mississippi Association of Broadcasters
Scholarship Committee, 855 S Pear Orchard Road, Suite 403, Ridgeland, MS 39157
Phone: 601-957-9121
Email: info@msbroadcasters.org
http://www.msbroadcasters.org/about-us/scholarships
Purpose: To support students involved in broadcasting.
Eligibility: Applicants must be Mississippi residents and be enrolled in an accredited broadcast curriculum at a Mississippi two- or four-year college.
Target applicant(s): College students. Adult students.
Amount: Varies.
Number of awards: Varies.
Deadline: March 1.
How to apply: Applications are available online. An application form, essay and up to three letters of recommendation are required.
Exclusive: Visit www.UltimateScholarshipBook.com and enter code MI201220 for updates on this award.

(2013) • Mississippi Eminent Scholars Grant (MESG)

Mississippi Office of Student Financial Aid
3825 Ridgewood Road, Jackson, MS 39211
Phone: 800-327-2980
Email: sfa@ihl.state.ms.us
http://www.ihl.state.ms.us
Purpose: To recognize academically high performing Mississippi students.
Eligibility: Applicants must be U.S. citizens or eligible noncitizens and current legal residents of Mississippi who are enrolled as full-time, first-time-in-college undergraduates. Applicants must have a high school GPA of 3.5 and a minimum ACT of 29. National Merit/National Achievement semifinalists with a 3.5 grade point average qualify without the test score.
Target applicant(s): High school students.
Minimum GPA: 3.5
Amount: $2,500.
Number of awards: Varies.
Scholarship may be renewable.
Deadline: September 15.
How to apply: Applicants must complete an MTAG/MESG application and either a FAFSA or a Statement of Certification (a waiver for completing the FAFSA).
Exclusive: Visit www.UltimateScholarshipBook.com and enter code MI201320 for updates on this award.

(2014) • Mississippi Scholarship

American Radio Relay League Foundation
225 Main Street, Newington, CT 06111-1494
Phone: 860-594-0348
Email: foundation@arrl.org
http://www.arrl.org/scholarship-program
Purpose: To provide financial assistance to Mississippi students who are amateur radio operators and are studying electronics or communications.
Eligibility: Applicants must be licensed amateur radio operators and residents of Mississippi who attend an institution of higher learning in Mississippi. They must be seeking a bachelor's degree or higher in electronics, communication or a related field, and they must be under 30 years old.
Target applicant(s): High school students. College students. Graduate school students. Adult students.
Amount: $500.
Number of awards: 1.
Deadline: January 31.
How to apply: Applications are available online.
Exclusive: Visit www.UltimateScholarshipBook.com and enter code AM201420 for updates on this award.

(2015) • Mississippi Tuition Assistance Grant (MTAG)

Mississippi Office of Student Financial Aid
3825 Ridgewood Road, Jackson, MS 39211
Phone: 800-327-2980
Email: sfa@ihl.state.ms.us
http://www.ihl.state.ms.us
Purpose: To assist financially needy Mississippi students to afford tuition.
Eligibility: Applicants must be current legal residents of Mississippi who are enrolled as full-time undergraduates. Applicants must have a high school grade-point average of 2.5 and a minimum ACT of 15.

Target applicant(s): High school students. College students. Adult students.
Minimum GPA: 2.5
Amount: $500-$1,000.
Number of awards: Varies.
Scholarship may be renewable.
Deadline: September 15.
How to apply: Applicants must complete an MTAG/MESG application and either a FAFSA or a Statement of Certification (a waiver for completing the FAFSA).
Exclusive: Visit www.UltimateScholarshipBook.com and enter code MI201520 for updates on this award.

(2016) • Missouri Oratorical Contest

American Legion, Department of Missouri
P.O. Box 179, Jefferson City, MO 65102
Phone: 800-846-9023
Email: bmayberry@missourilegion.org
http://www.missourilegion.org/
Purpose: To enhance high school students' experience with and understanding of the U.S. Constitution. The contest will help develop students' leadership skills and civic appreciation, as well as the ability to deliver thoughtful, insightful orations regarding U.S. citizenship and its inherent responsibilities.
Eligibility: Applicants must be high school students under the age of 20 who are U.S. citizens or legal residents and residents of the state. Students first give an oration within their state and winners compete at the national level. The oration must be related to the Constitution of the United States focusing on the duties and obligations citizens have to the government. It must be in English and be between eight and ten minutes. There is also an assigned topic which is posted on the website, and it should be between three and five minutes.
Target applicant(s): High school students.
Amount: $1,400-$18,000.
Number of awards: Varies.
Deadline: November 30.
How to apply: Application information is available by email.
Exclusive: Visit www.UltimateScholarshipBook.com and enter code AM201620 for updates on this award.

(2017) • Missouri State Thespian Scholarships

Missouri State Thespians
Attn.: Jennifer Forrest-James, 419 Sorrento Drive, Ballwin, MO 63021
Email: mstscholarships@gmail.com
http://www.mo-thespians.com/scholarship-applicants
Purpose: To support young Missouri thespians.
Eligibility: Applicants must be high school seniors, International Thespians members and delegates to the conference. Students must have a GPA of 2.5 or higher and audition in the category of performance, technical or theatre education.
Target applicant(s): High school students.
Minimum GPA: 2.5
Amount: Varies.
Number of awards: Varies.
Deadline: November 20.
How to apply: Applications are available online. An application form is required.
Exclusive: Visit www.UltimateScholarshipBook.com and enter code MI201720 for updates on this award.

(2018) • Mitchell Scholarship

Mitchell Institute
75 Washington Avenue, Suite 2E, Portland, ME 04101
Phone: 207-773-7700
Email: info@mitchellinstitute.org
http://mitchellinstitute.org/scholarship/
Purpose: To provide educational opportunities to students in Maine.
Eligibility: Applicants must be legal residents of Maine graduating from a public high school in Maine and attending a two- or four-year program at an accredited college. Scholarships are based on academic performance, community service and financial need. One scholarship is given out at every Maine public high school, with one extra scholarship per county intended for first-generation college students. While the deadline for the application is April 1, supporting materials have a deadline of May 1.
Target applicant(s): High school students.
Amount: $9,500.
Number of awards: 135.
Scholarship may be renewable.
Deadline: April 1.
How to apply: Applications are available online.
Exclusive: Visit www.UltimateScholarshipBook.com and enter code MI201820 for updates on this award.

(2019) • Monetary Award Program (MAP)

Illinois Department of Public Health
Center for Rural Health, 535 West Jefferson Street, Springfield, IL 62761
Phone: 217-782-1624
http://www.dph.illinois.gov
Purpose: To provide grants to eligible Illinois undergraduate students.
Eligibility: Applicants must be residents of Illinois, enrolled at a MAP-approved Illinois institution and carry a minimum of three hours per term. Applicants must also demonstrate financial need and maintain satisfactory academic progress.
Target applicant(s): High school students. College students. Adult students.
Amount: Varies.
Number of awards: Varies.
Scholarship may be renewable.
Deadline: September 30.
How to apply: Complete the Free Application for Federal Student Aid (FAFSA).
Exclusive: Visit www.UltimateScholarshipBook.com and enter code IL201920 for updates on this award.

(2020) • Money Sense Contest

North Dakota Jumpstart Coalition
P.O. Box 7113, Bismarck, ND 58507
Email: ndjumpstart@gmail.com
http://www.ndjumpstart.org
Purpose: To support North Dakota students pursuing post-secondary education.
Eligibility: Applicants must be graduating high school seniors in North Dakota planning to enroll in college. Students must create a YouTube video relating to a Money Sense topic.
Target applicant(s): High school students.
Amount: $1,000.
Number of awards: 1.
Deadline: November 17.

How to apply: Applications are available online.
Exclusive: Visit www.UltimateScholarshipBook.com and enter code NO202020 for updates on this award.

(2021) • Montana Cattlewomen Scholarship

Montana CattleWomen, Inc.
420 N. California, Helena, MT 59601
Phone: 406-442-3420
Email: lorrie@mtbeef.org
https://montanacattlewomen.org/programs/scholarships/
Purpose: To support a Montana university or college student whose major field of study benefits the livestock industry.
Eligibility: Applicants must be from Montana and currently enrolled as a sophomore or higher in an accredited university or college in Montana. Students must have a cumulative grade point average of 2.7 or more and demonstrate a need for financial assistance. Selection is based on demonstrated need and student's potential to benefit the livestock industry. Preference is given to students from an agriculture background and/or members or children of members of Montana CattleWomen.
Target applicant(s): College students. Adult students.
Minimum GPA: 2.7
Amount: $1,000.
Number of awards: 1.
Deadline: April 15.
How to apply: Application instructions are available online. A personal resume, academic resume, high school and college transcripts, essay, applicant photo, photo of family living situation and three recommendation letters are required.
Exclusive: Visit www.UltimateScholarshipBook.com and enter code MO202120 for updates on this award.

(2022) • Montana University System Honor Scholarship

Montana University System
Student Financial Services (SFS), Scholarship Department, P.O. Box 203101, Helena, MT 59620-3201
Phone: 800-537-7508
Email: mtscholarships@montana.edu
https://mus.edu/Prepare/Pay/Scholarships/
Purpose: To reward Montana high school seniors with outstanding academic achievement.
Eligibility: Applicants must have a 3.4 or higher GPA, meet specific college preparatory requirements and have been enrolled in an accredited Montana high school for at least three years prior to graduation, including their senior year. Applicants must also be accepted to and attend a Montana public university or community college.
Target applicant(s): High school students.
Minimum GPA: 3.4
Amount: Up to full tuition.
Number of awards: Up to 200.
Scholarship may be renewable.
Deadline: March 15.
How to apply: Applications are available from your high school guidance counselor.
Exclusive: Visit www.UltimateScholarshipBook.com and enter code MO202220 for updates on this award.

(2023) • Moody Scholar Program

Moody Foundation
600 North Pearl Street, Suite 2165, Dallas, TX 75201
http://moodyf.org
Purpose: To support students enrolled in a Texas college.
Eligibility: Applicants must be ranked in the top 25 percent of their graduating class. Award is renewable for up to four years of undergraduate work. Evidence of financial need is required.
Target applicant(s): High school students. College students. Adult students.
Minimum GPA: 3.0
Amount: $4,000.
Number of awards: 50.
Scholarship may be renewable.
Deadline: December 5.
How to apply: Applications are available online.
Exclusive: Visit www.UltimateScholarshipBook.com and enter code MO202320 for updates on this award.

(2024) • MSAA Scholarship Program

Minnesota State Archery Association
c/o Cheri Irlbeck, MSAA Secretary, 33266 County Hwy 4, Sanborn, MN 56083
Phone: 507-640-1683
Email: secretary.msaa@mnarchery.org
http://www.mnarchery.org
Purpose: To promote the sport of archery and encourage outstanding students to attend the college of their choice.
Eligibility: Students must apply as a senior in high school or within the first three years of college. The applicant must be a Minnesota State Archery Association member in good standing.
Target applicant(s): High school students. College students. Adult students.
Amount: $500.
Number of awards: 2.
Deadline: June 15.
How to apply: Applications are available online.
Exclusive: Visit www.UltimateScholarshipBook.com and enter code MI202420 for updates on this award.

(2025) • MSPE Kenneth B. Fishbeck, P.E., Memorial Grant

Michigan Society of Professional Engineers
P.O. Box 15276, Lansing, MI 48901-5276
Phone: 517-487-9388
Email: Scholarship@MichiganSPE.org
https://www.michiganspe.org/scholarships/
Purpose: To aid Michigan students who are planning to pursue higher education in engineering.
Eligibility: Applicants must be high school seniors who are Michigan residents and U.S. citizens. They must have a GPA of 3.0 or higher for the sophomore and junior years of high school and a composite ACT score of 26 or higher. Students must be accepted into a Michigan institution of higher learning that has an ABET-accredited engineering degree program. Selection is based on personal essay, awards and recognitions, GPA, ACT scores and any college-level coursework that has been completed.
Target applicant(s): High school students.
Minimum GPA: 3.0
Amount: Varies.
Number of awards: Varies.
Deadline: Second Friday in February.

How to apply: Applications are available online. An application form, transcript, personal essay and ACT score report are required.
Exclusive: Visit www.UltimateScholarshipBook.com and enter code MI202520 for updates on this award.

(2026) • Music Committee Scholarship

American Legion, Department of Kansas
1314 SW Topeka Boulevard, Topeka, KS 66612
Phone: 785-232-9315
http://www.ksamlegion.org
Purpose: To support Kansas students who have distinguished themselves in the field of music.
Eligibility: Applicants must be Kansas residents who are currently high school seniors or college freshmen or sophomores. They must have a proven talent and background in music and be planning to major or minor in music at an approved Kansas post-secondary institution. Applicants must also be average or better students. Three letters of recommendation with only one from a music teacher, a 1040 income statement, a high school transcript and a statement describing why they are applying for the scholarship are required. The scholarship will be awarded in two installments; recipients must maintain a C average to receive the second installment.
Target applicant(s): High school students. College students. Adult students.
Amount: $1,000.
Number of awards: 1.
Deadline: February 15.
How to apply: Applications are available online.
Exclusive: Visit www.UltimateScholarshipBook.com and enter code AM202620 for updates on this award.

(2027) • My Action Plan for College Young Scholars Initiative

My Action Plan for College
P.O. Box 121 , Hull, MA 02045
Phone: 508-631-0936
Email: ernest@mapforcollege.com
http://www.mapforcollege.com/
Purpose: To support 8th graders who plan to attend college.
Eligibility: Students must be current eighth graders with a goal to attend college one day. Applicants must submit a 250-300 word hand-written essay including the topics of academic and extra-curricular plans for college. Selection is based on the overall strength of the application.
Target applicant(s): Junior high students or younger.
Amount: $125-$750.
Number of awards: 6.
Deadline: August 1.
How to apply: Essays should be submitted by mail.
Exclusive: Visit www.UltimateScholarshipBook.com and enter code MY202720 for updates on this award.

(2028) • NACA Mid Atlantic Undergraduate Scholarship for Student Leaders

National Association for Campus Activities
13 Harbison Way, Columbia, SC 29212
Phone: 803-732-6222
Email: info@naca.org
https://www.naca.org/FOUNDATION/Pages/Scholarships.aspx
Purpose: To provide financial assistance to East Coast student leaders.
Eligibility: Students must hold a significant campus leadership position, demonstrate significant leadership skills and abilities and make significant contributions through on- or off-campus volunteering. Students must attend school in Delaware, New Jersey, Maryland, New York, eastern Pennsylvania or Washington, DC.
Target applicant(s): College students. Adult students.
Minimum GPA: 2.5
Amount: Varies.
Number of awards: 2.
Deadline: December 31.
How to apply: Applications are available online. Only the first 75 applicants are considered.
Exclusive: Visit www.UltimateScholarshipBook.com and enter code NA202820 for updates on this award.

(2029) • NACA Northern Plains Regional Student Leadership Scholarship

National Association for Campus Activities
13 Harbison Way, Columbia, SC 29212
Phone: 803-732-6222
Email: info@naca.org
https://www.naca.org/FOUNDATION/Pages/Scholarships.aspx
Purpose: To help students who are working toward undergraduate or graduate degrees that lead to careers in student activities or services.
Eligibility: Applicants must be undergraduate or graduate students taking at least six credits per semester and be enrolled in or have previously earned a degree from a college or university in Wisconsin or the Upper Peninsula of Michigan. Applicants must also have demonstrated leadership and service to their campus community.
Target applicant(s): College students. Graduate school students. Adult students.
Amount: Varies.
Number of awards: Varies.
Deadline: June 30.
How to apply: Applications are available online.
Exclusive: Visit www.UltimateScholarshipBook.com and enter code NA202920 for updates on this award.

(2030) • NACA South Student Leadership Scholarships

National Association for Campus Activities
13 Harbison Way, Columbia, SC 29212
Phone: 803-732-6222
Email: info@naca.org
https://www.naca.org/FOUNDATION/Pages/Scholarships.aspx
Purpose: To provide financial assistance to Southeast student leaders.
Eligibility: Students must hold a significant campus leadership position, demonstrate significant leadership skills and abilities and make significant contributions through on- or off-campus volunteering. Students must attend school in Alabama, Florida, Georgia, Mississippi, North Carolina, South Carolina, Tennessee, Virginia or Puerto Rico.
Target applicant(s): College students. Adult students.
Amount: Varies.
Number of awards: Up to 4.
Deadline: March 31.
How to apply: Applications are available online.
Exclusive: Visit www.UltimateScholarshipBook.com and enter code NA203020 for updates on this award.

(2031) • NACE Sandia Mountain Section Scholarship

National Association of Corrosion Engineers (NACE) International Foundation
15835 Park Ten Place, Houston, TX 77084-5145
Phone: 281-228-6205
Email: nace.foundation@nace.org
http://nace-foundation.org/programs/students/scholarships/

Purpose: To aid students interested in the careers of corrosion and engineering.

Eligibility: Applicants must an undergraduate enrolled full-time at an accredited college or university located in one of two states in the San Juan Basin which include Colorado and New Mexico. Applicants must have a serious interest in pursuing full-time employment in the corrosion industry. Selection is based on the overall strength of the application.

Target applicant(s): College students. Adult students.

Amount: $2,500.

Number of awards: 1.

Deadline: January 1.

How to apply: Applications are available online. An application form, two recommendation forms, academic transcripts and essay scholarship questions are required.

Exclusive: Visit www.UltimateScholarshipBook.com and enter code NA203120 for updates on this award.

(2032) • NADCA Indiana Chapter 25 Scholarship

Foundry Educational Foundation
1695 North Penny Lane, Schaumburg, IL 60173
Phone: 847-490-9200
Email: info@fefinc.org
http://www.fefinc.org/scholarships.html

Purpose: To aid Indiana region students who have a demonstrated interest in the die cast and cast metal industries.

Eligibility: Applicants must be residents of Indiana or of a state that is adjacent to Indiana. They must be enrolled at an Indiana school or at a Foundry Educational Foundation (FEF) member school located in a state that is adjacent to Indiana. They must have prior work experience in manufacturing, the die casting industry or the cast metal industry. Preference will be given to applicants who are studying a subject that is related to the die casting industry. Selection is based on the overall strength of the application.

Target applicant(s): High school students. College students. Adult students.

Amount: Varies.

Number of awards: Varies.

Deadline: June 2.

How to apply: Applications are available online. An application form and supporting documents are required.

Exclusive: Visit www.UltimateScholarshipBook.com and enter code FO203220 for updates on this award.

(2033) • Nancy Penn Lyons Scholarship Fund

Community Foundation for Greater Atlanta Inc.
50 Hurt Plaza, Suite 449, Atlanta, GA 30303
Phone: 404-688-5525
Email: info@cfgreateratlanta.org
http://www.cfgreateratlanta.org/community-impact/scholarships/

Purpose: To provide assistance to needy students who have been accepted to prestigious or out-of-state universities.

Eligibility: Applicants must be graduating high school seniors who have been Georgia residents for at least one year. They must have an ACT score of 22 or higher or an SAT composite score of 1000 or higher and a GPA of 3.0 or greater. They must have participated in community service and have financial need, and they must not be attending a public institution in the state of Georgia.

Target applicant(s): High school students.

Minimum GPA: 3.0

Amount: $5,000.

Number of awards: 5.

Scholarship may be renewable.

Deadline: March 15.

How to apply: Applications are available online.

Exclusive: Visit www.UltimateScholarshipBook.com and enter code CO203320 for updates on this award.

(2034) • Nathaniel A. Murray Scholarship

Alpha Phi Alpha Fraternity Inc.
Omicron Eta Lambda Chapter, P.O. Box 1844, Washington, DC 20013
http://www.ohlalpha1906.com

Purpose: To support graduating seniors of Washington, DC in pursuing post-secondary education.

Eligibility: A minimum GPA of 2.5 is required. Selection is primarily based on demonstration of leadership potential, excellent character and academic achievement.

Target applicant(s): High school students.

Minimum GPA: 2.5

Amount: Varies.

Number of awards: Varies.

Deadline: April 1.

How to apply: Applications are available online.

Exclusive: Visit www.UltimateScholarshipBook.com and enter code AL203420 for updates on this award.

(2035) • Nathaniel Alston Student Achievement Award

Pennsylvania Society of Physician Assistants
P.O. Box 128, Greensburg, PA 15601
Phone: 724-836-6411
Email: hohpac@windstream.net
http://www.pspa.net

Purpose: To aid outstanding physician assistant students attending school in Pennsylvania.

Eligibility: Applicants must be current students in good standing who are enrolled in an accredited physician assistant program in the state of Pennsylvania. They must be current Pennsylvania Society of Physician Assistants (PSPA) members who demonstrate outstanding leadership and participation in their schools and communities. Selection is based on the overall strength of the application.

Target applicant(s): College students. Graduate school students. Adult students.

Amount: $2,000.

Number of awards: Varies.

Deadline: July 30.

How to apply: Applications are available online. An application form and personal essay are required.

Exclusive: Visit www.UltimateScholarshipBook.com and enter code PE203520 for updates on this award.

(2036) · National Tour Association (NTA) La Macchia Family Undergraduate Scholarship

Tourism Cares
275 Turnpike Street, Suite 307, Canton, MA 02021
Phone: 781-821-5990
Email: scholarships@tourismcares.org
http://www.tourismcares.org/academic-scholarships/

Purpose: To aid those who are studying hospitality, tourism or travel at the undergraduate level in Wisconsin.

Eligibility: Applicants must be permanent residents of the U.S., full-time students and rising undergraduate juniors or seniors who are enrolled at an accredited four-year institution located in Wisconsin. They must be studying tourism, travel or hospitality and have a GPA of 3.0 or higher on a four-point scale. Applicants must have completed 60 or more credits by May of the application year. Selection is based on the overall strength of the application.

Target applicant(s): College students. Adult students.
Minimum GPA: 3.0
Amount: $2,000.
Number of awards: 1.
Deadline: April 3.

How to apply: Applications are available online. An application form, proof of residency, resume, two letters of recommendation, official transcript and personal essay are required.

Exclusive: Visit www.UltimateScholarshipBook.com and enter code TO203620 for updates on this award.

(2037) · NAWIC Granite State Chapter Scholarships

National Association of Women in Construction-Granite State Chapter #218
Attn: Peggy DeWever, 46 Heron Cove Road, Eliot, ME 03903
Phone: 603-659-4442
http://nawicnh.weebly.com

Purpose: To aid New Hampshire students who are preparing for careers in the field of construction.

Eligibility: Applicants must be New Hampshire residents who are entering the second, third or fourth year of an undergraduate program in a construction-related subject. They must have a GPA of 2.0 or higher. Selection is based on the overall strength of the application.

Target applicant(s): College students. Adult students.
Minimum GPA: 2.0
Amount: Varies.
Number of awards: Varies.
Deadline: April 1.

How to apply: Instructions for how to apply are available online. A personal essay and transcript are required.

Exclusive: Visit www.UltimateScholarshipBook.com and enter code NA203720 for updates on this award.

(2038) · NCRA Scholarship

North Carolina Racquetball Association (NCRA)
195 Hill Lane, Sneads Ferry, NC 28460
Phone: 910-327-4441
Email: ncra@ncracquetball.com
http://www.ncracquetball.com

Purpose: To support those NCRA junior racquetball participants who wish to pursue higher education after high school.

Eligibility: Applicants must be NCRA members in good standing, be a senior in high school or a college undergraduate and have a "B" overall grade point average.

Target applicant(s): High school students. College students. Adult students.
Minimum GPA: 3.0
Amount: $500.
Number of awards: 4.
Deadline: June 15.

How to apply: Applications are available online or by calling the NCRA office. The application includes a release form, at least one letter of reference, the teacher report form, a personal essay, an official transcript and a photo.

Exclusive: Visit www.UltimateScholarshipBook.com and enter code NO203820 for updates on this award.

(2039) · NDVA Waiver of Tuition

Nebraska Department of Veterans' Affairs
State Service Office, 3800 Village Drive, P.O. Box 85816, Lincoln, NE 68501-5816
Phone: 402-420-4021
Email: ndva@nebraska.gov
https://veterans.nebraska.gov/

Purpose: To provide assistance to children and spouses of Nebraska veterans.

Eligibility: Applicants must be the children, stepchildren, spouses or widows of veterans who died of a service-connected injury or illness, became totally and permanently disabled as a result of military service or was classified as MIA or POW during armed conflict after August 4th, 1964. They must be Nebraska residents and attend a state college, university or community college.

Target applicant(s): High school students. College students. Adult students.
Amount: Full tuition.
Number of awards: Varies.
Scholarship may be renewable.
Deadline: Prior to the start of any term.

How to apply: Applications are available from your County Veterans Service Officer.

Exclusive: Visit www.UltimateScholarshipBook.com and enter code NE203920 for updates on this award.

(2040) · Nebraska Academy of Sciences High School Scholarships

Nebraska Academy of Sciences, Inc.
302 Morrill Hall, 14th and U Streets, Lincoln, NE 68588-0339
Phone: 402-472-2644
Email: nebacad@unl.edu
https://nebraskaacademyofsciences.wildapricot.org/GrantsandScholarships

Purpose: To assist Nebraska high school students.

Eligibility: There are six scholarships given to Nebraska high school seniors including those who plan to study geology, earth sciences, prairie and soil conservation, climate and environmental change and business and the environment.

Target applicant(s): High school students.
Amount: $300-$1,500.
Number of awards: Varies.
Deadline: March 1.

How to apply: Applications are available online. Requirements vary by the individual award.

Exclusive: Visit www.UltimateScholarshipBook.com and enter code NE204020 for updates on this award.

(2041) • Nebraska Actuaries Club Scholarship

Nebraska Actuaries Club
c/o Laura Huscroft, Enterprise Risk Management, Mutual of Omaha, 3301 Dodge Street, Omaha, NE 68131
Email: Laura.Huscroft@MutualofOmaha.com
http://n-a-c.org/

Purpose: To aid Nebraska students who plan to major in actuarial science or a related subject.

Eligibility: Applicants must be U.S. high school seniors who are planning to attend an accredited college or university located in the state of Nebraska. They must be planning to major in actuarial science, economics, mathematics or statistics and must intend to pursue an actuarial career. Applicants must have demonstrated mathematical ability. Selection is based on the overall strength of the application.

Target applicant(s): High school students.
Amount: $2,000-$4,000.
Number of awards: 4.
Deadline: March 31.
How to apply: Applications are available online. An application form, recommendation letter and standardized test scores are required.
Exclusive: Visit www.UltimateScholarshipBook.com and enter code NE204120 for updates on this award.

(2042) • Ned McWherter Scholars Program

Tennessee Student Assistance Corporation
404 James Robertson Parkway, Suite 1510, Parkway Towers, Nashville, TN 37243
Phone: 800-342-1663
Email: tsac.aidinfo@tn.gov
http://www.tn.gov/collegepays/section/money-for-college

Purpose: To assist outstanding Tennessee students who are planning to attend a Tennessee college or university.

Eligibility: Applicants must be U.S. citizens or legal residents and Tennessee residents who are graduating high school seniors. They must have plans to attend an eligible Tennessee undergraduate institution full-time and have a GPA of 3.5 or higher. Applicants must have a combined math and reading SAT score of at least 1280 or an ACT composite score of 29 or higher. Selection is based on the overall strength of the application.

Target applicant(s): High school students.
Minimum GPA: 3.5
Amount: $6,000.
Number of awards: Varies.
Scholarship may be renewable.
Deadline: February 15.
How to apply: Applications are available online. An application form, official transcripts and standardized test scores are required.
Exclusive: Visit www.UltimateScholarshipBook.com and enter code TE204220 for updates on this award.

(2043) • Need Based Tuition Waiver Program

Massachusetts Department of Higher Education
Office of Student Financial Assistance, 454 Broadway, Suite 200, Revere, MA 02151
Phone: 617-727-9420
Email: osfa@osfa.mass.edu
http://www.mass.edu/osfa/students/forstudents.asp

Purpose: To support Massachusetts students who are in need of supplemental financial aid.

Eligibility: Applicants must live in the state of Massachusetts for at least one year prior to the beginning of the school year, and they must be enrolled in a state-funded college. They must be in an undergraduate program with at least three credits per semester. Students must not owe any refunds on prior scholarships and cannot have any defaulted government loans. They must also be able to show proof of financial need.

Target applicant(s): High school students. College students. Adult students.
Amount: Up to full tuition.
Number of awards: Varies.
Deadline: Varies.
How to apply: Applications are available at college financial aid offices.
Exclusive: Visit www.UltimateScholarshipBook.com and enter code MA204320 for updates on this award.

(2044) • Nevada Women's Fund Scholarships

Nevada Women's Fund
770 Smithridge Drive, Suite 300, Reno, NV 89502
Phone: 775-786-2335
Email: info@nevadawomensfund.org
http://www.nevadawomensfund.org

Purpose: To improve the lives of women and children in northern Nevada.

Eligibility: Northern Nevada residents and those attending northern Nevada schools receive preference. Applicants must be enrolled in an accredited two or four year degree or certifying program, will take a minimum of 6 to 8 credits per semester and have a cumulative GPA of 3.0.

Target applicant(s): High school students. College students. Graduate school students. Adult students.
Minimum GPA: 3.0
Amount: $500-$5,000.
Number of awards: Varies.
Deadline: February 28.
How to apply: Applications are available online or from several offices listed on the website.
Exclusive: Visit www.UltimateScholarshipBook.com and enter code NE204420 for updates on this award.

(2045) • New Century Scholarship

Utah System of Higher Education
New Century Scholarship, P.O. Box 145116, Salt Lake City, UT 84114-5116
Phone: 801-321-7221
Email: newcentury@ushe.edu
http://www.utahsbr.edu

Purpose: To assist Utah high school students.

Eligibility: Applicants must be high school students who have completed the equivalent of an associate's degree at a Utah state institution of higher education or completed a specific math and science curriculum by September 1 of their high school graduation year. The award provides assistance for the bachelor's degree at a state college.

Target applicant(s): High school students.
Amount: Up to $1,250.
Number of awards: Varies.
Scholarship may be renewable.
Deadline: February 1.
How to apply: Applications are available online.
Exclusive: Visit www.UltimateScholarshipBook.com and enter code UT204520 for updates on this award.

(2046) · New England Regional Student Program

New England Board of Higher Education
45 Temple Place, Boston, MA 02111
Phone: 617-357-9620
Email: rsp@nebhe.org
http://www.nebhe.org

Purpose: The program lowers tuition rates for New England students who must travel out of state for their desired major.
Eligibility: Students must be residents of Connecticut, Maine, Massachusetts, New Hampshire, Rhode Island or Vermont and attend a school in another of those states that offers an RSP program in their major. The major must not be available at an in-school state.
Target applicant(s): High school students. College students. Graduate school students. Adult students.
Amount: Varies.
Number of awards: Varies.
Scholarship may be renewable.
Deadline: Varies.
How to apply: Students should note that they are interested in the RSP program on their regular college application.
Exclusive: Visit www.UltimateScholarshipBook.com and enter code NE204620 for updates on this award.

(2047) · New Hampshire Charitable Foundation Statewide Student Aid Program

New Hampshire Charitable Foundation
37 Pleasant Street, Concord, NH 03301-4005
Phone: 603-225-6641
Email: info@nhcf.org
https://www.nhcf.org/how-can-we-help-you/

Purpose: To allow New Hampshire students to access over 50 scholarship and loan opportunities through a single application.
Eligibility: Applicants must be New Hampshire residents who plan to pursue a bachelor's degree or graduate students of any age. They must enroll at least half-time to qualify.
Target applicant(s): High school students. College students. Graduate school students. Adult students.
Amount: $100-$7,500.
Number of awards: Varies.
Deadline: April 14 (under 23); For those over 23: May 15, August 15, December 15.
How to apply: Applications are available online.
Exclusive: Visit www.UltimateScholarshipBook.com and enter code NE204720 for updates on this award.

(2048) · New Hampshire Society of CPAs Scholarship

New Hampshire Society of Certified Public Accountants
Attn.: Financial Careers Committee, 1750 Elm Street, Suite 403, Manchester, NH 03104
Phone: 603-622-1999
http://www.nhscpa.org

Purpose: To reward students with strong academic performance who will serve the CPA profession with honor.
Eligibility: Applicants must be a U.S. citizen, a New Hampshire resident and either entering their senior or a graduate student in an accredited four-year college or university studying accounting or business. Students may also be seeking their additional thirty hours of education to become eligible for their CPA license in New Hampshire. Applicants must be recommended by a teacher or person responsible for their accounting/business program where they are enrolled. Students must have ninety credits or senior standing and must have taken at least three courses of upper level accounting courses.
Target applicant(s): College students. Graduate school students. Adult students.
Amount: Varies.
Number of awards: Varies.
Deadline: December 1.
How to apply: Applications are available online.
Exclusive: Visit www.UltimateScholarshipBook.com and enter code NE204820 for updates on this award.

(2049) · New Jersey Open Scholarship

Eastern Region USA Roller Skating
30 Wyndham Road, Voorhees, NJ 08043
Phone: 610-328-1314
Email: dwalsh999@comcast.net
http://www.erusars.org/

Purpose: To support Eastern Region artistic roller skaters as they further their education beyond high school.
Eligibility: Applicants must be a high school senior who is a member of a USA Roller Skating club in New Jersey, Pennsylvania or Delaware and must compete in the New Jersey Open Invitational. Selection is based on skating achievements and participation, academic success and financial need.
Target applicant(s): High school students.
Amount: $500.
Number of awards: 1.
Deadline: June 14.
How to apply: Applications are available online.
Exclusive: Visit www.UltimateScholarshipBook.com and enter code EA204920 for updates on this award.

(2050) · New Jersey Oratorical Contest

American Legion, Department of New Jersey
135 W. Hanover Street, Trenton, NJ 08618
Phone: 609-695-5418
Email: adjudant@njamericanlegion.org
http://www.njamericanlegion.org

Purpose: To enhance high school students' experience with and understanding of the U.S. Constitution. The contest will help develop students' leadership skills and civic appreciation, as well as the ability to deliver thoughtful, insightful orations regarding U.S. citizenship and its inherent responsibilities.
Eligibility: Applicants must be high school students under the age of 20 who are U.S. citizens or legal residents and residents of the state. Students first give an oration within their state and winners compete at the national level. The oration must be related to the Constitution of the United States focusing on the duties and obligations citizens have to the government. It must be in English and be between eight and ten minutes. There is also an assigned topic which is posted on the website, and it should be between three and five minutes.
Target applicant(s): High school students.
Amount: Up to $4,000.
Number of awards: 5.
Deadline: January 22.
How to apply: Application information is available by email: ray@njamericanlegion.org.
Exclusive: Visit www.UltimateScholarshipBook.com and enter code AM205020 for updates on this award.

(2051) • New Jersey Physician Assistant Foundation/ New Jersey State Society of Physician Assistants Scholarship

New Jersey State Society of Physician Assistants
760 Alexander Road , P.O. Box 1, Princeton, NJ 08543
Phone: 609-275-4123
Email: scholarships@njsspa.org
http://www.njsspa.org
Purpose: To aid New Jersey physician assistant students.
Eligibility: Applicants must be enrolled in a physician assistant degree program at a school located in the state of New Jersey. They must be student members of the New Jersey State Society of Physician Assistants (NJSSPA). Selection is based on the overall strength of the application.
Target applicant(s): College students. Graduate school students. Adult students.
Amount: $1,000.
Number of awards: 1.
Deadline: September 20.
How to apply: Applications are available online. An application form, two reference letters and supporting materials are required.
Exclusive: Visit www.UltimateScholarshipBook.com and enter code NE205120 for updates on this award.

(2052) • New Jersey State Elks Special Children's Committee Scholarship

New Jersey State Elks
665 Rahway Avenue, P.O. Box 1596, Woodbridge, NJ 07095
Phone: 732-326-1300
Email: ndame788@aol.com
http://www.njelks.org/index.php/our-programs/scholarship-information
Purpose: To assist students with physical handicaps in obtaining higher education.
Eligibility: Applicants must be New Jersey residents and high school seniors with physical handicaps. They must demonstrate financial need and excellent academic standing.
Target applicant(s): High school students.
Amount: Up to $2,500.
Number of awards: 2.
Scholarship may be renewable.
Deadline: Mid-April.
How to apply: Applications are available online or by phone.
Exclusive: Visit www.UltimateScholarshipBook.com and enter code NE205220 for updates on this award.

(2053) • New Jersey World Trade Center Scholarship

New Jersey Higher Education Student Assistance Authority
P.O. Box 540, Trenton, NJ 08625
Phone: 800-792-8670
Email: clientservices@hesaa.org
http://www.hesaa.org
Purpose: To support the children and spouses of those who died as a result of the World Trade Center attack.
Eligibility: Applicants must be a dependent child or spouse of a New Jersey resident who was killed in the September 11, 2001 attack, died from resulting injuries or exposure to the attack site or are missing and presumed dead as a result of the attack. Students must be full-time undergraduates, and they may attend any eligible school in the U.S.
Target applicant(s): High school students. College students. Adult students.
Amount: Full tuition.
Number of awards: Varies.
Scholarship may be renewable.
Deadline: October 1 and March 1.
How to apply: Applications are available online.
Exclusive: Visit www.UltimateScholarshipBook.com and enter code NE205320 for updates on this award.

(2054) • New Mexico Scholars

New Mexico Higher Education Department
2044 Galisteo Street, Suite 4, Santa Fe, NM 87505-2100
Phone: 505-476-8400
Email: cesaria.tapia1@state.nm.us
http://www.hed.state.nm.us/students/
Purpose: To support New Mexico undergraduate students with financial need attend postsecondary institutions in New Mexico.
Eligibility: Applicants must be undergraduate students attending selected New Mexico public institutions or designated private non-profit colleges, meet family income requirements, be under the age of 22 and have graduated in the top 5 percent of their high school class, have a minimum ACT score of 25 or a minimum 1140 SAT score. Students must be enrolled full time.
Target applicant(s): College students.
Amount: Up to full tuition.
Number of awards: Varies.
Scholarship may be renewable.
Deadline: Varies.
How to apply: Contact your financial aid office. Must complete a FAFSA.
Exclusive: Visit www.UltimateScholarshipBook.com and enter code NE205420 for updates on this award.

(2055) • New York Legion Auxiliary Department Scholarship

American Legion Auxiliary, Department of New York
112 State Street, Suite 1310, Albany, NY 12207
Phone: 518-463-1162
Email: nyalaeducation@gmail.com
http://www.deptny.org/?page_id=2128
Purpose: To assist students whose parents, grandparents or great-grandparents served in the Armed Forces during wartime.
Eligibility: Applicants must be children, grandchildren or great-grandchildren of veterans who served in the Armed Forces during World War I, World War II, the Korean Conflict, the Vietnam War, Grenada/Lebanon, Panama, the Persian Gulf or War on Terrorism. Students must be high school seniors or graduates and be New York State residents and U.S. citizens.
Target applicant(s): High school students.
Amount: $1,000.
Number of awards: 1.
Deadline: March 1.
How to apply: Applications are available online.
Exclusive: Visit www.UltimateScholarshipBook.com and enter code AM205520 for updates on this award.

(2056) • New York Legion Auxiliary District Scholarships

American Legion Auxiliary, Department of New York
112 State Street, Suite 1310, Albany, NY 12207

Phone: 518-463-1162
Email: nyalaeducation@gmail.com
http://www.deptny.org/?page_id=2128
Purpose: To provide financial assistance to children, grandchildren and great-grandchildren of war veterans.
Eligibility: Applicants must be children, grandchildren or great-grandchildren of Armed Forces veterans of World War I, World War II, the Korean Conflict, the Vietnam War, Grenada/Lebanon, Panama, the Persian Gulf or War on Terrorism. Students must be high school seniors and must be U.S. citizens and New York State residents.
Target applicant(s): High school students.
Amount: $1,000.
Number of awards: 1.
Deadline: March 15.
How to apply: Applications are available online.
Exclusive: Visit www.UltimateScholarshipBook.com and enter code AM205620 for updates on this award.

(2057) • New York Oratorical Contest

American Legion, Department of New York
112 State Street, Suite 1300, Albany, NY 12207
Phone: 518-463-2215
Email: info@nylegion.org
https://nylegion.net/
Purpose: To enhance high school students' experience with and understanding of the U.S. Constitution. The contest will help develop students' leadership skills and civic appreciation, as well as the ability to deliver thoughtful, insightful orations regarding U.S. citizenship and its inherent responsibilities.
Eligibility: Applicants must be high school students under the age of 20 who are U.S. citizens or legal residents and residents of the state. Students first give an oration within their state and winners compete at the national level. The oration must be related to the Constitution of the United States focusing on the duties and obligations citizens have to the government. It must be in English and be between eight and ten minutes. There is also an assigned topic which is posted on the website, and it should be between three and five minutes.
Target applicant(s): High school students.
Amount: $2,000-$6,000.
Number of awards: 5.
Deadline: November 18.
How to apply: Application information is available by contacting the local American Legion Post.
Exclusive: Visit www.UltimateScholarshipBook.com and enter code AM205720 for updates on this award.

(2058) • New York State Association of Agricultural Fairs/New York State Showpeople's Association Scholarships

New York State Association of Agricultural Fairs
Norma W. Hamilton, Executive Secretary, 67 Verbeck Avenue, Schaghticoke, NY 12154
Phone: 518-753-4956
Email: carousels4@aol.com
http://www.nyfairs.org/scholarship.htm
Purpose: To aid New York students who are preparing for careers in agriculture, fair management or the outdoor amusement business.
Eligibility: Applicants must be New York state residents or must attend school in the state of New York and must be high school seniors or current undergraduate students. They can be enrolled in or planning to enroll in any degree program but additional consideration may be given to those pursuing degrees in agriculture, fair management or the outdoor amusement business. They must be attending or planning to attend an accredited postsecondary institution and must be active in local fairs. Selection is based on fair participation, leadership, citizenship and essay.
Target applicant(s): High school students. College students. Adult students.
Amount: $1,000.
Number of awards: 10.
Deadline: Second Friday in April.
How to apply: Applications are available online. An application form, personal essay, two recommendation letters and a transcript are required.
Exclusive: Visit www.UltimateScholarshipBook.com and enter code NE205820 for updates on this award.

(2059) • New York State Society of Physician Assistants Scholarship

New York Society of Physician Assistants
174 S. New York Road, P.O. Box 606, Oceanville, NJ 08231
Phone: 877-769-7722
Email: info@nysspa.org
http://www.nysspa.org
Purpose: To aid New York State Society of Physician Assistants (NYSSPA) student members.
Eligibility: Applicants must be NYSSPA members who are currently enrolled in an ARC-PA accredited physician assistant degree program in the state of New York. They must be in the professional phase of their degree program. Previous NYSSPA Scholarship winners, NYSSPA board members and NYSSPA committee chairs are ineligible. Selection is based on academic achievement, financial need and professional activities.
Target applicant(s): College students. Graduate school students. Adult students.
Amount: Varies.
Number of awards: Varies.
Deadline: Varies.
How to apply: Applications are available online. An application form, one reference letter, a personal essay and a financial aid award letter are required.
Exclusive: Visit www.UltimateScholarshipBook.com and enter code NE205920 for updates on this award.

(2060) • New York State USBC Scholarships

New York State USBC
55 Edgewood Drive, Batavia, NY 14020
Phone: 585-343-3736
Email: bowlny300@yahoo.com
https://www.bowlny.com/youth_scholarships.php
Purpose: To assist bowlers in New York.
Eligibility: Applicants must be members of a New York State USBC Youth certified league and be high school seniors. Selection includes academic and extracurricular achievement.
Target applicant(s): High school students.
Amount: $1,000-$5,000.
Number of awards: Varies.
Scholarship may be renewable.
Deadline: December 1.
How to apply: Applications are available online.
Exclusive: Visit www.UltimateScholarshipBook.com and enter code NE206020 for updates on this award.

(2061) • New York State USBC Spirit Awards

New York State USBC
55 Edgewood Drive, Batavia, NY 14020
Phone: 585-343-3736
Email: bowlny300@yahoo.com
https://www.bowlny.com/youth_scholarships.php
Purpose: To assist bowlers in grades 8-11 in New York.
Eligibility: Applicants must demonstrate sportsmanship, commitment and leadership.
Target applicant(s): Junior high students or younger. High school students.
Amount: $250-$750.
Number of awards: 3.
Deadline: February 1.
How to apply: Bowlers are nominated by their bowling coach.
Exclusive: Visit www.UltimateScholarshipBook.com and enter code NE206120 for updates on this award.

(2062) • New York Women in Communications Foundation Scholarships

New York Women in Communications Foundation
355 Lexington Avenue, 15th Floor, New York, NY 10017
Phone: 212-297-2133
http://www.nywici.org/students/scholarships
Purpose: To support high school, college and graduate students currently residing in New York, New Jersey, Connecticut or Pennsylvania with the pursuit of a degree in a communications-related field.
Eligibility: Applicants are required to have a minimum GPA of 3.2 and must be majoring, declaring a major or pursuing an advanced degree in a communications-related field at an accredited college or university in the United States. Graduate students must already be members of New York Women in Communications.
Target applicant(s): High school students. College students. Graduate school students. Adult students.
Minimum GPA: 3.2
Amount: $10,000.
Number of awards: 18-20.
Deadline: January 26.
How to apply: Applications are available online.
Exclusive: Visit www.UltimateScholarshipBook.com and enter code NE206220 for updates on this award.

(2063) • Nightingale Awards of Pennsylvania Scholarship

Nightingale Awards of Pennsylvania
2400 Ardmore Boulevard, Suite 302, Pittsburgh, PA 15221
Phone: 412-871-3353
Email: info@nightingaleawards.org
http://www.nightingaleawards.org/scholarships/
Purpose: To support Pennsylvania nursing students.
Eligibility: Applicants must be Pennsylvania residents who are enrolled in or have been accepted into a Pennsylvania nursing program in licensed practical nursing, registered nursing or graduate-level nursing practice. They must have completed at least one course in nursing and must have a B average or better. Previous recipients of this scholarship are ineligible. Selection is based on academic achievement, leadership ability, extracurricular activities and professional dedication to nursing.
Target applicant(s): College students. Graduate school students. Adult students.
Minimum GPA: 3.0
Amount: Varies.
Number of awards: Varies.
Deadline: March 28.
How to apply: Applications are available online. An application form, official transcript, two recommendation letters, a copy of the applicant's nursing program acceptance letter, a personal statement and a research proposal abstract (Ph.D. applicants only) are required.
Exclusive: Visit www.UltimateScholarshipBook.com and enter code NI206320 for updates on this award.

(2064) • Nissan Scholarship

Nissan North America
P.O. Box 685003, Franklin, TN 37068
Phone: 800-647-7261
Email: webmaster@nissanusa.com
http://www.nissanusa.com
Purpose: To assist Mississippi high school seniors in attending public two-year or four-year colleges.
Eligibility: Applicants must have a minimum GPA of 2.5 and a minimum ACT score of 20 or SAT score of 820, have demonstrated financial need and be accepted as a full-time student at a Mississippi public college or university.
Target applicant(s): High school students.
Minimum GPA: 2.5
Amount: Full tuition.
Number of awards: Varies.
Deadline: March 1.
How to apply: No application is necessary. However, students must mail an essay, resume, high school transcript with ACT or SAT score and FAFSA results to Mississippi Office of Student Financial Aid, 3825 Ridgewood Road, Jackson, MS 39211-6453.
Exclusive: Visit www.UltimateScholarshipBook.com and enter code NI206420 for updates on this award.

(2065) • NJ Student Tuition Assistance Reward Scholarship

New Jersey Higher Education Student Assistance Authority
P.O. Box 540, Trenton, NJ 08625
Phone: 800-792-8670
Email: clientservices@hesaa.org
http://www.hesaa.org
Purpose: To support community college students in New Jersey who graduated from high school with excellent academic standing.
Eligibility: Applicants must have graduated from a New Jersey high school in the top 20 percent of their class, and they must have been state residents for at least 12 months prior to graduation. Students must enroll full-time in their home county college by the fifth semester after graduating from high school.
Target applicant(s): High school students. College students. Adult students.
Minimum GPA: 3.0
Amount: Up to full tuition.
Number of awards: Varies.
Scholarship may be renewable.
Deadline: October 1 and March 1.
How to apply: Applications are available at college financial aid offices.
Exclusive: Visit www.UltimateScholarshipBook.com and enter code NE206520 for updates on this award.

(2066) • NJ Student Tuition Assistance Reward Scholarship II

New Jersey Higher Education Student Assistance Authority
P.O. Box 540, Trenton, NJ 08625
Phone: 800-792-8670
Email: clientservices@hesaa.org
http://www.hesaa.org

Purpose: To support NJ STARS students who are transferring to four-year colleges.
Eligibility: Applicants must be county college graduates with an associate's degree, and they must have a GPA of at least 3.0. They must either be NJ STARS recipients or have other full state or federal aid during the semester in which they graduate. Students must be enrolled full-time at a New Jersey four-year college within two semesters of graduation.
Target applicant(s): College students. Adult students.
Minimum GPA: 3.0
Amount: Up to $2,500 a year.
Number of awards: Varies.
Scholarship may be renewable.
Deadline: October 1.
How to apply: Applications are available at college financial aid offices.
Exclusive: Visit www.UltimateScholarshipBook.com and enter code NE206620 for updates on this award.

(2067) • NJCDCA Scholarship

New Jersey Cheerleading and Dance Coaches Association
Doug Linden, 276 Stamets Road, Milford, NJ 08848
Phone: 908-797-6262
Email: doug.linden@njcdca.com
http://www.njcheerleading.com/index.htm

Purpose: To recognize New Jersey senior cheerleaders and dancers for their academic achievements and athletic excellence.
Eligibility: Applicants must be a high school senior and member of a cheer or dance team that is a New Jersey Cheerleading and Dance Coaches Association member. Selection is based on academic and athletic achievement, community involvement, personal essay and coach recommendation.
Target applicant(s): High school students.
Amount: Varies.
Number of awards: Varies.
Deadline: March 17.
How to apply: Applications are available online and include the application form including a personal essay, an official high school transcript and a coach recommendation form.
Exclusive: Visit www.UltimateScholarshipBook.com and enter code NE206720 for updates on this award.

(2068) • NJSCA High School Scholarship

New Jersey School Counselor Association Inc.
Sheila Brewer, NJSCA High School Awards Chair, 5 Split Rock Place, Moorestown, NJ 08057
Phone: 609-893-8141
Email: sbrewer@pemb.org
http://www.njsca.org

Purpose: To spread awareness of the importance of the role of school counselors.
Eligibility: Applicants must be New Jersey residents who will be graduating in the year of application. They must have been accepted to and plan to enroll in an institution of higher learning. A 300-500 word essay is required.
Target applicant(s): High school students.
Amount: Varies.
Number of awards: Varies.
Deadline: March 15.
How to apply: Applications are available online.
Exclusive: Visit www.UltimateScholarshipBook.com and enter code NE206820 for updates on this award.

(2069) • NJVVM Scholarship Program

New Jersey Vietnam Veterans' Memorial Foundation
1 Memorial Lane, P.O. Box 648, Holmdel, NJ 07733
Phone: 732-335-0033
Email: scholarship@njvvmf.org
http://www.njvvmf.org

Purpose: To support high school seniors in New Jersey who have visited the New Jersey Vietnam Veterans' Memorial.
Eligibility: Applicants must be New Jersey residents, be a graduating high school senior and submit an essay on their experience visiting the New Jersey Vietnam Veterans Memorial.
Target applicant(s): High school students.
Amount: $2,500.
Number of awards: 2.
Deadline: April 14.
How to apply: Applications are available online.
Exclusive: Visit www.UltimateScholarshipBook.com and enter code NE206920 for updates on this award.

(2070) • NMASBO Scholarship

New Mexico Association of School Business Officials
P.O. Box 7535, Albuquerque, NM 87194-7535
Phone: 505-923-3283
Email: info@nmasbo.org
http://www.nmasbo.org

Purpose: To support graduating high school seniors in New Mexico.
Eligibility: Students must have at least a 3.0 GPA. Applicants must submit an essay and two letters of recommendation. Students must plan to attend a New Mexico college or university on a full-time basis.
Target applicant(s): High school students.
Minimum GPA: 3.0
Amount: $1,500.
Number of awards: 6-10.
Deadline: February 10.
How to apply: Applications are available online.
Exclusive: Visit www.UltimateScholarshipBook.com and enter code NE207020 for updates on this award.

(2071) • NNM American Society of Mechanical Engineers Scholarship

Los Alamos National Laboratory Foundation
1112 Plaza del Norte, Espanola, NM 87532
Phone: 505-753-8890
Email: tony@lanlfoundation.org
http://www.lanlfoundation.org

Purpose: To support undergraduate students from northern New Mexico who are majoring in mechanical engineering.
Eligibility: Students must have at least a 3.25 GPA, and they must have either an SAT score (combined Math plus Critical Reading only)

of at least 930 or an ACT score of at least 19. Applicants must submit an essay and two letters of recommendation.
Target applicant(s): High school students. College students. Adult students.
Minimum GPA: 3.25
Amount: $1,000.
Number of awards: Varies.
Deadline: January 22.
How to apply: Applications are available online.
Exclusive: Visit www.UltimateScholarshipBook.com and enter code LO207120 for updates on this award.

(2072) · Norman and Ruth Good Educational Endowment

Lincoln Community Foundation
215 Centennial Mall South, Suite 100, Lincoln, NE 68508
Phone: 402-474-2345
Email: robertm@lcf.org
http://www.lcf.org
Purpose: To assist Nebraska students.
Eligibility: Applicants must be attending a private college in Nebraska and must be in their junior or senior year. Applicants may not apply if the scholarship money is to be used for summer programs or schools that are not valid degree-granting institutions.
Target applicant(s): College students. Adult students.
Minimum GPA: 3.5
Amount: $2,500.
Number of awards: Varies.
Scholarship may be renewable.
Deadline: March 31.
How to apply: Applications are available online.
Exclusive: Visit www.UltimateScholarshipBook.com and enter code LI207220 for updates on this award.

(2073) · Norman E. Strohmeier, W2VRS Memorial Scholarship

American Radio Relay League Foundation
225 Main Street, Newington, CT 06111-1494
Phone: 860-594-0348
Email: foundation@arrl.org
http://www.arrl.org/scholarship-program
Purpose: To support students from western New York who are involved in amateur radio.
Eligibility: Applicants must have an amateur radio license of Technician Class or higher. Students must have at least a 3.2 GPA, and preference will be given to graduating high school seniors.
Target applicant(s): High school students.
Minimum GPA: 3.2
Amount: $500.
Number of awards: 1.
Deadline: January 31.
How to apply: Applications are available online.
Exclusive: Visit www.UltimateScholarshipBook.com and enter code AM207320 for updates on this award.

(2074) · Norman S. and Betty M. Fitzhugh Fund

Greater Kanawha Valley Foundation
1600 Huntington Square, 900 Lee Street, East, Charleston, WV 25301
Phone: 304-346-3620
Email: shoover@tgkvf.org
http://www.tgkvf.org
Purpose: To provide financial assistance to West Virginia residents wishing to earn a college education.
Eligibility: Applicants must be full-time students (12 hours) and demonstrate good moral character and academic excellence. Students must have a minimum 2.5 GPA and minimum ACT score of 20.
Target applicant(s): High school students. College students. Adult students.
Minimum GPA: 2.5
Amount: $750.
Number of awards: 1.
Scholarship may be renewable.
Deadline: January 15.
How to apply: Applications are available online or by email.
Exclusive: Visit www.UltimateScholarshipBook.com and enter code GR207420 for updates on this award.

(2075) · North American International Auto Show High School Poster Competition

North American International Auto Show
1900 West Big Beaver, Suite 100, Troy, MI 48084
Phone: 248-643-0250
Email: sherp@dada.org
http://www.naias.com
Purpose: To support students interested in participating in the NAIAS by creating unique posters that are automotive-themed to be entered in competition.
Eligibility: Contestants must be Michigan high school students currently in grades 10-12. Selection is based on the overall quality of the poster entry.
Target applicant(s): High school students.
Amount: $100-$1,000.
Number of awards: 16.
Deadline: November 22.
How to apply: Automotive-themed poster entry is required. Posters must be mailed.
Exclusive: Visit www.UltimateScholarshipBook.com and enter code NO207520 for updates on this award.

(2076) · North Carolina 4-H Development Fund Scholarships

North Carolina 4-H Youth Development
Shannon McCollum, Extension 4-H Associate, NCCES 4-H/FCS Team, NCSU Campus Box 7655, Raleigh, NC 27695
Phone: 919-515-8486
Email: shannon_mccollum@ncsu.edu
https://nc4h.ces.ncsu.edu/
Purpose: To help North Carolina students who have been involved with the 4-H Club who want to go to college in the state.
Eligibility: Applicants must be enrolling as undergraduates at a four-year North Carolina college or university or a junior or community college in the state, provided the program of study is transferable to a four-year college. Students must also have a strong record of 4-H Club participation, have an excellent high school academic record and show an aptitude for college work through SAT scores. An application form, transcript, photo page and two recommendation letters are required. For some of the awards, financial need is necessary. Some awards have geographic restrictions to regions of the state while others are for a

degree program or a specific college or university. Some scholarships are renewable.
Target applicant(s): High school students.
Amount: Varies.
Number of awards: Varies.
Scholarship may be renewable.
Deadline: February 1.
How to apply: Applications are available through each county cooperative extension office in North Carolina by phone or online.
Exclusive: Visit www.UltimateScholarshipBook.com and enter code NO207620 for updates on this award.

(2077) · North Carolina Community College Grant

North Carolina Division of Vocational Rehabilitation Services
2801 Mail Service Center, Raleigh, NC 27699-2801
Phone: 888-234-6400
Email: jterrell@ncbar.org
http://www.cfnc.org
Purpose: To assist North Carolina community college students.
Eligibility: Applicants must be North Carolina residents, demonstrate financial need and attend a North Carolina community college for at least six credit hours per semester. Selection is based on financial need.
Target applicant(s): College students. Adult students.
Amount: Varies.
Number of awards: Varies.
Deadline: Varies.
How to apply: Application is made by completing the FAFSA.
Exclusive: Visit www.UltimateScholarshipBook.com and enter code NO207720 for updates on this award.

(2078) · North Carolina Education Lottery Scholarship

North Carolina Division of Vocational Rehabilitation Services
2801 Mail Service Center, Raleigh, NC 27699-2801
Phone: 888-234-6400
Email: jterrell@ncbar.org
http://www.cfnc.org
Purpose: To provide financial assistance to North Carolina residents with financial need who are attending North Carolina colleges and universities.
Eligibility: Applicants must be enrolled for at least six credit hours per semester in an undergraduate degree-seeking program at an eligible North Carolina institution and meet satisfactory academic progress requirements. Students who meet the same criteria as the Federal Pell Grant and those with an Estimated Family Contribution of $5,000 or less are eligible for the scholarship.
Target applicant(s): College students. Adult students.
Amount: $100-$3,000.
Deadline: Varies.
How to apply: Qualified students who submit the Free Application for Federal Student Aid (FAFSA) will be considered.
Exclusive: Visit www.UltimateScholarshipBook.com and enter code NO207820 for updates on this award.

(2079) · North Carolina Oratorical Contest

American Legion, Department of North Carolina
4 N. Blount Street, P.O. Box 26657, Raleigh, NC 27611-6657
Phone: 919-832-7506
Email: nclegion@nc.rr.com
http://nclegion.org/
Purpose: To enhance high school students' experience with and understanding of the U.S. Constitution. The contest will help develop students' leadership skills and civic appreciation, as well as the ability to deliver thoughtful, insightful orations regarding U.S. citizenship and its inherent responsibilities.
Eligibility: Applicants must be high school students under the age of 20 who are U.S. citizens or legal residents and residents of the state. Students first give an oration within their state and winners compete at the national level. The oration must be related to the Constitution of the United States focusing on the duties and obligations citizens have to the government. It must be in English and be between eight and ten minutes. There is also an assigned topic which is posted on the website, and it should be between three and five minutes.
Target applicant(s): High school students.
Amount: $1,500-$18,000.
Number of awards: Varies.
Deadline: March 18.
How to apply: Application information is available by contacting the local post by email.
Exclusive: Visit www.UltimateScholarshipBook.com and enter code AM207920 for updates on this award.

(2080) · North Dakota Academic Scholarship

North Dakota Department of Public Instruction
600 E. Boulevard Avenue, Bismarck, ND 58505
Phone: 701-328-2260
Email: cte@nd.gov
https://www.nd.gov/dpi/SchoolStaff/SAO/grantscholar
Purpose: To assist North Dakota high school seniors pursuing post-secondary education at a North Dakota college or university.
Eligibility: Applicants must plan to enroll full-time at an accredited North Dakota postsecondary institution and maintain a minimum 2.75 college GPA. The scholarship may not exceed $6,000 nor extend beyond six years. For additional scholarship criteria, see the information at the website listed below.
Target applicant(s): High school students.
Minimum GPA: 2.75
Amount: Up to $6,000.
Number of awards: Varies.
Scholarship may be renewable.
Deadline: Varies.
How to apply: Application instructions are available from your counselor.
Exclusive: Visit www.UltimateScholarshipBook.com and enter code NO208020 for updates on this award.

(2081) · North Dakota Career and Technical Education Scholarship

North Dakota Department of Public Instruction
600 E. Boulevard Avenue, Bismarck, ND 58505
Phone: 701-328-2260
Email: cte@nd.gov
https://www.nd.gov/dpi/SchoolStaff/SAO/grantscholar
Purpose: To assist North Dakota high school seniors pursuing post-secondary education at a North Dakota college or university.
Eligibility: Applicants must plan to enroll full-time at an accredited North Dakota postsecondary institution and maintain a minimum 2.75 college GPA. The total scholarship value is $6,000 paid by semester or quarter but may not extend beyond six years. For additional scholarship criteria, see the information at the website listed below.
Target applicant(s): High school students.

Minimum GPA: 2.75
Amount: $6,000.
Number of awards: Varies.
Scholarship may be renewable.
Deadline: Varies.
How to apply: Application instructions are available from your counselor.
Exclusive: Visit www.UltimateScholarshipBook.com and enter code NO208120 for updates on this award.

(2082) • North Dakota Scholars Program

North Dakota University System
10th Floor, State Capitol, 600 East Boulevard Avenue, Dept. 215, Bismarck, ND 58505
Phone: 701-328-2960
Email: ndus.office@ndus.nodak.edu
http://www.ndus.edu
Purpose: To assist outstanding North Dakota high school students.
Eligibility: Applicants must be North Dakota high school seniors who have scored in the top 5 percent of all students in North Dakota who have taken the ACT by July 1 in the calendar year preceding college enrollment. They must have plans to attend a North Dakota postsecondary institution. Selection is based on academic merit.
Target applicant(s): High school students.
Amount: Full tuition.
Number of awards: Varies.
Scholarship may be renewable.
Deadline: Varies.
How to apply: Applications are available by written request. An application form and supporting documents are required.
Exclusive: Visit www.UltimateScholarshipBook.com and enter code NO208220 for updates on this award.

(2083) • North Dakota School Counseling Association

North Dakota School Counselor Association
1601 College Drive, Devils Lake, ND 58301
http://www.ndsca.us/awards.html
Purpose: To support North Dakota students pursuing post-secondary education.
Eligibility: Applicants must be graduating seniors from a North Dakota high school. Students must submit an application signed by their school counselor, write an essay and provide a letter of recommendation.
Target applicant(s): High school students.
Amount: $1,000.
Deadline: December 18.
How to apply: Applications are available online.
Exclusive: Visit www.UltimateScholarshipBook.com and enter code NO208320 for updates on this award.

(2084) • North Dakota State Student Incentive Grant

North Dakota University System
10th Floor, State Capitol, 600 East Boulevard Avenue, Dept. 215, Bismarck, ND 58505
Phone: 701-328-2960
Email: ndus.office@ndus.nodak.edu
http://www.ndus.edu
Purpose: To assist North Dakota students who have financial need.
Eligibility: Applicants must be U.S. citizens or permanent residents. They must be North Dakota residents who are high school graduates or GED recipients and enrolled as full-time students in a North Dakota undergraduate program that lasts for at least one academic year. They must be first-time undergraduate students who have no defaulted student loans and who owe no Title IV grant or loan refunds. Selection is based on financial need.
Target applicant(s): High school students. College students. Adult students.
Amount: Varies.
Number of awards: Varies.
Scholarship may be renewable.
Deadline: March 1.
How to apply: Application is made by completing the Free Application for Federal Student Aid (FAFSA).
Exclusive: Visit www.UltimateScholarshipBook.com and enter code NO208420 for updates on this award.

(2085) • North Texas State Fair Association Scholarship

North Texas Fair and Rodeo
2217 N. Carroll Boulevard, Denton, TX 76201
Phone: 940-387-2632
Email: nkimmey@ntfair.com
http://www.ntfair.com/p/get-involved/195
Purpose: To support high school senior students by investing in their future.
Eligibility: Applicants must be a high school senior who has actively participated in school, community, FFA, FHA or 4-H activities. Selection is based on academic success, extracurricular involvement and financial need.
Target applicant(s): High school students.
Amount: $2,000.
Number of awards: Varies.
Deadline: April 1.
How to apply: Applications are available online and should include two letters of recommendation and two photos.
Exclusive: Visit www.UltimateScholarshipBook.com and enter code NO208520 for updates on this award.

(2086) • Northrop Grumman Scholarship

Society of Women Engineers
130 East Randolph Street, Suite 3500, Chicago, IL 60601
Phone: 877-793-4636
Email: scholarships@swe.org
http://societyofwomenengineers.swe.org/scholarships
Purpose: To support high school seniors who reside in a community where Northrop Grumman has a major presence and who intend to pursue a career in engineering, computer science, mathematics or physics.
Eligibility: Scholarships are available for students living in each of Maryland's 23 counties, one scholarship for a student living in the city of Baltimore and two scholarships for applicants living in specific counties/communities from the following states: Alabama, California, Colorado, Florida, Illinois, New York, Ohio, Utah or Virginia. Applicants must have a minimum composite SAT score of 1150 or ACT score of 27 and a minimum GPA of 3.5.
Target applicant(s): College students. Adult students.
Minimum GPA: 3.5
Amount: $5,000.
Number of awards: 5.
Scholarship may be renewable.
Deadline: February 15.

How to apply: Applications are available online.
Exclusive: Visit www.UltimateScholarshipBook.com and enter code SO208620 for updates on this award.

(2087) • Northwest Danish Association Scholarships

Northwest Danish Foundation
Meridian Office Building, 1833 North 105th Street, Suite 101, Seattle, WA 98133-8973
Phone: 206-523-3263
Email: seattle@nwdanish.org
http://www.northwestdanish.org
Purpose: To support students who are residents of Oregon or Washington and studying Danish language, literature, history, arts and crafts or political science.
Eligibility: Applicants must be residents of or enrolled in accredited schools in Oregon or Washington. Applicants must also be NWDA members (or have a family membership if under 18 years of age). Through travel, field of study, study abroad, heritage or life experience, applicants must clearly be able to illustrate their connection to Denmark. The NWDA scholarship must be used in seeking an academic degree, vocational degree, re-training for employment or training for an career in the arts. Those who have participated in NWDA activities or programs will be given preference.
Target applicant(s): High school students. College students. Graduate school students. Adult students.
Amount: Varies.
Number of awards: Varies.
Deadline: May 1.
How to apply: Applications are available online. An application form, essay, two references, official transcript and completed FAFSA form are required.
Exclusive: Visit www.UltimateScholarshipBook.com and enter code NO208720 for updates on this award.

(2088) • NTA Ohio Undergraduate Scholarship

Tourism Cares
275 Turnpike Street, Suite 307, Canton, MA 02021
Phone: 781-821-5990
Email: scholarships@tourismcares.org
http://www.tourismcares.org/academic-scholarships/
Purpose: To aid Ohio residents who are studying hospitality, tourism and travel at the undergraduate level.
Eligibility: Applicants must be permanent residents of Ohio and be enrolled at an accredited two- or four-year postsecondary institution located in Ohio. They must be entering the second year of a two-year program or entering the third or fourth year of a four-year program. By May of the application year, they must have completed 30 or more credits if in a two-year program or 60 or more credits if in a four-year program. They must have a GPA of 3.0 or higher on a four-point scale. Selection is based on the overall strength of the application.
Target applicant(s): College students. Adult students.
Minimum GPA: 3.0
Amount: $2,000.
Number of awards: 1.
Deadline: April 3.
How to apply: Applications are available online. An application form, personal essay, two letters of recommendation, proof of residency, a resume and an official transcript are required.
Exclusive: Visit www.UltimateScholarshipBook.com and enter code TO208820 for updates on this award.

(2089) • NTA Pat and Jim Host Undergraduate or Graduate Scholarship

Tourism Cares
275 Turnpike Street, Suite 307, Canton, MA 02021
Phone: 781-821-5990
Email: scholarships@tourismcares.org
http://www.tourismcares.org/academic-scholarships/
Purpose: To aid Kentucky residents who are studying hospitality, travel and tourism.
Eligibility: Applicants must be permanent residents of Kentucky and be accepted or enrolled full-time at an accredited, four-year postsecondary institution located in the state. They must be entering or returning undergraduate or graduate students who are studying travel, tourism or hospitality and have a GPA of 3.0 or higher on a four-point scale. Selection is based on the overall strength of the application.
Target applicant(s): College students. Graduate school students. Adult students.
Minimum GPA: 3.0
Amount: $2,000.
Number of awards: 1.
Deadline: April 3.
How to apply: Applications are available online. An application form, two letters of recommendation, a personal essay, a resume, proof of residency, proof of enrollment (for entering undergraduates only) and an official transcript are required.
Exclusive: Visit www.UltimateScholarshipBook.com and enter code TO208920 for updates on this award.

(2090) • Nursing Education Scholarship Program

Illinois Department of Public Health
Center for Rural Health, 535 West Jefferson Street, Springfield, IL 62761
Phone: 217-782-1624
http://www.dph.illinois.gov
Purpose: To increase the number of nurses in Illinois.
Eligibility: Applicants must be Illinois residents, having lived in the state for one year prior to applying and be U.S. citizens or permanent residents. Applicants must be accepted to or enrolled in an approved nursing program and demonstrate financial need. Scholarship recipients must agree to work as a nurse in Illinois after graduation.
Target applicant(s): High school students. College students. Graduate school students. Adult students.
Amount: Up to full tuition.
Number of awards: Varies.
Scholarship may be renewable.
Deadline: April 30.
How to apply: Applications are available online.
Exclusive: Visit www.UltimateScholarshipBook.com and enter code IL209020 for updates on this award.

(2091) • Nursing Incentive Scholarship Fund

Kentucky Board of Nursing
312 Whittington Parkway, Suite 300, Louisville, KY 40222
Phone: 800-305-2042
https://kbn.ky.gov/nisf/Pages/default.aspx
Purpose: To support Kentucky students pursuing nursing education.
Eligibility: Applicants must be Kentucky residents accepted to a nursing program who are completing core nursing courses. Students in prelicensure and BSN completion programs must complete a minimum of 15 credit hours and nine credit hours if in a graduate nursing program.

Applicants must maintain a high enough GPA to allow continuation in the program. Recipients must work as a full-time nurse in Kentucky for one year for each academic year funded.
Target applicant(s): College students. Graduate school students. Adult students.
Amount: $3,000.
Number of awards: Varies.
Deadline: June 1.
How to apply: Applications are available online.
Exclusive: Visit www.UltimateScholarshipBook.com and enter code KE209120 for updates on this award.

(2092) • NYWEA Major Environmental Career Scholarship

New York Water Environment Association Inc.
525 Plum Street, Suite 102, Syracuse, NY 13204
Phone: 877-556-9932
Email: theresa@nywea.org
http://www.nywea.org
Purpose: To support New York students who are planning to pursue a bachelor's degree in an environment-related subject.
Eligibility: Applicants must be residents of the state of New York and must be high school seniors who plan to enroll full-time in an environment-related bachelor's degree program no later than the fall following graduation. The programs could include but are not limited to environmental engineering, civil engineering with an environmental minor, chemical engineering with an environmental minor, hydrogeology with an environmental emphasis or biology or microbiology with an environmental emphasis. Selection is based on the overall strength of the application.
Target applicant(s): High school students.
Amount: $10,000.
Number of awards: 1.
Deadline: March 8.
How to apply: Applications are available online. An application form, official transcript, two recommendation letters and two personal essays are required.
Exclusive: Visit www.UltimateScholarshipBook.com and enter code NE209220 for updates on this award.

(2093) • OB/GYN Group Scholarship

Revere Health OB/GYN Group
1886 West 800 North, Pleasant Grove, UT 84062
Email: elizabeth.hiles@reverehealth.com
http://reverehealth.com/
Purpose: To support students attending a college or university in Utah.
Eligibility: Applicants must be U.S. citizens enrolled or planning on enrolling full-time in an accredited college or university. Selection is based on an essay on one of the given prompts found on the website. Students may be pursuing a degree in any field.
Target applicant(s): High school students. College students. Graduate school students. Adult students.
Amount: $1,000.
Number of awards: 1.
Deadline: May 30.
How to apply: Applications are available online. Students must provide proof of enrollment.
Exclusive: Visit www.UltimateScholarshipBook.com and enter code RE209320 for updates on this award.

(2094) • OBTA Dr. Mearl R. Guthrie Scholarship

Ohio Business Teachers Association
c/o Stephen M. Lewis, Sr., OBTA Past President, 7321 Winfield Drive, Lewis Center, OH 43035-8483
Phone: 513-732-5212
Email: webmaster@obta-ohio.org
http://obta-ohio.org/OBTA/awards-and-scholarships/
Purpose: To aid Ohio students who are preparing for careers as business education teachers.
Eligibility: Applicants must be undergraduate juniors, undergraduate seniors or graduate students who are enrolled at an Ohio college or university and have a minimum 3.0 GPA. They must be full-time students who are majoring in business education. They must have plans to pursue careers as business education teachers. Selection is based on the overall strength of the application.
Target applicant(s): College students. Graduate school students. Adult students.
Minimum GPA: 3.0
Amount: Varies.
Number of awards: Varies.
Deadline: July 15.
How to apply: Applications are available online. An application form, transcript, resume, two recommendation letters, an applicant photo and a personal essay are required.
Exclusive: Visit www.UltimateScholarshipBook.com and enter code OH209420 for updates on this award.

(2095) • Ohio Classical Conference Scholarship for Prospective Latin Teachers

Ohio Classical Conference
c/o Kelly Kusch, Covington Latin School, 21 East Eleventh Street, Covington, KY 41011
Phone: 513-227-6847
Email: kelly.kusch@covingtonlatin.org
http://www.ohioclassicalconference.org
Purpose: To aid Ohio students who are planning for careers as Latin teachers.
Eligibility: Applicants must be undergraduate students who are residents of Ohio or who are enrolled at an accredited Ohio postsecondary institution, or can be graduates of Ohio high schools pursuing study at accredited colleges or universities elsewhere in the U.S. They must have sophomore standing or above and be taking courses that provide preparation for a career as a K-12 Latin teacher. Selection is based on the overall strength of the application.
Target applicant(s): College students. Adult students.
Amount: $1,500.
Number of awards: 1.
Deadline: April 1.
How to apply: Applications are available online. An application form, official transcript, two recommendation letters, course schedule and personal statement are required.
Exclusive: Visit www.UltimateScholarshipBook.com and enter code OH209520 for updates on this award.

(2096) • Ohio Newspaper Women's Association (ONWA) Annual Scholarship

Ohio News Media Foundation
1335 Dublin Road, Suite 216-B, Columbus, OH 43215
Phone: 614-486-6677
Email: ariggs@ohionews.org

https://www.ohionews.org/aws/ONA/pt/sp/foundation_scholarships
Purpose: To support male or female junior or senior students pursuing a journalism-related degree at an Ohio college or university.
Eligibility: Applicants must be enrolled in an Ohio college or university as a junior or senior and be majoring in a journalism-related field such as journalism, advertising or marketing. Students must have two professor recommendations and submit three or four newspaper clippings or work samples demonstrating their skills along with answers to questions given on application.
Target applicant(s): College students. Adult students.
Amount: $2,000.
Number of awards: 1.
Deadline: March 31.
How to apply: Applications are available online.
Exclusive: Visit www.UltimateScholarshipBook.com and enter code OH209620 for updates on this award.

(2097) • Ohio Section Scholarships

Institute of Transportation Engineers - Ohio Section
1391 West 5th Avenue, PMB 157, Columbus, OH 43212
Phone: 614-898-7100
Email: gburch@hntb.com
http://ohioite.org/Scholarship
Purpose: To aid students who are enrolled in a degree program that is related to transportation engineering.
Eligibility: Applicants must be full-time students who are attending an ABET-accredited college or university located in the state of Ohio. They must be enrolled in a civil engineering or other transportation-related degree program and have a GPA of 2.5 or higher. Selection is based on academic achievement, stated career goals and extracurricular activities.
Target applicant(s): College students. Graduate school students. Adult students.
Minimum GPA: 2.5
Amount: $1,000.
Number of awards: 1.
Deadline: November 2.
How to apply: Applications are available online. An application form, personal statement, official transcript and one recommendation letter are required.
Exclusive: Visit www.UltimateScholarshipBook.com and enter code IN209720 for updates on this award.

(2098) • Ohio State Association/AOTF Scholarships

American Occupational Therapy Foundation
Attn: Jeanne Cooper, 4720 Montgomery Lane, Suite 202, Bethesda, MD 20814
Phone: 240-292-1034
Email: jcooper@aotf.org
http://www.aotf.org/scholarshipsgrants
Purpose: To aid Ohio occupational therapy students who are members of the American Occupational Therapy Foundation.
Eligibility: Applicants must be Ohio residents who are enrolled in an accredited occupational therapy associate's or first professional degree program at a school located in Ohio. Selection is based on the overall strength of the application.
Target applicant(s): College students. Graduate school students. Adult students.
Amount: Varies.
Number of awards: 3.
Deadline: October 31.
How to apply: Applications are available online. An application form, two personal references and a letter from the student's academic program director are required.
Exclusive: Visit www.UltimateScholarshipBook.com and enter code AM209820 for updates on this award.

(2099) • Ohio Turfgrass Foundation Scholarships

Ohio Turfgrass Foundation
Scholarships Committee, 2710 North Star Road, Columbus, OH 43221
Phone: 614-285-4683
Email: info@ohioturfgrass.org
http://www.ohioturfgrass.org
Purpose: To aid Ohio students who are pursuing higher education in subjects related to the turfgrass industry.
Eligibility: Applicants must be Ohio undergraduate or graduate students who are enrolled in a degree program that is related to turfgrass science. They must have a cumulative GPA of 2.5 or higher and a major GPA of 2.75 or higher. Selection is based on academic merit, professional commitment to the turfgrass industry and financial need.
Target applicant(s): College students. Graduate school students. Adult students.
Minimum GPA: 2.5
Amount: Varies.
Number of awards: Varies.
Deadline: October 1.
How to apply: Applications are available online. An application form, transcript and two recommendation letters are required.
Exclusive: Visit www.UltimateScholarshipBook.com and enter code OH209920 for updates on this award.

(2100) • Oklahoma Foundation for Excellence Academic All-State Scholarships

Oklahoma Foundation for Excellence
101 Park Avenue, Suite 420, Oklahoma City, OK 73102-7201
Phone: 405-236-0006
Email: info@ofe.org
http://www.ofe.org
Purpose: To reward Oklahoma students who have high academic achievement.
Eligibility: Applicants must be high school seniors who are nominated by their school principals or superintendents. They must have an ACT score of 30 or higher or an SAT score of 1340 or higher or be a semi-finalist for a National Merit, National Achievement or National Hispanic Scholarship. An essay is required.
Target applicant(s): High school students.
Amount: $1,000.
Number of awards: 100.
Deadline: Varies.
How to apply: Applications are available from your school.
Exclusive: Visit www.UltimateScholarshipBook.com and enter code OK210020 for updates on this award.

(2101) • Oklahoma Society of Land Surveyors Scholarships

Oklahoma Society of Land Surveyors
13905 Twin Ridge Road, Edmond, OK 73034
Phone: 405-202-5792
Email: osls@osls.org
http://www.osls.org

Purpose: To aid those who are preparing for careers in land surveying.
Eligibility: Applicants must be high school seniors who are planning to study land surveying in college, or they must be working toward licensure under the direct supervision of a professional land surveyor. High school seniors must be Oklahoma residents who have a GPA of 2.5 or higher. Applicants who are already working in the field must be associate members of the Oklahoma Society of Land Surveyors (OSLS) and must be recommended by a registered professional land surveyor. Selection is based on citizenship, leadership and commitment to professional land surveying.
Target applicant(s): High school students. College students. Adult students.
Minimum GPA: 2.5
Amount: Varies.
Number of awards: Varies.
Deadline: May 15.
How to apply: Applications are available online. An application form, official transcript, ACT scores and one recommendation letter are required.
Exclusive: Visit www.UltimateScholarshipBook.com and enter code OK210120 for updates on this award.

(2102) • Oklahoma State Fair Inc. Scholarship Program

Oklahoma State Fair
Email: kkelly@okstatefair.com
http://www.okstatefair.com
Purpose: To encourage Oklahoma students to continue their education.
Eligibility: Applicants must be graduating seniors from an accredited high school or homeschool in Oklahoma. Students must attend a college, university, vocation or technical school in Oklahoma. Applicants must be U.S. citizens and legal residents of Oklahoma.
Target applicant(s): High school students.
Amount: $2,500.
Number of awards: 10.
Deadline: March 31.
How to apply: Applications are available online.
Exclusive: Visit www.UltimateScholarshipBook.com and enter code OK210220 for updates on this award.

(2103) • Oklahoma Tuition Aid Grant Program (OTAG)

Oklahoma State Regents for Higher Education/Oklahoma Tuition Aid Grant Program (OTAG)
655 Research Parkway, Suite 200, Oklahoma City, OK 73104
Phone: 800-858-1840
Email: studentinfo@osrhe.edu
https://secure.okcollegestart.org/Financial_Aid_Planning/Oklahoma_Grants/Oklahoma_Tuition_Aid_Grant.aspx
Purpose: To assist Oklahoma undergraduates who are pursuing higher education in Oklahoma.
Eligibility: Applicants must be Oklahoma residents who are attending eligible undergraduate institutions in Oklahoma. They must be graduates of Oklahoma high schools and must have resided with their parents in Oklahoma while attending high school for at least two years before graduating. They must demonstrate financial need. Qualified undocumented immigrants are eligible for this award. Selection is based on financial need.
Target applicant(s): High school students. College students. Adult students.
Amount: Up to $1,300.
Number of awards: Varies.
Deadline: Varies.
How to apply: Application is made by completing the FAFSA.
Exclusive: Visit www.UltimateScholarshipBook.com and enter code OK210320 for updates on this award.

(2104) • Oklahoma Tuition Equalization Grant Program (OTEG)

Oklahoma State Regents for Higher Education (OTEG)
655 Research Parkway, Suite 200, Oklahoma City, OK 73104
Phone: 800-858-1840
Email: studentinfo@osrhe.edu
https://secure.okcollegestart.org/Financial_Aid_Planning/Oklahoma_Grants/Oklahoma_Tuition_Equalization_Grant.aspx
Purpose: To provide financial assistance for Oklahoma residents who are attending private institutions in the state.
Eligibility: Applicants must be enrolled in an undergraduate program at a private institution of higher learning full-time. They must have a family income of no more than $50,000, make satisfactory academic progress and not have already earned a bachelor's degree.
Target applicant(s): High school students. College students. Adult students.
Amount: $2,000.
Number of awards: Varies.
Deadline: Varies.
How to apply: Eligible students who file a Free Application for Federal Student Aid (FAFSA) will be considered.
Exclusive: Visit www.UltimateScholarshipBook.com and enter code OK210420 for updates on this award.

(2105) • Oklahoma Youth with Promise Scholarship Fund

Oklahoma City Community Foundation
1000 North Broadway, Oklahoma City, OK 73102
Phone: 405-606-2917
Email: scholarships@occf.org
https://occf.org/
Purpose: To provide educational assistance to students who graduated while in foster care.
Eligibility: Applicants must be graduates of Oklahoma high schools who were in the custody of the Oklahoma Department of Human Services at the time of graduation. They must have a minimum GPA of 2.0. Financial need is considered.
Target applicant(s): High school students. College students. Adult students.
Minimum GPA: 2.0
Amount: $2,000.
Number of awards: Varies.
Deadline: May 15.
How to apply: Applications are available online.
Exclusive: Visit www.UltimateScholarshipBook.com and enter code OK210520 for updates on this award.

(2106) • Oklahoma's Promise

Oklahoma State Regents for Higher Education/Oklahoma's Promise
655 Research Parkway, Suite 200, Oklahoma City, OK 73104
Phone: 800-858-1840
Email: studentinfo@osrhe.edu
https://www.okhighered.org/okpromise

Purpose: To assist children of families with income below $50,000 in preparing for and paying for college.
Eligibility: Applicants must be Oklahoma residents who are enrolled in the eighth, ninth or tenth grade at an Oklahoma high school (or are homeschool students between the ages of 13 and 15) and whose parents' income is less than $50,000 per year. They must take certain college preparatory courses in high school, maintain a GPA of 2.5 or higher and "stay out of trouble" such as gangs, drugs or alcohol.
Target applicant(s): Junior high students or younger. High school students.
Minimum GPA: 2.5
Amount: Full tuition.
Number of awards: Varies.
Scholarship may be renewable.
Deadline: July 2.
How to apply: Applications are available online.
Exclusive: Visit www.UltimateScholarshipBook.com and enter code OK210620 for updates on this award.

(2107) • Oliver Joel and Ellen Pell Denny Healthcare Scholarship Fund

Winston-Salem Foundation
751 West Fourth Street, Suite 200, Winston-Salem, NC 27101-2702
Phone: 336-725-2382
Email: StudentAid@wsfoundation.org
http://www.wsfoundation.org
Purpose: To aid North Carolina allied health students.
Eligibility: Applicants must be residents of North Carolina. They must be studying a subject in the field of allied health at an accredited postsecondary institution and have a GPA of 2.5 or higher. They must be seeking a first-time certificate, diploma, associate's degree or bachelor's degree. Master's degree holders are ineligible. Applicants must demonstrate financial need. Preference will be given to residents of Davidson, Davie, Forsyth, Stokes, Surry, Wilkes and Yadkin counties. Selection is based on the overall strength of the application.
Target applicant(s): High school students. College students. Adult students.
Minimum GPA: 2.5
Amount: Up to $3,000.
Number of awards: Varies.
Deadline: August 15.
How to apply: Applications are available online. An application form, official transcript, tax forms and financial aid award letter are required.
Exclusive: Visit www.UltimateScholarshipBook.com and enter code WI210720 for updates on this award.

(2108) • One Family Scholars Program

One Family, Inc.
Watermill Center, 800 South Street, Suite 610, Waltham, MA 02453
Phone: 617-423-0504
Email: scholars@onefamilyinc.org
http://www.onefamilyinc.org
Purpose: To provide financial support, mentoring, leadership development and other resources for Massachusetts low income mothers who are returning to school.
Eligibility: Applicants must be a single parent with a child under the age of 18 and have family earnings which fall 200 percent or more below the poverty level. They should have clear and obtainable career goals as well as the proven desire and ability to complete the chosen academic program. Students must continue to remain residents of the state of Massachusetts throughout the program, and they must remain active in attendance at required meetings, workshops and retreats. Applicants must be referred by two organizations that they are currently involved with or be endorsed by a partnering organization from One Family's network.
Target applicant(s): College students. Adult students.
Amount: Varies.
Number of awards: Varies.
Scholarship may be renewable.
Deadline: June 30.
How to apply: Applications are available by phone.
Exclusive: Visit www.UltimateScholarshipBook.com and enter code ON210820 for updates on this award.

(2109) • Opportunity Award

Louisiana Office of Student Financial Assistance
605 N. Fifth Street, Baton Rouge, LA 70802
Phone: 800-259-5626 x1012
Email: custserv@la.gov
http://www.osfa.la.gov/
Purpose: To aid Louisiana student residents.
Eligibility: Applicants must be Louisiana residents, U.S. citizens, have a minimum 2.5 GPA, have a minimum ACT score of 20 or equivalent SAT score and apply during their senior year in high school. Applicants must use the award at a Louisiana college or university.
Target applicant(s): High school students.
Minimum GPA: 2.5
Amount: Up to full tuition.
Number of awards: Varies.
Scholarship may be renewable.
Deadline: July 1.
How to apply: The application is the Free Application for Federal Student Aid (FAFSA). ACT or SAT scores must also be reported.
Exclusive: Visit www.UltimateScholarshipBook.com and enter code LO210920 for updates on this award.

(2110) • Opportunity Grant

Washington State Board for Community and Technical Colleges
P.O. Box 42495, 1300 Quince Street SE, Olympia, WA 98504-2495
Phone: 360-704-4400
Email: kwheeler@sbctc.edu
http://www.sbctc.edu/
Purpose: To assist Washington adult students.
Eligibility: Applicants must be adult students with financial need who are attending a community or technical college and who have a minimum 2.0 GPA. The grant provides funding for up to 45 credits over a maximum of three years and up to $1,000 for books and supplies per year. In addition, there are support services such as tutoring, career advising, emergency transportation and emergency child care.
Target applicant(s): College students. Adult students.
Minimum GPA: 2.0
Amount: Full tuition.
Number of awards: Varies.
Scholarship may be renewable.
Deadline: Varies.
How to apply: Applicants must complete the Free Application for Federal Student Aid (FAFSA). Contact your college for more information.
Exclusive: Visit www.UltimateScholarshipBook.com and enter code WA211020 for updates on this award.

(2111) • Oratorical Contest Scholarship

American Legion - Nebraska
Department Headquarters, P.O. Box 5205, Lincoln, NE 68505
Phone: (402) 464-6338
http://www.nebraskalegion.net

Purpose: To encourage students to work hard to gain a comprehensive understanding of the Constitution of the United States of America. This contest also seeks to encourage high school students to become leaders, build effective communication skills and learn of and accept any and all responsibilities associated with being an American citizen.

Eligibility: Students, current and under age twenty, must be current attendees or residents of the state where they are to participate in the contest. Students must compete at the local American Legion Post level. The winner will then move on to the district contest, with the winners advancing to the area competition. Four winners will move forward to the state finals each January. Winners will be awarded for each of these competitions, however the national scholarship awards will be awarded to the top three students in the final round of the national contest.

Target applicant(s): Junior high students or younger. High school students.

Amount: $1,500-$18,000.

Number of awards: Varies.

Deadline: Varies.

How to apply: There is no application for this program.

Exclusive: Visit www.UltimateScholarshipBook.com and enter code AM211120 for updates on this award.

(2112) • Oregon Army National Guard

Oregon Army National Guard
Oregon Military Department, 1776 Militia Way SE, Salem, OR 97301
Phone: 800-452-7500
http://www.oregonarmyguard.com

Purpose: To support students from Oregon who are in the National Guard.

Eligibility: Students must serve in the Oregon Army National Guard. The educational program provides tuition and expenses for vocational school, distance learning, alternative credit programs or college. The Student Loan Repayment Program helps students in repaying up to $50,000. Students must take the Armed Services Vocational Aptitude Battery (ASVAB).

Target applicant(s): High school students. College students. Graduate school students. Adult students.

Amount: Varies.

Number of awards: Varies.

Scholarship may be renewable.

Deadline: Varies.

How to apply: Applications are available online.

Exclusive: Visit www.UltimateScholarshipBook.com and enter code OR211220 for updates on this award.

(2113) • Oregon Collectors Association Hasson-Newman Memorial Scholarship Fund

Oregon Collectors Association
Doug Jones, ORCA Scholarship Fund, 1814 NE 123rd Avenue, Vancouver, WA 98684
Phone: 503-201-0858
Email: dcj@pandhbilling.com
https://www.acainternational.org/units/or

Purpose: To provide financial assistance to Oregon students who are attending a college or university in Oregon.

Eligibility: Applicants must be high school seniors in the state of Oregon who are not children or grandchildren of owners or officers of Oregon collection agencies. Students must write an essay on a specific topic, and if selected as finalists must attend the Oregon Collectors Association Spring Convention and read their essays.

Target applicant(s): High school students.

Amount: $4,000-$6,000.

Number of awards: 2.

Deadline: April 1.

How to apply: Students must send an essay via mail or email to apply.

Exclusive: Visit www.UltimateScholarshipBook.com and enter code OR211320 for updates on this award.

(2114) • Oregon Farm Bureau Memorial Scholarships

Oregon Farm Bureau
1320 Capitol Street NE, Suite 200, Salem, OR 97301
Phone: 800-334-6323
Email: andrea@oregonfb.org
http://www.oregonfb.org

Purpose: To aid Oregon high school graduates who are preparing for careers in agriculture or forestry.

Eligibility: Applicants must be Oregon high school or home school graduates with a full year of completed college coursework. Students must be enrolled in a degree program that is related to agriculture or forestry. Selection is based on the overall strength of the application.

Target applicant(s): College students. Adult students.

Amount: Varies.

Number of awards: 10-16.

Deadline: May 15.

How to apply: Applications are available online. An application form, transcript and three letters of recommendation are required.

Exclusive: Visit www.UltimateScholarshipBook.com and enter code OR211420 for updates on this award.

(2115) • Oregon Opportunity Grant

Oregon Office of Student Access and Completion
1500 Valley River Drive, Suite 100, Eugene, OR 97401
Phone: 541-687-7422
Email: cheryl.a.connolly@state.or.us
https://oregonstudentaid.gov/

Purpose: To provide financial assistance to Oregon residents in need.

Eligibility: Applicants must have financial need and be enrolled at least half-time in an undergraduate program at a participating Oregon college or university. They must be Oregon residents and U.S. citizens or eligible noncitizens, and they must be eligible for a Federal Pell Grant.

Target applicant(s): College students. Graduate school students. Adult students.

Amount: $2,250.

Number of awards: Varies.

Deadline: February 1.

How to apply: Qualified students who submit a Free Application for Federal Student Aid (FAFSA) will be considered.

Exclusive: Visit www.UltimateScholarshipBook.com and enter code OR211520 for updates on this award.

(2116) • Oregon Scholarship Fund Community College Student Award

Oregon Office of Student Access and Completion
1500 Valley River Drive, Suite 100, Eugene, OR 97401
Phone: 541-687-7422
Email: cheryl.a.connolly@state.or.us
https://oregonstudentaid.gov/
Purpose: To assist Oregon community college students.
Eligibility: Applicants must be U.S. citizens or legal residents, enrolled at or planning to enroll at a community college in Oregon and enrolled at least part-time. They must owe no educational grant refunds and must have no defaulted student loans. Selection is based on financial need.
Target applicant(s): High school students. College students. Adult students.
Amount: Varies.
Number of awards: Varies.
Scholarship may be renewable.
Deadline: March 1.
How to apply: Applications are available online. An application form and completed FAFSA are required.
Exclusive: Visit www.UltimateScholarshipBook.com and enter code OR211620 for updates on this award.

(2117) • OROS Scholarship

Organization of Rural Oklahoma Schools
P.O. Box 199, Dewar, OK 74431
Phone: 918-694-1572
http://www.orosok.org/vnews/display.v/SEC/Scholarship
Purpose: To support students in rural Oklahoma schools.
Eligibility: Applicants must be graduating high school seniors whose school is a registered member of Organization of Rural Oklahoma Schools. Scholarship will be awarded to one student from each quadrant of the state of Oklahoma.
Target applicant(s): High school students.
Amount: $500-$1,000.
Number of awards: 5.
Deadline: March 1.
How to apply: Applications are available online and must be submitted through the high school.
Exclusive: Visit www.UltimateScholarshipBook.com and enter code OR211720 for updates on this award.

(2118) • Osher Scholarship

Maine Community College System
323 State Street, Augusta, ME 04330-7131
Phone: 207-629-4000
Email: info@mccs.me.edu
http://www.mccs.me.edu
Purpose: To aid liberal arts students at Maine community colleges.
Eligibility: Students must be Maine residents who are not currently enrolled in any college or university program and who have completed no more than 24 college credits. They must also qualify for and be accepted into the associate of arts degree program in liberal/general studies at a Maine community college.
Target applicant(s): High school students. College students. Adult students.
Amount: Varies.
Number of awards: Varies.
Deadline: Varies.
How to apply: Applications are available from community colleges.
Exclusive: Visit www.UltimateScholarshipBook.com and enter code MA211820 for updates on this award.

(2119) • Outrigger Duke Kahanamoku Scholarship

Outrigger Duke Kahanamoku Foundation
Scholarship Committee, PMB 202, 350 Ward Avenue, Suite106, Honolulu, HI 96814
Phone: 808-545-4880
Email: info@dukefoundation.org
https://dukefoundation.org/scholarships-and-grants/
Purpose: To support Hawaii students who are involved in water sports.
Eligibility: Applicants must be Hawaii residents, demonstrate financial need and athletic involvement and have a minimum 3.0 GPA. Preference is given to the water sports.
Target applicant(s): High school students. College students. Adult students.
Minimum GPA: 3.0
Amount: Varies.
Number of awards: Varies.
Deadline: March 1.
How to apply: Applications are available online.
Exclusive: Visit www.UltimateScholarshipBook.com and enter code OU211920 for updates on this award.

(2120) • Page Education Foundation Grants

Page Education Foundation
901 North 3rd Street, Suite 355, Minneapolis, MN 55458
Phone: 612-332-0406
https://www.page-ed.org/scholar-applicants/
Purpose: To support students of color in Minnesota.
Eligibility: Applicants must be students of color who graduated from a Minnesota high school. Students must be enrolling full-time at an accredited Minnesota post-secondary institution and be willing to complete a minimum of 50 hours of volunteer tutoring for children.
Target applicant(s): High school students. College students. Graduate school students. Adult students.
Amount: Up to $2,500.
Number of awards: Varies.
Deadline: May 1.
How to apply: Applications are available online.
Exclusive: Visit www.UltimateScholarshipBook.com and enter code PA212020 for updates on this award.

(2121) • Palmetto Fellows Scholarship Program

South Carolina Commission on Higher Education
1122 Lady Street, Suite 300, Columbia, SC 29201
Phone: 803-737-2262
Email: cbrown@che.sc.gov
http://www.che.sc.gov
Purpose: Monetary assistance is awarded to academically talented South Carolina high school seniors in an effort to encourage them to go to South Carolina colleges.
Eligibility: Applicants must have a minimum SAT score of 1200 or ACT score of 27, have a minimum 3.5 GPA, rank in the top 6 percent of their class, be residents of South Carolina, be enrolled in a public or private high school, be U.S. citizens or permanent residents and plan to attend a college in South Carolina.
Target applicant(s): High school students.
Minimum GPA: 3.5
Amount: Up to $10,000.

Number of awards: Varies.
Scholarship may be renewable.
Deadline: Varies.
How to apply: Applications are available through your high school guidance office.
Exclusive: Visit www.UltimateScholarshipBook.com and enter code SO212120 for updates on this award.

(2122) • Paraprofessional Scholarship

California School Library Association
6444 E. Spring Street #247, Long Beach, CA 90815-1553
Phone: 888-655-8480
Email: info@csla.net
http://www.csla.net
Purpose: To increase the number of trained and qualified library technicians in Southern California.
Eligibility: Applicants must be classified library media workers currently enrolled in a two-year paraprofessional program to become a certified library technician. Students must be Southern California residents planning to work in California as library media technicians after completing the program and be members of the California School Library Association. Three letters of recommendation are required.
Target applicant(s): College students. Graduate school students. Adult students.
Amount: Up to $500.
Number of awards: 1.
Deadline: December 1.
How to apply: Applications are available online.
Exclusive: Visit www.UltimateScholarshipBook.com and enter code CA212220 for updates on this award.

(2123) • Paraprofessional Teacher Preparation Grant

Massachusetts Department of Higher Education
Office of Student Financial Assistance, 454 Broadway, Suite 200, Revere, MA 02151
Phone: 617-727-9420
Email: osfa@osfa.mass.edu
http://www.mass.edu/osfa/students/forstudents.asp
Purpose: To assist Massachusetts public school paraprofessionals who wish to become certified as full-time teachers.
Eligibility: Applicants must be employed for at least two years as a paraprofessional in a Massachusetts public school and enroll in an undergraduate program leading to teacher certification, or be employed as a paraprofessional for less than two years and enroll in an undergraduate course of study leading to teacher certification in a high need discipline. Applicants must not have previously earned a bachelor's degree.
Target applicant(s): High school students. College students. Adult students.
Amount: Up to $7,500.
Number of awards: Varies.
Scholarship may be renewable.
Deadline: June 1.
How to apply: Applications are available online.
Exclusive: Visit www.UltimateScholarshipBook.com and enter code MA212320 for updates on this award.

(2124) • Part-Time Grant

Maryland Higher Education Commission
Office of Student Financial Assistance, 6 North Liberty Street, Baltimore, MD 21201
Phone: 800-974-1024
Email: osfamail@mhec.state.md.us
http://www.maryland.gov
Purpose: To assist part-time, degree-seeking undergraduates.
Eligibility: All applicants and their parents (if applicants are dependents of their parents) must be Maryland residents. Part-time applicants must complete the Free Application for Federal Student Aid (FAFSA) and contact the financial aid office of the college attending and request to be considered for the Part-Time Grant. Selection is based on financial need. Recommended to apply as soon after January 1 as possible.
Target applicant(s): High school students. College students. Adult students.
Amount: $200-$2,000.
Number of awards: Varies.
Scholarship may be renewable.
Deadline: Varies.
How to apply: Applications are available by request from the applicant's financial aid office. An application form and a completed FAFSA are required.
Exclusive: Visit www.UltimateScholarshipBook.com and enter code MA212420 for updates on this award.

(2125) • Part-Time Grants

Vermont Student Assistance Corporation
Scholarships, P.O. Box 2000, Winooski, VT 05404
Phone: 888-253-4819
Email: info@vsac.org
http://www.vsac.org
Purpose: To assist Vermont part-time undergraduate students.
Eligibility: Applicants must be Vermont residents enrolled in or planning to enroll in an undergraduate degree or certificate program part-time (for less than 12 credits per semester). Those who have earned a bachelor's degree previously are ineligible. Selection is based on financial need.
Target applicant(s): High school students. College students. Adult students.
Amount: Varies.
Number of awards: Varies.
Deadline: Varies.
How to apply: Applications are available online. An application form, a completed FAFSA and supporting documents are required.
Exclusive: Visit www.UltimateScholarshipBook.com and enter code VE212520 for updates on this award.

(2126) • Part-Time TAP Program

New York State Higher Education Services Corporation (HESC)
99 Washington Avenue, Albany, NY 12255
Phone: 888-697-4372
Email: scholarships@hesc.ny.gov
http://www.hesc.ny.gov
Purpose: To support undergraduate students in the state of New York.
Eligibility: Applicants may attend the State University of New York, the City University of New York or any other public New York school. Students must be enrolled in 6-12 credits per semester, and they must have at least a 2.0 GPA. Applicants must have earned 12 credits per semester in at least two consecutive prior semesters. Students must demonstrate financial need through the FAFSA.
Target applicant(s): College students. Adult students.
Minimum GPA: 2.0
Amount: Varies.

Number of awards: Varies.
Scholarship may be renewable.
Deadline: Varies.
How to apply: Applications are available online.
Exclusive: Visit www.UltimateScholarshipBook.com and enter code NE212620 for updates on this award.

(2127) • Part-Time Tuition Aid Grant

New Jersey Higher Education Student Assistance Authority
P.O. Box 540, Trenton, NJ 08625
Phone: 800-792-8670
Email: clientservices@hesaa.org
http://www.hesaa.org
Purpose: To support part-time students who are attending county colleges in New Jersey.
Eligibility: Applicants must be residents of New Jersey for at least 12 months prior to college enrollment. They cannot have any previous degrees or defaulted student loans. Students must be enrolled in 6-11 credits per semester at an approved New Jersey county college, and they cannot be majoring in theology or divinity.
Target applicant(s): High school students. College students. Adult students.
Amount: Up to full tuition.
Number of awards: Varies.
Scholarship may be renewable.
Deadline: September 15 (fall and full-year) and February 15 (spring).
How to apply: Applications are available through completion of the FAFSA.
Exclusive: Visit www.UltimateScholarshipBook.com and enter code NE212720 for updates on this award.

(2128) • Past Department Presidents' Junior Scholarship Award

American Legion Auxiliary, Department of California
401 Van Ness Avenue, Suite 319, San Francisco, CA 94102-4570
Phone: 415-861-5092
Email: calegionaux@calegionaux.org
http://calegionaux.org/scholarships.htm
Purpose: To reward American Legion Auxiliary Juniors.
Eligibility: Applicants must be California resident high school students planning to attend a California college or university, be American Legion Auxiliary members with three years as a Junior and be the children, grandchildren or great grandchildren of a veteran.
Target applicant(s): High school students.
Amount: Varies.
Number of awards: 1.
Deadline: Varies.
How to apply: Applications are available online.
Exclusive: Visit www.UltimateScholarshipBook.com and enter code AM212820 for updates on this award.

(2129) • Past Presidents' Parley Nursing Scholarships

American Legion Auxiliary, Department of California
401 Van Ness Avenue, Suite 319, San Francisco, CA 94102-4570
Phone: 415-861-5092
Email: calegionaux@calegionaux.org
http://calegionaux.org/scholarships.htm
Purpose: To provide support to the U.S. Armed Forces members and their spouses and children.
Eligibility: Applicants must be residents of California, enrolled or planning to enroll in a nursing program and be the wife, husband, widow, widower or child of a veteran or be veterans themselves.
Target applicant(s): High school students. College students. Graduate school students. Adult students.
Amount: $2,000.
Number of awards: 1.
Deadline: April - 1st Friday.
How to apply: Applications are available online.
Exclusive: Visit www.UltimateScholarshipBook.com and enter code AM212920 for updates on this award.

(2130) • Patty and Melvin Alperin First Generation Scholarship

Rhode Island Foundation
One Union Station, Providence, RI 02903
Phone: 401-274-4564
Email: rbogert@rifoundation.org
http://www.rifoundation.org
Purpose: To provide opportunities for students whose parents did not graduate from college.
Eligibility: Applicants must be Rhode Island high school seniors and first-generation college students. They must be enrolled in an accredited institution of higher learning that offers either two-year or four-year degrees.
Target applicant(s): High school students.
Amount: $1,000.
Number of awards: Varies.
Scholarship may be renewable.
Deadline: April 28.
How to apply: Applications are available online.
Exclusive: Visit www.UltimateScholarshipBook.com and enter code RH213020 for updates on this award.

(2131) • Paul Flaherty Athletic Scholarship

American Legion, Department of Kansas
1314 SW Topeka Boulevard, Topeka, KS 66612
Phone: 785-232-9315
http://www.ksamlegion.org
Purpose: To support student athletes.
Eligibility: Applicants must be high school seniors or college freshmen or sophomores and have participated in high school athletics. Students must be average or better students and submit three letters of recommendation, one of which must be from a coach, a high school transcript, a 1040 income statement and an essay on the topic, "Why I Want to Go to College."
Target applicant(s): High school students. College students. Adult students.
Amount: $250.
Number of awards: 1.
Deadline: July 15.
How to apply: Applications are available online.
Exclusive: Visit www.UltimateScholarshipBook.com and enter code AM213120 for updates on this award.

(2132) • Paulina L. Sorg Scholarship

Hawaii Community Foundation - Scholarships
827 Fort Street Mall, Honolulu, HI 96813
Phone: 888-731-3863

Email: scholarships@hcf-hawaii.org
https://www.hawaiicommunityfoundation.org
Purpose: To support nursing or physical therapy students in Hawaii.
Eligibility: Applicants must be college juniors, college seniors or graduate students attending full-time in a physical therapy degree program with a minimum 2.7 GPA.
Target applicant(s): College students. Graduate school students. Adult students.
Minimum GPA: 2.7
Amount: Varies.
Number of awards: Varies.
Deadline: January 31.
How to apply: To apply, register online, complete the online application and select the scholarships to which you wish to apply. In addition, mail the supporting materials: printed confirmation page from the online application, personal statement, copy of Student Aid Report (SAR) available at www.fafsa.ed.gov and official transcript.
Exclusive: Visit www.UltimateScholarshipBook.com and enter code HA213220 for updates on this award.

(2133) · Pennsylvania American Legion Essay Contest

American Legion, Department of Pennsylvania
P.O. Box 2324, Harrisburg, PA 17105
Phone: 717-730-9100
Email: hq@pa-legion.com
http://www.pa-legion.com
Purpose: To encourage Pennsylvania high school students to develop research and writing skills.
Eligibility: Applicants must be Pennsylvania students who are in grades 9 through 12. They must submit an essay of 500 to 1,000 words on a topic that is determined by the scholarship committee. Selection is based on essay grammar, spelling, originality and factual accuracy.
Target applicant(s): High school students.
Amount: $2,500-$3,500.
Number of awards: Varies.
Deadline: Varies.
How to apply: Entry instructions are available online. An essay and cover page are required.
Exclusive: Visit www.UltimateScholarshipBook.com and enter code AM213320 for updates on this award.

(2134) · Pennsylvania Business Education Association Scholarship

Pennsylvania Business Education Association
c/o Renee Hughes, PBEA Scholarship Chair, 506 Pine Hill Drive, Pine Grove, PA 17963
Email: rhughes@pgasd.com
http://www.pbea.info
Purpose: To aid Pennsylvania business teacher education students.
Eligibility: Applicants must be enrolled in a business teacher education program at a postsecondary institution located in Pennsylvania. They must be pursuing an undergraduate degree, master's degree or teaching certificate in the subject. They must have a GPA of 3.0 or higher. Selection is based on the overall strength of the application.
Target applicant(s): College students. Graduate school students. Adult students.
Minimum GPA: 3.0
Amount: Up to $1,000.
Number of awards: 1.
Deadline: October 15.
How to apply: Applications are available online. An application form, official transcript, personal statement and three recommendation letters are required.
Exclusive: Visit www.UltimateScholarshipBook.com and enter code PE213420 for updates on this award.

(2135) · Pennsylvania Educational Gratuity Program

Pennsylvania Department of Military and Veterans Affairs
Building P-0-47, Fort Indiantown Gap, Annville, PA 17003-5002
Phone: 717-861-8910
Email: Ra-eg@pa.gov
http://www.dmva.pa.gov
Purpose: To provide financial assistance to children of veterans.
Eligibility: Applicants must be dependents of honorably discharged veterans who served during wartime or armed conflict and have service-connected disabilities or who died in service during war or armed conflict. They must be 16 to 23 years of age and have lived in and attended school in Pennsylvania for five years prior to application, and they must demonstrate financial need.
Target applicant(s): High school students. College students.
Amount: Up to $500.
Number of awards: Varies.
Scholarship may be renewable.
Deadline: Varies.
How to apply: Applications are available from your local Department of Military and Veterans Affairs.
Exclusive: Visit www.UltimateScholarshipBook.com and enter code PE213520 for updates on this award.

(2136) · Pennsylvania Engineering Foundation Grant

Pennsylvania Society of Professional Engineers
908 North Second Street, Harrisburg, PA 17102
Phone: 717-441-6051
Email: jennifer@wannerassoc.com
https://www.pspe.org/
Purpose: To aid Pennsylvania students who are planning to major in engineering.
Eligibility: Applicants must be Pennsylvania residents and must be rising undergraduate freshmen who plan to attend a Pennsylvania college or university that has an ABET-accredited engineering degree program. They must have a GPA of 3.6 or higher, an SAT Verbal score (or ACT equivalent) of 600 or higher and an SAT Math score (or ACT equivalent) of 700 or higher. Selection is based on the overall strength of the application.
Target applicant(s): High school students.
Minimum GPA: 3.6
Amount: $1,000.
Number of awards: 2.
Deadline: April 15.
How to apply: Applications are available online. An application form, official transcript, personal essay and standardized test scores are required.
Exclusive: Visit www.UltimateScholarshipBook.com and enter code PE213620 for updates on this award.

(2137) · Pennsylvania Engineering Foundation Upperclassman Grant/Faber Scholarship

Pennsylvania Society of Professional Engineers
908 North Second Street, Harrisburg, PA 17102

Phone: 717-441-6051
Email: jennifer@wannerassoc.com
https://www.pspe.org/
Purpose: To aid Pennsylvania engineering students.
Eligibility: Applicants must be Pennsylvania residents who are entering their sophomore, junior or senior year enrolled in an ABET-accredited engineering degree program at a college or university located in Pennsylvania. Selection is based on the overall strength of the application.
Target applicant(s): College students. Adult students.
Amount: $2,000.
Number of awards: 1.
Scholarship may be renewable.
Deadline: April 17.
How to apply: Applications are available online. An application form, personal essay and one letter of recommendation are required.
Exclusive: Visit www.UltimateScholarshipBook.com and enter code PE213720 for updates on this award.

(2138) • Pennsylvania Knights Templar Educational Foundation Scholarships

Pennsylvania Masonic Youth Foundation
Masonic Conference Center, Patton Hall, 1244 Bainbridge Road, Elizabethtown, PA 17022-9423
Phone: 800-266-8424
Email: pmyf@pagrandlodge.com
https://pmyf.org/
Purpose: To assist students in pursuing higher education.
Eligibility: Applicants must be working toward a two- or four-year college degree, graduate degree or trade school education. This award is open to students regardless of financial circumstances, Masonic ties, age, race or religion.
Target applicant(s): High school students. College students. Graduate school students. Adult students.
Amount: Varies.
Number of awards: Varies.
Deadline: March 15.
How to apply: Applications are available by mail.
Exclusive: Visit www.UltimateScholarshipBook.com and enter code PE213820 for updates on this award.

(2139) • Pennsylvania Land Surveyors' Foundation Scholarships

Pennsylvania Society of Land Surveyors
801 East Park Drive, Suite 107, Harrisburg, PA 17111
Phone: 717-540-6811
Email: psls@psls.org
http://www.psls.org/scholarship
Purpose: To aid Pennsylvania students who are planning for careers as land surveyors.
Eligibility: Applicants must be U.S. citizens and residents of Pennsylvania. They must be accepted into or enrolled in a two- or four-year degree program in land surveying. Selection is based on academic merit, statement of purpose, extracurricular activities and recommendations.
Target applicant(s): High school students. College students. Adult students.
Amount: Varies.
Number of awards: Varies.
Deadline: Varies.
How to apply: Applications are available online. An application form, transcript, standardized test scores (high school applicants only) and a guidance counselor evaluation form are required.
Exclusive: Visit www.UltimateScholarshipBook.com and enter code PE213920 for updates on this award.

(2140) • Pennsylvania Oratorical Contest

American Legion, Department of Pennsylvania
P.O. Box 2324, Harrisburg, PA 17105
Phone: 717-730-9100
Email: hq@pa-legion.com
http://www.pa-legion.com
Purpose: To enhance high school students' experience with and understanding of the U.S. Constitution. The contest will help develop students' leadership skills and civic appreciation, as well as the ability to deliver thoughtful, insightful orations regarding U.S. citizenship and its inherent responsibilities.
Eligibility: Applicants must be high school students under the age of 20 who are U.S. citizens or legal residents and residents of the state. Students first give an oration within their state and winners compete at the national level. The oration must be related to the Constitution of the United States focusing on the duties and obligations citizens have to the government. It must be in English and be between eight and ten minutes. There is also an assigned topic which is posted on the website, and it should be between three and five minutes.
Target applicant(s): High school students.
Amount: $4,000-$7,500.
Number of awards: 3.
Deadline: December 9.
How to apply: Applications are available from school coordinators and online.
Exclusive: Visit www.UltimateScholarshipBook.com and enter code AM214020 for updates on this award.

(2141) • Pennsylvania Society of Tax and Accounting Professionals Scholarships

Pennsylvania Society of Tax and Accounting Professionals
20 Erford Road, Suite 200A, Lemoyne, PA 17043
Phone: 800-270-3352
Email: info@pstap.org
http://www.pstap.org/
Purpose: To aid Pennsylvania accounting students.
Eligibility: Applicants must be full-time undergraduate students who are enrolled at a college or university located in Pennsylvania. They must be majoring in accounting, must have completed 60 credits or more of their degree program and must have a GPA of 3.0. Selection is based on academic achievement, leadership, extracurricular activities and financial need.
Target applicant(s): College students. Adult students.
Minimum GPA: 3.0
Amount: $1,000-$2,000.
Number of awards: 3.
Deadline: June 1.
How to apply: Applications are available online. An application form and an official transcript are required.
Exclusive: Visit www.UltimateScholarshipBook.com and enter code PE214120 for updates on this award.

(2142) • Pennsylvania Society Scholarship Program with the Maguire Foundation

Pennsylvania Society Scholarship Program with the Maguire Foundation
Scholarship America, One Scholarship Way, Saint Peter, MN 56082
Phone: 800-537-4180
Email: pennsylvaniasociety@scholarshipamerica.org
http://www.scholarsapply.org/pennsylvaniasociety
Purpose: To support Pennsylvania students in their pursuit of post-secondary education.
Eligibility: Applicants must be high school seniors at a Pennsylvania high school with a minimum 3.0 GPA and be planning to enroll full-time at a four-year college or university for the upcoming academic year. Applicants must also plan on taking at least nine credits of government, civics and/or U.S. history by the fall term of their junior year. Students should provide proof of financial need.
Target applicant(s): High school students.
Minimum GPA: 3.0
Amount: Up to $8,000.
Number of awards: Up to 25.
Scholarship may be renewable.
Deadline: November 1.
How to apply: Applications are available online.
Exclusive: Visit www.UltimateScholarshipBook.com and enter code PE214220 for updates on this award.

(2143) • Pennsylvania State Bowling Association Scholarship Program

Pennsylvania State Bowling Association
100 Dutch Hill Road, Bloomsburg, PA 17815
Phone: 570-784-9142
Email: psbasect@ptd.net
http://www.psbabowling.com/
Purpose: To support those students who have participated in the USBC Youth or USBC league in Pennsylvania as they pursue a college education.
Eligibility: Students must be a graduating senior or have recently graduated with the intent to begin collegiate studies. Applicants must have a minimum GPA of 2.0. Selection is based on academic achievements, involvement in bowling and non-bowling activities and financial need.
Target applicant(s): High school students.
Minimum GPA: 2.0
Amount: $1,500.
Number of awards: 4.
Scholarship may be renewable.
Deadline: March 15.
How to apply: Applications are available online. In addition to the form, applicants must submit an official high school transcript and a brief autobiography detailing academic as well as extracurricular achievements.
Exclusive: Visit www.UltimateScholarshipBook.com and enter code PE214320 for updates on this award.

(2144) • Pennsylvania State Grant Program

Pennsylvania Higher Education Assistance Agency (PHEAA)
Pennsylvania State Grant Program, P.O. Box 8157, Harrisburg, PA 17105
Phone: 800-692-7392
http://www.pheaa.org
Purpose: To assist Pennsylvania undergraduates who demonstrate financial need.
Eligibility: Applicants must be current Pennsylvania residents who have lived in the state for at least 12 consecutive months. They must be graduates of an approved high school or GED recipients and be enrolled in or plan to enroll in a two-year or longer degree program at an approved college or university. They must be enrolled for at least six credit hours per academic term and must meet financial need criteria. Applicants who have earned a bachelor's degree previously or who have a defaulted student loan are ineligible. Selection is based on financial need.
Target applicant(s): High school students. College students. Adult students.
Amount: Varies.
Number of awards: Varies.
Deadline: May 1, August 1, August 15.
How to apply: Applications are available online. An application form, a completed FAFSA and supporting documents are required.
Exclusive: Visit www.UltimateScholarshipBook.com and enter code PE214420 for updates on this award.

(2145) • PenSPRA Scholarship

Pennsylvania School Public Relations Association
Shelly Belcher, Communications Coordinator, Peters Township School District, 631 East McMurray Road, McMurray, PA 15317
Phone: 724-941-6251 x7205
Email: belchers@pt-sd.org
http://www.penspra.org/AwardsContests.aspx
Purpose: To support Pennsylvania students pursuing a career in the communications field.
Eligibility: Applicants must be Pennsylvania public high school students with a 3.0 GPA who are pursuing a degree in communications or a related field such as public relations, journalism, English, advertising or graphic arts. Students must have been accepted to or applied to a college, university, technical school or other institution of higher learning. Applicants must live within one of PenSPRA's three regions (Eastern, Central and Western).
Target applicant(s): High school students.
Minimum GPA: 3.0
Amount: $1,000.
Number of awards: 3.
Deadline: March 9.
How to apply: Applications are available online.
Exclusive: Visit www.UltimateScholarshipBook.com and enter code PE214520 for updates on this award.

(2146) • PepsiCo Cesar Chavez Latino Scholarship

Cesar Chavez Foundation
PepsiCo Cesar Chavez Latino Scholarship Fund, Cesar Chavez Foundation, Leasing Office, 1655 E. California Avenue, Bakersfield, CA 93307
Phone: 602-272-0080
https://www.chavezfoundation.org
Purpose: To support Latino students of Arizona and California in pursuing post-secondary education.
Eligibility: Applicants must be of Latino descent accepted for enrollment or enrolled full-time in an undergraduate program in Arizona or California. A minimum GPA of 3.0 is required. Selection is primarily based on demonstration of academic achievement, leadership potential, community service, extracurricular involvement and financial need.
Target applicant(s): High school students. College students. Adult students.

Minimum GPA: 3.0
Amount: $5,000.
Number of awards: 10.
Deadline: May 25.
How to apply: Applications are available online.
Exclusive: Visit www.UltimateScholarshipBook.com and enter code CE214620 for updates on this award.

(2147) • PG&E Better Together STEM Scholarship Program

PG&E Better Together STEM Scholarship Program, Scholarship America
One Scholarship Way, Saint Peter, MN 56082
Phone: 800-537- 4180
Email: pge@scholarshipamerica.org
http://pge.com/educationprograms
Purpose: To encourage students from California to further their studies in STEM-related fields.
Eligibility: Applicants must be PG&E customers who are either high school seniors, current college students, veterans or adults returning to school studying one of the following STEM related careers: Engineering (electrical, mechanical, computer, industrial or environmental), computer science/information systems, cyber security or environmental sciences. Students must intend to be full-time undergraduate students for the entire upcoming school year working toward their first degree at a PG&E Partner School in California.
Target applicant(s): High school students. College students. Adult students.
Amount: Up to $10,000.
Number of awards: 40.
Scholarship may be renewable.
Deadline: February 5.
How to apply: Applications are available online.
Exclusive: Visit www.UltimateScholarshipBook.com and enter code PG214720 for updates on this award.

(2148) • Philip P. Barker Memorial Scholarship

Los Alamos National Laboratory Foundation
1112 Plaza del Norte, Espanola, NM 87532
Phone: 505-753-8890
Email: tony@lanlfoundation.org
http://www.lanlfoundation.org
Purpose: To support undergraduate students from northern New Mexico.
Eligibility: Students must have at least a 3.25 cumulative unweighted GPA, and they must have either an SAT score (combined Math plus Critical Reading only) of at least 930 or an ACT score of at least 19. Applicants must submit an essay and two letters of recommendation.
Target applicant(s): High school students. College students. Adult students.
Minimum GPA: 3.25
Amount: $1,000.
Number of awards: Varies.
Deadline: January 22.
How to apply: Applications are available online.
Exclusive: Visit www.UltimateScholarshipBook.com and enter code LO214820 for updates on this award.

(2149) • Phillips/Laird Scholarship

Minnesota Nurses Association
345 Randolph Avenue, Suite 200, Saint Paul, MN 55102
Phone: 651-414-2800
Email: linda.owens@mnnurses.org
https://mnnurses.org/resources/mnaf/
Purpose: To support Minnesota Nurses Association members who are nursing students.
Eligibility: Applicants must be members of the Minnesota Nurses Association (MNA) who are enrolled in a bachelor's or graduate degree program in nursing with a minimum 3.0 GPA. Preference will be given to applicants who live or work in MNA District 13. Selection is based on academic merit, extracurricular activities, stated career goals and leadership.
Target applicant(s): College students. Graduate school students. Adult students.
Minimum GPA: 3.0
Amount: $3,000.
Number of awards: Varies.
Scholarship may be renewable.
Deadline: June 1.
How to apply: Applications are available by request from the MNA. An application form and supporting materials are required.
Exclusive: Visit www.UltimateScholarshipBook.com and enter code MI214920 for updates on this award.

(2150) • Phyllis V. Roberts Scholarship

General Federation of Women's Clubs of Virginia
P.O. Box 8750, Richmond, VA 23226
Phone: 804-288-3724
Email: scholarships@gfwcvirginia.org
http://www.gfwcvirginia.org/forms.htm
Purpose: To support undergraduate and graduate students in the field of food and nutritional sciences.
Eligibility: Applicants must be Virginia residents and have a minimum 3.0 GPA. Students will need to submit a short essay explaining why they have chosen a degree in food science/nutritional science. Applicants should have a goal of helping to address food insecurity in our communities.
Target applicant(s): College students. Graduate school students. Adult students.
Minimum GPA: 3.0
Amount: $1,000.
Number of awards: 3.
Deadline: March 15.
How to apply: Application is available online and must include three letters of reference, a college verification of GPA, a resume and the short essay.
Exclusive: Visit www.UltimateScholarshipBook.com and enter code GE215020 for updates on this award.

(2151) • Pine Cone Foundation Scholarship

Pine Cone Foundation
5758 Geary Boulevard #164, San Francisco, CA 94121
Email: admin@pineconefoundation.org
http://pineconefoundation.org/apply/
Purpose: To encourage students with learning disabilities to pursue higher education.
Eligibility: Applicants must have a documented learning disability and plan on attending a California community college in pursuit of an

associate, bachelor, technical or vocational degree. Students must be graduating high school seniors and have at least a 2.5 GPA. Applicants must also be U.S. citizens and California residents who can demonstrate financial need. The application includes a 200-word essay on the provided topic.
Target applicant(s): High school students.
Minimum GPA: 2.5
Amount: Up to $5,500.
Number of awards: 5.
Deadline: April 14.
How to apply: Applications are available online and must include: BOGFW approval email, one reference letter, transcript, learning disability documentation, essay and photo.
Exclusive: Visit www.UltimateScholarshipBook.com and enter code PI215120 for updates on this award.

(2152) • Pinnacol Foundation Scholarship Program

Pinnacol Foundation
7501 E. Lowry Boulevard, Denver, CO 80230
Phone: 303-361-4775
Email: pinnacolfoundation@pinnacol.com
https://www.pinnacolfoundation.org/
Purpose: To provide assistance for students whose parent was killed or injured in a work-related accident.
Eligibility: Applicants must be dependents of workers killed or permanently injured in compensable work-related accidents during employment with Colorado-based employers. They must be between the ages of 16 and 25 and have a diploma or GED or be high school seniors in good standing with a minimum GPA of 2.0. Letter of recommendation, essay, transcripts and documentation of the parent's injury or death are required.
Target applicant(s): High school students. College students.
Minimum GPA: 2.0
Amount: Varies.
Number of awards: Varies.
Scholarship may be renewable.
Deadline: Feb 15.
How to apply: Applications are available online.
Exclusive: Visit www.UltimateScholarshipBook.com and enter code PI215220 for updates on this award.

(2153) • Plan NH Scholarship and Fellowship Program

Plan New Hampshire
P.O. Box 1105, Portsmouth, NH 03802
Phone: 603-452-7526
Email: info@plannh.org
http://plannh.org/the-scholarship-program
Purpose: To support students who foster excellence in the planning and design of New Hampshire's development.
Eligibility: Applicants must be residents of New Hampshire and be pursuing a degree in or related to: architecture, landscape architecture, studio art, engineering, interior design, construction-related field or trade, environmental science, land or community planning or historic preservation. Students must be current college undergraduate or graduate level students with a superior grade point average. Applicants must also prove leadership experience, work excellence and dedication to life's work in their field with a focus on the New England area. Note: We do not recommend applying to scholarships that charge application fees. However, some scholarships of this type charge fees and are included for completeness.
Target applicant(s): College students. Graduate school students. Adult students.
Amount: Varies.
Number of awards: Varies.
Deadline: April 12.
How to apply: Applications are available online.
Exclusive: Visit www.UltimateScholarshipBook.com and enter code PL215320 for updates on this award.

(2154) • PRSA-Hawaii/Roy Leffingwell Public Relations Scholarship

Hawaii Community Foundation - Scholarships
827 Fort Street Mall, Honolulu, HI 96813
Phone: 888-731-3863
Email: scholarships@hcf-hawaii.org
https://www.hawaiicommunityfoundation.org
Purpose: To support Hawaii students who are pursuing careers in public relations.
Eligibility: Applicants must be college juniors, college seniors or graduate students. They must be majoring in public relations, journalism or communications. A minimum GPA of 2.7 is required.
Target applicant(s): College students. Graduate school students. Adult students.
Minimum GPA: 2.7
Amount: Varies.
Number of awards: Varies.
Deadline: January 31.
How to apply: To apply, register online, complete the online application and select the scholarships to which you wish to apply. In addition, mail the supporting materials: printed confirmation page from the online application, personal statement, copy of Student Aid Report (SAR) available at www.fafsa.ed.gov and official transcript.
Exclusive: Visit www.UltimateScholarshipBook.com and enter code HA215420 for updates on this award.

(2155) • R. Flake Shaw Scholarship

North Carolina Farm Bureau
Attn: R. Flake Shaw Scholarship, P.O. Box 27766, Raleigh, NC 27611
Phone: 919-782-1705
http://www.ncfb.org
Purpose: To aid North Carolina students who are preparing for careers in agriculture.
Eligibility: Applicants must be North Carolina students who are pursuing an associate's or bachelor's degree in an agriculture-related subject. They must be planning to pursue a career in agriculture and demonstrate leadership ability and financial need. Preference will be given to applicants who are the family members of Farm Bureau members. Selection is based on academic merit, character, stated career goals and financial need.
Target applicant(s): High school students. College students. Adult students.
Amount: $1,000-$4,000.
Number of awards: 8.
Scholarship may be renewable.
Deadline: March 3.
How to apply: Applications are available online. An application form, transcript, personal statement and financial information are required.
Exclusive: Visit www.UltimateScholarshipBook.com and enter code NO215520 for updates on this award.

(2156) • R. Preston Woodruff, Jr. Scholarships

Arkansas Student Loan Authority
3801 Woodland Heights, Suite 200, Little Rock, AR 72212
Phone: 800-443-6030
Email: info@asla.info
https://www.asla.info/scholarships
Purpose: To support students who live in Arkansas or are planning to attend school there.
Eligibility: Students must be a resident of Arkansas and be enrolled or planning to enroll in an undergraduate program at a postsecondary education institution in Arkansas with at least a half-time schedule. Applicants must be a high school senior or current college student.
Target applicant(s): High school students. College students. Adult students.
Amount: $1,000.
Number of awards: Varies.
Scholarship may be renewable.
Deadline: April 1.
How to apply: Applications are available online.
Exclusive: Visit www.UltimateScholarshipBook.com and enter code AR215620 for updates on this award.

(2157) • R.W. Bob Holden Scholarship

Hawaii Hotel Industry Foundation
Attn: Scholarship Committee, 2270 Kalakaua Avenue, Suite 1506, Honolulu, HI 96815
Phone: 808-923-0407
http://www.hawaiilodging.org
Purpose: To reward students enrolled in a college or university majoring in hotel or lodging management program.
Eligibility: Applicants must be Hawaii residents. Students must be enrolled as full-time juniors or seniors attending an accredited university or college in the United States.
Target applicant(s): College students. Adult students.
Minimum GPA: 3.0
Amount: $1,000.
Number of awards: 5.
Deadline: August 31.
How to apply: Applications are available online.
Exclusive: Visit www.UltimateScholarshipBook.com and enter code HA215720 for updates on this award.

(2158) • Rae Lee Siporin Award

Los Alamos National Laboratory Foundation
1112 Plaza del Norte, Espanola, NM 87532
Phone: 505-753-8890
Email: tony@lanlfoundation.org
http://www.lanlfoundation.org
Purpose: To support undergraduate students from northern New Mexico.
Eligibility: Students must have at least a 3.25 GPA, and they must have either an SAT score (combined Math plus Critical Reading only) of at least 930 or an ACT score of at least 19. Applicants must submit an essay and two letters of recommendation.
Target applicant(s): High school students. College students. Adult students.
Minimum GPA: 3.25
Amount: $1,000.
Number of awards: Varies.
Deadline: January 22.
How to apply: Applications are available online.
Exclusive: Visit www.UltimateScholarshipBook.com and enter code LO215820 for updates on this award.

(2159) • Ranelius Scholarship Program

Minnesota Turkey Growers Association
Scholarship Selection Committee, 108 Marty Drive, Buffalo, MN 55313-9338
Phone: 763-682-2171
Email: info@minnesotaturkey.com
http://www.minnesotaturkey.com
Purpose: To aid Minnesota students who are preparing for careers in the poultry industry.
Eligibility: Applicants must be Minnesota residents. They must be enrolled in or planning to enroll in a postsecondary educational program that provides adequate preparation for a career in the turkey or poultry industry. Preference will be given to applicants who have not won the award previously, members of the Minnesota Turkey Growers Association (MTGA), family members of MTGA members and employees of MTGA members. Selection is based on academic merit, extracurricular activities and demonstrated interest in the poultry industry.
Target applicant(s): High school students. College students. Adult students.
Amount: Varies.
Number of awards: Varies.
Scholarship may be renewable.
Deadline: December 15.
How to apply: Applications are available online. An application form, personal essay and one recommendation letter are required.
Exclusive: Visit www.UltimateScholarshipBook.com and enter code MI215920 for updates on this award.

(2160) • Ray Anthony Peacock Scholarship

Ray A. Peacock Foundation
3874 Blodgett Street, Houston, TX 77004
Phone: 281-793-7358
http://www.rapscholarship.com
Purpose: To support graduating seniors of Texas in pursuing post-secondary education.
Eligibility: Applicants must demonstrate excellent writing skills, a history of community or public service and have unmet financial need. A minimum GPA of 3.0 is required. Students must submit an essay about their goals and accomplishments, transcripts and two letters of recommendation.
Target applicant(s): High school students.
Minimum GPA: 3.0
Amount: Varies.
Number of awards: Varies.
Deadline: March 31.
How to apply: Applications are available online.
Exclusive: Visit www.UltimateScholarshipBook.com and enter code RA216020 for updates on this award.

(2161) • Raymond F. Cain Scholarship Fund

Hawaii Community Foundation - Scholarships
827 Fort Street Mall, Honolulu, HI 96813
Phone: 888-731-3863
Email: scholarships@hcf-hawaii.org
https://www.hawaiicommunityfoundation.org

Purpose: To support students in Hawaii who are majoring in fields related to landscape architecture.
Eligibility: Applicants must have at least a 2.7 GPA, and they must have financial need.
Target applicant(s): High school students. College students. Graduate school students. Adult students.
Minimum GPA: 2.7
Amount: Varies.
Number of awards: Varies.
Deadline: January 31.
How to apply: To apply, register online, complete the online application and select the scholarships to which you wish to apply. In addition, mail the supporting materials: printed confirmation page from the online application, personal statement, copy of Student Aid Report (SAR) available at www.fafsa.ed.gov and official transcript.
Exclusive: Visit www.UltimateScholarshipBook.com and enter code HA216120 for updates on this award.

(2162) • Raymond J. Faust Scholarship

American Water Works Association - Michigan Section
Attn.: Faust Scholarship Committee, P.O. Box 150469, Grand Rapids, MI 49515
Phone: 517-292-2912
Email: feedback@mi-water.org
http://www.mi-water.org
Purpose: To aid Michigan Section American Water Works Association members who are preparing for careers in the water utility industry.
Eligibility: Applicants must be members of the Michigan Section of the American Water Works Association (AWWA). They must be current water utility employees, the dependents of current water utility employees or prospective water utility professionals. They must be pursuing or planning to pursue a college degree in a subject that relates to the drinking water field. Selection is based on commitment to the water supply industry.
Target applicant(s): High school students. College students. Adult students.
Amount: Varies.
Number of awards: Varies.
Deadline: July 1.
How to apply: Applications are available online. An application form is required.
Exclusive: Visit www.UltimateScholarshipBook.com and enter code AM216220 for updates on this award.

(2163) • Raymond T. Wellington, Jr. Memorial Scholarship

American Legion Auxiliary, Department of New York
112 State Street, Suite 1310, Albany, NY 12207
Phone: 518-463-1162
Email: nyalaeducation@gmail.com
http://www.deptny.org/?page_id=2128
Purpose: To provide financial assistance to students who are children, grandchildren and great-grandchildren of war veterans.
Eligibility: Applicants must be children, grandchildren or great grandchildren of Armed Forces veterans who served in World War II, the Korean Conflict, the Vietnam War, Grenada/Lebanon, Panama, the Persian Gulf or War on Terrorism. Students must be high school seniors or high school graduates and must be U.S. citizens and New York State residents.
Target applicant(s): High school students.
Amount: $1,000.
Number of awards: 1.
Deadline: March 1.
How to apply: Applications are available online.
Exclusive: Visit www.UltimateScholarshipBook.com and enter code AM216320 for updates on this award.

(2164) • RBC Wealth Management Colorado Scholarship

Denver Foundation
55 Madison, 8th Floor, Denver, CO 80206
Phone: 303-300-1790
Email: information@denverfoundation.org
http://www.denverfoundation.org/grants/page/scholarships
Purpose: To provide assistance to outstanding Colorado high school seniors who plan to pursue degrees in science, engineering or math.
Eligibility: Applicants must be graduating seniors at a Colorado high school who have a 3.75 or higher GPA and have completed college preparatory coursework.
Target applicant(s): High school students.
Minimum GPA: 3.75
Amount: $3,000.
Number of awards: 5.
Deadline: March 17.
How to apply: Applications are available online.
Exclusive: Visit www.UltimateScholarshipBook.com and enter code DE216420 for updates on this award.

(2165) • Reach Higher Montana Scholarships

Reach Higher Montana
40 West 6th Avenue, Helena, MT 59601
Phone: 406-422-1275
http://www.reachhighermontana.org/scholarships/
Purpose: To support students from Montana who are pursuing a higher education.
Eligibility: Applicants must be graduating high school seniors from Montana or residents of Montana who graduated from a Montana high school and are currently attending a college or university in Montana. Students must be attending at least half-time with a 2.5 GPA.
Target applicant(s): High school students. College students. Adult students.
Minimum GPA: 2.5
Amount: $1,000.
Number of awards: Varies.
Deadline: January 15.
How to apply: Applications are available online.
Exclusive: Visit www.UltimateScholarshipBook.com and enter code RE216520 for updates on this award.

(2166) • Real DEAL Scholarship

Bank of North Dakota
P.O. Box 5509, 1200 Memorial Hwy, Bismarck, ND 58506
Email: bnd@nd.gov
https://bnd.nd.gov/scholarship/
Purpose: To support North Dakota students pursuing post-secondary education.
Eligibility: Applicants must be North Dakota high school seniors with a minimum 2.5 GPA. Students must plan on attending an accredited college or university in North Dakota. Applicants must demonstrate involvement in at least three extracurricular activities.

Target applicant(s): High school students.
Minimum GPA: 2.5
Amount: $500.
Number of awards: 48.
Deadline: February 28.
How to apply: Applications are available online.
Exclusive: Visit www.UltimateScholarshipBook.com and enter code BA216620 for updates on this award.

(2167) • Red Boucher Scholarship

Alaska Community Foundation
3201 C Street, Suite 110, Anchorage, AK 99501
Phone: 907-334-6700
https://alaskacf.org/
Purpose: To support graduating seniors and graduates of Alaskan high schools in pursuing a degree in technology education and/or training.
Eligibility: Applicants must be enrolled full-time in a technology related program by the beginning of the semester in which the award is granted. A minimum GPA of 3.0 is required. Preference is given to students with demonstrated financial need.
Target applicant(s): High school students. College students. Adult students.
Minimum GPA: 3.0
Amount: $1,000.
Number of awards: Varies.
Deadline: February 2.
How to apply: Applications are available online.
Exclusive: Visit www.UltimateScholarshipBook.com and enter code AL216720 for updates on this award.

(2168) • Regional University Baccalaureate Scholarship

Oklahoma State Regents for Higher Education/Regional University Baccalaureate Scholarship
655 Research Parkway, Suite 200, Oklahoma City, OK 73104
Phone: 800-858-1840
Email: studentinfo@osrhe.edu
https://secure.okcollegestart.org/Financial_Aid_Planning/Scholarships/Academic_Scholarships/Regional_University_Baccalaureate_Scholarship.aspx
Purpose: To provide financial assistance to students of regional universities.
Eligibility: Applicants must be Oklahoma residents who are enrolled in a bachelor's degree program at one of the following schools: Cameron University, East Central University, Langston University, Northeastern State University, Northwestern Oklahoma State University, Oklahoma Panhandle State University, Rogers State University, Southeastern Oklahoma State University, Southwestern Oklahoma State University, University of Central Oklahoma or the University of Science and Arts of Oklahoma. They must also either have an ACT score of 30 or higher or be a National Merit Semifinalist or Commended Student.
Target applicant(s): High school students.
Amount: $3,000.
Number of awards: Varies.
Scholarship may be renewable.
Deadline: Varies.
How to apply: Applications are available from your university.
Exclusive: Visit www.UltimateScholarshipBook.com and enter code OK216820 for updates on this award.

(2169) • Rehabilitation Assistance for the Blind and Visually Impaired

North Carolina Division of Vocational Rehabilitation Services
2801 Mail Service Center, Raleigh, NC 27699-2801
Phone: 888-234-6400
Email: jterrell@ncbar.org
http://www.cfnc.org
Purpose: To assist North Carolina undergraduate and graduate students who are blind or visually impaired.
Eligibility: Applicants must be North Carolina residents who are enrolled full-time at a North Carolina college or university. They must be legally blind or have a condition that could result in blindness, and they must be in need of vocational rehabilitation services.
Target applicant(s): High school students. College students. Graduate school students. Adult students.
Amount: Up to full tuition.
Number of awards: Varies.
Deadline: Varies.
How to apply: Applications are available from the State Division of Services for the Blind at http://www.dhhs.state.nc.us/dsb/.
Exclusive: Visit www.UltimateScholarshipBook.com and enter code NO216920 for updates on this award.

(2170) • Retail Chapter Awards

Oregon Association of Nurseries
29751 SW Town Center Loop West, Wilsonville, OR 97070
Phone: 503-682-5089
Email: onf@oan.org
http://www.oan.org
Purpose: To aid students who are majoring in ornamental horticulture or a related subject.
Eligibility: Applicants must be majoring in ornamental horticulture or a related subject. Selection is based on the overall strength of the application.
Target applicant(s): College students. Adult students.
Amount: $1,000.
Number of awards: 3.
Deadline: March 1.
How to apply: Applications are available online. An application form, official transcript and three references letters are required.
Exclusive: Visit www.UltimateScholarshipBook.com and enter code OR217020 for updates on this award.

(2171) • Rhode Island Foundation Association of Former Legislators Scholarship

Rhode Island Foundation
One Union Station, Providence, RI 02903
Phone: 401-274-4564
Email: rbogert@rifoundation.org
http://www.rifoundation.org
Purpose: To assist Rhode Island high school seniors with an excellent track record of community service.
Eligibility: Applicants must be Rhode Island high school seniors who have been accepted into college, have demonstrated need and have a substantial amount of community service.
Target applicant(s): High school students.
Amount: $1,500.
Number of awards: Varies.
Deadline: April 28.
How to apply: Applications are available online.

Exclusive: Visit www.UltimateScholarshipBook.com and enter code RH217120 for updates on this award.

(2172) • RI Promise

RI Office of the Postsecondary Commissioner
560 Jefferson Boulevard, Suite 100, Warwick, RI 02886
Phone: 401-736-1100
https://www.riopc.edu
Purpose: To assist outstanding Rhode Island high school students.
Eligibility: Applicants must be graduating Rhode Island high school seniors who plan to attend a postsecondary institution full-time and demonstrate academic achievement and financial need.
Target applicant(s): High school students.
Amount: Varies.
Number of awards: Varies.
Scholarship may be renewable.
Deadline: March 1.
How to apply: Complete the Free Application for Federal Student Aid (FAFSA).
Exclusive: Visit www.UltimateScholarshipBook.com and enter code RI217220 for updates on this award.

(2173) • Richard A. Brown Memorial Scholarship for Students

Texas Computer Education Association
P.O. Box 18507, Austin, TX 78760
Phone: 800-282-8232
Email: tceaoffice@tcea.org
http://www.tcea.org
Purpose: To aid students who are preparing for careers in education.
Eligibility: Applicants must be full-time undergraduates who are attending an accredited college or university and must be preparing for a career in education. They must have completed 24 credits or more of their degree program and must have a GPA of 2.75 or higher on a four-point scale. Selection is based on the overall strength of the application.
Target applicant(s): College students. Adult students.
Minimum GPA: 2.75
Amount: $1,000.
Number of awards: Varies.
Deadline: October 14.
How to apply: Applications are available online. An application form, transcript, three recommendation letters and two personal statements are required.
Exclusive: Visit www.UltimateScholarshipBook.com and enter code TE217320 for updates on this award.

(2174) • Richard B. Combs Hospitality Scholarship Grant

Connecticut Commission on Culture and Tourism
One Constitution Plaza, Second Floor, Hartford, CT 06103
Phone: 860-256-2725
Email: rosemary.bove@ct.gov
http://www.ct.gov/cct/site/default.asp
Purpose: To aid Connecticut hospitality students.
Eligibility: Applicants must be Connecticut residents. They must be a senior at a Connecticut high school (public or private), a high school graduate who has not yet begun a college curriculum or an enrolled undergraduate or graduate student at an accredited university or college. Selection is based on academic merit and proven interest in the hospitality industry.
Target applicant(s): High school students. College students. Graduate school students. Adult students.
Amount: $1,000.
Number of awards: 1.
Deadline: March 30.
How to apply: Applications are available online. An application form and supporting materials are required.
Exclusive: Visit www.UltimateScholarshipBook.com and enter code CO217420 for updates on this award.

(2175) • Richard D. Johnson Memorial Post-Secondary Scholarship

American Legion - Alaska
1550 Charter Circle, Anchorage, AK 99508
Phone: 907-278-8598
http://www.alaskalegion.org
Purpose: To support graduating high school seniors facilitate post-secondary education for personal life preparation.
Eligibility: Applicants must be average students involved in school, church and community activities with strong beliefs in the importance of patriotic organizations such as the American Legion. They must have a GPA between 2.0 and 3.0 with an improving outlook on life. Students must show need and have set goals upon graduating from high school. A minimum 500-word essay is required.
Target applicant(s): High school students. College students. Adult students.
Minimum GPA: 2.0
Amount: $1,000.
Number of awards: 1.
Deadline: March 30.
How to apply: Applications are available online.
Exclusive: Visit www.UltimateScholarshipBook.com and enter code AM217520 for updates on this award.

(2176) • Richard D. Wiegers Scholarship

Illinois Real Estate Educational Foundation
P.O. Box 2607, Springfield, IL 62708
Phone: 866-854-7333
Email: ssundquist@ilreef.org
http://www.ilreef.org
Purpose: To aid Illinois students who are preparing for careers in business, law and finance.
Eligibility: Applicants must be Illinois residents who are attending an Illinois college or university. They must be graduate students who are majoring in business or undergraduate students who are majoring in business, finance or pre-law studies. Selection is based on academic merit, stated career goals, references and financial need.
Target applicant(s): College students. Graduate school students. Adult students.
Amount: Up to $1,000.
Number of awards: Varies.
Deadline: April 1.
How to apply: Applications are available online. An application form, official transcript, two reference letters, a personal statement and course of study outline are required.
Exclusive: Visit www.UltimateScholarshipBook.com and enter code IL217620 for updates on this award.

(2177) • Richard E. Bangert Business Award

Independent Colleges of Washington
600 Stewart Street, Suite 600, Seattle, WA 98101
Phone: 206-623-4494
Email: info@icwashington.org
http://www.icwashington.org/scholarships/

Purpose: To aid business students who are attending one of the Independent Colleges of Washington (ICW) member institutions.
Eligibility: Applicants must be attending an Independent Colleges of Washington (ICW) member institution, namely Whitworth University, St. Martin's University, Gonzaga University, Pacific Lutheran University, Whitman College, University of Puget Sound, Walla Walla University, Heritage University, Seattle University or Seattle Pacific University. They must be rising undergraduate juniors or seniors who are majoring in business or a related subject and must demonstrate financial need. Selection is based on the overall strength of the application.
Target applicant(s): College students. Adult students.
Amount: $1,500.
Number of awards: 2.
Deadline: March 17.
How to apply: Applications are available online. An application form, resume, one recommendation letter, transcript and personal essay are required.
Exclusive: Visit www.UltimateScholarshipBook.com and enter code IN217720 for updates on this award.

(2178) • Richard Goolsby Scholarship Fund

Foundation for the Carolinas
220 North Tryon Street, Charlotte, NC 28202
Phone: 704-973-4500
Email: mmccrorey@fftc.org
http://www.fftc.org

Purpose: To support students who are interested in the plastics industry.
Eligibility: Applicants must be full-time graduate students or rising undergraduate sophomores, juniors or seniors. They must have completed science, business or engineering coursework that is related to plastics and must be interested in the plastics industry. Selection is based on the overall strength of the application.
Target applicant(s): College students. Graduate school students. Adult students.
Amount: Varies.
Number of awards: Varies.
Deadline: April 28.
How to apply: Applications are available online. An application form and supporting materials are required.
Exclusive: Visit www.UltimateScholarshipBook.com and enter code FO217820 for updates on this award.

(2179) • Ritchie M. Gregory Fund

Hawaii Community Foundation - Scholarships
827 Fort Street Mall, Honolulu, HI 96813
Phone: 888-731-3863
Email: scholarships@hcf-hawaii.org
https://www.hawaiicommunityfoundation.org

Purpose: To support students who are majoring in art.
Eligibility: Applicants must be residents of Hawaii, demonstrate financial need and have a minimum 2.7 GPA. Students must also plan to attend an accredited two- or four-year college or university full-time as an undergraduate or graduate student.
Target applicant(s): High school students. College students. Graduate school students. Adult students.
Minimum GPA: 2.7
Amount: Varies.
Number of awards: Varies.
Deadline: January 31.
How to apply: To apply, register online, complete the online application and select the scholarships to which you wish to apply. In addition, mail the supporting materials: printed confirmation page from the online application, personal statement, copy of Student Aid Report (SAR) available at www.fafsa.ed.gov and official transcript.
Exclusive: Visit www.UltimateScholarshipBook.com and enter code HA217920 for updates on this award.

(2180) • Road to Safety Scholarship Contest

Metzger Wickersham Injury Lawyers
Attn: Road to Safety Scholarship Contest, 2321 Paxton Church Road, Harrisburg, PA 17110
Phone: 717-268-4288
Email: road2safety@mwke.com
https://www.mwke.com

Purpose: To encourage students to take a stand against dangerous driving.
Eligibility: Applicants must be graduating, college-bound high school seniors in Pennsylvania. Students must submit a project sending a message about the dangers of drunk driving and/or distracted driving.
Target applicant(s): High school students.
Amount: $500-$1,000.
Number of awards: 3.
Deadline: April 27.
How to apply: Applications are available online.
Exclusive: Visit www.UltimateScholarshipBook.com and enter code ME218020 for updates on this award.

(2181) • Rob Branham Scholarship

Advertising Club of Connecticut
P.O. Box 549, Wallingford, CT 06492
Phone: 860-295-8929
Email: admin@adclubct.org
http://www.adclubct.org

Purpose: To help students planning careers in advertising, marketing and supporting industries.
Eligibility: Applicants must attend or be accepted to an accredited university or technical or trade school. They must major in advertising, marketing, broadcast media or print production. They must be sponsored by a member of the Advertising Club of Connecticut. Selection is based on GPA (20 percent), essay (30 percent), work experience and activities (30 percent) and SAT/ACT scores (20 percent).
Target applicant(s): High school students. College students. Adult students.
Amount: Varies.
Number of awards: Varies.
Deadline: August 1.
How to apply: Applications are available online. An application form, referral letter, two letters of recommendation, essay, transcript and SAT/ACT scores are required.
Exclusive: Visit www.UltimateScholarshipBook.com and enter code AD218120 for updates on this award.

(2182) • Robanna Fund

Hawaii Community Foundation - Scholarships
827 Fort Street Mall, Honolulu, HI 96813
Phone: 888-731-3863
Email: scholarships@hcf-hawaii.org
https://www.hawaiicommunityfoundation.org
Purpose: To support Hawaii students who plan to work in health care.
Eligibility: Applicants must be in an undergraduate health-related program and have a minimum GPA of 2.7. Students must also demonstrate financial need and plan to attend an accredited two- or four-year college full-time.
Target applicant(s): High school students. College students. Graduate school students. Adult students.
Minimum GPA: 2.7
Amount: Varies.
Number of awards: Varies.
Deadline: January 31.
How to apply: To apply, register online, complete the online application and select the scholarships to which you wish to apply. In addition, mail the supporting materials: printed confirmation page from the online application, personal statement, copy of Student Aid Report (SAR) available at www.fafsa.ed.gov and official transcript.
Exclusive: Visit www.UltimateScholarshipBook.com and enter code HA218220 for updates on this award.

(2183) • Robert D. Blue Scholarship

Robert D. Blue Scholarship
Michael L. Fitzgerald, Treasurer of State, State Capitol Building, Des Moines, IA 50319
Phone: 515-281-7003
Email: rdbluescholarship@iowa.gov
http://www.rdblue.org/scholarship/
Purpose: To provide financial assistance to deserving Iowa students.
Eligibility: Applicants must be Iowa residents who plan to attend an Iowa institution of higher learning the following school year. They may be high school seniors or current college students. An essay and two references are required.
Target applicant(s): High school students. College students. Adult students.
Amount: $500-$1,000.
Number of awards: Varies.
Deadline: May 10.
How to apply: Applications are available online.
Exclusive: Visit www.UltimateScholarshipBook.com and enter code RO218320 for updates on this award.

(2184) • Robert R. Robinson Memorial Scholarship

Michigan Townships Association
512 Westshire Drive, Lansing, MI 48917
Phone: 517-321-6467
http://www.michigantownships.org
Purpose: To aid Michigan students who are planning for careers in public administration.
Eligibility: Applicants must be undergraduate juniors, undergraduate seniors or graduate students who are attending a Michigan college or university. They must be majoring in public administration and must have plans to pursue a career in that field. Selection is based on academic merit, extracurricular activities and stated career goals.
Target applicant(s): College students. Graduate school students. Adult students.
Amount: Varies.
Number of awards: Varies.
Deadline: May 31.
How to apply: Applications are available online. An application form, one letter of recommendation, a personal essay and a resolution of support from a Michigan township board are required.
Exclusive: Visit www.UltimateScholarshipBook.com and enter code MI218420 for updates on this award.

(2185) • Roberta B. Willis Scholarship - Need and Merit-Based Award

Connecticut Office of Higher Education
39 Woodland Street, Hartford, CT 06105-2326
Phone: 860-947-1855
Email: sfa@ctohe.org
http://www.ctohe.org
Purpose: To aid Connecticut residents with higher education expenses.
Eligibility: Applicants must be a high school senior or high school graduate with a high school junior year class rank of 20 percent or better. Students must have a minimum SAT score of 1800 or ACT score of 27 and plan to attend a Connecticut public or non-profit private college. Selection is based on financial need and academic merit.
Target applicant(s): High school students.
Amount: $4,650-$5,250.
Number of awards: Varies.
Deadline: February 15.
How to apply: Applications are available through high school guidance offices. An application form and Free Application for Federal Student Aid are required.
Exclusive: Visit www.UltimateScholarshipBook.com and enter code CO218520 for updates on this award.

(2186) • Roberta B. Willis Scholarship - Need-Based Award

Connecticut Office of Higher Education
39 Woodland Street, Hartford, CT 06105-2326
Phone: 860-947-1855
Email: sfa@ctohe.org
http://www.ctohe.org
Purpose: To aid Connecticut residents with higher education expenses.
Eligibility: Applicants must be attending a public or non-profit private Connecticut college or university and be enrolled in full-time study in a two- or four-year program. Students must have a federal Expected Family Contribution within the allowable range. Selection is based on need.
Target applicant(s): College students. Adult students.
Amount: Up to $4,500.
Number of awards: Varies.
Deadline: Varies.
How to apply: A Free Application for Federal Student Aid is required.
Exclusive: Visit www.UltimateScholarshipBook.com and enter code CO218620 for updates on this award.

(2187) • Rockefeller State Wildlife Scholarship

Louisiana Office of Student Financial Assistance
605 N. Fifth Street, Baton Rouge, LA 70802
Phone: 800-259-5626 x1012
Email: custserv@la.gov
http://www.osfa.la.gov/

Purpose: To assist Louisiana students in wildlife, forestry or marine science.
Eligibility: Applicants must be Louisiana residents for at least one year, be enrolled as full-time undergraduate or graduate students in a Louisiana public college or university, earn a degree in wildlife, forestry or marine science and have a minimum 2.5 GPA (3.0 if a graduate level student). Applicants must also submit the Free Application for Federal Student Aid (FAFSA) and be U.S. citizens.
Target applicant(s): College students. Graduate school students. Adult students.
Minimum GPA: 2.5 for undergraduate students, 3.0 for graduate students
Amount: $2,000-$3,000.
Number of awards: Varies.
Scholarship may be renewable.
Deadline: July 1.
How to apply: Applications are available online or by written request.
Exclusive: Visit www.UltimateScholarshipBook.com and enter code LO218720 for updates on this award.

(2188) • Rollie Hopgood Future Teachers Scholarship

AFT Michigan
2661 East Jefferson, Detroit, MI 48207
Phone: 313-393-2200
Email: tftlindamoore@gmail.com
http://aftmichigan.org/
Purpose: To aid students who are affiliated with AFT Michigan and who are planning to become teachers.
Eligibility: Applicants must be planning to become teachers. They must be affiliated with AFT Michigan through a parent or other member. Selection is based on the overall strength of the application.
Target applicant(s): High school students. College students. Adult students.
Amount: $1,000.
Number of awards: Varies.
Deadline: June 5.
How to apply: Applications are available online. An application form and supporting materials are required.
Exclusive: Visit www.UltimateScholarshipBook.com and enter code AF218820 for updates on this award.

(2189) • Rosa L. Parks Scholarships

Rosa L. Parks Scholarship Foundation
160 W. Fort Street, Detroit, MI 48226
Phone: 313-222-2538
Email: info@rosaparksscholarship.org
http://www.rosaparksscholarshipfoundation.org/
Purpose: To provide education funds for students who hold ideals close to those of Rosa Parks.
Eligibility: Applicants must be Michigan high school seniors who will graduate by August of the application year. They must have a GPA of 2.5 or higher and have taken the SAT or ACT. An essay is required.
Target applicant(s): High school students.
Minimum GPA: 2.5
Amount: $2,000.
Number of awards: 40.
Deadline: Varies.
How to apply: Applications are available online.
Exclusive: Visit www.UltimateScholarshipBook.com and enter code RO218920 for updates on this award.

(2190) • Rosedale Post 346 Scholarship

American Legion, Department of Kansas
1314 SW Topeka Boulevard, Topeka, KS 66612
Phone: 785-232-9315
http://www.ksamlegion.org
Purpose: To assist the children of members of the Kansas American Legion or American Legion Auxiliary.
Eligibility: Applicants must be high school seniors or college freshmen or sophomores who are enrolling or enrolled in an approved post-secondary school. They also must be average or better students who are the children of veterans. The children of deceased parents are also eligible if the parent was a paid member at the time of death. Applicants must submit three letters of recommendation with at least one from a teacher, an essay on "Why I Want to Go to College," a 1040 income statement, documentation of parent's veteran status and a certified high school transcript.
Target applicant(s): High school students. College students. Adult students.
Amount: $1,500.
Number of awards: 2.
Deadline: February 15.
How to apply: Applications are available online.
Exclusive: Visit www.UltimateScholarshipBook.com and enter code AM219020 for updates on this award.

(2191) • Rosemary and Nellie Ebrie Foundation

Hawaii Community Foundation
827 Fort Street Mall, Honolulu, HI 96813
Phone: 808-537-6333
Email: scholarships@hcf-hawaii.org
http://www.hawaiicommunityfoundation.org/
Purpose: To assist college and graduate students who have Hawaiian ancestry or were born or have been a long-time residents of the Island.
Eligibility: Applicants must be residents of the Island of Hawaii and be of Hawaiian or part-Hawaiian ancestry. Applicants must also submit a four-sheet application and financial form, personal statement, recommendations and transcript.
Target applicant(s): High school students. College students. Graduate school students. Adult students.
Minimum GPA: 2.7
Amount: Varies.
Number of awards: Varies.
Deadline: January 31.
How to apply: Applications are available by written request.
Exclusive: Visit www.UltimateScholarshipBook.com and enter code HA219120 for updates on this award.

(2192) • Rosewood Family Scholarship Program

Florida Department of Education
Office of Student Financial Assistance, State Scholarship and Grant Programs, 325 West Gaines Street, Suite 1314, Tallahassee, FL 32399-0400
Phone: 888-827-2004
Email: osfa@fldoe.org
http://www.floridastudentfinancialaid.org
Purpose: To help Florida minority students especially direct descendants of Rosewood families.
Eligibility: Applicants must be full-time, undergraduate students who attend state universities, public community colleges or public postsecondary vocational-technical schools. Direct descendants of Rosewood families affected by the incidents of January 1923 receive

preference. The descendants must provide family information on the Florida Financial Aid Application.
Target applicant(s): High school students. College students. Adult students.
Amount: Up to $6,100.
Number of awards: Up to 50.
Scholarship may be renewable.
Deadline: April 1.
How to apply: Applicants must submit the Initial Student Florida Financial Aid Applications online by April 1. Florida residents must submit the Free Application for Federal Student Aid (FAFSA) online by May 15. Non-residents must submit the FAFSA in time to receive the Student Aid Report (SAR) from the processor and send a copy of the SAR to the Office of Student Financial Assistance by May 15.
Exclusive: Visit www.UltimateScholarshipBook.com and enter code FL219220 for updates on this award.

(2193) • Roy W. Likins Scholarship

American Water Works Association - Florida Section
1300 Ninth Street, Suite B-124 , St. Cloud, FL 34769
Phone: 407-957-8448
Email: marjoriecraig@polk-county.net
http://www.fsawwa.org
Purpose: To aid Florida students who are preparing for careers in the drinking water industry.
Eligibility: Applicants must be undergraduate upperclassmen or graduate students who are enrolled at an accredited postsecondary institution located in Florida. They must be majoring in a subject that is related to the drinking water industry and have a GPA of 3.0 or higher on a four-point scale. Previous recipients of this award are ineligible. Selection is based on academic achievement, extracurricular activities, character and stated career goals.
Target applicant(s): College students. Graduate school students. Adult students.
Minimum GPA: 3.0
Amount: $2,500-$25,000.
Number of awards: Varies.
Scholarship may be renewable.
Deadline: May 15.
How to apply: Applications are available online. An application form, personal statement, official transcript and two recommendation letters are required.
Exclusive: Visit www.UltimateScholarshipBook.com and enter code AM219320 for updates on this award.

(2194) • Russ Brannen/KENT FEEDS Memorial Beef Scholarship

Iowa Foundation for Agricultural Advancement
Winner's Circle Scholarships, c/o SGI, 30805 595th Avenue, Cambridge, IA 50046
Phone: 515-291-3941
Email: linda@slweldon.net
http://www.iowastatefair.org/participate/competition/
Purpose: To aid incoming freshmen at Iowa four-year colleges and universities.
Eligibility: Applicants must be incoming freshmen at an Iowa four-year college or university. They must have been actively involved in FFA beef cattle projects. Preference will be given to applicants who have experience in cattle showmanship contest and expositions. Selection is based on livestock project participation, academic merit and leadership.
Target applicant(s): High school students.
Amount: $1,500.
Number of awards: 1.
Deadline: May 1.
How to apply: Applications are available online. An application form, extracurricular activities list and personal essay are required.
Exclusive: Visit www.UltimateScholarshipBook.com and enter code IO219420 for updates on this award.

(2195) • Russ Casey/Maine Restaurant Associates Scholarship

Maine Restaurant Association
Chairman, Scholarship Committee, 45 Melville Street, Suite 2, Augusta, ME 04332
Phone: 207-623-2178
Email: info@mainerestaurant.com
http://www.mainerestaurant.com
Purpose: To aid Maine students who are pursuing higher education in hospitality, restaurant management, culinary arts, hotel management and related subjects.
Eligibility: Applicants must be Maine residents. They must be enrolled in or planning to enroll in a degree program relating to hospitality, restaurant management, hotel management or culinary arts. Preference will be given to students who are attending school in Maine. Selection is based on the overall strength of the application.
Target applicant(s): High school students. College students. Adult students.
Amount: $1,000.
Number of awards: 3.
Scholarship may be renewable.
Deadline: April 28.
How to apply: Applications are available online. An application form, cover letter and one recommendation letter are required.
Exclusive: Visit www.UltimateScholarshipBook.com and enter code MA219520 for updates on this award.

(2196) • Ruth Lutes Bachmann Scholarship

Grand Lodge of Missouri: Ancient, Free and Accepted Masons
6033 Masonic Drive, Suite B , Columbia, MO 65202-6568
Phone: 573-474-8561
Email: grlodge@momason.org
http://momason.org/scholarships/
Purpose: To aid Missouri high school seniors who are planning to become nurses or school teachers.
Eligibility: Applicants must have plans to pursue higher education in nursing or school teaching. Selection is based on academic merit and promise.
Target applicant(s): High school students.
Minimum GPA: 3.0
Amount: $1,000.
Number of awards: 1.
Deadline: March 31.
How to apply: Applications are available online. An application form, personal statement, transcript and standardized test scores are required.
Exclusive: Visit www.UltimateScholarshipBook.com and enter code GR219620 for updates on this award.

(2197) • Sadie Adwon Memorial Scholarship

Oklahoma Association of Broadcasters
6520 N. Western, Suite 104, Oklahoma City, OK 73116

Phone: 405-848-0771
Email: struby@oabok.org
https://oabok.org/careerseducation/scholarships/
Purpose: To support students majoring in broadcasting at Oklahoma colleges and universities.
Eligibility: Applicants must be enrolled in an Oklahoma college or university broadcasting program, be majoring in broadcasting and have an intent to enter the broadcasting career upon graduation. Students must be a junior or senior for the upcoming school year and must maintain a "B" average.
Target applicant(s): College students. Adult students.
Amount: $2,000.
Number of awards: 1.
Deadline: February 9.
How to apply: Applications are available online.
Exclusive: Visit www.UltimateScholarshipBook.com and enter code OK219720 for updates on this award.

(2198) • Safety Essay Contest

American Legion, Department of New Jersey
135 W. Hanover Street, Trenton, NJ 08618
Phone: 609-695-5418
Email: adjudant@njamericanlegion.org
http://www.njamericanlegion.org
Purpose: To reward students for exceptional essays regarding safety.
Eligibility: Applicants must be in the 6th, 7th or 8th grade and enrolled in a New Jersey school.
Target applicant(s): Junior high students or younger.
Amount: Up to $250.
Number of awards: 4.
Deadline: January 21.
How to apply: Application information is available from the local Department.
Exclusive: Visit www.UltimateScholarshipBook.com and enter code AM219820 for updates on this award.

(2199) • Sallie Mae Bank Scholarship (Utah)

Sallie Mae Bank Utah
175 S. West Temple, Suite 600, Salt Lake City, UT 84101
Phone: 801-320-3775
Email: scholarshipssmb@salliemae.com
http://docdro.id/mAanZsT
Purpose: To assist Utah students in nursing, respiratory therapy, engineering or teaching.
Eligibility: Applicants must attend an accredited institution whose main office is located in the following Utah counties: Cache, Davis, Salt Lake, Tooele, Utah or Weber County. Students may also attend an online accredited institution but must physically live in one of the counties. Applicants must be completing a bachelor's degree in nursing associate (RN), nursing, respiratory therapy, teaching or engineering (chemical, civil, computer, electrical, environmental or mechanical) or a transfer program in pre-engineering. Students must be enrolled full-time (12 credits or more per semester during two consecutive semesters beginning in the fall (fall and winter/spring)) OR be enrolled full-time in classes for one semester and practicum for the other semester. A minimum 3.25 GPA is required. All applicants will receive a disposition letter. Those awarded a scholarship will be required to sign an acceptance letter/waiver form.
Target applicant(s): College students. Adult students.
Minimum GPA: 3.25
Amount: $1,000-$5,000.
Number of awards: 35.
Deadline: April 7.
How to apply: Applications are available online and must be submitted by mail by the deadline.
Exclusive: Visit www.UltimateScholarshipBook.com and enter code SA219920 for updates on this award.

(2200) • Schlutz Family Beef Breeding Scholarship

Iowa Foundation for Agricultural Advancement
Winner's Circle Scholarships, c/o SGI, 30805 595th Avenue, Cambridge, IA 50046
Phone: 515-291-3941
Email: linda@slweldon.net
http://www.iowastatefair.org/participate/competition/
Purpose: To aid Iowa entering undergraduate freshmen who have experience in beef projects.
Eligibility: Applicants must be rising undergraduate freshmen at an Iowa postsecondary institution. They must have experience in beef projects and activities. Preference will be given to applicants who demonstrate an interest in continuing an involvement in the beef cattle industry after graduation from college. Selection is based on the overall strength of the application.
Target applicant(s): High school students.
Amount: $1,000.
Number of awards: 1.
Deadline: May 1.
How to apply: Applications are available online. An application form and supporting materials are required.
Exclusive: Visit www.UltimateScholarshipBook.com and enter code IO220020 for updates on this award.

(2201) • Schneider-Emanuel American Legion Scholarship

American Legion, Department of Wisconsin
2930 American Legion Drive, P.O. Box 388, Portage, WI 53901-0388
Phone: 608-745-1090
Email: info@wilegion.org
http://www.wilegion.org
Purpose: To award scholarships to American Legion members and their children or grandchildren and members of the Sons of the American Legion or Auxiliary.
Eligibility: Applicants must have graduated from an accredited Wisconsin high school and plan to earn an undergraduate degree at a U.S. college or university. Applicants must also have participated in one or more American Legion-sponsored activities listed in the eligibility requirements.
Target applicant(s): High school students. College students. Adult students.
Minimum GPA: 3.0
Amount: $1,000.
Number of awards: 3.
Deadline: March 1.
How to apply: Applications are available online.
Exclusive: Visit www.UltimateScholarshipBook.com and enter code AM220120 for updates on this award.

(2202) • Scholar Athlete Program

Davis Law Group
2101 4th Avenue, Suite 630, Seattle, WA 98121

Phone: 206-727-4000
https://www.injurytriallawyer.com/library/davis-law-group-scholar-athlete-program-scholarship.cfm
Purpose: To support Washington student-athletes.
Eligibility: Applicants must be U.S. citizens or permanent residents and high school seniors at a high school in Washington. Students must participate in a school-affiliated sport at their high school and have a minimum GPA of 3.0 and plan on enrolling in a two- or four-year college or university.
Target applicant(s): High school students.
Minimum GPA: 3.0
Amount: $1,100.
Number of awards: 20.
Deadline: May 17.
How to apply: Applications are available online.
Exclusive: Visit www.UltimateScholarshipBook.com and enter code DA220220 for updates on this award.

(2203) · Scholars for Excellence in Child Care

Oklahoma State Regents for Higher Education/Scholars for Excellence in Child Care
655 Research Parkway, Suite 200, Oklahoma City, OK 73104
Phone: 866-343-3881
Email: gmcpherson@osrhe.edu
https://www.okhighered.org/scholars/
Purpose: To aid child care professionals in Oklahoma who wish to pursue credentials in child development and early childhood education.
Eligibility: Applicants must be child care professionals in Oklahoma. They must be pursuing or planning to pursue additional education or credentials in early childhood education or child development. Selection is based on the overall strength of the application.
Target applicant(s): College students. Adult students.
Amount: Varies.
Number of awards: Varies.
Deadline: Varies.
How to apply: Applications are available online. An application form and supporting materials are required.
Exclusive: Visit www.UltimateScholarshipBook.com and enter code OK220320 for updates on this award.

(2204) · Scholarships for Academic Excellence

New York State Higher Education Services Corporation (HESC)
99 Washington Avenue, Albany, NY 12255
Phone: 888-697-4372
Email: scholarships@hesc.ny.gov
http://www.hesc.ny.gov
Purpose: To assist outstanding New York State high school graduates.
Eligibility: Applicants must be New York residents who are high school graduates, enrolled full-time in an eligible undergraduate program in New York State and are U.S. citizens or eligible noncitizens. Selection is based on grades in Regents exams.
Target applicant(s): College students. Adult students.
Amount: $500-$1,500.
Number of awards: 8,000.
Scholarship may be renewable.
Deadline: Varies.
How to apply: Students are nominated by their high schools.
Exclusive: Visit www.UltimateScholarshipBook.com and enter code NE220420 for updates on this award.

(2205) · Scholarships in Mathematics Education

Illinois Council of Teachers of Mathematics
ICTM Scholarship, c/o Sue and Randy Pippen, 24807 Winterberry Lane, Plainfield, IL 60585
Email: scholarships@ictm.org
http://www.ictm.org/
Purpose: To aid Illinois mathematics education students.
Eligibility: Applicants must be enrolled at an accredited Illinois postsecondary institution in an undergraduate mathematics education curriculum that provides preparation for becoming a teacher. They must be rising juniors or seniors who have a GPA of 3.0 or higher on a four-point scale. Applicants must be pursuing a first bachelor's degree. Selection is based on the overall strength of the application.
Target applicant(s): College students. Adult students.
Minimum GPA: 3.0
Amount: $1,500.
Number of awards: 2-5.
Deadline: March 6.
How to apply: Applications are available online. An application form, lesson planning form, personal essay, two recommendation letters and a transcript are required.
Exclusive: Visit www.UltimateScholarshipBook.com and enter code IL220520 for updates on this award.

(2206) · Science or Other Studies Scholarship

Los Alamos National Laboratory Foundation
1112 Plaza del Norte, Espanola, NM 87532
Phone: 505-753-8890
Email: tony@lanlfoundation.org
http://www.lanlfoundation.org
Purpose: To support undergraduate students in northern New Mexico.
Eligibility: Students must have at least a 3.25 GPA, and they must have either an SAT score (combined Math plus Critical Reading only) of at least 930 or an ACT score of at least 19. Applicants must submit an essay and two letters of recommendation.
Target applicant(s): High school students. College students. Adult students.
Minimum GPA: 3.25
Amount: $1,000-$2,500.
Number of awards: 9.
Scholarship may be renewable.
Deadline: January 22.
How to apply: Applications are available online.
Exclusive: Visit www.UltimateScholarshipBook.com and enter code LO220620 for updates on this award.

(2207) · Science-Related Studies

Los Alamos National Laboratory Foundation
1112 Plaza del Norte, Espanola, NM 87532
Phone: 505-753-8890
Email: tony@lanlfoundation.org
http://www.lanlfoundation.org
Purpose: To support students of northern New Mexico pursuing studies in the science field.
Eligibility: Applicants must be permanent residents of northern New Mexico with a minimum GPA of 3.25 and a minimum ACT score of 19 or minimum combined math and critical reading SAT score of 930. Applicants must be enrolled in or currently attending a post-secondary institution of higher learning. Selection is based upon academic success, ability to utilize critical thinking skills and leadership skills.

Those pursuing a degree in a science-related field will be given priority. Financial need is also considered but not a requirement for eligibility.
Target applicant(s): High school students. College students. Adult students.
Minimum GPA: 3.25
Amount: $5,000.
Number of awards: Varies.
Scholarship may be renewable.
Deadline: January 22.
How to apply: Applications are available online. An application form, transcripts, SAT and ACT scores, two letters of recommendation, a 250-word essay and wallet-size photograph are required.
Exclusive: Visit www.UltimateScholarshipBook.com and enter code LO220720 for updates on this award.

(2208) · Senator Patricia K. McGee Nursing Faculty Scholarship

New York State Higher Education Services Corporation (HESC)
99 Washington Avenue, Albany, NY 12255
Phone: 888-697-4372
Email: scholarships@hesc.ny.gov
http://www.hesc.ny.gov
Purpose: To increase the number of nursing educators and clinical faculty members in the State of New York.
Eligibility: Applicants must be U.S. citizens or eligible non-citizens and residents of New York for one year or more. They must be registered nurses who are licensed in New York, and they must be accepted into a graduate nursing program at an approved college or university in New York. Students must also agree to four years of service as nursing faculty in the state.
Target applicant(s): Graduate school students. Adult students.
Amount: Up to $20,000.
Number of awards: Varies.
Scholarship may be renewable.
Deadline: Varies.
How to apply: Applications are available online after June of each year.
Exclusive: Visit www.UltimateScholarshipBook.com and enter code NE220820 for updates on this award.

(2209) · Senatorial Scholarship

Maryland Higher Education Commission
Office of Student Financial Assistance, 6 North Liberty Street, Baltimore, MD 21201
Phone: 800-974-1024
Email: osfamail@mhec.state.md.us
http://www.maryland.gov
Purpose: To assist Maryland undergraduate and graduate students who can demonstrate financial need.
Eligibility: Applicants must be U.S. citizens or eligible noncitizens, legal residents of the state of Maryland and complete the Free Application for Federal Student Aid (FAFSA). Some senators have supplementary forms. Contact your area's senator's office for complete details. All applicants must enroll at a two- or four-year Maryland college or university as degree-seeking undergraduate or graduate student, or attend certain private career schools. Applicants must show financial need. High school applicants must also take the SAT or the ACT.
Target applicant(s): High school students. College students. Graduate school students. Adult students.
Amount: $400-$11,250.
Number of awards: Varies.
Scholarship may be renewable.
Deadline: March 1.
How to apply: Complete and file the Free Application for Federal Student Aid (FAFSA). Contact senator for specific application forms. The Office of Student Financial Assistance (OSFA) can provide a list of all State legislators.
Exclusive: Visit www.UltimateScholarshipBook.com and enter code MA220920 for updates on this award.

(2210) · Service League Nursing Scholarship

Akron General Medical Center
Volunteer Services, 1 Akron General Avenue, Akron, OH 44307
Phone: 330-344-6000
http://www.agmc.org
Purpose: To aid Ohio nursing school students.
Eligibility: Applicants must be enrolled in or accepted into an accredited school of nursing located in Ohio. They must be pursuing a bachelor's degree in nursing and must have a GPA of 3.0 or higher. Selection is based on academic achievement and financial need.
Target applicant(s): High school students. College students. Adult students.
Minimum GPA: 3.0
Amount: Varies.
Number of awards: Varies.
Deadline: March 1.
How to apply: Applications are available online. An application form, personal statement, official transcript, income tax information and three reference letters are required.
Exclusive: Visit www.UltimateScholarshipBook.com and enter code AK221020 for updates on this award.

(2211) · SGT Felix Delgreco Jr. Scholarship

Connecticut National Guard Foundation Inc.
State Armory, 360 Broad Street, Hartford, CT 06105-3795
Phone: 860-241-1550
Email: scholarship.committee@ctngfoundation.org
http://www.ctngfoundation.org/
Purpose: To provide financial assistance to children of Connecticut National Guard members.
Eligibility: Applicants must be sons or daughters of a member of the Connecticut Army National Guard. They must be enrolled in or plan to attend an accredited degree or technical program.
Target applicant(s): High school students. College students. Adult students.
Amount: $4,000.
Number of awards: 2.
Deadline: March 15.
How to apply: Applications are available online.
Exclusive: Visit www.UltimateScholarshipBook.com and enter code CO221120 for updates on this award.

(2212) · Shipley Rose Buckner Memorial Scholarship

Funeral Service Foundation
13625 Bishop's Drive, Brookfield, WI 53005-6607
Phone: 877-402-5900
Email: info@funeralservicefoundation.org
http://www.funeralservicefoundation.org
Purpose: To aid female Tennessee students with tuition costs of mortuary science education programs.
Eligibility: Applicants must be enrolled as a funeral service student full- or part-time in an American Board of Funeral Service Education

accredited program. Selection is based on the overall strength of the application.
Target applicant(s): College students. Graduate school students. Adult students.
Minimum GPA: 2.0
Amount: $5,000.
Number of awards: Varies.
Deadline: March 30.
How to apply: Applications are available online. An application form, essay, academic transcript and video submissions are required.
Exclusive: Visit www.UltimateScholarshipBook.com and enter code FU221220 for updates on this award.

(2213) • Shirley McKown Scholarship Fund

Hawaii Community Foundation - Scholarships
827 Fort Street Mall, Honolulu, HI 96813
Phone: 888-731-3863
Email: scholarships@hcf-hawaii.org
https://www.hawaiicommunityfoundation.org
Purpose: To support Hawaii students who are majoring in journalism, advertising or public relations.
Eligibility: Applicants must be attending a four-year college or university with at least a 3.0 GPA. They must be college juniors, college seniors or graduate students.
Target applicant(s): College students. Graduate school students. Adult students.
Minimum GPA: 3.0
Amount: Varies.
Number of awards: Varies.
Deadline: January 31.
How to apply: To apply, register online, complete the online application and select the scholarships to which you wish to apply. In addition, mail the supporting materials: printed confirmation page from the online application, personal statement, copy of Student Aid Report (SAR) available at www.fafsa.ed.gov and official transcript.
Exclusive: Visit www.UltimateScholarshipBook.com and enter code HA221320 for updates on this award.

(2214) • Shook Construction Harry F. Gaeke Memorial Scholarship

Associated General Contractors of Ohio
1755 Northwest Boulevard , Columbus, OH 43212
Phone: 614-486-6446
Email: parker@agcohio.com
https://agcohio.com/scholarships
Purpose: To aid students preparing for careers in the construction industry.
Eligibility: Applicants must be U.S. citizens either living in or attending school in Ohio, Kentucky or Indiana. They must be in at least the second year of an undergraduate degree program that is related to construction and have a GPA of 2.5 or higher. Selection is based on the overall strength of the application.
Target applicant(s): College students. Adult students.
Minimum GPA: 2.5
Amount: $1,000.
Number of awards: 1.
Deadline: February 3.
How to apply: Applications are available online. An application form, transcript and personal essay are required.
Exclusive: Visit www.UltimateScholarshipBook.com and enter code AS221420 for updates on this award.

(2215) • Shuichi, Katsu and Itsuyo Suga Scholarship

Hawaii Community Foundation - Scholarships
827 Fort Street Mall, Honolulu, HI 96813
Phone: 888-731-3863
Email: scholarships@hcf-hawaii.org
https://www.hawaiicommunityfoundation.org
Purpose: To support Hawaii students who are majoring in math, physics or science and technology.
Eligibility: Applicants must have at least a 3.0 GPA.
Target applicant(s): High school students. College students. Graduate school students. Adult students.
Minimum GPA: 3.0
Amount: Varies.
Number of awards: Varies.
Deadline: January 31.
How to apply: To apply, register online, complete the online application and select the scholarships to which you wish to apply. In addition, mail the supporting materials: printed confirmation page from the online application, personal statement, copy of Student Aid Report (SAR) available at www.fafsa.ed.gov and official transcript.
Exclusive: Visit www.UltimateScholarshipBook.com and enter code HA221520 for updates on this award.

(2216) • Sioux Falls Area Retired Teachers Scholarship

Sioux Falls Area Community Foundation
The Depot at Cherapa Place, 200 N. Cherapa Place, Sioux Falls, SD 57103-2205
Phone: 605-336-7055
Email: pgale@sfacf.org
http://www.sfacf.org/scholarships/
Purpose: To aid South Dakota students who are majoring in education.
Eligibility: Applicants must be rising undergraduate juniors or seniors who are majoring in education at an accredited South Dakota college or university. They must have a GPA of 2.5 or better, demonstrate financial need, participate in extracurricular activities and display a commitment to the teaching profession. Selection is based on the overall strength of the application.
Target applicant(s): College students. Adult students.
Minimum GPA: 2.5
Amount: $1,500.
Number of awards: 1.
Deadline: March 15.
How to apply: Applications are available from the applicant's financial aid office or guidance counselor. An application form and supporting materials are required.
Exclusive: Visit www.UltimateScholarshipBook.com and enter code SI221620 for updates on this award.

(2217) • Sister Helen Marie Pellicer Scholarship

Florida Academy of Nutrition and Dietetics Foundation
Scholarship Chair, P.O. Box 12608, Tallahassee, FL 32317-2608
Phone: 850-386-8850
Email: cstapell@eatrightflorida.org
http://www.eatrightflorida.org
Purpose: To aid Florida dietetics students.
Eligibility: Applicants must be U.S. citizens or permanent residents, Florida residents and undergraduate upperclassmen who are majoring in

dietetics. They must have a GPA of 2.5 or higher on a four-point scale. Selection is based on the overall strength of the application.
Target applicant(s): College students. Adult students.
Minimum GPA: 2.5
Amount: $1,000.
Number of awards: 1.
Deadline: November 2.
How to apply: Applications are available online. An application form, official transcript and two recommendation letters are required.
Exclusive: Visit www.UltimateScholarshipBook.com and enter code FL221720 for updates on this award.

(2218) • Sister Mary Petronia Van Straten and Ethel A. Neijahr Scholarships

Wisconsin Mathematics Council Inc.
W175 N11117 Stonewood Drive, Suite 204, Germantown, WI 53022
Phone: 262-437-0174
Email: wismath@teamwi.com
http://www.wismath.org
Purpose: To aid Wisconsin teacher education students.
Eligibility: Applicants must be Wisconsin legal residents, be enrolled in a teacher education program and have completed or be in the process of completing a course in mathematics teaching methods. They must have a GPA of 3.0 or higher. Selection is based on the overall strength of the application.
Target applicant(s): College students. Adult students.
Minimum GPA: 3.0
Amount: $2,000.
Number of awards: 2.
Deadline: March 1.
How to apply: Applications are available online. An application form, official transcript, two letters of recommendation, a plan of study and a personal essay are required.
Exclusive: Visit www.UltimateScholarshipBook.com and enter code WI221820 for updates on this award.

(2219) • Six Meter Club of Chicago Scholarship

American Radio Relay League Foundation
225 Main Street, Newington, CT 06111-1494
Phone: 860-594-0348
Email: foundation@arrl.org
http://www.arrl.org/scholarship-program
Purpose: To support Illinois residents who are involved in amateur radio.
Eligibility: Applicants must have an active amateur radio license in any class. Students must be enrolled in an Illinois university or technical school for undergraduate study. A minimum GPA of 2.5 is preferred.
Target applicant(s): High school students. College students. Adult students.
Minimum GPA: 2.5
Amount: $500.
Number of awards: 1.
Deadline: January 31.
How to apply: Applications are available online.
Exclusive: Visit www.UltimateScholarshipBook.com and enter code AM221920 for updates on this award.

(2220) • Smart Choices Scholarship Program

Washington Interscholastic Activities Association (WIAA)
435 Main Avenue South, Renton, WA 98057
Phone: 425-687-8585
Email: smartchoices@wiaa.com
http://www.wiaa.com/
Purpose: To support graduating seniors who have proven excellence in activities, academics, leadership and community service.
Eligibility: Applicants must be high school seniors, have a minimum GPA of 3.2 and participate in a WIAA high school sport or activity during the current school year. Applicants must also be dairy consumers. Selection will be based on academic achievement, leadership and community service.
Target applicant(s): High school students.
Minimum GPA: 3.2
Amount: $1,000-$5,000.
Number of awards: 10.
Deadline: April 1.
How to apply: Applications are available online.
Exclusive: Visit www.UltimateScholarshipBook.com and enter code WA222020 for updates on this award.

(2221) • Smith Scholarship Program

Smith Scholarship Foundation
400 Caldwell Trace, Birmingham, AL 35242
Phone: 205-202-4076
Email: appsupport@smithscholarships.com
http://www.smithscholarships.com
Purpose: To provide assistance for students who face financial, physical or emotional challenges and who have participated in volunteer work or assisted their families.
Eligibility: Applicants must be seniors at an Alabama high school and plan to attend an Alabama four-year college the following fall. Students must also write two essays about their future plans and their community service or family assistance endeavors and provide three letters of recommendation. A minimum C+ GPA is required.
Target applicant(s): High school students.
Minimum GPA: 2.33
Amount: Varies.
Number of awards: Varies.
Deadline: December 1.
How to apply: Applications are available online or by mail.
Exclusive: Visit www.UltimateScholarshipBook.com and enter code SM222120 for updates on this award.

(2222) • Society of American Military Engineers, Albuquerque Post Scholarship

New Mexico Engineering Foundation
P.O. Box 3828, Albuquerque, NM 87190-3828
Email: scholarship@nmef.net
http://www.nmef.net
Purpose: To support New Mexico students who plan to pursue college degrees in science, engineering or mathematics.
Eligibility: Applicants must be high school seniors and residents of New Mexico. They must plan to enroll in a math, science or engineering undergraduate degree program. Selection is based on academic achievement, leadership experiences at school, involvement in the community and financial need.
Target applicant(s): High school students.
Amount: $2,000.

Number of awards: 2.
Deadline: January 31.
How to apply: Applications are available online. An application form, a transcript and one letter of recommendation are required.
Exclusive: Visit www.UltimateScholarshipBook.com and enter code NE222220 for updates on this award.

(2223) • Sons of Italy Grand Lodge of California College Scholarship

Order Sons of Italy in America, Grand Lodge of California
Attention: Scholarship Commission, 5051 Mission Street, San Francisco, CA 94112-3473
Phone: 415-586-1316
http://www.osiaca.org/
Purpose: To support students of Italian ancestry graduating from public or private high schools in California, Nevada and Klamath Falls, Oregon.
Eligibility: Applicants must be of at least partial Italian ancestry and be enrolled at a college or trade school for the upcoming fall semester. Selection is based upon academic performance, leadership activities, financial need, essay detailing Italian ancestry, a personal statement and letters of recommendation.
Target applicant(s): High school students.
Amount: $500-$5,000.
Number of awards: Varies.
Deadline: March 1.
How to apply: Applications are available online. An application, personal statement, SAT/PSAT/ACT scores, GPA, record of activities, transcript and two letters of recommendation are required.
Exclusive: Visit www.UltimateScholarshipBook.com and enter code OR222320 for updates on this award.

(2224) • Sons of Italy Grand Lodge of California Italian Language Study Grant

Order Sons of Italy in America, Grand Lodge of California
Attention: Scholarship Commission, 5051 Mission Street, San Francisco, CA 94112-3473
Phone: 415-586-1316
http://www.osiaca.org/
Purpose: To support students of Italian ancestry graduating from public or private high schools in California, Nevada and Klamath Falls, Oregon with a 30-day summer study abroad program in Italy.
Eligibility: Applicants must be of at least partial Italian ancestry and be enrolled at a college or trade school for the upcoming fall semester. Applicants must also have finished a foreign language course in high school. Selection is based upon academic performance, leadership activities, financial need, essay detailing Italian ancestry, a personal statement and letters of recommendation.
Target applicant(s): High school students.
Amount: Varies.
Number of awards: Varies.
Deadline: March 1.
How to apply: Applications are available online. An application, personal statement, SAT/PSAT/ACT scores, GPA, record of activities, transcript and two letters of recommendation are required.
Exclusive: Visit www.UltimateScholarshipBook.com and enter code OR222420 for updates on this award.

(2225) • South Carolina Farm Bureau Foundation Scholarships

South Carolina Farm Bureau Foundation
P.O. Box 754, Columbia, SC 29202-0754
Email: sanderson@scfb.org
http://www.scfb.org
Purpose: To aid agriculture students from South Carolina Farm Bureau member families.
Eligibility: Applicants must be from a South Carolina Farm Bureau member family. They must be rising undergraduate sophomores, juniors or seniors. They must be majoring in agriculture or a related subject. Selection is based on commitment to the field of agriculture, character and demonstrated leadership ability.
Target applicant(s): College students. Adult students.
Amount: $1,000.
Number of awards: 6.
Deadline: April 30.
How to apply: Applications are available by request from the South Carolina Farm Bureau. An application form and supporting materials are required.
Exclusive: Visit www.UltimateScholarshipBook.com and enter code SO222520 for updates on this award.

(2226) • South Carolina Hope Scholarship

South Carolina Commission on Higher Education
1122 Lady Street, Suite 300, Columbia, SC 29201
Phone: 803-737-2262
Email: cbrown@che.sc.gov
http://www.che.sc.gov
Purpose: Monetary assistance is provided to those freshmen who do not qualify for LIFE or Palmetto Fellows Scholarships.
Eligibility: Applicants must attend an eligible South Carolina public or private college full-time, be South Carolina residents and have a minimum 3.0 GPA. The award is only applicable to the first year of college.
Target applicant(s): High school students.
Minimum GPA: 3.0
Amount: Up to $2,800.
Number of awards: Varies.
Deadline: Varies.
How to apply: Your college will determine your eligibility based on your high school transcript. There is no application form.
Exclusive: Visit www.UltimateScholarshipBook.com and enter code SO222620 for updates on this award.

(2227) • South Carolina Nurses Foundation Nurses Care Scholarship

South Carolina Nurses Foundation Inc.
Chairperson, SCNF Awards Committee, 1821 Gadsden Street, Columbia, SC 29201
http://www.scnursesfoundation.org
Purpose: To aid South Carolina nursing students.
Eligibility: Applicants must be South Carolina residents and be enrolled in an undergraduate registered nurse (RN) degree program or a graduate degree program in nursing. They must be in good academic standing, have plans to practice nursing in South Carolina after graduation and must demonstrate financial need. Selection is based on the overall strength of the application.
Target applicant(s): College students. Graduate school students. Adult students.

Amount: Varies.
Number of awards: Varies.
Deadline: June 15.
How to apply: Applications are available online. An application form, personal statement, transcript and two recommendation letters are required.
Exclusive: Visit www.UltimateScholarshipBook.com and enter code SO222720 for updates on this award.

(2228) • South Carolina Tuition Grants Program

South Carolina Tuition Grants Commission
115 Atrium Way, Suite 102, Columbia, SC 29223
Phone: 803-896-1120
Email: info@sctuitiongrants.org
https://sctuitiongrants.org/
Purpose: To assist students who wish to attend independent South Carolina colleges.
Eligibility: Students must be legal residents of South Carolina with financial need. High school seniors must graduate in the top 75 percent of their class or score a minimum of 900 on the SAT or 19 on the ACT. College applicants must complete and pass a minimum of 24 semester hours each year.
Target applicant(s): High school students. College students. Adult students.
Amount: Up to $3,200.
Number of awards: Varies.
Scholarship may be renewable.
Deadline: June 30.
How to apply: Fill out the FAFSA, which is available online.
Exclusive: Visit www.UltimateScholarshipBook.com and enter code SO222820 for updates on this award.

(2229) • South Dakota Free Tuition for Veterans and Others Who Performed War Service

South Dakota Board of Regents
306 East Capitol Ave, Suite 200, Pierre, SD 57501-2545
Phone: 605-773-3455
Email: info@sdbor.edu
http://www.sdbor.edu
Purpose: To allow veterans and others who served in war the opportunity to receive higher education.
Eligibility: Applicants must be veterans or others who performed active war service. They must South Dakota residents who qualify for resident tuition and not be entitled to have their tuition or expenses paid by the United States.
Target applicant(s): College students. Adult students.
Amount: Full tuition.
Number of awards: Varies.
Scholarship may be renewable.
Deadline: Varies.
How to apply: Applications are available from your financial aid office.
Exclusive: Visit www.UltimateScholarshipBook.com and enter code SO222920 for updates on this award.

(2230) • Southern Scholarship Foundation Scholarship

Southern Scholarship Foundation
322 Stadium Drive, Tallahassee, FL 32304
Phone: 850-222-3833
Email: elee@southernscholarship.org
http://www.southernscholarship.org
Purpose: To provide rent-free housing scholarships to students attending specific Florida institutions.
Eligibility: Applicants must have financial need, have a minimum 3.0 GPA, demonstrate high character and attend or plan to attend Florida A&M University, Florida Gulf Coast University, Florida State University, the University of Florida, Tallahassee Community College or Santa Fe Community College.
Target applicant(s): High school students. College students. Adult students.
Minimum GPA: 3.0
Amount: Room and board.
Number of awards: Varies.
Scholarship may be renewable.
Deadline: March 1 priority deadline.
How to apply: Applications are available online.
Exclusive: Visit www.UltimateScholarshipBook.com and enter code SO223020 for updates on this award.

(2231) • Southwest Iowa Educational Foundation Scholarships

Southwest Iowa Educational Foundation
Toni Christie, Iowa Western Community College, 2700 College Road, Council Bluffs, IA 51503
https://sites.google.com/site/swiowaef/application
Purpose: To support southwest Iowa students pursuing post-secondary education.
Eligibility: Applicants must be graduating high school seniors from the southwest area of Iowa in one of the following counties: Cass, Fremont, Harrison, Mills, Montgomery, Page, Pottawattamie and Shelby.
Target applicant(s): High school students.
Amount: Varies.
Number of awards: 80.
Deadline: March 15.
How to apply: Applications are available online.
Exclusive: Visit www.UltimateScholarshipBook.com and enter code SO223120 for updates on this award.

(2232) • Stan Forrer Scholarship

Oklahoma Association of Broadcasters
6520 N. Western, Suite 104, Oklahoma City, OK 73116
Phone: 405-848-0771
Email: struby@oabok.org
https://oabok.org/careerseducation/scholarships/
Purpose: To support students majoring in broadcasting at Oklahoma colleges and universities.
Eligibility: Applicants must be enrolled in an Oklahoma college or university broadcasting program, be majoring in broadcasting and have an intent to enter the broadcasting career upon graduation. Students must be a junior or senior for the upcoming school year and must maintain a "B" average.
Target applicant(s): College students. Adult students.
Minimum GPA: 3.0
Amount: $2,000.
Number of awards: 1.
Deadline: February 9.
How to apply: Applications are available online.
Exclusive: Visit www.UltimateScholarshipBook.com and enter code OK223220 for updates on this award.

(2233) • Stanley O. McNaughton Community Service Award

Independent Colleges of Washington
600 Stewart Street, Suite 600, Seattle, WA 98101
Phone: 206-623-4494
Email: info@icwashington.org
http://www.icwashington.org/scholarships/

Purpose: To reward students who are committed to community service and who attend an independent college of Washington.
Eligibility: Applicants must be juniors or seniors who have participated in community service in high school and college. Students attending Gonzaga University, Heritage University, Pacific Lutheran University, Saint Martin's University, Seattle Pacific University, Seattle University, University of Puget Sound, Walla Walla University, Whitman College or Whitworth University are eligible.
Target applicant(s): College students. Adult students.
Amount: $2,000.
Number of awards: 1.
Deadline: March 17.
How to apply: Applications are available online or from your school's financial aid office.
Exclusive: Visit www.UltimateScholarshipBook.com and enter code IN223320 for updates on this award.

(2234) • Stanley Z. Koplik Certificate of Mastery Tuition Waiver Program

Massachusetts Department of Higher Education
Office of Student Financial Assistance, 454 Broadway, Suite 200, Revere, MA 02151
Phone: 617-727-9420
Email: osfa@osfa.mass.edu
http://www.mass.edu/osfa/students/forstudents.asp

Purpose: To support Massachusetts students who have demonstrated academic merit.
Eligibility: Applicants must be currently enrolled in a public high school in the state of Massachusetts. Students must receive an "Advanced" score on at least one part of the 10th grade MCAS test, and they must score "Proficient" on all of the other sections. They must also have good scores on at least two AP exams, two SAT II exams or combinations of one of those tests and other achievements determined by the Koplik program. Students must maintain a 3.3 GPA while participating in the scholarship.
Target applicant(s): High school students.
Minimum GPA: 3.3
Amount: Up to full tuition.
Number of awards: Varies.
Scholarship may be renewable.
Deadline: Varies.
How to apply: Applications are available from high schools.
Exclusive: Visit www.UltimateScholarshipBook.com and enter code MA223420 for updates on this award.

(2235) • State Contractual Scholarship Fund Program

North Carolina Division of Vocational Rehabilitation Services
2801 Mail Service Center, Raleigh, NC 27699-2801
Phone: 888-234-6400
Email: jterrell@ncbar.org
http://www.cfnc.org

Purpose: To provide financial assistance to needy students attending private colleges and universities in North Carolina.
Eligibility: Applicants must be North Carolina residents who are enrolled in an undergraduate program at an approved North Carolina private postsecondary institution and have unmet financial need. They must not be enrolled in a program that is designed primarily to prepare students for religious vocations. Licensure students may also apply if they have a bachelor's degree and are enrolled in undergraduate classes in a licensure program for teachers or nurses.
Target applicant(s): High school students. College students. Adult students.
Amount: Varies.
Number of awards: Varies.
Deadline: Varies.
How to apply: See your financial aid office for application details.
Exclusive: Visit www.UltimateScholarshipBook.com and enter code NO223520 for updates on this award.

(2236) • State Employees Association of North Carolina (SEANC) Scholarships

SEANC Scholarship Foundation
1621 Midtown Place, Raleigh, NC 27609
Phone: 919-833-6436
Email: cwilson@seanc.org
https://www.seanc.org/scholarship

Purpose: To provide financial assistance to SEANC members, their spouses and their children who plan to attend college.
Eligibility: Applicants must be the spouses or children of members and demonstrate either financial need or merit, or applicants must be members working full-time and enrolled in six or more semester hours of undergraduate work or three or more hours of graduate work. Students who are spouses or children must be enrolled full-time.
Target applicant(s): High school students. College students. Graduate school students. Adult students.
Amount: Varies.
Number of awards: Varies.
Deadline: April 15.
How to apply: Applications are available online or from your guidance counselor or financial aid office.
Exclusive: Visit www.UltimateScholarshipBook.com and enter code SE223620 for updates on this award.

(2237) • State Need Grant

Washington Student Achievement Council
917 Lakeridge Way SW, Olympia, WA 98502
Phone: 360-753-7850
http://www.wsac.wa.gov/financial-aid

Purpose: To assist low-income students to pursue undergraduate degrees or train for new careers.
Eligibility: Applicants must be Washington residents who have a family income of 70 percent or less of the state median, enroll at least half-time as an undergraduate student in an eligible program and be pursuing a certificate, associate's degree or bachelor's degree.
Target applicant(s): High school students. College students. Adult students.
Amount: Varies.
Number of awards: Varies.
Deadline: Varies.
How to apply: Eligible students who have filed a Free Application for Federal Student Aid (FAFSA) are considered.
Exclusive: Visit www.UltimateScholarshipBook.com and enter code WA223720 for updates on this award.

(2238) • State Need-based Grants

South Carolina Commission on Higher Education
1122 Lady Street, Suite 300, Columbia, SC 29201
Phone: 803-737-2262
Email: cbrown@che.sc.gov
http://www.che.sc.gov

Purpose: Monetary assistance for higher education is provided to South Carolina resident students.

Eligibility: Applicants must be obtaining their first baccalaureate or professional degree, complete the Free Application for Federal Student Aid (FAFSA) and be residents of South Carolina. Students must have a minimum 2.0 GPA and be enrolled in their first one-year program, first associate's degree, first program leading to a baccalaureate degree, first baccalaureate degree or first professional degree to be eligible.

Target applicant(s): High school students. College students. Adult students.

Minimum GPA: 2.0

Amount: Up to $2,500.

Number of awards: Varies.

Scholarship may be renewable.

Deadline: Varies.

How to apply: Complete the FAFSA and contact your college's financial aid office if you plan to attend a public college or the South Carolina Commission on Higher Education if you plan to attend a private college.

Exclusive: Visit www.UltimateScholarshipBook.com and enter code SO223820 for updates on this award.

(2239) • State of Maine Grant Program

Maine Education Assistance Division
Finance Authority of Maine (FAME), 5 Community Drive, P.O. Box 949, Augusta, ME 04332
Phone: 800-228-3734
Email: education@famemaine.com
http://www.famemaine.com

Purpose: To support Maine undergraduate students who have financial need.

Eligibility: Applicants must be U.S. citizens or eligible non-citizens, be Maine residents and submit the Free Application for Federal Student Aid (FAFSA) by May 1. They must have an Expected Family Contribution (EFC) of $5,000 or less. Selection is based on financial need.

Target applicant(s): High school students. College students. Adult students.

Amount: $1,700.

Number of awards: Varies.

Scholarship may be renewable.

Deadline: May 1.

How to apply: Application is made by completing the FAFSA.

Exclusive: Visit www.UltimateScholarshipBook.com and enter code MA223920 for updates on this award.

(2240) • State Work Study

Washington Student Achievement Council
917 Lakeridge Way SW, Olympia, WA 98502
Phone: 360-753-7850
http://www.wsac.wa.gov/financial-aid

Purpose: To help low and middle income students earn money for college while gaining work experience.

Eligibility: Applicants must have demonstrated financial need according to the FAFSA, enroll at least half-time in an eligible undergraduate or graduate program and not be seeking a degree in theology.

Target applicant(s): High school students. College students. Graduate school students. Adult students.

Amount: $2,000-$5,000 per year.

Number of awards: Varies.

Deadline: Varies.

How to apply: Eligible students who have filed a Free Application for Federal Student Aid (FAFSA) will be considered.

Exclusive: Visit www.UltimateScholarshipBook.com and enter code WA224020 for updates on this award.

(2241) • Stephen Phillips Memorial Scholarship Fund

Stephen Phillips Memorial Scholarship Fund
P.O. Box 870, Salem, MA 01970
Phone: 978-744-2111
Email: staff@spscholars.org
http://phillips-scholarship.org/

Purpose: To aid New England residents pursuing higher education.

Eligibility: Applicants must be U.S. residents or resident aliens who are permanent residents of Connecticut, Massachusetts, Maine, New Hampshire, Rhode Island or Vermont. They must be enrolled in a demanding undergraduate course of study pursuing their first degrees. A GPA of 3.0 or higher is required. Applicants must demonstrate citizenship, character, serious-mindedness and financial need.

Target applicant(s): High school students. College students. Adult students.

Minimum GPA: 3.0

Amount: $3,000-$18,000.

Number of awards: Varies.

Deadline: May 1.

How to apply: Applications are available online. An application form, essay, transcript, counselor or professor recommendation, additional letter of recommendation, FAFSA Student Aid Report, financial aid award letter, documentation of college costs and student's and parents' tax forms are required.

Exclusive: Visit www.UltimateScholarshipBook.com and enter code ST224120 for updates on this award.

(2242) • Sterbenz-Ryan Scholarship

Sterbenz-Ryan Scholarship Program
Scholarship America, One Scholarship Way, Saint Peter, MN 56082
Phone: 507-931-1682
Email: sterbenz-ryan@scholarshipamerica.org
https://scholarsapply.org/sterbenz-ryan

Purpose: To support students from Minnesota and Wisconsin who will be full-time college students in the upcoming school year.

Eligibility: Applicants must reside in Minnesota or Wisconsin and plan to enroll as a full-time student as an undergraduate or graduate student for the upcoming school year. Students must be either high school seniors or current undergraduate students with a GPA of 2.5 to 3.5.

Target applicant(s): High school students. College students. Adult students.

Minimum GPA: 2.5

Amount: Up to $15,000.

Number of awards: Up to 44.

Scholarship may be renewable.

Deadline: June 15.

How to apply: Applications are available online.

Exclusive: Visit www.UltimateScholarshipBook.com and enter code ST224220 for updates on this award.

(2243) • Sterling Scholar Awards of Utah

Deseret News-KSL Broadcast Group Sterling Scholar
55 North 300 West, Suite 800, Salt Lake City, UT 84145
Phone: 801-323-4223
Email: michaelsonj@deseretmgt.com
http://www.sterlingscholar.org

Purpose: To aid outstanding Utah students.
Eligibility: Applicants must be Utah public high school seniors. They must be nominated by their schools in one of 14 categories. Selection is based on scholarship (50 percent), leadership (25 percent) and community service/citizenship (25 percent).
Target applicant(s): High school students.
Amount: Varies.
Number of awards: Varies.
Deadline: January 6.
How to apply: Applications are available from your school's Sterling Awards organizer. An ID page, application form, transcript, proof of ACT scores, principal's report, standardized test data sheet and letter of recommendation are required.
Exclusive: Visit www.UltimateScholarshipBook.com and enter code DE224320 for updates on this award.

(2244) • Steve Dearduff Scholarship Fund

Community Foundation for Greater Atlanta Inc.
50 Hurt Plaza, Suite 449, Atlanta, GA 30303
Phone: 404-688-5525
Email: info@cfgreateratlanta.org
http://www.cfgreateratlanta.org/community-impact/scholarships/

Purpose: To aid students who are preparing for careers in the fields of medicine and social work.
Eligibility: Applicants must be legal residents of Georgia and be enrolled at or accepted into an accredited postsecondary institution. They must be majoring in medicine or social work, have a GPA of 2.0 or higher and have a demonstrated commitment to community service. They must demonstrate financial need. Selection is based on academic merit, career potential, community service involvement and financial need.
Target applicant(s): High school students. College students. Graduate school students. Adult students.
Minimum GPA: 2.0
Amount: Up to $2,500.
Number of awards: Up to 3.
Scholarship may be renewable.
Deadline: March 15.
How to apply: Applications are available online. An application form and supporting materials are required.
Exclusive: Visit www.UltimateScholarshipBook.com and enter code CO224420 for updates on this award.

(2245) • Steve Fasteau Past Presidents' Scholarship

California Association for Postsecondary Education and Disability
Disabled Student Programs and Services, San Bernardino Valley College, 701 South Mt. Vernon Avenue, San Bernardino, CA 92410
Phone: 909-384-8663
Email: capedscholarships@gmail.com
http://www.caped.io/

Purpose: To support disabled students.
Eligibility: Applicants must be college students with high academic achievement. They must demonstrate leadership and dedication to the advancement of students with disabilities in higher education. Undergraduate students must have a minimum GPA of 2.5 and at least six semester units, and graduate students must have a minimum GPA of 3.0 and at least three semester units from a public or private California college or university.
Target applicant(s): High school students. College students. Graduate school students. Adult students.
Minimum GPA: 2.5 for undergraduate students, 3.0 for graduate students
Amount: $1,000.
Number of awards: 1.
Deadline: August 31.
How to apply: Applications are available online. An application form, letter of application, letter of recommendation, verification of disability, transcript and proof of enrollment are required.
Exclusive: Visit www.UltimateScholarshipBook.com and enter code CA224520 for updates on this award.

(2246) • Student Incentive Grant

North Carolina Division of Vocational Rehabilitation Services
2801 Mail Service Center, Raleigh, NC 27699-2801
Phone: 888-234-6400
Email: jterrell@ncbar.org
http://www.cfnc.org

Purpose: To assist outstanding North Carolina high school graduates.
Eligibility: Successful applicants must be North Carolina residents enrolled full-time at a state college or university. Study programs cannot be in preparation for a religious career. Students must demonstrate financial need and maintain adequate academic progress.
Target applicant(s): High school students. College students. Adult students.
Amount: $700.
Number of awards: Varies.
Scholarship may be renewable.
Deadline: Varies.
How to apply: Contact your financial aid office.
Exclusive: Visit www.UltimateScholarshipBook.com and enter code NO224620 for updates on this award.

(2247) • Student Incentive Grants

New Mexico Higher Education Department
2044 Galisteo Street, Suite 4, Santa Fe, NM 87505-2100
Phone: 505-476-8400
Email: cesaria.tapia1@state.nm.us
http://www.hed.state.nm.us/students/

Purpose: To support New Mexico undergraduate students with financial need to attend postsecondary institutions in New Mexico.
Eligibility: Applicants must be New Mexico resident undergraduate students and attend public and selected private nonprofit postsecondary institutions in New Mexico at least half-time. Students must also be U.S. citizens.
Target applicant(s): College students. Adult students.
Amount: $200-$2,500.
Number of awards: Varies.
Deadline: Varies.
How to apply: Submit the FAFSA and contact your financial aid office. Deadlines are set by individual institutions.
Exclusive: Visit www.UltimateScholarshipBook.com and enter code NE224720 for updates on this award.

(2248) • Student Recycling Leadership Corps

Indiana Recycling Coalition, Inc.
708 E Michigan Street, Indianapolis, IN 46202
http://indianarecycling.org/project/student-recycling-leadership-corps/
Purpose: To support students who promote recycling.
Eligibility: Applicants must be in their junior or senior year of high school and be a resident of Indiana. Students must have a grade point average of 2.5 or better and be interested in increasing their school's recycling measures.
Target applicant(s): High school students.
Minimum GPA: 2.5
Amount: $1,000.
Number of awards: 10.
Deadline: September 30.
How to apply: Applications are available online.
Exclusive: Visit www.UltimateScholarshipBook.com and enter code IN224820 for updates on this award.

(2249) • Susan Bunch Memorial Scholarship

California Association on Postsecondary Education and Disability (CAPED)
10073 Valley View Street, #242, Cypress, CA 90630
Phone: 562-397-2810
Email: capedscholarships2018@gmail.com
http://www.caped.io/scholarships/
Purpose: To support students with a learning disability who are pursuing a higher education.
Eligibility: Applicants must have a verifiable learning disability and be currently enrolled as a student at a California college or university with a GPA of 2.5 for undergraduates or 3.0 for graduate students. Students must have completed at least six semester or eight quarter units as an undergraduate student or three semester or four quarter units as a graduate student.
Target applicant(s): College students. Graduate school students. Adult students.
Minimum GPA: 2.5 for undergraduate students, 3.0 for graduate students
Amount: $1,000.
Number of awards: 1.
Deadline: August 31.
How to apply: Applications are available online.
Exclusive: Visit www.UltimateScholarshipBook.com and enter code CA224920 for updates on this award.

(2250) • Susan Howard Community Service Award

British American Foundation of Texas
Email: info@baftx.org
https://www.baftx.org
Purpose: To support Texas students with a passion for community service.
Eligibility: Applicants must be residents of Texas or the U.K. enrolled as full-time students within the Texas or U.K. education systems. Students must demonstrate financial need, be 11 to 21 years old and be currently working on an inspiring community service project.
Target applicant(s): Junior high students or younger. High school students. College students.
Amount: $5,000.
Number of awards: 1.
Deadline: March 31.
How to apply: Applications are available online.
Exclusive: Visit www.UltimateScholarshipBook.com and enter code BR225020 for updates on this award.

(2251) • Susan Thompson Buffett Foundation Scholarship Program

Susan Thompson Buffett Foundation
222 Kiewit Plaza, Omaha, NE 68131
Phone: 402-943-1383
Email: Scholarships_App@stbfoundation.org
http://www.buffettscholarships.org
Purpose: To support Nebraska students.
Eligibility: Applicants must be Nebraska residents pursuing undergraduate studies at a Nebraska public institution of higher learning who have not yet earned a bachelor's degree. They must be in need of financial assistance in order to obtain education. Students must have applied for federal aid and have a 2.5 or higher GPA.
Target applicant(s): High school students. College students. Adult students.
Minimum GPA: 2.5
Amount: Varies.
Number of awards: Varies.
Scholarship may be renewable.
Deadline: February 1.
How to apply: Applications are available online. An application form, transcript, two letters of reference and essay are required.
Exclusive: Visit www.UltimateScholarshipBook.com and enter code SU225120 for updates on this award.

(2252) • Sussman-Miller Educational Assistance Award

Albuquerque Community Foundation (ACF)
P.O. Box 25266, Albuquerque, NM 87125-5266
Phone: 505-883-6240
Email: foundation@albuquerquefoundation.org
http://www.albuquerquefoundation.org
Purpose: To assist New Mexico high school graduates and college undergraduates.
Eligibility: Students must be New Mexico residents for a minimum of one year, have been awarded a financial package that does not satisfy demonstrated need and be accepted by and have chosen to attend a U.S. post-secondary, accredited, nonprofit educational institution full-time. High school applicants need to graduate from an accredited public or private high school and have a 3.0 minimum GPA. Undergraduate applicants must have completed a minimum of one semester of undergraduate study with a 2.5 minimum GPA and cannot be applying for residency in another state.
Target applicant(s): High school students. College students. Adult students.
Minimum GPA: 3.0 for high school students, 2.5 for undergraduate students
Amount: $500-$2,000.
Number of awards: Varies.
Deadline: April 24 and June 27.
How to apply: Applications are available online.
Exclusive: Visit www.UltimateScholarshipBook.com and enter code AL225220 for updates on this award.

(2253) • Swine Industry Scholarship

Iowa Foundation for Agricultural Advancement
Winner's Circle Scholarships, c/o SGI, 30805 595th Avenue, Cambridge, IA 50046
Phone: 515-291-3941
Email: linda@slweldon.net
http://www.iowastatefair.org/participate/competition/

Purpose: To aid Iowa 4-H and FFA students who are planning to go to college.
Eligibility: Applicants must be Iowa entering undergraduate freshmen. They must have a history of involvement in 4-H or FFA with experience in swine projects. Selection is based on the overall strength of the application.
Target applicant(s): High school students.
Amount: Varies.
Number of awards: Varies.
Deadline: July 1.
How to apply: Applications are available online. An application form and supporting materials are required.
Exclusive: Visit www.UltimateScholarshipBook.com and enter code IO225320 for updates on this award.

(2254) • Talent Incentive Program Grant

State of Wisconsin Higher Educational Aids Board
P.O. Box 7885, Madison, WI 53707
Phone: 608-267-2206
Email: heabmail@wisconsin.gov
http://heab.state.wi.us

Purpose: To assist Wisconsin students who have financial need.
Eligibility: Applicants must be Wisconsin residents who are first-time college freshmen at a Wisconsin postsecondary institution. They must be enrolled at least part-time and must demonstrate financial need. Selection is based on financial need.
Target applicant(s): High school students. College students. Adult students.
Amount: $600 to $1,800.
Number of awards: Varies.
Scholarship may be renewable.
Deadline: Varies.
How to apply: Applicants must complete the FAFSA and must be nominated for this award by their financial aid office or by a Wisconsin Educational Opportunities Program (WEOP) counselor.
Exclusive: Visit www.UltimateScholarshipBook.com and enter code ST225420 for updates on this award.

(2255) • Teacher Shortage Employment Incentive Program

Oklahoma State Regents for Higher Education
655 Research Parkway, Suite 200, Oklahoma City, OK 73104
Phone: 800-858-1840
Email: studentinfo@osrhe.edu
http://www.okhighered.org

Purpose: To encourage students who major in mathematics or science to serve as teachers of mathematics and science in Oklahoma public secondary schools.
Eligibility: Applicants must be willing to teach mathematics or science at an Oklahoma public secondary school for at least five years. Students must complete an approved professional teacher education program from an Oklahoma accredited teacher education unit which must include a student teaching requirement. Applicants must also hold a valid certificate to teach mathematics or science at the secondary level.
Target applicant(s): College students. Adult students.
Amount: Varies.
Number of awards: Varies.
Deadline: Varies.
How to apply: Applications are available online.
Exclusive: Visit www.UltimateScholarshipBook.com and enter code OK225520 for updates on this award.

(2256) • Tech High School Alumni Association/W.O. Cheney Merit Scholarship

Community Foundation for Greater Atlanta Inc.
50 Hurt Plaza, Suite 449, Atlanta, GA 30303
Phone: 404-688-5525
Email: info@cfgreateratlanta.org
http://www.cfgreateratlanta.org/community-impact/scholarships/

Purpose: To aid future college students who are planning to major in engineering, mathematics or one of the physical sciences.
Eligibility: Applicants must be U.S. citizens, Georgia residents and high school seniors who have been accepted at an accredited four-year postsecondary institution. They must be planning to major in mathematics, one of the physical sciences or engineering and must be full-time students who have a proven interest in community service. They must have an SAT composite (math and critical reading) score of 1300 or higher and must either be in the top 10 percent of their class or have a GPA of 3.0 or higher. Selection is based on the overall strength of the application.
Target applicant(s): High school students.
Minimum GPA: 3.0
Amount: $5,000 a year.
Number of awards: Up to 4.
Scholarship may be renewable.
Deadline: June 1.
How to apply: Applications are available online. An application form and supporting materials are required.
Exclusive: Visit www.UltimateScholarshipBook.com and enter code CO225620 for updates on this award.

(2257) • Technical Certification Scholarship

Texas 4-H Youth Development Foundation
4180 Highway 6, College Station, TX 77845
Phone: 979-845-1211
Email: texas4h@ag.tamu.edu
https://texas4-h.tamu.edu/scholarships/

Purpose: To support Texas high school seniors who plan to pursue a technical program.
Eligibility: Applicants must be current active members and have actively participated in a 4-H program for at least two of the past three years. They must have formally applied to a Texas college or university, and they must meet all requirements for admission. Students must not have any plans to continue their college education after completion of a technical program.
Target applicant(s): High school students.
Amount: Varies.
Number of awards: Varies.
Deadline: February 7.
How to apply: Applications are available online.
Exclusive: Visit www.UltimateScholarshipBook.com and enter code TE225720 for updates on this award.

(2258) • Ted and Nora Anderson Scholarships

American Legion, Department of Kansas
1314 SW Topeka Boulevard, Topeka, KS 66612
Phone: 785-232-9315
http://www.ksamlegion.org

Purpose: To support worthy and needy children of American Legion and American Legion Auxiliary members as they pursue their educations.

Eligibility: Applicants must be high school seniors or college freshmen or sophomores who are average or better students. They must be enrolling or enrolled in a post-secondary school in Kansas and the son or daughter of a veteran. At least one parent must have been a member of the Kansas American Legion or American Legion Auxiliary for the past three years. The children of deceased parents are also eligible as long as the parent was a paid member at the time of death. Applicants must submit three letters of recommendation with only one from a teacher, a 1040 income statement, documentation of parent's veteran status, an essay on "Why I Want to Go to College" and a high school transcript.

Target applicant(s): High school students. College students. Adult students.

Amount: $500.

Number of awards: 4.

Deadline: February 15.

How to apply: Applications are available online.

Exclusive: Visit www.UltimateScholarshipBook.com and enter code AM225820 for updates on this award.

(2259) • Ted Brickley/Bernice Shickora Scholarship

New Jersey Chapter of the American Society of Safety Engineers
Liberty Mutual Insurance Company, Attn.: Frank Gesualdo, 7 Becker Farm Road, 2nd Floor, Roseland, NJ 07068
Email: scholarship@njasse.org
http://nj.asse.org/

Purpose: To aid New Jersey students who are majoring in industrial hygiene, occupational safety, environmental science or a related subject.

Eligibility: Applicants must be New Jersey residents who are enrolled at an accredited New Jersey college or university and must be graduate students or rising undergraduate juniors or seniors. They must be majoring in industrial hygiene, occupational safety, environmental science or a related subject and must be involved in extracurricular activities pertaining to occupational safety. They must have a major GPA of 2.5 or higher on a four-point scale. Selection is based on the overall strength of the application.

Target applicant(s): College students. Graduate school students. Adult students.

Minimum GPA: 2.5

Amount: Varies.

Number of awards: Varies.

Deadline: April 14.

How to apply: Applications are available online. An application form, transcript and one reference letter are required.

Exclusive: Visit www.UltimateScholarshipBook.com and enter code NE225920 for updates on this award.

(2260) • Tennessee Funeral Directors Association Memorial Scholarship

Tennessee Funeral Directors Association
Scholarship Committee, 1616 Church Street, Suite A, Nashville, TN 37203
Phone: 615-321-8792
Email: office@tnfda.org
http://www.tnfda.org

Purpose: To aid funeral service and mortuary science students who are residents of Tennessee.

Eligibility: Applicants must be U.S. citizens and legal residents of Tennessee. They must be enrolled full time in a funeral service or mortuary science program at a school that has been accredited by the American Board of Funeral Service Education (ABFSE). They must have completed one term of their program and must have at least one term remaining in their program. They must have plans to practice in Tennessee after graduating. Selection is based on the overall strength of the application.

Target applicant(s): College students. Adult students.

Amount: Varies.

Number of awards: Varies.

Deadline: Varies.

How to apply: Applications are available online. An application form, transcript, copies of federal income tax forms, one recommendation letter and a personal essay are required.

Exclusive: Visit www.UltimateScholarshipBook.com and enter code TE226020 for updates on this award.

(2261) • Tennessee HOPE Access Grant

Tennessee Student Assistance Corporation
404 James Robertson Parkway, Suite 1510, Parkway Towers, Nashville, TN 37243
Phone: 800-342-1663
Email: tsac.aidinfo@tn.gov
http://www.tn.gov/collegepays/section/money-for-college

Purpose: To support students who do not qualify for the Tennessee HOPE Grant.

Eligibility: Applicants must be entering freshmen who have a minimum GPA of 2.75. They must also have either an ACT score between 18 and 20 or an SAT score between 860 and 970. Independent students or the parents of dependent students must have an adjusted gross income under $36,000.

Target applicant(s): High school students.

Minimum GPA: 2.75

Amount: Up to $1,375 per semester.

Number of awards: Varies.

Deadline: Varies.

How to apply: Applications are available through completion of the FAFSA.

Exclusive: Visit www.UltimateScholarshipBook.com and enter code TE226120 for updates on this award.

(2262) • Tennessee HOPE Lottery Scholarship

Tennessee Student Assistance Corporation
404 James Robertson Parkway, Suite 1510, Parkway Towers, Nashville, TN 37243
Phone: 800-342-1663
Email: tsac.aidinfo@tn.gov
http://www.tn.gov/collegepays/section/money-for-college

Purpose: To support undergraduate students in Tennessee.

Eligibility: Applicants must be entering freshmen and either have at least a 3.0 GPA, a score of 21 on the ACT or a score of 980 on the SAT. GED students must also score at least a 525 on the GED test. Home-schooled students and some private school students must meet additional requirements. Applicants must be Tennessee residents for at least one year prior to the application deadline.

Target applicant(s): High school students.

Minimum GPA: 3.0

Amount: Up to $6,000.

Number of awards: Varies.
Scholarship may be renewable.
Deadline: Varies.
How to apply: Applications are available through completion of the FAFSA.
Exclusive: Visit www.UltimateScholarshipBook.com and enter code TE226220 for updates on this award.

(2263) · Tennessee Need-Based Supplemental Aspire Awards

Tennessee Student Assistance Corporation
404 James Robertson Parkway, Suite 1510, Parkway Towers, Nashville, TN 37243
Phone: 800-342-1663
Email: tsac.aidinfo@tn.gov
http://www.tn.gov/collegepays/section/money-for-college
Purpose: To supplement the Tennessee HOPE Scholarship.
Eligibility: Applicants must have a minimum ACT score of 21 or SAT score of 980. Entering freshmen may substitute a GPA of 3.0 or higher. GED students must also have a GED test score of 525 or higher. Family adjusted gross income may not be more than $36,000.
Target applicant(s): High school students. College students. Adult students.
Minimum GPA: 3.0
Amount: $750 per semester.
Number of awards: Varies.
Scholarship may be renewable.
Deadline: Varies.
How to apply: Applications are available online. A Free Application for Federal Student Aid (FAFSA) is required.
Exclusive: Visit www.UltimateScholarshipBook.com and enter code TE226320 for updates on this award.

(2264) · Tennessee Student Assistance Awards

Tennessee Student Assistance Corporation
404 James Robertson Parkway, Suite 1510, Parkway Towers, Nashville, TN 37243
Phone: 800-342-1663
Email: tsac.aidinfo@tn.gov
http://www.tn.gov/collegepays/section/money-for-college
Purpose: To aid Tennessee students.
Eligibility: Applicants must be Tennessee residents who have applied for federal aid and have an Expected Family Contribution of $2,100 or less. They must be enrolled at least half time at an eligible Tennessee institution of higher learning and maintain satisfactory academic progress. They may not be in default on a loan or owe a refund on any grant previously received for education.
Target applicant(s): High school students. College students. Adult students.
Amount: Up to $4,000.
Number of awards: Varies.
Scholarship may be renewable.
Deadline: Varies.
How to apply: Applications are available online. A Free Application for Federal Student Aid (FAFSA) is required.
Exclusive: Visit www.UltimateScholarshipBook.com and enter code TE226420 for updates on this award.

(2265) · Tese Caldarelli Memorial Scholarship

National Association for Campus Activities
13 Harbison Way, Columbia, SC 29212
Phone: 803-732-6222
Email: info@naca.org
https://www.naca.org/FOUNDATION/Pages/Scholarships.aspx
Purpose: To provide financial assistance to student leaders.
Eligibility: Students must hold a significant campus leadership position and demonstrate significant leadership skills and abilities. Students must also be making significant contributions through on- or off-campus volunteering. Applicants must also be current undergraduate or graduate students in Kentucky, Michigan, Ohio, western Pennsylvania or West Virginia and have a minimum 3.0 GPA.
Target applicant(s): College students. Graduate school students. Adult students.
Minimum GPA: 3.0
Amount: Varies.
Number of awards: Varies.
Deadline: December 31.
How to apply: Applications are available online.
Exclusive: Visit www.UltimateScholarshipBook.com and enter code NA226520 for updates on this award.

(2266) · Texas 4-H Opportunity Scholarship Program - Baccalaureate Scholarships

Texas 4-H Youth Development Foundation
4180 Highway 6, College Station, TX 77845
Phone: 979-845-1211
Email: texas4h@ag.tamu.edu
https://texas4-h.tamu.edu/scholarships/
Purpose: To support Texas 4-H members who are planning to pursue a bachelor's degree.
Eligibility: Students must be high school seniors who have actively participated in a Texas 4-H program during the current year and at least two of the three previous years. They must have formally applied to a Texas college or university, and they must meet the school's admission requirements. Applicants must have a score of at least 1350 on the SAT or 19 on the ACT. Students must provide information about their 4-H achievements, financial need, community service participation and leadership skills.
Target applicant(s): High school students.
Amount: $3,000-$20,000.
Number of awards: Varies.
Deadline: February 3.
How to apply: Applications are available online.
Exclusive: Visit www.UltimateScholarshipBook.com and enter code TE226620 for updates on this award.

(2267) · Texas Association FCCLA Regional Scholarship

Family, Career and Community Leaders of America - Texas Association
1107 West 45th Street, Austin, TX 78756
Phone: 512-306-0099
Email: fccla@texasfccla.org
http://www.texasfccla.org
Purpose: To aid Texas students who are planning to major in family and consumer sciences.
Eligibility: Applicants must be members of Texas Association, Family, Career and Community Leaders of America (FCCLA). They must be

planning to major in family and consumer sciences in college. Selection is based on the overall strength of the application.
Target applicant(s): High school students.
Amount: $1,000.
Number of awards: 5.
Deadline: March 1.
How to apply: Applications are available online. An application form, transcript, personal essay and standardized test scores are required.
Exclusive: Visit www.UltimateScholarshipBook.com and enter code FA226720 for updates on this award.

(2268) • Texas Broadcast Education Foundation Scholarships

Texas Association of Broadcasters
502 E. 11th Street, Suite 200, Austin, TX 78701
Phone: 512-322-9944
Email: craig@tab.org
https://www.tab.org/scholarships
Purpose: To support promising Texas students.
Eligibility: Applicants must be TAB student members or attend a TAB member college or university. All eligible applicants must have a GPA of 3.0 or higher and enroll full-time in a program that emphasizes radio or television broadcasting or communications at a college or university in Texas.
Target applicant(s): High school students. College students. Graduate school students. Adult students.
Minimum GPA: 3.0
Amount: $3,000-$5,000.
Number of awards: 9.
Deadline: Varies.
How to apply: Applications are available online. An application form is required.
Exclusive: Visit www.UltimateScholarshipBook.com and enter code TE226820 for updates on this award.

(2269) • Texas Elks State Association Scholarship Program

Texas Elks State Association (TESA)
1963 FM 1586, Gonzales, TX 78629
Phone: 830-875-2425
Email: txelks@gvec.net
http://www.texaselks.org
Purpose: To support Texas students.
Eligibility: Applicants must be seniors in Texas high schools who are not in the top 5 percent of their class. They must be U.S. citizens and Texas residents.
Target applicant(s): High school students.
Amount: $1,250.
Number of awards: 6.
Scholarship may be renewable.
Deadline: February 17.
How to apply: Applications are available online. An application form, transcript, SAT or ACT scores, applicant statement and parent statement are required.
Exclusive: Visit www.UltimateScholarshipBook.com and enter code TE226920 for updates on this award.

(2270) • Texas Elks State Association Teenager of the Year Contest

Texas Elks State Association (TESA)
1963 FM 1586, Gonzales, TX 78629
Phone: 830-875-2425
Email: txelks@gvec.net
http://www.texaselks.org
Purpose: To support outstanding high school students.
Eligibility: Applicants must be graduating high school seniors from Texas. Selection criteria include SAT/ACT scores, honors and awards, participation and leadership in extracurricular activities and neatness and organization of application.
Target applicant(s): High school students.
Amount: $500-$1,500.
Number of awards: 6.
Deadline: February 17.
How to apply: Applications are available online. An application form and documentation of awards and activities are required.
Exclusive: Visit www.UltimateScholarshipBook.com and enter code TE227020 for updates on this award.

(2271) • Texas Elks State Association Vocational Grant Program

Texas Elks State Association (TESA)
1963 FM 1586, Gonzales, TX 78629
Phone: 830-875-2425
Email: txelks@gvec.net
http://www.texaselks.org
Purpose: To support students pursuing vocational education.
Eligibility: Applicants must be U.S. citizens and Texas residents 18 years of age or older. They must plan to enroll full-time in a two-year or less vocational or technical program that results in a certificate, diploma or associates degree.
Target applicant(s): High school students. College students. Adult students.
Amount: Varies.
Number of awards: Varies.
Deadline: March 31.
How to apply: Applications are available online. An application form, personal statement, letter from parent or other person with knowledge of family background, letter of recommendation and grade or work records for previous two years are required.
Exclusive: Visit www.UltimateScholarshipBook.com and enter code TE227120 for updates on this award.

(2272) • Texas Fifth-Year Accounting Student Scholarship Program

Texas Higher Education Coordinating Board
1200 East Anderson Lane, Austin, TX 78752
Phone: 512-427-6101
Email: pamela.harris@thecb.state.tx.us
http://www.collegeforalltexans.com/
Purpose: To aid Texas students who are preparing for careers as certified public accountants (CPAs).
Eligibility: Applicants must be Texas residents who are enrolled at an accredited, non-profit postsecondary institution located in Texas. By the time of award disbursement, they must have completed at least 120 credit hours of college coursework with at least 15 of those being from accounting courses. They must plan to take the exam to become a

certified public accountant (CPA), and they must demonstrate financial need. Selection is based on the overall strength of the application.
Target applicant(s): College students. Adult students.
Amount: Up to $5,000.
Number of awards: Varies.
Deadline: Varies.
How to apply: Applications are available from the applicant's college financial aid office or department of accounting. An application form and supporting materials are required.
Exclusive: Visit www.UltimateScholarshipBook.com and enter code TE227220 for updates on this award.

(2273) • Texas History Essay Scholarship

Sons of the Republic of Texas
1717 8th Street, Bay City, TX 77414
Phone: 979-245-6644
http://www.srttexas.org
Purpose: To aid high school students and promote awareness of Texas history.
Eligibility: Applicants must be graduating seniors. They must submit an essay exploring the relevance of Texas history in the building of the state. Selection is based on research, originality and organization.
Target applicant(s): High school students.
Amount: $2,000-$4,000.
Number of awards: 3.
Deadline: January 31.
How to apply: Applications are available online. An application form and essay are required.
Exclusive: Visit www.UltimateScholarshipBook.com and enter code SO227320 for updates on this award.

(2274) • Texas International Fishing Tournament Inc. Scholarship

Texas International Fishing Tournament
P.O. Box 2715, South Padre Island, TX 78597
Phone: 956-943-8438
Email: info@tift.org
http://www.tift.org
Purpose: To support college level anglers in their pursuit of completing undergraduate studies.
Eligibility: Applicants must be a college undergraduate (freshman through senior), have at least a 2.25 GPA and have been involved with the Texas International Fishing Tournament. Selection is based on past involvement with T.I.F.T., academic achievement and an essay.
Target applicant(s): College students. Adult students.
Minimum GPA: 2.25
Amount: $2,000.
Number of awards: Varies.
Scholarship may be renewable.
Deadline: March 31.
How to apply: Applications are available online.
Exclusive: Visit www.UltimateScholarshipBook.com and enter code TE227420 for updates on this award.

(2275) • Texas Occupational Therapy Association Scholarships

American Occupational Therapy Foundation
Attn: Jeanne Cooper, 4720 Montgomery Lane, Suite 202, Bethesda, MD 20814
Phone: 240-292-1034
Email: jcooper@aotf.org
http://www.aotf.org/scholarshipsgrants
Purpose: To aid Texas occupational therapy students.
Eligibility: Applicants must be members of the Texas Occupational Therapy Association (TOTA). They must be Texas residents who are enrolled in an occupational therapy certificate, associate's or professional degree program at an accredited Texas school. Selection is based on the overall strength of the application.
Target applicant(s): College students. Adult students.
Amount: Varies.
Number of awards: 2.
Deadline: October 26.
How to apply: Applications are available by request from Jeanne Cooper, who is the scholarship coordinator at the American Occupational Therapy Association. An application form and supporting materials are required.
Exclusive: Visit www.UltimateScholarshipBook.com and enter code AM227520 for updates on this award.

(2276) • Texas Oratorical Contest

American Legion, Department of Texas
P.O. Box 140527, Austin, TX 78714
Phone: 512-472-4138
Email: programs@txlegion.org
http://www.txlegion.org
Purpose: To enhance high school students' experience with and understanding of the U.S. Constitution. The contest will help develop students' leadership skills and civic appreciation, as well as the ability to deliver thoughtful, insightful orations regarding U.S. citizenship and its inherent responsibilities.
Eligibility: Applicants must be high school students under the age of 20 who are U.S. citizens or legal residents and residents of the state. Students first give an oration within their state and winners compete at the national level. The oration must be related to the Constitution of the United States focusing on the duties and obligations citizens have to the government. It must be in English and be between three and five minutes. There is also an assigned topic which is posted on the website, and it should be between three and five minutes.
Target applicant(s): High school students.
Amount: $500-$18,000.
Number of awards: Varies.
Deadline: December 30.
How to apply: Application information is available online or by contacting the local post.
Exclusive: Visit www.UltimateScholarshipBook.com and enter code AM227620 for updates on this award.

(2277) • Texas Public Educational Grant

Texas Higher Education Coordinating Board
1200 East Anderson Lane, Austin, TX 78752
Phone: 512-427-6101
Email: pamela.harris@thecb.state.tx.us
http://www.collegeforalltexans.com/
Purpose: To assist Texas students who have financial need.
Eligibility: Applicants must attend a public college or university in Texas and demonstrate financial need. Individual institutions determine additional eligibility criteria. Selection is based on financial need.
Target applicant(s): High school students. College students. Graduate school students. Adult students.
Amount: Varies.

Number of awards: Varies.
Deadline: Varies.
How to apply: Application is made by completing the FAFSA and contacting your school's financial aid office.
Exclusive: Visit www.UltimateScholarshipBook.com and enter code TE227720 for updates on this award.

(2278) • Thaddeus Colson and Isabelle Saalwaechter Fitzpatrick Memorial Scholarship

Community Foundation of Louisville
Waterfront Plaza, West Tower, 325 West Main Street, Suite 1110, Louisville, KY 40202
Phone: 502-585-4649
Email: ebonyo@cflouisville.org
https://www.cflouisville.org/scholarships/
Purpose: To aid female undergraduates in Kentucky who are majoring in environment-related subjects.
Eligibility: Applicants must be female Kentucky residents who are attending a public college or university in Kentucky. They must be full-time undergraduate students who are rising sophomores, juniors or seniors and be majoring in a subject that is related to the environment (such as agriculture, horticulture, environmental engineering, biology or environmental studies). They must have a GPA of 3.0 or higher. Selection is based on the overall strength of the application.
Target applicant(s): College students. Adult students.
Minimum GPA: 3.0
Amount: Up to $4,500.
Number of awards: Varies.
Deadline: March 15.
How to apply: Applications are available online. An application form and supporting materials are required.
Exclusive: Visit www.UltimateScholarshipBook.com and enter code CO227820 for updates on this award.

(2279) • Thomara Latimer Cancer Foundation Scholarship

Thomara Latimer Cancer Foundation
Franklin Plaza Center, 29193 Northwestern Highway #528, Southfield, MI 48034
Phone: 248-557-2346
Email: info@thomlatimercares.org
http://www.thomlatimercares.org
Purpose: To aid African-American students in Michigan who are preparing for careers in medicine or a related field.
Eligibility: Applicants must be African-American students between the ages of 17 and 30, have a minimum 3.0 GPA and be Michigan residents who are enrolled at or have been accepted to an accredited postsecondary institution. They must be studying or planning to study allied health, medicine, nursing, occupational therapy, physical therapy, physician assisting or a related subject. Selection is based on the overall strength of the application.
Target applicant(s): High school students. College students. Graduate school students. Adult students.
Minimum GPA: 3.0
Amount: Varies.
Number of awards: Varies.
Deadline: December 30.
How to apply: Applications are available online. An application form, official transcript, personal essay, two recommendation letters and proof of college acceptance or enrollment are required.
Exclusive: Visit www.UltimateScholarshipBook.com and enter code TH227920 for updates on this award.

(2280) • Thomas E. Desjardins Memorial Scholarship

Institute of Transportation Engineers - New England Section
Email: rod.emery@jacobs.com
http://www.neite.org
Purpose: To aid New England civil engineering students who are interested in transportation engineering.
Eligibility: Applicants must be civil engineering undergraduates or graduate students who are enrolled at an accredited postsecondary institution in Connecticut, Maine, Massachusetts, New Hampshire, Rhode Island or Vermont. They must demonstrate an interest in transportation engineering through their coursework or extracurricular activities. Selection is based on academic merit, character and extracurricular activities.
Target applicant(s): College students. Graduate school students. Adult students.
Amount: Varies.
Number of awards: 2.
Deadline: Varies.
How to apply: Applications are available by request from the New England section of the Institute of Transportation Engineers. An application form and supporting materials are required.
Exclusive: Visit www.UltimateScholarshipBook.com and enter code IN228020 for updates on this award.

(2281) • Timmins, Kroll & Jacobsen Scholarship

Iowa Foundation for Agricultural Advancement
Winner's Circle Scholarships, c/o SGI, 30805 595th Avenue, Cambridge, IA 50046
Phone: 515-291-3941
Email: linda@slweldon.net
http://www.iowastatefair.org/participate/competition/
Purpose: To aid Iowa students who have been active in 4-H or FFA.
Eligibility: Applicants must be Iowa residents, be incoming freshmen at an Iowa college or university and have experience in 4-H and/or FFA livestock projects. They must have plans to major in animal science, agriculture or a related subject. Preference will be given to applicants from Polk County. Selection is based on the overall strength of the application.
Target applicant(s): High school students.
Amount: $3,000.
Number of awards: 1.
Deadline: May 1.
How to apply: Applications are available online. An application form and supporting materials are required.
Exclusive: Visit www.UltimateScholarshipBook.com and enter code IO228120 for updates on this award.

(2282) • Tip Top Tux Scholarship

Tip Top Tux
500 Floyd Boulevard, Sioux City, IA 51101
Email: Scholarships@tttux.com
https://www.tttuxprom.com/scholarships/
Purpose: To support Midwestern students to pursue post-secondary education.
Eligibility: Applicants must be graduating high school seniors enrolling in a college or university and be residents of Iowa, Kansas, Minnesota, Missouri, Nebraska, North Carolina or South Dakota. Students must

complete an application, provide two letters of recommendation, transcripts and an essay describing their goals.
Target applicant(s): High school students.
Amount: Up to $5,000.
Number of awards: 4.
Deadline: May 1.
How to apply: Applications are available online.
Exclusive: Visit www.UltimateScholarshipBook.com and enter code TI228220 for updates on this award.

(2283) • Tongan Cultural Society Scholarship

Hawaii Community Foundation - Scholarships
827 Fort Street Mall, Honolulu, HI 96813
Phone: 888-731-3863
Email: scholarships@hcf-hawaii.org
https://www.hawaiicommunityfoundation.org
Purpose: To support students of Tongan ancestry.
Eligibility: Applicants must attend school in Hawaii and must maintain a minimum 2.7 GPA.
Target applicant(s): High school students. College students. Graduate school students. Adult students.
Minimum GPA: 2.7
Amount: Varies.
Number of awards: Varies.
Deadline: January 31.
How to apply: To apply, register online, complete the online application and select the scholarships to which you wish to apply. In addition, mail the supporting materials: printed confirmation page from the online application, personal statement, copy of Student Aid Report (SAR) available at www.fafsa.ed.gov and official transcript.
Exclusive: Visit www.UltimateScholarshipBook.com and enter code HA228320 for updates on this award.

(2284) • TOPS Performance Award

Louisiana Office of Student Financial Assistance
605 N. Fifth Street, Baton Rouge, LA 70802
Phone: 800-259-5626 x1012
Email: custserv@la.gov
http://www.osfa.la.gov/
Purpose: To aid Louisiana student residents.
Eligibility: Applicants must be Louisiana residents, U.S. citizens, apply during their senior year in high school, use the award at a Louisiana college or university, have a minimum 3.0 GPA and have a minimum ACT score of 23 or an equivalent SAT score.
Target applicant(s): High school students.
Minimum GPA: 3.0
Amount: Tuition plus $400 stipend.
Number of awards: Varies.
Scholarship may be renewable.
Deadline: July 1.
How to apply: The application is the Free Application for Federal Student Aid (FAFSA). ACT or SAT scores must also be reported.
Exclusive: Visit www.UltimateScholarshipBook.com and enter code LO228420 for updates on this award.

(2285) • TOPS Tech Award

Louisiana Office of Student Financial Assistance
605 N. Fifth Street, Baton Rouge, LA 70802
Phone: 800-259-5626 x1012
Email: custserv@la.gov
http://www.osfa.la.gov/
Purpose: To assist Louisiana resident students.
Eligibility: Applicants must be Louisiana residents, apply during their senior year in a public high school and pursue an industry-based occupational or vocational credential in a public college or university that meets certain standards. They must also have a minimum 2.5 GPA, score at least 15 on the English and Mathematics subsections of the ACT PLAN Assessment, have at least minimum passing scores in English and Mathematics on the GEE and have prepared a five-year education and career plan.
Target applicant(s): High school students.
Minimum GPA: 2.5
Amount: Up to full tuition.
Number of awards: Varies.
Scholarship may be renewable.
Deadline: July 1.
How to apply: Applications are available online or from guidance counselors.
Exclusive: Visit www.UltimateScholarshipBook.com and enter code LO228520 for updates on this award.

(2286) • Towards EXcellence, Access and Success (TEXAS) Grant Program

Texas Higher Education Coordinating Board
1200 East Anderson Lane, Austin, TX 78752
Phone: 512-427-6101
Email: pamela.harris@thecb.state.tx.us
http://www.collegeforalltexans.com/
Purpose: To assist Texas students who have financial need.
Eligibility: Applicants must be Texas residents and high school graduates. They must demonstrate financial need by having an Expected Family Contribution (EFC) of $4,000 or less. They must be enrolled at a public, non-profit Texas college or university and cannot have earned more than 30 semester credits at the time of application submission. Those who have earned an associate's degree at a Texas two-year institution and who intend to enroll in a Texas bachelor's degree program within 12 months of graduation are also eligible. Selection is based on financial need.
Target applicant(s): High school students. College students. Adult students.
Amount: Full tuition and fees.
Number of awards: Varies.
Scholarship may be renewable.
Deadline: March 15.
How to apply: Application is made by completing the FAFSA.
Exclusive: Visit www.UltimateScholarshipBook.com and enter code TE228620 for updates on this award.

(2287) • Township Officials of Illinois Scholarship

Township Officials of Illinois
3217 Northfield Drive, Springfield, IL 62702
Phone: 217-744-2212
Email: bryantoi@toi.org
http://www.toi.org
Purpose: To promote the ideas of quality local government and civic duty and to recruit young people into the TOI.
Eligibility: Applicants must be high school seniors attending an Illinois college or university in the fall and must have a minimum 3.0 GPA.
Target applicant(s): High school students.
Minimum GPA: 3.0

Amount: $1,500.
Number of awards: 7.
Deadline: March 1.
How to apply: Applications are available online in January.
Exclusive: Visit www.UltimateScholarshipBook.com and enter code TO228720 for updates on this award.

(2288) • Treacy Foundation Scholarship

Treacy Foundation
P.O. Box 1479, Helena, MT 59624
http://www.treacyfoundation.org
Purpose: To reward starting freshman and sophomore students from the states of Montana, Idaho and North Dakota.
Eligibility: Applicants must be either a starting freshman or sophomore. Students must be residents of either Montana, Idaho or North Dakota.
Target applicant(s): High school students. College students. Adult students.
Amount: $2,000.
Number of awards: Varies.
Scholarship may be renewable.
Deadline: May 1.
How to apply: Applications are available online.
Exclusive: Visit www.UltimateScholarshipBook.com and enter code TR228820 for updates on this award.

(2289) • Tuition Aid Grant

New Jersey Higher Education Student Assistance Authority
P.O. Box 540, Trenton, NJ 08625
Phone: 800-792-8670
Email: clientservices@hesaa.org
http://www.hesaa.org
Purpose: To support New Jersey students who are unable to pay the full cost of tuition.
Eligibility: Students must be residents of New Jersey for at least 12 months prior to college enrollment, enroll in an approved New Jersey school and remain in school full-time in an undergraduate program. Applicants cannot have any previous degrees, and they cannot be enrolled in theology or divinity programs.
Target applicant(s): High school students. College students. Adult students.
Amount: Up to full tuition.
Number of awards: Varies.
Scholarship may be renewable.
Deadline: September 15.
How to apply: Applications are available through completion of the FAFSA.
Exclusive: Visit www.UltimateScholarshipBook.com and enter code NE228920 for updates on this award.

(2290) • Tuition Assistance Program (TAP)

New York State Higher Education Services Corporation (HESC)
99 Washington Avenue, Albany, NY 12255
Phone: 888-697-4372
Email: scholarships@hesc.ny.gov
http://www.hesc.ny.gov
Purpose: To assist New York resident students in attending in-state postsecondary institutions.
Eligibility: Applicants must be U.S. citizens or eligible noncitizens, be legal residents of New York State, study full-time at an eligible New York State postsecondary institution as undergraduate or graduate students, meet income eligibility requirements and maintain a "C" average in college.
Target applicant(s): High school students. College students. Graduate school students. Adult students.
Minimum GPA: 2.0
Amount: Up to $5,165.
Number of awards: Varies.
Scholarship may be renewable.
Deadline: Varies.
How to apply: Complete the Free Application for Federal Student Aid (FAFSA), include a New York school on the application and then complete the Express TAP Application.
Exclusive: Visit www.UltimateScholarshipBook.com and enter code NE229020 for updates on this award.

(2291) • Tuition Equalization Grant Program

Texas Higher Education Coordinating Board
1200 East Anderson Lane, Austin, TX 78752
Phone: 512-427-6101
Email: pamela.harris@thecb.state.tx.us
http://www.collegeforalltexans.com/
Purpose: To assist students with financial need who are attending private, non-profit colleges or universities in Texas.
Eligibility: Applicants must be Texas residents or nonresident National Merit Finalists. They must be enrolled at a private, non-profit Texas institution in a first associate's, bachelor's, master's or doctoral degree program. Applicants cannot be athletic scholarship recipients and must demonstrate financial need. Applicants must maintain at least a 2.5 GPA and must complete 24 credit hours per year. Selection is based on financial need.
Target applicant(s): High school students. College students. Graduate school students. Adult students.
Minimum GPA: 2.5
Amount: Up to $3,364.
Number of awards: Varies.
Deadline: Varies.
How to apply: Application is made by completing the FAFSA.
Exclusive: Visit www.UltimateScholarshipBook.com and enter code TE229120 for updates on this award.

(2292) • Tuition Reduction for Non-Resident Nursing Students

Maryland Higher Education Commission
Office of Student Financial Assistance, 6 North Liberty Street, Baltimore, MD 21201
Phone: 800-974-1024
Email: osfamail@mhec.state.md.us
http://www.maryland.gov
Purpose: To support non-resident nursing students who are attending college in Maryland.
Eligibility: Applicants cannot be residents of the state of Maryland, but they must be enrolled in a two-year or four-year undergraduate nursing program in Maryland. Students must agree to work full-time at a Maryland hospital after graduation, for a period of four years for full-time students and two years for part-time students.
Target applicant(s): High school students. College students. Adult students.
Amount: Varies.
Number of awards: Varies.
Scholarship may be renewable.

Deadline: Rolling.
How to apply: Applications are available online.
Exclusive: Visit www.UltimateScholarshipBook.com and enter code MA229220 for updates on this award.

(2293) · Tuition Waiver for Foster Care Recipients

Maryland Higher Education Commission
Office of Student Financial Assistance, 6 North Liberty Street, Baltimore, MD 21201
Phone: 800-974-1024
Email: osfamail@mhec.state.md.us
http://www.maryland.gov
Purpose: To assist students who have resided in foster care in attending a public college.
Eligibility: Applicants must be under age 25 and have been in an out-of-home placement when they graduated from high school or have lived in foster care on their 14th birthday and subsequently been adopted.
Target applicant(s): High school students. College students.
Amount: Up to full tuition.
Number of awards: Varies.
Scholarship may be renewable.
Deadline: March 1.
How to apply: Students may apply by filing the FAFSA and contacting the financial aid office at the institution they plan to attend.
Exclusive: Visit www.UltimateScholarshipBook.com and enter code MA229320 for updates on this award.

(2294) · Tuttle Services Inc. Tiny Rauch Scholarship

Associated General Contractors of Ohio
1755 Northwest Boulevard , Columbus, OH 43212
Phone: 614-486-6446
Email: parker@agcohio.com
https://agcohio.com/scholarships
Purpose: To support students who are residents of Ohio pursuing degrees in construction-related fields or employees of Tuttle Services Inc. or immediate family.
Eligibility: Applicants must be a U.S. citizens and undergraduate students in at least the second year of a two-year, four-year or five-year degree seeking program. The minimum GPA requirement is 2.5. Selection is based on the overall strength of the application.
Target applicant(s): College students. Adult students.
Minimum GPA: 2.5
Amount: $1,000.
Number of awards: 1.
Deadline: February 3.
How to apply: Applications are available online. An application form, official college transcripts and essay are required and must be mailed.
Exclusive: Visit www.UltimateScholarshipBook.com and enter code AS229420 for updates on this award.

(2295) · Tweet Coleman Aviation Scholarship

American Association of University Women - Honolulu Branch
1888 Kalakaua Avenue, Suite C312-359, Honolulu, HI 96815
Phone: 808-537-4702
http://honolulu-hi.aauw.net/scholarships/
Purpose: To aid females in the state of Hawaii in earning a Federal Aviation Administration (FAA) Pilot Certificate.
Eligibility: Applicants must be a female living in Hawaii (only residence is Hawaii) or stationed in Hawaii with the military. Applicants must also be a college graduate (associate degree or higher) or currently enrolled in a college or university in Hawaii. Women from out of state attending a college in Hawaii are eligible. Selection is based on the overall strength of the application.
Target applicant(s): College students. Adult students.
Amount: Varies.
Number of awards: Varies.
Deadline: April 30.
How to apply: Applications are available by online request. An application form and supporting materials are required.
Exclusive: Visit www.UltimateScholarshipBook.com and enter code AM229520 for updates on this award.

(2296) · Twenty-first Century Scholars Program

State Student Assistance Commission of Indiana
W462 Indiana Government Center South, 402 West Washington Street, Indianapolis, IN 46204
Phone: 888-528-4719
Email: grants@ssaci.state.in.us
http://www.in.gov/che/
Purpose: To support Indiana middle school students from families with low to moderate incomes.
Eligibility: Applicants must be in 7th or 8th grade at a school recognized by the Indiana Department of Education. Students must be below the maximum income requirements, be wards of the state or county or be in foster care. Scholarship funds may only be used at eligible Indiana colleges or technical schools.
Target applicant(s): Junior high students or younger.
Minimum GPA: 2.5
Amount: Up to full tuition.
Number of awards: Varies.
Scholarship may be renewable.
Deadline: Varies.
How to apply: Applications are available at Indiana middle schools.
Exclusive: Visit www.UltimateScholarshipBook.com and enter code ST229620 for updates on this award.

(2297) · Two-year or Associate Degree Program

New Hampshire Charitable Foundation
37 Pleasant Street, Concord, NH 03301-4005
Phone: 603-225-6641
Email: info@nhcf.org
https://www.nhcf.org/how-can-we-help-you/
Purpose: To support New Hampshire students who are attending a two-year or short-term training program.
Eligibility: Applicants must have completed high school or earned a GED and plan to attend a short-term training program. Students will need to submit a copy of the Student Aid Report received from submitting the FAFSA. Preference is given to those who have successfully completed prior educational work or who are entering professions in the STEM fields such as: computer science, advanced manufacturing, clinical health care, engineering, engineering technology, graphic design (CAD), etc.
Target applicant(s): College students. Adult students.
Amount: $100-$3,500.
Number of awards: Varies.
Deadline: May 15.
How to apply: Applications are available online.
Exclusive: Visit www.UltimateScholarshipBook.com and enter code NE229720 for updates on this award.

(2298) · Tyler/Grandmaison MELMAC Scholarship

MELMAC Education Foundation
188 Whitten Road, Augusta, ME 04330
Phone: 866-622-3066
Email: info@melmacfoundation.org
http://www.melmacfoundation.org
Purpose: To assist Maine students and encourage them to continue their college education beyond the first year.
Eligibility: Applicants must be Maine high school students nominated by their school's principal. They must be accepted to a college or university and demonstrate exceptional financial need. They must face challenges or obstacles in their pursuit of an education and be committed to public service.
Target applicant(s): High school students.
Amount: $1,500.
Number of awards: Varies.
Deadline: Varies.
How to apply: Applications are made on the student's behalf by his or her high school principal.
Exclusive: Visit www.UltimateScholarshipBook.com and enter code ME229820 for updates on this award.

(2299) · Unitil Scholarship Fund

Unitil
Attn.: Kristen Anderson/Scholarship Committee, 6 Liberty Lane West, Hampton, NH 03842
Phone: 603-772-0775
http://unitil.com/our-community/unitil-scholarship-fund
Purpose: To support students who live in Maine, New Hampshire or Massachusetts.
Eligibility: Applicants must attend school and reside in one of the cities or towns in Unitil service territories and must have a declared major or concentration in science, technology, math or engineering.
Target applicant(s): College students. Adult students.
Amount: $5,000.
Number of awards: 6.
Deadline: March 15.
How to apply: Applications are available online.
Exclusive: Visit www.UltimateScholarshipBook.com and enter code UN229920 for updates on this award.

(2300) · University Journalism Scholarships

Ohio News Media Foundation
1335 Dublin Road, Suite 216-B, Columbus, OH 43215
Phone: 614-486-6677
Email: ariggs@ohionews.org
https://www.ohionews.org/aws/ONA/pt/sp/foundation_scholarships
Purpose: To support students pursuing a journalism-related major at an Ohio college or university.
Eligibility: Applicants must be enrolled in an Ohio college or university and be majoring in a journalism-related field such as journalism, advertising or marketing. Students must have at least a 2.5 GPA and write an essay as part of their application showcasing their writing skill along with including work samples related to degree.
Target applicant(s): College students. Adult students.
Minimum GPA: 2.5
Amount: $2,000.
Number of awards: 2.
Deadline: March 31.
How to apply: Applications are available online.
Exclusive: Visit www.UltimateScholarshipBook.com and enter code OH230020 for updates on this award.

(2301) · University Scholarship and Research Grant

Michigan Council of Women in Technology Foundation
Attn.: Scholarship Committee, 6 Parklane Boulevard, Suite 615, Dearborn, MI 48126
Phone: 248-218-2578
Email: scholarships@mcwt.org
https://mcwt.org/University_Programs_195.html
Purpose: To support female information technology students.
Eligibility: Applicants must be high school seniors or undergraduate or graduate students who are Michigan residents and U.S. citizens with a GPA of 3.0 or higher. Students must enroll in a degree program in information systems, business applications, computer science, computer engineering, software engineering or information security.
Target applicant(s): High school students. College students. Graduate school students. Adult students.
Minimum GPA: 3.0
Amount: $5,000.
Number of awards: Varies.
Scholarship may be renewable.
Deadline: Varies.
How to apply: Applications are available online. An application form, transcript, two letters of recommendation and research project description (for research grant applicants only) are required.
Exclusive: Visit www.UltimateScholarshipBook.com and enter code MI230120 for updates on this award.

(2302) · Upper Midwest Chapter Scholarships

National Academy of Television Arts and Sciences-Upper Midwest Chapter
4967 Kensington Gate, Shorewood, MN 55331
Phone: 952-474-7126
Email: info@midwestemmys.org
http://www.midwestemmys.org
Purpose: To aid students interested in television, broadcasting and electronic media careers.
Eligibility: Applicants must be high school seniors. They must have applied or been accepted to a college or university that offers a broadcasting, television or other electronic media curriculum and intend to pursue one of these fields. A GPA of 3.0 or higher is preferred, but not required.
Target applicant(s): High school students.
Amount: Varies.
Number of awards: Varies.
Deadline: February 6.
How to apply: Applications are available online. An application form is required.
Exclusive: Visit www.UltimateScholarshipBook.com and enter code NA230220 for updates on this award.

(2303) · Urban Scholars Award

New Jersey Higher Education Student Assistance Authority
P.O. Box 540, Trenton, NJ 08625
Phone: 800-792-8670
Email: clientservices@hesaa.org
http://www.hesaa.org
Purpose: To support New Jersey high school seniors from urban or economically depressed areas.

Eligibility: Applicants must be New Jersey residents for at least 12 months prior to college enrollment, and they must enroll full-time in an approved state college. Students must show outstanding academic achievement in high school through SAT scores and transcripts. Applicants must have a minimum 3.0 GPA and be in the top five percent of their class.
Target applicant(s): High school students.
Minimum GPA: 3.0
Amount: Varies.
Number of awards: Varies.
Scholarship may be renewable.
Deadline: Varies.
How to apply: Applications are available from high school guidance counselors.
Exclusive: Visit www.UltimateScholarshipBook.com and enter code NE230320 for updates on this award.

(2304) • Utah Association of Independent Insurance Agents Scholarship

Utah Association of Independent Insurance Agents
4885 South 900 East, Suite 302, Salt Lake City, UT 84117
Phone: 801-269-1200
Email: info@uaiia.org
http://www.uaiia.org
Purpose: To aid college-bound Utah high school seniors.
Eligibility: Applicants must be Utah high school seniors. They must have a GPA of 3.0 or higher and must be active in extracurricular activities. Selection is based on the overall strength of the application.
Target applicant(s): High school students.
Minimum GPA: 3.0
Amount: Varies.
Number of awards: At least 3.
Deadline: April 1.
How to apply: Applications are available online. An application form, transcript and applicant photo are required.
Exclusive: Visit www.UltimateScholarshipBook.com and enter code UT230420 for updates on this award.

(2305) • Utah Young Humanitarian Award

Youthlinc
1166 East Brickyard Road, Salt Lake City, UT 84106
Phone: 801-467-4417
https://www.youthlinc.org/young-humanitarian-award/
Purpose: To reward outstanding humanitarian service.
Eligibility: Applicants must be U.S. citizens, legal residents or have DACA status and be either Utah high school juniors or seniors or be enrolled as a full-time undergraduate student at an accredited college or university in Utah.
Target applicant(s): High school students. College students. Adult students.
Amount: Up to $5,000.
Number of awards: 10.
Deadline: March 1.
How to apply: Applications are available online.
Exclusive: Visit www.UltimateScholarshipBook.com and enter code YO230520 for updates on this award.

(2306) • Valedictorian Program Tuition Waiver

Massachusetts Department of Higher Education
Office of Student Financial Assistance, 454 Broadway, Suite 200, Revere, MA 02151
Phone: 617-727-9420
Email: osfa@osfa.mass.edu
http://www.mass.edu/osfa/students/forstudents.asp
Purpose: To provide comprehensive financial aid to Massachusetts valedictorians.
Eligibility: Applicants must be designated as a valedictorian by a public or private high school in the state of Massachusetts, and they must be residents of the state for at least one year prior to the beginning of the school year. Students must enroll in a Massachusetts public college and meet individual requirements for the program imposed by the school. They cannot owe refunds on previous financial aid or have any defaulted government loans.
Target applicant(s): High school students.
Amount: Full tuition.
Number of awards: Varies.
Scholarship may be renewable.
Deadline: Varies.
How to apply: Applications are available at college financial aid offices.
Exclusive: Visit www.UltimateScholarshipBook.com and enter code MA230620 for updates on this award.

(2307) • VCTA Virginia's Future Leaders Scholarship Program

Virginia Cable Telecommunications Association
1001 E. Broad Street, Suite 210, Richmond, VA 23219
Phone: 804-780-1776
Email: kvoxland@vcta.com
http://www.vcta.com/virginias-future-leaders-scholarship
Purpose: To support Virginia students seeking higher education.
Eligibility: Applicants must be Virginia residents. They must be attending or plan to attend a Virginia two- or four-year undergraduate program. Financial need is required.
Target applicant(s): High school students. College students. Adult students.
Amount: Varies.
Number of awards: Varies.
Deadline: Varies.
How to apply: Applications are available online.
Exclusive: Visit www.UltimateScholarshipBook.com and enter code VI230720 for updates on this award.

(2308) • Vermont Incentive Grants

Vermont Student Assistance Corporation
Scholarships, P.O. Box 2000, Winooski, VT 05404
Phone: 888-253-4819
Email: info@vsac.org
http://www.vsac.org
Purpose: To assist Vermont students who are attending college full-time.
Eligibility: Applicants must be Vermont residents who are accepted into or enrolled in an undergraduate degree program, a certificate program, a Doctor of Veterinary Medicine degree program or a University of Vermont College of Medicine degree program. They must attend or plan to attend school full-time. Applicants who have earned a bachelor's degree previously are ineligible. Selection is based on financial need.
Target applicant(s): High school students. College students. Adult students.

Amount: Varies.
Number of awards: Varies.
Deadline: Varies.
How to apply: Applications are available online. An application form and a completed FAFSA are required.
Exclusive: Visit www.UltimateScholarshipBook.com and enter code VE230820 for updates on this award.

(2309) • Vermont Oratorical Contest

American Legion, Department of Vermont
P.O. Box 396, 126 State Street, Montpelier, VT 05601-0396
Phone: 802-223-7131
Email: alvthq@myfairpoint.net
http://www.vtlegion.org
Purpose: To enhance high school students' experience with and understanding of the U.S. Constitution. The contest will help develop students' leadership skills and civic appreciation, as well as the ability to deliver thoughtful, insightful orations regarding U.S. citizenship and its inherent responsibilities.
Eligibility: Applicants must be high school students under the age of 20 who are U.S. citizens or legal residents and residents of the state. Students first give an oration within their state and winners compete at the national level. The oration must be related to the Constitution of the United States focusing on the duties and obligations citizens have to the government. It must be in English and be between eight and ten minutes. There is also an assigned topic which is posted on the website, and it should be between three and five minutes.
Target applicant(s): High school students.
Amount: Up to $18,000.
Number of awards: Varies.
Deadline: Varies.
How to apply: Applications are available from district representatives.
Exclusive: Visit www.UltimateScholarshipBook.com and enter code AM230920 for updates on this award.

(2310) • Vermont Sheriffs' Association Scholarship

Vermont Student Assistance Corporation
Scholarships, P.O. Box 2000, Winooski, VT 05404
Phone: 888-253-4819
Email: info@vsac.org
http://www.vsac.org
Purpose: To aid Vermont residents who are studying to become police officers.
Eligibility: Applicants must be Vermont residents. They must be enrolled in a law enforcement degree program at an accredited school that has been approved for federal Title IV funding. They must have plans to become police officers. Selection is based on academic merit, essay and financial need.
Target applicant(s): College students. Adult students.
Amount: $1,000.
Number of awards: 1.
Deadline: March 3.
How to apply: Applications are available online. An application form, official transcript, personal essay and financial aid information are required.
Exclusive: Visit www.UltimateScholarshipBook.com and enter code VE231020 for updates on this award.

(2311) • Vernon T. Swain, P.E./Robert E. Chute, P.E. Scholarship

Maine Society of Professional Engineers
Colin C. Hewett, P.E., Chairman, Scholarship Committee, P.O. Box 318, Winthrop, ME 04364
Email: chewett@ahgeng.com
http://www.mespe.org
Purpose: To aid Maine students who are preparing for careers in engineering.
Eligibility: Applicants must be Maine residents who are graduating high school seniors. They must have plans to enroll in an ABETEAC-accredited degree program in engineering and to pursue a career in engineering. Applicants have to have applied to at least one school that offers engineering degrees. These are the minimum acceptable standardized test scores: SAT Math 600, SAT Writing 500, SAT Critical Reading 500, ACT Math 29, ACT English 25, PAA Quantitative 750 and PAA Verbal 640. Selection is based on standardized test scores, GPA, personal essay, recommendations, extracurricular activities and work experience.
Target applicant(s): High school students.
Amount: At least $2,500.
Number of awards: 2.
Deadline: March 1.
How to apply: Applications are available online. An application form, official transcript, personal statement, two recommendation letters and official SAT or ACT scores are required.
Exclusive: Visit www.UltimateScholarshipBook.com and enter code MA231120 for updates on this award.

(2312) • Veterans Tuition Awards

New York State Higher Education Services Corporation (HESC)
99 Washington Avenue, Albany, NY 12255
Phone: 888-697-4372
Email: scholarships@hesc.ny.gov
http://www.hesc.ny.gov
Purpose: To assist veterans in obtaining higher education.
Eligibility: Applicants must be veterans from New York State who have been honorably discharged and served in Indochina between December 22, 1961 and May 7, 1975, the Persian Gulf on or after August 2, 1990 or Afghanistan on or after September 11, 2001. Applicants must also have applied for the Tuition Assistant Program if studying full-time and the Federal Pell Grant whether studying full-time or part-time, unless enrolled in a vocational training program.
Target applicant(s): College students. Graduate school students. Adult students.
Amount: Up to full tuition.
Number of awards: Varies.
Scholarship may be renewable.
Deadline: June 30.
How to apply: Applications are available from your institution's financial aid office or by phone from HESC.
Exclusive: Visit www.UltimateScholarshipBook.com and enter code NE231220 for updates on this award.

(2313) • VHSL Allstate Achievement Award

Virginia High School League Foundation
1642 State Farm Boulevard, Charlottesville, VA 22911
Phone: 434-977-8475
Email: lotoole@vhsl.org
http://www.vhsl.org/about.scholarships

Purpose: To support students who have made outstanding achievements in sports, academics or courageousness.
Eligibility: Students must be from a Virginia high school in Group 1A through 6A. Applicants must show participation in VHSL activities and other school or community activities. They must have at least a 3.0 GPA.
Target applicant(s): High school students.
Minimum GPA: 3.0
Amount: $1,500.
Number of awards: 19.
Deadline: March 15.
How to apply: Applications are available online.
Exclusive: Visit www.UltimateScholarshipBook.com and enter code VI231320 for updates on this award.

(2314) • Victoria S. and Bradley L. Geist Foundation

Hawaii Community Foundation - Scholarships
827 Fort Street Mall, Honolulu, HI 96813
Phone: 888-731-3863
Email: scholarships@hcf-hawaii.org
https://www.hawaiicommunityfoundation.org
Purpose: To support students who have been in the Hawaii foster care system.
Eligibility: Applicants must be residents of Hawaii. Students must not have been legally adopted before the age of 18.
Target applicant(s): High school students. College students. Adult students.
Amount: Varies.
Number of awards: Varies.
Scholarship may be renewable.
Deadline: January 31.
How to apply: Applications are available online. In addition, mail the supporting materials: confirmation letter from a case worker, personal statement and official transcript.
Exclusive: Visit www.UltimateScholarshipBook.com and enter code HA231420 for updates on this award.

(2315) • Vietnam Veterans' Scholarship

New Mexico Higher Education Department
2044 Galisteo Street, Suite 4, Santa Fe, NM 87505-2100
Phone: 505-476-8400
Email: cesaria.tapia1@state.nm.us
http://www.hed.state.nm.us/students/
Purpose: To support Vietnam veterans who are attending college in New Mexico.
Eligibility: Applicants must have been honorably discharged from the armed forces, and they must have received a Vietnam campaign medal for serving in Vietnam anytime between August 5, 1964 and the official end of the war. Students must be attending either a public school or one of the following private schools in New Mexico: the College of Santa Fe, St. John's College or the College of the Southwest. They must have been New Mexico residents when entering the armed forces or have lived in the state for at least 10 years.
Target applicant(s): College students. Graduate school students. Adult students.
Amount: Full tuition.
Number of awards: Varies.
Scholarship may be renewable.
Deadline: Varies.
How to apply: Applications are available at college financial aid offices.
Exclusive: Visit www.UltimateScholarshipBook.com and enter code NE231520 for updates on this award.

(2316) • Virginia Commonwealth Award

State Council of Higher Education for Virginia
101 N. 14th Street, 10th Floor, James Monroe Building, Richmond, VA 23219
Phone: 804-225-2600
Email: communications@schev.edu
http://www.schev.edu
Purpose: To assist Virginia students.
Eligibility: Undergraduate applicants must be admitted to a Virginia public two- or four-year college or university, be enrolled at least half-time, be residents of Virginia, be U.S. citizens or eligible noncitizens and demonstrate financial need. Graduate applicants must be enrolled full-time in an eligible Virginia graduate degree program. The selection process varies by school.
Target applicant(s): High school students. College students. Graduate school students. Adult students.
Amount: Up to full tuition.
Number of awards: Varies.
Scholarship may be renewable.
Deadline: Varies.
How to apply: Application instructions are available by request from the student's financial aid office.
Exclusive: Visit www.UltimateScholarshipBook.com and enter code ST231620 for updates on this award.

(2317) • Virginia Daughters of the American Revolution Scholarships

Virginia Daughters of the American Revolution
DAR Scholarship Committee, Brenda B. Atkinson, State Chairman, 4040 Snowgoose Circle, Roanoke, VA 24018-4865
Phone: 757-479-4167
Email: gandbatkinson@cox.net
http://www.vadar.org/scholarship.html
Purpose: To support Virginia high school students in pursuing higher education.
Eligibility: Applicants must be high school seniors and U.S. citizens who are sponsored by a Virginia DAR chapter. They may pursue an undergraduate degree in any field except nursing at any Virginia college or university.
Target applicant(s): High school students.
Amount: $2,500.
Number of awards: 4.
Deadline: January 12.
How to apply: Applications are available online. An application form, letter of sponsorship, written statement, transcript, financial need form and letter of recommendation are required.
Exclusive: Visit www.UltimateScholarshipBook.com and enter code VI231720 for updates on this award.

(2318) • Virginia Guaranteed Assistance Program

State Council of Higher Education for Virginia
101 N. 14th Street, 10th Floor, James Monroe Building, Richmond, VA 23219
Phone: 804-225-2600
Email: communications@schev.edu
http://www.schev.edu
Purpose: To provide a financial incentive for economically disadvantaged students to consider attending college.
Eligibility: Applicants must have graduated from a Virginia high school with at least a 2.5 GPA, and they must be enrolled full-time in

a two-year or four-year college in the state. Students must be classified as dependents. Preference will be given to students with the greatest financial need.
Target applicant(s): High school students. College students. Adult students.
Minimum GPA: 2.5
Amount: Up to full tuition.
Number of awards: Varies.
Scholarship may be renewable.
Deadline: Varies.
How to apply: Applications are available at college financial aid offices.
Exclusive: Visit www.UltimateScholarshipBook.com and enter code ST231820 for updates on this award.

(2319) • Virginia High School League Charles E. Savedge Journalism Scholarship

Virginia High School League Foundation
1642 State Farm Boulevard, Charlottesville, VA 22911
Phone: 434-977-8475
Email: lotoole@vhsl.org
http://www.vhsl.org/about.scholarships
Purpose: To support student journalists in Virginia.
Eligibility: Applicants must be active members of a high school newspaper, yearbook or other publication. Students must be in their senior year and have plans to study journalism in college.
Target applicant(s): High school students.
Amount: $500.
Number of awards: 1.
Deadline: Varies.
How to apply: Applications are available online.
Exclusive: Visit www.UltimateScholarshipBook.com and enter code VI231920 for updates on this award.

(2320) • Virginia Part-Time Assistance Program

State Council of Higher Education for Virginia
101 N. 14th Street, 10th Floor, James Monroe Building, Richmond, VA 23219
Phone: 804-225-2600
Email: communications@schev.edu
http://www.schev.edu
Purpose: To assist part-time Virginia students who have financial need.
Eligibility: Applicants must be Virginia residents. They must attend a school in Virginia's community college system part-time (one to eight credit hours per term) and must demonstrate financial need. Selection is based on financial need.
Target applicant(s): High school students. College students. Adult students.
Amount: Up to full tuition.
Number of awards: Varies.
Deadline: Varies.
How to apply: Applications are available from the student's financial aid office. An application form and supporting materials are required.
Exclusive: Visit www.UltimateScholarshipBook.com and enter code ST232020 for updates on this award.

(2321) • Virginia Police Chiefs Foundation College Scholarship Program

Virginia Police Chiefs Foundation
880 Technology Park Drive, Suite 100, Glen Allen, VA 23059
Phone: 804-709-1094
Email: stephanie@vachiefs.org
http://www.vapolicefoundation.org/
Purpose: To support the dependent children of current police officers working in the Commonwealth of Virginia.
Eligibility: Applicants must be the dependent children of active police officers on duty in the Commonwealth of Virginia, excluding children of sheriff's deputies and federal officers. They must be working towards their first undergraduate degree and be currently accepted or enrolled as a full-time student at a college or university. Selection is based upon financial need, academic success, 500-word essay and achievements in the community.
Target applicant(s): High school students. College students. Adult students.
Amount: Varies.
Number of awards: Varies.
Deadline: April 1.
How to apply: Applications are available online. An application form, typed essay, official transcripts, college acceptance letter, SAT/ACT scores, questionnaire and photograph are required.
Exclusive: Visit www.UltimateScholarshipBook.com and enter code VI232120 for updates on this award.

(2322) • Virginia PTA Annual Citizenship Essay Project

Virginia PTA
1027 Wilmer Avenue, Richmond, VA 23227
Phone: 804-264-1234
Email: info@vapta.org
http://www.vapta.org
Purpose: To promote citizenship awareness among Virginia students.
Eligibility: Applicants must be Virginia students in kindergarten through 12th grade who are attending a school that has a PTA or PTSA chapter in good standing. They must submit an essay on a sponsor-determined topic relating to citizenship. Selection is based on essay originality, clarity and grammar.
Target applicant(s): Junior high students or younger. High school students.
Amount: $50-$250.
Number of awards: 12.
Deadline: February 1.
How to apply: Entry forms are available online. An entry form and essay are required.
Exclusive: Visit www.UltimateScholarshipBook.com and enter code VI232220 for updates on this award.

(2323) • Virginia Sheriffs' Institute Scholarship

Virginia Sheriffs' Institute
951 East Byrd Street, Suite 905, Richmond, VA 23219
Phone: 804-225-7152
Email: vsavsi@virginiasherrifs.org
http://vasheriffsinstitute.org
Purpose: To aid Virginia criminal justice students.
Eligibility: Applicants must be residents of an eligible Virginia locality. They must be accepted or enrolled at a Virginia college or university and must be majoring in or planning to major in criminal justice. Selection is based on the overall strength of the application.
Target applicant(s): High school students. College students. Adult students.
Amount: Varies.
Number of awards: Varies.
Deadline: May 1.

How to apply: Applications are available online. An application form, transcript, letter of recommendation from applicant's local sheriff, personal essay, proof of college acceptance (incoming freshmen only) and standardized test scores (incoming freshmen only) are required.
Exclusive: Visit www.UltimateScholarshipBook.com and enter code VI232320 for updates on this award.

(2324) • Virginia Tuition Assistance Grant Program

State Council of Higher Education for Virginia
101 N. 14th Street, 10th Floor, James Monroe Building, Richmond, VA 23219
Phone: 804-225-2600
Email: communications@schev.edu
http://www.schev.edu
Purpose: To assist Virginia students who are attending eligible private postsecondary institutions in Virginia.
Eligibility: Applicants must be Virginia residents and enrolled full-time as undergraduate, graduate or professional school students at an eligible private, non-profit Virginia postsecondary institution. Applicants who are enrolled in a religious or theological degree program are ineligible as are graduate students who are enrolled in a degree program that is not related to health care. Selection is based on the overall strength of the application.
Target applicant(s): High school students. College students. Graduate school students. Adult students.
Amount: $1,600-$3,200.
Number of awards: Varies.
Scholarship may be renewable.
Deadline: July 31.
How to apply: Applications are available by request from the student's college financial aid office. An application form and supporting materials are required.
Exclusive: Visit www.UltimateScholarshipBook.com and enter code ST232420 for updates on this award.

(2325) • Vocational Nurse Scholarship

Health Professions Education Foundation
400 R Street, Suite 460, Sacramento, CA 95811
Phone: 916-326-3640
Email: stran@oshpd.ca.gov
http://www.oshpd.ca.gov
Purpose: To aid California vocational nursing students.
Eligibility: Applicants must be accepted or enrolled in an accredited California vocational nurse (VN) degree program and must be enrolled full-time. They must maintain a GPA of 2.0 or higher while enrolled in the degree program and must commit to two years of practice in an underserved area of California after graduation. Selection is based on academic merit, stated career goals, community involvement, work experience and financial need.
Target applicant(s): College students. Adult students.
Minimum GPA: 2.0
Amount: Up to $4,000.
Number of awards: Varies.
Deadline: February 28.
How to apply: Applications are available online. An application form, personal statement, official transcript, two recommendation letters and financial information are required.
Exclusive: Visit www.UltimateScholarshipBook.com and enter code HE232520 for updates on this award.

(2326) • Vocational Rehabilitation Program

North Carolina Division of Vocational Rehabilitation Services
2801 Mail Service Center, Raleigh, NC 27699-2801
Phone: 888-234-6400
Email: jterrell@ncbar.org
http://www.cfnc.org
Purpose: To provide financial assistance to students with mental and physical disabilities that hinder their ability to obtain employment.
Eligibility: The program provides assistance with counseling, job placement and some support services that is not based on financial need. Need is considered for assistance with tuition and fees, transportation and books.
Target applicant(s): High school students. College students. Graduate school students. Adult students.
Amount: Varies.
Number of awards: Varies.
Deadline: Varies.
How to apply: Applications are available from your local Vocational Rehabilitation Office or by mail or phone. The website for the office is www.dhhs.state.nc.us/docs/divinfo/dvr.htm.
Exclusive: Visit www.UltimateScholarshipBook.com and enter code NO232620 for updates on this award.

(2327) • W.P. Black Scholarship Fund

Greater Kanawha Valley Foundation
1600 Huntington Square, 900 Lee Street, East, Charleston, WV 25301
Phone: 304-346-3620
Email: shoover@tgkvf.org
http://www.tgkvf.org
Purpose: To aid West Virginia students.
Eligibility: Applicants must be residents of West Virginia who are full-time students, have a minimum 2.5 GPA, have a minimum ACT score of 20, be of good moral character and demonstrate significant financial need.
Target applicant(s): High school students. College students. Adult students.
Minimum GPA: 2.5
Amount: $2,000.
Number of awards: 62.
Scholarship may be renewable.
Deadline: January 15.
How to apply: Applications are available online.
Exclusive: Visit www.UltimateScholarshipBook.com and enter code GR232720 for updates on this award.

(2328) • Wallace S. and Wilma K. Laughlin Foundation Trust Scholarships

Nebraska Funeral Directors Association
Wallace S. & Wilma K. Laughlin Foundation Trust, 521 First Street, P.O. Box 10, Milford, NE 68405
Phone: 402-761-2217
Email: staff@nefda.org
http://nefda.org/career-services/
Purpose: To aid Nebraska students of mortuary science.
Eligibility: Applicants must be residents of Nebraska and must be graduating seniors at a Nebraska high school or they must be graduates of a Nebraska high school. They must be entering or current students of mortuary science, reside in Nebraska for at least three years after

completing their mortuary science degree programs and intend to practice mortuary science. Selection is based on applicant interview.
Target applicant(s): High school students. College students. Adult students.
Amount: At least $1,000.
Number of awards: Varies.
Deadline: June 30.
How to apply: Applications are available online. An application form, transcript, recommendation letter and proof that all pre-mortuary science state requirements have been met are required.
Exclusive: Visit www.UltimateScholarshipBook.com and enter code NE232820 for updates on this award.

(2329) · Walter Schoenknecht Tourism and Travel Scholarship Grant

Connecticut Commission on Culture and Tourism
One Constitution Plaza, Second Floor, Hartford, CT 06103
Phone: 860-256-2725
Email: rosemary.bove@ct.gov
http://www.ct.gov/cct/site/default.asp
Purpose: To aid Connecticut travel, tourism and hospitality students.
Eligibility: Applicants must be Connecticut residents. They must be enrolled in a degree program in hospitality, travel or tourism at an accredited college or university. Selection is based on the overall strength of the application.
Target applicant(s): College students. Adult students.
Amount: $1,000.
Number of awards: 1.
Deadline: March 23.
How to apply: Applications are available by request from the Connecticut Commission on Culture and Tourism. An application form and supporting materials are required.
Exclusive: Visit www.UltimateScholarshipBook.com and enter code CO232920 for updates on this award.

(2330) · Warner Norcross and Judd Paralegal Assistant Studies Scholarship

Grand Rapids Community Foundation
185 Oakes Street SW, Grand Rapids, MI 49503
Phone: 616-454-1751
Email: rbishop@grfoundation.org
http://www.grfoundation.org
Purpose: To aid Michigan minority students who are preparing for careers as paralegals or legal secretaries.
Eligibility: Applicants must be Michigan residents. They must be minority students who are enrolled in a paralegal or legal secretary degree program at an accredited school. They must demonstrate financial need. Selection is based on the overall strength of the application. Applicants who are not residents of Michigan may still apply if attending a Michigan law school.
Target applicant(s): College students. Adult students.
Amount: Varies.
Number of awards: Varies.
Deadline: April 1.
How to apply: Applications are available online. An application form and supporting materials are required.
Exclusive: Visit www.UltimateScholarshipBook.com and enter code GR233020 for updates on this award.

(2331) · Washington BPW Foundation Mature Woman Educational Scholarship

Washington Business and Professional Women's Foundation
Attn: Scholarship Committee Chairman, S. Tellock, 1914 NW 87th Circle, Vancouver, WA 98665
Phone: 360-714-8901
Email: WSBPW_Foundation@bpwwa.org
http://bpwwafoundation.org/scholarships/
Purpose: To assist non-traditional female students.
Eligibility: Applicants must be female students age 30 or older who are pursuing retraining or continuing education. Students must be U.S. citizens and Washington state residents for at least two years and must be accepted into a program at an accredited Washington state institution of higher learning or enrolled in an accredited online program from a Washington state school. They must demonstrate scholastic ability and financial need.
Target applicant(s): College students. Adult students.
Amount: $500.
Number of awards: Varies.
Deadline: May 10.
How to apply: Applications are available online. An application form, essay, proof of income, financial aid and expense estimates, three letters of recommendation, transcript and proof of acceptance or enrollment are required.
Exclusive: Visit www.UltimateScholarshipBook.com and enter code WA233120 for updates on this award.

(2332) · Washington College Bound Scholarship

Washington Student Achievement Council
917 Lakeridge Way SW, Olympia, WA 98502
Phone: 360-753-7850
http://www.wsac.wa.gov/financial-aid
Purpose: To provide an incentive for students and their families who might not consider college due to financial concerns.
Eligibility: Applicants must be Washington students in the seventh or eighth grades who are eligible for free or reduced-price lunch, and they must sign a pledge to participate in the program. The student's family income must be 65 percent or less of the state's median income when he or she graduates high school, and his or her GPA must be 2.0 or higher in order to receive the scholarship.
Target applicant(s): Junior high students or younger.
Minimum GPA: 2.0
Amount: Full tuition plus fee for books.
Number of awards: Varies.
Scholarship may be renewable.
Deadline: June 30.
How to apply: Applications are available online.
Exclusive: Visit www.UltimateScholarshipBook.com and enter code WA233220 for updates on this award.

(2333) · Washington Oratorical Contest

American Legion, Department of Washington
P.O. Box 3917, Lacey, WA 98509
Phone: 360-491-4373
Email: americanismchairman@americanism-alwa.org
http://www.walegion.org
Purpose: To enhance high school students' experience with and understanding of the U.S. Constitution. The contest will help develop students' leadership skills and civic appreciation, as well as the ability

to deliver thoughtful, insightful orations regarding U.S. citizenship and its inherent responsibilities.
Eligibility: Applicants must be high school students under the age of 20 who are U.S. citizens or legal residents and residents of the state. Students first give an oration within their state and winners compete at the national level. The oration must be related to the Constitution of the United States focusing on the duties and obligations citizens have to the government. It must be in English and be between eight and ten minutes. There is also an assigned topic which is posted on the website, and it should be between three and five minutes.
Target applicant(s): High school students.
Amount: Up to $5,000.
Number of awards: Varies.
Deadline: December 15.
How to apply: Application information is available online.
Exclusive: Visit www.UltimateScholarshipBook.com and enter code AM233320 for updates on this award.

(2334) · Washington State Auto Dealers Association Scholarship Program

WSADA Scholarship Program
c/o College Planning Network, 43 Bentley Place, Port Townsend, WA 98368
Phone: 206-433-6300
Email: info@wsada.org
http://www.wsada.org/community/scholarships
Purpose: To provide financial assistance for business majors.
Eligibility: Applicants must be high school seniors enrolled in a Washington State public or private high school, or are home-schooled and reside in Washington State. Students must plan to use their scholarship within the 12 months following the award by enrolling in any public or private school, vocational institution, community college or four-year college or university.
Target applicant(s): High school students.
Amount: $2,500.
Number of awards: 5.
Deadline: April 15.
How to apply: Applications available online and must also include two letters of reference, a resume and an essay.
Exclusive: Visit www.UltimateScholarshipBook.com and enter code WS233420 for updates on this award.

(2335) · Washington State Governors' Scholarship for Foster Youth

College Success Foundation
1605 NW Sammamish Road, Suite 100, Issaquah, WA 98027
Phone: 425-416-2000
Email: info@collegesuccessfoundation.org
http://www.collegesuccessfoundation.org
Purpose: To assist Washington state youth in an open dependency court order.
Eligibility: Applicants must be high school seniors, have a minimum 2.0 GPA, have resided in Washington for at least three years prior to graduation and plan to enroll full-time in an eligible Washington public or private college or university.
Target applicant(s): High school students.
Minimum GPA: 2.0
Amount: $2,000-$4,000.
Number of awards: 40-50.
Deadline: February 28.
Exclusive: Visit www.UltimateScholarshipBook.com and enter code CO233520 for updates on this award.

(2336) · Washington State PTA Scholarship

Washington State PTA
2003 65th Avenue West, Tacoma, WA 98466-6215
Phone: 253-565-2153
Email: wapta@wastatepta.org
http://www.wastatepta.org
Purpose: To provide financial assistance to graduates of Washington public high schools.
Eligibility: Applicants must meet maximum household income requirements and be entering their freshman year of college. Academic performance and community service are also considered.
Target applicant(s): High school students.
Minimum GPA: 3.2
Amount: $1,000-$3,000.
Number of awards: 4.
Deadline: March 1.
How to apply: Applications are available online.
Exclusive: Visit www.UltimateScholarshipBook.com and enter code WA233620 for updates on this award.

(2337) · Washington Women In Need

Washington Women In Need
232 5th Avenue South, Kirkland, WA 98033
Email: programs@wwin.org
https://www.wwin.org
Purpose: To support Washington women pursuing higher education.
Eligibility: Applicants must be female Washington residents and U.S. citizens or permanent residents admitted to a Washington college or university. Students must demonstrate financial need and exhibit qualities reflective of the WWIN program.
Target applicant(s): College students. Adult students.
Amount: $5,000.
Number of awards: Varies.
Scholarship may be renewable.
Deadline: March 31.
How to apply: Applications are available online.
Exclusive: Visit www.UltimateScholarshipBook.com and enter code WA233720 for updates on this award.

(2338) · Webber Group Career Advancement Scholarship

Futurama Foundation
c/o Marilyn Ladd, Office Manager, 103 County Road, Oakland, ME 04963
Email: mvladd@colby.edu
http://bpwmefoundation.org/scholarship-program/
Purpose: To provide financial assistance for women who want to advance their careers.
Eligibility: Applicants must be female Maine residents who are age 30 or older. They must need financial assistance to improve their skills or complete education for career advancement. They must have a definite plan to use their training to improve their chances of advancement, train for a new career or to enter or reenter the job market. Applicants must be officially accepted into their course of study or program.
Target applicant(s): College students. Adult students.
Amount: $1,200.

Number of awards: 1.
Deadline: April 13.
How to apply: Applications are available from your local BPW chapter or your financial aid office.
Exclusive: Visit www.UltimateScholarshipBook.com and enter code FU233820 for updates on this award.

(2339) · West Virginia Engineering, Science and Technology Scholarship

West Virginia Higher Education Policy Commission PROMISE Scholarship
1018 Kanawha Boulevard, East, Suite 700, Charleston, WV 25301
Phone: 304-558-2101
Email: canderson@hepc.wvnet.edu
https://secure.cfwv.com/Financial_Aid_Planning/Scholarships/_default.aspx
Purpose: To assist West Virginia students interested in obtaining a degree in engineering, science or technology and committed to the pursuit of a career in West Virginia.
Eligibility: Applicants must be enrolled or accepted for enrollment at time of application. Students must agree to work full-time in an engineering, science or technology field in West Virginia for one year for each year the scholarship was received or begin an approved program of community service related to specific fields. Applicants must demonstrate financial need.
Target applicant(s): High school students. College students. Adult students.
Minimum GPA: 3.0
Amount: Varies.
Number of awards: Varies.
Scholarship may be renewable.
Deadline: Varies.
How to apply: Applications are available online.
Exclusive: Visit www.UltimateScholarshipBook.com and enter code WE233920 for updates on this award.

(2340) · West Virginia Higher Education Grant

West Virginia Higher Education Policy Commission
1018 Kanawha Boulevard, East, Suite 700, Charleston, WV 25301
Phone: 304-558-2101
Email: Jacob.Abrams@wvhepc.edu
http://www.wvhepc.edu/
Purpose: To assist West Virginia students who have financial need.
Eligibility: Applicants must be U.S. citizens or permanent residents and West Virginia residents who have lived in the state for at least 12 months before the application submission date. They must be high school graduates or GED recipients who are enrolled full-time in an undergraduate degree program at a participating postsecondary institution located in West Virginia or Pennsylvania. They must demonstrate financial need. Applicants who have earned a bachelor's degree previously are ineligible. Selection is based on financial need.
Target applicant(s): College students. Adult students.
Amount: Up to $2,700.
Number of awards: Varies.
Scholarship may be renewable.
Deadline: May 1.
How to apply: Application is made by completing the FAFSA.
Exclusive: Visit www.UltimateScholarshipBook.com and enter code WE234020 for updates on this award.

(2341) · West Virginia PROMISE Scholarship

West Virginia Higher Education Policy Commission PROMISE Scholarship
1018 Kanawha Boulevard, East, Suite 700, Charleston, WV 25301
Phone: 304-558-2101
Email: canderson@hepc.wvnet.edu
https://secure.cfwv.com/Financial_Aid_Planning/Scholarships/_default.aspx
Purpose: To assist outstanding West Virginia high school students who are planning to attend college in the state.
Eligibility: Applicants must be West Virginia residents and high school seniors or GED recipients who are planning to attend a West Virginia postsecondary institution. They must have a GPA of 3.0 or higher or a GED score of 2500 or higher. Applicants must also have a combined reading and math SAT score of 1020 or higher or a composite ACT score of 22 or higher. Selection is based on academic merit and financial need.
Target applicant(s): High school students.
Minimum GPA: 3.0
Amount: Up to $4,750.
Number of awards: Varies.
Scholarship may be renewable.
Deadline: March 1.
How to apply: Applications are available online. An application form, supporting materials and a completed FAFSA are required.
Exclusive: Visit www.UltimateScholarshipBook.com and enter code WE234120 for updates on this award.

(2342) · West Virginia PTA Scholarship

West Virginia PTA
P.O. Box 3557, Parkersburg, WV 26103-3557
Phone: 304-420-9576
http://www.westvirginiapta.org/scholarship
Purpose: To support graduating seniors of West Virginia in pursuing post-secondary education.
Eligibility: A minimum GPA of 2.0 is required. Applicants must submit official transcripts, letters of recommendation and an essay describing their educational goals. Selection is primarily based on academic achievement, extracurricular involvement and community service.
Target applicant(s): High school students.
Minimum GPA: 2.0
Amount: $500.
Number of awards: Varies.
Deadline: Varies.
How to apply: Applications are available online.
Exclusive: Visit www.UltimateScholarshipBook.com and enter code WE234220 for updates on this award.

(2343) · Willa S. Bellamy Scholarship

Government Finance Officers Association of South Carolina
Attn.: Scholarship Committee, P.O. Box 8840, Columbia, SC 29202
Phone: 803-252-7128
Email: scholarship@gfoasc.org
http://gfoasc.org/
Purpose: To aid South Carolina students who are interested in government finance careers.
Eligibility: Applicants must be South Carolina residents who are rising undergraduate sophomores, juniors or seniors at an accredited public college or university located in South Carolina. They must be majoring in accounting, finance or business administration with a concentration in accounting or finance. They must have a GPA of 3.0 or higher and

must be full-time students. Selection is based on the overall strength of the application.
Target applicant(s): College students. Adult students.
Minimum GPA: 3.0
Amount: $1,500.
Number of awards: 1.
Deadline: April 5.
How to apply: Applications are available online. An application form, transcript and one recommendation letter are required.
Exclusive: Visit www.UltimateScholarshipBook.com and enter code GO234320 for updates on this award.

(2344) • Willard H. Erwin, Jr. Scholarship

Greater Kanawha Valley Foundation
1600 Huntington Square, 900 Lee Street, East, Charleston, WV 25301
Phone: 304-346-3620
Email: shoover@tgkvf.org
http://www.tgkvf.org
Purpose: To aid West Virginia state college and university students.
Eligibility: Applicants must be undergraduate students who are enrolled at a state-run college or university located in West Virginia. They must demonstrate financial need. Preference will be given to sophomores, juniors, seniors, part-time students, full-time students and health care finance students. Selection is based on the overall strength of the application.
Target applicant(s): College students. Adult students.
Amount: $600.
Number of awards: 1.
Scholarship may be renewable.
Deadline: January 15.
How to apply: Applications are available online. An application form, transcript, one recommendation letter and income tax information are required.
Exclusive: Visit www.UltimateScholarshipBook.com and enter code GR234420 for updates on this award.

(2345) • William and Gertrude Fradkin Memorial Scholarship

Los Alamos National Laboratory Foundation
1112 Plaza del Norte, Espanola, NM 87532
Phone: 505-753-8890
Email: tony@lanlfoundation.org
http://www.lanlfoundation.org
Purpose: To support students of northern New Mexico enrolled in or attending a post-secondary institution of higher learning.
Eligibility: Applicants must be permanent residents of northern New Mexico with a minimum GPA of 3.25 and a minimum ACT score of 19 or minimum combined math and critical reading SAT score of 930. Applicants must be enrolled in or currently attending a post-secondary institution of higher learning. Selection is based upon academic success, ability to utilize critical thinking skills and leadership skills. Financial need is also considered but not a requirement for eligibility.
Target applicant(s): High school students. College students. Adult students.
Minimum GPA: 3.25
Amount: $1,000.
Number of awards: Varies.
Deadline: January 22.
How to apply: Applications are available online. An application form, transcripts, SAT and ACT scores, two letter of recommendation, a 250-word essay and wallet-size photograph are required.
Exclusive: Visit www.UltimateScholarshipBook.com and enter code LO234520 for updates on this award.

(2346) • William and Sara Jenne' Scholarship

Montana State Elks Association
Robert J. Byers, Attn: Scholarship, P.O. Box 1274, Polson, MT 59860
Phone: 406-849-5276
Email: robert058@centurytel.net
http://www.mtelks.org
Purpose: To support undergraduate students in Montana.
Eligibility: Students must have completed one year of college or technical school with at least 30 semester hours, and they must have at least a 2.0 GPA. Applicants must show financial need and good character.
Target applicant(s): College students. Adult students.
Minimum GPA: 2.0
Amount: Varies.
Number of awards: Varies.
Deadline: June 1.
How to apply: Applications are available online.
Exclusive: Visit www.UltimateScholarshipBook.com and enter code MO234620 for updates on this award.

(2347) • William D. and Jewell Brewer Scholarship

American Legion, Department of Michigan
212 N. Verlinden Avenue, Ste. A, Lansing, MI 48915
Phone: 517-371-4720 x11
Email: programs@michiganlegion.org
http://www.michiganlegion.org
Purpose: To support Michigan students who are the sons, daughters or grandchildren of veterans.
Eligibility: Applicants must be sons, daughters or grandchildren of war-time veterans, residents of Michigan, have a minimum 2.5 GPA and plan to attend a college or university. Scholarships are based on financial need, academic standing and applicants' goals. Applicants must also provide proof of a parent's military service record. They should send scholarship information to the county district committee person.
Target applicant(s): High school students. College students. Graduate school students. Adult students.
Minimum GPA: 2.5
Amount: $500.
Number of awards: Varies.
Deadline: January 9.
How to apply: Applications are available online.
Exclusive: Visit www.UltimateScholarshipBook.com and enter code AM234720 for updates on this award.

(2348) • William D. Squires Scholarship

William D. Squires Educational Foundation
P.O. Box 2940, Jupiter, FL 33468-2940
Phone: 561-741-7751
Email: info@wmdsquiresfoundation.org
http://wmdsquiresfoundation.org/
Purpose: To provide financial assistance to needy Ohio students with specific career goals.
Eligibility: Applicants must be Ohio high school seniors with demonstrated financial need who have specific career goals and are highly

motivated. They must plan to enroll in a degree, diploma or certificate program at an accredited college or university, and they must have a minimum GPA of 3.2.
Target applicant(s): High school students.
Minimum GPA: 3.2
Amount: $3,000.
Number of awards: 15.
Scholarship may be renewable.
Deadline: April 5.
How to apply: Applications are available online.
Exclusive: Visit www.UltimateScholarshipBook.com and enter code WI234820 for updates on this award.

(2349) • William G. Saletic Scholarship

Independent Colleges of Washington
600 Stewart Street, Suite 600, Seattle, WA 98101
Phone: 206-623-4494
Email: info@icwashington.org
http://www.icwashington.org/scholarships/
Purpose: To provide financial assistance to students who are studying politics or history at an independent college of Washington.
Eligibility: Applicants must be juniors or seniors who are studying or majoring in politics or history. Students attending Gonzaga University, Heritage University, Pacific Lutheran University, Saint Martin's University, Seattle Pacific University, Seattle University, University of Puget Sound, Walla Walla University, Whitman College or Whitworth University are eligible.
Target applicant(s): College students. Adult students.
Amount: Up to $1,000.
Number of awards: 1.
Deadline: March 17.
How to apply: Applications are available online or from your school's financial aid office.
Exclusive: Visit www.UltimateScholarshipBook.com and enter code IN234920 for updates on this award.

(2350) • William James and Dorothy Bading Lanquist Fund

Hawaii Community Foundation - Scholarships
827 Fort Street Mall, Honolulu, HI 96813
Phone: 888-731-3863
Email: scholarships@hcf-hawaii.org
https://www.hawaiicommunityfoundation.org
Purpose: To support students who are majoring in physical sciences and related fields.
Eligibility: Applicants must be residents of Hawaii and be able to demonstrate financial need. Applicants must attend full-time an accredited, two or four year, not-for-profit institution in the U.S. (including U.S. territories) in an undergraduate or graduate level program in Physical Sciences (excluding Biological and Social Sciences). Applicants must have a minimum 3.0 GPA.
Target applicant(s): High school students. College students. Graduate school students. Adult students.
Minimum GPA: 3.0
Amount: Varies.
Number of awards: Varies.
Deadline: January 31.
How to apply: To apply, register online, complete the online application and select the scholarships to which you wish to apply. In addition, mail the supporting materials: printed confirmation page from the online application, personal statement, copy of Student Aid Report (SAR) available at www.fafsa.ed.gov and official transcript.
Exclusive: Visit www.UltimateScholarshipBook.com and enter code HA235020 for updates on this award.

(2351) • William L. Boyd, IV, Florida Resident Access Grant

Florida Department of Education
Office of Student Financial Assistance, State Scholarship and Grant Programs, 325 West Gaines Street, Suite 1314, Tallahassee, FL 32399-0400
Phone: 888-827-2004
Email: osfa@fldoe.org
http://www.floridastudentfinancialaid.org
Purpose: Provides monetary assistance to Florida undergraduate college students enrolled at eligible, private, non-profit Florida schools.
Eligibility: Applicants must attend an eligible private, nonprofit Florida college or university, be Florida residents and not be in default on any state or federal grant, loan or scholarship. Requirements vary by institution.
Target applicant(s): High school students. College students. Adult students.
Amount: $3,000.
Number of awards: Varies.
Scholarship may be renewable.
Deadline: Varies.
How to apply: Contact your financial aid office.
Exclusive: Visit www.UltimateScholarshipBook.com and enter code FL235120 for updates on this award.

(2352) • Win Cash for Class Scholarship Program

HFMA - Connecticut Chapter
Mary G. Messina, HFMA Scholarship Committee, c/o Yale - New Haven Health System, One Church Street, Fourth Floor, New Haven, CT 06510
Phone: 203-688-8543
Email: mary.messina@ynhh.org
http://www.cthfma.org
Purpose: To aid students pursuing higher education in a healthcare or financial management subject.
Eligibility: Applicants must be matriculated students attending an accredited college or university located in Connecticut; matriculated students attending a non-Connecticut school who are also the spouse or child of an HFMA Connecticut Chapter member; matriculated students who are Connecticut residents and who commute to an accredited school that is located in an HFMA Region 1 state or matriculated students who are permanent healthcare industry employees working in the state of Connecticut. They must be studying or planning to study financial management or a healthcare subject. Selection is based on the strength of the applicant's essay.
Target applicant(s): High school students. College students. Graduate school students. Adult students.
Amount: $1,000-$4,000.
Number of awards: 2.
Deadline: September 9.
How to apply: Applications are available online. An application form, essay, references and verification of enrollment are required.
Exclusive: Visit www.UltimateScholarshipBook.com and enter code HF235220 for updates on this award.

(2353) • Winifred R. Reynolds Educational Scholarship

Denver Foundation
55 Madison, 8th Floor, Denver, CO 80206
Phone: 303-300-1790
Email: information@denverfoundation.org
http://www.denverfoundation.org/grants/page/scholarships
Purpose: To support graduate students pursuing a degree related to early childhood education.
Eligibility: Applicants must have financial need, be residents of Colorado and have a 3.5 GPA for the graduate work they have completed. Students must be pursuing a graduate degree in early childhood education, child development or an equivalent field.
Target applicant(s): College students. Graduate school students. Adult students.
Minimum GPA: 3.5
Amount: $1,500-$7,000.
Number of awards: Varies.
Scholarship may be renewable.
Deadline: April 7.
How to apply: Applications are available online.
Exclusive: Visit www.UltimateScholarshipBook.com and enter code DE235320 for updates on this award.

(2354) • Wisconsin Amusement and Music Operators Scholarships

Wisconsin Amusement and Music Operators
P.O. Box 259506, Madison, WI 53725
Phone: 800-827-8011
http://wamo.net/
Purpose: To assist students of Wisconsin technical schools.
Eligibility: Applicants must be enrolled in or accepted for a minimum of six credits or plan to attend one of the 16 Wisconsin Technical College campuses. They must be family members, employees or players of a WAMO member business. They must have a recommendation from a WAMO member.
Target applicant(s): High school students. College students. Adult students.
Amount: Varies.
Number of awards: Varies.
Deadline: Open.
How to apply: Applications are available online. Two copies of application form, a transcript and two letters of recommendation are required.
Exclusive: Visit www.UltimateScholarshipBook.com and enter code WI235420 for updates on this award.

(2355) • Wisconsin Broadcasters Association Foundation Student Scholarship Program

Wisconsin Broadcasters Association
Linda Baun, WBA Foundation , 44 E. Mifflin Street, Suite 900, Madison, WI 53703
Phone: 608-255-2600
Email: contact@wi-broadcasters.org
http://www.wi-broadcasters.org
Purpose: To assist broadcasting students.
Eligibility: Applicants must attend a public or private college or university, a broadcast or media school or Wisconsin technical college. They must major in broadcasting, communications or a related field and have completed 60 credits by the application deadline. Students must have graduated from a Wisconsin high school or be attending a Wisconsin institution of higher learning. They must plan a career in radio or television broadcasting and must not have previously won a WBA scholarship.
Target applicant(s): College students. Adult students.
Amount: $1,000-$2,000.
Number of awards: 4.
Deadline: October 14.
How to apply: Applications are available online. An application form, transcript, essay and two letters of recommendation are required.
Exclusive: Visit www.UltimateScholarshipBook.com and enter code WI235520 for updates on this award.

(2356) • Wisconsin Higher Education Grant

State of Wisconsin Higher Educational Aids Board
P.O. Box 7885, Madison, WI 53707
Phone: 608-267-2206
Email: heabmail@wisconsin.gov
http://heab.state.wi.us
Purpose: To assist Wisconsin students who have financial need.
Eligibility: Applicants must be Wisconsin residents and certificate- or degree-seeking undergraduate students with financial need who are enrolled at least part-time. They must be attending a Wisconsin technical college, tribal college or University of Wisconsin system institution. Selection is based on financial need.
Target applicant(s): High school students. College students. Adult students.
Amount: $250-$3,000.
Number of awards: Varies.
Scholarship may be renewable.
Deadline: Varies.
How to apply: Application is made by completing the FAFSA.
Exclusive: Visit www.UltimateScholarshipBook.com and enter code ST235620 for updates on this award.

(2357) • Wisconsin National Guard Tuition Grant

Wisconsin Department of Military Affairs
WIAR-G1-ED, P.O. Box 8111, Madison, WI 53708-8111
Phone: 608-242-3159
Email: karen.behling@wisconsin.gov
http://dma.wi.gov
Purpose: To help Wisconsin National Guard members with their education.
Eligibility: Applicants must be Wisconsin National Guard enlisted members and warrant officers in good standing who do not have a bachelor's degree. Recipients may use the grant at any campus of the University of Wisconsin System, a public institution of higher education under the Minnesota-Wisconsin student reciprocity agreement or an accredited institution of higher education in Wisconsin.
Target applicant(s): High school students. College students. Adult students.
Minimum GPA: 2.0
Amount: Full tuition.
Number of awards: Varies.
Scholarship may be renewable.
Deadline: 90 days after completion of course/term.
How to apply: Applications are available online and are due no later than 90 days after the end of each course or term.
Exclusive: Visit www.UltimateScholarshipBook.com and enter code WI235720 for updates on this award.

(2358) • Wisconsin Oratorical Scholarship Program

American Legion, Department of Wisconsin
2930 American Legion Drive, P.O. Box 388, Portage, WI 53901-0388
Phone: 608-745-1090
Email: info@wilegion.org
http://www.wilegion.org

Purpose: To enhance high school students' experience with and understanding of the U.S. Constitution. The contest will help develop students' leadership skills and civic appreciation, as well as the ability to deliver thoughtful, insightful orations regarding U.S. citizenship and its inherent responsibilities.

Eligibility: Applicants must be high school students under the age of 20 who are U.S. citizens or legal residents and residents of the state. Students first give an oration within their state and winners compete at the national level. The oration must be related to the Constitution of the United States focusing on the duties and obligations citizens have to the government. It must be in English and be between eight and ten minutes. There is also an assigned topic which is posted on the website, and it should be between three and five minutes.

Target applicant(s): High school students.
Amount: Up to $5,000.
Number of awards: Varies.
Deadline: Varies.
How to apply: Application information is available by contacting the local American Legion Post.
Exclusive: Visit www.UltimateScholarshipBook.com and enter code AM235820 for updates on this award.

(2359) • Wisconsin Veterans Education Reimbursement Grants

Wisconsin Department of Veterans Affairs
201 West Washington Avenue, P.O. Box 7843, Madison, WI 53707-7843
Phone: 800-947-8387
Email: WDVAWeb@dva.wisconsin.gov
http://www.dva.state.wi.us

Purpose: To support Wisconsin veterans.

Eligibility: Applicants must be Wisconsin residents and must have served in the U.S. armed forces in active duty for two consecutive years, completed their initial active service obligations, accumulated at least 90 days of active duty during wartime or have received or become qualified to receive an expeditionary or service medal. Students must have received an honorable discharge and be working toward a degree or certificate. A minimum 2.0 GPA is required. Funds are awarded upon course completion.

Target applicant(s): College students. Adult students.
Minimum GPA: 2.0
Amount: Up to full tuition.
Number of awards: Varies.
Deadline: No later than 60 days after the start of classes.
How to apply: Applications are available online. An application form is required.
Exclusive: Visit www.UltimateScholarshipBook.com and enter code WI235920 for updates on this award.

(2360) • Wisconsin Women in Government Undergraduate Scholarship

Wisconsin Women in Government Inc.
P.O. Box 2543, Madison, WI 53701
Phone: 608-848-2321
Email: info@wiscwomeningovernment.org
http://wiscwomeningovernment.org/

Purpose: To aid Wisconsin women who are planning for careers in government and public service.

Eligibility: Applicants must be female Wisconsin residents who are undergraduate students at a participating Wisconsin college or university. They must be interested in government, public service or political careers and demonstrate financial need. Selection is based on academic merit, leadership, initiative, communication skills, extracurricular activities and commitment to public service.

Target applicant(s): College students. Adult students.
Minimum GPA: 2.0
Amount: Up to $3,000.
Number of awards: Varies.
Scholarship may be renewable.
Deadline: June 1.
How to apply: Applications are available online. An application form, transcript, two recommendation letters and financial aid information are required.
Exclusive: Visit www.UltimateScholarshipBook.com and enter code WI236020 for updates on this award.

(2361) • WISE Scholarship

Anderson Sobel Cosmetic
1632 116th Avenue NE, Suite A, Bellevue, WA 98004
Email: womeninstemscholarship@gmail.com
https://www.andersonsobelcosmetic.com/wise-scholarship/

Purpose: To support women in Washington to pursue STEM education.

Eligibility: Applicants must be female Washington residents pursuing a degree in a STEM-related field at an accredited institution.

Target applicant(s): High school students. College students. Graduate school students. Adult students.
Amount: $1,500.
Number of awards: 1.
Deadline: May 5.
How to apply: Applications are available online.
Exclusive: Visit www.UltimateScholarshipBook.com and enter code AN236120 for updates on this award.

(2362) • Wood Mackenzie - BAFTX Energy Award

British American Foundation of Texas
Email: info@baftx.org
https://www.baftx.org

Purpose: To support Texas students pursuing energy-related education.

Eligibility: Applicants must be Texas residents and full-time students within the Texas education system age 18 or above with demonstrated financial need. Students must be majoring in technology, energy, finance, mining and metals or research analysis and hold an undergraduate degree with a GPA of 3.5 or higher.

Target applicant(s): Graduate school students. Adult students.
Minimum GPA: 3.5
Deadline: March 31.
How to apply: Applications are available online.
Exclusive: Visit www.UltimateScholarshipBook.com and enter code BR236220 for updates on this award.

(2363) • Workforce Shortage Student Assistance Grant Program

Maryland Higher Education Commission
Office of Student Financial Assistance, 6 North Liberty Street, Baltimore, MD 21201
Phone: 800-974-1024
Email: osfamail@mhec.state.md.us
http://www.maryland.gov

Purpose: To support students in Maryland who plan to work in jobs which are needed on a statewide or regional basis.

Eligibility: Applicants must be currently enrolled or planning to enroll in a Maryland postsecondary school. Dependent students must have parents who also live in Maryland. Eligible majors are chosen to address current state or regional needs and usually include the following: child care, human services, teaching, nursing, physical and occupational therapy and public service. Students must agree to begin working within that employment field within one year of graduation at a rate of one year for every year that the scholarship was granted.

Target applicant(s): High school students. College students. Graduate school students. Adult students.

Amount: Up to $19,000.

Number of awards: Varies.

Scholarship may be renewable.

Deadline: July 1.

How to apply: Applications are available online in January.

Exclusive: Visit www.UltimateScholarshipBook.com and enter code MA236320 for updates on this award.

(2364) • World Trade Center Memorial Scholarship

New York State Higher Education Services Corporation (HESC)
99 Washington Avenue, Albany, NY 12255
Phone: 888-697-4372
Email: scholarships@hesc.ny.gov
http://www.hesc.ny.gov

Purpose: To support the families and dependents of those who were injured or died as a result of the attacks on September 11, 2001.

Eligibility: Applicants must be full-time undergraduate students. Students must attend school in the state of New York, but they may be residents of any state or country.

Target applicant(s): College students. Adult students.

Amount: Up to full tuition plus room and board.

Number of awards: Varies.

Scholarship may be renewable.

Deadline: June 30.

How to apply: Applications are available online.

Exclusive: Visit www.UltimateScholarshipBook.com and enter code NE236420 for updates on this award.

(2365) • WTS Minnesota Chapter Scholarships

Women's Transportation Seminar (WTS) - Minnesota Chapter
University of Minnesota, 200 Center for Transportation Studies, 511 Washington Avenue SE, Minneapolis, MN 55455
Email: Lyssa.Leitner@co.washington.mn.us
http://www.wtsinternational.org/minnesota//

Purpose: To aid women who are pursuing higher education in a transportation-related subject.

Eligibility: Applicants must be women who are enrolled in an undergraduate or graduate degree program that is related to transportation. They either must be attending a school located in Minnesota, or must be North Dakota, South Dakota or Iowa students who have lived in Minnesota at some point during the past five years. They must have plans to pursue a career in the transportation field, and must have a GPA of 3.0 or higher. Selection is based on academic merit, transportation-related activities and career goals.

Target applicant(s): College students. Graduate school students. Adult students.

Minimum GPA: 3.0

Amount: $500-$2,000.

Number of awards: 3.

Deadline: October 16.

How to apply: Applications are available online. An application form, official transcript, proof of enrollment, one letter of recommendation and a personal essay are required.

Exclusive: Visit www.UltimateScholarshipBook.com and enter code WO236520 for updates on this award.

(2366) • You've Got a Friend in Pennsylvania Scholarship

American Radio Relay League Foundation
225 Main Street, Newington, CT 06111-1494
Phone: 860-594-0348
Email: foundation@arrl.org
http://www.arrl.org/scholarship-program

Purpose: To support Pennsylvania students who are involved in amateur radio.

Eligibility: Applicants must have an amateur radio license in General Class or higher and an active American Radio Relay League membership. Applicants must have an "A" or equivalent GPA.

Target applicant(s): High school students. College students. Adult students.

Minimum GPA: 3.6

Amount: $2,000.

Number of awards: 2.

Deadline: February 16.

How to apply: Applications are available online.

Exclusive: Visit www.UltimateScholarshipBook.com and enter code AM236620 for updates on this award.

(2367) • Zagunis Student Leader Scholarship

National Association for Campus Activities
13 Harbison Way, Columbia, SC 29212
Phone: 803-732-6222
Email: info@naca.org
https://www.naca.org/FOUNDATION/Pages/Scholarships.aspx

Purpose: To provide financial assistance to student leaders.

Eligibility: Applicants must be current undergraduate or graduate students who hold a significant campus leadership position, demonstrate significant leadership skills and abilities and make significant contributions through on- or off-campus volunteering. Students must attend school in Kentucky, Michigan, Ohio, West Virginia or western Pennsylvania.

Target applicant(s): College students. Graduate school students. Adult students.

Minimum GPA: 3.0

Amount: Varies.

Number of awards: Varies.

Deadline: December 31.

How to apply: Applications are available online.

Exclusive: Visit www.UltimateScholarshipBook.com and enter code NA236720 for updates on this award.

MEMBERSHIP

(2368) · 4-H Youth in Action

National 4-H Council
7100 Connecticut Avenue, Chase, MD 20815
Email: youthinaction@4-h.org
https://4-h.org/parents/4-h-youth-in-action-awards/
Purpose: To recognize leadership among 4-H members.
Eligibility: Applicants must be current or former 4-H members between the ages of 16-19 years old. Students must create a one-minute video relating to their leadership in one of the 4-H pillar areas and provide the following: several short essays, photos supporting their entry and proof of 4-H involvement.
Target applicant(s): High school students. College students.
Amount: $5,000.
Number of awards: 4.
Deadline: October 22.
How to apply: Applications are available online.
Exclusive: Visit www.UltimateScholarshipBook.com and enter code NA236820 for updates on this award.

(2369) · AAST Scholarship

American Association of State Troopers (AAST), Inc.
1949 Raymond Diehl Road, Tallahassee, FL 32308
Phone: 800-765-5456
http://www.statetroopers.org
Purpose: To support dependents of AAST trooper members.
Eligibility: Applicants must be a dependent (child by natural birth, child legally adopted, stepchild or claimed dependent on income tax) of a trooper member. Student AAST member parent must have been a member in good standing for two consecutive years prior to application deadline.
Target applicant(s): High school students. College students. Adult students.
Minimum GPA: 3.0
Amount: $500.
Number of awards: 1.
Scholarship may be renewable.
Deadline: July 31.
How to apply: Applications are available online.
Exclusive: Visit www.UltimateScholarshipBook.com and enter code AM236920 for updates on this award.

(2370) · AFL-CIO Skilled Trades Exploring Scholarship

Explorers Learning for Life
1325 West Walnut Hill Lane, P.O. Box 152225, Irving, TX 75015-2225
Phone: 855-806-9992
Email: exploring@lflmail.org
http://www.exploring.org/scholarships/
Purpose: To assist explorers in obtaining an education that will help them start a career in skilled trades.
Eligibility: Applicants must be graduating seniors who plan to attend an accredited public or proprietary institution or a union apprentice program. They must provide three recommendations and a 500-word essay.
Target applicant(s): High school students.
Amount: $1,000.
Number of awards: 2.
Deadline: April 30.
How to apply: Applications are available online.
Exclusive: Visit www.UltimateScholarshipBook.com and enter code EX237020 for updates on this award.

(2371) · AFSA Financial Aid Scholarships

American Foreign Service Association (AFSA)
2101 East Street NW, Washington, DC 20037
Phone: 202-944-5504
Email: dec@afsa.org
http://www.afsa.org
Purpose: To provide financial aid to university students who are the children or dependents of Foreign Service employees.
Eligibility: Applicants must be dependents of U.S. government Foreign Service employees with a minimum 2.0 GPA. Students must attend or plan to attend full-time an undergraduate U.S. college, university, community college, art school, conservatory or other post-secondary institution. Applicants must submit applications, transcripts and financial need reports. Recipients must complete their undergraduate degree within four years and must demonstrate financial need.
Target applicant(s): High school students. College students. Adult students.
Minimum GPA: 2.0
Amount: $3,000-$5,000.
Number of awards: Varies.
Scholarship may be renewable.
Deadline: March 6.
How to apply: Applications are available after November 1.
Exclusive: Visit www.UltimateScholarshipBook.com and enter code AM237120 for updates on this award.

(2372) · AFSA/AAFSW Merit Awards

American Foreign Service Association (AFSA)
2101 East Street NW, Washington, DC 20037
Phone: 202-944-5504
Email: dec@afsa.org
http://www.afsa.org
Purpose: To recognize the academic and artistic achievements of high school seniors who are the children or dependents of Foreign Service employees.
Eligibility: Applicants must be dependents of U.S. government Foreign Service employees who are members of AFSA or AAFSW. Students must be high school seniors with a minimum 2.0 GPA. Applicants can also submit an art entry under the categories of visual arts, musical arts, drama, dance or creative writing. Awards are based on GPA, SAT scores, a two-page essay, letters of recommendation and extra-curricular activities.
Target applicant(s): High school students.
Minimum GPA: 2.0
Amount: $500-$2,500.
Number of awards: Varies.
Deadline: February 6.
How to apply: Applications are available online after November 1.
Exclusive: Visit www.UltimateScholarshipBook.com and enter code AM237220 for updates on this award.

(2373) • AFSCME Family Scholarship

American Federation of State, County and Municipal Employees (AFSCME), AFL-CIO
Attn: Education Department, 1625 L Street NW, Washington, DC 20036-5687
Phone: 202-429-5080
Email: education@afscme.org
https://www.afscme.org/members/scholarships
Purpose: To offer financial assistance to the dependents of AFSCME members.
Eligibility: Applicants must be graduating high school seniors who are the daughters, sons or financially dependent grandchildren of AFSCME members who intend to enroll in a full-time, four-year degree program in any accredited college or university. Applicants should submit applications, essays, transcripts, test scores and recommendation letters. Selection is based on information provided on the application form, high school transcript, SAT/ACT scores and a required essay.
Target applicant(s): High school students.
Amount: $2,000.
Number of awards: 10.
Scholarship may be renewable.
Deadline: December 31.
How to apply: Applications are available online and by written request.
Exclusive: Visit www.UltimateScholarshipBook.com and enter code AM237320 for updates on this award.

(2374) • AGCO Corporation FFA Scholarship

National FFA Organization
P.O. Box 68960, 6060 FFA Drive, Indianapolis, IN 46268-0960
Phone: 888-332-2668
Email: scholarships@ffa.org
https://www.ffa.org/participate/scholarships
Purpose: To support students in select majors who are in the FFA.
Eligibility: Applicants must be current FFA members and high school seniors or college students planning to enroll or currently enrolled full-time. They must have one of the following undergraduate majors: agronomy, crop science, general agriculture, agricultural communications, education, journalism, extension, public relations, business management, economics, sales and marketing, engineering, mechanization, agriculture power and equipment or welding. Students only need to complete the online application one time to be considered for all FFA-administered scholarships. The application requires information about the student's activities and a 1,000-word essay. Awards may be used for books, supplies, tuition, fees and room and board. Students must show financial need and evidence of community service participation.
Target applicant(s): High school students. College students.
Amount: $2,000.
Number of awards: 12.
Deadline: February 1.
How to apply: Applications are available online.
Exclusive: Visit www.UltimateScholarshipBook.com and enter code NA237420 for updates on this award.

(2375) • Allan Jerome Burry Scholarship

United Methodist Church
Office of Loans and Scholarships, P.O. Box 340007, Nashville, TN 37203-0007
Phone: 615-340-7342
Email: umscholar@gbhem.org
http://www.gbhem.org/loans-and-scholarships
Purpose: To support students in ministry or chaplaincy programs who are members of the United Methodist Church.
Eligibility: Applicants must be college undergraduates who show evidence of financial need, leadership qualities, academic excellence and church participation. They must have a GPA of 3.0 or higher. Students must have been active members of the United Methodist Church for at least three years and be nominated by the campus chaplain or minister.
Target applicant(s): College students. Adult students.
Minimum GPA: 3.0
Amount: $1,000.
Number of awards: Varies.
Deadline: March 7.
How to apply: Applications are available from campus ministers or chaplains.
Exclusive: Visit www.UltimateScholarshipBook.com and enter code UN237520 for updates on this award.

(2376) • ALPA Scholarship Program

Air Line Pilots Association
1625 Massachusetts Avenue NW, Suite 800, Washington, DC 20036
Phone: 703-689-2270
Email: Yvonne.Willits@alpa.org
http://www.alpa.org
Purpose: To support the children of medically retired, long-term disabled or deceased pilot members of the Air Line Pilots Association.
Eligibility: Applicants must be pursuing a baccalaureate degree. Selection is based on academic achievements and financial need. The award is renewable for four years with a minimum 3.0 GPA.
Target applicant(s): High school students. College students. Adult students.
Minimum GPA: 3.0
Amount: $12,000.
Number of awards: 1.
Scholarship may be renewable.
Deadline: April 1.
How to apply: Applications are available by mail.
Exclusive: Visit www.UltimateScholarshipBook.com and enter code AI237620 for updates on this award.

(2377) • American Legion Eagle Scout of the Year

American Legion
Attn.: Americanism and Children and Youth Division, P.O. Box 1055, Indianapolis, IN 46206
Phone: 317-630-1249
Email: acy@legion.org
http://www.legion.org
Purpose: To provide scholarships for Eagle Scouts.
Eligibility: Applicants must have received the Eagle Scout Award, be active members of their religious institutions, have received the appropriate Boy Scouts religious emblem, demonstrate citizenship, be at least 15 years old and be high school students. Nominations are due March 1.
Target applicant(s): High school students.
Amount: $2,500-$10,000.
Number of awards: 4.
Deadline: March 1.
How to apply: Applications are available online.
Exclusive: Visit www.UltimateScholarshipBook.com and enter code AM237720 for updates on this award.

(2378) • American Veterinary Medical Association FFA Scholarship

National FFA Organization
P.O. Box 68960, 6060 FFA Drive, Indianapolis, IN 46268-0960
Phone: 888-332-2668
Email: scholarships@ffa.org
https://www.ffa.org/participate/scholarships

Purpose: To support students who are pursuing degrees related to animal science.

Eligibility: Applicants must be current FFA members and high school seniors or college students planning to enroll or currently enrolled full-time. They must be pursuing a four-year degree in one of the following subject areas: animal nutrition; animal, dairy, equine or poultry science; animal breeding and genetics; animal pathology or veterinary sciences. Preference will be given to students who are planning to work in the fields of veterinary medicine and veterinary food supply. Students only need to complete the online application one time to be considered for all FFA-administered scholarships. The application requires information about the student's activities and a 1,000-word essay. Awards may be used for books, supplies, tuition, fees and room and board.

Target applicant(s): High school students. College students.
Amount: $1,000.
Number of awards: 3.
Deadline: February 1.
How to apply: Applications are available online.
Exclusive: Visit www.UltimateScholarshipBook.com and enter code NA237820 for updates on this award.

(2379) • AMVETS National Ladies Auxiliary Scholarship

AMVETS National Ladies Auxiliary Headquarters
Attn: Scholarship Officer, 4647 Forbes Boulevard, Lanham, MD 20706
Phone: 301-459-6255
http://www.amvetsaux.org/scholarships.html

Purpose: To promote educational opportunities for students interested in or involved with a national service organization.

Eligibility: Applicants must be a current member of or the child or grandchild of a current member of the AMVETS Ladies Auxiliary. Students must be at least sophomores at an accredited college or university.

Target applicant(s): College students. Adult students.
Amount: $750-$1,000.
Number of awards: 7.
Deadline: July 1.
How to apply: Applications are available by mail.
Exclusive: Visit www.UltimateScholarshipBook.com and enter code AM237920 for updates on this award.

(2380) • ARA Scholarship

ARA Scholarship Foundation Inc.
ARA Scholarship Advisor, 109 Defiant Way, Grass Valley, CA 95945
Phone: 703-385-1001
Email: arascholar@sbcglobal.net
http://www.a-r-a.org

Purpose: To support the children of Automotive Recyclers Association (ARA) members.

Eligibility: Applicants must be high school seniors and/or planning to attend college full-time and have earned a minimum 3.0 GPA in their last educational program. Applicants must also be the children of employees of a Direct Member of ARA who were hired at least one year prior to March 15 of the application year. Scholarships are based on academic merit, not financial need.

Target applicant(s): High school students. College students. Graduate school students. Adult students.
Minimum GPA: 3.0
Amount: Varies.
Number of awards: Varies.
Scholarship may be renewable.
Deadline: March 15.
How to apply: Applications are available online and by email request.
Exclusive: Visit www.UltimateScholarshipBook.com and enter code AR238020 for updates on this award.

(2381) • Archer Daniels Midland Company FFA Scholarship

National FFA Organization
P.O. Box 68960, 6060 FFA Drive, Indianapolis, IN 46268-0960
Phone: 888-332-2668
Email: scholarships@ffa.org
https://www.ffa.org/participate/scholarships

Purpose: To support students who are majoring in agriculture.

Eligibility: Applicants must be current FFA members and high school seniors or college students planning to enroll or currently enrolled full-time in an agriculture program. They must have at least a 3.0 GPA and a history of leadership and community service. Students only need to complete the online application one time to be considered for all FFA-administered scholarships. The application requires information about the student's activities and a 1,000-word essay. Awards may be used for books, supplies, tuition, fees and room and board.

Target applicant(s): High school students. College students.
Minimum GPA: 3.0
Amount: $1,000.
Number of awards: 80.
Deadline: February 1.
How to apply: Applications are available online.
Exclusive: Visit www.UltimateScholarshipBook.com and enter code NA238120 for updates on this award.

(2382) • Arthur M. and Berdena King Eagle Scout Scholarship

National Society, Sons of the American Revolution
1000 South Fourth Street, Louisville, KY 40203
Phone: 502-589-1776
Email: sdelong1@san.rr.com
http://www.sar.org

Purpose: To reward exceptional students who have reached the status of Eagle Scout.

Eligibility: Applicants must have reached Eagle Scout status, must currently be registered in an active unit and can't have reached their 19th birthday during the year of application. Applicants can apply multiple years as long as they are under the age limit, but the maximum award amount is $8,000. Applicants usually apply at the chapter level. Applicants will be required to submit an essay and four-generation ancestor chart with their application.

Target applicant(s): Junior high students or younger. High school students.
Amount: $2,000-$8,000.
Number of awards: 3.
Deadline: December 31.

How to apply: Applications are available online.
Exclusive: Visit www.UltimateScholarshipBook.com and enter code NA238220 for updates on this award.

(2383) • Ashby B. Carter Memorial Scholarship

National Alliance of Postal and Federal Employees (NAPFE)
1628 11th Street NW, Washington, DC 20001
Phone: 202-939-6325
Email: headquarters@napfe.org
http://www.napfe.com
Purpose: To aid the dependents of National Alliance members in furthering their education.
Eligibility: Applicants must be dependents of members of the National Alliance of Postal and Federal Employees who have been in good standing for at least three years. Applicants must take the Aptitude Test of the College Board Entrance Examination at their local high school before March 1 and be high school seniors.
Target applicant(s): High school students.
Amount: $2,000-$5,000.
Number of awards: 3.
Deadline: May 30.
How to apply: Applications are available online.
Exclusive: Visit www.UltimateScholarshipBook.com and enter code NA238320 for updates on this award.

(2384) • Association of Flight Attendants Annual Scholarship

Association of Flight Attendants
501 Third Street NW, Washington, DC 20001
Phone: 202-434-1300
Email: info@afacwa.org
http://www.afacwa.org/
Purpose: To provide financial assistance to the children of members of the AFA.
Eligibility: Applicants must be the dependents of AFA members in good standing. Applicants must also be in the top 15 percent of their class, have or expect to have excellent SAT/ACT scores, demonstrate financial need and provide a 300-word essay along with the completed application.
Target applicant(s): High school students.
Amount: Up to $5,000.
Number of awards: 1.
Scholarship may be renewable.
Deadline: April 10.
How to apply: Applications are available online.
Exclusive: Visit www.UltimateScholarshipBook.com and enter code AS238420 for updates on this award.

(2385) • Assured Life Association National Scholarship

Assured Life Association
Scholarship Committee, P.O. Box 3169, Englewood, CO 80155
Phone: 800-777-9777 x 3773
Email: scholarship@assuredlife.org
http://assuredlife.org
Purpose: To support students seeking a college education.
Eligibility: Applicants must be certificate holders or children or grandchildren of certificate holders of Assured Life Association of Greenwood Village, Colorado. Students must be seniors in high school, undergraduates or graduates students taking at least 12 credit hours. Applicants are required to submit a 250- to 500-word essay on the given topic.
Target applicant(s): High school students. College students. Graduate school students. Adult students.
Amount: $500-$2,500.
Number of awards: 60-70.
Deadline: March 15.
How to apply: Applications are available online and must include an official transcript, a current list of extracurricular activities, a recent photo of the applicant and the certificate information of the certificate holder.
Exclusive: Visit www.UltimateScholarshipBook.com and enter code AS238520 for updates on this award.

(2386) • Avon Scholarship Program for Representatives

Avon Foundation for Women
777 Third Avenue, New York, NY 10017
Phone: 866-505-2866
Email: info@avonfoundation.org
http://www.avonfoundation.org
Purpose: To aid Avon representatives who wish to pursue higher education.
Eligibility: Applicants must be U.S. residents who are age 18 or older. They must be Avon representatives in good standing who are enrolled in or who plan to enroll in an accredited U.S. undergraduate or graduate degree program with the aim of furthering their careers. Selection is based on academic merit, extracurricular activities, work experience and stated career goals.
Target applicant(s): High school students. College students. Graduate school students. Adult students.
Amount: $2,000-$4,000.
Number of awards: Varies.
Deadline: February 29.
How to apply: Applications are available online. An application form, statement of goals and transcript are required.
Exclusive: Visit www.UltimateScholarshipBook.com and enter code AV238620 for updates on this award.

(2387) • BCTGM International Scholarship Program

BCTGM International Union
Scholarship Program, 10401 Connecticut Avenue, Kensington, MD 20895-3961
Phone: 301-933-8600
http://www.bctgm.org
Purpose: To provide scholarships for the members and families of members of BTGCM.
Eligibility: Applicants must be members of the BCTGM in good standing or the children of such members. The scholarships are also open to office employees and children of those employed at the International Union office. Applicants must be high school students who will be attending an accredited college, technical college or vocational school for the first time, high school graduates who have never attended college or BCTGM members who have never applied to the program before who are currently enrolled or planning to begin or resume their studies in the fall. All applicants are required to take the SAT or an equivalent, such as the ACT.
Target applicant(s): High school students. College students. Graduate school students. Adult students.
Amount: $2,000.
Number of awards: 5.
Deadline: January 31.
How to apply: Applications are available through your local BCTGM union office.

Exclusive: Visit www.UltimateScholarshipBook.com and enter code BC238720 for updates on this award.

(2388) • Bernard Rotberg Memorial Scholarship Fund

Jewish War Veterans of the USA
1811 R Street NW, Washington, DC 20009
Phone: 202-265-6280
Email: jwv@jwv.org
http://www.jwv.org
Purpose: To provide scholarships for descendants of members of the Jewish War Veterans of the USA.
Eligibility: Applicants must be a direct descendant of a JWV member in good standing. Candidates must also have been accepted to an accredited college, university or nursing school, be in the upper 25 percent of their class and be active in activities at school and within the Jewish community.
Target applicant(s): High school students.
Amount: $1,000.
Number of awards: 1.
Deadline: May 1.
How to apply: Applications are available online and should be submitted by the applicant's school to the department commander in the local post.
Exclusive: Visit www.UltimateScholarshipBook.com and enter code JE238820 for updates on this award.

(2389) • Berrien Fragos Thorn Arts Scholarships for Migrant Farmworkers

Geneseo Migrant Center
3 Mt. Morris-Leicester Road, Leicester, NY 14481
Phone: 800-245-5681
Email: info@migrant.net
http://www.migrant.net
Purpose: To foster and encourage the creative talents of students with migrant histories.
Eligibility: Applicants must be at least 16 years old and must have a history of movement to obtain agricultural work. Applicants need not be enrolled in school at the time of application.
Target applicant(s): High school students. College students. Adult students.
Amount: $500-$2,500.
Number of awards: Varies.
Deadline: June 1 and November 1.
How to apply: Applications are available online.
Exclusive: Visit www.UltimateScholarshipBook.com and enter code GE238920 for updates on this award.

(2390) • Board of Director's Award

National Society of Collegiate Scholars (NSCS)
2000 M Street NW, Suite 600, Washington, DC 20036
Phone: 202-265-9000
Email: nscs@nscs.org
http://www.nscs.org/
Purpose: To help NSCS members attain their goals and to recognize their achievements in academics, service and leadership.
Eligibility: Applicants must be college undergraduates who show great enthusiasm, involvement and support for NSCS. Selection is based on the overall strength of the application.
Target applicant(s): College students. Adult students.
Amount: Varies.
Number of awards: Varies.
Deadline: March 16.
How to apply: Applications are available online.
Exclusive: Visit www.UltimateScholarshipBook.com and enter code NA239020 for updates on this award.

(2391) • Boys and Girls Clubs of America National Youth of the Year Award

Boys and Girls Clubs of America
1275 Peachtree Street NE, Atlanta, GA 30309
Phone: 404-487-5700
Email: info@bgca.org
http://www.youthoftheyear.org/
Purpose: To reward club members who demonstrate good academic performance, perform services for both their club and community and who are active in both family and spiritual life.
Eligibility: Applicants must be a member of a BGCA and be selected by their local club to compete for the regional and national scholarships.
Target applicant(s): High school students.
Amount: $5,000-$25,000.
Number of awards: Varies.
Deadline: Varies.
How to apply: Contact your local club for more information.
Exclusive: Visit www.UltimateScholarshipBook.com and enter code BO239120 for updates on this award.

(2392) • Bruce Van Ess Scholarship

International Union of Electronic, Electrical, Salaried, Machine and Furniture Workers-Communications Workers of America
2701 Dryden Road, Dayton, OH 45439
Phone: 937-298-9984
https://www.iue-cwa.org/
Purpose: To support IUE-CWA members and their families.
Eligibility: Applicants must be IUE-CWA members, employees of IUE-CWA or have a parent or grandparent who is employed by IUE-CWA. Students must already be accepted for admission or must be attending an accredited college, university, nursing or technical school as a full-time student.
Target applicant(s): High school students. College students. Adult students.
Amount: $2,500.
Number of awards: 1.
Deadline: March 31.
How to apply: Applications are available online.
Exclusive: Visit www.UltimateScholarshipBook.com and enter code IN239220 for updates on this award.

(2393) • Camp Counselor Appreciation Scholarship

Camp Network
1033 Demonbreun Street #303, Nashville, TN 37203
Email: areed@campnetwork.com
http://blog.campnetwork.com/home/scholarship-program
Purpose: To reward camp counselors who display humility, passion, unity, servanthood and thankfulness.
Eligibility: Applicants must be rising college freshmen and U.S. citizens. Selection is based on humility, passion, unity, servanthood and thankfulness. Applicants must create a short video (3-5 minutes) that explains your experience as a camp counselor, how you exhibit the five qualities and your academic goals.
Target applicant(s): High school students.
Minimum GPA: 3.0

Amount: $1,000.
Number of awards: 3.
Deadline: November 1.
How to apply: To apply, email your full name, school year, name of college you plan to or are already attending and a link to your video.
Exclusive: Visit www.UltimateScholarshipBook.com and enter code CA239320 for updates on this award.

(2394) • Carroll C. Hall Memorial Scholarship

Tau Kappa Epsilon Educational Foundation
7439 Woodland Drive, Suite 100, Indianapolis, IN 46278
Phone: 317-872-6533
Email: tkeogc@tke.org
http://www.tke.org/foundation/scholarships
Purpose: To reward a member of Tau Kappa Epsilon for outstanding academic achievement and for leadership within the organization, campus or community.
Eligibility: Applicants must have a minimum 3.0 GPA and be undergraduates seeking a degree in education or science with the intention of pursuing a career in teaching or the sciences.
Target applicant(s): High school students. College students. Adult students.
Minimum GPA: 3.0
Amount: $400.
Number of awards: 1.
Deadline: March 15.
How to apply: Applications are available online.
Exclusive: Visit www.UltimateScholarshipBook.com and enter code TA239420 for updates on this award.

(2395) • Catholic United Financial College Tuition Scholarship

Catholic United Financial
Scholarship Program, 3499 Lexington Avenue North, St. Paul, MN 55126
Phone: 800-568-6670
Email: engage@catholicunited.org
http://www.catholicunitedfinancial.org
Purpose: To reward members of the Catholic United Financial.
Eligibility: Applicants must be members of the Catholic United Financial for at least two years prior to the date of application, have completed high school and be entering their first or second year in any accredited college, university, state college or technical college other than a private, non-Catholic college/university. Those attending a Catholic college are eligible for a $300 award and those attending a non-Catholic college are eligible for a $500 award.
Target applicant(s): High school students. College students. Adult students.
Amount: $300-$500.
Number of awards: Varies.
Deadline: April 30.
How to apply: Applications are available online.
Exclusive: Visit www.UltimateScholarshipBook.com and enter code CA239520 for updates on this award.

(2396) • Chairman's Award

National Association of Blacks in Criminal Justice
1801 Fayetteville Street, 106 Whiting Criminal Justice Building, P.O. Box 20011-C, Durham, NC 27707
Phone: 919-683-1801
Email: Office@NABCJ.org
http://www.nabcj.org
Purpose: To support an individual who has shown leadership, dedication and made contributions to NABCJ at the chapter or regional level.
Eligibility: Applicants must be nominated by a member of NABCJ.
Target applicant(s): College students. Adult students.
Amount: Varies.
Number of awards: 1.
Deadline: March 15.
How to apply: Nomination applications are available online.
Exclusive: Visit www.UltimateScholarshipBook.com and enter code NA239620 for updates on this award.

(2397) • Champions for Christ Scholarship

Champions for Christ Foundation
P.O. Box 786, Greenville, SC
Phone: 864-294-0800
http://championsforchrist.us/
Purpose: To support students going into full-time Christian ministry.
Eligibility: Applicants must be enrolled at a U.S. educational institution. Selection is based on the overall strength of the application.
Target applicant(s): College students. Adult students.
Amount: Varies.
Number of awards: Varies.
Deadline: November 1.
How to apply: Applications are available online.
Exclusive: Visit www.UltimateScholarshipBook.com and enter code CH239720 for updates on this award.

(2398) • Charles R. Walgreen Jr. Leadership Award

Tau Kappa Epsilon Educational Foundation
7439 Woodland Drive, Suite 100, Indianapolis, IN 46278
Phone: 317-872-6533
Email: tkeogc@tke.org
http://www.tke.org/foundation/scholarships
Purpose: To honor Charles R. Walgreen's support of Tau Kappa Epsilon by recognizing academic achievement in members.
Eligibility: Applicants must be initiated Tau Kappa Epsilon members in good standing and full-time students. They must have a GPA of at least 3.0 and demonstrate leadership in their chapter, campus and community. Applicants must also include a statement describing how they have benefited from TKE membership.
Target applicant(s): High school students. College students. Adult students.
Minimum GPA: 3.0
Amount: $1,400.
Number of awards: 1.
Deadline: March 15.
How to apply: Applications are available online.
Exclusive: Visit www.UltimateScholarshipBook.com and enter code TA239820 for updates on this award.

(2399) • Charlie Logan Scholarship Program for Dependents

Seafarers International Union of North America
Seafarers Health and Benefits Plan, Scholarship Program, 5201 Auth Way, Camp Springs, MD 20746
Phone: 301-899-0675
http://www.seafarers.org

Purpose: To offer scholarships to the dependents of members of the SIU.
Eligibility: Applicants must be the dependent children or spouses of members of the Seafarers International Union. The union member must be eligible for the Seafarer's Plan and must have credit for three years with an employer who is obligated to make a contribution to the Seafarer's Plan on behalf of the employee. Recipients may attend any U.S. accredited institution. Selection is based upon review of secondary school records, SAT or ACT test scores, college transcripts, if any, character references, extracurricular activities and autobiography.
Target applicant(s): High school students. College students. Adult students.
Amount: $20,000.
Number of awards: 5.
Scholarship may be renewable.
Deadline: April 15.
How to apply: Applications are available by written request.
Exclusive: Visit www.UltimateScholarshipBook.com and enter code SE239920 for updates on this award.

(2400) · Chi Epsilon Scholarship

Chi Epsilon
c/o Dr. Robert L. Henry, University of Texas at Arlington, Box 19316, Arlington, TX 76019
Phone: 817-272-2752
http://www.chi-epsilon.org
Purpose: To reward undergraduate students who are members of Chi Epsilon.
Eligibility: Applicants must be members of the Chi Epsilon, Civil Engineering Honor Society.
Target applicant(s): College students. Adult students.
Amount: $2,000-$3,500.
Number of awards: Varies.
Deadline: October 15.
How to apply: Applications are available online.
Exclusive: Visit www.UltimateScholarshipBook.com and enter code CH240020 for updates on this award.

(2401) · Christina Madrigal Memorial Scholarship Fund

Shasta Head Start Child Development, Inc.
375 Lake Boulevard, Suite 100, Redding, CA 96003
http://www.shastaheadstart.org
Purpose: To support students who were members of Head Start and are now pursuing a higher education.
Eligibility: Applicants must have been members of a Head Start program who are now high school seniors enrolling in post-secondary institutions. Students must have a 3.0 GPA and have shown an interest in the welfare of the children and families in their community.
Target applicant(s): High school students.
Minimum GPA: 3.0
Amount: $1,000.
Number of awards: 1.
Deadline: April 17.
How to apply: Applications are available online.
Exclusive: Visit www.UltimateScholarshipBook.com and enter code SH240120 for updates on this award.

(2402) · Church and Dwight Company Inc. FFA Scholarship

National FFA Organization
P.O. Box 68960, 6060 FFA Drive, Indianapolis, IN 46268-0960
Phone: 888-332-2668
Email: scholarships@ffa.org
https://www.ffa.org/participate/scholarships
Purpose: To support FFA members who are pursuing degrees related to agricultural science or business.
Eligibility: Applicants must be current FFA members and high school seniors or college students planning to enroll or currently enrolled full-time. They must be majoring in one of the following areas: animal nutrition, animal or dairy science, agricultural business management, finance, sales and marketing or agricultural engineering. Students must have at least a 3.0 GPA. Preference will be given to applicants who show strong leadership skills and an interest in pursuing a dairy-related career. Students only need to complete the online application one time to be considered for all FFA-administered scholarships. The application requires information about the student's activities and a 1,000-word essay. Awards may be used for books, supplies, tuition, fees and room and board.
Target applicant(s): High school students. College students.
Minimum GPA: 3.0
Amount: $1,000.
Number of awards: 2.
Deadline: February 1.
How to apply: Applications are available online. The required signature page must be submitted by mail by February 22.
Exclusive: Visit www.UltimateScholarshipBook.com and enter code NA240220 for updates on this award.

(2403) · Community College Transition Award

National Society of Collegiate Scholars (NSCS)
2000 M Street NW, Suite 600, Washington, DC 20036
Phone: 202-265-9000
Email: nscs@nscs.org
http://www.nscs.org/
Purpose: To aid NSCS members in attaining their goals and to recognize their achievements in academics, leadership and service.
Eligibility: Applicants must be outstanding community college students transferring to a four-year college. Selection is based on the overall strength of the application.
Target applicant(s): College students. Adult students.
Amount: Varies.
Number of awards: Varies.
Deadline: June 8.
How to apply: Applications are available online.
Exclusive: Visit www.UltimateScholarshipBook.com and enter code NA240320 for updates on this award.

(2404) · Community Service Award

Golden Key International Honour Society
Scholarship Program Administrators, Golden Key Scholarships/Awards, 1040 Crown Pointe Parkway, Suite 900, Atlanta, GA 30338
Phone: 800-377-2401
Email: awards@goldenkey.org
https://www.goldenkey.org/scholarships-awards/overview/
Purpose: To recognize a Golden Key member for "outstanding and impactful service to the community."

Eligibility: Applicants must be undergraduate or graduate Golden Key members who are currently enrolled in a degree program. Selection is based on amount of service, impact of service and outside extracurricular involvement. To qualify, applicants much have 100 hours of community service through a nonprofit organization. Applicants must provide an essay of up to 500 words describing the community service project, recommendation letters and list of extracurricular activities.
Target applicant(s): College students. Graduate school students. Adult students.
Amount: $2,000.
Number of awards: Up to 10.
Deadline: June 15 and December 15.
How to apply: Applications are available online.
Exclusive: Visit www.UltimateScholarshipBook.com and enter code GO240420 for updates on this award.

(2405) • CWA Joe Beirne Foundation Scholarship

Communications Workers of America
Attn.: George Kohl, 501 Third Street NW, Washington, DC 20001
Phone: 202-434-1100
Email: kadams@cwa-union.org
http://www.cwa-union.org
Purpose: To provide scholarships for CWA members and their families.
Eligibility: Applicants may be Communications Workers of America (CWA) members, their spouses, their children or their grandchildren. Applicants must be high school graduates or at least high school students who will graduate during the year in which they apply. Winners are selected by a lottery drawing. This is a two-year scholarship.
Target applicant(s): High school students. College students. Graduate school students. Adult students.
Amount: $3,000.
Number of awards: 15.
Scholarship may be renewable.
Deadline: April 29.
How to apply: Contact a CWA Local or write (referencing CWA local number, member name and Social Security number) for an application. Applications are available online.
Exclusive: Visit www.UltimateScholarshipBook.com and enter code CO240520 for updates on this award.

(2406) • Delta Gamma Foundation Scholarship

Delta Gamma Foundation
3250 Riverside Drive, P.O. Box 21397, Columbus, OH 43221
Phone: 614-481-8169
Email: dgscholarships08@aol.com
http://www.deltagamma.org
Purpose: To support student members.
Eligibility: Applicants must be initiated members of Delta Gamma, have maintained a 3.0 GPA and have completed three semesters or five quarters of college coursework. Applicants should also be active participants in chapter, campus and community leadership activities. Awards are based on academic achievement and participation in activities.
Target applicant(s): College students. Adult students.
Minimum GPA: 3.0
Amount: Varies.
Number of awards: Varies.
Deadline: March 2.
How to apply: Applications are available online.
Exclusive: Visit www.UltimateScholarshipBook.com and enter code DE240620 for updates on this award.

(2407) • Delta Phi Epsilon Educational Foundation Scholarship

Delta Phi Epsilon Educational Foundation
16A Worthington Drive, Maryland Heights, MO 63043
Phone: 314-275-2626
Email: fausbury@dphie.org
http://www.dphie.org
Purpose: To reward members of Delta Phi Epsilon.
Eligibility: Applicants must be members or the sons or daughters of members of Delta Phi Epsilon who are applying for undergraduate or graduate study. The award is based on service and involvement, academics and financial need. Applicants should submit transcripts, letters of introduction and financial need, autobiographical sketches, two recent photos, at least two letters of recommendation and the contact information of the financial aid director for the school.
Target applicant(s): High school students. College students. Graduate school students. Adult students.
Amount: Varies.
Number of awards: Varies.
Deadline: January 15.
How to apply: Applications are available online.
Exclusive: Visit www.UltimateScholarshipBook.com and enter code DE240720 for updates on this award.

(2408) • Di Yerbury International Scholars Awards

National Society of High School Scholars
1936 North Druid Hills Road, Atlanta, GA 30319
Phone: 404-235-5500
https://www.nshss.org/scholarships/
Purpose: To support students who wish to participate in international study during college.
Eligibility: Applicants must be members of NSHSS and wish to study abroad while in college. Applicants must submit a personal statement explaining why they would like to study abroad, what they hope to gain from the experience, what field they are pursuing and how the study abroad will benefit their educational and career goals.
Target applicant(s): High school students. College students. Adult students.
Amount: $1,000.
Number of awards: 5.
Deadline: March 15.
How to apply: Applications are available online and must include: personal statement, resume, transcript, educator recommendation, location and dates of study abroad program and color headshot.
Exclusive: Visit www.UltimateScholarshipBook.com and enter code NA240820 for updates on this award.

(2409) • Diller Teen Tikkun Olam Awards

Helen Diller Family Foundation
121 Steuart Street, San Francisco, CA 94105
Phone: 415-512-6432
Email: dillerteenaward@sfjcf.org
http://www.dillerteenawards.org
Purpose: To assist Jewish teens who have demonstrated leadership and participation in community service projects that exemplify the value of tikkun olam (repair of the world).
Eligibility: Applicants must be Jewish teens, U.S. residents and between 13 and 19 years old. Two references and an application form are required. Teens' projects can help either the Jewish community or the general community as long as they have not been remunerated for their services.

Teens may be nominated by any community member who knows the importance of their project – except family members – or may also nominate themselves.
Target applicant(s): Junior high students or younger. High school students. College students.
Amount: $36,000.
Number of awards: Up to 15.
Deadline: January 4.
How to apply: Applications are available online.
Exclusive: Visit www.UltimateScholarshipBook.com and enter code HE240920 for updates on this award.

(2410) • Diocese of the Armenian Church of America (Eastern) Scholarships

Diocese of the Armenian Church of America (Eastern)
630 Second Avenue, New York, NY 10016
Phone: 212-686-0710
Email: mariab@armeniandiocese.org
https://armenianchurch.us/scholarships/
Purpose: To support young Armenian Church members who are seeking higher education.
Eligibility: Applicants must be Armenian Americans who are currently attending or plan to attend a four-year college or university. Preference is given to applicants who are U.S. citizens and are active in the Armenian Church.
Target applicant(s): High school students. College students. Adult students.
Amount: Varies.
Number of awards: Varies.
Deadline: Varies.
How to apply: Applications are available from the Diocese of the Armenian Church of America (Eastern).
Exclusive: Visit www.UltimateScholarshipBook.com and enter code DI241020 for updates on this award.

(2411) • Donald A. and John R. Fisher Memorial Scholarship

Tau Kappa Epsilon Educational Foundation
7439 Woodland Drive, Suite 100, Indianapolis, IN 46278
Phone: 317-872-6533
Email: tkeogc@tke.org
http://www.tke.org/foundation/scholarships
Purpose: To recognize academic achievement and leadership in honor of father and son members Donald A. and John R. Fisher.
Eligibility: Applicants must be initiated Tau Kappa Epsilon members in good standing and full-time students with a GPA of at least 3.0. They must demonstrate outstanding leadership in their chapter, campus and community. Applicants must also include a statement describing how they have benefited from TKE membership.
Target applicant(s): College students. Adult students.
Minimum GPA: 3.0
Amount: $800.
Number of awards: 1.
Deadline: March 15.
How to apply: Applications are available online.
Exclusive: Visit www.UltimateScholarshipBook.com and enter code TA241120 for updates on this award.

(2412) • Education Debt Reduction Award

Golden Key International Honour Society
Scholarship Program Administrators, Golden Key Scholarships/Awards, 1040 Crown Pointe Parkway, Suite 900, Atlanta, GA 30338
Phone: 800-377-2401
Email: awards@goldenkey.org
https://www.goldenkey.org/scholarships-awards/overview/
Purpose: To aid Golden Key alumni, graduate student and post-graduate members with the repayment of student loans.
Eligibility: Applicants must be Golden Key members. They must be alumni, graduate students or post-graduates. Selection is based on professional goals, listing of student loans and the financial impact this award would provide to the applicant.
Target applicant(s): Graduate school students. Adult students.
Amount: $10,000.
Number of awards: Up to 10.
Deadline: June 15 and December 15.
How to apply: Applications are available online. An application form, resume, personal statement and student financial assistance (loan debt, etc.) information are required.
Exclusive: Visit www.UltimateScholarshipBook.com and enter code GO241220 for updates on this award.

(2413) • Elizabeth Ahlemeyer Quick/Gamma Phi Beta Scholarship

National Panhellenic Conference Foundation
3901 W. 86th Street, Suite 398, Indianapolis, IN 46268
Phone: 317-872-3185
Email: dani@npcwomen.org
https://www.npcwomen.org/foundation/scholarships.aspx
Purpose: To support collegiate members of the National Panhellenic Conference.
Eligibility: Applicants must be members of an NPC member group in good standing, be nominated by their College Panhellenics and have displayed outstanding service. Students must be rising full-time juniors or seniors in college with a 3.0 or higher GPA.
Target applicant(s): College students. Adult students.
Minimum GPA: 3.0
Amount: $2,000.
Number of awards: 1.
Deadline: Varies.
How to apply: Applications are available online. An application form, transcript and two letters of recommendation are required.
Exclusive: Visit www.UltimateScholarshipBook.com and enter code NA241320 for updates on this award.

(2414) • Emergency Educational Fund Grants

Elks National Foundation Headquarters
2750 North Lakeview Avenue, Chicago, IL 60614
Phone: 773-755-4732
Email: scholarship@elks.org
https://www.elks.org/scholars/
Purpose: To assist children of deceased and incapacitated Elks.
Eligibility: Applicants must be the children of deceased or incapacitated Elks who were/are members in good standing for at least one year, unmarried, under 23 years old and full-time undergraduate students at a U.S. school. Applicants must also demonstrate financial need.
Target applicant(s): High school students. College students.
Amount: Up to $4,000.
Number of awards: Varies.

Scholarship may be renewable.
Deadline: December 31.
How to apply: Applications are available from the local Elks Lodge or by phone or e-mail request.
Exclusive: Visit www.UltimateScholarshipBook.com and enter code EL241420 for updates on this award.

(2415) • Emmett J. Doerr Memorial Scout Scholarship

National Catholic Committee on Scouting
P.O. Box 152079, Irving, TX 75015-2079
Phone: 972-580-2114
Email: nccs@scouting.org
http://www.nccs-bsa.org
Purpose: To help scouts in a Boy Scouts of America program with their college education.
Eligibility: Applicants must be practicing Catholics and full-time high school seniors who hold a leadership role in their scouting unit and are actively involved with a Scout Troop, Varsity Scout Team, Venturing Crew or Sea Scout Ship. Students must have provided service to their home parish and earned the Ad Altare Dei or Pope Pius XII Religious Award. Applicants must also have earned the Eagle Scout, Silver Award or Quartermaster Award and must currently hold a leadership role in a community or school organization other than scouting.
Target applicant(s): High school students.
Amount: $2,000.
Number of awards: 6.
Deadline: March 1.
How to apply: Applications are available online. An application form, official high school transcript, four letters of recommendation and a photo are required.
Exclusive: Visit www.UltimateScholarshipBook.com and enter code NA241520 for updates on this award.

(2416) • Engaging Race Award

National Society of Collegiate Scholars (NSCS)
2000 M Street NW, Suite 600, Washington, DC 20036
Phone: 202-265-9000
Email: nscs@nscs.org
http://www.nscs.org/
Purpose: To aid NSCS members and alumni with attaining their goals and to recognize their outstanding academic, leadership and service achievements.
Eligibility: Applicants must present a pitch for a creative and original service initiative and must be college undergraduates or alumni. Selection is based on the overall strength of the application.
Target applicant(s): College students. Adult students.
Amount: Up to $2,000.
Number of awards: 1.
Deadline: November 10.
How to apply: Applications are available online.
Exclusive: Visit www.UltimateScholarshipBook.com and enter code NA241620 for updates on this award.

(2417) • Eugene C. Beach Memorial Scholarship

Tau Kappa Epsilon Educational Foundation
7439 Woodland Drive, Suite 100, Indianapolis, IN 46278
Phone: 317-872-6533
Email: tkeogc@tke.org
http://www.tke.org/foundation/scholarships
Purpose: To reward a member of Tau Kappa Epsilon for outstanding academic achievement and leadership within the chapter, campus and community.
Eligibility: Applicants must have a minimum GPA of 3.0.
Target applicant(s): College students. Adult students.
Minimum GPA: 3.0
Amount: $300.
Number of awards: 1.
Deadline: March 15.
How to apply: Applications are available online.
Exclusive: Visit www.UltimateScholarshipBook.com and enter code TA241720 for updates on this award.

(2418) • Eva Johnson Memorial Scholarship Fund

Shasta Head Start Child Development, Inc.
375 Lake Boulevard, Suite 100, Redding, CA 96003
http://www.shastaheadstart.org
Purpose: To support students who were once participants of Head Start and are now pursuing a higher education.
Eligibility: Applicants must have been members of a Head Start program who are now high school seniors enrolling in post-secondary institutions. Students must have a 3.0 GPA and have shown an interest in the welfare of the children and families in their community.
Target applicant(s): High school students.
Minimum GPA: 3.0
Amount: $500-$1,000.
Number of awards: 2.
Deadline: April 17.
How to apply: Applications are available online.
Exclusive: Visit www.UltimateScholarshipBook.com and enter code SH241820 for updates on this award.

(2419) • Fadel Educational Foundation Annual Award Program

Fadel Educational Foundation
P.O. Box 212135, Augusta, GA 30917-2135
Phone: 484-694-1783
Email: secretary@fadelfoundation.org
http://www.fadelfoundation.org
Purpose: To support Muslim U.S. citizens and permanent residents.
Eligibility: Applicants must be non-incarcerated students pursuing higher education. Selection is based on need and merit. Applicants should provide application forms, two teacher recommendation forms, one masjid official recommendation letter and financial need reports.
Target applicant(s): High school students. College students. Graduate school students. Adult students.
Amount: Up to $3,500.
Number of awards: Varies.
Deadline: May 31.
How to apply: Applications are available online.
Exclusive: Visit www.UltimateScholarshipBook.com and enter code FA241920 for updates on this award.

(2420) • FEEA Scholarship Program

Federal Employee Education and Assistance Fund
1641 Prince Street, Alexandria, VA 22314
Phone: 202-554-0007x102
https://feea.org/our-programs/scholarships/

Purpose: The FEEA scholarship program aids postal employees and their family members.
Eligibility: Applicants must be current civilian federal and postal employees with three years of service or their children or spouses. Applicants must also be enrolled or plan to enroll in an accredited post secondary school, have a minimum 3.0 GPA and may be high school seniors, college students or graduate students.
Target applicant(s): High school students. College students. Graduate school students. Adult students.
Minimum GPA: 3.0
Amount: Up to $5,000.
Number of awards: At least 200.
Deadline: March 25.
How to apply: Applications are available online or by sending a self-addressed and stamped envelope.
Exclusive: Visit www.UltimateScholarshipBook.com and enter code FE242020 for updates on this award.

(2421) • First in the Family Scholarship

National Society of Collegiate Scholars (NSCS)
2000 M Street NW, Suite 600, Washington, DC 20036
Phone: 202-265-9000
Email: nscs@nscs.org
http://www.nscs.org/
Purpose: To aid NSCS members with achieving their goals and to recognize their academic, service and leadership achievements.
Eligibility: Applicants must be the first person in their family to attend college. Selection is based on the overall strength of the application.
Target applicant(s): College students. Adult students.
Amount: Varies.
Number of awards: Varies.
Deadline: December 15.
How to apply: Applications are available online.
Exclusive: Visit www.UltimateScholarshipBook.com and enter code NA242120 for updates on this award.

(2422) • Fleet Reserve Association Scholarship

Fleet Reserve Association (FRA)
FRA Scholarship Administrator, 125 N. West Street, Alexandria, VA 22314
Phone: 800-372-1924
Email: news-fra@fra.org
http://www.fra.org
Purpose: To provide financial support for post-secondary education to FRA members and their dependents and grandchildren.
Eligibility: Applicants must be either FRA members or the dependents or grandchildren of an FRA member who is in good standing or was in good standing at time of death. Applicants are judged on the basis of leadership skills, financial need, academic record and character.
Target applicant(s): High school students. College students. Graduate school students. Adult students.
Amount: Up to $5,000.
Number of awards: Varies.
Deadline: April 15.
How to apply: Applications are available online.
Exclusive: Visit www.UltimateScholarshipBook.com and enter code FL242220 for updates on this award.

(2423) • Ford Motor Company Fund and Ford Trucks Built Ford Tough - FFA Scholarship Program

National FFA Organization
P.O. Box 68960, 6060 FFA Drive, Indianapolis, IN 46268-0960
Phone: 888-332-2668
Email: scholarships@ffa.org
https://www.ffa.org/participate/scholarships
Purpose: To provide educational assistance to FFA members.
Eligibility: Applicants must be high school seniors who plan to pursue a two- or four-year degree in any major. They must apply online and obtain a signature and dealer code from a local participating Ford Truck dealer. If there is no participating Ford dealer in the applicant's area, he or she may obtain a signature from any local Ford dealer and be eligible for one of five national scholarships.
Target applicant(s): High school students.
Amount: $1,000.
Number of awards: Up to 500.
Deadline: February 1.
How to apply: Applications are available online.
Exclusive: Visit www.UltimateScholarshipBook.com and enter code NA242320 for updates on this award.

(2424) • Founders' Scholarship

American Atheists
P.O. Box 158, Cranford, NJ 07016
Phone: 908-276-7300
Email: info@athiests.org
http://www.atheists.org
Purpose: To support Atheist students who are activists.
Eligibility: Applicants must be high school seniors or college students who are Atheists, have a minimum 2.5 GPA and be student activists. The award is based on the level of activism and requires a 500- to 1,000-word essay. In addition to the scholarship, the winner will receive a free trip to the American Atheists National Convention.
Target applicant(s): High school students. College students. Graduate school students. Adult students.
Minimum GPA: 2.5
Amount: $500-$1,000.
Number of awards: 5.
Deadline: February 1.
How to apply: Applications are available online.
Exclusive: Visit www.UltimateScholarshipBook.com and enter code AM242420 for updates on this award.

(2425) • Fourth Degree Pro Deo and Pro Patria Scholarships

Knights of Columbus
Department of Scholarships, 1 Columbus Plaza, New Haven, CT 06510-3326
Phone: 203-752-4000
Email: info@kofc.org
http://www.kofc.org
Purpose: To provide aid to members or the children of members of the Knights of Columbus.
Eligibility: Applicants must be members or the children of current or deceased members of the Knights of Columbus or, in some cases, be members of the Columbian Squires. Applicants must be entering their freshmen year at a U.S. Catholic college.
Target applicant(s): High school students.
Amount: $1,500.

Number of awards: Varies.
Scholarship may be renewable.
Deadline: March 1.
How to apply: Applications are available by mail.
Exclusive: Visit www.UltimateScholarshipBook.com and enter code KN242520 for updates on this award.

(2426) • Frank Kamierczak Memorial Migrant Scholarship

Geneseo Migrant Center
3 Mt. Morris-Leicester Road, Leicester, NY 14481
Phone: 800-245-5681
Email: info@migrant.net
http://www.migrant.net
Purpose: To provide financial aid to migrant youth.
Eligibility: Applicants must be the children of migrant workers or migrant workers themselves and must have teaching as a career goal. Selection is based upon scholastic achievement, financial need and recent history of movement for agricultural employment, with priority given to applicants who have moved within the last three years before applying.
Target applicant(s): High school students. College students. Adult students.
Amount: $1,000.
Number of awards: 1.
Deadline: February 1.
How to apply: Applications are available online.
Exclusive: Visit www.UltimateScholarshipBook.com and enter code GE242620 for updates on this award.

(2427) • Frank S. Land Scholarships

DeMolay Foundation
10200 NW Ambassador Drive, Kansas City, MO 64153
Phone: 800-336-6529
Email: demolay@demolay.org
https://demolay.org/
Purpose: To reward DeMolay members.
Eligibility: Applicants must be active male members of DeMolay and be under the age of 21. DeMolay is an organization with more than 1,000 chapters in the world that helps prepare young men ages 12 to 21 to "lead successful, happy and productive lives." The group aims to help members develop civic awareness, personal responsibility and leadership skills.
Target applicant(s): Junior high students or younger. High school students. College students.
Amount: Varies.
Number of awards: Varies.
Deadline: April 1.
How to apply: Applications are available online.
Exclusive: Visit www.UltimateScholarshipBook.com and enter code DE242720 for updates on this award.

(2428) • Gaston/Nolle Scholarships

Alpha Chi
1210 East Race Avenue, Searcy, AR 72143-4656
Phone: 501-593-4810
Email: scholarships@alphachihonor.org
http://www.alphachihonor.org
Purpose: To assist Alpha Chi members who are entering their senior year of undergraduate study.
Eligibility: Applicants must be members of Alpha Chi who are enrolled full-time in a bachelor's degree program.
Target applicant(s): College students. Adult students.
Amount: $1,500-$2,500.
Number of awards: 12.
Deadline: February 15.
How to apply: Application requirements are available online, and applicants must be nominated by the faculty sponsor.
Exclusive: Visit www.UltimateScholarshipBook.com and enter code AL242820 for updates on this award.

(2429) • GCSAA Legacy Awards

Golf Course Superintendents Association of America
1421 Research Park Drive, Lawrence, KS 66049
Phone: 800-472-7878
Email: mwright@gcsaa.org
http://www.gcsaa.org
Purpose: To support the children and grandchildren of GCSAA members.
Eligibility: The applicant's parents or grandparents must have been GCSAA members for five or more consecutive years. Applicants must also be full-time college students or high school seniors already accepted into a postsecondary school.
Target applicant(s): High school students. College students. Adult students.
Amount: $1,500.
Number of awards: Varies.
Deadline: April 15.
How to apply: Applications are available by contacting Pam Smith, 800-472-7878, x3678.
Exclusive: Visit www.UltimateScholarshipBook.com and enter code GO242920 for updates on this award.

(2430) • GEICO Award

National Society of Collegiate Scholars (NSCS)
2000 M Street NW, Suite 600, Washington, DC 20036
Phone: 202-265-9000
Email: nscs@nscs.org
http://www.nscs.org/
Purpose: To aid NSCS members in attaining their goals and to recognize their achievements in academics, service and leadership.
Eligibility: Applicants must be college undergraduates. Selection is based on the overall strength of the application.
Target applicant(s): College students. Adult students.
Amount: Varies.
Number of awards: Varies.
Deadline: June 22.
How to apply: Applications are available online.
Exclusive: Visit www.UltimateScholarshipBook.com and enter code NA243020 for updates on this award.

(2431) • GEICO Graduate Award

National Society of Collegiate Scholars (NSCS)
2000 M Street NW, Suite 600, Washington, DC 20036
Phone: 202-265-9000
Email: nscs@nscs.org
http://www.nscs.org/
Purpose: To aid NSCS members and alumni in attaining their goals and to recognize their achievements in academics, service and leadership.

Eligibility: Applicants must be current or accepted graduate students. Selection is based on the overall strength of the application.
Target applicant(s): Graduate school students. Adult students.
Amount: Varies.
Number of awards: Varies.
Deadline: June 22.
How to apply: Applications are available online.
Exclusive: Visit www.UltimateScholarshipBook.com and enter code NA243120 for updates on this award.

(2432) · GEICO Life Scholarship

Golden Key International Honour Society
Scholarship Program Administrators, Golden Key Scholarships/Awards, 1040 Crown Pointe Parkway, Suite 900, Atlanta, GA 30338
Phone: 800-377-2401
Email: awards@goldenkey.org
https://www.goldenkey.org/scholarships-awards/overview/
Purpose: To support undergraduate students who balance family, career or other life commitments with pursuing a degree.
Eligibility: Applicants must be members of Golden Key, be enrolled in a baccalaureate program and have completed at least 12 hours at the time of application and have at least a 3.5 GPA. The award is based on academic achievement, educational and professional goals and family and/or career commitments.
Target applicant(s): High school students. College students. Adult students.
Minimum GPA: 3.5
Amount: $1,000.
Number of awards: 10.
Deadline: June 15.
How to apply: Applications are available online.
Exclusive: Visit www.UltimateScholarshipBook.com and enter code GO243220 for updates on this award.

(2433) · George Heller Memorial Scholarship Fund of the SAG-AFTRA Foundation

Screen Actors Guild - American Federation of Television and Radio Artists
5757 Wilshire Boulevard, 7th Floor, Los Angeles, CA 90036
Phone: 855-724-2387
Email: sagaftrainfo@sagaftra.org
https://sagaftra.foundation/assistance/scholarship-programs/
Purpose: To support AFTRA members and their children.
Eligibility: Applicants must be AFTRA members in good standing with five years of membership or the children of members. Scholarships are awarded based on academic achievement and financial need and can be used to study any academic field or for professional training in the performing arts at an accredited higher education institution.
Target applicant(s): High school students. College students. Graduate school students. Adult students.
Amount: Up to $2,500.
Number of awards: Up to 15.
Deadline: March 15.
How to apply: Applications are available online.
Exclusive: Visit www.UltimateScholarshipBook.com and enter code SC243320 for updates on this award.

(2434) · Girls Incorporated Lucile Miller Wright Scholars Program

Girls Inc.
120 Wall Street , New York, NY 10005-3902
Phone: 212-509-2000
Email: communications@girlsinc.org
http://www.girlsinc.org
Purpose: To support young members of Girls Incorporated.
Eligibility: Applicants must be young women who are in their junior or senior year of high school and members of a Girls Incorporated affiliate.
Target applicant(s): High school students.
Amount: $5,000-$20,000.
Number of awards: Varies.
Deadline: Varies.
How to apply: Applications are available by written request.
Exclusive: Visit www.UltimateScholarshipBook.com and enter code GI243420 for updates on this award.

(2435) · Glass, Molders, Pottery, Plastics and Allied Workers Memorial Scholarship Fund

International Scholarship and Tuition Services, Inc.
GMP Memorial Scholarship Fund, 1321 Murfreesboro Road, Suite 800, Nashville, TN 37217
Phone: 855-670-4787
Email: contactus@applyists.com
http://www.gmpiu.org
Purpose: To provide financial assistance to the children of members.
Eligibility: Applicants must be children, step-children or legally-adopted children of Glass, Molders, Pottery, Plastics and Allied Workers members.
Target applicant(s): High school students. College students. Adult students.
Amount: $2,000-$4,000.
Number of awards: 10.
Scholarship may be renewable.
Deadline: January 26.
How to apply: Applications are available by written request or by contacting your local union office.
Exclusive: Visit www.UltimateScholarshipBook.com and enter code IN243520 for updates on this award.

(2436) · Gloria Mattera National Migrant Scholarship Fund

Geneseo Migrant Center
3 Mt. Morris-Leicester Road, Leicester, NY 14481
Phone: 800-245-5681
Email: info@migrant.net
http://www.migrant.net
Purpose: To assist migrant youth in attending college.
Eligibility: Applicants must be enrolling in college or another institute of post-secondary education or be high school dropouts or potential dropouts who show promise in intending to pursue higher education. Recipients are chosen based upon scholastic ability, financial need and recent history of movement for agricultural employment, with priority given to current interstate migrant youth.
Target applicant(s): High school students.
Amount: Up to $250.
Number of awards: 100.
Deadline: April 1.
How to apply: Applications are available online.

Exclusive: Visit www.UltimateScholarshipBook.com and enter code GE243620 for updates on this award.

(2437) • Golden Key Graduate Scholar Award

Golden Key International Honour Society
Scholarship Program Administrators, Golden Key Scholarships/Awards, 1040 Crown Pointe Parkway, Suite 900, Atlanta, GA 30338
Phone: 800-377-2401
Email: awards@goldenkey.org
https://www.goldenkey.org/scholarships-awards/overview/

Purpose: To support Golden Key members' graduate studies at accredited universities in the U.S. or abroad.
Eligibility: Applicant must be a Golden Key member, be enrolled in a graduate program or an undergraduate who will be enrolled in a graduate program in the next academic year. Selection is based on future academic and career goals, as well as how the applicant plans to create change in the future. Applicants must display academic achievement, leadership, service and involvement with the local Golden Key chapter.
Target applicant(s): College students. Graduate school students. Adult students.
Amount: $10,000.
Number of awards: Varies.
Deadline: June 15.
How to apply: Applications are available online.
Exclusive: Visit www.UltimateScholarshipBook.com and enter code GO243720 for updates on this award.

(2438) • Golden Key Research Grants

Golden Key International Honour Society
Scholarship Program Administrators, Golden Key Scholarships/Awards, 1040 Crown Pointe Parkway, Suite 900, Atlanta, GA 30338
Phone: 800-377-2401
Email: awards@goldenkey.org
https://www.goldenkey.org/scholarships-awards/overview/

Purpose: To assist members in their thesis research or in presenting their research at a professional conference.
Eligibility: Applicants must be undergraduate, graduate or post-graduate student members currently enrolled in a degree program. Selection is based on academic achievement and the quality of the research.
Target applicant(s): College students. Graduate school students. Adult students.
Amount: $2,000.
Number of awards: Varies.
Deadline: December 15.
How to apply: Applications are available online.
Exclusive: Visit www.UltimateScholarshipBook.com and enter code GO243820 for updates on this award.

(2439) • Golden Key Study Abroad Scholarship

Golden Key International Honour Society
Scholarship Program Administrators, Golden Key Scholarships/Awards, 1040 Crown Pointe Parkway, Suite 900, Atlanta, GA 30338
Phone: 800-377-2401
Email: awards@goldenkey.org
https://www.goldenkey.org/scholarships-awards/overview/

Purpose: To aid Golden Key members who are studying abroad.
Eligibility: Applicants must be Golden Key members. They must be undergraduate, graduate or post-graduate students who are enrolled in or have been accepted into a study abroad program. Selection is based on academic merit and relevance of study abroad program to applicant's academic program of study.
Target applicant(s): College students. Graduate school students. Adult students.
Amount: $5,000.
Number of awards: Up to 7.
Deadline: June 15.
How to apply: Applications are available online. An application form, personal statement, study abroad program description and official transcript are required.
Exclusive: Visit www.UltimateScholarshipBook.com and enter code GO243920 for updates on this award.

(2440) • Golden Key Undergraduate Achievement Scholarship

Golden Key International Honour Society
Scholarship Program Administrators, Golden Key Scholarships/Awards, 1040 Crown Pointe Parkway, Suite 900, Atlanta, GA 30338
Phone: 800-377-2401
Email: awards@goldenkey.org
https://www.goldenkey.org/scholarships-awards/overview/

Purpose: To aid degree-seeking Golden Key members.
Eligibility: Applicants must be Golden Key members who are enrolled in an undergraduate degree program with a 3.5 minimum GPA. Selection is based on academic achievement, leadership skills and service to the community.
Target applicant(s): College students. Adult students.
Minimum GPA: 3.5
Amount: $5,000.
Number of awards: Varies.
Deadline: December 15.
How to apply: Applications are available online. An application form, official transcript, resume, personal statement and one recommendation letter are required.
Exclusive: Visit www.UltimateScholarshipBook.com and enter code GO244020 for updates on this award.

(2441) • Guistwhite Scholarships

Phi Theta Kappa Honor Society
1625 Eastover Drive, Jackson, MS 39211
Phone: 601-987-5741
Email: scholarship.programs@ptk.org
http://www.ptk.org

Purpose: To aid Phi Theta Kappa members who plan to pursue bachelor's degrees.
Eligibility: Applicants must be active members of Phi Theta Kappa who will remain enrolled at a community college through December of the application year. They must have completed at least 30 semester credits (or 45 quarter credits) over the past five years and must have maintained a GPA of 3.5 or higher on a four-point scale over the past five years. Students must have plans to transfer to a four-year postsecondary institution during the calendar year following the submission of the scholarship application and must have junior status at the time of transfer. Applicants must have a community college record that is free of any disciplinary action and must not have a criminal record. Selection is based on academic merit and Phi Theta Kappa participation.
Target applicant(s): College students. Adult students.
Minimum GPA: 3.5
Amount: $5,000.
Number of awards: Up to 15.
Deadline: December 1.

How to apply: Applications are available online. An application form, official transcript, two recommendation letters and personal essay are required.
Exclusive: Visit www.UltimateScholarshipBook.com and enter code PH244120 for updates on this award.

(2442) • Harold Davis Memorial Scholarship

National FFA Organization
P.O. Box 68960, 6060 FFA Drive, Indianapolis, IN 46268-0960
Phone: 888-332-2668
Email: scholarships@ffa.org
https://www.ffa.org/participate/scholarships
Purpose: To provide financial assistance to students who have livestock backgrounds and are seeking degrees in animal science, agricultural education and agribusiness.
Eligibility: Applicants must be current FFA members and high school seniors or college students planning to enroll or currently enrolled full-time. Students only need to complete the online application one time to be considered for all FFA-administered scholarships. The application requires information about the student's activities and a 1,000-word essay. Awards may be used for books, supplies, tuition, fees and room and board.
Target applicant(s): High school students. College students.
Amount: $400.
Number of awards: 1.
Deadline: February 1.
How to apply: Applications are available online.
Exclusive: Visit www.UltimateScholarshipBook.com and enter code NA244220 for updates on this award.

(2443) • Harvey and Laura Alpert Scholarship Award

International Flight Services Association (IFSA)
1100 Johnson Ferry Road, Suite 300, Atlanta, GA 30342
Phone: 678-298-1187
Email: cellery@kellencompany.com
http://www.ifsanet.com
Purpose: To aid hospitality students who are relatives of members of the International Flight Services Association.
Eligibility: Applicants must be hospitality management students who have completed at least 32 credits in their degree program and have a minimum 3.0 GPA. They must have a family member who is a member of the International Flight Services Association (IFSA). Selection is based on academic achievement and stated career goals.
Target applicant(s): College students. Adult students.
Minimum GPA: 3.0
Amount: $5,000.
Number of awards: 2.
Deadline: April 28.
How to apply: Applications are available online. An application form, official transcript, personal essay and three recommendation letters are required.
Exclusive: Visit www.UltimateScholarshipBook.com and enter code IN244320 for updates on this award.

(2444) • Helen B. and Lewis E. Goldstein Scholarship Fund

Jewish Community Federation & Endowment Fund
121 Steuart Street, San Francisco, CA 94105
Phone: 415-777-0411
http://www.jewishfed.org
Purpose: To support Jewish students who pursue continuing education.
Eligibility: Applicants must be Jewish undergraduate or graduate students currently enrolled at an accredited four-year institution in the U.S. Preference is given to immigrants and students enrolled in a professional school. Applicants must demonstrate academic merit.
Target applicant(s): College students. Graduate school students. Adult students.
Amount: $6,800.
Number of awards: 2.
Deadline: March 30.
How to apply: Applications are available online.
Exclusive: Visit www.UltimateScholarshipBook.com and enter code JE244420 for updates on this award.

(2445) • Himmel Scholarship

Circle K International
3636 Woodview Trace, Indianapolis, IN 46268
http://www.circlek.org
Purpose: This scholarship is in memory of Harry S. Himmel, deceased President Emeritus of the Kiwanis International Foundation. Recipients should demonstrate dedication and leadership within the organization.
Eligibility: Applicants must be Key Club or Circle K members who appear on the international roster, are currently enrolled in college or are college-bound and have completed 100 service hours with the organization. Key Club members must have also held an elected officer position within the organization.
Target applicant(s): High school students. College students. Adult students.
Minimum GPA: 3.0
Amount: $500.
Number of awards: 2.
Deadline: March 15.
How to apply: Applications are available online.
Exclusive: Visit www.UltimateScholarshipBook.com and enter code CI244520 for updates on this award.

(2446) • Hites Transfer Scholarship

Phi Theta Kappa Honor Society
1625 Eastover Drive, Jackson, MS 39211
Phone: 601-987-5741
Email: scholarship.programs@ptk.org
http://www.ptk.org
Purpose: To aid Phi Theta Kappa members who intend to transfer to a four-year postsecondary institution.
Eligibility: Applicants must be Phi Theta Kappa members who are in good standing, have a GPA of 3.5 or higher and have completed 50 or more semester credits over the past five years. They must be enrolled at an accredited community college through March of the application year, have plans to transfer to a four-year postsecondary institution in the fall and have plans to pursue a bachelor's degree on a full-time basis. Applicants cannot have a criminal record. Selection is based on the overall strength of the application.
Target applicant(s): College students. Adult students.
Minimum GPA: 3.5
Amount: $7,500.
Number of awards: Up to 10.
Deadline: December 1.
How to apply: Applications are available online. An application form and supporting documents are required.
Exclusive: Visit www.UltimateScholarshipBook.com and enter code PH244620 for updates on this award.

(2447) • Hoard's Dairyman FFA Scholarship

National FFA Organization
P.O. Box 68960, 6060 FFA Drive, Indianapolis, IN 46268-0960
Phone: 888-332-2668
Email: scholarships@ffa.org
https://www.ffa.org/participate/scholarships

Purpose: To support FFA members working toward four-year degrees in agricultural journalism or dairy science.
Eligibility: Applicants specializing in agricultural communications are preferred. Selection is based on the overall strength of the application.
Target applicant(s): High school students. College students.
Amount: $1,000.
Number of awards: 1.
Deadline: February 8.
How to apply: Applications are available online.
Exclusive: Visit www.UltimateScholarshipBook.com and enter code NA244720 for updates on this award.

(2448) • Howard Coughlin Memorial Scholarship Fund

Office and Professional Employees International Union
80 Eighth Avenue, Suite 610, New York, NY 10011
Phone: 212-367-0902
http://www.opeiu.org

Purpose: To offer scholarships to OPEIU members and their children.
Eligibility: Applicants must either be members of OPEIU in good standing, or the children, stepchildren or legally adopted children of an OPEIU member in good standing or associate members. Applicants must also be high school seniors, high school graduates entering a college, university or a recognized technical or vocational post-secondary school as full-time students or presently in a college, university or a recognized technical or vocational post-secondary school as a full-time or part-time student. Part-time scholarships are defined as a minimum of three credits and no more than two courses. Selection is based on transcripts, high school class rank and SAT/ACT scores or evidence of an equivalent exam by a recognized technical or vocational post-secondary school.
Target applicant(s): High school students. College students. Adult students.
Amount: $662-$6,500.
Number of awards: 19.
Scholarship may be renewable.
Deadline: March 31.
How to apply: Applications are available at the local union office, at the secretary-treasurer's office of the International Union or online.
Exclusive: Visit www.UltimateScholarshipBook.com and enter code OF244820 for updates on this award.

(2449) • Hy-Vee Foundation Scholarship Program

Hy-Vee
5820 Westown Parkway, West Des Moines, IA 50266
Email: hy-veeuniversity@hy-vee.com
https://www.hy-vee.com/corporate/our-company/community/scholarships/

Purpose: To support students employed by Hy-Vee.
Eligibility: Applicants must be high school seniors who are employed by Hy-Vee or whose parent is an employee of Hy-Vee or current full-time undergraduate college students who are employed with Hy-Vee.
Target applicant(s): High school students. College students. Adult students.
Amount: $1,000.
Number of awards: 80.
Deadline: February 8.
How to apply: Applications are available online.
Exclusive: Visit www.UltimateScholarshipBook.com and enter code HY244920 for updates on this award.

(2450) • IAM Scholarship

International Association of Machinists and Aerospace Workers Scholarship Program, 9000 Machinists Place, Room 204, Upper Marlboro, MD 20772-2687
Phone: 301-967-4708
Email: scholarship@iamaw.org
https://www.goiam.org/news/departments/hq/scholarships/

Purpose: To offer scholarships to members of the International Association of Machinists and Aerospace Workers (IAM) and their children.
Eligibility: Applicants must be an IAM member who has two years of continuous good standing membership or the child of a member who has two years of continuous good standing membership. Applicants may be entering college or vocational/technical school as a freshman or at a higher level with some college credits already completed. Grades, attitude, references, test scores, activities and participation in local lodge are considered in selecting scholarship recipients.
Target applicant(s): High school students. College students. Adult students.
Amount: $1,000-$2,000.
Number of awards: Varies.
Deadline: February 24.
How to apply: Applications are available by written request.
Exclusive: Visit www.UltimateScholarshipBook.com and enter code IN245020 for updates on this award.

(2451) • IFSA Foundation Scholarship Award

International Flight Services Association (IFSA)
1100 Johnson Ferry Road, Suite 300, Atlanta, GA 30342
Phone: 678-298-1187
Email: cellery@kellencompany.com
http://www.ifsanet.com

Purpose: To aid students whose parents are members of the International Flight Services Association.
Eligibility: Applicants must be the children of International Flight Services Association (IFSA) members who are enrolled or planning to enroll at an accredited college or university. They must be attending or planning to attend school on an at least part-time basis and have a GPA of 3.0 or higher on a four-point scale. Selection is based on academic achievement and the applicant's interest in pursuing higher education.
Target applicant(s): High school students. College students. Adult students.
Minimum GPA: 3.0
Amount: Varies.
Number of awards: Varies.
Deadline: April 30.
How to apply: Applications are available online. An application form, official transcript, three recommendation letters, a personal essay and proof of college acceptance or enrollment are required.
Exclusive: Visit www.UltimateScholarshipBook.com and enter code IN245120 for updates on this award.

(2452) • Induction Recognition Award

National Society of Collegiate Scholars (NSCS)
2000 M Street NW, Suite 600, Washington, DC 20036

Phone: 202-265-9000
Email: nscs@nscs.org
http://www.nscs.org/
Purpose: To help NSCS members achieve their goals and recognize their academic, service and leadership achievements.
Eligibility: Applicants must be new college undergraduate members who attend their induction ceremony and become actively involved in their chapter. Selection is based on the overall strength of the application.
Target applicant(s): College students. Adult students.
Amount: Varies.
Number of awards: Varies.
Deadline: February 17.
How to apply: Applications are available online.
Exclusive: Visit www.UltimateScholarshipBook.com and enter code NA245220 for updates on this award.

(2453) · International Association of Machinists and Aerospace Workers Scholarship for Members' Children

International Association of Machinists and Aerospace Workers Scholarship Program, 9000 Machinists Place, Room 204, Upper Marlboro, MD 20772-2687
Phone: 301-967-4708
Email: scholarship@iamaw.org
https://www.goiam.org/news/departments/hq/scholarships/
Purpose: To offer scholarships to children of the members of the IAM.
Eligibility: The applicant's parent member must have two years of continuous good standing membership, and applicants must be in their senior year of high school. Selection is based on grades, attitude, references, test scores and activities outside of school.
Target applicant(s): High school students.
Amount: $1,000-$2,000.
Number of awards: Varies.
Deadline: February 24.
How to apply: Applications are available by written request.
Exclusive: Visit www.UltimateScholarshipBook.com and enter code IN245320 for updates on this award.

(2454) · ISF National Scholarship Program

Islamic Scholarship Fund
2140 Shattuck Avenue, Suite 706, Berkeley, CA 94704
Phone: 650-995-6782
Email: contact@islamicscholarshipfund.org
https://islamicscholarshipfund.org/scholarships/
Purpose: To aid Muslim students in pursuing degrees in humanities, social sciences, liberal arts and law.
Eligibility: Applicants must be accepted by or attend a top-ranked four-year college or university for undergraduate or graduate studies. They must be practicing Muslims and U.S. citizens or permanent residents. They must have college junior standing or higher and maintain a minimum GPA of 3.0. Applicants should be active members of their communities. Selection is based on academic record, school and extracurricular activities, extenuating circumstances and a personal interview.
Target applicant(s): College students. Graduate school students. Adult students.
Minimum GPA: 3.0
Amount: $2,000-$5,000.
Number of awards: Varies.
Deadline: June 11.
How to apply: Applications are available online. An application form is required.
Exclusive: Visit www.UltimateScholarshipBook.com and enter code IS245420 for updates on this award.

(2455) · Islamic Development Bank Loan Scholarship

Islamic Society of North America
6555 S. County Road 750 E, Plainfield, IN 46168
Phone: 317-839-8157
http://www.isna.net/scholarships/
Purpose: To support Muslim American students in pursuing post-secondary education.
Eligibility: Applicants must be accepted into a program in one of the following fields: medicine, engineering, pharmacy, nursing, nutrition, veterinary medicine, dentistry, medical technology, agriculture, food technology, forestry, fisheries science or computer science. Preference is given to engineering and medical students.
Target applicant(s): College students. Graduate school students. Adult students.
Amount: $15,000.
Number of awards: 5.
Scholarship may be renewable.
Deadline: March 15.
How to apply: Applications are available online.
Exclusive: Visit www.UltimateScholarshipBook.com and enter code IS245520 for updates on this award.

(2456) · IUE-CWA International Paul Jennings Scholarship

IUE-CWA
1275 K Street NW, Suite 600, Washington, DC 20005
Phone: 202-513-6300
http://www.iue-cwa.org
Purpose: To provide scholarships for the children and grandchildren of local IUE-CWA union elected officials.
Eligibility: Applicants must be the children or grandchildren of IUE-CWA members who are now or have been local union elected officials. Applicants must also be accepted for admission or already enrolled as full-time students at an accredited college, university, nursing school or technical school offering college credit courses. All study must be completed at the undergraduate level. Applicants should demonstrate an interest in equality, improving the quality of life of others and community service. Applicants will also be evaluated on character, leadership and a desire to improve.
Target applicant(s): High school students. College students. Adult students.
Amount: $3,000.
Number of awards: 1.
Deadline: February 28.
How to apply: Applications are available online.
Exclusive: Visit www.UltimateScholarshipBook.com and enter code IU245620 for updates on this award.

(2457) · J. Robert Ashcroft National Youth Scholarship

Assemblies of God
1445 North Boonville Avenue, Springfield, MO 65802-1894
Phone: 417-862-2781
Email: colleges@ag.org
http://www.ag.org

Purpose: To provide financial assistance to college-bound seniors who attend Assemblies of God churches.
Eligibility: Applicants must be high school seniors who attend an Assemblies of God church, either in the United States or abroad as dependents of Assemblies of God missionaries or chaplains. Applicants must also attend an institution of higher learning that is endorsed by the Assemblies of God the fall immediately following their high school graduation.
Target applicant(s): High school students.
Amount: $2,000-$8,000.
Number of awards: 3.
Deadline: February 10.
How to apply: Applications are available online. Applications must be sent to their AG District Council first, and the top candidates are then sent to us for review.
Exclusive: Visit www.UltimateScholarshipBook.com and enter code AS245720 for updates on this award.

(2458) • James E. Breining Scholarship Award

Explorers Learning for Life
1325 West Walnut Hill Lane, P.O. Box 152225, Irving, TX 75015-2225
Phone: 855-806-9992
Email: exploring@lflmail.org
http://www.exploring.org/scholarships/
Purpose: To encourage Law Enforcement Explorers to attend college.
Eligibility: Applicants must be active Law Enforcement Explorers in good standing who demonstrate a meaningful contribution to society, impeccable character and ethics and leadership abilities in both Law Enforcement Exploring and the community.
Target applicant(s): High school students. College students. Adult students.
Amount: At least $1,500.
Number of awards: Varies.
Deadline: April 30.
How to apply: Applications are available online.
Exclusive: Visit www.UltimateScholarshipBook.com and enter code EX245820 for updates on this award.

(2459) • Joan Nelson Study Abroad Scholarship

Golden Key International Honour Society
Scholarship Program Administrators, Golden Key Scholarships/Awards, 1040 Crown Pointe Parkway, Suite 900, Atlanta, GA 30338
Phone: 800-377-2401
Email: awards@goldenkey.org
https://www.goldenkey.org/scholarships-awards/overview/
Purpose: To assist members who study abroad.
Eligibility: Applicants must be undergraduate, graduate and post-graduate members who plan to be or are currently enrolled in a study abroad program. Selection is based on academic achievement and relevance of the study abroad program to the applicant's major. Students must be enrolled in a degree-granting program at time of application.
Target applicant(s): College students. Graduate school students. Adult students.
Amount: $5,000.
Number of awards: Varies.
Deadline: December 15.
How to apply: Applications are available online.
Exclusive: Visit www.UltimateScholarshipBook.com and enter code GO245920 for updates on this award.

(2460) • John Kelly Labor Studies Scholarship Fund

Office and Professional Employees International Union
80 Eighth Avenue, Suite 610, New York, NY 10011
Phone: 212-367-0902
http://www.opeiu.org
Purpose: To offer scholarships to OPEIU members and associate members.
Eligibility: Applicants must be members of OPEIU in good standing or associate members for at least two years, and applicants must be either undergraduate or graduate students in one of the following areas of study: labor studies, industrial relations, union leadership and administration or non-degree programs sponsored by the National Labor College at the George Meany Center or similar institution. The selections shall be based on recommendations of an academic scholarship committee.
Target applicant(s): College students. Graduate school students. Adult students.
Amount: $3,250.
Number of awards: 10.
Deadline: March 31.
How to apply: Applications are available by phone or written request from the local union office, at the secretary-treasurer's office of the International Union or online.
Exclusive: Visit www.UltimateScholarshipBook.com and enter code OF246020 for updates on this award.

(2461) • John L. Dales Scholarship Fund

Screen Actors Guild Foundation
5757 Wilshire Boulevard, Suite 124, Los Angeles, CA 90036
Phone: 323-549-6649
Email: dlloyd@sag.org
http://www.sagfoundation.org
Purpose: To award scholarships to the families of the SAG.
Eligibility: Applicants must be a member of the Screen Actors Guild or a child of a member of the Screen Actors Guild. Transitional scholarships are open to members under the age of 26 must have been a member of the Screen Actors Guild for five years and have a lifetime earnings of $30,000. The parent of an applicant must have ten vested years of pension credits or a lifetime earnings of $150,000 earned in the Guild's jurisdiction. Children of members are eligible for standard scholarships and must also be under age 26. Applicants must submit an essay of 350 to 750 words on a topic of their choice. The award may be used during college or graduate school.
Target applicant(s): High school students. College students. Graduate school students.
Amount: Varies.
Number of awards: Varies.
Deadline: March 15.
How to apply: Applications are available online.
Exclusive: Visit www.UltimateScholarshipBook.com and enter code SC246120 for updates on this award.

(2462) • John Sarrin Scholarship

United Society of Friends Women, Inc.
Attn.: Dinah Geiger, Clerk, John Sarrin Scholarship Fund, 2757 S. CR 1050 E., Indianapolis, IN 46231
Phone: 515-729-1422
Email: dinageiger@att.net
http://usfwi.net/

Purpose: To support the education of ministers, missionaries, the children of ministers and other Friends who aspire to full-time Christian service.
Eligibility: Applicants must belong to the Society of Friends. They must be committed to staying drug and alcohol free, and they must agree to never join the armed forces of any country. Students must possess good moral character in order to receive and keep the scholarship.
Target applicant(s): Junior high students or younger. High school students. College students. Graduate school students. Adult students.
Amount: Varies.
Number of awards: Varies.
Deadline: January 31.
How to apply: Applications are available by written request.
Exclusive: Visit www.UltimateScholarshipBook.com and enter code UN246220 for updates on this award.

(2463) · John W McDevitt (Fourth Degree) Scholarship Fund

Knights of Columbus
Department of Scholarships, 1 Columbus Plaza, New Haven, CT 06510-3326
Phone: 203-752-4000
Email: info@kofc.org
http://www.kofc.org
Purpose: To provide financial assistance to college students who are Knights of Columbus members or family members of a member.
Eligibility: Applicants must be a Knights of Columbus member, or the wife, widow or child of a member in good standing. New applicants must also be entering their freshman year at a Catholic college or university.
Target applicant(s): High school students.
Amount: $1,500.
Number of awards: Varies.
Scholarship may be renewable.
Deadline: March 1.
How to apply: Applications are available by mail.
Exclusive: Visit www.UltimateScholarshipBook.com and enter code KN246320 for updates on this award.

(2464) · Jones-Laurence Award for Scholastic Achievement

Sigma Alpha Epsilon (SAE)
Dave Sandell, Sigma Alpha Epsilon Foundation Scholarships, 1856 Sheridan Road, Evanston, IL 60201-3837
Phone: 800-233-1856 x234
Email: dsandell@sae.net
http://www.sae.net
Purpose: To improve scholarship among active Sigma Alpha Epsilon members.
Eligibility: Applicants must be brothers of Sigma Alpha Epsilon in good standing and either must have junior standing or higher or must be pursuing full-time graduate study. This award is merit-based, with an emphasis on combining academic excellence, leadership, service and campus involvement. Applicants are nominated by their chapters and have a minimum 3.8 GPA.
Target applicant(s): College students. Graduate school students. Adult students.
Minimum GPA: 3.8
Amount: Varies.
Number of awards: Varies.
Deadline: March 1.
How to apply: Applications are available online.
Exclusive: Visit www.UltimateScholarshipBook.com and enter code SI246420 for updates on this award.

(2465) · Kappa Sigma Scholarship-Leadership Award

Kappa Sigma Endowment Fund
1610 Scottsville Road, Charlottesville, VA 22902
Phone: 804-295-3193
http://www.kappasigma.org/
Purpose: To reward young members on their outstanding journey of education.
Eligibility: Applicants must be a full-time undergraduate and have a minimum 2.5 cumulative GPA on a 4.0 scale.
Target applicant(s): College students. Adult students.
Minimum GPA: 2.5
Amount: Varies.
Number of awards: Varies.
Deadline: Varies.
How to apply: Applications are available online.
Exclusive: Visit www.UltimateScholarshipBook.com and enter code KA246520 for updates on this award.

(2466) · Kyutaro and Yasuo Abiko Memorial Scholarship

Japanese American Citizens League (JACL)
1765 Sutter Street, San Francisco, CA 94115
Phone: 415-921-5225
Email: jacl@jacl.org
http://www.jacl.org
Purpose: To aid National Japanese American Citizens League (JACL) members who are pursuing higher education.
Eligibility: Applicants must be National JACL members who are enrolled as full-time undergraduates at a U.S. institution of higher learning. Preference will be given to applicants who are studying agriculture or journalism. Selection is based on the overall strength of the application.
Target applicant(s): High school students. College students. Adult students.
Amount: Varies.
Number of awards: Varies.
Deadline: April 1.
How to apply: Applications are available online. An application form, official transcript, personal statement, one recommendation letter and proof of JACL membership are required.
Exclusive: Visit www.UltimateScholarshipBook.com and enter code JA246620 for updates on this award.

(2467) · Legacy Award

Elks National Foundation Headquarters
2750 North Lakeview Avenue, Chicago, IL 60614
Phone: 773-755-4732
Email: scholarship@elks.org
https://www.elks.org/scholars/
Purpose: To assist the descendants of Elk members.
Eligibility: Applicants must be children or grandchildren (including step-children/grandchildren and legal wards) of Elk members in good standing and be high school seniors planning to attend accredited U.S. postsecondary institutions (with the exception of some non-U.S. Elks Lodges). Applicants must also take or have taken the SAT or ACT. The selection committee will evaluate applicants on the core values of

knowledge, charity, community and integrity. Financial need is not a consideration.
Target applicant(s): High school students.
Amount: $4,000.
Number of awards: 300.
Deadline: February 2.
How to apply: Applications are available from local Elks Lodges, online or by written request.
Exclusive: Visit www.UltimateScholarshipBook.com and enter code EL246720 for updates on this award.

(2468) • Lillian and Arthur Dunn Scholarship

National Society Daughters of the American Revolution
Committee Services Office, Attn.: Scholarships, 1776 D Street NW, Washington, DC 20006-5303
Phone: 202-628-1776
Email: scholarships@dar.org
http://www.dar.org/national-society/scholarships
Purpose: To assist the children of members with their education.
Eligibility: Applicants must be sons or daughters of current women members of NSDAR, must be U.S. citizens and plan to attend an accredited U.S. college or university. All applicants must obtain a letter of sponsorship from their local DAR chapter.
Target applicant(s): High school students. College students. Adult students.
Amount: $2,500.
Number of awards: 2.
Scholarship may be renewable.
Deadline: February 10.
How to apply: Applications are available by written request with a self-addressed, stamped envelope.
Exclusive: Visit www.UltimateScholarshipBook.com and enter code NA246820 for updates on this award.

(2469) • Literacy Grants

Honor Society of Phi Kappa Phi
7576 Goodwood Boulevard, Baton Rouge, LA 70806
Phone: 800-804-9880
Email: awards@phikappaphi.org
http://www.phikappaphi.org
Purpose: To award grants to Phi Kappa Phi members and chapters to offer literacy programs.
Eligibility: The project leader must be a member of Phi Kappa Phi. Previous winners have provided books and book bags to literacy programs, organized literacy fairs and conducted research on literacy.
Target applicant(s): College students. Graduate school students. Adult students.
Amount: Up to $2,500.
Number of awards: Varies.
Deadline: April 1.
How to apply: Applications are available online.
Exclusive: Visit www.UltimateScholarshipBook.com and enter code HO246920 for updates on this award.

(2470) • Maids of Athena Scholarships

American Hellenic Education Progressive Association
1909 Q Street NW, Suite 500, Washington, DC 20009
Phone: 202-232-6300
Email: ahepa@ahepa.org
https://ahepa.org/Education-Scholarships.htm
Purpose: To support members of the Maids of Athena.
Eligibility: Students must demonstrate financial need and academic achievement. Applicants must be high school seniors, college undergraduates or graduate students. Selection is based on academic achievement, financial need and participation in the organization.
Target applicant(s): High school students. College students. Graduate school students. Adult students.
Amount: Varies.
Number of awards: Varies.
Deadline: June 15.
How to apply: Applications are available online.
Exclusive: Visit www.UltimateScholarshipBook.com and enter code AM247020 for updates on this award.

(2471) • Margaret Jerome Sampson Scholarship

Phi Upsilon Omicron Inc.
National Office , P.O. Box 50970, Bowling Green, KY 42102-4270
Phone: 270-904-1340
Email: national@phiu.org
http://www.phiu.org
Purpose: To aid Phi Upsilon Omicron members who are working toward bachelor's degrees in family and consumer sciences.
Eligibility: Applicants must be Phi Upsilon Omicron (Phi U) members. They must be full-time students who are enrolled in a family and consumer sciences degree program at the baccalaureate level. Preference will be given to applicants who are majoring in food and nutrition or dietetics. Selection is based on academic merit, participation in Phi U and stated career goals.
Target applicant(s): College students. Adult students.
Amount: $5,000.
Number of awards: Up to 7.
Deadline: February 1.
How to apply: Applications are available online. An application form, three recommendation letters, an official transcript and a financial statement are required.
Exclusive: Visit www.UltimateScholarshipBook.com and enter code PH247120 for updates on this award.

(2472) • Martin Luther King, Jr. Memorial Scholarship

California Teachers Association (CTA)
CTA Human Rights Department, P.O. Box 921, Burlingame, CA 94011-0921
Phone: 650-697-1400
http://www.cta.org/scholarships
Purpose: To encourage ethnic minority students to become teachers and support the continuing education of ethnic minority teachers.
Eligibility: Applicants must be African American, American Indian/Alaska Native, Asian/Pacific Islander or Hispanic students pursuing a teaching-related career in public education. Candidates must also be active members of the California Teachers Association or Student California Teachers Association or the dependents of an active, retired-life or deceased California Teachers Association member.
Target applicant(s): High school students. College students. Graduate school students. Adult students.
Amount: Up to $4,000.
Number of awards: Varies.
Deadline: February 17.
How to apply: Applications are available online.
Exclusive: Visit www.UltimateScholarshipBook.com and enter code CA247220 for updates on this award.

(2473) · Mary E. Bivins Religious Scholarship

Mary E. Bivins Foundation
2311 West 16th Avenue, Amarillo, TX 79102
Phone: 806-379-9400
Email: info@bivinsfoundation.org
https://www.bivinsfoundation.org/scholarship/scholarship-program/
Purpose: To assist students pursuing Christian ministry.
Eligibility: Applicants must be graduate students pursuing a master degree in a field which prepares them to preach the Christian religion.
Target applicant(s): Graduate school students. Adult students.
Amount: $3,500.
Number of awards: 1.
Deadline: January 5.
How to apply: Applications are available online.
Exclusive: Visit www.UltimateScholarshipBook.com and enter code MA247320 for updates on this award.

(2474) · Mary Macey Scholarship

Women Grocers of America
1005 N. Glebe Road, Suite 250, Arlington, VA 22201
Phone: 703-516-0700
https://www.nationalgrocers.org/foundation/
Purpose: To encourage students who are interested in the grocery industry.
Eligibility: Applicants must work in a grocery store (summer jobs are acceptable). The awards will go toward tuition at two-year or four-year institutions. Students must explain their interest in the grocery industry and obtain a letter of recommendation from their supervisor.
Target applicant(s): High school students. College students. Graduate school students. Adult students.
Minimum GPA: 2.0
Amount: $1,500.
Number of awards: 3-4.
Scholarship may be renewable.
Deadline: June 14.
How to apply: Applications are available online.
Exclusive: Visit www.UltimateScholarshipBook.com and enter code WO247420 for updates on this award.

(2475) · Michael Hakeem Memorial College Essay Contest

Freedom from Religion Foundation
P.O. Box 750, Madison, WI 53701
Phone: 608-256-8900
Email: info@ffrf.org
https://ffrf.org/outreach/awards
Purpose: To assist current college students who write an essay about freedom from religion.
Eligibility: Applicants must write a four- to five-page essay on the provided topic. Recent topic choices have been, "Why I am an atheist/agnostic/unbeliever," "Growing up a freethinker" or "Rejecting religion." More details about the topic are available online.
Target applicant(s): High school students. College students.
Amount: $200-$3,000.
Number of awards: Varies.
Deadline: July 1.
How to apply: There is no application form. In addition to the essay, applicants must submit a one-paragraph biography and should not include a resume.
Exclusive: Visit www.UltimateScholarshipBook.com and enter code FR247520 for updates on this award.

(2476) · Michael J. Quill Scholarship Fund

Transport Worker Union of American, AFL-CIO
Michael J. Quill Scholarship Fund , 501 3rd Street NW, 9th Floor, Washington, DC 20001
Phone: 202-719-3900
http://www.twu.org
Purpose: To provide financial assistance to the dependents of TWU members.
Eligibility: Applicants must be high school seniors and may be the children of present, retired or deceased TWU members in good standing or meet other eligibility requirements. Recipients are selected by a public drawing.
Target applicant(s): High school students.
Amount: $4,800.
Number of awards: 15.
Scholarship may be renewable.
Deadline: April 22.
How to apply: Applications are available from local unions and the union publication. They're also available online.
Exclusive: Visit www.UltimateScholarshipBook.com and enter code TR247620 for updates on this award.

(2477) · Migrant Farmworker Baccalaureate Scholarship

Geneseo Migrant Center
3 Mt. Morris-Leicester Road, Leicester, NY 14481
Phone: 800-245-5681
Email: info@migrant.net
http://www.migrant.net
Purpose: To assist students with migrant histories.
Eligibility: Applicants must have a recent history of movement for agricultural employment, a good academic record and financial need. Applicants must also have successfully completed one year of schooling at an accredited post-secondary institution and may also use the award in graduate school.
Target applicant(s): College students. Adult students.
Amount: Up to $20,000.
Number of awards: 1.
Scholarship may be renewable.
Deadline: July 1.
How to apply: Applications are available online.
Exclusive: Visit www.UltimateScholarshipBook.com and enter code GE247720 for updates on this award.

(2478) · Modern Woodmen of America Scholarship

Modern Woodmen of America
1701 1st Avenue, P.O. Box 2005, Rock Island, IL 61204
Phone: 309-786-6481
Email: memberservice@modern-woodmen.org
http://www.modernwoodmen.org
Purpose: To support beneficial members of Modern Woodmen.
Eligibility: Applicants must be high school seniors and be beneficial members of Modern Woodmen for at least two years. Applicants should be in the upper half of their graduating class. There are national, regional and one-time awards.
Target applicant(s): High school students.
Amount: Varies.

Number of awards: Varies.
Deadline: January 15.
How to apply: Applications are available online.
Exclusive: Visit www.UltimateScholarshipBook.com and enter code MO247820 for updates on this award.

(2479) • Morgan Smith Memorial Scholarship

Aviation Boatswain Mates Association (ABMA)
Scholarship Chairman, Mr. Terry L. New, 3193 Glastonbury Drive, Virginia Beach, VA 23453
Email: secretary@abma-usn.org
http://www.abma-usn.org
Purpose: To support family members of ABMA.
Eligibility: Applicants must be the spouses or dependent children of ABMA members who have paid dues for at least two years. In addition to the application, applicants must write a letter stating their professional goals and how they plan to reach them.
Target applicant(s): High school students. College students. Graduate school students. Adult students.
Amount: Varies.
Number of awards: Varies.
Deadline: June 1.
How to apply: Applications are available online.
Exclusive: Visit www.UltimateScholarshipBook.com and enter code AV247920 for updates on this award.

(2480) • Moris J. and Betty Kaplun Scholarship

Kaplun Foundation
Essay Contest Committee, P.O. Box 234428, Great Neck, NY 11023
http://www.kaplunfoundation.org
Purpose: To reward essays about Jewish-related topics.
Eligibility: Applicants must be in grades 7 through 12. Grades 7 through 9 are level one, and grades 10 through 12 are level two. Applicants must submit essays on Jewish-related topics listed on the website, and essays must be typed, double-spaced and a minimum of 250 words. Level one essays may not be more than 1,000 words. Level two essays may not be more than 1,500 words. A recent level one topic has been, "What person of importance to the Jewish people, past or present, would you like to meet and why?" A recent level two topic has been, "Antisemitism plagues all Jews regardless of religious adherence. How do you see yourself reacting to it?"
Target applicant(s): Junior high students or younger. High school students.
Amount: $750-$1,800.
Number of awards: 12.
Deadline: March 3.
How to apply: Essays must be submitted by mail.
Exclusive: Visit www.UltimateScholarshipBook.com and enter code KA248020 for updates on this award.

(2481) • Mortar Board National Foundation Fellowship

Mortar Board National Foundation
1200 Chambers Road, #201, Columbus, OH 43212
Phone: (614) 488-4094
http://www.mortarboard.org
Purpose: To support Mortar Board members pursuing post-graduate degrees who exemplify the tenets of scholarship, leadership and dedication to service at their college Alma Mater.
Eligibility: Applicants must be current or former members of Mortar Board entering a post-graduate degree program who have not previously been awarded a Mortar National Foundation Fellowship. They must complete the online application, submit two letters of recommendation and a current, official transcript. Fellowship recipients must be ready to begin and complete the year of post-graduate study upon acceptance of the fellowship award.
Target applicant(s): College students. Adult students.
Amount: $3,000-$5,000.
Number of awards: 12.
Deadline: March 1.
How to apply: Applications are available online.
Exclusive: Visit www.UltimateScholarshipBook.com and enter code MO248120 for updates on this award.

(2482) • Mortin Scholarship

Triangle Education Foundation
Chairman, Scholarship and Loan Committee, 120 S. Center Street, Plainfield, IN 46168-1214
Phone: 317-837-9641
Email: TEF@Triangle.org
http://www.triangleef.org/
Purpose: To help deserving active members of Triangle Fraternity in completing their education.
Eligibility: Applicants must be active members of the Triangle Fraternity enrolled in a course of study leading to a degree. Applicants must have at least a 3.0 GPA, have completed at least two full academic years of school and be undergraduates in the year following their application. Selection is based on financial need, grades and participation in campus and Triangle activities.
Target applicant(s): College students. Adult students.
Minimum GPA: 3.0
Amount: $2,500.
Number of awards: 1.
Deadline: February 15.
How to apply: Applications are available online.
Exclusive: Visit www.UltimateScholarshipBook.com and enter code TR248220 for updates on this award.

(2483) • National Eagle Scout Association Academic Scholarships

National Eagle Scout Association, Boy Scouts of America
1325 West Walnut Hill Lane, P.O. Box 152079, Irving, TX 75015-2079
Phone: 972-580-2000
Email: nesa@scouting.org
https://nesa.academicworks.com
Purpose: To support Eagle Scouts.
Eligibility: Applicants must be Eagle Scouts who have received credentials from the national office. They must be graduating high school and entering college in the year of application and have an SAT score of 1200 or higher or an ACT score of 28 or higher. Demonstrated leadership ability in scouting and record of participation in activities outside of scouting are required.
Target applicant(s): High school students.
Amount: $2,500-$50,000.
Number of awards: Varies.
Scholarship may be renewable.
Deadline: October 31.
How to apply: Applications are available online. An application form, transcript and letter of recommendation from a scout leader are required.

Exclusive: Visit www.UltimateScholarshipBook.com and enter code NA248320 for updates on this award.

(2484) · National Eagle Scout Association STEM Scholarship

National Eagle Scout Association, Boy Scouts of America
1325 West Walnut Hill Lane, P.O. Box 152079, Irving, TX 75015-2079
Phone: 972-580-2000
Email: nesa@scouting.org
https://nesa.academicworks.com
Purpose: To support Eagle Scouts who plan to major in a science, technology, engineering or math field based on academic achievement.
Eligibility: Applicants must be seniors in high school who are planning to enter college the year that they apply and must be active members of the Boy Scouts or Varsity Scouts who have received the Eagle Scout award.
Target applicant(s): High school students.
Amount: $50,000.
Number of awards: Varies.
Scholarship may be renewable.
Deadline: October 31.
How to apply: Applications are available online.
Exclusive: Visit www.UltimateScholarshipBook.com and enter code NA248420 for updates on this award.

(2485) · National Honor Society Scholarship

National Honor Society
c/o National Association of Secondary School Principals, 1904 Association Drive, Reston, VA 20191
Phone: 703-860-0200
Email: nhs@nhs.us
https://www.nhs.us
Purpose: To recognize NHS members.
Eligibility: Applicants must be senior National Honor Society members. Applicants must demonstrate character, scholarship, service and leadership.
Target applicant(s): High school students.
Amount: $2,325-$20,125.
Number of awards: 400.
Deadline: December 7.
How to apply: Application forms are available from your local NHS chapter adviser.
Exclusive: Visit www.UltimateScholarshipBook.com and enter code NA248520 for updates on this award.

(2486) · National Leadership Council (NLC) Award

National Society of Collegiate Scholars (NSCS)
2000 M Street NW, Suite 600, Washington, DC 20036
Phone: 202-265-9000
Email: nscs@nscs.org
http://www.nscs.org/
Purpose: To help NSCS members attain their goals and to recognize their achievements in academics, service and leadership.
Eligibility: Applicants must be college undergraduates. Selection is based on the overall strength of the application.
Target applicant(s): College students. Adult students.
Amount: Varies.
Number of awards: Varies.
Deadline: February 9.
How to apply: Applications are available online.
Exclusive: Visit www.UltimateScholarshipBook.com and enter code NA248620 for updates on this award.

(2487) · National Presbyterian College Scholarship

Presbyterian Church (USA)
100 Witherspoon Street, Louisville, KY 40202
Phone: 800-728-7228 x5224
Email: finaid@pcusa.org
https://www.presbyterianmission.org/what-we-do/grants-scholarships/
Purpose: To recognize young students preparing to enter as full-time incoming freshmen in one of the participating colleges related to the Presbyterian Church.
Eligibility: Applicants must be members of the Presbyterian Church, U.S. citizens or permanent residents and high school seniors planning to attend a participating college related to PCUSA. Applicants must also demonstrate financial need and take the SAT or ACT exam no later than December 15 of their senior year in high school. Applicants must have recommendations from both their church pastors and high school guidance counselors.
Target applicant(s): High school students.
Minimum GPA: 3.0
Amount: Up to $1,500.
Number of awards: 25-30.
Scholarship may be renewable.
Deadline: May 15.
How to apply: Applications are available online.
Exclusive: Visit www.UltimateScholarshipBook.com and enter code PR248720 for updates on this award.

(2488) · National Propane Gas Foundation

National Propane Gas Foundation
1899 L Street, NW, Suite 350, Washington, DC 20036
Phone: 202-355-1328
Email: jcasey@npga.org
http://www.npga.org
Purpose: To support the educational opportunities of dependent children of employees of National Propane Gas Association (NPGA) member companies.
Eligibility: Applicants must be high school seniors or undergraduate students and have a 2.6 or higher GPA. Selection is based on academic achievement, letters of recommendation, extra curricular activity involvement, employment experience and financial need.
Target applicant(s): High school students. College students. Adult students.
Minimum GPA: 2.6
Amount: $1,000-$2,000.
Number of awards: Varies.
Deadline: February 15.
How to apply: Applications are only available online. In addition to the application form, students must submit an official transcript and have two letters of recommendation mailed directly to NPGA.
Exclusive: Visit www.UltimateScholarshipBook.com and enter code NA248820 for updates on this award.

(2489) • NESA Hall/McElwain Merit Scholarships

National Eagle Scout Association, Boy Scouts of America
1325 West Walnut Hill Lane, P.O. Box 152079, Irving, TX 75015-2079
Phone: 972-580-2000
Email: nesa@scouting.org
https://nesa.academicworks.com
Purpose: To assist Eagle Scouts.
Eligibility: Applicants must have received credentials from the national office. They must be graduating high school seniors or college freshmen, sophomores or juniors. A minimum SAT score of 1200 or ACT score of 28 is required. Applicants must have demonstrated leadership ability in scouting and a record of participation in activities outside of scouting.
Target applicant(s): High school students. College students. Adult students.
Amount: $5,000.
Number of awards: Varies.
Deadline: October 31.
How to apply: Applications are available online. An application form, transcript and letter of recommendation from a scout leader are required.
Exclusive: Visit www.UltimateScholarshipBook.com and enter code NA248920 for updates on this award.

(2490) • NIADA Scholarship

National Independent Automobile Dealers Association
2521 Brown Boulevard, Arlington, TX 76006-5203
Phone: 817-640-3838
Email: rachel@niada.com
http://www.niada.com
Purpose: To support high school seniors with academic achievement and ties to NIADA members.
Eligibility: Applicants must be the son, daughter or grandchild of a NIADA member, have an excellent high school academic record and have high SAT or ACT scores. Applications, transcripts, test scores and a maximum of five recommendation letters are required.
Target applicant(s): High school students.
Amount: $3,500.
Number of awards: 4.
Deadline: March 17.
How to apply: Applications are available online and should be submitted to the state association.
Exclusive: Visit www.UltimateScholarshipBook.com and enter code NA249020 for updates on this award.

(2491) • Non-Traditional Student Scholarship

American Legion Auxiliary
8945 N. Meridian Street, Indianapolis, IN 46260
Phone: 317-569-4500
Email: alahq@legion-aux.org
https://www.alaforveterans.org/scholarships/
Purpose: To support students resuming formal schooling after an interruption.
Eligibility: Applicants must be members of The American Legion, the American Legion Auxiliary or Sons of The American Legion and be undergraduate students who are enrolled in at least six hours per semester or four hours per quarter. Applicants must also be students resuming formal schooling after an interruption or who have had at least one year of college schooling and need financial assistance to continue their degree. Selection is based on financial need, scholastic achievement, character and goals.
Target applicant(s): College students. Adult students.
Amount: $2,000.
Number of awards: 5.
Deadline: March 1.
How to apply: Applications are available online.
Exclusive: Visit www.UltimateScholarshipBook.com and enter code AM249120 for updates on this award.

(2492) • Opportunity Scholarships for Lutheran Laywomen

Women of the Evangelical Lutheran Church in America
8765 W. Higgins Road, Chicago, IL 60631
Phone: 800-638-3522 x2730
Email: women.elca@elca.org
http://www.womenoftheelca.org
Purpose: To assist Lutheran women in studying for careers other than ordained ministry.
Eligibility: Applicants must be U.S. citizens, members of the Evangelical Lutheran Church in America (ELCA) and at least 21 years of age. They must also have had an interruption in education of two years or more since graduating from high school. There are four scholarships awarded with individual criteria including for women of color; for women studying for ELCA service abroad; graduate students preparing for careers in Christian service and for undergraduate, graduate, professional or vocational study.
Target applicant(s): College students. Graduate school students. Adult students.
Amount: Varies.
Number of awards: Varies.
Deadline: February 15.
How to apply: Applications are available online.
Exclusive: Visit www.UltimateScholarshipBook.com and enter code WO249220 for updates on this award.

(2493) • Owens-Bell Award

National Association of Blacks in Criminal Justice
1801 Fayetteville Street, 106 Whiting Criminal Justice Building,
P.O. Box 20011-C, Durham, NC 27707
Phone: 919-683-1801
Email: Office@NABCJ.org
http://www.nabcj.org
Purpose: To reward an individual NABCJ member for outstanding chapter development and leadership.
Eligibility: Applicants must be nominated by a member of NABCJ.
Target applicant(s): High school students. College students. Adult students.
Amount: Varies.
Number of awards: 1.
Deadline: March 15.
How to apply: Nomination applications are available online.
Exclusive: Visit www.UltimateScholarshipBook.com and enter code NA249320 for updates on this award.

(2494) • Phi Delta Kappa International Scholarship Grants for Prospective Educators

Phi Delta Kappa International
P.O. Box 7888, Bloomington, IN 47407
Phone: 812-339-1156
Email: scholarships@pdkintl.org

http://www.pdkintl.org
Purpose: To aid future and current education majors who are affiliated with Phi Delta Kappa (PDK) or Educators Rising.
Eligibility: Applicants must be high school seniors who are planning to major in education in college or current undergraduates who are majoring in education. They must have a connection to Phi Delta Kappa (PDK) or Educators Rising. Selection is based on the overall strength of the application.
Target applicant(s): High school students. College students. Adult students.
Amount: Varies.
Number of awards: Varies.
Deadline: April 2.
How to apply: Applications are available online. An application form and supporting materials are required.
Exclusive: Visit www.UltimateScholarshipBook.com and enter code PH249420 for updates on this award.

(2495) • Phi Kappa Phi Fellowship

Honor Society of Phi Kappa Phi
7576 Goodwood Boulevard, Baton Rouge, LA 70806
Phone: 800-804-9880
Email: awards@phikappaphi.org
http://www.phikappaphi.org
Purpose: To provide fellowships for Phi Kappa Phi members entering their first year of graduate or professional studies.
Eligibility: Applicants may enter any professional or graduate field and must not have completed one full term of graduate study. Selection is based on academic achievement, service, leadership, letters of recommendation, personal statement and career goals.
Target applicant(s): College students. Graduate school students. Adult students.
Amount: $5,000-$15,000.
Number of awards: 57.
Deadline: April 15.
How to apply: Applications are available online.
Exclusive: Visit www.UltimateScholarshipBook.com and enter code HO249520 for updates on this award.

(2496) • Presbyterian Church USA Student Opportunity Scholarships

Presbyterian Church (USA)
100 Witherspoon Street, Louisville, KY 40202
Phone: 800-728-7228 x5224
Email: finaid@pcusa.org
https://www.presbyterianmission.org/what-we-do/grants-scholarships/
Purpose: To aid students pursuing disciplines that further the mission of the Presbyterian Church.
Eligibility: Applicants must be members of the Presbyterian Church (USA) who have completed their first year of college. They must be enrolled full-time and have a GPA of 2.5 or greater. Students must be pursuing a bachelor's degree in education, health service/science, religious studies, sacred music or social service/sciences. Financial need is required. Preference is given to members of racial and ethnic minorities.
Target applicant(s): College students. Adult students.
Minimum GPA: 2.5
Amount: Up to $2,000.
Number of awards: Varies.
Scholarship may be renewable.
Deadline: May 15.
How to apply: Applications are available by mail or email.
Exclusive: Visit www.UltimateScholarshipBook.com and enter code PR249620 for updates on this award.

(2497) • Priscilla R. Morton Scholarship

United Methodist Church
Office of Loans and Scholarships, P.O. Box 340007, Nashville, TN 37203-0007
Phone: 615-340-7342
Email: umscholar@gbhem.org
http://www.gbhem.org/loans-and-scholarships
Purpose: To help students who are members of the United Methodist Church.
Eligibility: Applicants must be active, full members of the United Methodist Church for at least a year before applying and enrolled or planning to enroll in an accredited institution working towards a degree full-time. The scholarship may be used for undergraduate, graduate or professional study. Applicants should provide application forms, transcripts, references, membership proof and essays. Applicant should prove financial need. Preference is given to students who enroll at a United Methodist-related college, university, seminary or theological school.
Target applicant(s): High school students. College students. Graduate school students. Adult students.
Minimum GPA: 3.5
Amount: Varies.
Number of awards: Varies.
Deadline: March 1.
How to apply: Applications are available online.
Exclusive: Visit www.UltimateScholarshipBook.com and enter code UN249720 for updates on this award.

(2498) • Religious Liberty Essay Scholarship Contest

Baptist Joint Committee for Religious Liberty
Essay Contest, 200 Maryland Avenue, NE, Washington, DC 20002
Phone: 202-544-4226
Email: cwatson@bjconline.org
https://bjconline.org/
Purpose: To reward students who have written outstanding essays on religious liberty.
Eligibility: Applicants must be high school juniors or seniors. Students must submit an essay relating to religious freedom. Selection is based on the overall strength of the essay.
Target applicant(s): High school students.
Amount: $500-$2,000.
Number of awards: 3.
Deadline: March 8.
How to apply: Applications are available online.
Exclusive: Visit www.UltimateScholarshipBook.com and enter code BA249820 for updates on this award.

(2499) • Rev. Dr. Karen Layman Gift of Hope Scholarship

United Methodist Church
Office of Loans and Scholarships, P.O. Box 340007, Nashville, TN 37203-0007
Phone: 615-340-7342
Email: umscholar@gbhem.org
http://www.gbhem.org/loans-and-scholarships

Purpose: To support United Methodist students who are leaders in the church.
Eligibility: Applicants must have been full, active members and leaders in the United Methodist Church for at least three years. They must be U.S. citizens, permanent residents or members of the Central Conferences. Students must be enrolled in a full-time undergraduate degree program at an accredited U.S. institution with a GPA of 3.0 or higher.
Target applicant(s): High school students. College students. Adult students.
Minimum GPA: 3.0
Amount: $1,000.
Number of awards: Varies.
Deadline: March 1.
How to apply: Applications are available online. An application form, transcript, essay and three letters of recommendation are required.
Exclusive: Visit www.UltimateScholarshipBook.com and enter code UN249920 for updates on this award.

(2500) • Richard F. Walsh, Alfred W. DiTolla, Harold P. Spivak Foundation Award

International Alliance of Theatrical Stage Employees, Artists and Allied Crafts of the U.S.
207 West 25th Street, 4th Floor, New York, NY 10001
http://www.iatse-intl.org
Purpose: To provide scholarships for the children of IATSE members.
Eligibility: Applicants must be the sons or daughters of IATSE members in good standing, be high school seniors and apply for admission to an accredited college or university full-time leading towards a bachelor's degree.
Target applicant(s): High school students.
Amount: $10,000.
Number of awards: 5.
Scholarship may be renewable.
Deadline: December 31.
How to apply: Applications are available by written request (through an online form).
Exclusive: Visit www.UltimateScholarshipBook.com and enter code IN250020 for updates on this award.

(2501) • Robert G. Porter Post-Secondary Scholarships

American Federation of Teachers
555 New Jersey Avenue NW, Washington, DC 20001
Phone: 202-879-4400
http://www.aft.org
Purpose: To provide scholarships to AFT members' dependents.
Eligibility: Applicants must be graduating high school seniors. The award is merit-based and will consider academics, community service and performance on the required labor-related essay. Applicants' parents or guardians must be AFT members for at least one year.
Target applicant(s): High school students.
Amount: $1,000-$2,000.
Number of awards: 14.
Scholarship may be renewable.
Deadline: March 31.
How to apply: Applications are available by written request.
Exclusive: Visit www.UltimateScholarshipBook.com and enter code AM250120 for updates on this award.

(2502) • Robert G. Porter Scholars Program for Members

American Federation of Teachers
555 New Jersey Avenue NW, Washington, DC 20001
Phone: 202-879-4400
http://www.aft.org
Purpose: To provide grants to AFT members.
Eligibility: Applicants must be AFT members who have been in good standing for at least one year and intend to pursue courses in their field of work. Applicants must submit an essay on a labor-related topic.
Target applicant(s): Graduate school students. Adult students.
Amount: $1,000.
Number of awards: 10.
Deadline: March 31.
How to apply: Applications are available by written request.
Exclusive: Visit www.UltimateScholarshipBook.com and enter code AM250220 for updates on this award.

(2503) • Robert Sheppard Leadership Awards

National Society of High School Scholars
1936 North Druid Hills Road, Atlanta, GA 30319
Phone: 404-235-5500
https://www.nshss.org/scholarships/
Purpose: To reward students who possess an outstanding commitment to community service.
Eligibility: Applicants must be NSHSS members and be high school sophomores, juniors or seniors. Students must submit a personal statement describing a volunteer project in which they feel they benefited from as much as the recipients, why they became involved in that project, what it entailed and the outcome. Applicants must also submit a list of service activities.
Target applicant(s): High school students.
Amount: $1,000-$2,500.
Number of awards: 5.
Deadline: March 15.
How to apply: Applications are available online and must include: personal statement, list of service activities, transcript, educator recommendation, principal and counselor's name and email and color headshot.
Exclusive: Visit www.UltimateScholarshipBook.com and enter code NA250320 for updates on this award.

(2504) • Rust Scholarship

Triangle Education Foundation
Chairman, Scholarship and Loan Committee, 120 S. Center Street, Plainfield, IN 46168-1214
Phone: 317-837-9641
Email: TEF@Triangle.org
http://www.triangleef.org/
Purpose: To help deserving active members of Triangle Fraternity in completing their education.
Eligibility: Applicants must be active members of the Triangle Fraternity who have completed at least two full academic years of school and will be undergraduates in the school year following their application. Selection is based on financial need, grades and participation in campus and Triangle activities. Preference is given to applicants in engineering and the hard sciences. Applicants must have at least a 3.0 GPA.
Target applicant(s): College students. Adult students.
Minimum GPA: 3.0
Amount: $6,000.

Number of awards: 1.
Deadline: February 15.
How to apply: Applications are available online.
Exclusive: Visit www.UltimateScholarshipBook.com and enter code TR250420 for updates on this award.

(2505) • S. Frank Bud Raftery Scholarship

IUPAT International Office
7234 Parkway Drive, Hanover, MD 21076
Phone: 410-564-5900
Email: mail@iupat.org
https://iupat.org/member-information/scholarships/
Purpose: To provide scholarships for the children of IUPAT members.
Eligibility: Applicants must be the children or legally-adopted dependents of an IUPAT member in good standing. Selection is based on a 1,000- to 2,000-word essay on a subject chosen by the IUPAT.
Target applicant(s): High school students. College students. Adult students.
Amount: $2,000.
Number of awards: 10.
Deadline: January 31.
How to apply: Applications are available by written request.
Exclusive: Visit www.UltimateScholarshipBook.com and enter code IU250520 for updates on this award.

(2506) • Sal Ingrassia Scholarship

International Union of Electronic, Electrical, Salaried, Machine and Furniture Workers-Communications Workers of America
2701 Dryden Road, Dayton, OH 45439
Phone: 937-298-9984
https://www.iue-cwa.org/
Purpose: To support IUE-CWA members and their families.
Eligibility: Applicants must be IUE-CWA members, employees of IUE-CWA or have a parent or grandparent who is employed by IUE-CWA. Students must already be accepted for admission or must be attending an accredited college, university, nursing or technical school as a full-time student.
Target applicant(s): High school students. College students. Adult students.
Amount: $2,500.
Number of awards: 1.
Deadline: March 31.
How to apply: Applications are available online.
Exclusive: Visit www.UltimateScholarshipBook.com and enter code IN250620 for updates on this award.

(2507) • Sam Rose Memorial Scholarship

Ladies Auxiliary of the Fleet Reserve Association
Gini Larson PNP, National Scholarship Chairman, 2187 Capeheart Street, Ingleside, TX 78362-6222
Phone: 361-442-5707
Email: lovedduck@aol.com
http://www.la-fra.org
Purpose: To support the descendants of Fleet Reserve Association members.
Eligibility: Applicants must have a deceased father or grandfather who was a member of the Fleet Reserve Association or was eligible for membership at the time of death.
Target applicant(s): High school students. College students. Adult students.
Amount: Varies.
Number of awards: Varies.
Deadline: April 15.
How to apply: Applications are available online.
Exclusive: Visit www.UltimateScholarshipBook.com and enter code LA250720 for updates on this award.

(2508) • Sandra Jo Hornick Scholarship

Kappa Delta Pi Educational Foundation
3707 Woodview Trace, Indianapolis, IN 46268-1158
Phone: 800-284-3167
Email: foundation@kdp.org
http://www.kdp.org
Purpose: To aid Kappa Delta Pi members who are studying education.
Eligibility: Applicants must be active members of Kappa Delta Pi. They must be undergraduate students who are majoring in education. Selection is based on the overall strength of the application.
Target applicant(s): College students. Adult students.
Amount: $1,000.
Number of awards: 2.
Deadline: May 1.
How to apply: Applications are available online. An application form, transcript, one reference letter, a personal essay and the applicant's Kappa Delta Pi membership number are required.
Exclusive: Visit www.UltimateScholarshipBook.com and enter code KA250820 for updates on this award.

(2509) • Service Employees International Union Scholarships

Service Employees International Union
c/o Scholarship Program Administrators Inc., P.O. Box 23737, Nashville, TN 37202-3737
Phone: 800-424-8592
http://www.seiu.org
Purpose: To give financial assistance to members of the SEIU and their children.
Eligibility: For the $1,000 scholarship, applicants must be members or the children of members of SEIU who have been in good standing for at least three years. Applicants must also be enrolled in an accredited college or university and should not have completed more than one year of college. For the $1,500 scholarship, applicants must be members or the children of members of SEIU returning full time to an accredited college or university as a sophomore, junior or senior or attending an accredited community college, trade or technical school. All applicants must read a report online and answer questions.
Target applicant(s): High school students. College students. Adult students.
Amount: $1,000-$1,500.
Number of awards: Varies.
Deadline: March 2.
How to apply: Applications are available online.
Exclusive: Visit www.UltimateScholarshipBook.com and enter code SE250920 for updates on this award.

(2510) • Sheet Metal Workers' International Scholarship Fund

Sheet Metal Workers' International Association
1750 New York Avenue NW, 6th Floor, Washington, DC 20006-5389

Phone: 202-662-0858
Email: scholarship@smart-union.org
https://smart-union.org/
Purpose: To provide scholarships for members of the SMWIA and their families.
Eligibility: Applicants must be SMWIA members, covered employees, or dependent spouses or children under the age of 25 of SMWIA members or covered employees. Applicants must also be full-time students or accepted to be full-time students at an accredited college or university. Only qualified applicants from local unions that participate in the one-cent check off are eligible for these four-year scholarships. Selection is based on information on SMWIA membership, including information on the local union's jurisdiction and family member's SMWIA membership, high school transcript, SAT/ACT scores or college transcript if already enrolled in college, an essay on the importance of SMWIA to the applicant's family and a letter of recommendation.
Target applicant(s): High school students. College students.
Amount: $6,000.
Number of awards: 34.
Scholarship may be renewable.
Deadline: March 1.
How to apply: Applications are available by email and written request.
Exclusive: Visit www.UltimateScholarshipBook.com and enter code SH251020 for updates on this award.

(2511) • Shopko Teammate and Family Scholarship Program

ShopKo Foundation
P.O. Box 19060, Green Bay, WI 54307-9060
Phone: 920-429-4054
Email: shopkofoundation@shopko.com
http://www.shopko.com
Purpose: To provide educational opportunities for Shopko employees and their families.
Eligibility: Applicants must be Shopko employees who have been with the company for at least one year or their dependents under the age of 24. Students should be planning to enroll or enrolled full-time at a post-secondary, accredited college, university, vocational or technical school. Factors considered include academic record, leadership and community activities, honors, work experience and future goals.
Target applicant(s): High school students. College students. Adult students.
Amount: Up to $2,500.
Number of awards: Varies.
Deadline: March 1.
How to apply: Applications are available online or from Shopko stores.
Exclusive: Visit www.UltimateScholarshipBook.com and enter code SH251120 for updates on this award.

(2512) • Shropshire Scholarship

Civitan
Civitan International Foundation, P.O. Box 130744, Birmingham, AL 35213-0744
Phone: 205-591-8910
Email: civitan@civitan.org
http://www.civitan.org
Purpose: The Shropshire Scholarship assists deserving Civitan members who will pursue careers that further the ideals of Civitan International, such as working toward world peace and unity, fighting for justice and building better citizenship.
Eligibility: Applicants must be a Civitan, Campus Civitan or Junior Civitan and must have been a member for at least two years, be enrolled in a college or university and pursue careers which help further the ideals of Civitan International.
Target applicant(s): High school students. College students. Graduate school students. Adult students.
Amount: $1,000.
Number of awards: Varies.
Deadline: January 31.
How to apply: Applications are available online.
Exclusive: Visit www.UltimateScholarshipBook.com and enter code CI251220 for updates on this award.

(2513) • Sigma Phi Epsilon Balanced Man Scholarship

Sigma Phi Epsilon Fraternity (National)
310 South Boulevard, Richmond, VA 23220
Phone: 804-353-1901
Email: scholarships@sigep.net
http://www.sigep.org/bms
Purpose: To reward students who balance academics with healthy living.
Eligibility: Applicants must be male incoming freshmen or current undergraduates at one of the universities offering the scholarship. Students must exhibit academic excellence, leadership skills and a commitment to health and well-being.
Target applicant(s): High school students. College students. Adult students.
Amount: Varies.
Number of awards: varies.
Deadline: Varies.
How to apply: Applications are available online.
Exclusive: Visit www.UltimateScholarshipBook.com and enter code SI251320 for updates on this award.

(2514) • Sikh Education Aid Fund

Association of Sikh Professionals
2917 Oak Brook Hills Road, Oak Brook, IL 60523
Phone: 804-541-9290
http://www.unitedsikhs.org/index.php
Purpose: To encourage Sikh students to pursue a higher education at prestigious universities.
Eligibility: Applicants must be members of the Sikh community. Students must be intending to enroll at a prestigious college or university.
Target applicant(s): High school students. College students. Graduate school students. Adult students.
Amount: Varies.
Number of awards: Varies.
Scholarship may be renewable.
Deadline: Varies.
How to apply: Applications are available online.
Exclusive: Visit www.UltimateScholarshipBook.com and enter code AS251420 for updates on this award.

(2515) • Spirit of Youth Scholarship for Junior Members

American Legion Auxiliary
8945 N. Meridian Street, Indianapolis, IN 46260
Phone: 317-569-4500
Email: alahq@legion-aux.org
https://www.alaforveterans.org/scholarships/

Purpose: To assist Junior members of the American Legion Auxiliary.
Eligibility: Applicants must be or have been Junior members of the American Legion Auxiliary for three years, be high school seniors, have a minimum 3.0 GPA and demonstrate character. Selection is based on character/leadership (30 percent), essay/application (30 percent) and scholarship (40 percent).
Target applicant(s): High school students.
Minimum GPA: 3.0
Amount: $5,000.
Number of awards: 5.
Scholarship may be renewable.
Deadline: March 1.
How to apply: Applications are available online.
Exclusive: Visit www.UltimateScholarshipBook.com and enter code AM251520 for updates on this award.

(2516) • Stanfield and D'Orlando Art Scholarship

Unitarian Universalist Association
24 Farnsworth Street, Boston, MA 02210
Phone: 617-742-2100
Email: uufp@uua.org
http://www.uua.org/giving/awards
Purpose: To help graduate and undergraduate Unitarian Universalist artists.
Eligibility: Applicants must be preparing for a career in fine arts which includes painting, drawing, photography and sculpture. Applicants must submit applications, transcripts, recommendations, slide portfolios and a list of works.
Target applicant(s): College students. Graduate school students. Adult students.
Amount: Varies.
Number of awards: Varies.
Deadline: February 15.
How to apply: Applications are available online.
Exclusive: Visit www.UltimateScholarshipBook.com and enter code UN251620 for updates on this award.

(2517) • Stanley A. Doran Memorial Scholarship

Fleet Reserve Association (FRA)
FRA Scholarship Administrator, 125 N. West Street, Alexandria, VA 22314
Phone: 800-372-1924
Email: news-fra@fra.org
http://www.fra.org
Purpose: To provide financial aid to the dependents of FRA members.
Eligibility: Applicants must be the dependent children of a member in good standing of the FRA or a member who was in good standing at time of death. Recipients are selected on the basis of academic achievement, leadership skills, financial need and character.
Target applicant(s): High school students. College students. Graduate school students. Adult students.
Amount: Up to $5,000.
Number of awards: Varies.
Deadline: April 15.
How to apply: Applications are available online.
Exclusive: Visit www.UltimateScholarshipBook.com and enter code FL251720 for updates on this award.

(2518) • Starfleet Scholarships

STARFLEET Scholarship Program
c/o Tammy Wilcox, Director, 316 Dublin Road, Asheboro, NC 27203
Email: scholarships@sfi.org
http://sfi.org
Purpose: To assist members of the International Star Trek Fan Association.
Eligibility: Applicants must have been members of Starfleet for at least one year prior to applying and must be attending or planning to attend a community college, four-year college, technical school, junior college or graduate school. Awards are given in the categories of medicine, engineering, performing arts, international studies, business, science, education, writing, law enforcement and general studies.
Target applicant(s): High school students. College students. Graduate school students. Adult students.
Amount: $1,000.
Number of awards: 5.
Deadline: June 15.
How to apply: Applications are available online. An application form, a personal essay, three letters of recommendation and a transcript are required.
Exclusive: Visit www.UltimateScholarshipBook.com and enter code ST251820 for updates on this award.

(2519) • Student CTA (SCTA) Scholarship in Honor of L. Gordon Bittle

California Teachers Association (CTA)
CTA Human Rights Department, P.O. Box 921, Burlingame, CA 94011-0921
Phone: 650-697-1400
http://www.cta.org/scholarships
Purpose: To support members of the Student California Teachers Association.
Eligibility: Applicants must be planning to work in public education and have a minimum 3.5 high school GPA or show high academic achievement in college coursework, explaining any special circumstances affecting their grades. Scholarships are based on a personal statement, school and community activities and letters of recommendation.
Target applicant(s): High school students. College students. Graduate school students. Adult students.
Minimum GPA: 3.5
Amount: $5,000.
Number of awards: Up to 3.
Deadline: February 3.
How to apply: Applications are available online.
Exclusive: Visit www.UltimateScholarshipBook.com and enter code CA251920 for updates on this award.

(2520) • Tall Club International Scholarship

Tall Clubs International Foundation, Inc.
c/o Carolyn Goldstein, 1555 CR 2103, Weimar, TX 78962
Phone: 888-468-2552
Email: tci-scholarships@tall.org
http://www.tall.org
Purpose: To support students of tall stature.
Eligibility: Applicants must be high school seniors under the age of 21 attending or planning to attend a two- or four-year institution of higher learning for their first year of college. Female applicants must meet the height requirement of 5'10" and male applicants must meet

the requirement of 6'2". Applicants must live within the geographic area of a participating club.
Target applicant(s): High school students.
Amount: Up to $1,000.
Number of awards: Varies.
Deadline: March 1.
How to apply: Applications are available by emailing the closest TCI club.
Exclusive: Visit www.UltimateScholarshipBook.com and enter code TA252020 for updates on this award.

(2521) • Tau Beta Pi Scholarships

Tau Beta Pi Association
Attn.: D. Stephen Pierre Jr., P.E., P.O. Box 2697, Knoxville, TN 37901-2697
Phone: 865-546-4578
Email: fellowships@tbp.org
http://www.tbp.org
Purpose: To assist members who are studying engineering.
Eligibility: Applicants must be undergraduate members of Tau Beta Pi and be juniors at the time of application who are planning to remain in or return to school for a senior year of full-time study in engineering.
Target applicant(s): College students. Adult students.
Amount: $2,000.
Number of awards: Varies.
Deadline: April 1.
How to apply: Applications are available online.
Exclusive: Visit www.UltimateScholarshipBook.com and enter code TA252120 for updates on this award.

(2522) • Terrill Graduate Fellowship

Phi Sigma Kappa International Headquarters
2925 E. 96th Street, Indianapolis, IN 46240
Phone: 317-573-5420
Email: vershun@phisigmakappa.org
http://www.phisigmakappa.org
Purpose: To award money to graduating senior and alumni members entering graduate school or members already enrolled in graduate school.
Eligibility: Applicants must graduate from college by August of the year during which they apply, plan to begin graduate or professional study during the next academic year or already be in graduate school and have a minimum B GPA for all undergraduate work. Scholarships are awarded based on scholastic performance.
Target applicant(s): College students. Graduate school students. Adult students.
Minimum GPA: 3.0
Amount: $5,000-$10,000.
Number of awards: 2.
Deadline: January 31.
How to apply: Applications are available online.
Exclusive: Visit www.UltimateScholarshipBook.com and enter code PH252220 for updates on this award.

(2523) • Tri Delta Undergraduate Scholarship

Tri Delta
Delta Delta Delta Foundation, 14951 North Dallas Parkway, Suite 500, Dallas, TX 75254
Phone: 817-633-8001
Email: info@trideltaeo.org
http://www.tridelta.org
Purpose: To offer scholarships to undergraduate members.
Eligibility: Applicants must be undergraduates enrolled full-time in good standing with the organization. Selection is based on academic achievement, chapter involvement, campus/community involvement, financial need and future promise.
Target applicant(s): College students. Adult students.
Amount: Varies.
Number of awards: Varies.
Deadline: March 1.
How to apply: Applications are available online.
Exclusive: Visit www.UltimateScholarshipBook.com and enter code TR252320 for updates on this award.

(2524) • Truckload Carriers Association Scholarship Fund

Truckload Carriers Association
c/o TCA Scholarship Fund, 555 East Braddock Road, Alexandria, VA 22314
Phone: 703-838-1950
Email: TCA@truckload.org
http://www.truckload.org
Purpose: To support college students affiliated with the trucking industry.
Eligibility: Applicants must attend or plan to attend college, be in good standing and be the children, grandchildren or spouses of an employee of a trucking company; applicants may also be the children, grandchildren or spouses of an independent contractor or independent contractors affiliated with a trucking company and attending a four-year college.
Target applicant(s): High school students. College students. Adult students.
Minimum GPA: 3.3
Amount: $2,000-$6,250.
Number of awards: Varies.
Deadline: June 23.
How to apply: Applications are available online.
Exclusive: Visit www.UltimateScholarshipBook.com and enter code TR252420 for updates on this award.

(2525) • Tuition Exchange Scholarships

Tuition Exchange
1743 Connecticut Avenue NW, Washington, DC 20009
Phone: 202-518-0135
Email: info@tuitionexchange.org
http://www.tuitionexchange.org
Purpose: To assist the children or other family members of the faculty and staff at participating colleges and universities to encourage employment of parents and guardians in higher education.
Eligibility: Eligibility varies by institution. Applicants must be family members of the home institution where they are applying. However specific details about employment status, years of service or other requirements are determined solely by the home institution.
Target applicant(s): High school students. College students. Adult students.
Amount: Up to full tuition.
Number of awards: 6,000.
Scholarship may be renewable.
Deadline: Varies.
How to apply: Applications are available from the liaison officer at the home institution.

Exclusive: Visit www.UltimateScholarshipBook.com and enter code TU252520 for updates on this award.

(2526) • UCC Seminarian Scholarship

United Church of Christ
Pat Lyden, Associate Director Grant and Scholarship Administration, 700 Prospect Avenue, Cleveland, OH 44115
Phone: 216-736-2166
Email: scholarships@ucc.org
http://www.ucc.org/scholarships
Purpose: To support members of the United Church of Christ who are preparing for ministry.
Eligibility: Applicants must be members of a United Church of Christ congregation for at least one year prior to receipt of the scholarship. They must be currently enrolled in an ATS accredited seminary in a course of study to become an ordained minister, and they must maintain at least a B average to receive and keep the scholarship. Applicants should be able to show that they have demonstrated leadership abilities in a church or academic environment. Students must also agree to serve the United Church of Christ or one of its partners after the completion of their studies.
Target applicant(s): High school students. College students. Graduate school students. Adult students.
Minimum GPA: 3.0
Amount: Varies.
Number of awards: 5.
Scholarship may be renewable.
Deadline: March 1.
How to apply: Applications are available by mail.
Exclusive: Visit www.UltimateScholarshipBook.com and enter code UN252620 for updates on this award.

(2527) • UFCW Scholarship Program

United Food and Commercial Workers Union
Scholarship Program - Education Office, 1775 K Street NW, Washington, DC 20006
Email: cfscholarship@ufcw.org
http://www.ufcw.org
Purpose: To provide financial assistance for members of the UFCW and their children.
Eligibility: Applicants must be members of good standing of the UFCW with a membership of one continuous year or more or the unmarried children of a member. Applicants must also be graduating high school in the year of the competition and be less than 20 years old. Academic achievement, community involvement and essays are part of the selection process.
Target applicant(s): High school students.
Amount: Up to $2,000.
Number of awards: Varies.
Scholarship may be renewable.
Deadline: January 31.
How to apply: Applications are available online.
Exclusive: Visit www.UltimateScholarshipBook.com and enter code UN252720 for updates on this award.

(2528) • UMWA-Lorin E. Kerr Scholarships

United Mine Workers of America/BCOA T.E.F.
18354 Quantico Gateway Drive, Suite 200, Triangle, VA 22172
Phone: 703-291-2400
Email: info@umwa.org
http://www.umwa.org
Purpose: To offer scholarships to UMWA members and their families.
Eligibility: Applicants must be UMWA members or dependents who pursue undergraduate degrees. Selection is based on academic potential and financial need.
Target applicant(s): High school students. College students. Adult students.
Amount: $2,500.
Number of awards: 2.
Deadline: February 17.
How to apply: Applications are available online.
Exclusive: Visit www.UltimateScholarshipBook.com and enter code UN252820 for updates on this award.

(2529) • Undergraduate Scholarship

Delta Sigma Pi
330 South Campus Avenue, Oxford, OH 45056-2405
Phone: 513-523-1907
Email: centraloffice@dspnet.org
http://www.deltasigmapi.org
Purpose: To assist student members.
Eligibility: Applicants must be members in good standing of Delta Sigma Pi with at least one semester or quarter of undergraduate studies remaining. Applicants are judged on scholastic achievement, financial need, fraternal service, service activities, letters of recommendation and overall presentation of required materials.
Target applicant(s): College students. Adult students.
Amount: $1,000.
Number of awards: 8.
Deadline: June 15.
How to apply: Applications are available online.
Exclusive: Visit www.UltimateScholarshipBook.com and enter code DE252920 for updates on this award.

(2530) • Undergraduate Scholarships

American Baptist Churches USA
P.O. Box 851, Valley Forge, PA 19482-0851
Phone: 800-222-3872
Email: financialaid.web@abc-usa.org
http://abhms.org/ministries/developing-leaders/education-scholarships/
Purpose: To support American Baptist students pursuing educational opportunities.
Eligibility: Applicants must be members of an American Baptist church for at least one year before applying for aid, be enrolled at an accredited educational institution in the U.S. or Puerto Rico, be U.S. citizens and retain a 2.75 GPA to remain eligible for the scholarships.
Target applicant(s): High school students. College students. Adult students.
Minimum GPA: 2.75
Amount: Varies.
Number of awards: Varies.
Scholarship may be renewable.
Deadline: May 31.
How to apply: Applications are available by request.
Exclusive: Visit www.UltimateScholarshipBook.com and enter code AM253020 for updates on this award.

(2531) • Union Plus Scholarship

Union Plus
1100 1st Street NE, Suite 850, Washington, DC 20002
http://www.unionplus.org
Purpose: To help the families of union members.
Eligibility: Applicants must be members of unions participating in a Union Plus program or the spouses or children of such union members. Applicants must be accepted to or attending an undergraduate course of study at an accredited college or university, community college or recognized technical or trade school. Selection is based on academic ability, social awareness, financial need and appreciation of labor. Minimum 3.0 GPA is required.
Target applicant(s): High school students. College students. Graduate school students. Adult students.
Minimum GPA: 3.0
Amount: $500-$4,000.
Number of awards: Varies.
Deadline: January 31.
How to apply: Applications are available online.
Exclusive: Visit www.UltimateScholarshipBook.com and enter code UN253120 for updates on this award.

(2532) • United Agribusiness League and United Agricultural Benefit Trust Scholarships

United Agribusiness League
54 Corporate Park, Irvine, CA 92606-5105
Phone: 800-223-4590
Email: membership@unitedag.org
https://www.unitedag.org
Purpose: To aid undergraduate students who are affiliated with the United Agribusiness League (UAL) or the United Agricultural Benefit Trust (UABT).
Eligibility: Applicants must be current undergraduate students at an accredited college or university and must be affiliated with the United Agribusiness League (UAL) or the United Agricultural Benefit Trust (UABT) through a member or an employee of a member. They must have a GPA of 2.5 or higher. Selection is based on the overall strength of the application.
Target applicant(s): College students. Adult students.
Minimum GPA: 2.5
Amount: Varies.
Number of awards: Varies.
Deadline: December 31.
How to apply: Applications are available online. An application form, three reference letters, a personal essay and a resume are required.
Exclusive: Visit www.UltimateScholarshipBook.com and enter code UN253220 for updates on this award.

(2533) • United Methodist General Scholarship

United Methodist Church
Office of Loans and Scholarships, P.O. Box 340007, Nashville, TN 37203-0007
Phone: 615-340-7342
Email: umscholar@gbhem.org
http://www.gbhem.org/loans-and-scholarships
Purpose: To support students who are members of a United Methodist Church.
Eligibility: Applicants must be active, full members of a United Methodist Church for at least one year prior to applying, be admitted to a full-time degree program in an accredited college or university and have a minimum 2.5 GPA. Students must also be U.S. citizens or permanent residents and be undergraduate, graduate or doctoral students. Supporting documents are due by May 1.
Target applicant(s): College students. Graduate school students. Adult students.
Minimum GPA: 2.5
Amount: $500-$2,000.
Number of awards: Varies.
Deadline: March 7.
How to apply: Applications are available online.
Exclusive: Visit www.UltimateScholarshipBook.com and enter code UN253320 for updates on this award.

(2534) • United Transportation Union Scholarships

United Transportation Union Insurance Association
UTUIA Scholarship Program, 24950 Country Club Boulevard, Suite 340, North Olmsted, OH 44070-5333
http://www.utuia.org
Purpose: To provide financial aid to the children and grandchildren of UTU/UTUIA members.
Eligibility: Applicants must be at least high school seniors or the equivalent and be age 25 or less. Applicants must also be UTU or UTUIA-insured members, the children or grandchildren of a UTU or UTUIA-insured member or the children of a deceased UTU or UTUIA-insured member. UTU or UTUIA-insured members must be U.S. residents. Applicants must be accepted for admittance or already enrolled for at least 12 credit hours per quarter or semester at a recognized institution of higher learning (university, college or junior college, nursing or technical school offering college credit). Scholarships are awarded on the basis of chance, not grades. A UTUIA scholar, however, is expected to maintain a satisfactory academic record to keep the scholarship for the full four years.
Target applicant(s): High school students. College students.
Amount: $2,000.
Number of awards: 50.
Scholarship may be renewable.
Deadline: March 31.
How to apply: Applications are available from the UTU news or by written request.
Exclusive: Visit www.UltimateScholarshipBook.com and enter code UN253420 for updates on this award.

(2535) • Utility Workers Union of America Scholarships

Utility Workers Union of America
1300 L Street NW, Suite 1200, Washington, DC 20005
Phone: 202-899-2851
Email: rfarley@aflcio.org
http://uwua.net/
Purpose: To offer scholarships to the children of UWUA members.
Eligibility: Applicants must be the sons or daughters of active Utility Workers Union members. Recipients are selected from those who participate in the National Merit Scholarship Competition by taking the PSAT/NMSQT as high school juniors, complete high school and are enrolled in a regionally accredited college in the United States.
Target applicant(s): High school students.
Amount: $500-$2,000.
Number of awards: Varies.
Scholarship may be renewable.
Deadline: December 31.
How to apply: Applications are available online.

Exclusive: Visit www.UltimateScholarshipBook.com and enter code UT253520 for updates on this award.

(2536) • VantagePoint Public Employee Memorial Scholarship Fund

ICMA-RC Vantagepoint
ICMA-RC Vantagepoint Public Employee Memorial Scholarship Fund, Scholarship Management Services, One Scholarship Way, Saint Peter, MN 56082
Phone: 202-962-8085
Email: anna.owen@vantagescholar.org
http://www.icmarc.org/

Purpose: To support spouses and children of local and state employees including police officers, firefighters and government workers who died in the line of duty.
Eligibility: Applicants must be spouses or children of local or state governmental employees who died in the line of duty and must be able to supply written documentation from the deceased's past employer stating such. At the time of application, individuals must be attending or planning to attend a two-year or four-year college or a vocational school and may be studying at the undergraduate, graduate or technical level. Selection is based on academic performance, community and school involvement, leadership, honors, work experience, goals, letter of recommendation and financial need.
Target applicant(s): High school students. College students. Graduate school students. Adult students.
Amount: Up to $10,000.
Number of awards: Varies.
Deadline: March 16.
How to apply: Applications are available online.
Exclusive: Visit www.UltimateScholarshipBook.com and enter code IC253620 for updates on this award.

(2537) • VFW Scout of the Year Scholarship

Veterans of Foreign Wars
406 W. 34th Street, Kansas City, MO 64111
Phone: 816-968-1117
Email: kharmer@vfw.org
https://www.vfw.org/community/youth-and-education

Purpose: To reward an outstanding Boy Scout, Venture Scout, Sea Scout or Girl Scout.
Eligibility: Applicants must have received the Eagle Scout Award, the Girl Scout Gold Award, the Venture Silver Award or the Sea Scout Quartermaster Award and demonstrated practical citizenship. Applicants must also have reached their 15th birthday and be enrolled in high school.
Target applicant(s): High school students.
Amount: Up to $5,000.
Number of awards: 3.
Deadline: March 1.
How to apply: Applications are available online.
Exclusive: Visit www.UltimateScholarshipBook.com and enter code VE253720 for updates on this award.

(2538) • Vocations Scholarship Funds

Knights of Columbus
Department of Scholarships, 1 Columbus Plaza, New Haven, CT 06510-3326
Phone: 203-752-4000
Email: info@kofc.org
http://www.kofc.org

Purpose: To support theology students on their path to the priesthood.
Eligibility: Applicants must be males studying with ecclesiastical approval at a major seminary for a diocese or religious institute in the United States, its territories and Canada. The Father Michael J. McGivney Vocations Scholarship Fund awards scholarships based on financial need, and applicants must provide proof of need. The Bishop Thomas V. Daily Scholarships Fund awards recipients on the basis of merit, and applicants must submit their most recent transcript and two letters of recommendation. Both funds give preference to Knights of Columbus members and their sons, but membership is not required.
Target applicant(s): High school students. College students. Graduate school students. Adult students.
Amount: $2,500.
Number of awards: Varies.
Scholarship may be renewable.
Deadline: June 1.
How to apply: Applications are available from seminary rectors and diocesan vocations directors starting in February.
Exclusive: Visit www.UltimateScholarshipBook.com and enter code KN253820 for updates on this award.

(2539) • Walgreens DECA Scholarships

DECA Inc.
1908 Association Drive, Reston, VA 20191
Phone: 703-860-5000
Email: kathy_onion@deca.org
http://www.deca.org

Purpose: To aid DECA members who demonstrate leadership and community involvement.
Eligibility: Applicants must be active members of DECA. They must demonstrate leadership ability and be active in their communities. Selection is based on the overall strength of the application.
Target applicant(s): High school students. College students. Adult students.
Amount: $1,000.
Number of awards: 4.
Deadline: January 13.
How to apply: Applications are available online. An application form, transcript and other supporting materials are required.
Exclusive: Visit www.UltimateScholarshipBook.com and enter code DE253920 for updates on this award.

(2540) • Walmart Associate Scholarship

Wal-Mart Foundation
c/o ACT Scholarship and Recognition Services Email: https://www.act.org/walmart/contact.html
http://www.walmartfoundation.org

Purpose: To assist Walmart associates with higher education.
Eligibility: Applicants must be U.S. citizens or permanent residents, be employed part-time or full-time with Walmart for at least six months prior to applying and have graduated from high school, obtained a GED or be a graduating high school senior. Students must also demonstrate financial need.
Target applicant(s): High school students. College students. Adult students.
Amount: Up to $3,000.
Number of awards: Varies.
Deadline: January 31.
How to apply: Applications are available online.

Exclusive: Visit www.UltimateScholarshipBook.com and enter code WA254020 for updates on this award.

(2541) • Walmart Dependent Scholarship

Wal-Mart Foundation
c/o ACT Scholarship and Recognition Services Email: https://www.act.org/walmart/contact.html
http://www.walmartfoundation.org
Purpose: To assist the dependents of Walmart associates.
Eligibility: Applicants must be U.S. citizens or legal residents and graduating high school seniors. Students must also demonstrate financial need.
Target applicant(s): High school students.
Amount: $3,250 per year.
Number of awards: Varies.
Scholarship may be renewable.
Deadline: April 1.
How to apply: Applications are available online.
Exclusive: Visit www.UltimateScholarshipBook.com and enter code WA254120 for updates on this award.

(2542) • Walter L. Mitchell Memorial Scholarship Awards

International Chemical Workers Union Council/UFCW
Research and Education Department, Walter L. Mitchell Memorial Scholarship Awards, 1655 West Market Street, Akron, OH 44313
Phone: 330-926-1444
http://www.icwuc.org
Purpose: To offer scholarships to the children or step-children of members of the UFCW.
Eligibility: Applicants must be children or step-children of members of at least a year who intend to enter college the fall following application. Recipients are selected on the basis of biographical information, ACT/SAT scores and high school records.
Target applicant(s): High school students.
Amount: $1,500.
Number of awards: 12.
Deadline: April 14.
How to apply: Applications are available online.
Exclusive: Visit www.UltimateScholarshipBook.com and enter code IN254220 for updates on this award.

(2543) • Warren Poslusny Award for Outstanding Achievement

Sigma Alpha Epsilon (SAE)
Dave Sandell, Sigma Alpha Epsilon Foundation Scholarships, 1856 Sheridan Road, Evanston, IL 60201-3837
Phone: 800-233-1856 x234
Email: dsandell@sae.net
http://www.sae.net
Purpose: To recognize collegians who have demonstrated outstanding leadership and service and have exemplified a dedication to the values established by the founders of Sigma Alpha Epsilon.
Eligibility: Applicants must be brothers of Sigma Alpha Epsilon in good standing, have a minimum 3.0 GPA and either must have junior standing or higher or must be pursuing full-time graduate study. This award is merit-based, with an emphasis on combining academic excellence, leadership, service and campus involvement.
Target applicant(s): College students. Graduate school students. Adult students.
Minimum GPA: 3.0
Amount: Varies.
Number of awards: Varies.
Deadline: March 1.
How to apply: Contact the coordinator of educational programs and services.
Exclusive: Visit www.UltimateScholarshipBook.com and enter code SI254320 for updates on this award.

(2544) • Wenderoth Undergraduate Scholarship

Phi Sigma Kappa International Headquarters
2925 E. 96th Street, Indianapolis, IN 46240
Phone: 317-573-5420
Email: vershun@phisigmakappa.org
http://www.phisigmakappa.org
Purpose: To give financial aid to college sophomore and junior members.
Eligibility: Applicants must be sophomores or juniors in college for the year that the scholarship will apply to, have completed two semesters or three quarters of study and have a minimum B GPA. Scholarships are awarded on the basis of academic accomplishments and essays.
Target applicant(s): College students. Adult students.
Minimum GPA: 3.0
Amount: $2,500-$5,000.
Number of awards: 2.
Deadline: January 31.
How to apply: Applications are available online.
Exclusive: Visit www.UltimateScholarshipBook.com and enter code PH254420 for updates on this award.

(2545) • William C. Doherty Scholarship Fund

National Association of Letter Carriers
100 Indiana Avenue NW, Washington, DC 20001-2144
Phone: 202-393-4695
Email: nalcinf@nalc.org
http://www.nalc.org
Purpose: To offer scholarships to the children of members of the Letter Carriers Union.
Eligibility: Applicants must be the children or legally adopted children of an active, retired or deceased letter carrier and high school seniors. Applicants' parents must be members in good standing at least one year prior to applying. Selection is based on SAT/ACT scores, high school transcript and questionnaire.
Target applicant(s): High school students.
Amount: $4,000.
Number of awards: 5.
Scholarship may be renewable.
Deadline: December 31.
How to apply: Preliminary applications are available online.
Exclusive: Visit www.UltimateScholarshipBook.com and enter code NA254520 for updates on this award.

(2546) • Wilson W. Carnes Scholarship

National FFA Organization
P.O. Box 68960, 6060 FFA Drive, Indianapolis, IN 46268-0960
Phone: 888-332-2668
Email: scholarships@ffa.org
https://www.ffa.org/participate/scholarships

Purpose: To support students who are majoring in agricultural communications.
Eligibility: Applicants must be current FFA members and high school seniors or college students planning to enroll or currently enrolled full-time. Students only need to complete the online application one time to be considered for all FFA-administered scholarships. The application requires information about the student's activities and a 1,000-word essay. Awards may be used for books, supplies, tuition, fees and room and board.
Target applicant(s): High school students. College students.
Amount: $300.
Number of awards: 1.
Deadline: February 1.
How to apply: Applications are available online.
Exclusive: Visit www.UltimateScholarshipBook.com and enter code NA254620 for updates on this award.

(2547) • Women in Aviation International Scholarship

Women in Aviation International
WAI Scholarships, Morningstar Airport, 3647 State Route 503 South, West Alexandria, OH 45381-9384
Phone: 937-839-4647
Email: dwallace@wai.org
http://www.wai.org
Purpose: To assist students pursuing aviation and aerospace education.
Eligibility: Applicants must be members of Women in Aviation International. Students must write a resume and an essay and provide two recommendation letters.
Target applicant(s): High school students. College students. Adult students.
Amount: Varies.
Deadline: November 13.
How to apply: Applications are available online.
Exclusive: Visit www.UltimateScholarshipBook.com and enter code WO254720 for updates on this award.

(2548) • Women in Sports Media Scholarship/ Internship Program

Association for Women in Sports Media
7742 Spalding Drive #377, Norcross, GA 30092
Email: awsminternship@gmail.com
http://awsmonline.org/internships-scholarships
Purpose: To encourage females interested in sports media careers.
Eligibility: Applicants must be female students working full-time toward a graduate or undergraduate degree with the goal of becoming a sports writer, editor, broadcaster or public relations representative. Applicants must submit a resume, an essay on a memorable experience in sports or sports media, three references, two letters of recommendation and up to five samples of their work. Application fee is waived for AWSM members.
Target applicant(s): College students. Graduate school students. Adult students.
Amount: $1,000 plus paid internship.
Number of awards: Varies.
Deadline: October 31.
How to apply: Applications are available online.
Exclusive: Visit www.UltimateScholarshipBook.com and enter code AS254820 for updates on this award.

(2549) • Women in United Methodist History Writing Award

General Commission on Archives and History, The United Methodist Church
P.O. Box 127, 36 Madison Avenue, Madison, NJ 07940
Phone: 973-408-3189
Email: research@gcah.org
http://www.gcah.org
Purpose: To reward research and writing on the history of women in The United Methodist Church.
Eligibility: Applicants must submit completed, original manuscripts no longer than 20 double-spaced, typewritten pages with footnotes and bibliography about the history of women in the United Methodist Church or its antecedents.
Target applicant(s): High school students. College students. Graduate school students. Adult students.
Amount: $500.
Number of awards: 1.
Deadline: December 31.
How to apply: Send manuscript to the General Secretary at the address listed.
Exclusive: Visit www.UltimateScholarshipBook.com and enter code GE254920 for updates on this award.

(2550) • WomenLead Community College Scholarship

inFaith Community Foundation
625 Fourth Avenue South, Suite 1500, Minneapolis, MN 55415
Phone: 800-365-4172
Email: consuelo.gutierrez-crosby@infaithfound.org
https://www.infaithfound.org/newsgrants/scholarships
Purpose: To support women of faith.
Eligibility: Applicants must be enrolling or plan to enroll in an accredited theological seminary or post-graduate institution. Students must have a minimum 3.0 grade point average. Applicants must demonstrate active Christian faith, civil engagement and leadership.
Target applicant(s): Graduate school students. Adult students.
Minimum GPA: 3.0
Amount: $3,000.
Number of awards: 1.
Deadline: April 30.
How to apply: Applications are available online.
Exclusive: Visit www.UltimateScholarshipBook.com and enter code IN255020 for updates on this award.

(2551) • Young Christian Leaders Scholarship

Young Christian Leaders
144 Woodbury Road, Woodbury, NY 11797
Phone: 516-693-5790
Email: info@yclscholarship.org
http://www.yclscholarship.org
Purpose: To support emerging young Christian students.
Eligibility: Applicants must be a high school senior or full-time current college student who is a permanent resident of New York, New Jersey or Connecticut and is an active member of their local church (college students who attend school away from their home will be evaluated on an individual basis). A minimum 3.0 GPA is required. The scholarship is awarded on a monthly basis with a deadline of the 15th of each month.
Target applicant(s): High school students. College students.
Minimum GPA: 3.0

Amount: $1,000.
Number of awards: 12.
Deadline: 15th of each month.
How to apply: Applications are available online.
Exclusive: Visit www.UltimateScholarshipBook.com and enter code YO255120 for updates on this award.

(2552) • Youth of the Year Award

National Exchange Club
3050 West Central Avenue, Toledo, OH 43606
Phone: 419-535-3232
Email: info@nationalexchangeclub.org
http://www.nationalexchangeclub.org
Purpose: To recognize students who excel in academics, leadership and community service.
Eligibility: Applicants are chosen by their local Exchange Clubs. The process begins with Youth of the Month Awards. At the end of the year, a Youth of the Year nominee is selected from Youth of the Month winners. Applicants are judged based on participation in activities, community service, special achievements/awards, grades and a required essay. To be eligible to win, applicants must be able to attend national convention to accept the award.
Target applicant(s): High school students.
Amount: Varies.
Number of awards: Varies.
Deadline: Varies.
How to apply: Applications are available online.
Exclusive: Visit www.UltimateScholarshipBook.com and enter code NA255220 for updates on this award.

(2553) • Youth Partners Accessing Capital

Alpha Kappa Alpha Educational Advancement Foundation Inc.
5656 S. Stony Island Avenue, Chicago, IL 60637
Phone: 800-653-6528
Email: akaeaf@akaeaf.net
https://akaeaf.org/scholarships
Purpose: To provide financial assistance to Alpha Kappa Alpha members with exceptional academic achievement or extreme financial need.
Eligibility: Applicants must be Alpha Kappa Alpha members who are in their sophomore year of college or higher with a GPA of 3.0 or higher. They must have either high academic achievement or extreme financial need, and they must participate in leadership, volunteer, civic or campus activities.
Target applicant(s): College students. Adult students.
Minimum GPA: 3.0
Amount: Varies.
Number of awards: Varies.
Deadline: April 15.
How to apply: Applications are available online.
Exclusive: Visit www.UltimateScholarshipBook.com and enter code AL255320 for updates on this award.

ETHNICITY/RACE/GENDER/FAMILY STATUS

(2554) • A.T. Anderson Memorial Scholarship

American Indian Science and Engineering Society
2305 Renard Place, Albuquerque, NM 87106
Phone: 505-765-1052
http://www.aises.org/scholarships
Purpose: To provide scholarships for Native American and Alaskan Native students majoring in science, engineering, medicine, natural resources, math and technology.
Eligibility: Applicants must be full-time undergraduate or graduate students at an accredited college or university. Applicants must also be members of a Native American tribe or Alaskan Native and members of AISES. A minimum GPA of 3.0 is required.
Target applicant(s): High school students. College students. Graduate school students. Adult students.
Minimum GPA: 3.0
Amount: $1,000-$2,000.
Number of awards: Varies.
Deadline: May 1.
How to apply: Applications are available online.
Exclusive: Visit www.UltimateScholarshipBook.com and enter code AM255420 for updates on this award.

(2555) • AAUW Educational Foundation Career Development Grants

American Association of University Women (AAUW) Educational Foundation
Dept. 60, 301 ACT Drive, Iowa City, IA 52243-4030
Phone: 319-337-1716 x60
Email: aauw@act.org
http://www.aauw.org
Purpose: To support college-educated women who need additional training to advance their careers, re-enter the workforce or change careers.
Eligibility: Applicants must be U.S. citizens, hold a bachelor's degree and enroll in courses at a regionally-accredited program related to their professional development, including two- and four-year colleges, technical schools and distance learning programs and have earned the degree at least five years prior to application. Special preference is given to women of color, AAUW members and women pursuing their first advanced degree or credentials in a nontraditional field.
Target applicant(s): College students. Adult students.
Amount: $2,000-$12,000.
Number of awards: Varies.
Deadline: November 15.
How to apply: Applications are available online from August 1-December 15.
Exclusive: Visit www.UltimateScholarshipBook.com and enter code AM255520 for updates on this award.

(2556) • Abe and Esther Hagiwara Student Aid Award

Japanese American Citizens League (JACL)
1765 Sutter Street, San Francisco, CA 94115
Phone: 415-921-5225
Email: jacl@jacl.org
http://www.jacl.org
Purpose: To aid students who otherwise would have to delay or terminate their education due to lack of financing.

Eligibility: Applicants must be National JACL members and must be attending a college, university, trade school, business school or any other institution of higher learning. A personal statement, letter of recommendation, academic performance, work experience and community involvement are considered. Applicants should have extreme financial need.
Target applicant(s): High school students. College students. Graduate school students. Adult students.
Amount: Varies.
Number of awards: Varies.
Deadline: April 1.
How to apply: Applications are available online.
Exclusive: Visit www.UltimateScholarshipBook.com and enter code JA255620 for updates on this award.

(2557) · Actuarial Diversity Scholarship

Actuarial Foundation
475 N. Martingale Road, Suite 600, Schaumburg, IL 60173-2226
Phone: 847-706-3581
Email: scholarships@actfnd.org
http://www.actuarialfoundation.org/scholarships/
Purpose: To promote diversity through an annual scholarship program for African American, Hispanic and Native American Indian students and encourage academic achievements by awarding scholarships to full-time undergraduate and graduate students pursuing a degree in the actuarial profession.
Eligibility: Applicants must have at least one birth parent who is a member of one of the minority groups listed and a minimum GPA of 3.0. High school seniors must have a minimum ACT math score of 28 or SAT math score of 600. An award will be provided in the recipient's name to any accredited U.S. educational institution to cover educational expenses. An application, a personal statement, two letters of recommendation and official school transcripts (sealed) are required.
Target applicant(s): High school students. College students. Graduate school students. Adult students.
Minimum GPA: 3.0
Amount: $1,000-$4,000.
Number of awards: Varies.
Scholarship may be renewable.
Deadline: May 1.
How to apply: Applications are available online.
Exclusive: Visit www.UltimateScholarshipBook.com and enter code AC255720 for updates on this award.

(2558) · Ada I. Pressman Memorial Scholarship

Society of Women Engineers
130 East Randolph Street, Suite 3500, Chicago, IL 60601
Phone: 877-793-4636
Email: scholarships@swe.org
http://societyofwomenengineers.swe.org/scholarships
Purpose: To support female engineering students.
Eligibility: Applicants may major in any type of engineering. They must be U.S. citizens and must be college sophomores, juniors, seniors or graduate students. A GPA of 3.0 or higher is required.
Target applicant(s): College students. Graduate school students. Adult students.
Minimum GPA: 3.0
Amount: $5,000.
Number of awards: 9.
Deadline: February 15.
How to apply: Applications are available online. An application form is required.
Exclusive: Visit www.UltimateScholarshipBook.com and enter code SO255820 for updates on this award.

(2559) · Admiral Grace Murray Hopper Memorial Scholarships

Society of Women Engineers
130 East Randolph Street, Suite 3500, Chicago, IL 60601
Phone: 877-793-4636
Email: scholarships@swe.org
http://societyofwomenengineers.swe.org/scholarships
Purpose: To support women in engineering.
Eligibility: Applicants must be females who are enrolled in their freshman year at an accredited engineering or computer science program. They must have a GPA of 3.5 or higher.
Target applicant(s): College students. Adult students.
Minimum GPA: 3.5
Amount: $1,500.
Number of awards: 3.
Deadline: May 1.
How to apply: Applications are available online. An application form is required.
Exclusive: Visit www.UltimateScholarshipBook.com and enter code SO255920 for updates on this award.

(2560) · Adolph Van Pelt Scholarship

Association on American Indian Affairs
Lisa Wyzlic, Director of Scholarship Programs, 966 Hungerford Drive, Suite 12-B, Rockville, MD 20850
Phone: 240-314-7155
Email: lw.aaia@indian-affairs.org
https://www.indian-affairs.org/scholarships.html
Purpose: To assist Native American/Alaska Native undergraduate students based on merit and financial need.
Eligibility: Applicants must be full-time students and provide proof of tribal enrollment, a Certificate of Indian Blood (showing 1/4 Indian blood) and an essay on educational goals.
Target applicant(s): High school students. College students. Adult students.
Minimum GPA: 2.5
Amount: Varies.
Number of awards: Varies.
Scholarship may be renewable.
Deadline: June 1.
How to apply: Applications are available online.
Exclusive: Visit www.UltimateScholarshipBook.com and enter code AS256020 for updates on this award.

(2561) · Afro-Academic, Cultural, Technological and Scientific Olympics (ACT-SO)

National Association for the Advancement of Colored People
c/o Poise Foundation, Two Gateway Center, Suite 1700, 603 Stanwix Street, Pittsburgh, PA 15222
Phone: 412-281-4967
Email: info@poisefdn.org
http://www.poisefoundation.org/scholarships-overview/
Purpose: To recognize and reward the academic and cultural achievements of African American high school students.

Eligibility: Students must be in grades 9 through 12, 19 years of age or younger and of African-American descent. They must compete in one of 26 categories including business, sciences, humanities and performing and visual arts. Winners receive scholarships, internships and apprenticeships.
Target applicant(s): High school students.
Amount: Varies.
Number of awards: Varies.
Deadline: Varies.
How to apply: Applications are available from the NAACP.
Exclusive: Visit www.UltimateScholarshipBook.com and enter code NA256120 for updates on this award.

(2562) • AGBU Fellowships for U.S. Based Study

Armenian General Benevolent Union (AGBU)
55 East 59th Street, 7th Floor, New York, NY 10022-1112
Phone: 212-319-6383
Email: scholarship@agbu.org
http://www.agbu.org
Purpose: To support graduate students of Armenian heritage.
Eligibility: Applicants must be of Armenian heritage, be a full-time student at a U.S. college/university and have earned a minimum 3.5 GPA in undergraduate study.
Target applicant(s): Graduate school students. Adult students.
Minimum GPA: 3.5
Amount: Up to full tuition.
Number of awards: Varies.
Scholarship may be renewable.
Deadline: April 30.
How to apply: Applications are available online.
Exclusive: Visit www.UltimateScholarshipBook.com and enter code AR256220 for updates on this award.

(2563) • AGBU Scholarship Program

Armenian General Benevolent Union (AGBU)
55 East 59th Street, 7th Floor, New York, NY 10022-1112
Phone: 212-319-6383
Email: scholarship@agbu.org
http://www.agbu.org
Purpose: To help students of Armenian descent.
Eligibility: Applicants should be international full-time students or high school seniors of Armenian descent who attend academic institutions and graduate programs. Applications, two recommendation letters, transcripts, college acceptance letters, financial award letters, resumes and photographs are required.
Target applicant(s): High school students. College students. Graduate school students. Adult students.
Amount: Varies.
Number of awards: Varies.
Scholarship may be renewable.
Deadline: Varies.
How to apply: Applications are available online.
Exclusive: Visit www.UltimateScholarshipBook.com and enter code AR256320 for updates on this award.

(2564) • Agnes Jones Jackson Scholarship

National Association for the Advancement of Colored People
c/o Poise Foundation, Two Gateway Center, Suite 1700, 603 Stanwix Street, Pittsburgh, PA 15222
Phone: 412-281-4967
Email: info@poisefdn.org
http://www.poisefoundation.org/scholarships-overview/
Purpose: To reward NAACP members with financial need.
Eligibility: Students must be members of the NAACP, U.S. citizens and attending an accredited U.S. college. Undergraduates must attend college full-time, while graduates may be full- or part-time students. High school seniors and undergraduates must have a minimum 2.5 GPA while graduate students must have a minimum 3.0 GPA. Applicants must demonstrate financial need according to the formula in the application form.
Target applicant(s): High school students. College students. Graduate school students.
Minimum GPA: 2.5 for high school and undergraduate students, 3.0 for graduate students
Amount: $2,000.
Number of awards: 20-40.
Scholarship may be renewable.
Deadline: April 28.
How to apply: Applications are available online.
Exclusive: Visit www.UltimateScholarshipBook.com and enter code NA256420 for updates on this award.

(2565) • Agnes Missirian Scholarship

Armenian International Women's Association
65 Main Street, #3A, Watertown, MA 02472
Phone: 617-926-0171
Email: aiwainc@aol.com
http://aiwainternational.org/
Purpose: To honor the memory of Professor Agnes Missirian and assist Armenian women in obtaining higher education.
Eligibility: Applicants must be full-time students at accredited colleges or universities who are females of Armenian descent. They must be juniors, seniors or graduate students. Awards are based on financial need and merit.
Target applicant(s): College students. Graduate school students. Adult students.
Amount: $2,000.
Number of awards: Varies.
Deadline: April 18.
How to apply: Applications are available online.
Exclusive: Visit www.UltimateScholarshipBook.com and enter code AR256520 for updates on this award.

(2566) • AHEPA Educational Foundation National Scholarship Program

American Hellenic Education Progressive Association
1909 Q Street NW, Suite 500, Washington, DC 20009
Phone: 202-232-6300
Email: ahepa@ahepa.org
https://ahepa.org/Education-Scholarships.htm
Purpose: To assist Hellenic students.
Eligibility: Applicants must be members of the AHEPA family or be related to someone who is a member. Students must be of Hellenic descent and/or Phil-Hellene, the son or daughter of a member in good standing of AHEPA, the Maids of Athena, the Daughters of Penelope or the Sons of Pericles.
Target applicant(s): High school students. College students. Graduate school students. Adult students.
Minimum GPA: 3.0
Amount: $2,000.

Number of awards: 1.
Deadline: March 31.
How to apply: Applications are available online.
Exclusive: Visit www.UltimateScholarshipBook.com and enter code AM256620 for updates on this award.

(2567) · AICPA Scholarship for Minority Accounting Students

American Institute of Certified Public Accountants
220 Leigh Farm Road, Durham, NC 27707
Phone: 919-402-4500
Email: service@aicpa.org
http://www.aicpa.org
Purpose: To encourage minority students to become certified public accountants (CPAs).
Eligibility: Applicants must be African-American, Native American, Latino or Asian American students who are majoring in accounting. They must be full-time students who have completed at least 30 credits overall and at least six credits in accounting. They must have a GPA of 3.0 or higher and must have plans to become a certified public accountant (CPA). Selection is based on academic merit, leadership, volunteer experience and commitment to becoming a CPA.
Target applicant(s): College students. Graduate school students. Adult students.
Minimum GPA: 3.0
Amount: Up to $5,000.
Number of awards: 80.
Scholarship may be renewable.
Deadline: April 1.
How to apply: Applications are available online. An application form and a personal essay are required.
Exclusive: Visit www.UltimateScholarshipBook.com and enter code AM256720 for updates on this award.

(2568) · AISES Intel Scholarship

American Indian Science and Engineering Society
2305 Renard Place, Albuquerque, NM 87106
Phone: 505-765-1052
http://www.aises.org/scholarships
Purpose: To support the advancement of AISES (American Indian Science and Engineering Society) members who are American Indian, Alaska Natives or Native Hawaiians working towards degrees in the STEM disciplines (science, technology, engineering and math).
Eligibility: Applicants must be AISES members who are also members of an American Indian tribe, are Alaska Natives or are Native Hawaiians. They must also be enrolled as full-time undergraduate or graduate students at a four-year academic institution or at a two-year institution working towards an academic degree. Students must major in one of the following fields: computer science, computer engineering, electrical engineering, chemical engineering or material science. The minimum GPA requirement is 3.0. Selection is based upon the quality of the application.
Target applicant(s): College students. Graduate school students. Adult students.
Minimum GPA: 3.0
Amount: $5,000-$10,000.
Number of awards: Up to 5.
Deadline: May 1.
How to apply: Applications are available online. An application form, official transcripts, an essay, two letters of recommendation, tribal enrollment documentation and resume are required.
Exclusive: Visit www.UltimateScholarshipBook.com and enter code AM256820 for updates on this award.

(2569) · Allison E. Fisher Scholarship

National Association of Black Journalists
1100 Knight Hall, Suite 3100, College Park, MD 20742
Phone: 301-405-7520
Email: iwashington@nabj.org
http://nabj.site-ym.com/?page=SEEDScholarships
Purpose: To aid print and broadcast journalism students.
Eligibility: Applicants must be student members of the National Association of Black Journalists (NABJ). They must be undergraduate or graduate students enrolled at a four-year institution majoring in broadcast or print journalism. They must have a GPA of 3.0 or higher and must demonstrate a commitment to community service. Selection is based on the overall strength of the application.
Target applicant(s): College students. Graduate school students. Adult students.
Minimum GPA: 3.0
Amount: $2,500.
Number of awards: 1.
Deadline: February 12.
How to apply: Applications are available online. An application form and supporting materials are required.
Exclusive: Visit www.UltimateScholarshipBook.com and enter code NA256920 for updates on this award.

(2570) · Allogan Slagle Memorial Scholarship

Association on American Indian Affairs
Lisa Wyzlic, Director of Scholarship Programs, 966 Hungerford Drive, Suite 12-B, Rockville, MD 20850
Phone: 240-314-7155
Email: lw.aaia@indian-affairs.org
https://www.indian-affairs.org/scholarships.html
Purpose: To assist Native American/Alaska Native undergraduate and graduate students from tribes that are not recognized by the federal government.
Eligibility: Applicants must submit a financial need analysis form, Certificate of Indian Blood or documents proving their lineal descent, proof of tribal enrollment, essay, two letters of recommendation, current financial aid award letter, transcripts and class schedule.
Target applicant(s): High school students. College students. Graduate school students. Adult students.
Minimum GPA: 2.5
Amount: Varies.
Number of awards: Varies.
Deadline: June 1.
How to apply: Applications are available online.
Exclusive: Visit www.UltimateScholarshipBook.com and enter code AS257020 for updates on this award.

(2571) · Allstate WBCA Good Works Team

Women's Basketball Coaches Association
4646 Lawrenceville Highway, Lilburn, GA 30047
Phone: 770-279-8027
Email: dtrujillo@wbca.org
https://wbca.org/recognize/player-awards
Purpose: To bring attention to women's college basketball student-athletes who make a difference on and off the court with their contributions to volunteering and civic involvement.

Eligibility: Nominees must be women's basketball student-athletes who are in good standing with their institution and academically a sophomore, junior, senior or graduate student for that basketball season. Nominating institutions must be an NCAA or NAIA member. Nominees must be free of any felony charges.
Target applicant(s): College students. Graduate school students. Adult students.
Amount: Varies.
Number of awards: 10.
Deadline: Fall.
How to apply: Nominees are selected by head women's basketball coaches with assistance from their sports information directors. Nominations are accepted in the fall.
Exclusive: Visit www.UltimateScholarshipBook.com and enter code WO257120 for updates on this award.

(2572) • American Chemical Society Scholars Program

American Chemical Society
Christie Robinson, Training and Development Director, Rubber Division, ACS, 411 Wolf Ledges Parkway, Suite 201, Akron, OH 44311
Phone: 800-227-5558
Email: crobinson@rubber.org
http://www.acs.org
Purpose: To encourage minority students to pursue careers in the sciences and to help them acquire the skills necessary for success in these fields.
Eligibility: Applicants must be African American, Hispanic/Latino or American Indian and graduating high school seniors or college freshmen, sophomores or juniors enrolled full-time at an accredited institution. Students must major in chemistry, biochemistry, chemical engineering or a chemically-related science and plan to work in a chemistry-related field. Those entering pre-med programs or pursuing pharmacy degrees are not eligible. A minimum GPA of 3.0 or "B" or better with high academic achievement in chemistry or science is required. Students must also demonstrate financial need through the Free Application for Federal Student Aid (FAFSA).
Target applicant(s): High school students. College students. Adult students.
Minimum GPA: 3.0
Amount: Up to $5,000.
Number of awards: Varies.
Scholarship may be renewable.
Deadline: March 1.
How to apply: Applications are available online.
Exclusive: Visit www.UltimateScholarshipBook.com and enter code AM257220 for updates on this award.

(2573) • American Indian Services Scholarship

American Indian Services
3115 E. Lion Lane, Suite 320, Cottonwood Heights, UT 84121
Phone: 801-375-1777
http://www.americanindianservices.org
Purpose: To support Native American students in pursuing post-secondary education.
Eligibility: Applicants must be one-quarter enrolled members of a Federally Recognized Native American Tribe. A minimum GPA of 2.25 is required. Students must be undergraduate students who have earned fewer than 150 credits.
Target applicant(s): College students. Adult students.
Minimum GPA: 2.25
Amount: Varies.
Number of awards: Varies.
Deadline: February 1, May 1, August 1, November 1.
How to apply: Applications are available online.
Exclusive: Visit www.UltimateScholarshipBook.com and enter code AM257320 for updates on this award.

(2574) • American Society of Criminology Fellowships for Ethnic Minorities

American Society of Criminology
1314 Kinnear Road, Suite 212, Columbus, OH 43212-1156
Email: ronet@udel.edu
http://www.asc41.com
Purpose: To encourage minorities to study criminology or criminal justice.
Eligibility: Applicants must be African American, Asian American, Latino or Native American. Recipients must have been accepted into a doctoral studies program. Selection is based on curriculum vitae, college transcripts, financial need, references and letter describing career plans, experiences and interest in criminology.
Target applicant(s): Graduate school students. Adult students.
Amount: $6,000.
Number of awards: 3.
Deadline: March 1.
How to apply: Applications are available by written request.
Exclusive: Visit www.UltimateScholarshipBook.com and enter code AM257420 for updates on this award.

(2575) • Anne Maureen Whitney Barrow Memorial Scholarship

Society of Women Engineers
130 East Randolph Street, Suite 3500, Chicago, IL 60601
Phone: 877-793-4636
Email: scholarships@swe.org
http://societyofwomenengineers.swe.org/scholarships
Purpose: To support female engineering students.
Eligibility: Applicants must be enrolled in an accredited engineering or computer science program. A minimum GPA of 3.5 is required.
Target applicant(s): High school students. College students. Adult students.
Minimum GPA: 3.5
Amount: $7,000.
Number of awards: 1.
Scholarship may be renewable.
Deadline: February 15 (all others); May 1 (freshmen).
How to apply: Applications are available online.
Exclusive: Visit www.UltimateScholarshipBook.com and enter code SO257520 for updates on this award.

(2576) • ARS Awards Scholarship

Armenian Relief Society, Western USA
517 West Glenoaks Boulevard, Suite 300, Glendale, CA 91202
Email: office@arswestusa.org
http://arswestusa.org/chapters/
Purpose: To provide merit and need-based scholarships for students of Armenian ancestry.

Eligibility: Applicants must be of Armenian ancestry and not related to the ARS Central Executive or Eremian Scholarship Committee members. Specific requirements may vary by region.
Target applicant(s): College students. Graduate school students. Adult students.
Amount: Varies.
Number of awards: Varies.
Deadline: Varies.
How to apply: Applicants should contact their local ARS Chapter. See website for list of local Chapters.
Exclusive: Visit www.UltimateScholarshipBook.com and enter code AR257620 for updates on this award.

(2577) • ARS Undergraduate Scholarship

Armenian Relief Society of Eastern USA (ARS)
80 Bigelow Avenue, Suite 200, Watertown, MA 02472
Phone: (617) 926-3801
http://arseastusa.org/about.html
Purpose: To support students of Armenian descent who are attending a four-year college.
Eligibility: Applicant must be of Armenian descent. Applicants must be an undergraduate student who has completed at least one college semester at an accredited four-year college or university in the United States or enrolled in a two-year college and transferring to a four-year college or university as a full time student in the fall. A letter from an Armenian community leader or representative that attests to the applicant's activity or contributions to the Armenian Community is required.
Target applicant(s): College students. Adult students.
Amount: $1,000.
Number of awards: 12.
Deadline: April 1.
How to apply: Applications are available online.
Exclusive: Visit www.UltimateScholarshipBook.com and enter code AR257720 for updates on this award.

(2578) • ASA Scholarships

Armenian Students' Association of America
333 Atlantic Avenue, Warwick, RI 02888
Phone: 401-461-6114
Email: asa@asainc.org
http://www.asainc.org
Purpose: To provide scholarships for students of Armenian descent.
Eligibility: Applicants must be college sophomores or beyond in the year of application and be of Armenian descent.
Target applicant(s): High school students. College students. Graduate school students. Adult students.
Amount: Varies.
Number of awards: Varies.
Deadline: Varies.
How to apply: Request forms for applications are available online.
Exclusive: Visit www.UltimateScholarshipBook.com and enter code AR257820 for updates on this award.

(2579) • Asian and Pacific Islander American Scholarships

Asian and Pacific Islander American Scholarship Fund
2025 M Street NW, Suite 610, Washington, DC 20036
Phone: 202-986-6892
Email: info@apiasf.org
http://www.apiasf.org
Purpose: To provide financial assistance to Asian and Pacific Island Americans.
Eligibility: Applicants must be of Asian or Pacific Islander ethnicity as defined by the U.S. Census, and they must be legal citizens, nationals or permanent residents of the United States. Citizens of the Marshall Islands, Micronesia and Palau are also eligible. Applicants must be enrolling full-time as a first-year degree-seeking student in an accredited college or university in the U.S. They must have a GPA of 2.7 or higher or have earned a GED, and they must apply for federal financial aid.
Target applicant(s): High school students.
Minimum GPA: 2.7
Amount: $2,500-$20,000.
Number of awards: Varies.
Deadline: January 11.
How to apply: Applications are available online.
Exclusive: Visit www.UltimateScholarshipBook.com and enter code AS257920 for updates on this award.

(2580) • Asian Women in Business Scholarship

Asian Women in Business
42 Broadway, Suite 1748, New York, NY 10004
Phone: 212-868-1368
Email: info@awib.org
http://www.awib.org
Purpose: To recognize Asian women who have demonstrated scholarship, leadership or commitment to the community.
Eligibility: Applicants must be women of Asian or Pacific Islander descent. They must be U.S. citizens or permanent residents, demonstrate leadership in the community, demonstrate entrepreneurial success, be a full-time undergraduate student at an accredited U.S. four-year institution and have a GPA of 3.0 or higher on a four-point scale. Selection is based on the overall strength of the application.
Target applicant(s): College students. Adult students.
Minimum GPA: 3.0
Amount: $2,500.
Number of awards: Varies.
Deadline: Varies.
How to apply: Applications are available online. An application form, transcript (if applicable) and at least one professional recommendation letter are required.
Exclusive: Visit www.UltimateScholarshipBook.com and enter code AS258020 for updates on this award.

(2581) • Aspiring Writer Scholarship

Go On Girl! Book Club Inc.
P.O. Box 3368, New York, NY 10185
http://goongirl.org
Purpose: To support minority college students pursuing post-secondary education.
Eligibility: Applicants must be U.S. citizens or resident aliens who identify with the African diaspora. Students must be enrolled full-time at a historically black college or university with a minimum grade point average of 2.5. Applicants must submit an essay on the topic of the power of the written word.
Target applicant(s): College students. Adult students.
Minimum GPA: 2.5
Amount: $1,000.
Number of awards: 1.
Deadline: March 31.

How to apply: Applications are available online.
Exclusive: Visit www.UltimateScholarshipBook.com and enter code GO258120 for updates on this award.

(2582) • Association of Cuban Engineers Scholarship Foundation Scholarships

Association of Cuban-American Engineers Scholarship Foundation
P.O. Box 941436, Miami, FL 33194-1436
Phone: 305-597-9858
https://www.cubanamericanengineers.com/students/applications-for-scholarships-and-membership/
Purpose: To help undergraduate and graduate students of Hispanic heritage who are pursuing degrees in engineering.
Eligibility: Applicants must be U.S. citizens or legal residents of Hispanic heritage who have completed at least 30 units of coursework towards a bachelor's degree or higher in engineering at an ABET-accredited institution located in the United States or Puerto Rico. They must have a GPA of 3.0 or higher and must be current, full-time students (carrying 12 or more semester hours if an undergraduate and 6 or more semester hours as a graduate student). Selection is based on the overall strength of the application.
Target applicant(s): College students. Graduate school students. Adult students.
Minimum GPA: 3.0
Amount: Varies.
Number of awards: Varies.
Deadline: December 16.
How to apply: Applications are available online. An application form, official transcript and financial aid award letter are required.
Exclusive: Visit www.UltimateScholarshipBook.com and enter code AS258220 for updates on this award.

(2583) • B.J. Harrod Scholarships

Society of Women Engineers
130 East Randolph Street, Suite 3500, Chicago, IL 60601
Phone: 877-793-4636
Email: scholarships@swe.org
http://societyofwomenengineers.swe.org/scholarships
Purpose: To aid female engineering students.
Eligibility: Applicants may major in any type of engineering at an accredited institution of higher learning. They must be freshmen and have a GPA of 3.5 or higher.
Target applicant(s): College students. Adult students.
Minimum GPA: 3.5
Amount: $1,500.
Number of awards: 2.
Deadline: May 1.
How to apply: Applications are available online. An application form is required.
Exclusive: Visit www.UltimateScholarshipBook.com and enter code SO258320 for updates on this award.

(2584) • B.K. Krenzer Reentry Scholarship

Society of Women Engineers
130 East Randolph Street, Suite 3500, Chicago, IL 60601
Phone: 877-793-4636
Email: scholarships@swe.org
http://societyofwomenengineers.swe.org/scholarships
Purpose: To support reentering female engineering students.
Eligibility: Applicants must have been out of school and out of the job market for at least two years. They must enroll in an accredited engineering or computer science program. A GPA of 3.0 or higher is required. Preference is given to degreed engineers.
Target applicant(s): College students. Adult students.
Minimum GPA: 3.0
Amount: $2,500.
Number of awards: 1.
Deadline: September 15.
How to apply: Applications are available online. An application form is required.
Exclusive: Visit www.UltimateScholarshipBook.com and enter code SO258420 for updates on this award.

(2585) • Bechtel Foundation Scholarship

Society of Women Engineers
130 East Randolph Street, Suite 3500, Chicago, IL 60601
Phone: 877-793-4636
Email: scholarships@swe.org
http://societyofwomenengineers.swe.org/scholarships
Purpose: To support female engineering students.
Eligibility: Applicants must be enrolled in an accredited engineering program in their sophomore, junior or senior year. They must be SWE members. A minimum GPA of 3.0 is required.
Target applicant(s): College students. Adult students.
Minimum GPA: 3.0
Amount: $1,400.
Number of awards: 2.
Deadline: February 15.
How to apply: Applications are available online. An application form is required.
Exclusive: Visit www.UltimateScholarshipBook.com and enter code SO258520 for updates on this award.

(2586) • Berbeco Senior Research Fellowship

United Negro College Fund (UNCF)
1805 7th Street NW, Washington, DC 20001
Phone: 800-331-2244
https://scholarships.uncf.org/
Purpose: To encourage African Americans to conduct independent research internationally.
Eligibility: Applicants must be college juniors who attend United Negro College Fund (UNCF) member colleges or universities. The need-based award is for students to work on their senior thesis or research projects outside the U.S. during the summer between their junior and senior years.
Target applicant(s): College students. Adult students.
Minimum GPA: 2.5
Amount: Up to $6,000.
Number of awards: Varies.
Deadline: March 3.
How to apply: Applications are available online.
Exclusive: Visit www.UltimateScholarshipBook.com and enter code UN258620 for updates on this award.

(2587) • Black EOE Journal Scholarship

Black EOE Journal
18 Technology Drive, Suite 170, Irvine, CA 92618
Phone: 800-487-5099

https://www.blackeoejournal.com/scholarship-opportunity/
Purpose: To support students who are African-American undergraduate students.
Eligibility: Applicants must be U.S. citizens, African-American and undergraduate level students. Students must submit an essay describing their college experience so far and future career plans. Graphic or creative presentations are also accepted. Selection is based upon a genuine desire to use the scholarship to advance in a selected field of study and an overall passion for knowledge.
Target applicant(s): High school students. College students. Adult students.
Amount: $500.
Number of awards: 1.
Deadline: August 15.
How to apply: Applications are available online.
Exclusive: Visit www.UltimateScholarshipBook.com and enter code BL258720 for updates on this award.

(2588) · Bob Fennell Point Scholarship

Point Foundation
5757 Wilshire Boulevard, Suite 370, Los Angeles, CA 90036
Phone: 323-933-1234
http://www.pointfoundation.org
Purpose: To support LGBTQ students pursuing an undergraduate or graduate degree.
Eligibility: Applicants must be a high school senior, undergraduate or graduate student who openly identifies as lesbian, gay, bisexual, transgender or queer. Students must provide evidence of leadership and community involvement working for the betterment of the LGBTQ community.
Target applicant(s): High school students. College students. Graduate school students. Adult students.
Amount: $3,000.
Number of awards: 1.
Scholarship may be renewable.
Deadline: January 30.
How to apply: Applications are available online.
Exclusive: Visit www.UltimateScholarshipBook.com and enter code PO258820 for updates on this award.

(2589) · Burlington Northern Santa Fe (BNSF) Foundation Scholarship

American Indian Science and Engineering Society
2305 Renard Place, Albuquerque, NM 87106
Phone: 505-765-1052
http://www.aises.org/scholarships
Purpose: To provide a four-year scholarship for an American Indian student attending an accredited four-year college or university in a state where Burlington Northern Santa Fe operates.
Eligibility: Applicants must reside in one of the following states: Arizona, California, Colorado, Kansas, Minnesota, Montana, New Mexico, North Dakota, Oklahoma, Oregon, South Dakota or Washington. Applicants must also major in one of the following areas: business, engineering, math, medicine/health administration, natural/physical sciences, technology or education and belong to AISES. Applicants must have a 2.0 minimum GPA.
Target applicant(s): High school students.
Minimum GPA: 2.0
Amount: $2,500 for 4 years.
Number of awards: 5.
Scholarship may be renewable.
Deadline: May 1.
How to apply: Applications are available online.
Exclusive: Visit www.UltimateScholarshipBook.com and enter code AM258920 for updates on this award.

(2590) · Cafe Bustelo El Cafe Del Futuro Scholarship

Hispanic Association of Colleges and Universities (HACU)
8415 Datapoint Drive, Suite 400, San Antonio, TX 78229
Phone: 210-692-3805
Email: scholarship@hacu.net
http://www.hacu.net/hacu/scholarships.asp
Purpose: To support students who are of Latino heritage.
Eligibility: Applicants must be at least 18 years old, a U.S. citizen or permanent legal resident and be of Latino descent. Students must be enrolled full-time in an undergraduate or graduate level program at a four-year HACU-member institution in the United States, Washington, DC or Puerto Rico. Students will submit a 500-word essay on the topic outlined on the website pertaining to Latino heritage, goals and future community service.
Target applicant(s): College students. Graduate school students. Adult students.
Amount: $5,000.
Number of awards: 10.
Deadline: May 25.
How to apply: Applications are available online.
Exclusive: Visit www.UltimateScholarshipBook.com and enter code HI259020 for updates on this award.

(2591) · California Chafee Grant for Foster Youth

California Student Aid Commission
Specialized Programs Operations Branch - Chafee, P.O. Box 419029, Rancho Cordova, CA 95741-9029
Phone: 888-224-7268
Email: studentsupport@csac.ca.gov
http://www.csac.ca.gov/
Purpose: To provide educational assistance for students who have been in foster care in California.
Eligibility: Applicants must be current or former foster youth who are under 22 years of age as of July 1 of the award year. Dependency must have been established by the court between the ages of 16 and 18. Financial need is required. Applicants must enroll at least half-time in a program that is at least one academic year long, and they must attend class regularly and maintain good grades.
Target applicant(s): High school students. College students.
Amount: Up to $5,000.
Number of awards: Varies.
Scholarship may be renewable.
Deadline: Varies.
How to apply: Applications are available online and applicants must also complete a FAFSA.
Exclusive: Visit www.UltimateScholarshipBook.com and enter code CA259120 for updates on this award.

(2592) · Carmen E. Turner Scholarship

Conference of Minority Transportation Officials
100 M Street SE, Suite 917, Washington, DC 20003
Phone: 202-857-8065
Email: info@comto.org
http://www.comto.org/page/Scholarships

Purpose: To support students who are members of COMTO.
Eligibility: Applicants must have been COMTO members in good standing for at least the past year. Students must be enrolling as an undergraduate student at an accredited institution of higher education or enrolled in an undergraduate or graduate program for at least six credits per semester with at least a 2.5 GPA.
Target applicant(s): College students. Graduate school students. Adult students.
Minimum GPA: 2.5
Amount: $3,500.
Number of awards: Varies.
Deadline: March 10.
How to apply: Applications are available online.
Exclusive: Visit www.UltimateScholarshipBook.com and enter code CO259220 for updates on this award.

(2593) · Casey Family Scholarship

Casey Family
21351 Gentry Drive, Suite 130, Sterling, VA 20166
Phone: 571-203-0270
Email: info@fc2success.org
http://www.fc2success.org/our-programs/information-for-students/
Purpose: To support foster care students pursuing a higher education.
Eligibility: Applicants must have been in foster care for the year prior to their 18th birthday; or have been adopted or placed into legal guardianship from foster care after their 16th birthday; or they must have been orphaned for at least one year at the time of their 18th birthday. Students must have been accepted into an accredited post-secondary school. Applicants must have been in foster care or orphaned while living in the United States.
Target applicant(s): High school students. College students. Graduate school students. Adult students.
Amount: $1,500-$6,000.
Number of awards: Varies.
Scholarship may be renewable.
Deadline: March 31.
How to apply: Applications are available online.
Exclusive: Visit www.UltimateScholarshipBook.com and enter code CA259320 for updates on this award.

(2594) · Catching the Dream Native American Scholarship Fund

Catching the Dream
Attn.: Scholarship Affairs Office, 8200 Mountain Road NE, Suite 103, Albuquerque, NM 87110
Phone: 505-262-2351
Email: nscholarsh@aol.com
http://www.catchingthedream.org
Purpose: To support American Indian students pursuing higher education.
Eligibility: Applicants must be undergraduate or graduate students who are 1/4 or more American Indian, enrolled in a U.S. tribe and attend or plans to attend an accredited institution on a full-time basis. Students must excel academically, have received high ACT or SAT scores and demonstrate a strong commitment to the Indian community. Selection is based on the strength of the overall application.
Target applicant(s): College students. Adult students.
Amount: $5,000.
Number of awards: Varies.
Deadline: April 30 and September 15.
How to apply: Applications are available online.
Exclusive: Visit www.UltimateScholarshipBook.com and enter code CA259420 for updates on this award.

(2595) · Catherine W. Pierce Scholarship

United Negro College Fund (UNCF)
1805 7th Street NW, Washington, DC 20001
Phone: 800-331-2244
https://scholarships.uncf.org/
Purpose: To help African American students majoring in art or history.
Eligibility: Applicants must have a minimum 2.5 GPA, be pursuing a degree in an art or history discipline, complete the Free Application for Federal Student Aid (FAFSA) and have unmet financial need that is verified by the college or university financial aid office. UNCF students are encouraged to complete the UNCF General Scholarship application to be matched with scholarships for which they meet the criteria.
Target applicant(s): High school students. College students. Adult students.
Minimum GPA: 2.5
Amount: Up to $5,000.
Number of awards: Varies.
Deadline: July 29.
How to apply: Applications are available online.
Exclusive: Visit www.UltimateScholarshipBook.com and enter code UN259520 for updates on this award.

(2596) · CBC Spouses Heineken USA Performing Arts Scholarship

Congressional Black Caucus Foundation
1720 Massachusetts Avenue NW, Washington, DC 20036
Phone: 202-263-2800
Email: info@cbcfinc.org
http://www.cbcfinc.org
Purpose: To support students who are pursuing careers in performing arts.
Eligibility: Applicants must be African American students who have at least a 2.5 GPA, and they must be enrolled or accepted into a full-time undergraduate degree program. Applicants must show leadership qualities and community service participation.
Target applicant(s): High school students. College students. Adult students.
Minimum GPA: 2.5
Amount: Up to $3,000.
Number of awards: Up to 10.
Deadline: April 21.
How to apply: Applications are available online.
Exclusive: Visit www.UltimateScholarshipBook.com and enter code CO259620 for updates on this award.

(2597) · CHCI United Health Foundation Scholar-Intern Program

Congressional Hispanic Caucus Institute Inc.
300 M Street SE, 5th Floor, Suite 510, Washington, DC 20003
Phone: 202-543-1771
Email: shernandez@chci.org
http://www.chci.org
Purpose: To reward Latino students who are interested in careers in the healthcare industry.

Eligibility: Applicants must be Latinos focused on the healthcare industry who are currently enrolled full-time at an accredited community college, four-year university or graduate or professional program. Students must have at least one more full year of their program remaining when they apply, must have a minimum 3.0 GPA and must demonstrate financial need.
Target applicant(s): College students. Graduate school students. Adult students.
Minimum GPA: 3.0
Amount: $2,500-$5,000.
Number of awards: Varies.
Deadline: April 28.
How to apply: Applications are available online.
Exclusive: Visit www.UltimateScholarshipBook.com and enter code CO259720 for updates on this award.

(2598) • Cherokee Nation Directed Studies Scholarship

Cherokee Nation
P.O. Box 948, Tahlequah, OK 74465
Phone: 918-453-5000
Email: communications@cherokee.org
http://www.cherokee.org/Services/Education/College-Resources
Purpose: To aid Cherokee college students.
Eligibility: Applicants must be citizens of the Cherokee Nation and reside in the Cherokee Nation jurisdictional area. They must be enrolled full-time in a graduate or upper-level undergraduate degree program. They must agree to work for the Cherokee Nation for two years following graduation. Selection is based on the overall strength of the application.
Target applicant(s): College students. Graduate school students. Adult students.
Amount: Full tuition, books and fees.
Number of awards: Varies.
Deadline: June 15.
How to apply: Applications are available online. An application form and supporting materials are required.
Exclusive: Visit www.UltimateScholarshipBook.com and enter code CH259820 for updates on this award.

(2599) • Cherokee Nation Registered Nursing Scholarship

Cherokee Nation
P.O. Box 948, Tahlequah, OK 74465
Phone: 918-453-5000
Email: communications@cherokee.org
http://www.cherokee.org/Services/Education/College-Resources
Purpose: To aid Cherokee students who are pursuing degrees in registered nursing.
Eligibility: Applicants must be citizens of the Cherokee Nation and must be residents of the Cherokee Nation jurisdictional area. They must be full-time students who are enrolled in a registered nurse (RN) degree program. They must sign an agreement to work for a Cherokee Nation Health Facility for two years after graduation. Selection is based on the overall strength of the application.
Target applicant(s): High school students. College students. Adult students.
Amount: Varies.
Number of awards: Varies.
Deadline: June 15.
How to apply: Applications are available online. An application and supporting materials are required.
Exclusive: Visit www.UltimateScholarshipBook.com and enter code CH259920 for updates on this award.

(2600) • Cherokee Nation Scholarship - Graduate

Cherokee Nation
P.O. Box 948, Tahlequah, OK 74465
Phone: 918-453-5000
Email: communications@cherokee.org
http://www.cherokee.org/Services/Education/College-Resources
Purpose: To aid graduate students who are members of the Cherokee Nation.
Eligibility: Applicants must be citizens of the Cherokee Nation. They must be graduate students who are attending a not-for-profit educational institution. Selection is based on the overall strength of the application.
Target applicant(s): Graduate school students. Adult students.
Amount: Varies.
Number of awards: Varies.
Deadline: June 15.
How to apply: Applications are available online. An application form and supporting materials are required.
Exclusive: Visit www.UltimateScholarshipBook.com and enter code CH260020 for updates on this award.

(2601) • Cherokee Nation Scholarship - Undergraduate

Cherokee Nation
P.O. Box 948, Tahlequah, OK 74465
Phone: 918-453-5000
Email: communications@cherokee.org
http://www.cherokee.org/Services/Education/College-Resources
Purpose: To aid undergraduate students who are members of the Cherokee Nation.
Eligibility: Applicants must be citizens of the Cherokee Nation. They must be undergraduate students who are attending a not-for-profit educational institution. Selection is based on the overall strength of the application.
Target applicant(s): College students. Adult students.
Amount: Varies.
Number of awards: Varies.
Deadline: June 15.
How to apply: Applications are available online. An application form and supporting materials are required.
Exclusive: Visit www.UltimateScholarshipBook.com and enter code CH260120 for updates on this award.

(2602) • Chickasaw Nation Education Foundation Program

Chickasaw Nation Education Foundation
P.O. Box 1726, Ada, OK 74821-1726
Phone: 580-421-9030
Email: ChickasawFoundation@chickasaw.net
http://www.chickasawfoundation.org/
Purpose: To assist Chickasaw students who demonstrate academic excellence, community service, dedication to learning and a commitment to Native Americans.
Eligibility: Applicants must be full-time Chickasaw students. Other eligibility requirements vary by scholarship.

Target applicant(s): High school students. College students. Graduate school students. Adult students.
Amount: Varies.
Number of awards: Varies.
Deadline: June 1.
How to apply: Applications are available online.
Exclusive: Visit www.UltimateScholarshipBook.com and enter code CH260220 for updates on this award.

(2603) • Chief Manuelito Scholarship Program

Office of Navajo Nation Scholarship and Financial Assistance
P.O. Box 1870, Window Rock, AZ 86515
Phone: 928-871-7444
http://www.onnsfa.org
Purpose: The scholarship was created to help high-achieving Navajo students.
Eligibility: Students must be enrolled members of the Navajo nation, submit a Certificate of Indian Blood, attend a regionally-accredited school and complete a FAFSA form. Students must also complete a Navajo Government course (available online).
Target applicant(s): High school students. College students. Graduate school students. Adult students.
Amount: $7,000.
Number of awards: Varies.
Scholarship may be renewable.
Deadline: June 25 (fall), November 25 (spring).
How to apply: Applications are available online and must be submitted to your agency, which is listed online.
Exclusive: Visit www.UltimateScholarshipBook.com and enter code OF260320 for updates on this award.

(2604) • Citizen Potawatomi Nation Tribal Scholarship

Citizen Potawatomi Nation
1601 S. Gordon Cooper Drive, Shawnee, OK 74801
Phone: 405-275-3121
Email: college@potawatomi.org
http://www.potawatomi.org/services/education/
Purpose: To assist Citizen Potawatomi Nation tribal members who are pursuing higher education.
Eligibility: Applicants must be Citizen Potawatomi Nation tribal members who are enrolled full or part-time in an undergraduate or graduate academic degree program at an accredited postsecondary institution. Selection is based on the overall strength of the application.
Target applicant(s): High school students. College students. Graduate school students. Adult students.
Amount: $750-$2,000 per semester.
Number of awards: Varies.
Scholarship may be renewable.
Deadline: February 15 (spring), June 15 (summer), September 15 (fall).
How to apply: Applications are available online. An application form, proof of enrollment, federal tax return information and transcript are required.
Exclusive: Visit www.UltimateScholarshipBook.com and enter code CI260420 for updates on this award.

(2605) • Colgate-Palmolive Company/UNCF Scholarship

United Negro College Fund (UNCF)
1805 7th Street NW, Washington, DC 20001
Phone: 800-331-2244
https://scholarships.uncf.org/
Purpose: To help African American sophomores, juniors and seniors majoring in business with a concentration in marketing.
Eligibility: Applicants must have a minimum 3.0 GPA and attend United Negro College Fund (UNCF) member colleges and universities. Students must complete the Free Application for Federal Student Aid (FAFSA) and have unmet financial need that is verified by the college or university financial aid office. UNCF students are encouraged to complete the UNCF General Scholarship application to be matched with scholarships for which they meet the criteria.
Target applicant(s): College students. Adult students.
Minimum GPA: 3.0
Amount: Up to $5,000.
Number of awards: Varies.
Deadline: November 13.
How to apply: Applications are available online.
Exclusive: Visit www.UltimateScholarshipBook.com and enter code UN260520 for updates on this award.

(2606) • Colgate-Palmolive Haz la U Educational Grant

Hispanic Heritage Foundation Colgate-Palmolive Haz la U
1001 Pennsylvania Ave NW, Washington, DC 20004
http://www.colgate.com/HazLaU
Purpose: To support Latino students who excel in the classroom and their community by providing them with funds to further their education.
Eligibility: Applicants must have Latino heritage, have a minimum 3.0 GPA and be graduating high school seniors. Students must be role models in their communities and must also be permanent residents, DACA, U.S. citizens or eligible non-citizens.
Target applicant(s): High school students.
Minimum GPA: 3.0
Amount: $2,000-$15,000.
Number of awards: 31.
Deadline: October 15.
How to apply: Applications are available online.
Exclusive: Visit www.UltimateScholarshipBook.com and enter code HI260620 for updates on this award.

(2607) • Congressional Black Caucus Spouses Education Scholarship

Congressional Black Caucus Foundation
1720 Massachusetts Avenue NW, Washington, DC 20036
Phone: 202-263-2800
Email: info@cbcfinc.org
http://www.cbcfinc.org
Purpose: To support students who are pursuing undergraduate or graduate degrees.
Eligibility: Applicants must be African American students attending or planning to attend school on a full-time basis. Students must have at least a 2.5 GPA, and they must demonstrate leadership and community service participation.
Target applicant(s): High school students. College students. Graduate school students. Adult students.
Minimum GPA: 2.5
Amount: Varies.
Number of awards: Varies.
Deadline: May 19.

How to apply: Applications are available online.
Exclusive: Visit www.UltimateScholarshipBook.com and enter code CO260720 for updates on this award.

(2608) • Congressional Black Caucus Spouses Visual Arts Scholarship

Congressional Black Caucus Foundation
1720 Massachusetts Avenue NW, Washington, DC 20036
Phone: 202-263-2800
Email: info@cbcfinc.org
http://www.cbcfinc.org
Purpose: To support students who are pursuing careers in visual arts.
Eligibility: Applicants must be African American students, have at least a 2.5 GPA and be enrolled at or accepted into a full-time undergraduate degree program. Applicants must show leadership qualities and community service participation.
Target applicant(s): High school students. College students. Adult students.
Minimum GPA: 2.5
Amount: Up to $3,000.
Number of awards: Varies.
Deadline: April 21.
How to apply: Applications are available online.
Exclusive: Visit www.UltimateScholarshipBook.com and enter code CO260820 for updates on this award.

(2609) • Department of Defense Scholarship

Thurgood Marshall Scholarship Fund
901 F Street NW, Suite 300, Washington, DC 20004
Phone: 202-507-4851
Email: deshuandra.walker@tmcf.org
https://tmcf.org/our-scholarships
Purpose: To promote the study of STEM topics at Historically Black Colleges and Universities.
Eligibility: Applicants must be U.S. citizens or legal residents graduating from high school with a minimum 3.25 GPA. Students must have earned a grade of "B" or better in pre-calculus or an equivalent math course. Applicants must plan to enroll at a Historically Black College or University to pursue a degree in a STEM discipline.
Target applicant(s): High school students.
Minimum GPA: 3.25
Amount: $15,000.
Number of awards: 1.
Scholarship may be renewable.
Deadline: Varies.
How to apply: Applications are available online.
Exclusive: Visit www.UltimateScholarshipBook.com and enter code TH260920 for updates on this award.

(2610) • Development Fund for Black Students in Science and Technology

Development Fund for Black Students in Science and Technology
2705 Bladensburg Road NE, Washington, DC 20018
http://www.dfbsstscholarship.org/dfb_sch.html
Purpose: To support African-American students studying scientific fields.
Eligibility: Applicants must be U.S. citizens or permanent residents and undergraduate African-American students at a Historically Black College majoring in a technical field such as engineering or math. Students must demonstrate financial need and provide an essay along with their application materials.
Target applicant(s): High school students. College students. Adult students.
Amount: Up to $3,000.
Number of awards: 1.
Deadline: June 15.
How to apply: Applications are available online.
Exclusive: Visit www.UltimateScholarshipBook.com and enter code DE261020 for updates on this award.

(2611) • Displaced Homemaker Scholarship

Association on American Indian Affairs
Lisa Wyzlic, Director of Scholarship Programs, 966 Hungerford Drive, Suite 12-B, Rockville, MD 20850
Phone: 240-314-7155
Email: lw.aaia@indian-affairs.org
https://www.indian-affairs.org/scholarships.html
Purpose: To provide assistance to Native American/Alaska Native undergraduate men and women in any curriculum who would be unable to complete college due to family responsibilities.
Eligibility: Applicants must be full-time students able to prove financial need, proof of tribal enrollment and Certificate of Indian Blood (showing 1/4 Indian blood). Applicants must be 35 years old or older.
Target applicant(s): High school students. College students. Adult students.
Minimum GPA: 2.5
Amount: $1,500.
Number of awards: Varies.
Deadline: July 16.
How to apply: Applications are available online.
Exclusive: Visit www.UltimateScholarshipBook.com and enter code AS261120 for updates on this award.

(2612) • Distinguished Young Women Scholarship Program

Distinguished Young Women
751 Government Street, Mobile, AL 36602
Phone: 251-438-3621
Email: lynne@ajm.org
http://distinguishedyw.org/scholarships/
Purpose: To provide scholarship opportunities and encourage personal development for high school girls through a competitive pageant stressing academics and talent as well as self-expression and fitness.
Eligibility: Teen girls are selected from state competitions to participate in a national pageant. Contestants are judged on a combination of scholastics, personal interview, talent, fitness and self-expression. Applicants should be a high school student at least in their sophomore year. Students must be U.S. citizens, have never been married and have never been pregnant.
Target applicant(s): High school students.
Amount: Varies.
Number of awards: Varies.
Deadline: Varies.
How to apply: Applications are available online.
Exclusive: Visit www.UltimateScholarshipBook.com and enter code DI261220 for updates on this award.

(2613) • Diversity Scholars Program

Milbank
1 Chase Manhattan Plaza, New York, NY 10005
Phone: 212-530-5000
http://www.milbank.com

Purpose: To support law school students in earning their Juris Doctor degree.

Eligibility: Applicants must be enrolled at an ABA accredited law school and have successfully completed their first year of a full-time law program. Selection is primarily based on demonstration of academic achievement, leadership potential, writing ability and interpersonal skills. Preference is given to students of culturally diverse backgrounds.

Target applicant(s): Graduate school students. Adult students.

Amount: $25,000.

Number of awards: Varies.

Deadline: August 15.

How to apply: Applications are available online.

Exclusive: Visit www.UltimateScholarshipBook.com and enter code MI261320 for updates on this award.

(2614) • Dr. Ivy M. Parker Memorial Scholarship

Society of Women Engineers
130 East Randolph Street, Suite 3500, Chicago, IL 60601
Phone: 877-793-4636
Email: scholarships@swe.org
http://societyofwomenengineers.swe.org/scholarships

Purpose: To aid female undergraduates who are majoring in engineering.

Eligibility: Applicants must be full-time students who are enrolled in an ABET-accredited engineering program. They must be rising juniors or seniors who have a GPA of 3.0 or higher on a four-point scale. Applicants cannot be currently receiving another scholarship awarded by the Society of Women Engineers (SWE), and they cannot be receiving full funding from another source (such as an employee reimbursement program or the U.S. military). Selection is based on academic merit and financial need.

Target applicant(s): College students. Adult students.

Minimum GPA: 3.0

Amount: $1,500.

Number of awards: 1.

Deadline: February 15.

How to apply: Applications are available online. An application form, official transcript and two letters of recommendation are required.

Exclusive: Visit www.UltimateScholarshipBook.com and enter code SO261420 for updates on this award.

(2615) • Dr. Juan Andrade, Jr. Scholarship

United States Hispanic Leadership Institute
431 S. Dearborn Street, Suite 1203, Chicago, IL 60605
Phone: 312-427-8683
http://www.ushli.org

Purpose: To support Hispanic students in pursuing post-secondary education.

Eligibility: Applicants must be enrolled or accepted for enrollment as a full-time student at an accredited educational institution in the U.S. Students must have demonstrated financial need and at least one parent of Hispanic ancestry. Applicants must submit letters of recommendation, grade transcripts, a resume and several essays.

Target applicant(s): High school students. College students. Adult students.

Amount: $500-$1,000.

Number of awards: Varies.

Deadline: December 29.

How to apply: Applications are available online.

Exclusive: Visit www.UltimateScholarshipBook.com and enter code UN261520 for updates on this award.

(2616) • Drs. James and Wanda Trefil Science Scholarship

Kosciuszko Foundation
15 East 65th Street, New York, NY 10021-6595
Phone: 212-734-2130
http://www.kosciuszkofoundation.org

Purpose: To support American students of Polish descent.

Eligibility: Applicants must be U.S. citizens or legal permanent residents of Polish descent who are full-time undergraduate freshmen, sophomores or juniors at the time of application. Students must have a minimum GPA of 3.5 and be pursuing a major in physics, chemistry, biology, astronomy, earth science or another similar area.

Target applicant(s): College students. Adult students.

Minimum GPA: 3.5

Amount: $5,000.

Number of awards: 1.

Deadline: January 15.

How to apply: Applications are available online.

Exclusive: Visit www.UltimateScholarshipBook.com and enter code KO261620 for updates on this award.

(2617) • EDSA Minority Scholarship

Landscape Architecture Foundation
1129 20th Street NW, Suite 202, Washington, DC 20036
Phone: 202-331-7070
Email: scholarships@lafoundation.org
https://lafoundation.org/scholarship/

Purpose: To aid minority students of landscape architecture.

Eligibility: Applicants must be members of an ethnic, cultural or racial minority. They must be landscape architecture students who are in the final two years of their undergraduate degree program or who are graduate students of landscape architecture. Selection is based on the overall strength of the application.

Target applicant(s): College students. Graduate school students. Adult students.

Amount: $5,000.

Number of awards: 1.

Deadline: February 15.

How to apply: Applications are available online. An application form, personal essay, three work samples, two recommendation letters and an applicant photo are required.

Exclusive: Visit www.UltimateScholarshipBook.com and enter code LA261720 for updates on this award.

(2618) • Education Support Award

Patsy Takemoto Mink Education Foundation
P.O. Box 769, Granby, MA 01033
http://patsyminkfoundation.org

Purpose: To support low-income mothers in pursuing post-secondary education.

Eligibility: Applicants must be at least 17 years old. Selection is primarily based on demonstration of financial need, personal circumstances, educational and professional goals and community involvement.

Target applicant(s): High school students. College students. Adult students.

Amount: $5,000.
Number of awards: 5.
Deadline: August 1.
How to apply: Applications are available online.
Exclusive: Visit www.UltimateScholarshipBook.com and enter code PA261820 for updates on this award.

(2619) · Elizabeth and Sherman Asche Memorial Scholarship

Association on American Indian Affairs
Lisa Wyzlic, Director of Scholarship Programs, 966 Hungerford Drive, Suite 12-B, Rockville, MD 20850
Phone: 240-314-7155
Email: lw.aaia@indian-affairs.org
https://www.indian-affairs.org/scholarships.html
Purpose: To provide financial assistance to American Indians who are seeking undergraduate or graduate degrees in public health or science.
Eligibility: Applicants must be American Indians who are studying full-time in public health or science programs. They must be full-time students and must not be enrolled in a technical or trade program or seminary. The scholarship is open to undergraduate and graduate students.
Target applicant(s): High school students. College students. Graduate school students. Adult students.
Minimum GPA: 2.5
Amount: $1,500.
Number of awards: Varies.
Deadline: June 1.
How to apply: Applications are available online.
Exclusive: Visit www.UltimateScholarshipBook.com and enter code AS261920 for updates on this award.

(2620) · Emerge Scholarships

Emerge
3535 Peachtree Road, Suite 520-121, Atlanta, GA 30326
Phone: 770-905-5175
Email: info@emergescholarships.org
http://www.emergescholarships.org
Purpose: To provide financial assistance to women who are returning to school to change or further their careers and to stay-at-home moms who need additional training.
Eligibility: Applicants must be women at least 25 years of age who plan to study in the United States. Students from other countries are eligible but must be referred by an educational institution or organization. Applicants should not be eligible for significant funding from other sources. Selection is based on financial need, other funding received, goals, essay, leadership and participation in community activities, honors and awards.
Target applicant(s): College students. Adult students.
Amount: $2,000-$5,000.
Number of awards: Varies.
Deadline: April 21.
How to apply: Applications are available online. An application form and essay are required.
Exclusive: Visit www.UltimateScholarshipBook.com and enter code EM262020 for updates on this award.

(2621) · Empowering Future Female Leaders to Change the World

Toptal
548 Market Street #36879, San Francisco, CA 94104
https://www.toptal.com/scholarships-for-women
Purpose: To empower aspiring female leaders.
Eligibility: Applicants must be female students age 16 years or older who are accepted at or enrolling in an education program and who are passionate about community service. Students must create a plan then write a blog post describing how they want to change the world and what resources and mentorship they will need to make it happen.
Target applicant(s): High school students. College students. Graduate school students. Adult students.
Amount: $10,000.
Number of awards: 1.
Deadline: March 31.
How to apply: Applications are available online.
Exclusive: Visit www.UltimateScholarshipBook.com and enter code TO262120 for updates on this award.

(2622) · ESA Foundation Scholarship Program

Entertainment Software Association Foundation
575 7th Street NW, Suite 300, Washington, DC 20004
Phone: 202-223-2400
http://www.esafoundation.org
Purpose: To support female and minority students working on degrees toward a career in computer and video game arts.
Eligibility: Applicants must be female or minority students, U.S. citizens and current full-time college students or graduating high school seniors enrolled or accepted in a full-time program at a four-year college or university in the U.S. A minimum 2.75 GPA is required. Selection is based on the overall strength of the application.
Target applicant(s): High school students. College students. Adult students.
Minimum GPA: 2.75
Amount: $3,000.
Number of awards: Up to 30.
Deadline: April 27.
How to apply: Applications are available online.
Exclusive: Visit www.UltimateScholarshipBook.com and enter code EN262220 for updates on this award.

(2623) · Eugene and Elinor Kotur Scholarship Trust Fund

Ukrainian Fraternal Association
371 N. 9th Avenue, Scranton, PA 18504-2005
Phone: 570-342-0937
http://www.members.tripod.com/~ufa_home
Purpose: To support Ukrainian students.
Eligibility: Applicants must be in their sophomore year of college or higher at one of 30 participating schools. They must be of Ukrainian descent and have been members of the Ukrainian Fraternal Association for two years.
Target applicant(s): College students. Graduate school students. Adult students.
Amount: At least $1,000.
Number of awards: Varies.
Deadline: Varies.
How to apply: Applications are available by mail or phone.

Exclusive: Visit www.UltimateScholarshipBook.com and enter code UK262320 for updates on this award.

(2624) • Florence Young Memorial Scholarship

Association on American Indian Affairs
Lisa Wyzlic, Director of Scholarship Programs, 966 Hungerford Drive, Suite 12-B, Rockville, MD 20850
Phone: 240-314-7155
Email: lw.aaia@indian-affairs.org
https://www.indian-affairs.org/scholarships.html
Purpose: To provide financial assistance to Native Americans who are working toward a master's degree in art, public health or law.
Eligibility: Applicants must be full-time students from the continental U.S. or Alaska.
Target applicant(s): Graduate school students. Adult students.
Amount: Varies.
Number of awards: Varies.
Deadline: June 1.
How to apply: Applications are available online.
Exclusive: Visit www.UltimateScholarshipBook.com and enter code AS262420 for updates on this award.

(2625) • Forum for Concerns of Minorities Scholarship

American Society for Clinical Laboratory Science
Alpha Mu Tau Scholarship, Attn: Joe Briden, AMTF Scholarship Coordinator, 7809 S. 21st Drive, Phoenix, AZ 85041-7736
Phone: 571-748-3770
Email: awards@ascls.org
http://www.ascls.org
Purpose: To assist minority students in becoming clinical laboratory scientists and clinical laboratory technicians.
Eligibility: Applicants must be minority students accepted to an NAACLS-accredited Clinical Laboratory Science/Medical Technology program or a Clinical Laboratory Technician/Medical Laboratory Technician program. They must also demonstrate financial need.
Target applicant(s): High school students. College students. Graduate school students. Adult students.
Amount: Varies.
Number of awards: 2.
Deadline: April 1.
How to apply: Applications are available online.
Exclusive: Visit www.UltimateScholarshipBook.com and enter code AM262520 for updates on this award.

(2626) • Foundation Scholarships

CIRI Foundation
3600 San Jeronimo Drive, Suite 256, Anchorage, AK 99508-2870
Phone: 800-764-3382
Email: tcf@thecirifoundation.org
http://www.thecirifoundation.org
Purpose: To provide financial aid for Alaska Natives.
Eligibility: Applicants must be qualified Alaska Native beneficiaries who plan to attend or are currently attending undergraduate or graduate institutions. There are a number of awards based on field of study or career goal. Applicants must submit applications, proof of eligibility, reference letter, transcripts, purpose statements and proof of enrollment.
Target applicant(s): High school students. College students. Graduate school students. Adult students.
Amount: Up to $20,000.
Number of awards: Varies.
Scholarship may be renewable.
Deadline: June 1.
How to apply: Applications are available online.
Exclusive: Visit www.UltimateScholarshipBook.com and enter code CI262620 for updates on this award.

(2627) • Franklin C. McLean Award

National Medical Fellowships Inc.
347 Fifth Avenue, Suite 510, New York, NY 10016
Phone: 212-483-8880
Email: scholarships@nmfonline.org
http://www.nmfonline.org
Purpose: To reward medical students with outstanding achievement.
Eligibility: Applicants must be a senior, underrepresented minority student enrolled in an accredited United States medical school. Students must demonstrate outstanding academic achievement, leadership and community service.
Target applicant(s): College students. Adult students.
Amount: $5,000.
Number of awards: 1.
Deadline: Varies.
How to apply: Applications are available online.
Exclusive: Visit www.UltimateScholarshipBook.com and enter code NA262720 for updates on this award.

(2628) • GAHCC Foundation Scholarship

Hispanic Scholarship Consortium
314 E. Highland Mall Boulevard #103, Austin, TX 78752
Phone: 512-368-2956
http://www.hispanicscholar.org/scholarship
Purpose: To support Hispanic graduating seniors who are pursuing a degree in science, technology, engineering or mathematics.
Eligibility: Applicants must be enrolled full-time. A minimum GPA of 3.0 is required. Selection is based on the overall strength of the application.
Target applicant(s): High school students. College students. Adult students.
Minimum GPA: 3.0
Amount: $2,000.
Number of awards: 1.
Scholarship may be renewable.
Deadline: April 30.
How to apply: Applications are available online.
Exclusive: Visit www.UltimateScholarshipBook.com and enter code HI262820 for updates on this award.

(2629) • Gates Millennium Scholars Program

Gates Foundation
P.O. Box 10500, Fairfax, VA 22031
Phone: 877-690-4677
http://www.gmsp.org
Purpose: To provide outstanding minority students with opportunities to complete their undergraduate college educations.
Eligibility: Applicants must be African American, American Indian/Alaska Native, Asian Pacific Islander American or Hispanic American students with a minimum 3.3 GPA, enter an accredited college or university and have significant financial need. Applicants must also be eligible for federal Pell Grants.
Target applicant(s): High school students.
Minimum GPA: 3.3

Amount: Varies.
Number of awards: 1,000.
Deadline: Varies.
How to apply: Students are nominated by teachers, principals or other education professionals. Nomination materials are available online.
Exclusive: Visit www.UltimateScholarshipBook.com and enter code GA262920 for updates on this award.

(2630) · GEM MS Engineering Fellowship Program

National GEM Consortium
1430 Duke Street, Alexandria, VA 22314
Phone: 703-562-3646
Email: info@gemfellowship.org
http://www.gemfellowship.org
Purpose: To provide fellowships for minority engineering and computer science students pursuing master's degrees.
Eligibility: Applicants must be college seniors or graduate students majoring in engineering or computer science and be members of one of the following minority groups: African American, Native American or Latino or other Hispanic American. Students must also be U.S. citizens or permanent residents, have a minimum 2.8 GPA and agree to intern for two summers with a GEM employer.
Target applicant(s): College students. Graduate school students. Adult students.
Minimum GPA: 2.8
Amount: $8,000.
Number of awards: Varies.
Deadline: October 1 and November 13.
How to apply: Applications are available online. The deadline for Part I is October 1, and the deadline for part II is November 13.
Exclusive: Visit www.UltimateScholarshipBook.com and enter code NA263020 for updates on this award.

(2631) · General Society of Mayflower Descendants (GSMD) Scholarship

General Society of Mayflower Descendants
P.O. Box 3297, Plymouth, MA 02361
Phone: 508-746-3188
Email: scholarships@themayflowersociety.org
https://www.themayflowersociety.org/
Purpose: To assist high school seniors who are Mayflower descendants.
Eligibility: Applicants must plan to attend a four-year college or university or a two-year community college and must obtain a valid GSMD membership number. Recipients typically are in the top 10 percent of their class and score in the 75th percentile or higher on the SAT or ACT.
Target applicant(s): High school students.
Amount: $2,500-$5,000.
Number of awards: 3.
Deadline: March 1.
How to apply: Applications are available online.
Exclusive: Visit www.UltimateScholarshipBook.com and enter code GE263120 for updates on this award.

(2632) · George Choy Memorial/Gay Asian Pacific Alliance (GAPA) Scholarship

Horizons Foundation
550 Montgomery Street, Suite 700, San Francisco, CA 94111
Phone: 415-398-2333
Email: info@horizonsfoundation.org
http://www.horizonsfoundation.org
Purpose: To assist Bay Area gay, lesbian, bisexual and transgender Asian and Pacific Islander graduating high school students.
Eligibility: Applicants should have at least 25 percent Asian/Pacific Islander ancestry, in the process of applying to or currently attending a college, university or vocational school and reside in one of the nine Bay Area counties (Alameda, Contra Costa, Marin, San Francisco, San Mateo, Santa Clara, Napa, Sonoma or Solano). Preference is given to those who are lesbian, gay, bisexual or transgender or who are involved in the LGBT community.
Target applicant(s): High school students. College students. Adult students.
Minimum GPA: 2.75
Amount: Up to $1,000.
Number of awards: Varies.
Deadline: Varies.
How to apply: Applications are available by phone.
Exclusive: Visit www.UltimateScholarshipBook.com and enter code HO263220 for updates on this award.

(2633) · Gerber Scholarship in Pediatrics Program

National Medical Fellowships Inc.
347 Fifth Avenue, Suite 510, New York, NY 10016
Phone: 212-483-8880
Email: scholarships@nmfonline.org
http://www.nmfonline.org
Purpose: To support pediatric medical students who are underrepresented minorities.
Eligibility: Applicants must be underrepresented minority student enrolled in an accredited United States medical school. Students must have an interest in pediatric medicine with an emphasis on nutrition and demonstrate outstanding achievement.
Target applicant(s): Graduate school students. Adult students.
Amount: $5,000.
Number of awards: 2.
Deadline: Varies.
How to apply: Applications are available online.
Exclusive: Visit www.UltimateScholarshipBook.com and enter code NA263320 for updates on this award.

(2634) · Glamour's Top Ten College Women Competition

Glamour
The Conde Nast Publications Inc., 4 Times Square, New York, NY 10036
Phone: 800-244-4526
Email: ttcw@glamour.com
http://www.glamour.com/about/top-10-college-women
Purpose: To recognize outstanding female college students.
Eligibility: Applicants must be college juniors at an accredited U.S. or Canadian college or university. They must be enrolled full-time and may not be scheduled to graduate before May of the year following application.
Target applicant(s): College students. Adult students.
Amount: $3,750-$20,750.
Number of awards: 10.
Deadline: October 1.

How to apply: Applications are available online. An application form, transcript, list of activities on- and off-campus, essay, photograph and letter of recommendation are required.
Exclusive: Visit www.UltimateScholarshipBook.com and enter code GL263420 for updates on this award.

(2635) • GlaxoSmithKline Company Science Achievement Award

United Negro College Fund (UNCF)
1805 7th Street NW, Washington, DC 20001
Phone: 800-331-2244
https://scholarships.uncf.org/
Purpose: To support graduate-level science students.
Eligibility: Applicants must be African American graduates of a UNCF member college with a science-related degree pursuing a graduate degree in science. They must have a GPA of at least 3.0 and demonstrate financial need.
Target applicant(s): Graduate school students. Adult students.
Minimum GPA: 3.0
Amount: $6,000.
Number of awards: 4.
Deadline: March 12.
How to apply: Applications are available online.
Exclusive: Visit www.UltimateScholarshipBook.com and enter code UN263520 for updates on this award.

(2636) • Goldie Bateson Scholarship

Ladies Professional Golf Association
100 International Golf Drive, Daytona Beach, FL 32124-1092
Phone: 386-274-6200
Email: info@lpgafoundation.org
http://www.lpga.com/lpga-foundation/scholarships
Purpose: To support junior age females who play golf or have an interest in learning the game of golf.
Eligibility: Applicants must be between 7 and 17 years of age and have an interest in playing golf or be currently involved in golf. Students must reside within one of the LPGA T&CP Midwest Section States. Selection is based on the personal essay and letters of recommendation.
Target applicant(s): Junior high students or younger. High school students.
Amount: $250.
Number of awards: 10.
Deadline: September 15.
How to apply: Applications available online and include a personal essay and two letters of recommendation.
Exclusive: Visit www.UltimateScholarshipBook.com and enter code LA263620 for updates on this award.

(2637) • Google Generation Google Scholarship

Google Inc.
1600 Amphitheatre Parkway, Mountain View, CA 94043
https://edu.google.com/scholarships/the-generation-google-scholarship/
Purpose: To encourage students who are aspiring computer scientists to become leaders in their field.
Eligibility: Applicants must either be a graduating high school senior or be currently enrolled as an undergraduate or graduate student. Students must be enrolled as computer science or computer engineering majors, exhibit strong leadership skills and demonstrate a passion for computer science and technology. Applicants must be from an underrepresented group in computer science such as African American, Hispanic, American Indian or Filipino/Native Hawaiian/Pacific Islander.
Target applicant(s): High school students. College students. Graduate school students. Adult students.
Amount: $10,000.
Number of awards: Varies.
Deadline: December 11 (university), Varies (high school).
How to apply: Applications are available online.
Exclusive: Visit www.UltimateScholarshipBook.com and enter code GO263720 for updates on this award.

(2638) • Graduate Studies Tuition Scholarship Program

Kosciuszko Foundation
15 East 65th Street, New York, NY 10021-6595
Phone: 212-734-2130
http://www.kosciuszkofoundation.org
Purpose: To support American students of Polish descent.
Eligibility: Applicants must be United States citizens and legal permanent residents of Polish descent who are beginning or continuing their graduate studies as full-time students and who have a minimum GPA of 3.0.
Target applicant(s): College students. Graduate school students. Adult students.
Minimum GPA: 3.0
Amount: Up to $7,000.
Number of awards: Varies.
Deadline: January 15.
How to apply: Applications are available online.
Exclusive: Visit www.UltimateScholarshipBook.com and enter code KO263820 for updates on this award.

(2639) • Harriet Fitzgerald Scholarship

Sunflower Initiative
P.O. Box 378, Bedford, VA 24523
https://www.thesunflowerinitiative.com/scholarship/
Purpose: To support female students seeking post-secondary education.
Eligibility: Applicants must be female and planning to start her undergraduate education at a women's college in the following academic year. Women who have already completed a semester of college or more are not eligible. A minimum 3.7 GPA and either a SAT composite score of 1900 (old scoring through 2016) or 1350 (new scoring since 2016) OR an ACT composite score of 27 or higher with no single ACT score below 25 are required.
Target applicant(s): High school students.
Minimum GPA: 3.7
Amount: $10,000.
Number of awards: 1.
Deadline: February 1.
How to apply: Applications are available online.
Exclusive: Visit www.UltimateScholarshipBook.com and enter code SU263920 for updates on this award.

(2640) • Health Professions Pre-Graduate Scholarship Program

Indian Health Service
Scholarship Program Office, 5600 Fishers Lane, Mail Stop: OHR (11E53A), Rockville, MD 20857
Phone: 301-443-6197
Email: dawn.kelly@ihs.gov

http://www.ihs.gov
Purpose: To aid Native Americans and Alaska Natives who are enrolled in selected health-related pre-professional degree programs.
Eligibility: Applicants must be U.S. citizens who are enrolled in or accepted into a pre-medicine, pre-dentistry, pre-optometry, pre-podiatry or other health-related pre-professional degree program. Applicants must have plans to work in the Native American or Alaska Native community as a health care provider in the chosen field of study. Selection is based on academic achievement, recommendation letters and the applicant's stated career goals. Applicant must have a minimum 2.0 GPA.
Target applicant(s): High school students. College students. Adult students.
Minimum GPA: 2.0
Amount: Full tuition and fees.
Number of awards: Varies.
Scholarship may be renewable.
Deadline: Varies.
How to apply: Applications are available online. An application form, course curriculum outline, two recommendation forms, proof of Native American/Alaska Native status, an official transcript, proof of acceptance into an academic program and other supporting documents are required.
Exclusive: Visit www.UltimateScholarshipBook.com and enter code IN264020 for updates on this award.

(2641) • Health Professions Preparatory Scholarship Program

Indian Health Service
Scholarship Program Office, 5600 Fishers Lane, Mail Stop: OHR (11E53A), Rockville, MD 20857
Phone: 301-443-6197
Email: dawn.kelly@ihs.gov
http://www.ihs.gov
Purpose: To aid Native Americans and Alaska Natives who are preparing for careers in one of the health professions.
Eligibility: Applicants must be U.S. citizens accepted into or enrolled in a compensatory or pre-professional general education course of study at an accredited college or university. The applicant must be studying or have plans to study a subject that has been designated as a priority career category by the Indian Health Service. Applicants must plan to serve Native American or Alaska Native communities as a professional healthcare provider after completing the necessary training. Selection is based on academic achievement, recommendation letters and stated career goals.
Target applicant(s): College students. Adult students.
Minimum GPA: 2.0
Amount: Varies.
Number of awards: Varies.
Scholarship may be renewable.
Deadline: March 28.
How to apply: Applications are available online. An application form, two letters of recommendation, proof of Native American or Alaska Native status, an official transcript, proof of acceptance into a postsecondary educational program and other supporting documents are required.
Exclusive: Visit www.UltimateScholarshipBook.com and enter code IN264120 for updates on this award.

(2642) • Helene M. Overly Memorial Graduate Scholarship

Women's Transportation Seminar (WTS) International
1701 K Street NW, Suite 800, Washington, DC 20006
Phone: 202-955-5085
Email: membership@wtsinternational.org
https://www.wtsinternational.org/
Purpose: To support women pursuing careers in the transportation industry with their higher education expenses.
Eligibility: Applicants must be women enrolled in graduate studies in transportation or the related fields of engineering, planning, finance or logistics. Selection is based on the applicant's academic record, transportation-related activities or job skills and specific transportation goals.
Target applicant(s): Graduate school students. Adult students.
Amount: $10,000.
Number of awards: 1.
Deadline: Varies.
How to apply: Applications are available through a local chapter.
Exclusive: Visit www.UltimateScholarshipBook.com and enter code WO264220 for updates on this award.

(2643) • Henry Salvatori Scholarship

Order Sons of Italy in America (OSIA)
219 E Street NE, Washington, DC 20002
Phone: 202-547-2900
Email: scholarships@osia.org
https://www.osia.org/sif
Purpose: To support students who demonstrate exceptional leadership, distinguished scholarship and respect for the principles upon which our nation was founded.
Eligibility: Applicants must be U.S. citizens of Italian descent who are graduating high school seniors who are planning to attend an undergraduate program at a four-year, accredited college or university for the upcoming fall semester. Students must write an essay as part of the application process.
Target applicant(s): High school students.
Amount: Varies.
Number of awards: 1.
Deadline: February 28.
How to apply: Applications are available online.
Exclusive: Visit www.UltimateScholarshipBook.com and enter code OR264320 for updates on this award.

(2644) • Herbert Lehman Education Fund Scholarship

NAACP Legal Defense and Educational Fund, Inc.
40 Rector Street, 5th Floor, New York, NY 10006
Phone: 212-965-2200
Email: scholarships@naacpldf.org
http://www.naacpldf.org/scholarships
Purpose: To support African American students who are attending college for the first time.
Eligibility: Applicants must have a strong academic record and clear educational goals, and they must show leadership potential through involvement in school and extracurricular activities. Students must show good character through positive recommendations from teachers, employers or community representatives.
Target applicant(s): High school students. College students. Adult students.
Amount: $2,000.
Number of awards: Varies.
Scholarship may be renewable.
Deadline: April 1.
How to apply: Applications are available by sending a written request.

Exclusive: Visit www.UltimateScholarshipBook.com and enter code NA264420 for updates on this award.

(2645) • Higher Education Grant

Bureau of Indian Education
Tony L. Dearman, Director, 1849 C Street NW, Mailstop 4657 MIB, Washington, DC 20240
Phone: 202-208-6123
https://www.bie.edu/

Purpose: To assist American Indian and Alaska Native students obtaining their undergraduate degrees.

Eligibility: Applicants must be members of a tribe or at least one-quarter degree Indian blood descendants of members of an American Indian tribe, be accepted into a college or another similar institution that provides an associate's or bachelor's degrees and show financial need.

Target applicant(s): High school students. College students. Adult students.

Amount: Varies.

Number of awards: Varies.

Deadline: June 1.

How to apply: Applications are available through tribes.

Exclusive: Visit www.UltimateScholarshipBook.com and enter code BU264520 for updates on this award.

(2646) • Hispanic Heritage Youth Awards

Hispanic Heritage Awards Foundation
1001 Pennsylvania Avenue NW, Washington, DC 20004
Phone: 202-861-9797
Email: contact@hispanicheritageawards.org
http://hispanicheritage.org/

Purpose: To promote Hispanic excellence and recognize the contributions of Hispanic American youth.

Eligibility: Applicants must be high school seniors who are U.S. citizens or permanent residents, reside in Atlanta, Chicago, Dallas, Houston, Los Angeles, Miami, New York City, Philadelphia, Phoenix, San Diego, San Jose and Washington, DC and have Hispanic parentage (Hispanic parentage can be one parent of Mexican, Central American, Cuban, Puerto Rican, South American, Spanish or Caribbean Hispanic descent). Selection criteria include achievement in the applicant's discipline, involvement in community, ability to overcome adversity and character. The disciplines are: Academic Excellence, Sports, the Arts, Literature/ Journalism, Mathematics, Leadership/Community Service and Science and Technology.

Target applicant(s): High school students.

Minimum GPA: 3.0

Amount: Varies.

Number of awards: Varies.

Deadline: October 2.

How to apply: Applications are available by request.

Exclusive: Visit www.UltimateScholarshipBook.com and enter code HI264620 for updates on this award.

(2647) • Hispanic Network Magazine

Hispanic Network Magazine
18 Technology Drive, Suite 170, Irvine, CA 92618
Phone: 800-433-9675
http://www.hnmagazine.com/scholarship-opportunity/

Purpose: To support Hispanic students pursuing an undergraduate education.

Eligibility: Applicants must be legal U.S. residents, Hispanic and either currently enrolled in or planning to enroll in an accredited U.S. college or university as an undergraduate. Students must provide a narrative about themselves and their goals.

Target applicant(s): High school students. College students. Adult students.

Amount: $500.

Number of awards: 1.

Deadline: August 15.

How to apply: Applications are available online.

Exclusive: Visit www.UltimateScholarshipBook.com and enter code HI264720 for updates on this award.

(2648) • Hispanic Scholarship Fund

Hispanic Scholarship Fund (HSF)
1411 W. 190th Street, Suite 700, Gardena, CA 90248
Phone: 877-473-4636
Email: info@hsf.net
https://www.hsf.net/

Purpose: To support students of Hispanic heritage.

Eligibility: Applicants must be high school seniors, entering college students or current college undergraduate or graduate students who are of Hispanic heritage and U.S. citizens or permanent residents. Students must have a GPA of 3.0 or higher and plan to enroll full-time in a degree program at a two- or four- year accredited institution in the U.S., Puerto Rico, the Virgin Islands or Guam in the upcoming academic year. Applicants must also apply for federal financial aid and be pursuing their first undergraduate or graduate degree.

Target applicant(s): High school students. College students. Graduate school students. Adult students.

Minimum GPA: 3.0

Amount: $500-$5,000.

Number of awards: Varies.

Deadline: April 2.

How to apply: Applications are available online. An application form, letter of recommendation, transcript, enrollment verification form and copy of FAFSA Student Aid Report are required.

Exclusive: Visit www.UltimateScholarshipBook.com and enter code HI264820 for updates on this award.

(2649) • Honeywell International Inc. Scholarships

Society of Women Engineers
130 East Randolph Street, Suite 3500, Chicago, IL 60601
Phone: 877-793-4636
Email: scholarships@swe.org
http://societyofwomenengineers.swe.org/scholarships

Purpose: To aid female students planning to pursue undergraduate degrees in computer science and engineering.

Eligibility: Applicants must be female U.S. citizens. They must be rising undergraduate sophomores, juniors or seniors and must plan to major in computer science, computer engineering, electrical engineering, chemical engineering, manufacturing engineering, mechanical engineering, architectural engineering, aerospace engineering, industrial engineering or materials science and engineering. Applicants must demonstrate financial need. Selection is based on the overall strength of the application. Minimum 3.5 GPA required.

Target applicant(s): College students. Adult students.

Minimum GPA: 3.5

Amount: $5,000.

Number of awards: 3.

Deadline: February 15.

How to apply: Applications are available online. An application form and supporting documents are required.
Exclusive: Visit www.UltimateScholarshipBook.com and enter code SO264920 for updates on this award.

(2650) · Hopi Scholarship Program

Hopi Tribe Grants and Scholarship Program
P.O. Box 123, Kykotsmovi, AZ 86039
Phone: 800-762-9630
Email: heef@hopieducationfund.org
http://www.hopieducationfund.org
Purpose: To help Hopi students with academic achievement.
Eligibility: Applicants must be enrolled members of the Hopi tribe, be high school graduates or have earned a GED, have been accepted to a regionally accredited college and plan to attend full-time and have completed the Free Application for Federal Student Aid. Students must be in top 10 percent of their high school class or score 930 on the SAT or 21 on the ACT as entering freshmen; have a minimum 3.0 GPA as undergraduates or have a minimum 3.2 GPA as graduate, post graduate or professional degree students. Applications, statements of goals, financial needs analysis, proof of Hopi enrollment and transcripts are required.
Target applicant(s): High school students. College students. Graduate school students. Adult students.
Minimum GPA: 3.0 for undergraduate students, 3.2 for graduate students
Amount: $3,000.
Number of awards: Varies.
Deadline: August 30, November 1, January 15.
How to apply: Applications are available by mail.
Exclusive: Visit www.UltimateScholarshipBook.com and enter code HO265020 for updates on this award.

(2651) · Howard County PFLAG Academic Scholarship

PFLAG Columbia-Howard County, Maryland
Attention: Scholarship Committee, P.O. Box 1479, Columbia, MD 21044
Phone: 443-718-0474
Email: info@pflagmd.org
http://www.pflaghoco.org/
Purpose: To support outstanding gay, lesbian, bisexual and transgendered students and their straight allies.
Eligibility: Applicants must be Maryland residents who are attending or plan to attend an institution of higher learning during the upcoming academic year. They must not be receiving a scholarship or other assistance that pays their tuition in full. Prior Howard County PFLAG scholarship recipients may not apply.
Target applicant(s): High school students. College students. Adult students.
Amount: $2,000.
Number of awards: 1.
Deadline: April 14.
How to apply: Applications are available online. An application form, questionnaire, transcript and two letters of recommendation are required.
Exclusive: Visit www.UltimateScholarshipBook.com and enter code PF265120 for updates on this award.

(2652) · HSF Scholarship

Hispanic Scholarship Fund (HSF)
1411 W. 190th Street, Suite 700, Gardena, CA 90248
Phone: 877-473-4636
Email: info@hsf.net
https://www.hsf.net/
Purpose: To support students of Hispanic heritage who want to obtain a college degree.
Eligibility: Students must be of Hispanic heritage, have a minimum 3.0 GPA for high school students and at least a 2.5 GPA for college or graduate students, plan to enroll in an accredited four-year university or graduate school, meet citizenship requirements and complete the FAFSA or other financial aid applications.
Target applicant(s): High school students. College students. Graduate school students. Adult students.
Minimum GPA: 3.0 for high school students, 2.5 for college and graduate school students
Amount: $500-$5,000.
Number of awards: Varies.
Deadline: April 2.
How to apply: Applications are available online.
Exclusive: Visit www.UltimateScholarshipBook.com and enter code HI265220 for updates on this award.

(2653) · HSF/Association of Latino Professionals in Finance and Accounting (ALPFA) Scholarship Program

Hispanic Scholarship Fund (HSF)
1411 W. 190th Street, Suite 700, Gardena, CA 90248
Phone: 877-473-4636
Email: info@hsf.net
https://www.hsf.net/
Purpose: To aid outstanding Latino students who are majoring in finance, accounting, economics, business administration or management.
Eligibility: Applicants must be of Latino descent and be U.S. citizens or legal permanent residents. They must be enrolled full-time at an accredited postsecondary institution located in the U.S. or Puerto Rico. They must be entering a master's degree program or be rising undergraduate sophomores, juniors or seniors. Applicants must be majoring in accounting, business administration, economics, finance, hospitality management, human resources management, international relations, information technology (IT/MIS), management (including supply chain and information systems) or marketing and have a GPA of 3.0 or higher on a four-point scale. Selection is based on the overall strength of the application.
Target applicant(s): College students. Graduate school students. Adult students.
Minimum GPA: 3.0
Amount: $500-$5,000.
Number of awards: Varies.
Deadline: April 26.
How to apply: Applications are available online. An application form, supporting materials and submission of the Free Application for Federal Student Aid (FAFSA) are required.
Exclusive: Visit www.UltimateScholarshipBook.com and enter code HI265320 for updates on this award.

(2654) • HSF/Marathon Oil Corporation College Scholarship Program

Hispanic Scholarship Fund (HSF)
1411 W. 190th Street, Suite 700, Gardena, CA 90248
Phone: 877-473-4636
Email: info@hsf.net
https://www.hsf.net/

Purpose: To aid minority undergraduates who are studying selected subjects.

Eligibility: Applicants must be U.S. citizens or legal permanent residents who are Hispanic, African-American, Native American, Asian, Pacific Islanders or Alaska Natives and who are undergraduate sophomores or seniors. Sophomores must be majoring in accounting, chemical engineering, computer engineering, computer science, electrical engineering, environmental engineering, geology/geosciences, information technology (IT/MIS), mechanical engineering, petroleum engineering or supply chain management (management). Seniors must have plans to pursue a master's degree in geology or geophysics. Applicants must have a GPA of 3.0 or higher on a four-point scale. Selection is based on the overall strength of the application.

Target applicant(s): High school students. College students. Adult students.

Minimum GPA: 3.0

Amount: $5,000.

Number of awards: Varies.

Scholarship may be renewable.

Deadline: April 6.

How to apply: Applications are available online. An application form, submission of the Free Application for Federal Student Aid (FAFSA) and other supporting materials are required.

Exclusive: Visit www.UltimateScholarshipBook.com and enter code HI265420 for updates on this award.

(2655) • Hubertus W.V. Wellems Scholarship for Male Students

National Association for the Advancement of Colored People
c/o Poise Foundation, Two Gateway Center, Suite 1700, 603 Stanwix Street, Pittsburgh, PA 15222
Phone: 412-281-4967
Email: info@poisefdn.org
http://www.poisefoundation.org/scholarships-overview/

Purpose: To aid male students who are studying certain math and science subjects at the undergraduate and graduate levels.

Eligibility: Applicants must be U.S. citizens who are high school seniors, undergraduates or graduate students. They must be enrolled in or plan to enroll in a mathematics, chemistry, physics or engineering degree program at an accredited four-year institution of higher learning located in the U.S. Undergraduate applicants must be full-time students. High school seniors and undergraduate students must have a GPA of 2.5 or higher, and graduate students must have a GPA of 3.0 or higher. All applicants must demonstrate financial need. Selection is based on the overall strength of the application.

Target applicant(s): High school students. College students. Graduate school students. Adult students.

Minimum GPA: 2.5 for high school and college students, 3.0 for graduate students

Amount: $3,000.

Number of awards: 20-40.

Deadline: July 31.

How to apply: Applications are available online. An application form, personal essay, official transcript and two letters of recommendation are required.

Exclusive: Visit www.UltimateScholarshipBook.com and enter code NA265520 for updates on this award.

(2656) • Ida M. Pope Memorial Scholarship

Hawaii Community Foundation - Scholarships
827 Fort Street Mall, Honolulu, HI 96813
Phone: 888-731-3863
Email: scholarships@hcf-hawaii.org
https://www.hawaiicommunityfoundation.org

Purpose: To assist female students of Hawaiian ancestry in obtaining higher education.

Eligibility: Applicants must attend an accredited college or university and have a GPA of 3.5 or higher. Students must also major in health, science, education, counseling or social work.

Target applicant(s): High school students. College students. Adult students.

Minimum GPA: 3.5

Amount: Varies.

Number of awards: Varies.

Deadline: January 31.

How to apply: To apply, register online, complete the online application and select the scholarships to which you wish to apply. In addition, mail the supporting materials: printed confirmation page from the online application, personal statement, copy of Student Aid Report (SAR) available at www.fafsa.ed.gov and official transcript.

Exclusive: Visit www.UltimateScholarshipBook.com and enter code HA265620 for updates on this award.

(2657) • Jack and Jill of America Foundation Scholarship

Jack and Jill of America Foundation
1930 17th Street NW, Washington, DC 20009
Phone: 202-232-5290
http://jackandjillfoundation.org/scholarships/

Purpose: To help African American high school seniors attend college.

Eligibility: Applicants must plan to attend college full-time, have a minimum 3.0 GPA, complete the Free Application for Federal Student Aid (FAFSA) and have unmet financial need that is verified by the college or university financial aid office. UNCF students are encouraged to complete the UNCF General Scholarship application to be matched with scholarships for which they meet the criteria.

Target applicant(s): High school students.

Minimum GPA: 3.0

Amount: Up to $2,500.

Number of awards: Varies.

Deadline: July 14.

How to apply: Applications are available online.

Exclusive: Visit www.UltimateScholarshipBook.com and enter code JA265720 for updates on this award.

(2658) • Jackie Robinson Foundation Scholarship Program

Jackie Robinson Foundation
3 W. 35th Street, 11th Floor, New York, NY 10001
Phone: 212-290-8600
Email: general@jackierobinson.org

http://www.jackierobinson.org
Purpose: To help minority students who have shown leadership skills in their communities.
Eligibility: Applicants must be minority high school seniors with demonstrated financial need, leadership potential and academic achievement and who have already been accepted to a four-year college or university. Students must also be U.S. citizens and have a minimum SAT score of 1000 or composite ACT score of 22.
Target applicant(s): High school students.
Amount: Up to $28,000.
Number of awards: Varies.
Deadline: February 1.
How to apply: Applications are available online.
Exclusive: Visit www.UltimateScholarshipBook.com and enter code JA265820 for updates on this award.

(2659) • Japanese American Citizens League Creative and Performing Arts Awards

Japanese American Citizens League (JACL)
1765 Sutter Street, San Francisco, CA 94115
Phone: 415-921-5225
Email: jacl@jacl.org
http://www.jacl.org
Purpose: To recognize and encourage performing arts and creative projects among JACL members.
Eligibility: Applicants must be National JACL members and must be attending a college, university, trade school, business school or any other institution of higher learning. A personal statement, letter of recommendation, academic performance, work experience and community involvement are considered. Professional artists are not allowed.
Target applicant(s): High school students. College students. Graduate school students. Adult students.
Amount: Varies.
Number of awards: 30.
Deadline: March 1 (high school seniors), April 1 (all other levels).
How to apply: Applications are available online or by sending a self-addressed, stamped envelope.
Exclusive: Visit www.UltimateScholarshipBook.com and enter code JA265920 for updates on this award.

(2660) • Japanese American Citizens League Entering Freshman Awards

Japanese American Citizens League (JACL)
1765 Sutter Street, San Francisco, CA 94115
Phone: 415-921-5225
Email: jacl@jacl.org
http://www.jacl.org
Purpose: To recognize and encourage education as a key to greater opportunities among JACL members.
Eligibility: Applicants must be National JACL members and must be planning to attend a college, university, trade school, business school or any other institution of higher learning at the undergraduate level. A personal statement, letter of recommendation, academic performance, work experience and community involvement will all be considered.
Target applicant(s): High school students.
Amount: Varies.
Number of awards: Varies.
Deadline: March 1.
How to apply: Applications are available through local JACL chapters, regional offices, National JACL Headquarters and website.
Exclusive: Visit www.UltimateScholarshipBook.com and enter code JA266020 for updates on this award.

(2661) • Japanese American Citizens League Graduate Awards

Japanese American Citizens League (JACL)
1765 Sutter Street, San Francisco, CA 94115
Phone: 415-921-5225
Email: jacl@jacl.org
http://www.jacl.org
Purpose: To provide monetary assistance for graduate studies to JACL members.
Eligibility: Applicants must be National JACL members and must attend a college or university at the graduate level. A personal statement, letter of recommendation, academic performance, work experience and community involvement are considered.
Target applicant(s): Graduate school students. Adult students.
Amount: Varies.
Number of awards: 7.
Deadline: April 1.
How to apply: Applications are available online and by sending a self-addressed, stamped envelope.
Exclusive: Visit www.UltimateScholarshipBook.com and enter code JA266120 for updates on this award.

(2662) • Japanese American Citizens League Law Scholarships

Japanese American Citizens League (JACL)
1765 Sutter Street, San Francisco, CA 94115
Phone: 415-921-5225
Email: jacl@jacl.org
http://www.jacl.org
Purpose: To help JACL members who are studying law.
Eligibility: Applicants must be National JACL members and must be studying law at a college or university. A personal statement, letter of recommendation, academic performance, work experience and community involvement will all be considered.
Target applicant(s): Graduate school students. Adult students.
Amount: Varies.
Number of awards: 4.
Deadline: April 1.
How to apply: Applications are available online and by sending a self-addressed, stamped envelope.
Exclusive: Visit www.UltimateScholarshipBook.com and enter code JA266220 for updates on this award.

(2663) • Japanese American Citizens League Undergraduate Awards

Japanese American Citizens League (JACL)
1765 Sutter Street, San Francisco, CA 94115
Phone: 415-921-5225
Email: jacl@jacl.org
http://www.jacl.org
Purpose: To recognize and encourage education as a key to greater opportunities among JACL members.
Eligibility: Applicants must be National JACL members and must be attending a college, university, trade school, business school or any other

institution of higher learning at the undergraduate level. A personal statement, letter of recommendation, academic performance, work experience and community involvement will all be considered.
Target applicant(s): College students. Adult students.
Amount: Varies.
Number of awards: 7.
Deadline: April 1.
How to apply: Applications are available through local JACL chapters, regional offices, National JACL Headquarters and website.
Exclusive: Visit www.UltimateScholarshipBook.com and enter code JA266320 for updates on this award.

(2664) • Jean Charley-Call Nursing Scholarship

Hopi Tribe Grants and Scholarship Program
P.O. Box 123, Kykotsmovi, AZ 86039
Phone: 800-762-9630
Email: heef@hopieducationfund.org
http://www.hopieducationfund.org
Purpose: To aid Hopi Indian nursing students.
Eligibility: Applicants must be enrolled members of the Hopi Indian tribe and be full-time students who are pursuing a degree in nursing at an accredited college or university. They must have a GPA of 2.5 or higher and have completed the Free Application for Federal Student Aid (FAFSA). Selection is based on the overall strength of the application.
Target applicant(s): College students. Adult students.
Minimum GPA: 2.5
Amount: $1,000.
Number of awards: Varies.
Scholarship may be renewable.
Deadline: September 1.
How to apply: Applications are available online. An application form, official high school and college transcripts, a personal essay, plan of study and proof of college enrollment are required.
Exclusive: Visit www.UltimateScholarshipBook.com and enter code HO266420 for updates on this award.

(2665) • Jeannette Rankin Women's Scholarship Fund

Jeannette Rankin Foundation
1 Huntington Road, Suite 701, Athens, GA 30606
Phone: 706-208-1211
Email: info@rankinfoundation.org
http://www.rankinfoundation.org
Purpose: To support the education of low-income women 35 years or older.
Eligibility: Applicants must be women 35 years of age or older, plan to obtain an undergraduate or vocational education and meet maximum household income guidelines.
Target applicant(s): College students. Adult students.
Amount: Varies.
Number of awards: Varies.
Scholarship may be renewable.
Deadline: March 1.
How to apply: Applications are available online or by sending a self-addressed and stamped envelope to the foundation.
Exclusive: Visit www.UltimateScholarshipBook.com and enter code JE266520 for updates on this award.

(2666) • Judith Resnik Memorial Scholarship

Society of Women Engineers
130 East Randolph Street, Suite 3500, Chicago, IL 60601
Phone: 877-793-4636
Email: scholarships@swe.org
http://societyofwomenengineers.swe.org/scholarships
Purpose: To help female undergraduates who are majoring in astronautical, aeronautical or aerospace engineering.
Eligibility: Applicants must be rising undergraduate sophomores, juniors or seniors and have a GPA of 3.0 or higher on a four-point scale. They must be enrolled in an ABET-accredited degree program in aeronautical engineering, aerospace engineering or astronautical engineering. They cannot be receiving a renewable scholarship from the Society of Women Engineers. Applicants who are receiving full funding from another source (such as the U.S. military or an employee reimbursement plan) are ineligible. Selection is based on the overall strength of the application.
Target applicant(s): College students. Adult students.
Minimum GPA: 3.0
Amount: $3,500.
Number of awards: 1.
Deadline: February 15.
How to apply: Applications are available online. An application form, official transcript and two recommendation letters are required.
Exclusive: Visit www.UltimateScholarshipBook.com and enter code SO266620 for updates on this award.

(2667) • Julianne Malveaux Scholarship

National Association of Negro Business and Professional Women's Clubs Inc.
1806 New Hampshire Avenue NW, Washington, DC 20009-3298
Phone: 202-483-4206
Email: info@nanbpwc.org
http://www.nanbpwc.org
Purpose: To award scholarships to college students majoring in journalism, economics or a related field.
Eligibility: Applicants must be enrolled as sophomores or juniors at an accredited college or university and have a minimum 3.0 GPA. Students may major in related fields such as public policy or creative writing.
Target applicant(s): College students. Adult students.
Minimum GPA: 3.0
Amount: Varies.
Number of awards: Varies.
Deadline: March 1.
How to apply: Applications are available online.
Exclusive: Visit www.UltimateScholarshipBook.com and enter code NA266720 for updates on this award.

(2668) • Knights of Lithuania Scholarship Program

Knights of Lithuania Scholarship Program
c/o Mikalina Tambasco, Committee Chair, 14 Pine Avenue, Johnstown, NY 12095
Phone: 518-705-1165
Email: mikalina@hotmail.com
http://knightsoflithuania.com/scholarship/
Purpose: To assist Lithuanian-Americans in obtaining higher education.
Eligibility: Applicants must be members of the Knights of Lithuania for at least two years. They must receive recommendations from their council president or vice president, a pastor or spiritual adviser and a former teacher in addition to a separate character reference.

Target applicant(s): High school students. College students. Graduate school students. Adult students.
Amount: Varies.
Number of awards: Varies.
Deadline: June 23.
How to apply: Applications are available online.
Exclusive: Visit www.UltimateScholarshipBook.com and enter code KN266820 for updates on this award.

(2669) • Korean Ancestry Grant

William Orr Dingwall Foundation
P.O. Box 57088, Washington, DC 20037
Email: kag@dingwallfoundation.org
http://www.dingwallfoundation.org
Purpose: To aid students of Asian ancestry.
Eligibility: Applicants must be of Asian ancestry and have at least one Asian grandparent. They must be entering or current undergraduate students. Preference will be given to applicants of Korean ancestry. Selection is based on the overall strength of the application.
Target applicant(s): High school students. College students. Adult students.
Amount: Up to $10,000.
Number of awards: At least 7.
Scholarship may be renewable.
Deadline: March 31.
How to apply: Applications are available online. An application form, official transcript, personal statement and two recommendation letters are required.
Exclusive: Visit www.UltimateScholarshipBook.com and enter code WI266920 for updates on this award.

(2670) • LAGRANT Scholarship Program

LAGRANT Foundation
633 W. 5th Street, 48th Floor, Los Angeles, CA 90071
Phone: 323-469-8680
http://www.lagrantfoundation.org
Purpose: To support minority students who are seeking degrees in advertising, graphic design, marketing or public relations.
Eligibility: Applicants must be African American/Black, Asian American/Pacific Islander, Hispanic/Latino or Native American/Alaskan Native. Students must be U.S. citizens, permanent residents, AB-540 students or DACA recipients. Applicants must be full-time students at an accredited four-year institution in the U.S. A minimum 3.0 GPA or higher is required. Students must submit an essay with their application.
Target applicant(s): College students. Graduate school students. Adult students.
Minimum GPA: 3.0
Amount: $2,500-$3,750.
Number of awards: 50.
Deadline: February 28.
How to apply: Applications are available online.
Exclusive: Visit www.UltimateScholarshipBook.com and enter code LA267020 for updates on this award.

(2671) • Larry Whiteside Scholarship

National Association of Black Journalists
1100 Knight Hall, Suite 3100, College Park, MD 20742
Phone: 301-405-7520
Email: iwashington@nabj.org
http://nabj.site-ym.com/?page=SEEDScholarships
Purpose: To assist students who are planning for careers in sports journalism.
Eligibility: Applicants must be student members of the National Association of Black Journalists (NABJ). They must be graduate students or rising undergraduate juniors or seniors at an accredited four-year institution who are planning to pursue careers in sports journalism. They must be majoring in journalism or communications or must have demonstrated an interest in journalism by working for a media outlet. They must have a major GPA of 2.5 or higher. Selection is based on the overall strength of the application.
Target applicant(s): College students. Graduate school students. Adult students.
Minimum GPA: 2.5
Amount: $3,000.
Number of awards: 1.
Deadline: February 12.
How to apply: Applications are available online. An application form, resume, official transcript, personal essay, three writing samples and three references are required.
Exclusive: Visit www.UltimateScholarshipBook.com and enter code NA267120 for updates on this award.

(2672) • LatPro Scholarship

LatPro
3980 N. Broadway, Suite 103-147, Boulder, CO 80304
Phone: 954-727-3844
http://www.latpro.com
Purpose: To support Hispanic students in pursuing post-secondary education.
Eligibility: Applicants must be enrolled full-time in an undergraduate or graduate program at a LatPro registered school. Students must submit an essay explaining their educational goals. Selection is based on the overall strength of the overall strength of the application.
Target applicant(s): College students. Adult students.
Amount: $3,000.
Number of awards: 1.
Deadline: April 30.
How to apply: Applications are available online.
Exclusive: Visit www.UltimateScholarshipBook.com and enter code LA267220 for updates on this award.

(2673) • Lillian Moller Gilbreth Memorial Scholarship

Society of Women Engineers
130 East Randolph Street, Suite 3500, Chicago, IL 60601
Phone: 877-793-4636
Email: scholarships@swe.org
http://societyofwomenengineers.swe.org/scholarships
Purpose: To aid female students who are majoring in engineering.
Eligibility: Applicants must be rising undergraduate juniors or seniors who are enrolled in an ABET-accredited engineering degree program. They must have a GPA of 3.0 or higher on a four-point scale. Applicants cannot be receiving full academic funding from another source, and they cannot be receiving another renewable SWE scholarship at the time of award disbursement. Selection is based on the overall strength of the application.
Target applicant(s): College students. Adult students.
Minimum GPA: 3.0
Amount: $14,500.
Number of awards: 1.
Scholarship may be renewable.

Deadline: February 15.
How to apply: Applications are available online. An application form, official transcript and two letters of recommendation are required.
Exclusive: Visit www.UltimateScholarshipBook.com and enter code SO267320 for updates on this award.

(2674) • Live Your Dream Awards Program

Soroptimist International of the Americas
1709 Spruce Street, Philadelphia, PA 19103
Phone: 215-893-9000
Email: siahq@soroptimist.org
http://www.soroptimist.org/awards/live-your-dream-awards.html
Purpose: To assist women entering or re-entering the workforce with educational and skills training support.
Eligibility: Applicants must be attending or been accepted by a vocational/skills training program or an undergraduate degree program. Applicants must be the women heads of household who provide the primary source of financial support for their families and demonstrate financial need. Applicants must submit their application to the appropriate regional office.
Target applicant(s): High school students. College students. Adult students.
Amount: Up to $10,000.
Number of awards: Varies.
Deadline: November 15.
How to apply: Applications are available online.
Exclusive: Visit www.UltimateScholarshipBook.com and enter code SO267420 for updates on this award.

(2675) • Lockheed Martin Corporation Scholarship

Society of Women Engineers
130 East Randolph Street, Suite 3500, Chicago, IL 60601
Phone: 877-793-4636
Email: scholarships@swe.org
http://societyofwomenengineers.swe.org/scholarships
Purpose: To aid female students who are planning to pursue higher education in engineering.
Eligibility: Applicants must be undergraduate students who are majoring in computer science, computer engineering, software engineering or electrical engineering. Students must have a minimum 3.2 GPA. Selection is based on the overall strength of the application.
Target applicant(s): College students. Adult students.
Minimum GPA: 3.2
Amount: $2,000.
Number of awards: 8.
Deadline: May 15.
How to apply: Applications are available online. An application form and supporting materials are required.
Exclusive: Visit www.UltimateScholarshipBook.com and enter code SO267520 for updates on this award.

(2676) • Loreen Arbus Foundation Scholarship

Alliance for Women in Media
2365 Harrodsburg Road, Suite A325, Lexington, KY 40504
Phone: 202-750-3664
Email: info@allwomeninmedia.org
https://allwomeninmedia.org/foundation/scholarships/
Purpose: To support female undergraduate and graduate students studying media, journalism, English, communications and related fields.
Eligibility: Applicants must be attending an accredited college or university in the United States in the fall of application year. Students must submit a 750- to 1,000-word essay on a suggested topic.
Target applicant(s): College students. Graduate school students. Adult students.
Amount: $2,500.
Number of awards: 1.
Deadline: May 4.
How to apply: Applications are available online.
Exclusive: Visit www.UltimateScholarshipBook.com and enter code AL267620 for updates on this award.

(2677) • Louise Moritz Molitoris Leadership Scholarship for Undergraduates

Women's Transportation Seminar (WTS) International
1701 K Street NW, Suite 800, Washington, DC 20006
Phone: 202-955-5085
Email: membership@wtsinternational.org
https://www.wtsinternational.org/
Purpose: To aid female undergraduates who are pursuing transportation-related degrees.
Eligibility: Applicants must be currently enrolled in a transportation-related degree program, have a GPA of 3.0 or higher and have plans to pursue a career in the field of transportation. Selection is based on academic merit, proven leadership in transportation-related activities and stated career goals.
Target applicant(s): College students. Adult students.
Minimum GPA: 3.0
Amount: $5,000.
Number of awards: 1.
Deadline: Varies.
How to apply: Applications are available from local WTS chapters by request. An application form and supporting materials are required.
Exclusive: Visit www.UltimateScholarshipBook.com and enter code WO267720 for updates on this award.

(2678) • Lucy Kasparian Aharonian Scholarship

Armenian International Women's Association
65 Main Street, #3A, Watertown, MA 02472
Phone: 617-926-0171
Email: aiwainc@aol.com
http://aiwainternational.org/
Purpose: To aid female students of Armenian descent who are studying selected subjects.
Eligibility: Applicants must be full-time undergraduate juniors, undergraduate seniors or graduate students who are enrolled at an accredited postsecondary institution. They must be pursuing a degree in architecture, computer science, engineering, mathematics or technology. Selection is based on academic merit and financial need.
Target applicant(s): College students. Graduate school students. Adult students.
Amount: $1,000.
Number of awards: 1.
Deadline: April 21.
How to apply: Applications are available online. An application form and supporting materials are required.
Exclusive: Visit www.UltimateScholarshipBook.com and enter code AR267820 for updates on this award.

(2679) • LULAC General Awards

League of United Latin American Citizens
1133 19th Street NW, Suite 1000, Washington, DC 20036
Phone: 202-835-9646
Email: scholarships@lnesc.org
http://www.lnesc.org

Purpose: To provide assistance to Latino students who are seeking or plan to seek degrees.

Eligibility: Students must have applied to or be enrolled in a two- or four-year college or graduate school and be U.S. citizens or legal residents. Grades and academic achievement may be considered, but emphasis is placed on motivation, sincerity and integrity as demonstrated by the interview and essay.

Target applicant(s): High school students. College students. Graduate school students. Adult students.

Amount: $250-$1,000.

Number of awards: Varies.

Deadline: March 31.

How to apply: Applications are available online.

Exclusive: Visit www.UltimateScholarshipBook.com and enter code LE267920 for updates on this award.

(2680) • LULAC Honors Awards

League of United Latin American Citizens
1133 19th Street NW, Suite 1000, Washington, DC 20036
Phone: 202-835-9646
Email: scholarships@lnesc.org
http://www.lnesc.org

Purpose: To provide assistance to Latino students of all levels of education.

Eligibility: Applicants must be U.S. citizens or legal residents, have applied to or attend a college or graduate school and have a GPA of 3.0 or better. Applicants who are entering freshmen must also have an ACT score of 23 or higher or an SAT score of 1100 or higher.

Target applicant(s): High school students. College students. Graduate school students. Adult students.

Minimum GPA: 3.0

Amount: $500-$2,000.

Number of awards: Varies.

Deadline: March 31.

How to apply: Applications are available from LULAC.

Exclusive: Visit www.UltimateScholarshipBook.com and enter code LE268020 for updates on this award.

(2681) • MAES Scholarship Program

Society of Mexican American Engineers and Scientists Inc. (MAES)
711 W. Bay Area Boulevard, Suite #206, Webster, TX 77598-4051
Phone: 281-557-3677
Email: execdir@maes-natl.org
http://mymaes.org/

Purpose: To assist Hispanic students in the fields of science and engineering.

Eligibility: Applicants must be current Hispanic MAES student members who are full-time undergraduate and graduate students in an accredited U.S. college or university majoring in science or engineering. Community college applicants must be enrolled in majors that are transferable to a four-year institution offering bachelor's degrees. There are various scholarships in the program. Some sponsors require students to be U.S. citizens or permanent residents. Awards are based on financial need, academic achievement, personal qualities, strengths and leadership abilities. Applicants should submit applications, financial information, recommendations and transcripts.

Target applicant(s): High school students. College students. Graduate school students. Adult students.

Amount: Varies.

Number of awards: Varies.

Deadline: April 30.

How to apply: Applications are available online.

Exclusive: Visit www.UltimateScholarshipBook.com and enter code SO268120 for updates on this award.

(2682) • Malcolm X Scholarship for Exceptional Courage

United Negro College Fund (UNCF)
1805 7th Street NW, Washington, DC 20001
Phone: 800-331-2244
https://scholarships.uncf.org/

Purpose: To assist students who attend UNCF member colleges and universities and have overcome extreme circumstances and hardships.

Eligibility: Applicants must be African American students, have a minimum 2.5 GPA, complete the Free Application for Federal Student Aid (FAFSA) and have unmet financial need that is verified by the college or university financial aid office. Students are encouraged to complete the UNCF General Scholarship application to be matched with scholarships for which they meet the criteria. Academic excellence and leadership on campus and in the community are also required.

Target applicant(s): College students. Adult students.

Minimum GPA: 2.5

Amount: $4,000.

Number of awards: Varies.

Deadline: September 29.

How to apply: Applications are available online.

Exclusive: Visit www.UltimateScholarshipBook.com and enter code UN268220 for updates on this award.

(2683) • MALDEF Law School Scholarship

Mexican American Legal Defense and Educational Fund
634 South Spring Street, Los Angeles, CA 90014
Phone: 213-629-2512
http://maldef.org

Purpose: To support law school students in funding their education.

Eligibility: Applicants must be enrolled full-time at an accredited U.S. law school. Selection is primarily based on demonstration of academic achievement, extracurricular involvement, financial need and commitment to the advancement of Latino civil rights. Students must submit transcripts, letters of recommendation and a personal statement.

Target applicant(s): College students. Graduate school students. Adult students.

Amount: $5,000.

Number of awards: Varies.

Deadline: December 18.

How to apply: Applications are available online.

Exclusive: Visit www.UltimateScholarshipBook.com and enter code ME268320 for updates on this award.

(2684) • Marcia Silverman Minority Student Award

Public Relations Student Society of America
33 Maiden Lane, 11th Floor, New York, NY 10038
Phone: 212-460-1474

Email: prssa@prsa.org
http://prssa.prsa.org/scholarships-and-awards/
Purpose: To aid minority students who are preparing for careers in public relations.
Eligibility: Applicants must be of African-American, Latino, Asian, Native American, Pacific Islander or Alaska Native ancestry. They must be rising undergraduate seniors who are majoring in journalism, public relations or a related subject and be planning to pursue a career in public relations. They must have a GPA of 3.0 or higher. Selection is based on academic merit, stated career goals, relevant work experience, writing ability, recommendations and leadership skills.
Target applicant(s): College students. Adult students.
Minimum GPA: 3.0
Amount: $5,000.
Number of awards: 1.
Deadline: May 9.
How to apply: Applications are available online. An application form, resume and one recommendation letter are required.
Exclusive: Visit www.UltimateScholarshipBook.com and enter code PU268420 for updates on this award.

(2685) • Marcus Garvey Scholarship

Malcolm Frierson Foundation
P.O. Box 271221, Flower Mound, TX 75027
Email: mfrierson@gmail.com
https://www.malcolmfrierson.com/
Purpose: To encourage students who identify as being of African descent and who demonstrate leadership and service.
Eligibility: Applicants must identify as being of African descent and plan on enrolling as a first-time student at an accredited U.S. college or university. Students must have a minimum high school GPA of 3.0 and demonstrate leadership and commitment to service.
Target applicant(s): High school students. College students. Adult students.
Minimum GPA: 3.0
Amount: $1,000.
Number of awards: 1.
Deadline: July 16.
How to apply: Applications are available online.
Exclusive: Visit www.UltimateScholarshipBook.com and enter code MA268520 for updates on this award.

(2686) • Margaret Mcnamara Memorial Fund Fellowships

Margaret Mcnamara Memorial Fund
1818 H Street NW, MSN H2-204, Washington, DC 20433
http://www.mmeg.org/
Purpose: To provide financial assistance to women from developing countries who are currently studying to earn a college degree in the U.S., Canada or developing countries in Africa.
Eligibility: Applicants must be from an eligible nation, have a record of community service in their country and be U.S. or Canadian residents at the time of application, while intending to return to their country of origin within two years. Individuals under the age of 25 and relatives of World Bank employees are not eligible.
Target applicant(s): College students. Graduate school students. Adult students.
Amount: $4,000-$12,000.
Number of awards: Varies.
Deadline: January 15.
How to apply: Applications are available online.
Exclusive: Visit www.UltimateScholarshipBook.com and enter code MA268620 for updates on this award.

(2687) • Maria Elena Salinas Scholarship Program

National Association of Hispanic Journalists
Scholarship Committee, 1050 Connecticut Avenue NW, 10th Floor, Washington, DC 20036
Phone: 202-662-7145
Email: nahj@nahj.org
http://nahj.org/next-generation-nahj/
Purpose: To support Spanish-speaking students who plan to become broadcast journalists.
Eligibility: Applicants must be high school seniors, undergraduates or first-year graduate students who plan to pursue careers in journalism in Spanish-language television or radio. The award includes an opportunity to intern with the news division of Univision or an affiliate. Applicants must write an essay in Spanish outlining their career goals and provide Spanish-language samples of their work.
Target applicant(s): High school students. College students. Graduate school students. Adult students.
Amount: Up to $5,000.
Number of awards: 1.
Scholarship may be renewable.
Deadline: February 24.
How to apply: Applications are available online.
Exclusive: Visit www.UltimateScholarshipBook.com and enter code NA268720 for updates on this award.

(2688) • Marilynn Smith Scholarship

Ladies Professional Golf Association
100 International Golf Drive, Daytona Beach, FL 32124-1092
Phone: 386-274-6200
Email: info@lpgafoundation.org
http://www.lpga.com/lpga-foundation/scholarships
Purpose: To support female high school senior golf participants who wish to play competitive golf in college.
Eligibility: Applicants must have played at least 50 percent of their high school team's schedule or played competitive junior golf for the past two years. Students must also be a U.S. citizen or legal resident, have a 3.2 GPA or higher, be accepted to attend a college or university and plan on playing competitive golf while attending college. Selection is based on the personal essay, letters of reference and financial need.
Target applicant(s): High school students.
Minimum GPA: 3.2
Amount: $5,000.
Number of awards: 20.
Deadline: April 30.
How to apply: Applications are available online and must include the official application form, three letters of reference, official high school transcript and the personal essay.
Exclusive: Visit www.UltimateScholarshipBook.com and enter code LA268820 for updates on this award.

(2689) • Mark Ando and Ito Family Scholarship

Far West Athletic Trainers' Association/District 8
Ned Bergert, Committee Chair
Phone: 714-501-3858
Email: nhbergert@gmail.com
http://www.fwatad8.org/

Purpose: To aid students of Asian descent in California, Hawaii and Nevada who are pursuing higher education in athletic training.
Eligibility: Applicants must be District 8 student members of the National Athletic Trainers' Association (NATA) who are of Asian descent. They must be enrolled in an undergraduate- or graduate-level athletic training program. Community college applicants and all other applicants must have a GPA of 3.2 or higher on a four-point scale. Non-community college undergraduates must be sponsored by a certified athletic trainer and must have junior standing. All applicants must have plans to pursue a career in athletic training. Selection is based on academic merit, extracurricular activities, leadership potential and athletic training achievement.
Target applicant(s): College students. Graduate school students. Adult students.
Minimum GPA: 3.2
Amount: Varies.
Number of awards: Varies.
Deadline: March 1.
How to apply: Applications are available online. An application form, an official transcript and a personal essay are required.
Exclusive: Visit www.UltimateScholarshipBook.com and enter code FA268920 for updates on this award.

(2690) • Mary Gunther Memorial Scholarship

Society of Women Engineers
130 East Randolph Street, Suite 3500, Chicago, IL 60601
Phone: 877-793-4636
Email: scholarships@swe.org
http://societyofwomenengineers.swe.org/scholarships
Purpose: To aid students who plan to major in engineering.
Eligibility: Applicants must be female rising undergraduate freshmen, sophomores, juniors or seniors who intend to major in engineering at an ABET-accredited school. They must be full-time students who have a GPA of 3.5 or higher on a four-point scale. Preference will be given to students majoring in architectural engineering or environmental engineering. Selection is based on the overall strength of the application.
Target applicant(s): High school students. College students. Adult students.
Minimum GPA: 3.5
Amount: $3,000.
Number of awards: 4.
Deadline: May 1.
How to apply: Applications are available online. An application form, transcript, proof of college acceptance and two recommendation letters are required.
Exclusive: Visit www.UltimateScholarshipBook.com and enter code SO269020 for updates on this award.

(2691) • Mary Moy Quan Ing Memorial Scholarship

Asian American Journalists Association
5 Third Street, Suite 1108, San Francisco, CA 94103
Phone: 415-346-2051
Email: naov@aaja.org
http://www.aaja.org
Purpose: Monetary assistance is awarded to a high school senior pursuing college studies that lead to a journalism career.
Eligibility: Applicants must be high school seniors intending to major in journalism. Applicants must also demonstrate a commitment to the field of journalism, sensitivity to Asian American issues as demonstrated by community involvement, journalistic ability, scholastic ability and financial need.
Target applicant(s): High school students.
Amount: $2,000.
Number of awards: 1.
Deadline: April 16.
How to apply: Applications are available online.
Exclusive: Visit www.UltimateScholarshipBook.com and enter code AS269120 for updates on this award.

(2692) • Mary R. Norton Memorial Scholarship Award for Women

ASTM International
100 Barr Harbor Drive, P.O. Box C700, West Conshohocken, PA 19428-2959
Phone: 610-832-9585
Email: awards@astm.org
https://www.astm.org/studentmember/Student_Awards.html
Purpose: To aid female students who are pursuing graduate studies in materials science or physical metallurgy.
Eligibility: Applicants must be full-time undergraduate seniors or first-year graduate students. They must be enrolled in or planning to enroll in a graduate program in physical metallurgy or materials science, with an emphasis on the relationship between properties and microstructures. Selection is based on faculty recommendation and personal statement.
Target applicant(s): College students. Graduate school students. Adult students.
Amount: $1,000.
Number of awards: 1.
Deadline: Varies.
How to apply: Applications are available online. An application form, one faculty recommendation, personal statement and transcripts are required.
Exclusive: Visit www.UltimateScholarshipBook.com and enter code AS269220 for updates on this award.

(2693) • Mas Family Scholarships

Jorge Mas Canosa Freedom Foundation
Attn: Mas Family Scholarships, P.O. Box 14-1898, Coral Gables, FL 33114
Phone: 305-507-7323
http://masscholarships.org/
Purpose: To aid undergraduate and graduate students of Cuban descent who are studying selected subjects.
Eligibility: Applicants must be majoring in or have plans to major in business, communications, economics, engineering, international relations or journalism. They must demonstrate leadership potential and a commitment to success in a democratic, free enterprise society. Selection is based on academic merit, personal essay, leadership ability, professional potential and character.
Target applicant(s): High school students. College students. Graduate school students. Adult students.
Amount: Up to $8,000.
Number of awards: Varies.
Scholarship may be renewable.
Deadline: January 9.
How to apply: Applications are available online. An application form, official transcript, SAT scores, personal essay, three recommendation forms, proof of Cuban descent, proof of college acceptance (for incoming freshmen only), cost of tuition statement and statement of financial need are required.
Exclusive: Visit www.UltimateScholarshipBook.com and enter code JO269320 for updates on this award.

(2694) • Maureen L. and Howard N. Blitman, P.E., Scholarship

National Society of Professional Engineers
1420 King Street, Alexandria, VA 22314-2794
Phone: 703-684-2885
Email: students@nspe.org
https://www.nspe.org/resources/students/scholarships
Purpose: To encourage minority students to pursue careers in engineering.
Eligibility: Applicants must be African-American, Hispanic or Native American high school seniors who have been accepted into an accredited engineering program at a four-year institution. Students are evaluated based on academic achievement, community involvement and recommendations and must have a minimum 3.5 GPA.
Target applicant(s): High school students.
Minimum GPA: 3.5
Amount: $5,000.
Number of awards: 1.
Deadline: March 1.
How to apply: Applications are available online.
Exclusive: Visit www.UltimateScholarshipBook.com and enter code NA269420 for updates on this award.

(2695) • MCCA Lloyd M. Johnson, Jr. Scholarship Program

Minority Corporate Counsel Association (MCCA)
1111 Pennsylvania Avenue, NW, Washington, DC 20004
Phone: 202-739-5901
Email: contactus@applyists.com
http://www.mcca.com/resources/scholarship-program/
Purpose: To support first-year entering law students.
Eligibility: Applicants must be diverse students entering their first year of law school full-time at an accredited institution. They must have a GPA of at least 3.2 and demonstrate financial need.
Target applicant(s): College students. Graduate school students. Adult students.
Minimum GPA: 3.2
Amount: $10,000.
Number of awards: Up to 10.
Scholarship may be renewable.
Deadline: August 31.
How to apply: Applications are available online.
Exclusive: Visit www.UltimateScholarshipBook.com and enter code MI269520 for updates on this award.

(2696) • Medicus Student Exchange

Swiss Benevolent Society of New York
Scholarship Committee, 500 Fifth Avenue, Room 1800, New York, NY 10110
https://www.sbsny.org/
Purpose: To provide need and merit-based scholarships for students from Swiss-American backgrounds.
Eligibility: Applicants or one of their parents must be a Swiss national. The Medicus grant for study in Switzerland is only open to U.S. residents and is a need-based award. Applicants must be college juniors or seniors or graduate-level students accepted to a Swiss university or the Federal Institute of Technology.
Target applicant(s): College students. Graduate school students. Adult students.
Amount: Varies.
Number of awards: Varies.
Deadline: March 31.
How to apply: Applications are available online.
Exclusive: Visit www.UltimateScholarshipBook.com and enter code SW269620 for updates on this award.

(2697) • Medtronic Foundation Scholarship

United Negro College Fund (UNCF)
1805 7th Street NW, Washington, DC 20001
Phone: 800-331-2244
https://scholarships.uncf.org/
Purpose: To support African American sophomores and juniors at UNCF member colleges and universities majoring in a science, engineering or medical field.
Eligibility: Applicants must be college juniors majoring in one of the following: biochemistry, biology, biomedical engineering, biotechnical, chemistry, computer engineering, computer science, electrical engineering and mechanical engineering. Applicants must have a GPA of at least 3.0 and demonstrate financial need.
Target applicant(s): College students. Adult students.
Minimum GPA: 3.0
Amount: $4,500.
Number of awards: Varies.
Deadline: March 24.
How to apply: Applications are available online.
Exclusive: Visit www.UltimateScholarshipBook.com and enter code UN269720 for updates on this award.

(2698) • Michael Jackson Scholarship

United Negro College Fund (UNCF)
1805 7th Street NW, Washington, DC 20001
Phone: 800-331-2244
https://scholarships.uncf.org/
Purpose: To assist students majoring in communications, English or performing arts.
Eligibility: Applicants must be African American students at a UNCF member college or university majoring in communications, English or performing arts. Applicants must have a GPA of at least 3.0 and demonstrate financial need.
Target applicant(s): High school students. College students. Adult students.
Minimum GPA: 3.0
Amount: Up to $5,000.
Number of awards: Varies.
Deadline: October 21.
How to apply: Applications are available online.
Exclusive: Visit www.UltimateScholarshipBook.com and enter code UN269820 for updates on this award.

(2699) • MillerCoors National Scholarship

Adelante U.S. Educational Leadership Fund
8415 Datapoint Drive, Suite 400, San Antonio, TX 78229
Phone: 877-692-1971
Email: info@adelantefund.org
https://www.adelantefund.org/scholarships
Purpose: To assist Latino students attending participating institutions who are pursuing degrees in business, economics, marketing or communications.
Eligibility: Applicants must be college juniors or seniors pursuing a business, marketing, economics or communications degree. Students

must have a 3.0 GPA or above and be full-time students attending one of the partnering universities.
Target applicant(s): College students. Adult students.
Minimum GPA: 3.0
Amount: Varies.
Number of awards: Varies.
Deadline: May 25.
How to apply: Applications are available online starting March 1.
Exclusive: Visit www.UltimateScholarshipBook.com and enter code AD269920 for updates on this award.

(2700) • Minority Affairs Committee Award for Outstanding Scholastic Achievement

American Institute of Chemical Engineers - (AIChE)
120 Wall Street, Floor 23, New York, NY 10005-4020
Phone: 800-242-4363
Email: awards@aiche.org
https://www.aiche.org/community/awards
Purpose: Recognizes outstanding achievements by a chemical engineering student who serves as a role model for minority students.
Eligibility: Applicants must be ethnic minorities, major in chemical engineering and be undergraduate students.
Target applicant(s): College students. Adult students.
Amount: $1,000.
Number of awards: 10.
Deadline: June 16.
How to apply: Applications are available online or by telephone or written request.
Exclusive: Visit www.UltimateScholarshipBook.com and enter code AM270020 for updates on this award.

(2701) • Minority Scholarship

National Strength and Conditioning Association (NSCA) Foundation
1885 Bob Johnson Drive, Colorado Springs, CO 80906
Phone: 800-815-6826
http://www.nsca.com/foundation/
Purpose: To encourage minorities to enter the field of strength and conditioning.
Eligibility: Applicants must be African American, Hispanic, Asian American or Native American students working toward a graduate degree related to strength and conditioning. Students must be NSCA members for one year before applying and be pursuing careers in strength and conditioning. Applications are evaluated based on grades, courses, experience, honors, recommendations and involvement in the community and with NSCA.
Target applicant(s): High school students. College students. Graduate school students. Adult students.
Amount: $1,500.
Number of awards: Varies.
Deadline: March 15.
How to apply: Applications are available with membership.
Exclusive: Visit www.UltimateScholarshipBook.com and enter code NA270120 for updates on this award.

(2702) • Minority Scholarship

Brown and Caldwell
Attn.: HR/Scholarships Program, 1527 Cole Boulevard, Suite 300, Lakewood, CO 80401
Phone: 800-727-2224
Email: scholarships@brwncald.com
http://www.brownandcaldwell.com
Purpose: To support minority students interested in pursuing a career in the environmental profession.
Eligibility: Applicants must attend an accredited college or university as an undergraduate junior or senior or as a graduate student. Students must also provide two letters of recommendation, official transcripts and complete a 250-word essay on predetermined topic.
Target applicant(s): College students. Graduate school students. Adult students.
Minimum GPA: 3.0
Amount: $5,000.
Number of awards: Varies.
Deadline: April 15.
How to apply: Applications are available online.
Exclusive: Visit www.UltimateScholarshipBook.com and enter code BR270220 for updates on this award.

(2703) • Minority Scholarship Award for Physical Therapy Students

American Physical Therapy Association
1111 North Fairfax Street, Alexandria, VA 22314
Phone: 703-684-2782
Email: honorsandawards@apta.org
http://www.apta.org
Purpose: To aid minority physical therapy students.
Eligibility: Applicants must be U.S. citizens or legal permanent residents. They must be African-American, Hispanic, Native American, Pacific Islander, Native Hawaiian or Alaska Native. They must be in the final year of an accredited or developing professional physical therapist program at the time of award disbursement. Students must demonstrate academic excellence, service to minority affairs and career potential. Selection is based on the overall strength of the application.
Target applicant(s): Graduate school students. Adult students.
Amount: Varies.
Number of awards: Varies.
Deadline: December 1.
How to apply: Applications are available online. An application form, official transcript, personal essay and three letters of reference are required.
Exclusive: Visit www.UltimateScholarshipBook.com and enter code AM270320 for updates on this award.

(2704) • Minority Scholarship Awards for College Students

American Institute of Chemical Engineers - (AIChE)
120 Wall Street, Floor 23, New York, NY 10005-4020
Phone: 800-242-4363
Email: awards@aiche.org
https://www.aiche.org/community/awards
Purpose: To aid minority students who are majoring in chemical engineering.
Eligibility: Applicants must be members of a minority group that is underrepresented in the field of chemical engineering (African-American, Latino, Native American, Alaska Native or Pacific Islander). They must be student members of the American Institute of Chemical Engineers (AIChE) and must be undergraduates who are majoring in chemical engineering. Selection is based on academic merit, stated career goals, AIChE participation and financial need.
Target applicant(s): College students. Adult students.

Amount: $1,000.
Number of awards: Varies.
Deadline: July 1.
How to apply: Applications are available online. An application form and supporting materials are required.
Exclusive: Visit www.UltimateScholarshipBook.com and enter code AM270420 for updates on this award.

(2705) • Minority Scholarship Awards for Incoming College Freshmen

American Institute of Chemical Engineers - (AIChE)
120 Wall Street, Floor 23, New York, NY 10005-4020
Phone: 800-242-4363
Email: awards@aiche.org
https://www.aiche.org/community/awards
Purpose: To offer financial aid to minority students in chemical engineering.
Eligibility: Applicants must be members of a minority group (i.e. African American, Hispanic, Native American or Alaskan Native) that is underrepresented in chemical engineering. Applicants must also be high school graduates during the academic year of application and plan to enroll in a four-year college or university. Applicants are encouraged to major in science or engineering. Selection is also based on academic record, reason for choosing science or engineering, work or activities and financial need.
Target applicant(s): High school students.
Amount: $1,000.
Number of awards: 10.
Deadline: August 15.
How to apply: Applications are available online or by telephone or written request.
Exclusive: Visit www.UltimateScholarshipBook.com and enter code AM270520 for updates on this award.

(2706) • Minority Serving Institution Grants

Council on International Educational Exchange (CIEE)
300 Fore Street, Portland, ME 04101
Phone: 207-553-4000
Email: studyinfo@ciee.org
http://www.ciee.org
Purpose: To aid underrepresented students who wish to study abroad.
Eligibility: Applicants must be CIEE Study Center participants. They must be students who are self-identified as being from a group that is underrepresented in study abroad programs. Selection is based on the overall strength of the application.
Target applicant(s): College students. Adult students.
Amount: Up to $2,000.
Number of awards: Varies.
Deadline: Varies.
How to apply: Applications are available online. An application form, financial aid information and an essay are required.
Exclusive: Visit www.UltimateScholarshipBook.com and enter code CO270620 for updates on this award.

(2707) • Morgan Stanley Richard B. Fisher Scholarship Program

Morgan Stanley
1585 Broadway, New York, NY 10036
Email: richardbfisherprogram@morganstanley.com
http://www.morganstanley.com/
Purpose: To assist minority students with outstanding academic achievement.
Eligibility: Applicants must be African American, Hispanic, Native American or LGBT current juniors at an accredited four-year college. The award includes a summer internship.
Target applicant(s): College students. Adult students.
Amount: $15,000.
Number of awards: Varies.
Deadline: February 15.
How to apply: Applications are available by email.
Exclusive: Visit www.UltimateScholarshipBook.com and enter code MO270720 for updates on this award.

(2708) • Morris K. Udall Scholarship

Morris K. Udall Foundation
130 S. Scott Avenue, Tucson, AZ 85701-1922
Phone: 520-901-8500
Email: info@udall.gov
http://www.udall.gov
Purpose: To aid students committed to careers related to the environment, tribal public policy or Native American health care.
Eligibility: Students must be juniors or sophomores studying full-time for an associate's or bachelor's degree at an accredited two- or four-year institution. They must be U.S. citizens, nationals or permanent residents and be committed to a career related to the environment, tribal public policy or Native American health care. Students must be nominated by a college or university faculty representative and must have a grade point average equivalent to a "B" or higher. Selection is based on demonstrated commitment to the environment, tribal public policy or Native American healthcare. Selection is also based on potential of applicant to make significant contributions, leadership, character, desire to make a difference and demonstration of diverse interests and activities.
Target applicant(s): College students. Adult students.
Minimum GPA: 3.0
Amount: Up to $5,000.
Number of awards: 50.
Scholarship may be renewable.
Deadline: March 5.
How to apply: Applications are available online. An application form, essay, college transcript(s) and three recommendation letters are required.
Exclusive: Visit www.UltimateScholarshipBook.com and enter code MO270820 for updates on this award.

(2709) • Mutual of Omaha Actuarial Scholarship for Minority Students

Mutual of Omaha
Mutual of Omaha Plaza, Strategic Staffing - Actuarial Recruitment, Omaha, NE 68175
Phone: 402-351-3300
http://www.mutualofomaha.com
Purpose: To support undergraduate students who are preparing for actuarial careers.
Eligibility: Applicants must be African-American, Native American, Hispanic, Asian American or from another underrepresented minority group. They must be U.S. citizens, permanent residents, temporary residents, asylees or refugees and must be full-time undergraduate students who have completed 24 or more credit hours (including 18 or more graded hours). They must be pursuing a degree in mathematics or an actuarial-related subject and must have a GPA of 3.4 or more. Applicants must have plans to pursue a career in an actuarial field and

must have passed at least one actuarial exam. Scholarship recipients must be willing to complete a summer internship at the Mutual of Omaha offices in Omaha. Selection is based on the overall strength of the application.
Target applicant(s): High school students. College students. Adult students.
Minimum GPA: 3.4
Amount: $5,000.
Number of awards: Varies.
Scholarship may be renewable.
Deadline: October 20.
How to apply: Applications are available online. An application form, personal statement, one recommendation letter and a resume are required.
Exclusive: Visit www.UltimateScholarshipBook.com and enter code MU270920 for updates on this award.

(2710) • NABJ/Carole Simpson Scholarship

National Association of Black Journalists
1100 Knight Hall, Suite 3100, College Park, MD 20742
Phone: 301-405-7520
Email: iwashington@nabj.org
http://nabj.site-ym.com/?page=SEEDScholarships
Purpose: To aid broadcast journalism students.
Eligibility: Applicants must be student members of the National Association of Black Journalists (NABJ). They must be undergraduate or graduate students who are enrolled in a degree program in broadcast journalism and have a GPA of 2.5 or higher. Selection is based on the overall strength of the application.
Target applicant(s): College students. Graduate school students. Adult students.
Minimum GPA: 2.5
Amount: $2,500.
Number of awards: 1.
Deadline: February 13.
How to apply: Applications are available online. An application form and supporting materials are required.
Exclusive: Visit www.UltimateScholarshipBook.com and enter code NA271020 for updates on this award.

(2711) • NAHJ General Scholarships - Rubén Salazar Fund

National Association of Hispanic Journalists
Scholarship Committee, 1050 Connecticut Avenue NW, 10th Floor, Washington, DC 20036
Phone: 202-662-7145
Email: nahj@nahj.org
http://nahj.org/next-generation-nahj/
Purpose: To support Hispanic students who plan to enter the broadcast journalism field.
Eligibility: Applicants must be high school seniors, college undergraduate or graduate students who plan to pursue careers in English or Spanish-language broadcast journalism.
Target applicant(s): High school students. College students. Graduate school students. Adult students.
Amount: $1,000-$2,000.
Number of awards: Varies.
Deadline: March 15.
How to apply: Applications are available online.
Exclusive: Visit www.UltimateScholarshipBook.com and enter code NA271120 for updates on this award.

(2712) • NAHN Scholarship

National Association of Hispanic Nurses
1500 Sunday Drive, Suite 102, Raleigh, NC 27607
Phone: 919-573-5443
Email: info@thehispanicnurses.org
http://www.nahnnet.org
Purpose: To aid Hispanic nursing students who demonstrate the potential to make contributions to the nursing profession and who will act as positive role models for other nursing students.
Eligibility: Applicants must be members of the NAHN and be enrolled in a diploma, associate, baccalaureate, graduate or practical/vocational nursing program.
Target applicant(s): College students. Graduate school students. Adult students.
Minimum GPA: 3.0
Amount: Varies.
Number of awards: Varies.
Deadline: April 15.
How to apply: Applications are available online or by mail.
Exclusive: Visit www.UltimateScholarshipBook.com and enter code NA271220 for updates on this award.

(2713) • NAJA Scholarship Fund

Native American Journalists Association
University of Oklahoma at Gaylord College, 395 W. Lindsey Street, Norman, OK 73019-4201
Phone: 605-677-5282
Email: info@naja.com
http://www.naja.com
Purpose: To assist Native American students pursuing journalism degrees.
Eligibility: Applicants must be current members of NAJA and be either high school seniors, undergraduate or graduate level students.
Target applicant(s): High school students. College students. Graduate school students. Adult students.
Amount: $500-$3,000.
Number of awards: 3-9.
Deadline: August 31.
How to apply: Applications are available online.
Exclusive: Visit www.UltimateScholarshipBook.com and enter code NA271320 for updates on this award.

(2714) • NANBPWC National Scholarships

National Association of Negro Business and Professional Women's Clubs Inc.
1806 New Hampshire Avenue NW, Washington, DC 20009-3298
Phone: 202-483-4206
Email: info@nanbpwc.org
http://www.nanbpwc.org
Purpose: To provide assistance to African American students who wish to pursue higher education.
Eligibility: Applicants must be graduating African American high school seniors with a GPA of 3.0 or higher. A 300-word essay is required.
Target applicant(s): High school students.
Minimum GPA: 3.0
Amount: Varies.
Number of awards: Varies.

Deadline: March 1.
How to apply: Applications are available online.
Exclusive: Visit www.UltimateScholarshipBook.com and enter code NA271420 for updates on this award.

(2715) · National and District Scholarships

American Hellenic Education Progressive Association
1909 Q Street NW, Suite 500, Washington, DC 20009
Phone: 202-232-6300
Email: ahepa@ahepa.org
https://ahepa.org/Education-Scholarships.htm
Purpose: To support projects furthering the goals of AHEPA: studies concerning Hellenism, Hellenic culture or Greek-American life.
Eligibility: Applicants must be high school seniors, college students, post-graduate students or adult students of Greek descent.
Target applicant(s): High school students. College students. Graduate school students. Adult students.
Amount: Up to $2,000.
Number of awards: Varies.
Scholarship may be renewable.
Deadline: March 31.
How to apply: Applications are available online.
Exclusive: Visit www.UltimateScholarshipBook.com and enter code AM271520 for updates on this award.

(2716) · National Association of Black Accountants National Scholarship Program

National Association of Black Accountants
7249-A Hanover Parkway, Greenbelt, MD 20770
Phone: 301-474-NABA
http://www.nabainc.org
Purpose: To support African Americans and other minorities in the accounting and finance professions.
Eligibility: Applicants must be ethnic minorities currently enrolled as full-time undergraduates in accounting, finance or business or as graduate students in a Master's of Accountancy program. Applicants must also be NABA members and have a minimum 3.5 major GPA and 3.3 cumulative GPA.
Target applicant(s): College students. Graduate school students. Adult students.
Minimum GPA: 3.3
Amount: $1,000-$5,000.
Number of awards: 50.
Deadline: January 31.
How to apply: Applications are available online.
Exclusive: Visit www.UltimateScholarshipBook.com and enter code NA271620 for updates on this award.

(2717) · National Association of Black Journalists Scholarship Program

National Association of Black Journalists
1100 Knight Hall, Suite 3100, College Park, MD 20742
Phone: 301-405-7520
Email: iwashington@nabj.org
http://nabj.site-ym.com/?page=SEEDScholarships
Purpose: To support African American students who are planning to pursue careers in journalism.
Eligibility: Applicants must be African American high school seniors, college students or graduate students who plan to pursue careers in journalism and who are journalism majors or in staff positions on the school newspaper or campus television, radio or website.
Target applicant(s): High school students. College students. Graduate school students. Adult students.
Minimum GPA: 2.5
Amount: Up to $2,500.
Number of awards: 7.
Deadline: April 16.
How to apply: Applications are available online.
Exclusive: Visit www.UltimateScholarshipBook.com and enter code NA271720 for updates on this award.

(2718) · National Foster Parent Association (NFPA) Youth Scholarship

National Foster Parent Association (NFPA)
2313 Tacoma Avenue South, Tacoma, WA 98418
Phone: 253-683-4246
Email: scholarships@nfpaonline.org
http://www.nfpaonline.org/nfpascholarship
Purpose: To support foster youth.
Eligibility: Applicants must be foster children, adopted children or biological children of currently licensed foster parents who are high school seniors planning to attend a college or university.
Target applicant(s): High school students.
Amount: Varies.
Number of awards: Varies.
Deadline: March 15.
How to apply: Applications are available online.
Exclusive: Visit www.UltimateScholarshipBook.com and enter code NA271820 for updates on this award.

(2719) · National Gymnastics Foundation Men's Scholarship

USA Gymnastics
Men's Scholarship Program, 132 E. Washington Street, Suite 700, Indianapolis, IN 46204
Phone: 317-237-5050
Email: dmcintyre@usagym.org
http://www.usagym.org
Purpose: To support competitive USA Gymnastics athlete members by helping to fund college or post-secondary education.
Eligibility: Applicants must be USA Gymnastics members and pursuing college or post-secondary education.
Target applicant(s): High school students. College students. Adult students.
Amount: Varies.
Number of awards: Varies.
Deadline: May 15.
How to apply: Applications are available online.
Exclusive: Visit www.UltimateScholarshipBook.com and enter code US271920 for updates on this award.

(2720) · National Hispanic Health Professional Student Scholarship

National Hispanic Health Foundation
The New York Academy of Medicine, 1216 Fifth Avenue, Room 457, New York, NY 10029
Phone: 212-419-3686
Email: nhhf@nhmafoundation.org

http://www.nhmafoundation.org
Purpose: To support Hispanic students who are planning to pursue careers in health care.
Eligibility: Applicants must be Hispanic students who are enrolled in a postsecondary degree program in allied health, dentistry, medicine, nursing, health research, public health or health management and policy analysis. Selection is based on academic achievement, leadership skills and commitment to improving health care in the Hispanic community.
Target applicant(s): College students. Graduate school students. Adult students.
Amount: Varies.
Number of awards: 20.
Deadline: October 6.
How to apply: Applications are available online. An application form and supporting materials are required.
Exclusive: Visit www.UltimateScholarshipBook.com and enter code NA272020 for updates on this award.

(2721) • National Italian American Foundation Scholarship

National Italian American Foundation
1860 19th Street NW, Washington, DC 20009
Phone: 202-387-0600
Email: scholarships@niaf.org
https://www.niaf.org/programs/scholarships-overview/
Purpose: To support Italian American students.
Eligibility: Applicants must be Italian American students who demonstrate outstanding academic achievement and must either be a member or child of a member. Applicants must also plan to be or currently be enrolled in an accredited institution of higher education, have a minimum 3.5 GPA and be U.S. citizens or permanent residents.
Target applicant(s): High school students. College students. Adult students.
Minimum GPA: 3.5
Amount: $2,500-$12,000.
Number of awards: Varies.
Deadline: March 1.
How to apply: Applications are available online.
Exclusive: Visit www.UltimateScholarshipBook.com and enter code NA272120 for updates on this award.

(2722) • National Medical Fellowships Emergency Scholarship Fund

National Medical Fellowships Inc.
347 Fifth Avenue, Suite 510, New York, NY 10016
Phone: 212-483-8880
Email: scholarships@nmfonline.org
http://www.nmfonline.org
Purpose: To aid minority medical students who are in need of emergency funding.
Eligibility: Applicants must be African-American, Latino, Native American, Alaska Natives, Native Hawaiians, Vietnamese or Cambodian. They must be third- or fourth-year medical students who are in need of immediate, emergency funding for living expenses and/or tuition. Selection is based on the overall strength of the application.
Target applicant(s): Graduate school students. Adult students.
Amount: Up to $5,000.
Number of awards: Varies.
Deadline: Varies.
How to apply: Applications are available by request. An application form, two personal essays, financial information and one letter of support are required.
Exclusive: Visit www.UltimateScholarshipBook.com and enter code NA272220 for updates on this award.

(2723) • National Pathfinder Scholarship

National Federation of Republican Women
124 North Alfred Street, Alexandria, VA 22314
Phone: 703-548-9688
Email: mail@nfrw.org
http://www.nfrw.org
Purpose: To honor former First Lady Nancy Reagan.
Eligibility: Applicants must be female college sophomores, juniors, seniors or master's degree students. Two one-page essays and three letters of recommendation are required. Previous winners may not reapply.
Target applicant(s): College students. Graduate school students. Adult students.
Amount: $2,500.
Number of awards: 3.
Deadline: June 1.
How to apply: Applications are available online. An application form, three letters of recommendation, transcript, two essays and State Federation President Certification are required.
Exclusive: Visit www.UltimateScholarshipBook.com and enter code NA272320 for updates on this award.

(2724) • National Scholarship

National Association of Negro Business and Professional Women's Clubs Inc.
1806 New Hampshire Avenue NW, Washington, DC 20009-3298
Phone: 202-483-4206
Email: info@nanbpwc.org
http://www.nanbpwc.org
Purpose: To award scholarships to aspiring business and professional college or university students.
Eligibility: Applicants must be African American graduating high school seniors and have a minimum 3.0 GPA. Students must submit a transcript, an application form, two letters of recommendation and an essay that is at least 300 words on "Why is education important to me?"
Target applicant(s): High school students.
Minimum GPA: 3.0
Amount: Varies.
Number of awards: Varies.
Deadline: March 1.
How to apply: Applications are available online.
Exclusive: Visit www.UltimateScholarshipBook.com and enter code NA272420 for updates on this award.

(2725) • Native American Education Grant

Presbyterian Church (USA)
100 Witherspoon Street, Louisville, KY 40202
Phone: 800-728-7228 x5224
Email: finaid@pcusa.org
https://www.presbyterianmission.org/what-we-do/grants-scholarships/
Purpose: To aid Alaska Natives and Native Americans pursuing full-time post-secondary education.
Eligibility: Applicants must be U.S. citizens who are high school graduates or G.E.D. recipients and demonstrate financial need and

must have a minimum 2.5 GPA. Applicants must present proof of tribal membership, and preference will be given to active members of the Presbyterian Church. Students are selected based on the availability of funds and best match to donor restrictions. The deadline for students applying to renew the grant is May 1. Awards for new students will be offered on a funds available basis after May 1.
Target applicant(s): College students. Adult students.
Minimum GPA: 2.5
Amount: Up to $1,500.
Number of awards: Varies.
Scholarship may be renewable.
Deadline: May 15.
How to apply: Applications are available online.
Exclusive: Visit www.UltimateScholarshipBook.com and enter code PR272520 for updates on this award.

(2726) · NCWIT Award for Aspirations in Computing

National Center for Women and Information Technology (NCWIT)
University of Colorado, Campus Box 322 UCB, Boulder, CO 80309
Phone: 303-735-6671
Email: aspirations @ncwit.org
http://www.ncwit.org
Purpose: To recognize young women who are interested in technology-related pursuits.
Eligibility: Applicants must be U.S. residents and be female high school students. They must be interested in technology-related subjects. Selection is based on aptitude for computing and internet technology, leadership skills, academic merit and educational goals.
Target applicant(s): High school students.
Amount: $500.
Number of awards: Varies.
Deadline: November 7.
How to apply: Applications are available online. An application form and supporting materials are required.
Exclusive: Visit www.UltimateScholarshipBook.com and enter code NA272620 for updates on this award.

(2727) · NMF National Alumni Council Scholarship Program

National Medical Fellowships Inc.
347 Fifth Avenue, Suite 510, New York, NY 10016
Phone: 212-483-8880
Email: scholarships@nmfonline.org
http://www.nmfonline.org
Purpose: To support minority medical students demonstrating community service dedication.
Eligibility: Applicants must be fourth-year medical students at an accredited U.S. medical school and members of an underrepresented minority group. Students must demonstrate community service and leadership potential.
Target applicant(s): Graduate school students. Adult students.
Amount: $5,000.
Number of awards: 8.
Deadline: Varies.
How to apply: Applications are available online.
Exclusive: Visit www.UltimateScholarshipBook.com and enter code NA272720 for updates on this award.

(2728) · NOAA Educational Partnership Program Undergraduate Scholarships

NOAA Educational Partnership Program - Office of Education
Herbert C Hoover Building, 14th Street and Constitution Ave NW, Room 6863, Washington, DC 20230
Phone: 202-482-3384
Email: EPP.USP@noaa.gov
http://www.epp.noaa.gov
Purpose: To aid undergraduates who are attending a minority serving institution and are pursuing undergraduate degrees in subjects related to the atmospheric, oceanic or environmental sciences.
Eligibility: Applicants must be U.S. citizens and full-time undergraduates who are in the second year of a four-year degree program or in the third year of a five-year degree program. They must be attending an accredited minority serving institution (MSI), and they must have a GPA of 3.2 or higher on a four-point scale. Applicants must be majoring in a discipline that is related to environmental, atmospheric or oceanic sciences. Selection is based on relevant coursework completed, stated career goals, recommendations and extracurricular activities.
Target applicant(s): College students. Adult students.
Minimum GPA: 3.2
Amount: Varies.
Number of awards: Varies.
Scholarship may be renewable.
Deadline: January 31.
How to apply: Applications are available online. An application form, two personal essays, two recommendation letters and an official transcript are required.
Exclusive: Visit www.UltimateScholarshipBook.com and enter code NO272820 for updates on this award.

(2729) · Northrop Grumman/HENAAC Scholars Program

Great Minds in STEM (HENAAC)
602 Monterey Pass Road, Monterey Park, CA 91754
Phone: 323-262-0997
Email: jcano@greatmindsinstem.org
http://www.greatmindsinstem.org
Purpose: To aid Hispanic undergraduates who are studying naval architecture, computer science, computer engineering, electrical engineering or systems engineering.
Eligibility: Applicants must be undergraduates who have completed at least one academic year of college and must have a minimum 3.0 GPA. They must demonstrate leadership experience. Selection is based on the overall strength of the application.
Target applicant(s): High school students. College students. Graduate school students. Adult students.
Minimum GPA: 3.0
Amount: Up to $10,000.
Number of awards: Varies.
Deadline: April 30.
How to apply: Applications are available online. An application form, personal essay, transcript, letters of recommendation and resume are required.
Exclusive: Visit www.UltimateScholarshipBook.com and enter code GR272920 for updates on this award.

(2730) · OCA-AXA Achievement Scholarship

OCA (formerly Organization of Chinese Americans)
1322 18th Street NW, Washington, DC 20036

Phone: 202-223-5500
Email: oca@ocanational.org
http://www.ocanational.org
Purpose: To help Asian Pacific American students.
Eligibility: Applicants must be entering their first year of college and be U.S. citizens or permanent residents. They must have a GPA of 3.0 or higher and demonstrate academic achievement, leadership ability and community service.
Target applicant(s): High school students.
Minimum GPA: 3.0
Amount: Up to $25,000.
Number of awards: 52.
Deadline: December 15.
How to apply: Applications are available online. An application form, resume, essay, transcript, copy of acceptance letter, summary of college costs and Student Aid Report are required.
Exclusive: Visit www.UltimateScholarshipBook.com and enter code OC273020 for updates on this award.

(2731) • OCA/UPS Gold Mountain Scholarship

OCA (formerly Organization of Chinese Americans)
1322 18th Street NW, Washington, DC 20036
Phone: 202-223-5500
Email: oca@ocanational.org
http://www.ocanational.org
Purpose: To support first generation Asian American students.
Eligibility: Applicants must be Asian Pacific Americans who intend to begin college in the fall of the year of application and must demonstrate significant financial need. Applicants must also be the first in their family to attend college and have a minimum 3.0 GPA.
Target applicant(s): High school students.
Minimum GPA: 3.0
Amount: $2,000.
Number of awards: 15.
Deadline: January 10.
How to apply: Applications are available online or by written request.
Exclusive: Visit www.UltimateScholarshipBook.com and enter code OC273120 for updates on this award.

(2732) • Olive Lynn Salembier Memorial Reentry Scholarship

Society of Women Engineers
130 East Randolph Street, Suite 3500, Chicago, IL 60601
Phone: 877-793-4636
Email: scholarships@swe.org
http://societyofwomenengineers.swe.org/scholarships
Purpose: To aid female engineering students.
Eligibility: Applicants must be females who have been out of the engineering work force and out of school for a minimum of two years prior to reentry, Applicants must have a GPA of 3.0 or higher on a four-point scale except for first year reentry. Selection is based on the overall strength of the application.
Target applicant(s): High school students. College students. Graduate school students. Adult students.
Minimum GPA: 3.0
Amount: $1,500.
Number of awards: 1.
Deadline: February 15.
How to apply: Applications are available online. An application form and supporting materials are required.
Exclusive: Visit www.UltimateScholarshipBook.com and enter code SO273220 for updates on this award.

(2733) • P.A. Margaronis Scholarships

American Hellenic Education Progressive Association
1909 Q Street NW, Suite 500, Washington, DC 20009
Phone: 202-232-6300
Email: ahepa@ahepa.org
https://ahepa.org/Education-Scholarships.htm
Purpose: To support undergraduate and graduate students who are of Greek descent.
Eligibility: Applicants must have a minimum 3.0 GPA and submit an essay and two letters of recommendation.
Target applicant(s): High school students. College students. Graduate school students. Adult students.
Minimum GPA: 3.0
Amount: Up to $2,000.
Number of awards: Varies.
Deadline: March 31.
How to apply: Applications are available online.
Exclusive: Visit www.UltimateScholarshipBook.com and enter code AM273320 for updates on this award.

(2734) • P.E.O. Program for Continuing Education

PEO International
3700 Grand Avenue, Des Moines, IA 50312
Phone: 515-255-3153
http://www.peointernational.org
Purpose: To assist women whose education has been interrupted.
Eligibility: Applicants must be women who are resuming studies to improve their marketable skills due to changing demands in their lives. They must have financial need and cannot use the funds to pay living expenses or repay educational loans. They must be sponsored by a P.E.O. chapter and be citizens and students of the United States or Canada. They must have had at least two consecutive years as a non-student in their adult lives and be able to complete their educational goals in two consecutive years or less. Doctoral degree students are not eligible.
Target applicant(s): College students. Graduate school students. Adult students.
Amount: $3,000.
Number of awards: Varies.
Deadline: 10 weeks before the start of classes.
How to apply: Applications are available from your local P.E.O. Chapter. An application form, income and expense statement and chapter recommendation are required. See website to locate nearest P.E.O. Chapter.
Exclusive: Visit www.UltimateScholarshipBook.com and enter code PE273420 for updates on this award.

(2735) • P.O. Pistilli Undergraduate Scholarship for Advancement in Computer Science and Electrical Engineering

Design Automation Conference/Association for Computing Machinery
Professor Andrew B. Kahng, P.O. Pistilli Scholarship Director, Department of Computer Science and Engineering, UCSD, 9500 Gilman Drive #0404, La Jolla, CA 92093
Phone: 858-822-4884
Email: abk@cs.ucsd.edu
http://www.dac.com

Purpose: To promote professions in electrical engineering, computer engineering and computer science among underrepresented groups.
Eligibility: Applicants must be high school seniors who are from an underrepresented group (African American, Hispanic, Native American, women or disabled). Students must have a minimum 3.0 GPA, have demonstrated high achievement in math and science courses and have financial need. Applicants must also intend to pursue a career in electrical engineering, computer engineering or computer science.
Target applicant(s): High school students.
Minimum GPA: 3.0
Amount: $4,000.
Number of awards: Up to 7.
Scholarship may be renewable.
Deadline: March 10.
How to apply: Applications are available online. An application form, three letters of recommendation, an official transcript, a personal letter, a copy of tax returns and a copy of the FAFSA are required.
Exclusive: Visit www.UltimateScholarshipBook.com and enter code DE273520 for updates on this award.

(2736) • Parents, Families and Friends of Lesbians and Gays General Scholarships

Parents, Families and Friends of Lesbians and Gays (PFLAG)
1828 L Street NW, Suite 660, Washington, DC 20036
Phone: 202-467-8180
Email: info@pflag.org
http://www.pflag.org
Purpose: To provide educational opportunities for the LGBTQ community.
Eligibility: Applicants must identify themselves as gay, lesbian, bisexual or transgender or be an ally of the LGBTQ community. Students must be graduating from high school in the year of application or have graduated the previous year. They must have applied to an accredited college or university to attend for the first time, and they must demonstrate interest in serving the LGBTQ community.
Target applicant(s): High school students.
Amount: Varies.
Number of awards: Varies.
Deadline: May 15.
How to apply: Applications are available online.
Exclusive: Visit www.UltimateScholarshipBook.com and enter code PA273620 for updates on this award.

(2737) • Paumanauke Native American Indian Scholarship

Paumanauke Native American Festival, Inc.
2005 Merrick Road, Suite 221, Attn.: Tony Moon Hawk Langhorn, Merrick, NY 11566
http://www.paumanauke.org
Purpose: To encourage Native American Indians to finish their college educations.
Eligibility: Applicants must be members of a Native American Indian tribe who are enrolled full-time at a college, university or other accredited post-secondary institution. Selection is based on the overall strength of the application.
Target applicant(s): College students. Graduate school students. Adult students.
Amount: $500.
Number of awards: 6.
Deadline: June 1.
How to apply: Applications are available online.
Exclusive: Visit www.UltimateScholarshipBook.com and enter code PA273720 for updates on this award.

(2738) • PEO International Peace Scholarship

PEO International
3700 Grand Avenue, Des Moines, IA 50312
Phone: 515-255-3153
http://www.peointernational.org
Purpose: Women from countries other than the U.S. or Canada are assisted in their graduate studies within North America.
Eligibility: Applicants must be female, attend a North American graduate school or Cottey College and be from a country other than the U.S. or Canada. Eligibility must be established by submitting an eligibility form between August 15 and December 15.
Target applicant(s): College students. Graduate school students. Adult students.
Amount: Up to $12,500.
Number of awards: Varies.
Scholarship may be renewable.
Deadline: December 15.
How to apply: Applicants must first submit an eligibility form, available online. If found eligible, students will be mailed application materials.
Exclusive: Visit www.UltimateScholarshipBook.com and enter code PE273820 for updates on this award.

(2739) • Phyllis G. Meekins Scholarship

Ladies Professional Golf Association
100 International Golf Drive, Daytona Beach, FL 32124-1092
Phone: 386-274-6200
Email: info@lpgafoundation.org
http://www.lpga.com/lpga-foundation/scholarships
Purpose: To support a female high school senior golf participant of a recognized minority background in pursuit of a college education.
Eligibility: Applicants must have a 3.0 GPA and be a U.S. citizen or legal resident. Students must also have been accepted to a college or university and plan to play competitive golf at the collegiate level. Selection is based on financial need.
Target applicant(s): High school students.
Minimum GPA: 3.0
Amount: $1,250.
Number of awards: 1.
Deadline: April 30.
How to apply: Applications available online.
Exclusive: Visit www.UltimateScholarshipBook.com and enter code LA273920 for updates on this award.

(2740) • Polish National Alliance Scholarship

Polish National Alliance
Educational Department, 6100 Cicero Avenue, Chicago, IL 60646
Phone: 800-621-3723
Email: pna@pna-znp.org
http://www.pna-znp.org
Purpose: To assist members of the Polish National Alliance with their undergraduate studies.
Eligibility: Applicants must be college sophomores, juniors or seniors and have been paying members in good standing with the Polish National Association for at least three years and must have a minimum 3.0 GPA. If the applicant has been in good standing with the PNA

for at least two years, his or her parents must have been paying PNA members for at least five years.
Target applicant(s): College students. Adult students.
Minimum GPA: 3.0
Amount: Varies.
Number of awards: Varies.
Scholarship may be renewable.
Deadline: April 15.
How to apply: Applications are available by email at mary.srodon@pna-znp.org.
Exclusive: Visit www.UltimateScholarshipBook.com and enter code PO274020 for updates on this award.

(2741) • Prince Kuhio Hawaiian Civic Club Scholarship

Prince Kuhio Hawaiian Civic Club
P.O. Box 4728, Honolulu, HI 96812
Phone: 808-678-0321
Email: andreahamilton808@gmail.com
http://www.pkhcc.com
Purpose: To provide funds for higher education to Hawaiians.
Eligibility: Applicants must be high school seniors or current college students from Hawaii. Preference is given to students who have some Hawaiian ancestry and have participated in community service or volunteer work. Studies of Hawaiian language, studies and culture, journalism and education are encouraged. Applicants must enroll full-time at a two- or four-year institution.
Target applicant(s): High school students. College students. Adult students.
Amount: $500-$1,000.
Number of awards: Varies.
Scholarship may be renewable.
Deadline: April 1.
How to apply: Applications are available online or by mail.
Exclusive: Visit www.UltimateScholarshipBook.com and enter code PR274120 for updates on this award.

(2742) • Professional Woman's Magazine Scholarship Opportunity

Professional Woman's Magazine
18 Technology Drive, Suite 170, Irvine, CA 92618
Phone: 888-562-9662
https://www.professionalwomanmag.com/scholarship-opportunity/
Purpose: To support students who are female undergraduate students.
Eligibility: Applicants must be U.S. citizens, female and undergraduate level students. Students must submit an essay describing their college experience so far and future career plans. Graphic or creative presentations are also accepted. Selection is based upon a genuine desire to use the scholarship to advance in a selected field of study and an overall passion for knowledge.
Target applicant(s): High school students. College students. Adult students.
Amount: $500.
Deadline: August 15.
How to apply: Applications are available online.
Exclusive: Visit www.UltimateScholarshipBook.com and enter code PR274220 for updates on this award.

(2743) • PRSA Diversity Multicultural Scholarship

Public Relations Student Society of America
33 Maiden Lane, 11th Floor, New York, NY 10038
Phone: 212-460-1474
Email: prssa@prsa.org
http://prssa.prsa.org/scholarships-and-awards/
Purpose: To aid minority communications students.
Eligibility: Applicants must be of African-American, Latino, Asian, Native American, Alaska Native or Pacific Islander descent. They must be undergraduates of at least junior standing who are majoring in communications at an accredited four-year institution. They must be full-time students who have a GPA of 3.0 or higher on a four-point scale. Selection is based on the overall strength of the application.
Target applicant(s): College students. Adult students.
Minimum GPA: 3.0
Amount: $1,500.
Number of awards: 2.
Deadline: May 9.
How to apply: Applications are available online. An application form, official transcript, essay and one recommendation letter are required.
Exclusive: Visit www.UltimateScholarshipBook.com and enter code PU274320 for updates on this award.

(2744) • Que Llueva Cafe Scholarship

Chicano Organizing and Research in Education
P.O. Box 160144, Sacramento, CA 95816
Email: jdelrazo@ca-core.org
http://www.ca-core.org
Purpose: To aid undocumented Latino students who wish to attend college.
Eligibility: Applicants must be graduating high school seniors, high school graduates or GED recipients who are legally undocumented residents of the U.S. They must have plans to enroll at an accredited postsecondary institution located in the U.S. or Puerto Rico. They must show academic promise and demonstrate financial need. Selection is based on the overall strength of the application.
Target applicant(s): High school students.
Amount: Varies.
Number of awards: Varies.
Deadline: February 25.
How to apply: Applications are available online. An application form, transcript, one letter of recommendation, a personal essay and a financial need statement are required.
Exclusive: Visit www.UltimateScholarshipBook.com and enter code CH274420 for updates on this award.

(2745) • Richard R. Tufenkian Memorial Scholarship

Armenian Educational Foundation Inc.
600 W. Broadway, Suite 130, Glendale, CA 91204
Phone: 818-242-4154
Email: aef@aefweb.org
http://www.aefweb.org
Purpose: To support Armenian undergraduate students.
Eligibility: Applicants must be full-time undergraduate students of Armenian descent at U.S. universities, have a minimum 3.0 GPA, demonstrate financial need and be involved in the Armenian community. Tax returns, transcripts, two reference letters, essays and applications are required.
Target applicant(s): High school students. College students. Adult students.

Minimum GPA: 3.0
Amount: $3,000.
Number of awards: 3.
Deadline: July 31.
How to apply: Applications are available online.
Exclusive: Visit www.UltimateScholarshipBook.com and enter code AR274520 for updates on this award.

(2746) • Rockwell Automation Scholarship

Society of Women Engineers
130 East Randolph Street, Suite 3500, Chicago, IL 60601
Phone: 877-793-4636
Email: scholarships@swe.org
http://societyofwomenengineers.swe.org/scholarships
Purpose: To aid female undergraduates who are studying engineering, computer science or engineering technology.
Eligibility: Applicants must be sophomores who are majoring in computer engineering, computer science, electrical engineering, engineering technology, industrial engineering, mechanical engineering, manufacturing engineering or software engineering. They must have a GPA of 3.0 or higher on a four-point scale and must demonstrate leadership ability. Selection is based on the overall strength of the application.
Target applicant(s): College students. Adult students.
Minimum GPA: 3.0
Amount: $2,500.
Number of awards: 2.
Deadline: February 15.
How to apply: Applications are available online. An application form and supporting materials are required.
Exclusive: Visit www.UltimateScholarshipBook.com and enter code SO274620 for updates on this award.

(2747) • Rockwell Collins Scholarship

Society of Women Engineers
130 East Randolph Street, Suite 3500, Chicago, IL 60601
Phone: 877-793-4636
Email: scholarships@swe.org
http://societyofwomenengineers.swe.org/scholarships
Purpose: To aid female undergraduates who are majoring in engineering, engineering technology or computer science.
Eligibility: Applicants must be sophomores, juniors or seniors who are majoring in mechanical engineering, industrial engineering, manufacturing engineering, software engineering, computer engineering, electrical engineering, engineering technology or computer science. They must have a GPA of 3.0 or higher on a four-point scale. Selection is based on the overall strength of the application.
Target applicant(s): College students. Adult students.
Minimum GPA: 3.0
Amount: $2,500.
Number of awards: 2.
Deadline: February 15.
How to apply: Applications are available online. An application form and supporting materials are required.
Exclusive: Visit www.UltimateScholarshipBook.com and enter code SO274720 for updates on this award.

(2748) • Ron Brown Scholar Program

CAP Charitable Foundation
Ron Brown Scholar Program, 1160 Pepsi Place, Suite 206, Charlottesville, VA 22901
Phone: 434-964-1588
Email: franh@ronbrown.org
http://www.ronbrown.org
Purpose: To award scholarships to academically talented, highly motivated African American high school seniors.
Eligibility: Applicants must be African American collegebound high school seniors. Selection is based on academic promise, leadership, communication skills, school and community involvement and financial need.
Target applicant(s): High school students.
Amount: $40,000.
Number of awards: Varies.
Scholarship may be renewable.
Deadline: January 9.
How to apply: Applications are available online.
Exclusive: Visit www.UltimateScholarshipBook.com and enter code CA274820 for updates on this award.

(2749) • Rosa L. Parks Scholarship

Conference of Minority Transportation Officials
100 M Street SE, Suite 917, Washington, DC 20003
Phone: 202-857-8065
Email: info@comto.org
http://www.comto.org/page/Scholarships
Purpose: To support graduating high school students whose parents are COMTO members and college or graduate students who are studying fields related to transportation.
Eligibility: Applicants must have at least a 3.0 GPA. High school students must be accepted into a college or technical school, and their parents must have been COMTO members in good standing for at least the past year. College students must have at least 60 credits, and graduate students must have at least 15 credits.
Target applicant(s): High school students. College students. Graduate school students. Adult students.
Minimum GPA: 3.0
Amount: $4,500.
Number of awards: Varies.
Deadline: March 10.
How to apply: Applications are available online.
Exclusive: Visit www.UltimateScholarshipBook.com and enter code CO274920 for updates on this award.

(2750) • RRHolmes Scholarship

RRHolmes Scholarship Organization for Caribbean Advancement Inc.
P.O. Box 810, Snellville, GA 30078
Phone: 678-612-4161
Email: rrholmes@rrhsoca.com
http://www.rrhsoca.com/scholarship-application/
Purpose: To support students with ties to the Caribbean.
Eligibility: Applicants must hail from the Caribbean or be of Caribbean descent and be attending a U.S. college or university. Students must complete the application in full and provide proof of heritage along with transcripts and letters of recommendation.
Target applicant(s): High school students. College students. Graduate school students. Adult students.

Amount: $1,500.
Number of awards: 2.
Deadline: September 1.
How to apply: Applications are available online.
Exclusive: Visit www.UltimateScholarshipBook.com and enter code RR275020 for updates on this award.

(2751) • Scholarships for Social Justice

Higher Education Consortium for Urban Affairs
2233 University Avenue W, Suite 210, St. Paul, MN 55114
Phone: 651-287-3300
Email: hecua@hecua.org
https://hecua.org/logistics/scholarships/
Purpose: To support students from low-income families, students from ethnic minorities and students who are the first in their families to attend college.
Eligibility: Students must have submitted an application to one of HECUA's semester programs, and they must be enrolled at an HECUA member institution. A list of member institutions is available online.
Target applicant(s): College students. Adult students.
Amount: $1,500.
Number of awards: Varies.
Deadline: April 15 (fall), December 1 (spring).
How to apply: Applications are available online. An essay, letter of recommendation and Student Aid Report from completing the Free Application for Federal Student Aid are required.
Exclusive: Visit www.UltimateScholarshipBook.com and enter code HI275120 for updates on this award.

(2752) • Sequoyah Graduate Scholarships

Association on American Indian Affairs
Lisa Wyzlic, Director of Scholarship Programs, 966 Hungerford Drive, Suite 12-B, Rockville, MD 20850
Phone: 240-314-7155
Email: lw.aaia@indian-affairs.org
https://www.indian-affairs.org/scholarships.html
Purpose: To provide graduate fellowships for students of American Indian and Alaskan Native heritage.
Eligibility: Applicants must be full-time students who can provide proof of tribal enrollment and an essay on educational goals.
Target applicant(s): Graduate school students. Adult students.
Amount: $1,500.
Number of awards: Varies.
Deadline: May 1.
How to apply: Applications are available online.
Exclusive: Visit www.UltimateScholarshipBook.com and enter code AS275220 for updates on this award.

(2753) • Sharon D. Banks Memorial Undergraduate Scholarship

Women's Transportation Seminar (WTS) International
1701 K Street NW, Suite 800, Washington, DC 20006
Phone: 202-955-5085
Email: membership@wtsinternational.org
https://www.wtsinternational.org/
Purpose: To help women pursuing transportation careers with their higher education expenses.
Eligibility: Applicants must be women enrolled in undergraduate programs related to transportation studies. Selection is based on the applicant's academic record, transportation-related activities, job skills and specific transportation goals.
Target applicant(s): College students. Adult students.
Amount: $5,000.
Number of awards: Varies.
Deadline: Varies.
How to apply: Applications are available through a local chapter.
Exclusive: Visit www.UltimateScholarshipBook.com and enter code WO275320 for updates on this award.

(2754) • SHPE Scholarship Program

Society of Hispanic Professional Engineers
13181 Crossroads Parkway North, Suite 450, City of Industry, CA 91746
Phone: 323-725-3970
Email: scholarships@shpe.org
http://scholarships.shpe.org/
Purpose: To aid Hispanic students who are majoring in science, engineering or construction-related subjects.
Eligibility: Applicants must be members of the Society of Hispanic Professional Engineers (SHPE). They must be current undergraduates or entering graduate students who are pursuing degrees in engineering, science or a construction-related discipline. They must have a GPA of 3.0 or higher. Selection is based on the overall strength of the application.
Target applicant(s): College students. Graduate school students. Adult students.
Minimum GPA: 3.0
Amount: Varies.
Number of awards: Varies.
Deadline: July 31.
How to apply: Applications are available online. An application form, official transcript, resume, personal statement and two recommendation letters are required.
Exclusive: Visit www.UltimateScholarshipBook.com and enter code SO275420 for updates on this award.

(2755) • Snapology STEM Studies Scholarship

Snapology
1699 Washington Road, Pittsburgh, PA 15228
Phone: 412-780-2996
Email: scholarship@snapology.com
https://www.snapology.com/scholarships
Purpose: To support female students in STEM studies.
Eligibility: Applicants must be female graduating high school seniors and be enrolling at an accredited institution to pursue a STEM education. Applicants must demonstrate academic achievement and financial need.
Target applicant(s): High school students.
Amount: $1,000.
Number of awards: 1.
Deadline: April 15.
How to apply: Applications are available online.
Exclusive: Visit www.UltimateScholarshipBook.com and enter code SN275520 for updates on this award.

(2756) • St. Andrew's Society of Washington, DC Scholarship

St. Andrew's Society of Washington, DC
Chairman, Scholarships Committee, P.O. Box 7849, Washington, DC 20044

Email: scholarships@saintandrewsociety.org
http://www.saintandrewsociety.org/scholarships/
Purpose: To assist students of Scottish birth or descent.
Eligibility: Applicants must be of Scottish birth or descent and be able to cite their Scottish descent. U.S. citizens must be permanent residents of the District of Columbia, Delaware, Maryland, New Jersey, North Carolina, West Virginia, Pennsylvania or Virginia. Students must also demonstrate financial need and academic achievement. Attention will be given to work that enhances the "knowledge of Scottish history or culture."
Target applicant(s): College students. Graduate school students. Adult students.
Amount: Varies.
Number of awards: Varies.
Deadline: April 30.
How to apply: Applications are available online.
Exclusive: Visit www.UltimateScholarshipBook.com and enter code ST275620 for updates on this award.

(2757) · SWE Exelon Corporation Scholarship

Society of Women Engineers
130 East Randolph Street, Suite 3500, Chicago, IL 60601
Phone: 877-793-4636
Email: scholarships@swe.org
http://societyofwomenengineers.swe.org/scholarships
Purpose: To aid female students who plan to major in electrical engineering or mechanical engineering.
Eligibility: Applicants must be female and must be rising undergraduate freshmen who are planning to major in electrical engineering or mechanical engineering at an ABET-approved college or university. They must plan to enroll on a full-time basis and must have a GPA of 3.5 or higher on a four-point scale.
Target applicant(s): High school students.
Minimum GPA: 3.5
Amount: $5,000.
Number of awards: 5.
Deadline: May 1.
How to apply: Applications are available online. An application form, transcript, two recommendation letters and proof of college acceptance are required.
Exclusive: Visit www.UltimateScholarshipBook.com and enter code SO275720 for updates on this award.

(2758) · SWE Past Presidents Scholarship

Society of Women Engineers
130 East Randolph Street, Suite 3500, Chicago, IL 60601
Phone: 877-793-4636
Email: scholarships@swe.org
http://societyofwomenengineers.swe.org/scholarships
Purpose: To aid female engineering students.
Eligibility: Applicants must be U.S. citizens and be graduate students or undergraduate sophomores, juniors or seniors. They must be enrolled in an ABET-accredited engineering degree program and have a GPA of 3.0 or higher on a four-point scale. Selection is based on the overall strength of the application.
Target applicant(s): College students. Graduate school students. Adult students.
Minimum GPA: 3.0
Amount: $2,000.
Number of awards: 2.
Deadline: February 15.
How to apply: Applications are available online. An application form and supporting materials are required.
Exclusive: Visit www.UltimateScholarshipBook.com and enter code SO275820 for updates on this award.

(2759) · Taiwanese American Scholarship Fund

Taiwanese American Scholarship Fund
1145 Wilshire Boulevard, Suite 105, First floor, Los Angeles, CA 90017
Phone: 213-624-6400 x 6
Email: scholarships@apcf.org
http://tascholarshipfund.org
Purpose: To assist Taiwanese American students with financial need.
Eligibility: Applicants must be U.S. citizens or permanent residents and direct blood descendants of a Taiwanese citizen. Students must also be a high school senior or first-year college student with a minimum 3.0 GPA and have a household income level below the federal, state or county low-income level.
Target applicant(s): High school students. College students. Adult students.
Minimum GPA: 3.0
Amount: $5,000.
Number of awards: 10.
Deadline: March 27.
How to apply: Applications are available online. The application form, three references and official transcript are required.
Exclusive: Visit www.UltimateScholarshipBook.com and enter code TA275920 for updates on this award.

(2760) · TheDream.US Scholarship

TheDream.US
One Scholarship Way, Saint Peter, MN 56082
Phone: 507-931-1682
http://thedream.us
Purpose: To support immigrant students in pursuing post-secondary education.
Eligibility: Applicants must be graduating seniors who intend to enroll full-time in an associate's or bachelor's degree program at one of TheDream.US Partner Colleges. Students must have come to the U.S. before their 16th birthday and must demonstrate significant unmet financial need.
Target applicant(s): High school students.
Minimum GPA: 2.5
Amount: $25,000.
Number of awards: Varies.
Scholarship may be renewable.
Deadline: March 1.
How to apply: Applications are available online.
Exclusive: Visit www.UltimateScholarshipBook.com and enter code TH276020 for updates on this award.

(2761) · Thurgood Marshall College Scholarship Fund

Thurgood Marshall Scholarship Fund
901 F Street NW, Suite 300, Washington, DC 20004
Phone: 202-507-4851
Email: deshuandra.walker@tmcf.org
https://tmcf.org/our-scholarships
Purpose: To provide support to the nation's 47 historically black public colleges and universities by offering merit-based scholarships.

Eligibility: Applicants must be currently enrolled or planning to enroll as full-time students at one of the 47 TMSF member schools and have a minimum 3.0 high school GPA. Applicants must demonstrate a commitment to academic excellence and community service and show financial need. Winners need to maintain a 3.0 GPA for the duration of the scholarship. Applicants must submit a head shot photograph, letters of recommendation, essay and resume.
Target applicant(s): High school students. College students. Graduate school students. Adult students.
Minimum GPA: 3.0
Amount: $3,100.
Number of awards: Varies.
Scholarship may be renewable.
Deadline: Varies.
How to apply: Applications are available through the member schools.
Exclusive: Visit www.UltimateScholarshipBook.com and enter code TH276120 for updates on this award.

(2762) · Tom Joyner Foundation Denny's Hungry for Education Scholarship

Tom Joyner Foundation
P.O. Box 630495, Irving, TX 75063
Email: info@tomjoynerfoundation.org
http://tomjoynerfoundation.org
Purpose: To encourage students attending black colleges and universities to combat childhood hunger in their community.
Eligibility: Applicants must be currently enrolled at a Historically Black College or University (HBCU). Students must submit an idea for a program to combat childhood hunger in their HBCU communities.
Target applicant(s): High school students. College students. Adult students.
Amount: $2,000.
Number of awards: 9.
Deadline: Varies.
How to apply: Applications are available online.
Exclusive: Visit www.UltimateScholarshipBook.com and enter code TO276220 for updates on this award.

(2763) · Trailblazer Scholarship

Conference of Minority Transportation Officials
100 M Street SE, Suite 917, Washington, DC 20003
Phone: 202-857-8065
Email: info@comto.org
http://www.comto.org/page/Scholarships
Purpose: To support undergraduate and graduate students in the field of transportation.
Eligibility: Students must be in an undergraduate or graduate program enrolled in at least six credits per semester, and they must have at least a 2.5 GPA.
Target applicant(s): High school students. College students. Graduate school students. Adult students.
Minimum GPA: 2.5
Amount: $2,500.
Number of awards: Varies.
Deadline: May 8.
How to apply: Applications are available online.
Exclusive: Visit www.UltimateScholarshipBook.com and enter code CO276320 for updates on this award.

(2764) · Traub-Dicker Rainbow Scholarship

Stonewall Community Foundation
446 W. 33rd Street, New York, NY 10001
Phone: 212-367-1155
https://stonewallfoundation.org
Purpose: To support female LGBTQ students in pursuing post-secondary education.
Eligibility: Applicants must be incoming or current college students in any year of study, including graduate school. Selection is primarily based on demonstration of academic achievement, community service and desire to make a difference.
Target applicant(s): High school students. College students. Graduate school students. Adult students.
Amount: $3,000.
Number of awards: Varies.
Deadline: April 15.
How to apply: Applications are available online.
Exclusive: Visit www.UltimateScholarshipBook.com and enter code ST276420 for updates on this award.

(2765) · Truman D. Picard Scholarship

Intertribal Timber Council
Attn.: Education Committee, 1112 NE 21st Avenue, Suite 4, Portland, OR 97232
Phone: 503-282-4296
Email: itc1@teleport.com
http://www.itcnet.org/about_us/scholarships.html
Purpose: To promote the field of natural resources.
Eligibility: Applicants must be high school seniors or college students and must pursue the natural resources field. Applicants must submit a resume, letters of reference, validated enrollment in Tribe/Native Alaska Corporation and a letter about their interest in natural resources, educational background, academic achievements and financial need.
Target applicant(s): High school students. College students. Graduate school students. Adult students.
Amount: $2,000-$2,500.
Number of awards: Varies.
Deadline: February 7.
How to apply: There is no official application form.
Exclusive: Visit www.UltimateScholarshipBook.com and enter code IN276520 for updates on this award.

(2766) · U.S. Lacrosse Native American Scholarships

Tewaaraton Foundation
1135 16th Street NW, Washington, DC 20036
Phone: 202-255-1485
Email: sarah@tewaaraton.com
http://www.tewaaraton.com
Purpose: To acknowledge and reward students' academic and athletic achievement in the sport of lacrosse.
Eligibility: Applicants must be a member of the Iroquois community, enrolled in a secondary school and in good academic standing. Scholarships are awarded based on academic achievement, athletic performance and ambition.
Target applicant(s): High school students.
Amount: $5,000.
Number of awards: 2.
Deadline: April 20.

How to apply: Applications are available online. An application form, an essay, two letters of recommendation, a high school transcript and a photograph of the applicant are required.
Exclusive: Visit www.UltimateScholarshipBook.com and enter code TE276620 for updates on this award.

(2767) • UBS/PaineWebber Scholarship

United Negro College Fund (UNCF)
1805 7th Street NW, Washington, DC 20001
Phone: 800-331-2244
https://scholarships.uncf.org/
Purpose: To help African American sophomores and juniors attending United Negro College Fund (UNCF) institutions and majoring in the field of business.
Eligibility: Applicants should demonstrate leadership skills and may major in accounting, business administration, economics, finance or any business-related major. Students should submit two recommendation letters, an essay, a resume, two small photos and a transcript. Applicants must have a minimum 3.0 GPA, complete the Free Application for Federal Student Aid (FAFSA) and have unmet financial need that is verified by the college or university financial aid office. Students are encouraged to complete the UNCF General Scholarship application to be matched with scholarships for which they meet the criteria.
Target applicant(s): College students. Adult students.
Minimum GPA: 3.0
Amount: $8,000.
Number of awards: Varies.
Scholarship may be renewable.
Deadline: December 8.
How to apply: Applications are available online.
Exclusive: Visit www.UltimateScholarshipBook.com and enter code UN276720 for updates on this award.

(2768) • UNCF-Foot Locker Foundation Inc. Scholarship

United Negro College Fund (UNCF)
1805 7th Street NW, Washington, DC 20001
Phone: 800-331-2244
https://scholarships.uncf.org/
Purpose: To support African American students attending UNCF member schools.
Eligibility: Applicants must be high school seniors or current college students planning to attend or attending a UNCF member college or university. Students must also have a minimum 2.5 GPA, complete the Free Application for Federal Student Aid (FAFSA) and have unmet financial need that is verified by the college or university financial aid office. Students are encouraged to complete the UNCF General Scholarship application to be matched with scholarships for which they meet the criteria.
Target applicant(s): High school students. College students. Adult students.
Minimum GPA: 2.5
Amount: Up to $5,000.
Number of awards: Varies.
Deadline: May 12.
How to apply: Applications are available online.
Exclusive: Visit www.UltimateScholarshipBook.com and enter code UN276820 for updates on this award.

(2769) • United Parcel Service Scholarship for Minority Students

Institute of Industrial and Systems Engineers
3577 Parkway Lane, Suite 200, Norcross, GA 30092
Phone: 800-494-0460
Email: bcameron@iienet.org
http://www.iise.org/
Purpose: To help minority undergraduate students in industrial engineering.
Eligibility: Applicants must be full-time undergraduate minority students enrolled in a college in the United States, Canada or Mexico with an accredited industrial engineering program, have at least a 3.4 GPA, major in industrial engineering and be active members. Students may not apply directly for this scholarship and must be nominated. The award is based on academic ability, character, leadership, potential service to the industrial engineering profession and financial need.
Target applicant(s): College students. Adult students.
Minimum GPA: 3.4
Amount: $4,000.
Number of awards: 1.
Deadline: November 15.
How to apply: Nomination forms are available online.
Exclusive: Visit www.UltimateScholarshipBook.com and enter code IN276920 for updates on this award.

(2770) • Upakar Foundation Indian American Community College Scholarship

Upakar Foundation
9015 Shady Grove Court, Gaithersburg, MD 20877
http://www.upakarfoundation.org
Purpose: To support Indian-American graduating seniors in pursuing post-secondary education at a community college.
Eligibility: Applicants must have been born in India or have at least one parent born in India. Students must be U.S. citizens or U.S. Green Card holders. A minimum GPA of 3.6 is required.
Target applicant(s): High school students.
Minimum GPA: 3.6
Amount: Varies.
Number of awards: Varies.
Scholarship may be renewable.
Deadline: April 30.
How to apply: Applications are available online.
Exclusive: Visit www.UltimateScholarshipBook.com and enter code UP277020 for updates on this award.

(2771) • UPS Hallmark Scholarship

U.S. Pan Asian American Chamber of Commerce
1329 18th Street NW, Washington, DC 20036
Phone: 800-696-7818
Email: info@uspaacc.com
http://uspaacc.com/
Purpose: To provide financial assistance to Asian American students.
Eligibility: Applicants must be high school seniors at least 16 years of age who are of Asian or Pacific heritage. They must be U.S. citizens or permanent residents and plan to enroll full-time at an accredited college or university in the United States in the fall following graduation. A minimum GPA of 3.3 is required, and applicants should demonstrate academic excellence, leadership, community service involvement and financial need.
Target applicant(s): High school students.

Minimum GPA: 3.3
Amount: Varies.
Number of awards: 2.
Deadline: March 13.
How to apply: Applications are available online.
Exclusive: Visit www.UltimateScholarshipBook.com and enter code U.277120 for updates on this award.

(2772) • USA Funds Scholarship

United Negro College Fund (UNCF)
1805 7th Street NW, Washington, DC 20001
Phone: 800-331-2244
https://scholarships.uncf.org/
Purpose: To help African American students attain a post-secondary education at a UNCF member college or university.
Eligibility: Applicants must have a minimum 2.5 GPA, complete the Free Application for Federal Student Aid (FAFSA) and have unmet financial need that is verified by the college or university financial aid office. Students are encouraged to complete the UNCF General Scholarship application to be matched with scholarships for which they meet the criteria.
Target applicant(s): High school students. College students. Adult students.
Minimum GPA: 2.5
Amount: Up to $5,000.
Number of awards: Varies.
Deadline: February 10.
How to apply: Applications are available online.
Exclusive: Visit www.UltimateScholarshipBook.com and enter code UN277220 for updates on this award.

(2773) • Visual Task Force Scholarship

National Association of Black Journalists
1100 Knight Hall, Suite 3100, College Park, MD 20742
Phone: 301-405-7520
Email: iwashington@nabj.org
http://nabj.site-ym.com/?page=SEEDScholarships
Purpose: To aid visual journalism students.
Eligibility: Applicants must be student members of the National Association of Black Journalists (NABJ). They must be enrolled in a four-year undergraduate degree program or a graduate program and must be concentrating in visual journalism. They must have a GPA of 2.75 or higher, have experience working in an on-campus media outlet and have completed an internship. Selection is based on the overall strength of the application.
Target applicant(s): College students. Graduate school students. Adult students.
Minimum GPA: 2.75
Amount: $1,500.
Number of awards: 2.
Deadline: March 21.
How to apply: Applications are available online. An application form and supporting materials are required.
Exclusive: Visit www.UltimateScholarshipBook.com and enter code NA277320 for updates on this award.

(2774) • William and Charlotte Cadbury Award

National Medical Fellowships Inc.
347 Fifth Avenue, Suite 510, New York, NY 10016
Phone: 212-483-8880
Email: scholarships@nmfonline.org
http://www.nmfonline.org
Purpose: To reward minority medical students with outstanding achievement.
Eligibility: Applicants must be senior minority medical students at an accredited U.S. medical school. Students must demonstrate outstanding academic achievement, leadership and community service.
Target applicant(s): Graduate school students. Adult students.
Amount: $5,000.
Number of awards: 1.
Deadline: April 21.
How to apply: Applications are available online.
Exclusive: Visit www.UltimateScholarshipBook.com and enter code NA277420 for updates on this award.

(2775) • William Wrigley Jr. Scholarship/Internship

United Negro College Fund (UNCF)
1805 7th Street NW, Washington, DC 20001
Phone: 800-331-2244
https://scholarships.uncf.org/
Purpose: To support African American engineering, business and chemistry students with scholarships and paid internships.
Eligibility: Applicants must be sophomores or juniors at a UNCF member college or university. They must demonstrate financial need and have a GPA of at least 2.5.
Target applicant(s): College students. Adult students.
Minimum GPA: 2.5
Amount: Up to $5,000.
Number of awards: Varies.
Deadline: October 21.
How to apply: Applications are available online.
Exclusive: Visit www.UltimateScholarshipBook.com and enter code UN277520 for updates on this award.

(2776) • Women's Independence Scholarship Program (WISP)

Women's Independence Scholarship Program
4900 Randall Parkway, Suite H, Wilmington, NC 28403
Phone: 910-397-7742
Email: nancy@wispinc.org
http://www.wispinc.org
Purpose: To assist formerly battered women.
Eligibility: Applicants must plan to attend an accredited program full-time or part-time. Preference is given to undergraduate programs and programs in this order of priority: state supported community colleges, state supported colleges or universities, technical/vocational schools, private colleges or universities or for-profit schools. Students must have been direct survivors of intimate partner abuse, with priority given to women who have been parted from their partner for at least one year. Students must also be U.S. citizens or legal residents and demonstrate financial need.
Target applicant(s): High school students. College students. Adult students.
Amount: $2,000.
Number of awards: Varies.
Scholarship may be renewable.
Deadline: At least two months before start date of schooling.
Exclusive: Visit www.UltimateScholarshipBook.com and enter code WO277620 for updates on this award.

(2777) • Working Parent College Scholarship Award

Job-Applications.com
6615 Promway Street, North Canton, OH 44720
http://www.job-applications.com/scholarships
Purpose: To assist working parents with costs for post-secondary education.
Eligibility: Applicants must be part- or full-time students at an accredited U.S. post-secondary institution, have a minimum 3.0 GPA and have worked an average of at least 12 hours per week for the previous four weeks. Students must also be the residential parent of at least one minor child, be a legal U.S. resident and be at least 18 years old.
Target applicant(s): College students. Adult students.
Minimum GPA: 3.0
Amount: $1,000.
Number of awards: 1.
Deadline: August 19.
How to apply: Applications are available online. An essay is required.
Exclusive: Visit www.UltimateScholarshipBook.com and enter code JO277720 for updates on this award.

(2778) • Worthy Women's Professional Studies Scholarship

Worthy
551 5th Avenue, 20th Floor, New York, NY 10176
Phone: 888-222-0208
Email: scholarships@worthy.com
https://www.worthy.com/about/scholarship
Purpose: To assist women who have enrolled in continuing education professional studies to pursue their passion.
Eligibility: Applicants must be a permanent resident of the U.S., identify as a female, be over the age of 30 and be enrolled in a continuing education professional studies program. A 300- to 500-word essay is required on one of three provided topics.
Target applicant(s): College students. Adult students.
Amount: $1,000-$2,500.
Number of awards: 3.
Deadline: November 26.
How to apply: Applications are available online. A 300- to 500-word essay on one of three topics provided is required.
Exclusive: Visit www.UltimateScholarshipBook.com and enter code WO277820 for updates on this award.

(2779) • Young Women in Public Affairs Award

Zonta International
1211 West 22nd Street, Suite 900, Oak Brook, IL 60523
Phone: 630-928-1400
Email: zontaintl@zonta.org
http://www.zonta.org
Purpose: To encourage young women to participate in politics and public service.
Eligibility: Applicants must be young women between the ages of 16 and 19. District award winners receive at least $1,000, and international award winners receive $4,000. Selection is based on volunteerism, volunteer leadership and dedication to "advancing the status of women worldwide." Club deadlines vary. The April 1 deadline is the date by which applications must be received by the District Governor.
Target applicant(s): High school students.
Amount: $1,000-$4,000.
Number of awards: Varies.
Deadline: Varies.
How to apply: Applications are available online or from your local Zonta Club.
Exclusive: Visit www.UltimateScholarshipBook.com and enter code ZO277920 for updates on this award.

DISABILITY/ILLNESS

(2780) • AbbVie Immunology Scholarship

AbbVie Immunology Scholarship
Scholarship America, One Scholarship Way, Saint Peter, MN 56082
Phone: 507-931-0651
Email: abbvieimmunology@scholarshipamerica.org
https://abbvieimmunologyscholarship.com
Purpose: To support students who are living with chronic inflammatory diseases.
Eligibility: Applicants must be legal residents of the U.S. who have been diagnosed with one of the following conditions: ankylosing spondylitis, Crohn's disease, hidradenitis suppurativa, juvenile idiopathic arthritis, psoriasis, psoriatic arthritis, rheumatoid arthritis, ulcerative colitis or uveitis. Students must plan to enroll in an undergraduate or graduate level program at an accredited college, university or technical school in the U.S. for the upcoming school year.
Target applicant(s): High school students. College students. Graduate school students. Adult students.
Amount: Up to $15,000.
Number of awards: Varies.
Deadline: January 9.
How to apply: Applications are available online.
Exclusive: Visit www.UltimateScholarshipBook.com and enter code AB278020 for updates on this award.

(2781) • AG Bell College Scholarship Program

Alexander Graham Bell Association for the Deaf and Hard of Hearing
Youth and Family Programs Manager, 3417 Volta Place NW, Washington, DC 20007
Phone: 202-337-5220
Email: financialaid@agbell.org
http://www.agbell.org
Purpose: To recognize students with moderate to profound hearing loss who have academically excelled.
Eligibility: Applicants must have moderate to profound hearing loss since birth or before learning to speak with a hearing loss of 60 dB or greater. Students must use spoken communication as their primary means of communicating and be enrolled in an accredited mainstream university and must also have a minimum unweighted cumulative 3.25 GPA. The TTY phone number is 202-337-5221.
Target applicant(s): High school students. College students. Graduate school students. Adult students.
Minimum GPA: 3.25
Amount: $1,000-$10,000.
Number of awards: Varies.
Deadline: March 11.
How to apply: Applications are available online.
Exclusive: Visit www.UltimateScholarshipBook.com and enter code AL278120 for updates on this award.

(2782) • American Council of the Blind Scholarships

American Council of the Blind
Scholarship Program , 1703 North Beauregard Street, Suite 420, Alexandria, VA 22311
Phone: 202-467-5081
Email: info@acb.org
http://www.acb.org
Purpose: To reward outstanding blind students.
Eligibility: Students must be legally blind in both eyes and admitted full-time to a post-secondary academic or vocational program. A minimum GPA of 3.3 is required, except in extenuating circumstances. Students who work full-time and attend school part-time may apply for the John Hebner Memorial Scholarship. Scholarship recipients are expected to attend a national convention if they are over 18.
Target applicant(s): High school students. College students. Graduate school students. Adult students.
Minimum GPA: 3.3
Amount: $1,000-$2,500.
Number of awards: Up to 20.
Deadline: March 1.
How to apply: Applications are available online and by phone.
Exclusive: Visit www.UltimateScholarshipBook.com and enter code AM278220 for updates on this award.

(2783) • Andre Sobel Award

Andre Sobel River of Life Foundation
Andre Sobel Award Submission, 8581 Santa Monica Boulevard #80, West Hollywood, CA 90069
Phone: 310-276-7111
Email: aswire@andreriveroflife.org
http://andreriveroflife.org/
Purpose: To provide financial assistance for young survivors of catastrophic illness.
Eligibility: Applicants must be between the ages of 12 and 21 as of June 30 of the year of application. They must be survivors of cancer or some other critical or life-threatening illness. Friends, family members and caregivers of those who meet these qualifications may also participate. All applicants must be United States residents. An essay is required.
Target applicant(s): Junior high students or younger. High school students. College students.
Amount: Varies.
Number of awards: Varies.
Deadline: January 31.
How to apply: Applications are available online.
Exclusive: Visit www.UltimateScholarshipBook.com and enter code AN278320 for updates on this award.

(2784) • Anne Ford Scholarship Program

National Center for Learning Disabilities
381 Park Avenue South, Suite 1401, New York, NY 10016-8806
Phone: 888-575-7373
Email: afscholarship@ncld.org
http://www.ncld.org
Purpose: To provide financial assistance to high school seniors with learning disabilities who plan to pursue undergraduate degrees.
Eligibility: Applicants must be U.S. citizens who are academically successful in public or private secondary schools and with an identified learning disability. Students must have a minimum 3.0 GPA. Financial need is considered.
Target applicant(s): High school students.
Minimum GPA: 3.0
Amount: $10,000.
Number of awards: 2.
Deadline: November 13.
How to apply: Applications are available online.
Exclusive: Visit www.UltimateScholarshipBook.com and enter code NA278420 for updates on this award.

(2785) • Baer Reintegration Scholarship

Baer Reintegration Scholarship
P.O. Box 259, Lafayette Hill, PA 19444
Phone: 800-809-8202
Email: baerscholarships@reintegration.com
http://www.reintegration.com

Purpose: To provide aid to students with schizophrenia or similar disorders who are seeking to advance themselves academically and vocationally.
Eligibility: Applicants must have been diagnosed with schizophrenia, schizophreniform, schizoaffective disorder or bipolar disorder, be undergoing medical treatment for their disease(s) and be involved in other rehabilitative efforts, such as working part-time or volunteering with a civic organization.
Target applicant(s): High school students. College students. Graduate school students. Adult students.
Amount: Varies.
Number of awards: Varies.
Deadline: January 29.
How to apply: Applications are available online or by phone, mail or email.
Exclusive: Visit www.UltimateScholarshipBook.com and enter code BA278520 for updates on this award.

(2786) • Bernice McNamara Memorial Scholarship Fund

Ulman Cancer Fund for Young Adults
1215 East Fort Avenue, Suite 104, Baltimore, MD 21230
Phone: 410-964-0202
Email: scholarship@ulmanfund.org
http://ulmanfund.org/scholarships/

Purpose: To support the educational pursuits of young people affected by cancer through the diagnoses of a parent and committed to making a difference in the areas of science, research or healthcare.
Eligibility: Applicants must be U.S. citizens accepted to or attending a four-year college or university and majoring in the sciences. Applicants must also have been 15 years old or older during their parent's active treatment for cancer and must be age 25 or younger at the time of application. Scholarship winners are required to complete a minimum of 40 hours of community service. Selection is based on a letter of recommendation and the overall strength of the application.
Target applicant(s): High school students. College students.
Amount: $2,500.
Number of awards: 1.
Deadline: March 1.
How to apply: Applications are available online. An application form, physician's verification or death certificate and letter of recommendation are required.
Exclusive: Visit www.UltimateScholarshipBook.com and enter code UL278620 for updates on this award.

(2787) • BMO Capital Markets Lime Connect Equity Through Education Scholarship

Lime Connect
590 Madison Avenue, 21st Floor, New York, NY 10022
Phone: 212-521-4469
http://www.limeconnect.com

Purpose: To support undergraduate and graduate students with disabilities in pursuing a career in financial services.
Eligibility: Applicants must be enrolled full-time in a finance, business, engineering, mathematics, physics, statistics or related program in the U.S. or Canada. Students must submit university transcripts, resume, an essay explaining their career goals and a letter of recommendation. Selection is based on the overall strength of the application.
Target applicant(s): College students. Graduate school students. Adult students.
Amount: $10,000.
Number of awards: 1.
Deadline: September 30.
How to apply: Applications are available online.
Exclusive: Visit www.UltimateScholarshipBook.com and enter code LI278720 for updates on this award.

(2788) • Boomer Esiason Foundation General Academic Scholarship

Boomer Esiason Foundation
c/o Chris McEwan, 483 10th Avenue, Suite 300, New York, NY 10018
Phone: 646-292-7930
Email: jcahillbef@aol.com
http://www.esiason.org/cf-living/scholarships

Purpose: To provide assistance to students with cystic fibrosis.
Eligibility: Applicants may be pursuing undergraduate or graduate degrees. They must demonstrate financial need. Selection is based on scholastic achievement, character, leadership, community service and financial need. Scholarships are awarded in April, July, September and December of each year.
Target applicant(s): High school students. College students. Graduate school students. Adult students.
Amount: $500-$2,500.
Number of awards: 10-15.
Deadline: March 31, June 30, September 29, December 29.
How to apply: Applications are available online. An application form, recent photo, letter from doctor, essay, transcript, tuition breakdown and W2 from both parents are required.
Exclusive: Visit www.UltimateScholarshipBook.com and enter code BO278820 for updates on this award.

(2789) • Bristol-Myers Squibb Scholarship for Cancer Survivors

Bristol-Myers Squibb
Scholarship America, One Scholarship Way, Saint Peter, MN 56082
Phone: 507-931-1682
Email: cancer-survivors@scholarshipamerica.org
https://learnmore.scholarsapply.org/cancer-survivors

Purpose: To assist cancer survivors pursue post-secondary education.
Eligibility: Applicants must be cancer survivors age 25 years or younger. Students must be high school seniors or post-secondary undergraduates with at least a 3.5 grade point average. Applicants must plan to enroll as full-time students at an accredited college, university, vocational or technical school.
Target applicant(s): High school students. College students.
Minimum GPA: 3.5
Amount: $10,000.
Number of awards: Up to 25.
Deadline: March 31.
How to apply: Applications are available online.
Exclusive: Visit www.UltimateScholarshipBook.com and enter code BR278920 for updates on this award.

(2790) • Business Plan Scholarship

FitSmallBusiness.com
315 Madison Avenue, 24th floor, New York, NY 10017
http://fitsmallbusiness.com/learn-how-to-write-a-business-plan/
Purpose: To support students enrolled in an undergraduate or graduate program at any accredited college, university or trade school who have a documented disability.
Eligibility: Applicants may have any type of disability, including but not limited to physical disabilities, medical conditions, mental and psychiatric conditions, speech and language, learning disabilities, behavioral conditions and all other disabling conditions. Students must compose essay on the topic provided related to business plans.
Target applicant(s): High school students. College students. Graduate school students. Adult students.
Amount: $1,000.
Number of awards: 2.
Deadline: April 1 and November 1.
How to apply: Applications are available online.
Exclusive: Visit www.UltimateScholarshipBook.com and enter code FI279020 for updates on this award.

(2791) • Cancer for College Scholarships

Cancer for College
981 Park Center Drive, Vista, CA 92081
Phone: 760-599-5096
Email: applications@cancerforcollege.org
https://www.cancerforcollege.org/
Purpose: To support current and former cancer patients and amputees.
Eligibility: Applicants must be U.S. residents. They must be enrolled in an accredited university, community college or trade school. Recipients must agree to attend regional events and be available for interviews and media coverage.
Target applicant(s): High school students. College students. Adult students.
Amount: $1,000-$5,000.
Number of awards: Varies.
Scholarship may be renewable.
Deadline: January 31.
How to apply: Applications are available online. An application form, summary of cancer treatment, personal statement, details of college financing and two letters of recommendation are required.
Exclusive: Visit www.UltimateScholarshipBook.com and enter code CA279120 for updates on this award.

(2792) • CFSF Standard Scholarship

Cystic Fibrosis Scholarship Foundation
1555 Sherman Avenue #116, Evanston, IL 60201
Phone: 847-328-0127
Email: mkbcfsf@aol.com
http://cfscholarship.org/scholarships/
Purpose: To aid to students with cystic fibrosis.
Eligibility: Applicants must be high school seniors or college undergraduates who have cystic fibrosis. Recipients are chosen on the basis of academic achievement, leadership skills and financial need.
Target applicant(s): High school students. College students. Adult students.
Amount: $1,000.
Number of awards: Varies.
Deadline: March 24.
How to apply: Applications are available online.
Exclusive: Visit www.UltimateScholarshipBook.com and enter code CY279220 for updates on this award.

(2793) • Challenge Met Scholarship

American Radio Relay League Foundation
225 Main Street, Newington, CT 06111-1494
Phone: 860-594-0348
Email: foundation@arrl.org
http://www.arrl.org/scholarship-program
Purpose: To provide assistance to amateur radio operators with learning disabilities.
Eligibility: Applicants must be licensed amateur radio operators who are accepted to or enrolled in a two- or four-year college, technical school or university. Preference is given to students with documented learning disabilities who are putting forth effort.
Target applicant(s): High school students. College students. Adult students.
Amount: $500.
Number of awards: Varies.
Deadline: January 31.
How to apply: Applications are available online.
Exclusive: Visit www.UltimateScholarshipBook.com and enter code AM279320 for updates on this award.

(2794) • Cystic Fibrosis Scholarships

Cystic Fibrosis Scholarship Foundation
1555 Sherman Avenue #116, Evanston, IL 60201
Phone: 847-328-0127
Email: mkbcfsf@aol.com
http://cfscholarship.org/scholarships/
Purpose: To provide educational opportunities for young adults with cystic fibrosis.
Eligibility: Applicants may be high school seniors or current college students. A doctor's note indicating a diagnosis of cystic fibrosis is required. Criteria for selection include financial need, academic achievement and leadership.
Target applicant(s): High school students. College students. Adult students.
Amount: $1,000.
Number of awards: Varies.
Scholarship may be renewable.
Deadline: March 24.
How to apply: Applications are available online.
Exclusive: Visit www.UltimateScholarshipBook.com and enter code CY279420 for updates on this award.

(2795) • Disabled Student Scholarship

Disability Care Center
2875 South Orange Avenue #500, Orlando, FL 32806
Phone: 888-504-0035
Email: scholarship@disabilitycarecenter.org
http://www.disabilitycarecenter.org
Purpose: To support students who have a physical or mental impairment that are pursuing a college education.
Eligibility: Applicants must have a medically diagnosed physical or mental impairment that interferes with everyday activities or quality of life and can provide a physician's statement regarding their impairment. A minimum GPA of 2.5 is required. Students must be a legal resident of the U.S. and enrolled full time for the upcoming fall semester. Applicants will need to submit a short essay describing an obstacle or hardship

incurred due to their medical condition, how the student overcame that obstacle, how it influence the student's life and how it will impact them in the future. Selection is based on the essay.
Target applicant(s): High school students. College students. Adult students.
Minimum GPA: 2.5
Amount: $500.
Number of awards: 1.
Deadline: August 1.
How to apply: Applications are available online and must also include proof of college acceptance or college ID, proof of registration for the fall semester, copy of most recent transcript, proof of U.S. citizenship, a physician's letter and the essay.
Exclusive: Visit www.UltimateScholarshipBook.com and enter code DI279520 for updates on this award.

(2796) • DIVERSEability Scholarship Opportunity

DIVERSEability Magazine
18 Technology Drive, Suite 170, Irvine, CA 92618
Phone: 949-398-5296
https://www.diverseabilitymagazine.com/scholarship-opportunity/
Purpose: To support students who are undergraduate students with a disability.
Eligibility: Applicants must be U.S. legal residents and have a disability. Students must submit an essay, graphic or creative presentation on their college experience and future goals. Selection is based upon the applicant's genuine desire and goal of using the scholarship to help advance in their field and an overall passion for knowledge.
Target applicant(s): College students. Graduate school students. Adult students.
Amount: $500.
Number of awards: 1.
Deadline: August 15.
How to apply: Applications are available online.
Exclusive: Visit www.UltimateScholarshipBook.com and enter code DI279620 for updates on this award.

(2797) • Duane Buckley Memorial Scholarship

American Council of the Blind
Scholarship Program , 1703 North Beauregard Street, Suite 420, Alexandria, VA 22311
Phone: 202-467-5081
Email: info@acb.org
http://www.acb.org
Purpose: To assist students who work to overcome challenges.
Eligibility: Applicants must be legally blind college freshmen. A letter of recommendation, autobiographical sketch and copies of transcripts are required.
Target applicant(s): College students. Adult students.
Amount: $1,000.
Number of awards: 1.
Deadline: February 15.
How to apply: Applications are available online.
Exclusive: Visit www.UltimateScholarshipBook.com and enter code AM279720 for updates on this award.

(2798) • Elizabeth Nash Foundation Scholarship Program

Elizabeth Nash Foundation
P.O. Box 1260, Los Gatos, CA 95031-1260
Email: info@elizabethnashfoundation.org
http://www.elizabethnashfoundation.org
Purpose: To support students with cystic fibrosis.
Eligibility: Applicants must be current or entering graduate or undergraduate students at an accredited U.S. institution of higher learning. They must be U.S. citizens, and they must be pursuing a bachelor's degree or higher. Selection criteria include scholastic achievement, character, leadership, community service, service to cystic fibrosis-related causes and financial need.
Target applicant(s): High school students. College students. Graduate school students. Adult students.
Amount: $1,000-$2,500.
Number of awards: Varies.
Deadline: April 3.
How to apply: Applications are available online. An application form, essay, letter of recommendation, documentation of cystic fibrosis diagnosis, transcript, copy of FAFSA and details of tuition costs are required.
Exclusive: Visit www.UltimateScholarshipBook.com and enter code EL279820 for updates on this award.

(2799) • Eric Dostie Memorial College Scholarship

NuFACTOR
41093 County Center Drive, Temecula, CA 92591
Phone: 800-323-6832
http://www.kelleycom.com
Purpose: To assist students who suffer from hemophilia or related bleeding disorders as well as their immediate families.
Eligibility: Applicants must be individuals with hemophilia or related to said individuals, enrolled full-time in an accredited college or university and demonstrate academic achievement, financial need and a history of community service.
Target applicant(s): High school students. College students. Adult students.
Amount: $1,000.
Number of awards: 10.
Deadline: March 1.
How to apply: Applications are available after November 1 by telephone or mail.
Exclusive: Visit www.UltimateScholarshipBook.com and enter code NU279920 for updates on this award.

(2800) • Eric Marder Scholarship Program of The Immune Deficiency Foundation

Eric Marder Scholarship Fund
1912 Rolling Green Circle, Sarasota, FL 34240
Email: annieb3907@gmail.com
http://www.ericsfund.org
Purpose: To provide financial assistance to undergraduate students afflicted with a primary immune deficiency disease.
Eligibility: Applicant must have been admitted or must currently be enrolled in an accredited college or university as an undergraduate student. Applicants must also have demonstrated financial need and a record of community involvement.
Target applicant(s): High school students. College students. Adult students.

Amount: Varies.
Number of awards: Varies.
Scholarship may be renewable.
Deadline: May 1.
How to apply: Applications are available online, by email or by telephone.
Exclusive: Visit www.UltimateScholarshipBook.com and enter code ER280020 for updates on this award.

(2801) • Flicker of Hope Foundation Scholarships

Flicker of Hope Foundation
8624 Janet Lane, Vienna, VA 22180
Phone: 703-698-1626
Email: info@flickerofhope.org
http://www.flickerofhope.org
Purpose: To support burn survivors.
Eligibility: Applicants must be current high school seniors or graduates or current college students. Winners must be accepted to an accredited college or university prior to disbursement of funds. Selection is based on severity of burn injury, academic performance, community service and economic need.
Target applicant(s): High school students. College students. Adult students.
Amount: Varies.
Number of awards: Varies.
Deadline: June 1.
How to apply: Applications are available online. An application form, list of other sources and amounts of financial aid, transcript, college acceptance letter, listing of college costs, two letters of recommendation, letter from a medical professional and a copy of most recent tax return on which student is claimed as a dependent are required.
Exclusive: Visit www.UltimateScholarshipBook.com and enter code FL280120 for updates on this award.

(2802) • Fred Scheigert Scholarships

Council of Citizens with Low Vision International
1155 15th Street NW, Suite 1004, Washington, DC 20005
Phone: 800-733-2258
Email: ncclv@yahoo.com
http://www.cclvi.org
Purpose: To provide educational assistance for students with low vision.
Eligibility: Applicants must be registered in a full-time undergraduate or graduate course of study at a college, trade or vocational school. They must have a GPA of 3.2 or higher. Those with extenuating circumstances may be exempt from these requirements. Applicants must have 20/70 or worse vision in the better eye with the best possible correction, or a field of vision of 30 degrees or less.
Target applicant(s): High school students. College students. Graduate school students. Adult students.
Minimum GPA: 3.2
Amount: $3,000.
Number of awards: 3.
Deadline: March 1.
How to apply: Applications are available online.
Exclusive: Visit www.UltimateScholarshipBook.com and enter code CO280220 for updates on this award.

(2803) • George H. Nofer Scholarship for Law and Public Policy

Alexander Graham Bell Association for the Deaf and Hard of Hearing
Youth and Family Programs Manager, 3417 Volta Place NW, Washington, DC 20007
Phone: 202-337-5220
Email: financialaid@agbell.org
http://www.agbell.org
Purpose: To assist graduate students with a moderate to profound hearing loss.
Eligibility: Applicants must attend or be accepted to attend full-time an accredited law school or a master's or doctoral program in public policy or public administration and must use spoken language as the primary mode of communication. Students must also have a pre-lingual and bilateral hearing loss. Applications are available online.
Target applicant(s): Graduate school students. Adult students.
Amount: $5,000.
Number of awards: Up to 3.
Deadline: April 22.
How to apply: Applications are available online.
Exclusive: Visit www.UltimateScholarshipBook.com and enter code AL280320 for updates on this award.

(2804) • Graeme Clark Scholarship

Cochlear Americas
The Graeme Clark Scholarship, 13059 East Peakview Avenue, Centennial, CO 80111
Phone: 303-790-9010
http://www.cochlearamericas.com
Purpose: To support cochlear implant recipients.
Eligibility: Applicants must have received a Nucleus cochlear implant. They may be high school seniors, current college students or students who have been accepted into an institution of higher learning. Students must pursue a minimum of a three-year undergraduate degree at an accredited university. Criteria for selection include academic achievement and commitment to leadership and humanity. A minimum GPA of 2.5 is required for all applicants.
Target applicant(s): High school students. College students. Adult students.
Minimum GPA: 2.5
Amount: $2,000.
Number of awards: Varies.
Deadline: September 30.
How to apply: Applications are available online. An application form, transcript, proof of university admission, list of activities and awards, personal statement, proof of age and citizenship and three letters of reference are required.
Exclusive: Visit www.UltimateScholarshipBook.com and enter code CO280420 for updates on this award.

(2805) • Guthrie-Koch PKU Scholarship

National PKU News
6869 Woodlawn Avenue NE #116, Seattle, WA 98115
Phone: 206-525-8140
Email: scholarship@pkunews.org
https://pkunews.org/guthrie-koch-scholarship/
Purpose: In honor of the doctor who created the newborn screening test for PKU, the scholarship gives support to bright students living with PKU.

Eligibility: Students must have PKU, follow the diet and attend an accredited school. Financial need is considered along with academic excellence.
Target applicant(s): High school students. College students.
Amount: Varies.
Number of awards: Varies.
Deadline: October 15.
How to apply: Applications are available online after July 1 each year.
Exclusive: Visit www.UltimateScholarshipBook.com and enter code NA280520 for updates on this award.

(2806) • HIV-Positive Scholarship

STDcheck.com
Phone: 800-456-2323
https://www.stdcheck.com/scholarship-application.php
Purpose: To support students who are HIV-positive.
Eligibility: Applicants must be U.S. citizens who are currently enrolled or will be enrolled the following semester full-time at an accredited college or university in the U.S. Students will need to provide proof that they are HIV-positive. Applicants must also submit an essay on how HIV was contracted, how it has affected their life and what they wish those living without HIV knew about living with the virus. The scholarship is awarded monthly.
Target applicant(s): High school students. College students. Adult students.
Amount: $250-$5,000.
Number of awards: Varies.
Deadline: Varies.
How to apply: Applications are available online and must include the essay, proof of HIV-positive status and an official transcript.
Exclusive: Visit www.UltimateScholarshipBook.com and enter code ST280620 for updates on this award.

(2807) • Incight Scholarship

Incight Education
111 SW Columbia Street, Suite 1170, Portland, OR 97201
Phone: 971-244-0305
Email: questions@incight.org
http://incight.org/education/scholarship
Purpose: To support students with physical or learning disabilities who are residents of Oregon, Washington or California.
Eligibility: Applicants must have a documented disability that may include physical, learning or cognitive. Students must also attend a trade school, college or university on a full-time basis. Recipients are placed with internships related to their field of study.
Target applicant(s): High school students. College students. Graduate school students. Adult students.
Amount: $500-$2,500.
Number of awards: Varies.
Scholarship may be renewable.
Deadline: April 1.
How to apply: Applications are available online.
Exclusive: Visit www.UltimateScholarshipBook.com and enter code IN280720 for updates on this award.

(2808) • Independence Foundation Scholarship

Independence Foundation
2220 Hall Road, Elma, NY 14059
Phone: (716) 685-3976
http://theindependencefoundation.org
Purpose: To support students with physical disabilities in pursuing post-secondary education.
Eligibility: Applicants must use wheelchairs in their daily lives. Students must submit an essay explaining how they have overcome challenges posed by their physical limitations and their educational/professional goals and aspirations. Selection is based on the overall strength of the application.
Target applicant(s): High school students. College students. Adult students.
Amount: $500.
Number of awards: Up to 3.
Deadline: February 15.
How to apply: Applications are available online.
Exclusive: Visit www.UltimateScholarshipBook.com and enter code IN280820 for updates on this award.

(2809) • Kermit B. Nash Academic Scholarship

Sickle Cell Disease Association of America
3700 Koppers Street, Suite 570, Baltimore, MD 21227
Phone: 800-421-8453
Email: scdaa@sicklecelldisease.org
https://www.sicklecelldisease.org/programs/
Purpose: To encourage individuals with sickle cell disease to pursue their educational goals.
Eligibility: Applicants must be U.S. citizens or permanent residents who have sickle cell disease and are members of SCDAA. They must be graduating high school seniors with a GPA of 3.0 or higher (unless they can demonstrate special hardship), a record of leadership and community service and SAT scores. An essay is required.
Target applicant(s): High school students.
Minimum GPA: 3.0
Amount: $5,000.
Number of awards: 1.
Scholarship may be renewable.
Deadline: Varies.
How to apply: Applications are available online.
Exclusive: Visit www.UltimateScholarshipBook.com and enter code SI280920 for updates on this award.

(2810) • Kevin Child Scholarship

National Hemophilia Foundation
7 Penn Plaza, Suite 1204, New York, NY 10001
Phone: 212-328-3700
Email: ssarode@hemophilia.org
http://www.hemophilia.org
Purpose: To support students who have been diagnosed with hemophilia A or B.
Eligibility: Applicants must be high school seniors or enrolled undergraduate students.
Target applicant(s): High school students. College students. Adult students.
Amount: $1,000.
Number of awards: 1.
Deadline: June 15.
How to apply: Applications are available online.
Exclusive: Visit www.UltimateScholarshipBook.com and enter code NA281020 for updates on this award.

(2811) • L.I.F.E. Scholarship

Lupus Inspiration Foundation For Excellence
P.O. Box 64088, Tucson, AZ 85728
http://www.lifescholarship.org

Purpose: To support students diagnosed with lupus in pursuing post-secondary education.

Eligibility: Applicants must be enrolled for a minimum of six credits for the upcoming fall semester after the award is granted. A minimum GPA of 3.0 is required. Selection is primarily based on extracurricular involvement, community service and leadership ability.

Target applicant(s): High school students. College students. Adult students.

Minimum GPA: 3.0

Amount: $500.

Number of awards: Varies.

Deadline: July 1.

How to apply: Applications are available online.

Exclusive: Visit www.UltimateScholarshipBook.com and enter code LU281120 for updates on this award.

(2812) • Lighthouse Guild Scholarships

Lighthouse Guild
Scholarship Awards, 15 West 65th Street, New York, NY 10023
Phone: 212-769-7801
Email: scholars@lighthouseguild.org
https://www.lighthouseguild.org/

Purpose: To assist blind or partially-sighted collegiate or college-bound students.

Eligibility: Applicants must be legally blind. Visual requirements include a best corrected visual acuity of 20/200 or less in the better eye and/or a visual field of less than 20 degrees in the better eye and be in one of three categories: college-bound high school student, undergraduate college student or graduate student. They must also be U.S. citizens and residents and attend an accredited college or university in the U.S. or its territories. Selection is based on academic and personal achievements.

Target applicant(s): High school students. College students. Graduate school students. Adult students.

Amount: Up to $10,000.

Number of awards: Up to 21.

Deadline: March 31.

How to apply: Applications are available online.

Exclusive: Visit www.UltimateScholarshipBook.com and enter code LI281220 for updates on this award.

(2813) • Lisa Higgins Hussman Scholarship

Organization for Autism Research
2000 N. 14th Street, Suite 240, Arlington, VA 22201
Phone: 703-243-9710
http://researchautism.org

Purpose: To support students with an autism diagnosis in pursuing post-secondary education.

Eligibility: Applicants must plan on enrolling full-time at an accredited educational institution for the upcoming academic year. Selection is primarily based on challenges the applicant has overcome, future goals and aspirations and chosen field of study.

Target applicant(s): High school students. College students. Adult students.

Amount: $3,000.

Number of awards: 40.

Deadline: May 7.

How to apply: Applications are available online.

Exclusive: Visit www.UltimateScholarshipBook.com and enter code OR281320 for updates on this award.

(2814) • Little People of America Scholarships

Little People of America
250 El Camino Real, Suite 218, Tustin, CA 92780
Phone: 888-572-2001
Email: info@lpaonline.org
http://www.lpaonline.org

Purpose: To aid those affected by dwarfism.

Eligibility: Applicants may be junior high, high school or college students who have been involved with Little People of America. Preference is given in the following order: LPA members with medically diagnosed dwarfism, immediate family members of LPA members diagnosed with dwarfism and non-LPA members with dwarfism.

Target applicant(s): Junior high students or younger. High school students. College students. Adult students.

Amount: $250-$1,000.

Number of awards: 3.

Deadline: April 30.

How to apply: Applications are available online. An application form, personal statement and three letters of recommendation are required.

Exclusive: Visit www.UltimateScholarshipBook.com and enter code LI281420 for updates on this award.

(2815) • Living With Dyslexia Scholarship

Gemm Learning
877 Post Road E., Suite 2, Westport, CT 06880
Phone: 203-292-5410
https://www.gemmlearning.com/about/scholarship-opportunities

Purpose: To support students with dyslexia in pursuing post-secondary education.

Eligibility: Applicants must be enrolled or planning on enrolling at a U.S. or Canada based educational institution. Students must submit an essay explaining what it's like to live with dyslexia. Selection is based on the overall strength of the submission.

Target applicant(s): High school students. College students. Adult students.

Amount: $1,000.

Number of awards: 1.

Deadline: July 15.

How to apply: Applications are available online.

Exclusive: Visit www.UltimateScholarshipBook.com and enter code GE281520 for updates on this award.

(2816) • Marilyn Yetso Memorial Scholarship

Ulman Cancer Fund for Young Adults
1215 East Fort Avenue, Suite 104, Baltimore, MD 21230
Phone: 410-964-0202
Email: scholarship@ulmanfund.org
http://ulmanfund.org/scholarships/

Purpose: To support students who have a parent with cancer and those who have lost a parent to cancer.

Eligibility: Applicants must reside in the Baltimore/Washington metro area. Students must show financial need, community service participation, commitment to education and career goals and how they have used their experience to help others. Applicants must be age 39 or younger.

Target applicant(s): High school students. College students. Adult students.
Amount: $2,500.
Number of awards: Varies.
Deadline: March 15.
How to apply: Applications are available online.
Exclusive: Visit www.UltimateScholarshipBook.com and enter code UL281620 for updates on this award.

(2817) • Marion Huber Learning Through Listening Awards

Learning Ally
20 Roszel Road, Princeton, NJ 08540
Phone: 800-221-4792
Email: naa@LearningAlly.org
https://www.learningally.org/
Purpose: To assist learning-disabled high school seniors.
Eligibility: Applicants must demonstrate leadership skills, scholarship and a desire to help others and attend a two- or four-year college or vocational school. Students must have a specific learning disability and be registered with RFB&D for at least one year prior to the application deadline.
Target applicant(s): High school students.
Minimum GPA: 3.0
Amount: $2,000-$6,000.
Number of awards: 6.
Deadline: May 31.
How to apply: Applications are available online.
Exclusive: Visit www.UltimateScholarshipBook.com and enter code LE281720 for updates on this award.

(2818) • Mary P. Oenslanger Scholastic Achievement Awards

Learning Ally
20 Roszel Road, Princeton, NJ 08540
Phone: 800-221-4792
Email: naa@LearningAlly.org
https://www.learningally.org/
Purpose: Assistance for graduate study is awarded to blind college senior students or graduate students who have shown leadership skills, scholarship and a desire to help others.
Eligibility: Applicants must be blind or visually impaired, Learning Ally members and college seniors and graduate students.
Target applicant(s): College students. Graduate school students. Adult students.
Minimum GPA: 3.0
Amount: $1,000-$6,000.
Number of awards: 9.
Deadline: May 31.
How to apply: Applications are available online.
Exclusive: Visit www.UltimateScholarshipBook.com and enter code LE281820 for updates on this award.

(2819) • Michael A. Hunter Memorial Scholarship Fund

Orange County Community Foundation
4041 MacArthur Boulevard, Suite 510, Newport Beach, CA 92660
Phone: 949-553-4202
Email: cmontesano@oc-cf.org
http://www.oc-cf.org
Purpose: To support those who have been affected by leukemia as they pursue an education.
Eligibility: Applicants must be high school seniors or current college students who are leukemia patients and/or are the children of non-surviving leukemia patients. Applicants must be full-time students with a GPA of at least 3.0 and demonstrate financial need. They must submit an essay describing how leukemia has impacted their life, a doctor's note verifying the leukemia diagnosis and two letters of recommendation.
Target applicant(s): High school students. College students. Adult students.
Minimum GPA: 3.0
Amount: $2,000-$3,000.
Number of awards: Varies.
Deadline: March 15.
How to apply: Applications are available online.
Exclusive: Visit www.UltimateScholarshipBook.com and enter code OR281920 for updates on this award.

(2820) • Mike Hylton and Ron Niederman Scholarships

Factor Support Network Pharmacy
900 Avenida Acaso, Suite A, Camarillo, CA 93012-8749
Phone: 877-376-4968
Email: maria.vetter@matrixhealthgroup.com
http://www.factorsupport.com/
Purpose: To support men with hemophilia or von Willebrand disease and their families.
Eligibility: Students must provide proof of diagnosis by a physician. Applicants must submit an essay and two letters of recommendation.
Target applicant(s): High school students. College students. Adult students.
Amount: $1,000.
Number of awards: 2.
Deadline: August 1.
How to apply: Applications are available online.
Exclusive: Visit www.UltimateScholarshipBook.com and enter code FA282020 for updates on this award.

(2821) • Millie Brother Scholarship

Children of Deaf Adults, International
Dr. Jennie E. Pyers, Assistant Professor of Psychology, Wellesley College, 106 Central Street, SCI480, Wellesley, MA 02481
Phone: 781-283-3736
Email: scholarships@coda-international.org
http://www.coda-international.org/scholarship
Purpose: To assist hearing children of deaf parents to pursue post-secondary educational opportunities.
Eligibility: Applicants must be graduating high school seniors and the hearing children of deaf parents. Applicants must submit a transcript, letters of recommendation and essay. Essays should describe applicants' Coda experience and future career goals.
Target applicant(s): High school students. College students. Graduate school students. Adult students.
Amount: $3,000.
Number of awards: 2.
Deadline: First Friday in April.
How to apply: Applications are available online.
Exclusive: Visit www.UltimateScholarshipBook.com and enter code CH282120 for updates on this award.

(2822) • Millie Gonzales Memorial Scholarships

Factor Support Network Pharmacy
900 Avenida Acaso, Suite A, Camarillo, CA 93012-8749
Phone: 877-376-4968
Email: maria.vetter@matrixhealthgroup.com
http://www.factorsupport.com/
Purpose: To support women with hemophilia or von Willebrand Disease.
Eligibility: Students must provide proof of diagnosis by a physician. Applicants must submit an essay and two letters of recommendation.
Target applicant(s): High school students. College students. Adult students.
Amount: $1,000.
Number of awards: 2.
Deadline: August 1.
How to apply: Applications are available online.
Exclusive: Visit www.UltimateScholarshipBook.com and enter code FA282220 for updates on this award.

(2823) • National Collegiate Cancer Foundation Scholarship

National Collegiate Cancer Foundation
4858 Battery Lane, #216, Bethesda, MD 20814
Phone: 240-515-6262
Email: info@collegiatecancer.org
http://www.collegiatecancer.org
Purpose: To provide financial assistance to college students who have been diagnosed with cancer.
Eligibility: Applicants must demonstrate financial need. Selection is based on financial need, quality of essay and recommendations, demonstrating a "will win" attitude and overall story of cancer survivorship.
Target applicant(s): High school students. College students. Graduate school students. Adult students.
Amount: $1,000.
Number of awards: Varies.
Deadline: May 15.
How to apply: Applications are available online.
Exclusive: Visit www.UltimateScholarshipBook.com and enter code NA282320 for updates on this award.

(2824) • National Federation of the Blind Scholarship

National Federation of the Blind
200 East Wells Street, Baltimore, MD 21230
Phone: 410-659-9314
Email: scholarships@nfb.org
http://www.nfb.org
Purpose: The National Federation of the Blind offers thirty scholarships to exceptional blind scholars.
Eligibility: Applicants must be legally blind and pursue a full-time postsecondary study in the following semester in the U.S. One scholarship may be given to a part-time student. There are no additional restrictions for most of the scholarships. However, a few require study in certain fields or other special traits. Awards are based on academic excellence, community service and financial need. Applicants must reside in the United States or Puerto Rico and attend college in the United States or Puerto Rico. Students make one application for any of the 30 awards; the members of the NFB Scholarship Committee choose the 30 winners and decide which person will receive which award. Legally blind means one is blind in both eyes according to the legal definition, which is available on the organization's website.
Target applicant(s): High school students. College students. Graduate school students. Adult students.
Amount: $3,000-$12,000.
Number of awards: 30.
Deadline: March 31.
How to apply: Applications are available online.
Exclusive: Visit www.UltimateScholarshipBook.com and enter code NA282420 for updates on this award.

(2825) • National MS Society Scholarship Program

National Multiple Sclerosis Society
733 Third Avenue, New York, NY 10017
Phone: 800-344-4867
http://www.nationalmssociety.org
Purpose: To provide educational opportunities for students affected by multiple sclerosis.
Eligibility: Applicants must be high school seniors or graduates who have MS, or who have a parent with MS and will be attending college for the first time. They must be U.S. citizens or legal residents who plan to enroll in an undergraduate program at an accredited institution of higher learning. Applicants must take at least six credit hours per semester, and the courses taken must lead to a degree, license or certificate.
Target applicant(s): High school students.
Amount: $1,000-$3,000.
Number of awards: Up to 400.
Deadline: January 18.
How to apply: Applications are available online.
Exclusive: Visit www.UltimateScholarshipBook.com and enter code NA282520 for updates on this award.

(2826) • National Scholarship Competition for Disabled College Students

disABLEDperson, Inc.
P.O. Box 230636, Encinitas, CA 92023
Phone: 760-420-1269
http://www.disABLEDperson.com
Purpose: To support disabled students in pursuing their undergraduate studies.
Eligibility: Applicants must be enrolled full-time in an two- or four-year college. Students must provide proof of disability through the Disability Student Services department at their school. Applicants must also include an essay with their application. Selection is based on the overall strength of the application.
Target applicant(s): College students. Adult students.
Amount: $2,000.
Number of awards: 1.
Deadline: October 23.
How to apply: Applications are available online.
Exclusive: Visit www.UltimateScholarshipBook.com and enter code DI282620 for updates on this award.

(2827) • NFMC Hinda Honigman Award for the Blind

National Federation of Music Clubs (NC)
Bobbye Guyton, 2400 Coronado Drive, Hoover, AL 35226
Phone: 205-822-6117
Email: rag2400@aol.com
http://www.nfmc-music.org/competitions-awards/

Purpose: To support blind instrumentalists or vocalists.
Eligibility: Applicants must be between the ages of 16 and 25, be an instrumentalist or vocalist and submit an affidavit from an ophthalmologist stating that they are blind. Applicants must also be affiliated with the National Federation of Music Clubs.
Target applicant(s): High school students. College students. Graduate school students. Adult students.
Amount: $500-$1000.
Number of awards: 2.
Deadline: February 1.
How to apply: Applications are available online.
Exclusive: Visit www.UltimateScholarshipBook.com and enter code NA282720 for updates on this award.

(2828) · Optimist International Communications Contest

Optimist International
4494 Lindell Boulevard, St. Louis, MO 63108
Phone: 314-371-6000
Email: programs@optimist.org
http://www.optimist.org
Purpose: To reward students based on their communications performance.
Eligibility: Applicants must be students up to grade 12 in the U.S. and Canada, to CEGEP in Quebec and to grade 13 in the Caribbean who are recognized by their schools as deaf or hard of hearing.
Target applicant(s): High school students.
Amount: $2,500.
Number of awards: Varies.
Deadline: June 15.
How to apply: Contact your local Optimist Club.
Exclusive: Visit www.UltimateScholarshipBook.com and enter code OP282820 for updates on this award.

(2829) · P. Buckley Moss Endowed Scholarship

P. Buckley Moss Foundation for Children's Education
74 Poplar Grove Lane, Mathews, VA 23109
Phone: 800-430-1320
Email: foundation@mossfoundation.org
http://mossfoundation.org
Purpose: To support students with learning disabilities to pursue visual arts education.
Eligibility: Applicants must be graduating high school seniors with a language-related learning disability who are enrolling in an accredited two- or four-year college or university. Students must be pursuing a career in the visual arts and demonstrate financial need.
Target applicant(s): High school students.
Amount: $1,000.
Number of awards: 1.
Deadline: March 31.
How to apply: Applications are available online.
Exclusive: Visit www.UltimateScholarshipBook.com and enter code P.282920 for updates on this award.

(2830) · Paul and Ellen Ruckes Scholarship

American Foundation for the Blind Scholarship Committee
1000 Fifth Avenue, Suite 350, Huntington, WV 25701
Phone: 800-232-5463
Email: afbinfo@afb.net
http://www.afb.org
Purpose: To support visually impaired engineering, computer science, life sciences or physical sciences students.
Eligibility: Applicants must be U.S. citizens who are blind or visually impaired. They must be undergraduate or graduate students who are majoring in computer science, life sciences, physical sciences or engineering. Selection is based on the overall strength of the application.
Target applicant(s): High school students. College students. Graduate school students. Adult students.
Amount: $2,000.
Number of awards: 2.
Deadline: April 1.
How to apply: Applications are available online. An application form, official transcript, personal statement, two reference letters, proof of college acceptance, proof of U.S. citizenship and proof of legal blindness are required.
Exclusive: Visit www.UltimateScholarshipBook.com and enter code AM283020 for updates on this award.

(2831) · Rudolph Dillman Memorial Scholarship

American Foundation for the Blind Scholarship Committee
1000 Fifth Avenue, Suite 350, Huntington, WV 25701
Phone: 800-232-5463
Email: afbinfo@afb.net
http://www.afb.org
Purpose: To aid blind or visually impaired students who are preparing for careers in the rehabilitation or education of the blind or visually impaired.
Eligibility: Applicants must be U.S. citizens who are blind or visually impaired. They must be undergraduate or graduate students who are preparing for careers in the education or rehabilitation of visually impaired or blind people. Previous recipients of this award are ineligible. Selection is based on the overall strength of the application.
Target applicant(s): College students. Graduate school students. Adult students.
Amount: $2,500.
Number of awards: 4.
Deadline: April 1.
How to apply: Applications are available online. An application form, official transcript, personal essay, two recommendation letters, proof of legal blindness and proof of U.S. citizenship are required.
Exclusive: Visit www.UltimateScholarshipBook.com and enter code AM283120 for updates on this award.

(2832) · Scholarships for Survivors

Patient Advocate Foundation
Ruth Anne Reed, Vice President of Special Programs, 700 Thimble Shoals Boulevard, Suite 200, Newport News, VA 23606
Phone: 800-532-5274
Email: help@patientadvocate.org
http://www.patientadvocate.org
Purpose: This group of scholarships seeks to assist students who have been diagnosed with cancer or another life-threatening illness.
Eligibility: Students must be under the age of 25 and have been diagnosed with or be actively treated for their life-threatening illness in the past five years. If awarded a scholarship, the student must maintain a 3.0 GPA, be enrolled full time and perform 20 hours of community service each year.
Target applicant(s): High school students. College students. Graduate school students.
Minimum GPA: 3.0

Amount: $3,000.
Number of awards: 12.
Scholarship may be renewable.
Deadline: February 25.
How to apply: Applications are available online.
Exclusive: Visit www.UltimateScholarshipBook.com and enter code PA283220 for updates on this award.

(2833) · Sean Silver Memorial Scholarship Fund

Ulman Cancer Fund for Young Adults
1215 East Fort Avenue, Suite 104, Baltimore, MD 21230
Phone: 410-964-0202
Email: scholarship@ulmanfund.org
http://ulmanfund.org/scholarships/
Purpose: To support young people in active treatment for cancer in their pursuit of a degree in higher education.
Eligibility: Applicants must be U.S. citizens accepted to or attending a two- or four-year U.S. institution and have financial need. Applicants must currently be residents of Chicago, in active treatment for cancer and must be between the age of 15 and 30 at the time of application. Scholarship winners are required to organize and run a bone marrow registry drive with the support of Delete Blood Cancer and There Goes My Hero. A physician's verification is required. Selection is based on a letter of recommendation and the overall strength of the application.
Target applicant(s): High school students. College students. Adult students.
Amount: $2,500.
Number of awards: 2.
Deadline: March 15.
How to apply: Applications are available online. An application form, physician's verification and letter of recommendation are required.
Exclusive: Visit www.UltimateScholarshipBook.com and enter code UL283320 for updates on this award.

(2834) · Sertoma Scholarship for Students Who Are Hard of Hearing or Deaf

Sertoma International
1912 E. Meyer Boulevard, Kansas City, MO 64132
Phone: 816-333-8300
Email: infosertoma@sertomahq.org
http://www.sertoma.org
Purpose: The organization's focus is to concentrate on communicative disorders.
Eligibility: Applicants must be entering or continuing as full-time undergraduates in the U.S., show proof that they have a clinically significant (40dB) bilateral hearing loss and have a minimum 3.2 GPA for all high school and college courses.
Target applicant(s): High school students. College students. Adult students.
Minimum GPA: 3.2
Amount: $1,000.
Number of awards: Varies.
Deadline: May 1.
How to apply: Applications are available online.
Exclusive: Visit www.UltimateScholarshipBook.com and enter code SE283420 for updates on this award.

(2835) · Soozie Courter Hemophilia Scholarship Program

Pfizer
Hemophilia Scholarship Program, 235 East 42nd Street, New York, NY 10017
Phone: 888-999-2349
http://www.hemophiliavillage.com
Purpose: To provide financial assistance to students with hemophilia.
Eligibility: Applicants must be high school seniors or graduates, GED recipients or college or vocational school students who have been diagnosed with hemophilia A or B.
Target applicant(s): High school students. College students. Adult students.
Amount: $2,500-$4,000.
Number of awards: 15.
Deadline: May 5.
How to apply: Applications are available online.
Exclusive: Visit www.UltimateScholarshipBook.com and enter code PF283520 for updates on this award.

(2836) · Student Award Program of FSD

Foundation for Science and Disability
503 N.W. 89 Street, Gainesville, FL 32607
http://stemd.org
Purpose: To support students with disabilities in completing a science project or thesis in any field of mathematics, science, medicine, engineering or computer science.
Eligibility: Applicants must be graduate students or senior undergraduates who have been accepted to graduate school. Students must submit two letters of recommendation and an essay outlining their professional goals and aspirations and the purpose for which the grant would be used. Selection is based on the overall strength of the application.
Target applicant(s): College students. Graduate school students. Adult students.
Amount: $1,000.
Number of awards: 1.
Deadline: December 1.
How to apply: Applications are available online.
Exclusive: Visit www.UltimateScholarshipBook.com and enter code FO283620 for updates on this award.

(2837) · Susanna DeLaurentis Memorial Scholarship

Susanna DeLaurentis Charitable Foundation
SDCF, P.O. Box 11208, Elkins Park, PA 19027
Phone: 215-635-9405
http://thesusannafoundation.org/scholarships/apply.php
Purpose: To support graduating seniors who have faced chronic disease or other serious health issues in pursuing post-secondary education.
Eligibility: Applicants must submit high school transcripts, verification of health condition from a medical professional, a letter of recommendation and a personal statement. Selection is primarily based on academic achievement and extracurricular involvement.
Target applicant(s): High school students.
Amount: $1,000.
Number of awards: 1.
Deadline: April 21.
How to apply: Applications are available online.
Exclusive: Visit www.UltimateScholarshipBook.com and enter code SU283720 for updates on this award.

(2838) • Tony Coelho Media Scholarship

American Association of People with Disabilities (AAPD)
2013 H Street, NW, 5th Floor, Washington, DC 20006
Phone: 800-840-8844
http://www.aapd.com

Purpose: To support students with disabilities pursuing a career in the entertainment industry.

Eligibility: Applicants must be second year associate's degree students, undergraduate students in their sophomore year or higher or graduate students with disabilities who are interested in pursuing a career in the communications, media or entertainment industry.

Target applicant(s): College students. Graduate school students. Adult students.

Amount: $5,625.

Number of awards: 8.

Deadline: April 10.

How to apply: Applications are available online.

Exclusive: Visit www.UltimateScholarshipBook.com and enter code AM283820 for updates on this award.

(2839) • TPA Scholarship Trust for the Hearing Impaired

TPA Scholarship Trust for the Deaf and Near Deaf
2041 Exchange Drive, Saint Charles, MO 63303
Phone: 314-371-0533
Email: support@tpahq.org
http://www.tpahq.org

Purpose: To provide financial aid to children and adults who are deaf or hearing impaired and who need assistance in obtaining mechanical devices, treatment or specialized education.

Eligibility: Applicants must suffer from deafness or hearing impairment. Completed applications must be returned to the Trust by the end of each quarter. Applications are reviewed on the last day of each quarter and recipients will be notified within 30 days of the decision.

Target applicant(s): Junior high students or younger. High school students. College students. Graduate school students. Adult students.

Amount: Varies.

Number of awards: Varies.

Deadline: March 31, June 30, September 30, December 31.

How to apply: Applications are available by written request or online.

Exclusive: Visit www.UltimateScholarshipBook.com and enter code TP283920 for updates on this award.

(2840) • UCB Family Epilepsy Scholarship Program

UCB Family Epilepsy Scholarship Program
120 White Plains Road, Tarrytown, NY 10591
Phone: 866-825-1920
Email: ucbepilepsyscholarship@summitmedcomm.com
https://ucbepilepsyscholarship.com

Purpose: To provide financial assistance to people with epilepsy who wish to obtain higher education.

Eligibility: Applicants must be U.S. citizens or legal and permanent residents who have epilepsy, or family members or caregivers of persons with epilepsy. They must be graduating high school in the year of application or have already graduated and be enrolled in or awaiting acceptance from a U.S. institution of higher learning. They must have demonstrated academic achievement, participate in extracurricular activities and be positive role models.

Target applicant(s): High school students. College students. Graduate school students. Adult students.

Amount: $5,000-$10,000.

Number of awards: 32.

Deadline: April 3.

How to apply: Applications are available online.

Exclusive: Visit www.UltimateScholarshipBook.com and enter code UC284020 for updates on this award.

(2841) • Vera Yip Memorial Scholarship

Ulman Cancer Fund for Young Adults
1215 East Fort Avenue, Suite 104, Baltimore, MD 21230
Phone: 410-964-0202
Email: scholarship@ulmanfund.org
http://ulmanfund.org/scholarships/

Purpose: To support students who are cancer survivors and students whose parents have been afflicted with cancer.

Eligibility: Students must show financial need, community service participation, personal or family medical hardship, commitment to education and career goals and how they have used their experience to help others. Applicants must have been between the ages of 15 and 39 during the diagnosis/treatment of their parent or sibling or during their own diagnosis/treatment.

Target applicant(s): High school students. College students. Adult students.

Amount: $2,500.

Number of awards: Varies.

Deadline: March 15.

How to apply: Applications are available online.

Exclusive: Visit www.UltimateScholarshipBook.com and enter code UL284120 for updates on this award.

(2842) • Vitality Medical's Student Disability Scholarship

Vitality Medical
Attn.: Vitality Medical Scholars, 7910 S. 3500 E., Suite C, Salt Lake City, UT 84121
Phone: 800-397-5899
http://www.vitalitymedical.com/

Purpose: To encourage outstanding students who make an impact on their school and community.

Eligibility: Applicants must be a high school senior or currently enrolled undergraduate student. Students should be 16 years old or older and have at least a 3.0 GPA. Applicants do not have to have a disability to enter. A poem and personal statement on how using disability aids have added vitality to your life are required.

Target applicant(s): High school students. College students. Adult students.

Minimum GPA: 3.0

Amount: $500.

Number of awards: varies.

Deadline: September 15.

How to apply: Application information available online. Poem, personal statement and transcript must be submitted by mail.

Exclusive: Visit www.UltimateScholarshipBook.com and enter code VI284220 for updates on this award.

(2843) • VSA International Young Soloists Awards

John F. Kennedy Center for the Performing Arts
2700 F Street NW, Washington, DC 20566
Phone: 800-444-1324
Email: vsainfo@kennedy-center.org

http://education.kennedy-center.org/education/vsa/programs/
Purpose: To reward promising young musicians with disabilities with scholarship funds and a chance to perform in Washington, DC, at the John F. Kennedy Center for the Performing Arts.
Eligibility: Applicants must be instrumentalists or vocalists between the ages of 14 and 25 years of age and have physical or mental disabilities that limit one or more of their major life activities. Applicants need to include audio or video recordings of three musical selections along with a one-page biography explaining why they feel they should be selected for the award. Awards are based on technique, tone, intonation, rhythm and interpretation from the taped performances.
Target applicant(s): Junior high students or younger. High school students. College students. Graduate school students.
Amount: $2,000.
Number of awards: Varies.
Deadline: Varies.
How to apply: Applications are available online.
Exclusive: Visit www.UltimateScholarshipBook.com and enter code JO284320 for updates on this award.

(2844) · Wells Fargo Scholarship Program for People with Disabilities

Wells Fargo Scholarship Program for People with Disabilities, Scholarship America
One Scholarship Way, Saint Peter, MN 56082
Phone: 844-402-0357
Email: pwdscholarship@scholarshipamerica.org
https://scholarsapply.org/pwdscholarship/
Purpose: To support students with disabilities in the career path of their choice.
Eligibility: Applicants must have an identified disability, a long-term or recurring issue that impacts one or more major life activities. Students must be either high school seniors or current undergraduate students enrolled full- or half-time at an accredited two- or four-year college or university in the U.S. A GPA of 2.5 or higher is required.
Target applicant(s): High school students. College students. Adult students.
Minimum GPA: 2.5
Amount: Up to $2,500.
Number of awards: Up to 25.
Scholarship may be renewable.
Deadline: December 6.
How to apply: Application available online.
Exclusive: Visit www.UltimateScholarshipBook.com and enter code WE284420 for updates on this award.

(2845) · William and Dorothy Ferrell Scholarship

Association for Education and Rehabilitation of the Blind and Visually Impaired
AER Scholarship Committee, 1703 N. Beauregard Street, Suite 440, Alexandria, VA 22311
Phone: 703-671-4500
Email: scholarships@aerbvi.org
https://aerbvi.org/resources/aer-scholarships/
Purpose: To assist visually-impaired students who plan to assist others who are visually impaired.
Eligibility: Applicants must be legally blind, with a vision of 20/200 or less in the best eye or 20 degrees or less in the visual field. Applicants must also study in college or a similar institution in the field of services for the blind or visually impaired. Scholarships are only awarded in even-numbered years.
Target applicant(s): College students. Graduate school students. Adult students.
Amount: $1,000.
Number of awards: 2.
Deadline: Varies.
How to apply: Applications are available online or by phone request.
Exclusive: Visit www.UltimateScholarshipBook.com and enter code AS284520 for updates on this award.

Scholarship Indexes

What would you rather do: read the description of every single scholarship in this book or use an index to quickly zero in on scholarships that fit you? That's what we thought, which is why we put together a set of indexes that make it easy for you to find the perfect scholarships. We strongly recommend that you use all of the indexes. This is because every scholarship can be categorized in numerous ways and often the decision is unavoidably subjective. So to make sure that you don't miss out on a great scholarship, spend the time to consult each of the following indexes:

GENERAL CATEGORY INDEX

This is one of the most useful indexes since it organizes the scholarships by common fields of study or career areas. It does not list any state specific scholarships since there is another index just for state of residence.

Academics/General

Also See Scholarships Listed Under:
Leadership
Public Service/Community Service

Accounting/Finance

Aerospace/Aviation

Biological Sciences/Life Sciences

English/Writing

Also See Scholarships Listed Under:
Academics/General
Education/Teaching
Communications
Journalism/Broadcasting
Library Science

Hospitality/Travel/Tourism

Also See Scholarships Listed Under:
Business/Management

Journalism/Broadcasting

Also See Scholarships Listed Under:
Communications

Law

Also See Scholarships Listed Under:
Leadership

Leadership

Also See Scholarships Listed Under:
Academics/General
Public Service/Community Service
Public Administration/Social Work

Military/Police/Fire

Also See Scholarships Listed Under: Leadership

Organizations/Clubs/Employers

Also See Scholarships Listed Under: Unions

Performing Arts/Music/Drama/Visual Arts

Also See Scholarships Listed Under:
English/Writing
Graphic Arts

Psychology

Also See Scholarships Listed Under:
Social Science/History

Public Administration/Social Work

Also See Scholarships Listed Under:
Leadership
Education/Teaching
Public Service/Community Service

Public Service/Community Service

Also See Scholarships Listed Under:
Academics/General
Leadership
Education/Teaching

Race/Ethnicity/Gender/Family Status

Also See Scholarships Listed Under: Academics/General

FIELD OF STUDY INDEX

This index organizes the scholarships by fields of study. It lists both general areas of study (in bold) as well as specific areas of study. If you cannot find a specific area of study that matches your major simply look at the scholarships under the closest matching general area.

In addition to this index be sure to use the Career Index since many scholarships are targeted to specific careers but do not have specific field of study requirements.

COMMUNICATION AND JOURNALISM -- BROADCAST JOURNALISM

COMMUNICATION AND JOURNALISM -- JOURNALISM

COMMUNICATION AND JOURNALISM -- MASS COMMUNICATION / MEDIA STUDIES

COMMUNICATION AND JOURNALISM -- PHOTOJOURNALISM

COMMUNICATION AND JOURNALISM -- PUBLIC RELATIONS / IMAGE MANAGEMENT

COMMUNICATION DISORDERS, GENERAL

See: HEALTH PROFESSIONS AND RELATED CLINICAL SCIENCES

COMPUTER AND INFORMATION SCIENCES

COMPUTER AND INFORMATION SCIENCES -- COMPUTER SCIENCE

ENGINEERING -- AEROSPACE, AERONAUTICAL AND ASTRONAUTICAL ENGINEERING

ENGINEERING -- AGRICULTURAL / BIOLOGICAL ENGINEERING AND BIOENGINEERING

ENGINEERING -- BIOMEDICAL / MEDICAL ENGINEERING

ENGINEERING -- CHEMICAL ENGINEERING

ENGINEERING -- CIVIL ENGINEERING

ENGINEERING -- COMPUTER ENGINEERING, GENERAL

ENGINEERING -- ELECTRICAL, ELECTRONICS AND COMMUNICATIONS ENGINEERING

ENGINEERING -- ENGINEERING SCIENCE

ENGINEERING -- ENVIRONMENTAL / ENVIRONMENTAL HEALTH ENGINEERING

ENGINEERING -- INDUSTRIAL ENGINEERING

ENGINEERING -- MATERIALS ENGINEERING

ENGINEERING -- MECHANICAL ENGINEERING

ENGINEERING -- METALLURGICAL ENGINEERING

ENGINEERING -- NUCLEAR ENGINEERING

ENGINEERING -- POLYMER / PLASTICS ENGINEERING

HEALTH PROFESSIONS AND RELATED CLINICAL SCIENCES -- ATHLETIC TRAINING / TRAINER

HEALTH PROFESSIONS AND RELATED CLINICAL SCIENCES -- CHIROPRACTIC

HEALTH PROFESSIONS AND RELATED CLINICAL SCIENCES -- CLINICAL / MEDICAL LABORATORY SCIENCE AND ALLIED PROFESSIONS

HEALTH PROFESSIONS AND RELATED CLINICAL SCIENCES -- COMMUNICATION DISORDERS, GENERAL

HEALTH PROFESSIONS AND RELATED CLINICAL SCIENCES -- DENTAL SUPPORT SERVICES AND ALLIED PROFESSIONS

HEALTH PROFESSIONS AND RELATED CLINICAL SCIENCES -- DENTISTRY

HEALTH PROFESSIONS AND RELATED CLINICAL SCIENCES -- DIETETICS / DIETITIAN

HEALTH PROFESSIONS AND RELATED CLINICAL SCIENCES -- EMERGENCY MEDICAL TECHNOLOGY / TECHNICIAN

HEALTH PROFESSIONS AND RELATED CLINICAL SCIENCES -- FAMILY PRACTICE NURSE / NURSE PRACTITIONER

HEALTH PROFESSIONS AND RELATED CLINICAL SCIENCES -- HEALTH AND MEDICAL ADMINISTRATIVE SERVICES

HEALTH PROFESSIONS AND RELATED CLINICAL SCIENCES -- LICENSED PRACTICAL / VOCATIONAL NURSE TRAINING

CAREER INDEX

This index organizes the scholarships by common career fields. If you cannot find your specific career listed simply look at the scholarships under the closest matching career area.

In addition to this index be sure to use the Major Index since many scholarships are targeted to fields of study but do not have specific career requirements.

INTERESTS / HOBBIES INDEX

This index lists awards that are geared toward students who are active in specific pastimes and hobbies.

Science

Speech / Debate

Sports

Star Trek

Student Government

Study Abroad

Teaching

Technology

Ukulele

Volunteer firefighter

Writing

Yearbook

SPECIAL CIRCUMSTANCES

This index lists a variety of special circumstances that are used as eligibility limits for these scholarships.

STATE OF RESIDENCE INDEX

This index lists awards that are restricted to students who are residents of the state or territory or who are planning to study in the state or territory.

Colorado

Connecticut

DC

Delaware

Florida

Georgia

Hawaii

MILITARY RELATED INDEX

Most of the awards in this index require that you have a parent, grandparent or spouse who has served in the military. There are also awards if you want to enter the armed services or if you have served.

ETHNICITY AND RACE INDEX

This index lists awards for members of minority and non-minority ethnic groups.

African-American

ESKIMO

FILIPINO

GREEK

HAWAIIAN

HISPANIC / LATINO

Italian

Japanese

Korean

Lithuanian

Mexican

Middle Eastern

Mongolian

Native American

Pacific Islander

RELIGION INDEX

This index lists awards from various churches and religious organizations.

DISABILITY INDEX

This index lists awards for students with physical, hearing, vision, mental and learning disabilities. It also includes awards for students who have been afflicted with certain illnesses.

MEMBERSHIP INDEX

If you or your parents are members of any of the groups in this index, you may qualify for a scholarship.

INDEX BY SPONSOR

SCHOLARSHIP NAME INDEX

GET THE MONEY YOU NEED TO PAY FOR COLLEGE!

- Insider tips from top scholarship winners and judges
- Secrets to writing applications and essays that win
- Where to find the best scholarships
- Techniques for maximizing your financial aid package

ISBN13: 978-1-61760-135-4

Price: $19.99

EVERY CONCEIVABLE WAY TO PAY FOR COLLEGE

- Where to find the best scholarships
- Pay in-state tuition even if you're an out-of-state student
- Jump-start your college savings
- Get your share of the $252 billion in financial aid available
- Have your state pay for your college education
- Get your student loans forgiven
- And much, much more!

ISBN: 978-1-61760-149-1

$19.99

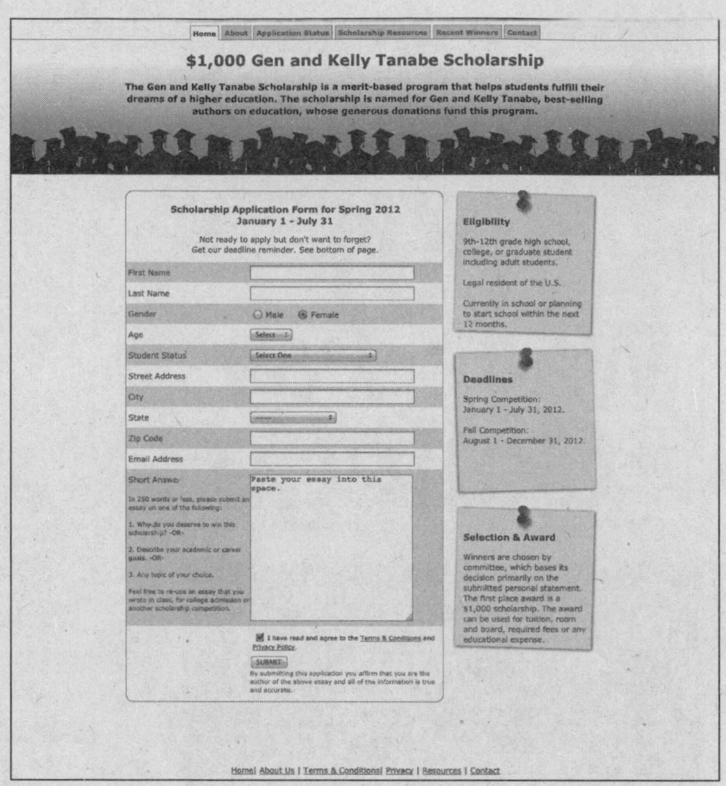

APPLY FOR THE GEN AND KELLY TANABE SCHOLARSHIP

The Gen and Kelly Tanabe Scholarship is a merit-based program that helps students fulfill their dreams of a higher education. The program is open to 9th-12th grade high school, college, or graduate students including adult learners. Visit **www.gkscholarship.com** to apply.

GET MORE TOOLS AND RESOURCES AT SUPERCOLLEGE.COM

Visit **www.supercollege.com** for more free resources on college admission, scholarships and financial aid. And, apply for the SuperCollege Scholarship.

ABOUT THE AUTHORS

Harvard graduates and husband and wife team Gen and Kelly Tanabe are the founders of SuperCollege and award-winning authors of 14 books including: *Get Free Cash for College*, *1001 Ways to Pay for College*, *How to Write a Winning Scholarship Essay*, *The Ultimate Guide to America's Best Colleges*, *Get into Any College*, *Accepted! 50 Successful College Admission Essays*, *501 Ways for Adult Students to Pay for College* and *Accepted! 50 Successful Business School Admission Essays.*

Together, Gen and Kelly were accepted to every school to which they applied, including all the Ivy League colleges and won over $100,000 in merit-based scholarships. They were able to graduate from Harvard debt-free.

Gen and Kelly give workshops across the country and write the nationally syndicated "Ask the SuperCollege Experts" column. They have made hundreds of appearances on television and radio and have served as expert sources for *USA Today*, the *New York Times*, *U.S. News & World Report*, *New York Daily News*, *San Jose Mercury News*, *Chronicle of Higher Education*, *CNN* and *Seventeen.*

Gen grew up in Waialua, Hawaii. A graduate of Waialua High School, he was the first student from his school to be accepted at Harvard, where he graduated magna cum laude with a degree in both History and East Asian Studies.

Kelly attended Whitney High School, a nationally ranked public high school in her hometown of Cerritos, California. She graduated magna cum laude from Harvard with a degree in Sociology.

The Tanabes approach financial aid from a practical, hands-on point of view. Drawing on the collective knowledge and experiences of students, they provide real strategies students can use to pay for their education.

Gen and Kelly live in Belmont, California with their sons Zane and Kane.